Mahatma Gandhi

Political Saint & Unarmed Prophet

By The Same Author

English Edition

- Dr. Babasaheb Ambedkar: Life and Mission (1954) (Fifth Edition)
- Lokamanya Tilak: Father of the Indian Freedom Struggle (1959) (Third Edition)
- Mahatma Jotirao Phooley: Father of Our Social Revolution (1964) (Third Edition)
- Veer Savarkar (1966) (Fourth Edition)
- Shahu Chhatrapati: A Royal Revolutionary (1976)
- Dr. Ambedkar: A Memorial Album (1982)

Marathi Edition

- Dr. Babasaheb Ambedkar (1966) (Fifth Edition)
- Mahatma Jotirao Phooley: Amachya Samaj Krantiche Janak (1968) (Fifth Edition)
- Swatantryaveer Savarkar (1972) (Third Edition)
- Rajarshi Shahu Chhatrapati (1979) (Third Edition)
- Krutagya Mi, Krutartha Mi (1987) (Second Edition)
- Lokamanya Tilak (2015)

Hindi Edition

- Dr. Babasaheb Ambedkar: Jeevan-Charit (1996) (Third Edition)

Other Publishers

- Tilak aani Rajarshi Shahu Maharaj: Ek Mulyamapan (1971)
- Teen Mahan Saraswat (1979)
- Vishvabhushan Dr. Babasaheb Ambedkar: Manas Ani Tatwa Vichar Yani Itihas Ghadvila (1980)
- Mahatma Phooley Samagra Wangmaya, edited in collaboration with Dr. S. G. Malshe (1969)
- Shetakaryacha Asud by Mahatma Jotirao Phooley (Marathi), edited in collaboration with Dr. S. G. Malshe
- Guruvarya Krushnrav Arjun Keluskar: Atma Charitra ani Charitra, edited by Dhananjay Keer

Mahatma Gandhi

Political Saint & Unarmed Prophet

DHANANJAY KEER

Published by Harsha Bhatkal for
Popular Prakashan Pvt. Ltd.
301, Mahalaxmi Chambers
22, Bhulabhai Desai Road
Mumbai – 400026
www.popularprakashan.com

(4529)
ISBN: 978-81-7991-995-8

First Published January 1973
Second Edition March 2020

Printed in India
by India Printing Works
Wadala, Mumbai - 400 031

To

My grandmother, Lakshmi

Publisher's Note

NIRMALA SADANAND SERIES is being published as a Popular Prakashan imprint to commemorate Nirmala (1924-2011) and Sadanand Bhatkal (1922-2011) who assisted Ganesh Ramrao Bhatkal (1896-1972) in establishing Popular Book Depot (Established in 1924) and its publishing division Popular Prakashan.

Sadanand played an important role in establishing book trade organisations and in putting Indian publishing on the world map. He planned a number of important books in English and nurtured the G. R. Bhatkal Foundation. Through the Foundation he co-edited a three-volume Encyclopaedia of Marathi Literature.

Apart from their sterling contribution to the book trade, particularly as editors of *The Indian Publisher and Bookseller* (1950-1985), they had both participated in India's freedom movement.

While reissuing biographical works by Dhananjay Keer in this series we have added bibliography and chronology for works on Savarkar, Ambedkar, Tilak, Phooley and Rajarshi Shahu. This practice has not been followed for this title, since there is more than one volume on Gandhi bibliography and Gandhi chronology.

In this edition, the English translation of Tilak's foreword for the first Marathi biography on Gandhi titled, *Mahatma Gandhi: Charitra Vishesh Parichay* (1918), is being made available to the English reader for the very first time.

Dhananjay Keer's works have enabled scholars to explore sources hitherto not available to them. The biographies of Lokamanya Bal Gangadhar Tilak (1856-1920), Mahatma Gandhi (1869-1948) and Vinayak Damodar Savarkar (1883-1966) trace the political developments in India while those of Mahatma Jotirao Phooley (1827-1890), Rajarshi Shahu Chhatrapati (1874-1922) and Dr. Babasaheb Ambedkar (1891-1956) document important socio-political events. Together these biographies give a different perspective on modern Indian history.

Mumbai, August 2019

Preface

IT IS WITH great pleasure and no less eagerness that, having written biographies of Gandhi's great contemporaries and opponents like Tilak, Savarkar and Ambedkar, I present this biography of Mahatma Gandhi. We of our generation are still near to the times in which Gandhi worked and preached. According to Gandhi, it is not in the fitness of things to measure the worth of a great man's work before we have seen it in its entirety; and even after his death it takes some time to assess it.[1] Gandhi is separated from us by a period of almost twenty-five years and it is not too early to write his life at this distance of time.

Several useful biographies of occasional interest appeared during the birth centenary of Gandhi. His disciples, too, have written his biographies, but Gandhi has truly said that a disciple cannot write a critical biography: "What could a disciple however write about his master? How could he write it? It would be presumptuous for a disciple to do so. The true disciple merges himself in the Guru and so can never be a critic of the Guru. Bhakti or devotion has no eye for shortcomings."[2]

I have painstakingly gone through the voluminous material relating to Gandhi, consisting of about forty thousand pages, and in addition to it a number of newspaper files and other contemporary records. Having done this, I have applied myself to depicting not only the outer life of Gandhi's work and activity, but the inner emotion and passion, evolution, development and the working of his mind.

I am not without admiration for the Mahatma. Yet, I have been frequently critical of him in this biography. This is inevitable if a biographer is to speak his mind freely about the man and his institutions, his politics and his public work.

No great man has a blameless record, and he must also take his share of reproach. Devotion or hero-worship takes to exalt a man into a blameless hero and the prejudice of his opponents casts a longer shadow over his failings and errors. While regard must be shown to the memory of the dead, more respect is to be paid to history without exalting fame or aggravating infamy. My approach is analytical. And analytical criticism is not antagonism; nor does it exclude appreciation.

In this biography I have tried to present a critical estimate and appreciation of this great man. In doing so it was necessary to shed light on the myriad sides of the man. An awareness of the sexual life of Gandhi is essential to an understanding of his career and of the extraordinary drama of his life. I have dealt with it briefly whenever it was necessary.

My object in writing this biography is also to try to focus the attention of students, historians, psychologists and sociologists on this life which gives a faithful portrait of a soul in its adventures through life. Besides attempting to present a true and correct picture of the various events and incidents in Gandhi's life, this biography gives a comprehensive survey of his activities and movements in South Africa and in India.

Mine was a formidable task. Many persons helped me to complete it. Chief among them is Prof. Nissim Ezekiel. I acknowledge my deep debt of gratitude to him for his critical reading of the entire manuscript and for making useful suggestions. My sincere thanks are also due to Ramdas Bhatkal and G. D. Khanolkar for minutely reading the manuscript. I am grateful to Prof. S. G. Malshe and his friend, P. G. Ketkar, for making available to me most of the files of Gandhi's *Young India* and *Harijan* and to S. R. Tikekar and Subhash Surve for supplying me with *The Collected Works of Mahatma Gandhi* and to Madhavrao Bagal and D. R. Samant, Director of Publicity, Government of Maharashtra, and to the Librarian, Mani Bhavan Gandhi Sangrahalaya Library, Bombay, for supplying me with some files of *Harijan.* Mention must be made of the assistance of my brother Vinayak and the timely assistance of C. Y. Sinkar in typing the manuscript. I am thankful to them and also to V. R. Patil, Padmakar Edwankar and G. K. Vaitee for their help in this work.

I sincerely acknowledge my deep debt of gratitude to all the authors, editors and publishers from whose books, journals and other publications I have drawn excerpts. Gandhi is a universally popular subject and the gigantic amount literature that is growing around his name should be open to all scholars and research workers. I am grateful to the Publications Division, Government of India, for making a great contribution in this field. Gandhi's thought is the property of the world.

I need not add that my publisher's patriotic and sympathetic attitude towards national literature has played an important role in the production of this biography.

My thanks are due to V. D. Limaye and his staff for their minute reading of the typescript and their excellent printing.

77 Bhageshwar Bhuvan
Dilip Gupte Road
Bombay 16
September 9, 1972

DHANANJAY KEER

Contents

CHAPTER I

Background and Boyhood

MOHANDAS KARAMCHAND GANDHI was born at Porbandar on October 2, 1869. This was nearly twelve years after the unsuccessful War of Independence (1857) in which about one lakh Indians fought and fell and about forty thousand British soldiers and civilians were killed. Porbandar is a seaside 'white city' in Kathiawad on the west coast of India, The Gandhis belong to the Modh sub-caste of the Bania community and were originally grocers. The Banias constitute one of the leading communities of Kathiawad. They are known for their enterprise, industry, prudence and thrift.

The Peninsula of Kathiawad, also known as Saurashtra, has been the home of a strong and sturdy people. They differ from the people of Gujarat, of which Kathiawad is a sub-province. In the puranic days it was the land of the Yadavas to whose clan Lord Krishna belonged, and in modern times it has produced two powerful and illustrious men of religion. The first is Swami Dayanand Saraswati who was born at Morvi in 1824. He was a saint, sage and seer as well as a social reformer who dominated the Indian scene during the seventies and eighties of the last century. The other is Gandhi, hero of this biography.

The home province of the Gandhis is situated Dwarka. Founded by Lord Krishna, it has been a place of pilgrimage for the Hindus and is traditionally linked with Sudamapuri called Porbandar, the home town of Lord Krishna's poor classmate Sudama. The other salient feature of this part of India is that it has been tremendously influenced by Jainism and Vaishnavism. The supreme and exalted principle of the former is ahimsa (nonviolence) which preaches respect for all forms of life, and the latter embodies tolerance and humanitarianism. Both prescribe strict vegetarianism. The Gandhis were Vaishnavas and, like others in Kathiawad, they too were influenced by Jainism. This region overflowed with milk and butter at that time.

Uttamchand Gandhi *alias* Ota Gandhi, the grandfather of Mohandas, was in the beginning of his career an ordinary employee of the Rana of Porbandar. Kathiawad was at that time a conglomeration of about two hundred small states. Most of them were smaller than Porbandar and were controlled by the British Agent for Kathiawad. The population of Porbandar State in those days was 72,000. Ota Gandhi was a resolute, thoughtful and dutiful officer and by dint of merit rose to be Dewan. He was a self-respecting man, who possessed remarkable organising ability and conducted state affairs with unstinted loyalty, absolute integrity and fearless independence. The Rana led a sensual and indolent life, but was a shrewd judge of men. After his death, his widow Rupaliba began to take an active interest in state affairs as her son Vikramjit was a minor.

During Rupaliba's regency a store clerk, who had earned her displeasure, took refuge in the house of Ota Gandhi. A few days later she came to know the whereabouts of the clerk and asked the Dewan to hand him over to the Court. He doggedly refused to do so. She had his big house fired at by her troops and Ota Gandhi fled to Junagadh, which was a Muslim state. The house, which had sheltered three generations of the Gandhis, bore the cracks of canon-balls. It is now known as Kirti Mandir of Porbandar.

On being presented at the Junagadh Court, Ota saluted the Nawab, to the bewilderment of the courtiers, with the left hand. This was an act of outrage, pure and simple, against all decorum and convention. Asked to explain his apparent discourtesy, Ota replied with his usual candour that the right hand was already pledged to Porbandar; and although he had left that state owing to the displeasure of and differences with the dowager, his pledge of loyalty remained unchanged. He did not mean, he added, to insult Junagadh. The Nawab highly appreciated this spirited reply and gave him an honoured place in his Court. Some time later, through the good offices of the Nawab, a rapprochement was brought about and, at the request of the dowager, Ota Gandhi resumed his work in Porbandar as Dewan.

Ota Gandhi married twice. His first wife bore him four sons, and the second two, Karamchand *alias* Kaba and Tulsidas. Of these six sons, the fifth—Kaba Gandhi—succeeded at the age of twenty-five to the Dewanship of Porbandar on his father's retirement. He had studied only upto the fifth Gujarati standard and knew little or nothing about history and geography. But he had common sense to a high degree, had a talent for organization and could manage men and affairs efficiently. Above all, he had no love of money or property.

Like his father, Kaba Gandhi was a resolute, loyal, impartial and absolutely incorruptible minister. He was truthful, brave and generous, but short-tempered. He did not like interference in his work and so he left the Dewanship of Porbandar to be a member of the Rajasthanik Court. His brother Tulsidas succeeded him as Dewan of Porbandar. For some time Kaba Gandhi worked at the Rajasthanik Court which was an influential body for settling disputes between tribal chiefs and their fellow clansmen. Thereafter, in 1874, he became the Dewan of Rajkot, another state smaller than Porbandar. During this Dewanship he had a conflict with the Assistant Political Agent at Rajkot as the latter spoke rudely and insultingly about the Thakore Saheb of Rajkot. The Agent was angry and asked Kaba Gandhi to apologize. He stoutly refused. The Agent ordered him to be detained under a tree till he apologized. Some hours later, seeing that Kaba Gandhi was adamant, the Agent ordered him to be released.

Now a noted minister, Kaba Gandhi was commissioned to act as Dewan of Vankaner on condition that if he found it difficult to carry on, he should be paid a salary for five years on his resignation. He resigned after two months; but declined to accept the salary which was offered to him in accordance with the bond. He then resumed his work as Dewan of Rajkot.

UNFORTUNATELY KABA GANDHI lost three wives. He married for the fourth time when he was over forty. Two daughters survived the three wives. His fourth and last wife Putlibai bore him a daughter named Raliatbehn afterwards Gokibehn, and three sons Laxmidas, Karsandas and the youngest, Mohandas.

Kaba Gandhi sometimes visited temples and listened to religious discourses. Later, at the instance of a Brahmin friend he recited aloud some verses from the Gita every day at the time of worship. But religion was the very breath of Putlibai. She would take the hardest vows and keep them without flinching. Illness was no excuse for relaxing them. She observed long religious fasts with utmost rigidity. Going every day to the Haveli, the Vaishnava temple, was one of her sacred duties. She could not bear the sight of starving people in her neighbourhood. "The outstanding impression", said Mohandas in later life, "my mother has left on my memory is that of saintliness".

The impact of this remarkable woman proved to be profound and ineffaceable on the character of her son Mohandas. He inherited his father's stubbornness, incorruptibleness and practical sense and his mother's life of religion, devotion and asceticism. His life was influenced both by Jainism and by Vaishnavism. He grew in the midst of a population which would not kill even wild animals that daily destroyed their crops.[1] Mohandas accompanied his mother to the temples, but their glitter and pomp did not appeal to him. He would accompany her when she paid visits to the widowed mother of the Thakore Saheb. Putlibai, though unlettered, was well-informed about all matters of state. A darling of his mother, Mohandas often massaged her legs when she was tired or unwell.

When Kaba Gandhi moved his family to Rajkot, Mohandas was seven years old. At Porbandar he had attended an elementary school and had gone through the multiplication tables with difficulty, his intellect being sluggish and memory weak. He was a coward and haunted as he was by the fear of bandits, ghosts and serpents, he would not step out of doors at night. He was so oppressed with the fear of bandits that at the age of seventy-eight he once said that he came from Kathiawad which was notorious for bandits.[2] He had learnt *Ramaraksha Stotra,* and to remove the fear of ghosts he would repeat *Ramanama* as suggested by his nurse and housemaid Rambha. He was also taught to repeat what in Hindu scriptures are known as the thousand names of Lord Vishnu, He remembered Rambha so well that later he named one of his grand-daughters Rambha.

At Rajkot Mohandas was sent to school. A shy, mediocre and companionless boy, he attended the school in dhoti, long coat and a cap which he soon changed for a turban. As a student he was regular and punctual. He was even afraid lest anyone should poke fun at him. From the primary school he was transferred to the "Suburban School" called the City Taluka School and was admitted to Gujarati standard III. His elder brother Karsandas was admitted to Gujarati standard IV. After he completed his primary education Mohandas was admitted to Kathiawad High School, Rajkot, known since 1907 as Alfred High School. On the day of the first annual inspection, the teacher prompted him with the point of his boot to copy the spelling of the word 'Kettle' from his neighbour's slate, but he would not be prompted. Although he knew the faults of his elders and teachers, he carried out their orders and did not criticize their actions.

As a rule Mohandas had a distaste for reading beyond his school books. "School books", he later observed, "alone gave me enough food for thought, for it was natural for me to reduce to practice what I learnt at school. For home reading I had an intense dislike!"[3] From a school book he learnt a simple yet grand doctrine. It forbade him to hate anybody.[4] He read also a book *Shravana Pitribhakti Nataka*, a play about Shravan's devotion to his parents, and saw the pictures depicting his life shown by itinerant showmen. He was overpowered by the pathos in the agonized lament of the blind parents over the death of Shravana who, while bringing water for his thirsty parents, met his tragic death by an arrow inadvertently shot at him by the king Dasharath. The parents of Shravana cursed Dasharath that he would die a broken-hearted father. Mohandas played the melting tune on the concertina presented by his father.

Just about this time Mohandas saw a play called *Harishchandra*. He was a king of Ayodhya, known for his unflinching devotion to truth. In order to fulfil his word, he even sold his wife and son and undertook to serve himself. The play fascinated him. "I must have acted Harishchandra to myself times without number. Why should not all be truthful like Harishchandra?" he said to himself. Thereupon he resolved to follow truth and to go through all the ordeals Harishchandra went through, although he did not believe that Harishchandra was an historical character. Thus Shravana and Harishchandra became the lodestars of his character.

The human sympathy awakened in Mohandas exerted itself even at this stage. Against caste rule, he deliberately touched Uka the scavenger who cleansed the latrines of the Gandhi house. On touching him, he, as a dutiful son, performed ablutions, but he told his mother that he did not consider his touch to be sinful and added that untouchability was not sanctioned by religion[5]; even Rama was taken across the Ganges by an Untouchable. His mother would tell him that the shortest cut to purification after the unclean touch of an Untouchable was to cancel the touch by touching any Muslim passing by![6]

Mohandas wore the sacred thread. He was invested with it in his boyhood. At that time a movement had been started for making the sacred thread obligatory[6] on the first three *varnas* although the practice of wearing the sacred thread was not common among the Vaishya families in Kathiawad. He had envied Brahmin lads sporting bunches of keys tied to their sacred threads. He got a key tied to his own and showed it off to others.

During one mango season he stopped eating mangoes as he had failed to invite a friend to a mango party given in his house. The friend and the parents tried to dissuade him from his resolve, but to no purpose.

Mohandas was married at Porbandar to Kasturbai at the age of thirteen. She was the daughter of Gokuldas Makanji, who was a close friend of Kaba Gandhi and was a merchant. According to the records preserved by Laxmidas Gandhi, she was born in April 1869, being about six months older than Mohandas. Her mother's name was Vrajkuvar. Kasturbai was her third child, the earlier children having died. Kasturbai and her younger brother Madhavdas survived her. Kasturbai was a lovely girl with black hair, a fine nose, delicate lips, well-formed chin and dark large eyes. She wore bracelets, anklets, earrings, rings on her fingers and a nose-ring, precious stones at the temples and gold ornaments in her hair. To the bridegroom the wedding meant an occasion for good clothes, for drum beating, marriage processions and sumptuous feasts, and an opportunity to have an unknown playmate. In those days child marriage was the rule, and a boy bridegroom would often inquire of his parents whether the elders would take him to his wedding!

Before his marriage took place, two girls chosen for and betrothed to Mohandas had died. The third betrothal had led to the marriage. On the same day, the marriages of his elder brother Karsandas and one of his cousins were performed. In later life Mohandas condemned such preposterously early marriages. After the marriage ceremony was over, the new couple was taken to all the Hindu temples in the neighbourhood, of Shiva and Vishnu, and even to the Dargah of the Muslims, to invoke God's blessings.

An incident that had taken place on the eve of these marriages had more or less marred their happiness. Kaba Gandhi, while coming post-haste from Rajkot to Porbandar in a coach, met with an accident. The coach toppled over and he received severe injuries. Soon he gave up the Dewanship, accepted with great reluctance as reward a small part of the vast land offered him by the Thakore Saheb and became a pensioner of the Rajkot State.

The Thakore Saheb was wholly engrossed in the gratification of his desires, in drinking and meat-eating. Mohandas asked his father why he did not give up the service of such a ruler. The old man replied that his family was indebted to the prince for their livelihood[7] and he could not be ungrateful. In later life Mohandas as Mahatma Gandhi was sorry that the family was supported by such a ruler.

As a result of the engrossing wedding festivities and their stay at Porbandar, Mohandas failed in the second standard. His elder brother Karsandas, who failed in standard III, bade goodbye to school.

Devoted as he was to his parents, Mohandas tenderly nursed his father during his long illness. But his life was disturbed at this stage as he found himself in the grip of lust and in the vortex of bad company. He was oversexed and devouring passions haunted him. At school he used to think of his girl-wife and his lustful love for her, and the thought of his nightly encounters with her seized his mind during the day. He was a devoted but jealous husband; and his friend fanned the flame of suspicion about his wife. He wanted to make her an ideal wife. Guideless, illiterate, bold, independent and persevering, Kasturbai could not brook restraints. Yet like a true Hindu wife, she tolerated the hardships Mohandas imposed on her.

BY NOW INDIA had begun to react to the influence of western ideas and education. The new pattern of Government, the new kind of education, the new branches of science, the new types of machines, which accompanied British rule, deeply, impressed the first two generations of Indians. They suffered from an inferiority complex. As a result, a violent reaction set in against Hinduism and against all the meaningless accretions of customs and prejudices it had hugged for centuries. The will of Indian leaders to reform religion and society found expression in institutions like the Brahmo Samaj, the Paramahansa Sabha, the Prarthana Samaj, the Satya-Shodhak Samaj and the Arya Samaj. The Indian demand for political reform was voiced prayerfully by the British Indian Association of Calcutta, the Sarvajanik Sabha of Poona, the Bombay Branch of the East India Association and by a similar political Association in Madras.

These ideas were spreading in Kathiawad also. The young reformers, teachers and educated men in Kathiawad, in their zeal to reform Hinduism and to attack out-worn social customs, turned, to meat-eating, decried the gods and denigrated religion.

Sheikh Mehtab, a Muslim friend of Karsandas who had left school, began to influence Mohandas. He was the son of a jailer at Gondal. This classmate led Mohandas to believe that meat-eaters were always bolder and stronger than others. And because he was a meat-eater, he was hardier and more daring than Mohandas and was adept in high and long jumping. The English, he said, ruled over Indians because they were meat-eaters. Mohandas was cowardly by nature and was frightened to sleep in the dark. To sleep alone in a room was an act of bravery for him.[8] Mohandas, therefore, wished to be strong, healthy and daring, and he wanted Indians to be the same, so that they might defeat the English and make India free. In those days a stanza of the Gujarati poet Narmad was in vogue. It said:

> Behold the mighty Englishman
> He rules the Indian small,
> Because being a meat-eater
> He is five cubits tall.

All this had its effect on Mohandas who wished to transform the coward in him into a brave man; and he turned to meat-eating. A boy from a family dominated by Vaishnavism becoming a meat-eater! It was sacrilege, for Vaishnavism and vegetarianism go hand in hand. When he first ate meat, he had a very bad night. Every time he dropped off to sleep it would seem as though a live goat were bleating inside him. Thereafter the demoralization started rapidly. The elder brother, Mohandas and the Muslim friend cooked meat in secluded places. Such meat-feasts were clandestinely arranged about half a dozen times a year. Mohandas had to lie to his mother that he had no appetite and so he did not eat at home whenever he had had the meat-feast.

This mental strain, however, proved too much for Mohandas. Besides, he had no taste for flesh either. He thought that he would abjure meat-eating rather than lie to his parents. His attachment for his mother and the innate love of truth proved stronger than his fear of confessing sin. He would eat meat, he said, if he liked when he was independent. And he gave up meat-eating! "Restrained by my love for my mother", he later said, "I stopped eating meat and saved myself from sin. Had this not happened, I would have been today among the most wicked men in the world".[9]

The Muslim friend even took him to a brothel, but Mohandas saved himself by the skin of his teeth. He was almost struck dumb and blind in the den of vice. On four more similar occasions, he later said, God interceded and saved him in spite of himself. His mother, his eldest brother and his wife warned him that he was in bad company, but he had obstinately turned a deaf ear to them.

Nevertheless, Mohandas did not forsake his friend. He said he wanted to reform him. But instead of being able to reform him he again fell under his spell. He took to smoking, pilfering stumps of cigarettes thrown away by his uncle. To purchase *bidis* he required money. So he stole coppers from the servants' pocket money. As the boys could not smoke openly, they had to do so secretly and the sense of guilt smothered them. They, therefore, decided to leave home and commit suicide with *dhatura* seeds which were an effective poison, they swallowed two or three seeds each, but courage failed them and they returned. At last, they gave up smoking. In later life Mohandas regarded the habit of smoking as barbarous, dirty and harmful.

This, however, was not the last phase. The climax was reached when Mohandas stole a bit of gold from the solid armlet of his meat-eating brother to pay off the debt they had incurred. This tormented his soul. The twinge of conscience prevailed. Although he did not know at that time that truth is the highest thing, he certainly had attachment enough for his father to feel that he should do a certain thing to please him.[10]

So Mohandas wrote out a confession and with a trembling hand gave it to his father who was bed-ridden. In the note he implored his father not to punish himself for the offence of his son and promised not to steal in future. His father read the note, and tears trickled down his cheeks. They washed his son's sin away.

The sublime forgiveness resulted in a solemn resolve. Mohandas vowed never to commit the sin again. And the little Mahatma in Mohandas was born. The making of a superman is not a one-sided development. It is a long, hard process. It is the result of action and reaction between man and his destiny.

Meanwhile Mohandas studied in the third standard, and on his good performance in the terminal examination he was promoted to standard IV in 1884. Although he was an average student at the high school, he jealously guarded his character, and the least little lapse drew tears from his eyes. As he neglected his handwriting, he repented of this neglect in later life. Sports he disliked, but he formed the habit of taking walks, which remained with him till his last days.

One day, having failed to attend sports practice in time, Mohandas was marked absent, and Dorabji Edulji Gimi, the Headmaster, who was a strict disciplinarian, fined him. Mohandas's truthfulness, however, got the fine remitted and his father secured him exemption from sports as he wanted Mohandas to serve as nurse after school hours. Mohandas found it very difficult to study geometry through the medium of English, but in the end he succeeded in doing so.

Mohandas and his brothers now wore trousers. His mother was not happy to see them in trousers She thought they were not fully dressed in them. [11]

Mohandas could not get rid of his ties with Sheikh Mehtab completely; nevertheless he gave up his bad habits. But he could not control his sexual passion. The thought of lustful meetings with his wife obsessed him. The Shravana in him massaged his father's legs and looked after him with great devotion, but with inner restlessness.

One day Mohandas went to the theatre against the will of his father who wept bitterly and beat his breast. So he was called back and he stood by the sick bed of his father. With repentance in his eyes he saw his father weeping and repeatedly striking his forehead in grief.[12] Punish yourself for the sin of others to bring about a change of heart in them was the lesson Mohandas derived from this incident. It cast a long shadow over the life and mission of Mohandas.

Years later, he wrote feelingly to his son Manilal: "When I was younger than you are, my keenest enjoyment was to nurse my father. Of amusement after I was twelve, I had little or none".[13] The long service he rendered to his sick father, however, was rewarded in more ways than one. Besides knowing the importance of nursing a sick man, the love of healing and its virtue, he learnt important lessons in religious tolerance.

A Brahmin named Ladha Maharaj devotionally read Tulsidas's *Ramayana* to Mohandas's father. Mohandas was profoundly influenced by it, and he regarded the *Ramayana* as the greatest book in all devotional literature. This did not mean that in boyhood he had any living faith in God. He was somewhat inclined towards atheism or agnosticism. But from the discourses his father had with the priests on other religions, he learnt to be tolerant to other religions, and from his mother he learnt to worship all gods.

Kaba Gandhi was suffering from fistula. On the last night of his father's earthly existence, Mohandas nursed him as usual. After some hours his uncle relieved him. The lustful husband immediately ran to his pregnant wife who was asleep and woke her up. But within a few minutes the servant came and told him that his father was no more. Kaba Gandhi had a premonition of the coming event. A few minutes before his death, he called for a piece of paper and wrote on it that they should 'prepare for the last rites'.

At the age of sixteen, Mohandas lost his father who was sixty-three. Mohandas later said that because of carnal desire he could not be present at the last moment of his father's earthly existence. It was, he added, a blot on his life he had never been able to efface or forget. Kasturbai soon gave birth to a child, but it breathed scarcely more than three or four days.

Kaba Gandhi was Dewan of more than one state, but had left no big property or much cash. By nature he was no hoarder of wealth. All that he earned he spent on charity and on the education and marriages of his children. He had also sold some of his property.[14] When asked why he did not amass wealth for his children, he would reply that his children represented his wealth, and if he hoarded much money, he would spoil them.[15]

MOHANDAS NOW LEANED on his mother, who was the prop and shelter of his life. His studies continued. In November 1887 he went to Ahmedabad to appear for the Matriculation Examination. He was to stay with a man recommended by his eldest brother. This man met Mohandas at the station and took him to his house in a *tonga*. The host was a miser. He went into his house leaving Mohandas at the door with the *tonga*-driver! He came out after Mohandas had paid the fare. In December 1887 Mohandas passed the examination obtaining 89 marks out of 200 in English, 45 out of 100 in the Second Language, 59 out of 175 in Mathematics and 54 out of 150 in History, Geography and Natural Science. He obtained 247 marks out of 625 which was quite an ordinary performance, but not uncommon with boys who became great heroes later.

In January 1888 Mohandas joined Samaldas College at Bhavnagar. There he studied for about four months, but found it difficult to concentrate on his studies. He suffered from constant headaches and nose-bleeds, supposed to be caused by the hot climate. While at Bhavnagar, he had a chat with Jayashankar Buch, who suggested to him the idea of proceeding to London. Mohandas left Bhavnagar on

April 13 for a vacation at Rajkot.

A fortnight later, with his eldest brother, Mohandas met Mavji Dave who was priest, adviser and a friend of the family and was called Joshiji. Dave advised Laxmidas to send Mohandas to London to become a barrister, so that some day he would be a dewan or would perhaps attain an even higher position. The idea caught the imagination of Mohandas. He thought that after three more years he would graduate, but that would not bring him much income. "If I go to London", he said to himself, "not only shall I become a barrister (of whom I used to think a great deal), but I shall be able to see England, the land of philosophers and poets, the very centre of civilization".[16] He wanted to be a doctor, but his father had once said that dissection of dead bodies was against religion and so he had intended him for the bar.

There were three difficulties in his way — mother's consent, the caste objections and the cost. "The object of sending me to England", said Mohandas afterwards, "was that, we all the three of us (brothers) might thereby maintain the status of the father more or less, be well-off and enjoy the good things of life".[17]

His eldest brother Laxmidas, who loved him as his son, up held the idea and decided to arrange for a loan. In his eagerness to meet some persons, Mohandas met with a serious accident and was unconscious for some hours. Mohandas left for Porbandar. The thought of going to London had emboldened him to take the journey. The uncle at Porbandar was not ready to support his nephew's going to London, as it was against Hindu religion to cross the seas, nor was he co-operative in securing him a scholarship from the Porbandar State. Mohandas saw Lely, the British Agent, who supervised state affairs for the Government of India, and asked for some aid. The Agent bluntly declined it. He asked Mohandas to be a graduate first. Paramanandbhai, cousin of Mohandas, promised him Rs. 5,000. With great joy, he went to Bhavnagar, and disposing of his furniture and giving up his rooms, he returned to Rajkot.

At Rajkot Mohandas saw Colonel Watson, the Political Agent of Kathiawad and the Thakore Saheb of Rajkot. He grossly flattered both but to no avail. Sheikh Mehtab had forged a letter with his signature to Meghjibhai, cousin of Mohandas, and secured a promise of help. But the result was disappointing. Mohandas, however, did not lose heart.[18] He was the pet of his mother. But his mother and the eldest brother too sometimes changed their mind. They knew well that once Mohandas resolved to do a thing he would accomplish it! At last, he and his brother decided to take the risk. "The risk", he said in later life, "was indeed great as we had decided to stake whatever we had on my education".[19]

Mother was not happy with her eldest son, and she feared that Mohandas would be morally lost in England. She did not like the idea of parting from her son. So she asked him to take vows before Becharji Swami, a learned Jain monk, who was her spiritual guide and originally a Modh Bania. He, too, was their family adviser. He administered the oath and Mohandas vowed not to touch wine, woman and meat. Thereupon he was granted permission to go to London. With great patience and persuasion he secured the consent of his father-in-law.

On July 4, 1888, his fellow-students of Kathiawar High School gave Mohandas Gandhi a send-off. He rose to make his maiden speech. His head reeled. His whole frame shook and he scarcely stammered out the words of thanks which he had written on a piece of paper. "I hope", he said in a trembling voice, "that some of you will follow in my footsteps and after your return from England you will work whole-heartedly for big reforms in India."[20]

On the eve of his departure to London, Mohandas got rid of the tuft of hair on his head, so that in England he should not expose himself to ridicule and make himself look 'a barbarian in the eyes of Englishmen'![21] August 10, the day of departure to Bombay, dawned. He heard the sobbing of his mother. His heart too was breaking, but he did not weep. His wife had begun sobbing long before. "I went to her", he said, "and stood like a dumb statue for a moment. I kissed her, and she said, 'Don't go'. What followed I need not describe."[22]

With the blessings of his mother, Mohandas Gandhi, in the company of his elder brother and his bosom friend Sheikh Mehtab and others, left for Bombay. His little son Harilal remained with his wife. The heads of the Modh Bania caste in Bombay were against his going to London. He was surrounded and hooted at by members of his caste when they came across him in the street. They pestered him with deputations. They even held a meeting in Bombay and threatened to out-caste him if he went to London.

Mohandas, a stripling of eighteen, mustering all his courage, defiantly replied that people of his caste, should not interfere in the matter. Thereupon they resolved to treat him as an outcaste from that day and declared that "he who will support him in any way or go to see him off will be treated as an outcaste". Upon this Laxmidas too faltered, but Mohandas did not flinch. His castemen, however, somehow succeeded in putting off his departure to London for a fortnight through a captain who told his brother that in August the sea was rough and so Mohandas should not undertake the voyage.

Soon after this, Gandhi learnt that a Junagadh lawyer named Tryambakrai Mazmudar was planning to sail for London. This news came to him as a godsend. He arranged for a loan, as his brother-in-law would not give him the money his brother had kept with him. One Jagmohandas Samaldas gave him a substantial loan[23] and helped him to go to London. Mohandas. booked a second-class passage, his friends bought clothes, and with a supply of fruit and sweets he left Bombay for London on September 4, 1888, by the steamer *Clyde* in the company of Mazmudar who was going to London to qualify himself for the bar.

CHAPTER II

Law Student in London

On Board The ship, Gandhi wore a black suit. The necktie he disliked and the short jacket he looked upon as immodest. He was quite ignorant of the use of knives and forks. He did not feel seasick but was fidgety. As he was shy, Mazmudar told him that lawyers should have a long tongue; yet he hid himself in the cabin. He lived for three days on the sweets and fruits he had brought with him. He refused to eat meat and naively secured from a fellow passenger a certificate of his having kept strictly to a vegetarian diet during the journey. Whenever possible he went ashore at some ports for sightseeing.

On board Gandhi played the piano. He enjoyed the scene around him. To him the reflection of the stars in the water looked like fireworks. He fancied himself to be standing on the storey of a bungalow watching the fireworks performed before him. For the first time in his life he saw the electric light in the front of the ship.[1]

The steamer reached London on October 28, 1888. Gandhi was the only passenger to land in white flannels. With Mazmudar and Abdul Masjid, a fellow passenger, he went to the Victoria Hotel in London. They entered the lift and Gandhi thought that it was a room in which they had to sit for some time. But, to his surprise, they were taken to the second floor. Next day they moved to rented rooms.

Gandhi was a sensitive youth, nearly five feet five inches tall, with a long massive head, low forehead, large eyes, huge slanting ears, prominent pointed nose, sensuous thick, big lips, protruding chin, broad chest, bony arms and well-shaped fingers. This face was an index to the obstinacy, suppressed anger and the sensual life of the man, and yet he had a certain awareness of inner strength, self-denial and self-reliance crying for an outlet. He was homesick and unhappy and a stranger to British life and culture. His mother's love haunted him, and at night tears often rolled down his cheeks.

A Maharashtrian friend had given Gandhi four letters of introduction to Dr. P. J. Mehta, Dalpatram Shukla, the great cricketer Ranjitsinh, and Dadabhai Naoroji. Dr Mehta saw him and gave him instructions in English etiquette: "Don't touch other people's things. Don't ask questions on first acquaintance. Don't talk loudly and don't address people as 'Sir'. " Gandhi could not relish boiled vegetables cooked without salt or spices. His landlady was puzzled. Although he was persistently pressed by friends to take meat, he stuck to his vow irrevocably. To him a vow was sacred.

On November 6, 1888, Gandhi was admitted to the Inner Temple. After his admission he wrote to Lely and Watson for aid. He thought that it would be impossible for him to pull on for three years on £666 which was all he had.

In the new world of London, Gandhi read a newspaper for the first time in his life. *The Daily News*, *The Daily Telegraph* and *The Pall Mall Gazette* he read with a thrill. Agnostic, inquisitive and active, he was in search of a cheap vegetarian hotel. He walked about ten miles and to his joy found one on Farrington Road. The restaurant supplied its customers with vegetarian food, and offered books on vegetarianism for sale.

This restaurant was also the centre for men who held there weekly talks on diet, sexual behaviour, religion, economics and politics. Some of them were not only nature-cure zealots and extremist simple-lifers, but also connected with the Fabian Society and other institutions. Their leader was Henry Salt who was the only vegetarian of his day at Eton. There Gandhi bought Henry Stephens Salt's *Plea for Vegetarianism*, devoured it avidly and found in Salt the salt of the earth.

In England the term vegetarianism came in use about 1847 and was applied to the practice of living on food from which fish, flesh and fowl were excluded. Some sects even denied themselves all animal products, such as milk and eggs, confining their food to nuts, fruits and cereals. Health, economy and kindness to animals, were the reasons adduced in favour of vegetarianism. There were several vegetarian societies and restaurants in London.

In September 1890 Gandhi joined the London Vegetarian

Society which published a weekly journal of its own. He soon found himself on its Executive Committee and came in contact with those who were regarded in those days as the pillars of vegetarianism. He was glad to note that all philosophers and prophets from 'Pythagoras and Jesus' down to those of the present, were vegetarians. So he feverishly started his dietary experiments. Sometimes he gave up starchy foods and lived on bread and fruit. One day his friend, perturbed by the scene Gandhi created over a soup at a restaurant, flared up and passionately said to him: "You are too clumsy for decent society!" This remark hurt him to the quick and he decided to be polished and to make up for his vegetarianism by acquiring other accomplishments which fitted one for polite society. In a word, he decided to be an English gentleman.

Gandhi, therefore, went in for a chimney-pot hat at a high price, and wasted ten pounds on an evening suit made in Bond Street, the centre of fashionable life in London. He got a double watch-chain from his noble-hearted eldest brother in India. And Gandhi, who in India hardly ever used a mirror, now frequently looked into one and carefully adjusted his hair. He took lessons in dancing, elocution, violin playing and French. This infatuation lasted, he says in his autobiography, for about three months. But on introspection and on the minute inspection of accounts which he scrupulously maintained, he decided to be a gentleman not by clothes but by character.

Gandhi now applied himself to his studies. He saved much time and money by taking rooms in a house from which he was able to reach his place of business on foot in half an hour. To save money, he cooked "his own food, dined at home and lunched out. He did not spend more than half an hour in the morning and in the evening for cooking. In the morning he sometimes prepared porridge and in the evening soup. After putting the pot on the fire, he would sit by and read. Thus he managed to live simply and economically, on a shilling and three pence a day. This deliberate choice of plain living gave him plenty of time for study and his soul seemed now in harmony with his outward life.

Gandhi was very careful in keeping his accounts. One day he bought fruits at Tottenham Court Road in London for two pence. By mistake he perhaps paid three pence to the fruiterer. At home the balance would not tally. He rushed back to the fruiterer for the over-paid penny. The fruiterer replied that he knew nothing of it. Gandhi never got it back. He would talk of the penny he had never been able to account for in his life.[2]

GANDHI'S WEAK ENGLISH was a perpetual worry to him in his student days. In December 1889 he appeared for the London Matriculation examination which required a good deal of hard work. Latin and a modern language were compulsory. Latin was useful for understanding law-books and mastering the English language. He took the examination but failed in Latin. He had no liking for Chemistry and so he took Physics (Heat and Light) instead. In June 1890 he was successful in the London Matriculation examination.

Gandhi soon founded at Bayswater, in west London, a vegetarian society with the enthusiasm of a new convert. Dr. Joshiah Oldfield, editor of *The Vegetarian*, was its President, Sir Edwin Arnold was invited to be its Vice-President, and Gandhi was its Secretary. This society closed down when Gandhi left the locality. This was the first institution founded by Gandhi. He was now a confirmed vegetarian not only by choice but by mission. At first, health, hygiene and economy were the considerations for his dietic experiments, but later in South Africa, the religious aspect of it became predominant.

Meanwhile, there was a furore in the Vegetarian Society, in February 1891, over the anti-puritanic opinions of Dr. T. R. Allinson, who was noted for his writings on health and hygiene. Because Dr. Allinson was an advocate of the then new birthcontrol movement, A. F. Hills, President of the Vegetarian Society, decided to oust him. Hills was an ironmaster and a puritan who spent much on the Society, whose object was the promotion of vegetarianism. A majority of the members were his proteges. Although he did not like Dr. Allinson's views on artificial methods of birth control, Gandhi thought it wrong to exclude a man from the Vegetarian Society because he did not regard puritan morals as one of the objects of the Society. He therefore opposed the motion. His speech was read by another member as Gandhi felt, at the last moment, very nervous. But he found himself with the losing party, and on Allinson's expulsion, Gandhi resigned from the Society. That showed his spirit of independence.

The mind of young Gandhi was struggling with ideas of inner spirituality and truthfulness. According to the doctrine of some vegetarian sects, there was no injury done to living creatures in taking eggs. So he was inclined to put a new interpretation on his vow to his mother. He included eggs in his diet for about a month and a half, but in the end gave them up. This promise to his mother, the friendship of vegetarians and the early influence of Jainism kept him away from wine and meat.

The third part of the vow he kept with great difficulty. The shackles of untruth and sexual passions were encircling his youthful mind. A woman of new acquaintance shrewdly ensnared him into indulging in sweet talks with a young girl who stayed with her. He managed to pass off as a bachelor though he was the father of a son. He later admitted that in order 'to be able to have exciting friendships with young girls which a married man could not do', he pretended to be unmarried.

He was, Gandhi writes, about to fall a victim to lust. But before his entering into deep waters, the memory of the vow triumphed over the temptation. He then revealed to the women that he was already a married man, and they forgave him for his frankness. There was another occasion when he was saved from a moral lapse. He had gone to attend a Vegetarian Conference at Portsmouth in 1890. While playing bridge with the landlady there, he was about to go beyond the limit with her, but he said, God, who was the helper of the helpless, saved him from, the pitfall.

Gandhi, while in England, or for that matter throughout his life, was never drawn to men of science, rationalists, Fabian socialists or intellectuals. He was shy and nervous. His poor reading and lack of intellectual pursuits favoured anti-intellectual trends in his convictions. He kept himself aloof, from the radical intellectual and political movements of Labour and Socialist leaders. Yet he accompanied Narayan Hemchandra when, towards the end of September 1889, he called on Cardinal Manning, who had successfully intervened in the labour strike and attained some prominence.

This Narayan Hemchandra, with whom he had made friends in London, was a bold and ambitious young man who had never been to school but knew Marathi, Gujarati and Bengali. He was a linguist and scholar from Gujarat. This youth, with a clumsy pair of trousers, a dirty coat, without a necktie and collar, shook hands with Manning and congratulated him on his good work in the labour strike. Gandhi acted as his interpreter. The flaming youth, while bidding good-bye to the dignitary, did not fail to add that it was his custom to visit the sages of the world. While in England, Narayan Hemchandra was once locked up in a prison for wearing a dhoti.[3]

In London Gandhi had made friends with Pestonji Padshah who was a vegetarian and known for his erudition. It was, however, vegetarianism, not scholarship, that attracted him to Pestonji. He had also developed a close friendship in London with Keshavrao Deshpande who later conducted a national school in the Baroda State, where Kaka Kalelkar was once a teacher.

Gandhi went to Paris on a seven-day visit to see the exhibition held in the middle of 1890. The huge new iron Eiffel Tower had then aroused wide interest and had become a major attraction for tourists.

Leo Tolstoy of Russia had spoken disparagingly of the Tower. According to this philosopher-novelist, it was a monument of folly and not of wisdom. This remark had led to a bitter controversy. Gandhi saw the Tower, but was not impressed either by its novelty or by its unique dimensions. On the other hand, he was pleased to see the wonderful construction of Notre Dame and its sculpture.

To Gandhi, who later came to regard religion as self-realization or knowledge of self, religion was not at that time a living reality. All that he learnt of religion in his impressionistic age was acquired from the religious atmosphere of the home. The second phase of his religious development began when he met some theosophists in London who introduced him to Sir Edwin Arnold's *Song Celestial*. It was a translation of the Gita and Gandhi had not till then read the Gita either in Gujarati or in Sanskrit. So he began reading it with his theosophist friends. He also read *The Light of Asia* by Sir Edwin Arnold with greater interest. He was introduced in November 1889 to Madame Blavatsky (1831-91) and Mrs. Annie Besant (1847-1933). A Russian by birth, Helena & Petrovna Blavatsky lived for many years in North America and in India, and at the age of forty-four she founded in New York the Theosophical Society (1875). Her books *The Secret Doctrine* and *The Key to Theosophy* were published in 1888 and 1889 respectively.

Mrs. Besant's conversion from Atheism to Theosophy had roused a great controversy in London. Hailed in England as the finest platform orator of her generation, she was a person of great power and capacity of mind, a person born to lead and serve. She travelled from one continent to another, changing her god each time. She propagated atheism under the influence of Charles Bradlaugh (1833-1891), evolution under the influence of Edward Aveiling, socialism under Bernard Shaw and since 1899 theosophy under Madame Blavatsky. In 1877 she was prosecuted along with Bradlaugh for publishing a pamphlet on birth-control, but was acquitted. As she look pride in India's cultural heritage, she came afterwards to India to serve it.

Mrs. Besant's conversion from atheism to theosophy strengthened, Gandhi says, his aversion to atheism. Professor Max-Muller's books and lectures on India's sacred books had aroused great interest in England. Thousands of copies of his books were sold and they had riveted the attention of leading men in Britain on Indian history and culture.

A good Christian from Manchester, who met Gandhi at a vegetarian boarding house, pressed him to read the Bible. Dr. Josiah Oldfield, editor of *The Vegetarian*, tried hard to interest Gandhi in Christianity. During his student days at Rajkot, Gandhi had turned against the Christian faith as the new convert to it was obliged to eat meat, drink liquor and change his mode of dress. Converts to Christianity abused the religion of their ancestors and the customs of their country. Gandhi's reading of the Old Testament, however, did not make much progress. The message in the Sermon on the Mount from the New Testament, on the other hand, went straight to his heart. He even attended service in some Christian churches at the instance of his Christian friends. He heard famous preachers like Spurgeon and Farrar. He took special interest in the services of Dr. Parker which were given in City Temple.[4]

The Gita, *The Light of Asia*, and the Sermon on the Mount had a tremendous effect on Gandhi. He tried to unify the teachings of these three great religious classics, the first two being Indian. He drew a lesson from the three, that renunciation was the highest form of religion. He read also a chapter from Carlyle's *Heroes And Hero-Worship* on the Prophet, and came to know of Mohammed's greatness, his bravery and his austere living.

Charles Bradlaugh died on January 30, 1891. He was an uncompromising atheist and champion of women's suffrage, birth control and trade unionism. A great fighter, he was one of the very few selfless men who were in the forefront wherever oppression and tyranny were grinding the faces of the poor. For his fearless championship of the rights of the Indian people, he was contemptuously described in England by Conservatives as the Member for India.

Bradlaugh had attended the session of the Indian National Congress in 1889 in Bombay when he told the delegates that the Congress was the dawn, and he saw the day, and he did not count the rays which were yet below the horizon. Indians in London gratefully attended his funeral, miles away from London, at Woking, and young Gandhi was one of them. Forty years later, Gandhi who talked and worked in the name of God, said that although Bradlaugh delighted to call himself an atheist, he would call him a god-fearing man.[5] At one of the political meetings in London, Gandhi saw Dadabhai Naoroji whom he had not met before although he had a letter of introduction to him. Dadabhai said, "You can come and have my advice whenever you like,"

GANDHI'S STUDY OF law was progressing. He kept twelve terms, and during these got fruits and vegetables at his table. On every occasion, two bottles of wine were served to each group of four, and Gandhi, a teetotaller, was always in great demand every time. He read all the text-books and not much beyond them. He read Roman Law in Latin which he later found useful in South Africa where Roman Dutch was the Common Law. The reading of Justinian helped him a great deal later to understand South African Law. It took him nine months of fairly hard work to read Broom's *Common Law*, which he found interesting. To him Snell's *Equity*, too, was full of interest. Whereas White and Tudor's *Leading Cases* was, he says, full of instruction, Williams' and Edward's *Real Property*, read like a novel. He read also Goodeve's *Personal Property* and, later in India, Mayne's *Hindu Law*.

In the first quarter of 1891, Gandhi was busy with his law studies and with other activities. He wrote six articles for *The Vegetarian* which the editor published in February and March 1891. In India, he observed in one of the articles, that thousands of people were compulsorily vegetarians because they had to live on one pice (1/3rd pence) a day and were too poor to buy meat.

The Hindus, he continued, as a rule were notoriously weak, and child marriage and its attending evils were the reasons for their proverbial weakness. The Kshatriya princes were, in spite of their meat-diet, weak owing to debauchery. What was gained in mental power must be lost in bodily power. The Kshatriyas as a race were very weak. The Hindu weakness, he concluded, was not due to vegetarianism which was conducive to bodily strength.

Of course, these articles were against meat-eating. These were probably the first articles by Gandhi who, in his classic way, declared to the world that the "Hindus as a rule are notoriously weak" and discussed their "proverbial weakness".[6] Another point noted in these articles is the reference to the utter poverty of the Indian people. These were the vague glimmerings of his psychological preoccupations.

Gandhi wrote three more articles in *The Vegetarian*, two on the Diwali festival and one on the Holi festival. He also wrote a speech which he was scheduled to read at the Vegetarian Conference on May 2, 1891, in Bloomsbury Hall. He apologised for his paper which he called 'The Foods of India' and began to read it. But he could not read more than a few sentences. He was nervous and sat down. On every such occasion when he stood to read a speech, he trembled, his vision reeled and he sat down. Then someone from the audience would read his speech. Accordingly, the aforesaid speech was re-read by somebody else at the Portsmouth Conference.

Gandhi, in justification of his constitutional shyness and hesitancy in speech, observes that its greatest benefit was that it taught him economy of words and the habit of restraining his thoughts. The result, he added, was that in future a thoughtless word scarcely escaped his tongue or pen.

Gandhi made a speech for about a quarter of an hour at the meeting of the members of the Band of Mercy, an institution for the prevention of cruelty to animals. He said that to be logical, the members should be vegetarians.

Gandhi passed the law examination. He was called to the Bar on June 10, 1891. Next day he enlisted in the High Court and gave a farewell party to his vegetarian friends at the Holborn Restaurant. It was a strictly vegetarian dinner with music and speeches. When Gandhi's turn came to speak, his head reeled and memory failed as usual and he could not go beyond saying. "I thank you, gentlemen, for having responded to my invitation." There was no sorrow, reported *The Vegetarian* of June 13, 1891, as all felt that though Gandhi was going back to India, he was going to do still greater work for vegetarianism. Gandhi did not fail to speak in a touching way of what he owed to Dr. Josiah Oldfield.

Gandhi had completed his law studies. Much credit was due to his eldest brother Laxmidas, for when those who had promised to help Mohandas did not keep their word, his brother worked hard even at the cost of his health and ungrudgingly gave him as much money as he asked for. That showed his magnanimity and his affection for his younger brother.[7] He spent a sum of Rs. 13,000 on him during his stay in London.

On the eve of his departure, Gandhi saw Frederick Pincutt

and sought his advice. He told the young barrister that facts were three-fourths of the law and that common honesty and industry were enough to make a living. Gandhi should, Pincutt added, try to read a man's character from his face and, though it had no connection with the profession, he should read Indian history and books on physiognomy by Lavator and Shemmelpennick. Like his father, Gandhi was innocent of Indian history!

With the thought that it was easy to be called to the bar, but difficult to practise at the bar, the young barrister left for India by the Australian steamer *Oceana* and at Aden embarked the S.S. *Assam*. London had left an imprint on his mind.

"So much," Gandhi said, "attached was I to London and its environments; for who would not be? London with its teaching institutions, public galleries, museums, theatres, vast commerce, public parks and vegetarian restaurants, is a fit place for a student and a traveller, a trader and a 'faddist'— as a vegetarian would be called by his opponents. Thus, it was not without deep regret that I left dear London."[8] Afterwards he told the Rev. Josheph J. Doke, "Even now, next to India, I would rather live in London than in any other place of the world."[9] Gandhi was so fascinated by London that he later wrote a little hand-book *Guide to London*, but it remained unpublished.

On board the ship there was F. S. Taleyarkhan, another newly qualified barrister. Gandhi wanted to make a speech on vegetarianism at a concert on board and he was asked to be humorous. Gandhi said he would be nervous and not humorous. But the concert did not come off and the speech was not delivered. He landed at Bombay safely on July 5, 1891, with mixed feelings of joy and anxiety; joy for the return home and anxiety about the future. A barrister with average intellect, he had a flaming passion for vegetarianism, but not a visible trace of patriotism. He had made a resolve that he would earn enough to satisfy his eldest brother and enable him to forget the hardships he had undergone for his sake.

Meanwhile, on June 20, 1891, *The Vegetarian* published a reply given by Gandhi to a question. Gandhi, who had taken a vow not to touch three things—wine, women and meat, observed in his reply: "In conclusion, I am bound to say that, during my nearly three years' stay in England, I have left many things undone, and have done many things which perhaps I might better have left undone, yet I carry one great consolation with me that I shall go back without having taken meat or wine."[10]

Perhaps, Gandhi forgot to mention the third vow about women.

CHAPTER III

Gandhi Finds Himself

ON HIS ARRIVAL in Bombay, Gandhi was received at the dock by his brother Laxmidas and taken to Dr. P. J. Mehta who had helped him in London. At Dr. Mehta's house he told his brother that he was very eager to go to Rajkot to see his mother. Upon this, his brother broke to him the sad news of their mother's death. The death had occurred while Gandhi was still in London. His grief was even greater than over his father's death. It was a great shock to him. Yet he did not give himself up to any wild expression of grief. He checked his tears and went on with his normal life as if nothing had taken place.

Much later in life, when Mahadev Desai, his personal secretary, asked him whether austerity and not saintliness was the appropriate word he should have used to describe his mother, Gandhi replied, "No. I have used the word saintliness deliberately. Austerity implies," he added, "external renunciation, endurance and sometimes even hypocrisy. But saintliness is an inner quality of the soul. My mother's austerity was only an echo of her inner life." If you notice, he concluded, "any purity in me, I have inherited it from my mother, and not from my father. Mother died at the early age of forty. I have been a witness of her behaviour in the flower of youth, but never did I see in her any frivolity, any recourse to beauty aids or interest in the pleasures of life. The only impression she ever left on my mind is that of saintliness."[1]

To please one of the sections of the caste, which was divided on the issue of Gandhi's going to London, Laxmidas took him to Nasik before they went to Rajkot. Gandhi had a ritual bath in the sacred river Godavari. In Rajkot his brother hosted a dinner to some people of his caste. The trouble about Gandhi's readmission to one section of his caste was over. The other section boycotted Gandhi. His relations would not entertain him and he would not touch even water at their houses. He neither agitated for his admission to the section which was hostile to his re-admission, nor attempted to divide the caste on his account.

His eldest brother Laxmidas was formerly secretary and adviser to the son of the Rana of Porbandar before he was installed on the *gadi.* Being out of favour with the Rana, he had lost his job and became a petty pleader in Rajkot and was now a partner of an established lawyer. On his young brother's career he had built high hopes and the anticipation of his brother's successful practice had led him to increase his household expenses. At home he had created some sort of English atmosphere by introducing crockery and such other things. Gandhi added cocoa and oatmeal porridge, completing the Europeanisation of the household by taking to European dress, socks and shoes. He had planned to reform the education of his children and used his sister's son and his own four son's as subjects for his experiments.

But where and how to begin life again? On November 16, 1891, Gandhi applied for enrolment as advocate of the High Court, Bombay. In May 1892 he was allowed to practise in the Kathiawad Agency Courts. But he found it difficult to get any work. He was afraid that Jagmohandas Samaldas, who had favoured him with a loan, might ask for an instalment.[2] Friends in Rajkot advised him to go to Bombay for some time to study Indian Law and to gain experience of work in the High Court. So he went to Bombay and started his household with a Brahmin cook who was as dirty as he was ignorant of his calling.

Gandhi continued his squeamishness and jealousy in respect of his wife and although he intended to teach her to read and write, he observes, lust came in his way and she had to suffer for his weakness in this respect. One day he broke her bangles to bits which were a gift from her mother. He went to the length of sending her back to her parents, and she was quite miserable at this stage of her life with Gandhi. In his old age Gandhi, the Mahatma, however, described the bangle incident and said he broke the bangles 'not out of hate but love-ignorant'![3]

Friends in Bombay told him that he would have to vegetate for about six years. He made it a rule to walk to the High Court. It took him forty-five minutes, and he invariably returned home on foot. He attended the Court daily, but, being unable to follow the cases, he often dozed off in the High Court. Although a briefless barrister, he refused, on principle, to pay a commission to any tout. Yet a case came his way. He made his *debut* in the Small Causes Court on receiving a payment of Rs. 30 as his fees. As he appeared for the defendant, he stood up to cross-examine the plaintiff's witnesses. But his heart sank, in his boots. He sat down, returned the fees to his client and never went to any court in Bombay till he went to South Africa.

It would be interesting to mark a contrast. Unlike Gandhi, Mohamed Ali Jinnah, who became a barrister in 1896 at the age of twenty-one, on his arrival in India, had to face litigation arising out of some transaction done in his name by his father. He conducted and won the case and thus registered his first triumph in the practice of the law.

The only thing Gandhi could do was to draft a memorial gratis for a Muslim of Porbandar. But he could not live in Bombay on drafting memorials without fees. So he applied for the post of a teacher. His application was rejected as he was not a graduate. He wrung his hands in despair. In a reminiscent mood, later, he said: "I had no ambition at all. The only idea was to maintain myself somehow or other and to render some service to the public wherever I was."

COOLING HIS HEELS for six months, Gandhi became tired of his stay in Bombay. The only benefit he reaped in Bombay was the long walks which kept him physically fit. In the city he attended a number of public meetings. He heard a lecture on a pilgrimage to Kashi at the Prarthana Samaj Hall, Bombay. Another benefit he derived there lasted him a lifetime. He met in Bombay Rajchandra or Raychandbhai Ravjibhai Mehta, a young Jain philosopher who became the prop of his spiritual life. He was the son-in-law of Revashankar Mehta, the elder brother of Dr. Pranjivan Mehta. A connoisseur of pearls and diamonds, he was a poet, a man of strong character as well as a religious philosopher. He was deeply absorbed in godly pursuits in the midst of mundane affairs and had a burning passion for self-realization.

No other person influenced Gandhi more profoundly than this religious luminary who was then hardly twenty-five. In his autobiography Gandhi later said that he could not enthrone Raychandbhai as his Guru in his heart though he regarded him as a guide and helper. Raychandbhai, better known as Kavi Rajchandra, profoundly influenced the youth of his generation in Gujarat and created a new spirit particularly among the Jains. Gifted with marvellous powers of memory, teen-age Rajchandra had impressed Sir Charles Sargent, the then Chief Justice of the Bombay High Court, Dr. Peterson, Poet Malbari and several others. Sir Charles wanted Raychandbhai to accompany him to Europe; but he refused to cross the seas and to be 'an animal for show.'[4] He was preparing himself for leading a religious revival.

At last Laxmidas took Gandhi to Rajkot where he set up his legal office. Gandhi's quarrel with his wife was as usual shortlived and he now helped her to make certain changes in their life. As regards the practice of law, he drafted memorials and earned about Rs. 300 a month. He drafted a memorial on behalf of the Rana of Porbandar and succeeded in regaining some of his power and prestige. But unfortunately, like his father, he came into collision with the British Political Agent in Rajkot. In 1892 Laxmidas had been charged with having given wrong counsel while he was secretary and adviser to the Rana of Porbandar before he was installed in the *gadi*. Gandhi, at the instance of his elder brother, though with much reluctance, went to the British Agent to put in a word for his brother.

That officer was a London acquaintance of Gandhi. He did not like interference in his work and asked Gandhi to leave his office instantly. As Gandhi lingered, the Agent asked his peon to eject him out 'with just enough force'. Gandhi fumed and frowned at this dire insult. He threatened the Agent with legal action. But Pherozeshah Mehta, who at that time happened to be in Rajkot, advised him to give up the thought of giving battle to the British Agent and not to resent personal wrongs if he would serve India.[5] So Gandhi rightly restrained his youthful ardour, pocketed the insult and drew in his horns. He learnt the lesson of his life. Fight against authority was smouldering in his blood. His grandfather and father had done it. A Britisher in authority drove the man out, who resolved later to end British rule in India!

Now Gandhi was in a fix. He knew that if he continued his practice in Rajkot, he would find it embarrassing to appear before the English officer whom he had offended. "This shock" Gandhi said, "changed the course of my life."

Just at this point, there came a chance of Gandhi's being sent to the dark continent, A Meman firm from Porbandar inquired of his brother whether Gandhi would go to South Africa to help in a big case Dada Abdulla and Co. was fighting in a Court there. Gandhi saw Abdul Karim Zaveri, the partner of the company.

He told the young barrister that there he would have to instruct their counsel and also to help them in their English correspondence.

Gandhi closed the offer without any bargaining. He was promised first-class return fare and a sum of £105, all found. He was, he felt, going there not so much as a barrister but as a servant of the company. He wanted to leave India as it was disgusting to him to pay commission to touts and the intriguing atmosphere of Kathiawad was stifling to him. "I loved to see," he afterwards said, "fresh fields and pastures anew." So he left India in April 1893 to try his luck in South Africa, leaving in India his wife and two little sons. Destiny was shaping his future. Sir F. C. O. Beaman, retired Judge of the Bombay High Court, who knew Gandhi the young barrister, said in 1925 that Gandhi would never have been a successful barrister.[6]

Gandhi, as mentioned earlier, had said that during these days he had no ambition at all. Although politics was in his blood, he was then not inspired to devote his life to the liberation of his nation as Tilak, Agarkar and Savarkar had done in their youth. The Indian National Congress had met eight times, placed the mild and bare demands of the Indian people before their god-sent and enlightened rulers, and pleaded for them once in a year with the force and prayerfulness of their masterful minds. They sincerely declared that their highest patriotism and best interests demanded the continuation of British rule in India.

Tilak as a leader of the younger generation, scholar and educationist was coming to the forefront in Maharashtra. Ranade's Social Conference was meeting yearly in the Congress Pandal whenever the Congress met. Pherozeshah Mehta, Subramanian lyer and Surendranath Banerjee were the great stalwarts of the Congress.

In Maharashtra, Mahatma Jotirao Phooley led an agitation of the farmers at Junnar to boycott the cultivation of land until Government had given them protection against landlords and money-lenders. Founding the Satya Shodhak Samaj in 1873, Phooley launched a social equality movement to liberate women, the depressed classes and the down-trodden. He was the first Indian to start, in 1848, a girls' school for the untouchables of India, and the first Indian leader to proclaim in modern India the dawn of a new age for the common man. He inspired a, barbers' movement and they refused to shave Hindu widows. He and his lieutenant Lokhande had inaugurated the Indian labour movement in 1884 to voice the grievances of the workers.

Phooley's Satya-Shodhak Samaj (Truth-seeking Society) had

proclaimed war on priests and the other parasites who exploited the ignorant masses. The Mahar workers of the Alibag Municipality had struck work in 1888, and the sweepers employed by the Bombay Municipality had struck work in 1889 'to get their grievances redressed'. At both places they were successful. Jotirao Phooley was the first leader of modern India to receive the title Mahatma in 1888 at the hands of people. His letterheads bore the eternal message of Bharat, 'Truth ultimately prevails'.

On March 16, 1890, an advertisement appeared in the *Indu-prakash*, an Anglo-Vernacular weekly in Bombay, which gives an indication of the difficulties in the field of social reforms in those days. "Wanted an earnest Gujarati-speaking preacher whose duty will be to travel through Gujarat and to induce the various castes to give up the practice of premature marriage and to take legally enforceable pledges in this behalf. The Hindu Social Association of Gujarat undertakes to pay his expenses and to provide a fair remuneration. Native of Gujarat preferred. Apply to Mahipatram Rupram, Esq., C.I.E., Ahmedabad."

These were the political and social conditions of India in general and in particular of the Bombay Presidency which then included Gujarat and most of Maharashtra.

ON ITS VOYAGE to South Africa the steamer put in at Zanzibar for about ten days. Gandhi went on an outing with the Captain accompanied by an Englishman. A pimp took them to some Negro women's quarters. They were each shown into a room. 'Gandhi thanked God that the sight of the prostitute did not move him in the least. He came out as he had gone in. This was the third trial of its kind and he was saved. Towards the close of May 1893 he landed at Durban, the port of Natal.

Although he had been a briefless barrister in India, Gandhi had a due sense of the dignity of his profession and his own importance. He wore a fine frock coat, a top hat, pressed trousers and shining shoes. Beneath the modern dress, he wore his usual Vaishnava necklace of tulsi-beads which his mother had put round his neck out of love, in the belief that it would be conducive to his welfare. He wore also a golden chain with a locket containing pictures of his brother and father. At the dock Gandhi was received by Dada Abdulla, partner of the Dada Abdulla Company.

Natal had a population of about 400,000 zulus and about 40,000 Europeans as against 60,000 indentured, 10,000 ex-indentured and

10,000 free Indians. Slavery had been abolished and so the white men in black Africa could not make the zulus work hard on their plantations. The white men wanted a stable labour force. So they entered into an agreement with the Government of India for the supply of labour. Accordingly, the first batch of indentured labourers came to Natal on November 16, 1860.

The British officers, who negotiated on behalf of the Government of India, were partial to their white brethren in Natal. Naturally they did not make adequate provision to safeguard the interests of the ignorant and illiterate Indian labourers. They were cheated by the recruiting agents. If an indentured labourer left his job, he was liable to be proceeded against in a criminal court and to be imprisoned on conviction. Thus these Indian labourers worked there in a state of semi-slavery. It meant that the indentured labourer was the property of his master.

Indentured labourers were called coolies or *samis* by the Europeans. A coolie means a porter. Sami is a corrupted form of Swami meaning a master; but the Europeans used it as a term of "contempt for the Indians in South Africa. They called Indian lawyers coolie-lawyers and traders coolie-traders. All Indians were treated with scant respect. The Indian Parsis, therefore, called themselves Persians and the Indian Muslims chose to pass themselves off as Arabs! Europeans apologised to the Muslims if they called them coolies. In the courts, the Muslims were allowed to keep their turbans on. But the Hindus who, true to their tradition and to their country, called themselves Indians, had to take off their turbans on entering a court! There were some Christians. Born of indentured labourers, most of them worked as waiters in white hotels.

There was now an agitation started by white colonists in South Africa to restrict the indentured labourers by providing their compulsory return to India at the expiry of their term of service if they did not renew their indenture. By hook or by crook they wanted to make it impossible for the ex-indentured labourers to live as free men in Natal. A minority of the labourers were Tamilians and Telugus and some were North Indians.

The Indian free traders could trade with the indentured, labourers and Negroes. Being frugal and simple, they could undercharge, undersell and underbid the British and Dutch traders. Before 1893, Indians were being hounded out in the Transvaal and in the Orange Free State. These two colonies were Dutch, and they had brought labour for their use from Malaya and Java. In the Crown Colony of Zululand, the Transvaal and the Orange Free State the Indians were not allowed to own land. They could not even use footpaths and pavements. They were required to carry a pass if they had to go out after 9 p.m. The Cape Colony was no better, in this respect.

In Natal the Government had appointed in 1885 an Indian Immigration Commission under Justice Wragg, whose findings revealed that the white men regarded the free Indians as a rival or competitive community in both agricultural and commercial pursuits. The indentured labourers were given free boarding and lodging and their families lived with them.

Dada Abdulla was virtually unlettered, knew a smattering of English for conversational purposes and was fond of discourses on Islamic philosophy. On the second or third day of Gandhi's arrival in Durban, Dada Abdulla took him to the Durban court, introduced him to several lawyers and to some important persons and seated him next to his attorney. The Magistrate kept staring at the new man and finally asked him either to take off his turban or leave the Court. Gandhi preferred to leave the Court rather than remove his turban. This was the first round of insult that he experienced in South Africa.

Gandhi wrote to the press about the incident and defended his wearing of a turban in Court. The matter was discussed in Natal papers, some of which described him as an unwelcome guest. Opposition to authority thus became the first source of publicity for Gandhi. But to avoid further trouble he told Dada Abdulla that he would give up wearing his turban and begin wearing an English hat. Upon this Dada Abdulla, half seriously and half jocularly, said that in that event he would pass for a waiter! And waiter was a contemptuous term because Indian-born Christians, who worked as waiters, too, were not respected in South Africa.

Gandhi made some acquaintances in Durban, Rustomji Ghorkhodoo, a Parsi trader, and Paul, the court interpreter being among them. The case in which Gandhi was to help the lawyers was being fought at Pretoria, the capital of the Transvaal. The rival party was Tyeb Haji Khan Muhammad who was a near relative of Dada Abdulla. They belonged to the same place in India. The clerk of Dada Abdulla explained the case to Gandhi, but the young barrister knew nothing about book-keeping on which the case had much bearing. Gandhi purchased a book on book-keeping and studied it. With detailed instructions from

Dada Abdulla about men, matters and places, Gandhi started for Pretoria on the seventh or eighth day after his arrival.

THE TRAIN REACHED Maritzburg at 9 p.m. It was the capital of Natal. A European entered the compartment in which Gandhi was sitting. He saw that Gandhi was a coloured man and felt that his presence was an outrage on his civility and culture. Going out, he brought in two officials. One of them asked Gandhi to move to the van compartment. Gandhi cooly protested: "I have a first class ticket." They persisted, Gandhi refused. They called a police constable who pitched Gandhi out with his luggage. Yet he refused to go to the van compartment. The train steamed off without him.

Keeping his handbag with him and leaving the other luggage where it was lying, Gandhi sat in a waiting room. The railway authorities took charge of his luggage. It was an extremely cold night. His overcoat was in his suit case, but for fear of being insulted again, he sat shivering in the dark room, At midnight a passenger entered the room and wanted to talk to him. But he was in no mood to talk. In the bitter cold night, he sat quivering with fear and regret. Again it was a man in authority that insulted him!

According to Gandhi, this was the most creative experience in his life. He was afraid for his very life. He said to himself: "What is my duty? Should I go back to India or should I go forward, with God as my helper and face whatever was in store for me?"

Out of that darkness, light came to him in the dark continent. To defy an unjust authority was in his blood. His father and grandfather had defied princes. He decided to stay and suffer rather than be a coward and run back to India. "My nonviolence," said Gandhi later, "began from that date." He passed a wakeful night. He felt carpingly the indignity and insult of apartheid and the colour bar. He would use now his own suffering for righting the wrong, for removing the colour bar. He, therefore, made an unflinching resolve to suffer hardships and brave the situation himself and to take the train to Pretoria.

Gandhi's lifelong obsession for travelling third class probably originated in this incident. It must have perhaps awakened him to the reality of the scorching rigours of untouchability!

Morning came. He sent a long telegram to the General Manager of the Railway and another to Dada Abdulla. The Muslim merchant saw the Railway Manager who justified the conduct of his men, but instructed the station master at Maritzburg to see that Gandhi reached his destination safely. On a telegram from Dada Abdulla, the merchants of Maritzburg saw him at the station and coldly narrated to him their similar humiliating experiences and tale of woes. The next day a berth was reserved for him and he took a 'bedding ticket' too. He then reached Charlestown by train without any further trouble.

The journey between Charlestown and Johannesburg was to be made by a stage-coach, there being no railway connecting these two towns. Gandhi had a ticket for the coach. The conductor of the coach told Gandhi that his ticket was cancelled. Gandhi gave him a suitable answer. He realized that the conductor regarded him as a coolie and so was unwilling, perhaps to avoid unpleasantness with the other passengers, to allow him to sit with the white passengers. There were two seats, one on either side of the coach-box. He asked Gandhi to occupy either and he himself sat inside. Gandhi helplessly accepted the situation.

On the way, at Pardekoph, the conductor felt that he should sit on his usual seat and smoke and enjoy the fresh air. So, coming out, he spread a piece of sacking for Gandhi on the footboard of the coach and asked him to sit at their feet. Gandhi said he would either sit inside or sit where he was already sitting. His refusal angered the conductor who tried to drag him out. The conductor was a strong man. Gandhi was weak; yet he stubbornly clung to the brass rails of the coach. The brute then began both thrashing and dragging him. Gandhi would neither retaliate nor give in. He looked like a man who was determined to suffer. The other passengers were moved to pity. They frankly said that Gandhi was not to blame. At this the ruffian stopped beating him and asked the Hottentot servant to sit on the footboard and he himself occupied the seat on the other side of the coach-box.

The coach started, but the conductor all the while looked at Gandhi with murderous eyes and swore at him. The poor barrister feared that he would not reach Standerton, the next destination, alive. In his heart of hearts he was praying to God while the coach was on the move. He was, however, not thrashed any more on the way. He reached Standerton safely. He was received by Dada Abdulla's men as directed by him. At the request of Gandhi, the agent of the Coach Company at Standerton promised to give him a seat along with other passengers and added that the manager of that coach to Johannesburg would be a different man. Accordingly he was given a good seat the next day, and he reached Johannesburg safely at night.

At Johannesburg the man who came to receive Gandhi could not recognise him. The Grand National Hotel in the city would not accept him. So he asked a cabman to take him to the friend of Dada Abdulla. He narrated to the merchant his recent experiences; but the latter only laughed heartily. He said it was not a country where a man like Gandhi should stay. They could live there because, for making money, they did not mind pocketing insults.

Next day Gandhi appeared before the station master of Johannesburg in faultless English dress, wearing his frock coat, top hat and neck-tie. He talked with Gandhi sympathetically and gave him a first-class railway ticket. But Gandhi would have to travel, he warned him, at his own risk and if any trouble arose during the journey, he should not involve the station master's name in the affair. Gandhi agreed. The train started with Gandhi and a European passenger in a first class compartment. At Germiston the guard entered and asked Gandhi to move to the third class. Gandhi refused. The European passenger intervened. He told the guard that he had no objection to travelling with a man who held a first-class ticket and asked Gandhi to remain where he was. Upon this the guard muttered: "If you want to travel with a coolie, what do I care?" And he went away. Gandhi was saved further humiliation. Without further trouble he reached Pretoria.

LIGHTS WERE BURNING dim in Pretoria station. Gandhi wanted to ask the ticket collector whether he could direct him to a hotel. But he half feared, a rebuff. Nevertheless, he courteously made inquiries with him. But the ticket collector was not of much help. Seeing him in a hopeless predicament, an American Negro cheered him up and took him to a hotel run by an American. The proprietor said he had no colour prejudice and accepted Gandhi on condition that he would eat in his room and not in the dining room where his European customers had their meals. This condition was, however, waived as the other customers did not object to Gandhi having his meals in the dining room. Gandhi had a hearty meal there soon after his arrival.

The next morning Gandhi met in the city A. W. Baker, the attorney of Dada Abdulla. He received Gandhi warmly. The young barrister explained to Baker as much as he could about himself. The attorney reassuringly said 'that he had not much work for the young barrister. The case was a prolonged and complex one. So he would ask his assistance only to the extent of getting some necessary information from time to time.

The white men in the land of gold were men of iron heads and stony hearts. The Transvaal Government had levied on Asiatics a tax of £3 as registration fee per head for entry into the Transvaal and denied them the right to own land or to vote and compelled them to live in locations. The Government forbade them to move outdoors after 9 p.m. Gandhi began to study the social, political and economic condition of Indians in the Transvaal. He met Tyeb Haji Khan Muhammad who was a public figure among the Indians in Pretoria. Gandhi decided to organise the Indians and asked for his help in the matter.

With Tyeb Haji's help Gandhi called and addressed a meeting of all Indians in Pretoria. As a well-wisher of the community, Gandhi made his first public speech. He appealed to them to observe truthfulness in their business dealings. According to the business community, truth was a matter of religion but inconsistent with business which was a practical affair. The young barrister told them that their responsibility to be truthful was all the greater in a foreign land. He drew their attention to the insanitary condition of their houses and surroundings and emphasised the necessity of personal hygiene. He impressed upon them the importance of the English language in their business dealings and asked them to learn English. It was no wonder that he taught English to a Muslim barber, a Muslim clerk and a Hindu shopkeeper who responded to his suggestion. Gandhi now knew virtually every Indian in Pretoria.

The success of the first meeting encouraged Gandhi to hold similar weekly or monthly meetings and emboldened him to make the acquaintance of Jacobus de Wet, the British Agent, in Pretoria who had shown some sympathy for the Indians. The railway authorities also agreed to issue first and second class tickets to Indians who were properly dressed.

It was unlikely for a man like Gandhi to meet with insulting behaviour in Pretoria. Through a common friend he happened to know the State Attorney Dr. Karuse. They both turned out to be barristers of the same Inn. Dr. Karuse gave Gandhi a letter authorising him to go out of doors, if he so desired, even after 9 p.m. without police interference. Gandhi always went out for a walk along President Street in which President Kruger lived. Indians were not allowed to use the footpath. One day while Gandhi was going out for a walk, the police before the President's house, without even asking him to leave the footpath, pushed him and kicked him into the street. Gandhi was dismayed. His Quaker friend Michael Coates, who happened to be passing by, pressed him to proceed against the police. But Gandhi refused to do so as he had made it a rule not to go to court in respect of his personal grievances. It was, Coates replied, just like Gandhi, but the Quaker wanted to teach the police a lesson. All the same Gandhi never went walking again on that street. The incident created a deeper sympathy in him for the Indians of South Africa.

One A. C. Pillay wrote a letter to the *Transvaal Advertiser* bringing this incident to the notice of the public. The *Natal Advertiser*, a European daily in Durban, reproduced the letter with comments on it. Gandhi wrote to the *Natal Advertiser* that he was the unfortunate Indian barrister who was pushed off the foot-path, not Pillay. After two days Gandhi replied to the *Natal Advertiser* which had, in a leading article, described Indian merchants in South Africa as "the wily wretched Asiatic traders, the real canker that is eating into the very vitals of the community, these parasites who live a semi-barbaric life".[7]

The young defender of the Indian community in a succinct reply said that if no beer, no tobacco, no ornamental walking stick, no golden watch chain, no luxuriously fitted sitting-rooms, be a semi-barbaric life,[8] the Indian traders must plead guilty to the charge. No Indian merchant, Gandhi proceeded, had been imprisoned for theft or robbing. Their simplicity, their total abstinence from intoxicants, their peaceful and above all their business-like and frugal habits which should serve as a recommendation, were really at the bottom of all the white contempt and hatred for the poor Indian traders.

In October 1893 Gandhi wrote a letter to the *Natal Advertiser*[9] informing its readers that there was no possibility of Indians swamping the British vote. Refuting the charge that the Indians were semi-barbarians, he cited the glory of the rule of Akbar and the land system introduced by Todarmal. He stated also that some Indians were working as judges and one of the Indians was a Member of the British Parliament. He asked his readers whether these facts did not indicate the existence of an Indian civilization.

Gandhi's enthusiasm for vegetarianism was not cooled. On the contrary, it was dominating his mind. Early in the year 1894, he wrote to *The Vegetarian*, London, about his experiments in vital diet. This theory of vital food was originally propounded by A. F. Hills, Chairman of the Vegetarian Society. It prescribed foods consisting of fruit, grain, nuts and pulses which provided vitality and energy.

Gandhi's experiment lasted eleven days. As a result of the experiment, he felt very weak and his teeth began to ache. He gave up the experiment as it had failed. The reason, he observed, which led him to try "vital food", was its extreme simplicity. One could do without cooking, avoid uncleanness and carry one's food about in travelling. In such a country, as South Africa, vital food, he thought, would be ideal food.

CHAPTER IV

Christian Influence

WHILE GANDHI WAS gaining experience as a lawyer under Dada Abdulla's attorney and was educating himself to express public grievances and to lead the Indians in Pretoria, he was learning a most valuable lesson in his life in another field. His association with Christian men and missionaries kindled his religious spirit, and the religious quest began to be a dominant feature of his life.

Dada Abdulla's attorney A. W. Baker, under whom Gandhi was working, was a Christian preacher and a religious zealot. He had built a church at his own expense, and with his co-workers he prayed every day in it for a few minutes for peace and light. It was his belief that unless one accepted Jesus as the only Son of God and the saviour of mankind, it was impossible for one to find eternal peace. He prevailed on Gandhi to attend the noon prayers at the church.

Gandhi, as a young man of twenty-five, knew little of Hinduism, and since he had to work under Baker, he yielded to his wish. He decided to go to church, but made up his mind to make a study of comparative religion and not to embrace any other religion unless he had understood his own. He went to the church of Baker and prayed with him with great hopes. Baker introduced him to Christians of all denominations such as Quakers, Roman Catholics, Protestants and Plymouth Brethren. Michael Coates was a frank and staunch Quaker, and he, took Gandhi to other Christians for religious discourses. As all of them intended to convert Gandhi, they provided him with many books on Christianity. Among the several books he read, he found Dr. Parker's *Commentary* morally stimulating, Butler's

Analogy profound but difficult and Pearson's *Many Infallible Proofs* not very effective. He avidly read about eighty books on religion and philosophy which dominated his mind for a number of years.

One day the Quaker friend Coates impatiently expressed his desire to break the necklace of tulsi-beads which Gandhi wore as a memento of his mother. Respect for the memory of his mother made Gandhi overcome his usual meekness. He did not allow Coates to have his way. Coates then asked him if he really believed in the religious efficacy of the necklace. Gandhi replied that he did not believe he would come to any harm if he gave up wearing it; but he was not prepared to part with the gift which his mother had given him. No matter, the Quaker continued, whether there was some truth in other religions, salvation was impossible for Gandhi unless he accepted the Christian faith. The Plymouth Brethren said that Jesus was the only sinless Son of God. Gandhi boldly answered that he did not seek redemption from the consequences of sin, but from the very thought of sin.

Baker took Gandhi to the conference of Keswick Christians which was held at Wellington in April 1894. He listened to discourses on the efficacy of prayer with unbiased attention and assured Baker that nothing could prevent him from accepting Christianity if his inner voice gave him such a call.

This is the third phase of his religious development when Christian missionaries made persistent efforts to convert him.

Finding himself amidst Christian preachers, missionaries and zealots, Gandhi thought it would be wise to correspond with his brilliant guide and philosopher Raychandbhai, The Jain philosopher answered his questions and resolved his doubts about his religious quest. That provided proper ballast to Gandhi's sinking faith. The outcome of these discussions was that Gandhi refused to believe that Jesus was the only incarnate Son of God. If Jesus was like God, or God Himself, he observed, then all men were like God and could be God. Furthermore, according to Christianity, only human beings had souls and not other living beings; but Gandhi believed that all other beings also had souls. He regarded Jesus Christ as a martyr, an embodiment of sacrifice and a divine teacher, but not as the most perfect man ever born. His reason refused to believe that Jesus by his death or blood reduced the sins of the world.

Gandhi later came to believe that philosophically, there was nothing extraordinary in Christian principles. From the point of view of sacrifice the Hindus greatly surpassed Christians. The Christian belief that God was a Christian and He had preserved heaven for Christians alone, Gandhi felt, must assail any man of ordinary common sense. Many such doubts assailed him. Nor did he believe that the Vedas were the inspired word of God. If those sacred works were inspired, why not, he asked, the Bible and the Koran too? He read also the translation of the Koran.

The Muslim with whom Gandhi was associated tried to convert him to Islam, but failed. No Christian priest or preacher ever entertained thoughts of converting men like Ranade, Tilak, Vivekanand, Telang, Surendranath, Tagore, Lajpatrai and Savarkar when they were young. Gandhi's love for the association of Christian friends and his ignorance of his own religion which perhaps bordered on inferiority complex, were responsible more than his meekness for their attempt to convert him.

Gandhi had also corresponded with Edward Maitland, who sent him *The Perfect Way* and *The New Interpretation of the Bible*. But the book that had an abiding influence on Gandhi was Leo Tolstoy's *The Kingdom of God Is Within You* which was published in 1893 as a sequel to *What I Believe*. The greatness of the book lay in the fact that its author had given a new meaning to Christ's precept: 'Resist not him that is evil but whosoever smiteth thee on thy right cheek turn to him the other also'. Tolstoy meant by this that it laid down the law of non-resistance to evil by violence.

Tolstoy preaches abandonment of physical violence as a means of settling human affairs. As soon as Tolstoy began to repeat the 'real message of Christ' and appealed to the world to apply it to everyday life, the precept attracted both scorn and denunciation.

Tolstoy sings the glory of William Llyod Garrison (1805-79), who was a famous American champion of the emancipation of the Negroes. Garrison had founded in 1835 a society called the 'Society for Non-Resistance' in open acceptance of the doctrine of non-resistance to evil by violence. He was non-resistant and a believer in moral persuasion. A spearhead of American abolitionism he called through his weekly *The Liberator*, for immediate abolition of slavery and the enfranchisement of all American Negroes and propagated his doctrine of non-resistance. After his death, Adam Ballou, another American preacher, propagated this doctrine of non-resistance for fifty years and died in 1890.

Tolstoy's book overwhelmed Gandhi. He felt possessed by it.

Gandhi became a disciple of Tolstoy and learnt many things from him. Tolstoy was not only a great Russian novelist, but also a mystic, a religious enthusiast, and an ardent believer in non-violence. Small in stature, he had a broad, flat nose, small grey eyes and thick lips, and though ugly, his face revealed the strength of his spirituality. Tolstoy rejected the divinity of Christ. According to him, love, self-denial and the returning of good for evil was the essence of Christianity.

In his youth Tolstoy had taken to gambling, drinking and dissipation, had contracted syphilis and had had a flock of children. He later renounced earthly pleasures, made boots which nobody could wear, and took to dressing like a peasant. Becoming a total abstainer and a thorough vegetarian, he left home to live among peasants, fetched water and washed his own clothes. Tolstoy was grieved to find that the Russians called Napoleon a great man. He came to think that manual labour was nobler than mental labour; and that love between the sexes a worthless animal desire.

After becoming a disciple of Tolstoy, Gandhi was perhaps again assailed by doubts. So he wrote to Raychandbhai, his guide and philosopher, plying him with a series of questions on religion, God, the Vedas, the Gita, the soul and rebirth. Replying to his queries Raychandbhai opined that no other religion had the subtle and profound thought of Hinduism, its vision of the soul or its charity. These replies from Raychandbhai and the Indian books on religion such as *Panchikaran*, *Mumukshu*, *Prakaran* of *Yogavasishtha*, *Maniratnamala* and *Shad-darshana Samuchchaya*, which he sent Gandhi, decidedly gave a turn to Gandhi's thinking, enabling him to escape the net of Christians around him and saving him from the Christian clergymen who tried to convert him.

Later, in a reminiscent mood, Gandhi said: "There was a time when I was wavering between Hinduism and Christianity. When I recovered my balance of mind, I felt that to me salvation was possible only through the Hindu religion and my faith in Hinduism grew deeper and more enlightened".[1]

THE MAIN WORK for which Gandhi had come to Pretoria was progressing. With great diligence and study he prepared the case. His knowledge of book-keeping and his ability in translation improved greatly. He gave his days to reading of the law and to looking up cases and consulted the senior attorney Leonard. His advice was that if Gandhi took care of the facts of the case, the law would take care of itself. Gandhi dived deep into the facts of the Abdulla case. The result was that he now found an entirely new light. He not only realised the dictum 'that facts are three-fourths of the law and facts mean truth;' but was now convinced that the facts were in favour of Dada Abdulla.

The suit was for £40,000. It was full of intricacies concerning accounts. Both parties had engaged the best attorneys and counsel. Gandhi felt sorry that both parties were wasting money and time. He, therefore, tried to befriend both parties and to bring them together. With all his heart he struggled to bring about a compromise. Tyeb Sheth agreed. An arbitrator was appointed. The case was argued before him and Dada Abdulla won, Gandhi made sure that Tyeb Sheth was not harassed to pay the money at once. He fixed up instalments and the suit ended well. Thus the long law-suit ended.

Gandhi now returned to Durban sometime in April 1894 to sail for India. At the farewell party held at Sydenham by Dada Abdulla, someone put a copy of the *Natal Mercury* into Gandhi's hands. It contained a news item under the caption 'Indian Franchise'. The Natal Legislative Assembly was about to introduce a Bill to disfranchise the Indians in Natal. They were being deprived of what little rights they had. Gandhi read the report to the traders and those present and explained to them its meaning. He suggested that the Indians should strenuously resist the Bill.

The Indians present at the meeting said they were helpless and unlettered people who would not be strong enough to give battle to their oppressors without his help. The other Indians, they said to the surprise of Gandhi, being Christians, would not help them. So they urged him to stay on.

And 'Gandhibhai' agreed to stay on for a month. A fateful decision indeed!

Gandhi wanted funds to start his work. Money would be necessary for telegrams and printing, petitions and memorials, travel and the purchase of law books. The fight for self-respect began and Gandhi found himself extending his stay in South Africa.

"Thus", Gandhi said, "God laid the foundation of my life in South Africa and sowed the seed of the fight for national self-respect".

By now two Indians, B. G. Tilak and Swami Vivekanand, had won international fame. Tilak published his thesis *Orion* in October 1893 and raised the reputation of Indian scholarship and research in the world of learning. In September 1893 Vivekanand unfurled in Philadelphia at the Parliament of Religions the banner of Hindu religion and Vedanta and impressed the world with its message. The former was acclaimed, as a scholar and the latter was applauded as a saint all over the world. In India the one was hailed as scholar-patriot and the other was acclaimed as saint-patriot.

CHAPTER V

The Leader

GANDHI STARTED A campaign for civil and political rights in Natal. He was hardly twenty-five. A meeting was held under the presidentship of Haji Mohammed Haji Dada who was a well-known public figure in Natal. The meeting resolved to offer opposition to the Franchise Bill. Gandhi at once drafted a telegram and sent it in the name of Haji Mohammed to the Speaker of the Natal Assembly, the Prime Minister Sir John Robinson and Attorney-General Harry Escombe, urging them to postpone consideration of the Franchise Bill till the Indian petition was submitted. As a result of this telegraphic appeal, further reading of the Bill was postponed by two days. This gladdened the hearts of the Natal Indians.

On June 28, 1891, Gandhi submitted a petition signed by five-hundred Indians to the Natal Legislative Assembly, opposing the Bill. It was the contention of the Government of Natal that the Indians were not fit for the exercise of franchise and in their own land they had never exercised it. In the petition[1] to the Assembly, Gandhi drew the attention of the Assembly to Sir Henry Sumner Maine's *Village Communities* and pointed out how Indians had been familiar with representative institutions almost from time immemorial. He explained in it the meaning of the word *Panchayat* which, he said, had been a household word throughout India. There were 892 Local Boards in India and the Mysore State had an Assembly in 1891.

To support his viewpoint Gandhi quoted Sir George Birdwood, Sir Thomas Munro who was sometime Governor of Madras, and Professor Max-Muller on the characteristics and culture of India and fervently appealed to the Assembly either to reconsider the decision or to appoint a Commission to inquire into the question whether the Indians were fit to exercise the privilege of franchise.

The next day Gandhi waited in deputation on Sir John Robinson and asked for a week's time to present the case exhaustively. He led a deputation to the Governor of Natal and urged him not to give sanction to the Bill. He wrote to Dadabhai Naoroji, then a Member of the British Parliament, requesting him to intervene on behalf of the Indians in Natal and added that in ten years the position of Indians in South Africa would be intolerable. He petitioned the Legislative Council to reject the Bill, but it received the third reading on July 7 in the Council. He, therefore, petitioned the Governor not to despatch the Bill to the Imperial Government for Royal Assent till the petition of the Indians had been submitted.

A thrill of enthusiasm passed through the Indians of Natal. It was a new kind of experience. Volunteers, supporters and workers were busy collecting funds, doing copying work and obtaining signatures to the petition. They worked hard, ungrudgingly and without remuneration. Numerous meetings were held. Dada Abdulla's house turned into a caravanserai and centre of social workers. Gandhi worked untiringly and energized his co-workers to get the signatures within a fortnight. And on July 17, Gandhi submitted a monster petition signed by 10,000 Indians, addressed to Lord Ripon, the Secretary of State for Colonies.

A thousand copies of the petition were printed for circulation and distribution. The petition acquainted the Indian public and the British newspapers with conditions in Natal. *The Times of India* and the *The Times*, London, supported the stand of the Indians in Natal.

Young Gandhi was a practical leader and a plodding propagandist. He soon realised that mere petitioning was not enough. A permanent organization was essential for educating the Indian opinion. It would give vent to their feelings, make an impression on the Natal Government and the Imperial Government, and above all carry on a sustained agitation against the Franchise Bill. So, with the assistance of his co-workers, he established the Natal Indian Congress in Durban on August 22, 1894. He who paid five shillings a month was enrolled as a member. Gandhi was its Secretary and Abdulla Haji Adam, its President.

These workers established another organization called the Colonial-born Indians Association under the auspices of the

Natal Indian Congress. It served to ventilate their needs and grievances and served also as a debating society. Members spoke or read papers on different subjects. They drew the attention of the members to the importance of domestic sanitation and personal hygiene. They inculcated in them the love of their motherland as well.

After doing this tremendous job of agitation and organization, Gandhi said his promise to work for a month in Natal had been fulfilled. His co-workers and supporters urged him to extend his stay. But he refused to remain there at public expenses. He said if he chose to stay on, he would have to set up a household befitting a barrister-at-law. The leaders, merchants and workers agreed to entrust their legal work to him, and about twenty merchants gave him retainers for a year. Gandhi then applied to the Supreme Court of Natal for admission as an advocate. As the application was to be submitted through a member of the Bar, it was submitted through Harry Escombe, who was Attorney-General and also legal adviser to Dada Abdulla Company.

By now Gandhi had become a well-known Indian leader who had attracted the attention of the Colony and especially the European section of it. In the Supreme Court his application was, therefore, opposed by the Law Society of Natal. But the Chief Justice admitted his application saying that "the law makes no distinction between white and coloured people".

When Gandhi took the oath in the court, he was asked to remove his turban. He obeyed. Naturally Dada Abdulla and Gandhi's coworkers were displeased with him. Gandhi was nettled by their arguments. So he replied that he had preserved his strength for fighting bigger battles!

This act was indeed a come-down prognosticating a slippery tendency. Thirty years later Gandhi tried to explain it away, but the justification was not very convincing.

GANDHI SETTLED DOWN in Durban to continue public work and to practise as lawyer. In his office, drawing room and bedroom he had hung up the photographs of his father. His clerk was a Tamilian. During the first month Gandhi appeared in the Gopi Maharaj case and won it. He was successful in transferring the indenture of a labourer Balasundaram from one European employer to another. His old boss had beaten him up and broken two of his teeth. Gandhi had lodged a complaint with a magistrate, but on a compromise he withdrew it. The labourers were happy to note this. They felt assured that Gandhi was there to defend their rights and champion their cause.

Gandhi took much interest in Esoteric Christianity. What is more, he became an agent for selling its literature. In November 1894 he advertised[2] its books in the *Natal Mercury* under his signature as agent for the Esoteric Christian Union and the London Vegetarian Society. As in London, so in Durban and Pretoria, the influence of Christianity on Gandhi at this stage was profound. So he enthusiastically acted as an agent for the spread of Christianity. And the more he entered into deliberations and discussions with Christian priests, preachers and friends, the more they hoped for his conversion. He thus gave them a handle to bring pressure on him to yield to their pleadings.

With the object of spreading the mission of the Esoteric Christian Union, Gandhi as its agent recommended the books written by Dr. Anna Kingsford and Edward Maitland to those who found that present-day materialism and all its splendour was insufficient for the needs of their soul. Under the dazzling and bright surface of modern civilization, he observed, there was much contrary to what one expected and that modern luxuries afforded no relief.[3] Two months later he again advertised the books of the Esoteric Christian Union in the *Natal Advertiser*. These were the seeds of anti-materialism and anti-modern civilization that sprouted vigorously in his *Hind Swaraj* and his future work in India.

It seems that Gandhi's Muslim boyhood friend Sheikh Mehtab had doggedly followed him to Natal. Gandhi's infatuation for Mehtab had completely blinded him to his friend's weaknesses. His relations with this evil genius, it seems, were closer than those of a friend. Vicious as he was, Mehtab soon turned Gandhi's residence into a place for prostitutes to visit when Gandhi was away in his office. He poisoned Gandhi's ears against his clerk who ultimately left his master. One day Mehtab was found with a prostitute in Gandhi's house. Instantly Gandhi drove him out. He was at last relieved from the coils of an evil influence which had led him astray in his boyhood and had been dogging his footsteps for years.

Gandhi's work of issuing circulars and writing letters to the press and to public men was going on unabated. In December 1894 he wrote an 'Open Letter' to the Members of the Assembly and Council of Natal. Appealing to them to consider the disabilities the Indians were suffering, he requested them to mould public opinion so that both the communities might live peacefully. He did so not from selfish motives or from a spirit of self-aggrandizement. He humbly requested them to state "whether they were going to regard the Indian as a despicable being in the colony and whether the treatment they gave him was in accordance with British traditions, or with their ideals of justice and morality or with the principles of Christianity.

In support of his statement that the Hindus were a civilised race, Gandhi cited the opinions of William Hunter, Arthur Schopenhauer, Andrew Carnegie, Goethe, Victor Hugo, F. Pincott and others on the philosophy and religion of the Hindus.

The facts in Gandhi's statement were admitted by some newspapers and contradicted by none. Commenting on it, the *Star*, the leading paper in Johannesburg, said "Mr. Gandhi writes forcibly, moderately and well. He has himself suffered some slight measure of injustice since he came into the colony, but that fact does not seem to have coloured his sentiment".[5] The *Natal Mercury*, the Government organ, observed that Gandhi wrote with calmness and moderation and that he was as impartial as anyone could expect him to be. The Indian National Congress, at its tenth session at Madras, in December 1894, passed a resolution entreating Her Majesty's Government to grant the prayer of Indians in South African Colonies by turning down the Bill of the Colonial Government which aimed at disfranchising them.

In April 1895 Gandhi visited the Trappist Monastery near Durban. There he noted that vegetarianism was practised from the spiritual point of view and was much impressed by it. Gandhi's propaganda and pamphlets had a desirable effect in India. Towards the middle of 1895, the Natal Government sent a deputation to the Governor-General of India to urge him to agree to a poll tax of £25. The Natal Indian Congress protested against this, agitated and appealed to the British and Indian Governments not to approve of it. The Viceroy, therefore, disapproved it and reduced it to £3. Besides the indentured labourer and his wife, every Indian boy over 16 and every Indian girl over 13 was to be taxed when the income of every labourer was not more than 14 shillings a month. This was an atrocity unheard of in any other country. This £3 tax remained an open sore for many years. The Natal Indian Congress tried to cure it and later had to prescribe a drastic remedy for it.

On August 11, 1895, Gandhi addressed a long memorial to Joseph Chamberlain, Colonial Secretary, objecting to the imposition of £3 as licence fee. He also requested Dadabhai Naoroji to intervene. Dadabhai led a deputation to the Colonial Secretary. Thereupon Chamberlain conveyed to the Natal Government his "refusal to sanction the Franchise Bill. Gandhi published two more pamphlets, *The Indian Franchise*, and *An Appeal to Every Briton in South Africa.*

About this time Gandhi read Tolstoy's *Gospels in Brief* and his other books which made an indelible impression on his mind about universal love. It may be mentioned here that while he was carrying on propaganda against the Natal Government he applied for an appointment as a Gujarati interpreter[7] in the Natal Court. It seems he was not appointed.

The Natal Government again submitted in November 1895 a fresh Franchise Bill to the Colonial Secretary and introduced it in April 1896 in its modified form, depriving the natives of other countries of the franchise who did not enjoy parliamentary franchise in their own countries. Gandhi, therefore, again cabled to Chamberlain and the British Committee of the Indian National Congress against accepting the Bill or any alteration thereto till the Indian memorial was presented.

The Natal Legislative Assembly passed the Bill on May 13, 1896. Immediately after this, Gandhi waited in deputation on the British Agent in Pretoria requesting the Government to bear the cost of the test case the Indians were planning to lodge against the Law 3 of 1885. Gandhi was in contact with the leaders of the Indian National Congress. It protested in December 1895 against the disabilities sought to be imposed on Indian settlers in South Africa and earnestly appealed to the British Government and the Government of India to guard "the interests of those settlers as they were British subjects."

It may be noted here that the basis of Gandhi's argument was the Indians were British subjects and so they were entitled to the rights of citizenship including equality before the law with others in a British Colony. Gandhi's untiring energy, his boundless capacity for work and his deep love for his countrymen were seen in this struggle. He was, however, an avowed loyalist at that time and had infinite faith in the British Government, the British Empire and the Government of India. His mission was supported by the British Government as well as the Indian Government, and leading newspapers like, *The Times*, London, and *The Times of India* because he fought for the rights of 'British Indians' as a devoted son of the British Empire.

Gandhi partly played the role of a patriotic Indian leader and partly that of a loyalist. He was neither a staunch patriot nor a supporter of all humanity in as much as he took no notice of the poverty and indignity under which the Negroes and other oppressed communities in South Africa were labouring, though he may have expressed at that time some lip sympathy for the Negroes.

The Christian missionaries, who had influenced him in religious matters, were the supporters of his political stand because he was a loyalist. His Muslim clients and colleagues had a preponderance in his organization and some influence on his mental make-up. This aspect of his leadership was unique in that no other Hindu leader had started his public work with Muslims as his supporters. Their love of identity as a separate community was reflected in their letter welcoming the New Governor of Natal. In their letter the Muslims said that the members of the Mohammedan[6] and Indian community welcomed him. They were thus Muslims first and separate from the Indian community.

Gandhi had now established a fairly good legal practice. After his incessant agitational work, he was granted leave for six months. On May 26, 1896, he was commissioned by twenty representative men and institutions to represent the grievances of the Indians in South Africa before the Indian authorities, public men and public bodies in India. On June 4, 1896, the Tamil and Gujarati Indians of Durban along with other communities met in the Congress Hall and presented him with an address under the presidentship of Dada Abdulla. In reply Gandhi thanked them for their kindness and asked them to show an interest in the common purposes of the Natal Indian Congress by deeds and not mere words.

Gandhi then sailed for India on June 5, by the *s. s. Pongola*, studying Tamil and Telugu during the journey. He landed at Calcutta on July 4, 1896, and took the train for Bombay.

THE TRAIN STOPPED for a quarter of an hour at Allahabad. Gandhi went out to enjoy a drive in the city. Purchasing there some medicines, he returned to the station and found that the train had left and his luggage was left on the platform.

Gandhi utilized the day in furthering the cause he was championing. He saw Chesney, editor of *The Pioneer*, and requested him to do some minimum justice to the cause of the Indians in South Africa. But the editor frankly told him that, he would give due weight to the view-point of the white Colonists.

On reaching Rajkot on July 9, 1896, Gandhi started writing a pamphlet which he named *The Grievances of the British Indians*. After a month's ceaseless work, he published it at Rajkot on August 14. He took the help of the children in the locality in posting the pamphlet, promising to give them the used stamps he had collected. One thousand copies of the pamphlet were posted to public men, institutions and newspapers. The *Pioneer* was the first to notice the pamphlet editorially.

The pamphlet was called *Green Pamphlet* because its covers were green. It had no shades of red, yet it proved to be a red rag to the Europeans in South Africa.

In this *Green Pamphlet* Gandhi shrewdly gave a subdued picture of the grievances of the Indians. The language was moderate. It was a summary of the several petitions, memorials, circulars, and leaflets he had issued to the authorities of Natal and the authorities in London and in Calcutta, then the capital of India. In it he observed: "There is rooted prejudice against the Indians; sufferance is the badge of the Indians, and colonists' hatred has crystallized in the legislation. The law, many a time, is used as an engine of oppression. There the lavatories are marked 'Natives and Asiatics'. The whites describe an Indian as a thing black and lean, the Asiatic dirt to be heartily cursed. The Indians are British subjects and in a British colony. In future the presence of Indians might become an impossibility there. The goal of the Natal Government is not merely disfranchisement. Their object is total extinction of the Indians. They are compelled to live in separate localities. The railway officials treat the Indians as beasts".

The remedy? The pamphlet said: "Our method in South Africa, is to conquer this hatred by love".

Meantime, plague broke out in Bombay, A committee was appointed to take precautionary measures in Rajkot. Gandhi worked on the committee, which launched a campaign for cleanliness of the latrines. He found dirty latrines in a rich locality, huge heaps of refuse behind a temple and, surprisingly, the houses and utensils of the poor untouchables clean and shining. This was the first visit of Gandhi to a locality of the untouchables.

On September 11, Gandhi met Justice Mahadev Govind Ranade and Justice Badruddin Tyabji in Bombay in connection with his pamphlet. Ranade and Tyabji were sympathetic, but directed him to Phirozeshah Mehta who arranged a meeting for the purpose. Gandhi's sister Raliatbehn's husband was seriously ill.

So he took his ailing brother-in-law to Rajkot to nurse him. Unfortunately he died. Kasturbai consoled and helped Raliatbehn in the funeral rites. Gandhi could not wait some more days for the funeral rites to be completed.

Just at this time Reuter cabled from London to Durban a brief summary of Gandhi's '*Green Pamphlet*'. The cable appeared in Natal newspapers on September 14, 1896. Reuter's report said: "A pamphlet published in India declares that the Indians in Natal are robbed and assaulted and treated like beasts, and are unable to obtain redress. *The Times of India* advocates an inquiry into these allegations". This news appeared in Natal newspapers, and it ignited a spark in South Africa. As a violent reaction to the report of Reuter, the colonists established on September 18, 1896, the European Protection Association at Maritzburg to endeavour to further reform the laws regulating the introduction of Asiatics into the colony and to have the Australian laws regarding immigration made applicable to Natal.

The *Natal Mercury*, however, said in its issue of September 18, 1896: "Mr. Gandhi, on his part and on behalf of his countrymen, has done nothing that he is not entitled to do, and from his point of view the principle he is working for is an honourable and a legitimate one. He is within his rights and so long as he acts in a straightforward manner, he cannot be blamed nor interfered with. So far as we know, he has always done so, and his latest pamphlet, we cannot honestly say, is an unfair statement of the case from his point of view. Reuter's cable is a gross exaggeration of Mr. Gandhi's statement. He enumerates only a number of grievances, but these by no means justify anyone in stating that his pamphlet declares that the Indians in Natal are robbed and assaulted and treated like beasts, and are unable to obtain redress." [7]

The *Natal Advertiser* of the same date said: "A perusal of Mr. Gandhi's pamphlet, recently published in Bombay, leads to the conclusion that the telegraphic description of its objects and contents was considerably exaggerated."[8]

From Rajkot Gandhi returned to Bombay to address a meeting. On the previous day Pherozeshah Mehta had asked him to write out his speech. At the meeting which was held on September 26 at the Sir Cowasji Jehangir Institute, Gandhi began reading his speech. All the while he trembled and felt nervous. His voice failed. His old friend Keshavrao Deshpande stood up to read Gandhi's speech, but the audience clamoured for D. E.

Vacha. So Vacha read it. The speech dealt fully with the grievances of the Indians in South Africa.

Gandhi was fortunate in having Pherozeshah Mehta, the lion of Bombay, to occupy the chair. The importance of the meeting was thereby doubly heightened. The question of grievances, Gandhi said in his written speech, affected the future well-being of the Indians in South Africa. The feeling of hatred towards Indians was encouraged by the African newspapers and was connived at, even encouraged by, the legislators. "We," he appealed in the end, "are hemmed in on all sides in South Africa. We are yet infants. We have a right to appeal to you for protection."

In Poona Gandhi met Gokhale, Tilak and Bhandarkar and went to Madras to address a meeting. Meanwhile, he had tried to persuade some lawyers to go to Natal with him. F. S. Taleyarkhan was one of them. Gandhi sincerely hoped that Taleyarkhan would be able to join him in Natal and added that it was a cause worth fighting for. This appeal was in conformity with a promise Gandhi had made at a meeting held at Durban on October 1, 1895, that he would endeavour to persuade a number of good Indian barristers to come to Natal. He made three attempts to induce barristers to go to South Africa but in vain. On the contrary, his friend Pestonji Padshah tried to dissuade him from returning to South Africa. But to Gandhi 'to die performing duty was no ill'.

The Natal Agent-General had denied the charges underlined in Reuter's message. So Gandhi asserted in a letter to *The Times of India* his statement that railway and tram-car officials treated Indians as beasts. He also wrote to Gokhale to ask some questions about it in the Imperial Council at Calcutta. Gandhi reached Madras and met G. Subrahmaniam Aiyar, editor of the *Hindu*, and G. Parameshwaran Pillay, editor of the *Madras Standard*, and other public leaders such as Bhashyam lyengar and Eardley Norton.

At Madras Gandhi entered his remark in the visitor's book when he visited the Hindu Theological High School on october 26, 1896. "Being a Gujarati Hindu myself," he remarked, "I feel proud to know that this institution was started by a Gujarati gentleman... I only wish that such institutions will crop up all over India and be the means of preserving the Aryan religion in its purity."[9]

Gandhi addressed a meeting on October 26, 1896, under the

auspices of the Mahajan Sabha at Pachaiyappa's Hall in Madras. In his rejoinder he replied to the Agent-General of Natal who had contradicted his statement. "You have heard," he concluded, "our cry. The blame will now lie on your shoulders if the yoke is not removed from our necks." Thereupon the meeting adopted a resolution protesting against the ill-treatment of South African Indians. Gandhi was overwhelmed with the enthusiasm shown by the people of Madras and thanked them for their cordial support. The case of Balasundaram which Gandhi had defended in South Africa had impressed them greatly. He issued a second edition of the Green Pamphlet as it was in great demand.

Gandhi then went to Calcutta, where the leaders and editors did not take much interest in his campaign. Surendranath Banerjee, the idol of Bengal, said he was afraid people would not take an interest in Gandhi's work. Raja Sir Pyarimohan Mukerji and Maharaja Jyotindra Mohan Tagore referred Gandhi to Surendranath. The hands of the editors of the *Amrita Bazar Patrika* and the *Bangabasi* were full. The editors of the *Statesman* and the *Englishman* realized the importance of his work. Saunders, editor of the *Englishman*, supported Gandhi's mission in his columns. Gandhi addressed a meeting of the Committee of the British India Association. The result was that it decided to address a memorial to the Secretary of State for India in regard to the grievances of the Indians in Natal. Gandhi was about to succeed in holding a meeting at Calcutta when he received on November 12, a cable from Dada Abdulla of Durban saying, "Parliament opens January. Return soon."

Cancelling all his appointments, Gandhi, therefore, returned to Bombay and addressed a meeting at Poona on November 16 under the auspices of the Sarvajanik Sabha. Prof. R. G. Bhandarkar, a non-partisan public man and a scholar, presided. The meeting passed a resolution moved by Tilak sympathising with the Indians in South Africa and authorising a committee composed of Bhandarkar, Tilak, Gokhale and six others to submit a memorandum to the Government of India on the disabilities imposed on the Indians in South Africa.

Later, in his recollections Gandhi said that Pherozeshah Mehta appeared to him like the Himalayas, Tilak like the ocean and Gokhale like the holy Ganges.[10]

Reuter's cable had ignited the spark of white opposition, and distorted reports of Gandhi's Indian speeches had inflamed them. A mass meeting of Durban Europeans held on November

26, 1896 added fuel to the flames by condemning Asiatic immigration. The audience hissed at the mention of Gandhi's name. They established an association called the Colonial Patriotic Union to prevent further influx of Asiatics into their country. And the stage was set for the next act.

Gandhi was a real representative of the people and an exemplary public man. He carefully kept the accounts of the money he spent in India, correct to a pie! From July 5 to November 29, 1896, he spent Rs. 1,766-12-7 on his tour in India. It was his practice to take vouchers for soda-water bottles when acting as the secretary of any deputation. Barring Tilak, very few Indian leaders cared to keep accounts of public funds with such scrupulous exactness.

With his wife, two sons and the son of his widowed sister, Gandhi left Bombay for Durban on November 30, 1896, by the *Courland* which Dada Abdulla and Co. had recently purchased. Another steamer *Naderi* had sailed for Durban on November 28. It belonged to the Persian Steam Navigation Co. and its agents were Dada Abdulla and Co. The two steamers carried about eight hundred passengers.

The Calcutta Congress of 1896 recorded a solemn protest against the disabilities imposed on Indian settlers in South Africa. Gandhi's tour had borne this much fruit, though his work in South Africa had so far brought no tangible results.

CHAPTER VI

An Escape from Lynching

DURING THE VOYAGE a terrible gale overtook the *Courland.* The passengers were seized with panic. Gandhi was a good sailor. He was cheering up the passengers and instilling courage in them. He observed that God was on every lip when the danger was on, and as soon as the danger passed off the lip put off God.

Gandhi now changed the mode of dress of his wife and children from the Western to the Parsi style. The Parsis were regarded in South Africa as the most civilized community among the Indians. Gandhi thought their style of dress would help him gain prestige and influence in society. Much against her will, he compelled Kasturbai to don a rich Parsi sari. His sons wore long coats and trousers. Everyone used shoes and stockings, and also forks and knives at table. Shoes cramped their feet. Stockings stank with perspiration. Being pregnant, Kasturbai was somewhat restless. Yet like a dutiful Hindu wife, she rendered, though unhappily, implicit obedience to her husband.

Kasturbai, now in her twenty-sixth year, was a beautiful woman, her dark hair, immense dark eyes, delicate lips, fine oval face, soft mouth and well-formed nose all made her an attractive personality. Her charm fascinated her husband in spite of his rages and fits of rigour and renunciation.

The *Courland* and *Naderi* reached Durban on December 18, 1896. The news of the coming of these two steamers had already reached Durban. The newspapers and the Town Council had urged that Bombay should be declared a plague-infected port. Gandhi's fears came true. The steamers were put in quarantine, but the proclamation concerning it was issued on December 19.

The medical officer imposed five days' quarantine. As he was dismissed, another medical officer took over. He extended it to twelve days from the expiry of the first quarantine.

A committee was set up to report as to how the two ships were to be treated. The report recommended twelve days' quarantine after fumigation. According to instructions, fumigation and disinfection were carried out. The clothes and blankets of the passengers were burnt. The Natal Government did not care to supply them with substitute clothes or blankets. So the Indians in Durban, guided by Mansukhlal Hiralal Nazar and F. A. Laughton, raised a Quarantine Relief Fund and provided all the passengers with blankets, clothes and food.

The solicitors of Dada Abdulla and Company appealed by telegrams and letters to the Natal authorities for assistance to the passengers. But these were ignored. On top of it all, Dada Abdulla and Company were threatened with dire consequences if they did not repatriate the passengers. Neither the Company flinched nor the passengers cowered down. They bravely faced the inconvenience and the hardship. They were determined to land in Durban.

Gandhi knew well and truly that he was the real target of the attack and what the agitation in Durban meant. Because of him, Dada Abdulla and Company, the other passengers and his family were in danger.

At Christmas the captain of the steamer gave a party, and the Gandhis were invited to it. In Parsi dress the Gandhi family looked up-to-date. It added to their prestige and made them freer and lighter having cast off the tinsel of 'civilization'! At the dinner Gandhi made a speech on Western civilization. After the speech the captain asked Gandhi what he would do if the people beat him on landing. He replied that he would face it non-violently and hoped that God would give him the courage and sense to forgive his oppressers.

Meantime a local butcher and captain, Harry Sparks, published a notice in the *Natal Advertiser* under his signature calling "every man in Durban to attend a public meeting to be held on January 4, 1897, for the purpose of arranging a demonstration to proceed to the Point, and to protest against the landing of the Asiatics."[1] Neither the Associations mentioned above nor the sober section of the whites took part in this meeting which was held in the Durban Town Hall. Dr. Mackenzie and J. S. Wylie were the other chief movers to back up the butcher. Inflammatory speeches were made at this meeting and everybody present bound himself to help the Government to repatriate the passengers at the Colony's cost.

The Government replied telegraphically that they had no power, to prevent the landing in the Colony of Her Majesty's subjects. Wylie said that if the Committee failed to prevent the passengers from landing, Durban itself would do it. The Government officers was supporters of the Demonstration Committee. Harry Escombe, Attorney-General and Minister of Defence, said that the Government was with them, and they would not use force to oppose them. Thus the two Harry's made the atmosphere uneasy for Gandhi.

On January 7, 1897, Harry Sparks, Chairman of the Demonstration Committee, called another meeting in the Town Hall, where fiery speeches were made. Sparks took the law into his own hands. He wrote to the captains of the two ships that the passengers should avoid a conflict with Durban men who were ready and waiting to oppose their landing.

On the morning of Wednesday, January 13, 1897, Gandhi was interviewed on the *Courland* by a representative of the *Natal Advertiser* when he refuted all the charges levelled against him. He said he had not brought the other passengers with him; some of them were old residents of Natal and others were proceeding to the Transvaal. Neither had blackened the character of the white colonists as had been wrongly imagined. It was not his intention to swamp Natal with Indians. The object of his agitation was to have the Imperial Question decided once for all; namely, "What status will the Indians outside British India have?" The attitude of the Demonstration Committee, he added, was intolerant.

Wiser counsel, however, prevailed. Harry Escombe addressed a meeting of the people who had collected at the dock to oppose the landing of the passengers. He shrewdly pacified the demonstrators by appreciating their courage and unity. But he added that if they prevented a single person from landing they would injure their own interests and place the Government in an awkward position. In the end he told them that further immigration would be stopped by legislation. On hearing this, the mob dispersed. Escombe also sent word to Gandhi that he should not leave the steamer until evening when the Superintendent of Water Police would escort him to his place.

AT LONG LAST the passengers were permitted to land. On the morning of January 13, 1897, Gandhi's wife and sons landed and safely reached the house of Parsi Rustomji, who was his friend and client in Durban. Laughton, legal adviser of Dada Abdulla and Company, came up and said to Gandhi that if he entered the city at night like a thief, he would stand humiliated. So Gandhi decided to leave the steamer with Laughton. He took leave of the captain and left the steamer.

It was now half past four in the evening. The sky was slightly overcast. Gandhi landed with Laughton. It would take him an hour to reach Rustomji's house where Kasturbai was anxiously awaiting his arrival. Her little sons were making anxious inquiries with their mother about their father. Parsi Rustomji was cheering them up and promising them every moment that their father would come soon. As soon as Gandhi came out of the wharf, two boys recognised him by his turban. They began to shout, "Gandhi, Gandhi, thrash him, surround him". At this some elders enthusiastically joined them, and the number of rioters went on swelling every moment.

They pelted Gandhi with stones, rotten eggs and brickbats. Laughton hailed a rikshaw. But the rikshaw boy howled, 'Kha', meaning 'no'. Then Laughton was torn away by the rioters from Gandhi. A burly fellow slapped Gandhi in the face and kicked him. Gandhi almost fainted, but somehow held on to the railings of a house near by. His head reeled. But in a moment he came to and ploughed his way through the mob.

Just at that moment Mrs. Alexander, wife of the Police Superintendent, happened to be passing by. Noticing the mad acts of the mob, she came up briskly, opened her parasol and stood between Gandhi and the mob. Meanwhile, an Indian youth had run to the police station, and Alexander sent a posse of men to escort Gandhi to his destination.

The police station was on their way. The Superintendent of Police offered him asylum in the police station. But Gandhi declined the offer and said he had faith in the fair play of the citizens and in the rightness of his cause. They, therefore, escorted him to Parsi Rustomji's house. He was battered and bruised all over. Fortunately he had no injury except at one place. The ship's doctor, Dadi Barjorji, who happened to be at Rustomji's, attended him. Kasturbai, though fearful, was much relieved to see him.

Gandhi was thus thrice insulted and kicked in South Africa; twice by men in authority and once by a white mob.

The whites again collected outside and surrounded the house of Rustomji. "We must have Gandhi", they angrily shouted. The Superintendent joined the crowd and tried to keep it under control. He posted detectives at several places. While trying to distract the crowd, he took possession of the entrance of the house of Rustomji. The mob was relentless. It was thirsty for Gandhi's blood. Hours rolled by. Alexander sent in word to Gandhi that he should escape by disguising himself as an Indian constable and save the property of his friend, his guests and his own family.

With great distress Gandhi agreed. He put on an Indian constable's uniform and wrapped his head with a Madrasi scarf. Then, with two detectives, one disguised as an Indian merchant and the other in some similar disguise, Gandhi left Rustomji's house. They reached a neighbouring shop by a by-lane, escaped by the gate of the shop and threaded their way through the crowd to a carriage kept ready for them at the end of the street. And swiftly the carriage rolled up to the police station. Gandhi escaped.

After Gandhi's escape, the Police Superintendent asked the rioters what they would do to Gandhi if they caught him. They said in anger that they would burn him. They shouted, "Hang old Gandhi: on the sour apple tree". He then disclosed to them the news that Gandhi had escaped and said that the police had done their duty. On a promise that they would not hurt any other person in the house, he took three or four representatives of the crowd inside to show them that Gandhi had escaped. They searched for him in every nook and corner, but were disappointed at not finding Gandhi. So they dispersed, fuming and fretting. Alexander handled the situation tactfully and succeeded in saving the life of Gandhi.

Like most men of principle in similar crises, Gandhi preferred to sacrifice half of his principles to save his life. Had he faced the murderous attack in the belief that "whom God wishes to save, cannot fall even if he will",[2] it would have perhaps proved fatal. On such occasions humanity sometimes gained what brutality failed to claim.

On receiving a telegram from Joseph Chamberlain, Harry Escombe politely invited Gandhi to his office. He said in an apologetic tone that Chamberlain had ordered the prosecution of the men who had belaboured him. Gandhi replied that although he could recognize in the crowd one or two men who had beaten him, he had no desire to prosecute them. His anger was not against them. It happened, he added, through ignorance and misapprehension on their part. Accordingly he gave Harry Escombe in writing on January 20, 1897, that he did not want to prosecute his assailants. He thanked the

Government for the kind inquiries they made about him. He, however, admitted that he went on shore on his own responsibility without informing the Water Police of his intention to land.[3]

In three or four days Gandhi took his family to his residence. The newspapers declared him innocent and condemned the mob. Good Europeans were ashamed of the conduct of the fanatics. "Thus", said Gandhi afterwards, "the lynching ultimately proved to be a blessing for me, that is for the cause". "It enhanced", he said, "the prestige[4] of the Indian community". This incident, however, fanned the flames of the white opposition to the Indians.

Gandhi informed Wedderburn, Dadabhai Naoroji and Bhownaggree about the landing incident. He then resumed his normal activities. At that time India was going through a terrible famine. Thousands were dying from hunger. So he raised a fund in Natal to help the famine-stricken people of India. He approached the people, the press and the missionaries for funds and sent the money to Calcutta.

On April 6, 1897, Gandhi submitted a memorial to the Governor of Natal. It was addressed to Her Majesty's Principal Secretary of State for the Colonies. On June 22 he participated in the Diamond Jubilee Celebrations of Queen Victoria and made a speech at the opening of the Diamond Jubilee Library inaugurated by J. P. Waller, the Resident Magistrate. An address inscribed on a silver shield and bearing twenty-one signatures including that of Gandhi was forwarded for presentation to the Queen-Empress. It echoed the sentiment and devotion of Indians for peace, security of life and prosperity of 'Indians in India and abroad. But later, for want of sufficient care and supervision, this library closed down. Gandhi described books as mute, noble friends.

At that time, Gandhi, a loyal member of the British Empire, taught his little sons the British anthem which he would solemnly sing at public functions and meetings in South Africa. As his concept of ahimsa developed, he began to smell violence in the lines of the British anthem:

> 'Scatter her enemies, And make them fall;
> Confound their politics; Frustrate their knavish tricks'.

DESPITE THIS, HIS loyalty to the British Empire was unsullied.

The question of the education of his sons became difficult in Durban. Schools conducted for European children were not open to Indians. As a favour Gandhi could have got his sons admitted to one of such schools, but he did not like the idea. It was difficult for him to get a suitable Gujarati teacher. So he engaged a governess to teach his sons and nephew. That arrangement could not carry them far. He then himself taught them Gujarati at home. While in Africa, he could not send his sons, to a public school. Later, they could get some regular schooling in an impoverished school which he started for the children of satyagrahis. His sons, therefore, had complaints to make against him in this matter.

Nevertheless the disadvantages his sons suffered, said Gandhi, were compensated by learning simplicity and the spirit of service. According to him, their artificial ways of living would have been a serious handicap in his public work.[5] Yet he was not sure, he observed as he looked back, whether his inability to give them a literary education to their satisfaction was not to the best of his ability and duty. He said the traits he found in his eldest son were the outcome of his own indisciplined and unformulated early life.[6] That son thought he was the victim of his father's experiments. When friends asked Gandhi why he deprived his sons of an academic education and what right he had to clip their wings, Gandhi replied that between liberty and learning he chose liberty and self-respect for his sons, though he painfully justified his stand. Admittedly, he looked at that question from the point of view of his public work. Later, he appealed to the youth in India to choose liberty instead of learning.

Gandhi was now becoming simpler and simpler, following Tolstoy's footsteps. He had already learnt to cut his own hair since in Durban a white barber refused to cut it. He began to believe in self-help. Like Tolstoy, he washed his own clothes and ironed them. He was now above ridicule. He afterwards ironed Gokhale's valuable scarf which he had carefully preserved as a memento of his Guru Ranade. Gokhale jovially said that Gandhi was good at ironing. Gandhi planted a number of pineapple trees and persuaded his friends and visitors each to plant one so that he could remember them.[7]

As a barrister, Gandhi was progressing fairly well. Khan, a lawyer, was his assistant and was living with him. He attended Court work in his absence. Most of Gandhi's work was confined to his Chambers conveyancing and arbitrating and he had a few cases in the Magistrate's Court.

With the support of his legal work, Gandhi now concentrated his energy on the organization of the Natal Indian Congress. Adamji Miakhan and Mansukhlal Nazar were assisting him in the work of the Congress. He could raise a building for the Congress with the subscriptions and funds he had collected. A few days later, internecine quarrels arose over the property of the Congress, and the rent collected in the Court. Yet the work of the Natal Congress was going smoothly. Gandhi kept informing Dadabhai Naoroji, Mancherji Bhownaggree, Wedderburn and the Indian leaders about the condition of the South African Indians. He sent Mansukhlal Nazar to London to acquaint fully the British statesmen with the situation. Sir William Hunter stoutly supported the cause of the Indians in South Africa. Gandhi also sent Mohanlal Ray to India to mobilize public opinion in its favour.

A man with phenomenal energy, Gandhi longed for some humanitarian work. For a few days he had nursed a leper at his house. He started an Indian hospital with the charities of his friend Parsi Rustomji under the supervision of Dr. Booth, who was head of the St. Aidan's Mission and treated his patients free. Gandhi served in the Indian hospital for two hours a day as medical assistant. There he came in closer contact with the indentured labourers and came to know of their grievances directly.

The Transvaal High Court ruled in the test case, which the Indians had instituted, that Indians must reside and trade in locations specified by the Transvaal Government. Gandhi cabled to the Viceroy of India communicating the decision of the Transvaal High Court and appealed to him to intervene. He wrote to the leaders of the Indian National Congress, the Secretary of State for the Colonies and to Bhownaggree about it and stated that everything depended on Chamberlain's intercession. He sent petitions to the Natal Government complaining against the location orders and the Dealers Licence Act of 1897 and sent a memorial to Chamberlain regarding the Transvaal Government's steps to enforce Law 3 of 1885. He called on the State Secretary, waited in deputation on the British Agent in Pretoria and petitioned the Natal Governor to amend the Licensing Law.

JUST THEN BRITAIN went to war with the Boers on October 11, 1899. Dr. Jameson with the help of some British millionaires had tried to capture Johannesburg in 1895 but failed. The British, acquisitive and imperialist, thought that Britain was not safe in South Africa while the Boers had the Transvaal and its gold in their hands. On the pretext of reforming the Government and of redressing the grievances of Uitlanders and the Boers' ill-treatment of the Indians, the war was launched upon the Boers by Joseph Chamberlain, who was actually egged on by Sir Alfred, afterwards Lord Milner, the unrepentant imperialist.

The Boers were Bouwers-farmers. They were the descendants of Dutch, French and other little groups that had come to the Cape of Good Hope. Their language is modelled after that of Holland. According to Gandhi, who had believed since his boyhood that the Hindus were a weak and cowardly race, every Boer was a good fighter. Their leaders were great farmers, great lawyers and great soldiers. For their liberty they fought as one man. Boer women were, according to Gandhi, as brave as Boer men.

Gandhi would not sit silent when ruin stared the British Empire in the face. To show his individual loyalty he rushed to the British Government. He wanted to show that the Indians were not mere money-grabbers, cowards and self-seekers, they too were brave and loyal men. So he enforced his loyalty on the other Indians. He lost no time in forming, with the help of Dr. Booth who trained the Indians in ambulance work, a corps of 1,100 strong with nearly forty group leaders.

Early in December 1899 the Indian Ambulance Corps went to the front but was disbanded soon after on December 19. It was, however, reformed and sent again to the front. The Indian Corps served the British Army for about six weeks there at the critical moment and worked within the firing line. They brought the wounded from the battle-field, even marching about twenty-five miles a day and carrying soldiers like General Woodgate. Gandhi carried the only son of Lord Roberts out of action at Spion Kop under fire. He was mentioned in General Buller's despatch and won distinction for his work in the war. Later, Gandhi proudly recalled how he served the British loyally during the Boer War and put his life in peril. The Indian Ambulance Corps was present at the battle of Colenso, Spion Kop and Vaalkranz.

At one stage of the war the Boers had inflicted a severe defeat on the British troops in January 1900. Jan Christian Smuts, a brilliant scholar and barrister, who was a legal officer in the Government of President Paul Kruger, fought the British Army heroically to the bitter end. The Indians proved their fortitude Vere Stent, editor of the *Pretoria News*, said about the work of the Indian Ambulance Corps: "After a night's work, which had shattered men with much bigger frame, I came across Gandhi in the early morning, sitting by the roadside - eating a regulation army biscuit. Every man in Buller's force was dull and depressed, and damnation was heartily invoked on everything. But Gandhi was stoical in his bearing, cheerful and confident in his conversation, and had a kindly eye".[8]

Their unassuming dauntlessness cost the Indians many lives. When in the moment of triumph Gandhi hosted a dinner to Europeans who had supported the Indian movement, they and hundreds of Indians paid him glowing tributes. In reply Gandhi said with great modesty that he had only done his duty. As he was a believer in the myth that the British Empire existed for the welfare of the world, his heart knew no bounds when the Natal papers published laudatory rhymes with the refrain: "We are sons of Empire after all". The atmosphere of war had melted for the time being many proud, rude white hearts into genial creatures of God.

Gandhi very enthusiastically felicitated the British General on their victory in the Boer War, he wrote to *The Times of India* giving a detailed account of the work of the Indian Ambulance Corps and loyally conveyed to Queen Victoria Indians' felicitations on her birthday. Gandhi also sent an address of felicitations to the Sultan of Turkey on the Silver Jubilee of his reign, obviously to please his Muslim colleagues and Muslim followers.

The war over, the British erected a monument on one of the Hills of Johannesburg which bore an inscription on three of its sides in English, Hindi and Urdu in memory of those who had died during the Boer War.[9] For his services as assistant superintendent of the Indian Volunteer Stretcher-bearer Corps, Gandhi was presented with a war medal. The other Indian officers of the corps were also awarded medals.

Gandhi wrote afterwards in unstinted praise of the Boers who fought bravely for their very existence. His personal sympathies were, he added, with the Boers, but he had no right to enforce his individual convictions on others. This was indeed a flimsy justification.

Gandhi's ambition to be a doctor had not left him. It urged him to serve the people in many ways. He studied Dr. Tribhuvandas's *Ma-ne Shikkaman* (Advice to a Mother) and nursed his son Ramdas who was born in May 1897. At the time of the birth of his last son Devdas who was born on May 22, 1900, neither a doctor nor a nurse was available. Gandhi had to act boldly as midwife and see his wife safe through the delivery.

Gandhi's frequent letters and circulars, appeals and petitions attracted the attention of the Indian leaders and revived their interest in the welfare of the Indians in South Africa. They had passed a resolution in the Madras session of the Congress in December 1898 appealing to the British and Indian Governments to guard the interest of the Indian settlers in South Africa. In the Lahore session of December 1900 the Congress expressed the hope that since the Boer Republics were incorporated in the British Empire, Indians' disabilities, which were inconsistent with the British constitution, would now be removed.

QUEEN VICTORIA OF Britain died in January 1901. Gandhi sent a condolence message to the Colonial Secretary on her death. Laying a wreath on the pedestal of the Queen's statue in Durban, he paid tributes to her at the memorial meeting. He got into contact with schools in Durban and enthusiastically distributed the souvenir-portrait of the deceased Queen. A man of such devotional loyalty was bound to be mentioned in the war despatches when he served the British in the Boer War.

The Indians in South Africa were regarded by the whites as a slovenly people. Gandhi tried to teach them to keep their houses and surroundings clean. In doing this he met with insults in some localities and in others with indifference. They praised Gandhi who fought for their rights, but they disliked Gandhi the sanitary reformer. He came to the conclusion that "it is the social reformer who is anxious for the reforms and not society". In every country, the real reformer expects nothing better than opposition, abhorrence and mortal persecution.

In May 1901 Raychandbhai passed away at the early age of thirty-two. Gandhi expressed his grief in a letter of condolence he sent to Revashankar Zaveri. Raychandbhai left an indelible impression on him.

Gandhi now felt that he had no more work in South Africa. In October 1901 he persuaded his colleagues and workers to consent to his departure for India. They consented to his leaving when he promised them that he would return if his presence was necessary. On October 15, 1901, the Indians in Natal gratefully showered valuable presents on Gandhi and presented him with an address. It expressed their profound sense of gratitude for "the valuable services you have so untiringly and cheerfully rendered, and the exemplary self-sacrifice you have ever-willingly undergone, to watch and further the interests of your fellow-countrymen since your arrival in the Colony over eight years ago".[10] The Natal Indian Congress, while accepting the resignation of its Secretary, praised him for his unflinching devotion and immense sacrifice. In his farewell speech Gandhi said, "What was wanted in South Africa was not a white man's country, not a white brotherhood, but an imperial brotherhood".[11]

At this stage Gandhi was passing through a new phase of introspection and decided to live a life of utter simplicity and self-denial. Naturally, he decided to return all the gifts for the use of public work. He got his sons to agree to his will. But it was difficult for him to get Kasturbai's consent to this new mood of renunciation. She argued with him, wishing to preserve the necklace and other things given her as gifts. She said she would preserve these things for her daughters-in-law. He asked her straightway whether the necklace was given her for her service or for his service. Service, she rejoined, done by him was as good as done by her as she had toiled for him and had served all and sundry he had forced on her. Yet he deposited the gifts given to him in 1896 and 1901 in a bank under a trust with instructions to utilise the gifts for public work in South Africa.

This was, however, not the first major clash Gandhi had had with his wife. Some months earlier, Kasturbai had refused to clean the chamber-pot of a Christian clerk who was born of untouchable parents. Helpless as she was, one day she came downstairs with the pot in her hand, arguing with and defying her husband. Tears rolled down her cheeks. Her eyes were red with anger. Gandhi was not satisfied with the act of her carrying the pot. So he shouted, "I will not stand this nonsense in my house". She shouted back; "Keep your house to yourself and let me go".

Gandhi, beside himself with anger, dragged her to the gate and began pushing her out. In a flood of tears she said: "Have you no sense of shame? Must you so forget yourself? I have no parents or relatives here to harbour me. Being your wife, you think I must put up with your cuffs and kicks? For heaven's sake behave yourself, and shut the gate!" Gandhi came to his senses and the scene was closed!

The blind infatuated husband that he was, Gandhi did not tell the clerk to do his duty, but he exacted it mercilessly from his wife. Her sufferings contributed to the Mahatmaship of Gandhi. Mary Todd made Lincoln's life miserable, and Xanthippe that of Socrates. Gandhi was fortunate that Kasturbai was gifted with the remarkable powers of endurance of an ideal Hindu wife. With all these troubles and insults beyond endurance, she followed in his footsteps dutifully and patiently though his friends often caused her bitter tears and she had many trials on his account. Yet Gandhi proudly said he had a feeling that theirs was a life of contentment, happiness and progress.

With his family Gandhi sailed for India on October 18, 1901. He landed at Mauritius as the steamer had made a halt there. He was the guest of Sir Charles Bruce, Governor of Mauritius, and was given a public reception by the Indian community. He left Mauritius on November 19 and reached Rajkot on December 14, 1901 via Porbandar.

Soon after, on December 17, Gandhi left for Bombay *en route* to Calcutta. He attended the Calcutta Congress which was held during the last week of December 1901. During the journey to Calcutta Pherozeshah Mehta frankly told him that the condition of South African Indians would not improve unless Indians had power in their own land. At this Wacha cast a pathetic look at Gandhi!

Gandhi wanted to do some useful work for the Congress. So he saw Babu Bhupendranath Basu who was one of the two secretaries of the Congress. Basu said he had no work for him and directed him to Ghosal who was one of the secretaries of the Reception Committee. Without making full inquiries about him, Ghosal asked Gandhi to attend to his correspondence and Gandhi worked there as a personal secretary to him. He ably disposed of the correspondence and even humbly buttoned the shirt of the secretary once without revealing his identity. Work was the great force in his life. He was ready to play any role however humble, with untiring energy and boundless sincerity. That was the striking characteristic of Gandhi.

Gandhi was disgusted with the dirt and insanitary condition of the places where the Congress delegates and visitors put up. He listened with great interest to the talks between Tilak and Motilal Ghose. He himself addressed two public meetings at Calcutta, one on the question of the Indians in South Africa and the other on the work of the Indian Ambulance Corps.

Writing about the session of the Congress, Gandhi said that he was a feeble pipe amongst the veteran drums. When he moved the resolution on South Africa entreating His Majesty to secure for the Indian settlers a just and equitable treatment, he trembled and his head reeled. In his brief speech he told the familiar tale of Indian grievances as a petitioner on behalf of the hundred thousand British Indians in South Africa.

A. Pillai seconded the resolution. All this was done under the guiding and patronizing care of G. K. Gokhale. The young leader noted that the Congress met for three days every year and then went to sleep for the rest of the year. A three-day show! There were caste-wise dinners. To the Tamil delegates even the sight of others, while they were dining, meant pollution. Nobody minded the stench and dirt.

Curzon was awaiting the burial of the Congress. He thought that it was tottering to its fall! Gandhi had written to Curzon in May 1901 describing him as 'the strong sympathetic Viceroy'.[12] At this juncture he expressed his desire to wait in deputation on Curzon, but the Viceroy felt that if he received Gandhi it might be resented as an undue pressure. So they never met![13] Later, in 1905, when almost all Indian leaders, moderate as well as extremist, attacked Curzon's autocratic policy, Gandhi was wooing his 'watchful guardianship'![14]

During his month's stay at the India Club in Calcutta, Gokhale introduced Gandhi to many eminent public men. One of them was Dr. P. C. Ray who earned Rs. 800 a month out of which he spent Rs. 30 for himself and devoted the balance to public purposes. Gandhi was pleased to see Gokhale at work. To see him at work, he said, was as much a joy as an education. Gokhale went to the India Club to play billiards. He saw how Gokhale grew eloquent about his master Ranade whom his great disciple considered to be a versatile genius towering above all.

It was during this stay that Gokhale told Gandhi how he, on his arrival in Bombay from London in 1897, threw the letters of Ranade and Wacha into the sea when Wacha met him on the steamer at Bombay.[15] Wacha, who had been to England, was during his return voyage on the same steamer from Brindisi to Bombay. Gandhi's account as stated by Mahadev Desai is clear. These were the letters on the strength of which Gokhale had made the serious statement about the excesses Rand's soldiers had committed in Poona during the plague days of 1897. As a result Gokhale withdrew the charges he had made against the Plague Administration, tendered an unconditional apology to the Bombay Government and for months his heart burnt with agony.

The intimacy with his Guru grew and Gandhi asked Gokhale why he did not go about in tram-cars. Gokhale replied that it was difficult, if not impossible, to do so if one was the victim of as wide a publicity as he was. The disciple was sorry that the Guru did not take any exercise. The Guru said that he had no time for exercise. Gandhi visited notable places and personalities in Calcutta. He visited the Kali temple. Rows of beggars lined the lane leading to the temple. Gandhi was opposed to giving alms to sturdy beggars. He was horrified by the sight of the pools of blood in the temple of Kali. It made him restless. To him the life of a lamb was no less precious than that of a human being. He read the life of Keshab Chandra Sen and read and heard a good deal about the Brahmo Samaj. He went to see Maharashi Devendranath Tagore, but was not allowed to meet him. Instead he was invited to a function of the Brahmo Samaj. There one thing pleased him most. It was the Bengali music.

Gandhi then paid a brief visit to Burma, reaching Rangoon on January 19, 1902, by steamer. He saw that the Indians in Burma were helping the Europeans to exploit the Burmese. According to him the Burmese men were lazy, the women energetic, the monks lethargic and the pagodas dirty.

On his return to Calcutta, Gandhi decided to go to Benares to pay his respects to Mrs. Annie Besant who was one of his London acquaintances. Gokhale, accompanied by Dr. Ray, saw him off at Calcutta station. Gokhale had given him a metal tiffin-box filled with sweetballs and puris. Gandhi had bought a canvas bag worth twelve annas and a long coat made of *chhaya* wool. The bag contained this rough woollen coat, a dhoti, and a towel. He had also a blanket and a water jug. At Benares he had a dip in the holy Ganga in the orthodox manner. He bowed devotionally to Kashi Vishwanath. The stinking heaps of flowers nearby pained him.

There Gandhi gave a pie to a Brahmin who cursed him saying that the insult would take him straight to hell. Gandhi pocketed both the insult and the coin. The Brahmin, however, overpowered Gandhi's calculating generosity and took back the pie after a homily by Gandhi. The dirt, noise, hypocrisy and irreligion he found to be the features of Benares at the time of his next visit also. The relieving feature of this visit to Benares was the glimpse he could catch of Annie Besant who was ill. Intensely proud of India's glorious past, culture and scriptures, Mrs. Besant had come to India on November 16, 1893, to do religious, educational and social work. Her headquarters was Benares. She had founded the Central Hindu College in Benares and her theosophist friends from England and America helped her in this educational work. Gandhi paid his respects to her and left.

Staying a day each at Agra, Jaipur and Palanpur, Gandhi

reached Rajkot on February 26, 1902. There he set up his legal office and began to practise. He conducted some cases successfully. During the plague days in May 1902, he worked as secretary of the volunteer committee in Rajkot. He wanted to do public work under the guidance of Gokhale and to earn his livelihood as a barrister. So he decided to leave for Bombay. On receiving money from Natal, he took chambers in July 1902 in the offices of Payne, Gilbert and Sayani and started practice. During the previous months he had studied Indian law, and his friends from Rajkot had promised him legal work. He did some work in the lower courts, entrusted to him by the persons who were his Natal acquaintances.

While in Bombay, his son Manilal was taken seriously ill with typhoid. Gandhi refused to give him eggs and chicken soup although the doctor insisted on his doing so. He applied the hydropathic treatment recommended by Kunhe in his book. One night, during this illness of his son, sorely tired and plunged in thought, he was taking a walk on the Chaupatty sands of Bombay and praying to God "My honour is in thy keeping, Oh Lord, in this hour of trial". He repeated Ramanam several times to himself, and the boy recovered. After some days he moved from Girgaum to Santa Cruz where he rented a good house. The slaughter house at Bandra was too horrible for him. From his new residence Gandhi travelled first class by train on his way to the court and took pride in being the only first class railway passenger in the compartment. A barrister must keep his dignity and prestige. As a social worker, Gandhi had suggested to Gokhale that he should travel third class or by tram-car!

Gandhi enjoyed the soporific breezes in the Bombay High Court along with the other young briefless barristers. He utilized his time in the library, reading law books. Gokhale peeped in at his chambers once or twice a week. But with whatever income he had, it seems he cleared all the debts his brother had contracted.[16]

During these days Gandhi had continued his work for the Indians in South Africa. He wrote to *The Times of India*, *The Voice of India* and other papers furnishing them with notes on the situation in South Africa. He wrote to his friends in South Africa and, on receiving information from them, he kept the Indian leaders informed about the situation. In March 1902 he informed his colleagues in South Africa that he would go there if his presence was necessary. It was better to be the head of a suppressed people in a foreign land than to be the tail in one's own. And the call came. "Chamberlain expected here. Please start", wired the Natal colleagues.

On Receiving Funds from Natal, Gandhi left Bombay for Durban by steamer on November 20, 1902, keeping his family in the rented house at Santa Cruz, Bombay, and taking with him four young men including Maganlal Gandhi. Breaking up his establishment and going away from the family was rather painful to him. He was now inured to an uncertain life. "I think," he sighed, "it is wrong to expect certainties in the world where all else but God that is Truth is an uncertainty. . . . The quest for that Truth is the *summum bonum* of life."[17]

Gandhi arrived in Durban in the third week of December 1902 and on December 28, led the deputation of Natal Indians to Joseph Chamberlain presenting a memorial regarding their grievances. Chamberlain wanted money from the South African Colonies, the Orange Free State and the Transvaal, which had after the Boer War become British Colonies. He was lukewarm in respect of the demands of the Indians. He suavely told the deputation that he would confer with the Natal Government on the subject, but added that the British Government had very little control over the self-governing colonies. In the end Chamberlain asked them to placate the whites amongst whom the Indians had to live.

Spokesman of the British Indians as he was, Gandhi was in a hurry to go to Pretoria too. But after the war, entry into the Transvaal was controlled by passes. Gandhi used at this time the influence of the Police Superintendent of Durban to force his entry into the Transvaal by gaining a permit. He reached Pretoria on the first day of the new year 1903.

The Asiatic Department, just established to deal with the affairs of the Asiatics, was surprised to see Gandhi there. The officers of the Department wanted to exclude Gandhi from the delegation. The Chief Officer would not even ask him and Tyeb Sheth, who took him to the office, to take a chair. He was told that he would not be allowed to wait on Chamberlain. All the officers of the Asiatic Department were against his inclusion in the Transvaal deputation.

Insulted, Gandhi returned and pacified his friends. The Indian deputation was therefore led by George Godfrey, an Indian barrister, who handed over to Chamberlain the memorial drafted by Gandhi. Chamberlain referred to Gandhi and said that it was better to hear a fresh local representative than to hear the same one again. It was not that he wss unaware of Gandhi's work in Natal and the Transvaal.

Gandhi then decided to settle down in Johannesburg. He wrote to Gokhale that there was more work than he had expected. In the middle of February 1903, he applied to the Supreme Court for admission to practise in the Transvaal. He decided to maintain himself by legal practice. With the help of L. W. Ritch, a theosophist merchant, he obtained suitable rooms for his office in the legal quarters of the city.

Gandhi's office became the headquarters of the social workers. His work began in right earnest. He issued a spate of appeals and reports to the Transvaal, Natal and British authorities, and to leaders like Dadabhai Naoroji and G, K. Gokhale as well as to the British Committee of the Indian National Congress in London. He wrote to the Indian newspapers about the anti-Indian laws and bills which affected the Indian traders' licences, immigration, residential locations, bazaars, indentured labour, permits and franchise. He referred these matters to the Viceroy of India also.

In the Transvaal he held meetings to protest against these unjust laws and put forth the grievances of the Indian communities in the local press.

The Governor of the Transvaal, Lord Milner, the unmitigated imperialist, set up a committee to make a list of the Transvaal laws that were prejudicial to the interests of the British community. He then repealed them by a stroke of the pen, but he did not repeal the anti-Indian laws. Perturbed at this, Gandhi's colleagues were indignant with him for the zealous help he had asked the Indians to render to the British Government during the Boer War. They sarcastically said that it was the right reward for his loyalty to the British Empire. Gandhi replied that as a British subject he simply did his duty by the Empire and so he did not regret his advice. When his colleagues made a wry face at this he evaded the issue by saying: "Let us forget the past and think of the task before us."[18] Shyamji Krishna Varma, too, had severely attacked Gandhi in his *Indian Socialist* for having served the British against the Boers who fought for their independence.

The first thing Gandhi wanted to do was to establish an institution to voice the grievances of the people. So he immediately founded the British Indian Association, of which he became the Secretary and Abdul Gani, the President.

Gandhi now felt the necessity of starting a newspaper devoted to the cause of the Indians. Madanjit Vyavaharik was a Nagar Brahmin from Junagadh. He went from Zanzibar to Durban and lived with Gandhi. In 1898, at the instance of Gandhi, he set up a press called International Printing Press in Durban.

With Gandhi's help Madanjit founded on June 4, 1903, a weekly called *Indian Opinion* with Mansukhlal H. Nazar as its first editor. Mansukhlal Nazar was the son of an engineer who was Kayasta by caste. While he was a student of Elphinstone College, Bombay, he left it and studied at Grant Medical College for four years. But he gave up the studies as he was influenced by the patriotic ideals of Dadabhai Naoroji, On entering upon business, he travelled widely in Europe. A scholar-politician known to several politicians and litterateurs in England and India he discussed with them the political problems. He, however, wanted to lead a peaceful life and so he went to South Africa and lived at Sydenham, a suburb of Durban.

Events and political problems, however, again drew Nazar into the vortex of politics and he appeared on the scene when the steamers bringing Indian passengers were not allowed to land at Durban in 1897. Nazar was then sent to London as a special delegate by South African Indians to represent their case to the British Government. When *Indian Opinion* was started, he volunteered to act as an unpaid editor.

Madanjit threw the responsibility of writing editorials on Gandhi as he himself could not write on intricate problems. Gandhi was naturally responsible for the editorial contents of *Indian Opinion* although he was not its avowed editor. While declaring its aims and objects, the first editorial said: "We need offer no apology for making an appearance. The Indian community in South Africa is a recognised factor in the body politic, and a newspaper, voicing its feelings, and specially devoted to its cause, would hardly be considered out of place: indeed, we think, it would supply a longfelt want."[19] At another place Gandhi, to whom the sole aim of journalism was service, said: "The object of *Indian Opinion* was to bring the European and the Indian subjects of King Edward closer together. It was to educate public opinion, to remove causes for misunderstanding; to put before the Indians their own blemishes; and to show them the path of duty while they insisted on securing their rights. This was an Imperial and pure ideal, towards the fruition of which anyone could work unselfishly."[20]

The weekly was first published in four languages, Tamil, Gujarati, Hindi and English. Later, from February 3, 1906, the Tamil and Hindi sections were stopped for want of the services of the necessary editors and compositors. In the beginning only 400 copies were sold, and Gandhi had to incur a monthly loss of about £75.

CHAPTER VII

Ruskin and Islam

GANDHI'S OFFICE IN Johannesburg was at the corner of Rissik and Anderson streets. From its appearance it seemed that it was intended for work and not for show. The windows and doors had the name of Gandhi with the denomination of Attorney attached to it. In the first room an English woman typist worked and there were four Indian clerks. The second room was the *sanctum sanctorum*, meagerly furnished and dusty, some chairs and shelves were filled with books. Some photographs and pictures of the Indian Strecher-Bearer Corps and photographs of Mrs. Besant, Sir William Hunter and Justice Ranade hung on the walls. A beautiful picture of Jesus Christ adorned the wall over Gandhi's desk. No picture of Krishna or Buddha was to be seen.

In this room Gandhi worked, a slenderly built man with a bold masterful face, mildly dark skin and a small dark moustache. His kindly eyes not only heightened the power of the man, but also reflected the spirituality of the face and partly overcame its ugliness. He was hardly thirty-three, yet his hair had grown grey. His voice was soft and musical. His speech showed his earnestness and strength, the greatness of his heart and his transparent honesty. In those days he moved his fingers to emphasize his thoughts. He lived in a double-storied house with eight rooms, and the house stood on the outskirts of the town. His wife and four sons were now with him. This was a new establishment. A large photograph of Dadabhai Naoroji hung on a wall of Gandhi's bedroom.

At this stage Gandhi entered another phase of introspection in his life. He was gradually getting control over his inner self and divesting himself of passion and possessions, of the lust and greed for money. Moderation was coming after the excesses. He allowed a life assurance policy to lapse which he had taken out for Rs. 10,000 while in India. The insurance agent was an American. He said people in America regarded it as a religious obligation to get insured. Gandhi had sold the ornaments of his wife and thought it was wiser to make provision for his family in case of his death.

But now he felt that life assurance implied fear and want of faith in God. As the spirit of self-sacrifice and self-reliance was increasingly dominating his mind, he thought that in getting his life insured he was depriving the members of his family of their self-reliance. He said that God who had created them would take care of them.

Gandhi now began to think of taking the vow of celibacy even in respect of his wife. His main object was to escape having more children and that too without using contraceptives, the outward means. Self-control was the most difficult method, and he tried it without much success by sleeping in a separate bed and retiring only after he was thoroughly exhausted. But the final phase in this connection was to come three years later.

By *brahmacharya* Gandhi meant realization of *Brahman*. It means control of the senses in thought, word and deed. In it lay the protection of the body, the mind and the soul. Control of the palate was the first essential in observance of the vow. "A brahmachari's food", he said, "should be limited, simple, spiceless, and if possible, uncooked. His ideal food is fresh fruits and nuts. Milk diet makes the *brahmacharya* vow difficult to observe; fasting is necessary as selection and restriction in diet; extinction of the sexual passion is as a rule impossible without fasting". For many, admitted Gandhi, this was an ideal and was impossible to attain by mere human effort. He criticized the method of contraceptives propagated by Dr. Allinson. Needless to say, it is impossible for a common man to bear the pressures of the diet, money and fast prescribed by Gandhi for the attainment of *brahmacharya*.

At this time, in 1903, Gandhi entered the fourth phase of religious development and introspection. He now turned to theosophical literature as a result of his friendship with L.W. Ritch. Gandhi's thoughts on religion were maturing. He had his differences with the theosophists but addressed their meetings. It was Gandhi's charge against them that their conduct did not agree with their ideal of cultivating and promoting universal brotherhood.

Theosophical literature is replete with Hindu influence. Gandhi's knowledge of Sanskrit was not much to speak of, and he had not read the Hindu scriptures in the original. So he read *Rajayoga* by Swami Vivekanand, M. N. Dvivedi's *Rajayoga*, Patanjali's *Yoga Sutras* and the Bhagvad Gita. He committed to memory thirteen chapters of the Gita, which became an infallible guide of conduct, a dictionary of daily reference, providing 'a ready solution of all my troubles and trials'. All these helped him to deepen his belief in his faith and since then no efforts were made to convert him to Christianity.

Ritch gave up his business and became an articled clerk to Gandhi. He later went to London for legal studies in 1905. A man of broad outlook, he held strong pro-Indian views.

While in South Africa, Gandhi was called Bhai, a brother. He had not yet become Mahatma or Bapu. There was, Gandhi says, a sweet flavour about the appellation 'Bhai' when the ex-indentured Indians uttered it. At this stage he made experiments in earth and water treatment. He used to have three square meals daily in addition to the afternoon tea. He was never a spare eater and enjoyed varieties of vegetarian and spiceless dishes. When he stopped having breakfast, the headaches from which he frequently suffered disappeared. He read Adolf Just's *Return to Nature* which prescribed fresh fruit and nuts as the natural diet of man and advocated earth treatment. Although Gandhi's opinion was that man need not consume any milk at all, he could not stick to his resolve and often drank milk. He tried to find out whether there was any vegetable substitute for milk.

In March 1904 plague broke out in Johannesburg. Gandhi had warned Dr. Porter and other Municipal officers that plague symptoms had developed. He took measures to fight the dreadful disease. With the help of Dr. William Godfrey, the missionary, he started a temporary hospital and served the plague stricken Indians promptly.

Before the outbreak of plague, Gandhi had discussed the question of sanitation fully and impressed upon the minds of the Indians that "cleanliness is next to godliness". He blamed the authorities and the employers for keeping the Indians in unhealthy and insanitary locations, which Gandhi likened to the Ghettos of the Jews or the *Dhedvadoes* of the Untouchables in India.

The plague, however, served as a peg for the Transvaal authorities. Under the cover of taking plague precautions, the issuing of permits to British Indian refugees from the Colonies in South Africa was stopped. Discussing this, Gandhi said that the plague rats were pressed into service by the Transvaal Government![1] Corruption was rampant in the Asiatic Department, and an entry permit was issued on a payment of £100. Fearless and ruthless, Gandhi resolved to stamp out this evil. He saw the Police Commissioner and the suspects were arrested, but the jury let them off. In the official inquiry, however, they were found guilty and were dismissed. Gandhi felt pity for them and secured them new jobs. He said one should hate the sin and not the sinner. He was grieved that the legal profession should have been used to screen the culprits. The case raised Gandhi's prestige and brought him more business. But dishonesty continued to play its role in the Asiatic Department.

Gandhi, who wanted to display Indian heroism to African Europeans and to enthuse the British Indians, eulogised the bravery of an Indian sepoy who fought in the British ranks in Tibet. Isolated and alone, he stuck to his post with heroic courage and fell after shooting down a number of Tibetan soldiers. Gandhi was thrilled by the sepoy's spirit of heroism and quoted Lord Tennyson's[2] *Charge of the Light Brigade* to describe the Indian sepoy.

About this time Pherozeshah Mehta was knighted. A new livery was added to the mane of the Bombay Lion. Gandhi felicitated him on his being knighted by the British Government and said, "The conferring of the knighthood, therefore, is no less a compliment to the Congress than to the honourable gentleman himself." He proudly mentioned that Gokhale was another Congress leader who had already received the distinction of C.I.E.

President Kruger passed away in July 1904. Gandhi said in the obituary that his demeanour on the continent was worthy of a great and godly man, a brave man. "The one lesson," he concluded, "that he has left behind him is his simple-minded, though at times misguided, patriotism, and we venture to think that it will be as a staunch patriot that he will be best known to posterity."

It was here that Gandhi first used his favourite but ungenerous epithet 'misguided'[3] to condemn great men in his own peculiar style.

In October he wrote to Gokhale that there ought to be an articulate and persistent agitation in favour of justice being done to Indians in the Transvaal. He noted that *The Times*, London, too, had expressed its opinion to the effect that harsh treatment to Indians would be very bad on the Indian mind and that it would be a great strain on Indian loyalty.

Gandhi, a votary of vegetarianism, met one Miss Ada M. Bissicks, who was conducting a vegetarian restaurant. She wanted to expand the venture and approached Gandhi for a loan. He lent her about a thousand pounds from the account of one Mr. Badri, his client. The woman was fond of art, but was extravagant and ignorant of accounts. The result was that Gandhi lost the money and he had to make good the loss from his own pocket.

It was at the vegetarian restaurant in Johannesburg that Gandhi made friends with Albert West and Henry Saloman Leon Polak. West was running a press in Durban. He gave up this work and handing over his press to Gandhi, worked on a salary of £10 month for *Indian Opinion* which was in trouble. Polak hailed from a peasant family in Lincolnshire and had received an ordinary education. According to Gandhi, West was a pure, sober, god-fearing, human Englishman. Polak was born at Dover in 1882 and studied at London University. He held certificates in literary and economic subjects issued by the London Chamber of Commerce. He also received some education in Switzerland and came to South Africa in 1903 for reasons of health. To him religion and ethics were convertible terms.

Polak was working as a sub-editor of the *Transvaal Critic* and promised Gandhi to join *Indian Opinion* as a sub-editor. Thereafter he became identified with the Indian cause. His attraction to Indian culture had begun even before he went to South Africa in 1903 through Romesh Chandra Dutt's summaries of the *Mahabharata* and the *Ramayana* and later through the Bhagavad Gita. The inspiration he derived from the study of Indian culture was profound.[4]

The third man was Herbert Kitchin who was a theosophist. He later became editor of *Indian Opinion* after the premature death of Mansukhlal Nazar. According to Gandhi these three Englishmen were good, capable and selfless and they early expressed their opinions against the oppression of Indians in South Africa.

As his practice was growing, Gandhi had to employ more assistants. Of the Indian clerks none could do his typewriting because of their poor English. It was impossible for him to cope with the professional and public work alone. So he was in search of a European clerk. An agent brought him a Scottish girl called Miss Dick. She was a good steno-typist and the very image of loyalty and honesty. She handled big funds and kept their accounts ably and faithfully. After her marriage, Gandhi employed another European girl named Miss Sonja Schlesin introduced to him by Hermann Kallenbach. She, too, was loyal, suitable, and had no colour prejudice. Her courage was equal to her spirit of self-sacrifice. A girl of high character, she was also a good steno-typist. But her impetuosity often landed Gandhi in difficulties. She refused to receive more than £10 a month. She devoted herself to the cause and mission of her master.

ALTHOUGH DOING CONTINUOUS public service with great enthusiasm and devotion, *Indian Opinion* was in trouble. Madanjit, with the financial help of Gandhi, had struggled strenuously to make it a success. But he failed. Gandhi had handed over to him £1,600 received by him as fees in the cases of Indians against the Johannesburg Corporation and yet the deficit was not covered.

All knew that Gandhi was responsible for the conduct of *Indian Opinion*. He spent a lot of money on it, and it would have been a loss and a disgrace if it had been discontinued. The changes in the life of the journal marked the changes in the life of Gandhi as at that stage it was a mirror of his life. He poured out his soul in its columns. It was a fine education for him to study and digest and reply to friendly, critical or angry letters. Over five hundred complimentary copies were sent out.

This was a financial drag on the journal. There was some help from the British Indian Association and the Natal Indian Congress. They came to its rescue and voted certain funds towards the payment of the expenses of printing and porting the complimentary copies. To study the situation, Gandhi was leaving for Durban where the Weekly was published. At the station Polak gave Gandhi a copy of Ruskin's *Unto This Last* to read. And Gandhi fell under the magic spell of the book.

John Ruskin (1819-1900) was a precocious child. He read chapters of scriptures to his mother till the age of fifty-two. His book *Modern Painters* brought him fame as an art critic. As art lecturer he assisted F. D. Maurice, the great divine and preacher who wrote in the *Christian Socialist* in 1851, and Charles Kingsley, in their new Working Men's College which was a centre of *Christian Socialism*. His lectures at the Working Men's College gave him a more intimate understanding of the problems of working men, and his interest in men ousted his interest in art. Consequently he left the study not only of architecture, but virtually of all art.

The Industrial Revolution had wrought vast changes in the lives of the masses. England had become the richest country at the cost of thousands of young children who had been reduced to the condition of helpless slaves. Ruskin was moved by their sad lot. The life of the average worker was brief, one of toil, hunger, disease and dirt and with the oblivion of drunkenness as its chief relief. The more he reflected on the life of the average labouring man who led a life of ugliness and mechanical drudgery, the more clearly he realized that the current social ideals were at fault.

In 1860 Ruskin flung a challenge to the political economists of his day when he published his essays on political economy in the *Cornhill Magazine* edited by William Makepeace Thackeray. Ruskin was opposed to the current economic theories of Adam Smith, who was the founder of political economy as a separate branch of human knowledge and chief propagandist of free trade. Ruskin also attacked the political theories of Mill and Ricardo. The current economic theories, he opined, treated men as a non-moral machine. The opposition to Ruskin's theory was violent. So the editor discontinued the publication of the series. Ruskin then published the essays in a book entitled *Unto This Last* in 1862. It contained four essays and they bore quaint titles.

Ruskin's *Unto This Last* appeals for justice to the workers, who were being exploited by the new capitalism. He wanted the industrialists to treat the workers as their sons and to use wealth in the service of mankind. He did not desire, as the socialist did, to break the arm of the strong man who oppressed the weak, but to teach him to use it to better purpose. According to Ruskin, "The rich not only refuse food to the poor; they refuse wisdom; they refuse virtue; they refuse salvation." Ruskin thought that *Unto This Last* was his greatest work and added, "It would stand if anything stand surest and longest of all work of mine".

The title, *Unto This Last*, is taken from Matthew XX-14, and the book echoes the phrasing and rhythm of the Bible and that of John Bunyan. Ruskin's theory defines "value as the power of anything to support life". He says that profit is not the only motive of human action. "Happiness in life," he continues, "must, besides, be measured by other things than money. People, to be ideal men and women, not only must have food, clothes and places to sleep, but must have also beautiful and ennobling surroundings. Machine-tending tends to dehumanise men and that means must be sought to make man the master and not the servant of the machine."

Unto This Last became the gospel of the English working man. Ruskin was a practical social reformer and not merely a sentimental preacher. He had made experiments in social reform. The St. George's company or Guild was an example. His supporters failed to give one-tenth of their wealth to support this institution while he gave away the sum of £157,000 left by his father and lived only on money from the sales of his books. He refused to invest his money and take interest. The vital law of St. George's company was that there must be "no use of steam power, nor any machine where arms would serve."

Ruskin's rule of life and the motives of his action were such that he took pleasure in washing with his own hands unclean stairways and muddy crossings. He took great pleasure in working with the builder's pickaxe, carpenter's plane or house painter's brush.

Many of Ruskin's ideas have taken shape in the present welfare state of England and Ruskin proved to be its prophet. The idealistic philosophy of his life, the nobility of his heart, his love of the dignity of labour, the beauty of his spiritual charity, his pity for the victims of injustice and ignorance, and above all the religious and moral earnestness of this indignant prophet naturally captivated the mind of Gandhi.

Three decades later Gandhi said that while Tolstoy condemned his former literary activity, Ruskin[5] crowned it with *Unto This Last* and *Fors Clavigera.*

Inspired with the message of Ruskin, Gandhi arose with the dawn, ready to translate the principles of Ruskin into practice. He understood the teaching of *Unto This Last* to mean that 'the good of the individual is contained in the good of all, that life of labour is the life worth living and that a lawyer's work has the same value as the barber's. He discovered some of his deepest convictions[6] reflected in this great book and he said in later years that the one book that brought about an instantaneous and practical transformation in his life was Ruskin's *Unto This Last.* He once told Vallabhbhai Patel that a time was coming when those who had not listened to Ruskin and had neglected his teaching would turn to him.

GANDHI AT ONCE decided to launch upon a project which was novel and revolutionary, as he called it. Did not Ruskin work with his hands? Did not Tolstoy live on a farm, with his disciples? According to his project, Gandhi bought with the help of Parsi Rustomji a piece of land covering a hundred acres, two and a half miles from Phoenix station and fourteen miles from Durban. In less than a month a shed, 75 ft. long and 50 ft. broad, was erected to house the press. When he took over the management of *Indian Opinion*, the number of subscribers was 887 and the advertisement revenue had greatly decreased.

Gandhi's plan was this. Each worker could have a piece of three acres of land at the cost price and he could live on it. The workers could receive per mensem an advance sufficient to cover their necessary expenses. The profits could be divided amongst them at the end of each year. "Living under such conditions and amidst the beautiful surroundings, the workers could live a more simple and natural life and the ideas of Ruskin and Tolstoy be combined with strict business principle".[7]

Each could be his own agriculturist and there would be brotherhood between the European and Indian workers. Each was to make a living by manual work and find the joy of service. The farming was to be done by hand. A piece of three acres of land fell to the lot of Gandhi. Non-killing was a fundamental principle in Phoenix Farm, as it was named. Yet a snake was killed without any complaint from Gandhi although he said that man should fear nothing that God had created.

West agreed to work on £3 a month. Although still editor, Mansukhlal Hiralal Nazar did not accept the scheme. Madanjit disapproved of it, fortelling disaster, and dissociated himself from it. Maganlal, Gandhi's nephew, who had cast his lot with Gandhi accepted it with his characteristic zeal and devotion. By December 1904 the Phoenix settlement was started and *Indian Opinion* was published on December 24, 1904, from Phoenix. For some days the settlers used machines, but later they worked with hand-power only, and the paper was reduced to foolscap size. They learnt typesetting. They built houses with corrugated iron.

Gandhi wanted gradually to retire from legal practice and go to live in the settlement. Polak was glad that the loan of the book *Unto This Last* had been so fruitful and he joined the settlement after a month. But in the meanwhile Ritch went to England towards the end of March 1905 to finish his law studies. So Polak was called back to Johannesburg to join Gandhi's office as an articled clerk along with one Mr. Maclntyre who also joined Gandhi with the same object.

The Indian Congress, which met in Bombay in December 1904, fervently prayed that the British Parliament would insist on a just and equal treatment of Indians in the Crown Colony of Transvaal.

Early in the year Gandhi wrote to 'Dear Prof, Gokhale' inviting him to make a tour of the main cities of South Africa, obviously to help the Indians put their problem before the Transvaal and Natal Governments. But Gokhale, who was then in London, declined the offer of his disciple who ended his letter with "I remain: Yours truly".

Polak began to live with Gandhi like a blood-brother. As he had no money, he had so far remained unmarried. Gandhi persuaded him to marry by saying that if poverty was a bar, poor men could never marry. So one Miss Douns was brought to Johannesburg. Polak was Jewish and Miss Douns Christian. Gandhi was interested in getting his friends married and Polak married Miss Douns at the end of the year. West, too, married at his native place and came back with a beautiful young woman, who was a daughter of a shoemaker working in a Leicester factory. By this time about a dozen families lived at Phoenix.

A year later Gandhi brought his family to Johannesburg. He wanted to live according to the philosophy of Ruskin. So they depended upon manual labour for everything in the household. Gandhi purchased a hand-mill for £7 and Polak and Gandhi, Mrs. Polak and the children worked at it. They prepared bread at home. This was done to ensure health, simplicity and economy. Gandhi had some exercise regularly and he was an adept at skipping. At table, various kinds of vegetable dishes were served as the first course, accompanied by a kind of lentil dish, hard-baked wholemeal bread, nuts, butter, and various dishes of raw salad. The second course consisted of a milk dish and raw fruit. Thereafter, a kind of cereal coffee or lemonade. Gandhi did not smoke.

Polak suggested to Gandhi that he should give an English education to his sons, so that they would easily gain considerable advantage over others in the race of life. To Gandhi, education was just a means. If it was not accompanied by truthfulness, firmness and patience it was sterile. The object of education was to improve oneself and serve the community and not to be able to earn money.

Gandhi seemed to think that book-knowledge obscured—if, indeed, it did not destroy—the capacity to perceive the inner vision[8] and he considered history a record of the wars of the world.[9] So he opined : "Indian parents who train their children to think and talk in English from their infancy betray their children and their country. They deprive them of the spiritual and social heritage of the nation".[10] Gandhi, who denied his sons an English education, added that it had been the regret of his sons and also his that he failed to ensure them enough literary training, and although he was not heart-broken over it, his regret, if any, was that he did not prove an ideal father.

Yet, strangely enough, Gandhi, while congratulating James Godfrey on his becoming a Barrister-at-law, observed that if Indian parents were to follow the example of Godfrey in large numbers the fetters that bound the Indians would soon break. All of them, he added, were in pressing need of education,[11] but they were slow to act in acquiring it.

From contact with Mrs. Polak and other European guests, who lived with the family, Kasturba had learnt bits of conversational English such as, "What the matter Mr. Polak? What for he (Gandhi) cross? What for he cross Bapu? What Bapu done?" After some time Gandhi sent his family to Phoenix and he lived with the Polaks. He now gave up taking milk and using onion in his diet as he thought that these stimulated the passions. Mother's milk, he said, was the correct food for babies, but it was not meant for adults.

When Mrs. Millie Polak tried to wean her baby, Gandhi took the child every night for about two weeks to sleep on a mattress near him, and the weaning was completed. In his behaviour with a stranger Gandhi was very attractive personally, full of courtesy, sympathy and buoyancy, but he did not show that much courtesy to his own men.[12] Asked about this, he replied that just as arms constituted a part of our very selves, so were those nearest to us. This trait reflected in his future dealings with the foreigners, foreign journalists and foreign leaders as against his behaviour with Indian journalists and leaders. Forty years later, K. Rangaswami, an eminent Indian journalist, experienced this difference and severely blamed Gandhi for his weakness for foreign journalists.[13]

Now a well-established and well-known lawyer in South Africa, Gandhi earned about £3,600 annually. He invariably took the fees in advance from a person not known to him. He never filed a suit against anybody for default of payment and conducted deserving cases gratis.

On more than one occasion Gandhi threw over his brief and left the court when he discovered that his client had betrayed him by giving false information. Every client was forewarned of this. Once he asked the accused why he had committed a theft. When the accused replied that he had committed it because he had to live, Gandhi simply asked him: "Why?" A most thrilling case was the one in which Gandhi's lieutenant Parsi Rustomji was involved. He was an expert smuggler, but was caught. Gandhi saved him by compelling him to confess his guilt to the customs officers and paying a penalty equal to twice the amount on goods he had confessed to having smuggled. The lesson was not lost upon Parsi Rustomji, who blared it out to all from a frame which contained the story!

IN MARCH 1905 Gandhi delivered a series of lectures on Hinduism at the Masonic Temple, Plein Street, in Johannesburg, under the auspices of the Johannesburg Theosophical Society, Major Peacocke, Vice-President, was in the chair.

In his four lectures Gandhi explained that one of the remarkable characteristics of Hinduism was self-abnegation, and unlike most of the great world religions, Hinduism did not derive its name from any person. Buddhism, he said, had a reforming effect on Hinduism, somewhat similar to that of Protestantism on Catholicism. Although Buddhism was said to have declined in India, the spirit of Buddhists remained in the country. The Hindus seemingly worshipped sticks and stones. He was not one of those who believed that the religion of Islam was a religion of the sword. The keynote of Islam was, however, its levelling spirit.

Kabir tried to bring about a fusion of Hindus and Muslims by keeping intact the chief tenets of Hinduism and by borrowing somewhat from Islam. But the attempt was not quite successful. Guru Nanak drew upon Kabir for his doctrine and added to it militant Hinduism. He offered the olive branch by respecting Muslim susceptibilities, but was ready to defend Hinduism from Muslim aggression, and so Sikhism was a direct result of Islam. It was Hinduism that gave Mohammedanism its Akbar. Hinduism arose out of the struggle braced with warm glow.

In spite of the assaults on Hinduism coming from Buddhism, Islam and Christianity, Gandhi continued, it had come out of them unscathed. According to Gandhi, the tenets of Hinduism are : "God exists and is without attribute or form and is omnipresent and omniscient. His original form is Brahman. The soul exists and is distinct from the body. To be free from the cycles of birth and death and be merged in Brahman is *Moksha* or liberation."

Zeal or passion, he added, was a great speciality, a mighty force, of Islam. It had been the cause of many good deeds, and sometimes of bad ones too. In India the majority of converts to Islam came from the lower classes. "All religions", he concluded, "teach that we should live together in love and mutual kindness."

Gandhi's opinions on Islam caused a stir among the Muslims and they wrote several letters of protest to him. Replying to them, Gandhi said that all the facts stated by him were drawn from history, and observed : "That Islam was spread by force is a historical fact." To him personally there was no distinction between a Brahmin and a Bhangi (scavenger). He explained that he used the word 'fervour' in a complimentary sense and fervour was as necessary as in other tasks as it was in war. It was a positive virtue. Japan, he observed, was able to take the Fort of Port Arthur only because she had been fighting with fervour. Edison and Watt made inventions because of passion.

In conclusion, Gandhi said: "I maintain that Hindu religion teaches us to look upon all with an equal eye without making distinctions between Hindu and Muslim, Brahmin and Bhangi and that is the religion I follow." Yet certain Muslims resented Gandhi's views and the Young Men's Mohammedan Society continued for a whole year criticizing Gandhi for referring to the conversion of lower class Hindus to Islam. In reply Gandhi quoted.[14] *The Encyclopaedia Britannica* and Hunter's *History of India* and added that as he had presented the historical facts with the intention of doing good, nobody should take offence.

In an apologetic tone Gandhi, however, said at the meeting of the Natal Indian Congress at Durban that he had no intention in his speeches on the Hindu religion to hurt the susceptibilities of Mohammedans. He said that the Indians had lost their country to foreigners through disunity. Though Indians, he observed, professed different religions, they should regard themselves as one in the matter of public work.

In June 1905 Gandhi apologized to the Muslims and said that he did not want to prolong the controversy. Yet their bitter protests continued. At last, in April 1906, Gandhi reiterated his apology and sorrowfully appealed to the Muslims to forgive[15] him if he had committed an error in what he had said.

It seems that Gandhi had learnt one of the important lessons of his life, and in future he took the utmost care never to wound the susceptibilities of Muslims. He did not refer to this early experience with Muslims in his autobiography.

On the advice of Gandhi the managers of the International Printing Press published a reprint of the translation of the Bhagavad Gita, without the permission of Annie Besant, the authoress, for distribution among Hindu boys and others. A portrait of Annie Besant was also included. Mrs. Besant was annoyed. Gandhi apologized to her for the offence and added that if she considered any public statement necessary or complete withdrawal of the book from further circulation, or taking out of the portrait from the book, her wishes would be carried out.

With his fervour and passion Gandhi was now enthusing his people. He cited to them the progress Sayajirao Gaikwad, the Maharaja of Baroda, had made in the fields of education, revenue and self-government. He described Sayajirao as one of the most cultured princes of India. The village panchayats, instead of being hereditary, would now be elected by the people in Baroda, and Gandhi praised it as a great experiment and added that "a state like Baroda ought to serve as a help to dispel prejudices and illusions about India."

With the same fervour Gandhi praised 'the epic heroism' of Japan which had defeated the great Russian fleet. "This unity," Gandhi pointed out, "and patriotic spirit together with a heroic indifference to life (or death) have created an atmosphere in Japan the like of which is nowhere else to be found in the World. Of death, they do not entertain any fear. To die in the service of the country, they have always regarded as wholly good." He asked the Indians in South Africa to emulate the example of Japan.

The victory of Asiatic Japan over European Russia had an inspiring effect on Indian leaders like Lokamanya Tilak and Surendranath Banerjee. Tilak congratulated the Japanese people at a meeting in Poona and Surendranath said : "All Asia is astir with the pulsations of a new life. The sun has arisen in the East. Japan has saluted the rising sun. That sun, in its meridian splendour, will pass through our country."[18]

At this time Gandhi was taking much interest in learning Tamil and in making efforts to collect funds for the earthquake relief in India. Plague, too caused terrible havoc in India, and the average number of deaths a year was 1,20,000.

Gandhi wrote in *Indian Opinion* on numerous topics.

He opined that Bhai Parmanand who was then on a lecture tour in South Africa on behalf of the Arya Samajists, should be honoured at Durban by both Hindus and Muslims as a man of learning. Prof. Parmanand delivered at various places discourses on religion and education to crowded audiences. Gandhi praised the Arya Samaj for its useful and practical work and for producing earnest patriots and a band of self-sacrificing teachers, and said that the Arya Samaj represented a reformation of Hinduism.[17] He added that they in South Africa, were not yet ripe for vigorous enterprise on religious lines. At Johannesburg, Bhai Parmanand was presented with an address obviously by Hindu leaders alone, Gandhi, Patel and Pillay, for no Muslim signature appeared on that address. The address described Parmanand as a self-sacrificing worker and one who had given his lifetime to the cause of religion and education.

Later, in 1915, Bhai Parmanand was sentenced by the Government of India to transportation for life. Writing an article in *Young India* in November 1919 in which he appealed to the Government to release Parmanand, Gandhi observed that he was a man of sterling character and lofty patriotism, and had left on his mind a deep impression as a man full of truth and nobility.

Gandhi was above caste and creed. He wrote also an article on Hali, an Urdu poet who had made a name in north India. His full name was Maulvi Sayed Altaf Hussain Ansari. A translation of his poems was made by one Mr. Ward.

In order to inspire the Indians with courage and sacrifice, Gandhi wrote a series of articles on historic personalities. He described Lord Charles Metcalfe, the Governor-General of India, as the liberator of the Indian press. He hailed Mountstuart Elphinstone, who was a popular Governor of Bombay, as a great man, described Sir Thomas Munro, Governor of Madras, as the friend of the Ryot and appreciated his selfless and dutiful conduct.

Gandhi extolled Tolstoy to the skies. There was, he said,[18] no man so talented, learned and as ascetic as Count Tolstoy, and though eighty years old, he was quite healthy, industrious and mentally alert. Words fell short to express adequately the power of his goodness and godly living. Gandhi had even translated into Gujarati a story by Tolstoy "God sees the truth but waits" for the benefit of his readers. He traced Maxim Gorky's life from poverty to eminence, from an apprentice to a shoemaker, and described him as a champion of the people's rights.

Gandhi praised George Washington for his devotion to truth, his courage and the bravery he had displayed in war, in introducing land reform, in keeping the American people united and in enhancing his country's reputation. "The name of Washington", he observed, "will live as long as America lives. May India too produce such heroes." Later, on his becoming the Mahatma,

Gandhi, in April 1925 measured Washington's greatness by the standard of non-violence and declared him to be a misguided patriot.[19]

ABOUT THIS TIME Bengal was partitioned, the western half made a Hindu Province and the eastern a Muslim one. The Bengal Hindus, lawyers, leaders and landlords opposed the partition carried out by Lord Curzon, the Governor-General of India. Hundreds of meetings were held in protest and thousands attended them. Curzon, though he outwardly justified partition from the administration point of view, was determined to give a blow to the power of the Bengal press and its leadership. So he divided the Muslims from the Hindus by creating for them a separate province.

Surendranath Banerjee gave a call to the country and said the whole nation should support them. Tilak gave them full support and the partition of Bengal became an all-India question.

Men like Muncherji Bhownaggree differed from the Bengalis on the partition issue and so an effigy of Muncherji was burnt at the College Square in Calcutta. It was with great sorrow, observed Gandhi, that *Indian Opinion* noticed the insult to Muncherji Bhownaggree, the friend to the unrepresented thousands in South Africa and a friend in the cause of India. "Indians" Gandhi warned from South Africa, "will do very wrong to value a man according to the power of his invective and the bitterness of his denunciation of Britain's perfidy. The more moderate opinions of a man like Muncherji have a far greater weight than the extravagances of hot-bed radicals. It is the conviction of calm reasoning alone that will get the full measure of justice for India,"[20] Later, the hot-headed Gandhists did the same thing in India to liberals and to those who differed from Gandhi, as the Bengalis did in the case of Muncherji. An admirer of the worshippers of the British Empire, Gandhi was gratefully defending his supporter. That is all.

Gandhi, however, supported the boycott movement in Bengal and said that it would be productive of only good to India, and if the resolve to use only Indian goods was maintained. It would be no small help, he added, in developing the national spirit and in giving a stimulus to national industries. He noted that even Chinese merchants in Bengal had taken part in the agitation against partition. If the people really acted accordingly there would be nothing surprising if "our troubles came to a speedy end'. The boycott was so complete that the Collector of Barisal District in East Bengal had to request Aswini Kumar Dutt, leader of Barisal, to allow a shopkeeper to sell salt to him.

When Bengal observed a general strike and a lakh of people gathered demonstrating their solidarity, Gandhi cheered Bengal as 'brave Bengal' and appreciated the unity of the Hindus and Muslims. He saw in the agitation the unification of different communities. Later, while commenting on Morley's speech in which he had said that the partition was a settled fact, Gandhi said that the hope that Morley would act boldly and fearlessly and do what was necessary, was belied.

Gandhi also supported Dadabhai Naoroji's candidature when he contested from North Lambeth in October 1905. He praised his pioneer work and self-sacrificing devotion to the cause of India.

At this time Gandhi expressed his opinion on some of his contemporaries and some historical figures. Horatio Nelson, according to him, was worshipped not because he was a naval hero, but because he was a living embodiment of duty. His patriotism was of the purest type. Gandhi prayed for a long life for King Edward and said that the British Indians in South Africa were the humblest of his subjects but not the least in loyalty and devotion. He described Lajpatrai as the recognised leader of the Punjab and said on Gokhale was centered the hope of India.

While commenting on the Russian revolution of 1905 Gandhi said that even the most powerful could not rule without the cooperation of the ruled and added that if the Russian people succeeded, the revolution in Russia would be regarded as the greatest victory, the greatest event of the present century.[21] Later Lenin, however, described it as a rehearsal for the 1917 revolution. Comparing Russia with India, Gandhi said that, "We, too, can resort to the Russian remedy against tyranny. The movement in Bengal for the use of Swadeshi goods is much like the Russian movement." This shows how Gandhi's mind was gradually working towards a solution to the Indian problem.

On November 29, 1905, Gandhi led a deputation to Lord Selborne. Previously, on October 14, Gandhi had led a deputation to Lord Selborne at Patchefstroom. He explained to him the position of British Indians in the Transvaal.

Gandhi put before Lord Selborne the serious consequences of the restrictions on Indian trade, explained how the Law 3 of 1885 was equally unjust and dangerous, and lastly put forward the demands of the Indians. Selborne admitted the extreme reasonableness of the statement.

About this time news came that the salt tax was to be abolished in India. Gandhi was extremely glad about it. He had already noted the reduction of the salt tax as a good point for Curzon. He quoted the opinion of Dr. Hutchinson that the salt tax was a barbarous practice and was a great shame for the British Government in India to continue the salt tax while a similar tax previously in force in Japan had been abolished. "The tax," Gandhi observed in *Indian Opinion* of July 8, 1905, "should be immediately abolished. Salt is an essential article in our dietary. It could be said that to a certain extent, the increasing incidence of leprosy in India was due to the salt tax." This gives an indication of what was going on in Gandhi's mind.

On every important question of nationalism Gandhi expressed his opinion through *Indian Opinion.* In a note he observed that 'Bande Mataram', the heroic song of Bengal, had come to be our national anthem. "It is nobler in sentiment and sweeter than the songs of other nations. While other anthems contain sentiments that are derogatory to others, Bande Mataram is quite free from such faults. Its only aim is to arouse in us a sense of patriotism. It regards India as the mother and sings her praise. The poet attributes to Mother India all the good qualities one finds in one's own mother,"[22]

The words used, Gandhi concluded, were mostly Sanskrit but easy to understand and the language, though Bengali, was simple. The song was of a high order.

Lakhs of people later underwent flogging for either singing or shouting 'Bande Mataram'. It proved a veritable red rag to the British Bulldog.

What Gandhi, as the all-powerful Congress leader, did to the Bande Mataram when later the determined Muslim opposition to this song was voiced, would be given at the proper place.

At this time Gandhi expressed his opinion that Hindustani was sweet, polite and spirited, and it should be adopted for achieving nationhood in India. It suited Hindus and Muslims alike, he added, being derived from Sanskrit and Persian.[23]

After carrying the responsibility of *Indian Opinion* for over fourteen months, Gandhi once defined in a note the duty of the press. He said it was its duty to serve the people, but while doing so, the press should not suppress their faults, but bring them to their notice. If it flattered them, it would be playing the part of the enemy. If their opponents spoke ill of them, they should boldly defend them, but should fearlessly expose their faults to public gaze and urge their removal.

The Indian National Congress held its session at Benares in December 1905 under the presidentship of G. K. Gokhale. It reiterated its usual resolution on South Africa.

Gandhi consoled Indians in South Africa by saying that every just cause was its own strength and people should not give way to despair and consequential lethargy. Their position, he observed, was not entirely cheerful but self-help could be the primary cause for any amelioration in that position. In the end, he appealed to them to continue their struggle with reasonableness, as acknowledged by Lord Selborne, with patience, and yet with persistence.

Madanjit, the founder of *Indian Opinion*, had returned to India and was serving like a true patriot. His name had been retained as its printer and publisher. He was expected to send reports of his work for *Indian Opinion* and to keep in touch with it for which he was to be paid some remuneration. He later went to Rangoon and early in the year 1907 started an English journal entitled *United Burma* with the object of uniting the Burmese and persuading them to take part in the activities of the Indian National Congress.

Gandhi again appealed to the Indians in South Africa to help *Indian Opinion*. The objects of the Journal, he said, were to make Indian grievances known to the Government, to the whites in South Africa and in England and to people in India, to tell Indians of their shortcomings and to exhort them to overcome them and principally to eliminate the distinctions between Hindus and Mohammedans, as also those among Gujaratis, Tamilians and 'Calcuttawallas' and essay an experiment in achieving unity. To him the journal was a great instrument of education. Lastly, he appealed to the Gujaratis who numbered 20,000 in South Africa and expected 25 per cent of the number to become subscribers.

The new year 1906 opened with distress for Gandhi. Mansukhlal Hiralal Nazar, his colleague and the editor of *Indian Opinion*, passed away on January 20, 1906. A brilliant and moderate-minded journalist, he served the cause of the Indians through *Indian Opinion*. After his death, Herbert Kitchin, Gandhi's English friend, became editor. Then the post of editor was long filled by Henry S. L. Polak and during his incarceration, the Rev. Joseph Doke acted as its editor.

CHAPTER VIII

Deputation to London

Just When Disabilities were being heaped upon the Indians in the Transvaal, the Zulus rose in revolt against the Natal Government in February 1906. There are various tribes among the African Negroes, such as the Zulus, the Swazis, the Basutos and the Bechuanas. They speak different languages. Among the Negroes, the tallest and the most 'handsome' are the Zulus. Their legs and arms are muscular, lips large and thick, nose flat and large, their hair curled, and skin shining black like ebony.

The Zulu chief had advised non-payment of a new tax imposed upon his tribe. This resulted in a sergeant being assassinated and the clash that followed developed into a rebellion.

Many Europeans joined the Natal Army as volunteers. Gandhi thought that he must do his bit in the war as he was a loyal British citizen. During the Boer War he had justified his stand by saying that he did not like to enforce his personal opinion on others. Naturally, this time also he did not stop to consider which party had justice and right on its side. His lip sympathy was for the Zulus, but his head was with the British Empire.

The Indians in Natal held a meeting and declared their intention of helping the Natal Government. They raised a Soldiers' Fund and formed an Indian Stretcher-Bearer Corps. Gandhi, who considered himself a citizen of Natal, said that the Natal Government had put the Indian community on its mettle and had given the Indians an opportunity of taking their share in the defence of the country.

The sacrifices, Gandhi observed, would be insignificant; yet the consequences in the future were great. His advice to the Indian community was to bear the brunt of colonial defence and to obey the laws designed for the defence of the country they lived in.

Gandhi asked them to give their lives in defence of Natal. Even if every shop offered one man, many men could be trained. They would gain in strength and energy and would be deemed to have done their duty as citizens. They would learn to discipline their mind and body. There were not greater risks to life in going to the battlefield than in everyday life. More men died of plague, fever and other diseases than in war. The experience in every war had been similar. They should therefore participate in the war if they wanted to live happily and with self-respect in Natal.

Meanwhile Gandhi fought the Johannesburg Municipality on the issue of restrictions on the use of tram-cars by Indians. He had also led a deputation to wait on the Constitution Committee of the Transvaal. Just then the British Indian Committee in London suggested that Gandhi alone should go to London to represent the Indian case. But Gandhi had written to the Governor of Natal expressing his readiness to form an Indian Ambulance Corps. The Governor accepted the offer. So he informed Dadabhai Naoroji that he had postponed his departure as he was going to the front along with the Indian Stretcher-Bearer Corps.

Immediately Gandhi broke up his home at Johannesburg, sent some of his things to Phoenix and left some with Polak who rented a smaller house in Johannesburg. He sent his family to settle at Phoenix and, reaching Durban, he formed the Indian Stretcher-Bearer Corps.

The ideas of non-possession increasingly influenced Gandhi's mind. A year earlier, in July 1905, he had written to Revashankarbhai Jhaveri that as the financial burden on him was very heavy, it was difficult for him to meet the expenditure which was being incurred over his son Harilal and his sister Raliatbehn who were in India. He expressed his desire that his son should be sent back to Africa and requested Revashankarbhai to write to Raliatbehn that she should limit her expenses to Rs. 25 and added that he too had written to her to cut down her expenses. He wrote also to his eldest brother Laxmidas that whatever savings he had, he had given him, but thenceforth he should expect nothing. Savings, if any, he said, would be utilized for the benefit of the Phoenix community. Laxmidas was offended. He wrote back sternly and said that it was Gandhi's duty to support the family as their father had done.

Upon this Gandhi wrote to Laxmidas in May 1906 that he

had no idea of separating from him. He claimed nothing from the property nor did he want anything as his own. All that he had was being utilized for public purposes and he would have satisfied Laxmidas's desire for money if he had not dedicated his all to the service of the people. In case of Laxmidas's death, he said, he would support the family. He had ceased to think of Harilal as his son.

"My mind," he concluded, "is now quite clear, my aspirations are higher and I have no desire for worldly enjoyments of any type whatever. I am engaged in my present activities as I look upon them as essential to life. If I have to face death while thus engaged, I shall face it with equanimity. I am now a stranger to fear."

Laxmidas, however, replied charging Gandhi with selfish motives and demanded a share in his income. Reacting to this very sharply, Gandhi said in April 1907: "Between you two brothers I have already paid nearly Rs. 60,000. I cleared all the debts while I was there. From this you will see that I have paid back much more than Rs. 13,000 spent on me during my stay in England. In saying this I do not mean to suggest that I have done you a favour. I only state the bare facts to pacify your anger." He further said that Laxmidas sought peace and happiness through money and had squandered a lot of money on pleasures, and on pomp and show. He had handed over to Laxmidas all his savings in Natal and that "I had not kept a penny for myself". He added that he might have to go to jail in the course of the impending struggle, and as he was running the Phoenix press with borrowed money he was unable to send him a hundred Rupees a month. He pointed out that his family included not only his relatives but all living beings. He would use whatever money was left after meeting his expenses, for the benefit of the people. As regards the possibility of his not being able to get caste girls to marry his sons and nephews, he said, "I repeat that it is the divine law that one gets fruits according to one's faith." In this letter Laxmidas was addressed as 'Respected Sir,' not as brother.

Thereafter Laxmidas virtually stopped all communication with Gandhi. His heart burnings and misunderstandings persisted for some years.

The Indian Stretcher-Bearer Corps was ready to go to the front; Gandhi, its leader, was given the rank of Sergeant-Major by the Government of Natal. He wrote to Gokhale about the Corps and informed Dadabhai that his departure to London was postponed as the formation of the Corps was far more important than a visit to London.

Under the leadership of Gandhi, the Indian Stretcher-Bearer Corps worked at the front and dressed the wounds of the Zulus. The Natal European leaders, who were in the military service, were agreeably surprised at Gandhi's grateful attitude and thanked him. Gandhi, who had received for a year training in compounding and dispensing prescriptions and in nursing at Dr. Booth's little hospital did that work for the white soldiers. Sometimes the Corps marched forty miles a day.

Zulu rebellion was put down ruthlessly. It was not a war, observed Gandhi, but was a man-hunt! Being a believer in the myth that the British Empire existed for the welfare of all, Gandhi miserably failed to react to the human tragedy in Zulu-land.

The Indian Stretcher-Bearer Corps was disbanded on July 19. It worked from June 23 to July 18 at the front. Gandhi and other members of the staff were feted at Stanger and were given receptions and awarded medals in Durban. Sir Henry MacCallum, the Governor of Natal, specially thanked them heartily for their services. Gandhi made a suggestion that the leaders of the Corps should receive five shillings a day.

As mentioned above, these meritorious and loyal services of Gandhi were rewarded with medals. Gandhi had not become Mahatma yet. When he became one he reflected upon this Red Cross work and seriously, though with an air of philosophy, observed: "There is no defence for my conduct in doing ambulance work, weighed only in the scales of ahimsa. I draw no distinction between those who wield the weapons of destruction and those who do Red Cross work. Both participate in war and advance its course; both are guilty of the crime of war."[1] Yet he added that under the circumstances in which he found himself he was bound to adopt the course he did.

Life is full of complexities and contradictions and a man, great or small, keeps defending, justifying and rationalising them. That is human nature. And Gandhi was not an exception to it.

WHAT WAS THE effect of the Zulu War on Gandhi?

The Zulu rebellion over, Gandhi quietly hurried to Phoenix settlement and took two vows, the vow of celibacy, of course having gained the consent of his wife to the vow, and the vow of poverty. Was this the lesson he derived from the travails of the

Zulu War? He was thirty-seven when he took the vow of celibacy. Self-control, he thought, would give him the power of self-sacrifice. It seems, however, that with all his fasts, control of the palate, and giving up of a milk diet he could not succeed in curbing his sexual passion until he was forty-five.

In a letter to Mahadev Desai, Gandhi said on September 15, 1919, that his *tapascharya* (self-suffering accepted as moral discipline), his *brahmacharya* (purity of mind and body in regard to sex) were extolled to the skies, but he himself felt that both were imperfect. "One who started sex gratification with his wife at the age of 15," he admitted, "and continued to indulge in it fairly often for 30 years, what praise does such a one's brahmacharya merit? It is like the cat which after having killed several hundreds of mice, decided to go on a pilgrimage to Mecca."[2]

Just at this time, in the first week of August 1906, the Colonial Secretary, Duncan, informed the Transvaal Legislation of Government's intention to introduce a Bill to re-register Asiatics in the Transvaal. The Ordinance was published in the Government Gazette Extraordinary of August 26, 1906.

The Ex-Boer Government had deprived the Indians of burgher rights and land ownership except in locations and wards specially set apart for Indians. Under their Law 3 of 1885 only those of the Indians who wanted to settle for purposes of trade or otherwise had to be registered and pay a fee of £3. On the advent of British rule, on the advice of Lord Milner, the Indians were registered. They held certificates bearing the details of their family, business, place of birth, the distinctive marks and thumb-prints.

According to the new ordinance, every Indian, man, woman and child of eight years or upwards must register his or her name and give finger-prints at the office on the pass which he would have to carry on his person. At the final stage, however, the Government declared that it would not apply to women.

It was the contention of the Government that they had done this to prevent impersonation and infiltration although the Indians at that time were holding registration certificates.

The Malays were exempted from the operation of the new ordinance. The Kaffirs, who carried passes, were not required to produce identification particulars. But Kaffirs with some status were exempted from the liability of carrying passes.

The ordinance threw a new challenge to the leaders of the British Indians. Denouncing it outright, Gandhi said the Black Ordinance would spell ruin for the Indians as it was the first step to hound the Indians out of the Transvaal. He therefore raised a cry of alarm in *Indian Opinion*, wrote to Dadabhai Naoroji to intervene, cabled protests to the Secretary of State for India and the Viceroy of India; and addressed a meeting of the Hamidiya Islamic Society in Johannesburg where he appealed to the Indians not to put up with the intolerable, wicked and vicious Draft Ordinance. He also said that there was no alternative to sending a deputation to London. He advised them that they should cheerfully suffer imprisonment, but they should not seek fresh registration.

Even the half-castes[3] and Kaffirs, he added, who were less advanced than Indians had resisted the Government. "If the Government," he went on with resolute will, "sends me to jail, I shall be the first to incur imprisonment." And if any Indian was put to trouble because of his non-registration he would defend him free of charge. In the end he urged them to close their shops on the following Tuesday and to attend the mass meeting convened at the Empire Theatre. Gandhi unconsciously compromised his belief in human dignity and equality as he referred to the poor people as half-castes.

Accordingly a mass meeting was held on September 11, 1906, at the Empire Theatre in Johannesburg, under the presidentship of Abdul Gani, Chairman of the British Indian Association. Not less than three thousand people attended the meeting. Representatives from neighbouring places like Pietermaritzburg, Klerksdorp, Krugersdorp and Pretoria attended, and letters expressing sympathy and agreement with the views of the meeting were also received from Klerksdorp and other places.

Addressing the meeting, Gandhi solemnly said that he had done the right thing in advising them to take the step as loyal British subjects, and no shadow of disloyalty could rest upon them. He hoped that when occasion required they would take the heroic step. One ounce of practice, he observed, was worthwhile tons of speeches and writings. Herein lay the power of a maker of history, the power of Gandhi, one of the greatest men of action in the twentieth century.

Haji Habib proposed that they should take a solemn vow to oppose the ordinance. Upon this Gandhi, explaining the significance of the vow, said that pledges and vows were taken on rare occasions, and if having taken such a pledge they violated it, they would be guilty before God and man. Suffering, jail, starvation, poverty and hardships they would have to endure. 'But,' he gravely added, "even if everyone else flinched leaving me alone to face the music, I am confident that I would never violate my pledge."[4]

Another speaker, Abdul Gani, said that under the Union Jack no one should suffer any disability; all must have equal rights. When in his eloquent and brief speech he spoke of jail-going, the audience shouted in one voice, "We shall go to jail, but will not register ourselves again." Dr. George Godfrey said that if the Bill was passed, they would storm the courts and say, 'arrest us'. Haji Ojeer Ally said in a thundering speech that they had a right to live in peace and happiness under the Union Jack. Like the Boers, he added, they would not take the rifles but would go to jail.

Four resolutions were passed. One resolution said that the Ordinance reduced the British Indians to a status lower than that of the Kaffirs and other coloured persons. By another resolution the meeting authorised the British Indian Association to send a deputation to London in order to put their grievances before the Imperial Government. The main resolution proclaimed that "should the Legislative Council, the Local and the Imperial Governments, reject the humble prayer of the Indian Community against the Asiatic Ordinance, every Indian present at the meeting solemnly and sincerely resolves that, rather than submit to this tyrannical law and abide by its un-British provisions, he will prefer to go to jail and will continue to do so until it pleases His Majesty and the King-Emperor to grant relief."

Then three cheers were called for the King-Emperor Edward; God Save the King was sung and the meeting dispersed.[5] It was indeed a memorable meeting.

An indefatigable worker, Gandhi did not allow his colleagues and co-workers to stop at that point. He got the pledges circulated, and signatures were obtained on them at different places. Gandhi, a plodding propagandist, approached the press explaining the Indian stand. The *Rand Daily Mail*, and the *Star* echoed it, attracting the attention of the whites.

Just then the arrest of an Indian woman called Punia, who was travelling with her husband without a separate pass, worsened the situation. The husband knew nothing about a permit being required for his wife. Gandhi drew the attention of the press to the injustice and asserted that the Government was adding difficulties and indignities to the trouble of the Indians.

Lord Elgin, Secretary of State for the Colonies, and Lord Selborne both had clearly informed the leaders of the British Indian Association that no useful purpose was likely to be served by their sending a deputation. Still, a deputation consisting of Gandhi and H. O. Ally started on October 1 by train for Cape

Town. Three persons were named for the deputation, but Abdul Gani withdrew at the last moment. A Muslim was included in the deputation at the instance of Gandhi. During the railway journey Ally was taken ill and Gandhi attended on him. A sum of £900 was handed over to the deputation of which £300 was sanctioned for Ally's domestic and other expenses.

They embarked the *Armadale Castle*. Its passengers included the acting Governor of the Transvaal Sir Richard Solomon and Lady Solomon. Yuk Lin Lew, Chinese Consul-General in the Transvaal was going to represent the Chinese case in South Africa through the Chinese Embassy in London.

Haji Ojeer Ally was born in 1853 in Mauritius. He was educated and brought up there. His mother was a Malay and his father an Indian Muslim. Ally knew Dutch, Hindustani and English well. He had worked as painter and clerk, had visited Mecca and become a Haji. Coming to South Africa in 1884, he became a very influential merchant and public man in Cape Town. Then he moved to Johannesburg. A man of liberal views, he was a good speaker in English. During the journey to London his illness troubled him greatly.

On board the ship Gandhi had milk, potatoes, soda-water and ginger. He ate stewed fruit in the morning, cream at 1 p.m., cocoa at four and potatoes, boiled vegetables, stewed fruit, soda-water and ginger at 6.30 p.m. He had had no bread, or raw fruit or nuts as a loose molar had been hurting him.

Sir Richard Solomon took part in the sports on the deck. Gandhi reluctantly paid subscriptions towards the sports but did not take part in them. He was reading Forbes's *Rasamala* or *A History of Gujarat*, and the *Alien Immigration Report*.

Ally was reading Justice Ameer Ali's *Spirit of Islam* and Washington Irving's *Mahomet And His Successors*. Gandhi met Sir Richard and discussed the whole question of the Indians in South Africa. Sir Richard said that he would consider the possibility of appointing a commission. Next day, however, he told Ally that he had given up the idea. Gandhi said that Sir Richard wanted to be Prime Minister of the Transvaal under responsible Government. Sir Richard probably thought that granting the request for a commission would be thwarting his ambition.

The deputation reached England on October 20, 1906, On their arrival in London, Ally and Gandhi went to stay at India House of Pandit Shyamji Krishna Varma and were very well looked after. But this House was rather remote, or perhaps the atmosphere was uncongenial. So they moved to the Hotel Cecil after two days.[6]

As Soon As they came to the Hotel Cecil, Gandhi got Ally admitted to hospital as a rheumatic patient and asked his old friend Dr. Josiah Oldfield to look after his health daily. Ally was ill for about a fortnight. Gandhi worked strenuously day and night. He left the hotel in the morning immediately after his breakfast. Paying visits to eminent public men and retired Indian civil servants, he sought their advice. He wrote to fix appointments with them, and obtained their consent to join the deputation, enlisting the support of some or assuaging the differences of others. He gave interviews to newsmen saying that the new Ordinance had reduced the Indians to a position lower than that of the Kaffirs.

The deputation worked under the guidance of Dadabhai Naoroji. On November 7 a meeting of the Liberal, Labour and Nationalist Members of the British Parliament was addressed by Gandhi and Ally in the Grand Committee Room of the House. Gandhi fully explained the grievances of the British Indians and the stand taken by them. Sir Henry Cotton, the Chairman of the meeting, protested against the treatment meted out to the British Indians and said that the question had become one of Imperial importance. The meeting unanimously supported the objectives of the deputation.

Next day the deputation waited on Lord Elgin, the Secretary of State for Colonies, at the Colonial Office at 3 p.m. The deputation consisted of Sir Henry Cotton, T. H. Thornton, Sir George Birdwood, F. H. Brown, Sir Muncherji Bhownaggree, Lord Stanley, Syed, Ameer Ally, Harold Cox, J. D. Reeds, Dadabhai Naoroji, Gandhi and Ally. Sir William Wedderburn did not take part as he differed on the personnel of the deputation. When Sir Lepel Griffin insisted that Wedderburn should join the deputation, Gandhi wrote to Wedderburn saying "I forgot at the time to tell him (Sir Lapel Griffin) of the objection you raised to your joining the deputation."[7] It was led by Sir Lapel Griffin who was the Chairman of the East India Association of which Lord Elgin was Vice-President.

Introducing the deputation Sir Lapel said that Ally was the representative of the Mohammedan part of the Indian Community in the Transvaal and the leader of the deputation brilliantly explained the justness of the grievances of the British Indians. Gandhi said that the British Indians ought to be treated as

British subjects, and the new ordinance, should not be applied to them. Finally, he appealed to Lord Elgin for appointing a commission to report on the situation. Ally said that the lot of British Indians was at the time infinitely worse than under the Boer regime. Dadabhai Naoroji said that the principle involved was the freedom of British subjects under the British Flag.

Elgin calmly replied that he agreed that the matter should not be regarded as a party question. He said that it was the view of the Transvaal Government that whatever they had done was to improve the condition of the British Indians. He then coldly added that he was stating the view which had been put before him. He stated, however, that the previous pass bore the thumb mark and so he did not see why it should not be affixed to the registration certificate without prejudice. It could not be debasing.

This statement got Gandhi in the trap.

Gandhi: It is the ten-finger mark.

Elgin: Is it more debasing with ten fingers?

Henry Cotton: It is required in the case of criminals.

Elgin: I do not want to argue it.

Then Lord Elgin drew out his claws. He referred to the telegrams and letters and memorials he had received against the deputation led by Gandhi. In the end he said he would give the best consideration to their representation. Before leaving, Gandhi spontaneously said, "Nothing short of a Commission would place our position accurately before your Lordship."

Thus Lord Elgin spoke much; but said nothing. The deputation also met Lord Hamilton and John Morley, the Secretary of State for India. The leader of the deputation pledged his word that Gandhi's methods and motives were disinterested. This he purposely did to nullify the propaganda against Gandhi carried on by the whites. Gandhi appealed to Morley to give the British Indians the protection they were entitled to. Morley promised to support them against the harsh and humiliating indignities. Then a second meeting of the M.Ps was held and they waited on the Prime Minister Sir Henry Campbell-Bannerman who said that he did not approve of the Asiatic Ordinance and would speak to Lord Elgin.

On November 27, the deputation also waited on Winston Churchill, the under-Secretary of State for the Colonies. Gandhi had not then become a naked fakir and so Churchill agreed to meet him. One sentence in the letter which Gandhi wrote while making the appointment with Churchill was typical of both Churchill and Gandhi. He wrote that "the deputation ventures to request an appointment with you." Later Gandhi said that Churchill spoke nicely and promised to do all he could, if the delegates could send him a report. Gandhi had also drafted a representation for the Chinese Ambassador and sent it to him. It was addressed to the Foreign Secretary Sir Edward Grey.[8]

Gandhi met John Edward Redmond, the leader of the Irish Party, and gained his sympathy. Gandhi then established a committee called the South Africa British Indian Committee to watch the interests of the British Indians in South Africa and to unite all the well-wishers and sympathisers in an organization. L. W. Ritch acted as its secretary. Gandhi wrote to Gokhale to form a similar committee in India although, he added, Pherozeshah Mehta did not see eye to eye with him in the matter.[9]

With his self-sacrificing zeal Gandhi could attract some of the Indian students like Ruthnum Pather to help him to despatch letters and in many other ways. Polak's father J. H. Polak, George V. Godfrey, Manilal Mehta, Adam Gool and Bhai Parmanand did useful work voluntarily. For a few days Miss Edith Lawson acted as secretarial assistant to the deputation.

While engaged day and night in the work of the deputation, Gandhi found out the addresses of certain old acquaintances, saw Dr. Josiah Oldfield, Mrs. Freeth, Mrs. Barnes and the relatives of his associates in South Africa. He visited Polak's sisters, found them most lovable, and fondly wrote to Polak that "if I was unmarried, or young, or believed in mixed marriage, you know what I would have done!" He arranged for the boarding and education of M. M. Pather who afterwards became a staunch member of Savarkar's Abhinava Bharat. Gandhi had the waiter of Hotel Cecil treated by Dr. Josiah Oldfield for an ailment, secured a nurse to give a massage to his colleague Ally, but found no time to undergo an operation at a hospital for his own painful molar and had to cancel the appointment made for the purpose.

Writing about the painful molar to Dr. Josiah Oldfield, Gandhi said: "When I was in Bombay last, I had lost my sense of smell; as the doctor put it, I am supposed to be suffering from chronic ozena. I have chronic catarrh. ... I think it was when I was carrying on a fruit and nut diet experiment that I damaged my teeth. I believed that I had permanently damaged two molars and thought that I was going to lose one of them on board. I certainly tried hard to pull one out but I did not succeed".[10] He had asked his friend Dr. Oldfield to come professionally, for it was his opinion that whatever a Doctor received went to a humanitarian purpose. This story of the molars and the loss of smell did not find a place in the *Guide to Health* Gandhi later wrote for the use of the people. This admission was a sequel to it.

As A New rising leader, Gandhi followed in the footsteps of English politicians. He gave a farewell breakfast on November 29, 1906, to friends, well-wishers and sympathisers of the British Indians in South Africa, expressing gratitude to all. And on the eve of his departure to South Africa, he issued a statement to the press, declaring that they asked neither for political power in the Transvaal nor for unrestricted immigration of British Indians. They claimed, he added, ordinary rights of citizenship for those Indians who were already in the Transvaal.

It was characteristic of Gandhi that he kept proper accounts of the expenses. He was very punctilious in keeping receipts and vouchers. As a rule no sundries figured in the accounts. It was his guiding principle "that a public man should account for every single pie he spends from public funds."

After a stay of forty-one days, the deputation left England on December 1, 1906 and reached Capetown on December 20, 1906. Gandhi had a bottle of hair-restorer in his bag. While having his hair cut at the Hotel Cecil, he unattentively nodded an assent to the suggestion of the barber that he should use a hair restorer. The barber sent it and to his utter surprise a bill for £2 followed! Gandhi presented Mrs. Polak with it at Johannesburg, and, the hair-restorer of Gandhi became a joke with the Polaks!

During his return journey Gandhi had received a telegram on board the ship that the Imperial Government had refused assent to the Ordinance. Gandhi, who was a raw politician at conferences, was overjoyed. He said a prayer to God and exclaimed: "This was more than we had hoped for. But God's ways are inscrutable. Well-directed efforts yield appropriate fruit. The case of the Indian community was just, and the circumstances turned out to be favourable." But he again cautiously added: "It is a happy outcome, but we may not exult over it. Much of the struggle still lies ahead."[11]

On his arrival Gandhi thanked all for the messages of greetings and humbly and devoutly said: "It is God who has to be thanked, not the delegates who have done no more than their duty."

Meanwhile the Transvaal was granted self-Government on December 6, 1906. Gandhi knew now that his hopes were frustated and the struggle was inevitable. So he was reminded of Dr. Oldfield's remark that strength and justice were dear to the British people. But now it dawned upon him that "under British rule, justice is often not to be found without some show of strength, whether of the pen, of the sword, or of money. For our part we are to use only the strength that comes from unity and truth."[12]

The stage of prayers and petitions, memorials and meetings had passed. Gandhi had been preparing himself for a struggle although he was trying for a compromise. He was raising the spirit of resistance and sacrifice among the Indians. He woke them to their resolve and vow and warned them not to yield to the humiliating Ordinance. He cited to them the example of British women who were fighting for their right of vote and asked whether Indian men would be effeminate or would they emulate the manliness shown by English women. In a few days, he said, the mettle of the Indians would be tested.[13]

Gandhi had paid glowing tributes to the brave women leaders of Britain, Miss Cobden and Mrs. Lawrence, who went to jail during their struggle to obtain the right to vote. In England the movement of woman suffrage began in 1851. Its advocates were Cobden, John Stuart Mill and Disraeli. Its leaders were Mrs. Millicent Garett Fawcett, Mrs. Emmeline Pankhurst and a group of suffragettes, as women suffragists were called.

Gandhi mentioned some of them and pointed out that those brave women were bound to succeed and gain the franchise. "Deeds", he concluded, "after all are better than words. All other things are unavailing. . . . The only way therefore is to sacrifice oneself and take the plunge. We have much to do yet, no doubt of that." Action was becoming the breath of his nostrils and he was heading for great deeds.

Many receptions were held in honour of the deputation. At one such reception Gandhi said that Ally and he had been successful because they acted as father and son and remained united in the struggle. "Secondly," he said solemnly. "Truth and justice were on our side. I believe God is always near me. He is never away from me. May you also act in this faith. Believe me that God is near you and always follow the truth."

Gandhi once narrated a story. When Prophet Mohammed,

the founder of Islam, was defeated and took shelter in a cave, his disciples saw a troop coming towards the cave. They cried out in fear, "O Prophet! We are only three, and the army consists of hundreds of men. How shall we save ourselves?" The two disciples trembled. Mohammed, encouraging them, serenely said: "We are not just three: God, who is a match for all, is with us."[14] The soldiers passed by the cave without looking into it, and the danger was averted. Leaders of great movements always infuse courage and inspire hope in their followers by showing irrevocable faith and undying hope in the success of their mission. So did Gandhi.

At the close of the year 1906, the Indian National Congress placed on its records, at its Calcutta session under Dadabhai Naoroji, its sense of deep regret and indignation that the people of the country should be subjected to harassing and degrading restrictions and denied the ordinary rights of British citizenship in His Majesty's Colonies.

CHAPTER IX

God-based Civil Resister

GANDHI TRIED TO instil courage and right conduct in his followers by publishing translations or summaries of English books which were likely to be useful to Indians in South Africa. He intended publishing Justice Ameer Ali's world-famous book, *The Spirit of Islam*. He had sought the permission from the publisher, but it is not known whether the translation was ever published.

Gandhi summarized into Gujarati *Ethical Religion* by William MacIntyre Salter, the founder of the Society for Ethical Culture, Chicago. The book was issued by the Nationalist Press Association in America in March 1889 and was published later in English in 1905. In the Gujarati series, Gandhi summarized only eight of the fifteen chapters and published them serially in January and February, 1907 in *Indian Opinion* and in book form sometime in 1912.

In the summary Gandhi observed: "Hypocrisy has now a days increased in the world. Whatever a man's religion, he thinks only of its outward form and fails in his real duty. All religions are based for the most part on ethical principles and they teach morality." Although, said Gandhi, Salter's book did not teach any particular religion, it contained religious teachings of universal application.

Gandhi further observed: "The different sciences show us the world as it is; ethic tells us what it ought to be. The ethical idea is like an architect's plan. God is omnipotent. He is perfect. If a (moral) man does some good deed, he does not do it to win applause, he does it because he must. The ethical religion means that we should become a little more diligent, a little better educated, a little cleaner and neater. Without morality, religion cannot subsist. True morality, true civilization and true progress are always to be found together. Pursuit of mere self-interest is immoral. Improve yourselves and do good to others.

"A moral act must spring from our own will and we must believe that God within us, the God of all, is ever witness to all our acts. The motive should be duty and not pity to win prestige. That action is moral which is done only for the sake of doing good."

"Jeremy Bentham was truly moral. Wendell Phillips was a great hero. Alexander was termed great, but moral he cannot be called.

"Plain, simple living would be moral if, one, though wealthy, lives a plain, simple life and not one of ease and luxury. To preserve morality demands a brave man prepared to face even death. Moral laws are immutable.

"Morality is the basis of religion. Some regard religion as more than morality. But when there is morality, there is no need for religion." This chapter, observed Gandhi, "seeks to consider morality as a religion."

"Bismark's morality was not grounded in morality. Darwin shows that moral strength is even superior to physical and intellectual strength. A man who has moral qualities lasts longer than one who is devoid of it. Nations are sustained neither by wealth nor by arms, but by righteousness alone. Man should practise altruism, which is the highest form of morality.

"Prophets have caused the world's wheels to change the course. It is a universal experience that God always saves the man who wholeheartedly devotes himself to the service of others. Higher morality embraces all men. All men are equal. Call not man God, for man is not God.

"A man's value depends upon his way of life, not his status. It must not be judged by his visible outward actions, but by his inner leanings. He alone is religious, he alone is happy and he alone is wealthy, who is sincere in himself, bears no malice, exploits no one and always acts with a pure mind. A damp match cannot kindle a log of wood. Emerson says: 'Adversity is the prosperity of the great'."

It is obvious that W. M. Salter's book had a profound effect on Gandhi.

Gandhi deplored the backwardness of Indian women in education. "The modern age," he observed in *Indian Opinion*, "is such that it does not allow anyone to remain in the same position. Indian men have deliberately kept their women backward. If this state of affairs continues, India will remain in its present abominable condition even if she were to secure all her rights from the British Government."

Meantime Lord Elgin disallowed, to the dismay of Lord Selborne, the Asiatic Registration Act. But he secretly gave an assurance that if on the grant of Responsible Government to the Transvaal on January 1, 1907, the Transvaal Government passed an identical measure it would not be refused the royal assent.

The statesmanship of Sir Henry Campbell-Bannerman's Liberal Government generously restored the independence of the defeated Boers.

Accordingly, Responsible Government was inaugurated in the Transvaal and fresh elections were held on February 20, 1907. The Dutch under the leadership of General Botha and General Smuts won in the elections what they had lost in the Boer War. As a result, General Botha became Prime Minister of the Transvaal and General Smuts its Colonial Secretary. Expressing its views on this new development, *Indian Opinion* said that from the point of view of the Indians in South Africa there was not much either to rejoice in or to reject.

About this time Winston Churchill, Under-Secretary of State for Colonies, declared in the British Parliament that the Natal Government was refused leave to introduce the legislation which excluded Asiatics from trading licences.

This was apparently a good gesture, but the main problem of the Transvaal was left as it was. So Gandhi convened meetings of the British Indian Association in March 1907 and protested against the taking of finger-prints. The New Government of the Transvaal was determined to carry through the Asiatic Registration Bill. It was gazetted on March 19, 1907 and introduced in the assembly on March 20. Within two hours it went through all the three readings and was sent to the Legislative Council which passed it on March 22. It was then sent to Lord Elgin for approval.

For the inauguration of the struggle, Gandhi decided to establish a new institution. The British Indian Association had a large membership, but he did not want to involve all its members in the struggle. He shrewdly kept it aloof from satyagraha. He did not like to risk its reputation by making it a party to the struggle. So he founded a new body called the 'Passive Resistance Association' with the help of the Indian workers. A large number of people joined it. The Anti-Indian-Law-Fund Committee furnished it with funds.

It was Gandhi's belief that when men of sterling character were at the helm of any institution, it was bound to get the requisite funds. "A movement," said Gandhi, "takes its downward course from the time that it is afflicted with a plethora of funds! . . . An institution run with the interest of accumulated capital ceases to be amenable to public opinion and becomes autocratic and self-righteous."[1] Through the new association the oath of jail-going was re-administered and re-affirmed. The pulse of the community was felt, and the spirit was found as high as it was in September 1906.

Cables were sent to Lord Elgin and Morley requesting them to defer their consent to the Act. Smuts refused to forward to Lord Elgin the cablegram sent to him. Smuts said that the whole white population of the Transvaal was of one mind. Selborne said he refused to interfere with the local Government! The entire Indian population in the Transvaal was about 13,000 of whom over 10,000 lived in Johannesburg and Pretoria.

Several meetings were held all over the Transvaal. A mass meeting, attended by delegates from all parts of the Transvaal, was held at Johannesburg on March 29, 1907, under the chairmanship of Abdul Gani, who was also the President of the B.I.A. H.O. Ally said the labours of the deputation to London had been reduced to naught. Though a law-abiding people, he declared, they were harassed. Pandit Ram Sundar said that the Government was like a step-mother. They must follow the example of Japan and unite. Milner wrote in a letter to *The Times*, London, in favour of the Indians. The Natal Indian Congress sympathised.

As directed by the mass meeting under its fourth resolution, Gandhi, accompanied by Gani, Mian and Ally, called on Smuts at Pretoria and presented the resolutions adopted at the mass meeting. He explained all the facts to Smuts. In his written reply Smuts warned the Indian leaders not to advise the people to disobey the law by not registering themselves. The Indian community, he hoped, which was always considered law-abiding, would co-operate with the Government in every way by registering themselves lawfully, gracefully and expeditiously. Otherwise, he concluded, Government would take more stringent measures to prevent the Asiatics from entering South Africa without a permit. It was a courteous threat! A polite but firm reply was made to it. The Indian community resolved to vindicate its honour and prestige.

Gandhi wrote to newspapers refuting their allegations against the Indians and also addressed a meeting of the Chinese leaders in his office. In London, a deputation led by Lord Ampthill waited on General Botha who denied having any intention of hurting British Indian feelings in the colony. Lord Ampthill was Governor of Madras in 1899-1905 and had acted as Viceroy of India during Lord Curzon's absence from India. Gandhi repeated his pledge in *Indian Opinion* that he would oppose the Act and appealed to the Indians to be firm in their resolve to fight it. Sir Henry Cotton waited on Morley, who agreed to address General Botha in the matter.

DURING GENERAL BOTHA'S absence from Pretoria, Smuts acted as Prime Minister of the Transvaal. The Indians at Klerksdorp presented him with an address. Their leaders reaffirmed the view that the Indian community should under no circumstances submit to the Act. Just at this psychological moment Gandhi repeated his pledge and said he would prefer to go to jail rather than submit to the Act. He said if he retreated at that stage, he would be deemed unfit to serve the Indian community. "I believe," concluded Gandhi, "the Indians will rise in public esteem if all of them remain staunch in not submitting to the law, and that moreover, it will evoke sympathy in India also for the cause of the Transvaal Indians."

The British Government accorded its royal consent to the Registration Act on May 7. The voice of men like Lionel Curtis prevailed. He wrote in *The Times*, London, that Englishmen and Indians ought never to have equal rights. The Act was to take effect from July 1. The British Indians were required to apply for registration before July 31, 1907. The Act excluded Malays and the Chinese who had come to the Transvaal as indentured labourers as also Turkish Christians and Jews, but brought the Turkish Muslims within the purview of the law.

All over the Transvaal Indians were discussing the jail-going resolution at public meetings. Then leaders said that jail was a palace and a paradise, and they fervently appealed to their followers not to swerve from the jail-going resolution. When the *Star* threatened the leaders of the Indian community with deportation, Gandhi replied that on implementing the new law the Government should do so. As the Indians residing in the Transvaal had no right to vote, he added, the resolution about going to jail was the only means to oppose any particular law.

To enthuse the people, *Indian Opinion* quoted a verse from the Gujarati poet Narmadashanker.

Forward ye all to battle, the bugles sound
Raise the cry and take the plunge, for victory's around.

The leader urged them to be free from doubt as doubt was like a ghost. They should be free from selfishness, which was like a witch.

Soon after, Gandhi addressed meetings in Durban. One was held in honour of the retiring Superintendent of Police, Officer Alexander who had once saved his life. At another, Gandhi advised boycott of the permit office. On Botha's arrival in Pretoria, Gandhi wrote to him requesting acceptance of a compromise formula; but Botha was adamant. Botha was then at the height of his fame and power and had been given a royal reception in London and was awarded 'the Freedom of the City of London.'

Gandhi also addressed the Chinese Association on anti-Asiatic laws and championed the cause in various newspapers. In the first week of June 1907 the British Indian Association decided to send a deputation to General Botha; but he declined to meet it.

Indian Opinion voiced its master's inspiring message to the British Indians.

'Take up arms, and march together,
Spear in hand, roaring a challenge to the foe.'

Gandhi warned that the new law would burst as well as thunder. He cited to them how the Boers fought for their independence and how John Hampden fought and freed the people. He also cited to them how Karl Blind, a German litterateur and friend of Mazzini and Garibaldi, suffered imprisonment five times in the cause of freedom and for the rights of the people. A prize of £1 for the finest poem on the imminent struggle in Gujarati, Urdu or Hindi was announced. If the Indian community really disapproved of the Act, Gandhi said, it would not submit to it. No matter what calamities befell it, it would accept imprisonment for not submitting to it.

Some of the members of the South Africa British Indian Committee became restless at the thought of the jail-going and law-breaking programme. J. D. Rees resigned. It was suggested that instead of finger-prints photographs should be appended to the permits. This suggestion too failed. Upon this *Indian Opinion* solemnly said that knowing God always protected the righteous, the community would feel happy in accepting imprisonment and keep to the straight path!

Some liberal-minded British statesmen like Lord Ampthill were moved. He initiated a debate in the House of Lords on the Asiatic Registration Act. He opined that a British subject was a British subject all over the world! Pleadings like these were of no avail. So Gandhi wrote sadly in *Indian Opinion*: "Rama sent Angada on a peace mission to Ravana. What Rama did with Ravana, the Indian Committee has done with the Transvaal Government. But to no avail!"

While organizing the struggle, Gandhi took precautions against hurting the feelings of the Imperial Government. He was of the opinion that "we stand to lose by ending British rule." While eulogising patriots like Lala Lajpatrai for the hardships they suffered for the sake of the country, he apologetically opined that those patriots appeared to be in error in so far as they wanted to end British rule. "We have," he averred, "no quarrel with British rule but instead of desiring the end of British rule,[2] let us aspire to be as able and spirited as the colonists are Public spirit," the loyalist in Gandhi continued, "is not likely to grow among us without western education and contacts with the West. If that spirit grows, the British may grant our demands even without a fight, and may leave India if we want them to do so."

Laziness always provoked Gandhi's anger. He showed a dislike for the parasites which grow on society. Many *bavas* and *fakirs*, he observed, maintained themselves by begging but served neither themselves nor the community. He praised those who worked selflessly and spoke highly of D. K. Karve, who later founded a women's university.

Gandhi also approvingly quoted a statement on the Indian Princes by Amir Abdur Rahman, King of Afghanistan, in which he held their dress and ornaments to ridicule. The King of the Afghans said: "Their trouser-belts were studded with jewels and the pendants, hanging from their waist-ribbons, almost reached their feet. They little knew what was happening in the world or what it contained. They passed their time in consuming wine and opium."[3]

Commenting on this, Gandhi said not only the princes but also the people lived in such a base manner. But he took care to say that "our comment mainly refers to the Hindus in India!" [4]

Gandhi avoided referring to the Muslim princes. This is characteristic of Hindu leaders who always go by the name of Indian leaders. They call themselves Indian but never try to reform Indian Muslims. Gandhi's hatred of the gilded princes grew with age and it later burst at Benares in February 1916.

A mass meeting was addressed by Gandhi at Pretoria on June 30. Although the Imperial Government, he observed, had given assent to the Act, it could not be considered to have been passed until the Indian community had accepted it. Even if some Indians were to take out the title-deeds of slavery, those who were free would win in the end.

On the following day the Government Registration offices were opened. Volunteers, pickets, watchmen and patriotic workers were posted by the Indian leaders at different places. They devoted their time to keeping watch on the offices. The volunteers plunged into any service that was needed. Indian traders stopped importing goods from Britain. The volunteers told the weak-minded Indians that it was cowardly to say, "We would do what others do." They should say, "I dislike the law. I have taken an oath in the name of God. I would rather go to jail than submit to the law." If the Indians perjured before God, said Gandhi, the ghettos of old would be their proper and deserved lot.

Their petition, said Gandhi, was no longer addressed to men, but to God Himself![5] If the whole of the white Transvaal was against the Indians, God was with them, said another leader, Hajee Habib. Law-abiding instinct, he added, did not mean acceptance of any measure howsoever distasteful.

Several poems came in as a response to the call of *Indian Opinion*. The prize-winning poem declared:

> Placing your trust in the Master,
> Full and sincere,
> Be glad in your heart,
> That to gaol you'll go, certainly to gaol you'll go.

ON JULY 28 the Indian workers and traders struck work all over the Transvaal. It was now July 31, the last day for filing applications under the Registration Act. A meeting of British Indians from all over the Transvaal was held at Pretoria on that day.

The Hamidia Society of Johannesburg sent 600 men by special train to help the Indians of Pretoria to organize the meeting. William Hosken, who was a member of the Transvaal Assembly, was known all over South Africa as a friend of the non-white races. He had met Gandhi in the morning and expressed his desire to address the meeting. He said he was doing it at the instance of General Botha. Hosken, the messenger of peace, told the meeting that their struggle proceeded from a right mind, and passive resistance was a legitimate method of securing redress of their grievances. But their oath was ill-taken and was not binding on them. The Act was sanctioned by Parliament and was in the nature of an Act of God. He would, if he could, grant their request, but they should submit to the inevitable. He had his say and left the meeting.

The next speaker was Gandhi. He calmly said that he claimed to be one of the most peaceful men in South Africa and had served his fellow countrymen for thirteen years. They had put up with some indignities, some insults, but now the cup was filled to overflowing. If the Asiatics, he continued, submitted to the new law, they would be in a state of slavery. So they should not wear the badge of slavery on their arm and forehead. They should resign themselves to the inevitable, to the will of God, not to submit to the insult and the degradation that the law sought to impose on them. Thus ended the historic meeting.

In Pretoria, a few persons registered, but in general Pretoria put up a good show. Pietersburg was beyond praise as none there registered. Its bravery was praised everywhere in the Transvaal. The Registration Office moved from Pretoria to Pietersburg and then to other places. It was declared that November 30 would be the last date for registration. So the Registration Office, said *Indian Opinion*, like the tail of Hanuman, which grew heavier in weight as it went further, moved from place to place!

How Gandhi was organizing his forces and leading the Indians to the struggle can be seen from the comments of the Press. The *Star* observed: "Mr. M. K. Gandhi, the well-known Indian barrister, is the leader of the Passive Resistance Movement. He has certainly marshalled his forces well, and the Indians as a rule are prepared to follow him to the extreme."

On August 11 Gandhi gave an impetus to the movement by making another fervent speech at Pretoria where weekly meetings had been held for the previous two months.

Meanwhile, in August 1907, Gandhi received another shock from Muslim fanaticism in South Africa. He serialised in Gujarati a translation of the life of the Prophet Mohammed by Washington Irving in *Indian Opinion* for the benefit of its Muslim readers. He said he did so in good faith and out of great regard for Islam. But some of his Muslim readers entered emphatic protests against the publication as they were pained to read the account of the Prophet's marriage in Chapter V. Upon this Gandhi declared in *Indian Opinion* that the editor had no desire to needlessly injure the feelings of anyone, and so he stopped publishing further instalments of the 'life'.[6]

While Gandhi issued pamphlets and statements representing the cause of all Indians, his Muslim colleagues felt the necessity of addressing independently a circular letter to Muslim individuals and organizations in India and in England. They sought their help in the struggle they were carrying on in South Africa.[7]

When the time for the actual struggle came, Gandhi's colleague H.O. Ally left the Transvaal with his family, protesting apparently against the Act rather than facing it manfully! Later, Gandhi revealed, "Ally could not continue to trust me fully because I was a Hindu."[8] Ally had written to Syed Ameer Ali that Gandhi's campaign against the Registration Act "would ruin[9] thousands of my coreligionists who are all traders while the Hindus are mostly hawkers."

All African newspapers were not, however, against the Indian struggle. There were some which sympathised with the Indians in their heroic struggle for self-respect. The *Friend* of Bloemfontein, for example, said that the British Indians were perfectly justified in protesting, by means of passive resistance, against a humiliating law. The *Friend* was edited by the Rev. Dewdney Drew, one of the finest speakers in South Africa and an M.P. from the Orange Free Colony.

Gandhi's *Indian Opinion* with only 1,100 subscribers proved to be a symbol of education and patriotism among the Indians. Both the paper and the press made their contribution to the struggle. The paper resolved the doubts of the opponents and repelled all attacks frankly, fearlessly and forensically. It declared that the Transvaal fight was a fight for the whole of South Africa. It therefore appealed to the Natal Congress to send more money to help the struggle and reminded the Cape Colony that it had not at all done its duty by their brethren in the Transvaal.

Meanwhile Gandhi suggested some amendments to Smuts, but he did not entertain them. Sir Raymond West suggested to the Indian leaders that they should refer the case to the Privy Council. Thereupon Gandhi said that the Indians could build no hopes on Sir Raymond's opinion. The real Privy Council of Indians was the courage of the community.

"And God," Gandhi observed, "is the only Judge who will redress our grievances. Trust in him is a great counsel whose pleadings will never go in vain." In resisting the wretched Act, he added, Indians would be seeking the "kingdom of God."

The leader was leading the people in the name of God, By this repeated expression of his unshakable faith in God, Gandhi showed the Indians that his moral stature was above theirs. He impressed upon their mind that God was with him. He was near him, in effect Gandhi was the messenger of God! He acted and lived in the name of God. Gandhi without God was nothing. He wanted to put people under God's control. Was he adding to their faith or superstition?

Several meetings were held all over the Transvaal, memorials and monster petitions were addressed to the Transvaal authorities, Gandhi now declared that he would defend the arrested pickets.

THUS THE FIRST phase of the struggle was over. Now an active struggle was impending. Gandhi searched for the Gods of passive resisters, the lovers, originators and the givers of passive resisters. He cited the case of the Archbishop of Canterbury who had issued orders prohibiting marriages with a deceased wife's sister although such unions were recognized as legal by the law of the land. Gandhi also quoted Thoreau who had said that "we should be men before we are subjects, and that no obligation imposed upon us by our conscience to give blind submission to any law, no matter what force or majority backed it."[10]

While Gandhi was thus in search of moral support to his cause he found another Guru, a new teacher in Henry David Thoreau who preached resistance to Civil Government in his famous *Civil Disobedience*[11] if its law was unjust. He published it in 1849 at the age of thirty-two, under the title *Resistance to Civil Government.* Thoreau was arrested for refusing to pay poll tax as long as it went to the support of the Mexican War and the extension of slavery.

This great American had built a modest house in the woods near Waldon Pond. He put no lock on his door. He was against materialism and against the idea that happiness consisted of counting money or material possessions.

Some of Thoreau's major ideas were as follows: "Under a government which imprisons any man unjustly, the true place for a just man is also a prison. If unjust laws exist, civil disobedience is an effective way to oppose and change them. That Government is best which governs least." Thoreau practised what he preached. He was poet, writer, essayist, individualist, transcendentalist philosopher, naturalist and a practical man.

Gandhi said that Thoreau was one of the greatest and most moral men America had ever produced. His essay on Civil Resistance, he added, was sanctified by suffering. Gandhi had secured a copy of a pocket book called *Simple Life Series* published by Arthur C. Fifield, London, which included this essay spread over thirty pages. In the light of Thoreau's principles, the Asiatic law, said Gandhi, was degrading to their manhood and offensive to their religion. It was evil legalized.

"When we shall have resisted the law to the last," Gandhi observed enthusiastically, "we shall be regarded as so many Thoreaus in miniature."[12] When once they were inspired by such a noble spirit, Gandhi observed, people would see how glorious their struggle could be. Such persons, like the brave Thoreau, would find jail to be a palace and the cry of challenge from Indians in prison would pierce Smuts[13] through and through.

Gandhi was now the spirit of Thoreau personified. It is well known that he was tremendously influenced by Thoreau's philosophy of Civil Resistance. In his autobiography Gandhi mentions Raychandbhai as his Guide, Tolstoy and Ruskin as his Gurus. He does not mention Thoreau. Not only that, he later ungraciously said his disciple might drop Thoreau's name from the list of heroes who had influenced him.

The movement was launched by Gandhi with the help of his colleagues Ahmad Mahammad Kachhalia and Thambi Naidu. Kachhalia was a Surati Meman, A man of his word, he was known for his simplicity, humility and courage. He said he would be hanged, but would not submit to the Black Act. It was greatly to his credit that he observed his pledge during the struggle without flinching. Thambi Naidu was a Tamilian born in Mauritius. He spoke and wrote English very well and spoke Tamil and Hindustani fluently. Although he had never seen India, his love for the homeland was boundless. He was a man of fervid patriotism, patient firmness and tireless energy. Though irascible, he was a pillar of strength to the movement.

Secrecy had no place in the movement. Volunteers were not to threaten those who took out permits.

The Chinese supported the stand taken by the Indian

leaders. But eventually many of the Chinese fell away as their leader turned out to be insincere.

At this stage Gandhi, impressing upon the peoples' mind the importance of the method of their struggle, said at the H. I. Society: "This is a new kind of step for us in the present age. There is a deep-rooted superstition that a law cannot be disobeyed. It would be no small step forward for the commnunity if this superstition were rooted out."

It was indeed a new step for the Indians in Africa; but discussions on the practice of passive resistance were going on in other countries too. The idea of passive resistance was in the air. Savarkar, the leader of Indian revolutionaries, wrote about it in one of his letters from London. During his recent stay in London, Gandhi had discussed the Indian problem with Shyamji Krishna Varma and Savarkar. A revolutionary writer and a matchless orator, Savarkar had founded a revolutionary Party, Abhinav Bharat, having branches in important places all over Maharashtra and at other places such as Baroda, Indore and Gwalior. He had gone to England apparently to study law, but his real aim was to spread the seeds of revolution in the minds of the best brains of India that came to London for studies.

Of course there were talks on means and ends between Gandhi and Savarkar during the 1906 visit of Gandhi. Savarkar, who was planning an armed revolt against British rule, and Gandhi, a disciple of Tolstoy, who was thinking of a non-violent weapon, exchanged views. In his famous letters from London, Savarkar explained in February 1907 that passive resistance[14] became ultimately ineffective and futile. In July 1907 he wrote that the twentieth century rightly boasted that it had founded a weapon to work out a revolution without bloodshed or without resort to sedition; but since none up to that day had used it successfully, it was difficult to predict its future usefulness.[15] In support of his stand Savarkar cited the example of the passive resistance struggle launched by the Southern French farmers and workers. Hundreds of cities and villages resorted to passive resistance. Children abandoned their schools, clerks their offices, Municipality their work. Parliament members from that part of France tendered their resignations. Above all the police refused to carry out their duties. This was a lesson in passive resistance, observed Savarkar, who was to be Gandhi's future opponent in Indian politics.

But the human mind, Savarkar proceeded, was addicted to

the dictum 'might is right!' Soon martial law was proclaimed. Meetings and marches were stopped. Drawing the logical conclusion, Savarkar said: 'In the end passive resistance fails because it has no backing of the army and because it presupposes all men to be selfless and believes that all men will not co-operate with the aggressor. It does not take into consideration the difficulties in the way, the limitations and inability of poverty-striken men to stick to noble resolve of self-sacrifice."

"Besides," continued Savarkar[16] "it blindly presumes that the aggressor has a high sense of morality and will not resolve to arms or promulgate new ordinances." This was Savarkar's opinion on the passive resistance staged by the French farmers and workers of Narbonne early in the year 1907.

In that year the idea of passive resistance as a method for solving political questions was being discussed also in Irish newspapers. When the British Parliament passed the Education Act, the non-conformists had offered passive resistance under the leadership of Dr. Clifford. The English women during their struggle for the franchise, had offered passive resistance.

THE MAIN OBJECTIVE of Gandhi's struggle was to remove the humiliation under which the Indians in South Africa were smarting. His fight did not aim at securing the right of vote or other political rights for the Indians. His fight was against the discrimination based on racialism. His fight was not against imperialism. The British Government was sympathetic; the Indian Government was on his side. Moreover he was fighting as a loyal British subject and that too non-violently. So the fight involved no great risks as did the fight against British rule in India.

India was then in turmoil. Tilak was driving the Indian National Congress away from the policy of petition towards the politics of pressure and boycott, swadeshi and Swaraj. The fiery doctrine of boycotting foreign goods, the propagation of swadeshi and the hatred of foreign rule were spreading all over India. Lajpatrai and his lieutenant Ajit Singh had been deported. Lajpatrai was released and the Punjab succeeded in getting the Punjab Land Act repealed. Strangely enough, this success in the Punjab, was described by Gandhi, as "a strong proof of the effectiveness of passive resistance".[17]

The Transvaal Government started taking action against the defaulters. On November 8 it arrested Pandit Ram Sundar at Germiston for "unlawfully entering and remaining in the Transvaal" after expiry of his temporary permit. He refused to be bailed out though scores of Indians had offered to stand security for him.

A thrill of excitement went through the Indians all over the Transvaal. Telegrams poured in offering congratulations and cheers to the Pandit in jail. Leaders, Hindu and Muslim, gathered from various places at Germiston. Gandhi pleaded before the magistrate to release Ram Sundar on his personal recognizance. On his release, the Pandit received a tremendous ovation as a hero. He was sentenced to one month's imprisonment on November 14, and the sentence was greeted with a hartal all over the Transvaal by the Indians. Gandhi met Ram Sundar in jail. After his release Ram Sundar bade good-bye to the Transvaal and went into oblivion. It was found afterwards that he was an indentured labourer who had deserted before completing his term.

Gandhi defended the pickets who were arrested. On November 30, the last date for registration, it was found that only 511 out of 13,000 Indians had registered themselves.

As the struggle advanced, Gandhi felt the necessity of giving a name to the movement. At a meeting in Germiston, William Hosken, while introducing him to the audience, said that passive resistance was a weapon of the weak. Gandhi wrote afterwards that he had replied that his movement depended on soul force, and force, arms or violence had no place in it. There was no intention of hurting the opponent. "If they (the Indians) had the franchise," Gandhi later observed in his *Satyagraha in South Africa*, "probably there would not have been any scope for satyagraha."[18]

It follows that for a people with the franchise there is no necessity to resort to satyagraha. Gandhi wanted to use a Gujarati term for 'passive resistance'. So he sought for a term which would precisely describe his movement.

Accordingly *Indian Opinion* in its issue of December 28, 1907, announced a prize for the person who would suggest suitable equivalents for 'passive resistance', 'passive resister'. 'cartoon' and 'civil disobedience'. Maganlal Gandhi suggested the word 'sadagraha' meaning firmness in a good cause. Gandhi liked the word but corrected it to 'Satyagraha'. Truth (Satya) implies love and firmness (Agraha) engenders force, but a force born of truth and love or non-violence.

The Colonial Secretary, General Smuts, obtained royal

consent to the Transvaal Immigration Act and announced it in the Gazette on December 27. Being now empowered to deport the Indians, he laid his hands on their leaders. The same day the police Commissioner of Johannesburg called Gandhi to the police station and informed him of the orders for his arrest and the arrest of other leaders. Gandhi promised to attend the Court the next day.

Gandhi conducted his own case on December 28 and told the Magistrate that he conscientiously objected to the law. He also appeared in defence of the pickets. Jordan, the Magistrate, curtly ordered him to leave the Transvaal within 48 hours. Gandhi was a fearless leader. He made a speech in Johannesburg and two days later also addressed a meeting of the Chinese Association there. He gave an interview to Reuter. On the last day of the year 1907 he was informed that his appearance in the Court was not required until further notice.

On the first day of the year 1908, Gandhi protested at a mass meeting in Fordsburg against both the T.I.R.A. (Transvaal Immigrants Registration Act) and the T.A.R.A. (Transvaal Asiatic Registration Act). Smuts declared that no Parliament in the country would repeal T.A.R.A. Gandhi gave interviews to several newspapers and tried to meet Smuts.

On the morning of January 10, Gandhi made a speech at the New Town mosque and exhorted the congregation to cling to God and to their vow; for 'it was a struggle for religious liberty and there was neither terror nor fear for a man who believed in God'.

The Times, London, called upon the British Government to do everything in its power to secure justice for the Indians.

The term satyagraha was coined at this stage, in the words of Gandhi, "to respect our own language, speak it well and use in it as few foreign words as possible—this is also a part of patriotism."[19] He later felt the necessity of differentiating between passive resistance and satyagraha. So he adopted the word satyagraha for the struggle.

As he did not leave the Transvaal, he was called upon to attend the Court at 2 p.m. on January 10, 1908. A regular cordon was formed by mounted and foot police around the entrance to the Court. Jordan, the Magistrate of B Criminal Court in Johannesburg, asked Gandhi if he had any questions to ask. Gandhi pleaded guilty and said that he had heard that at Pretoria his compatriots had been sentenced to three months' imprisonment with hard labour, and since he had committed a greater offence the Magistrate should impose, upon him the heaviest penalty. Six months' hard labour with a fine of £500 was the proper sentence; but Jordan sentenced him to two months' imprisonment without hard labour. Thus after a period of sixteen months' agitation, the slim central figure of Gandhi was removed from the scene and put behind bars.

On that day, in his last interview to the press, Gandhi said that he had undertaken the struggle prayerfully and in all humility. His removal would show whether the position was real or unreal. His colleague P. K. Naidu, C. M. Pillay, M. Easton, John Fortoen, the last two being Chinese, were sentenced to two months' imprisonment without hard labour for having disobeyed the earlier order of the Court. Thambi Naidu and Quinn, Chairman of the Chinese Association, were sent to jail later on January 14.

Thus the new year 1908 opened with a gift to the world of the weapon of satyagraha for the solution of its political questions by non-violent struggle. The Transvaal Government on its part made a present of Gandhi to the world as a civil resister!

When men go to prison for a principle their imprisonment advertises their cause. And the cause which Gandhi represented was well-advertised throughout the world. He became a subject for a series of cartoons in African papers and Smuts was caricatured along with Gandhi.

In the jail Gandhi fell into deep thought, and all the recent scenes of his life passed before his mind's eye like a dream. If the people failed 'two months' would be as tedious as an age. But soon he recalled how he had asked his followers to regard jails as His Majesty's Hotels. This second thought cheered him. On January 21 Gandhi petitioned to the Government on behalf of his twenty colleagues for a change in diet. Eighteen prisoners were British Indians and three were Chinese. None of them was accustomed to taking maize meal. Suitable diet, according to European standard, the application prayed, should be provided for them. On that very day, seventy-six new satyagrahis were lodged in the same jail.

At their request Gandhi and Naidu were supplied with clippers and scissors, and with great pleasure, they cut the hair of their co-prisoners.

A prisoner wore black trousers, a shirt, a jumper, a cap, socks and a pair of closed sandals. He was given a wooden plank, two blankets and an apology for a pillow!

The jailor and the doctor were kind. In the morning Gandhi read the Gita with a commentary by Manilal Nathubhai Desai, who was a Gujarati poet, author, scholar and philosopher. In the afternoon he read the Koran in English. He read Huxley's lectures, Carlyle's biographies of Burns, Johnson and Scotts, Bacon's essays on civil and moral counsel and the writings of Tolstoy, Ruskin and Socrates. He had also some Tamil books and one in Urdu. He read the Bible to Fortoen. He had intended to complete the translation of one of the books by Carlyle and that of another by Ruskin. At this time he must have started writing his Gujarati series 'Story of a Soldier of Truth', a version of Plato's Dialogue.

The prisoners also learnt drill from the warden and all the satyagrahis enjoyed it for some days. They worked on the sewing machine. Naidu and Easton, who had an aptitude for it, learned the work quickly. No prisoner, observed Gandhi, found his confinement irksome! On the contrary, he came out a better-informed and abler man.

There had been, Gandhi added, instances of conscientious men who achieved great things while in jail like John Bunyan who wrote his *Pilgrim's Progress*. Tilak wrote, Gandhi pointed out wrongly, his *Orion* in jail. "I believe," Gandhi said, "that anyone who enjoys reading good books can easily bear to be alone anywhere." He quoted a proverb from the book *Arab Wisdom* which says he who enjoys no respect has no religion.

Later, on his release, Gandhi wrote some articles entitled: "My experience in jail." In those articles he said: "It is by defending their honour over a long period of time that nations achieve greatness. Honour does not mean arrogance. Real honour consists in a state of mind that does not countenance the loss of a right, and in action flowing from such a state of mind. He alone can attain to such honour who really trusts, depends on God."

Albert Cartwright, editor of the *Transvaal Leader*, was of the opinion that the T.A.R.A. should be repealed. He was called an angel of peace, and he had suffered imprisonment for reasons of conscience. Pressure for the removal of Indian grievances was being exerted by English statesmen. Botha wanted a loan of five million pounds for his Government. So the pressure prevailed. At the instance of General Smuts, Albert Cartwright saw Gandhi in jail on Tuesday, January 21, 1910. It was agreed that T.A.R.A. should be repealed and Indians should register voluntarily. Cartwright[20] himself drafted a letter to that effect and brought it to Gandhi in jail on January 28. But Gandhi later stated in his *Satyagraha in South Africa* that the letter was either drafted or approved of by

General Smuts.

Gandhi made some changes in the draft, and Gandhi, Quinn and Naidu signed the letter at 12.30 p.m. Cartwright left for Pretoria and at 5 p.m. rang up to say that General Smuts had accepted the terms of the letter. Smuts was allowed to change only one word. "There are some things," added *Indian Opinion*, "that can be put down in writing, and for others one has to rely on oral understanding." Here was the rub! The terms were never reduced to writing as Gandhi himself later admitted in his interview to the *Natal Mercury* that "with regard to the compromise there was nothing written in so many words[21] as to the repeal of the Asiatic Act of 1907."

ON JANUARY 30, 1908, Gandhi was taken to Pretoria and he discussed the draft with General Smuts who believed in making South Africa a white man's country. General Smuts, observed Gandhi, deliberately[22] but verbally, promised to repeal the Act. The draft was approved by the Cabinet. The Government letter promised to lay the matter before Parliament at its next session and added that the Indian leaders should appeal to their compatriots to make the registration effective and final, Gandhi was set free. He borrowed money for the train fare from the Secretary of General Smuts. Gandhi told representatives of newspapers that the compromise was honourable to both sides. His head was closely cropped and his moustache was cut. This was his own doing as the use of brushes and combs was not allowed in jail.

After the interview Gandhi reached Johannesburg by the last train. He addressed a midnight meeting on the grounds of the Mosque at Fordsburg. There he declared that God had given them that unexpected victory.

Not all were satisfied with the compromise Gandhi had made. The critics said that Smuts should have repealed the Act first and then the Indians should have been called upon to register. They warned Gandhi not to trust General Smuts. Gandhi said that even if the opponent played them false twenty times, a satyagrahi should trust him for the twenty-first time.[23]

Mir Alam, a Pathan, at once assailed Gandhi with a volley of questions at the meeting. He said Gandhi had betrayed the people and sold them to General Smuts for £15,000, and added, "I swear with Allah as my witness, that I will kill the man who takes the lead in applying for registration." "To die,"

Gandlhi replied gravely, "by the hand of a brother, rather than by disease or in such other way, cannot, be for me a matter of sorrow,"[24] With this passage-at-arms the meeting ended.

All satyagrahis numbering about 220 were released the next day.

At the meeting of the B.I.A. held on February 2. Gandhi said that God helped the cause of truth, and a campaign that was carried on in the name of God could not but end in success. Even God was won over by humility. However, Gandhi cautiously told them that under the proposed agreement Government would accept signatures by educated men and by owners of property, but unlettered people would have to give their finger-prints on the application forms. And if violence was to be used against anyone, let it be first used against him. He would thank the person who assaulted him. Finally, he said that he was doing nothing for the community for the sake of reward or fame.

On February 3 Gandhi saw General Smuts in the presence of Chamney, the Registrar of Asiatics, and appealed to him to repeal the T.A.R.A. Afterwards Gandhi said that Smuts had agreed in Chamney's presence that he would do it if the Asiatics abided freely and frankly by the terms of the compromise.

The controversy over the compromise began. The condemnatory letters he received were all from Muslims who believed that Gandhi had brought ruin upon the Muslims in South Africa. Yet Gandhi declared that the victory was for truth.

"Truth is God," Gandhi observed, "or God is nothing but truth. It is a divine law that he who serves that truth—that God—will never suffer defeat. Sometimes men of truth appear to have failed, but that is no more of a fleeting appearance. If this is a victory for truth, it is also a victory for satyagraha. Every Indian should by now be convinced that satyagraha, or passive resistance, is an infallible remedy. It must be also realized that there are evils to which satyagraha cannot be applied, For instance, if the Government does not allow us to acquire land, satyagraha will be of no avail. This was not a struggle against digit-impressions. Once the law is gone, there is no harm in our having to give the ten fingerprints. Doing so certainly does not amount to a violation of our pledge." Thus the slogan, "Ten impressions if you give, humbled will your manhood be," now lost its edge.

Mir Alam, accompanied by his colleagues, followed Gandhi and his colleagues who were going to the Registry office on February 10, 1908, to apply for registration. Just when Gandhi, Essop Mia and Naidu were three minutes' walk from the Registration office, Mir Alam accosted Gandhi and asked him, "where are you going?" He replied that he was going to take out a certificate of registration giving the ten finger-prints. He had scarcely finished the sentence when a heavy cudgel blow fell on his head from behind. Gandhi fell down with the words 'He Rama' (Oh God) on his lips. Then he was struck with an iron pipe and a stick and was also kicked. Naidu and Mia also were beaten up and injured.

The Pathans were running away, but were caught by a European passers-by. The police took them into custody. Gandhi was picked up and taken into an office nearby. No sooner did he regain consciousness than he inquired about Mir Alam and said that the Pathan and his colleagues should be let off. He was then taken to the Rev. J. J. Doke's house. Chamney, the Registration officer, arrived on the scene. He brought the papers and took Gandhi's finger-prints. Mir Alam and one of his colleagues were sentenced to three months' imprisonment with hard labour although Gandhi had written to the Attorney-General not to prosecute them.

A doctor stitched the wounds in the forehead and on the upper lip and advised Gandhi to take rest for two months. He had received severe blows on his left ribs. Three of his upper teeth were injured. Even after a fortnight be found breathing difficult. With a clay poultice the wounds healed without becoming septic. The Rev. J. J. Doke took care of his health. He was a Baptist minister and had worked as a priest in New Zealand. When he first met Gandhi, the latter thought that like other Christian missionaries he had come to convert him to Christianity or to advise him to give up the struggle or to express patronizing sympathy with the movement. But he then realized that Doke was a real follower of Christ who aimed at lightening the load of those who were heavily laden. Gandhi's admirers flocked to Doke's house to inquire after his health.

There were about fifty Pathans in Johannesburg. They and some other Muslims had sent a telegram to Mohammed Ali Jinnah, protesting against the compromise. Gandhi said he regarded both Ameer Ali and M. A. Jinnah with respect. Some Muslims now said that Gandhi had totally ruined the Muslims and had been doing so for the previous fifteen years.[25]

Gandhi feared that because the assailants were Muslims the Hindus would feel aggrieved. So he said that his assailants knew not what they were doing. He prayed that the blood spilt would cement the Hindu and Muslim communities indissolubly. The lesson they should draw, he said, was that "if anyone wants to serve the community, and always do the right by it, he must be prepared for physical assaults. Such assaults should really be looked upon as rewards."

Although men of liberal views from England congratulated the Indian leaders on the compromise and heroic fight, the controversy continued. Critics from Natal also poured abuse on Gandhi. When he went to Durban, he found misunderstanding prevalent there. At a meeting in Durban a Pathan tried to assault him. But Parsi Rustomji brought the Police Superintendent and took Gandhi away from the disturbed meeting. In deprecatory letters some harshly criticized. So he wrote a fine dialogue on the compromise and with the skill of a barrister gave justification for his stand, but ended by saying, "Even supposing that giving in on the question of finger impressions was a mistake, satyagraha remains unsullied. Its success is complete. You may, if you wish, blame those who gave in on the question of finger-impressions."

About this time another attempt was made on Gandhi's life. After a meeting was over, Gandhi and Mrs. Polak came out of the public hall. They noticed a man lurking in the shadow. Gandhi went up to him, linked his arm in his and talked to him in a low voice. The effect was magical. The man took out his weapon and handed it to him and went away.

Again Gandhi cited the examples of Thoreau, Luther, Galileo and Columbus as satyagrahis since they faced the Government, or the society or difficult situations like true satyagrahis! He further explained: "Satyagraha is really an attitude of mind. He who has attained to the satyagraha state of mind will remain ever victorious, at all times and places and under all conditions irrespective of whether it is a government or a people that he opposes, whether they be strangers, friends or relatives. It is only because we do not appreciate the marvel of satyagraha that we live in India as a poor and cowardly race!"[26]

Gandhi was grateful for the support Ritch, Mancherji, Ampthill and Curtis gave in England in propagating the cause of the Indians. These stalwarts were gratefully presented either with addresses or purses.

CHAPTER X

Again Jailed Twice

ON FEBRUARY 22, 1908, Gandhi sent to General Smuts a Draft Bill requesting him to amend the Immigration Registration Act No. 15 of 1907. This he did in accordance with the permission given by Smuts himself. Yet there were some who asserted that Gandhi had effected the compromise in undue haste and in ignorance. They said the community had to suffer for his credulity in public matters.

At this stage Gandhi revealed the causes that led him to the compromise. Firstly, he said that the thought that elderly and respectable businessmen were to seek jail on January 31, 1908, had worried him. Secondly, those who followed him to jail had told him there seriously that some people had been losing courage and the hawkers were pressing for a compromise. Lastly, those who went to jail lost their nerve in a few days and some of them hinted that they would not go to jail again. Even Smuts told him the same thing. Gandhi told his accusers that he had enjoyed being in jail and would welcome jail again if the occasion demanded.

The Chinese gave only thumb impressions in accordance with a compromise arrived at between Gandhi and Smuts. About ninety-five per cent of the Indians gave finger-impressions and five per cent gave thumb impressions.

While discussing the Gujarati equivalent for passive resistance, Gandhi gave a definition of it. "Passive resistance means resistance of evil with inner force instead of physical force. A passive resister cannot remain passive to everything that happens." In the first week of March Gandhi gave an account of his jail life, believing firmly as he did "that incarceration may often be the means of opening the gateway to freedom, liberty, and reform."

Flushed with victory, Gandhi referred to the deathless heroism of the Spartans who defended the pass at Thermopylae and called upon the Indians to raise a memorial hall in Johannesburg to the heroic satyagraha struggle which was the first example of its kind. At a dinner given by grateful Indians, William Hosken admitted that he had wrongly advised them to accept the law. He saw that Gandhi's words had come true. Doke said that satyagraha was a true battle.

With a zeal for organization, Gandhi took much care in developing contacts with important people. He wrote to Maganlal: "I hope you gave Hassan Mia a treat before he left." A rising leader is always warm and grateful for assistance and Gandhi was no exception to this rule. Hassan Mia was the son of Dawood Mia, President of the Natal Indian Congress. He was leaving for England to study for the Bar. Inconsistently enough, he denied an English education to his sons, but praised other Indian boys going in for it!

Leader of the satyagraha movement as he was, Gandhi was always justifying his action or quoting examples to support it or to inspire his followers to courageous deeds. It was this motive that led him to write in April 1908 a series of articles on Socrates whom he called a satyagrahi. The title of the articles was "Story of a Soldier of Truth." In concluding the trial speech of Socrates, Gandhi exhorted his readers to have the moral strength which enabled Socrates to follow virtue to the end and to embrace death as if it were one's beloved.

Just then the Transvaal Government ruled that Asiatics who entered the Transvaal after May 9, 1908, would have to apply for registration under the Act. A crisis began to brew. Gandhi was rudely shocked. He wrote to Cartwright that he had signed the document because Cartwright was associated with it. Fight began through telephones, telegrams, interviews and articles. Smuts wired that the terms of the settlement had been fulfilled and added that those who arrived after May 9 would be obliged to apply for registration under the law.

Gandhi asked him to refer to his letter written from jail. Smuts rightly said that Gandhi's interpretation of the letter was wrong. In one of his letters Gandhi (with two others) had said: "We recognise that it is not possible during the Parliamentary recess to repeal the Act, and we have noted your repeated public declarations that there is no likelihood of the Act being repealed."[1] Yet Gandhi insisted on his interpretation and

Smuts persisted in his view. Thinking that Smuts had departed from his oral promise, Gandhi described his reply as a 'frightful reply' and accused him of 'foul play'.

Gandhi had an interview with Cartwright and decided to meet General Smuts with Cartwright. He also gave a signal for a fight with increased and more effective strength. "The satyagraha," he said, "which yielded the settlement could force the implementation."

Essop Mia, President of the B.I.A. too was struck by a Pathan. Mia fell down unconscious. Gandhi wrote to Montford Chamney, the Registration officer, to return his application for registration as he was once more prepared to submit to the punishment involved in non-submission to the Asiatic Act. He declared in *Indian Opinion*: "I will fight it unto death, even if I should be the only one to do so." Leung Quinn, Chairman of the Chinese Committee, also recalled his application for registration.

Essop Mia had given evidence about the attack on Gandhi. "One should," Gandhi said, "accept blows with courage rather than run away. If such courage was beyond one's reach, one should strike back in self-defence." On May 21 he again appealed to Smuts to repeal the Act. There was a possibility of an attack on his person or an arrest. His lieutenants were worried about it. So he wrote to Maganlal Gandhi that he would have to sacrifice himself and if he had to give his life for a cause which he considered to be good, what better death[2] could there be?

Simultaneously Gandhi published from May to July 1908 a series of nine articles on the message of John Ruskin whom he regarded as one of the three moderns to make a deep impression on him. In the introduction Gandhi said he was opposed to the theory which preached the greatest good of the greatest number. He opposed it on moral grounds. He said that the exclusive quest for physical and material happiness of the majority at the cost of the minority has no sanction in the divine law. The object of Ruskin's work was, the welfare or the advancement of all and not merely of the greatest number. He entitled his articles 'Sarvodaya'.

Gandhi delivered a lecture on 'Are Asiatics and the coloured races a menace to Empire?' at the Y.M.C.A., Johannesburg, in May 1908. At the outset he said that originally the term 'coloured people' meant offspring of mixed marriages, but the term was then made to include the coloured people proper, the Africans and the Asiatics. Both the Africans and the Asiatics had advanced the interests of the Empire as a whole. His observations and experiences, he said, were confined very largely to British Indians, his own countrymen. But in studying the Indian question, he had endeavoured to study it as it affected the Africans and the Chinese.

Gandhi then stated that there were some who held that physical might was right and supreme. Some of them combined intellectual strength with physical strength, but he was of the opinion that nobody with merely physical strength or intellectual might could ever enjoy that strength which proceeded from the heart.

According to him, Western civilization represented tremendous activity whereas Eastern represented contemplativeness and sometimes lethargy. The former was destructive while the latter was constructive. Western civilization was centrifugal while Eastern was centripetal. Western civilization, he believed, was without a goal whereas Eastern civilization had always had a goal before it.[3] He believed as a loyal subject of the British Empire, that the mission of the Empire was to raise the subject races to equality with themselves, to give them free institutions and make them absolutely free men.

ON JUNE 6, 1908, Gandhi interviewed Smuts. The interview was not satisfactory; Smuts did not yield. He did not give an assurance that he would repeal the Act. Gandhi told Smuts that he would approach the Supreme Court for an order compelling the return of the documents. He asked Cartwright to play the role of an angel of peace. On June 24 a mass meeting was held under the auspices of the B.I.A. at Johannesburg where Gandhi declared repentantly that some of his countrymen said that he had not taken them into his confidence before he approached General Smuts.

"I believe," he affirmed, "that, in seeing General Smuts as I saw him, I acted correctly and in accordance with my conscience, but time has shown that they were right, time has shown also that I need not have gone to General Smuts as I did, . . . but I believed too much."[4]

This was the reply he gave to the unkind charge that he had misled his countrymen and sold them for selfish purposes. The Pathan had a perfect right to do what he did, Gandhi went on, as he found now from the consequences that had been entailed on the whole of the Asian community.

To make decisions without taking his colleagues into confidence was Gandhi's significant trait which he developed into a political style.

On June 23 Ibrahim Ismile Aswat made an application to the Supreme Court alleging breach of trust by General Smuts and demanding the return of his registration papers. Gandhi and Essop Mia too filed affidavits. Chamney and Smuts too filed affidavits to the effect that Smuts had never promised to repeal the Act.

On July 2, 1908, the Supreme Court rejected the application. Mr. Justice Solomon truly said that Gandhi's letter from jail and Smuts' reply to it did not throw any light on the repeal of the Act.[5] But Gandhi had declared already, "I state most emphatically and definitely that General Smuts did promise that he was going to repeal the Act in the presence of the Registrar of the Asiatics."[6]

Gandhi, therefore, gave a call for the renewal of satyagraha to give a taste of their strength, for the sword of satyagraha was superior to the steel sword. Having lost the case in the Supreme Court, the Indian leaders decided at a meeting held on the grounds of the Hamidia Mosque to burn the registration certificates. Newspapers advised Smuts not to carry the dispute further.

At this time Gandhi, giving his views on the Indian situation, expressed his disapproval of the bomb explosion in which two English ladies were killed. Khudiram Bose threw the bomb on April 30, 1908, at Muzaffarpur. Gandhi opined that they had no reason to rejoice at the introduction of Russian methods in India. The Indian people would not win their freedom by these methods.

They had no reason, Gandhi added, to believe that what was effective in Russia would be so in India too. He said it was a horrifying thought. He was surprised that many people exulted at the explosion of bombs. The bombs with which the British would have been killed would fall on India after the British left. They could neither achieve real Swaraj by following the path of evil, i.e. by killing the British nor by establishing factories. If every Indian made it a point to follow truth always, India would achieve Swaraj as a matter of course. That, according to Gandhi, was the message of Ruskin's book.

General Smuts started taking action against defaulters and Sorabji Shapurji, a youth from Natal, was sentenced to one month's imprisonment with hard labour. The second phase of the struggle began with Sorabji's arrest. Four years later he was sent to London to become a barrister and to take

Gandhi's place on his return to South Africa. Dr. Pranjivan Mehta paid for his education. He practised at Johannesburg and served the people for a while, but he soon died.

Thambi Naidu and Gandhi's son Harilal were sent to jail. The leading Indians started collecting licences and registers for a bonfire. Hawkers without licences were jailed. Gandhi addressed several mass meetings. Shops were closed and hartals were observed. By August 14 as many as sixty leaders and workers were re-arrested. They refused to accept release on bail. The families of jail-going satyagrahis were maintained by a system of monthly allowances in cash according to their needs.

Meanwhile Lokamanya Tilak was arrested in Bombay because of three articles that appeared in the *Kesari* regarding the bomb explosion at Muzaffarpur. He was sentenced on July 22, 1908, to six years' transportation. Gandhi wrote in *Indian Opinion* an article about the 'Sentence on the Great Tilak'. Pungent, bitter and penetrating writing, Gandhi curtly observed, was Tilak's object. He aimed, Gandhi proceeded, at inciting Indians against British rule. The rulers were justified, from their point of view, in taking action against them.

"Mr. Tilak, however," Gandhi added, "deserves our congratulations. He has, by his suffering, attained undying fame and laid the foundations of India's freedom."

Yet Gandhi further remarked: "What we need to consider is whether Indians should accept the views of Mr. Tilak and his party. We submit, after great deliberation, that Mr. Tilak's views should be rejected."[7]

Gandhi, a British loyalist and a devotee of British Imperialism, was far away from the Indian scene and among illiterate Indians and that is why he could afford to pass such an impertinent remark. Gokhale, his Guru, would have counselled restraint. Indeed, Tilak was the first leader who boldly stood up in Asia to uproot the British Empire while Gandhi loyally devoted years of his life to reform British Imperialism.

Gandhi tried to justify his remark by saying that freedom gained through violence would not endure. One might say it was historically incorrect to say so. He bristled with over-confidence when he said that the outcome of his exertions would be a thousand times better. Gandhi, the devotee of satyagraha, who attacked Tilak for his views, openly and unprincipally praised, in the same breath, the Young Turks who worked through secret societies and publications for the resumption of a parliamentary Government in Turkey![8] As it was, Turkey was a Muslim state, and to please his Muslim followers in South Africa he applied to the Young Turks a different moral standard!

On August 16, 1908, the registration certificates were publicly burnt at a mass meeting. Intimation had been given to Smuts about it. Essop Mia set fire to the certificates which had been thrown into a large cauldron saturated with paraffin. The bonfire contained about 2,300 certificates. The crowd hurrahed and shouted themselves hoarse and there was a scene of the wildest enthusiasm. The Chinese also put their certificates in the fire. Gandhi made a stirring speech at the bonfire. *The Daily Mail*, London, compared the act of the Indians in burning the certificates with that of the Boston Tea Party.

Gandhi then attended a meeting called by Botha, Smuts and members of their party. But no compromise was reached. On August 21 the Transvaal Assembly passed the Asiatics Registration Amendment Bill which fell short of the terms proposed by the Indian leaders. On August 23 Gandhi again burnt certificates and his assailant Mir Alam, who was in a repentant mood, burnt his own.

THE ASIATIC REGISTRATION Amendment Act was gazetted on September 2, 1908, without repealing the offensive Act of 1907. On September 10 Gandhi tried to reach a settlement through Hosken, but failed. There was now no alternative but to openly resume the non-violent struggle which had already been in operation with the arrests of the workers. This time the Government became sterner and the satyagrahis were given hard labour.

Gandhi's lieutenants Thambi Naidu, Nadirsha Cama, Polak and A. M. Andrews filed affidavits affirming that the authorities had promised a repeal of the Registration Act. The British Indian Association took over Gandhi's financial responsibilities, and Kallenbach, the Jewish architect, stood by Gandhi. The leader defended traders charged with trading without grocer's licences and demanded legal equality for Indians.

In the heat of the struggle, Gandhi charged Smuts with foul play and breach of his definite but verbal promise to repeal the Registration Act. But later he himself wrote with a greater sense of detachment in his *Satyagraha in South Africa* that "it is possible that in behaving to the Indians as he did in 1908, General Smuts was not guilty of a deliberate breach of faith."[9]

The New Asiatic Act came into force from September 21, 1908. Incessant demands were made by prisoners inside jail and by leaders outside for improving jail diet and requesting the jail authorities to give ghee instead of fat.

While Gandhi was returning from Durban, he was arrested on October 7, 1908, for being without his registration certificate and for refusing to give his thumb impression. There were six Natal Indians with him and they also were arrested. They declined to offer bail. The hearing of the case was postponed for a week. On October 14 they were charged with being prohibited immigrants entering the Transvaal. Gandhi defended them; but they were sentenced to a fine of £20 or 6 weeks' hard labour. Gandhi himself was then charged under the new Act with failure to produce his register and to give his thumb and finger impressions on demand.

Gandhi pleaded guilty. But as the Act, he added, offended his conscience he had asked his followers to refuse submission to it. The Assistant Resident Magistrate De Villiers said he was sorry to see Gandhi in that situation and sentenced him to pay a fine of £25 or go to jail with hard labour for two months.

Gandhi gladly accepted to go to jail. Just before his trial, Gandhi had sent a message to Indian youth. In it he said: "We are engaged in raising men who will give a good account of themselves in any part of the world." Adding that passive resistance was always infinitely superior to physical force, he concluded that it would be a calamity to break the connection between the British people and the people of India.[10]

The message reveals Gandhi's faith in passive resistance and his loyalty to the British Empire and his budding and nascent ambition to play a future role in it.

After the Magistrate pronounced the sentence, Gandhi said in a message to his followers that they should stand firm to the end. From the Volksrust jail on November 7, he sent a cablegram on behalf of the Indian prisoners to the Secretary of State for the Colonies expressing his loyal felicitations on the 57th birthday of King Emperor Edward VII and, inviting his attention to the circumstances that led to their imprisonment. Reuter's Volksrust correspondent wrote that "Mr. Gandhi expressed himself as being the happiest man in the Transvaal."

In a message from jail, Gandhi said that the people should remain steadfast even though the struggle might last eight months or eight years or even longer, and added that if they made a conscious effort to remove the causes, everything could be over even that day.[11]

This is typical of Gandhi. All great leaders always create hopes in their followers. Gandhi later said that Swaraj could be won within a year. Comparatively this was a long period he fixed for the fulfilment of the promise! For a satyagrahi, he often said later, nothing was impossible!

Sir Pherozeshah Mehta cabled Lord Ampthill about the maltreatment of Indians in South Africa. In London a meeting was held protesting against Gandhi's arrest. Lala Lajpatrai, Savarkar and B. C. Pal made stirring speeches and Sir Muncherji Bhownaggree presided. Lord Minto, the Viceroy of India, conveyed to the India Office Indian resentment of the treatment given to passive resisters in the Transvaal and urged a considerate attitude to the Indian problem. Mrs. Annie Besant sent a message of hope, of consolation and of friendship to Gandhi and his colleagues.

While in Volksrust Jail, Gandhi was made to work increasingly hard along with other prisoners on the site of the agricultural show-ground which was close to the road. The warden shouted at him incessantly although he worked hard. Gandhi picked up earth to rub on the blisters of his palms. Lymph was oozing out of his palms. When he returned to his cell, his whole body was so stiff with pain and fatigue that he could scarcely move. Along with other prisoners he too dug holes for trees for more than nine hours a day and worked on Municipal water-works, cleaning a cemetery and tending soldiers' graves.

On October 25 Gandhi was removed for some days from Volksrust Jail to Johannesburg Jail in a prisoner's dress to give evidence in a case. The jail authorities had given him no food packet for the journey. The station master offered him some money, but he declined. He borrowed 10 shillings from a Kazi who was present at the station and bought food for himself and for the warden.

The warden in charge repeatedly offered to take him in a cab; but prisoner Gandhi chose to march on foot from Park Station to the jail, carrying a prison knapsack. He carried a bundle of clothes in a bag and a basket of books. Polak walked along with him from the station for some minutes on their way to the jail. Gandhi accepted no preferential treatment as a prisoner and so he had to go through the street as a convict was required to do. But the sight was shocking.

So some Europeans, admirers and lieutenants of Gandhi

raised a hue and cry against the Government, denouncing the shameful act as monstrous and nothing short of a disgrace.

But the friends and admirers did this without knowing the facts of the case. Frankly, this situation was of Gandhi's own making, and he deliberately used it to do propaganda for the struggle, for he had much in his make-up to daze and dazzle. Yet *Indian Opinion* commented that "it was typical of the anti-Asiatic policy of the Transvaal Government that no instructions were issued to jail officers to transfer Gandhi in civil dress and to take Gandhi in a cab to the jail."

In Johannesburg Jail there was a common ward for the Kaffir and Indian prisoners sentenced to hard labour. There the lavatories had open access and no doors. As soon as Gandhi occupied one of them there came along a strong, heavily-built, fierce-looking Kaffir. He asked Gandhi to get out and started abusing him. Gandhi said he would leave very soon. "Instantly," Gandhi later said, "he lifted me up in his arms and threw me out. Fortunately, I caught hold of the door-frame and saved myself from a fall." The Indian prisoners who saw the sight wept as they felt helpless and miserable.

In this jail Gandhi was given the work of stitching caps with a sewing machine. Although he was doing the work for the first time, he picked it up in no time. He requested the officers to give him the work of pounding gravel. At the time of medical examination Kaffir prisoners were kept standing undressed for 15 minutes so as to save the physician's time. Indian prisoners however, were asked to lower their breeches only when the doctor approached.

Gandhi was of the opinion that "there should be no need to conceal any parts of our anatomy when in the presence of men only. There is no reason to believe, moreover, that others will keep staring at the parts which we generally hide. We need not have any false sense of shame." Gandhi sometimes gave up this false sense of shame later in his Indian Ashrams. That phase originated in this early experience. "If," he observed, "we are, pure in our own minds, where is the need to be particular about hiding what is a part of our natural endowment?" He said that the Indians should learn to take that right view.

Some difficulties arose in the jail. According to the prison rules, a prisoner must be vaccinated. The Indian prisoners refused to be vaccinated on grounds of conscience. The Government yielded on this point. Then another problem arose. Hindu prisoners were not prepared to eat food cooked by Muslims although they raised no objection when any Kaffir or white man touched the food. They feared excommunication in India. Gandhi observed that Indians who joined the movement should not cling to false distinctions and quarrel among themselves.

On his return to Volksrust jail, Gandhi was informed in the first week of November that Kasturbai Gandhi was taken seriously ill. Some days before the arrest of Gandhi she had undergone an operation at Durban without chloroform. The doctor and his wife nursed her and allowed Gandhi to go to Johannesburg. But she grew worse and the doctor telephoned to Gandhi for permission to give her meat or wine. Both Kasturbai and Gandhi refused. Kasturbai was reduced to a skeleton. She was removed to Phoenix and under hydropathic treatment she felt better.

Kasturbai was now again suffering from haemorrhage and her condition was grave. West informed Gandhi from Natal about it. But he replied from jail that "it cuts me but does not surprise me." He added that he would not pay the fine for his release and that he had counted the cost when he embarked upon the struggle. Concluding, he said that he hoped she would be alive and conscious to receive and understand the letter which he enclosed.

The jailer asked Gandhi whether he would pay the fine and go. Gandhi refused as he regarded his love for the motherland as an aspect of his religion. There was no cruelty in it, it was his duty to do so.

In a pathetic but courageous letter Gandhi wrote to 'Beloved Kasturba'. "I have received West's telegram today about your illness. It eats my heart. I am very much grieved but I am not in a position to go to nurse you. I have offered my all to the satyagraha struggle. My coming there is out of the question. I can come only if I pay the fine which I must not. If you keep courage and take the necessary nutrition, you will recover. If, however, my ill luck so has it that you pass away, I should only say that there would be nothing wrong in your doing so during your separation from me while I am still alive. I love you so dearly that even if you are dead, you will be alive to me. Your soul is deathless."

"I repeat," he added, "what I frequently told you that if you do succumb to your illness, I will not marry again. Time and again I have told you that you may quietly breathe your last with faith in God. If you die, even that death of yours will be a sacrifice to the cause of satyagraha. My struggle is not merely political. It is religious and therefore quite pure. It does not matter much whether one dies in it or lives. I hope and expect that you will also think likewise and not be unhappy. I ask this of you. Mohandas."[12]

ON DECEMBER 12, 1908, Gandhi was released from Volksrust Jail. On his way to Johannesburg he gave an interview to the press in which he said he enjoyed every minute in jail and his complaint was not against the jail officers but against the jail regulations. At a reception in Johannesburg he said, "Where there is God, there is truth. I love truth only, and so God is with me. Therefore I will do what pleases God, even if the community should turn against me. ... If you fight truthfully with Him as witness, your bonds will be loosened in eight days, according to your Chairman, but in less than 24 hours according to me. God is present everywhere; He sees and hears everything. I am sure that we shall be free when that God stirs our opponents' conscience."

Thus God was the main pillar of Gandhi's satyagraha philosophy. Next day he said at another meeting he was glad that of a population of 7,000 as many as 1,500 had been to jail. He considered it a victory!

The philosophy of satyagraha was taking shape and Gandhi was explaining it. 'A satyagrahi should have regard for truth, have little regard for his body and must resist till the end without fear of death. He must be content to think himself rich in his poverty. If he owns any wealth, he must hold it in some other country!'[13] His precautionary advice on wealth, however, is not consistent with the Philosophy of satyagrahi. It was partly materialistic and partly spiritualistic.

"Securing one's rights is one of the results, but satyagraha can be offered without thinking of the result. The invaluable education received through the strengthening of will power which results from one's adherence to truth and suffering hardships for its sake is never lost." When cases of the satyagrahis failed in the court, Gandhi said, the people must apply to God alone. He who left everything to God, he believed, could never know defeat in the world.[14]

Replying to the charge that the pickets terrorised those who wanted to register, Gandhi said it was not terrorism; it was ostracism.

At Phoenix, Cordes, a German theosophist friend of Gandhi, was for some time in charge of a school started to teach the children of the settlers. Teaching was in both Gujarati and English. Attention was paid to the simultaneous development of mind and body. Special emphasis was laid on strengthening the moral character of the pupils. It was no good, said the founders of the school, for children to have one standard of behaviour in school and another at home. The diet of the children did not include tea, coffee or cocoa as these things were considered harmful to them also and because slaves or indentured labourers were used in their production.

Children were to follow their respective religious observances as desired by their parents. Education was fruitless without religious instruction. Both religious and secular education was provided. According to Gandhi, secular education strengthened religious instruction. Boys were to be taught the history of ancient and modern India so as to inculcate in them love of India and help them grow patriotic.

At this stage Gandhi published a summary of Tulsidas's *Ramayana*, as according to him the general spirit of Hinduism reflected in the *Ramayana*. Hinduism was an essentially ethical religion. Gandhi sent a copy of Tolstoy's *The Kingdom of God is Within You* to the warden in Volksrust jail for his many kindnesses within the law during his incarceration. The country, said Gandhi, and religions could not advance by a step that would not lead to spiritual growth.

After his release on December 12, 1908, Gandhi as usual wrote a series of articles, this time on 'My second experience in jail.' Everything and every experience was used for the propagation of the cause. It was good education for him personally and he observed that "a campaign of satyagraha may take many forms, but it is found that jail-going is the most effective means of fighting political disabilities." He said he had read Thoreau's essays in jail.

Gandhi went to Phoenix to see Kasturbai who was by that time much improved. While returning to Johannesburg, he was again arrested at Volksrust on January 16, 1909 and released on bail on his own recognizance. He wrote a letter to his daughter-in-law Chanchal, wife of Harilal, whom he regarded as his daughter. Harilal had a daughter named Rami. Gandhi wrote Chanchal that love for her did not mean that Harilal should stay only with her. Her husband would stay at Johannesburg till the struggle was over. As the young girl was living in separation, Gandhi was trying to change her mental attitude. He wrote telling her how Damayanti, Taramati and Draupadi each had become immortal on account of separation from the husband, and the, entire Hindu nation sang the praises of Draupadi's resoluteness. "Don't think," he continued,. "that these instances have not taken place." Here he does not say that these stories were apocryphal!

The struggle now entered upon its third stage. At this stage some men were giving in and there were some rifts among the Indians. Gandhi said that they should get training in organizing a movement, learn to be resourceful and demonstrate that they were not cowards. And to inspire them he added: "The great Thoreau said that one sincere man is more than a hundred thousand insincere men." There were some Pathans who wickedly charged Gandhi with insulting the Prophet of Islam. He replied that he had not even dreamt of such a thing. "My enthusiasm," he said longingly, "is such that I may have to meet death in South Africa at the hands of my own countrymen. If that happens, you should rejoice. It will unite the Hindus and the Mussalmans."[15]

The European merchants brought pressure to bear on Indian merchants not to support the satyagraha. Merchants like Adam Mahomed Cachalia, who were fearless leaders of the satyagraha, were forced into liquidation although his assets were insured by sums larger than the liabilities.

After Gandhi's arrest at Volksrust on January 16, the trial was postponed to February 4, 1909. But it actually took place at Volksrust on February 25. The charges were read. Gandhi pleaded guilty. But addressing the Court, he said that it was his misfortune that he had to appear before the Court for the same offence the second time. As he was a man who respected conscience above everything, he asked the Magistrate to impose on him the highest penalty The Magistrate said he acted in accordance with the law and sentenced him to a fine of fifty pounds or to undergo imprisonment for three months with hard labour. Gandhi was sentenced for the third time. In a parting message to the Indians, Gandhi said that his only regret was that he received only three months' imprisonment whereas other satyagrahi patriots had received six months'. He appealed to the Indians to continue the struggle and sacrifice wealth and life for it, for it was a fight on behalf of the religion which underlined all religions.

In a message to his Tamil brethren, who were the vanguard of his movement, he said that they were descendants of Prahlad and Sudhanva, both passive resisters of the purest type. They disregarded the dictates of their parents when they were asked to deny God. They suffered extreme torture rather than inflict suffering on their persecutors. So he appealed fervently not to deny their manhood, not to go back upon their oath and deny God as they were asked to do by the Transvaal Government.

On March 3 Gandhi was removed to Pretoria Prison. The jail authorities did not allow him to write in Gujarati to his wife. He could use his right hand with difficulty. So he wrote to West with his left hand. It was here that he first wrote with the left hand. He applied to the jail Governor for ghee otherwise the petitioner feared that he would suffer in health for want of sufficient nutrition.

Gandhi wrote to Manilal that if he practised the three virtues Truth, Ahimsa and Brahmacharya and if the virtues became part of his life, he would have completed his education as far as his father was concerned.

In the jail Gandhi read a book given by Swami Shankaranand, a Hindu Missionary, who was then touring South Africa. It made him inquisitive about the life of Swami Dayanand, the founder of the Arya Samaj. He hesitated to accept the revolutionary meaning given by Swami Dayanand to the *gayatri* and several other *mantras*. Besides, Gandhi was of the opinion that the adoption of the sacred thread by those who had for ages given it up was a mistake. The sacred thread was in those days rather a hindrance than a help. It seems, however, that there was one more reason in his mind which acted against the wearing of the thread. In his autobiography he says: "In fact this cowardly feeling carried me so far that in South Africa I got my cousin Chhaganlal Gandhi, who was religiously wearing the *shikha* (tuft of hair on the head), to do away with it. I feared that it might come in the way of his public work and so, even at the risk of paining him, I made him get rid of it."[16]

Gandhi read and considered the Upanishads an invaluable work. He thanked Keshavram Bhatt who presented him with the book. He read Emerson, Ruskin and Mazzini. They all confirmed, the view, said Gandhi, that education did not mean knowledge of letters, but it meant character building, a knowledge of duty.

He asked Manilal to write out in good hand passages, hymns and verses from English, Gujarati and Hindi books and to make a valuable collection for himself. In Gandhi's opinion Emerson's essays contained the teaching of Indian wisdom in a Western garb. Strangely enough he asked his son to send him a copy of an Algebra text-book. It may be that he was teaching Algebra to some prisoner.

Just then the Transvaal Liquor Commission was considering the issue of prohibition. Early in April 1909 Gandhi sent a representation from Pretoria Jail saying that both Hindus and Mohomedans were prohibited by their religions from taking intoxicating liquors. He opined, however, that partial prohibition would not be useful and unless those who preached abstinence were themselves ready to practise it, all liquor legislation must be largely a make-shift.

At this time the Phoenix settlement was in debt, and Gandhi asked Polak to sell his law and other books and to raise money. Kasturbai was improving in health, and Gandhi inquired from jail whether she was taking part in household work.

ON COMPLETION OF his sentence, Gandhi was released on May 24, 1909, from Pretoria Jail. A crowd greeted him at the jail. The hero marched at their head to the Pretoria Mosque and addressed a meeting. He said that because the people were cowed down they did not fill the jails. As for him, he said, his pleasures and his happiness were in jail. He would try to see that he was imprisoned again. He called upon them to help the movement financially and fill the jails. There was no other course that he could advise.

On his way to Johannesburg, Gandhi was given, at Park Town, a hero's welcome by a vast gathering including Indians, Chinese and Europeans like the Rev. J. J. Doke. Gandhi had now done five months and three weeks in jail, having served three sentences.

At the meeting he was greeted with a new slogan: "Salute the King of Hindus and Muslims." Referring to this slogan Gandhi said he was their servant and humbly added: "My aspiration will be fulfilled only if I have to lay down my life in the very act of serving the community."[17]

From this repeated desire for immolation it seems that Gandhi's soul was craving for immolation and immortality! He was aching to give life for a cause, to lay down his life in action! With the mental frame of a masochistic-martyr he seemed to be in search of a killer!

Writing about his third experience in jail, Gandhi said he was kept in an isolated cell, was given no pillow or bedboard and was given the work of polishing the floor of his cell and the cell-doors of the corridor and also of blanket-quilting.

Gandhi said he was brutally treated and intentionally added that General Smuts wanted to bend him, but he was not likely to succumb. Again he had battled for the supply of ghee and remained on one meal a day. After a month and a half, ghee was allowed to all Indian prisoners and Gandhi was given a bed-board, a felt-mattress, a night shirt and a handkerchief. When General Smuts sent two books for him to read, he admitted that Smuts personally entertained no ill-will against him.

Gandhi read over thirty books during this period. The books saved him much dejection, despair and unpleasant thoughts. These books were in English, Hindi, Gujarati, Sanskrit and Tamil. Reading the book by Carlyle on the *French Revolution*, Gandhi came to the conclusion that it was not from the white nations that India could learn the way out of her present degradation. It was his belief that the French people had gained nothing of value through the Revolution. Gandhi thought that Mazzini was also of the same opinion.

According to Gandhi, Tamil was a very fine language and his opinion was that Tamil had produced and would produce a larger number of intelligent, thoughtful and wise men. Moreover, since India was going to be one country, observed Gandhi, Indians outside Madras also should learn Tamil. Concluding the account of his jail experience, Gandhi said that he was growing more convinced every day that no-one who did not know his religion could have true patriotism in him.

Once again Gandhi explained on June 7, 1909, 'the ethics of passive resistance' at the Germiston Library. Passive resistance, he said, was a misnomer. But the expression had been accepted as it was popular. It had been for a long time used by those who carried out in practice the idea denoted by the term. The idea was more completely and better expressed by the term "soul-force."

Jesus Christ, Daniel and Socrates represented the purest form of passive resistance or soul-force. Tolstoy was its best and brightest exponent and lived according to it. Soul-force was infinitely superior to body-force. It only injured the users and not those against whom it was used. If people in order to secure redress of wrongs resorted to soul-force, most of their present sufferings would be avoided. "Resist not evil" meant that evil was not to be repelled by evil but by good. According to Gandhi, the same idea was expressed in Indian philosophy by the expression, 'freedom from injury of every living thing.'

CHAPTER XI

A Satyagrahi's Mission

The Proposals About the formation of the Union of South Africa were being discussed between African leaders and British statesmen. General Botha and General Smuts were about to visit England in connection with the unification of the colonies. The European Committee in the Transvaal suggested to the Indian leaders that they should send a deputation to represent their cause when the Transvaal leaders would be in London. Besides the satyagrahis were not in a position to put up a strong fight, as some of them had been either deported or imprisoned four or five times. Every movement has its ebb and tide. So had Gandhi's. The deportations, imprisonments and a number of difficulties had blunt the edge of the satyagraha movement.

The leaders of the British Indian Association therefore decided on June 13, 1909, to send a deputation to England consisting of A. M. Cachhalia, V. A. Chettiar, Haji Habib and Gandhi, and another deputation to India consisting of Polak, Gopal Naidu, N. A. Cama and E. S. Coovadia. But the next day Cachalia, Chettiar and Naidu were arrested. At a public meeting in Johannesburg on June 16, the name of the two deputations were announced. The deputation to England was to place before the Imperial authorities and the British public the true situation with regard to the Asiatic struggle and the British Indian view of the proposed union of South Africa. The deputation to India was to place before the Indian authorities and the Indian public the true situation with regard to the Asiatic struggle in the Transvaal.

According to Gandhi, a satyagraha must suffer and depend upon God, and his success consisted in the very fact of his offering satyagraha. But many Indians did not desire to continue the satyagraha and wanted to put an end to the struggle as early as possible. So Gandhi had to justify the idea of sending these deputations. The Transvaal Government was unyielding, and the so-called victory of the new weapon of satyagraha was not so very effective and tangible. Deputations to two countries, Gandhi argued, would shorten the duration of the struggle. However, the task of the deputation, he observed, was difficult, and sending it did not imply the end of satyagraha. Going to jail was the only remedy. The repeal of the Black Act could be secured, he held, only through the satyagraha.

Here Gandhi was playing the role of an apostle of satyagraha. Yet he played the role of a barrister also and offered arguments to justify his deviation from satyagraha and the unexpected stand or gesture he had to resort to.

Gandhi tried to get the delegates-elect released on parole but failed, Smuts replying that he could not interfere with the law. And although Gandhi himself half expected to be arrested, he and Hajee Habib who was a Muslim merchant from Gandhi's native place Porbandar, left Johannesburg on June 21 and started for London by the S.S. *Kenilworth Castle* which left Cape Town on June 23, 1909. Haji Habib had not received an English education, but knew English, Dutch, Urdu and other languages.

As the other delegates-elect of the deputation were not released, a one-man deputation in the person of Polak left Johannesburg on June 25 and sailed for India on July 7. Polak had acted as Assistant Secretary of the British Indian Association since 1906 and had been admitted as Attorney of the Supreme Court of the Transvaal. He had studied the Indian problem in detail from all its angles and propagated it with unremitting zeal and devotion. He was 27. His wife Millie was organizing Indian women in the Transvaal with the help of Miss Schlesin and Mrs. Vogal, both European women.

On the day Gandhi left Johannesburg he replied to a letter of a Muslim named Habib Motan who had asked him whether the demand for the inclusion of a Muslim in the Viceroy's Council in India was reasonable or not. The demand had been put forward by the Muslim League delegation which waited on Morley, the Secretary of State for India. Gandhi's co-workers and followers in the Transvaal were predominantly Muslims. He had learnt at great cost that it was not easy for any non-Muslim leader to express his opinion on any problem concerning the Muslim religion and Muslim demands. So he replied:

"I think it reasonable that a Muslim should be appointed to the Viceroy's Council. If Lord Morley has ordered such an appointment, I think he is justified. I make no distinction between Hindus and Muslims. To me both are sons of Mother India."

"My personal view is that," he added, "since numerically Hindus are in a great majority, and are, as they themselves believe, better-placed educationally, they should cheerfully concede to their Muslim brethren the utmost they can. As a satyagrahi, I am emphatically of the view that the Hindus should give to the Muslims whatever they ask for, and willingly accept whatever sacrifice this may involve. Unity will be brought about only through such mutual generosity."[1]

This is a key to Gandhi's future policy regarding Hindu-Muslim unity. As a satyagrahi, Gandhi never felt his duty to tender advice to Muslims, and the word 'mutual' remained always one-sided and had no meaning except that it involved sacrifice on the part of Hindus. What Gandhi wrote on June 21, 1909, he kept on saying later in India for thirty-eight years, adding a rider to it to the effect that without Hindu-Muslim unity there would not be Swaraj for India.

On board the ship, the famous African authoress Mrs. Olive Schreiner and her sister Mrs. Lewis, who had great sympathy for the cause of the British Indians in South Africa, shook hands with Gandhi in the presence of a huge crowd. Mrs. Schreiner's charming and refined manners and progressive views made her personality exceptionally impressive. This authoress of *Dreams* and *The Story of an African Farm* paid a tribute to passive resistance. The whole Schreiner family was exceptional.

It was Gandhi's opinion that the South African Indians could not oppose the formation of a Union of South Africa merely on the ground that they would be ruined. When the enemies were united, Gandhi added, they were bound to increase their pressure on them, but the Indians could not certainly prevent them from being united.

Of the representatives of the coloured deputation consisting of Dr. Abdur Rahman, Frederick, Londors and Mavela, the first three travelled second class and the last, third class. Mr. Schreiner had gone ahead to plead their case in London. He did this work at his own expense and did not charge the coloured people a farthing. He was a legal celebrity in Cape Town.

The white leaders on board the ship were John Xavier Merriman, Prime Minister of Cape Colony and Botha from the Orange Free River Colony.

Gandhi, a passenger in the first-class, was soon disgusted with its delicacies and luxuries and decorum. He envied the lot of the servants. He said those who wanted to serve God should not run after luxury. Ten years earlier Gandhi, who had asked Gokhale why the great Indian leader did not travel by tram-car, was now himself travelling first-class although he was for simplicity and solitude.

In justifying his action, Gandhi said that travelling by first class was not wrong always and in all circumstances. In South Africa there were several reasons why he would prefer Indians to travel first or second class. They must rebut, he observed the charge of miserliness that was levelled against the Indians.

He did not eat pudding because it contained eggs. He avoided tea and coffee as these were the products of slave labour. On board the ship most of his day was spent in reading. He prepared also the statement which was to be submitted in England. It was entitled 'Statement of Transvaal Indian case'.

He discussed the British Indian problem with Merriman who was in sympathy with it. From a work named *Kasassul Ambia*, which Gandhi read with the help of Haji Habib, he learnt that "we can make no conditions with God, we must live as He may order us." He saw the necessity for every Hindu to have a knowledge of Sanskrit. In order to emphasise the significance of his movement, he always wrote in his letters that because they had gone to jail people cared to listen to them.

ON HIS ARRIVAL in London on July 10, Gandhi, in an interview with a Reuter representative, said that the Transvaal Immigration Law insulted the whole of India and created a racial bar for the first time in the history of colonial legislation. They conveyed their luggage to the Hotel Cecil, saw Ritch and set to work. Polak's sister Miss Maud did the typing. The deputation was to work in accordance with the advice of Lord Ampthill and his South Africa British Indian Committee. Gandhi's leg was swollen; it was a legacy of Pretoria Jail. The swelling had continued for many days.

Miss Florence Winterbottom, Secretary of the Union of Ethical Societies, London, took keen interest in the Indian Problem. She boiled with rage when she knew of poor Nagappen's death which had occurred just after his release from jail as a satyagrahi. Gandhi inquired after the health of Mrs. Ritch and came to know that his old friend Dr. Josiah Oldfield whom he had held so many years in high esteem, had deviated from the path of virtue. Upon this Gandhi said, "We have often to break our idols."

Lord Ampthill charmed Gandhi with his transparent honesty, courtesy and humility. Gandhi saw Lord Curzon, to whom he had submitted a representation when the former paid a visit to South Africa in January 1909. Just then the *South Africa* in its leading article alleged that Gandhi was guided by sympathisers in London, who were associated "with the dangerous movement in India." He disarmed his critic by stating that he was guided by Ampthill[2] and his Committee. Besides, he said that he was a satyagrahi and the test of true passive resistance was 'sacrifice of self and not of others.'

Gandhi meant that the business of satyagrahis was to get killed by an aggressor and not to kill him. Their aim was to pacify the killers and tyrants and aggressors! Violence exists in the scheme of things, but it is willed upon oneself !

Gandhi issued this statement against 'the dangerous movement in India' because Madanlal Dhingra, one of the Indian revolutionaries, had given a shock to British statesmen by killing, on July 1, 1909, Sir Curzon Wyllie, Morley's aide-de-camp. Wyllie was the eye and brain of the India Office and was shot by Dhingra at a function held in the Jehangir Hall of the Imperial Institute by the National Indian Association in London. Dr. Cawas Lalcaca, an Anglicized Parsee zealot from Shanghai, who tried to save the life of Wyllie, also was killed in the action. Gandhi, like other moderate leaders in India, felt that the killing of Sir Curzon Wyllie had done India much harm, and he thought that his deputation's efforts too had received a setback. Even should the British leave in consequence of such murderous acts, he feared, the murderers would rule in their place.[3] Those who commended the murder were, according to him, guilty of a heinous sin. India would never prosper unless its men invited the utmost suffering on themselves.

Madanlal Dhingra was a student at an engineering college in London. Smartly dressed, he looked like a dandy. He was a member of the London branch of the Abhinava Bharat Society established by Savarkar in 1899 at Nasik. He was a devoted follower of Savarkar and was proud of India.

In India British repression had reached its climax. A great many revolutionaries of the Maniktola Revolutionary Society had been either sentenced to transportation or hanged. Savarkar's elder brother had been sentenced to transportation for having published a revolutionary poem in which the poet sang, 'pray tell, who has attained independence without a war?' A number of editors in the Punjab, Maharashtra and Bengal were jailed. India's greatest and most popular leader Tilak had been already sentenced to transportation for six years. This had provoked the Indian revolutionaries in London and they had started to answer with equal violence the challenge of the furious and reckless British bureaucrats. Gandhi was not fully aware of the serious situation prevailing in India.

When on his arrest the police searched Dhingra and his residence, they seized some copies of a certain statement. A meeting held on July 5, by Indians Sir Muncherji Bhownaggaree, the Aga Khan, Surendranath Banerjee, B. C. Pal and G. S. Khaparde at the Caxton Hall, ended in pandemonium as Savarkar, who voted against the resolution condemning Dhingra, said that the meeting had no right to do so in advance while the case was *sub judice*. A Eurasian struck Savarkar a blow on his forehead and his face became besmeared with blood. Gandhi's ideal leader Sir Muncherji rushed rashly at Savarkar. The Aga Khan did not like Muncherji's rashness which was responsible for the turn the meeting had taken.

In the Court Dhingra, despite the advice of some that he should feign madness, boldly asserted that he wished that the English Court of law should sentence him to death; for in that case the vengeance of his countrymen would be all the keener. He further said: "Just as the Germans have no right to occupy this country, so the English people have no right to occupy India; and it is perfectly justifiable on our part to kill the Englishman who is polluting our sacred land. I am surprised at the terrible hypocrisy, the farce and the mockery of the English people." Dhingra made this *extempore* statement as the written statement found on his person was suppressed by the police. Savarkar, the author of that statement, arranged for its publication through David Garnet, later a famous author in England, who took the journalistic scoop to Robert Lynd, and Lynd published it in the *Daily News*, London. Like a bombshell, it exploded on the morning of August 16.

The statement said: "I admit, the other day, I attempted to shed English blood as a humble revenge for the inhuman hangings and deportations of patriotic Indian youths. I believe that a nation held in bondage with the help of foreign bayonets is in a perpetual state of war. Since open battle is rendered impossible to a disarmed race, I attacked by surprise; since guns. are denied to me, I drew forth my pistol and fired. The war of Independence will continue between India and England so long as the English and Hindu races last (if this present unnatural relation does not cease.)" Dhingra gloried in his own martyrdom. His statement is given in detail so that the views Gandhi criticized should be known fully as a part of history. Gandhi, indignantly criticizing Dhingra, observed:[4] "Dhingra's defence is inadmissible. In my view, he has acted like a coward. All the same, one can only pity the man. He was egged on to do this act by ill-digested reading of worthless writings. His defence of himself, too, appears to have been learnt by rote. It is those who incited him to this that deserve to be punished. The analogy of Germans and Englishmen is fallacious. If the Germans were to invade (Britain), the British would kill only the invaders. They would not kill every German whom they met."

According to Gandhi, Dhingra's statement argued mere childishness or mental derangement. Gandhi wanted the leader of the Indian revolutionaries punished and so he put a wrong interpretation on the analogy of Germans and Englishmen to suit his own views. He had held discussions on several occasions in India House with Savarkar and the Indian revolutionaries led by him.

The 'worthless writings' mentioned by Gandhi were Savarkar's famous books *Mazzini* and *The Indian War of Independence of 1857* and his fiery pamphlets which inspired the Indian revolutionaries. Savarkar's *Mazzini* had been taken out in procession in palanquin in Maharashtra and enjoyed immense popularity in Maharashtra. And his *Indian War of Independence of 1857* was proscribed both by the British and Indian Governments before it was published. Like Carlyle's *French Revolution, Savarkar's Indian War of Independence of 1857* was itself a revolution. The latter book was sometimes sold at Rs. 300 and was praised with mixed feelings of admiration and hatred by eminent Englishmen like Sir Valentine Chirol and was presented to one another by them on auspicious occasions!

While Gandhi, the apostle of non-violence and an avowed worshipper of British imperialism, was thus ruthlessly condemning Dhingra, Irish newspapers paid glowing tributes to Dhingra declaring loudly: "Ireland honours Madanlal Dhingra who was proud to lay down his life for the sake of his country."

W. S. Blunt observes in *My Diaries*:[5] "People talk about political assassination as defeating its own end, but it is nonsense, it is just the shock needed to convince selfish rulers that selfishness has its limits of imprudence. It is like that other fiction that

England never yields to threats. My experience is that when England has her face well slapped she apologises, not before."

Blunt further wrote in his *Diaries* that no Christian martyr ever faced his judges more fearlessly or with greater dignity, and remarked that the day of Dhingra's execution would be regarded as one of martyrdom in India for generations. Blunt also revealed in his *Diaries* that Lloyd George expressed to Winston Churchill his highest admiration of Dhingra's attitude as a patriot. Churchill shared the same views and quoted with admiration Dhingra's last words as the finest ever made in the name of patriotism. They both compared Dhingra with Plutarch's immortal heroes.

Dhingra's spirit revolted against imperialism and imperialist exploitation, and Gandhi condemned him in the name of nonviolence, but supported an imperialist war of British imperialists by recruiting Indians for use as cannon-fodder.

IT IS NECESSARY to give here some details to shed light on these opposing philosophies which held the stage of Indian politics for over four decades. As Gandhi soon wrote a book in reply to Savarkar, Indian Home Rule or the Indian Swaraj, it would be in the fitness of things to know to what ideology he replied. Gandhi was then a promising Mahatma and Savarkar the spirited Shivaji. Gandhi arrogated the religion of God to himself and imputed the irreligion of the devil to the revolutionaries and to those leaders who opposed him.

Savarkar represented the rebellious force of a subject people. He replied to Gandhi and men of his persuasion:[6] "We feel no special love for secret organizations or surprise and secret warfare. We hold that whenever the open preaching and practising of truth is banned by enthroned violence, then alone secret societies and secret warfare are justified as the inevitable and indispensable means to combat violence by force. Whenever the natural process of national and political evolution is violently suppressed by the forces of wrong, then revolution must step in as a natural reaction and ought to be welcomed as the only effective instrument to re-enthrone Truth and Right."

"You rule," Savarkar further observed, "by bayonets and under those circumstances it is mockery to talk of constitutional agitation when no constitution exists at all. But it would be worse than a mockery, even a crime to talk of revolution when there is a constitution that allows the fullest and freest development of a nation. Only because you deny us a gun, we pick up a pistol. Only because you deny us light, we gather in darkness to compass means to knock out the fetters that hold our Mother down."

This was the concise doctrine of the revolutionary philosophy of Savarkar. He was in line with thinkers and men of action like President Thomas Masaryk who later said: "Revolution is a moral act when it is the only means left for the defence of liberty and justice."

The controversy over the doctrine of absolute non-violence and the principle of relative non-violence is age-long. The same continued between Gandhi and Savarkar, like the one that took place between Thomas Paine and the Quakers during the American War of Independence. Thomas Paine then said: "I am thus for a Quaker that I would gladly agree with all the world to lay aside the use of arms and settle matters by negotiation, but unless the whole world wills, the matter ends and I take my musket and thank Heaven He has put it in my power. . . . We live not in a world of angels. The reign of satan is not ended, neither can we expect to be defended by miracles."

Paine further replies to the Quakers, the early apostles of nonviolence, "Wherefore, if you really preach from conscience and mean not to make a political hobby-horse of your religion, convince the world thereby proclaiming your doctrine to our enemies for they likewise bear arms. Preach repentance to your king and warn him of eternal ruin. You should not spend your invectives against the injured and insulted only but like faithful ministers cry aloud and spare none."[7] Non-violence is taught to the defeated and downtrodden, and not to an aggressor, a conqueror or a tyrant. So is resignation.

Through *The Indian War of Independence of 1857* Savarkar replied to the apostles of non-violence and he anticipated Gandhi. Savarkar observed: "When humanity will reach the goal of universal justice, of ultimate beatitude, when the millennium preached by the incarnations, by the Messiahs, and by religious preachers will be an accomplished fact on earth, when the resignation taught by Christ in the glorious words 'whosoever shall smite thee on the right cheek turn to him the other also' will be impracticable because, there will be no one to hit on the right cheek, in such a divine age, if anyone even whispers the word revenge, then at once, the sinner by this act, by his very utterance would be eternally damned. For, when truth reigns in every heart, revolt must be a serious sin. When everyone abhors killing, to shed a drop of blood must be a sin."

"But as long as," Savarkar continued, "that divine age has not arrived so long as the highly auspicious end remains only in the lines of saintly poets and in the prophecies of the divinely inspired, and so long as, even to make that state of universal justice possible, the human mind has to be busy eradicating sinful and aggressive tendencies, so long, rebellion, bloodshed and revenge cannot be purely sinful."[8]

The young leader of Abhinava Bharat (New India) believed that revolt, bloodshed and revenge had often been instruments created by nature to root out injustice and introduce an era of justice. Savarkar, therefore, said in his famous book: "And when justice uses these terrible means for her salvation, the blame of it does not lie on justice but on the preceding cruel injustice, the power and insolence of which called forth the means. We do not hold the justice, which gives the death sentence, responsible for bloodshed, but rather the injustice which is taken to the gallows. Therefore, the sword of Brutus is holy. Therefore, the *Waghnakh* of Shivaji is sacred. Therefore the beheading of Charles I is a just deed. Therefore the arrow of William Tell is divine. And the sin of brutality falls heavily on the heads of those who committed the provoking injustice."

Savarkar believed that had the world had no fear of revolt, bloodshed and revenge, the earth would have been bent under the devil-dance of unchecked robbery and oppression. "If the oppressors were to be secure," he concluded, "from the fear that Nature would, sooner or later, create the avenger of temporary injustice, the whole world would have swarmed today with tsars and robbers! But because every Hiranyakashipu has his Narasimha; because every Dushshasana has his Bheema, because every evil-doer has his avenge there is still some hope in the heart of the world that injustice cannot last."

According to Gandhi, these thoughts were worthless. So he planned a book to refute them.

The work of the deputation was going on as directed by Lord Ampthill, and Polak acted in India according to Gandhi's instructions. Gandhi asked him to meet Dr. R. G. Bhandarkar, B. M. Malbari, a journalist, poet and social reformer, G. K. Gokhale, Pherozeshah Mehta and others. Gokhale tremendously helped though he was not hopeful; Pherozeshah held back. In London, Gandhi attended some banquets. He described the banquet given in London in honour of the Ottoman Parliament as refined savagery because of the cigarette fumes and wine glasses.

Gandhi wrote to Lord Crewe, the Secretary of State for

Colonies, asking for an appointment. Lord Crewe asked him to state reasons why he wanted to see him. Gandhi was depressed. He said those who occupied positions of power showed little inclination to do justice; they were preoccupied with their own problems.

Gandhi was out to please Lord Ampthill who had asked him whether passive resistance was financed or fomented from India, In reply Gandhi earnestly and soothingly wrote on July 29, 1909, to him to excuse him for saying that[9] "I know of no Indian, whether here, in South Africa or in India, who had so steadily, even defiantly, set his face against sedition—as I understand it— as 1 have. It is part of my faith not to have anything to do with it, even at the risk of my life." English statesmen and rulers always wanted men of his persuasion to condemn the extremists, and revolutionaries in India and so Gandhi was emphasizing the distinction and importance of his role. He now and then affirmed that a satyagrahi did not inflict suffering on others, but he invited it on himself. He swore by the self-sacrificing heroism which invites only sufferings.

The influence of the doctrine of non-killing was thus having the upper hand of Gandhi. "May I add too," he wrote to Lord Ampthill, "that the idea of passive resistance originated in South Africa was independent of any movement in India?" He asserted that he never received help from 'the party of sedition' in India or elsewhere. On the contrary, they were assailed by some of their Indian friends for pinning their faith to passive resistance, pure and simple.

Gandhi saw Lord Morley. He was surprised to learn that Morley did not know that General Smuts was in London. Gandhi praised Schreiner for his strenuous efforts and his philanthropic zeal in fighting the case on behalf of the coloured people of Africa. Mrs. Ritch was seriously ill and Gandhi appealed to Indians through *Indian Opinion* to address a letter of sympathy to Ritch and gave also Ritch's address. He humoured Ameer Ali by saying that the bracing climate of the Swiss mountains had done him and Mrs. Ameer Ali a great deal of good. Gandhi accompanied Dr. Mehta to put the latter's son to Warrel's Grammar School at Louth. He wrote to Manilal who wanted to go to London, that people in England were degenerate.

Gandhi was anxious to secure an introduction to a biography of him, *M. K. Gandhi: An Indian Patriot in South Africa*, written by the Rev. Mr. Joseph Doke. Requesting Lord Ampthill to write the introduction soon he wrote on August 9; "I have not received the somewhat delayed proof of the Rev.

Mr. Doke's book which I am very anxious to see published as early as possible. I might mention in passing that I have received a number of subscriptions from subscribers in advance. I know you are very busy and I have hesitated to burden you further with the perusal of this proof and with the writing of the introduction, which you were good enough to promise, if the proof should meet with your approval. Nevertheless you will, I hope, find time—as I am sure you have the desire—to give this matter your very kind attention."[10]

These two letters make amply clear how and why Gandhi was impressing upon Ampthill's mind the importance of his role and differentiating it from that of other Indian politicians and was decrying the Indian revolutionaries and criticizing Tilak.

On August 10, 1909, the deputation had an interview with Lord Crewe. His Lordship was very sympathetic and gave it a patient hearing. He promised to pass on the Amendment suggested by Gandhi to General Smuts and would let him know what should be done in the circumstances. When Smuts left London in August 1909, he said that the majority of Transvaal Indians were sick to death of the agitation. Gandhi, however, remained stubborn and unbent.

GANDHI WAS FINANCIALLY hard up and wanted money. He wrote to Polak, who was in India, to recover money from his life policy for about £660 which was lying with Revashankar Mehta. It was long preying on his mind. He would like, he said, to give up the policy and receive back a large portion of the premium paid. He asked him to convince moneyed men that Phoenix was intended to be a nursery for producing the right men and the right kind of Indians. It was a suitable place, Gandhi added, for making experiments and providing proper training and that passive resistance was a sovereign remedy for most of the ills of life.

The Bill declaring the Union of Africa was passed and the coloured deputation led by Schreiner and Dr. Abdur Rahman failed in their efforts to get it modified. The Natal Indian delegation was also struggling. Gandhi sympathised with them for the failure of the Coloured deputation and offered congratulations on the work they had done. He promised to send Dr. Abdur Rahaman a copy of Thoreau's *Duty of Civil Disobedience*. Having praised others for obtaining degrees or diplomas and put other men's children in schools in England, he wrote to his son Manilal from London that there was no reason to believe that

London was particularly suited for any type of better education. People there appeared to be very degenerate.[11]

While London was jubilant over the achievement of Louis Bleriot, French aviator and inventor, who was the first to fly across the English Channel on July 25, 1909, Gandhi alone was sad and sorrowfully said that no one pointed out what good it would do to mankind if planes flew in the air. "While Western civilization,"[12] he further lamented, "is still young, we will find things have come to such a pass that unless its whole machinery is thrown overboard people will destory themselves like so many moths."

He expressed his opinion also on sex and dissection. He said that few Indians need marry at the present time and a person who married in order to satisfy his carnal desire was lower than even the beast. It was considered proper to have sexual intercourse only for having progeny. He said he would not go in for medical studies if a frog was to be used for dissection and more if it was killed for that purpose.

During his sojourn in London, Gandhi read a very illuminating book by Edward Carpenter, *Civilization, Its Cause and Cure*. He found the author's analysis good and his condemnation of civilization entirely deserved, and the cure suggested by him was good. But he found Carpenter afraid of his own logic as he was not sure of his ground. Gandhi opined that no man would be able to give an accurate forecast of the future and prescribe a proper cure, unless he had seen the heart of India. To do good to others and serve them without any sense of egotism—this was real education. The body should not be dearer than the soul.

Just then the *Advocate of India*, Bombay, had depicted Polak as a paid agent. Gandhi felt the insult as directed against the Transvaal Indians. He explained to the editor that Polak was a regular delegate and it was the duty of the Transvaal Indians to provide him with the passage and hotel expenses as they would have done in the case of other delegates if they had not been arrested by General Smuts. The editor did not publish the letter. So it was published in *Gujarati*.

While papers like the *Advocate of India* were unable to grasp the importance of the African problem, Gokhale was trying his best to impress its importance upon the minds of the Indian people, and how Indians' honour, dignity and prestige were involved. He made a very stirring speech at the Town Hall, Bombay, on September 9, 1909, stating that the Transvaal struggle was led by the indomitable Gandhi, a man of tremendous spiritual power, one who was made of the stuff of which great heroes and martyrs were made.

Referring to passive resistance, Gokhale said that "passive resistance to an unjust law or an oppressive measure is a refusal to acquiesce in that law or measure and a readiness to suffer the penalty which might be prescribed as an alternative."[13]

A long time passed and there was no news from Lord Crewe. Gandhi was doing his best to speed him on, but the work was slow. So Gandhi wrote a letter on October 1, 1909, to his Guru, Tolstoy, inviting his attention to what had been going on in the Transvaal. He said that he considered submission to the Asiatic Law Amendment Ordinance degrading and inconsistent with the spirit of true religion. "I and some of my friends," Gandhi further observed,[14] "were and still are firm believers in the doctrine of non-resistance to evil. I had the privilege of studying your writings also, which left a deep impression on my mind." Accordingly, he said, about 2,500 British Indians suffered imprisonment for conscience's sake.

Stating that he had gone to London with a friend to see the Imperial authorities and to explain the position to them with a view to seeking redress, Gandhi gently said that the deputation was there at the instance of the weaker members of the community. He also said that he wanted to declare a general competition for an essay on the ethics and efficacy of passive resistance, but a friend had raised the question of morality in connection with the proposed competition, as the friend felt that such an invitation would be inconsistent with the true spirit of passive resistance. He, therefore, requested Tolstoy to favour him with his opinion on the subject of morality and also to give the names of those whom he should specially approach to write on the subject.

Gandhi referred to another subject in his letter to his Russian Guru. Tolstoy had written a reply to a letter addressed to him by the editors of *Free Hindustan* issued from Vancouver in Canada. Its chief editor was Tarak Nath Das. Gandhi desired to reprint Tolstoy's letter addressed to the editor and added: "I would also venture to make a suggestion. In the concluding paragraph you seem to dissuade the reader from a belief in reincarnation. I do not know whether (if it is not impertinent on my part to mention this) you have specially studied the question. Reincarnation or transmigration is a cherished belief with millions in India, indeed, in China also. With many, one might almost say, it is a matter of experience, no longer a matter of academic acceptance. It explains reasonably the many mysteries of life. With some of the passive resisters who have gone through the jails of the Transvaal, it has been their solace. My object in writing this is not to convince you of the truth of the doctrine, but to ask you if you will please remove the word 'reincarnation' from the other things you have dissuaded your reader from."

Concluding his letter, Gandhi said that he had taken the liberty of addressing that communication in the interest of truth and in order to have his advice on problems the solution of which Tolstoy had made his life-work.

Replying to Gandhi on October 7, 1909, from Yasnaya Polyana, Tolstoy said: "God help our dear brothers and co-workers in the Transvaal. That same struggle of the tender against the harsh, of meekness and love against pride and violence, is every year making itself more and more felt here among us also. As to the word reincarnation," observed the old philosopher, "I should not myself like to omit it, for, in my opinion, belief in reincarnation can never be as firm as belief in the soul's immortality and in God's justice and love. You may, however, do as you like about omitting it."

Tolstoy further said that he was glad that the translation into and the circulation of his letter in 'the Hindu language' could only be a pleasure to him. A competition, i.e. an offer of a monetary inducement, he went on, in connection with a religious matter would be out of place. Concluding his letter, Tolstoy said,[15] "I greet you fraternally, and I am glad to have intercourse with you."

As pressed by Gandhi, Lord Ampthill wrote a preface to Doke's biography of Gandhi. In it he seriously observed: "Mr. Gandhi has been denounced in this country, even by responsible persons, as an ordinary agitator; his acts have been misrepresented as mere vulgar defiance of the law; there have not even been wanting suggestions that his motives are those of self-interest and pecuniary profit. . . . The Indian community in the Transvaal are struggling for the maintenance of a right and the removal of a degradation. The Colonial Government can remove both grievances without sacrificing an ounce of principle or losing a grain of dignity."

So far the biography had, however, remained unpublished. Gandhi expected that it would be out in the first week of October 1909. He wrote to Polak on September 17, that "for reasons I need not go into this week, I am thinking of buying out the whole of the edition, more for the sake of Mr. Doke than anything else. He will be very much cut up if there is a fiasco, and there might be. The publisher has not put his heart into it, and as many copies will have to be distributed free of charge, I thought I should pocket my own personal feelings and deal with the thing myself. I fancy that Dr. Mehta will guarantee any deficit."[16]

Gandhi also asked Polak to be on the look-out for any bookseller who would care to take up the book; but he added that books should not be given on credit to booksellers on whom he could not rely implicitly. Natesan of Madras, Polak replied, would take 250 copies for distribution among booksellers for sale.

Great men are often not free from self-praise. But that Gandhi, an ascetic and spiritualist, intent on achieving *moksha* should take keen interest in the preparation, publication and propagation of his own biography and be the sole distributor of the copies was self-propaganda *par excellence*. This sort of self-propaganda is unthinkable on the part of a real ascetic man who does not covet publicity or advertisement. Gandhi's later daily public prayers and speeches at the prayer meetings have deep roots in this trait.

About this time Gandhi approvingly quoted the opinion of G. K. Chesterton who said that Indian youths wanted to pollute their ancient villages and poison their kindly homes by introducing Spencer's philosophy into them. Polak was trying to get a poem by Sarojini Naidu on the Transvaal affair and moved the organization led by Ramabai Ranade, wife of M. G. Ranade, and the Seva Sadan in Bombay to support the Transvaal Indian women. Gandhi was glad that the suffragettes in London had remained faithful to their pledge and sacrificed their all to secure the right to vote, but he was sorry that their agitation was drifting to violence. The women had served notice that they would commit arson or murder should they be denied the franchise. He opined that they should eschew violence.

The *Bande-Mataram*, an organ of the Indian revolutionaries published from Switzerland, attacked Gokhale and Pherozeshah Mehta for their weak-kneed policy. Gandhi said that such criticism did not do them credit, but betrayed their own unworthiness. At a dinner given in honour of Syed Ali Imam, a Bihar Muslim leader, Gandhi, who was always carried away by his feelings for Hindu-Muslim unity, said that the Indian Nation was being formed in South Africa where the Hindu-Muslim problem was as good as solved. From London Gandhi wrote to Narandas on October 3, that the Gandhi family had done good deeds as well as bad ones. "However," he added, "we are known for our good conduct. If we can add to it, that will be our real service to the family."

Gandhi expressed his opinion at a Gujarati Conference in London that every Indian should turn his attention to his own language. India should have one single language, but that would take time. "So the basis of my pride as an Indian, I must have pride in myself as a Gujarati, otherwise we shall be left without any moorings," he added. N. M. Cooper, editor of the *Indian Chronicle*, London, published Doke's biography of Gandhi. Gandhi asked Cooper to send copies to Dr. Mehta in Rangoon, to Natesan in Madras and to Durban.

Gandhi made a speech at Hampstead on October 13, 1909, on East and West. C. E. Maurice presided. Gandhi said that he would have to break up many idols which he, his countrymen and his audience had worshipped. 'East is East and West is West' was a doctrine of despair. If he had believed in Kipling's doctrine, he would have never lived in London. The chief spirit of modern civilization was that it worshipped the body more than the spirit. Their railways, telegraphs and telephones did not tend to help them forward to a moral elevation. The modern travelling facilities had reduced their holy places to unholy places. If India adopted the modern civilization, it would be the football of the world[17], he concluded.

Gandhi asked his son to tell people that he was in Bapu's class and added that as they wanted to die in Phoenix or some similar mission, there should not be any thought of earning at all. In one of his letters to Gokhale, Gandhi said that, "Although I have your kind message through Polak that I should not address you as Professor, my reverence for you will not enable me to adopt a more familiar style." Gandhi further informed Gokhale that there was extreme bitterness against the latter among the Indians in London. He appealed to Gokhale to participate in the satyagraha struggle and said that if Gokhale did so, he would give it a world-wide significance. If Gokhale was imprisoned he should be delighted.

On the *Dassara* day a dinner was arranged by Hindus in London, to which non-Hindus were also invited. The dinner was cooked in the underground kitchen cellar of a London restaurant and served by volunteers from among young Indian revolutionaries who were students of medicine and law. Gandhi who was called to preside over the dinner, had laid a condition that the students should themselves cook vegetarian dishes.[18] He strenuously worked in the kitchen for over four hours and helped the students to lay the tables.

The gathering was entertained by Hussain Dawud with some songs about jail life which were set to music. Small, thin and wiry, Gandhi attended the dinner in a swallow-tail coat and stiff-front shirt. Gandhi had laid down another condition that no controversial politics were to be touched upon. His real object, however, in accepting the invitation was to dissuade the revolutionaries from the use of violence for reforms. Nearly seventy Indians attended. Presiding over the function Gandhi said: "Everyone, whether Hindu, Muslim or Parsee, should be proud of belonging to a country which produced a man like Shri Ramachandra. To the extent that he was a great Indian, he should be honoured by every Indian. If India again produced a Ramachandra, a Sita, a Lakshmana and a Bharat, she would attain prosperity in no time." He was very proud, Gandhi added, to have the honour of sitting by the side of Savarkar. He expressed the hope that India would reap the fruits of Savarkar's sacrifice and patriotism. Asaf Ali, who attended the dinner, narrated that while formally introducing Savarkar that evening to the audience, Gandhi said, "But Mr. Savarkar, the speaker of the evening is to follow me and I should not like to stand between you and him."

Savarkar delivered a spirited speech on the excellence of the *Ramayana* and said that every Indian should realize the significance of the fast, that *Vijaya Dashmi* was preceded by a nine-day-fast observed to propitiate the goddess Durga. A great orator, he impressed upon his audience that without Shri Ramachandra life in India would be nothing. He asked them to remember that Rama established Rama Raj after slaying Ravan, the symbol of tyranny, aggression and injustice and concluding his speech, he said: "Hindus are the heart of Hindustan. Nevertheless, just as the beauty of the rainbow is not impaired but enhanced by its varied hues, so also Hindustan will look the more beautiful across the sky of future by assimilating all the best from the Muslim, Parsi, Jewish and other civilizations."

Of course Gandhi in his report on this meeting dropped the reference made by Savarkar to the slaying of Ravan! Asaf Ali described this speech by Savarkar as one of the finest speeches he had ever listened to.

In the last week of October 1909, Gandhi sent copies of his own biography *M. K. Gandhi, An Indian Patriot in South Africa* by Doke to Polak with a list of complimentary copies to be sent to newspapers in India; no complimentary copies were to be given to public men. Doke intended to name his book 'Path-finder' or 'Jungle breaker'[19] but he gave up the idea and named the book as mentioned above at the instance of Polak. Gandhi would have frankly ridiculed such an attempt as vanity, but it was to be done for a cause, he might have thought. He himself distributed 81 complimentary copies in London to newspapers for review and four to public men. He asked Polak to arrange for cuttings containing reviews to be sent to Doke.

It was now the end of October and there was no final reply yet from Lord Crewe. So Gandhi was thinking of leaving without making any moves in public. In a letter to Natesan, Gandhi said that Indians in the Transvaal were fighting for the rights of cultured Indians and had eschewed violence as they believed that self-suffering was the only true and effective means to procure lasting reforms. They held that loyalty to an earthly sovereign or an earthly constitution was subordinate to God and His constitution.

Incidentally, he added that the Hindu-Mohammedan problem had been solved in South Africa. He believed that passive resistance was an infallible panacea for the many ills they suffered from in India, It was the best weapon that was suited to the genius of the Indian people and their land, which was the nursery of the most ancient religions and had very little to learn from modern civilization.

Gandhi made several speeches at various places in London in defence of his stand in the Transvaal. He received a letter from Lord Crewe informing him that General Smuts was unable to accept the claim that Asiatics should be placed in a position of equality with Europeans in respect of the right of entry or otherwise. Herein lay the crux of the matter and the end of the deputation. So Gandhi issued a letter to the Press, addressed a farewell meeting and gave an interview to Reuter on November 9 declaring the failure of negotiations with General Smuts.

On November 10 Gandhi tendered thanks to Tolstoy for his letter. "I beg," Gandhi said,[20] "to send you herewith a copy of a book (his biography) written by a friend—an Englishman, who is at present in South Africa, in connection with my life, in so far as it has a bearing on the struggle with which I am so connected, and to which my life is dedicated. As I am very anxious to engage your active interest and sympathy, I thought that it would not be considered by you as out of the way for me to send you the book!"

If Tolstoy was satisfied with the facts mentioned in Doke's book, Gandhi said, he should use his influence to popularise the movement in any manner he thought fit. The negotiations for a settlement of the question had practically fallen through.

Concluding his letter, Gandhi said: "I may add that my son has happily joined me in the struggle and is now undergoing imprisonment with hard labour for six months. This is his fourth imprisonment in the course of the struggle."

This was a tribute to Harilal Gandhi. He sacrificed his life for the principles of his father who wished him to embrace poverty in the prime of his life. Many great leaders thus sacrifice their kith and kin for their principles.

Gandhi released a statement to the British press declaring the failure of negotiations on the Transvaal Asiatic Legislation, although the Colonial office Minute recorded that Gandhi's claim to equality was indisputable. Smuts was prepared to give permits of permanent residence to Indians, and also to repeal the obnoxious Act. But he was not prepared to concede equal rights in theory.

Gandhi addressed the farewell meeting on November 12, called by the Rev. F. B. Mayer and addressed also by Motilal Nehru, Ritch and Sir Raymond West. "As subjects of an Empire," Gandhi said, "they should have equal rights. In resisting the law we are rendering a service not only to British India but also to the whole British Empire." The Indian struggle was one of the greatest in modern times. They wanted, he concluded, equality in the eyes of law which General Smuts refused to grant. So they wanted to tear off the bond of slavery. At last, after waiting for a long month, Gandhi and Haji Habib left London for South Africa on November 13 by the S.S. *Kildonan Castle*.

CHAPTER XII

Ideal Manifesto: Guru Tolstoy

ON BOARD THE *Kildonan Castle* Gandhi began writing a booklet in Gujarati called *Hind Swaraj later translated as Indian Home Rule* in dialogue in answer mainly to the arguments of Indian revolutionaries led by Savarkar, and completed it on November 22. The booklet is divided into twenty small chapters and contains sixty-four pages. This Gujarati booklet was serialised in the issues of *Indian Opinion* dated December 11 and December 18, 1909, and was published in book form in January 1910.

The booklet was proscribed by the Government of Bombay on March 28, 1910. In the meanwhile Gandhi had, at the instance of Kalenbach, hurriedly done a faithful rendering of the original into English and, with a new preface to the English booklet, published it at the end of March 1910.

In the preface to the Gujarati booklet, Gandhi said that he was venturing to ventilate publicly the views he had expressed in private on the condition of India. The views were, he observed, his own in that they were a part of his being and not his own as they were formed after reading several books. He had discussed the subject with Englishmen and with his countrymen in England. In the preface to the English edition of the book he said that while his views were his own he had endeavoured to follow his old teachers—Tolstoy, Thoreau, Emerson and other writers besides the masters of Indian philosophy.

According to Gandhi, modern civilization represented by the British Government was the kingdom of Satan and the ancient civilization of India was the kingdom of God. Giving the object of his writing in the booklet, he observed: “Had I not known that there was a danger of methods of violence becoming popular, even in South Africa, and had it not been called upon by hundreds of my countrymen and not a few English friends, to express my opinion on the nationalist movement in India, I would have even refrained, for the sake of the struggle, from reducing my views to writing."

Later, Ganesh and Co., Madras, brought out the first Indian edition in 1919 with Gandhi's foreword dated May 28, 1919. In the preface to this edition he said: "I have re-read this booklet more than once. The value at the present moment lies in reprinting it as it is. But if I had to revise it, there is only one word I would alter in accordance with a promise made to an English friend. She took exception to my use of the word 'prostitute' in speaking of Parliament. Her fine taste recoiled from the indelicacy of the expression."

Gandhi, however, made the object of the book more clear when he wrote in *Young India* dated January 26, 1921. "The book was written in 1908 (it is wrong: it should be 1909) during my return voyage from London to South Africa in answer to the Indian school of violence and its prototype in South Africa. I came in contact with every known Indian anarchist in London. Their bravery impressed me, but I felt that their zeal was misguided. I felt that violence was no remedy for India's ills, and that her civilization required the use of a different and higher weapon for self-protection." The result, Gandhi added, was that it stopped the rot that was about to set in among some Indians in South Africa.

In the booklet Gandhi pays tribute to Dadabhai Naoroji as the father of the nation, to Gokhale as a parent and adds that a nation that is desirous of securing Home Rule cannot afford to despise its ancestors. He protested against the several newspapers which wrote disrespectfully of his Guru, Gokhale. It was natural that he should not mention Tilak, his Guru's great opponent! It is surprising enough that he who condemns the writings of the revolutionaries or similar writers should opine that "it is a bad habit to say that another man's thoughts are bad and ours only are good and that those holding different views from ours are the enemies of the country." Gandhi emphasizes the fact that the Bengal partition of 1905 brought about the real awakening of India and the day of Bengal's partition might be considered the day of the partition of the British Empire. Great events produce great results.

Then he represents the British Parliament, the Mother of Parliaments, as a sterile woman and a prostitute and calls it a costly toy of the nation. Her Prime Minister's energy, he observes, is concentrated upon securing the success of his Party. His care is not always that Parliament shall do right. As are the people, so is their Parliament. Parliaments are really emblems of slavery.

"Under modern civilization the nations of Europe are becoming degraded and ruined day by day. The object of modern civilization is bodily happiness or welfare. It is a disease. Its emblems are European clothing, better-built houses, agriculture by means of steam engines, hospitals and doctors, writing of books by any Tom, Dick and Harry, travelling by air and the possibility to travel in airships, work without the use of the hands and delicately served food. Men are enslaved by the temptation of money and of the luxuries that money can buy. This civilization takes note neither of morality nor of religion. It is irreligion.

"It is truer to say that we gave India to the English than that India was lost." It was his deliberate opinion that India was being ground down, not under the English heel, but under that of modern civilization. "We," he observes, "are turning away from God. All religions, Hinduism, Islam, Zoroastrianism, Christianity teach us that we should remain passive about worldly pursuits and active about godly pursuits. Railways, lawyers and doctors have impoverished the country. But for the railways, the English could not have such a hold on India as they have. The railways have spread the bubonic plague. Because of the railways, people sell out their grain and it is sent to the dearest markets. Railways accentuate the evil nature of man. The holy places of India have become unholy. Nowadays rogues visit them to practise roguery. Railways propagate evil.

"We were one nation before the English came. Many Hindus and Muslims have the same ancestors and the same blood. People should not become enemies because they change their religion. The cow is the protector of India. I should approach my Mohammedan brother and urge him for the sake of the country to join me in protecting her. If he would not listen to me, I should let the cow go for the simple reason that the matter is beyond my ability. If I were overfull of pity for the cow, I should sacrifice my life to save her but not take my brother's. This, I hold, is the law of our religion and cow-protecting societies may be considered cow-killing societies.

"We Hindus and Muslims would have to blame our own folly rather than the English if we allow them to put us asunder. The Muslims ask for concessions from Morley and the Hindus should not oppose this. Lawyers have enslaved India, have accentuated Hindu-Muslim dissensions and have confirmed English authority. They take up that profession in order to enrich themselves. So they advance quarrels and multiply disputes.

"Diseases arise through our negligence or indulgence. The business of a doctor is to rid the body of diseases that may afflict the body. Hospitals are institutions for propagating sin. Sometimes the quacks are better than highly qualified doctors, the European doctors being the worst of all. They kill annually thousands of animals for the sake of a mistaken care of the human body. They practise vivisection. No religion sanctions this. They violate our religious instinct. To study European medicine is to deepen our slavery. There is no real service of humanity in the profession, and it is injurious to mankind. It is better that bodies remain diseased than that they are cured through the instrumentality of the diabolical vivisection that is practised in European schools of medicine.

"Civilization is that mode of conduct which points out to man the path of duty. Civilization means good conduct. The rich are often seen to be unhappy, the poor to be happy. Millions will always remain poor. It was not that the forefathers of the Indians did not know how to invent machinery, but they did not set their hearts on such things because they would become slaves and lose their moral fibre. They reasoned that large cities constituted a snare of thieves, robbers and prostitutes. Western civilization propagates immorality and is godless whereas the Indian civilization propagates elevation of the moral being and is based on a belief in God. It is Swaraj when we learn to rule ourselves. It is not necessary for us to have as our goal the expulsion of the English. If the English become Indianized, we can accommodate them.

"Mazzini was a great and good man. Garibaldi was a great warrior. Garibaldi gave, and every Italian took arms. The machinations of Minister Cavour disgrace that portion of the history of Italy. According to Emanuel, Cavour and even Garibaldi, Italy meant the king of Italy and his henchmen. According to Mazzini, it meant the whole of the Italian people. The gain after the withdrawal of Austrian troops was only nominal. By patriotism I mean the welfare of the whole people. To arm India on a large scale is to Europeanize it. This means, in short, that India must accept European civilization. But the fact is that the Indian nation will not adopt arms, and it is well that it does not."

To those who said that they would undertake guerrila warfare and defeat the English, Gandhi replies: "That is to say, you want to make the holy land of India unholy. What we need is to sacrifice ourselves. It is a cowardly thought, that of killing others. Those who will rise to power by murder will certainly not make the nation happy. Those who believe that India has gained by Dhingra's act and other similar acts in India make a serious mistake. Dhingra was a patriot, but his love was blind. He gave his body in a wrong way; its ultimate result can only be mischievous. The English are both a timid and a brave nation. It is possible that Lord Morley has granted the reforms through fear, but what is granted under fear can be retained only so long as the fear lasts."

To those who said that they should obtain their goal, which was good, by any means whatever, even by using violence Gandhi replies: "As is the God, so is the votary. The means may be likened to a seed, the end to a tree. If the thief is armed from top to toe, I shall simply remain quiet. Your duty is not to drive away the thief by any means you like. Keep your things in a manner most accessible to a robber. He comes to learn about your broad and loving heart, he repents, he begs your pardon, returns you your things, and leaves off the stealing habit. One negative cures thirty-six diseases. The force implied in this may be described as love-force, soul-force, or, more popularly but less accurately, passive resistance. The force of arms is powerless when matched against the force of love or the soul."

What is the definition of history? According to Gandhi, "History as we know it, is a record of the wars of the world, and so there is a proverb among Englishmen that a nation which has no history, that is, no wars, is a happy nation. Those that take sword shall perish by the sword. With us, the proverb is that professional swimmers will find a watery grave. History, then, is a record of an interruption of the course of nature. Soul-force, being natural, is not noted in history."

"PASSIVE RESISTANCE Is a method of securing rights by personal suffering; it is the reverse of resistance by arms. It involves sacrifice of self. Everybody admits that sacrifice of self is infinitely superior to sacrifice of others. No man who has realized his manhood, who fears only God, will fear anyone else. Man-made laws are not necessarily binding on him. This is the key to self-rule or Home Rule."

"Soul-force is superior to the force of arms. A passive resister will say he will not obey a law that is against his conscience even though he may be blown to pieces at the mouth of a cannon. A man devoid of courage and manhood can never be a passive resister. Passive resistance is an all-sided sword, it can be used anyhow; it blesses him who uses it and him against whom it is used. Peasants have never been subdued by the sword, and never will be. That nation is great which rests its head upon death as its pillow. Real Home Rule is possible only when passive resistance is the guidance force of the people. Any other rule is foreign rule. Those who want to become passive resisters for the service of the country have to observe perfect chastity, adopt poverty, follow truth, and cultivate fearlessness.

"Chastity is one of the greatest disciplines without which the mind cannot attain the requisite firmness. When a husband and wife gratify the passions, it is no less an animal indulgence on that account. Such an indulgence, except for perpetuating the race, is strictly prohibited. Just as there is necessity for chastity, so is there for poverty. One who is free from hatred requires no sword.

"Education does not mean a knowledge of letters." Gandhi quotes Huxley who said that an educated man was he whose body was the ready servant of his will. "Elementary education or higher education does not make men of us. I do not for one moment believe that my life would have been wasted, had I not received higher or lower education. It is not necessary to make this education compulsory. Our ancient school system is enough. Character-building has the first place in it and that is primary education. A building erected on that foundation will last. To give millions a knowledge of English is to enslave them. Religious, that is ethical, education will occupy the first place. A universal language for India should be Hindi, with the option of writing it in Persian or Nagari characters. We cannot do without religious education. India will never be godless. Rank atheism cannot nourish in this land. One effort is required and that is to drive out Western civilization. All else would follow."

"It is machinery that has impoverished India. It is true that Bengal encourages the mill-industry of Bombay. If Bengal had proclaimed a boycott of all machine-made goods, it would have been much better. Machinery has begun to desolate Europe. Ruination is knocking at the English gates. Machinery is the chief symbol of modern civilization; it represents a sin. If the machinery craze grows in our country, it will become an unhappy land. Both money and sexual vice are poison. People can cease to use machine-made goods. We cannot condemn millowners; we can but pity them."

"We can do without matches, pins and glassware and tramcars. We will make wicks, as of old, use hand-made earthern saucers for lamps. Machine is not a boon, it is an evil.

"I do not think of a third party. I would serve both the Moderates and the Extremists. To Extremists I would say, 'British force is not natural to India' and to the Moderates I would say 'Mere petitioning is derogatory. We thereby confess inferiority.' To say that British rule is indispensable is almost a denial of the Godhead. To the British I would respectfully say: 'I have no objection to your remaining in my country but although you are the rulers, you will have to remain as servants of the people. Your function will be to police India. We consider our civilization to be far superior to yours. We consider your schools and law courts to be useless.' The common language of India is not English but Hindi. Deportation for life to the Andamans is not enough expiation for the sin of encouraging European civilization. Real Home Rule is self-rule or self-control. The way to it is passive resistance; that is soul-force or love-force. To exert that force, Swadeshi in every sense is necessary. I bear no enmity towards the English, but I do towards their civilization."

THIS UTOPIA Of Gandhi is called by his devotees 'Sermon On The Sea' and one of his acquaintances called it the production of a fool. He thus denounced all that is modern, scientific and progressive in human civilization. It is remarkable that Gandhi condemned Western or modern civilization while he was acting as a loyal subject of that very British Empire which was at that time one of the biggest centres of modern civilization. On top of this, his wholesale condemnation of Western civilization is hardly justifiable. He does not make any distinction between culture and civilization. The history of civilization is itself the history of secularization. When Europe had seen the twilight of God, Gandhi was dealing in God, religion and hope. He ennobles ascetism, poverty and ignorance rather than material welfare, culture and knowledge. Modern education has an ennobling influence on morality and religion.

Gandhi described during these days his role to Polak: "Men say," observed Gandhi, "that I am a saint losing myself in politics. The fact is that I am a politician trying my hardest to be a saint."[1]

In the booklet Gandhi condemned Parliamentary Democracy, but in the preface of 1921 he said that he was working for Parliamentary Swaraj in accordance with the wishes of the people of

India. It was a paradox that he should help to introduce a system that he himself considered ruinous. And yet he asserted that he withdrew nothing from his original booklet.

Gandhi's mind and attitude was not scientific. That Western civilization lacks religion and morality is not true. It, too, has produced men of noble patriotism, truth and courage. Gandhi's views are one-sided. So also is his interpretation and definition of history and the loss of the freedom of India. He attributes the loss of Indian freedom to absence of selflessness and the prevalence of baseness. Another of his attacks is against modern education because it is divorced from religion. He seems to propound that when religion prevails, there is no injustice, there is no poverty, no wars; peace and beatitude rule the country. Indian history does not support this. When religion prevailed and ruled there were wars, poverty and injustice. Gandhi's diatribes against railways, doctors, hospitals, machines and lawyers are equally strange and faddish. From this book the foreigners may think that India had fought no battles, made no scientific progress, was against the machine and that there were no courts before the advent of the British. Who is not devoid of the greed of money? If doctors and lawyers are blamed, so must merchants and others. According to Gandhi, celibacy is the essence of civilization. With this aim no country will ever prosper.

People would be reduced to *bairagis* and they would fall a victim to foreign rule. Gandhi's views that in ancient time people broke civil laws if they disliked them or that farmers were never subdued by the sword are all dubious. His views ennoble poverty and illiteracy. His statement that a patient should remain diseased rather than be treated by a doctor is perverse. Even he himself could never follow this as his own life was saved by doctors though he called them men who practised diabolical dissection. Biologically, socially, psychologically, the thoughts of Gandhi are not favourable to the growth of a people.

If no animal is killed, the universe will be overcrowded by animals and man would face extinction. Darwin calculated that the progeny of a single pair of elephants would in about 750 years number 19 million. If all the progeny of one oyster survived and multiplied, their number until there were great great grandchildren, would be 66,000,000,000,000,000 ,000,000,000,000, 000,000, and the heap of shells would be eight times the size of the earth. Gandhi's philosophy is a comfort to the weak in their inevitable subjection to the aggressor, the tyrant, the unscrupulous, the powerful.

Hind Swaraj was a Utopian manifesto of Gandhi sent in advance to India. Gandhi never outgrew it. His disciples were not men of great intellect or calibre. So they also could not grow beyond it.

About fourteen years after the publication of this booklet, Gandhi again threw more light in the *Satyagraha in South Africa* on the object of his writing the booklet. He revealed that he had also discussed the main points of the book with Lord Ampthill who did not agree with Gandhi's views. But the discussions he had with him had always remained imprinted on his memory. He must have discarded Gandhi's views on Western civilization and encouraged him to write against the Indian extremists and revolutionaries in India.

Brij Narain, criticizing the principle of non-violence in his *Marxism is Dead*, observes: "In Mahatma Gandhi's Utopia no violence will be committed by man against man. If any goondas are left in this ideal state of affairs, they will be allowed to kill honest folk. I can imagine an exponent of non-violence saying to a goonda in the satyagraha to come. 'You want to kidnap my little girl? I have another at home. Kidnap both', or 'It will give you pleasure to burn down my house? You may burn down the whole street. All of us in this street are completely non-violent. And our non-violence is not non-violence of the weak, but that of the bravest of the brave."

"Or have we misunderstood Mahatma Gandhi? Does he permit one to commit violence as a measure of self-defence against unjust aggression? If he does, then it is not my duty to allow myself to be killed by goondas, but to knock the goondas on the head. And since an individual, on account of physical weakness, or other circumstances, may not be able to defend himself, it is the duty of the state to use the police and the military for the protection of law-abiding citizens."[2]

While on board the *Kildonan Castle*, Gandhi wrote on November 24, 1909, a letter to Maganlal Gandhi saying, "I wish that my name is forgotten, and only my work endures. The work will endure only if the name is forgotten." This time there were some suggestions that the name of Phoenix should be changed. Gandhi did not yield to the suggestions. "The word *Math* or *Ashram*", Gandhi observed, "has a particularly Hindu connotation and therefore may not be used. Phoenix is a very good word which has come to us without any effort on our part. . . . Its significance is that the bird Phoenix comes back to life again and again from its own ashes." "The aims of Phoenix," Gandhi concluded, "will not vanish even we are turned to dust."[3]

Manilal, who was very eager to receive a regular education wrote to his father about Phoenix. Gandhi, as he was tired of writing with the right hand, wrote to his son with the left. He said to this young boy: "First of all, we shall have to consider how we can realize the self and how to serve our country. . . . Morality means the acquisition of virtues such as fearlessness, truth, celibacy and so on. ... I believe it is very difficult to preserve morality in cities where people live in congestion and there are many temptations. Experience is the real school. The (Phoenix) school is a means to achieve our end. I understand your eagerness to learn. My advice to you is to have patience. Meanwhile have faith in Bapu." He thus asked his young son to realize his self and put off his request for a regular education.

ON HIS ARRIVAL in Cape Town, Gandhi was enthusiastically received by the Indians. He was given at Park Town on December 2, 1909, a tremendous ovation by the Transvaal Indians and on the way at all other stations. Flowers were showered on him.

While at Cape Town, Gandhi received a cable from Gokhale on November 30 informing him that Ratanji Jamshedji Tata of Bombay had given Rs. 25,000 in aid of the Transvaal struggle. Tata was a leading Indian industrialist and philanthropist. Moved by this gesture, Gandhi gratefully mentioned to the Transvaal Indians that the motherland was fully alive to their problem. It required the passive resisters to show that they were prepared to die for a cause that was righteous, godly and national. Ratan Tata donated another sum of Rs. 25,000 for the satyagraha campaign in December 1910. Later, the Maharaja of Bikaner and the Maharaja of Mysore also helped the satyagraha struggle. Gandhi thanked also the Government for their courtesy in allowing the delegates re-entry into the Transvaal without interference.

Gandhi expressed his total disagreement with the atmosphere and methods of the Servants of India Society established by G. K. Gokhale on June 12, 1905, to train men to devote their lives to the cause of the country. "It is a matter of regret," said Gandhi, "that a great man like Prof. Gokhale is engrossed in it." He was very critical of the Society as these 'servants' had kept servants and cooks, had large buildings and only an M.A. or B.A. could become a 'servant'. Gandhi wrote to his disciple Maganlal: "According to the stand indicated by me in *Hind Swaraj* the work of Gokhale's 'servants' cannot be regarded as proper. It is likely to add to our slavery. We do not aspire to improve India; we want to improve ourselves. That alone can be our aspiration, the rest is all false. He who has not realized his self has not known anything. The position taken by the 'servants' was materialistic and not spiritualistic. We have to rid ourselves of the fetish of literacy and mundane knowledge." "Yet, comparatively," Gandhi added, "it (Phoenix) is better than the pomp and show of Poona."[4]

Gokhale was not aware of his disciple's secret attack on his institution and on its aims and objectives. And after the death of Gokhale, Gandhi said: "Gokhale's best achievement was the establishment of the Servants of India Society".[5] Whatever Gandhi said about Gokhale's institution, Gokhale was extolling him to the skies. While speaking on the resolution concerning the African struggle at the Lahore Congress session in December 1909, he said; "It is one of the privileges of my life that I know Mr. Gandhi intimately and I can tell you that a purer, a nobler, a braver and a more exalted spirit has never moved on this earth. He is a man who may be well described as a man among men, a hero among heroes, a patriot among patriots, and we may well say that in him, Indian humanity at the present time has really reached its high-water mark."[6]

In another letter Gandhi said: "We ought to prepare ourselves here so that we may spread our bed there. ... I always feel that I should be strong enough to welcome death in any form and at any time."[7]

The British Prince of Wales was due to arrive in Cape Town and Dr. Abdur Rahman, the leader of the coloured people, refused to be associated with the rejoicings. Gandhi congratulated him on his fearless declaration and hoped that Dr. Abdur Rahman would have the courage to follow out his programme when the time came. Gandhi was described at this stage as Deshbhakta (patriot) M. K. Gandhi. On February 25, 1910, Gokhale moved a resolution in the Legislative Council of India in favour of prohibiting the recruitment of indentured labour for Natal. The resolution was carried. Gandhi said Gokhale had rendered a service to the Indians in South Africa and to India generally by stopping the indentured labour.

Early in March 1910 Gandhi noted with pride that "our struggle is producing a profound effect on the coloured people. Dr. Abdur Rahman has commented on it in his journal at great length and has held up the example of the Indian community to every coloured person. Some of them have also passed a resolution in Johannesburg to defy the laws of the Government and take to satyagraha." Action against and resistance to evil is always inspiring. Gandhi's active struggle and the increasing pressure of the whites were bound to effect a change in the mind of the coloured people and rouse them to action. The Zulu rebellion was the first to act like a torch in the dark continent.

According to Gandhi, the first attribute of the divine heritage was fearlessness and in that context he asked Narandas to remember the lives of Prahlad, Sudhanva and others and not to think that all these were legends. It was the vision of the satyagraha, he was sure, which would teach the heart of mankind. The tyranny of Parliament was much greater than that of Chengiz Khan, Tamerlane and others.

About this time the Maharaja of Baroda passed an order for the admission of members of the Bhangi (scavenger) castes to public schools and he was opposed and criticized by the higher classes. Writing on this, Gandhi quoted the carping criticism made by K. Srinivasa Rao, a South Indian Judge of Madras. The Judge said: "We look down upon our own people, think ourselves defiled by their touch, keep them at a distance from us and grind them under our heels. Why do we not, instead of lashing out at the whites, rain lashes on our own backs?"

As the Government of Bombay had proscribed Gandhi's *Hind Swaraj*, *Universal Dawn*, *Mustafa Kemal Pasha's Speech*, *Defence of Socrates* or *the Story of a True Warrior*—all Gujarati pamphlets as they contained matter declared to be seditious, Gandhi sent a typed copy of *Hind Swaraj* to Gokhale through Polak and feared that he might dislike the book. So he requested Gokhale to keep the merits of the struggle entirely separate from his views should any prejudice arise in him against himself personally or the pamphlet. He also added that the views expressed by him in *Hind Swaraj* had not been formed without much thought and consideration.

It seems Gokhale did not express his opinion on *Hind Swaraj* till he went to Africa. There he said that it was "crude and hastily conceived" and that Gandhi himself would destroy the book after spending a year in India."[8] But it was very strange that while giving the news of the proscribed books Gandhi was very happy to support the Government of India in its sanguinary fight with the Indian revolutionaries saying, "We sympathise with the Government of India in their desire to stop the spread of methods of violence."[9] His passive resistance sought to reform politics and religion, to test every one of his actions in the light of ethical principles and above all to annihilate the Indian revolutionaries!

Gokhale and J. B. Petit left the disbursement of the

satyagraha fund to Gandhi's discretion. He used part of it to clear off the debts incurred on account of *Indian Opinion*, to meet the expenditure on the office of the Association as well as the office in London and to maintain the families of poor satyagrahis. The end of the struggle was not in sight. None could tell how long it would last. According to Gandhi, a satyagrahi struggle was impossible without men of character who were pledged to fight unto death or victory. Gandhi desired now to have a centre for the satyagrahis where they should live a new and simple life, and all the families should be kept at one place and become members of a sort of co-operative commonwealth.

Phoenix was three hundred miles away from Johannesburg and was thirty hours by train. So Gandhi's friend Hermann Kallenbach bought a farm of about 1,100 acres and gave the use of it to the satyagrahis, free of any rent or charge, on May 30, 1910. There were nearly a thousand orange, apricot and plum trees and a small house at the foot of the hill. There were two wells as well as a spring. Lawley, the nearest railway station, was about a mile from the farm and Johannesburg was 21 miles. The farm was infested with snakes.

A chawl was constructed fifty feet long. It was made of corrugated iron. Carpenters put in voluntary work. A small house was built for Kallenbach. The farm was named after Gandhi's Russian Guru, Tolstoy. Gandhi and his family came to live on Tolstoy Farm. Thrift is in the blood of a Kathiawadi and Gandhi was the symbol of it. There were no servants. Everything from cooking to scavenging was done with their own hands. There were no meat-eaters or beef-eaters. They were all vegetarians. Drinking and smoking were totally prohibited. For bed everyone was given two blankets, one for spreading on the floor and the other for covering. A wooden pillow was also provided. There were no chairs and no beds.

Bread was home-baked. It was made from coarse wheat flour ground at home from which the bran was not removed. There was only one kitchen, and all dined in a single row. Groundnut butter prepared at home was used and home-made marmalade was served. Everyone cleaned his own dishes. Gandhi's presence in the kitchen and the farm prevented petty bickerings. They had rice, dal, vegetables, and roti with porridge occasionally superadded. During illness earth and water treatment was given or changes in diet were made.

They shaved and cut the hair of one another. Rubbish was buried in trenches; leavings of food and vegetable refuse were utilized as manure. The use of shoes in a hot climate is harmful. So feet were protected against thorns and stones with sandals. Kallenbach acquired the art of making sandals, taught it to Gandhi and Gandhi in his turn taught it to other workers. They sold these to friends. There was a workshop. Carpentry was introduced in it. Kallenbach was fond of fruit trees and he took to gardening. There was a school run by Gandhi and Kallenbach. Gandhi gave up his legal practice.

Gandhi travelled third class now as the money was spent from the Satyagraha Fund. Except on work, everybody was to go on foot to Johannesburg. After hard work on the farm in the morning, they worked in the school every day between two and five except on Mondays and Thursdays. The teachers as well as the taught dozed. Their body ached for rest. But the classes were conducted in spite of the dozings. Gandhi knew a little Tamil but no Telugu. He taught Tamil and Urdu. Hindi, Gujarati and English were also taught.

Gandhi never felt the want of text-books. He read to the students passages from books on moral training. Gandhi had written out the fundamental doctrines of all religions and taught them in accordance with the religions of the students belonging to Hinduism, Zoroastrianism, Christianity and Islam. They were about thirty, of whom four or five were girls.

Gandhi decided to experiment in co-education. He allowed boys and girls, some of them grown up, to bathe at the spring at the same time. His eyes, he said, followed the girls as a mother's eye follows a daughter. At night everybody slept on an open veranda and the beds were only three feet apart. And Gandhi, who himself had experienced the thrill of sex since his thirteenth year, explained the duty of self-restraint to them. But he burnt his fingers badly and had bitter experience. He had to cut the long hair of two girls to teach them a lesson and give a warning to every man that no evil eye might be cast upon them and to every girl that no one dare assail her purity. Yet he says he did not repent having made the experience. He was opposed to corporal punishment; but one day with a trembling hand he gave a blow on the arm of an unruly wild boy.

Gandhi and Kallenbach gave up cooked food in 1912 and lived a "fruitarian" life. Kallenbach was brought up in the lap of luxury. For his fads and renunciations the Europeans called him a fool. Yet he was prepared to go through these experiments. They lived on a pure fruit diet consisting of raw groundnuts, bananas, dates, lemons, and olive oil. He gave up milk, as cows in Calcutta, Gandhi learnt from newspapers, were milked very cruelly to the last drop. There was a total prohibition against killing and yet Gandhi allowed a student to kill a snake on the farm.

"A mind consciously unclean," Gandhi observed, "cannot be cleaned by fasting. Modifications in diet have no effect upon it, although dietic restrictions and fasting are very helpful." As regards his famous earth and water treatment, he later said in 1928: "But I have now lost the courage, and in view of my two serious illnesses I feel that I have forfeited even that right, to make such experiments."[10]

On the whole the experiments at Tolstoy Farm, observed Gandhi, proved to be a source of spiritual purification and penance for the final struggle.

GANDHI MOURNED THE death of King Edward VII and praised him as a sovereign who followed in the footsteps of his mother of revered memory. He made a speech at the Socialist Hall in Johannesburg on 'Modern as compared with Ancient Civilization.' He expressed the view that the simple life was better than the complex. The body was not the be-all and end-all of life. The rush of modern life left little time for higher pursuits. In ancient civilization people looked upwards to heaven; in modern civilization they looked downwards to the earth.

The elections to the Union Parliament were held. No party attached any importance to the Indian problem, and encouragement of European and the prevention of Asiatic immigration into South Africa was the object of both the Unionist Party and General Botha's Party.

On August 15, 1910, Gandhi wrote a letter to Tolstoy requesting him to favour him with his detailed criticism of *Indian Home Rule* which he had been so kind as to promise in his letter. Kallenbach, Gandhi added, had gone through most of the experiences that Tolstoy had so graphically described in his work *My Confessions* and as a spur to further effort in living up to the ideals held before the world by him. Kallenbach had taken the liberty, he continued, after consultation with him of naming his farm after Tolstoy. According to Gandhi, Tolstoy, as all world-teachers had done, preached "that every man has to obey the voice of his own conscience and be his own master, and seek the kingdom of God from within."[11]

Tolstoy was on the verge of death. Yet he replied to Gandhi on September 7, in Russian, about *Hind Swaraj*. The letter went to a friend of his in England to be posted to Gandhi, who received it after Tolstoy's death. "Tolstoy", wrote his friend V. Chertkov, "sends you and your co-workers his heartiest greetings and warmest wishes for the success of your work, his appreciation of which you will gather from the enclosed translation of his letter to you."

Chertkov further said that Tolstoy's letter and Gandhi's letter would be published in a small periodical and a copy of its issue would be sent to Gandhi. Fyvie Mayo, of Glasgow, he added, who was well known as an authority, was being requested to write about Gandhi's movement as he thought it desirable that more should be known about his movement in England. He asked Gandhi to send her all material concerning his movement.

Tolstoy in his letter said: "The more I live—and especially now that I am approaching death—the more I feel inclined to express to others the feelings which so strongly move my being, and which, according to my opinion, are of great importance. That is, what one calls non-resistance is in reality nothing else but the discipline of love undeformed by false interpretation. . . . That love is the supreme and unique law of human life, which everyone feels in the depth of one's soul. We find it manifested most clearly in the soul of the infants. Man feels it so long as he is not blinded by the false doctrines of the world. . . . That law of love has been promulgated by all philosophers—Indian, Christian, Hebrew, Greek and Roman. . . . That the employment of violence is incompatible with love."

"Consequently", Tolstoy said with a prophetic voice, "your work in the Transvaal, which seems to be far away from the centre of our world, is yet the most fundamental and the most important to us supplying the most weighty practical proof in which the world can now share and with which must participate not only the Christians but all the peoples of this world."[12]

Tolstoy the great Russian religious philosopher and the advocate of the cult of non-violence and non-resistance to evil, died on November 20, 1910. In an obituary note, Gandhi described his Guru as the late lamented Tolstoy the Great. "It is truer," Gandhi observed, "to say that he has quit this corporeal frame than that he has died. There can be no death for Tolstoy's soul. His name will ever remain immortal. Only his body, which was of dust, has returned to dust. ... In India, we would have described him as a Maharshi, 'Great Seer' or 'Fakir.' He did not denounce any religion. He pointed out that selfish priests,

Brahmins and Mullas had distorted the teaching of Christ and other religions and mislead the people."

There was some important distinction between Tolstoy and Gandhi. Tolstoy never suffered as did Gandhi for his views. Gandhi amply possessed practical sense and the qualities that made a political leader. Tolstoy was a great literary figure and essentially a thinker. Their philosophy had its origin, not in reason, but in faith and religion.

As arranged by Tolstoy's friends, Mrs. Mayo did write an article against the colour bar in South Africa.

The Allahabad Congress held in December 1910 expressed its great admiration of the intense patriotism, courage and self-sacrifice of the Indians in the Transvaal, who, heroically suffering persecution in the interests of their countrymen, were carrying on their peaceful and selfless struggle for elementary civil rights against heavy and overwhelming odds. G. A. Natesan moved the resolution praising the heroism of the passive resisters. Manilal Doctor seconded it; Raghunandan Prasad and Debi Prasad supported it.

GANDHI EXPRESSED In January 1911 his opinion on the custom of wearing ornaments. "The first and real ornament," he said, "for both men and women is purity of character. Custom of wearing ornaments on the nose and the ears seems to me barbarous. I mean barbarous, not in comparison with the whites, but according to our own ideas". In a letter to Narandas he came out with "an axiomatic truth that even if a single satyagrahi remains, he will win."[13]

But it seemed that the Indians were winning the battle. A new Bill was published by the Union Government on February 23, 1911 and though the Bill was unsatisfactory from the viewpoint of the Natal and Cape Town Indians the end of the struggle was in sight. A letter received by Polak from General Smuts and *The Times* report both pointed to the same conclusion.

On April 1, 1911, the Government of India officially notified that emigration of indentured labour to South Africa was to cease from July 1. This seemed to be a triumph for Gandhi and Gokhale and the Indian South African League at Madras. But the problem lingered long.

On March 27 Gandhi went to Cape Town and spent virtually the whole of April 1911 discussing the New Bill and canvassing support for the modifications he proposed. He was in touch with events in the Transvaal, Natal and the Cape. Ritch was now in Johannesburg in charge of the BIA office and Polak was busy in Durban. The negotiations were being carried on with the support of the entire Indian community in South Africa.

The Bill seemed to concede the basic demands of the Indians for the removal of the racial bar from the immigration law of the Union. But it retained the racial bar in the Orange Free State. General Smuts could not or would not prevail upon that State to agree to the line followed by other States. Smuts wanted the passive resistance to cease. So Gandhi relieved him from his predicament by offering to suspend satyagraha when Smuts assured him of repealing the Transvaal Asiatic Registration Act. This provisional settlement was effected on May 20, 1911. Gandhi conveyed to Smuts acceptance of the provisional settlement on behalf of the BIA and gave a list of passive resisters to be released. He declared in *Indian Opinion* of May 27, that "a provisional settlement of the Asiatic trouble in the Transvaal has at last been reached and the Indians and Chinese of the Transvaal are free to resume their ordinary occupations."

When the final stage had been reached, Gandhi said in an interview with the *Star* that he would leave public life and retire to his farm in Natal.[14] He would provide for the care and education of the satyagrahis and be in closer touch with the philosophic musings of Tolstoy. To those who asked if the satyagraha had achieved anything, he replied that the entire world had learnt of their struggle and a law was passed in India prohibiting the emigration of indentured labour. As a sign of gratitude, addresses and receptions were given to benefactors like Hosken, Kallenbach and others.

Gandhi expressed his loyalty to the throne of England on the occasion of the coronation of the British King George V and said: "The Indian residents of this country sent congratulatory cablegrams on the occasion, thus declaring their loyalty."

Gandhi wanted now to turn to farming and weaving, Ritch was to take his legal practice and replace him by and by. He wanted to hand over Phoenix to a Trust. Just then Harilal Gandhi desired to leave Gandhi in protest against his father who neglected the worldly interests of those nearest to him. Gandhi tried his spiritual methods and practice of renunciation on his young sons and young relatives. Harilal left for India in May 1911.

Yet Gandhi said he went with a clean mind. "He was," Gandhi observed, "much unsettled in mind. He was angry with me, really. He gave vent to all his pent-up feelings on Monday evening. He feels that I have kept all the four boys very much suppressed, that I did not respect their wishes at any time, that I have treated them as of no account, and that I have often been hard-hearted."[15] It was Gandhi's general behaviour he protested against. His charge was that his father had not respected his sons or done anything special for them but always put them and Kasturba last.

On his way to India Harilal was honoured at Zanzibar as a satyagrahi. Gandhi was pleased. He wrote a note on it in *Indian Opinion*. On July 3, 1911, Gandhi wrote to him that "*The Star* publishes every week a biographical sketch of some well-known persons and they have published mine, too. I send you a cutting. Please pass it on to Sorabji after reading it."[16] How appreciative are even the spiritual leaders of publicity and praise! A human heart indeed!

Gandhi further wrote to Harilal that he should live in any way that suited him, but strive to realize God anyhow. If their destination is the same, they would meet there. His son was infatuated with the Matriculation Examination and wanted to go to England for education but his father asked him to overcome that desire. The time was not yet. The son wanted to be a barrister, but Gandhi discouraged him. If he sent him to become one, all his ideas would go by the board. Instead he encouraged Sorabji Shapurji Adajania to become one and said it befitted a Hindu to encourage a Parsi![17] Besides, according to Gandhi, Sorabji was the greatest of the satyagrahis, a mild amicable Parsi with the finest qualities of the Parsis. As a satyagrahi he was without a compeer. Harilal failed in his Matriculation Examination. Gandhi wanted him to grow up in freedom. But the ties were broken never to be mended again.

Gandhi zealously taught in the school at Tolstoy Farm. This is how things went on at the Farm. "Physical labour on the farm up to 10 a.m., teaching work at the school from 1 to 4-30 p.m., a meal at 5-30 p.m. and office and other correspondence at night. As I do everything single-handed, I have no time left and I do writing work till late at night." Now and then he referred in *Indian Opinion* to the inequitable £3 tax which continued on ex-indentured Indians and to the attempts of the Municipalities there to shifting the Indians from established locations. He protested against the segregation of Indians and other coloured people as a remedy against small-pox then raging in the Transvaal.

Gandhi's name and fame had spread among the political workers in India. His name was proposed for the presidentship of the Indian National Congress for the Calcutta Session in

December 1911. Gandhi said that he would accept it if his freedom was not compromised and if his presence was especially necessary.[18] But there was no response. In his place Bishan Narayan Dhar was elected President. At the Congress J. Chaudhari moved the resolution on South Africa and C. Y. Chintamani seconded. Dr. Manilal and Sorabji Shapurji, who had been to jail eight times during the South African Struggle, and Polak, the gallant emissary of the Indians and lieutenant of Gandhi, supported the resolution. The Congress cordially congratulated Gandhi and the Transvaal Indian community on the repeal of the anti-Asiatic legislations of the Transvaal. The Congress showered its praise on Lord Hardinge and the Government for annulling the partition of Bengal! The settled fact was unsettled!

Towards the end of 1911 the Provisional settlement expired. A new Immigration Registration Bill was drafted and shown to Gandhi, but it was seen that some changes had been made in it afterwards. General Smuts removed some clauses and gave an assurance concerning others. When the Bill had passed only its second reading Gandhi was informed that the Provisional settlement would continue pending the passage of the Bill and the Union Parliament was prorogued until September 23, 1912.

Thus the Bill was shelved. The Immigration Law oppressed women and minor children of domiciled Indians. The matter was fought in the Supreme Court where Justice Sir John Wessels ruled in the case of Bai Rasul Jussat that if a person had more than one wife the court could grant right of entry into the Transvaal only to one of them, that is, the first wife. This judgment was a terrible shock to the entire Indian community.

Another Muslim wife named Fatima Jussat was denied entry into the Transvaal. The Registrar of Asiatics did not admit two out of the six names proposed by Gandhi as per the provisional settlement. The Ministers did not care to carry out their assurances and so Gandhi threatened to resume satyagraha. Gandhi's disappointment grew bitterer as the resolution introduced in March 1912 by Gokhale in the Imperial Legislative Council of India was thrown out by a majority. The twenty-two non-official members, who had voted for the resolution, took a pledge that they would bring forward the resolution every year till the indenture system was abolished.

As the struggle was drawing near, Gandhi thought it proper to publish in September 1912 the Phoenix Trust deed under which he made over the hundred acres land and all other property including the International Printing Press and *Indian Opinion* to the Trust he had formed. The

Trustees were his co-workers Kallenbach, Parsi Rustomji, Omar Hajee, Amod Johari, L. W. Ritch and Dr. Pranjivandas Mehta of Rangoon. The settlers were to follow the ideals set forth by Tolstoy and Ruskin in their works. Gandhi reserved to himself the use of two acres of land and buildings on it and £5 a month from the Phoenix Trust. In case of his death, the two acres of land and buildings on it and £5 a month from the Phoenix Trust to be given to Kasturba and his minor sons. When Tolstoy Farm was closed down the pupils who wished to, came over to Phoenix.

Just Then Gokhale, who was in England, informed Gandhi that he was visiting South Africa and sailing on October 5, 1912. On July 30 Gokhale had been appointed Member of the Royal Commission on Indian Public Services. Gokhale informed the Secretary of State for India of his intention to proceed to South Africa and to acquaint himself with the facts of the Indian case at first hand. The Secretary of State for India informed the Government of South Africa of his visit and his position in the empire and saw that the best cabin was at his disposal.

All wished Gokhale a peaceful voyage and a royal welcome, Gokhale asked Gandhi to arrange for a six-week programme. Gandhi and his co-workers were overjoyed. They put up decorations at important railway stations to give a rousing ovation to the great leader. Gandhi made a special request to Muslims to take a lead in honouring Gokhale. He had also published a booklet *The Hon. Mr. Gokhale and the Indenture System* which contained a sketch of his public life and a full report of the debate on the resolution he had introduced but was defeated in March 1912 in the Imperial Legislative Council, Calcutta.

During his voyage Gokhale learnt the game of quoits and played it with patriotic zeal to show that Indians were the equals of Europeans if not their superiors.

Gokhale landed at Cape Town on October 22, 1912, with the knowledge of the Indian Government, but entirely on his own initiative, to investigate the Indian question in South Africa for himself. Gandhi, welcoming Gokhale at Cape Town, said that the name of Gokhale was sacred to him and he was his political teacher. He had come, he added, to keep them to bring the two peoples close together.

Gokhale made a triumphal tour throughout South Africa, This great servant of India and outstanding Indian parliamentary speaker, was pressed by Gandhi to make speeches in Marathi, and Gandhi became the interpreter with his scanty and sketchy knowledge of Hindi and little or no knowledge of Marathi. The British Indian Association presented Gokhale with an address engraved on solid gold plate.

Gandhi took his Guru to Tolstoy Farm where he lived a very simple life for two days. He slept on the floor, took soup which his disciple prepared and bread made by Kotwal without uttering a syllable, and humbled the pride of the apostle of simplicity. Gandhi wanted to serve his master, to massage his feet and to iron his clothes. Gandhi wanted Gokhale to be what Shri Krishna was to Arjun. Gokhale allowed him to do anything but massage his legs. He made important speeches at Cape Town and Johannesburg, interviewed Botha, Smuts and other Members of the Union Government, and had a luncheon with Lord Gladstone, the Governor-General of the Union. Gandhi took Gokhale to the diamond mines. During his twenty years of stay in South Africa, he never once thought of visiting the diamond mines there, partly because he was afraid lest as an 'Untouchable' he should be refused admission and insulted.[19] There was no fear, he thought, when he accompanied Gokhale.

On November 15, 1912, Gokhale, while making a farewell speech at the Pretoria Town Hall, said: "Your future is largely in your own hands. But whatever happens, do not lose faith or give way to despair. But if it (the struggle) has to be resumed, or if you have to enter struggles of a like nature for justice denied or injustice forced upon you, remember that the issue will largely turn on the character you show, on your capacity for combined action, on your readiness to suffer and sacrifice in a just cause. India will no doubt be behind you."[20]

Gokhale, accompanied by Gandhi and Kallenbach, boarded the S.S. *Cronprinz* on November 18, 1912. They landed at Beera, Mozambique and Zanzibar. At all these places Gokhale was presented with addresses. On board the ship Gokhale played the game of quoits with Kallenbach, who was a famous player at the game, and defeated him. Gokhale pressed Gandhi to go to India, mapped a programme for him and said: "We lack in India character; we need religious zeal in the political field." From Dar-es-Salaam he wrote to Gokhale on December 4, 1912, "I want to be a worthy pupil of yours. We may have many differences of opinion, but you shall still be my pattern in political life." On his way back Gandhi was detained by officials. He said: "I kept smiling but rage flared in my heart."

Gokhale's visit gave a stimulus to the Indian struggle and rivetted the attention of the world on it. Lord Ampthill raised questions about his successful visit and wanted to know what the Government had done to acknowledge and encourage and to take advantage of the resulting spirit of reasonableness and conciliation and goodwill. Lord Emmot, Under Secretary of State for the Colonies, said that Gokhale's visit was unofficial and his representations to the Union Ministers were informal.

It seems Gokhale told Lord Gladstone that the grievances of Indians in South Africa were productive of grave mischief and danger in India. After his talks with Smuts and others Gokhale told Gandhi that the Black Act would be repealed, the £3 tax would be abolished and the necessary legislation would be introduced in the ensuing session of the Union Parliament. He added that Gandhi must return to India in a year.

Although Gandhi replied to his Guru that he was not optimistic, he wrote to Dr. Pranjivan Mehta that he was thinking of returning to India. He wrote to his son that he was arranging to go there in six months. He should certainly be able to go if a law satisfactory to their demands was passed. He did not wish to stir out of Phoenix for five months. He had, he said, assured his master that he would not return to India until he had found someone to replace him. Polak, who had returned in August 1912 from India, would be probably chosen for the task. The call of his motherland, he felt, irresistible.

During the return journey Gokhale lost his umbrella and his cap. Gandhi wrote to Gokhale on February 14, 1913, that the umbrella had been traced and was being sent with Joshi while his cap was sent with Kotwal! Gandhi sent a copy of *Return to Nature* to Gokhale and asked him to read it. Gokhale, on his return to India, made speeches at Bombay, Poona and Bankimpore, giving a spirited account of and defence of the struggle and stand of the Indians in South Africa. He said neither Gandhi nor he ever surrendered one particle of the rights of the Indians. He declared that Indians did not want political rights for the present, that India would not object if the Union Government were to disallow further immigration and that in matters of franchise Indians should have equal rights with the whites.

In India the revolutionaries were active and Ras Behari Bose threw a bomb at the Viceroy Lord Hardinge. The Viceroy was wounded. Gandhi treated this as a dastardly act. "We as Indians," declared Gandhi angrily, "deplore that this nefarious institution of cold-blooded satanic murder should find its votaries in India. In the midst of this darkness we can but pray for India's deliverance from the curse of assassination."[21] He prayed for Hardinge's quick recovery!

CHAPTER XIII

Satyagraha: A Partial Success

GANDHI NOW SENSED that a new struggle was coming on. Early in January 1913 Gandhi closed down Tolstoy Farm as it was easier for him to lead the struggle from Phoenix. Every year when he found leisure he gave lessons in moral and physical health through *Indian Opinion*. That year, on January 4, he began a series called General Knowledge about Health. It consisted of thirty-four articles and continued till August 18, 1913. In the conclusion he said that most medical science was quackery. "The body can remain in health only by obeying the laws of God. Rama is not in the *Ramayana*, nor Krishna in the Gita. Khuda is not in the Koran, nor Christ in the Bible. They all live and have their being in a purity of human conduct, which springs from morality." These articles were published in book form. It was then translated into Hindi and other Indian languages. The Hindi version was again translated into English by A. Rama lyer and published by S. Ganesan in July 1921 as *A Guide to Health*.

The one wish Gandhi could not fulfil in his life was to qualify himself as a doctor. During his stay in England in 1909, he had a mind to do so, but he gave up the idea as medical study was practically impossible without dissection. He fulfilled his wish partly by attacking the medical profession and partly by issuing such booklets as *A Guide to Health*.

The new Immigration Bill was published on March 3, 1913. It conceded some of the points for which the satyagraha struggle had been launched. But it failed to carry out the provisional settlement as it took away some of the existing rights.

On March 14, 1913, Justice Searle of the Cape Supreme Court

ruled that Indian marriages performed in accordance with non-Christian rites or not registered before the marriage officer, could not be recognised in the Union of South Africa. The result was that Hindu and Muslim married women were reduced to the status of concubines. Upon this *Indian Opinion* sarcastically observed that in the eye of the law, Mrs. Cachhalia, Mrs. Naidu, Mrs. Cama and Mrs. Gandhi were concubines, and their off-spring were not honoured and beloved sons or daughters of their parents but illegitimate children!

The British Indian Association called a meeting at Johannesburg on March 30 and gave a storm signal. Cachhalia gave a firm warning to the South African Government that there were some Indians in South Africa who were prepared to give their all for the sake of their honour and their country's. They protested against the Searle Judgment. It was a test case. At the meeting L. W. Ritch too thundered against the judgment. Next day Gandhi wrote to the Minister of the Interior, Cape Town, drawing his attention to the intolerable position, and said that Mr. Justice Searle's decision and the statement made by the Immigration Officer in Natal took away the rights exercised by Indians to that day.

Thus, to the list of demands was added the new issue of marriage. The minister replied to Gandhi on April 10, that no new principle was introduced as regards the registration of marriages. In spite of Gandhi's repeated appeals, in spite of the unanimous opposition of the Unionist Party, the Immigration Bill was read on April 30 a second time when Fisher, the Minister of the Interior, openly said that it was the intention of South Africa to exclude Asiatics.

The Bill was passed on June 11, 1913, and enforced soon after. Gandhi was to leave for India in June 1913, but he postponed his visit and finally put forward his demands. He appealed to the Government to repeal the Asiatic Act, to modify the marriage laws, to amend the Immigration Bill, to restore the existing rights and to abolish the £3 tax which the Union Government had promised Gokhale to abolish during his visit to Africa. In case the Government failed to meet these demands, the Indian community would have to resort to passive resistance throughout South Africa. A revival of the awful struggle was a certainty, he concluded.

As the sanctity of Indian marriages was questioned and threatened by the Union Government, Gandhi deliberately decided to include women among the passive resisters. He was much influenced in this by the British women who were agitating for woman suffrage. Gandhi encouraged and inspired the Indian women to break with the ancient social traditions and take up the challenge. In England women had been fighting desperately for the franchise. That was indirectly an inspiration to women all over the world. There was consternation and indignation at the new legislation among the Indian women in South Africa. Kasturba said angrily to Gandhi. "Then I am not your wife according to the laws of this country!"

Gandhi—It is so and our children are not our heirs.

Kasturba—Then let us go to India.

Gandhi—It would be cowardly and that would not solve the difficulty.

Kasturba—Could I not, then, join the struggle and get imprisoned myself?

Gandhi—You can but it is not a small matter. Your health is not good. You have not known the type of hardship and it would be disgraceful if, after joining the struggle you weaken.

Kasturba—I have nothing to think but I am fully determined.

The other Phoenix women prepared themselves to follow Kasturba. The invading batch of women with Kasturba at their head became ready to march. Gokhale asked about the number of satyagrahis and their needs. But Gandhi requested him neither to send money nor to appeal to Indians in India for funds. Later, however, he asked him to do something for the London Committee and pleaded for funds also.

Preparations for the fight were going on. Towards the end of April 1913 Gandhi told a public meeting at Vrededrop that it would be a third campaign and he had no doubt that it would be the most brilliant of all, though it would involve much greater suffering and would be a protracted ordeal. It was resolved to launch the struggle. Several meetings were held all over South Africa, declaring their intention to resume the struggle, not in the Transvaal alone but in the whole of South Africa. They should demonstrate their unity by their actions. Instructions were given to those who were prepared to court jail and also to those who would not be able to go to jail. The Committee of the Transvaal Indian Women's Association threatened the Government with passive resistance if it did not amend the marriage laws. Its secretary was Miss Sonja Schlesin.

The negotiations between the Union Government and Gandhi failed. The inevitable happened. And the satyagraha was resumed, Kasturba leading with great courage the first invading batch of 16 satyagrahis, twelve men and four women, on Monday the 15th September 1913. But for the white workers' strike in July the struggle would have been launched immediately.

Here Gandhi lost the opportunity to help the working class in South Africa and kill two birds with one stone. He did not want to embarrass the Union Government when it was involved in the strike.

The satyagrahis left Durban for Volksrust by train to cross the border of the Transvaal. Gandhi wanted his son Harilal to join the struggle, but Gokhale intervened and detained him in India to continue his studies. On September 23, 1913, the satyagrahis were sentenced to three months' imprisonment with hard labour. Gandhi advised Indians to court arrest by hawking or trading without licences or by declining to produce them when demanded. This satyagraha was pitted against the Transvaal Government, the European population and the Imperial Government.

The Transvaal Government had given a promise to Gokhale that it would abolish the £3 tax which was universally condemned during Gokhale's tour and was now the crux of the new struggle. The passive resisters were deported to the Natal border, but they recrossed the border and were re-arrested. The re-crossing and re-arresting went on for some time.

Soon the satyagraha developed with rapidity into a mass movement, as the indentured Indian labourers were asked to strike and over 2,000 of them responded to the call. Without propaganda and much organization the entire Indian community rose like a surging wave! Gandhi started a grand march into the Transvaal. A wave of excitement passed through South Africa and India. Lord Hardinge openly sympathised with the satyagraha movement in South Africa. Thus it was the Indian workers in South Africa who gave a decisive turn to the struggle.

Twenty-two railway workers struck work at Dannhauser on October 20 and about 3,000 Indian workers from the Newcastle, Cambrian and Durban Navigation Collieries struck work. Next day eleven Indian women were arrested at Newcastle. They admitted having peacefully advised miners to suspend work. So they were sentenced to three months' hard labour. On October 22, fifteen hundred strikers at Dannhauser decided to walk to the border and court arrest. Gandhi cabled Gokhale that the strikers would resume work if the Government promised to repeal the £3 tax and informed General Botha accordingly. Nine coal mines closed down owing to the strike. Gandhi addressed meetings at several places asking the workers to strike. On October 28 the march from Newcastle began. General Smuts denied at a South African Party that he had promised Gokhale to repeal the £3 tax. The next day Gokhale contradicted Smuts' statement and confirmed that a definite promise had been made to him.

ON THE MORNING of October 29, 1913, Gandhi left Ingogo with some strikers for Volksrust to court arrest. At Charlestown he had 1,500 passive resisters under his command on November 2. Next day he informed Reuter that he contemplated moving 1,500 men into the Transvaal and court arrest. Accordingly, on November 4, 1,700 passive resisters started the march from Newcastle. On November 6, at 6.30 a.m., Gandhi led the 'great march' of 2,037 men, 127 women and 57 children from Charlestown. He addressed marchers halfway between Charlestown and Volksrust. The police superintendent and the immigration officer questioned Gandhi and Kallenbach. The marchers broke through the police cordon and crossed the border. On November 6, 1913, Gandhi was arrested at 8-30 p.m. at Palmford railway station. Yet the march continued. He was released on £50 bail in Volksrust Court and the case was remanded till November 14. He motored 33 miles and rejoined the marchers. More workers struck work.

During the march tea and shelter were offered to the marchers by enthusiastic and patriotic Indians. A thousand tins of jam were generously offered for the use of the old among the marchers; the sick were treated and attended to. Bread was kept ready for them. Some arranged for the transport of stores and others for medicine. The strikers were treated as if they were on a pilgrimage!

Gandhi was arrested near Pickford on November 7, 1913, and charged with having brought unauthorised persons into the Transvaal. He was produced before the Magistrate at Volksrust and was released on bail. He telegraphed the Government that either he should be allowed to go with the marchers or Government should arrange for their dispatch by railway to Tolstoy Farm and provide full rations for them. On November 8 Gandhi arrived at Standerton with about 2,000 passive resisters. Eighty-five Indians who had left Hattingh Spruit Colliery were arrested.

Here Gandhi was charged with aiding or abetting prohibited persons to enter the Transvaal. When he was produced befove the Magistrate he stated that he was already on bail and was asking for bail in order to enable himself to take the marchers to their destination. The Prosecutor opposed bail unless the accused would refrain from taking further part in the demonstration. The accused replied that he was not prepared to give such an assurance. The Magistrate released Gandhi on his own recognizance of £50 and the case was remanded till November 21. On his release a representative of Reuter asked him what he thought would be the outcome of his demonstration. He said he felt sure that the Government would repeal the £3 tax. As soon as Gandhi was released the passive resisters continued their march.

Gandhi was as inspiring as a victorious General. He infused courage into his brave, non-violent soldiers. They had marched 24 miles a day on one and a half pounds of bread and a little sugar. They suffered horses' kicks silently, endured kicks and blows from the whites. Women walked in the heat of the noon, some of them carrying two-month-old babies in their arms and bundles of clothes on their heads. Everyone braved the rigours of weather, heat, cold and rain. "Such sacrifice," Gandhi emphatically declared, "will no doubt result in repeal of the £3 tax and what is more, it will enhance India's prestige." He appealed to Indians to provide the marchers and strikers with food and shelter.

On November 9, 1913, Gandhi was arrested for the third time at Teakworth. He was taken to Heidelberg and produced before the Magistrate. On November 11 he was charged on three counts, before the Resident Magistrate, J. W. Cross of Dundee, with inducing indentured immigrants to leave the Province. J. W. Godfrey appeared for Gandhi. The accused pleaded guilty to the charges and expressed his desire that the Magistrate should not hesitate to impose the highest sentence upon him. Gandhi declared in the Court that it was a worthy cause and he was sorry for the serious losses being caused to the employers and that the heavy tax should be removed.

The Magistrate said that the Government had not broken faith with the Indians and the defendant was, by his threatening conduct, only bringing ruination to the men and harshness upon them. The Magistrate sentenced him to 9 months' imprisonment with hard labour or a fine of £60.

Gandhi boldly elected to go to jail. Crowds waited outside the jail but Gandhi was secretly removed to Dundee jail. No end to the strike without the repeal of the £3 tax was his message. He was sentenced at Volksrust on November 14, to a further 3 months' imprisonment when he said, "I claim to be a sane and law-abiding citizen."

Now in jail Gandhi was happy; for going to jail had become,

he said, holidaying for passive resisters. The march was a wonderful experience and he took a pledge on the day of the sentence that he would live on one meal a day till the repeal of the tax was promised. He would take only lemon or orange squash. His food consisted of 12 bananas, 12 dates, 3 tomatoes and 3 selected groundnuts and 2 ounces of olive oil.

In Gandhi's absence Polak led the march and he too was sentenced to three months' simple imprisonment. Kallenbach was also sent to jail. From jail Gandhi gave instructions to his followers. Anxious about Kasturba's health he hoped that her old trouble had not revived and that she had kept good health. He implored her not to be anxious about him. She would help him, he added, to keep better by looking after her own health. She should keep to the diet prescribed for her.

The struggle had reached its climax. It echoed throughout India and England. Two Tamilians[1] were shot during the struggle. About forty thousand[2] men and women courted imprisonment out of which nearly ten thousand were actually imprisoned. Lord Hardinge, Governor-General of India, who was wholly sympathetic, made a fervent speech at Madras on November 24, 1913, supporting the struggle and urging an inquiry into the problem of the Indians in South Africa. The Government of India soon moved the Imperial Government and appealed to it to bring pressure on the Union Government to mend its ways.

SOON AN INDIAN Inquiry Commission was set up by the Union Government on December 11, 1913, to inquire into the causes of the strike and the disturbances in connection with it. On the recommendations of the commission, Gandhi, Polak and Kallenbach were released unconditionally on December 18. They were given an ovation at Johannesburg. The commission was called the Solomon Commission after the name of its Chairman Sir William Solomon. Ewald Esselen and Lord J. S. Wylie were members. As there was no representative of the Indians on the commission, it was unanimously resolved, at a meeting held in Johannesburg on December 18, that they should neither tender evidence before the commission nor co-operate with it. The meeting was addressed by Gandhi, Kallenbach, Polak and William Hosken.

At Durban Gandhi told a meeting on December 21, 1913, that he repeated his charge against the appointment of the commission. The Indian community was not consulted as to the nomination of its members. Esselen and Wylie were anti-Indians and so he desired that at least one member acceptable to Indians should be added.

When Gandhi heard of the shooting of his fellow countrymen, he changed his European dress which he had worn for the previous 20 years. He felt, he proceeded, how glorious it would have been if one of those bullets had struck him also, because might he not be a murderer himself, by having participated in that event, by having aroused them to strike?[3]

Gokhale, who had been exerting himself feverishly and was playing a vital role in the last stage of the struggle, feared that a boycott of the commission might alienate the Viceroy of India who all the while felt that the inquiry had been secured after great efforts. Lord Ampthill also tendered similar advice and asked Ritch to tell Gandhi not to place his friends in India and England in a false position. He added that a peremptory note was not in accordance with the spirit of passive resistance. Gokhale over-exerted himself and Gandhi wrote to him that "nothing would grieve me more than to find that our troubles hastened your departure from the earth."

The Indian National Congress, at its session in December 1913, at Karachi, made an emphatic protest against the Immigration Act and disapproved of the personnel of the commission, since two of its members were known to be biased against Indians. The pressure from India and England compelled the South African Government to take a conciliatory view.

The Indian Government deputed Sir Benjamin Robertson to bring about a settlement. With Gokhale's approval, a mission consisting of C. F. Andrews and W. W. Pearson, both noted missionaries in India, landed at Durban on January 2, 1914. At the first glimpse of Gandhi's ascetic personality, Andrews touched his feet. Gandhi wore a *dhoti* and a *kurta.*

When Gandhi had despaired of negotiating with General Smuts, Andrews came and proved to be of great help in the negotiations whereas Sir Benjamin Robertson proved to be 'weak and by no means sincere' although the other side said that he was tactful, judicious and reasonable. To Lord Gladstone, the Governor-General of South Africa, and to Smuts, Gandhi seemed to be an unusual type of human being, a curious combination of mysticism and astuteness that baffled the ordinary process of thought.[4]

Gandhi and General Smuts met in January 1914, and it was agreed between them that the commission would consider and make recommendations on the issues of marriage, voluntary registration and abolition of the £3 tax together with the other unresolved issues. Non-co-operation with the commission apparently continued, but the Indian demands were strongly pressed by their friends and supporters. In March 1914 Kasturbai was taken seriously ill. Gandhi read the *Ramayana* to her. He had given up hopes about her recovery. He said: "I have made preparations and inquired about everything in case she dies. There is a cremation ground here equipped with the necessary facilities. It is four miles away."[5]

To Gokhale he wrote: "I doubt whether she will survive the settlement." She survived, but Gandhi's eldest brother Laxmidas passed away on March 8, 1914, at Porbandar. In the end Laxmidas wrote a very pathetic letter of reconciliation to Gandhi. He commended his sons to his care and wanted to meet him but that was not to be. Gandhi could not mould them. "It is idle," he observed, "to expect one's children and wards necessarily to follow the same course of evolution as oneself."

Gandhi had now the responsibility of having to look after five widows in his father's family and of course their children. As the news of his brother's death spread people sympathised with Gandhi.

From Andrews Gandhi learnt about the work of Mahatma Munshiram who later became known as Swami Shraddhanand. The Gurukul students had sent monetary help to the Passive Resistance Movement which they had collected by denying themselves milk and by working as labourers. On March 27, 1914, Gandhi wrote a letter to Shraddhanand addressing him as 'Dear Mahatmaji'. Andrews had told him that three persons had influenced him, namely, Tagore, Mahatma Munshiram and Sushil Kumar Rudra, an Indian Christian educationist, Principal of St. Stephens College, Delhi. Overwhelmed with feelings of respect for Shraddhanand, Gandhi proceeded: "I am impatient to pay my respects to the three grand sons of India who are at the head of those institutions."

In March 1914 the commission reported favourably, practically conceding all the demands of Gandhi. Smuts climbed down. The Union Government accepted the recommendations and passed the Indian Relief Act on June 26. Gandhi wrote to Smuts and accepted it as a complete settlement of all the issues for which the satyagraha had been fought. The £3 tax was removed, Indian marriages performed in accordance with Indian rites were accepted and the Asiatic Act was repealed. Glory to the heroic working people who played a decisive part in the struggle and to satyagrahis like Valliamma R. Munuswami and Herbat Singh who had died as a result of their hard life in jail!

If there was a settlement in March 1914, Gandhi wrote to Gokhale, he wanted to leave for India in April to learn at his feet and gain the necessary experience. He promised that "he would scrupulously observe the compact of silence for one year after his arrival in India." On July 1 Gandhi wrote to Gokhale that "my one desire is now to meet you and see you, take my orders from you and leave at once for India." On July 6, in a triumphant mood, he wired to Gokhale tendering "heartfelt thanks and congratulations on final settlement which without your self-sacrificing services would not have been reached so early. We ask you as our spokesman to convey by cable to Lord Hardinge our humble thanks for his great help and for fearless manner in which he facilitated settlement." And indeed it was true that but for the help of the Indian Government and the agitation in India the struggle would not have achieved success to the extent it had done.

Gandhi had another achievement to his credit. Throughout the struggle he could keep the British Indian Association aloof and used its influence and reputation to make representations and negotiate peace and the settlement. This was so important an achievement that years after he said at a meeting in Madras on September 6, 1927, "If I had made the blunder of dragging the British Indian Association into the agitation, I would have cut the association into pieces and there would have been no South African victory. And I would have missed Mahatmaship."[6]

THUS ENDED AN epic struggle launched by Indians and fought so gloriously "which cost them much suffering and pecuniary loss and to the Government much anxious thought and consideration". Later Gandhi gratefully acknowledged on his arrival in India that it was true that pressure was exerted on the Union Government, but it was the favourable European public opinion in the Colony which made it possible for the Passive Resistance Movement to succeed.

General Jan Christian Smuts with whom Gandhi fought was soldier, statesman, and philosopher. He was born on May 24, 1870, and had a brilliant academic career in England. A lover of simple life, he neither smoked nor played cards. Music and films had no attraction for him. A barrister-at-law, he devoted his entire life to politics and made several contributions to botany, archaeology and philosophy. He was well known for his theory of Holism by which he meant that the whole is something above the sum of its constituent parts, and that no part is sufficient for complete fulfilment by itself. He left Cape Town and practised at Johannesburg and became Attorney-General of the Transvaal. During the Boer War he became a Commandant General.

On the strength of his theory of Holism, Smuts advocated the unification of the Boer Republics of the Transvaal and the Orange Free River with the two British Colonies Natal and Cape. He had a spiritual awe of Gandhi and venerated Gandhi and Thomas Woodrow Wilson as men who could do what they thought right in the teeth of a nation's opposition.[7]

Smuts, as a responsible leader of a democracy, helped Gandhi to develop his political and spiritual weapons and his power. Under a dictatorship there would not have been an opportunity for Gandhi to develop it.

"As a passive resister," Gandhi gratefully and frankly admitted, "I discovered that I could not have that free scope which I had under the British Empire."[8] He was thus doubly grateful to the British Empire for helping him to develop his personality and weapon. The British as well as the Indian Government helped him as his agitation was not directed against them.

Smuts later promoted the idea of commonwealth and the League of Nations and the U.N.O. He became thrice Prime Minister of the Union of South Africa which he put on the map of the world and was given twenty honorary doctorates by Universities from different countries.

During 1913 and 1914 Gandhi was going through intense spiritual introspection. The letters he wrote to Manilal Gandhi, Jamnadas Gandhi and others are witnesses to it. About the existence of God he said: "There is no need, however, to deny the existence of God. We may try to define God in accordance with the limits of our knowledge. At any rate God is no dispenser of awards and punishments, nor is He an active agent. But, if one *atman* can be conceived after the embodied *atman* have become free, it is God. He is no material thing, but pure consciousness. This is also the view of the *advaitavadis*. The self in man is not distinct from the Brahman, the Absolute."

After a few days he writes to Jamnadas that God exists, and yet does not. He does not, in any literal sense. The *atman* that has attained *moksha* is God and therefore omniscient. The true meaning of *bhakti* (devotion) is search for the *atman*. When the *atman* realizes itself, *bhakti* is transformed into Jnana. Krishna, Rama and others were divine incarnations, but we, too, can be like them when immense *punya* (accumulated merit) has accrued to us. It is difficult to say who was the greatest among Krishna, Rama, the Buddha and Jesus. Their achievements differed, because they lived in different times and under different circumstances. In point of character alone, possibly the Buddha was the greatest."[9] Gandhi shrewdly does not include the founder of Islam for comparison.

"Those who deny the existence of God," Gandhi proceeded, "will end up on the wrong path; for they will be obliged to deny the existence of the *atman*. *Avatar* (incarnation) is and will always remain, a necessity. . . . The criterion of a religion is compassion. There are as many paths as there are human beings. Caste distinctions are both necessary and unnecessary. Their forcible observation is unnecessary."

Gandhi asked Jamnadas to marry. "All the same," he said, "if you have no sexual union with your wife, this cannot but conduce to the welfare of both of you. It will also be an excellent example to others. It is more difficult to observe unbroken *brahmacharya* in marriage than without marrying." About his own *brahmacharya* he said: "I dare not assert that the desire for sexual pleasure will never get the better of me in whatever state I may be. Love for the wife, the sons and other members of the family has not yet melted away. All that can be said about me is that I am one who is striving earnestly to attain *moksha* (spiritual liberation). And when the *atman* is free from bondage to body, it is said to have attained *moksha*."

The settlers in Phoenix were experimenting in many fields and while doing so two of them had moral lapses. Gandhi does not, understandably, mention the names but says in his autobiography that he undertook a fast for seven days as a penance. His son Manilal was one of the sinners. Manilal[10] wrote in 1955 that he himself was the cause of his father's having had to undertake a fast for seven days in 1912 as he had tried to deceive him. Gandhi wanted an admission of guilt from him, and his son persisted in denying it.

At last Manilal enclosed a letter confessing his guilt with a letter to Kallenbach. Gandhi forgave Manilal, but wrote immediately to the parents of the other children informing them of the episode and asked them to withdraw their children if they so wished. But none did so.

Gandhi, Manilal and Kallenbach undertook a fast for seven days. But this action was taken after the deed. Kasturba had warned Gandhi in the matter, but he had ignored the warning. A circumstance arising out of this seven-day fast over the moral fall of his son and some other children compelled Gandhi a little later to undertake another fast for fourteen days. This second fast went hard with Gandhi and he became terribly weak.

THE TIME had come for Gandhi to leave South Africa and to take up his work in India which he had been preparing for and planning for three years. He was to leave Phoenix on July 11, and to sail for London *en route* to India with Kasturba and Kallenbach. During that week innumerable farewell meetings were held, addresses were presented, public dinners were given amidst deep emotions and gratitude and abiding love at Kimberley, Durban, Verulam, Park Station and Pretoria. The Indians in South Africa poured out their hearts to him. At Vrededorp a section of the Muslim population had opposed the settlement and they were critical of Gandhi. He replied that he had accepted the settlement as Secretary of the British Indian Association.

He explained also issues arising out of the hospital funds and the accounts of the British Indian Association about which they had raised unseemly questions on the occasion.[10] The Europeans too expressed their respect and admiration for the great work and service Gandhi had done; and General Botha and Smuts shared their sentiments. "I shall forever cherish," Gandhi solemnly declared, "the sacred memory of European friends and the love my countrymen have borne towards me." I am, he added, "going to India to try to perfect myself, for I believe that it is in India that the nearest approach to perfection is most possible." His parting message was: "Whether you are Hindus or Muslims, Parsis or Christians, work unitedly as Indians. If, during my stay in South Africa, I have harmed anyone, maybe unknowingly, please forgive me."

Before leaving for London *en route* to Cape Town, Gandhi sent General Smuts a gift of a pair of leather sandals he had made in prison. After wearing them on his farm for some years, Smuts returned them to Gandhi in 1939 adding that he was not worthy to stand in the shoes of so great a man.

At Cape Town, Dr. J. H. Gool and Dr. Abdur Rahman, Cape Town leaders, eulogized his services. Hundreds of telegrams containing messages of love and sympathy were showered on Gandhi from all parts of South Africa. Lord Hardinge had lost his wife and Gandhi did not fail to sympathise with the Viceroy for his loss. He described Lord Hardinge as 'the noble Viceroy and faithful friend of ours'. He described the settlement 'as the Magna Carta of our liberty in this land'.

Polak was now to carry on his practice. Miss Schlesin, who played a vital part in the passive resistance movement and who was also publicly honoured for her services, had already started work elsewhere. Miss West was at Phoenix. Gandhi said he could not say where he would settle down permanently. The Rev. Doke had died in August 1913. Gandhi had praised him as one of the truest friends of the Indian community.

So the 'most arresting figure' in the Indian community in South Africa crowded with experience and work was leaving South Africa after twenty-one years, a figure so frail could house so vigorous a character. He left Cape Town by S.S. *Kinfauns Castle* for London on July 18. "I sailed for England," he wrote in *Satyagraha in South Africa*, "to meet Gokhale on my way back to India, with mixed feelings of pleasure and regret— pleasure because I was returning home after many years and eagerly looked forward to serving the country under Gokhale's guidance, regret because it was a great wrench for me to leave South Africa, where I had passed twenty-one years of my life sharing to the full in the sweets and bitters of human experience, and where I had realized my vocation in life."

On board the ship Gandhi, who had accepted costly gifts at Cape Town contrary to his principles, asked Kallenbach to throw his pair of binoculars into the sea because this set of costly things was inconsistent with the ideal of simplicity that they aspired to reach! He had not recovered from the physical consequences of the fast he had undertaken for 15 days. Though there was a pain in his calves, he could take a stroll on deck every day.

When Gandhi reached London on August 6, he learnt that a war had broken out on August 4, 1914. Gokhale was stranded in Paris where he had gone for reasons of health. On August 13 Gandhi issued a circular affirming his resolve to tender unconditional service to the British Empire and sent it around for signatures. He offered to raise an Indian Volunteer Corps for ambulance work. An Indian Volunteer Committee was set up with Gandhi as Chairman. V. V. Giri and Dr. Jivraj Mehta joined him but Giri resigned as he thought it sinful to help the British. Gandhi attended classes for nursing wounded soldiers. He met Gokhale in London on September 18, 1914.

Gandhi could not bear the idea that the British masters' difficulty was India's opportunity. A loyal subject should unselfishly cooperate with the master in the hour of his need. Non-violently violent towards the Indian revolutionaries, he was violently loyal to the British master. He thought it was more becoming and far-sighted not to press the Indian demands. Sarojini Naidu then in London was a member of the Lyceum, a ladies' club. She enthusiastically threw herself into the work of serving wounded British soldiers. She placed before Gandhi heaps of clothes which had been cut to pattern and he got them sewn up and returned them to her. He had differences with the commanding officer who did not care to deal with the corps through Gandhi the chairman. But ultimately Charles Roberts, Under Secretary of State for India, appointed Gandhi's men to work at Netley Hospital independently but directly under the Commanding Officer there.

Gandhi took part in the drill and had to walk a long distance. That gave him pleurisy and he was bed-ridden. Dr. Jivraj Mehta treated him, but Gandhi refused to act in accordance with his advice. He refused to take milk, cereals or meat. Gokhale intervened, but the disciple would not yield. He obeyed the dictates of his inner voice.

Gokhale left for home as he could not stand the October fogs of London. Gandhi called in Dr. Allinson, his old acquaintance of London. Dr. Allinson advised him to bathe in tepid water, have an oil massage on the affected parts, and a walk in the open for fifteen minutes every day when he went out. He wore European dress; at home he wore his satyagrahi dress. Lady Cecilia Roberts gave him malted milk and Gandhi found it to be a preparation of milk. So he gave it up. But here he took salt and pulses although he had given them up two years earlier. Kasturba too had a relapse of an old ailment. Roberts advised Gandhi to leave for India and help in the war there.

At a farewell party in London, Gandhi said that 'The India of his imagination was an India unrivalled in the world, and an India where the most spiritual treasures were to be found'.

On December 19, 1914, Gandhi with Kasturba sailed for India, parting with a wrench from Kallenbach, who, being a German, was not allowed to go to India. He died in Africa in 1945. Dr. Jivraj Mehta had bandaged his affected ribs but soon Gandhi removed the bandage. By and by, he felt better. During the voyage he made considerable progress in the study of Bengali.

In the last week of December 1914 the Congress session held at Madras thanked the Viceroy Lord Hardinge for the able and courageous stand taken by him in the cause of the Indians in South Africa, placed on record its warm appreciation of, and admiration for, the heroic endeavours of Gandhi and his followers and the unparalleled sacrifice in their struggle. It also expressed its gratitude to Polak and Kallenbach for their sacrifice and suffering and to the Rev. Andrews for his help. It recorded appreciation of Gokhale's invaluable services in bringing about the settlement. Moving the resolution, Natesan said that it was a partial settlement! Mrs. Annie Besant too considered it a partial settlement. Sir Pherozeshah Mehta totally disapproved of the settlement with which Gandhi was satisfied.

Gandhi reached Bombay on January 9, 1915. It was a great joy to get back to the homeland after ten years. "I was filled with joy," he wrote jubilantly, "when, reaching Bombay, I sighted the coast."

Gandhi landed at Bombay at eight in the morning. Gokhale arranged for his reception. Gandhi ardently desired to merge himself in Gokhale. But that was not all. He arrived in a simple dress of a Gujarati peasant with a Kathiawadi turban, a dhoti, a shirt and a long loose cloak reaching to the knees, a white scarf, all made of Indian mill-cloth. He was armed with the weapon of non-violent satyagraha.

A batch of his dedicated followers had left for India in August 1914 under the leadership of Maganlal Gandhi. He had drilled a batch of devoted followers to follow him implicitly in the intensely ascetic life he had chosen for himself. They had discarded all European habits; they had learnt to squat on the floor for meals. They had given up all animal food including milk, salt, condiments and other things that were likely to tempt the palate and prevent spiritual growth. At one stage Gandhi was inclined to give up wheat, roots and rice as they were capable of producing life. Actually, he had been living entirely on fruit, subsisting mostly on bananas, groundnuts and lime. He knew he was to take up political work. But he was more anxious to bring about a moral and spiritual transformation in India.

Gandhi arrived with a philosophy of his own and a new technique of social and political agitation. He was a man who had been struggling for the mastery of spirit over flesh and who looked upon celibacy as a way of life. His views on nonviolence, his idea of women's liberation, his pro-Muslim policy, his obsession with Hindu-Muslim unity, his love for religious tolerance, his profound faith in God and his love for and insistence on leading an ascetic life were settled, fixed and predominant. It was his experience that the world took no note of abstract principles but only of action.

The one thing noticeable about his mental make-up was that he never planned for the success of the struggle he launched. He was a superb and supreme propagandist. He launched upon direct action, of course non-violent, and conducted it enthusiastically, but then suddenly called off the struggle making compromises with the authorities without the consent or knowledge of the people who participated in the struggle. It was his belief that "a struggle which has to be previously planned is not a righteous struggle. In a righteous struggle God Himself plans campaigns and conducts battles." Such a man with his boundless energy, capacity for fearless action, immense if uncritical faith and iron will was bound to play a historic role in the affairs of the nation.

CHAPTER XIV

Feeling the Way

Gandhi Was Received by Gokhale and his colleagues, the master being present despite ill-health. On landing at Bombay on January 9, 1915, Gandhi said in an interview to the Press that he would, as he had promised Gokhale his guide and leader, pass some time as an observer and a student before he formed any definite conclusions about Indian problems. As regards the problem of Indians in South Africa, he admitted that not all the disabilities had been removed, but the bulk of them had. However, he added that he would not return to the scene of his former activities unless some unforeseen call was made upon him.

During the decade, the political situation in India had greatly deteriorated. The arrests, transportations and deaths on the gallows of several gallant revolutionaries in Bengal and Maharashtra resulted in the break-up of the revolutionary forces in Bengal, the Punjab and Maharashtra. The Prevention of Seditious Meetings Act, the press Act, the Explosive Substances Act, the Criminal Law Amendment Act, all these had suppressed and gagged the freedom of the press and platform. Under the Press Act no less than 208 prosecutions took place between the years 1910 and 1913, and numerous editors were thrown behind bars. Tilak, the mighty leader of India, had been released at the age of fifty-eight in June 1914 after undergoing imprisonment for six years in Mandalay Jail. Savarkar was arrested in London in March 1910 and he escaped at Marseilles while he was being repatriated in a steamer to India. He was re-arrested at Marseilles and sentenced at Bombay by a Special Tribunal to fifty years' transportation for life in January 1911.

The constitution of the Congress was drafted in 1908 and amendments were accepted at Bankipur in 1912. Since 1907 the Extremists or the New Party had stood aloof, from the Moderates. Almost all of Tilak's eminent contemporaries and colleagues had receded into the background. Bipin Chandra Pal and Lala Lajpatrai had resorted to self-imposed exile. Bengal's great leader Aurobindo Ghose retired to Pondicherry in pursuit of divine life. Since the Delhi Darbar of 1911, Surendranath Banerjee, now in his sixty-seventh year, had relapsed into inactivity. The lion of Bombay, Pherozeshah Mehta, being in his seventieth year, had not the old fervour, and so he had not attended Congress sessions for the previous three or four years. Hume, who was the real Prometheus of the Congress, had died in 1912.

Besides, the illness of Gokhale and consequent decreased activity had weakened the Congress, and it had lost its grit and ballast. This was the sad state to which the Congress was reduced after Tilak's removal from the political field. With the entry of Mrs. Annie Besant in Indian politics in 1913, a new force developed in the freedom struggle of India. She was sixty-eight, but her vigour and valour were undiminished by age. There was no eminent leader of all-India stature in Gujarat. The way to leadership in Gujarat was open. Verily, Gujarat awaited its leader.

About this time a great change was seen in the creed of the Muslim League. It accepted in 1913 the attainment of Self-Government for India as its goal, and so the Aga Khan relinquished its permanent presidentship. New Muslim leaders like Dr. Ansari, Mahomed Ali and Hakim Ajmal Khan in North India, Abul Kalam Azad in Bengal and Khan Abdul Ghaffar Khan in the North-West Provinces were rousing Muslims to their new goal.

Patriot Gandhi was welcomed enthusiastically by the Moderates but more so because he styled himself a disciple of Gokhale. As he had opposed a foreign Government and was a leader of satyagraha and a great mass movement, Tilak's followers, too, accorded him a warm welcome. People of all religions, of all parties, of all castes participated in welcoming him. Even Government officers contributed their mite to the functions and offered their meed of praise to the hero of South Africa.

Gandhi looked like the Bania that he was with a sandal mark on his forehead and a *kumkum* dot besides, indicating marks of high-caste Hindu! The residents of Santa Cruz, Bombay, accorded him a warm reception on January 10, 1915 and he said he would try to be worthy of their compliments. Gandhi met Swami Anand when the former saw his own relatives. He was honoured also by his Modh community. Amidst the flutter and flush of the receptions Gandhi wrote to Maganlal Gandhi on January 11, 1915, only two days after his arrival, that he felt suffocated by all the public honouring. He had not known, he added, a moment's peace as he had an endless stream of visitors.

On the evening of January 10, 1915, Gandhi was presented with an address by the Bombay National Union at Hirabag, Bombay. The meeting was organized by Dr. D. D. Sathe and presided over by C. V. Vaidya. Tilak was invited to attend, but he said he would do so only if Gandhi had no objection to his presence. As things were, Tilak's presence was likely to embarrass all the loyalists. But Gandhi agreed to Tilak's presence. Accordingly, when Tilak arrived, Gandhi got down from the platform, welcomed and embraced him in Indian fashion. He seated the father of Indian unrest in a chair on the platform and bowed to him by touching his feet.

At the meeting Tilak said that they were doing their duty in honouring Mr. and Mrs. Gandhi who had fought for the honour of the country. He said India ought to produce more men and women of the self-sacrificing spirit of the honoured guest. After the meeting Tilak thanked Dr. Sathe for organizing the function with a view to winning Gandhi over to their side.

In Bombay Gandhi was warmly welcomed by the Imperial Citizenship Association of India at Mount Petit in palacial surroundings full of pomp, splendour and glitter. On his arrival at this party, Gandhi fell prostrate at the feet of Sir Pherozeshah Mehta. It was the ancient practice of Indians to greet elderly persons in this manner. Sir Pherozeshah presided at the party although he had not appreciated Gandhi's settlement in South Africa. Gandhi, thanking all including Sir Pherozeshah for their guidance, instructions and advice, said that the life of Dadabhai Naoroji, to whom he had paid his respects that morning, was an inspiration to him. He added that Gokhale's life was more than an inspiration to him as the latter was his guide and political leader. It was peculiar to Gandhi, the speaker, that he moved and raised the forefinger of his left hand while he developed the theme of his address. Kasturba Gandhi was welcomed as the wife of the great Gandhi. The Moderate leaders must have been flushed with the tributes Gandhi paid to their leaders.

On the morning of January 14, Gandhi, at the instance of Gokhale, called on Lord Willingdon, Governor of the Bombay Presidency, and promised him that as a satyagrahi he would not take any steps concerning Government unless he understood its viewpoint. The Governor in turn told him that his Government would not willfully do anything wrong.

Immediately after the interview with the Governor, Government informed the police department that it did not desire M. K. Gandhi to be shadowed by detectives.

That same evening a garden party was given in honour of Gandhi by the members of the Gurjar Sabha, Bombay, on the grounds of Mangaldas House. M. A. Jinnah, Chairman of the Sabha, presided. K. M. Munshi hailed Gandhi as the greatest son of modern Gujarat. Jinnah praised his struggle in South Africa and frankly added that the Indians in South Africa were not at the end of their difficulties. Gandhi said he was glad to find a Mohammedan a member of the Gurjar Sabha and the Chairman of the function. Observing that he and his wife had to serve their country faithfully, Gandhi narrated the account of his interview with the Governor, adding that even the Governor said he was absolutely confident that under the guiding spirit of Gokhale he would be adopting the right course.

As regards the Hindu-Muslim question, Gandhi said that he would always keep before his eyes his twenty-one years' experience in South Africa. He referred to a sentence uttered by Sir Syed Ahmed Khan that the Hindus and Mohammedans were the two eyes of Mother India. Gandhi, not a student of history, did not know that Sir Syed Ahmed Khan, the educationist, religious reformer and founder of the Mohammedan-Anglo-Oriental College established in 1877 at Aligarh, had afterwards changed his stand and regarded the Indians as two peoples, two nations. He had warned the Muslims of the evils which they would suffer from majority rule in India. Consequently, he asked the Muslims to boycott the Congress, and he was thus against the harmonious evolving of a new nation in India.

Yet Sir Syed Ahmed was frank enough to declare that slaughtering cows for the purpose of annoying Hindus was the height of cantakerous folly and that Hindu friendship was far to be preferred to the slaughter of cows.

GANDHI'S RELATIVES Were eager to see him. His sister Raliatbehn was eager to have a glimpse of him. But he wrote that she should have patience. He would meet her when God willed it. He was taken up, he said, with many difficult tasks. Thereafter he left for Kathiawad. At Wadhwan station, Motilal, a social worker, a tailor by profession, met him and complained about the Viramgam customs and the hardships the railway passengers had to suffer on account of it. Gandhi asked abruptly, "Are you prepared to go to jail?" Motilal replied, "We will certainly go to jail, provided you lead us." The local workers swore that they would go to jail if necessary. Thereupon Gandhi decided to take up the matter and promised to secure the removal of the customs cordon kept between Kathiawad and British Indian territory.

At Rajkot, while replying to the Citizens' Address, Gandhi asked them to keep up unimpaired, the love which they had shown that day. He said he considered the address given at Rajkot as a form of blessing. He called on Thakor Saheb. Gandhi was happy beyond words at Rajkot, in accepting the Modh Community's blessings at the place of his education and boyhood days. Although he was in poor health, he went there to pay a call on his brother's widow and other relatives at Rajkot and Porbandar.

It was on January 27 that Gandhi was given an address on behalf of the Rasa Shala Aushadhashram at Gondal by Jivram Kalidas Shastri. In the Sanskrit address the Pandit described Gandhi as a *Jagat Vandaneeya Mahatma* meaning the Great Soul worthy of being worshipped by the world. The Dewan Ranchhoddas Patwari, speaking on the occasion, said that Gandhi had brought honour to India by his struggle in South Africa. Thus the Pandit of Gondal was the first man to use the appellation Mahatma for Gandhi in an address. On February 2 Gandhi was given a reception at Ahmedabad. There he said that Ahmedabad was the capital of Gujarat where he had appeared for his matriculation. Besides it was a place, he added, which had made an important contribution to the satyagraha in South Africa and so he was on a pilgrimage to it.

Gandhi then visited Poona where he was entertained on February 11 by the members of the Deccan Sabha and on February 12 by the Sarvajanik Sabha. At both the places the conversation was interesting and illuminating. Asked why some people said that the Indian problem in South Africa was not so far finally and satisfactorily settled, Gandhi replied that the grievances relating to accommodation, and to racial distinctions on tramways and railways remained to be removed and attempts must be made to remove them. There was a settlement so far as the grievances were concerned for which the satyagraha had been launched.

On February 13, 1915, Poona honoured Gandhi at a public meeting in the Kirloskar Theatre, where Dr. R. G. Bhandarkar, H. N. Wadia and Tilak spoke. Sardar Nowroji Padamji presided. In his reply Gandhi said that Poona was a place of learning and culture, noted for the spirit of self-sacrifice of its citizens, a city which, whether he made his future 'Home' there or not, would be considered by him and his wife to be a sacred place of pilgrimage. As instructed by his Guru and guide Gokhale, he added, he would keep his lips closed and eyes open for some time. He prayed that he should be judged generously if he slipped up at any time in future and disappointed them.

During this visit of Gandhi, Gokhale asked him to read a lot of important works from his library. Gandhi replied that a few works would serve instead of such a vast number. This upset some members of the Servants of India Society. The other thing that upset them was the work of sweeping and cleaning the latrines which Gandhi did in the compound of the Society. Being perturbed at this, Gokhale asked him to stop the work! Yet he said that "sweeping and scavenging was part of his daily routine!" Gokhale replied that it was not a part of his regimen! And Gandhi stopped scavenging in his Guru's compound!

With the members of the Servants of India Society, Gandhi then had a frank talk on many important subjects, but he found there was a great difference between his ideals and methods of work and theirs. Naturally, they feared that it would not be proper for Gandhi to join the Society. Realizing this, Gokhale told him that the members did not lack in respect or love for him. Gandhi, too, told his leader frankly that he wanted to have an Ashram of his own whether he was admitted as a member or not. He would establish it preferably somewhere in Gujarat, as, being a Gujarati, he thought he was best fitted to serve the country through serving Gujarat.

The Guru agreed and asked Dr. Dev to open an account for Gandhi in the Society's books and give Gandhi whatever money he required for the Ashram and other public expenses. The question of membership, however, was postponed. Was it an exigency or expediency or the change of opinion about the Servants of India Society that Gandhi was seeking its membership? Had he not attacked the institution unworthily while in Africa?

On the eve of Gandhi's departure, Gokhale arranged a party for selected friends. Although ill, he attended it but fainted while it was going on. So he was removed from the scene. When he came to, he asked them to go on with the party.

During that fortnight a controversy raged between Tilak and Gokhale over the misrepresentation of Tilak's views regarding the question of re-union of the nationalists with the Congress by Gokhale in his letters to the Bengal Congress leader Bhupendranath Basu. Tilak insisted that Gokhale should publish his letters to the Bengali leader. As Gokhale thought that it would harm the cause of the country, he did not publish them. Gokhale was in great pain at this time. So Gandhi called on Tilak and expressed his displeasure at the violent article he had written in the *Kesari* against his Guru. Tilak said it was a reply to his Guru's men who had written several articles against him whereas he had written only one. After Gandhi left, Tilak remarked, "Oh! he is a seasoned missionary!" This was Gandhi's first encounter with Tilak.

On February 15 Gandhi left Bombay for Calcutta as his boys from Phoenix had been shifted from the Gurukul of Mahatma Munshiram, later known as Swami Shraddhanand at Kangri, to Ravindranath Tagore's Brahmacharya Ashram at Santiniketan. Gandhi travelled third class.

At this stage Gandhi made some changes in his dress. He gave up using the scarf, the turban and the cloak and wore a Kashmiri cap worth about ten annas. Gandhi thanked Mahatma Munshiram for the trouble he had taken in looking after the Phoenix boys and the affection he had showered on them. At Santiniketan the Phoenix boys, in all eighteen, were given quarters at Nutanwadi near Tagore's own residence.

Gandhi reached Bolpur on February 17. At the station, those who went to receive him searched for him in the first and second class carriages. Not finding him there, they were about to leave disappointed when they were surprised to find Gandhi getting down from a third class carriage. At Santiniketan, Gandhi was received warmly in Indian style. The inmates and students overwhelmed him with affection. Gurudeo Tagore, who was not at Santiniketan, had already thanked Gandhi for allowing "your boys to become our boys and thus form a living link in the sadhana (accomplishment) of both of our lives." He had also written to Andrews hoping that "Mahatma and Mrs. Gandhi had arrived in Bolpur and Santiniketan has accorded them such welcome as befits her and them."

Amidst the boys, Gandhi said, he was very happy and although he and Kasturba were received at Bombay with pomp, they were not happy there. He told the inmates of Santiniketan that they would proceed to their goal in the eastern ways and would grow up in the beautiful manners and customs of India. In the absence of Tagore, Gandhi introduced in Santiniketan the principle of self-help and urged the enthusiastic inmates to start a common kitchen for the two-hundred of them. Kaka Kalelkar, then known as Brahmachari Dattatraya, had arrived at Santiniketan in search of a spiritual Guru, after moving in Poona revolutionary circles and through the Himalayas. He took up charge of the common kitchen with great hesitation. The servants including cooks were discharged, and for some days the new experiment was made with great fervour.

Tagore soon consented, but the fervour diminished. The experiment came to an end after forty days as the common kitchen, it was realized, took much of the students' time and energy. But in memory of this event every year, March 10 is observed as Gandhi day when all work at Santiniketan is done by teachers and students. As Tagore was not present Gandhi solemnly said: "We feel his presence in our hearts."

Gandhi could not stay there till the arrival of Tagore, for he received the sad news of his Guru's death. Gokhale succumbed to his malady on February 19, 1915, at the age of forty-nine.

At a meeting held in Santiniketan to mourn the death of Gokhale, Gandhi said that Gokhale was dead, but his work was not dead, for his spirit lived. Few knew of his religious life. Truth was the spring of all his actions. Gokhale had said that Gandhi was going to be the leader of India when they were all gone.[1]

DURING GANDHI'S RETURN journey, Andrews was with him upto Burdwan. With great curiosity he asked Gandhi whether there would be any occasion for him to resort to satyagraha in India. He quietly replied that he did not think that such an occasion would arise for another five years.

Gandhi returned to Poona and felt that on account of his Guru's death he was left without support. He made a speech at a condolence meeting held on March 3, at the Kirloskar Theatre, Poona, under the presidentship of Lord Willingdon, the Governor of Bombay. Gandhi's desire to be a member of the Servants of India Society was not viewed with favour by the majority of the members as they differed from him on many vital points. It was decided that Gandhi should study Indian problems for a year and then the question of his admission would be decided. As a mark of respect to the memory of his Guru, Gandhi gave up wearing sandals for a year.

Gandhi now decided that he should start an Ashram at Ahmedabad, acquiring land and buildings from the people of Ahmedabad and money from the entire country. There they would do without machinery and they need not concern themselves whether that would lead to the stopping of the mills. He wrote to Maganlal that if Keshu, Maganlal's son, with the right type of education they were giving him, did not marry, he would acquire a light that would shine over the world. Gandhi reared many such Brahmacharies on leaves and liquid diet and such education, but none of them shed the light that shone over the world, nor did the mills stop coming up in India! Vinoba Bhave's learning and dedication was his own. It was not the creation of Gandhi. For Gandhi had admitted in June 1916 that when Vinoba joined him, he had "acquired at so tender an age such high-spiritedness and asceticism as took me years of patient labour."[2]

In the first week of March 1915, Gandhi again went to Santiniketan and met Tagore. All the students and teachers there were very eager to see the meeting of the Nobel prize-winner and Gandhi of African fame. Andrews was the man to introduce his 'Mohan' to 'Gurudev'. Pearson also was present. When they entered the hall, Tagore who was sitting on a sofa, rose to greet Gandhi. The Poet's tall, stately figure with his silver hair, his long white flowing beard, his rich gown stood magnificently against the background of Gandhi's lean figure with his scanty dhoti, his thin simple shirt and his Kashmiri cap.

One was a great poet, the other was a great man of action. Although their paths and temperaments were different, they were spiritually inheritors and representatives of India's age-long culture and traditions. Being rebels, both denounced what they considered evil. Both had great affection and admiration for each other. One was an out-and-out boycotter of Western civilization while the other, a man of wide culture, refused to reject it!

As Gandhi sat on the carpet spread over the floor, Gurudev, too, had to do so. The teachers saw the two great men greet each other and making a few polite enquiries, they left the hall. The two great men then discussed food and diet. The fruitarian Gandhi said, "To fry bread in ghee or oil to make puris is to turn good grain into poison!" With a smile the

Poet said that he had been eating *puris* for the whole of his life and it had done him no harm so far! The poet lived a simple life, but was free from the rigidity of asceticism.

Gandhi met Kaka Kalelkar's friend J. B. Kripalani at Santiniketan. Kalelkar and Kripalani were, in those days, fire-brand revolutionaries. Kripalani was a professor at Muzaffurpur and had visited Santiniketan on several occasions to see his nephew who was studying there. These two friends had a talk with Gandhi. They kept talking while he was having his meal of nuts and masticating it slowly. This style of eating while talking, the deputy Gandhis followed later on. Gandhi told Kripalani and Kalelkar with spontaneous confidence that he did not believe in following history but in creating[3] it! Perhaps Gandhi was not aware of Prof. Seely's dictum that history without politics bears no fruit while politics without history has no roots!

At Calcutta Harilal saw him and parted from him permanently. On his return to Calcutta from Santiniketan, Gandhi was honoured publicly at Calcutta under the presidentship of Motilal Ghose. Eulogizing Gandhi's services, Surendranath Banerjee said that his name would find its place in the enduring places of history. Replying, Gandhi said that Gokhale's life had inspired him and would do so throughout the work that lay before him. Moulvi Leaqat Hussein called for shouts of Bande Mataram, for those were the times when Indian politics was not Muslimised.

Gandhi, accompanied by his wife, son Ramdas, and Chaganlal, then left Calcutta for Rangoon and stayed with his friend Dr. Pranjivan Mehta. He returned to Calcutta on March 28 from Rangoon and was given an address by the local Hindu Sabha. On the last day of March he addressed a meeting of the students at the Students' Hall, College Square, under the presidentship of P. C. Lyons. He told them that there was no reason why students should not study and also take part in politics. Politics, however, should not be divorced from religion. Literary education was of no value, if it was not able to build up a sound character. He believed that some of them resorted to nefarious means because they did not work in fear of God, but in the fear of man. The young men who resorted to dacoities and assassinations were misguided youths with whom they should have absolutely no connections. They were a foreign growth in India. They proved, he concluded, that assassinations had done no good.[4]

During World War I Gandhi, a British loyalist, wanted to

make India safe for the British Empire. So, as a loyalist, he delivered the first blow against Indian revolutionaries at a meeting of Bengal youth whom Gandhi wished to be 'the hope of India, nay perhaps of the Empire'. On April 1 Gandhi saw Gurudev Tagore with Dr. Mehta and discussed some problems with him.

Just then Gandhi received a telegram from Hridaynath Kunzru asking him to go to Hardwar and assist the volunteers of the Servants of India Society in sanitary arrangements there on the occasion of the Kumbha Mela fair which is held every twelve years. Kunzru led the volunteer corps for service at the fair. With his Phoenix boys from Santiniketan Gandhi reached Hardwar on the evening of April 5. The next day he visited Gurukul at Kangri. He fell prostrate at the feet of Mahatma Munshiram. He visited also Rishikesh, walked to Laksman Jhoola and saw the hanging bridge.

There a sanyasin pressed him to grow a tuft of hair on his head and to wear thread. Gandhi regrew the tuft of hair on the back of his head but declined to wear the thread as millions of his countrymen had to go without it. Later he noted with regret that people were ashamed to grow the tuft of the hair on their heads. On April 8 Gandhi was given an address by the Gurukul students where Gandhi told the students that he had gone to the Gurukul to pay his respects to Mahatma Munshiram, as Andrews had pointed out that he was one of the three great men whom he ought to meet in India. He said he was prepared to lay down his life in the service of his country and hoped that Mahatmaji (Swami Shraddhanand) would be a brother to him. The address described Gandhi as a Mahatma as Gurudev Tagore had done earlier in a letter.

It may be remembered that a staunch supporter of Hindi as lingua franca of India, Mahatma Munshiram asked Gandhi, to correspond with his countrymen in Hindi.[5] Later Gandhi asked Tilak to address the people in Hindi!

It may be noted here that Jotirao Phooley was the first man, Shishir Kumar Ghose was the second, Munshiram (Swami Shraddhanand) was the third and Gandhi was the fourth man on whom the appellation Mahatma was bestowed by the Indian people in modern India.

Gandhi said that at Hardwar he was disgusted with the hypocrisy and slovenliness practised at the Kumbha fair and was sick of the swarms of Sadhus who enjoyed the good things of life. It was here on April 9 that Gandhi took the vow of not taking more than five articles of food in twenty-four hours and of never eating after dark. These vows, Gandhi said later, served him as his shield, added a few years to his life and saved him from many an illness.

Leaving the Phoenix boys at Gurukul, Gandhi visited Delhi to meet the third great man whom Andrews wished him to see. It was Susil Kumar Rudra, Principal of St. Stephen's College, Delhi. He had received the Phoenix boys on their way to the Gurukul at Kangri. On April 13 Gandhi addressed a meeting in the Sangam Theatre and spoke on Unity and Perseverance. Mahomed Ali eulogised Gandhi's modesty and self-sacrifice and called upon the Indians to be prepared like him to suffer every hardship in the cause of their fellowmen and country. Hakim Ajmal Khan presided at the meeting.

Maulana Mahomed Ali (1878-1931) was a product of the Mohammedan Anglo-Oriental College at Aligarh (now the Aligarh Muslim University). His brother Shaukat Ali was younger than him by two years. They were the sons of a small landowner in the Rampur State in the United Provinces. Mahomed Ali, after completing his studies at Aligarh in 1898, matriculated at Lincoln College, Oxford, but failed in the I.C.S. examination. In 1902 he served the Nawab of Rampur and for some time, also the Baroda State. He started a Muslim weekly called the *Comrade* in English and published it first from Calcutta and then from New Delhi.

GANDHI THEN WENT to Madras on April 17, 1915 and made speeches at the Gokhale Club, and at the receptions given by the Madras Mahajan Sabha and the Madras Provincial Congress Committee. To the members of the Gokhale Club he said that he was against all machinery and would use only hand-made articles. Passive resistance, he observed, was a difficult weapon to use and should be used as a last resort in defence of the dearest interests, like national honour.

At the public meeting Gandhi took an opportunity to thrill the Madrasis by paying warm and grateful tributes to Nagappen, Naryanswamy and Valliamma, the Madrasis who had sacrificed their lives in the satyagraha struggle in South Africa. The meeting was filled with excitement. He also mentioned the name of Harbat Singh, the martyr. He said he knew that he had a corner in their hearts.

Gandhi, with an eye to building a centre of sympathisers, touched the sentiments of the Tamilians. Everywhere he declared Gokhale as his Raja Guru—political Guru—so that he might utilise the services of Gokhaleites as his own men.

Gandhi then made on April 24 the most important speech in his tour. He was proposing the toast of the British Empire at a meeting held under the auspices of the Madras Bar Association. He proudly declared: "It gives me the greatest pleasure this evening at this very great and important gathering to redeclare my loyalty to the British Empire and my loyalty is based upon very selfish grounds. As a passive resister I discovered that I could not have that free scope which I had under the British Empire . . . and I discovered that the British Empire has certain ideals with which I have fallen in love, ('Hear, hear.') and one of those ideals is that every subject of the British Empire has the freest scope possible for his energies and efforts and whatever he thinks is due to his conscience."[6]

Gandhi said railways propagated evil, but it seemed that he used them in these earlier years to propagate loyalty to the British Empire of which he was proud for an unbroken period of twenty-five years.

On April 25 the members of the Social Service League met Gandhi. Srinivas lyengar, C. Vijayaraghavachariar, Srinivas Sastri and V. T. Krishnamachariar and G. A. Natesan were present. Gandhi said that all social work must be undertaken in a spirit of utter humility and self-sacrifice and must be carried on strenuously and whole-heartedly to a successful conclusion in spite of the absence of recognition or appreciation. Asked about the policy of mingling Panchama (untouchable) boys with caste boys in night schools, he said that there was nothing bad in it at least in night schools.

Gandhi was given a reception by the Indian Christians, Arya Vaishya Mahasabha and also by the Gujarati community in Madras. The speech which he delivered at the Y.M.C.A. Madras on April 27 in reply to a students' address was significant. He asked the students to give up political assassinations and political dacoities and conquer the conquerors not by shedding blood but by sheer force of spiritual predominance. They should be guided by the message of Gokhale who wanted to spiritualize political life and the political institutions of the country. "Politics," he concluded, "is as essential to them as religion. Politics cannot be divorced from religion. Politics divorced from religion becomes debasing."

The following day, Gandhi attended a function held in his honour at Mrs. Besant's. She described Gandhi as a great man. "I looked," she said in her *New India*, "into his eyes and, instead saw through his eyes Jesus of Nazareth who stooped down in order to lift others. About Him it was said: "He tried to save others but could not save himself? May it not be repeated of this great man."[7]

Gandhi then went to Mayavaram to see the two widows of men who were shot during the struggle in South Africa. He saw Selvan's widow but the widow of the other Tamilian he could not find. There he declared that if untouchability was a part of Hinduism, and he believed it was not, he would rebel against it. He said he seemed to be at war with his leaders. He spoke in favour of the native languages and swadeshi clothing and asked if swadeshi was to be confined only to women, as only sarees were woven on handlooms. He had not himself seen a handloom or a spinning wheel till the year 1909.

Gandhi then went to Nellore to attend the Madras Provincial Conference which was held in the first week of May 1915. There he said that Gokhale's life, his message, his words and his methods had been a guiding star to him.

At the students' meeting in Nellore, Gandhi said that unless the leaders and workers translated their words into action and offered encouragement to local indigenous industries, such conferences were of no use. On his return to Madras he thanked, at the meeting of the South African League, G. A. Natesan and all the Indian donors. Thereupon this League dissolved itself and placed the balance of its funds at his disposal for the assistance of the passive resisters' families.

At Bangalore Gandhi unveiled a portrait of Gokhale in the Government High School at the instance of the Social Service League. There he said that Gokhale inspired his life and was still inspiring it and that he wished to purify himself and spiritualise himself. The meaning of spiritualising the political life of the country and of spiritualising oneself, he observed, was that political life must be an echo of private life and there could not be any divorce between the two.

In a talk at Bangalore, Gandhi said that India was becoming poor on account of the gradual disappearance of handloom industries, violent competition from abroad and export of raw materials. He was sorry that Indians thought and spoke in English. They had lost much of their self-respect on account of their being Europeanised. A knowledge of English was not essential to the service of the motherland. Caste was the great power and secret of Hinduism. Modern civilization was a curse in Europe as well as in India. Money, land and women were the sources of evil. Jagatguru Sankaracharya did not deserve the appellation Jagatguru because he had no more force in him. Emigration did no good to the country from which people emigrated. There was, he concluded, much good in the Theosophical Society; irrespective of individuals, it had stimulated ideals and thought.

At the last meeting in Bangalore, Gandhi said that if Indians acted on the political platform from a spiritual motive, they would conquer the conquerors. During his Madras tour he witnessed *Prahaladakhyan* performed in Telugu at Nellore and also *Harischandra* (Telugu play) by Sagun Vilas Sabha.

GANDHI RETURNED TO Bombay on May 10 and in a letter thanked G. A. Natesan profusely, saying he would endeavour to prove himself worthy of his affection. He added that Madras remained his favourite city.

Gandhi then returned to Ahmedabad, visited Limdi and Rajkot where his eldest brother's wife and his sister, perhaps by their worldly views, disappointed him. On his return to Ahmedabad, with cap as headcover he performed the house-entering ceremony of the Satyagraha Ashram at Kocharab village near Ahmedabad on May 20, 1915. The working of the Kocharab Ashram started regularly from May 25. Gokhale had wanted him to continue using the name 'Phoenix' for the Ashram he would establish. Some of his friends suggested names such as 'Sevashram' or 'Tapovan', but Gandhi chose the name Satyagraha Ashram as it conveyed both his goal and his method of service.

Jivanlal Desai, a barrister in Ahmedabad, let his Kochrab bungalow to Gandhi. The object of the Ashram was to learn how to serve the motherland one's whole life. The Ashram started with about twenty-five persons out of whom thirteen were Tamilians including his Phoenix disciples who came to the Ashram from the Gurukul, Kangri on May 23. The Ashram consisted of three classes: controllers, novitiates and students.

Before finalising the rules he had prescribed for his Ashramites, he had sent them to some eminent leaders and social workers for opinions. R. P. Paranjpye, social reformer, liberal and rationalist, was one of them. Giving his opinion on the vows, Paranjpye said that his ascetic ideal was impracticable and even if it were practicable, it would not be desirable. Gandhi credited ordinary humanity with a degree of self-denial it did not possess. He added that moral forces were bound to go to the wall if they were alone and so "we must use our moral forces to organize our material forces and therein lies our salvation."[8]

The rules and observances included vows of truth, nonviolence, celibacy, control of the palate, fearlessness, non-stealing, non-possession and education through the vernaculars. Milk and its products were virtually taboo. Chillies and condiments were excluded, but salt, pepper and turmeric were allowed. A vow of Swadeshi was taken and according to it machine-made cloth was taboo. This vow was dropped in the third edition of the constitution of the Ashram which was issued on November 7, 1915.

The vow against untouchability and a paragraph on Varnashram Dharma were added. The vow against untouchability was adopted because Gandhi admitted Dudabhai Malji Dafda (Dhed) an untouchable on the recommendation of Amritlal Thakkar. There was much resentment and some Ashramites gave up their evening meal as a protest against his admission. On September 26, 1915, Dudabhai brought his family to the Ashram. The Dhed family consisted of Dudabhai who was a Municipal teacher in Bombay, his wife Danibehn and their daughter Laxmi who was two-and-a-half years old. The admission of the Dhed family landed the Ashram in trouble. There was a flutter among Gandhi's sympathisers. No man from the Ashram was allowed to draw water from the well in the compound as it was partly controlled by the owner of the bungalow. All monetary help was stopped.

Even Kasturba and Gandhi's chief disciple Maganlal, did not like the idea. Kasturba fulminated against the admission of the untouchable family. She smouldered inside herself for months! However, she yielded eventually as she was told by Gandhi that she could leave him and they would part as good friends. She was convinced that she incurred no sin in obeying her husband. Gandhi held that a wife or a husband had no right to obstruct the other in pursuit of a worthy aim. Maganlal was in Madras learning a trade.

It seems, according to Government records, that Kaka Kalelkar, who had joined Gandhi a little earlier, felt uneasy and left him soon after the untouchable family had joined the Ashram. He had told Gandhi that he was a Tilakite and believed in the possibility of winning independence by armed revolt. In leaving Gandhi on this count, he really proved to be a Tilakite if the report is correct. The servant of the owner of the bungalow swore at the Ashramites and threatened to molest Dudabhai. There was excitement in Ahmedabad.

Consequently no monetary help came and the funds ran out. Gandhi decided to remove his Ashram to the untouchable quarters. But a mill-owner, Ambalal Sarabhai, who did not reveal his identity at the time, rendered, without any inquiries or visits, help to the value of Rs. 30,000. The financial crisis was overcome.

This incident, however, led Gandhi to re-define his stand in respect to the caste system and the untouchables. While doing so he said in the revised constitution of the Ashram in November 1915 that "some revisions have been made in this edition in the light of suggestions from friends or experience." Although he desired to eradicate the evil of untouchability, in the vow against untouchability he laid down that: "This vow does not extend to association for purposes of eating."[9]

As regards the Varnashram Dharma, he said that there was no scope for Varnashram Dharma in the Ashram as the inmates, were in the stage of *sanyasins*—those who renounced the world—and he further observed: "The Ashram has a firm belief in the Varnashram Dharma. The discipline of caste seems to have done no harm to the country; on the contrary, rather. There is no reason to believe that eating in company promotes brotherhood ever so slightly. In order that the Varnashram Dharma and caste[10] discipline might in no way be undermined, the Ashram inmates are under obligation, whenever they stir out, to subsist on fruits if they cannot cook their own food."

So Gandhi believed implicitly in the Varnashram Dharma which is a vital part of Gandhism, and he did not want to undermine caste discipline. Moreover, his vow against untouchability did not extend to association for purposes of eating, that is, the untouchables were not to take their food from the common kitchen and to eat it in the company of other inmates. Gandhi religiously believed in the Varnashram Dharma, i.e. in caste division determined by birth and in the caste system based on birth. This is all that Gandhi meant by removal of untouchability. The caste system is a doctrine of inequality. It is the very negation of democracy. It is graded untouchability. These orthodox and reactionary views of Gandhi were no better than those of Tilak who defended the caste system and asked the Hindus to utilize the existing institution of caste to improve the moral and material conditions of the working classes. It was Tilak's pet theory that political progress did not depend upon social progress. Gandhi, like all Hindu saints, denounced untouchability, not on a rational basis but on humanitarian grounds. He jealously guarded caste which was the root cause of untouchability. Gandhi wrote to a friend that he would sacrifice his life itself to uphold the Sanatana Dharma as he understood it.

Dudabhai hailed from Amreli in Saurashtra. Amreli was then under the rule of Maharaj Sayajirao Gaikwad, the enlightened and benevolent ruler of Baroda. A champion of the removal of untouchability he promoted education of the untouchables. He had even attended the wedding of Dudabhai. After the incident at the Ashram, Dudabhai went back to Bombay with his family and child. Gandhi told Dudabhai that he would adopt the girl when she was a little grown-up. Laxmi was handed over to Gandhi on October 5, 1920, and he adopted her in 1921.

In the Ashram, Gandhi used to grind food grains and draw water from the well and cook. Thoreau's book on *Civil Disobedience* was read every evening. At this stage he said he observed *brahmacharya* (celibacy) but not in all its subtle aspects. "I cannot say", he proceeded, "that my mind, or eyes are never disturbed. I maintain truthfulness, but I cannot say that I am never guilty of exaggeration, consciously or unconsciously". The students of the Ashram were in the stage of *brahmacharya* and were not to attend marriages. Andrews vehemently attacked Gandhi for the vow of celibacy and he described it as moral tyranny. It made him consider getting married but he did not. Later, after a visit to the Satyagraha Ashram, W. W. Pearson and Andrews went to the Fiji Islands to inquire into the conditions of indentured Indian labour.

The Satyagraha Ashram recorded its first event on June 1, 1915. Gandhi fasted for a day because of falsehood among the boys. On June 3 the Award of Kaiser-i-Hind medal to Gandhi for his loyal service to the British Empire was announced in the King's birthday honours. When Ranchhodbhai congratulated him, Gandhi replied that there need be no congratulations on the award of the Kaiser-i-Hind medal. "One may," he added, "get it and also lose it. I do want a medal, but of a different kind altogether. There is no knowing when I shall get it, if ever."

IN THE SECOND week of June Gandhi submitted a detailed statement of the income and expenditure to Jehangir Bomanji Petit who was the secretary of the South African Indian Fund. In that report, Gandhi again laid emphasis on the point that the satyagrahis had achieved all the objects for which they fought, although he did not mean, he added, that everything had been gained. This he did as there were some mild but discordant notes at many meetings held to honour him.

One A. H. West indicted him for his method of allocations in the accounts. Gandhi replied that relief allocations needed no discussion. "As to books," Gandhi added, "you are quite wrong. Our books contain all the receipts and disbursements. We need no audit, we owe nobody anything and no one has a legal right to ask us to do anything except the committee."[11] Surprisingly enough, a selfless man like Gandhi resented the idea of getting the accounts audited. Not only that he also added that auditing, if it was to cost anything appreciable, was useless!

On June 26 Gandhi went to Poona as desired by the Governor and attended the Government function held at Ganeshkhind where he received at the hands of Lord Willingdon, Governor of Bombay, the Kaiser-i-Hind (first class) medal. His Guru's disciple Gopal Krishna Deodhar was the recipient of the Kaiser-i-Hind (second class) and Sir Prabhashankar Pattani was another to receive the Knight Commandership of the most Eminent Order of the Indian Empire! The British Government conferred the Kaiser-i-Hind (first class) also on Lady Willingdon along with Gandhi!

Gandhi, the satyagrahi, became openly and frankly a British loyalist and medalist like the eminent Moderates who in those days became Knights. Neither the newspapers nor the Indian leaders took note of Gandhi's decoration as he was not then considered an important leader in the political struggle of India. The Indian Government could not have dreamt of asking Tilak or Lajpatrai or B. C. Pal or C. R. Das to receive such a decoration. Gandhi was considered a faithful co-operator, and being a disciple of Gokhale he was considered a safe politician.

In the second week of July Gandhi attended the 15th Bombay Provincial Conference at Poona. During his two-day stay in Poona Gandhi had two interviews with Tilak whose name he had taken particular care not to mention in any of his speeches during his tour. Tilak was his Guru's opponent and a mighty leader of nationalist India, but was an extremist. Mrs. Besant was then trying to bring about a union of the two wings of the Congress, the Moderates and the Nationalists.

It was during these interviews that Gandhi also acted as an

intermediary between the two groups. He tried to persuade Tilak to accept the creed as formulated in article No. 1 of the Congress and added that Tilak would be doing a national service if he surrendered to it completely.

Tilak replied that the Congress rules were to regulate discussion and not to stifle it. And in case the majority in the Congress was against him, he would wait till opinion was created in his favour. He concluded by saying that he and his followers would not join the conventionists as mere slaves. It was reported by the Moderate newspapers that from the talks of Tilak with Gandhi it appeared that Tilak was obstinate and unreasonable and hence the compromise with him was impossible.

Tilak, therefore, sent to 'My dear Gandhi' an account of his talks with Gandhi for confirmation. On July 27 Gandhi wrote to 'Dear Mr. Tilak' that the conversations were private and that he had not given anyone any authority to use his name in connection with the interviews. He never said, he added, that he spoke for the Congress party or with its authority, and the draft sent by Tilak hardly did justice to the interview. "I hope," Gandhi concluded his reply, "you will respect my wish not to be drawn in a newspaper controversy and that you will in no case publish the interview."[12]

Gandhi, who said he came to Tilak as a friend and admirer, had neither the will to correct the draft nor the desire to do justice to Tilak. He had been cautiously ranging himself against him. He had vigorously denounced his view while in Africa.

Towards the end of October, Gandhi delivered at the Empire Theatre a speech under the auspices of the Girgaon District Committee, Bombay. He objected to the indenture system as the labourers remained in a state bordering on slavery, a state which stunted the national growth and deprived them of their national dignity. J. B. Petit announced at this meeting that they had, under the guidance and able advice of Gandhi, founded an institution called the Imperial Indian Citizenship Association. Its object was to obtain for the people of India the full rights and privileges of the citizens of the British Empire. It had sent Andrews and Pearson to Fiji with a view to obtaining the abolition of the pernicious system of indentured labour.

Gandhi asked students and social workers to correspond in Hindi or in their mother tongue, but when he could not receive his letters in time because of this, he wrote to Maganlal to write the address in English.

Just then another great Indian leader passed away. Pherozeshah Mehta died on November 5, 1915, a few weeks before the session of the Congress was held. A legal celebrity and a stormy leader he had dominated Indian public life for over two decades. Lord Willingdon, Governor of Bombay, presiding over a condolence meeting as he had done in the case of Gokhale's death, declared that "I have lost in him a sincere adviser, a frank critic, a staunch supporter".

At Ahmedabad Gandhi spoke on philosopher Rajchandra's birth anniversary on November 21, 1915. He said the deceased was one of the best religious philosophers of modern times in India. He was a universalist and had no quarrel with any religion in the world. In the West, the speaker found Tolstoy and Ruskin among the best philosophers, and he did not hesitate to put Rajchandra above both. The philosopher in the businessman and jeweller outdid Tolstoy and Ruskin in religious experience. Rajchandra, he concluded, exercised a powerful influence on him. But he refused to call him Tirthankar as he in his earthly pilgrimage suffered from headaches which a Tirthankar never did.[13]

Gandhi attended a meeting called to congratulate N. C. Mehta alias Bhai Nanalal on his being admitted to the Indian Civil Service. He said Bhai Nanalal deserved to be honoured for his hard work, but he did not like other students to follow his example. Indians needed character and no labels.

During the first fortnight of December 1915, Gandhi toured Kathiawad collecting funds for the Gokhale memorial. He made speeches at Viramgaon Station, Jetpur, Bhavnagar, Amreli and Bagasra. When he was presented with an address, he said that the casket containing it would be used for the Ashram.

In the Congress session which was held in Bombay in the last week of December 1915 the new constitution was passed and membership was thrown open to the Nationalists. Sir S. P. Sinha, later Lord Sinha, was the last of the Moderates to preside over the Congress. His speech proved to be the swansong of the Moderates as Congressmen. Gandhi spoke at the Congress on 'India and Colonies' and said that the Imperial Citizenship Association should provide Lord Hardinge with a detailed solution to the problem of the colonies.

The Muslim League also held its session in Bombay at the

same time and Gandhi, Besant, Malaviya and Surendranath Banerjee attended it. The Muslim League under Jinnah's leadership set up a committee to frame, in consultation with the Congress, a scheme of reform. Jinnah, with Umar Sobhani as his brilliant lieutenant, braved the opposition in the League with his usual courage and determination and brought the Muslim League in line with the Congress to present a united demand to the Government of India.

CHAPTER XV

A Loyalist

THE NEW YEAR 1916 began with a speech by Gandhi at Salej where he said that they should honour men who had faith. At Surat he declared open the Arya Samaj temple and hoped the fragrance the members would acquire would endure even after the temple had come down some day. Next day, January 3, 1916, he attended the annual celebration of the Arya Samaj at Surat. He said he was not an Arya Samajist although he had come under the influence of Dayanand. "Although the names differ, the Arya Samaj, the Sikh Samaj and the Brahmo Samaj express the truths of Hinduism and a time would come certainly when all the sects of Hindus would be included under the single term Hinduism. There was much speaking and little work and people were fed on speeches and discourses."

Whenever Gandhi visited the native towns and villages of the Indian satyagrahis in Gujarat and Kathiawad, he said the places of their birth were places of pilgrimages for him and paid high tributes to those satyagrahis.

Likewise he reminded Surat also of Ahmad Mahammad Kachhalia and Sorabji Shapurji Adajania who belonged to Surat. He wanted to visit Surat first, but unforeseen circumstances prevented it. At the latter place, he pleased the Parsis by paying tributes to Parsi Rustomji. Whenever he spoke before a Muslim audience, he told them that Hindus and Muslims had fought together in South Africa and at Surat he said so, but unwittingly added that "in a right cause, a community, can win even if it fights single-handed"!

Towards the middle of January 1916, Gandhi learnt that the members of the Servants of India Society were coming to a decision in not having him as a member and he himself admitted to Sastri that he would be a disturbing factor. So he informed Sastri, the president of the Society, that "our common discipleship would constitute an indissoluble bond though we would be following out Gokhale's work from different viewpoints." Gandhi, as he observes in his autobiography, withdrew his application for admission he had made, and after much wooing he was content to say that "the withdrawal of my application made me truly a member of the society"! And epitomizing his frustration in his autobiography in a spiritual manner he said, "Spiritual relationship is far more precious than physical. Physical relationship divorced from spiritual is body without soul."

Later, adding a postscript to this, he humourously observed: "I was to have the honour of Gokhale's successor, but I found a worthy usurper to whom I made willing surrender—I had and have no gifts which Gokhale had and Sastri has in luxurious abundance."[1] On his part Gokhale, Sastri revealed later, had a misgiving about him (Sastri) that he was an extremist in disguise.[2] Yet Gokhale being a man of greater wisdom and greater faith than most men, Sastri added, left the selection of his successor to the judgment of his people. Sastri became President of the Servants of India Society after Gokhale's death. Senior to Gandhi by nine days, he was a poor lad who sat shirtless in the college class and whose mother had no money to buy even salt. During his academic career he won several prizes and became scholar, teacher, social reformer and legislator. He had joined the Society on January 6, 1907.

Gandhi was now free from his promise to his Guru Gokhale that he would close his lips for one year and study the conditions in India. On February 5 he attended the anniversary celebrations of Kashi Nagari Pracharini Sabha and asked the students to use Hindi in their correspondence; for freedom could not be gained without literature. He then attended the lectures in connection with the opening of the Benares Hindu University. Lord Hardinge laid the foundation stone of the University on February 4. The idea of the University was mooted in 1904, the Benares Hindu University Bill was passed on October 1, 1915, and now the University was established amidst a veritable galaxy of ruling princes, a constellation of Lieutenant-Governors and the flower of India's intellect!

On the morning of February 6, Besant, Harold Mann and Dr. P. C. Ray spoke. In the evening Gandhi was specially requested by Madan Mohan Malaviya, the builder of the

Benares Hindu University, to address the gathering. On the platform were sitting the princes and noblemen who had contributed much to the building of the University. At the outset Gandhi emphasised the point of the medium of instruction. He said he expected the Benares Hindu University to teach the students through Hindi.

As regards the resolution of Self-Government passed by the Bombay Congress of 1915, he said that no paper contribution would ever give the Indians Self-Government. No amount of speeches would ever make them fit for Self-Government. Their duty was to fit themselves by their own action for Self-Government.

At this point Gandhi must have sensed a stir in the audience. So, by way of precaution, he said that if they thought that he seemed to transgress the limits that courtesy imposed upon him, he should be pardoned for the liberty he might be taking. He referred to the poverty of India on which some speakers had dealt the previous day, and comparing the millions of the poor with the richly bedecked noblemen in the pandal he said he would like saying to those noblemen: "There is no salvation for India unless you strip yourselves of this jewellery and hold it in trust for your countrymen in India."

There he referred to the distrust shown by Government and to the stationing of detectives in every nook and corner of Benares and said, "Is it not better that even Lord Hardinge should die than live a living death? He finds it necessary even to live a living death. We may foam, we may fret, we may resent, but let us not forget that India of today in her impatience has produced an army of anarchists. I myself am an anarchist but of another type. And if I was able to reach them, I would say to them that their anarchism has no room in India if India is to conquer the conqueror. I honour the anarchist for his love of the country. I honour him for his bravery in being willing to die for his country; but I ask him: Is killing honourable? Is the dagger of an assassin a fit precursor of an honourable death? I deny it. There is no warrant for such methods in any scriptures. The bomb-thrower creates secret plots, is afraid of coming into the open, and when caught pays the penalty of misdirected zeal."

"I have been told," Gandhi observed, "had we not done this, had some people not thrown bombs, we should never have gained what we have got with reference to the partition movement."

At this stage Mrs. Besant appealed to the Chairman to stop

him. Turning to the Chairman, the Maharaja of Darbhanga, Gandhi said, "If I am told to stop, I shall obey." There were cries of 'Go on' from the audience. The Chairman said: "Please explain your object briefly". There was, however, further objection. Gandhi said that he wanted to purge India of the atmosphere of suspicion on either side and added that there was no reason for anarchism in India.

Gandhi then put in a word for the civil service, because a noble, broadminded member of it had requested him to do so. It was five minutes to eight, the usual hour for closing the meeting. The princes, who were sitting on the other side of the Chairman, rose and left the meeting. Gandhi in the words of S. S. Setlur, a former judge of the Chief Court of Mysore, neither cared for time nor for the feeling of his audience. So the Maharaja of Darbhanga also left. The meeting automatically ended. Mrs. Besant was discussing the matter with someone on the platform and then left.

According to Setlur, who was present at the Benares meeting, Gandhi was responsible for the incident as there was no relevancy of his discourse on Self-Government, jewellery of the princes and anarchism at the time of the university foundation ceremony. Setlur denounced Gandhi's speech as one made by a Kaiser-i-Hind Medalist, an ungracious and indecent attack on the ruling princes.[3]

The next morning Gandhi wrote a letter of explanation to the Maharaja of Darbhanga expressing his regret at the incident and added that his sole object was to express the strong views he held against all acts of violence and so "called anarchy." He felt, he concluded, deeply humiliated that extraordinary precautions should have been rendered necessary for the protection of the person of one of the noblest of viceroys who was in a sense, their honoured guest in that sacred city.

Gandhi had some prejudice against Mrs. Besant, for her correspondent, according to Gandhi, had misrepresented his statement in which he had said that man continually did an injustice to woman by using her for his lust. Now a controversy took place between Gandhi and Besant over the Benares incident. He wanted to put the blame of the failure of the Benares meeting on Besant. So, he said, that she left along with the princes and but for her hasty and ill-conceived interruption he would have concluded his speech.

Besant replied that there was only one prince at the far end of the chairman where she was sitting and that prince did not move till after the rest had gone and that it was impossible for

Gandhi to hear her whisper. It was very strange that Gandhi should state that she left along with the princes and in the same breath charged her with discussing the matter with a group on the dais! Moreover, she said it was unwise on the part of Gandhi to say boldly, "I am an anarchist' in a country where anarchism meant bombs while Gandhi was a philosophic anarchist of the type of Prince Kropotkin, Edward Carpenter and Walt Whitman."

Gandhi had no good opinion about the Indian princes especially those from Kathiawad who had not helped him in his education. One knows how he had also approvingly quoted the views of the Afghan King about Indian princes and ridiculed them all. He broke his silence of one year but broke the meeting as well.

GOVERNMENT DID NOT misunderstand Gandhi when he made such speeches against the revolutionaries. Gandhi knew it well that he was serving their cause although on ethical grounds. Gandhi had solemnly averred in England that "I know of no Indian, whether here (England), in South Africa or in India, who had so steadily, even defiantly, set his face against sedition —as I understand it—as I have. It is a part of my faith not to have anything to do with it, even at the risk of my life." Besant was not aware of this.

While Gandhi was carrying on propaganda against the Indian revolutionaries, the war situation was worrying the Government of India. "During these months," writes Lord Hardinge, the Governor General of India in *My Indian Years*, "the internal situation began to grow menacing, due to the anarchists realizing our military weakness owing to the depletion of our troops."

Describing this critical situation, J. C. Ker observes: "Early in the War a serious situation developed in the Punjab, arising out of the return from America of Sikhs who had been demoralized by the teaching of the Ghadr party. During the first three years of the War some 8,000 Sikhs came back from the United States, Canada, and the Far East.... Several risings were attempted and efforts were made in two or three instances to seduce the Indian regiments. A large number of dacoities and murders were committed in many of the Punjab districts, and efforts were made to raise a rebellion."[4] Revolutionary strongholds and conspiracies were discovered at Delhi, Lahore and Meerut. Some days earlier, the *Komagatamaru*, a chartered steamer with 500 revolutionaries from Vancouver, was seized when she called at the mouth of Hugli. The Ghadr party had planned to enter Burma through Siam and after gaining over the military police to proceed to the conquest of India.

Armed with extensive powers and with the help of the 6000 troops from Nepal, the British Government ruthlessly suppressed the heroic risings in the Punjab. There was a holocaust of victims at the altar of freedom. Some five thousand were put on trial for treason in the Punjab alone. Five hundred revolutionaries were tried by court martial and executed, eight hundred were sentenced to transportation for life, ten thousand were interned without trial, and a large number had to remain underground for years. 'There was trouble with the 10th Baluchies of which the Mahsud company shot their officer on embarking at Bombay for Mesopotamia. Several of the company were "tried and shot"! Rivers of blood thus flowed; yet the historians of Gandhi persuasion have been dinning into the ears of the people that India won independence without shedding blood! These risings may be aptly called the Second War of Independence of India.

Naturally on both grounds, ethical as well as loyalist, Gandhi was making British India free from the revolutionaries. In the name of moral values and non-violence he condemned the revolutionaries who fought against British Imperialism, but he supported without qualms of conscience the violence of British Imperialism by sending men for being used as cannon fodder!

Immediately after, Gandhi went to Madras. There on February 14, he read a paper on swadeshi at a Missionary Conference at the Y.M.C.A. Auditorium, where he defined swadeshi as 'the spirit in us which restricts us to the use and service of our immediate surroundings to the exclusion of the more remote and it might not be abandoned even though it might not be fully attained for generations to come.' As regards the Christian religion, he passionately said that India owed a deep debt of gratitude for what the missionary bodies had done and were doing. They would do still better and serve the spirit of Christianity better, by dropping the goal of proselytising and by continuing their philanthropic work.

He considered, he devotionally observed, the Bible to be part of his scriptures, the spirit of the Sermon on the Mount competed at most on equal terms with the Bhagwad Gita for domination of his heart. With great pleasure he further told them that he had come under the influence of noted Christian missionaries and that he was an impartial student of religion with great leanings towards Christianity.[5] It seems, on Gandhi's arrival in India, the spirit of the Sermon on the Mount, which had been struggling for domination over him since his African career, grew weaker and weaker as he was away from the influence of the noted missionaries. And at long last he declared at the Y.M.C.A. in Calcutta on July 28, 1925, that "Hinduism, as I know it, entirely satisfies my soul, fills my whole being, and I find a solace in the Bhagwad Gita and Upanishads that I miss even in the Sermon on the Mount. My life has been full of external tragedies, and if they have not left any visible and indelible effect on me, I owe it to the teachings of the Bhagwad Gita."[6] It thus took him twenty-five years to get rid of the missionary influence!

While dealing with the political question he said in this speech that much of the poverty of the masses was due to the ruinous departure from swadeshi in the economic and industrial life. India could not live for Lancashire or any other country before she was able to live for herself. Lord Curzon set the fashion for tea-drinking. India was a country of nonsense.[7] It was after all Gandhi who described India as a country of nonsense!

Gandhi explained the Ashram vows to students at the Y.M.C.A. As soon as he entered the hall, a slip was handed over to him by a student requesting him to throw light on the Benares incident. But Gandhi, giving a gentle rebuke, said, "These are but passing waves that come and go." "Politics," he said, "are a part of our being". The students should study political institutions instead of crowding the platforms. He asked them not to be a party to the great and indelible crime of untouchability.

Gandhi then went to Poona and on February 19, made a speech on the death anniversary of his Guru. During the whole year he had laid emphasis on swadeshism in language, in education, in trade and in politics and on the oneness of the country. He said that during the past year he found that the country was vibrating with a passionate spirit of patriotism, but the bugbear of fear loomed large on the horizon. Behind all the work of Gokhale, he observed, lay his great spirituality.

Gandhi referred to Gokhale's spiritualised politics and advertised his spirituality with such gusto and vehemence that the members of the Servants of India Society must have been dumbfounded.

Gandhi spoke of Gokhale as if none of his co-workers knew much about the master who observed neutrality in matters religious and followed the policy of least resistance in matters social and never made much of God, religion and metaphysics. His country was his God. He called himself agnostic. He neither performed *sandhya* nor *shraddha*; never visited shrines, or observed fasts and wore no sacred thread. H. W. Wadia, president of the meeting, frankly told the audience that he did not agree with Gandhi on his apprehensions and hopes.

About This Time Gandhi expressed his views on women's education. While supporting Prof. D. K. Karve, who was canvassing support in Ahmedabad for the founding of a Women's University in India, Gandhi said that according to Gokhale, Karve was truth incarnate. "In Gujarat," Gandhi observed, "we do not have the spirit of self-sacrifice that we find in Poona." As regards his own ideas of the education for women, he said, "We shall accept equality of rights for women, but 1 think their education should differ from men's, as their nature and functions do."[8]

Andrews and Pearson returned to India from Fiji completing their enquiry. Malaviya gave in March notice for leave to move a resolution in the Imperial Council for the abolition of indentured labour. Gokhale had tried by a resolution for the abolition of that system, but his resolution had been outvoted by Government. Gandhi again raised a hue and cry against the inhuman system.

Early in March 1916, on a pressing invitation from the Sind Congress, Gandhi toured Sind. He visited Hyderabad, Karachi and many other towns and villages, talking with Muslim pirs, speaking on Gokhale, Swaraj and Swadeshi. At Karachi, while giving his impressions about his tours in India, Gandhi said that he saw in Poona that there were men who could identify themselves with the common people and it did not seem so in Madras.

At Hyderabad he declared that "vaccination is against religion and to allow the injection of calf-serum in the blood is as good as eating calf-flesh. Vaccination produces many diseases and does not give freedom from small-pox. Compulsory vaccination is therefore highly tyrannical. Such a thing is against God and must be protected against". The Government sensibly did not allow this summary of his speech to be telegraphed to newspapers.

As Sind had a Muslim majority, Gandhi talked to them about Sir Syed Ahmed's old theory that India must see through both the Hindu eye and the Muslim eye otherwise she was partly blind. The impression of a Khalifa Haji Mehmud of Lurwani was that Gandhi was really a Mohammedan.[9] Such was the impression he could produce on his mind. At every station people were disappointed to see their great man turning out of a third class carriage dressed like a coolie.

Then Gandhi attended the Gurukul anniversary meeting at Kangri on March 16, 1916. He said that the Arya Samaj could do much good. He found no difference between Arya Samajists, Sanatan Dharmists and Brahmo Samajists as they all sprang from the common religion of ancient India. He said that he believed that "through our civilization we have a message to deliver to the world and I would like to use the British race for transmitting the mighty message of ahimsa to the whole world." He recommended that the institution should impart knowledge to the students in agriculture, hygiene, sanitation and give industrial training.

Swami Shraddhanand, who was a staunch champion of the movement for abolition of untouchability, held a conference. Gandhi told the conference that "we have to attain not the salvation of the untouchables but ours by treating them as equals." He quoted Sir Sankaran Nair who said that they had lost India through inequality to the untouchables. Gandhi was unwell but visited Dehradun.

After the Congress had amended its constitution, the nationalists led by Tilak held the Bombay Provincial Congress at Belgaum from April 29 to May 1, 1916. D. V. Belvi and D. V. Gokhale pressed Gandhi, at the instance of Tilak, to attend the conference and Gandhi replied that only death would prevent him from going to Belgaum.

On April 28, 1916, the Home Rule League was founded by the Nationalists. This institution accepted the creed of the Indian National Congress. Besant started her Home Rule League on June 12, 1916 in London and on September 1, 1916 at Madras.

During the days of the conference D. V. Gokhale and G. S. Khaparde had discussions with Gandhi. After the talk Gangadharrao Deshpande asked Tilak about the views of Gandhi. Khaparde intervened and said, "He does not belong to our party." Tilak did not pass any remark. He knew the power of Gandhi who had shaken the Union Government of South Africa. After much hesitation Gandhi became a delegate to the conference. He agreed to be one when Deshpande told him that the delegates would have an opportunity to know his views.

The Provincial Conference was held and it passed the resolution moved by Tilak recommending the entry of the Nationalists into the Congress. Gandhi heartily supported the resolution and said that had the wording of the resolution been in his own hands, he would probably have omitted some expressions. They should overlook the faults and defects of the erstwhile opponents and seek points of agreement.

Political circles knew that by making that resolution, Tilak had captured the Congress. Tilak held that the strong party needed a magnetic leadership, a rallying point and a war cry. He provided the nation with the first, furnished it with the second by organizing the Home Rule League and supplied the party with a war cry, "Swaraj is my birth right and I will have it."

During the days of the conference, Gandhi addressed a meeting in connection with the Depressed Classes. He was ill. He walked long distances barefoot in the scorching heat, standing on one leg while the other rested for a moment. Allaying the suspicion of certain communities, he said that if Home Rule should be granted, no particular class would dominate; otherwise, it would not be Home Rule. His religion taught him to consider all men alike, without distinction of caste and creed. He deprecated their opposition to the holding of the Provincial Conference at Belgaum. Lingayats and Untouchables attended the meeting.

In April Gandhi was, on his application for a life-membership, nominated as an honorary life-member of the Gujarati Vernacular Society (now Vidya Sabha). In his application he had stated that he was a teacher living on his labour. As regards his own perfection, he wrote to a disciple in May 1916 that he might, sometimes, be guilty of partiality and he sometimes did get unworthy thoughts. During this period he used to discuss with his disciples life of Thoreau.

GANDHI THEN ATTENDED on June 12, the anniversary of the Servants of India Society at Poona. Srinivas Sastri presided. Gandhi spoke there about India's right to Self-Government or Home Rule, but he did not think it proper to hurt the enemy when he was engaged in a life-and-death struggle.

Gandhi's insistent talks on ahimsa began to irritate some of the Indian leaders and it was given to Lala Lajpatrai, reformer, scholar, educationist and patriot, and first rate leader to raise his voice against it. This great leader whose mother was from a Jain family, wrote an article from America in the *Modern Review* of July 1916 under the title 'Ahimsa Paramo Dharmah.' "There is no religion higher than truth, nor a course of conduct nobler than 'Ahimsa Paramo Dharmah.' "Rightly understood and rightly applied to life," observed Lajpatrai, "the latter makes a man saint and hero. Misunderstood and misapplied, it makes a man cowardly and craven, base and stupid." When well-intentioned and otherwise saintly people made a fad of it and the sole test of a good life, honour and self-respect were thrown into the shade. Patriotism, love of country, love of family, honour of the race were all extinguished. "It was," he continued, "this perverted use or misuse of ahimsa (non-killing), or its exaggerated importance at the cost of everything else, that brought about the social, political and moral downfall of the Hindus. Ahimsa," he graphically described, "overdone and misapplied is a gangrene that poisons the system, enervates the faculties and converts men and women into half-lunatic, hysterical, unnerved creatures, good for nothing that requires the energetic pursuits of noble ends and noble virtues. It converts men into monomaniacs and cowards. The worst, he concluded with a warning, "is that people who profess an absolute faith in the doctrine, prove by their own practice that a perverted use of such a truth necessarily leads to a life of hypocrisy, unmanliness and cruelty."

Lajpatrai's volcanic article was given wide publicity in Gujarati papers and magazines. So Gandhi had to explain his position. He replied in October 1916 that the elevation of the doctrine of ahimsa did not contribute to the downfall of India. The Hindus as a nation had given ample proof of physical courage. The fact was that the internal dissensions and love of self instead of love of country had contributed to her downfall. He said he was a Vaishnavite and it was true that he had derived much benefit from Jain religious works and other great faiths of the world and that his guide Rajchandra was a Jain by birth. Ahimsa required deliberate self-suffering, not a deliberate injuring of the supposed wrong-doer. Ahimsa was, in his humble opinion, a panacea for all evils, mundane and extra-mundane.[10]

Gandhi knew little of Indian history. Whatever anecdotes he quoted from the Puranas and history were such as to justify his stand. Knowing his views on ahimsa, Tilak also once inquired whether Gandhi was a Jain, because he felt that Gandhi's teachings were full of absolute non-violence, satyagraha and fasting which were more in keeping with Jainism than Hinduism. Tilak's great commentary on the Gita was a masterpiece and a great contribution to Indian philosophy. So his views on Gandhi's interpretation of the doctrine of absolute non-violence were significant.

Another great opponent of Gandhi was Dr. Ambedkar, scholar, thinker, social revolutionary and democrat. He loved the principle of absolute non-violence as an end and believed in relative violence as a means. He was of the opinion that Gandhi's non-violence sprang from Jainism and not from Buddha who never stretched it to the extreme view of Jainism.

It is then not surprising that Bernard Shaw[11] should have thought Gandhi to be a Jain at heart. Jainism had made an indelible impression on his teaching. Edward Thompson suggested that Gandhi's emphasis on non-violence was a badge of his unmartial origins, he being a Gujarati. Gandhi's disciple K. G. Mashruwala, who once referred to this remark of Edward Thompson, raised a question whether his own love for non violence was the indication of his congenital Bania-timidity.

A study of Indian history and scriptures without bias and prejudice will hardly support Gandhi's views on absolute nonviolence.

Gandhi and historians of Gandhi's persuasion turned to history for sustaining or supporting Gandhian ideals. They lacked scientific outlook and approach and relied on historical catchwords and assumptions favourable to Gandhian ideals. India in her past did not preach and practise the doctrine of absolute non-violence. It would be perversion of Indian history to say that her course had not run through war and bloodshed. The Mauryas and the Guptas, let alone other emperors, were votaries of the blood and iron policy. Gautama Buddha and Mahaveer preached the doctrine of ahimsa which resulted in some sections of society taking to a vegetarian diet. But the Jain and Buddhist rulers never hesitated to take to the sword, war and bloodshed.

Just at this time Tilak's Diamond Jubilee was celebrated by people on a nationwide scale and he was given a purse of one lakh of rupees. On the same day he was served with a notice by the District Magistrate of Poona and a few days later prosecuted at Poona for his Home Rule speeches. The District Magistrate decided the case against Tilak. Tilak filed an appeal in the Bombay High Court and the court admitted the appeal.

On October 21, 22 and 23 the Provincial Conference was held at Ahmedabad. Jinnah was the President-elect of the conference. So proposing formally the election of the President Gandhi said that the conference, which was a gathering of the Moderates and the Nationalists, should give birth to a temperate party. He added that the President, Jinnah, was an eminent lawyer, a member of the legislature but the President of the Muslim League and prayed to God to grant Jinnah the necessary strength, wisdom and ability to guide the work of the conference. Tilak said that they were all nationalists.

The next day Gandhi moved a resolution protesting against the working of the Defence of India Act and against the orders placed on Mrs. Besant under which she was prohibited from entering the Bombay Presidency. On the third day he moved at the conference resolutions urging the abolition of the indenture system and removal of customs cordon at Viramgaum railway station and at other places on Kathiawad frontier. On the same day Gandhi spoke at the First Gujarati Education Conference on education through mother-tongue.

GANDHI THEN LEFT for Lucknow to attend the Congress session and to give a talk at Muir College in Allahabad.

Gandhi delivered his talk on December 22, 1916 in the Physics Lecture Theatre of Muir College, Allahabad, under the auspices of its Economic Society. The subject of his talk was "Does economic progress clash with real progress?" Although the subject was rather odd and dull from Gandhi's standpoint, he introduced liveliness in it. He spoke in terms of eternal values and put moral progress above material progress. He said: "How hardly shall they that have riches enter into the kingdom of God."

"Let us," he concluded, "seek first the kingdom of God and his righteousness and the irrevocable promise is that everything will be added to us." Polak had revised his speech before he delivered it. In those days Gandhi used to take 'mombai halva' in good quantity and adequate arrangements were made for it at Allahabad.

Gandhi's economics had not gone farther than Tolstoy's 'Kingdom of God' and the charkha. Much later when G. K. Chesterton wrote in the *Fortnightly Review* to the effect that Gandhi had a tool belonging to an age of flint-arrow or stone-axe, there was much sense in it; for a similar opinion, Gandhi said during his talks, was expressed by a civilian friend of his when he attacked him with a spate of questions 'on his crankism'. Gandhi observed in this very talk that since he knew very little of economics, his intrusion should be treated as a welcome diversion from the trodden path.

He spoke also on education on December 23, 1916 at Allahabad. A few days earlier he had said in an article that the existing methods of education did not improve the standard of traditional vocations and the present education was disloyal to caste. Education was not an end in itself, he added, but only a means and that alone could be called education which made people men of character.

Now at Allahabad he said that education through English had created a wide gulf between the educated few and the masses. Much greater progress would have been made if they had been taught in their mother tongue. In ancient times, the basis of life was self-restraint, but now it was enjoyment. India was pre-eminently the land of religion and the forces born of spirituality the bedrock of Indian civilization, were more than a match for material forces.

Meantime, Tilak had won the case in the High Court on November 9, 1916 and propaganda for Home Rule became legal! It was a great triumph for the national movement. The Indian sky reverberated with the slogan of Home Rule given by the Home Rule Leagues of Tilak and Besant. And amidst thundering cheers Tilak, like a conqueror, started with his followers by a special train decorated with flowers and bunting to attend the Congress and capture it. At Lucknow a vast crowd gave him a rousing royal reception and in the procession his car was drawn by volunteers! Tilak and Besant were both acclaimed almost the incarnations of the deity. Babu Ambica Charan Mazumdar presided over the Congress session.

THE CONGRESS LEAGUE Scheme of Reforms was ratified on December 29 by the Congress demanding that India should be lifted from the position of a dependency to that of an equal partner in the Empire with the self-Governing Dominions. The Hindu-Muslim pact called the Lucknow pact was signed by Tilak and Jinnah and others. The Muslim League which held its session at Lucknow on December 30 and 31, under the presidentship of Jinnah wearing a Turkish Fez, agreed to the demand for Swaraj, and the Hindu leaders in the Congress headed by Tilak agreed to separate electorates for the Muslims and weightages in the bargain. The Lucknow Pact was ratified by the Muslim League at its Lucknow session on December 31, 1916.

DR. B. S. Moonje, Tej Bahadur Sapru, Madan Mohan Malaviya and some Moderates had opposed Tilak for granting sanction to the anti-national and antidemocratic separate electorates and the weightages.

Tilak wanted to take advantage of the war situation and was eager for a compromise with the Muslims to present a united demand to the British. There was no go, he said to a fellow delegate, but to avoid a triangular fight. He added that the Hindus had overthrown Muslim rule in the past and would do so again if such a situation arose. Gokhale had, in his testament, supported the need for separate and direct representation of Mohammedans, and other minority communities.

Whatever Tilak's arguments, he gave sanction to the anti-national separate electorates and the separate political entity introduced by the Morley-Minto Reforms and a national recognition to the Muslim League as the accredited spokesman of the Muslims.

Aurobindo Ghose, criticizing the policy of Hindu-Muslim unity, observed: "that it was not swadeshi but the acceptance of the communal principle that created the Hindu-Muslim split and here Tilak made his great blunder." Aurobindo was also of the opinion that "the greatness of India's past or her spirituality should not be thrown into the waste paper basket in order to conciliate the Moslems who would not at all be conciliated by such policy".[12]

The Lucknow Pact was accepted as a settlement (and not as a compromise) which, however, was to remain in force for a period of ten years[13] only, so that the Muslim community should realise in that short experimental period the mischief and the harm of the communal electorates and come back to democratic common sense and national unity.

It is history, however, that after Tilak's death the Lucknow Pact proved to be a rift in the lute. Tilak's subtle intellect could not foresee it.

It is interesting to note how Gandhi got into the Subjects Committee at Lucknow. There was a contest between the Nationalists and the Moderates, every time a Nationalist candidate being pitted against a Moderate. In each case the former was elected. When a Nationalist name was pitted against Gandhi, the Kaiser-i-Hind Medalist was voted down. Tilak, however, declared that Gandhi was elected.

Sir James Meston, Lt. Governor, attended the Congress session and was given a warm welcome. Jawaharlal Nehru, then a young barrister, saw Gandhi at this Congress session for the first time. He, however, was not much impressed. He said: "all of us admired him for his heroic fight in South Africa, but he seemed very distant and different and unpolitical to many of us young men."[14]

It was at Lucknow that Gandhi, presiding over the All-India Common Script and Common Language Conference, on December 29, advised the conference to popularise Hindi in Southern India by sending some men to Madras for the spread of Hindi. Tilak, B. C. Pal, Besant and Gandhi attended the Muslim League session held at Lucknow on December 30 and 31. Speaking at this session, Gandhi asked the Muslims to conduct their proceedings in Urdu if they wished to carry out their resolution to maintain Urdu as the lingua franca of India. Two days earlier he had said during an interview that so long as the Congress did not use Hindi for all its work, Swaraj was not possible. He also told the Muslims that the English bowed before the strong and ruled over the weak.

It is interesting to note that the Lucknow Congress passed a very important resolution dealing with the relation between the Indian ryot and the European planters in North Bihar, and urging the advisability of a mixed committee of officials and non-officials to inquire into the causes of the agrarian trouble.

It was at this session that Rajkumar Shukla, a leader of the labourers on the Indigo plantation in Champaran, saw Gandhi and requested him to move the foregoing resolution. As Gandhi had no personal knowledge of the problem, he refused to move it. Babu Brajkishore, the leader of Bihar and a member of the Legislative Council, moved the resolution and Rajkumar Shukla seconded it. One more resolution was passed. It demanded repeal of the Arms Act. Speaking on it, Sarojini Naidu said that the mothers of men whom they wished to make men and not emasculated machines, raised a voice to demand the birthright of their sons to be given to them. "The refusal of the privilege," the Nightingale of India sung, "that gifted privilege and inalienable right to carry arms, is to insult the very core of their valiant manhood."[15] A woman demanded the right to carry arms!

During the session of the Congress Gandhi spoke also on indentured labour resolution. Another item of important work he did at the time of the Congress was that he published a letter written to Philip Kerr, Secretary of the Round Table Group by Lionel Curtis in which he had suggested proposals for the consideration of the group to which he belonged. Curtis, who was then in India, was known to Gandhi as the former Assistant Colonial Secretary for Urban Affairs in the Transvaal and was member of the Transvaal Legislative Council.

His scheme subordinated India to the control of the dominions. The letter came to Gandhi through mistake of some pressman, along with a book which he purchased at Agra. The letter was printed in the Government Press and was marked private. Gandhi exposed the conspiracy before the Congress. Swami Shraddhanand was arranging a meeting between Curtis and Gandhi, but Polak intervened.

CHAPTER XVI

The Welfare of Labour

THE IMPERIAL CITIZENSHIP Association decided to launch an agitation if the Government did not abolish the indentured labour system by July 31, 1917. Gandhi spent the first quarter of the year addressing meetings at Godhra, Ahmedabad, Bombay, Surat and Karachi, creating an atmosphere in favour of the abolition of the system. At one meeting he demanded that it should be abolished by May 31, 1917. Gandhi said he had seen the Viceroy Lord Chelmsford who promised to help. A ladies' deputation led by Mrs. Jaiji Petit waited on the Viceroy Lord Chelmsford and pleaded for the abolition of the indenture system. During one of Gandhi's visits to Bombay, Kishorlal Mashruwala met him in February 1917 and joined the Ashram in June or July 1917.

On February 1, 1917, Tilak, too, addressed a meeting in Poona protesting against indentured labour in the Fiji Islands. Gandhi left Karachi for Calcutta *via* Lahore. There he found it impossible to get into the train. So he paid twelve annas to a porter who shoved him in bodily through the window. He was shadowed by detectives throughout his journey. He was dead tired and his head often reeled. When his identity came to be known the passengers made room for him. At Calcutta he made a speech on March 6 declaring that India would not tolerate indentured emigration a minute longer than May 31, 1917. The president of the meeting was Maharaja M. C. Nandi.

On his return to Ahmedabad, Gandhi stayed for a few days at the Ashram. He then left for Calcutta to attend a meeting of the All-India Congress Committee to be held on April 8. Gandhi stayed with Bhupendranath Basu.

As promised, Gandhi left Calcutta with Rajkumar Shukla for Patna to make inquiries into the condition of the Indigo labourers in North Bihar. On April 10 he reached Patna. Babu Rajendra Prasad had just then started law practice at the High Court which had been newly established at Patna and he was doing social work there under the guidance of Brajkishore, an eminent leader of Bihar.

Rajkumar took him to the house of Rajendra Prasad who was not at home. Rajendra Prasad's servant thought them to be village clients. Gandhi had put on a dhoti, an *achkan* and a Kathiawadi turban although ordinarily he wore a dhoti, a *kurta* and a cap. He asked Gandhi to sit in the out-house, but he did not allow him to use his master's latrine or to bathe at the well. There was strict untouchability in Bihar. Drops of water from the bucket, the servant thought, would pollute him. Gandhi ate what he had with him, and Rajkumar brought him dates from the bazaar. Mazharul Haq met him at Patna and as directed by him, Gandhi got down at Muzaffarpur with his luggage under his arm and a small tin-box containing some dates and ground-nuts. Kripalani received him at the station with a crowd of students.

Gandhi stayed with Prof. Malkani at whose place Kripalani was staying, as he had just resigned his post at the Government College in Muzaffarpur.

A pressing invitation made Gandhi stay at Gaya Babu's place. Brajkishore Babu and Rajendra Prasad both met him there. Brajkishore acquainted Gandhi with the facts of the case. Barrister's fees in Bihar and Bengal in those days staggered Gandhi, in each case nothing less than four figures merely for an opinion. Before studying the cases, Gandhi thought that he would be able to leave the place in two days, but later he realized that the work might take even two years. The lawyers promised to work under him and even to face imprisonment if it fell to their lot!

Gandhi met Morshead, the Commissioner of the Division, and Wilson, the Secretary of the Planters' Association, and explained to them the object of his visit. They protested against his visiting Champaran and making inquiries into the matter as, according to them, he was an outsider. They considered it an anti-European agitation, and so they feared the excitement as well. It was a century-old grievance. The Indigo concerns, known as Nil Kothis, came into existence in the eighteenth century and by the end of it there were nine concerns in North Bihar under non-official Europeans.

In the first decade of the twentieth century strong feelings were expressed by the ryots against forced indigo cultivation and the feelings burst in. The degradation of the tenantry in Champaran was such that a tenant could not walk with an umbrella opened within a mile of the house of a European.

A secret opposition was set up to fight the tyranny of the planters. The ryots refused to grow indigo. Their leaders were prosecuted but acquitted by the Calcutta High Court. There was a compromise in 1910, but the promises made by the European planters were not kept.

Now it was Gandhi's turn to take up the question. Seeing Macpherson, Chief Secretary, he intimated L. F. Morshead, the Commissioner, that he would visit Motihari and Bettiah to look into the condition of the ryots. A batch of workers gathered round him. Gandhi started for Motihari on elephant back, an elephant being a common conveyance in Champaran.

While Gandhi was on his way to Jasaulipatti W. B. Heycock, the District Magistrate, served a notice on April 16, 1917, directing him to leave the district of Champaran by the first available train. Gandhi replied that he felt bound not to obey that order and added that the Magistrate might take such action as he deemed fit.

Gandhi, however, gave definite instructions to his colleagues to go on with the work of inquiry. A summons was therefore served on him and he was called upon to be present in Court the following morning. The administration was bewildered. Crowds now fearlessly followed Gandhi to the Court. On the same day Gandhi wrote a letter to the Private Secretary of the Viceroy Lord Chelmsford and threatened him with the return of the Kaiser-i-Hind Medal if his humanitarian motive in making the inquiries in Champaran was questioned. He would feel honoured to receive it back when his motive was no longer questioned. Accordingly Gandhi instructed his Ashram men at Ahmedabad to return the Kaiser-i-Hind Medal which they despatched on April 20.

Defying the order politely, Gandhi replied to the notice of George Chandra, S.D.O., that the Commissioner had totally misinterpreted his position. "Out of a sense of public responsibility," he observed, "I feel it to be my duty to say that I am unable to leave this district, but if it so pleases the authorities I shall submit to the order by suffering the penalty of disobedience."

In the Court Gandhi declared on April 18: "I have done so on a pressing invitation to come and help the ryots, who urge that they are not being fairly treated by the Indigo planters I could not render any help without studying the problem. I have, therefore, come to study it with the assistance, if possible, of the administration and planters. I have no other motive and I cannot believe that my coming here can in any way disturb public peace or cause loss of life."

Gandhi added that he could not obey the order without doing violence to his sense of duty to those for whom he had come, and so he had decided to submit without protest to the penalty of disobedience. He disregarded the order not for want of respect for lawful authority, but in obedience to the higher law of being—the voice of conscience. Gandhi pleaded guilty, but the Magistrate would not impose the punishment.

THE CASE WAS adjourned till April 21. And the Government climbed down. The Viceroy intervened and asked the Commissioner to allow Gandhi to continue his work of hearing the ryots. The Government withdrew the case on April 21. Gandhi continued his work and the ryots fearlessly narrated their grievances to him. By this time, a number of social workers from different provinces had gathered round Gandhi. The administration desired Gandhi to dispense with his colleagues, but he did not agree to it. It wanted to malign Brijkishore Prasad whereas his colleague's prestige was a point of honour with him.

By this time Gandhi's co-workers like Rajendra Prasad, Brijkishore, Kripalani and others swelled the ranks. The inquiry confirmed Gandhi in his opinion that the condition of labour in Champaran, was in many respects worse than that of labour in Fiji. When Gandhi was asked to terminate his work, he submitted on May 19 a summary of the preliminary inquiry into the condition of the ryots of Champaran. He requested the Government either to accept the grievances as genuine and redress them or institute an official inquiry. As a result of this, Government was obliged to appoint, on June 10, a committee to go into the matter, Gandhi being the fifth and last member. This committee was called the Sly Committee after its chairman Sir Francis Sly. It submitted its report on October 3, 1917, giving clear recommendations.

Consequently the Champaran Agrarian Bill was passed on November 29 and it became an Act.

Sir Edward Gait, Lieutenant-Governor of Bihar, stood firmly

by the Act. The *tinkathia* system was abolished and the enhancement of rent was cancelled to the extent recommended.

After the appointment of the Sly Committee, the Viceroy had returned to Gandhi the Kaiser-i-Hind Medal towards the end of June 1917.

There were many incidents that cast a sidelight on this struggle. A Government servant secretly provided Rajendra Prasad and his colleagues with a copy of the report he had sent to Government. They took it to Gandhi who refused to read it as it had come to him in a secretive manner. Another incident reveals the depth of Gandhi's respect for truth. The Collector of Champaran had written him a stiff letter, but on second thoughts withdrew it. Gandhi's young followers wanted to make a copy of it, but he did not allow them to do so saying that in that case the letter could not be said to have been withdrawn.[1] While Rajendra Prasad and Gandhiji were returning from a village, the former asked him which Province had the greatest number of persons devoted to the service of the people. He said: "The people of the South are sentimental and clever; the people of Bengal are very sentimental, they have a great capacity for sacrifice, and they have made tremendous sacrifices; but the place of pilgrimage for a person who wants to devote himself to the service of the people is Poona. No other place in the country has so many public institutions run entirely by a selfless body of workers. In Poona, you will come across a great many people who have pledged their lives to the service of the country, and who are fulfilling their pledge with great firmness. I, therefore, look upon it as a place of pilgrimage."[2]

Gandhi devoted himself to the work of education, cleanliness and sanitation in villages in Champaran. He opened schools in which Gujarati and Maharashtrian teachers taught. Mahadeo Desai and his wife, Narhari Parikh and his wife, Kasturba and Anandibai Vaishampayan of Poona, Avantikabai Gokhale of Bombay and Dr. Dev of the Servants of India Society, Soman and Pundalik from Belgaum, joined Gandhi in his social work. Champaran and Bihar throbbed with a new vitality, and the workers who had gathered in Champaran carried back with them new ideals, new thoughts and new aims. And such a campaign required not more than three thousand rupees! It was a model agitation indeed!

Gandhi had to spend a lot of energy. Although he thought he would never fall ill he was laid up with fever which attacked him on alternate days and in the afternoon; still, he carried on his work. While in Champaran he would have boiled rice with the vegetable gravy of the Karaila, a vegetable with a bitter taste.

It was in Bihar that Gandhi gave an impetus to the propaganda of Hindi. He wanted to spread Hindi in South India. While in Champaran, Gandhi was happy that he was working where Rama and Janaki lived and he was hopeful of finding out his Naidus and Sorabjis. His struggle rallied under his banner some selfless and courageous lieutenants to fight for people's demands. And indeed he found them in Rajendra Prasad and Kripalani, the latter proving a matchless scarecrow to *darshan*-seekers of Gandhi.

There was criticism of Gandhi's clothes by one Irwin of Motihari Sugar Factory in the *Pioneer* and the *Statesman*. Gandhi said that except for a short period in India he had worn the dress he was wearing in Champaran and that it was the natural and national dress he wore. He did not go about Champaran barefoot although he avoided shoes for religious reasons.

Gandhi neither worked in the name of the Congress, nor allowed newspapers to harp on the Indigo labourers' grievances and to work upon the feelings of the parties concerned.

Gandhi won his first victory when the Government put an end to the customs cordon between Kathiawad and Bombay Presidency. The second victory came with the abolition of the indenture system. Champaran was the third victory, although some criticized the terms of the Champaran compromise which Gandhi had arrived at. The oppression ceased and the European planters, a short while after the implementation of the report of the commission, sold their lands, factories and livestock and left Champaran. This was the first mass struggle Gandhi led in India, not against British imperialism but against European planters. All these struggles, it may be noted, were political, but were not against British imperialism.

In the meanwhile the political situation in India had deteriorated. In February 1917 Tilak was prohibited from touring the Punjab or going to Delhi to spread his mission of Home Rule.

On June 16, 1917, Besant and her two lieutenants G. S. Arundale and B. P. Wadia were interned at Ootacamund and securities of Rs. 2,000 deposited by Besant on June 5, 1916, for her Press were forfeited. In June 1916 Besant had asked Gandhi to work with her in the Home Rule League. Gandhi refused saying that he did not want to embarrass the British Government which was fighting the Germans. Jawaharlal

Nehru joined both the Home Rule Leagues but worked for Annie Besant's league. Jinnah became President of Besant's Bombay Branch of the Home Rule League in June 1917. Umar Sobani and Shankarlal Banker were secretaries, Kanji Dwarkadas, its treasurer.

These secretaries and treasurer, with Indulal Yajnik and Jamnadas Dwarkadas saw Gandhi in connection with Besant's internment when he had returned for a short while from Bettiah to Ahmedabad for about ten days. But Gandhi told them that he wanted 100 volunteers to walk from Bombay to Coimbatore, a distance of about 1,000 miles, where Besant had been transferred from Ootacamand. So far Gandhi had not taken any active part in the agitation for her release. But on July 7 he wrote a letter to Maffey, Personal Secretary to the Governor-General of India, letting them know his views on the arrest of Besant, as he had gauged the situation while he passed through Bombay and Allahabad. Gandhi, the faithful servant of the British Empire, reveals his real feelings in his letter: "I myself do not like much in Mrs. Besant's method. I have not liked the idea of the political propaganda being carried on during the War. In my opinion, our restraint will have been the best propaganda. The whole country was against me." Then praising Besant's powers of organization and devotion to India he observed, "The Congress was trying to 'capture' Mrs. Besant, the latter was trying to capture the former. Now they have almost become one." He avowed that his life was devoted to preventing the spread of the cult of violence and its uprooting in so far as it had gained a foothold. If his presence, he concluded, was necessary, he was at the disposal of the Viceroy!

Kanji Dwarkadas says[3] that Gandhi wrote this letter to the Government without taking his friends into confidence about it, neither did he give a copy of it to the press. He considered the Viceroy and himself on the same side, impressing upon him that the whole country was against him and that his real worry was that the Congress and Besant had come together! He pleaded with the Government to withdraw the order of internment on Besant not because it was fundamentally wrong but because that act would be a demonstration of strength.

The views expressed in the letter mentioned above were worthy of a Kaiser-i-Hind Medalist and maker of the loyalty speech. The All-India Congress Committee and the Muslim League met at Bombay in the last week of July and passed a resolution demanding the release of Mrs. Besant and the Ali

Brothers. It shows how the two chief political institutions were coming nearer.

At This Time E. S. Montagu, who described the Government of India as 'too wooden, too iron, too inelastic,' to be of any use for modern purposes, was appointed on July 17, Secretary of State for India. And in view of his proposed visit important Indian leaders including some Congress leaders opposed the idea of passive resistance against the Government. The British Government was now compelled to pay adequate attention to the Indian problem. They were depressed by reverses in the war, hard-pressed by the Indian Home Rule Movement and oppressed by the forces of the Indian revolutionaries. So on August 20 the British Government proclaimed through E. S. Montagu, Britain's policy of gradual development of self-governing institutions with a view to progressive realization of responsible Government in India as an integral part of the British Empire.

On August 24 Gandhi addressed a meeting of businessmen held at Ahmedabad to demand the release of Besant. During his stay at Ahmedabad Gandhi met Mahadev Desai 'just the type of young man for whom I have been searching for the last two years.' On September 2 Gandhi spoke at the meeting of the All-India Congress Committee on "passive resistance" and said that it could not be carried on by an institution like the Congress. Tilak spoke in favour of passive resistance. But ultimately an amendment drawn up in agreement with Tilak was passed.

The resolution so amended declared that the measures to put the principles of passive resistance might be held in abeyance and it expressed the hope that the Government would take the necessary steps to allay the bitter feelings aroused among the people by internments and coercive measures. That very day Gandhi wrote to Shankarlal Banker that only men inclined to the ethical way could use the weapon of satyagraha since it was essentially an ethical weapon. During this week it was resolved by the Congress leaders at the instance of Gandhi, to present a public memorandum to Montagu demanding Swaraj, and the work of obtaining signatures of the people to the Congress-League Scheme was begun by the All-India Home Rule Leagues. In Gujarat this work was done by the Gujarat Sabha under its President Gandhi.

Gandhi contributed a paper to the Bombay Provincial

Co-operative Conference held on September 17, 1917. Explaining his new viewpoint in his paper 'The Moral Basis of Cooperation' he said that the co-operative movement would be a blessing to India only to the extent that it was a moral movement strictly directed by men fired with religious fervour. That without character there is no co-operation is a sound maxim, he added. The success of the movement should not be measured by the number of co-operators.

As a good example, he referred to his Satyagraha Ashram which was described by the critics 'as a soul-less soul-force and merely mechanical.'

On October 2 Besant unveiled the portrait of Gandhi in the Gokhale Hall, Madras. Besant and Gandhi differed on their methods but recognised the greatness of each other. On October 6 the All-India Congress Committee and the Muslim League decided at their joint session in Allahabad to send a deputation to E. S. Montagu and to the Viceroy in support of the Congress-League Scheme. The question of passive resistance was dropped, Besant herself being opposed to the idea. It was a great disappointment to the younger leaders.

By October 1917 Gandhi shifted his Ashram from Kochrab to a piece of land on the banks of the Sabarmati, four miles from Ahmedabad. Plague had broken out at Kochrab and it was a danger to the safety of the inmates. The Ashram was now near the Sabarmati Jail and a proper place for a satyagrahi to live by! It was beautifully situated on the banks of the Sabarmati and the site covered a plot of about twenty acres registered under a document on June 13, 1917. The situation and the solitude it offered were appealing. Children bathed in the river. There were no buildings or trees on the land. It was a waste land infested with rats. Gandhi could use it through the help of one Punjabhai Hirachand, a selfless merchant of Ahmedabad. They started living in bamboo huts and had a tin shed for a kitchen till permanent houses were ready. The buildings cost the Ashram about three lakhs of rupees. Dr. Pranjivan Mehta, as usual, spent a considerable amount on it. A shed for hand-weaving was erected and, later, spinning-wheels thrived in it, the spinning which aimed at deposing the satanic mills. Gandhi considered this institution to be the finest thing in the world. It gave him great inspiration although critics told him that it represented a soul-less soul-force and that its severe discipline had made it merely mechanical. "I suppose," Gandhi said once, "both the critics and I are wrong. It is, at best, a humble attempt to place at the disposal of the nation a home where men and women may have scope for free and unfettered development of character in keeping with the national genius."

Dr. Hariprasad Desai told Gandhi that his Ashram stood at a place where the Ashram of Dadhichi had once stood. Gandhi asked Desai who Dadhichi was. Desai replied that he was a sage who supplied Indra, the king of the gods, with his bones to be forged into weapons which the gods used against the demons. Gandhi inspiringly said he would play the role of Dadhichi, mythological hero, when an opportunity offered itself.[4] And indeed he proved himself to be one.

In the second week of October 1917 Gandhi was in Bettiah where he made a speech on cow-protection in which he said that if Hindu society desired others to stop sinning against the cow, they must not sin themselves; they should neither milk it to the last drop nor keep it ill-nourished. Besides, the Hindus should carry on an agitation among the British in India to close down slaughter houses and then persuade the Muslims to stop killing of cows on occasions like Bakri-Id, which was not obligatory. The Hindus should take a pledge that they would bear no ill-will or malice towards Muslims or fight with them. They should bring about a change of heart in the Muslims. It is here that Gandhi introduced the cow question into Indian politics which Congress secular politics had avoided.

In other countries do Muslims kill cows to please God ? The Hindus consider the cow sacred and so the Muslims kill it. Islamic law does not insist upon the slaughter of the cow in Mecca or Medina. So also music is played in all Muslim countries without any objections being raised against it. One of Gandhi's characteristics was that he never rendered advice to or tried to reform the Muslim community although he played the role of an Indian leader. He always poured out his advice to the Hindus. Sir Syed Ahmed, on the other hand, had asked the Muslims to refrain from cow-killing.

Gandhi regarded cow-protection as a religious problem as well as an economic one. He noted that the income from the milk of cows was less than the cost of their maintenance. So *Gaushalas* should be put up, he said, in the neighbourhood of cities and should be made economically independent. Gandhi's emphasis, of course, was on the religious aspect of the question as he considered cow-protection a religious duty. Naturally he later said that the central fact of Hinduism was cow-protection, described the cow as a poem of pity and asserted that Swaraj would be incomplete without cow-protection.

At the reception given to Gandhi on October 11, in Broach, he rightly told the Gujarati merchants that the Bengalis complained that the prices of *dhotis* had been abnormally increased. He further said that patriotism was necessary even for religion and swadeshi was one of the golden keys which would unlock Swaraj to them, he concluded.

On October 20, 1917, Gandhi made a thought-provoking speech at the Second Gujarati Educational Conference in Broach. He observed: "A language mirrors the character of the people who use it, and takes its form from the character and life from the people who speak it." "To impart," he continued, "education without first considering the question of medium of instruction will be like raising a building without a foundation. All education must aim at building character. Harmonious music has the power to soothe the anguish of the soul. Education through a foreign language entails an excessive strain and waste of energy and years. It creates a gulf between the masses and the educated classes."

Even Lord Chelmsford, the Viceroy, Gandhi pointed out, described the prevailing method of imparting education through English as a vicious system. It was wrong, Gandhi said, to keep women in ignorance and suppression, but he thought it a sign of decadence and it was tyrannical to burden them with work which was ordinarily done by men. "A state of affairs," Gandhi opined rather strangely, "in which women have to work as telegraph clerks, typists or compositors can be, I think, no good, such a people must be bankrupt and living on their capital."

Gandhi considered Hindi and Urdu not two different languages but one. He regarded Hindi as the national language written either in Devanagari or Urdu script. Muslim Kings, he noted, could not make Persian or Arabic the national language.

On the following day Gandhi ended a speech to the conference with these words: "Only if I die for India shall I know that I was fit to live." So the craving to die for India always existed at the bottom of his heart.

On the same day, Gandhi described Anandashankar Dhruva, President of the Humanitarian League, as a priceless jewel of Gujarat and told the League that "Jainism and Hinduism are not so different as to justify our treating them as distinct religions. The religion named after Gautam Buddha cherishes the same ideals as Hinduism."

Gandhi made a very important speech as President of the First Gujarat Political Conference which was held on November

3, 1917, at Godhra. Lokamanya Tilak arrived late for the conference and Gandhi, who always insisted on punctuality, was naturally perturbed. He jokingly said that one should not mind if Swaraj too came correspondingly late. He said, "I am but a baby of two years and a half in Indian politics. I cannot trade here on my experience in South Africa." He said: "The conference was the first of its kind in Gujarat and a most important event for Gujarat. The air in the country was thick with cries of Swaraj, which was the goal of the Congress. The ideal of Swaraj did not originate with Besant, but the credit of pressing it to the Indians as a goal realizable in the immediate future belonged to her alone."

The work of taking signatures, he observed, on the Congress-League Scheme was to educate the people about Swaraj. The scheme was not Swaraj, but was a great step towards it. The freedom to err and the power to correct errors was one definition of Swaraj. When India decided to acquire military strength, she would do so in no time. It was painful that the Government had debarred the Indians from military training and had their policy been shaped differently from the beginning they would have that day an unconquerable army. To say that literacy was essential for achieving Swaraj betrays ignorance of history.

"At the time the British rule was established," he proceeded, "it was considered a wise policy for the governance of crores of men to deprive them of arms and military training. But it is never too late to mend, and both the rulers and the ruled must immediately repair the omission."

Meetings and speeches could not make a nation. Instead of killing the Muslim brethren, the Hindus should be ready to die themselves, and if their attempts were pure they would succeed in saving the cow. He hoped that "India will never respect the principle of might being right. She will ever reserve her allegiance to the principle,[6] 'Truth alone triumphs'." Swaraj was useless, concluded Gandhi, at the sacrifice of truth.[5]

GANDHI WAS NOW the effective leader of Gujarat. He was the only effective politician in India after Tilak. In the presence of Tilak, Gandhi purposely gave Besant the credit of pressing the goal of Home Rule. He was all the while being cautious not to say anything about Tilak. He called himself a baby in politics, but he was the *enfant terrible*. He wanted military training for the Indians and yet he deprecated those who fought and killed the enemy and increased hatred of foreign rule and the spirit of revenge. He asked Tilak to engage a Gujarati teacher and pick up Gujarati. But Gandhi could not make a speech in Marathi during his thirty-four years of public life in India. The conference passed a resolution to the Government to release the Ali Brothers.

On November 5 Gandhi addressed the Social Conference at the same place and asked the upper classes to subscribe towards opening and maintaining a school for the Untouchables. Vithalbhai Patel, who held radical social views and was therefore no believer in the caste system, spoke at the meeting. It was here that Gandhi declared that untouchability was a stain on India's forehead. A critic said that in course of time Gandhi's views might change. Gandhi replied that before such a time came, he would have forsaken not only Hinduism but all religion. Hinduism had been burdened with a load of sin in the name of religion and if in the attempt to free Hinduism of this blot, he had to lay down his life, it would be no great matter.

In a message to the Gujarati Stri Mandal (Women's institution) Gandhi said that modern education failed utterly to prepare women for their distinctive role. Women, he rightly added, should not spend their time in a temple unmindful of their tasks. They should not wait on men of holy life who stood in no need of services from others, and should not serve them in all manner of ways. It was unwholesome for both parties and waste of one's time.

At Godhra, Gandhi replied rudely to one of the delegates and then apologised to him in public. When he lost his temper with Kasturba, he confessed at this time, he gave himself 'condign punishment' for doing so. What that condign punishment was none knows. At this time he was in correspondence with Miss Esther Faering who was a member of the Danish Missionary Society. She was drawn to Gandhi as though to a father.

Working in Champaran for a fortnight, Gandhi had an interview with Montagu and Chelmsford at Delhi on November 26 and again with Montagu on November 27, 1917. The Congress delegation and the Home Rule delegation saw them and submitted their memorandum. Montagu was impressed by Besant's personality. She was in white-and-gold embroidered Indian clothes, with short, white hair and the most beautiful voice he had ever heard. Montagu described Tilak as "the

Great Tilak" and observed: "He (Tilak) is at the moment probably the most powerful man in India."

Of Gandhi he says: "Afterwards we saw the renowned Gandhi. He is a social reformer; he has a real desire to find grievances and to cure them, not for any reason of self-advancement, but to improve the conditions of his fellow men." Montagu then refers to his work in South Africa and Champaran and proceeds, "He dresses like a coolie, forswears all personal advancement, lives practically on air and is a pure visionary. He does not understand details of schemes; all he wants is that we should get India on our side. He wants the millions of India to leap to the assistance of the British throne."[6]

Gandhi, wearing a white *kurta*, a *dhoti* and a cap, made a speech at Aligarh on November 28, 1917, where he referred to the Arrah riots and expressed the view that the barbarism exhibited by the Hindus was contemptible and detestable. He advised the Hindus to bridge the gap. Gandhi attended the Calcutta Congress session in the last week of December 1917 where Besant and Tilak were worshipped as heroes. Besant delivered a brilliant speech which was an elaborate thesis on India's self-government.

At the Subjects Committee, the question of the formation of provinces on the basis of language was keenly discussed. Gandhi was of the opinion that the question might await the implementation of the reforms. But Tilak said that the linguistic provinces constituted an essential prerequisite for real Provincial Autonomy and the principle was accepted.

Gandhi spoke at the Congress on British Indians in South Africa. It was at this session that the Congress formally raised the tricolour flag which had been adopted by the Home Rule League. In the Social Service Conference held at Calcutta on December 30, 1917, Gandhi moved a resolution requesting Government and social reform bodies to enforce equality of treatment and provide greater facilities for the education of the depressed classes. M. R. Jayakar supported it. Gandhi told the Bengali Agriculturists' Conference which met under the presidentship of C. R. Das, that he would try to improve the lot of peasants.

Gandhi made a speech at the National Language Conference which was held on December 30, 1917, at the Alfred Theatre in Calcutta under the presidentship of Tilak. Tilak addressed the Conference in English. Gandhi, with the permission of Tilak, asked the listeners to raise their hands if they had understood Tilak's speech in English. Few raised their hands.

Gandhi said it would be a great pleasure if Lokamanya Tilak would speak in Hindi. Gandhi then requested Malaviya to see that at the next Congress no speeches were made in a language other than Hindi. Tilak promised that he would make speeches in Hindi within two months' time. Gandhi himself had a working knowledge of Hindi.

At the Muslim League session held on the last day of December 1917, Gandhi assured the Muslims, amidst loud cheers that Hindus were, to a man, with them in their agitation for the release of the Ali Brothers. He presided over a meeting held on the same day at the University Institute under the auspices of the Bengal and Bombay Humanitarian Funds and appealed to the Hindus to stop the cruel practice of animal sacrifice which was incompatible with the principles of Hinduism. It was at the All-India Social Service Conference that he said that if he wanted to hear music and poetry he would go to Bengal, but he spoke strongly against Bengali provincialism. The audience did not resent it. He said that social service was best performed when the left hand knew not what the right was doing and added that social service to be effective had to be rendered without noise.

Writing about the Calcutta Congress to Rudra, Gandhi said that he had had a very nice time in Calcutta, but not at the Congress. It was all outside the pandal. He was enraptured to witness *Post-office*, a play by Tagore, performed by Tagore and his company. The exquisitely sweet voice of Tagore and equally the exquisite acting by the sick-boy, who is the main character in it, charmed him for a long time. Bengali music had for him, he said, a charm all its own. It had a most soothing effect upon his nerves. He proudly added that he had spoken against Bengali provincialism!

CHAPTER XVII

A Recruiting Sergeant

On The First day of the year 1918 Gandhi made an appeal to the Viceroy to release the Ali Brothers. In his appeal to the Secretary of the Viceroy he said that Government's refusal to discharge them was creating greater and greater dissatisfaction. He was prepared to give an assurance to the Government about their future conduct and to get a public declaration of their loyalty. They would be devoted to their religion and India.

Gandhi wrote to Maganlal Gandhi that he would have to battle with the Government over the release of Mahomed Ali. So, like a man of the world, he asked Maganlal to transfer everything standing in his name to Maganlal so that "in the storm that will follow we do not lose, whether in our wisdom or folly, the money that we have received for the Ashram."[1] He should also replace Gandhi's name by his own wherever money was deposited in the joint names of Gandhi and some other person. Money was deposited in the joint names of Gandhi and Revashankarbhai in a Bombay bank. Gandhi, however, had no tussle or battle over the release of the Ali Brothers and his money was safe!

During the first week of January 1918, he discussed in Bombay with the leaders of the Meghwal (untouchable) community about the conversion and other grievances. Two or three Khojas also were present. The Khojas said, "We are Hindus-Satpanthis." Thereupon Gandhi, true to his philosophy, replied: "Aga Khan was President of the Muslim League. How can you be called Hindus?"

Gandhi spent the latter half of January 1918 in Champaran supervising his social work. In the scheme of this loyalist there was then no serious thought of achieving national independence. He was, in his own words, taking up activities as they came to him. He was dealing with cow-protection, sanitation, a national system of education, hand-weaving and acceptance of Hindi as the lingua franca of India.

At this time two problems in Gujarat were clamouring for solution. The first was the question of the payment of land revenue by the Kheda peasants. The second was the demand for an increase in salary by the Ahmedabad mill workers. For the solution of the first the Gujarat Sabha had been making efforts, but the Collector of Kheda District and the Commissioner of that division did not respond to its demands sympathetically although the Government had declared that due exemptions would be granted in worthy cases. The workers in the Kheda District had kept Gandhi in touch with the developments in Kheda and sought his advice.

Gandhi returned to Ahmedabad from Champaran and took up these questions. Anasuyabehn Sarabhai had sought his advice regarding the rise in the wages of the mill workers. She herself favoured a rise in wages against the will of her brother Ambalal who was a leading mill-owner.

Gandhi, who happened to be in Bombay discussing the Kheda problem with Gokuldas Parekh, Vithalbhai Patel and Dinshaw Wacha and the Governor of Bombay, met Ambalal Sarabhai. Gandhi apprised him of the discontent that was spreading among the mill workers of Ahmedabad over the issue of bonus. The mill-owners had stopped giving the plague bonus and therefore the workers demanded in its place an increase of 50 per cent in dearness allowance.

Gandhi addressed the first meeting of Ahmedabad workers on February 8 and suggested to them that they should follow the path of justice and seek a solution without bitterness by agreeing to arbitration. They should learn to be clean, get rid of their various addictions and see that their children get education. Again, on February 19 he explained to them their responsibility in regard to their problem. Like Ruskin, he advised also the employers to bind the workers to them with the silken thread of love. The right use of money, he said, was to spend on the country.

Meanwhile Gandhi made a speech at the annual gathering of the Bhagini Samaj, a women's welfare organization of Bombay, on February 20, 1918. He paid tributes to Karsandas Chitalia who had dedicated himself to the service of women and expressed his opinion that women should elect their office-bearers from among themselves and give a better account of themselves. The point for them to consider was the degeneration of Indian women relatively to men. Legislation had been mostly the handiwork of men; and man had not been fair and discriminate in performing that self-appointed task.

Child-marriage, the restrictions on widows and such other evils owed their origin to the injunctions in the *Smritis*. That women had been placed on a level with Sudras had done unimaginable harm to Hindu society. The occasional attacks by Christians on the *Smritis* were made with a view to striking at the roots of Hinduism and to showing that its scriptures were imperfect and ordinary books. His own attempt was to show that the imperfection of the Smritis came from interpolated passages and to rid Hinduism of its defects and restore it to pristine glory.

"Woman," Gandhi observed, "is the companion of man gifted with equal mental capacities. She has the right to participate in the very minutest detail in the activities of man and she has an equal right of freedom and liberty with him. She is entitled to a supreme place in her own sphere of activity as man is in his. This ought to be the natural condition of things and not as a result only of learning to read and write. By sheer force of a vicious custom, even the most ignorant and worthless men have been enjoying a superiority over women which they do not deserve and ought not to have. Many of our movements stop half-way because of the condition of our women."[2]

He requested educated Indian women to go out and educate their ignorant sisters about their real condition, the benefits of clear air, clean water, clean and simple food and exercise. There was no justification for men to deprive women of anything they needed or to deny to them equal rights on the grounds of their illiteracy; but education was essential for enabling women to uphold those natural rights, to improve on them and to spread them. Education, therefore, was necessary for women as it was for men. Not that the methods of education should be identical in both cases. Man and woman were of equal rank but they were not identical. They were a peerless pair, being supplementary to one another. Anything that would impair the status of either of them would involve the equal ruin of both. Man was supreme in outward activities and home life was entirely the sphere of woman and therefore in domestic affairs, in the upbringing and education of children, women ought to have more knowledge. Not that knowledge should be divided into watertight compartments or that some branches of knowledge should be closed to anyone. But unless courses of instruction were based on a discriminating appreciation of these basic principles, the fullest life of man and woman could not be developed.

In the end Gandhi sounded a warning to the literary men in India. He said that the habit of deriving pleasure only from a foreign literature was, if they would pardon him the simile, like the thief's habit of deriving pleasure from stolen goods; for that would leave the Indian languages poor.

This was surely a better view of things concerning women than that taken by other contemporary Indian political leaders. It gave a stimulus to the growth and independence of women who soon played a heroic part in the freedom movement of the country. Mahatma Phooley and Mahatma Gandhi were great liberators who helped to break the shackles of Indian women, the third vital force exerted in the field being that of Karve.

On his return from Nadiad to Ahmedabad on February 25, 1918, Gandhi learnt that the Ahmedabad mill-owners had declared general lock-out on February 22. He issued leaflets, seventeen in all, on the mill-hands' struggle, addressed meetings under a *babul* tree on Sabarmati bank and advised his co-workers to feed and clothe the strikers in need. About ten thousand workers were on strike, and another ten thousand came to listen to him on the river bank. He used to narrate his experience in South Africa on the value of non-violence and truth. He frequently discussed the lock-out situation with the co-workers.

AMBALAL SARABHAI WAS the leader of the mill-owners. Gandhi's relations with him were cordial and for some days he stayed with this multi-millionaire in his palatial house in the Mirzapur locality of Ahmedabad. He was the man who had favoured Gandhi's Ashram with money when it was in dire need of help. The mill-owners did not agree to refer the dispute to arbitration.

Gandhi, therefore, asked the mill-workers to go on strike but not to resort to violence or to molest the blacklegs. In the meantime they should earn bread by some other honest means, and should not depend on alms. The workers paraded the streets peacefully.

The lock-out was lifted and the strike was started on March 12. Besant, who was on her way to Bhavnagar, addressed two meetings of the workers. But after a while the workers' faith began to falter. Their enthusiasm began to flag. When Gandhi found that some of the workers were about to return to work on the mill-owners' terms, he asked his followers to picket the mills. Ambalal challenged this behaviour on Gandhi's part and said that if he began picketing, the mill-owners would be driven to unfair means in self-defence.

Gandhi, who always took a decision by intuition, was tricked into advising the workers to return to work on employers' terms if they thought it right to do so. This enraged the majority of his followers to such an extent that they nearly mobbed him and Miss Anasuyabehn Sarabhai, who considered sending for the police. The workers assailed Gandhi for being a friend of the mill-owners, riding in their motor-cars and enjoying meals with them while they were starving. Their faith in Gandhi was weakening. Stung by their taunts, Gandhi declared on March 15, on the spur of the moment, that he would neither eat nor sit in a motor-car until the workers' terms were granted by the mill-owners. It was a moral but coercive measure against Ambalal Sarabhai, his beloved mill-owner, his patron. It frightened both the workers and the mill-owners. And on March 18 they hastily agreed to the appointment of A. B. Dhruva as arbitrator. Gandhi's role as mediator in this wage-struggle brought the workers some relief in the long run.

Gandhi did not fight for the rights of labour. He merely wanted the capitalists to liberalise their policy towards the mill-hands. It was not his intention to free them entirely from exploitation. The Gandhian ideal of peaceful relations between landlords and tenants, capital and labour, preached brotherly love between the exploiter and the exploited. It did not seek to establish a new social order based on new modes of industrial and social relations. The struggle ended with the distribution of sweets among the workers and with the breaking of Gandhi's fast which was a way of expressing his suppressed anger against a beloved person. During this strike Vallabhbhai Patel and Shankarlal Banker, the latter a passionate lover of the Sinn Fein movement, were drawn to Gandhi.

One more point concerning the fast Gandhi undertook deserves mention here. While fasting, he revealed to his disciples in the Ashram the motive behind it. He wanted to convey his message to India that he differed from Tilak in his mode of action. He told his disciples that there was only one person in India over whom millions were "crazy," for whom millions of his countrymen would lay down their lives. That person was Tilak Maharaj. That was a great asset of him, his great treasure. Tilak had written on the inner meaning of the Gita, but Gandhi felt that Tilak had not understood the age-old spirit of India, her soul, and that was the reason why the nation had come to its present pass. Tilak would like Indians to be what Europeans were.

If Tilak, said Gandhi to his disciples, had undergone the sufferings of internment with a spiritual motive, things would not have been as they were, and the results of his internment would have been different. Gandhi thus unburdened his soul to his disciples and tried to impress on their mind his moral and spiritual superiority over Tilak. It was Gandhi's belief that his vow and fast had awakened Indians to the reality of their soul and spread a new consciousness. If that truth were mastered by a few disciples, Gandhi proudly asserted, it would give these few a mastery over the world! He thus revealed the inner side of his soul! His secret target was Tilak. His rival was Tilak! He displayed his moral superiority over Tilak by making the Ahmedabad mill-owners agree to arbitration by means of a fast! Did it ever occur to Tilak to resort to a fast to effect such a change?

And yet Gandhi confessed the next day that the mill-owners acted under pressure of his fast and under duress. He found that his fast was open to criticism from many points of view! For a time a feeling of despair came over him and he bitterly said that if such a feeling came over him again, he would go where they would never be able to seek him out![4] In times of despair, introspection is a great purifier and great men increase their strength by its constant use.

Anxious to recruit disciples, Gandhi, on February 12, 1918, wrote to Vinoba, who had not returned to the Ashram for a whole year, that his character and love fascinated him. He added that he was not fit to measure the worth of Vinoba. He assumed the position of the adoptive father to Vinoba and said that a father was only a father when he had a son who surpassed him in virtue. To Mahadev Desai he said Vinoba was a great man. At the same time, to his sister Raliyatbehn, Gandhi wrote, "I am not in the least ashamed that you have to find the extra money you need by grinding corn for others." The world, Gandhi added, did not regard him as defiled while he was so to her. He asked her to come over and live with him and join him in his work; for, on seeing her he would at least have some recollections of his mother. Another shock came to him from Harilal. He was charged with theft and Gandhi asked him to explain everything to the advocate on the other side. The episode was a terrible blow to him. In anguish he wrote to Harilal that "he was no child. He had lived a thoughtless and self-willed life. He would have died broken-hearted if he had no other sons." To West he wrote that Mrs. West should not consider for one moment that he had forgotten her. New ties and new acquaintances could not make him forget old ones. Early in the year Gandhi suffered from pain in the left side but wrote that he ate too much and was ill at ease and sorry that although 49 he could not bring his palate under control. Nor could he follow his principles in respect of thieving. When thieves attempted to steal things from the Ashram, Gandhi instead of asking, as he did in *Hind Swaraj*, 'to keep your things in the manner most accessible to him' instructed Maganlal to ask someone to sleep in the verandah and send others also to do so.[5]

Gandhi wrote in February 1918 an introduction to Gokhale's speeches which were published in Gujarati. In it he observed that "the true disciple merges himself in the Guru and so can never be a critic of the Guru. *Bhakti* or devotion has no eye for shortcomings. . . . The relationship between the master and the disciple is purely spiritual." Gandhi was Gokhale's disciple and wrote a few days later to Kasturba that it was Maganlal, if anyone, who could carry on his work after him! He was discussing with his disciples non-violence and truth. He said: "Non-violence and truth are convertible terms. . . . Truth and non-violence are the same thing. If anyone vowed to non-violence speaks or acts untruth, he will be violating his vow and if a man dedicated to truth commits violence, he sacrifices truth."[6] This is a reply to those who wrongly believe that when the choice is between non-violence and truth, Gandhism chooses the latter.

About This Time Gandhi wanted to be a member of the Ahmedabad Municipality. He wanted to clean up the city and set an example to other municipalities. He was not a voter. So he asked Hariprasad Desai to enrol him as a practising barrister and even asked him to have a signboard of his name at his dispensary![7] But in the meanwhile the Kheda trouble engaged him and he gave up the idea of becoming a Municipal councillor.

The problem of the Kheda peasants proved to be aggravating. Owing to heavy rains most of the Kharif crops were seriously damaged. Somabhai Kashibhai of Nadiad started a campaign for the total remission of land revenue. In November 1917 a deputation of the agriculturists waited on the Collector of Thasra. After a full discussion, it was decided that 39 villages should be granted suspension of half the revenue, one village full suspension, and the rest full revenue. It was claimed on behalf of the peasants that the suspension was not adequate to the realities of the situation. The orders were resisted by the agitators, and on January 10, 1918, under advice from Gandhi the Gujarat Sabha advised non-payment of the revenue. The Servants of India Society also held an independent inquiry in the matter and reported that some relief was necessary in Matai Taluka only. The Commissioner and the Collector threatened action against defaulters.

Gandhi held discussions with the leaders, and led a deputation to the Governor of Bombay. The Government did not yield. Gandhi then used his European emissary C. F. Andrews to intercede, but to no avail. Finally, he issued an ultimatum to F. G. Pratt, Commissioner, who had asked the workers of Ahmedabad to obey Gandhi during the strike!

On March 22 Gandhi inaugurated satyagraha at a meeting in Nadiad which had been for a long time the headquarters of the Home Rule agitation. The satyagrahis were enjoined to stick to truth, to be fearless and to keep in mind that real bravery lay in receiving rather than in giving blows and that it was mean to run away in the face of danger. The satyagrahis pledged not to pay land revenue and to face the consequences. Propaganda for the satyagraha spread over the district. Supplies of food, drink and shelter to Government servants were stopped. No labourer helped the Government officers. They were socially ostracized. Warnings by bugle were given to villages as soon as an officer arrived. Barbers, potters and priests were dissuaded from doing the customary service for the Government servants. Gandhi encouraged the peasants to keep up satyagraha, walking about barefooted in the scorching sun.

Mohanlal K. Pandya removed onion crop from a field on June 4. He and his co-satyagrahis were sentenced to imprisonment varying from ten to twenty days. Their leader Pandya was later nicknamed onion thief. Vallabhbhai Patel nearly gave up his practice, and Gokuldas Parekh, Mahadeo Desai, Shankarlal Banker and Rajendra Prasad took keen interest in the agitation. Sir Gokuldas Parekh and Vithalbhai Patel led deputations and waited upon the Governor. In a speech Gandhi said the presence of Dr. Rajendra Prasad made him forget the loss of his brothers. Anandibai, a widow, had made up for his want of a daughter.

The peasants were eventually exhausted and Gandhi was waiting for an opportunity to terminate the struggle in a way that would be acceptable to a satyagrahi. He wrote to Sastri in the matter, but he replied curtly that he was not satisfied with the expediency of passive resistance in the Kheda affair. And when at a Bombay meeting a resolution was moved by Gandhi on the Kheda satyagraha, Sastri, the President, ruled it out on the ground that seven days' notice of the resolution had not been given. All except Sastri had agreed to the resolution. Yet Gandhi wrote to Sastri that his 'no' had a real value for him. The 'Ayes' had no value at all!

On April 20 the Collector had given orders granting total remission to those who were poor. But it was left to the Government officers to determine who were poor, and the terms were repeated on May 22 to Mamlatdars in the district. Gandhi avidly clung to the offer and agreed to it.

On June 6 Gandhi exhorted the peasants at Nadiad to pay up the land revenue without delay. When he left the place, nobody went to see him off! Only 8 per cent of the land revenue was in arrears and most of it was subsequently recovered. Yet Gandhi thought he had won a victory! Later he wrote in his autobiography that although the termination was celebrated as a triumph of satyagraha, he could not enthuse over it, as it lacked the essentials of a complete triumph! Which satyagraha by Gandhi fulfilled the essentials of a complete triumph? His much-trumpeted victory did not bring any material remission of land revenue. But in one respect it was indeed a moral victory for the struggle, since it inspired the people of Gujarat with a new spirit. They became bolder than ever, prepared themselves for sacrifices and lost their fear of jail! During the struggle, processions escorted the prisoners to jail. It taught the workers and leaders to establish contact with the rural life of the peasants and develop the capacity for sacrifice. "It is our firm belief," concluded Gandhi, "that the people of Kaira have truly served their own cause, as well as the cause of Swaraj and the Empire." The Empire was in danger and he promised to recruit men for it. On April 30 he had written to the Viceroy to relieve him from the Kaira struggle for recruitment by removing the grievances of the peasants.

Gandhi was thinking of giving a further stimulus to the spread of Hindi. He wrote to Gurudev Tagore seeking his views on the lingua franca of India. Tagore replied that Hindi was certainly the possible national language for inter-provincial communication in India. But he thought that they could not enforce it for a long time. Gandhi's interest in the spread of Hindi was unflagging. He had deputed Swami Satyadev to spread the knowledge of Hindi in Southern India. So in recognition of his service to Hindi, Gandhi was elected President of the Hindi Sahitya Sammelan held at the Town Hall in Indore on March 29, 1918, for three days. This was the eighth session, the first being presided over by Pandit Madan Mohan Malaviya at Benares in 1910. Purushottamdas Tandon and Rajendra Prasad were among its leaders. In his presidential address Gandhi urged the people to abandon the use of English entirely and to raise Hindi to the high status of a national language. The people in India should do their correspondence and conversation in Hindi and their official language should be Hindi.

Although he defined Hindi as the language which was spoken in the North by Hindus and Muslims, written in the Nagari or the Persian script, neither too Sanskritised nor too Persianised. To him, the 'village Hindi' was the best. He asked the Sammelan to train good Hindi teachers to take up the work of spreading Hindi in Southern India, to insist on Hindi being used in national councils and in the Congress session. The lead Gandhi gave to the spread of Hindi showed his emphasis on national unity and integration.

At Indore Gandhi also spoke on Indian civilization. He urged the people to have faith in it and not to adopt the ways of the West, for Western civilization, he observed, was satanic. Truth and non-violence should be their goal. Without an unshakable faith in them they would make no progress, nor would they save the cow by killing Muslims.

The Indore Government officers served the guests rich food in silver plates. Gandhi ate simple food and asked the officers to serve his men simple food. In a statement issued to the press Gandhi said that he had faith enough in the patriotism, selflessness and sagacity of the Tamil and Telugu people and knew that those who wanted to render national service or to be in touch with the other Provinces, could undergo the sacrifice, if it was one, of learning Hindi. What did the Tamilians do?

Obsessed with Hindu-Muslim unity, Gandhi thought that his ahimsa would be put to the test on that question and that God was putting him on his trial. Naturally, the thought of the release of the Ali Brothers was on Gandhi's mind for the previous four months. Shuaib Qureshi, editor of *New Era*, met him in the first week of April 1918 in connection with it.

Mahomed Ali used to write long letters to Gandhi from Betul and Chhindwada where the Ali Brothers were interned. On April 10 Gandhi wrote again to J. L. Maffey, Secretary of the Viceroy, urging the Viceroy to release them, and said if they should betray his trust he would lay down his life for it.

In the letter, Gandhi expressed his sorrow at the worry he was causing the Government. He humbly and loyally added: "I seem to be ever worrying the administrators in the country when as a respectable citizen of the Empire I should be taking my share in the war. I should have felt happier being in Mesopotamia or France. I twice offered my services but they were not accepted. I feel ashamed that since my arrival in India I can show no war work record in the conventional sense of the term."[8]

NATURALLY GANDHI WAS invited to the War Conference which the Viceroy Lord Chelmsford held on April 26, 1918. Tilak and Besant were not invited. On April 26 Gandhi wrote to Sir Claude Hill that the conference would not be successful as Tilak, Besant and the Ali Brothers were excluded from it. He also warned the Government against accepting or initiating conscription.

Gandhi rightly insisted upon the inclusion of leaders like Besant and Tilak. Writing about the exclusion of Tilak, Montagu said: "With regard to Tilak if I were the Viceroy I would have had him at Delhi at all cost. He is at the moment probably the most powerful man in India."

The next day Gandhi wrote to Maffey, the Secretary of the Viceroy, urging the release of the Ali Brothers and having a prolonged interview with Maffey and the Viceroy, he agreed to join the War Conference as a matter of duty as well as out of his great regard for Lord Chelmsford. On April 28 he wrote to Maffey to obtain the permission of the Viceroy to allow him to deliver his speech in Hindi. The Viceroy was very keen on Gandhi's supporting the resolution regarding recruiting. He consented. So making a speech on April 28 at the War Conference, Gandhi said briefly: "I considered myself honoured to find my name among the supporters of this resolution. I realize its meaning and I tender my support to it with all my heart." Tilak's lieutenant G. S. Khaparde tried to move the Home Rule resolution at the War Conference, but it was not included in the Agenda.

Gandhi said that many congratulated him on his having spoken in Hindustani. That was, they said, the first instance within living memory of anyone having spoken in Hindustani at such a meeting. Although he supported the imperialist war and gave the go-by to his moral values of non-violence, Gandhi seemed to have been much elated at this achievement at the War Conference. Writing about it to Harilal, he warmly observed: "I have done something very big in Delhi." That big something was the ungrudging, unequivocal and unconditional support he lent to the Empire through Hindi!

After the conference was over, Gandhi wrote two letters to the Viceroy. In the first he promised to make India offer all her able-bodied sons as a sacrifice to the Empire at its critical moment, and added that nothing less than a definite vision of Home Rule to be realized in the shortest possible time would satisfy the Indian people. In the second he pleaded for allowing him to interview the Ali Brothers. He sent these letters with the Rev. Mr. Ireland, a missionary of the Cambridge Mission, to the Viceroy at Simla. It was now an established practice with Gandhi to use European messengers to carry his message or letters to British Governors or Governor-General.

Having promised the Government at the War Conference to offer able-bodied Indians as a sacrifice to the Empire the votary of non-violence reached Nadiad and held discussions with Vallabhbhai Patel and others regarding the recruiting campaign. In Delhi, Sir William Vincent had asked him point-blank whether he had brought the authorities a single recruit. Gandhi felt the insult keenly and the next day wrote to him that it was not a fair question, one might truly serve the Empire and yet not bring a single recruit!

Gandhi, the votary of non-violence, who discovered a weapon of non-violence to end violent strife in the world, supported a war and promised to recruit men to fight the war to end war. On his return to Delhi he had a talk with Vallabhbhai and other workers regarding the recruitment.

Gandhi's optimism for military recruitment, however, received a rude shock. It was now difficult to get a car on hire in Nadiad, to say nothing of volunteers. He travelled along in the district about 20 miles a day, carrying his food in his satchel, for it was idle to expect people to feed him and his recruiting assistants. He addressed meetings at Nadiad, Kathlal, Karamsad, Godhra, Jambusar and Vadlhai. He addressed a meeting for military recruitment under the presidentship of Pratt, the Commissioner. The people asked him, "You are a votary of ahimsa, how can you ask us to take up arms? What good has Government done for India to deserve our co-operation?"

But Gandhi was not a man to lose face and heart. He used leaflets and made speeches asking people to enlist as recruits to fight the war to end war. Vallabhbhai Patel worked as a recruiting sergeant. Gandhi said at Patna on May 25 that some seven or eight lakhs were serving outside India and another five lakhs were to be recruited. The opportunity of obtaining self-government, he added, did not mean dismissal of the British from India. The English race had two outstanding characteristics: they lived in friendship with those who knew how to die and those who knew how to kill. Cats could not be friends of mice. In the first place then they must learn to die, but if they could not do that, they should learn to die while killing. Two essentials were necessary for self-government, power over the army and power over the purse. So they should not miss military training and opportunities to assist the empire! At another place he said that voluntary recruiting was a key to Swaraj and would give the Indians honour and manhood. On June 24 he fervently exhorted the people of Ahmedabad to take to careers in the army in order to wipe out the blot on Gujarat. Criticizing this Patna speech, the *Modern Review* asked Gandhi, a thorough-going ahimsaist, whether the suggestion and the exhortation were consistent with ahimsa and soul-force.

The fact was that Gandhi's doctrine of non-violence so far fluctuated with his feeling and emotion rather than reason. European pacifists would try to base their doctrine on reason. That the discoverer of the weapon of satyagraha would show such fluctuations and should promote the war to end war was the tragedy of the author of satyagraha!

At this time Gandhi was called to direct many activities. Attending a Depressed Classes Conference convened by Karmaveer Vithal Ramji Shinde on May 5, 1918, at Bijapur, he was surprised to see that no Untouchable was present at the Conference. He told the gathering that it was useless to waste their time, and that they were like parrots endlessly repeating Narayan, Narayan. He added that he would advise Bhai Shinde to give up calling such conferences and engage himself in solid work. Genuine feeling alone, he added, would ensure results, not any unnatural efforts.

On June 23, 1918, Gandhi issued from Nadiad his famous appeal to the people of Kheda District in particular and of Gujarat in general: "If we want to learn the use of arms with the greatest possible despatch, it is our duty to enlist ourselves in the army. There can be no friendship between the brave and the effeminate. We are regarded as a cowardly people. If we want to become free from that reproach, we should learn the use of arms."

"The easiest and straightest way to win Swaraj," Gandhi declared, "is to participate in the defence of the Empire. If the Empire perished, with it perishes our cherished aspirations. Some will say that if we do not secure those rights just now, we would be cheated of these afterwards. The strength we employ in defending the Empire now can secure those rights. If we want Swaraj, it is our duty to help the Empire and we shall undoubtedly get the reward for that help."[8]

Gandhi offered the services of five persons from the Ashram, but he excluded from recruitment Devdas as he was doing the work of spreading Hindi. Manilal was doing important work in South Africa. Harilal was not likely to go, and Ramdas did not feel happy if he had to leave one job and take up another. Gandhi thus excluded all his sons from being recruited!

Gandhi's friend Charles Andrews did not approve of Gandhi's recruiting campaign. He criticized Gandhi, saying that he was deluding himself, and his activity might injure the service to the cause of ahimsa.

Gandhi justified his *volte-face* and said, "There was a danger of those who put faith in my word becoming or remaining utterly unmanly, falsely believing that it was ahimsa. We must have the ability in the fullest measure to strike and then perceive the inability of brute force and renounce the power. Jesus had the power to consume his enemies to ashes, but he refrained and permitted himself to be killed for he so loved."[9] If ability to strike was the prerequisite for being a satyagrahi, did any satyagrahi ever prove the ability to strike in the fullest measure?

Logic, consistency and reason were not the strong points of Gandhian thinking. Whenever he was cornered, he later said, "My aim is not to be consistent with my previous statements on a given question but to be consistent with truth as it may present itself to me at a given moment."[10]

Some months earlier Gandhi had defied humanitarianism. According to him, it did not mean saving a definite number of lives. It was the property of the soul. There was no room for arithmetic in humanitarianism. "Unclean flour," he proceeded, "is infested with numberless lives. To preserve such flour is no humanitarianism. Numberless vermin perish even in the process of keeping our bodies clean."

On June 10, 1918, the Government of Bombay also held a War Conference at the Town Hall in Bombay. Among the invitees were B.G. Tilak, M.K. Gandhi, M.A. Jinnah, Jamnadas Dwarkadas, B.G. Horniman, N.C. Kelkar and others. On the previous night Tilak and Gandhi had a discussion at which Gandhi said that Tilak's methods were devilish. Tilak answered that had Gandhi undergone the tribulations and trials he had, he would have been more devilish than he was. Gandhi, however, at the instance of Tilak, decided not to attend the Conference. Accordingly, he wrote to L. Robertson, the Secretary of the Governor, that as men like Tilak were not included on the Man-Power Committee, he feared that his usefulness would be materially curtailed if he could not have the benefit of his co-operation and that of the other Home Rule leaders of his calibre. Yet Gandhi changed his opinion and attended. The conference began under the chairmanship of Lord Willingdon, the Governor of Bombay, on June 10. The chairman interrupted Tilak when he said that defence and Swaraj were interlinked. He gagged Kelkar, B. G. Horniman, Jamnadas Dwarkadas and S. R. Bomanji, who silently 'walked out.' Jinnah and Gandhi did not leave the conference. Jinnah did not vote when the resolution was put to vote.

The next day Gandhi wrote to the Governor that his gagging all the leaders would be resented as an insult to a great and growing party in the country. His action had made the position of the workers delicate and difficult, and if Tilak was the enemy of the Empire, the Governor had undoubtedly strengthened his hands in the pursuit of his course.

As a result of this walk-out, the Chief Secretary of the Bombay Government was thinking of interning these leaders. Later Jinnah, however, avenged the insult by routing a proposal for raising a public memorial to Lord Willingdon for which the latter never forgave him.

On June 16, 1918, Gandhi made a speech in Bombay when he said that Tilak was the idol of the people and his word was law to them. The insult offered to him and through him to the Home Rule Leagues, was, therefore, an insult to the nation at large.

Tilak told Gandhi that Government was not sincere about its offer. He said that recruits enlisted in India for the army should be eligible for training in the military colleges and for higher posts, and commissions should be open to them. If Indian youths were given such an assurance, he would secure 5,000 recruits within six months. If he failed to do so, he would forfeit a sum of Rs. 50,000 for which he enclosed a cheque.

Gandhi's help was unconditional while Tilak's was conditional, So Gandhi returned the cheque to Tilak.

Early in July 1918, the report of the Montagu-Chelmsford Reforms was published. Tilak, the foremost leader of India, described the reforms as 'a sunless morning,' a useless and unacceptable scheme. Besant declared that the reforms were "unworthy of England to offer and unworthy of India to accept." On August 1 Gandhi declared that it was good in parts but also strange in some parts and added that Indians were not entitled to Swaraj till they came forward to enlist in the Army!

Gandhi made strenuous efforts to supply the Government with military recruits and spent his energy, time and goodwill in the propagation of army recruitment. The strain proved unbearable. While at Nadiad, he was taken seriously ill with dysentery on August 11, 1918. Dr. Talwalkar and Dr. Kanuga examined him. On August 23, he was brought back from Nadiad to Ahmedabad and kept in the palatial bungalow of Ambalal Sarabhai. His faith in God was boundless and undying. He said he followed his will and no other; for Nature was God and God was love. Later he wrote to C. F. Andrews that his illness was a just punishment for his recruiting campaign.

As his illness took a serious turn, he said "If I am to die, it is best to be in my Ashram." So he was taken to the Ashram on September 7.

During his illness Gandhi was depressed and dejected. One day he bitterly wept in the Ashram as he said he had no peace of mind. He thought for a while that he was spending his life in incomplete jobs. Before he completed his work at the Ashram, he went to Champaran; before he completed it he went to take up the problem of the Kheda peasants and before he was half-way through that he took to recruiting, and then he fell ill! Rajendra Prasad, his lieutenant, calmly listened to his outburst! As he was unwell and also had differences of opinion with the Congress leaders as also with the Moderate leaders, he could not attend the special session of the Congress which was held on August 29, 1918, to consider the Montagu-Chelmsford Reforms. V. J. Patel was the chairman of the Reception Committee and Hasan Imam presided over the Congress session. The resolution on the reforms proposals declared that they were disappointing and unsatisfactory and suggested some modifications. After the Congress session was over, the Moderates parted company and started the All-India Moderates Conference to work out the reforms that had been offered. Their first President was Surendranath Banerjee. From their third session at Madras they assumed the name The National Liberal Federation.[11]

Gandhi was extremely weak and suffered an excruciating pain from piles. One day, after the Ashram prayers, parts of the *Pilgrim's Progress* were read out, Gandhi, spoke on the greatness of this commentary on the Bible and said it was as good as Tulsidas's *Ramayana.* He said Tilak Maharaj wrote his *Gita-Rahasya* in jail, as Bunyan wrote his *Pilgrim's Progress* in jail.

On October 1, 1918, he was at death's door. All the inmates of the Ashram gathered round his sick-bed, said prayers and recited his favourite verses from the second chapter of the Gita. According to the Indian calendar, Gandhi's birthday was on that day.

Gandhi told his disciples that it was not possible for anyone to measure the worth of a man before his death. Even after his death it took some time to assess it.

Gandhi's erstwhile colleagues Kachalia and Sorabji S. Adajania were dead. He publicly grieved over their loss. His illness was protracted. His doctors were helpless before his cranky ideas about curing the malady. At this critical moment Dr. Talwalkar introduced Kelkar to him. Kelkar had studied at the Grant Medical College, Bombay, but not taken a degree. He was a Brahmo Samajist. Kelkar, whom Gandhi described as a crank like himself, applied his ice treatment. It infused a new hope and a new energy in Gandhi and a strong desire to live. He soon thought he was out of danger. On doctors' advice Gandhi left Ahmedabad on November 29 and went to Matheran for a change of air and returned to Bombay in the second week of December. He stayed in Mani Bhavan owned by Revashankar Jhaveri, on Laburnum Road, Gamdevi, Bombay.

During his illness there were ups and downs. He took fifteen hypodermic injections and his appetite improved, but the needle pricks were unpleasant. He was now gradually ignoring his vow not to use Western medicines. He wrote to Srinivas Sastri, P. C. Ray, Mahomed Ali and Sarojini Naidu that he would not get out of his self-imposed restrictions. "I should be false to God and man and to myself," he solemnly explained to them, "if I disregarded my vow taken after the fullest deliberation and in anticipation of all the consequences that have followed it." He regarded the sickness as a trial and temptation for him. If he broke the restrictions he felt that he would be perfectly worthless. These restrictions restricted the body, but they freed the soul.

But at last the human mind of the Mahatma yielded. The will to live proved stronger than the devotion to truth and nature cure, let alone the remedies he insisted upon in the illnesses of others. Piles tormented him. Physical weakness and mental torpor overpowered him. Kasturba's soul was in torment. She stood by the sick-bed speechless. The doctors persisted in their appeal that Gandhi should take milk. Kasturba anxiously and gently said that when he took the vow, goat's milk was not in his mind at all. He yielded. He said his vow related only to cow's milk, and when he took the vow, he was not thinking of the goat at all. Although he did not think of the buffalo either, he did not take buffalo's milk as it would have broken his vow. He said by taking goat's milk he now relieved his friends of much of their concern. He let the doctor inject arsenic, strychnine and iron and drank goat's milk which he now discovered to be richer than that of the cow. When Narahari Parikh said he should have given up the vow straightway instead of putting a new interpretation upon it and gradually breaking it, and when others charged him with self-deception, Gandhi confessed at the first blush that his vow did not retain its full value.[10] But after ten days he doggedly observed that "personally I feel convinced that I have fully succeeded in observing my vows with the utmost strictness."

On January 27, 1919, he declared: "And I would even go so far as to maintain that the fact of big loopholes being left in both my vows is evidence of their utter sincerity." Narahari Parikh, his co-worker, still criticized him. It was the practice of Gandhi to allow his friends and co-workers to fondly criticize him and to drown their criticism in the divine justification of his lapses and foibles. In his autobiography, however, he confessed that he adhered to the letter of the vow and killed the spirit of the vow, the soul of the vow. It was a breach of the vow. The ideal of truth, he added sorrowfully, required that vows taken should be fulfilled in the spirit as well as in the letter. He rigidly adhered to his fads and faiths in respect of the illness of his wife, sons and relatives, but he compromised his principles whenever his own life was in danger. This was a prelude to many such lapses on the part of Gandhi.

On January 20, 1919, Gandhi was operated upon by Dr. Dalal for fissures. At the time of the operation he was given morphia by injection. Gandhi, the author of *Hind Swaraj*, who condemned European medicine and its practice of vivisection, himself embraced it to save himself from the clutches of death.

Besides the violation of the milk vow, this was another violation of his principles!

The Congress was held at Delhi in December 1918. Owing to illness, Gandhi could not attend. Tilak, although elected President, could not attend either. He was in England. The Congress under the presidentship of Malaviya demanded self-determination for India and elected Lokamanya Tilak, Gandhi and Syed Hasan Imam to represent India at the Peace Conference.

CHAPTER XVIII

Miscalculations and Massacres

MEANWHILE, GERMANY HAD been defeated and Britain and the Allies won World War I declaring armistice on November 11, 1918. Gandhi said that the Germans were defeated not because they were necessarily in the wrong, but because the Allied Powers had greater brute force. The conflagration in Europe ended but was smouldering in Turkey.

At this juncture the Government of India was busy with the Rowlatt Committee's Report and its recommendations. The Committee, known as the Sedition Committee, was appointed on December 10, 1917, and was headed by Mr. Justice Rowlatt to investigate and report on the nature and extent of the criminal conspiracies connected with the revolutionary movement in India and to advise as to legislation to enable Government to deal effectively with them. The Sedition Committee presented its report to the Government on April 15, 1918. Tilak was depicted in it as the source of all revolutionary deeds and the brain behind them.

The report and recommendations of the Sedition Committee were denounced by the Special Congress held in Bombay on August 29, 1918. The Defence of India Act was to cease existing six months after the expiry of World War I. Naturally the Indian Government was in a hurry to replace it by some measures which would empower them to curtail the freedom of the people. The two Rowlatt Bills embodying the recommendations of the Rowlatt Committee were published on January 18, 1919 in the *Gazette of India*, and on February 6 and 10 were introduced in the Central Legislative Council to the horror of the Indian people.

Indians, who believed that the war was waged for the freedom of all, helped the British in their time of need. A wave of demands for self-determination for the nations and of democracy was sweeping over the old world and everywhere there was clamour for a new international order. The future of Turkey, the revolt of Ireland and the Russian revolution exerted a tremendous influence on Indian public opinion. At such a time the British Government threw at the people the two drastic Rowlatt Bills, depriving them of their most elementary human rights—Bills unparalleled in the laws of any modern civilized State. Conditions were favourable for an agitation. Through her opposition to the Rowlatt Bills, India was entering upon the third stage of her struggle. India had already gone through the stages of awakening and organization and the third stage of rising in revolt had come.

Tilak was in England. He had lost his case against Chirol, as the jury and the judge looked upon it as a Government case. If Tilak succeeded, they thought, it would be a disaster for the Indian Government.

Now Gandhi was, besides Tilak and Das, the only leader of stature in a position to give a lead to the nation. To him this was a lifetime's opportunity! The road to leadership was almost open, there being Mrs. Annie Besant in the way who could be removed without much trouble! The Home Rule workers and others looked to Gandhi for a lead. Shankarlal Banker announced at a Bombay meeting on February 2, 1919, presided over by Pandit Madan Malaviya, the message of Gandhi who was convalescing in Bombay. Through his message Gandhi declared that if the Rowlatt Bills were passed and became law, the Montagu-Chelmsford Reforms, whatever their value, would be absolutely worthless.

Gandhi wrote to Madan Mohan Malaviya, Srinivas Sastri and Vijayaraghavachariar seeking their views on the Rowlatt Bills. He stated that if Government brought in the obnoxious law, the people would be entitled to defy their other laws also. He declared that the Bills were the aggravated symptoms of a deep-seated disease. Mrs. Annie Besant called on Gandhi on January 20, 1919, to inquire after his health. She requested him to join the deputation sponsored by her to give evidence before the Joint Select Committee in London. Malaviya wanted him to join the Congress deputation to England.

Gandhi refused to join either as he said he had lost faith in the efficacy of deputations. The Rowlatt Bills agitated his mind and he decided to start a civil disobedience movement.

Gandhi had not recovered from his illness. He was advised to take a three-month holiday and for some time he even thought of a sea-voyage. But now he gave up that idea and was about to return to his Ashram in Ahmedabad. Besant spoke at a meeting held in Bombay to protest against the Rowlatt Bills. There, she voiced her fears and anxiety about the proposed civil disobedience movement. The audience interrupted her speech which they did not like. The next day the nationalist papers harshly criticized her for her discordant note. From that day she began to gradually lose her popularity.

On February 10, 1919, Gandhi returned to his Sabarmati Ashram and gently remonstrated with the Ashramites who were displeased with Maganlal on many counts. Gandhi replied to them that Maganlal was wedded to an ideal. If he sent away Maganlal, one of his creations, he would be the only person left in the Ashram.

Gandhi then wrote to Maffey, the Secretary of the Viceroy, that if the Government did not release the Ali Brothers, he would embark on satyagraha. According to Gandhi, the Ali Brothers were brave and perfectly straightforward. They were outspoken, God-fearing and able men, commanding the respect alike of the Mohammedans and the Hindus.

Gandhi now sensed satyagraha in the air. He summoned a meeting of Home Rule workers at his Sabarmati Ashram on February 24, 1919. Vallabhbhai Patel, Sarojini Naidu, B. G. Horniman, Umar Sobani, Shankarlal Banker, Anasuyabehn Sarabhai and Jamnadas Dwarkadas attended it. They issued a satyagraha pledge, Gandhi's manifesto and leaflets containing extracts from Thoreau and advice to volunteers.

Among the more important signatories to the satyagraha pledge were Gandhi, Vallabhbhai Patel, Anasuyabehn Sarabhai, Indulal Yagnik, B. G. Horniman, the editor of *Bombay Chronicle*, Jamnadas Dwarkadas, Sarojini Naidu, Umar Sobani, Shankarlal Banker, Dr. D. D. Sathe and Dr. N. D. Savarkar.

Gandhi then sent a strongly-worded telegram to the Secretary of the Viceroy asking the Government to reconsider the decision on the Rowlatt Bills. At first Gandhi wanted to restrict the movement to a few selected individuals and he wanted them to take the pledge of speaking the truth and developing soul-force. A new institution called Satyagraha Sabha was formed and Gandhi became its president. At its meeting Horniman opposed the condition in the pledge to speak the truth because, he said, an editor could not always speak and write the truth.

L. R. Tairsee ridiculed the idea of soul-force. This ridicule and criticism at first upset Gandhi. But the others eventually put up with Gandhi's peculiar views. He was, however, outvoted at one of the meetings in regard to his proposed restrictions, changed his original intention and accepted the resolution without the pledges! Branches of the Satyagraha Sabha were established all over India.

Besant was against a mass movement. She came again to Bombay to dissuade Gandhi from launching such a movement as she feared that it would lead to violence and rioting and every kind of violent upheaval and end in mob frenzy. She added that the spirit of lawlessness would result in loss of respect for the laws even in self-governing India. So on March 5 she again addressed a meeting in Bombay and spoke fervently against the agitation and became unpopular. Gandhi never forgot or forgave her for this opposition, although he presided over her birthday-meeting just to show his condescending magnanimity. Wacha, Banerjee, Sastri, Shafi and others too issued a joint manifesto against passive resistance. But the Bengal nationalists as well as the nationalists at Allahabad and Delhi supported Gandhi.

The Home Rule workers, who had been drawn to Gandhi, decided to overthrow Besant's leadership. They seized an early opportunity to do so. Just then Besant, as she wanted to lead a deputation to London, saw the Home Secretary, Sir James Dubolaix, in connection with her passport. Her meeting was misconstrued and at a Bombay meeting of the Home Rule workers attended by Jinnah, C. P. Ramaswami Aiyer, Umar Sobani, Shankarlal Banker, P. K. Telang and Kanji Dwarkadas, Jinnah and Aiyar made it clear that Besant should leave the Home Rule League. She said that if her erstwhile colleagues did not want her any more she would gladly leave and fight alone. She left the meeting after making that statement. Telang, Kanji Dwarkadas and Jamnadas Dwarkadas left with her. On her resignation, Besant started her own National Home Rule League. How these leaders soon installed Gandhi, a Swadeshi leader, in the gadi of the Home Rule League in place of Mrs. Besant's "foreign leadership" will be seen at the proper place.[1]

On March 3, 1919, Gandhi left Bombay for Delhi. On March 5 he interviewed the Viceroy Lord Chelmsford at Delhi. Describing his talk with the Viceroy, he said that the talk was cordial, but he added, an Englishman would not be argued into yielding; he yielded only under compulsion. Gandhi then saw the Ali Brothers and the Nawab Saheb at Rampur and returned to Delhi. During his stay in Delhi Gandhi attended the proceedings of the Legislative Assembly on the occasion of the debate on the Rowlatt Bill and heard Sastri's spirited and eloquent attack on the Bill. He saw the Viceroy listening attentively to Sastri's speech. This was the only time Gandhi attended the Council debates.

GANDHI THEN STARTED his campaign against the Rowlatt Bills in right earnest. At Delhi he declared at a meeting that satyagraha alone could rid India of violence and the patient suffering of the Indian people was bound to bend the mightiest power. He revealed his mind to Srinivas Sastri in a letter dated March 8, 1919, saying that he and others would soon think with Gandhi that nothing but an energizing activity which satyagraha certainly was, could have prevented the ambitious and high-spirited youths of the country from taking up a questionable activity for want of a better one. Gandhi's hand shook as he wrote, at this stage in his life. And he soon got fatigued. This weakness persisted. But activity was Gandhi's unfailing medicine. Despite the weakness he toured the country. As he could not deliver his speeches, they were read out in his presence at Allahabad, Lucknow and Bombay.

On March 14, 1919, Gandhi's speech was read out at a meeting in Bombay in which he declared that six hundred men had signed the pledge in the Presidency. Satyagraha, he added, was not a threat, it was a fact, and even the mighty Government of India would have to yield if they were true to their pledge.

The pledge meant a change of heart. It was an attempt to introduce the religious spirit into politics. "We may no longer believe," he proceeded, "in the doctrine of tit for tat; we may not meet hatred by hatred, violence by violence, evil by evil; but we have to make a continuous and persistent effort to return good for evil." Swami Shraddhanand attended the meeting and was to go to Gandhi's Sabarmati Ashram. Gandhi instructed Maganlal to 'drench him with love'.

Two days later, Gandhi left for Madras on a tour of the Presidency to prepare the people for the coming struggle. On March 18 the Rowlatt Bill was passed despite the opposition from non-official members and the united opposition of all sections in the country. Surendranath Banerjee spoke vigorously against it; Srinivasa Sastri attacked it angrily, and Jinnah attacked it mercilessly. All this gave an edge to Gandhi's speeches aimed at driving the people towards the struggle.

Gandhi spoke at Madras, Tanjore, Trichinopoly, Madurai,

Tuticorin and Nagapattam. He tried to impress upon the people that satyagraha was a religious movement and an attempt to introduce the religious element in politics, as he thought that the people of India would be best appealed to by religion. Gandhi, like Tilak before him, knew that religion and renunciation were the sources of power in India. And well did he utilize these sources. The examples of Pralhad and the three South Indians—Nagappan, Narayanswami, Valliamah—heroes in the South African struggle, were cited. People were asked to fast on April 6, 1919, to suspend all business and to hold meetings asking the Secretary of State for India to veto the Rowlatt Act. At Madras he said that if Sir William's fear as to violence was realized, it would undoubtedly be a disaster. In the parting message to the people of Madras, at a meeting held on March 30, he replied to those who argued that satyagraha movement would only accentuate the fear they had of the onrush of Bolshevism. "The fact," he observed, "however, is that if anything can possibly prevent this calamity descending upon our country, it is satyagraha. Bolshevism is the necessary result of modern materialistic civilization. Self-indulgence is the Bolshevic creed, self-restraint is the satyagraha creed."[2]

Gandhi flatteringly said that he always felt at home in the South. The extreme religiosity of the South appealed to him. He met Vijayaraghavachariar and S. Kasturiranga Ayyangar but he found in C. Rajagopalachari (Rajaji) an asset to his struggle. Gandhi was his guest at Madras. Mahadev Desai asked Gandhi to cultivate the man. Rajaji had started law-practice at Madras. He was a man whose mind was as sharp as a razor blade. From his boyhood Rajaji had been a prodigy, though myopic. He was scholar, tactician and politician, and enjoyed a lucrative practice.

While Gandhi was Rajaji's guest, they discussed plans for the satyagraha. Gandhi told Rajaji early the next morning that the idea came to him the previous night in a dream, that they should call upon the country to carry out a general *hartal* and observe the day as one of fast and prayer. Most of Gandhi's decisions came to him suddenly. It happened in that way in South Africa when he gave a call for the struggle there and again when he declared he would fast during the mill-hands' struggle at Ahmedabad. His ideas broke upon him on the spur of the moment which might be described as intuition.

Accordingly, a statement was issued to the nation from Madras appealing to the people to observe fast, to pray and to suspend all business on April 6, 1919, instead of March 30 which was already fixed. The Muslims, Gandhi said, might not fast more than a day; so the duration of the fast should not be twenty-four hours. He expected Bombay, Bihar, Madras and Sind to respond to the call.

At Delhi, however, March 30 was observed as the day of *hartal*. Big processions were taken out. The military opened fire on the processionists, causing a number of casualties.

In Bombay, over a lakh of people gathered on April 6, at Chowpati, for a purificatory immersion in the sea. Gandhi was present with about a hundred satyagrahis. His speech was read out by Jamnadas Dwarkadas. Sarojini Naidu and Horniman were present. Referring to the deaths at Delhi, Gandhi said that no nation had arisen without sacrifice and asserted that the people of Delhi should not have insisted upon the release of the arrested men. It was arrest and imprisonment they sought by civil disobedience. Gandhi addressed a meeting at a mosque in Bombay and Shraddhanand spoke at Jumma Masjid in Delhi.

There was a meeting of women at China Bagh. Mrs. Jayakar presided. The meeting recorded its emphatic protest against the Rowlatt Act. There was some disturbance at the Market in Bombay. That day there was a suggestion that people should take a vow of swadeshi and a vow of Hindu-Muslim unity. Gandhi explained that there was a world of difference between boycott and swadeshi, for boycott was a sort of punishment and the swadeshi vow was a religious duty. It was decided to take the first vow on the birth anniversary of Rama and the vow of Hindu-Muslim unity was administered the next day. To the surprise of the leaders the attendance was negligible on the second day.

Hartal was observed in important cities and towns throughout India, the pledge was taken, and a fast was observed at Lahore, Calcutta, Amritsar and Allahabad. The common man gained the unique experience of participation in the national struggle. It was decided to break some laws till the Rowlatt Act was repealed. People were asked to prepare salt from sea-water in their own houses in disregard of the salt laws. The second suggestion was about the sale of proscribed books. Two proscribed books *Hind Swaraj* and *Sarvodaya* and two other pamphlets by Gandhi were selected for sale. Gandhi and Sarojini Naidu went out in a car selling them. People purchased copies and paid liberally for them. Even the Maharaja of Baroda. purchased some of them in the street.

On April 7 Gandhi started a weekly called *Satyagrahi* in defiance of the Indian Press Act, giving guidance to people involved in the struggle. It was decided to publish it every Monday from Mani Bhavan, Gamdevi, Bombay. Gandhi asked Griffith, Commissioner of Police, Bombay, whether he should send him a copy of the unregistered *Satyagrahi* edited by him. Its publication stopped on April 21.

Gandhi, accompanied by Mahadev Desai, left for Delhi by train. On April 9, at Kosi, he was served with an order prohibiting him from entering the Punjab and Delhi, and he was asked to restrict himself to the Bombay Presidency. On his disobedience of the order, he was asked by the police to get down at Palwal station and was put under police custody. He was taken to Mathura. Gandhi asked Mahadev Desai to convey to Swami Shraddhanand the news about his arrest. While he was being brought back to Bombay, at Baroda station, on April 11, he was served with an order not to leave the Bombay Presidency. He reached Bombay at a time when the police and the people were engaged in a fight at the Market. The crowds were out of Gandhi's control, but the police behaved with restraint and the danger of violence was averted.

During those two months, Gandhi said, he had experienced boundless love and was happy. "I am," he wrote to Esther Faering on April 10, 1919, in the flush of enthusiasm "the one man who can today preserve the peace in India as no other man can."[3] These were the stirrings of his boundless self-confidence. Gandhi's satyagraha movement was a novel experience even for the police officers. He gave interviews freely to the police officers at his place, visited their offices to give information about his tours and visits, and discussed with them the behaviour of his lieutenants. He told police that 'Horniman was an advocate of violence' who believed that a revolution might be justifiable if justifiable ends could be achieved by no other means. He promised the British police officers[4] that if Umar Sobani revealed his mind to him he would tell them about it. It does not become any national leader to give such information against his followers in a country struggling for its freedom. Unfortunately Gandhi was at this stage torn between truth and loyalty and he did so in his truthful way. He also told the police that his campaign was an experiment, and if it failed he would withdraw it.

TAGORE EXPRESSED APPREHENSIONS about the principle of satyagraha. On April 12, 1919, he conveyed to Gandhi his opinion that passive resistance was a force which was not necessarily moral in itself, it could be used against truth as well as for it. ... "I know your teaching is to fight against evil by the help of the good. But such a fight is for heroes and not for men led by the impulses of the moment. Evil on one side naturally begets evil on the other, injustice leading to violence and insult to vengefulness."

Gandhi said, continued Tagore, what Buddha had done in his time and for all time to come 'conquer anger by the power of non-anger and evil by the power of good'. Tagore prayed that martyrdom for the cause of truth might never degenerate into fanaticism for mere verbal forms.

The prophesy made by Besant, Tagore and the Liberal leaders came true. Satyagraha ended in violence, bloodshed and destruction of property at Ahmedabad, the home town of Gandhi, and at Nadiad and other places. Telegraph wires were cut, rails were removed and property was destroyed. The news of disturbances at the places which observed the *hartal* on March 30 and the arrest of Gandhi increased the hostility of the people who had observed the *hartal* on April 6, 1919.

Amritsar observed the *hartal* on March 30; it passed off without any public trouble, disturbance or disorder. The Hindus, Sikhs and Mohammedans were united. Amritsar was the venue of the Congress for the ensuing annual session in December 1919. Dr. Satyapal and Dr. Kitchlew were their most active and influential leaders. As doubts arose whether the *hartal* had taken place on the right date, a second *hartal* observed on April 6 also went off quietly, and again all business was stopped. The Moderate leaders in Amritsar were alarmed by the Delhi incidents and were against the second *hartal*.

On the morning of April 10, the leaders, Dr. Satyapal and Dr. Kitchlew, were deported. The news of their arrest spread in the city, and crowds in an angry and excited mood went to the civil lines to see Irving, the Police Commissioner. At Hall Bridge, the crowd was stopped by a small mounted picket and the Deputy Police Commissioner and the Liberal leaders. The crowd pressed forward. Irving arrived and sent for more reinforcements; orders were also given for the protection of the station.

Connor, an Assistant Commissioner, who was making his way to the police station in the city, met Lieutenant Dickie and told him that he must stop the mob from reaching the civil lines at all costs. So two of his soldiers dismounted and fired three or four shots inflicting that number of casualties. Infuriated by the sight of their dead and wounded, the crowd, which had swelled to 30,000, rushed back to the city. Determined, the violent crowd pressed forward and paid no heed to warnings.

In the city, the mob took charge and murdered some British bank officials. Their bodies were burnt in the street. Much damage was done to property connected with British activities. The Town Hall and the Indian Christian Church were destroyed. Telephone and telegraph wires were cut. Unrest spread to the neighbouring villages.

On April 11 the situation quietened down. Funeral processions were taken out of the ten Indians who were killed on the previous day. Notices were given to the leaders of the processionists for circulation that processions and gatherings were prohibited and that gatherings would be fired on, as would also persons leaving the city in groups of more than four.

Brigadier-General Dyer arrived and took control in the evening. He was a fighting soldier, full of determination and initiative, excitable and eccentric and over-confident of his judgement.

On April 12, 1919, some arrests were made in the city in connection with the riots of April 10. Although martial law had not been declared, a proclamation announcing by beat of drum that violence would be punished by martial law and prohibiting all meetings and gatherings was issued; but according to the Hunter Committee, the records did not show that steps were taken to ensure its publication on the morning of April 13. General Dyer issued another proclamation which was read out mostly in the Western parts of the city, prohibiting citizens from leaving the city or leaving their house after 8 p.m. and prohibiting processions and gatherings of four men or more.

Despite this the people decided to hold a meeting on that day at Jallianwala Bagh to mourn the victims of the Hall Gate Bridge incident. The Bagh was an enclosed open space which was frequently used for large gatherings. Although the Bagh was in the eastern part of the city, it was widely known that the proposed meeting was illegal and liable to lead to a clash with the Government authorities. At 4 o'clock General Dyer posted troops designed to disperse the meeting.

On arrival at the Bagh, Dyer found about 10,000 persons (according to some estimates it was 6,000) gathered. The Bagh was not a public garden, but simply a piece of rectangular waste land, possibly the remains of a lake. It was filled with debris and was surrounded by the back walls of buildings. Jallian was the surname of its original owner. It was now the joint property of about 40 persons.

The entrances and exits to Jallianwala Bagh were few, narrow and imperfect. As the people had defied his orders, General Dyer, within 30 seconds of his arrival, ordered his 50 men armed with rifles to open fire on the crowd without warning or calling on it to disperse. The crowd was on the lower ground listening to an address delivered from a platform some 100 yards from the troops. Firing was continued for about ten minutes and in all 1,650 rounds were fired, the soldiers completely exhausting the supply of ammunition they carried with them. Panic-stricken, the crowd were unable to disperse. Thousands escaped by jumping the walls. But about 380 persons were killed. The troops were immediately marched away without attending to the wounded of whom there were 1,137, or making arrangements for their treatment. Dyer later said, the dying men did not apply for help!

Lord Chelmsford published on April 14 a resolution authorising Government officers to employ available forces to put a speedy end to the disaster. On April 14, two days after the massacres, martial law was proclaimed. Amritsar, Lahore, Gujaranwalla and Kasur were kept under martial law for six weeks and unarmed people were shot at. Dyer, the brutal soldier and murderer, wrought vengeance on Amritsar. The Martial Law administration cut its electric and water supplies. But worse than the butchery was his inhuman order under which he compelled people to crawl on their bellies at a spot where a Miss Sherwood was attacked, though she was rescued by some Indians. A public platform for whipping was raised near the fort, and a number of triangular structures were erected in various parts of the city for flogging. After the failure of the revolution of 1857, people were likewise, forced to lick the blood on the ground, were flogged and publicly hanged from trees.

The Martial Law Tribunal and the Civil Magistrates tried, under Martial Law, 298 and 100 persons respectively, on several major charges out of whom the Tribunal sentenced 51 persons to death and 167 to various terms of imprisonment. The Civil Magistrates sentenced the accused to various terms of imprisonment. The vindictive and inhuman crawling order was cancelled by the Government after a week.

It is probable that the stirring and patriotic speeches King Amanulla made on his accession to the throne of Afghanistan on February 20, 1919, the impending Third Afghan war consequent upon this upsurge in Afghanistan and the discontent fomented by the agents of Afghans and emissaries of the Third International at Moscow on the north-west frontier of India, impelled the British imperialists to these drastic and inhuman atrocities.

General Dyer informed his headquarters that he continued the fire to produce an unforgettable moral effect and it was deliberate. At other places, fierce rioting had occurred but no officer followed the method of butchery used by General Dyer. During one of his journeys, Pandit Jawaharlal Nehru heard him say that he wanted to reduce the city to a heap of ashes. Dyer was condemned in India as a brutal soldier and as a murderer.

Dyer was praised by the British imperialists as a saviour of India from a second mutiny. Strictly speaking, General Dyer had formed an extreme and positive opinion on the situation and consulted no other. The perpetrators of these heinous acts were Col. Johnson, Bosworth-Smith, Col. O'Brien and Capt. Doveton. The news of their horrible atrocities was not allowed to reach England. It was censored.

Many have expressed their opinions on this tragedy. But the judgement passed on it by Major-General Sir Charles W. Gwynn in his book *Imperial Policing* is notable from the point of view of military principles. He observes that fire without specific warning is only justified when the mob is actively endangering life or property.[5] Here the mob was listening to a speech and the firing without specific warning was not justified. Prolonged firing also violated the principle that minimum amount of force only should be used. His motive to teach a lesson to Indians was also unjustified.

The whole country was filled with horror and resounded with protests against the Amritsar massacres and the bloodcurdling barbarities in the Punjab. The people put the blame on Sir Michael O'Dwyer, the Lieutenant Governor of the Punjab, who approved the terrible work of General Dyer.

Gandhi was at Ahmedabad where a sergeant was done to death by the mob and martial law was proclaimed under which more than 50 persons were killed and more than 250 were wounded. He wrote to the Viceroy that the atrocities in Amritsar were, as far as he could see, unconcerned with satyagraha and his arrest, he felt sure that had he been able to proceed to Delhi, Lahore and Amritsar, these awful occurrences could have been avoided. Amidst those harrowing tales of massacre and disorders, Gandhi, writing on April 14, 1919, proudly drew the attention of the Viceroy to the fact that rightly or wrongly, he seemed to command, at that moment, in an excessive degree the respect and affection of the people all over India.[6] He was thus impressing on the Government that he was on his way to becoming Indian leader No. 1. He asserted this belief in his growing strength when he, as mentioned earlier, spiritedly observed in his letter to Esther Faering, "I am the one man today who can preserve the peace of India as no other man can."

Gandhi returned to Ahmedabad on April 13. He was horrified by the violent acts done by his followers at Ahmedabad and Nadiad. At a meeting held on April 14, at the Ashram, Gandhi said repentantly: "A rapier run through my body could hardly have pained me more. I have said times without number that satyagraha admits of no violence, no pillage, no incendiarism, and still in the name of satyagraha we burnt down buildings, forcibly captured weapons, extorted money, stopped trains, cut off telegraph wires, killed innocent people and plundered shops and private houses." Gandhi added that some educated clever man or men were behind the disturbances at Viramgam, Ahmedabad and other places!

Terribly grieved, he undertook a fast for three days and asked the people of Gujarat to go on a fast for a day. He advised the Ashramites to give evidence in the identification of rioters. Although they had to follow their conscience and consistently refused to give evidence incriminating others, they should see that the guilty made full confessions.

On April 18, much to the chagrin of his co-workers and followers, Gandhi temporarily suspended the satyagraha and postponed it to July. Gandhi now admitted he had launched the satyagraha struggle before people were qualified for such an agitation and repented that he could not perceive what was obvious. He wrote repentantly to the Viceroy that he over-calculated the measure of permeation of satyagraha among the people and underrated the power of hatred and ill-will and the forces of evil.

Gandhi admitted at Nadiad that he had made "a blunder of Himalayan dimensions which had enabled ill-disposed persons, not true passive resisters at all, to perpetuate disorders". Later, on August 18, 1921, confessing his grave error, Gandhi said: "When I launched out light-heartedly on civil disobedience in 1919, I saw that I erred grievously. As soon as I perceived at Nadiad the want of foresight, I called it a

Himalayan miscalculation."

It was now decided that Gandhi should be editor of *Young India* and *Navajivan.* This was the first time that Gandhi appeared in public as an editor. Although he had edited *Indian Opinion* while in Africa, his name never appeared on it as its editor. *Young India,* an English weekly, published from Bombay, was started by Jamnadas Dwarkadas in November 1915 with a view to making it an organ of the Home Rule League Movement. After Horniman's deportation on April 26 the *Chronicle* was muzzled as a result of the forfeiture of its security, and by pre-censorship. For a fortnight thereafter it appeared with comments and then it was allowed to appear without censorship after a fresh security of Rs. 10,000 had been deposited by the proprietors. Gandhi with Syed Brelvi looked after its publication during the crisis.

In the meanwhile *Young India* was run as a bi-weekly from May 7, 1919, in Bombay under Gandhi's supervision and when the *Chronicle* resumed its regular work it was transferred to Ahmedabad by Banker and Sobani who controlled it. There it was published as a weekly from October 7, 1919, with Gandhi as editor.

Navajivan and *Satya,* a Gujarati monthly, conducted by Indulal Yagnik and financially backed by Banker and Sobani was published from Ahmedabad. It was turned into a weekly and Gandhi became its editor dropping *Satya* from the title. Yagnik offered to work on *Navajivan* and the first issue was published on September 7, 1919. A modern political leader is powerless if he does not have at his disposal an organ to propagate and defend his views. Gandhi always took care to have one.

The first issue of *Young India* appeared on October 8, 1919. Gandhi appealed to the Tamilians to see to it that the requisite number of subscribers was found, if they wished to see *Young India* continued. *Young India* had then a little more than 12,000 subscribers. It had stopped publishing advertisements. Gandhi wrote to Jinnah at the end of June 1919 that he had not studied the Montagu-Chelmsford Reforms. In a letter to the Viceroy, Gandhi appealed for an independent inquiry to examine the causes of disturbances in the Punjab and the administration of Martial Law in the Provinces, including the sentences passed by the Martial Law Tribunal.

Gandhi now turned the attention of the people to swadeshi and began to educate the people by issuing leaflets to them on the principles of satyagraha. When defeated on one front he at once shifted to another very swiftly. He attended the Hindi

Sahitya Sammelan which was held in Bombay on April 20. At a meeting held in Bombay on May 31, he upheld the proposal mooted by the Tilakites for presenting a purse to Tilak to enable him to defray the expenses of the Chirol case. Victory in law courts, Gandhi said, did not depend upon the truth of one's case but on the judge, the counsel and the venue of the court. He wished that Tilak was a satyagrahi like himself!

Gandhi appealed to the people to purchase swadeshi goods. He did not lay emphasis on the boycott of foreign goods as he felt at the time that boycott was entirely inconsistent with satyagraha. He felt that boycott was based on hatred and swadeshi on love. He wanted to save India Rs. 60 crores a year which went to foreign countries for imported cloth, and he desired to give work in spinning and weaving to the farmers in villages who remained idle for the major part of the year. To Gandhi swadeshi was a religion, India's primary dharma. It meant a fiscal economy as it implied India's economic independence. Swadeshi therefore might be called Swaraj. And swadeshi was satyagraha! It was irreligious to neglect our own Indian artisans and to encourage the foreign ones. If legislation were in his hands he would penalize the labour-saving machines used in India. Mill-made cloth could not be treated as pure swadeshi. Machine-made cloth had no soul in it.

Gandhi also sent the swadeshi pledge to the Governor of Bombay for his endorsement so that the fact might be emphasized that the swadeshi vow was not taken in hostility but as an economic necessity. He sent the swadeshi vow to the Viceroy also and said it would be a great thing if the Viceroy took the vow! On October 7 the Governor of Bombay replied that he was in sympathy with the swadeshi movement but his view was that better facilities for economic and technical education were the best methods of assisting Indian industrial development.

In a speech at the Fergusson College, Gandhi said, "Only a revival of swadeshi industries, viz. hand-spinning and hand-weaving could work their economic salvation." Thanking Gandhi for his speech, R. P. Paranjpye, Principal of the College, asked Gandhi whether he wished that the railways should be destroyed and the primitive means of trade and communications should be restored instead. It was vain, he maintained, to strive to turn back the tide of time and to seek solution to an economic question in a sentimental way.

Speaking at another meeting in Poona on the same topic, Gandhi said that if Poona saw eye to eye with him in the matter of swadeshi, it would relieve him from half his task. What

Poona lacked, in his opinion, was faith and self-confidence. It was the misfortune of Gandhi that not only Poona but the whole of Maharashtra had no faith in Gandhism and was highly critical of its principles. Even at that time, it was bubbling and boiling with opposition to Gandhism. All the same Gandhi gave a concrete shape to his movement. He established in Bombay a Shuddha Swadeshi Vastra Bhandar and on July 1 founded the Swadeshi Sabha the branches of which were established all over India just as his Satyagraha Sabhas.

In the several leaflets he issued on satyagraha, Gandhi impressed upon the minds of the people its true meaning. "The foundation of satyagraha is based on truth and non-violence. He who abides by truth and does not wish to harm anybody can be called a satyagrahi.[7] There is no religion other than truth. Religion is love. So truth is love and love is truth. A father, far from getting angry with his son, often expresses his disapproval of wrong action by taking suffering on his person." Thus the origin of Gandhian satyagraha was in the anger of his father who suffered himself for the wrong actions of his son. Gandhi asserted often that satyagraha had a universal application. Time might show, he observed, that neither India nor the world could have anything better than satyagraha as a restraining force ranged on the side of law and order. "*Hartal* shows," Gandhi said in one of the leaflets, "popular disapproval whereas hardest hearts are impressed by a fast. Those who voluntarily fast became gentle and purified by it. A pure fast is a very powerful prayer."

Gandhi's statement that some educated man or men were behind the disturbances was quoted by Montagu in London. The Governor-General in his speech before the Legislative Council on September 3, mentioned it in proof of the charge that the satyagraha movement had Bolshevist brains and money behind it. Displeased with Gandhi's statement, the Delhi satyagrahis sent a remonstration to him and protested against his view. In order to allay Government fears and suspicions, Gandhi stressed the point that his satyagraha aimed at ridding Indian political movement of terrorism and violent methods by which he meant the revolutionary movement. If, he added, the rapidly widespread growth of Bolshevism which was attacking one nation after another in Europe was to be successfully arrested in India, it was necessary that the people should be reminded of their civilization and culture, which was compressed in the one word, satyagraha, the highest *mantra* one could know of. [8] Civil resistance was, he repeated on many occasions, a most powerful antidote against Bolshevism.[9]

Meantime Gandhi Wrote to E. S. Montagu, who had approved of the Rowlatt Act, and explained to him why he had launched a movement against it. He also sent messages and appeals to him through Sir Prabhashankar Pattani, Sastri and Sir Stanley Reed. Montagu cabled to the Governor of Bombay to interview Gandhi and dissuade him from resuming the satyagraha movement. Liberal leaders like Sir Narayan Chandavarkar also advised him to give up the struggle.

As suggested by Montagu, the Governor of Bombay had an interview with Gandhi at Poona on July 12, 1919 and told him that according to Montagu it would be a crime for Gandhi to resume civil resistance. Through the Governor of Bombay, the Viceroy, too, conveyed to Gandhi on July 20 a grave warning of the consequences which would result from resumption of the satyagraha. As a result of the warning and in response to these appeals, Gandhi issued a statement from Bombay on July 21, suspending the civil disobedience, to hasten, as he declared, the end of the Rowlatt Act! Next day from Ahmedabad he wrote to the Viceroy informing him that he had suspended the satyagraha. In his statement he said that he was accused of throwing lighted matches, but he expressed the opinion that the Rowlatt Act and persistence in retaining it on the statute book were a thousand matches scattered over India.

Gandhi justified his come-down by informing his critics that a satyagrahi was the strongest when he appeared to outsiders to have weakened! Thus the Rowlatt Act remained on the statute book and Gandhi gave up his struggle without the consent or knowledge of the thousands of people who had participated in it, as he had done earlier in South Africa. Leaders like Swami Shraddhanand and Jamnadas Dwarkadas did not like Gandhi's policy, and they resigned from the Satyagraha Sabha.

The non-violent struggle failed because Gandhi never planned it properly as it was his belief that a struggle which had to be planned was not a righteous struggle![10] Moreover, as Gandhi's opponents said, "The non-violent struggle ultimately fails because it presupposes all men to be selfless, believes that all men will not co-operate with the tyrant or aggressor and blindly presumes that the tyrant or aggressor has a sense of morality and will not resort to arms and ordinances." For the outbreak of violence the Government put the blame on Gandhi and he in turn put the blame partly on Government and partly on "educated and clever men" to whom he imputed the charge, although he swore that he had assumed the leadership of the revolt against the Rowlatt Act just "to divert the movement from violence".[11]

Hundreds of innocent men were killed, telegraph and railway and post offices were burnt and damage to property was untold. The blood of hundreds of men was spilt in the first phase of the satyagraha struggle which was claimed to be a bloodless struggle. The sun of satyagraha dawned on April 6, 1919, but it went under an eclipse in the Punjab and Gujarat! In the Indian revolutionary movement, which Gandhi wanted to suppress, generally no innocent Indian people were killed and comparatively very little violence was perpetrated! Gandhi said he wanted to get rid of violence, but his satyagraha was against the violence of the people and not against that of the Government. On its part, the Government too said that by instituting the Rowlatt Act, it wanted to put an end to the violence committed by revolutionaries!

The satyagraha struggle was a mass movement. A leader of a mass movement is a man of one idea and capable of sustained action. A mass movement comprises both noble and base elements. Crime accompanies it with the malcontent, self-seekers, perjurers and others who attach no value to the sanctity of life and property. These trouble-makers join any mass movement to escape individual responsibility.

Yet the gain from the satyagraha struggle was tremendous. The movement gave for the first time thousands of common men all over the country the joy of active participation in the national struggle. Although non-violent, it was no doubt a fight. It gave expression to the growing discontent and anti-British feeling among the people. The people who were involved in such a mass action, workers, lawyers and students, became the recruits of Gandhi in the national struggle. He gave them a new purpose, a new weapon and a new identity. And he became a symbol of national resistance, representing the spirit of revolt in the Indian masses and their great new awakening.

CHAPTER XIX

The Khilafat and Amritsar

The Atmosphere In the country was surcharged with discontent, distrust and disaffection, and the anti-British feeling was growing intense. Sir Sankaran Nair resigned office as a Member of the Viceroy's Council on July 23, 1919, protesting against the Rowlatt Act.

The All-India Congress Committee held at Allahabad on June 8 demanded an inquiry into the Punjab occurrences. Cables were sent to the British Premier and to the Secretary of State for India requesting suspension of all sentences passed under martial law pending the proposed inquiry. The A.I.C.C. appointed a sub-committee to inquire into the Punjab occurrences and accordingly Malaviya, Motilal Nehru and Shraddhanand went to Amritsar to hold an inquiry into the atrocities there.

On September 3, 1919, the Government appointed a committee under Justice Hunter to make inquiries into the Punjab and Ahmedabad disorders. Out of the eight members Sultan Ahmed, Sir Chimanlal and Pandit Jagat Narayan were Indians. But before the committee started its work, the Government of India passed an Indemnity Act granting immunity to its officers against civil or criminal proceedings. In the Council this was opposed and there was a good deal of protest against it outside, but Gandhi supported it! A sub-committee of the Congress was appointed to lead evidence before the Hunter Committee. Gandhi saw Lord Hunter at Delhi, but Hunter refused to secure the temporary release of the Punjab leaders who were undergoing sentences, even for a short time, for the collection of the evidence. So the Congress Committee refused to co-operate with it.

The Punjab sub-committee of the A.I.C.C. appointed on November 14, 1919, Motilal Nehru, C. R. Das, Abbas Tayabji, Fazlul Haq and Gandhi as commissioners and K. Santanam as Secretary for preparing an independent Congress report on the Punjab disturbances. The restrictions imposed on Gandhi were removed on October 15, and he was allowed to go to the Punjab. He went to Lahore on October 24. He then toured extensively in the Punjab, addressed gatherings and meetings and collected evidence. In December 1919 Motilal Nehru resigned as he was elected President of the forthcoming Congress session, and M. R. Jayakar was selected a member of the inquiry committee in place of Haq. In the meantime a petition demanding the repeal of the Rowlatt Act was forwarded to the Government by the All-India Home Rule League!

The Congress Committee had engaged Neville, a London solicitor, to help in its inquiry work, and he came and helped the committee. Gandhi now said he did not join the cry for the recall of the Viceroy as he was not so much concerned with that as with securing justice.

While Gandhi was carrying the tremendous responsibility of the committee's work, people gathered for his *darshan*. Inwardly elated at this, he wrote: "At present even when people come for *darshan*, I continue to write and do other work. Even as I write this, people come and go but I do not interrupt my work. I salute them and go on with my writing." Gandhi proudly added that it was the miracle wrought by even a small measure of devotion to truth and service.[1]

Gandhi secured the removal of Miss Esther Faering from Madras to his Ashram with the permission of the Governors of Madras and Bombay. He supported her petition for nationalization and asked Andrews to use his good offices in the matter. He said Miss Faering was truthful and lived in the fear of God, and he promised the Government that he would not avail himself of her services in the political field as the major part of his work was social and moral or religious. Miss Faering stayed at the Satyagraha Ashram, and on one occasion complained against Kasturba. Gandhi, who was always rather partial to foreigners, observed, "Ba has not an even temper. She is not always sweet. And she can be petty."

Gandhi again expressed his orthodox views on caste. Speaking on untouchability and caste, on August 31, 1919, he told a meeting of the weavers at Dohad that to him, even to think that it was pollution to touch any creation of God was sinful. But he cautiously added that he did not want to put the prejudice of untouchability on a level with food and marriage regulations based on caste distinctions. "For", he concluded, "it is a question of choice. We are not bound to subscribe to promiscuous inter-dining and inter-marriage."[2]

Tilak evaded the question of inter-dining by stating that he would dine in the company of anybody if he won Swaraj. Gandhi went one step further and condemned inter-dining and inter-marriage as promiscuous! As regards the remarriage of child widows, Gandhi, who did not consider the sight of a widow an ill-omen, said that to live a widow's life was a holy thing, but it was not entirely sinful for a widow to remarry. He said that love could marry only once. It is enough to say here that Tilak had opposed the Age of Consent Bill which prohibited the consummation of marriage before the age of twelve!

About this time Gandhi had unwittingly a tussle with the High Court of Bombay. He had published a private letter addressed by Kennedy, District Judge of Ahmedabad, to the Registrar of the Bombay High Court in the issue of *Young India* of August 6. The Bombay High Court wanted him to attend the chamber of the Chief Justice on October 20, 1919. On October 22 Gandhi replied that he was in a hurry to go to the Punjab, but explained that in his humble opinion he was within the rights of a journalist in publishing the letter in question and making comments on it. He believed, he added, the letter to be of great public importance and one that called for public criticism.

The Registrar demanded an apology, and Gandhi replied that he could not conscientiously offer one. The satyagrahi lawyers of Ahmedabad were given a warning by the Bombay High Court. Gandhi said that lawyers should be guardians of law and liberty and as such were interested, in keeping the statute-book of the country "pure and undefiled". Later, on March 3, 1920, Gandhi and Mahadev Desai appeared in person in the High Court. On March 12, 1920, this question was decided. Justice Marten and Justice Hayward and Justice Kajiji of the High Court severely reprimanded Gandhi, the editor and Mahadev Desai, the publisher for contempt of Court.

DURING THE FIRST World War, Indian Muslims suffered severe mental strain as they were torn between conflicting loyalties, their religious loyalty to the Caliph of Turkey who was fighting the British and their political loyalty to Britain whom they had helped. The Khilafat movement aimed at seeing the temporal and spiritual powers of the Caliph (the Sultan of Turkey) restored to their pristine glory. The Muslims of India were now protesting against the threatened dismemberment of defeated Turkey and removal of the holy places of Islam from the Khalifat's control.

Lloyd George, Prime Minister of England, had promised to fulfil this request. The Muslim leaders were agitating for a solution to the question which they called the Khilafat question. The Caliph was the ruler and religious head of Turkey which was in the throes of a revolution. A nationalist revolution had captured the Young Turks and they wanted to end the Caliphate and his Sultanate, the rotten structure of a dead institution. Their revolutionary leader, Gazi Mustafa Kemal Pasha, had declared that "Islam, this theology of an immortal Arab, is a dead thing". He wanted to tear out religion from the body politic of Turkey.

Gandhi, himself a religious-minded man, took up the cry of the Muslims without understanding its implications and significance and the conditions in Turkey. He addressed a meeting of Muslims in Bombay on September 18, 1919, declaring that Khilafat was the question of questions. He was sorry that the Viceroy gave only one out of fifty-five minutes of his speech in the Imperial Legislative Assembly to the question of the Khilafat. It was the question among questions and on the right solution to it depended the future peace of India. He therefore asked the Muslims to be ready to sacrifice their ease, comfort, commerce and even their life for the cause. To die for a cause was the law of man, to kill was that of the beast.

Gandhi appealed to every Hindu man and woman to observe October 17, as Khilafat day, a day of national fasting and prayer, and proposed suspension of business as expected by the Khilafat Conference at Lucknow. The Hindus should show that they were one with the Muslims in their sorrow and thus put a sacred seal on the Hindu-Muslim bond. If the Khilafat disappeared, Islam would lose its vitality. This the Muslims would not tolerate. Gandhi's followers said that Montagu and Chelmsford should resign over the Khilafat question.

The Khilafat day was celebrated peacefully! Upon this Gandhi said that a Government was an instrument of service only so far as it was based upon the will and the consent of the people. It was an instrument of oppression when it enforced submission at the point of the bayonet. He opined, however, that he did not believe in the boycott of foreign goods as it bred ill-will, was a subterfuge for boycott of the Government and spelt disloyalty. "The boycott of British goods, while we retain the British connection, is, in our opinion, a blunder of the first magnitude," he concluded.

The first Khilafat Conference met at Delhi on November 23, 1919. Its leaders were Reza Ali, Syed Hussain, Hakim Ajmal Khan, Dr. Ansari and Maulana Abdul Bari Saheb. Its secretary was Asaf Ali. Motilal Nehru, C. R. Das, Swami Shraddhanand and Dr. Choithram of Sind had extended their moral support to the conference. Jinnah kept himself aloof as he always stood for secularism and real nationalism.

On the first day of the Khilafat Conference, Gandhi was the only Hindu leader who was asked to attend. Addressing the conference, he said their cause was just, but they should not resort to boycott as it meant economic punishment to the British people. Some Hindu leaders wanted to combine the issue of the Punjab massacres with the Khilafat question, but Gandhi opposed it, saying that 'he would resign the whole campaign if they pressed for it.'[3]

The next day the conference was attended by Hindus, Parsis and Christians. Gandhi presided and addressed the meeting. He said the Hindus could save the cow only by doing their duty and helping the Muslims unconditionally. Conditional co-operation, he added, is like adulterated cement which does not bind. The readiness of thirty crores of people for sacrifices could obtain the fulfilment of their desires in the world. If the question was satisfactorily solved, all Indians would join the victory celebrations and rejoicings on December 13. However, Gandhi asked the Muslims to cancel their boycott resolution. Boycott was a form of revenge and indicated their weakness, non-co-operation proved their strength. It was during this speech that Gandhi coined the phrase 'non-co-operation'!

The conference urged Muslims not to participate in the victory celebrations, and further resolved to progressively withhold all cooperation from the British Government and to boycott British goods in case the Turkish question was not satisfactorily solved.

In the conference Maulana Abdul Bari said that in refraining from cow slaughter of their own free will, Muslims in no way went against their faith.

In the conference money was collected for propaganda and Gandhi was requested to contribute one pice. Gandhi had no pice on him. It was lent by Khwaja Sahib Hussan Nizami. This coin, wrote Gandhi, was auctioned by Syed Hussain, and one

Mia Chhotani bought it for Rs. 501! With this gesture Gandhi brought the Muslims into his religious politics and added the cow question to it, thus abandoning the secular politics of Gokhale, Dadabhai Naoroji and others!

Gandhi appealed to the Viceroy and to the Punjab Government to reconsider the sentences passed upon Karamchand, Gurdial Singh, Mahomed Bastur, Bhai Parmanand and Durgadas Advani by the Military Tribunal.

The Congress Session was held at Amritsar in the last week of December 1919. Tilak had returned from London on November 27, 1919, after doing much work in England. Jinnah, Besant and Srinivas Sastri also returned to India after giving evidence before the Joint Select Committee appointed to examine the provisions of Montagu's India Bill. The India Bill got though the Houses of Parliament about the middle of December and the Royal Proclamation was issued on December 23, 1919.

Motilal Nehru presided over the Amritsar session and Shraddhanand was the Chairman of the Reception Committee.

On his way to Amritsar, Tilak wired from Bharatpur railway station to the King Emperor thanking him for the Proclamation and amnesty and assuring him responsive co-operation. This created a sort of consternation in the mind of Tilak's colleagues, one of them being C. R. Das. The session was the biggest one held up to that time. Motilal said that if the ordinary rights of human beings were denied to Indians, then all talk of reforms was a mockery. Then the President added that all would join with him in offering a most cordial welcome to Tilak after his arduous labour in England for the country's cause. The Ali Brothers and the Punjabi leaders, who were released, rushed to Amritsar to attend the session. Up till now the Ali Brothers were not Congressmen. They were first interned and then imprisoned on May 15, 1915, when they represented the unprovoked invasion of India by the Amir of Afghanistan and now released after nearly five years at the end of 1919.

The main resolution on the Montagu-Chelmsford Reforms proved to be a battle royal. C. R. Das moved the resolution which declared that the reforms were inadequate, unsatisfactory and disappointing, the last adjective being inserted on Tilak's insistence. Das was a poet, a brilliant barrister, a patriot and defender of Bengal revolutionaries. As a leader he had come to the forefront during the previous three years especially after the Montagu Declaration, displacing Surendranath Banerjee and receiving the homage and allegiance of Young Bengal. The irony of the situation was that Gandhi, Malaviya, Sastri, Besant and Motilal Nehru were for working the reforms, and they offered co-operation to the Government. Das was a thorough non-co-operator. Tilak supported the Das resolution and said that people should accept what they had been offered and agitate and work for further reforms. Nothing favourable, he added, had happened during the past year that required them to change the adjective 'disappointing'.

Malaviya and Motilal Nehru used Gandhi to lead their opposition to Tilak and Das. Gandhi was then the apostle of co-operation. He was a loyal and devoted co-operator. Tilak wanted to work out the reforms in a spirit of responsive co-operation; but was for declaring that the reforms were inadequate, unsatisfactory and disappointing. Gandhi, who was in favour of working the reforms in a spirit of co-operation, moved an amendment suggesting omission of the word disappointing, and adding to the resolution of Das a fourth paragraph which entreated the Congress to add the expression "Congress begs loyally to respond" and "warmest thanks to Montagu."

This amendment was hotly debated. The party led by Gandhi said that the Congress should not say that the reforms were disappointing; for he feared that the people would then not show any interest in them. He later declared that he did not consider the reforms to be an evil or unjust, but a progressive step towards Responsible Government. Besant moved an amendment welcoming the reforms and appealing to the people to work them out. She said the new scheme was a *Kamadhenu.* Bomanji supported Besant and so did Telang. B. C. Pal moved an amendment and was supported by Mahomed Ali.

Gandhi, moving the amendment, said, "If Tilak Maharaj tells you that we are going to make use of the Reforms Act as he must, and as he has already told Montagu, as he has told the country that we are going to take the fullest advantage of the reforms, then I say, be true to yourself, be true to the country and tell the country that you are going to do it. But if you were to say, after having gone there, you will put obstruction, say that also. But on the question of propriety and obstruction, I say, Indian culture demands that we shall trust one who extends a hand of fellowship." He added that they should cooperate by accepting the reforms and not say one thing when they meant another. Tilak viewed the problem from a different angle. It was not improper, he said, to express disappointment. That attitude gave added vigour to the efforts and fight.

Jinnah seconded Gandhi as he was for co-operation and the working of the reforms. Malaviya and Motilal Nehru were supporters of Gandhi.

The resolution was discussed for three days. The Maharashtrian delegates left and reached Amritsar station on their way homewards. When Tilak saw that no compromise was reached and that voting was inevitable, he called back the delegates and they returned to the sessions from the station. At such a psychological moment, Gandhi put his white cap[4] on the platform before Tilak, who was sitting on the platform, as a token of his acceptance of the compromise. Tilak had a majority in the subjects committee; but in order to maintain unity and to respect the feeling of Motilal Nehru, Malaviya and Gandhi, Das and Tilak agreed to the compromise.[5] It was also paying in a way the debt of gratitude to Gandhi for the lead he gave to the nation during the agitation against the Rowlatt Act.

Then the five leaders—Das, Tilak, Gandhi, Malaviya and Pal—arrived at a compromise. The original resolution proposed by Das with Gandhi's amendment, shorn of the expression 'Begs to loyally respond' and the word 'warmest', was passed.

It was a victory for Tilak. His policy of responsive co-operation meant both constitutional co-operation and obstruction. The resolution declared in favour of responsive co-operation. It was in the right direction. The Congress declared that the people were fit for Swaraj and urged that Parliament should take early steps to establish full responsible Government in India in accordance with the principle of self-determination. Pending this, it trusted that so far as possible the people would so work the reforms as to secure an early establishment of full responsible Government.

The Congress passed fifty resolutions on various topics; one of them demanded recall of Lord Chelmsford. It may be noted that the Congress did not adopt Gandhi's agitation for the nation although it appreciated it.

The Moderates at their second conference in Calcutta in December 1919 declared ungrudging and whole-hearted cooperation in working the reforms.

At Amritsar, Besant's amendment failed. The Amritsar Congress hastened the eclipse of Besant and witnessed the emergence of Gandhi. Besant had said early that "the scheme was unworthy of England to offer and unworthy of India to accept". Gandhi, N. C. Kelkar, Vithalbhai Patel, Rangaswami Iyengar and I. B. Sen were selected members of a sub-committee to examine the Congress constitution and to consider necessary changes in it. That shows the power and personality of Gandhi. Yet Gandhi said in his peculiar humble way that his participation in the proceedings at Amritsar was not his real entry into Congress politics. Resolutions on swadeshi and Khilafat were passed. It was also decided to raise a memorial column in Jallianwala Bagh.

After the Congress session, leaders like C. P. Ramaswami Aiyar thought that but for Gandhi's intervention the Congress would have taken a violent turn. Indeed it was so for liberals and loyalists!

Gandhi fulminated against those who used discourteous and unmannerly language about Lord Chelmsford and concluded a review of the session by saying: "I am sure that if we use all the provisions of the reforms wisely and secure appropriate improvements in them, we should achieve full Swaraj in no more than a few years!" So he was not only for Council entry but envisaged the possibility of full Swaraj through those reforms! At Amritsar Gandhi declared that the Humanitarian Conference was closed down. During the days of the Amritsar Congress, the Muslim League held its session, and the Khilafat Conference met in the same place.

It was in this session that Gandhi came in closer contact with the Nehrus. N. C. Kelkar, Tilak's chief lieutenant, observes in his autobiography that he saw for the first time how on account of a certain reason Motilal Nehru and Gandhi had developed a close and admirable relationship.[6] Kelkar mentioned in another book of his that Gandhi wanted to condemn the people as they also, like the Government, had committed atrocities. As it was improper, Tilak and Das did not agree to it.

THE PROCEEDINGS OF the Amritsar Congress, which was dominated by Tilak and Das, left Pandit Malaviya and Gandhi very unhappy. The first open clash with Tilak weighed heavy upon Gandhi. Writing about this session in his *Liberator*, Swami Shraddhanand observed that these two leaders, Malaviya and Gandhi, were then thinking of purging the Congress of its 'diplomatic and crooked policy.'[7] Malaviya wanted Shraddhanand to go out of the Congress with them and to work for the reform of the Congress. It seems that Gandhi was arranging his forces against the formidable leadership of Tilak. Every party was trying to assert itself.

So immediately after the Amritsar Congress where Gandhi said that Tilak should not say one thing when he meant another, he joined issue with him in *Young India*: "For as party formation progresses, we suppose it would be considered quite the proper thing for party leaders to use others as tools so long as there are any to be used. Care will have therefore to be taken rather to purify our politics than for fear of being used as tools to hesitate to take the right course. Lokamanya Tilak represents a definite school of thought of which he makes no secret. He considers that everything is fair in politics. We have joined issue with him in that conception of politics. We consider that political life of the country will become thoroughly corrupt if we import Western tactics and methods."

Tilak's reply to this article of Gandhi appeared in *Young India* of January 28, 1920, and is given below:

"I am sorry to see that in your article on 'Reform Resolution' in the last issue you have represented me as holding that I considered everything fair in politics. I write this to you to say that my view is not correctly represented herein. Politics is a game of worldly people and not of sadhus and instead of the maxim: 'One should conquer anger by opposing it with tranquillity, non-anger' as preached by Buddha, I prefer to rely on the maxim of Shri Krishna: 'My response to the devotees is in perfect harmony with the manner of their approach.' Both methods are equally honest and righteous, but the one is more suited to this world than the other. Any further explanation about the difference will be found in my *Gita-Rahasya*."

Gandhi's rejoinder to Tilak was as follows:

"With deference to the Lokamanya I venture to say that it betrays mental laziness to think that the world is not for sadhus. The epitome of all religions is to promote Purushartha, and Purushartha is nothing but a desperate attempt to become a sadhu, i.e. to become a gentleman in every sense of the term. Finally, when I wrote the sentence about everything being fair in politics according to Lokamanya's creed I had in mind his oft-repeated quotation 'tit for tat'. To me it enunciates bad law. I shall not despair of the Lokamanya with all his acumen agreeably surprising India one day with a philosophical dissertation proving the falsity of the doctrine."

It is crystal clear from the foregoing letters how Tilak writes with dignity and tranquillity, how Gandhi charges his acumen with mental laziness in the same breath. Although the bitterness is couched in moral clothing, yet the human heart of

Gandhi, the great man, reveals its inside. He is damning his adversary with faint praise!

Gandhi, however, did not come out successful in this controversy. Tilak said: "Politics is a game of the worldly people and not of sadhus." Gandhi put a wrong interpretation on Tilak's remarks when he said: "Sadhus have no place in this world!" Tilak suggested that sadhus should not pollute themselves by contact with the worldly game of politics. However high on the moral plane a man might be, it would be impossible for him to achieve the desired goal in this matter-of-fact world without sacrificing at some stage his saintliness, but in so doing the object of the saintly man ought to be selfless. This is what Tilak meant. This was Tilak's guiding principle. It is a fact that the politician in Mahatma Gandhi himself could not be an exception to this.

CHAPTER XX

The Hindu Defender of the Khilafat

The Hunter Commission worked from October 1919 to January 1921. On January 9 its members examined Gandhi at Ahmedabad when he explained that the satyagraha movement was an extension of the domestic law on the political field. Satyagraha would be open even to the masses when India had her own ministers. A minority would certainly bring down the tallest ministry by offering stubborn civil resistance in free India also. He further said that he was not prepared to give the names of those who gave him the information as to who organized the acts at Ahmedabad, as his principles and law forbade him to do so. Whether the principles of truth or those of non-secrecy prevented him from revealing the names of the miscreants, none knew. Perhaps he was giving evidence as a leader and not as a satyagrahi!

The Khilafat question was coming to the fore. A Khilafat deputation was to wait on the Viceroy, and Gandhi joined it. With the Muslim leaders Abdul Bari, Abul Kalam Azad, Hakim Ajmal Khan, Dr. Ansari and Mahomed Ali, Gandhi waited on the Viceroy at Delhi on January 19, 1920. The Viceroy received the delegation with courtesy, but Gandhi said that behind the courtesy there was the determination to punish Turkey.

Under the royal amnesty a number of political prisoners were released by the Provincial Governments in the last week of January 1920 and during the first fortnight of February. Some were released even from Andaman Jail, but not the Savarkar brothers. Lajpatrai arrived in Bombay on February 20, and Tilak eagerly welcomed him. About this time it was declared that the Jallianwala Bagh was acquired for the nation by the Indian National Congress at Rs. 5.4 lakhs.

During the first quarter of 1920, Gandhi was of the opinion that the reforms were a progressive step towards responsible Government. To him the idea of boycott was still anathema.

Gandhi said the Indians were engaged in a spiritual war. Answering the question whether he was putting back the hand of the clock of progress, he replied that he would not weep over the disappearance of machinery or consider it a calamity. To him swadeshi meant production and distribution of articles manufactured in one's own country. Swadeshi was a constructive programme, but boycott was a punishment, punishing the wrong-doer and evoking his anger. He said his opposition to boycott was based on spiritual conception.

It seems Gandhi, as leader of the non-violent, non-co-operation movement, was developing a unit at Bardoli to stage a non-violent struggle and set an example to the whole country. The women and men of Bardoli resolved at a conference in February 1920 to launch a struggle.

The main activity to which Gandhi now devoted his energy and attention was the Khilafat agitation. His propaganda was gathering momentum and strength and giving a stimulus to the Khilafat movement. The Khilafat was a decrepit and moribund institution. It belonged to a dead past. Neither the Turks nor the Arabs wanted it. They were thoroughly disgusted with it. The smaller nations, crushed under the heels of the Turkish Ottoman Empire, were struggling to throw off the Turkish yoke. Gandhi neither cared about the struggle of those nations nor understood their ambitions. So in the beginning of the Khilafat struggle, partly with a desire to foist the extra-territorial ambitions of the Indian Muslims on the Middle-Eastern Muslim nations and partly with a view to making his favourite experiments on the Muslims regarding the doctrine of non-violent non-co-operation, Gandhi threw himself energetically into the Khilafat struggle.

It was thus the wrong side Gandhi took up and the wrong people he chose to make experiments on. On Khilafat, "the question of questions", as he described it, he issued on March 7, 1920, a statement, advocating non-co-operation without boycott of English goods as he thought that boycott was a form of violence. He wanted Turkey not to be deprived of her suzerainty over Arabia. He asked those who were holding offices of honour or emolument to give them up. Those who belonged to the menial services under Government should do likewise. Advice to the soldiers to refuse to serve, he added, was premature. He would cease to co-operate with the Khilafat movement if there was violence actually done and in that case he would resist anger, hatred, ill-will and violence on the part of the Khilafatists with his life even if he should stand alone. There was no reference to the Punjab wrongs at this stage. He refrained from amalgamating it with the Khilafat issue.

While Gandhi publicly advocated non-co-operation on March 7, in his letter of March 20 to Sastri, he mentioned that future aspirants for the membership of the Council should be asked to pledge themselves to an out-and-out protection of the country's interests. This was not in keeping with the foregoing resolve. It seems he was at this stage in favour of Council entry.

Some leaders warned Gandhi against launching the non-co-operation movement. They raised questions as to his motives, wisdom and action. They said he exploited unjustly an unreasonable religious sentiment to embarrass the British Government. But a leader of a mass movement often does not give heed to such warnings. His vision is always one-sided, fixed on the goal. Sastri, Besant and Tilak remained aloof, and Besant and Sastri even issued warnings to Gandhi. They gave him one word before the deed rather than two afterwards.

Tilak wanted the national movement to be kept away entirely from all contamination with theological or foreign political questions. He foretold that the Hindu leaders would find they had deceived themselves and not the Muslims who were shrewd at diplomatic negotiations. He was of the opinion that the co-operation of the Muslims should be sought on the broader national question of Swaraj by offering them special privileges, and added: "Never seek to introduce theology into our politics."

Srinivas Sastri, referring to Gandhi's statement, observed on April 13 that he feared[2] the Khilafat movement was going to land the country in disaster. He pictured the Mohammedans breaking out here and there in futile demonstrations. Hindus, he foretold, would foolishly join and when the punishments came, the latter would fare the worst.

Aurobindo Ghose said that the recognition of the communal principle at Lucknow made the Muslims permanently a separate political entity in India and the Khilafat affair made that separate political entity of the Muslims an organized separate political power. He opined that the attempt at bringing the Muslims into the national struggle by joining the Khilafat movement was on the wrong lines.[3] Besant also warned against the dangers arising out of the panacea of passive resistance.

Andrews, too, was not in agreement with the Indian Muslim viewpoint.

So far India had followed an orthodox nationalism. Although vague in many respects, it was secular. Gandhi was now definitely furnishing it with an obscurantist ideology in the name of spiritualism. He stood for decayed medieval institutions and was in favour of the caste system which, he said, was not a harmful institution. He believed in the divine dispensation, according to which God shaped events in the world. He often impressed upon the mind of his followers that God was with him. He was near him, in effect he was the new messenger of God. He claimed to work, act and live in the name of God. While in the twentieth century religious influence was declining and freedom of the individual was growing, Gandhi was committing the Indian nationalist movement to a reactionary, religious, emotional and socially outdated outlook.

Gandhi's movement had no vital social purpose to clear away the established order of a decayed society and to establish a new social order. It inspired loyalty to the traditions of a dead past and advocated return to some old position. It did not mean progress which means a forward movement. In fact, it was a counter-revolutionary movement for it wanted to preserve the established social order and to revive older institutions, although politically it aimed at a revolution.

GANDHI SAID THAT with satya (truth) combined with ahimsa (non-violence) one could bring the whole world to one's feet. According to him, satyagraha was nothing but introduction of truth and gentleness in national life. A genuine fast, he said, cleansed body, mind and soul. A sincere prayer could work wonders. When *Gayatri jap* was performed with a humble and concentrated mind in an intelligent manner in times of national difficulties and calamities, it became a most potent instrument for warding off danger![4] He proudly told Sastri that he had reduced fasting and prayer to an exact science. With them he would do millions of things pertaining to the nation! This was one aspect of his spiritual ideology.

In the last week of February 1920, Gandhi addressed the Bengal Provincial Khilafat Conference at Calcutta. The Committee proposed March 19 as the second Khilafat day, a day of *hartal*. The conference appealed to Muslims to renounce titles, resign seats in councils and Government employment, the Police and the Army! But there was little response! The Khilafat delegation led by Mahomed Ali had already arrived in England in the last week of February 1920.

The deputation was received by Fisher on behalf of Montagu. Lloyd George, Prime Minister of England, was blunt in the interview he gave on March 17, 1920, to the Khilafat deputation. He told them that like Germany and Austria, Turkey must pay the penalty for defeat. He also debarred the delegation from appearing before the Supreme Council of the Peace Conference.

As a result of this frustration, the Indian skies were filled with Khilafat slogans. The Khilafat Committee gave a call to observe Khilafat day on March 19. Gandhi, who had made the Khilafat agitation his main concern in the political field, completely identified himself with that agitation and was fanatically and desperately fighting for the cause of the Khilafat.

The magic of the slogan 'Khilafat in danger' worked on the Muslim masses and they enthusiastically joined the struggle. The result was that for nearly six or seven years, till the abolition of the Khilafat, the Khilafat Committee outshone the Muslim League. The agitation now reached its crescendo. Hundreds of meetings were held all over India, and people observed *hartal* by complete cessation of work on March 19. There was fasting and prayer and Hindus participated in observing the Khilafat Day, as Gandhi in his message to his countrymen had said that if the Khilafat movement failed, revolution might come in. A week before this Khilafat Day, Police had raided the Khilafat offices at Calcutta and the Nawab of Rampur arrested the relatives of the Ali Brothers. The Aga Khan told the Central Khilafat Committee that the Turks as a race were being exterminated for the previous ten years and the Arabs were being incited to revolt against them.

Gandhi was overjoyed at the success of the Khilafat Day and gave a veiled threat to the Government that the Muslims reserved to themselves the right in the event of the failure of the non-co-operation-cum-non-violent movement to resort to all such methods as might be enjoined by Islamic scriptures. He described the success of the Khilafat Day as a magnificent spectacle and felt no hesitation in guaranteeing a proper solution to the Khilafat question purely on the strength of that prayer. He witnessed in it the glory and splendour in a revival of the institutions of fasting and prayer. Because people thought, spoke and wrote openly, he proudly said, they had no secret revolutionary movement, and they seemed to have outlived the evil day.

Gandhi then completed his tour of the Punjab in connection with the inquiry. The Punjab Sub-Committee of the Congress paid visits to several places, sifted through evidence and examined the statements of over 1,700 witnesses, out of which it selected about 650 statements for incorporating in the report. The task of writing the report fell on Gandhi. After working ceaselessly for a fortnight, he finished the report incorporating some of the suggestions made by Jayakar. Gandhi did the work with commendable industry, evident moderation and strict accuracy. He put before the public bare facts and truth. He did not accept, he said, the view taken by Motilal Nehru, C. R. Das and M. R. Jayakar that Dyer had laid a trap to drive the people into the Jallianwala Bagh with a view to giving them condign punishment. The report was published on March 25, 1920, and was signed by Gandhi, C. R. Das, Abbas S. Tyabji and M. R. Jayakar. In it the committee demanded the removal of Dyer and the repeal of the Rowlatt Act, suggested that the officers guilty of atrocities should be prosecuted for corruption and that fines imposed on the people should be withdrawn. The committee demanded that the Viceroy should be recalled to England, though Gandhi had earlier thought otherwise. There was a hot discussion on the point whether they should demand impeachment or dismissal of Dyer. They unanimously recommended his dismissal on the grounds of humanity.[5]

GANDHI INVITED TAGORE to address the sixth Gujarati Literary Conference held in Ahmedabad on April 2, 1920. Tagore, an ardent champion of the autonomy of the aesthetic life, remarked very frankly in the course of his address that the search after gold must be subservient to the search after God. Gandhi told the literary conference that literature should reflect national aspirations and further the national effort. Literary men should write for the masses and should unite the saint and the peasant. Gandhi had no patience with literature as an expression of imagination, pure and simple. The next day the poet addressed the inmates of the Satyagraha Ashram at Sabarmati.

The national week was observed all over India from April 6 to 13 to commemorate the Jallianwala Bagh massacres. Gandhi addressed meetings in Bombay during the national week and wired to the Viceroy and the British Government seeking permission for his going to England to acquaint the British Cabinet Ministers with Muslim sentiment over the Khilafat question. Gandhi, the Hindu defender of the Khilafat, was granted permission, but the general view was that he should give up the idea of going to England, and the proposal was dropped.

The Mahatma's so-called Muslim elder brother Shaukat Ali, who was disappointed at the result of the Khilafat Conference at Calcutta, was fomenting the agitation in Madras. Presiding over the Madras Khilafat Conference on April 17, he suggested progressive abstention from co-operation with Government; first, to renounce honorary posts and titles and membership of the Legislative Council; secondly, to resign from remuneratory posts under Government; thirdly, to give up service in the Police and the Army and fourthly to refuse to pay taxes to the Government. Criticizing this move, Besant said that it meant India would have to face aimless rioting, rapine and bloodshed and then Gandhi would again dissociate himself from it![6]

The All-India Home Rule League, after Besant's resignation from it, lacked a leader of action. Tilak's Home Rule League was independent. The Home Rule Leaguers requested Gandhi to accept the presidentship of the Home Rule League. In spite of Jayakar's opposition, Jinnah, too, approached Gandhi to accept the leadership of the Home Rule League. On receiving their invitation, Gandhi wrote to Sastri that he could join an organization to effect its policy and not to be affected by it. Besant, the founder of the All-India Home Rule League, had been already deprived of her position and now a 'swadeshi leader' was enthroned in place of a 'foreign leader'.

Gandhi joined the All-India Home Rule League with the object of promoting swadeshi, Hindu-Muslim unity with special reference to the Khilafat question, and Hindustani—a blend of Hindi and Urdu—and redistribution of provinces on a linguistic basis. When Gandhi deliberately changed the creed and name of the Home Rule League to Swaraj Sabha at Calcutta on September 4, 1920, all the leading members including Jinnah and Jayakar resigned. They accused him of changing the creed of the organization arbitrarily. Gandhi truly and calmly replied that the country was moving so fast that those who had resigned could not keep pace with it. As the legality of the proceedings was challenged, another meeting of the Home Rule Leaguers was called on October 3, 1920, and the name Swaraj Sabha was confirmed.

Jinnah and Umar Sobani tried to win Gandhi over to their side and save him from the thoughtlessness of encouraging the religious fanaticism of the communal leaders, the Ali Brothers, the Moulvis, the Ulemas and their equally ignorant and superstitious Muslim followers, but Jinnah was himself dislodged from the Home Rule League. He could not save Gandhi from his unholy alliance with the Ali Brothers. Gandhi was at that time more pro-Muslim than Jinnah and a fanatic Khilafatist at that. Jinnah wisely kept aloof from the fanaticism of the Khilafatists.

THE IDEOLOGICAL DIFFERENCE between Tilak and Gandhi was weighing on the minds of some of their devotees. Swami Anand had reverence for both leaders. He arranged a meeting between the two at Sinhagad towards the end of April 1920. Sinhagad is eighteen miles from Poona and is a hill station. Sometimes Tilak used to take a rest there. Gandhi arrived in Poona on the morning of April 29 by train and motored to Sinhagad. Gandhi, Mahadev Desai, Dr. Jivraj Mehta, Swami Anand, Prabhudas, Dipak, Dr. Kelkar the naturopath and Balkoba Bhave were at Sinhagad.

Gandhi stayed there from April 29 to May 4, 1920. He was ill and had a pain in his left leg. He had a most torturing and splitting headache for two days but enjoyed luscious mangoes.

Tilak and Gandhi met two or three times at Sinhagad. At one of the meetings, Gandhi expressed his displeasure to Tilak for stigmatizing Besant as Putana and added that she was doing her work in her own way honestly though in private conversation Gandhi's circle described Besant as a foreign leader. Tilak replied that Putana, the demoness, also did her work in her own way, honestly, to kill Krishna!

During that week Dr. Bhandarkar was seriously ill. Tilak inquired of Dr. Kelkar about Bhandarkar's health and said a man should not live in this world until he had lost his eyes, ears and the strength to walk. He should not become a burden to his relatives. There was no meaning in such an existence. Upon this Gandhi asked Tilak whether such a man should put an end to his life and opined that life or death was not in one's hands. Tilak answered that in such a situation one should necessarily commit suicide. For such acts there was scriptural authority. Gandhi said this was improper. Tilak asserted that it was proper. A person had no right to pull on with life and become a nuisance to society; he should make room for worthy people.

Then they turned to Buddhism which Tilak described as refined Hinduism, a branch of Hinduism. When they came to philosophy, Tilak said that logic had no end and when one reached the Pole and wanted to go ahead, one began his return voyage! Synthesis was the end. The Buddhists mixed with the people and worked among them on the basis of friendship, sympathy and joy. Like the Brahmins, they did not keep themselves aloof on high pedestals. Yet the *Darshanas* of Buddhists and Jains, though on a higher plane, were imperfect and lopsided. They did not understand the value of synthesis.

Good and evil raised a duel in man's mind. "In different circumstances," Tilak observed, "man has to use different means and ends, even opposite and contradictory." The duty of a householder differed from that of a recluse. Pavanaharibuva, Tilak added, treated the serpent-bite as the message of God whereas Tukaram said: 'To Serpent, Scorpion, Narayan, one should bid farewell from a distance.'

Of course there was discussion on some of the aspects of the Gita, and Tilak put his usual interpretation on it and emphasized his point that Arjun ultimately resorted to war when the question of good and evil was resolved by Krishna. These were the answers Tilak gave to Gandhi, Swami Anand and Dr. Kelkar who enjoyed the talk of Tilak. Gandhi always suffered from an inferiority complex in such discussions as he was neither a scholar nor a debater.

At about this time Maganlal Gandhi was very critical of Gandhi. His acceptance of a motor-car as a gift and his shouldering of additional responsibilities like the Khilafat movement upset Maganlal. From Sinhagad, Gandhi tried to defend himself and said, "My staunchness has not disappeared. My ideas have grown more tolerant. It is true," he continued, "that I have lost my former fire. My illness has disabled me. . . . The steel-like strength of my body having given place to softness, I put up with many things. Did anyone ever see me going for a change of air? ... I feel ashamed when travelling second class. My soul suffers on such occasions and to be sure, it loses its lustre. There is no way out of it. My best time is over. People may take now what they can from my ideas. I have ceased to be the ideal man of action which I used to be. I am to be pitied for being in this state. There is no exaggeration in this."[7]

Two years earlier, when Gandhi was in high spirits and the times looked propitious and promising, he had written to this devoted disciple: "I feel that, while my star is in the ascendant, I should do all I can to spread my ideals."[8] Even men of great action or mission are of course sometimes depressed and dejected in spirit. But the call of duty soon awakens them to action. For, to them action and adventure is the salt of life.

GANDHI LEFT SINHAGAD as he was called to Ahmedabad to attend negotiations on the system of arbitration for solving the disputes between mill-workers and mill-owners. There was some misunderstanding about the line taken up by Gandhi.. He therefore wrote to Mangaldas Parekh, a mill-owner, who had helped Gandhi to establish the Kochrab Ashram, that the line of action he recommended was based on pure justice. "For," he added, "I want neither money nor honour. I had had enough of wealth and gave up its pursuit. God meets all my needs through friends. I would not take a single step which would do injustice to the workers." He then addressed meetings of mill-hands at Ahmedabad on the settlement of their strike.

Gandhi once again declared that Indian Muslims wanted Turkish suzerainty over Arabia and that Turkey should guarantee complete self-rule for Arabia. He admitted that non-cooperation was attended with danger but added that without non-co-operation violence was a certainty, with it only a possibility. He said he had joined the Khilafat movement because the cause was just and was supported by scriptural authority. If he did not support the Muslims, it would be a cowardly breach of brotherhood and he would be unworthy of the position he claimed. When he was charged with involving India in an international struggle over the Khilafat question, he said he was doing it because he shared the sufferings and trials of Indian Muslims. Replying to a question Gandhi stated that he wanted "to buy their friendship".

Writing about Hindu-Muslim unity on April 11, 1920, Gandhi said that unity is strength and not merely a copy-book maxim but a rule of life. Hindu-Muslim unity meant not only unity between Hindus and Muslims but between all those who believed India to be their home, no matter to what faith they belonged. He also declared that Pan-Islamism was not anti-Indian or anti-Hindu.[9] Although he knew the Muslims might adopt non-co-operation in a spirit of retaliation and a Karachi leader drew his attention to the alarming speeches of Shaukat Ali made at Madras, Gandhi said he understood what Shaukat Ali meant! Gandhi was out "to buy the friendship of the Muslims', so he never stopped to think whether the Muslims regarded India as their home. He began offering a price for their love. The bargaining began.

Gandhi asked the Hindus not to insist on playing music while passing by a mosque. He did not want them to quote precedents on this question. The Muslims should accommodate their Hindu brothers; they should not slaughter the cow which was as dear as life to a Hindu. Yet Gandhi admitted that the Muslims were under no religious obligations to slaughter cows.

Gandhi had suggested the establishment of panchayats of unimpeachable probity and imperturbability whose decisions must be binding on both parties. But neither Gandhi nor his lieutenants worked for it.

A few months earlier Jinnah had earnestly suggested a remedy for communal clashes. While giving evidence before the Joint Select Committee after the passing of the Reforms Act of 1919, he said, "If I was the minister, I would make bold to say that nothing would weigh with me except justice, and what is right. . . . Communal riots occur, because the police take one side or the other."[10]

About this time Gandhi's attention was drawn to the case of the Savarkar brothers who were rotting in the Andamans although all political prisoners from Indian jails and from the cellular jail in the Andamans were released under the royal amnesty. Dr. Narayanrao Savarkar was in touch with Gandhi, and at his instance he wrote an article on May 26, 1920, in *Young India*. Therein he said that no act of violence was proved against the Savarkar brothers. The cult of violence had, at that moment, no following in India. Unless there was absolute proof that the discharge of these two brothers could be a danger to the State, the Viceroy was bound to give them their liberty. Savarkar was however, not released till 1937.

At this time Gandhi's policy was being discussed in England. In the April 1920 issue of the *East and West*, a writer said: "Gandhi has the reputation of a saint, but it seems that the politician in him often dominates his decisions." He added that like Buddha and Christ, Gandhi should take up the larger mission of uniting the world. Gandhi replied that the word saint should be ruled out as he was a humble searcher after truth, making experiments about some "of the external varieties of life", but he could not even claim to be a scientist because he could show no tangible proof of scientific accuracy in his methods or such tangible results of his experiments as modern science demanded. He disclaimed sainthood, avowed that the politician in him never dominated a single discussion of his and added: "If I seem to take part in politics, it is only because politics encircles us today like the coil of a snake from which one cannot get out no matter how much one tries".

He was, Gandhi concluded, following in the footsteps of the great teachers Buddha and Christ.[11] It may be remembered here that he had told Polak while in South Africa that "I am a politician trying my hardest to be a saint". This was indeed true of Gandhi. In Gandhi's opinion Jesus was a prince among the politicians and the politics of his time consisted in securing the welfare of the people by teaching them not to be seduced by the trinkets of the priests and the Pharisees.[12]

The Khilafat question was more political than religious, more international than national, for it affected the politics of many countries in Europe and Asia. It particularly affected the North-West Frontier of India. During the preceding year the Bolsheviks and the Afghans had joined hands to exert pressure on Indian politics and were working against British rule in their own way. In the British Parliament, Montagu was asked to state whether the tribal risings of April and May 1919 had any connection with the disturbances throughout India and especially in the Punjab. He was asked also about Bolshevik activities in those areas. Because of its sympathy with the Pan-Islamic policy, Afghanistan, although defeated by the British in the third Afghan War in May 1919, sympathised with the agitation of the Indian Muslims, and the Ali Brothers were suspected of disloyalty. On August 8, 1919, a Treaty of Peace was signed between Afghanistan and British India. The way was paved for further talks.

Meanwhile the Indian Government started giving Nepal a subsidy to the extent of Rs. 10 lakhs a year, its object being to secure the frontier against Bolshevik and Afghan inroads, with the help of Nepal troops. Their help to the British in World War I was remembered. The Indian Government had stopped giving a subsidy to the Afghan Government as it had lost the friendship of the Afghans.

As fresh talks were about to be resumed, the Afghan delegation under H.E. Mohammed Tazzi Beg came to open preliminary parleys with the Indian Government on a treaty of friendship. The delegates came on April 9, 1920, and the parleys opened at Mussoorie on April 16, 1920. The talks continued intermittently till January 4, 1921, and the next day Beg went to Afghanistan.

While the talks were proceeding between the Afghan and British envoys at Mussoorie, Pandit Jawaharlal Nehru occupied some rooms in the hotel in which the members of the Afghan delegation were staying. On May 16, 1920, Nehru was externed under the Defence of India Act and he had to quit the hotel, leaving behind his ailing mother and his ailing wife. The Simla authorities wanted an undertaking from Nehru that he would not have any dealings or contacts with the Afghan delegation. Nehru refused to give such an undertaking.

When the news about the externment of Jawaharlal Nehru became known, Gandhi denounced it as insanity and stated that the Afghan delegation was also in complete accord with Indian Mohammedan feeling. The Hunter Committee's Report was published on May 28, 1920. It was sent to the Indian Government in December 1919 by the British Government, but it was kept a secret. In its majority report the Hunter Commission blamed Dyer for the atrocities and massacres. The military council found him guilty only of an error of judgment. The report was denounced and justly censured by Indians of all shades of opinion as entirely disappointing, whitewashing the criminal action of the officers and exonerating the Viceroy. The European Association at Calcutta and other European institutions in India passed resolutions praising and exonerating Dyer and other officers who perpetrated the horrible atrocities. On top of it all, a Dyer Fund was also started in India.

The British Congress Committee expressed its indignation at the massacres and urged the British Government to recall the Viceroy and bring the incriminated officers to book. The Labour Conference of Britain passed resolutions regarding the Punjab affairs, urged the recall of the Viceroy and pressed for the impeachment of O'Dwyer and punishment to Punjab officials. Yet the British Parliament was satisfied with Dyer's removal only. In the British Parliament, Churchill and Asquith raised their voice against the atrocities, but the majority of the Members upheld the action of the Punjab Government.

The House of Lords, carrying Lord Finlay's motion by a majority, acquitted General Dyer! The age of Burke and Sheridan was over a century earlier, and Montagu, though well inclined to India, was no Burke. Yet he asked the supporters of Dyer whether they were going to keep a hold on India by terrorism, racial humiliation and subordination or were they going to rest it upon the growing goodwill of the people of their Indian Empire.

The only silver lining to the darkest cloud of disgrace was the defeat of Sir Edward Carson who callously moved an amendment justifying the atrocities perpetrated by Dyer. The British people presented Dyer with a purse of three lakhs of Rupees and added insult to injury. O'Dwyer was puffed. So he sued Sir Sankaran Nair for damages as he thought Nair's statements defaming and won the case in June 1924. H. G. Wells, criticizing the judgment of Mr. Justice McCardie, observed: "It is treachery to Indians to go talking liberally to them, to seek their friendship and attempt co-operation with Dyer's impenitent rifles re-loaded and our Justice McCardie ready and eager to tear up our poor attempts to make amends."[13]

Sir Michael O'Dwyer, the defender of Dyer escaped scot-free in 1919 but fell a victim to the bullets of a Punjabi youth named Sardar Udamsingh. He shot him in London on March 13, 1940, and avenged in his own way the deaths of the martyrs at Jallianwala Bagh. Dyer died a natural death peacefully and unrepentingly on July 23, 1927.

On May 14, 1920, the Indian Government published the Turkish Peace Terms and asked the Muslims to bear with resignation the misfortunes of the Turks. The Peace Terms were denounced indignantly by Indian newspapers. The meeting of the All-India Khilafat Committee held in Bombay accepted the policy of non-co-operation. The Central Khilafat Committee adopted non-co-operation on May 28, 1920, as the only means left to them. Few renounced titles as the first step towards non-co-operation. Batches of Muslims started emigrating and left Peshawar for Kabul in protest against the Turkish Peace Terms which were considered to be against the tenets of Islam.

The All-India Congress Committee met at Benares on May 30. Gandhi and Tilak were present. Heated debates on non-co-operation took place. Gandhi proposed that the Congress should recommend to the country a programme of non-cooperation without further delay as a protest against the Turkish Peace Treaty and the decision of the Government in respect of Punjab affairs. Gandhi, who opposed the Khilafat being bracketed with the Punjab wrongs, now joined both in order to make it attractive to the Hindus. The decision, however, was left to the Congress which was scheduled to meet in August 1920, but actually met in September.

A joint Hindu-Muslim Conference was held at Allahabad on June 1, 1920. Gandhi, Besant, Motilal, Malaviya and Sir Tej Bahadur Sapru were against non-co-operation. Other Hindu leaders saw many difficulties in it, and they feared complications arising from Indian Muslims welcoming the invasion of India by the Afghans. These leaders, however, approved of the non-co-operation policy in theory. The Muslim leaders declared they would fight any invasion made with a view to conquering India, but would non-co-operate with it if it was made to uphold the prestige of Islam and to vindicate justice.

Shaukat Ali requested Tilak to attend the meetings of the

Council of the All-India Muslim League and that of the Khilafat Committee, held to discuss the Khilafat question, but he said he would not attend any meeting other than that of the Congress. The Muslims, he added, should take the initiative in respect of the decisions on the Khilafat, and Hindus would support them. Gandhi addressed the meetings of both the League and the Central Khilafat Committee and spoke on non-co-operation. On June 3 the Central Khilafat Committee resolved to resort to non-co-operation with the Government.

GANDHI WAS DETERMINED to launch the struggle. Strangely enough, he said that his experience of the previous year showed him that in spite of the aberrations in some parts of India the country was entirely under control. Ample provision was being made this time to avoid the mistakes of the past. He would risk, he added, if necessary, a million lives[14] so long as they were voluntary sufferers and were innocent, spotless victims. This was the declaration of a non-violent Napoleon or a Caesar or an Alexander who violently sacrificed millions of men for the sake of their ambition whereas the non-violent Napoleon in Gandhi was prepared to sacrifice passively and non-violently a million innocent people as victims for the sake of his principles. Loss of a million lives was nothing to Gandhi for the vindication of his principles! Accordingly, on June 30, a representation signed by Abul Kalam Azad, Abdul Bari, the Ali Brothers and Yakub Hassan was sent to the Viceroy notifying him that they and the people would be obliged from August 1 to withdraw co-operation from the Government! They considered loyalty to an earthly sovereign to be subservient to their loyalty to Islam. So their loyalty to Islam enjoined upon every Mussalman to consider those who want only injured the status of the Khilafat to be enemies of Islam and to resist them with arms if necessary.

As a member of the Sub-Committee appointed by the Khilafat Committee, Gandhi said that, according to some, he was no doubt 'a superior person' but after all a crank and an interloper at that. Yet he was leading the movement of the Khilafatists in the sense that he was their adviser and interpreter. But he added he did not represent Muslim opinion. He was there on the committee as a specialist and not as a Hindu leader. He said he was a sagacious worker who never travelled beyond his limits. He considered the step of non-co-operation perfectly consistent with his loyalty to the British connection. Although the Muslim leaders made an equivocal statement at Allahabad, he declared that the Muslim leaders promised to fight to a man any invader who wanted to conquer India. But they were, Gandhi admitted, equally frank in asserting that any invasion from without undertaken with a view to upholding the prestige of Islam and vindicating justice would have their full sympathy if not their actual support.[15]

The *Modern Review*,[16] putting the nation's leaders on their guard, asked them whether the upholding of the prestige of Islam required an invasion of India and how justice would be vindicated by inflicting on the unoffending men of India the indignity and misery for an offence committed by the Allies. The *Modern Review* further observed: "Who is to judge whether an invasion is for purposes of conquest and plunder or for upholding of Islamic prestige and the vindication of Justice? In former ages Mohammedan invaders of India like Mahomed of Ghazni claimed that their expeditions into India were undertaken in the interests of Islam."

Gandhi then declared that he would neither go with the Muslims on any campaign of violence nor help them to promote, for instance, an invasion of India through Afghanistan. He wanted to prevent any such armed conflict. It was, he said, the duty of every Hindu to resist any inroad on India.

During the early twenties, Gandhi tried to encourage the Dravidians to learn Hindi and said that he had the greatest faith in the Dravidians some day taking up the study of Hindi seriously. He made appeal after appeal to push forward swadeshi, wishing that the music of the spinning wheel might permeate the masses and princes. He himself had learnt to spin at the age of fifty. Some of the noted families in India and even some princes took to spinning as a patriotic gesture and found solace in the music of the spinning wheel! While Gandhi was stirring up the non-co-operation struggle, surprisingly enough, he was, up to June 9, 1920, in favour of the Council elections being contested by those who wished to serve the nation. He hoped that when people did exercise their vote, they would give it to the best man no matter to which party he belonged.[17]

The Ali Brothers proposed *hijrat* (emigration) to Muslims. In their opinion India had ceased to be Dar-ul-Aman (holy land) and become Dar-ul-Harab (enemy land), and so the only alternative for a true Muslim was between *jehad* (a holy war) or *hijrat* (emigration). So the active part of the Khilafat movement began early in July when about 18,000 Muslims started on *hijrat* and migrated to Afghanistan leaving Peshawar for Kabul in protest against the Turkish Peace Terms which were thought to be against the tenets of Islam. The Amir of Afghanistan, however, having forbidden entry of more emigrants, those who tried to enter had to come back facing confusion and hardships. Abdul Ghaffar Khan was one of those who returned from Afghanistan.

Just then Lajpatrai vehemently denounced Council entry which he himself later enthusiastically advocated! That pushed Gandhi one step ahead and he said he was in entire accord with Lala Lajpatrai, declaring that for him it was but one step in the campaign of non-co-operation. So Gandhi declared that to enter the Councils was to co-operate.

Commenting on this, N. C. Kelkar said that "Gandhi was a loyal co-operator and this champion of non-co-operation had recently declared in favour of working out the reforms even though the Rowlatt Act stood on the statute book and the massacres in the Punjab had taken place. Gandhi knew what the outcome of the Hunter Committee would be, and the fate of the Khilafat was in the balance. Yet at the Amritsar Congress, in trying to be a whole-hearted co-operator, he was prepared to tolerate humiliation on these three scores."[18] At that time, Gandhi later said, his knowledge was limited and he could not judge the Government. Gandhi was thus unpredictable at any crucial time.

About this time the British Government was thinking of sending the Prince of Wales to India and the Government wanted the Indians to give the Prince of Wales an enthusiastic welcome. Gandhi said that if the Government wanted the people to do so, they should remove the Khilafat and Punjab grievances; otherwise they would boycott his visit. The visit was then postponed.

On July 12, 1920, Tilak went to Bombay as the application he had made to the Bombay High Court, for allowing Jagannath Maharaj the possession of his property at Kolhapur, was about to come up before the High Court. He was staying at Sardar Griha where Gandhi and Shaukat Ali met him and held some discussions on the Khilafat question. Tilak did not show any active interest in the Khilafat question. Writing about this discussion, Gandhi later observed: "About Hindus and Mussalmans, Tilak, turning to the Maulana, said, 'I will sign anything that Gandhi suggests because I have full faith in him on the question.' About non-co-operation he significantly repeated to me what he had said to me before. 'I like the programme well enough, but I have my doubts as to the country being with us in the self-denying ordinance which non-co-operation presents to the people. I will do nothing to hinder the progress of the movement. I wish you every success, and if you gain the popular ear, you will find in me an enthusiastic supporter!' Tilak added that if the Muslims boycotted the councils he and his party would follow suit."

This report of the discussion, like truth, has many sides. The details of the discussion between Tilak and Gandhi will not be complete unless its other side, which Gandhi has not narrated, is given here. Tilak was sceptical of the success of both the satyagraha and the Khilafat movement. As regards the satyagraha, he said to Gandhi. "I consider an armed revolt also constitutional. The only difficulty is, at present it is not possible. If anyone were to assure me that armed revolt would be successful to the extent of even eight annas in the rupee, I would start the revolt, trusting God to give success to the extent of the remaining eight annas. But today to the extent of even four annas we are not prepared and there is no certainty."

A few days earlier, Tilak had told J. R. Ajgaonkar, an eminent Marathi author, that up to that moment he had thought that Gandhi was a Jain, and because Gandhi was a Jain his teachings were tinged with non-violence, satyagraha, fasting and such other things, which were more in keeping with Jainism than Hinduism. But these means and methods were of no use in politics which required a change of attitude from time to time. Tilak further said that exalted religious principles or abstract doctrines about truth were not of much value in the existing political game. Satyagraha would have the least effect upon the rulers and even *hartal* would lead to bloodshed when the officers would try to break it.

A leader holds the leadership of a nation so long as his qualities and message meet the need and mood of the people. The ambivert in Tilak had rightly sensed that this was the time for a change. Tilak, who had towered in the forefront of politics and played so decisive and cardinal a part in the affairs of his nation, would have found it rather difficult to reconcile himself or to gravitate to Gandhian methods of non-violence and a jail-courting programme. He had courageously borne the brunt of the freedom struggle for over twenty years and given the Congress the *mantra* of Swaraj. So perhaps to allow the Gandhian movement to have a chance, he was considering a visit to London.

Gandhi toured the Punjab in the middle of July 1920,

speaking on the Khilafat, non-co-operation and Hindu-Muslim unity and on the decision of the House of Lords on Dyer. Tilak was still in Bombay. He fell ill with fever on July 20. On July 21 he won the Tai Maharaj case and thus brought it to a successful conclusion after nineteen years. The next day fever did not abate. On July 23 congratulations on his sixty-fourth birthday flowed in from every corner of the country.

Towards the end of July Gandhi toured Sind which was leading the way in *hijrat* and expostulated with the Khilafatists there but in vain. On his return to Bombay on July 28, he issued a statement in which he said that many people dreaded the advent of non-co-operation. They feared madness from the mob and consequent repetition of the previous year's reprisals. He admitted that it was easier to oust a Government that had rendered itself unfit to govern than it was to cure unknown people in a mob of their madness. No general worth the name gave up a battle because he had suffered reverses. Determined as he was to sacrifice a million men, Gandhi declared that the 1st August 1920 would be as important an event in the history of India as was the 6th April 1919.

CHAPTER XXI

Leader of the Nation

THE 1ST AUGUST 1920, said Gandhi, was to be marked by fasting and prayer, suspension of business and by meetings to pass resolutions praying for revision of the Turkish Peace Terms, justice for the Punjab and the inculcation of non-co-operation until justice had been done. On July 28 making a stirring call to the country, Gandhi said, "Islam must rise now or be fallen if not for ever, certainly for a century." He could not imagine, he added, a graver wrong than the massacres of Jallianwala Bagh, the whitewash of it by the Hunter Committee, Montagu's defence of the Viceroy and the refusal to remove the guilty officers. During the preceding year, Gandhi had made a sacred promise to the nation that he would obtain the repeal of the Rowlatt Act, and the removal of the Punjab grievances, and both were so far unremedied. He now promised to remove the Khilafat grievances, and all these by means of a non-violent struggle! So Gandhi, the Hindu defender of the Khilafat, along with the Muslim leaders gave a clarion call to the Hindus and Muslims with the slogans 'Khilafat in danger' and 'Islam in danger'!

Since the morning of July 29, 1920, Tilak had become delirious and unconscious at Sardar Griha in Bombay. Among those who went that day to inquire after his health were Gandhi, Baptista, R. P. Paranjpye, Jayakar and Jamnadas Dwarkadas. In the first hour of August 1920, Tilak, whom the Government feared and the people worshipped and who held the stage of Indian politics for over two decades, breathed his last. Never before in the history of modern India was such nation-wide grief witnessed.

It was the dawn of the first hour of Gandhi's Khilafat

movement, the dawn of a new age, the inauguration of his country-wide non-violent struggle which was sanctioned neither by the Congress nor by any political party except the Khilafat Committee.

Gandhi, paying a glowing tribute to Tilak, said that Tilak knew no religion but love of his country. He was unquestionably the idol of his people. No man preached the gospel of Swaraj with the consistency and the insistence of Lokamanya. He certainly brought it nearer by many a year. For the Indians, concluded Gandhi, Tilak would go down to the generations yet unborn as a maker of modern India.

Destiny worked its miracle. Now no leader except C. R. Das, the next great leader after Tilak, could either challenge Gandhi or give a lead to the country. Gandhi was the only full-time politician and perhaps the only man of action on the Indian political scene. His shrewd alliance with the Ali Brothers and the prestige and popularity he had gained so far through his struggles, were powerful enough to overpower the leadership of Das.

Gandhi gave emphasis on swadeshi as he considered it a plank of non-co-operation. Not increase of mills was the remedy for supplying the deficiency of cloth but manufacturing thousands of spinning wheels and distributing home-spun cloth. Thus the people would be able to partially solve the problem of India's grinding poverty. He advocated boycott of schools and courts. Just to give a stimulus to the movement he cited the example of Ambrose, the Bishop of Milan, who refused to see the face of Theodosius the Great, whose officers had massacred innocent people. He also quoted the example of Ramshastri Prabhune, the judge of the Peshwa Court, who boycotted the Peshwa and declined to serve under him while he conducted the Government. Money could hardly be allowed to count where honour or religion was at stake. He wrote that no country had ever risen or made progress towards freedom, enlightenment and progress without being purified by the fire of suffering at some stage or other.

The proposal about boycotting the schools was described by many leaders as mischievous, harmful and opposed to the best interests of the country. Malaviya was its most uncompromising opponent. His influence began to wane with the students of Benares Hindu University. For the first time in the history of India the student force was requisitioned and brought on the battle front of direct action. Gandhi's guru Gokhale did not want students to participate in politics.

Malaviya, whose approbation and blessings Gandhi was ever eager to receive, appealed to Gandhi to desist from non-cooperation and requested him to suspend action till the Congress gave its verdict on the question of non-co-operation. A manifesto was issued by Sir Narayan Chandavarkar and many other leaders against the launching of non-co-operation. To this Gandhi replied that a higher duty required him not to turn from the course mapped out by the Non-co-operation Committee!' "There are moments," he serenely observed, on August 4, 1920, "in your life when you must act, even though you cannot carry your best friends with you. The 'still small voice' within you must always be the final arbiter when there is a conflict of duty."[1]

As regards the question of suspension of non-co-operation, Gandhi observed, "In my humble opinion it is no Congressman's duty to consult the Congress before taking an action in a matter in which he has no doubts. To do otherwise may mean stagnation. The Congress," he argued, "is after all the mouthpiece of the nation. And when one has a policy or programme which one would like to see adopted, one naturally asks the Congress to discuss it and form an opinion. But when one has an unshakable faith in a particular policy or action, it would be folly to wait for the Congress pronouncement. On the contrary one must act and demonstrate its efficacy so as to command acceptance by the nation."

Previously Gandhi had opined that the Congress, like the British Parliament, was not a party organization. He had hoped that all parties would cherish the Congress as a national organization providing a platform for all parties to appeal to the nation with a view to moulding its policy. As regards himself, he said that he belonged to no party and wished to belong to none thereafter. He knew that most of the Congress leaders were not in favour of non-co-operation and he might be defeated at the Congress. "My loyalty to Congress," he now fearlessly stated, "requires me to carry out its policy when it is not contrary to my conscience. If I am in a minority I may not pursue my policy in the name of the Congress. The decision of the Congress on any given question therefore does not mean that it prevents a Congressman from any action to the contrary, but if he acts, he does so at his own risk and with the knowledge that the Congress is not with him."[2]

Upon this Chandavarkar replied to Gandhi and in a rejoinder, Gandhi said that he did not believe that the Gita taught violence for doing good. Gandhi had a novel interpretation of his own. His reading of the Gita was diametrically opposite to Tilak's.

Now that Tilak was gone, Gandhi backed by the Muslims, gave a threat to the Congress leaders that he would carry on his movement in spite of them. He declared that for him to suspend non-co-operation would be to prove untrue to his Mussalman brethren. The Muslims could not wait till the Congress took a decision. They could only expect the Congress to ratify their action and share their sorrows and their burdens. The governing passion of Gandhi's political life was direct action. He believed that nothing had ever been achieved on the earth without direct action. He was in direct touch with the masses and had previously led militant struggles. This was the vital difference between the Congress old leaders and Liberals and Gandhi. The man of action was aware of this weakness of theirs and gave them an ultimatum. The disciples of Gokhale had already left the Congress. Gandhi now resumed the role of Tilak in the Congress as well as in the country.

Gandhi made a winning gesture towards the Tilakites. He soon went to Tilak's house in Poona, consoled the relatives of Tilak and asked for one of the articles Tilak had used to preserve as a memento. Tilak's tiny silver box in which he kept crushed bettlenut was presented to Gandhi. None of Tilak's lieutenants had made such a request to the family of Tilak.

GANDHI THEN STARTED on his tour of Southern India. He had support from those parts of India where the Khilafat movement had been organized—U.P., Bengal and Madras. He addressed public meetings in Madras, Kumbakonam, Trichinopoly, Calicut, Bezwada and at several other places, on the theme of non-violent non-co-operation.

At this time Gandhi wrote in *Young India* of August 11, 1920, his famous epistle on the doctrine of the sword. He was plied with silly questions, privately as well as publicly and asked whether he was waiting for the right moment for declaring open violence. Gandhi knew that the Muslims had no faith in non-violence; but they were following it as a policy or as a matter of expediency. Shaukat Ali, too, held that Gandhi was a shrewd Bania, not an out-and-out believer in non-violence and was preparing the country for guerilla warfare. Replying to various queries, Gandhi said that he regarded secrecy as a sin and observed: "I do believe that where there is only a choice between cowardice and violence, I would advise violence." "I would," he continued, "rather have India resort to arms in order to defend her honour than that she should in a cowardly manner become or remain a helpless witness to her own dishonour."

Gandhi considered non-violence infinitely superior to violence and forgiveness more manly than punishment. "But abstinence," he added, "is forgiveness only when there is the power to punish. ... A mouse hardly forgives a cat when it allows itself to be torn to pieces by her."

Gandhi further said he was not a visionary, he claimed to be a practical idealist. The religion of non-violence was not meant merely for Rishis and saints. It was meant for the common people as well. Non-violence was the law of our species as violence was the law of the brute. He, therefore, ventured to put the ancient law of self-sacrifice, for satyagraha and its off-shoots. Non-co-operation and civil resistance were nothing but new names for the law of suffering. The religion of non-violence was the root of Hinduism. Gandhi invited even believers in violence to give the peaceful non-co-operation a trial.

Concluding his epistle, Gandhi gave a message to India and to the world as he believed that his religion had no geographical limits. He said:[3] "If India takes up the doctrine of the sword, she may gain momentary victory. Then India will cease to be the pride of my heart. I am wedded to India, because I owe my all to her. I believe absolutely that she has a mission for the world. She is not to copy Europe blindly. India's acceptance of the doctrine of the sword will be the hour of my trial. I hope I shall not be found wanting." Gandhi's interpretation of Hinduism is over-stretched and over-emphasized to suit his theory. A study of Indian history and the history of Hindu, Buddhist and Jain religions would show how these religions allowed their followers to fight with lethal weapons for liberty and self-defence. Gandhi's knowledge of these scriptures and of the history of India was limited.

Towards the middle of August 1920, Gandhi toured the Madras Presidency, speaking in English and propagating the principle of non-co-operation. With great feeling he said his voice was stronger than it was a year earlier but his body was weak. He spoke sitting at all meetings in Madras, Kumbakonam, Trichinopoly, Calicut, Mangalore and Bangalore. He told the people that the Government used schools and colleges to produce servants, and lawyers interpreted law to the people and thus supported authority. They might be called honorary officeholders. If they desired to bend the Government to the will of the people, they must suspend their legal practice.

Gandhi saw that the people were better disciplined than they were before, but some leaders had no faith in non-co-operation and those who had it lacked the capacity for self-sacrifice. There were those who believed one thing and said another. Gandhi said he could not wait till the decision of the special Congress. He thought that he held the honour of the Muslims in his hands and the Muslims could not eat their own words and withdraw from the honourable position they had taken up. Even if the Congress voted against the movement, he would still advise the Muslims to stand single-handed and fight rather than yield to the attempted dishonour of their religion.

Meanwhile the Bengal Congress Committee accepted the principle of non-co-operation with some modifications. The Bombay Provincial Congress Committee, too, approved it. Gandhi, who believed that sword-force was brute-force, reiterated his faith in wresting justice by sacrifice of self and not by violence. He added that as soon as India accepted the doctrine of the sword his life as an Indian would be finished. And yet Gandhi wrote in the *Navajivan* of August 15, 1920, that he once told his son Harilal in South Africa that "if you could not protect me by taking the danger upon yourself, you should undoubtedly do so by attacking the other man. It is any day better to use brute-force than to betray cowardice."

On his return from Madras, Gandhi attended the Gujarat Political Conference at Ahmedabad in the last week of August. It was held to decide the question of non-co-operation, to educate public opinion and to place Gujarat's view before the Congress session. The Gujarat Political Conference passed a resolution on non-co-operation, but Rao Bahadur Ramanbhai warned that non-co-operation would lead to lawlessness.

The Indian Government had begun gradually to make appealing gestures towards the people. It appointed Sir Tej Bahadur Sapru, Member of the Executive Council of the Viceroy, and Lord Sinha, Governor of Bihar and Orissa.

Although Gandhi was desperately telling the country that the Muslims had launched the struggle without the sanction of the Congress, and he had decided to give them a lead single-handed, he knew also that it would not be a really national struggle. So he was bound to try desperately to win over the Congress to the Khilafatists.

Thus it was under the auspices of the Khilafat Committee

that Gandhi inaugurated the non-co-operation movement on August 1, 1920. Naturally non-co-operation was initiated not for winning Swaraj, but for getting Khilafat wrongs redressed. Gandhi now wanted the Congress to adopt non-co-operation and strengthen the Khilafat movement, which, in fact, represented Muslim extra-territorial loyalty and ambition and Muslim chauvinism. The Khilafat movement was undoing the work of educated and modernist Muslims. It was leaping forward and a large number of fanatic Muslims resorted to *hijrat* or emigration in August 1920, but were repulsed by the Afghan Government.

Mrs. Besant, C. R. Das, Pandit Motilal Nehru, N. C. Kelkar, Jinnah and Kasturiranga lyengar were opposed to Gandhi's, non-co-operation movement. Motilal, who was a co-operator at Amritsar, came to Howrah station to see Jinnah and told him that they should combine to defeat Gandhi's resolution on non-co-operation.[4] A few days earlier he had warned Das that they must be prepared for a big tussle with Gandhi. He said Gandhi placed too much trust on popularity. In June 1920 Motilal was thinking of contesting election to the Council and of fixing a constituency also for Jawaharlal.[5] He was sure that Congress would not bind itself to non-co-operation. Motilal Nehru and C. R. Das had just come from Arrah (Bihar), where they had been fighting, since the beginning of the year, the celebrated Dumraon case, Das representing the Maharaja, who was the plaintiff, and Motilal Nehru and N. N. Sircar his opponents, the Dewan's sons. Motilal received Rs. 25,000 as fees a month, and Das more than a thousand rupees a day. Lajpatrai, who was to preside over the historic Congress, was at this juncture drawn to Gandhi while he was in favour of the stalwarts of the Congress.

THE CONGRESS MET at Calcutta in the first week of September 1920. Before the Subjects Committee met, it was not difficult for Gandhi to win over Motilal Nehru to his side through Jawaharlal Nehru. Then Gandhi's colleagues and staunch supporters did superb manoeuvrings in the composition of the Subjects Committee. N. C. Kelkar, who was then the spokesman of the Maharashtra Congress and had been drafting the constitution for the Congress along with Gandhi, wrote in the *Kesari* that questionable methods were used by Gandhi's associates to gain a majority in the Subjects Committee. Care was taken to see that the Subjects Committee was predominantly filled with Muslim delegates. For example 14 Madras delegates were elected to the Subjects Committee from Rajagopalachari's list which included seven Muslims, and not a single member was elected from the list of Satyamurti.[6]

On Sunday, the 5th September, C. R. Das, the next great leader after Tilak, was the first to place a resolution before the Subjects Committee. His draft resolution recommended non-co-operation till the attainment of Swaraj, boycott of Government levies, *Durbars* and other official and semi-official functions, establishment of national schools and establishment of private arbitration courts for settling private disputes. It also advocated entry into Councils to oppose the Government. Kasturiranga Iyengar supported the resolution. Shyam Sunder Chakrabarti opposed it.

Then Gandhi placed before the Subjects Committee the draft resolution which he had prepared at the instance of Shaukat Ali. While Gandhi was preparing the draft resolution in the morning, the word 'non-violent' had escaped him. Shaukat Ali had no hesitation in agreeing to the addition of the adjective 'non-violent' before the word non-co-operation. The resolution recommended non-violent non-co-operation until the Khilafat and Punjab grievances were redressed, besides recommending immediate boycott of schools, colleges, courts and councils. It made no mention of the attainment of Swaraj or the boycott of British goods. Gandhi felt convinced now, he observed, though he felt otherwise at Amritsar, that the reforms were a dangerous trap which concealed gilded chains that enslaved the country. He assured the members that if they would start the movement in the right spirit he was confident that they would secure Swaraj in a year. A lifelong loyalist became a staunch enemy of the Empire. A leader who ridiculed Tilak and Besant in private talks for having "dinned the poison of Home Rule into the ears of the people of the country and raising false hopes of their liberation in a short time", now came forward at the age of fifty-one to promise Swaraj in a year! It may be noted here that Gandhi had, at the first Khilafat Conference in Delhi, opposed the Khilafat question being combined with the Punjab issue. He now joined both to make it attractive to the Hindus.

Lajpatrai, the President of the Congress, said that he was as eager as anybody to achieve absolute political independence of India, but as long as the creed of the Congress was not changed it should be observed. As regards the giving up of titles, he said that even the Muslims were not unanimous on the question of non-co-operation; only two persons from the Punjab had renounced titles and they were Hindus. So Gandhi should not, for the present, impose his resolution on the Congress. Upon this, Shaukat Ali admitted that there were a few Muslims for non-co-operation, but the Muslims would not give up the movement till the last inch of the sacred land of the Muslims was taken from the possession of the enemy. Baptista and Kelkar laid emphasis on the Council entry.

Just to pacify Das, who recommended non-co-operation with the Government till the attainment of Swaraj, Motilal Nehru moved an amendment to Gandhi's resolution recommending adoption of the policy of non-violent non-co-operation till the said wrongs were righted and Swaraj was established. He recommended also the terms 'gradual' and 'progressive' to qualify the boycott of schools and courts.

Gandhi considered school and college students to be soldiers in the national army and he thought that once they were out they would participate in public activities and would be trained in national service. So he wanted immediate boycott of schools and colleges. Yet Gandhi accepted the amendment.

In a fiery speech Yakub Hassan supported Gandhi. On Monday, September 6, Besant opposed the Gandhi resolution. Jinnah, too, opposed it saying that he was doubtful whether India, even if all the programmes laid down by Gandhi were carried out, would win Swaraj in one year.

On Tuesday, September 7, B. C. Pal moved an amendment proposing a deputation to England and in the event of its failure Gandhi's non-co-operation movement should be carried out. Khaparde supported it.

Gandhi was allowed to reply to the debate. He said that even if his resolution was thrown out, he would try to turn the minority into a majority. He said he agreed to graduality in the withdrawal of school children and lawyers. He accepted the amendment regarding full self-government in his proposal, but not on the ground that the Khilafat question was subservient to the question of Swaraj. To him the Khilafat question and the Punjab wrongs were greater than Swaraj. The Councils were a death trap, he concluded.

Das was allowed to reply to the debates. He said the Councils were not a trap to those who knowingly entered it. He was surprised that Motilal Nehru, who had gone over to the Gandhi camp only twenty-four hours earlier, asked them whether they were sure of a majority in the Councils. He said that the principle of graduality should be applied to the boycott of the

Councils also. 'Mahatma Gandhi said so' was no reply to his question, he thundered.

The nationalists were in favour of Council entry and so the opposition had mainly centred on this question. After the reply of Das, Gandhi's resolution with Motilal Nehru's amendment was passed by a majority of seven votes in the Subjects Committee. All the Muslim delegates except Jinnah voted for Gandhi's resolution. Among the stalwarts nobody except Motilal Nehru supported Gandhi. Then "Vijayaraghavachariar moved his amendment recommending boycott of foreign goods, and in spite of the determined opposition of Gandhi, his followers and lieutenants it was passed by the Subjects Committee. Thus, boycott of foreign goods and the word Swaraj were tagged to the Khilafat and Punjab wrongs in spite of Gandhi.

Notice was given by B. C. Pal to the effect that he would oppose Gandhi's resolution in the open session. It was signed by Baptista, Jayakar, Jinnah, Kasturiranga lyengar, Satyamurti, Kelkar, Das, Chakrabarti, Lahiri, Shyamlal Nehru, T. Prakasam, A. Rangaswami, Dr. Moonje and others.

Realizing the significance of this great move and the bare majority in the Subjects Committee, the Gandhi party resorted to improper measures and methods. Umar Sobani and Shankarlal Banker managed to add over a hundred[7] delegates from the streets, some of them being Muslim taxi-drivers of Calcutta, to vote for the non-co-operation resolution. Jamnalal Bajaj, who was shortly to be an adopted son of Gandhi, too, spent a lot of money on bringing delegates to vote for non-co-operation. And Gandhi later described this fight at the Congress session as a fair fight!

On September 8 Gandhi moved his resolution in the open session. He was requested to speak in Hindi, but he spoke in English. With the great preparations and manoeuvrings which had been made on his behalf, Gandhi, sure to win the day, gave up his threatening attitude and adopted a conciliatory tone with commendable restraint. He said he was charged with saintliness and a desire for dictatorship and that by his mad resolution he was wrecking the Congress. A minority need not leave the Congress but might look forward to translate itself into a majority. And if they condemned his policy he would not go away from the Congress but would plead with them to convert the minority into a majority. He made bold, he said, to reiterate his statement that he could gain Swaraj in the course of a year provided they gave effect to the enforcement of the resolution in a progressive manner.

As regards the boycott of foreign goods, Gandhi said he was sorry that it found a place in his resolution. He firmly opposed Council entry which was the bone of contention between him and the nationalists. However, he helplessly swallowed the suggestion about the boycott of foreign goods which he had depicted as morally wrong, impractical and unworthy although he felt that those words did mar the symmetry of the programme. He claimed laborious industry and great thought behind his programme and unflinching determination to bring it about.

The amendments moved to delete the word "gradual" from the resolution were lost. Pal moved his amendment, was backed strongly by Das, Jinnah, Baptista and Pandit Madan Mohan Malaviya. Das asked in a sarcastic tone whether the boycott of schools and colleges and courts had any sense when they were qualified by the terms 'gradual' and 'progressive'. Besant opposed the Pal and the Gandhi resolution. Gandhi again explained that the expression gradual was inserted just to allow time for making preparations. He said it was his impression upto the Amritsar Congress that Government officers were repentant, but at that time found that they were unrepentant and that non-co-operation was the only reply to their challenge.

After six days of discussion, Gandhi's resolution as amended by the Subjects Committee was passed in the open session by 1,852 against 908 votes, the total delegates being 4,702. Pal's amendment was thrown out. It may be noted that 1,942 delegates did not vote. The resolution said: "This Congress is further of opinion that there is no course left open for the people of India but to approve of and adopt the policy of progressive non-violent non-co-operation until the said wrongs are righted and Swaraj is established." Gandhi's success was spectacular and his moves were tactful. A quiver of enthusiasm went through young India. A quick flame leaped in Gandhi's eyes. A faint, fleeting smile lighted his lips. He stood before the august assembly as a man of decision and action. He was taking the country into a new political revolution beyond Tilak.

THE NATIONALISTS, WHO routed the moderates at Surat, now compromised with the Gandhian policy as a majority decision. They proved to be moderate and Gandhi and his lieutenants turned out to be extremists. The men of premeditated prudence, decorum and dignity looked flabbergasted, although, with the exception of Motilal Nehru, all nationalist leaders were on their side. They thought that although the policy was approved, it was not a final and irrevocable settlement. Gandhi gave up 'satyagraha' and stood now before the country as a champion of non-co-operation. He said he shifted to non-co-operation as he had found to his cost that civil disobedience required far greater preliminary training and self-control. All could non-co-operate but few only could offer civil disobedience. He always said he derived inspiration from Gokhale whom he called his Guru, and his Guru was a great parliamentarian and had been a Council-goer. Yet, in the Subjects Committee Gandhi declared that had Tilak been a Council-goer he would not have been able to do one-tenth of the work he had done.

The idea of non-violent non-co-operation was a novel one, simple, thrilling, attractive and appealing to the youth of India. It caught their imagination. To hazard a guess, even Tilak would have found it difficult to resist Gandhi at Calcutta.

The non-co-operation resolutions adopted at Calcutta by the Muslim League and the Khilafat Conference were practically the same as the non-co-operation resolution adopted by the Congress. The Congress resolution touched upon neither a no-tax campaign nor resignation of services in the military although it appealed to people not to offer clerical and labour services to the military in Mesopotamia.

The Muslim mind tried to assert itself once again in India. Since the War of Independence of 1857 the Muslims had begun to assess the position and prestige of their society in India. Their grim struggle for the Muslimization of India had failed and their political power had been smashed thoroughly by the Marathas. Sir William Hunter, a historian of note, says: "The British won India, not from the Mughals but from the Hindus".[8] Grant Duff, historian of the Marathas, described the Marathas as "our predecessors in conquest in India".[9]

The Muslims were trying to organize themselves and found an opening in the partition of Bengal in 1905. The partition of Bengal blessed them in 1905 with a Muslim majority Province and whetted their appetite for political power. They demanded separate electorates and established a separate political institution called the Muslim League in 1906. The establishment of the Hindu Sabha movement in 1907 was a direct reaction to this new Muslim ideology. But the partition of Bengal being annulled in 1911 through the attempts of Hindu landlords, leaders and lawyers, the Muslims now found an opportunity through the Khilafat movement to organize themselves and tried once again to assert themselves in India.

The Khilafat leaders shrewdly kept their Khilafat Committee apart from the Indian National Congress although the latter adopted its cause and propounded it. Gandhi, however, did not oppose its independent existence.

The progressive Muslim element was in retreat and the orthodox section aided by Gandhi's equally orthodox views was coming to the front. Not the men of broader and more modern outlook among the Muslims, but the Maulanas and fanatical element among them were now capturing the mind of the Muslim masses.

Thus it was evident that the leaders of the Khilafat movement fought for one cause whereas the Congress fought for another. Naturally the collaboration of the Khilafat Committee and the Congress was an alliance based on expediency and not on the unity of purpose, ideas or culture. The collaboration undoubtedly created an anti-imperialist front but introduced dangerous communalism into the national politics.

In the beginning Gandhi regarded the Khilafat movement as the churning of the sea and was not concerned, as he said, with what it would produce. He was pampering the orthodox Muslims with the object of drawing them into the orbit of the national struggle. Their collaboration gave him in the bargain a unique chance to capture the leadership of India. Besides, as a counterpoise against Das, he was successful in winning the Nehrus to his side. Gandhi and Motilal Nehru came together through Jawaharlal Nehru. The Nehrus made a tryst with destiny!

Accompanied by Jawaharlal Nehru, Gandhi then paid a visit to Santiniketan, the abode of peace. Tagore was away on a visit to Europe. The play *Valmiki Pratibha* was staged by the students for the guests. This was a return visit by Gandhi after Tagore's visit to Ahmedabad when Gandhi's Ashram, according to Maganlal Gandhi, had spent some unnecessary extra money on it. Maganlal was in distress on another count also. Gandhi was thinking of receiving a motor-car as a gift as economically a car was an advantage and Gandhi said that he was not at that time opposed to using a car as much as he used to be. Personally he took advantage of railways, cars and surgery while he was opposed to machinery and modern medicine and surgery. Gandhi, however, justified the spending of money on Tagore's reception as he was, he said, an exceptional man and stood for poetry, goodness and patriotism.

On an appeal from Andrews, Gandhi had appealed to Gujaratis on July 11, 1920, to assist Santiniketan in building some houses there. He was sorry that Tagore's tour in Gujarat and Kathiawad in April 1920 had failed to evoke any response to his appeals for funds. "Before we help a man," observed Gandhi charitably in *Navajivan*, "it is not necessary to be in complete agreement with everything he does. It is quite possible that we see defects or imperfections in the actions of the great. None the less, if their motives are sincere it is our duty to help them." And some help was sent to Andrews. It was in this context that Gandhi referred to the missionary work of Pandita Ramabai. She was a Brahmin lady who had embraced Christianity. Gandhi remarked that she carried on her work with the help of American money and her object was the propagation of Christianity in India.[10]

Gandhi was at Santiniketan from September 13 to 17, 1920. In a speech there he said that he had much improved his broken health. For him personally, he said, there was only one religion and that was Hinduism. He took pride in calling himself a Hindu, but he was no dogmatic, ritual-bound Hindu. "As I understand Hinduism it is an extremely comprehensive faith. It has tolerance and respect for other faiths."

As regards his friendship with Shaukat Ali, Gandhi said he had become a brother to him, though they had differences on some matters. Shaukat Ali always addressed Gandhi as 'Sarkar'. "I believe," said Gandhi, "in the principle of non-violence. He seems to believe in violence." Gandhi said that he continued to work with Shaukat Ali as he was a man of his word, a perfectly loyal friend and extraordinarily brave. Shaukat Ali had great faith in God. Gandhi hoped that his success in employing non-violence would convince him of its beauty.

Gandhi, now a master of the Congress and leader of the nation, gave three national slogans. They were 'Allah ho Akbar' (God alone is great), 'Bande Mataram' (Hail Motherland), or 'Bharatmata Ki Jai' (Victory to the Motherland) and 'Hindu Mussalman Ki Jai'. Gandhi had now thoroughly captivated the masses. In South Africa it so happened that he had to take the chair at a meeting when only two or three persons were on the platform and only one person in the audience.[11] Now thousands crowded to hear him. But the crowds were unruly. Gandhi wrote against mobocracy and the behaviour of the unruly crowds. It was in this month that Gandhi opined that *ahimsa* and the English term 'innocence' might be regarded as equivalent.

JUST BEFORE THE Calcutta session of the Congress, Willoughby, a Deputy Commissioner, was assassinated in U.P. by a Muslim. Gandhi wrote in September 1920, that the murder was a cruel, thoughtless and fanatical act, but, he added, the fact must not be disguised that the murder would be regarded by many Mohammedans as a pious act worthy of a martyr, just as, he said sorrowfully, many considered Dhingra to have been a martyr. He noted with grief that the Sinn Feinners openly practised murder and other forms of violence for the purpose of freeing their country. *The Times of India* described the murder as the first fruits of the Khilafat propaganda.

Gandhi had promised the Hindus and the Government that he would resist with his life if violence and recklessness were to reign supreme in the Khilafat movement. But did Gandhi do anything more than deploring the act? He wished simply that it had been possible for him to take that blow upon himself and in that case he would have rendered service to Islam and India!

Thereafter Gandhi, the Ali Brothers and Maulana Abdul Bari made speeches at Lucknow on October 15, 1920. Abdul Bari and Shaukat Ali described Willoughby as a *Kaffir* and hailed his murderer as a *shahid*, a martyr. H. P. Douglas, a Christian barrister, who had suspended practice and joined the non-co-operation movement, was present at the meeting. He resigned from the movement in protest against Maulana Shaukat Ali's speech. Gandhi tried to defend Bari and even blamed poor Mahadev Desai for doing injustice to Bari in his report in the *Navajivan*, asserting that the Maulana had not said that the murderer was a martyr. But it was, Gandhi hastened to add, a different thing when Bari was asked, as he was by some of his friends, to condemn the murderer to (*jahanam*) hell. Bari, as a religious man, Gandhi observed, found it impossible to do so. Gandhi admitted that it would have been better had the term *Kaffir* not been used. But Gandhi again defended Bari by saying that even Bishop Heber called Hindus heathens.

Replying to Gandhi in November 1920, Douglas said he was surprised that a man of the eminence of Gandhi should have gone so wide off the mark. He said it was a national platform, the occasion was for the preaching of the doctrine of non-violent non-co-operation, and the Muslim leaders, though they did not approve of the murder from a mundane point of view, did so from the religious aspect because the person murdered was a Christian. The murderer being a Mohammedan he was ipso facto a *shahid*!

It was a fact that whenever a murderer was Muslim, Gandhi unfortunately took this view and he was disposed to extenuate his guilt. The Muslim leaders of course openly exonerated the murderer. Gandhi never protested against the murderers when they were Muslims. He never called them to account when they were guilty of gross crimes against Hindus or Christians, although he had been very punctilious in condemning every act of violence done by Indian revolutionaries. This was a prominent feature and characteristic of Gandhi's politics.

Gandhi was often asked questions on the boycott of schools and colleges. He was asked whether schools were any the worse at that time than they were before the Punjab wrongs or the Khilafat breach, and how he tolerated them before those events. He replied that so far as he was concerned, the knowledge of the Punjab and the Khilafat betrayal had revolutionised his view of the existing Government. He said that at the Calcutta special Congress much laughter was indulged in at his expense for having told the Congress that if there was sufficient response to his programme of non-co-operation, Swaraj, would be attained in one year, Gandhi felt that they ignored the condition and laughed because of the impossibility of getting Swaraj anyhow within a year. "Others have spelt the 'if in capitals," said Gandhi sorrowfully, "and suggested that if 'ifs' were permissible in argument any absurdity could be proved to be a possibility." But Gandhi, a week after publishing this statement, told a representative of *The Times of India* that he would win Swaraj within nine months. It would be the Parliamentary Government of India in the modern sense. The existing Government like a lion, would lie with the lamb. He said that good government was no substitute for self-government. According to him, "Swaraj means a state such that we can maintain our separate existence without the presence of the English."

During the Calcutta session a Sub-Committee consisting of Gandhi, Motilal Nehru and Vithalbhai Patel was appointed to prepare draft instructions on the non-co-operation resolution. The Sub-Committee published its report on September 26, 1920, with Gandhi and Nehru on one side and Patel dissenting. The Sub-Committee said in its report that "the Congress has approved of Mr. Gandhi's full programme of progressive non-violent non-co-operation but has adopted for immediate use the items of the first stage only." Patel said "he regretted he could not see his way to accept the suggestion contained in the report that the Congress has approved of Mr. Gandhi's full programme of non-co-operation."[12]

Lala Lajpatrai also took strong exception to the statement that the Congress had approved of the whole of Gandhi's programme although he said he agreed with the policy of non-co-operation. B. C. Pal, too, opposed the report as he also differed on some points. Patel suggested that the Congress would have to amend the first article of its constitution by replacing the word 'constitutional means' by 'peaceful means' before they approved of all the stages of Gandhi's full programme.

At the All-India Congress Committee meeting held on October 2, 1920, to consider the report, Gandhi was charged with interpreting the resolution of the Calcutta Congress to suit his purpose, indicating that his individual opinion was the opinion of all and that the programme as inaugurated and formulated by Gandhi had been adopted by the Congress.

In the report the term 'gradual' was misconstrued and besides Motilal Nehru had the temerity to say that the boycott of foreign goods was an unfortunate interpolation due to a misapprehension. Gandhi purposely kept silent on these points. He did not contradict Motilal Nehru. Patel said fearlessly that it was not an interpolation. Lajpatrai asserted that it was not an interpolation. Nor was it passed under a misapprehension. Gandhi must have felt quite embarrassed! The fact was that the policy and not the programme of Gandhi was approved by the Calcutta Congress. The report was shorn by N. C. Kelkar and Rangaswami lyengar of its exuberance and misstatements before it was passed.[13]

In the last week of September 1920 Gandhi submitted a draft of the new constitution of the Congress. He had completed the drafting in collaboration with the members of the Sub-Committee, N. C. Kelkar, V. J. Patel, G. Mishra and Rangaswami lyengar entrusted by the Congress at Amritsar in December 1919 with the drafting of a new constitution.

AFTER THE CALCUTTA Congress, Gandhi began to consolidate his party while the nationalists did nothing beyond waiting for the Nagpur session. In spite of the fact that they did not vote for Gandhi's resolution, in their individual conduct they conformed to its terms because they wanted to obey the Congress-mandate and wished not to break the solidarity of the Congress. They were confused for a while. Tilak, their man of action, had departed the world. At this time Das did not make an all-India tour for the support of his views. Neither did the Tilakites. Baptista helplessly accepted the majority decision and did not conduct any agitations against it. Khaparde, another lieutenant of Tilak, though an effective speaker, had no genius for organization and had no initiative. Kelkar was editor of the *Kesari*, the mouthpiece of Tilak's policy, but he was not a man of action. He was trying to organize Tilak's followers but could not give enough time to organizing the nationalist forces.

The Congress having gone under his grip, Gandhi strove untiringly to dominate it. Gandhi, the Ali Brothers and Motilal Nehru toured north India explaining the non-violent non-cooperation resolution, addressing students' meetings on boycott of schools and colleges at Surat, Rohatak, Moradabad, Aligarh, Kanpur, Lucknow, Bareilly, Amritsar and Lahore. Gandhi addressed conferences held at Moradabad and Bhiwani. A man of boundless energy, he toured also his home province making speeches at Nadiad and Broach on non-co-operation and the necessity for national schools and colleges.

At Broach Gandhi said that he believed that the British Government was satanic and he had been spreading that idea ever since he awoke to the truth. At Surat he advised the students to politely refuse to comply with their parents' orders if they found them unreasonable. They should sacrifice, if need be, their parents and relations as did Pralhad his father. According to Gandhi, it was a sin to enter Councils and attend courts and an altogether heinous sin to attend schools. If all Government schools were left empty, he promised that they would find the face of India changed within a month. They should even boycott Municipal Primary Schools if they did not repudiate their connection with the Government. He was, Gandhi added, a practical idealist and so he did not ask them to boycott trains.

The existing Government was no Rama Rajya, it was Ravan-rajya. During the Diwali they celebrated the victory of Rama over Ravana. But they truly celebrated that victory only when they destroyed the monster with not ten but a thousand heads. If the Hindus wanted cows to be saved, they should show large-heartedness. The British ate beef every day and the British soldiers could not do without beef for a single day. Why then should the Hindus hate Muslims alone for beef-eating? He asked. Muslims were god-fearing and if the Hindus made common cause with them, Swaraj would not be long in coming. Thus Gandhi added one more rider to the goal of Swaraj.

Gandhi again issued an appeal for Hindu-Muslim unity when Hakim Ajmal Khan settled the dispute between the Hindus and the Muslims at Agra. Gandhi said there was nothing in the holy Koran enjoining upon the followers of Islam to treat Hindus as their natural enemies nor was there anything in Hinduism to warrant a belief in the eternal enmity between the two. It was true that fanatical priests in both religions set the one against the other. It was equally true that Muslim rulers, like Christian rulers, had used the sword for the propagation of their respective faiths. He wanted a union of hearts based on a definite recognition of the indubitable proposition that Swaraj for India must be an impossible dream without an indissoluble union between the Hindus and Muslims of India.

Gandhi's Guru, Gokhale was disappointed at the thought of unity. He once told Sarojini Naidu that Hindu-Muslim unity could never come in her lifetime or in his. *The Modern Review* described Gandhi's Hindu-Muslim unity as a camouflage and added that it was a house of cards. Gandhi replied that it was just becoming a permanent reality although unfortunately the communal spirit was predominant and mutual distrust was still there. In offering to lay down his life for the Khilafat, he was ensuring the safety of the cow. To him, the attainment of Khilafat through India's power was the attainment of Swaraj. He asserted that the unity was not a camouflage but it was a lasting friendship.

As regards Gandhi's repeated advice to children to leave the parental roof if a father did an injustice, the *Modern Review* observed that Gandhi had unintentionally enunciated an antisocial principle.

The fact was that Gandhi and his colleagues like Motilal Nehru were not so much intent on national education as they were on turning the students into propagandists for the national movement. Exorting the students to join the national movement, Motilal Nehru said at Benares that if non-cooperation was to succeed, it would be due to Aligarh and Benares; and as the masses only could change the fate of any country, he asked the students to do propaganda work among the masses and to train them. They must forget their careers and prospects just as English youth did in the last war.[14]

At Lucknow Gandhi said that he used the Post Office and the Telegraph Office as he considered them his own property. Theoretically all Indian institutions belonged to Indians and so Gandhi was asked why he did not consider law courts and public schools and colleges his own property. There was no reply. Besant had suggested to the Government that Government should refuse to deliver postal articles to Gandhi[15] and Shaukat Ali, to issue them railway tickets, and so on. Gandhi replied that if the Government did it, it would be a great day indeed.

THE KHILAFAT DEPUTATION returned to Bombay on October 4, 1920, after meeting statesmen in France and Italy. The delegation obtained an audience with the Pope. Welcoming them back at a meeting in Bombay the same day, Gandhi said that it was a happy day for him and for them all as their brother Mohomed Ali and his colleagues had returned to the motherland safe and sound.

In the first week of October 1920 Gandhi issued another appeal to the lawyers in the country to free themselves from the hallucination of the law courts. The atmosphere about the courts was foetid and the worst was that besides the economic drain they caused, they supported the authority of the Government. Without its Law Courts, he observed, the Government must perish in a day. And Gandhi, who earned about Rs. 40,000 a year in South Africa, realized now that the best legal talent must be available to the poorest at reasonable rates. Gandhi knew well that lawyers were not willing to give up the armchair and the motor-car. The lawyers were leaders of public opinion and public activity. That work they did, he said, during the few leisure hours they got from their tennis and billiards. So he revealed his real intention to a barrister of the Patna Bar when he said, "I want at least the public workers among them to be whole-timers, and when that happy day comes, I promise a different outlook before the country."[16] Gandhi wanted an army of propagandists to carry the idea of non-co-operation to villages and this was an astute plan.

Gandhi then appealed to the trustees of the Aligarh College, the Hindu University and the Khalsa College to get their institutions converted into national institutions. Aligarh was the centre of Muslim culture, Benares of Hindu culture and the Khalsa College, of the Sikh. Inasmuch as Islam was in peril at English hands, Hinduism and Sikhism too, were in peril. In his opinion it was a sin for the nation to receive education in schools which were financed by or were under the influence or control of the Government. When the nation was marching forward, the scholastic institutions should not lag behind. They should disaffiliate themselves and withdraw all voluntary association with the Government.

In his appeal to the trustees of the Aligarh College, Gandhi said that he did not want to suspend secular education for a moment, but it should be given in consistence with the law of Islam and the honour of India. The majority of the Trustees, however, turned down the students' demand for Aligarh College to become a national institution and on October 29, 1920, the National University of Aligarh was inaugurated by the Ali Brothers.

Gandhi then came out on October 27, 1920, with a statement addressed to every Englishman in India explaining why he who put his life in peril four times for the sake of the Empire and devoted some time in a recruiting campaign during World War I, had now inaugurated non-co-operation with the Government, which had glorified the Punjab administration and flouted Mussalman sentiment. Gandhi wanted them to compel Lloyd George to redeem British promises and force the Viceroy to retire in favour of a better one or persuade him to make common cause with the people of India whose salt they were eating. The thwarting of their aspirations was disloyalty to the country. Every Britisher in India knew what Gandhi meant. But Gandhi, better late than never, thought it was wise to give notice and advertise the cause though he had inaugurated the non-co-operation movement almost three months earlier!

For the previous two years Gandhi had been trying to stimulate hand-spinning and hand-weaving and his efforts were bearing fruit at many places. For want of suitable occupations thousands were dying of starvation and under-feeding, and so Gandhi was impressing upon them the need for that primitive industry. The Marwaris and Bhatias who respected and worshipped Gandhi took advantage of this movement by raising the prices of swadeshi goods during the swadeshi movement inaugurated in Bengal. The Marwaris and Bhatias were dealers in foreign piece-goods. Under-production, profiteering and speculation by them made the lot of the poor in India very miserable. So some suggestions and appeals were made to Gandhi to exercise his influence on the profiteers and speculators, so that they might not aggravate and exploit the situation. To Gandhi's shame and sorrow those merchants sold Japanese cloth in swadeshi stores as khaddar and proved that capital knows no morality. It talks of the love of country only when it is profitable.

The Gujarati multi-millionaires took keen interest in Gandhi's leadership. With his emergence as a national leader, their provincial pride was satisfied. Gujarat had no leader of stature for several decades. Naturally they furnished him with men and money but at the same time exploited Gandhi's influence and movement for their own economic interests and Gandhi exploited them, his movements being financially backed by them. The Bengal nationalists led by Das and the Maharashtrian nationalists led by Kelkar were representatives of the middle class. So there was an invisible rivalry between the nationalists and Gandhi's associates and supporters who were backed by business magnates functioning in the background.

CHAPTER XXII

Defender of the Caste System

IN THE FIRST week of November 1920, Gandhi made a tour of Western Maharashtra up to Belgaum, inaugurating national schools, denouncing the British Government as satanic and expressing his views on the Brahmin and non-Brahmin problem which had assumed dangerous proportions in Madras and Maharashtra. During his Madras tour he had an informal talk with the students of the Law College on the Brahmin-non-Brahmin question on August 22, 1920. He told them that the Brahmins should surrender to the demands of the non-Brahmins. The demand of the non-Brahmins was the result of their distrust towards the Brahmins who had for long contributed their best, but in their arrogance, the distinction they had drawn between themselves and the other castes was as diabolical as the distinction drawn by the European races between themselves and the darker races. In short, as he repeated a few days later in *Young India*, in his opinion the treatment of non-Brahmins by the Brahmins was as satanic as the treatment given to Indians by the British.[1]

Gandhi explained that his foregoing remarks were never intended to encourage the powerful non-Brahmins of Maharashtra and Madras, or the mischievious element among them to overcome the so-called Brahmins. He advisedly used the word 'so-called', Gandhi said, because the Brahmins who had freed themselves from the thraldom of superstitious orthodoxy had not only no quarrel with non-Brahmins as such but were in every way eager to advance the cause of the non-Brahmins wherever they were weak. Gandhi warned the non-Brahmins who were coquetting with the British Government that no

Indian worthy of his birth should cut off his nose to spite the face.

When he spoke at Bhavani Peth, a non-Brahmin locality in Poona, on November 5, he referred to his Madras speech. He said the problem of non-Brahmins in Madras was different and very acute. Gandhi proceeded: "Giving an example, I said that the Brahmins' treatment of the Panchamas was as satanic as the treatment meted out by the bureaucracy to us."[2] Gandhi desired to win the leaders of the Maharashtra Congress, who were Brahmins, over to his side in the non-co-operation movement. In order to assuage the Brahmin leaders and soften his Madras statement, he now used the word 'Panchamas' instead of 'non-Brahmins' which he had used at Madras and also in his article in *Young India*. "So long", he added, "we had not got rid of the satanism in us, we were not fit to overcome it in others." "I am," he concluded, "an orthodox Hindu. I am a Vaishnava. I am a staunch believer in Varnashram." At Wai Gandhi said that he was a non-Brahmin, but he did not hate any Brahmin.

Some days later Gandhi admitted that the non-Brahmin movement owed its vitality, not to religious or social disabilities, but to the political ascendency of the Brahmins which the latter undoubtedly enjoyed by right of merit. Gandhi advised the nationalists, who were almost all Brahmins, to boycott Government posts, councils, and nominated seats of Municipality. He urged them not to use haughty language towards the non-Brahmins, or belittle them or treat them with contempt. The non-Brahmins, on the other hand, were told to note that their exploitation and emasculation was due to English rule. They should not help to tighten the hold of the Government on the masses.

All the while from Broach to Belgaum, from Nasik to Nipani, Gandhi denounced the British Government as satanic, described it as *Ravanarajya* and exhorted the people to end that Rajya and to establish *Ramarajya* and that *Ramarajya* was Swaraj. He said he had been speeding that idea since he awoke to the truth. He was, he observed, not against the British people but against the Empire. It was not his intention, he added, to suggest that every Englishman or English officer was a devil. Every officer, however, working as part of a satanic machine and, therefore, whether intentionally or unintentionally, became an instrument of injustice, deception and repression.

Like Gandhi, Indian revolutionaries, too, regarded every

British officer as a part of a Satanic machine and an instrument of injustice, deception and repression. Later Gandhi denounced the British Empire as a Godless empire and added that loyalty to such an Empire was disloyalty to God. But a few days earlier he had cautiously added that "even after we have won Swaraj, fraud, robbery and Dyerism will flourish. I am not naive or hypocritical enough to say that with Swaraj will come satyayuga (the age of truth). After all it will be Swaraj in kaliyug (the age of strife) and not in satyayuga." But power will be in our hands, he said, "so that at the most, we ourselves will have abused it, or will have allowed it to be abused."[3]

Gandhi wanted to utilize women for the national struggle. He addressed their meetings and awoke them to their prime duty. His advice to them was that all women should always spend one hour every day in spinning yarn. Gandhi impressed upon their minds the great idea that without freedom it was impossible for them to protect religion. So the first reform for them should be to understand the important idea of freedom and cherish it as a part of Dharma.

On November 15, 1920, the Gujarat National University was founded by the co-workers of Gandhi. Gandhi, as Chancellor of the University, said in his inaugural address: "Many people conceived of our universities and colleges as so much of brick and mortar, so many buildings, so many other equipments. The university or college had much less of these than any existing university or college." The Vidyalaya, he declared, was founded not only with an educational, but also with a national aim in view. It was imbued with the best patriotic ideals and had on its staff outstanding Sindhi, Maharashtrian and Gujarati professors. Gandhi asked Principal A. T. Gidwani, the professors, teachers and organizers of the college to devote the institution to building up true character in their students with the best possible influence and ideals, to sow the seed of true freedom in the students and make them into a nation of brave, fearless and patriotic men and women. If their Principal or any of their preceptors, Gandhi concluded, failed them they should burn him to ashes in the fire of their righteousness, replace them from among themselves and go ahead with their work.[4] Vinoba Bhave was the teacher of Religion. R. B. Athavale and R. C. Parikh taught Sanskrit, and Gidwani and P. V. Pathak taught English. Kishorelal Mashruwala was Registrar of the University.

GANDHI SAID THAT the Gujarat National University was founded not only with an educational but also with a national aim in view. Although his idea of education had for its object the formation of character, his emphasis was on the national and not on the educational aspect of the University.

The prominent and distinct feature of national education, said Prof. Vijapurkar, who was one of the pioneers of national education in Maharashtra, was the preservation of the Chaturvarnya, the caste system, and the belief in rebirth. That education, Tilak said, was national which enabled the youth to develop and maintain the political, industrial and social power of the nation. Like Lajpatrai, Tilak's emphasis was on scientific, technological and industrial education. Lajpatrai wanted every Indian to know one European language and handle European mechanical appliances. He wanted Indians to be modern, up-to-date, progressive, proud of their past and aspiring to a greater and a nobler future.

Judging from the social aspect of the political movement of Gandhi, it was different from this. The special characteristic of Gandhi's movement was that it was indifferent to academic values and it had a dread of intellectualism. It was this fear which had made Gandhi tell Gokhale that he need not read a lot of books, a selected few would serve his purpose. He seemed to learn more from men than from books. The movement had derived from Gandhi, a sort of abhorrence for doctors, lawyers, scientists and specialists of all kinds.

Two days later Gandhi further explained the object in founding the university. The ideal of a united India, the revival of Indian languages, a systematic study of Asiatic culture, synthesis of the different cultures that had come to stay in India and the study of Hindustani which he regarded as a national blend of Sanskrit, Hindi and Persianised Urdu, and bridging the gulf between the educated and uneducated classes constituted the aims of the new university. He expected education to 'filter down'[5] to the masses. It seems Gandhi, too, was a supporter of the theory of filtration to which spokesmen of the common man like Mahatma Jotirao Phooley were opposed.

The Gujarat National University resolved to admit depressed class children to its colleges, and this created a sensation all over Ahmedabad. The discussion raged furiously for months in Gujarat! The Hindu Dyers harassed Gandhi and the *Gujarati* attacked him. Some critics said that the University was not national because no Muslim was on its senate. Gandhi replied that 'no higher educated' Muslim, able to give his time, was found to take sufficient interest in the national education movement.

Thus, the non-co-operation movement gave, an impetus to national education which had been inaugurated under the resolution of the Calcutta Congress of 1906.

Gandhi then started touring north India once again, inspiring the people with his rebellious spirit. He visited Benares, Allahabad, Patna, Gaya, Muzaffarpur, Monghyr, Calcutta and Dacca, opening national schools, addressing women's meetings on their duties and on co-operation and exhorting the students to respond to the call of the nation to boycott the Government controlled schools and colleges. There were disturbances at Benares Hindu University and at Khalsa College in Amritsar when the students adopted non-co-operation and demanded that their respective colleges should be transformed into national institutions.

In the second week of December, Gandhi, in his reply to Lord Ronaldshay's comments on *Hind Swaraj*, defined his conception of Swaraj as being synonymous with *moksha*. Gandhi's definitions of Swaraj varied with the time, the tide of the movement and the mind of the questioner! He has given as many as twenty definitions! Each time the definition either obscures the previous definition or heightens its mysticism! Swaraj means rule over oneself; swadeshi is Swaraj; Swaraj is self-reliance; Swaraj is *moksha* (salvation); Swaraj means the rule of *Dharma*; Government over self is the truest Swaraj!

On November 6, the Government of India published its resolution on the 'Non-co-operation movement' and said that the avowed object of the principal exponents of the movement was to destroy the present Government. But the full consummation of their hopes would leave India defenceless both against foreign aggression and internal chaos. It hoped that India would attain progress under the Reform scheme. The policy of non-repression, it concluded, would depend largely on the success the moderates achieved in checking the extension of the movement and keeping its dangers within bounds. Gandhi described this fleeting attitude of non-repression on the part of the Government as a triumph of non-violence. Gandhi significantly said: "Everybody knows that the danger of an outbreak of violence is the greatest if we (Gandhi and the Ali Brothers) are imprisoned. I am aware that this is a humiliating confession." But he expected that the people, if they were truly strong and self-reliant, would remain unperturbed by their or any leader's imprisonment. As regards the defence of India, he said that he should very much like the gods to witness a duel between the powers of all the world who wanted to trade with her at the point of the bayonet and the martial races of India voluntarily fighting for their hearth and home.[6] Indeed this was not a non-violent view of the situation!

Gandhi had a passage of arms with the Sikh League which was sore over the 'pernicious' effects of the doctrine of non-violent, non-co-operation on the martial Sikh masses. He had said in October 1920 that "if despite his warning the Sikhs became violent, he would not regret if the British crushed them by force."[7] In that case Hindus or Muslims would not come to their aid. This statement was much discussed and Gandhi explained, that it was torn from its context. In fact he repudiated nothing but reaffirmed much the same opinion. If Gandhi wished to witness a fight between the martial races and the aggressors, the proper way was not to emasculate, discourage and devalue the tradition of the Sikhs but to ask them to keep and develop their martial spirit.

Meanwhile Gandhi had to express his views on the removal of untouchability and on the caste system. During his tour of Madras, he was heckled by the Untouchables and pressed to say something about their sad lot. They appealed to him to get the agelong, immemorial social disabilities removed by starting a campaign similar to that of non-co-operation for the removal of social injustice. Gandhi replied in *Young India* of October 27, 1920, that the Hindus had suppressed the Untouchables and become themselves pariahs of the empire. If he had a truly national legislature, he would answer Hindu insolence by building special and better wells for the exclusive use of the suppressed classes and by erecting numerous and better schools for them.

There were, Gandhi observed, three courses open to the Untouchables: Government assistance, conversion to Islam or Christianity and self-help. They should reject Government aid for it would be used against their kith and kin; the second course was rejection of Hinduism and wholesale conversion to Islam or Christianity. And if a change of religion could be justified for worldly betterment, he would advise it without hesitation. But religion, he said, was a matter of heart. According to Gandhi, conversion was no remedy because he believed that untouchability was no part of Hinduism; it was rather its excrescence to be removed by every effort. They should choose self-help and join the great national movement; for non-cooperation with the Government presupposed co-operation between sections forming the Indian nation. The Hindus must make common cause with them as they had done with the Muslims.

Gandhi believed that untouchability was a blot on Hinduism. If untouchability was no part of Hinduism, how could it be a blot on it? Pandits, like Madan Mohan Malaviya, who were well versed in *Shastras*, admitted that the Antajas were Untouchables according to *Shastras*.[8]

One Mr. S. M. Michael condemned Gandhi's arguments in the foregoing article as admirable dialectics which might deceive the shallow superficial reader. Gandhi replied to Michael that when Swaraj was established by the method of non-co-operation there would be no pariah or non-Brahmin problem left to be solved. Michael also quoted Tagore in support of his stand who had said that, "No enduring political freedom can be built in this country on the quick sands of social slavery, and the real problem of the country is social and not political." Gandhi said he adhered to his statement that amelioration of radical social evils meant attainment of Swaraj, but the British Government was the greatest of all social evils with which society was cursed.

It may be noted here that Rajarshi Shahu, the Maharaja of Kolhapur, was the first prince in modern India to fight untouchability and liberate the Untouchables by opening to them schools and public water-places, appointing them to Government posts, giving them lands, and employing them in his palace. A true follower of Mahatma Phooley, he presided at the first All-India Untouchable Conference at Nagpur in May 1920 and gave a stimulus to this movement.

GANDHI WAS NOW facing the problem of non-Brahmins and Untouchables. He had been explaining his social philosophy for the previous four years. At Madras he told the Missionary Conference on February 14, 1916, that the vast organization of caste answered not only the religious wants of the community, but it answered too its political needs. He had made a speech on the caste system at the conference of communities held in Ahmedabad on June 5, 1916. In his speech he said: "I have devoted much thought to the subject of the caste system and come to the conclusion that Hindu society cannot dispense with it, that it lives on because of the discipline of caste. Societies all over the world are organized on the principle of caste or *Varnavyavastha* (division of society into classes on the basis of vocations).

Our society was organized in this manner for the purpose of self-control, that is, for self-denial. Certainly, there is a difference between *Varnavyavastha* in the West and among us; but there is *Varnavyavastha* everywhere." He again justified his stand against inter-dining and inter-marriage by saying that "if friendly relations depended on eating together and inter-marriage, the German and the British would not be fighting against each other. The Rajputs of Kathiawad did sit together at meals and marry among themselves but have no end of internecine strife and fighting. Of course these caste restrictions have something of value in them."

A few days later, in October 1916, Gandhi explained his ideas on caste in an article. He said that the caste system contained the seed of Swaraj and they could carry out social reform with ease through the agency of the caste system. "I am," he observed, "opposed to the movements which are being carried on for the destruction of the system."[9] He opposed inter-dining and inter-marriage because there was a good chance that thereby loose conduct would be kept down. He believed in his mystic way that the process of eating was as unclean as excretion. "Prohibition of marriage," he continued, "with anyone not belonging to one's community promotes self-control and self-control is conducive to happiness in all circumstances. . . . The caste system has struck such deep roots in India that I think it will be far more advisable to try to improve it rather than uproot it. The more numerous the communities, the better it would be. ... The Hindu caste system is not merely an inert, lifeless institution but a living one and has been functioning according to its own law. . . . We cannot conclude from it that the system is itself bad."

"*Varnashram* (caste)," he said, "is, in my opinion, inherent in human nature, and Hinduism has simply reduced it to a science. It does attach to birth. A man cannot change his varna by choice. Not to abide by one's varna is to disregard the law of heredity."[10] On May 8, 1915, he said at Bangalore that caste was the great power and secret of Hinduism. His Ashram had firm belief in Varnashram Dharma and he thought that the discipline of caste seemed to have done no harm to the country; on the contrary, rather.[11] And then he said it was necessary to improve the condition of the Untouchables. He believed in caste and at the same time wished to abolish untouchability!

As the pressure of the problem of non-Brahmins and Untouchables was increasing, Gandhi again gave expression in February 1920 to his views on the caste system. Gandhi was always careful to remove the fears of his orthodox followers. He said: "For years I have taken nothing but fruit in Mohammedan or Christian households." During his tour in U.P. Maulana Bari, he said, had engaged a Brahmin cook and made special arrangements for the Hindus of the party. A month earlier he had observed: "I am one of those who do not consider caste to be a harmful institution. In its origin caste was a wholesome custom and promoted national well-being.[12] In my opinion the idea that inter-dining or inter-marrying is necessary for national growth, is a superstition borrowed from the west." He further said in the same article that inter-marriage and inter-dining were not necessary factors in friendship and unity though they were often emblems thereof. He was of the opinion the eating should be done in private as one performed the other necessary functions of life in private. Inter-marriage and inter-dining were not a bar to dissensions and quarrels. The Pandavas and the Kauravas, Gandhi argued, flew at one another's throat although they inter-dined and inter-married! He held it to be utterly impossible for Hindus and Muslims to inter-marry and yet to retain intact their religion.

In his article on the caste system Gandhi observed: "They argue that retention of the caste system spells ruin for India and that it is caste which has reduced India to slavery. In my opinion, it is not caste that has made us what we are. It was our greed and disregard of essential virtues which enslaved us. I believe that caste has saved[13] Hinduism from disintegration. ... I consider the four divisions alone to be fundamental, natural and essential. The innumerable sub-castes are sometimes a convenience, often a hindrance. The sooner there is fusion the better." "Social pressure," he proceeded, "and public opinion can be trusted to deal with the problem. But I am certainly against any attempt at destroying the fundamental divisions. The caste system is not based on inequality, there is no question of inferiority, and so far as there is any such question arising as in Madras, Maharashtra, or elsewhere, the tendency should undoubtedly be checked. But there appears to be no valid reason for ending the system because of its abuse. It lends itself easily to reformation."

"The spirit of democracy," he asserted, "which is fast spreading throughout India and the rest of the world, will, without a shadow of doubt, purge the institution of the idea of predominance and subordination. It (the spirit of democracy) requires change of the heart. If caste is a bar to the spread of that spirit, the existence of five religions in India—Hinduism, Islam, Christianity,

Zoroastrianism and Judaism—is equally a bar. The spirit of democracy requires inculcation of the spirit of brotherhood .... and Hinduism that is responsible for the doctrine of the caste is also responsible for the inculcation of the essential brotherhood, not merely of man but even of all that lives."

Some suggested, Gandhi went on, that the idea of heredity in caste should be rejected. "I am inclined," he said, "to think that the law of heredity is an eternal[14] law and any attempt to alter that law must lead us, as it has before led, to utter confusion. I can see very great use in considering a Brahmin to be always a Brahmin throughout his life. ... If Hindus believe, as they must believe in reincarnation, transmigration, they must know that nature will, without any possibility of mistake, adjust the balance by degrading a Brahmin, if he misbehaves himself, by reincarnating him in a lower division, and translating one who lived the life of a Brahmin in his present incarnation to Brahminhood in his next." "Inter-drinking, inter-dining, inter-marrying," he concluded, "I hold, are not essential for the promotion of the spirit of democracy."

He, however, said, that he considered untouchability to be a heinous crime against humanity and if Hinduism was to be recognised as an honourable and elevating religion, the sooner it purged itself of the sin, the better it was for itself.

Gandhi defended and gave justification for caste, the caste system, reincarnation, transmigration of souls, and the doctrine of heredity, opposing inter-marriage and inter-dining. He pointed out that Europe had class, and if caste produced certain evils, class had not been productive of anything less. The beauty of caste was that it did not base itself upon distinctions of wealth and possession. Caste was an extension of the principle of the family. Both were governed by blood and heredity. This was true though experience of many lands went against the doctrine of western scientists, who were busy trying to prove that heredity was an illusion and that milieu was everything. Yet it was very easy, said Gandhi, to prove that milieu could be conserved and developed more through caste than through class. Caste was the best possible adjustment of social stability and progress.[15] It was a system of culture!

This was the social content of the political movement of Gandhi whose social philosophy was not much discussed during the hectic days of the struggle against British imperialism. Socially, Gandhi belonged to a caste which stood high in the social hierarchy. He defended the caste system and the doctrine of heredity which kept the Brahmins and Vaishyas at the top of the ladder (there being, according to them, no Kshatriyas but all Shudras) but kept large masses at the bottom of it to rot, depriving them of any chance to grow.

Gandhi was thus an orthodox reformer who white-washed a dilapidated house! Frankly, he shared the views of the ignorant masses on whose credulity he banked for the support of his leadership.

What Gandhi's Guru, Gokhale, thought about the caste system will prove whether or not Gandhi was his disciple in respect of political and social views. "It is sometimes urged," said Gokhale in 1903, "that if we have our castes, the people in the West have their classes, and after all, there is not much difference between the two. A little reflection will, however, show that the analogy is quite fallacious. The classes of the West are a perfectly elastic institution, and not, rigid or caste-iron like our castes. Mr. Chamberlain, who is the most masterful personage in the British Empire today, was at one time a shoemaker and then a screw-maker."

"Will a shoemaker," Gokhale proceeded, "ever be able to rise in India in the social scale in a similar fashion, no matter how gifted by nature he might be? A great writer has said that castes are eminently useful for the preservation of society, but that they are utterly unsuited for purposes of progress. And this I think is perfectly true. If you want to stand where you were a thousand years ago, the system of castes need not be modified in any material degree. If, however, you want to emerge out of the slough in which you have long remained sunk, it will not do for you to insist on a rigid adherence to caste. Modern civilization has accepted greater equality for all as its watchword, as against privilege and exclusiveness, which were the root ideas of the old world."[16]

Comments on the views of the disciple and those of the Guru are superfluous. Evidently Gokhale's views stood for the new world of progress, social equality and social justice whereas Gandhi defended and justified the defective, unjust and decaying old institution of caste and stood for the old world. With Gandhi *varna* was determined not by a man's innate qualities but by birth and the profession of a *varna* was determined by the principle of heredity. In ancient Indian society *Varnavyavastha* could maintain harmony so long as it continued to be non-hereditary and flexible. When it accepted heredity as its base it became rigid, intolerant, narrow-minded, and a religion of inequality. Gandhi used *varna* as another name for caste.

Thus after Tilak, Gandhi was the second great leader of modern India to justify the caste system and give a fresh lease of life to it as did Shankaracharya. The foregoing speech was the blue print of the socio-religious policy of Gandhi who was hailed as a veritable incarnation of Buddha and Christ! A man who believed in the gospel of caste by birth-cum-hereditary vocation and disapproved of inter-caste marriages, under the soothing but deceptive balm of the principle that all professions were equal, but shoemakers must remain shoemakers, scavengers must remain scavengers, carpenters must remain carpenters, washermen must remain washermen from father to son, from generation to generation so that the God-ordained caste system might prevail can hardly be called a lover of social equality and social justice. The governing fact about Gandhi was that he looked at society from the angle of a humanitarian and not from the angle of a social revolutionary. He arrived at the problem of the removal of untouchability through humanitarianism and not through the social and rationalistic angle.

Gandhi thus came forward to put back the hand of the clock of progress made by the Hindu leaders. Indeed he hampered the past and the contemporary work of the galaxy of social reformers and evolutionaries like Ram Mohan Roy, Mahatma Jotirao Phooley, Swami Dayanand Saraswati, Swami Shraddhanand, Acharya P. C. Ray, R. C. Dutta, B. C. Pal, Jadunath Sarkar, Aurobindo Ghose, Ramanand Chatterjee, Bhai Parmanand, Hardayal, Shahu Chhatrapati, Veer Savarkar and Dr. Ambedkar who raised their hammer against the caste system which deprived the Hindus of a strong feeling of patriotism and nationality, of social equality and solidarity and denied opportunity to develop fully and freely. They all said to the effect that "caste grows by fusion and is antagonistic to national union and democracy; caste is the curse of India, the bane of Hindus." It is the verdict given by historians, philosophers, sociologists, leaders of thought and social reformers. And yet Gandhi said he was opposed to the destruction of caste which was fraught with social injustice, inequality and misery and deprived large masses of any chance of growth. Instead of helping the progressive social forces that were working for the reorganization of society on deeper and broader foundations, he, like Tilak, defended the antiquated and unjust, defective and decaying institution of caste which was injurious to growth, solidarity of the people and contradictory to or conflicting with the aspirations of true nationalism and democracy.

AFTER THE CALCUTTA Congress some Muslim leaders were arrested and sentenced to various periods of imprisonment. Gandhi said that he saw no gateway to liberty save the doors of His Majesty's prisons. He was preparing his workers and associates to face imprisonment. Yet he himself avoided, he added, disregarding the Madras Government's order and courting arrest as he had to move cautiously. In case he was arrested, he wrote in November in *Young India*, they should not resort to violence and play into the hands of the Government. Government would ruthlessly use force. India, he concluded, could not win Swaraj by force.

The election to the Reformed Councils were held in November 1920. The nationalists, true to their word, withdrew their candidates. The public boycott of the elections was almost entirely successful. More than two-thirds of the voters abstained from voting. At Delhi and in Bengal much harassment was caused to co-operators. Night soil was thrown at a candidate, and the right to burial of a corpse was denied to a man whom the non-co-operator hated. Gandhi said they must concede to their opponents the freedom they claimed.

In November and upto the middle of December 1920, Gandhi made another whirlwind tour from Agra to Dacca for his non-co-operation movement, explaining its significance, stressing the idea of nationality and oneness of the people and preaching non-violent revolt. It was a campaign on a nation-wide scale carried on with valour and vigour by a conquering hero. After it, Gandhi went directly to Nagpur to attend the Nagpur session of the Congress.

On his arrival in Nagpur, Gandhi delivered a lecture to women at the Chitnavis Park. He asked them not to learn English. They should learn weaving as he wanted to revive the handloom industry in every home. Gandhi was criticized for this. Women, his critics pointed out, were human beings like men. English was necessary for knowledge of different modern subjects which were required for the attainment of even ordinary culture.

The Congress met in the last week of December 1920 at Nagpur. At the time of the Amritsar Congress, Dr. B. S. Moonje had invited the Congress to hold its session at Nagpur. He wanted to fulfil his long-cherished dream of seeing Tilak on the *gadi* of the Congress. But Tilak had passed away. Gandhi, who knew that the nationalists were not wholly on his side, wanted a Gandhian to be Chairman of the Reception Committee. So he insisted upon Jamnalal Bajaj's acceptance of the chairmanship of the Reception Committee. In his youth Jamnalal Bajaj was an admirer of Tilak and his *Kesari*. As he had received an ordinary education, he was hesitant to accept such a heavy responsibility. But ultimately he yielded to Gandhi's wish.

Another feature of the Nagpur Congress was that the British politicians Col. Wedgwood, Benjamin Spoor and Halford Knight attended the Congress and were allowed to participate in the debates of the Subjects Committee by the President, C. Vijayaraghavachariar. In his welcome speech in Hindi Jamnalal Bajaj appealed to his fellow-businessmen to participate in the national endeavour for Swaraj so that trade, industry and commerce might flourish a hundred-fold. So far there were landlords and professional classes in the Congress. With the emergence of Gandhi the capitalists entered it.

Das had brought a contingent of 250 Bengali delegates and wanted to oppose the non-co-operation resolution. In the initial stages he tried to scuttle it but found it difficult to do so. There were acute differences between the Das group and the group of Jitendra Lal Banerjee who was in favour of non-co-operation. On December 27 both parties had come to blows in the Bengali camp at Nagpur. When the news came to Gandhi, who was having a chat with Vallabhbhai Patel, he ran to the Bengali camp, stood on a table and pleaded for peace. He said that as he was the cause of their dissension and strife his head should be blown to pieces. He then had a long talk with Das and they arrived at a secret compromise which was known as the Das-Gandhi Pact, "by which each promised the other freedom of propaganda in his own sphere, for the future."[17] As soon as this pact was entered into, Gandhi became the undisputed leader of India and Das became a convert to the non-co-operation idea, coming forward to move the resolution. Jitendra Lal Banerjee was professor of English, a fiery orator who had gone to jail so often that he was later known as Jail-Banerjee!

It may be noted here that on the eve of the Nagpur session, Das had visited Nagpur and discussed with Maharashtrian leaders a draft signed by Lajpatrai, Das, Pal and Madan Mohan Malaviya.[18] They differed from the resolution of the Calcutta Congress over the boycott of schools and colleges. Kelkar told Das that it was proper for them to allow Gandhi one year to work out his scheme. The Nagpur leaders had invited the Congress to Nagpur and so they remained neutral. Das returned disappointed.

C. Vijayaraghavachariar, President of the Congress, differed with Gandhi on the boycott of schools and courts and opined that instead emphasis should be laid on universal primary education which was the prime need of the country. He gave a timely warning to the nation against regimentation which implied absolute and universal surrender of private judgment and gradual emasculation of the capacity for it. He cited the examples of Pericles of Athens and Bismark of Germany who became great but left their countries small owing to regimentation. It was a pointer to those enthusiasts who left the thinking in every field to Gandhi and were fast accepting regimentation of thought!

The British Government and the Moderates expected a fight between the nationalists and Gandhi's followers. There was, however, not much trouble. As stated earlier, Das came forward to move the resolution on non-co-operation, and the scene changed. The Maharashtrian nationalist old leaders were not men of action, and most of the younger leaders now went over to Gandhi's side. Only Malaviya and Jinnah, who wanted the Congress to limit the goal of Swaraj within the British Empire, opposed the resolution on the new creed of the Congress. In the Subjects Committee Malaviya and Jinnah were heckled, especially Jinnah, who refused to call Gandhi 'Mahatma' and Mahomed Ali 'Maulana' and referred to them as 'Mr. Gandhi' and 'Mr. Mahomed Ali', Jinnah refused to be dictated to in that way and added that he had the liberty to refer to any man in any way he wanted to.

Col. J. C. Wedgwood opposed in the Subjects Committee the resolution on the new creed of the Congress, deploring the fact that it would make the task of India and of India's friends in England such as the Labour members more difficult if not impossible. He emphasized the need of liberty of speech and said it pained him to remember the bad treatment accorded to Jinnah and Malaviya. Pattabhi Sitaramayya, Kelkar and Mahomed Ali replied to Wedgewood and supported the goal of Swaraj. There were amendments suggesting that the word Swaraj be qualified by the word 'democratic' or replaced by the words 'full responsible Government within the British Commonwealth' or by asking for a debate on the clause by 'all legitimate and peaceful means.' But the new creed was passed. The new creed declared: "That the object of the Congress is the attainment of Swaraj by the people of India by all legitimate and peaceful means." The creed the Congress had adopted in 1907 said: "The object of the Indian National Congress shall be to promote by constitutional means the interests and the well-being of the people of the Indian Empire."

Gandhi declared that the Indian people desired to retain the British connection if they could rise to their full height within it, but if it was necessary for them to get rid of the British connection for their national development, they would dispense with it. So Gandhi purposely kept Swaraj undefined. Whether the pressure from the Muslim leaders, who were expecting an invasion of India by the Afghan ruler Amanulla, prevailed, is a point worth consideration.

In the open session Gandhi carried the day. The Calcutta resolution on non-co-operation was adopted with slight changes in respect of the appeal to students below 16. The Congress ratified and clarified, amplified and reaffirmed the Calcutta declaration. It appealed to all people in Government employment, pending the call of the nation, to resign and offer their service to the national cause. It called upon all public associations to advance Hindu-Muslim unity. It requested Hindu leaders to settle all disputes between Brahmins and non-Brahmins wherever they might be existing and to make special efforts, to rid Hinduism of the reproach of untouchability. It appealed for the raising of a national fund to be called the All-India Tilak Memorial Swaraj Fund for the purpose of financing the non-co-operation movement.

Gandhi, who believed in self-help and had faith in self-reliance, pressed for the abolition of the British Committee and the closure of their mouthpiece *India*. He pointed out that the Congress had to incur the heavy expenditure of £3,300 a year on the committee, which was, according to Gandhi, a needless waste of public money. Congress could ill spare a single worker for foreign work, he added. At that time Syed Hussain worked as editor-secretary and Fenner Brockway as co-editor-secretary on the British Committee, each getting £550 a year! Gandhi had the confidence of bringing the world to India to witness the non-co-operation movement and so wanted to abolish the British Committee. The attempt at appointing a committee in India to do propaganda work in foreign countries failed. But two years later, when the tide of non-co-operation had receded it was Motilal Nehru who gave an impetus to foreign propaganda.

GANDHI SOUGHT TO give the movement a mass basis and so, under the new constitution, he rightly widened its base and influence to suit the new goal and new circumstances.

Gandhi thus completely revolutionised the Congress, spreading its message and organization to the remote villages, bringing the lower middle class into the Congress and converting the organization of goody-goody talkers and intellectuals, richly dressed landlords and lawyers belonging to the upper strata of society into dedicated patriotic workers belonging to the masses. With four-anna franchise it was now a peoples' organization possessing the will of the masses. It now became a revolutionary body with an effective weapon. The provincial units of the Congress were formed on a linguistic basis. The Congress Working Committee came into being.

The Nagpur Congress was a complete triumph for Gandhi. The only opponent worthy of consideration was Das, but he moved the main resolution on non-co-operation! A voice from the audience asked him whether he had suspended his legal practice. He replied that Chitta Ranjan Das practised what he preached. From that day he became one of the stoutest crusaders for some time of the new movement. On his return to Calcutta from Nagpur, he declared on January 19, 1921, the suspension of his legal practice and gave up his life and property to the non-co-operation movement amidst scenes filled with rapture and reverence. Das gave up smoking and drinking and luxurious living and began to live the life of a political and spiritual ascetic. Das was a poet by temperament. Emotion was the governing characteristic of his personality. For a while he gave up his smouldering resistance to the rising cult of Gandhism. The Gandhi-Muslim alliance completely overwhelmed him. That was the touch of Gandhi, the trick was done and the opponent became a supporter of his own volition!

ANOTHER NOTABLE FEATURE of the Nagpur Congress was that the Muslim League, which held its session under the presidentship of Dr. Ansari in the Congress pandal, accepted the Congress creed of Swaraj. Pandit Motilal Nehru and Gandhi attended the session. The Muslim League passed a resolution entreating Amanulla, the Amir of Afghanistan, to reject any advance on the part of the Government of India for a treaty with Great Britain and declaring that both Afghanistan and India would cultivate friendly relations between them.

Gandhi attended the Khilafat Conference which met at Nagpur under the Presidentship of Abul Kalam Azad during the same week. "The Ayats (verses)", Shraddhanand narrates, "of the Koran recited by Maulanas on that occasion contained frequent references to Jihad against and the killing of Kaffirs. But when I drew his attention to this phase of the Khilafat movement, Mahatmaji smiled and said: 'They are alluding to the British Bureaucracy.' In reply I said that it was all subversive of the idea of non-violence."[19]

It was at this session of the Khilafat Conference that Shaukat Ali announced amidst acclamation that Amir Amanulla had sent a message of condolence at the death of Sheikh-ul-Hind Mohammad-ul-Hussain. Thereupon it was decided to thank the Amir for his message on behalf of all communities of India. Both the Khilafat Conference and the Muslim League independently passed a resolution begging Amir Amanulla not to make a treaty with the British Government as any such alliance would strengthen Britain's hold on India. The resolutions hoped that both India and Afghanistan would develop friendly relations between themselves. In the Khilafat Conference this resolution on the Afghan affair was moved by Gandhi and seconded by Shaukat Ali. Gandhi would not dare to move such a resolution in the Congress.

The Depressed Class Conference also met at Nagpur under the Presidentship of Gandhi who said that untouchability was the greatest sin of India under the guise of Hinduism and a great satanism in Hinduism. Chhaganlal Fakirjee described untouchability as "our own Rowlatt Act". The Social Conference also held its session at Nagpur during the Congress session under the Presidentship of Vithalbhai Patel. In his presidential address he said that the caste system must go root and branch. He regretted to find that Gandhi ranged himself in that matter on the side of reaction.[20] Democracy, he added, would be nothing but a dream if in the same breath caste distinctions were observed.

Whatever criticism Patel made of Gandhi's social views, his political movement and leadership impressed the Britishers. And Ben Spoor, who attended the Nagpur session, was one of them. Giving his impressions about the Nagpur Congress, he said that although some irresponsible persons in Britain described Gandhi as a madman, he found Gandhi to be a man of transparent sincerity, moral courage and spiritual intensity. "The West," he observed, "has produced a Lenin, strong, masterful, relentless alike in logic and methods. The East has given birth to Gandhi, equally strong, masterful and relentless. But while the former pins his faith on force, the latter relies on non-resistance. The one trusts the sword, the other trusts the spirit. In an ordinary manner these men appear to incarnate those fundamentally opposing forces that—behind all the surface struggles of our day—are fighting for supremacy."[21]

What Ben Spoor's estimate of Gandhi lacked, S. A. Dange soon furnished in his pamphlet *Gandhi vs. Lenin* which he published a few days later. Lenin followed science and economic theory, reason and rationalism. Whereas Gandhi followed God and Varnashram Dharma. Gandhi's aversion to modern civilization and adherence to caste system were well known.

CHAPTER XXIII

Swaraj in One Year

THE NEW YEAR 1921 witnessed great unrest in India. Students emptied the Government-aided and Government-controlled schools and colleges in cities and towns. Bengal, the Punjab and the United Provinces echoed the national cries of students. Gandhi undertook a tour of eastern and northern India to inspire the youth with the spirit of nationalism, to instill courage into the new generation and fearlessness into the old guard. Everywhere he was received like a god!

On the eve of his visit to Bengal, Gandhi deliberately made an appeal to the youth in Bengal through *Young India*. "Bengal," he said, "has great intelligence, it has a greater heart, it has more than its share of the spiritual heritage for which our country is noted. You have more imagination, more faith and more emotion than the rest of India. You have falsified the calumny of cowardice on occasions more than one." He asked Bengali youth to remember that non-violence was the cornerstone of the edifice of non-co-operation. He urged them to suspend their studies and added that suspension of studies need not extend even to a year. Government would not yield, he asserted, to the logic of words but to brave and true deeds.

Gandhi then visited Calcutta. He was there from January 23 to February 4, 1921. On January 19 C. R. Das had given up his enormous legal practice. This gave a tremendous momentum to the national movement in Bengal, and as Gandhi observed, it hastened events. Thousands of students left their high schools and colleges. Eminent lawyers like Motilal Nehru followed suit. Srinivas Iyengar resigned the Advocate-Generalship in Madras and Bhulabhai Desai his in Bombay. Rajaji and several other provincial lawyers like L. B. Bhopatkar gave up their lucrative practices. The old leaders of the national movement were receding into the background. They gave place to new ones. Surendranath Banerjee, the former 'Sir Surrender-Not' was knighted in January 1921 and this voice of India unfortunately became a muzzled drum.

Gandhi told the Bengali students that it was a sin to pursue their studies in institutions run with Government aid. They were entering upon a new life and turning a new leaf. He advised them to translate into their mother-tongue the knowledge they had gained through English literature, find equivalent expressions in their mother-tongue for the richest thoughts they had learnt from English poets and authors. This advice was indeed a great stimulus fo the growth of Indian languages and had a powerful effect upon the development of the regional languages.

Gandhi further asked the students of high schools and colleges including medical and law colleges to suspend their education, throw in their lot with the millions of their countrymen and gain Swaraj within one year. It was absolutely necessary that they should not return to the colleges and schools they had abandoned. He advised them to shun the modern civilization which, according to him, was a modern curse. The young men of Bengal, he observed, had given him great hope and greater strength and he earnestly prayed to God. "Shaukat Ali and Mahomed Ali and I will live to erect this flag of Swaraj inside this year! But if it is the will of God that my ashes should be placed in the Ganges water before the eight months of the year are out, I shall die with the conviction that you will see to it that Swaraj is secured before this year is out."[1]

Feeling that the Bengal students' enthusiasm was likely to get out of control, Gandhi emphasized the need for discipline and respectful behaviour on the part of students towards their elders. He then impressed upon their minds that to have Swaraj was everyone's *Dharma.* He asked them to ply the spinning wheel for some hours a day, to practise truthfulness, tolerance and non-co-operation.

Education under Swaraj, Gandhi said, should aim at making pupils self-reliant right from the early years. The students should live for others and not for themselves. They should have the capacity to die for India and should not live as witness to her shame.

Gandhi said that the more he thought the more numerous grew the conditions for Swaraj. He often defined Swaraj and mentioned the conditions for the attainment of it. "Swaraj means rule over one's self." "Swaraj," he observed, "in my opinion hangs on a thread, the spinning 'thread.' Swaraj means the rule of *Dharma*. On Charka alone the Swaraj depends. Boycott is an indispensable condition for the attainment of Swaraj. When large numbers of wholly innocent men are in jail, we may take it that Swaraj is at hand. Swaraj is the abandonment of the fear of death. Removal of (untouchability), the blot on Hinduism, is necessary for the attainment of Swaraj. To get rid of the infatuation for English is one of the essentials of Swaraj. Swaraj is democratic Government. The real meaning of Swaraj is that every poor person in the country must have food and clothing. Swaraj means conditions in which a young girl could, without danger, move about alone at dead of night. For me the attainment of the Khilafat through India's power is the attainment of Swaraj." "It meant promising Hindu-Muslim unity, setting up Congress organization, introducing the spinning wheel. Swadeshi means Swaraj and Swadharma." The last definition he made during this period was: "Love is Swaraj."

Two years earlier Gandhi had said: "It is through swadeshi that we will get Swaraj. Swadeshi movement holds the key to Swaraj. It is through students that we can achieve independence." He now declared in Calcutta that the attainment of Swaraj depended on the workers and the agriculturists. According to him the spinning wheel protected a woman's virtue, fed and clothed the poor, and would solve the problem of India's chronic poverty. And it was an insurance against famine as well. So he said, "I can only think of India's *kamdhenu*[2] and the spinning wheel is that for India." The next day he declared that Khilafat was *kamdhenu*.[3] Gandhi then declared open the National College started by the Board of Education led by C. R. Das.

Gandhi addressed a women's meeting in Calcutta. Lessons in patriotism and sacrifice were being given to women. They were being awakened to the new role and responsibility in their life. Gandhi asked them to donate to the Tilak Swaraj Fund and to promote swadeshi. At that meeting Gandhi spread his shawl and there was a spontaneous shower of gifts which literally covered the shawl.

On January 30, 1921, Gandhi addressed a meeting on the birthday anniversary of Swami Vivekanand at the Belur Math, Calcutta, the headquarters of the Ramkrishna Mission. Gandhi told the audience that he had great respect for Swami Vivekanand. He had studied many of Vivekanand's books and added that his ideals agreed in many respects with those of the great man. If Vivekanand were alive that day, he concluded, he would be a great help to the national awakening.

While he was in Calcutta some students blocked by sitting *dharna* the passage of their fellow-students who wanted to go to the university for paying their fees or doing some such work. Gandhi condemned this act and described it as a form of barbarity, a crude way of using coercion. The *Modern Review*, Calcutta, sounded a warning to Gandhi that if the thousands "of student-strikers, who could neither be educated in national institutions, nor utilized for propaganda, teaching or social work in villages, were either obliged to idle away their time or to go back to their former institutions, the non-co-operation movement would experience a set-back in Bengal.[4] Gandhi therefore warned the students that they were being accused of emotional behaviour and impulsiveness. As they were the makers of new India they should approach the task with a religious faith, with industry and perseverance, eschew violence and *dharna* and falsify the fears of those who had expressed a sense of nervous fear about their future.

THE DUKE OF Connaught, who was to inaugurate the new reformed councils, arrived in Calcutta on January 28, 1921, to inaugurate the Bengal Legislative Council. He had arrived in Madras on January 10, and inaugurated the Madras Legislative Council. In the first week of February he proclaimed the Royal message in which the King Emperor had said: "For years, it must be for generations, patriotic and loyal Indians have dreamed of Swaraj for their motherland, an opportunity for progress to the liberty which my other dominions enjoy."

On February 8, 1921, the Duke inaugurated the Chamber of Princes at Delhi and on February 9, he formally inaugurated the bicameral legislature composed of the Legislative Assembly and the Council of State. The Legislative Assembly had 106 elected members of whom 40 were nominated members and 25 official. The Council of State having 61 members commanded an unofficial majority. The Legislative Assembly sat for three years and the Council of State for five years.

When the Duke arrived in Calcutta, people observed complete *hartal*. Gandhi wrote to the Duke explaining that the public demonstration was not against his high personage but against the system he had come to uphold. The non-co-operationists would not be deceived by the reforms that tinkered with the problems of India's distress and humiliation. On February 28 the Duke left Bombay for England with India's message of despair, disaffection and discontent.

On the eve of the Duke's visit to Bombay, Gandhi had wired from the Punjab that Bombay should certainly boycott the Duke's visit as it had been in other cities. On March 24 Gandhi was officially informed at Lahore that his telegram had been held up at Ahmedabad as objectional under the rulings of the Department and that a refund would be granted on his applying for it.

Gandhi again emphasized the non-violent character of his movement. He explained that non-violence meant reliance on God. It was undoubtedly a religious movement. Non-co-operation meant self-purification. Non-co-operation was not a movement of brag, bluster or bluff. It required solid and silent sacrifice. By violence, Ireland might gain her freedom and Turkey her lost possessions. Islam decayed when its followers dangled the sword in the face of man and lost sight of the godliness, the humanity and austerity of its founder and his disciples.

About this time Gandhi was charged with being a dictator. He replied that he was not a dictator. In the Subjects Committee he yielded on many points, but it was true that in matters of conscience, he added, he was uncompromising. He, therefore, tolerated the charge of being a dictator and said that unity did not mean identity of views.

While in Calcutta, Gandhi began observing silence on Monday and spending the whole day in meditation with his soul.[5] The untiring work, the extensive travels, the unending speeches, the constant interviews exasperated him. He wanted to rest for one day a week and so instituted the day of silence. Later, in his mystic way, he clothed it with spiritual virtues.

The Rev. Mr. Gillespie blamed Gandhi for his non-cooperation movement and said Jesus co-operated with all to win the evil-doers to righteousness. Gandhi replied that it was true Jesus had done so, but he wiped the dust off his feet of those places which did not listen to his word. He denounced Pharisees and seducers and hypocrites. So Gandhi said he was denouncing as satanic a Government which had been guilty of fraud, murder and wanton cruelty.

A few days earlier Gandhi had said that although he did not stand comparison with Buddha and Christ, even so he aspired to be their equal in love.[6] He requested the readers not to think him presumptuous on that account. The highest ideal he had set before him was a Mehta of Gujarat as he thought that Narsinha Mehta's love was no less than that of Buddha. He also said: "I have not accepted anyone as my dharma-guru (spiritual mentor), and don't think myself, either, to be worthy of the honour of being such (to anyone else)." He had accepted Gokhale, who was older than him by three years, "as his political Guru, but he accepted no one as his spiritual Guru. His *Dharma* or spiritual Guru was his inner voice. He was his self-conceived Guru.

Gandhi then left Calcutta and visited Patna, Benares and several other places, advising the national schools to impart instruction in Hindi and Urdu and to use the Devanagari and Urdu scripts. His appeal moved the classes, the masses and the sadhus as well. On his way to Benares Gandhi was harassed by the slogans and shouts of *jai* raised by the devotees who insisted on having his *darshan*. Mahadev Desai and Kasturba tried to keep them quiet and requested them not to disturb Gandhi who was thoroughly exhausted. Gandhi, too, appealed to the devotees to have pity on him, but in vain. At last he beat his forehead three times which had its effect on the people and they left him alone.

This was the fourth occasion in Gandhi's life when he beat his forehead. "When a person," Gandhi explained, "simply cannot control his anger, the best way to work it off is to strike oneself. Of the four incidents I mentioned, on three occasions my grief was due to the misdeeds of those dear to me and I could not bear. On one occasion I atoned for my own lapse. I had committed such a sin that I felt suddenly shocked at it and was aflame with anger with myself. I rose and struck myself hard blows and only then did I have peace."[7]

Psychologically, it was a way to show one's suppressed hatred of beloved persons. He had inherited this trait from his father.

Gandhi spoke at the opening ceremony of the Bihar National University and also at the opening ceremony of a National College. At Benares he spoke at the founding of Kashi Vidyapith and reached Delhi, laying down the foundation stones of several national high schools, at several places on the way.

While FORMALLY DECLARING open Tibbia Medical College in Delhi on February 13, 1921, Gandhi unveiled the portraits of Lord and Lady Hardinge, treasuring the memory of their good deeds. Lord Hardinge had supported Gandhi's struggle in South Africa. To sing praise of a Governor-General and to unveil his portrait was an inconsistent act for a non-co-operator and Gandhi alone could perform the feat and yet fit it in the scheme of non-co-operation. Attempt at proving the purity of heart and the debt of gratitude proved stronger than the ephemeral applause of the followers. But the queerest act for him was to express his strange opinion on medicine at a medical college which he was declaring open. He believed that a multiplicity of hospitals was no test of civilization. It was rather a symptom of decay. The present science of medicine was divorced from religion. "A man," he added, "who attends to his daily *namaz* or his *gayatri* (Vedic prayer to the Sun-god for illumination) in the proper spirit need not ever get ill."[8]

Yet Gandhi paid his humble tribute to the spirit of research that inspired modern scientists and concluded his speech with the words: "The condition of indigenous medicine is truly deplorable. Not having kept abreast of modern research their profession has fallen largely into disrepute."[9] He was glad that the institution had a Western wing for the benefit of the students. Gandhi had faith in the prophylactic virtues of prayer and yet he could not help resorting to Western medicine in times of his own illness.

Gandhi, the leader of the non-co-operation movement, agreed to co-operate with the Government on a vital point. It was in the matter of the census. Explaining and defending this stand, he said: "My loyalty has triumphed in the matter of census. I am convinced that it strengthens the cause."

About this time Gandhi published an article in *Young India* advising practising lawyers not to figure as leaders on public platforms. He asked them to be silent social workers, and help the movement with money. They should not have touts or exploit clients but insist on private arbitration.

Gandhi was in fact moulding the half-day politicians into full-time politicians with a view to shifting the initiative in politics from lawyers to social workers and to eliminating those who opposed his policy. He was breaking with the established ways of thinking and acting. The result was that the leadership in cities and towns shifted to those who gave their time and energy to the non-co-operation movement, and a new class of leaders emerged from the urban areas.

The second aspect of this policy became visible. The ideal patriot was considered the one who professed absolute, blind faith in Gandhi, flirted with orthodox and fanatic Muslims and discarded the idea of an armed revolt. This new class of patriots thought that the non-Gandhians were not real patriots.

They were either stooges of the British Empire or misguided patriots or communalists. So, to become ideal patriots, landlords and wealthy lawyers donned rough Khadi clothes and became Gandhians.

The third aspect of this movement was that the new leadership of the Congress was developing a dictatorial tendency.

Gandhi left Delhi to make a tour of the Punjab. He addressed rural conferences at Bhiwani and Rohtak and a meeting at Gujaranwala. He pleased the Punjabis by telling them that the Punjab had become a second Gujarat to him. He received an unprecedented ovation, the faces of his audiences shining at sight of him. While he was in the Punjab, the enthusiasm of Bengali students ebbed and towards the end of February 1921 their boycott of schools and colleges collapsed. A majority of students returned to their old institutions. Gandhi admitted that the vast majority of the students went back after the first flush of enthusiasm. But he added that the recantation was proof rather of the extent of our degradation than of the wrongness of the step! During the first flush of success he always provided justifications for his moves and when retreat was unavoidable he admitted the blunder!

ON MARCH 3, Gandhi, accompanied by Shaukat Ali, visited Nankana Saheb where one hundred and six Akali Sikhs had been massacred on February 20, 1921, on the Gurudwara premises by a faction led by Mahant Narandas. The Akali Dal had come to take possession of the Gurudwar at Nankana. The Akalis wanted to rid the Gurudwaras of the abuses that had crept into them. The movement had been going on for some years.

In his speech Gandhi said that, were it not for the futility of suicide to end grief, he should long before have done away with his life. Their grief was his. When he heard of the tragedy of Nankana he felt like wanting to be among the victims. It was his view that the martyrs had died to save not only their own faith but also other religions from impurity.

He asked the Sikhs to keep the Kirpan sheathed and to dedicate all their matchless bravery to the service of the country and her redemption. He praised the martyrdom of Lachhmen Singh and Dulip Singh who sacrificed their lives at Nankana Saheb without raising a finger.

Shortly after, Gandhi wrote in *Young India* that the purest way of seeking justice against the murderers was not to seek it as the perpetrators, whether they were Sikhs, Pathans or Hindus, were our countrymen. Their punishment could not recall the dead to life. Upon this a reader of *Young India* asked him why he then incessantly recalled Jallianwalla Bagh and Dyer. Gandhi replied that his letter as addressed to the Sikhs would have lost its force somewhat if he had broadened the appeal from patriotism to humanity. Gandhi described the perpetrators of the murders as 'our countrymen'. Here the national leader in Gandhi dominated the truth seeker in him.

Later, Gandhi swiftly resumed his great role in life and nobly declared: "For me patriotism is the same as humanity. I am patriotic because I am human and humane. It is not exclusive. I will not hurt England or Germany to serve India. Imperialism has no place in my life. The law of a patriot is not different from that of the patriarch. And a patriot is so much the less a patriot if he is a lukewarm humanitarian."[10]

Another important principle Gandhi enunciated at this time expressing his thoughts on the would-be constitution of India. He observed: "No one can produce a swaraj scheme because it is not one man's swaraj that is wanted, nor can a scheme be framed in advance. What may satisfy the nation today may not satisfy it tomorrow. Our evolution is, and must be, an organic growth. National will is, therefore, subject to change from day to day. But some broad outlines can certainly be laid down in advance for any scheme of swaraj. The nation's representatives must have full control over education, law, police and military. We must have full financial control. And if we are to be self-governing, not a soldier can leave India without our consent."[11]

The Nankana murderers were prosecuted and in October 1921, the Mahant and seven others were sentenced to death, eight were sentenced to transportation for life and seventeen to seven years' rigorous imprisonment.

Having completed his tour through Lyallpur, Lahore, Multan, Jullunder, Hoshiarpur, Hariana and Ambala, Gandhi returned to Bombay. He fixed one crore of rupees as the sum to be collected in the name of the great patriot Tilak. Seventy-five per cent of the money so collected was to be spent on provincial items by every province. His friends Parsi Rustomjee and Dr. Mehta had donated Rs. 40,000 and 1,50,000 respectively towards Gandhi's different activities, and the latter amount "was purely, he said, an answer to the soul's prayers.

Gandhi was always practical in his organizational work and knew the power of both purse and prayer. He wrote to Maganlal

Gandhi instructing him how he should keep the accounts and spend this money on certain items and how he should draw money from Revashankarbhai.

Gandhi was indeed an ascetic man who relied on God rather than on money, but he rolled in funds and spent crores of rupees on political propaganda.

Meanwhile, as Gandhi's non-co-operation movement grew, the Government began to counteract. The U.P. Government declared the non-co-operation movement revolutionary and anarchical and instructed its servants to combat it. The Bihar Government, too, started an offensive against the non-cooperation movement. The Madras Government had thrown Yakub Hassan behind bars. The Punjab Government prohibited Lajpatrai from entering or remaining in the North-West Frontier. There were riots in Nagpur and Bareilly, and Rajashai jail had been broken.

Referring to this repression, Gandhi said that it was a sure sign of the approaching victory. Every movement, he added, passed through five stages: indifference, ridicule, abuse, repression and respect. He again declared that the primary motive of non-co-operation was self-purification by withdrawing cooperation from an unrighteous and unrepentant Government. The secondary object was to rid ourselves of the feeling of helplessness by being independent of all Government control.

CHAPTER XXIV

The Afghan Bogey

GANDHI THEN TURNED to the Khilafat movement of the Muslims. There was a demand for a change in the Treaty of Sevres. In an article in *Young India* he said that by no canon of ethics or war could Palestine be given to the Jews as a result of the war. Gandhi added that the Zionists must either revise their ideal about Palestine or, if Judaism permitted the arbitrament of war, engage in a holy war with the Muslims of the world, the Christians throwing in their weight on their side. He wanted unequivocal Muslim control over Arabia which included Mesopotamia, Syria and Palestine. To the end of his life Gandhi did not give up this stand. He was opposed to Palestine being given to the Jews. He sided with the Muslims and later opposed even the partition of Palestine.

Gandhi now shifted the centre of gravity of the national movement to the village. The All-India Congress Committee was held on March 31, 1921, at Bezwada in Andhra. Gandhi was carrying the national movement right down to the cottages. The members of the A.I.C.C. who attended were only fifty, but more than a lakh of villagers from a radius of 40 miles had come on foot to have a glimpse of the Mahatma. The huge crowd was divided into many groups and the Mahatma addressed them from one platform after another.

Gandhi moved four important resolutions at this A.I.C.C. He declared that the nation should collect one crore rupees for the Tilak Swaraj Fund, enlist one crore members on the Congress registers and introduce twenty lakhs of spinning wheels. Gandhi was the first Indian leader to launch such a huge scheme for political propaganda. Das upheld it, called for men, money and munition, and backed Gandhi's demands. Mrs. Besant and Surendranath Banerjee were critical of Gandhi's movement and they preached resistance to it.

Just at this moment Lord Reading assumed the Viceroyalty of India on April 2, 1921. He was a former Attorney-General and Chief Justice of England and a former British ambassador to Canada. Lord Chelmsford embarked for London. Few Viceroys left with such a record of unrest, discontent and ill-will. Gandhi, impressed by Reading's high judicial standing and his antecedents, did not want any hostile demonstrations to be made on his landing.

The Congress had formally accepted the tri-colour flag of the Home Rule League at the Calcutta session in 1917 and it virtually became the Congress flag. At the Bezwada meeting of the A.I.C.C. the tri-colour flag with the Charkha as its chief emblem was accepted as a new National Flag.

P. Venkayya of the National College, Masulipatam, had kept before the public a suggestive booklet offering designs for an Indian National Flag. He had been championing the cause of the National Flag at the Congress sessions for four years. It was Lala Hansraj of Jullunder who suggested that a spinning wheel should be placed on the National Flag. Red was a Hindu colour, green was Muslim and white represented all the other faiths. The weakest numerically occupied the first place, the Islamic colour came next and the Hindu one last. The Sikhs who wanted black on the flag, were told that they had no differences with the Hindus and moreover white included all other colours.

On April 13, 1921, another conference of the suppressed classes was held at Ahmedabad. A few Untouchables attended it. Addressing the conference, Gandhi said that he believed untouchability was no part of Hinduism, and true Hinduism did not regard untouchability as a sin. "I do want," he observed, "to attain *moksha.* I do not want to be reborn. But if I have to be reborn, I should be born an Untouchable so that I may share their sorrows, sufferings, and the affronts levelled at them."[1] He urged the Untouchables to give up drinking and gambling, and to cultivate cleanliness. They should not accept leavings from the meals of others; they should accept only good food. He told the Untouchables that they would never be able to obtain redress for their grievances by discarding the Hindu religion.

"Two of the strongest desires," Gandhi concluded, "that keep me in flesh and bone are the emancipation of the Untouchables and the protection of the cow. When these two desires are fulfilled, there is my own *moksha.* In January 1921 he opined that removal of the blot of untouchability on Hinduism was necessary for the attainment of Swaraj; it was a reform not to follow Swaraj but to precede it. A few days earlier he had written to Andrews that "it is a bigger problem than that of gaining Indian Independence but I can tackle it better if I gain the latter on the way. It is not impossible that India may free herself from English domination before India has become free of the curse of untouchability." "I have felt," he added, "that I could not remain a Hindu if it was true that untouchability was a part of Hinduism."

Gandhi often called himself a Sanatani Hindu. And according to him "a Hindu is anyone who, born in a Hindu family in India, accepts the *Vedas*, the *Upanishads* and the *Puranas*' as holy books, who has faith in the five Yamas of truth, nonviolence, etc., and practises them to the best of his ability; who believes in the existence of the *atman* (self) and the *parmatman* (supreme self) and believes, further, that the *atman* is never born and never dies but, through incarnation in the body, passes from existence to existence and is capable of attaining *moksha*; who believes that *moksha* is the supreme end of human striving and believes in *Varnashram* and cow-protection."[2]

For him the *Vedas* were divine and 'unwritten'. He believed in the Varnashram Dharma, and defended the usefulness and dignity of the caste system, but he now gilded his Varnashram Dharma with the saintly thought that Varnashram was not a religion of superiority or inferiority. No man of God could consider another man to be inferior to himself. In fact this was the religion of "men of God."

GANDHI TURNED AGAIN to the Brahmin-non-Brahmin question which had assumed a very serious turn in southern India. In Madras he had remonstrated with the Brahmins. But he knew that those who supported him in the south were mostly Brahmins. The Brahmins who formed only three per cent of the total population in the south had monopolized the majority of the posts under Government. Brahminism which was the essence of the caste system and Varnashram Dharma had crushed the non-Brahmins for ages. So when the Brahmin politicians turned to Gandhi's movement, the non-Brahmins turned to the British Government for support to their claims.

So now Gandhi made a speech at Madras on April 8, 1921 saying that he himself, a non-Brahmin, would request the non-

Brahmins not to decry the Brahmins who had accepted poverty and self-effacement and were silently but surely showing every class in India their rights and privileges. He appealed to the non-Brahmins not to interfere with the non-co-operation movement by intriguing with the British Government. Whether Gandhi referred to the Brahmins of old or those of the present was not clear! The southern Brahmins of Gandhi's time treated the non-Brahmins as inferior beings and the Untouchables as social lepers and even unapproachables. Nowhere was the rigidity and inhumanity of caste experienced in India as in southern India!

Just at this time the Tatas were planning to erect a dam across the rivers Nira and Mula at Mulshi in Poona District. For this the Government had, under the Land Acquisition Act, to acquire land from the neighbouring villages. Fifty-one villages were involved in the project and about 1,100 farmers refused to be turned out of their land. So they resorted to satyagraha on April 16, 1921, but suspended it at N. C. Kelkar's intervention.

Gandhi, who thought that the people so dispossessed never got the exact equivalent of their land, appealed to the Tatas to confer the boons it claimed to confer upon India by deferring to the wishes of the weak. He even said that he dreaded the Rockefeller spirit that seemed to be overtaking the great House of Tatas. It was appropriating poor people's properties for the doubtful benefit of making India industrial. Gandhi did not know that what the Tatas were trying to do at that time, the Government of independent India would do at treble the cost in free India!

P. M. Bapat, a famous revolutionary, led the satyagraha, which was at first pure and passive. Gandhi had no sympathy for industrialization, and Bapat, firebrand patriot that he was, sympathised with the poor farmers, took their side and fought fearlessly with the then Government as he perhaps would have done also in independent India in similar situations. Bapat then led an active and violent struggle and ultimately in 1924 suffered a long imprisonment, gaining the title 'Senapati' (General) for his valiant though fruitless fight. In the end the farmers gave up the struggle and sold their lands.

Later, in April 1924, Gandhi asked Dastane to drop the movement as according to him there seemed no ideal behind it, and the leader Bapat was not an out-and-out believer in non-violence.

Gandhi appealed to the Parsis to support the temperance

movement that was spreading in India. The nationalist leaders like Tilak had launched this movement in 1908. Gandhi's non-co-operation movement aimed at "comprehensive purification and so it gave a fillip to the idea. Gandhi said that the farmers should not steal and gamble, they should sell corn at a reasonable price without making unduly large profits. He said that betting at the races was a curse. Gandhi further said: "As journalist and reformer, my function is to call public attention to these vices. I must own that I had not the courage to bring the drink traffic in the campaign of purification. It has come unsought. The people have taken it up of their own accord."

Sir Chunilal V. Mehta, Member for Excise in the Bombay Governor's Council, who knew Gandhi's views on prohibition, met Gandhi in June 1921 at the house of Kanji Dwarkadas and made definite suggestions for the gradual eradication of the drink evil. Gandhi wanted the Government to introduce complete prohibition at once, and did not want it step by step. So Gandhi did not agree to Chunilal's proposal. Upon this Sobani said that Gandhi did not want prohibition. He had in mind only its political aspect, namely to embarrass and harass the Government.

WHILE GANDHI WAS shaping and purifying the political movement and making history in India, his image was casting a shadow over the world. His politics and philosophy were being discussed in Britain, France and in America. By now Indian leaders and leaders of thought had declared him to be the greatest Indian of their times. Tagore spoke of him as "the greatest of living men." Lajpatrai, describing him, had said: "I challenge the whole world to produce another man like Mahatma Gandhi!" And C. F. Andrews described him as a moral genius of the first order and added that he was a surgeon rather than a physician. *The New York Call* of April 11, 1921, summarised a sermon preached by Rev. Dr. John Haynes Holmes on April 10, 1921, in which "M. K. Gandhi, leader of the non-co-operation movement of India, was declared to be the greatest man now living in the world." The Rev. Dr. Holmes was preaching to his people on the subject: "Who is the Greatest Man in the World?".

There was confusion in the congregation when the priest named Gandhi, for few had heard of him or knew that he was an Indian, and fewer still knew anything about his career.

Gandhi was named by Holmes in preference to Nicolai Lenin and Remain Rolland, as according to Holmes, Gandhi combined the practical achievement of the one and the idealism of the other. Holmes said that Gandhi's method would succeed in freeing India, it would paralyse the British Government, and that Gandhi would build up a new social structure.

In Holmes's opinion Lenin, an intellectual giant, moved through practical affairs with the stride of a Hercules but he fell short of the highest human ideals because he had no moral principles and did not even see the need for them. Holmes believed that Lenin's failure to recognize the moral law would, unless it was repaired, lead to the overthrow of communism. Holmes characterized Rolland as the successor of Tolstoy and added that he was an intellectual but not a leader of men.

Although there were persons, Holmes continued, superior to Gandhi as scholars, intellectuals, thinkers, teachers and spiritual artists, and in the loftiness, depth, range and comprehensiveness of their idealism, there were few who practised what they professed and preached with greater consistency and thoroughness than Gandhi, though even Gandhi was not free from inconsistencies. "When I think of Gandhi," Holmes concluded, "I think of Jesus. He lives his life, he speaks his word; he suffers, strives and will some day nobly die for his kingdom upon earth."[3]

Holmes felt that Gandhi would build up a new social structure. Ten years later, it was Dr. B. R. Ambedkar, leader of the suppressed people in India, who told Gandhi bluntly that "History tells that Mahatmas, like fleeting phantoms, raise dust but raise no level."

It is interesting to note how Gandhi appeared to Englishmen during this period. Percival Landon of the *Daily Telegraph*, London, described Gandhi as an amazing and dangerous man who alone bestrode the field of Indian sedition like a Colossus. He bewildered the Indians with his pure utopianism. He preached to the heart and disliked the head.

Percival Landon further said that Gandhi had the typical head of the idealist and his skull was well-formed and finely modelled, his face narrowing to the pointed chin. He found Gandhi's eyes deep, kindly, entirely sane, his hair greying a little over the forehead. He spoke gently and well and in his voice was a note of detachment which lent uncanny force to his strange doctrines that he had given up his life to teach. In answer to a remark of Percival Landon that Christ strictly abstained from interfering in politics, Gandhi answered, "I do not think so, but if you are right, the less Christ in that was He."

Listening to Gandhi, Percival Landon stated, one was again and again reminded of the beautiful vision of a world of selfless kindliness that Gautam inculcated twenty-four centuries earlier—a world that never existed, a vision which had left human nature unchanged. Summing up his impression of Gandhi, Percival Landon observed: "A pure idealist, whom the people of India reverenced as a god, must, through the very qualities which enthroned him, end by delivering them over to bloodshed and misery." He made this forecast as if he were visualizing the killing of two lakhs of Indians in the partition of India!

Wedgewood said in *Nation* that one did not feel blasphemous to compare Gandhi with Christ. For Gandhi was a philosopher anarchist and a new edition of Tolstoy without Tolstoy's past.[5] In the *Daily Mail* a writer said that Gandhi had the disarming sweetness of a saint and all the arts of an advocate. The key to Gandhi and Gandhism was wrapped in his self-revealing sentence, "Most religious men I have met are politicians in disguise. I, however, who wear the guise of a politician, am at heart a religious man."[6] Previously he had said that he was a politician trying to be a saint.

Col. Yate suggested in the House of Commons that Gandhi, in view of his recent declaration that he preferred Bolshevik to British rule, should be deported as a Soviet agent.[7] Montagu replied that he left the problem of India to the authorities in India. The fact was that Gandhi had shown his dislike of Bolshevism. Woodrow Wilson's fourteen points were a reply to the Bolsheviks and Gandhi by his satyagraha posed a challenge to both!

While some writers and thinkers in the world were depicting Gandhi as the greatest man of the day, Gandhi in his own way was diminishing the greatness of the great Indians of modern India. While Gandhi was denouncing English education, he had been asked at Cuttack whether it was not a mixed evil inasmuch as Lokamanya Tilak, Ram Mohan Roy and Gandhi himself were the products of English education. In reply Gandhi in his inimitable style humbly asked them to leave aside his case as he was a miserable pigmy, and added that Ram Mohan Roy and Tilak were so many pigmies who had no hold upon the people compared with Chaitanya, Shanker, Kabir and Nanak. He once again asserted, "Ram Mohan, Tilak were pigmies before these giants." He asked the audience whether Ram Mohan Roy had produced a single martyr of the type of Dulip Singh who embraced death during the massacre of Nankana. To diminish the greatness of these two great men and to support his theory he cited the fact that British rule had not produced any Pratap or Shivaji.

Gandhi published the speech referred to above in *Young India* of April 13, 1921, and repeated his opinion in *Young India* of April 27, saying, "I do believe that Chaitanya, Kabir, Nanak, Guru Govind Singh, Shivaji and Pratap were greater men than Ram Mohan Roy and Tilak." But three years later Gandhi without any hesitation declared in *Young India* on April 9, 1925, that Shivaji and Pratap, too, were misguided patriots!

Gandhi wanted a crore of rupees in the name of Tilak but throughout his career he had been trying to diminish Tilak's greatness and to demolish his platform. Incidentally, he slighted the name of Ram Mohan Roy, another great man of Modern India, and hurt Bengal's pride. The Tilakites, who had given Gandhi a chance to take the freedom movement to its destination, perhaps ignored this attack on Tilak. But Bengal was disturbed, and Tagore, who had been striking now and then a discordant note over the ways of the non-co-operation movement, pulled up Gandhi for his harsh denigration of Ram Mohan Roy. Tagore was in Europe, travelling. He protested against Gandhi's remark. Tagore had his differences with Gandhi although he too did not believe in the physical body as the highest truth of man. But still less did he believe in the devaluing of the physical body, and the ignoring of the material necessities of life. He said: "We from the East have to come to her (the West) to learn whatever she has to teach us, for by doing so we hasten the fulfilment of this age." Now Tagore came out and said: "I strongly protest against Mahatma Gandhi's trying to cry down such great personalities of modern India as Ram Mohan Roy in his blind zeal for crying down our modern education. It shows that he is growing enamoured of his own doctrines, which is a dangerous form of egotism, that even great people suffer from at times."[8] *The Modern Review* of July 1921 also replied to Gandhi: "Mr. Gandhi says that he reads English as a nationalist should do. Ram Mohan read English, after attaining manhood as a nationalist and a cosmopolitan lover of humanity." It further pointed out that Ram Mohan Roy was one of the first Bengalees to write Bengali text-books for students.

Replying to Tagore, Gandhi said that Indians talking with and writing to their children or wives or husbands in English was a sign of slavery and degradation. He added that he was as great a believer in free air as the great poet. Undoubtedly this was true, but to prove that point he had no reason to run down Tilak and Roy. The controversy between Gandhi and Tagore went on for years.

Meanwhile Gandhi made a tour of Gujarat and Sind. In Karachi he advised the leaders to draw lots and decide which pleaders ought to suspend practice. Those on whom the lot fell should non-co-operate and the rest should maintain the families of the non-co-operators. Gandhi then attended the Political Conference of Maharashtra which was held at Bassein on May 7 after the reorganization of Provinces by the Congress on the basis of language. Gandhi declared at the conference: "I know that my work will be done when Maharashtra comes to have complete faith in the movement. Nowhere else have I seen the like of Maharashtra's capacity for self-reliance and its knowledge. Where knowledge is combined with the spirit of self-sacrifice, the *Yajna* is perfect." He added that it was only as long as Maharashtra was not awakened that there was need for him to work. If the educated men who had drunk deep of the philosophy of Bentham and Mill had no faith in his movement, he concluded, they should declare that what Gandhi said was all madness. Dr. Moonje was president of the conference at which Gandhi made this declaration.

POLITICAL UNREST IN India was on the increase. In Bihar, a mob of ten thousand tried to storm a jail and looted a police station, and mob violence by the armed Khilafatists at Malegaon in the Bombay Presidency resulted in the murder of five police officers. There was labour unrest in Assam. The Khilafat Movement was gaining momentum. Gandhi preached that Hindu-Muslim unity was essential to gaining Swaraj. The Khilafat leaders said: "Islam first and everything else afterwards." They added fuel to the fanaticism of the Muslim masses by their fanatical and fiery speeches. A conference called Majhs-ul-Ulema Conference was held on April 2, 1921, at Erode in the Madras Presidency. It was attended by the Ali Brothers, Abul Kalam Azad and Hakim Ajmal Khan. It was at this conference that Mahomed Ali made his famous speech in which he said that if the Amir of Afghanistan invaded India, it would be the duty of the Indian Muslims to assist him. And the Ali Brothers openly tried to seduce the Indian army and police from their allegiance to the British Government.

How the menace of the Afghan war developed is interesting to study. Gandhi had promised on March 10, 1920, that he would resist violence with his life even if he stood alone. According to a statement of Montagu, during the year ending April 1921, the total number of casualties included 5,169 killed, 2,474 injured, and 829 missing on the North-West Frontier of India. Gandhi wrote in *Young India* of April 13, 1921: "It is no use isolating me from the rest. The critics who continue to suspect the Ali Brothers do themselves and the cause a great injustice. The Brothers' position is perfectly clear and intelligible. To them violence is lawful under given circumstances. As Maulana Mahomed Ali often puts it, war is bad but there are worse things than war. The British Government has no two opponents more honourable than the Brothers. They mean no ill in a spirit of wantonness. They are honestly and industriously endeavouring to secure a peaceful settlement. But should their effort prove vain, either for want of response from the Government or the people, as lovers of their faith, they will not hesitate to precipitate war if they could. I refuse to be considered so simple as to be readily taken in by my companions. I believe my companions to be incapable of deceiving me. I believe them to be god-fearing, brave, and honourable men whose association I prize as a privilege."

"As for my own attitude," Gandhi proceeded, "whilst my faith would not permit me to invite or encourage a war of violence, I do contemplate with equanimity a state of war in preference to the present state of effeminate peace imposed by force of arms. And it is for that reason that I am taking part in this movement of non-violent non-co-operation even at the risk of anarchy being the ultimate result."

Gandhi *ipso facto* admitted that the faith of the Ali Brothers permitted them to invite or encourage a war of violence and he also preferred anarchy to the then effeminate peace. At the Nagpur Muslim League session held in December 1920, Gandhi had moved a resolution advising Amir Amanulla not to make a treaty with the British Government. Sir William Vincent, the then Home Member, had referred to these suggestions and the Ali Brothers' speeches about preventing friendly negotiations between the Amir of Afghanistan and the British Government.

Lajpatrai, Sastri, Malaviya and B. C. Pal were all disturbed by this menace. Some Afghan agent had met Malaviya and Shraddhanand. Sastri said that a powerful movement designed to overthrow Government though only by peaceful means, was regarded by aliens as a propitious occasion, for their aggressive schemes. Gandhi gave an interview to the *Daily Express* in April 1921 in which he referred "to preparations that were then made in Afghanistan as being really in support of the Khilafat."

At the end of April or at the beginning of May 1921, one Ahfad Hussain wrote to Gandhi: "You know that Maulana Mahomed Ali has publicly declared from a platform in the Madras Presidency that he would assist the Amir of Afghanistan if he came towards India against those who have emasculated Islam and who are in wrongful possession of the Holy place, etc." Ahfad Hussain further said that it might be high treason to show sympathy and give open assistance to the king's enemy but in those days of frank talk and candid speech one was eager to hear the decision of leaders."

Gandhi published his reply to this letter in *Young India* of May 4, 1921, under the title 'The Afghan Bogey'. "I have not read," said Gandhi which he sometimes found convenient to say on such occasions, "Maulana Mahomed Ali's speech referred to by the correspondent. But whether or not, I would, in a sense, certainly assist the Amir of Afghanistan if he waged war against the British Government, that is to say I would openly tell my countrymen that it would be a crime to help a Government which had lost the confidence of the nation to remain in office."

The Muslim leaders were thus forcing Gandhi to resort to drastic action, and the Government thought that the threat to it was more serious from the Mohammedans than from the Hindus. Lord Reading wrote to Montagu that some executive action was necessary and obtained consent from Montagu to deal with the situation. He decided on May 6 to prosecute the Ali Brothers as they had overstepped the limits of dissent. Malaviya, Sastri, Pal, Lajpatrai, and Andrews were worried by the Ali Brothers' references to Afghanistan and by a rumour current amongst Mohammedans that the Amir was ready to move against India in May or June 1921. Malaviya had impressed Reading with his character and intellect and later the Viceroy opined that Malaviya was a subtler brain than Gandhi. Malaviya thought it wise to bring about a meeting of Reading and Gandhi, The second intermediary was, it seems, Andrews. It was likely that he met Reading with the consent or knowledge of Gandhi.

The opportunity came. Gandhi went to Allahabad to attend the marriage ceremony of Motilal Nehru's daughter Swarup Rani Nehru who later became famous as Vijayalaxmi Pandit. Mahomed Ali and Swami Shraddhanand came to Allahabad by the same train. During the journey Mahomed Ali complained about political leaders taking him to task for sending a telegram to the Amir of Kabul urging him not to make peace with the British Government. He also gave Shraddhanand the draft of a telegram to read. Shraddhanand said: "What was my astonishment when I saw the draft of the self-same telegram in the peculiar handwriting of the Father of the non-violent non-co-operation movement."[9]

While Gandhi was at Allahabad, he received a letter and a telegram from Malaviya asking him to go to Simla and have a meeting with the Viceroy. Shraddhanand told Gandhi that he should not talk to the Viceroy without consulting the Working Committee, which was to meet the next day at Allahabad. But Gandhi ignored this advice. Before leaving Allahabad for Simla, he addressed, on May 10, the Allahabad District Conference, which was presided over by Mahomed Ali. There Gandhi said: "I cannot understand why the Ali Brothers are going to be arrested as the rumour goes, and why I am to remain free. They have done nothing which I would not do. If they had sent a message to the Amir I also would send one to inform the Amir, that if he came no Indian, so long as I can help it, would help the Government to drive him back. If a man is true to his religion, no Afghan or any power on earth can make him transgress his religious precepts."[10]

GANDHI'S ASSURANCE THAT the Hindus need not necessarily lose their religion on account of Afghan rule implied the possibility of the invasion. He was aware of the impending arrest of the Ali Brothers before he went to Simla. On May 6, Government had decided to arrest the Ali Brothers. From Gandhi's decision and action in this context, a characteristic hastiness was once again revealed, that he arrived at policies without taking his colleagues into confidence. Gandhi was not a student of history and he once observed that he wanted to make history and not to follow it. Otherwise he would have come across the lesson historians like Jadunath Sarkar had drawn from the Muslim domination of India. Sarkar said: "According to the Quaranic Law, there cannot be peace between a Mahommadan King and his neighbouring 'infidel' States. The latter are Dar-ul-Harb or legitimate seats of war, and it is the Muslim King's duty to slay and plunder in them, till they accept the true faith and become Dar-ul-Islam, after which they will become entitled to his protection."[11]

Andrews was in high spirits after his interview with the new Viceroy. He met Gandhi at Allahabad before the Mahatma left for Simla. Gandhi reached Simla on May 12. He was made to sign a typed application asking for an interview with Lord Reading. The Viceroy said he had taken a firm stand against sending for him. Gandhi went to the Viceregal Lodge in a white loin-cloth and a cap woven on a spinning wheel, with bare feet and legs. In Simla he used a rickshaw which he had not done in South Africa. As he was no longer physically able to travel third class, he travelled first class! The interview with the Viceroy lasted for four hours and five other meetings followed. According to the Viceroy, who was an astute diplomat, the general purpose of the interview was to induce Gandhi to abandon the dangerous non-co-operation agitation, but the immediate object was to give to the Ali Brothers through him, a last opportunity to withdraw publicly their seditious utterances and incitements.

Lord Reading said there was nothing to arrest attention in Gandhi's appearance. He said that he would have passed Gandhi in the street without a second look at him. Gandhi was direct and knew the value of words. Reading felt a ring of sincerity in all Gandhi uttered, save when discussing some political questions.[12] His religious views were genuinely held and on a remarkably high altitude. Gandhi was convinced, Reading observed, to a point bordering on fanaticism that non-violence and love would give India independence and enable it to withstand the British Government.

The Viceroy wrote to his son giving the foregoing impressions made on him by Gandhi and added: "A critical point came towards the end of the second interview when I, for the first time, adopted a firm and rather severe attitude. He seemed surprised, and I think his attitude changed from the moment." The Viceroy offered Gandhi tea, but he asked for hot water and would not think of drinking it until the Viceroy had sipped his own cup of tea.

The topics discussed during the six interviews were: the Punjab disturbances of 1919, the treaty of Sevres, the meaning of Swaraj and Gandhi's own attitude in the event of an Afghan invasion of India. The Viceroy failed to grasp the meaning of Swaraj, for Gandhi took refuge in vague generalities and kept the word undefined.[13]

The Viceroy asked Gandhi a direct question: What definite proposals did he wish to make to avert the arrest of the Ali Brothers? Gandhi replied that he had come to endeavour to avoid the disturbances which were bound to follow the arrests. The Viceroy bluntly said that all those considerations were before his Government but he demanded satisfactory assurances from the Ali Brothers that there would be no repetition of the offence, together with a public expression of regret.[14]

The Viceroy was bent on putting down Mahomed Ali in some way as he considered him the most important figure in the situation and at the moment a far more dangerous factor than Gandhi. He thought that if there was trouble between Mahomed Ali and Gandhi, it would be the collapse of the bridge over the gulf between Hindus and Mohammedans. If Mahomed Ali did what Gandhi desired him to and tendered a public apology, he would be lowered in the public esteem and his position as a leader would be seriously impaired. Gandhi had given Lord Reading a pledge of secrecy and he adhered to it.

The Viceroy approved the draft of the apology, and with a little change Mahomed Ali issued the apology to the Press on May 29. The Ali Brothers promised in their apology that as long as they were associated with the movement of non-cooperation they would not directly or indirectly advocate violence at that time or in future, nor create an atmosphere for violence. Immediately after this galling apology the Government let off the Ali Brothers!

Naturally, Gandhi was harshly criticized by his colleagues for letting down the Ali Brothers. The Viceroy's sardonic speech on this subject on May 30, at the Chelmsford Club in Simla lowered the prestige of Gandhi. The public apology made the affair humiliating and put a strain on Hindu-Muslim unity. Gandhi had fallen a victim to the seductive diplomacy of the Viceroy and to his own theories.

Montagu, the Secretary of State for India, was mightily pleased with Reading's statecraft and wrote to him: "We are all delighted with your skilful treatment of Gandhi. You gained a great victory." Both the Ali Brothers and Gandhi lost face for which Gandhi was as responsible as they were. Even Motilal Nehru wrote to him that he (Gandhi) had secured the suspension of the prosecution of the Ali Brothers by inducing them to give a public apology, and the whole principle of non-co-operation had been abandoned.

Another notable and instant effect of the Viceregal interviews on Gandhi was that he counteracted the statement he had made to the effect that he would assist Amanulla if he waged war against the British Government. This was an indirect apology by Gandhi to the Viceroy! Immediately after his second interview with the Viceroy, he published in *Young India* of May 18 a statement that Andrews had asked him whether his article on the 'Afghan bogey" was not an invitation to the Afghans to violate the Indian border. Gandhi repeatedly and apologetically explained in his article of May 18, that his previous article was written for Indians and for the Government. "I do not believe," he added, "the Afghans to be so foolish as to invade India on the strength of my article. But I see that it is capable of bearing the interpretation put upon it by Mr. Andrews. I therefore hasten to inform all whom it may concern, that not only do I not want to invite the Afghans or anybody else to come to our assistance but I am anxious for them not to come to our assistance."

During the trial of Mahomed Ali, it was revealed that he had written a letter to the Amir, and a letter by Amir's Foreign Minister instructing his envoy at Simla to incite Indian leaders and create disaffection in the minds of Indians was found among the papers of the envoy. That revealed the roots of the conspiracy. On June 1, 1921, Gandhi wrote in *Young India* that if India, as non-co-operating India, did not assist the British Government, it would make terms with the people. Quoting this opinion of Gandhi's, the *Citizen of Madras* said, "We admire Gandhi's chivalry but deplore his political degeneracy."

What Shraddhanand wrote in his *Liberator* about this Afghan affair which Gandhi's bitter critics colourfully depicted as a Gandhi-Muslim conspiracy, his Allahabad speech of May 10 and his own admission of 18 May in *Young India* fairly prove, that Gandhi was not free from blame in this intrigue. After his interview with the Viceroy, Gandhi speedily wriggled himself out of this dangerous trap and regained his balance. Referring to the project of the invasion of India by the Amir of Afghanistan, Dr. Ambedkar in his famous book *Thoughts on Pakistan* observes: "It needs no saying that the project of an invasion of India was the most dangerous project and every sane Indian would dissociate himself from so mad a project. What part Mr. Gandhi played in this project it is not possible to discover. But he did not certainly dissociate himself from it. On the contrary his misguided zeal for Swaraj and his obsession of Hindu-Muslim unity as the only means of achieving it led him to support the project." And he further stated that Gandhi not only advised the Amir not to enter into any treaty with the British Government but also did not stop to enquire what he was really doing in this mad endeavour.[15]

CHAPTER XXV

Moplah Fanatics and Tagore

As Gandhi was being criticized for his interview with the Viceroy and blamed for the galling apology, he turned the attention of the people from it to the Tilak Swaraj Fund, swadeshi and the evil of drink.

Gandhi toured Maharashtra in May and June to give a fillip to his non-co-operation movement, create faith in the minds of Maharashtrians about his programme and to collect subscriptions for the Tilak Swaraj Fund. During this period he expressed his views on zamindars and ryots, his ideas on the middle class revolution and the relations between labour and capital. In the United Provinces the peasants had overstepped the mark and taken the law into their hands. Gandhi said that though he would not hesitate to advise the kisans to suspend payment of taxes to the Government when the moment came, it was not contemplated that at any stage of non-co-operation the leaders would seek to deprive the zamindars of their rent. The kisan movement must be confined to the improvement of the status of the kisans and the betterment of the relations between the zamindars and them. The kisans must be advised scrupulously to abide by the terms of their contracts with the zamindars.[1]

Gandhi, who believed in mass action, regarded the masses as the mainstay of Swaraj. It was neither the sole concern of moneyed men nor that of the educated classes. Both must subserve their interests to the scheme of Swaraj.

The avowed policy of non-co-operation had been not to make political use of disputes between labour and capital. They had endeavoured, Gandhi added, to hold the balance evenly between the two. We would be fools, he said, if we wantonly set labour against capital.[2]

While preaching the doctrine of non-co-operation, Gandhi referred to the case of the Savarkar brothers, as it had a bearing on the issue before the country. The Savarkar brothers had been brought back to India from the Andamans in the first week of May 1921 and locked in jail. "The Savarkar Brothers' talent," Gandhi observed, "should be utilized for public welfare. As it is, India is in danger of losing her two faithful sons, unless she wakes up in time. One of the brothers (V. D. Savarkar) I know well. He is brave. He is clever. He is a patriot. He was frankly a revolutionary. The evil, in its hideous form, of the present system of Government, he saw much earlier than I did. He is in the Andamans for having loved India too well. Under a just Government he would be occupying a high post. I therefore feel for him and his brother. Had it not been for non-co-operation, Mr. Horniman would have returned and the brothers would have been discharged long ago."[3] A few days later he again referred to the case of the Savarkar brothers when he said that the non-co-operators should not defend themselves before a British court of law.

In June Gandhi was engaged in feverish activities for the Tilak Swaraj Fund in Bombay. As declared by him at Bezwada, people were to subscribe to the funds to the tune of rupees one crore. That such a gigantic sum was collected for political purposes in eight weeks at the behest of a single man was a thing unheard of in the history of the Indian National Congress. The wonder of it was that over eighty lakhs of rupees was collected in sixteen days from June 14, and on June 30, the collection amounted to rupees one crore and five lakhs. From July 10 to August 3, Gandhi addressed meetings in Bombay and in the towns in its neighbourhood on the Tilak Swaraj Fund, swadeshi and the evil of drink. The Bombay capitalists had promised Gandhi's lieutenants that they would subscribe Rs. 20 lakhs. Although the Government had styled the non-co-operation movement anarchical, the subscribers from the class of millowners and wealthy merchants were in preponderance. The middle-class also subscribed its mite to it. It was a great personal triumph for Gandhi, a unique achievement.

Gandhi created the machinery for the Congress, won the masses for it and provided it with funds to carry on its mass agitation. He now turned to swadeshi and to the anti-drink campaign. He exhorted the people to regard foreign cloth as no better than beef or liquor.[4] There was no Swaraj without swadeshi which meant a permanent boycott of foreign cloth. Gandhi issued an appeal to the mill-owners to conduct their business on national lines and not on selfish ones, and also not to raise the prices of cloth. In his anti-drink campaign, Gandhi proposed to use Dheds and Bhangis as picketers, if necessary, in the expectation that no decent Hindu would use violence against the picketers through fear of defiling themselves.[5] According to him, drink was more a *disease* than a vice.

Gandhi visited Poona on July 20, 1921, on the occasion of Tilak's death anniversary according to the new Hindu calendar. Before his visit he had said in *Young India* that it was Tilak who breathed into Indians the spirit of Swaraj. Although his method was not Tilak's, he added, he would march side by side with the foremost of the Lokamanya's disciples in the pursuit of Swaraj. In Poona he unveiled a bust of Tilak at the *Kesari* office, opened the buildings of the Tilak Mahavidyalaya and said that its system of education and its organisation was superior to its counterparts in Gujarat and Bengal. He asked the audience to take to swadeshi in right earnest and to have faith in his programme.

At a meeting in Poona, Gandhi said that Maharashtra was wise; it possessed learning and would spare no sacrifice, but it lacked faith. While thanking Gandhi, N. C. Kelkar said that to say Maharashtra lacked faith was not correct. Otherwise, men like Ranade, Gokhale and Tilak would not have been elevated to the positions they held. Maharashtra had political faith and it believed in non-co-operation but the fault lay with those who would not make it definite and practicable and included in it several unrealistic details.

Kelkar referred to this charge in the *Kesari* and asked Gandhi whether his home Province was following him closely. He asked Gandhi to state the number of lawyers and Councillors from Gujarat who had given up their practice and Council, and how many national colleges he had established in Gujarat!

While Gandhi was in Bombay engrossed in the movement for boycott of foreign cloth, Subhas Chandra Bose, who had resigned from the Indian Civil Service a month earlier, met Gandhi on his arrival in Bombay from London at Laburnum Road, Bombay, on July 16, 1921. He wanted a clear conception of Gandhi's plan of action. He heaped question upon question on Gandhi and Gandhi replied with patience. Bose felt that there was a deplorable lack of clarity in Gandhi's plan and that the Mahatma himself did not have a clear idea of the successive stages of the campaign which would bring India to her cherished goal of freedom. Bose's first interview with Gandhi ended in disagreement which recurred at intervals in the future. He left Gandhi with disappointment, met his hero C. R. Das and became his lieutenant.

GANDHI WAS RAISING the movement for the boycott of foreign cloth to a high pitch. In his view, destruction was the best method of dealing with foreign cloth. He compared foreign cloth to beef, liquor and refuse. It was impossible, he observed, to retrace steps, to reform and to purify without some destruction and some hurt being caused somewhere. As a champion of the boycott of foreign cloth, Gandhi now said that one was not responsible for the suffering one might cause to others while doing one's duty![6] He therefore made a bonfire of a large collection of expensive and fine foreign cloth on July 31, 1921, at Parel in Bombay. Savarkar had made the first huge bonfire of foreign cloth at Poona on October 7, 1905, and the bonfire had lighted up the Indian skies! Gandhi's *Indian Opinion*, however, had then made a wry face at it. But now after nearly sixteen years, Gandhi had not only come to believe in the use of the boycott and the bonfire but also paid a glowing tribute to Savarkar by saying that he was frankly a revolutionary and had been able to see much earlier the evil in its hideous form of the existing system of Government. Gandhi agreed that there was some violence in those bonfires. He said the shastras told them that some violence was unavoidable and breathing too involved violence! The object of burning the cloth, he stated, was to create a greater aversion to it.

Andrews was pained at the sight of the bonfire. He said sadly: "The picture of you lighting that great pile, including beautiful fabrics, shocked me intensely." Andrews added that the bonfire would lead to a rise in the mill-made cloth prices and it smacked of racial feeling. Gandhi replied that destruction was the quickest method of stimulating production. His emphasis was on the boycott of foreign cloth and "if the emphasis were on all foreign things, it would be racial, parochial and wicked".

The Muslim leaders, however, preferred to send their foreign clothes to Muslim countries. They pressed Gandhi to allow them to despatch the clothes made of foreign cloth to Smyrna. As it was a Muslim demand, he was willing to deviate from his rule. So Gandhi came out with a moral and practical reason in favour of their demand and yielded to it. He helplessly said that there were things which might be sinful, not always and everywhere. In countries which did not grow cotton, foreign cloth was not a sin. "It would not be proper, for me," he frankly admitted, "to enter into argument with Muslim friends on this point, so I yielded and allowed the option of sending the cloth discarded by us to Smyrna. Our primary duty, however, is to make a bonfire of such cloth."[7] He wanted the elite to take to spinning as a part of their dharma (duty) so that the common man might do likewise!

Gandhi's message of the boycott of foreign cloth caught the imagination of the people all over India and gave a rude shock to British merchants in Liverpool and Manchester. Several firms there went into liquidation. The courts there granted immediate discharge in bankruptcy cases. In one such case, counsel for the firms said: "His client had the misfortune to meet conditions in India, which no merchant could have foreseen. Just after he shipped a large quantity of goods, Mr. Gandhi started boycott of British goods, as the result of which Mouradian lost nearly £3,200."[8] The judge said these circumstances had ruined many Manchester firms during the previous three or four years.

Non-co-operators were neither to defend themselves in the court nor to give evidence. On July 29 Gandhi sent a telegram to a non-co-operator in Hyderabad (Sind) saying that "non-co-operators cannot give evidence". But, contrary to this advice, the very next day Gandhi himself appeared in the court of the Acting Second Presidency Magistrate of Bombay. He was called as a witness for the defence by the accused who was being prosecuted for cheating. The case against the accused was that he had extracted money from the complainant promising him to remove picketers from his tea-shops but had not kept his word. In his deposition Gandhi told the court that he did not remember hearing at the meeting the accused advising the boycott of the complainant's tea-shops and added that if he had heard him he would have rebuked him.[9]

Gandhi's swadeshi had awakened the people from torpor and there was a high tide of swadeshism and patriotism. Undoubtedly it gave an incentive to swadeshi enterprise. The white cap captivated young and old all over the country. It became a red rag to John Bull. The Provincial Governments put a ban on the use of the white cap. Everywhere khaddar was seen. Formerly, political workers wore khaddar only during conferences. Now their daily clothes were khaddar-made. They looked holier than other patriots! Wearing a white cap became illegal, and the possession of a spinning wheel was regarded as a crime.

These were the different facets of non-co-operation which looked for a while like an evolutionary revolution! They sharply awoke the Indian mind in villages to the basic problem of Swaraj.

While Gandhi was collecting money for the Tilak Swaraj Fund in Bombay, Mohammad Ali addressed a Khilafat Conference at Karachi on July 8. Gandhi, who did not attend the Khilafat Conferences which met at Broach and at Belgaum in June, did not attend also the one at Karachi. It seems he was cautiously keeping aloof from the fanatical speeches of the Khilafatists. Mahomed Ali told the Karachi Conference that his apology was meant for Pandit Madan Mohan Malaviya who entertained fears of an Afghan invasion. The cordial relations of unity between Mahatma Gandhi and themselves were like a magic drug which cured all diseases. The assurance that he had given was meant for all those who feared violence.

The Khilafat Conference congratulated Gazi Mustafa Kemal Pasha of Turkey on the courage and suffering the Turks had endured to save Islam. It declared it unlawful for any of the faithful to serve from that very day in the Indian Army or help or acquiesce in recruitment to it. It added that if the British fought the Angora Government, the Muslims of India would start civil disobedience and declare complete independence at the next session of the Indian National Congress to be held at Ahmedabad and hoist the flag of the Indian Republic.

Achieving success in collecting the Tilak Swaraj Fund, Gandhi visited with Mohammed Ali prominent cities and towns in U.P. and Bihar. He visited Calcutta and went to Assam. His energy was phenomenal and his frail body was indefatigable. Starting his untiring tours he inculcated his doctrines in the minds of the people and the masses responded to them as never before.

WHILE GANDHI WAS touring Dibrugarh, Sylhet, Silchar and Chillagon of Assam, the Moplahs rose in revolt in Malabar, a district on the coast of the then Madras Presidency. Ernad and Wallavanad, two Talukas of this District, were the seats of Moplah disturbances and a hot-bed of Muslim fanaticism. Out of a population of a little over three million in the district, nearly a million were Mohammedans sprung from Arab traders and sailors and native women. As a rule they were frugal and industrious, but hot-headed and primitive. They worked on the estates of the Nambudri Brahmins or on leaseholds. The rent was often raised at each renewal of their contracts. The uncertainty of tenure of their holdings made for agrarian discontent. Since British rule was established, Malabar had witnessed thirty-five serious Moplah outbreaks, but their causes were rooted in religious fanaticism. As a result, two special Acts were in force designed to provide for the disarming of and the levying of fines on Moplah villages when outrages occurred.

The Khilafat movement and the non-co-operation movement had sharpened the fanaticism of the Moplahs. They preached that the satanic British Government was the enemy of Islam and that it had to be paralysed. The non-violent character of the non-co-operation movement had no effect on the religious teachers of the Moplahs. They believed that the British Government was nearing its end, and the day would dawn when they would have neither to pay taxes to the Government nor rent to the landowners. The failure of the monsoon had that year added to their economic distress which was capped by the religious fanaticism generated by the cry of the Khilafat, and the explosion came on August 20, 1921: The demobilised Moplahs added to its ferocity and brutality.

The rebellion was directed against the Hindus, and a bloodthirsty and blood-curdling campaign of terror, murder, arson, rapine, loot and incendiarism resulted. Under this Khilafat Raj, the violation of Hindu women, forced conversion, desecration of temples, destruction of railways, courts and communications stalked the land.[10] For cruelty, ferocity and recklessness it had no parallel in this century. Hindus were given the option of "Islam or death".

There were pitched battles between the armed Moplahs led by the dreadful Ali Musaliar and other leaders and the British regiment in August, September, November and December 1921. Martial law, which was declared on August 24, 1921, was withdrawn on February 24, 1922, when the police and civil authorities finally resumed charge. Reflecting on the massacres and conversions, Gandhi later said: "Forcible conversions are horrible things. But Moplah bravery must commend admiration." Was it bravery or barbarity? Fanaticism is religion caricatured and not bravery. Yet in the name of humanity Gandhi dissuaded the Hindus from retaliation. He humanly said it was bad enough for one to commit rape or murder, but it was equally bad if not worse to flog the rake or murderer and to rape his women or murder the rest of his family. Gandhi later supported enthusiastically the fund started to help the flood-stricken Moplahs.

The approximate number of casualties suffered by the Moplah rebels during the rebellion were 2300 killed and 1,650 wounded. The casualties to the troops numbered 137, but great numbers of the innocent Hindu population were massacred. The Madras Government reported to the Government of India that the number of forcible conversions probably ran into thousands.[11] On November 19, 1921, one hundred prisoners from these murderous gangs were being sent to Coimbatore by a goods train. Seventy of these died of asphyxiation at Podunur. This train tragedy, too, horrified the land.

Gandhi, who had been placating the Muslims, was held responsible for the massacres of the Hindus in Malabar. The Liberals said that the misguided Moplahs rendered a distinct disservice to the sacred cause of Islam and Swaraj. Gandhi stated: "The Moplahs are among the bravest in the land. They are god-fearing. Their bravery must be transformed into purest gold."[12] He represented the perpetrators of vile deeds as godfearing people! Was it not a travesty of religion to describe men who murder and rape in the name of religion as godfearing? True religion makes one meek, merciful, just, pious and devout. The Moplahs killed in the name of religion and the Hindus died for their religion.

Many mercilessly criticized Gandhi for his lenient and exonerating attitude to the Moplah atrocities. The editor of *Modern Review* described Hindu-Muslim unity as a camouflage. Later, Gandhi said that the Moplah revolt was a test for Hindus and Mussalmans. A verbal disapproval by the Mussalmans of Moplah madness was no test of Mussalman friendship. The Mussalmans must naturally feel the shame and humiliation of the Moplah conduct in forcible conversions and looting. Gandhi described the Moplah ferocity as the ignorant fanaticism of the Moplah brother, and the Hindu mentality as cowardice.

Gandhi had dubbed the Frontier Hindus cowards and now he described the Malabar Hindus as cowards. In his boyhood he was infatuated by the strength of Sheikh Mehtab. In his youth, he had said in his article in *The Vegetarian* that Hindus vere proverbially a weak race. So his theory of Hindu cowardice developed. Hindus, under the spell of the opiate of his non-violence, were becoming proverbially so. It was the reflection of Gandhi's own mind, the mind that had been unconsciously struggling against the cowardice in himself since his boyhood.

Maulana Hazrat Mohani declared publicly that the Moplahs had fought for their religion and so said almost all of the Muslim leaders. Gandhi, who off and on pledged himself to resist such violence with his life, did not feel much for the rapes and murders and forcible conversions. He had declared that he would sacrifice a million men for his principles! Three months earlier he had said: "I think that only god-fearing people can become true non-co-operators." And now he hailed the murderous Moplahs as god-fearing men!

SEVERAL SWADESHI STORES were opened with the Tilak Swaraj Fund to promote swadeshi, hand-spun khadi, but cloth which was neither hand-spun nor hand-woven was sold in the name of pure khadi. Mill-cloth or Japanese cloth was sold in the name of khaddar. In August 1921 Gandhi said that it was a pity that such stuff was being sold in swadeshi stores and added that the people must be prepared for such frauds.

At this time another shock came to Gandhi. He made a confession, similar to the one which he had called a Himalayan miscalculation. He said it was a mistake that he did not make hand-spinning an integral part of education in all national institutions. Boys did not take to hand-spinning, and so the spinning wheel remained more or less an excrescence or an idle pastime in most non-co-operation schools. A soldier was considered a sinner and a spinner was hailed as a holier man and a liberator of his country. Gandhi wrote that he read the message of the spinning wheel in the Gita and that the "best national education for India was undoubtedly an intelligent handling of the spinning wheel. Yet, to his dismay, the music of the spindle and the charkha had begun to fade.

The most painful shock to Gandhi came from Tagore who had returned from a world tour on July 16, 1921. Tagore was perturbed by some of the items in the scheme of non-co-operation, although he was not hostile to the main idea. He differed from Gandhi in his views on modern science and medicine, and Gandhi did aim at breaking with Western science, culture and civilization.

On August 15 Tagore gave expression to his views at the University Institute, Calcutta. During his speech he observed: "It was due to no external cause that the West now occupied a principal place in the modern world. She had achieved that eminence because she had realized some great truth in her mind and carried it out in action." As regards the non-co-operation programme, Tagore said: "I have no little respect for Mahatma Gandhi. He has preached a doctrine of love and truth. But he talks of Swaraj in a year, I fail to fall in with him. I cannot believe that it is a commodity on sale and that it can be had on such easy terms. A nation must deserve freedom before she can desire to have it, and to be free a nation requires not a few preliminary preparations. We must free our country not only from aliens but from quagmire of indolence and ignorance in which she is now submerged. When my nation has turned a deaf ear to the dictates of reason and good advice and believes in the chimera of Swaraj in a year, I cannot help entertaining some fears for her. The days of oracles are past and yet my nation believes in the existence of Alladin's lamp!"

"In preaching the doctrine of burning clothes," he proceeded, "the Mahatma has set to naught all economic principles and taken recourse to pseudo-religious doctrines. But" he concluded, "I must be convinced of the truth of Swaraj coming in a year. I believe in no oracles from men."[13]

It was a bitter antidote to Gandhi's criticism of Western civilization and an attack on his non-co-operation movement. Sarat Chandra Chhattopadhyaya, Bengal's great novelist, who was a strong supporter of Gandhi's non-co-operation movement, furiously replied to Tagore. The poet published his article, entitled "The Call of Truth" in the *Modern Review* of October 1921, clarifying his position and his thoughts. Gandhi, who was that day at Patna, came to Calcutta on August 17 and left for Assam.

Gandhi was enchanted by the Assamese landscape and said Assam was a region of magnificent vegetation and gorgeous scenery. The Assamese women were accomplished weavers. Some Government officials disclosed to the Assamese people that Gandhi in his booklet *Hind Swaraj* had bracketed the Assamese with the Pindharis and other tribes. Gandhi had to make amends to them. He addressed meetings of the tea plantation labourers who were on strike. To secure justice for them the Assam-Bengal railway workers were on sympathetic strike.

It seems Mahadev Desai, who was then working with Nehru on the *Independence* at Allahabad, wrote to Gandhi saying that Tagore was envious of Gandhi. On September 1, 1921, Gandhi replied that he could not imagine that either Malaviya or Tagore could be envious of him. Both of them "lacked fearlessness" but they were confused by the novelty and simplicity of his ideas. Tagore and Malaviya he concluded, could not overlook the shortcomings of the non-co-operators as he himself did. On his return to Calcutta, Gandhi met Tagore on September 6, 1921. Andrews, who had arranged for a possible reconciliation, was present at this meeting. It was a secret interview. The differences were not resolved. Each adhered to his views.

In reply to Tagore's "Call of Truth", Gandhi wrote an article in *Young India* of October 13, entitled "The Great Sentinel" in which he tried to passify Tagore and disarm his suspicion, but not without a sting in the tail. He replied to Tagore that it was impossible to soothe suffering patients with a song from Kabir. The hungry millions asked for one poem—invigorating food! In that upsurge of the non-co-operation movement everything coming in its way was pushed aside. C. R. Das too had attacked Tagore for his criticism of the non-co-operation movement and said it did not befit Tagore to criticize the movement, keeping himself away from the heat of the movement.

The indignant Mahatma, giving a desperate reply to his critics and especially to Tagore's 'Chimera of Swaraj in one year', declared in *Navajivan* of October 23, 1921, that he believed that he would definitely get Swaraj before the end of December 1921 and then would retire to a solitary place or would welcome an opportunity to help the country to draft the constitution of Swaraj. "I should not like," Gandhi concluded, "to remain alive next year if we have not won Swaraj by then. I am, in that event, likely to be pained so deeply that the body may perish—I would desire that it should."

Gandhi tried for some years to passify Tagore and win the confidence of Tagore's elder brother, Barodada. Tagore was silent and kept aloof although he did not like the intolerance and violence of the Gandhian zealots who burnt foreign cloth in front of his residence just to annoy him. His warning had a chastening influence upon Gandhism which ignored the influence of science, the challenge of the age.

Gandhi and Tagore differed fundamentally in their outlook although both were champions of freedom. But Tagore was in favour of science which was utilized to remove material suffering and poverty and he also stood for the victories of the human mind and soul over the earthly environment. To Gandhi, Western civilization was anathema. Tagore was a deadly enemy of outworn traditions and conceited prejudices. He regarded the organization of caste as inconsistent with the truth of the spirit, while Gandhi defended caste and the Vanashram Dharma. Tagore spoke of the joy of life, the freedom of the spirit and the delight of existence. Gandhi took a grim and austere attitude: that life was suffering and restraint. Tagore was a sterling patriot and resigned his knighthood immediately after the horrible massacres at Amritsar. Gandhi, who was then a loyalist, returned his medals much later, on August 1, 1920.

Many devotees credited Gandhi with supernatural powers and even called him a messenger of God. Some likened him to Lord Krishna, but Gandhi meekly said he did not have supernatural powers; he was seeking only God's truth and had lost all fear of man. He realised God's omnipresence, but said that it was a blasphemy to represent him as Shrikrishna. He had no desire to found a sect. He represented no new truth and he repudiated all claims to divinity.

After touring Assam, Gandhi returned to Calcutta and held talks behind closed doors with many revolutionaries. C. R. Das and Subhas Bose were present at these meetings.

Gandhi and Mahomed Ali started to tour Madras and especially to restore peace in Malabar district where the Moplah rebellion had played havoc. A week before the commencement of the tour, Gandhi wrote in *Young India* expressing the hope that the rumour about the impending prosecution of the Ali brothers was untrue. He wanted the Government to note that the incarceration of the Ali Brothers would make the task of the preservation of peace more difficult than it had always been. Gandhi and Mahomed Ali visited Midnapur and Kharagpore. At Kharagpore, a messenger from Shaukat Ali gave a letter to Gandhi in which Shaukat Ali had said that he had information of the impending arrest of himself as well as of his brother. Yet Mahomed Ali and Gandhi started for Malabar.

ON SEPTEMBER 14, 1921, Mahomed Ali was arrested under the orders of the District Magistrate of Vizagapattam at Waltair before Gandhi's eyes. Mahomed Ali was quite calm. So was his brave wife, the Begum Sahiba. She accompanied Gandhi. Gandhi addressed a meeting soon after the arrest. Gandhi said in his message to the Bombay citizens that there was no cause for sorrow. He regarded the arrest as a prelude to Swaraj and later added that it was a victory; it had come to them as godsend. Happily, Gandhi continued, he saw signs about himself every day that God was with them. In his message to the ex-Aligarh college students, Gandhi said: "Never mind, we will soon get him back free." Gandhi was warned by the Government of Madras not to proceed to Malabar. On September 16, 1921, Shaukat Ali was arrested at Bombay and Pir Gulam Masjid, Maulana Hassan Ahmed, Maulavi Nissar Ahmed,

Dr. Kitchlew and Shri Venkatraman Shankaracharya were also arrested and taken to Karachi.

Gandhi silently gave up his visit to Malabar and toured the Madras Province making speeches on Hindu-Muslim unity, swadeshi and the removal of untouchability. He found that swadeshi had made the least headway in Madras and the Madras Province was the worst regarding untouchability. However, in order to pacify Hindus, he made a reference, during the tour to the madness of the Moplahs.

At Trichinopoly Gandhi said on September 19, that under the existing conditions it was a sin for any Indian to serve either in the Army or in any of the civil departments of the Government, and added that if it was an offence to say it, he had been guilty of that offence times without number. Mahomed Ali was released on September 17 but was re-arrested and taken to Karachi for trial:

While Gandhi was at Madura, the holy city in southern India, he was much depressed. The country had not responded to his khaddar programme adequately. He wrote to Mahadev Desai that Bengal had indeed depressed him. But Madras did so even more. He felt weak and exhausted. He said his legs required oiling and massaging. Prabhudas and Krishnadas did that for him. In a mood of utter frustration, Gandhi decided to inflict a penalty on himself by way of expiation. On September 21, at 10 p.m., a barber was called to shave his head. He came and reverently shaved the massive head of Gandhi with all possible care. A wave of fear passed through the hearts of his associates and followers. There was a shadow of anxiety on every face. With heavy hearts they sat around Gandhi during the night, attempting by a word or two to divert him from the thoughts of becoming a *sanyasin* (ascetic).

Early next morning, before Gandhi started his journey in a motor-car, he discarded his cap and vest. He took a little khaddar bag to carry the things he used to put in the pocket of his vest. Then he donned a loin-cloth and put on a *chaddar*. Dr. Rajan and Rajagopalachari tried to dissuade him from giving up his usual clothes and the cap. But he persuaded them to withdraw the request. He told them that he was not going to turn a *sanyasin*, and besides the new style of dress he had adopted was not strange to the people who went about with bare bodies. He said his heart was bleeding, and the new style of dress was but an expression of the intense pain he was feeling.

Gandhi said his new dress would shock the Gujaratis. His

idea was to give up the cap and the vest upto the 31st October 1921, but he changed his mind and said that he would do so until Indians rich and poor alike would be able to get an adequate supply of clothes. Later Gandhi declared that previously on two occasions the thought of dispensing with the cap and shirt had seized him, first in Khulna and the second time soon after the arrest of Mahomed Ali, but he restrained himself fearing that he might create a scene. During this Madras tour he started using a fountain pen. It was Satish Babu who first presented him with one.

Gandhi started *Hindi Navajivan* on August 19, 1921, to propagate non-co-operation. That no language, he observed, except Hindustani could be the national language was beyond doubt. He wrote an article in *Young India* of September 29 under the title "Tampering with Loyalty" and encouraged the people to tamper with loyalty. "We must reiterate from a thousand platforms!" he said, "the formula of the Ali Brothers regarding the sepoys and we must spread disaffection openly and systematically till it pleases the Government to arrest us." The Government of India drew the attention of the Bombay Government to this article and the wheels for the prosecution of Gandhi began to move.

Gandhi returned to Bombay and met a number of prominent Indian leaders in Bombay on October 4. He and forty-seven others issued the next day a manifesto on the Ali brothers' arrest and reiterated the substance of the Karachi resolution for which the Ali brothers were arrested. The manifesto advised every Indian soldier and civilian to sever his connection with the Government. The next day the A.I.C.C. met and urged Indians to withdraw from Government services and to boycott foreign cloth, but it postponed the civil disobedience movement. The Karachi resolutions of the Khilafat Committee were repeated and reaffirmed at important places all over India.

The Government had proscribed the religious *fatwas* issued by the Ulemas of India and Gandhi proposed publication of the *fatwas*. In *Young India* Gandhi declared that in India everything was armed, peace, loyalty and opinion! Only the people were disarmed! In April 1921 the Khilafat Committee requested the A.I.C.C. to formulate a clear and definite foreign policy for India. Accordingly, on October 5, 1921, the A.I.C.C. declared that India as a self-governing country had nothing to fear from the neighbouring states and that her foreign policy would naturally be always guided so as to respect the religious obligations imposed upon Mussalmans by Islam!

The Trial Of the Ali Brothers and five others opened on September 26, 1921. They were charged with spreading disaffection in the Indian Army. The sessions trial began on October 24 and continued over the next six days. On November 1 they were sentenced to two years' rigorous imprisonment on each of the charges, the sentences to run concurrently in all cases. One of the accused, Bharaty Krishna Tirthaji, was acquitted. As soon as the judgment was pronounced, Mahomed Ali stood up, raised his voice above the din and shouted that they would be free men under Swaraj before the expiry of the sentence. The Malegaon rioters' trial, too, ended on November 2. Five were sentenced to death, sixty-one variously sentenced and forty-seven were acquitted.

Gandhi was depressed. The Government was becoming drastic. The pressure of the movement was growing. Friends like Andrews were expressing discordant ideas over the bonfires. Gandhi said he would not survive December 1921, but as the dead-line was drawing near he declared in October 1921 in an article under the title "Optimism": "The optimist lives in fear of God and believes that God ordained everything for the best. He would not kill or harass anybody. The pessimist had no such thing as the inner voice, he flitted from pleasure to pleasure and finally died unloved, unwept and unsung."

About this time somebody asked Gandhi whether he was really a Mahatma. Gandhi replied that he did not feel like being one and observed that he could not give any definition of the word Mahatma as he was not acquainted with one. As regards the soldiers, Gandhi said that their services were utilized more often for enslaving Indians than for protecting them; but under Swaraj the soldiers would not be hirelings. They would form the national militia for defence and protective purposes alone.[14] They would have a voice in the moulding of the affairs of the nation. And they would certainly never be sent to cut down inoffensive Turks or Arabs in the West or equally inoffensive Chinese or Burmese in the East.

The Prince of Wales was due to arrive in Bombay on November 17, 1921. Gandhi said that the people must organize a complete boycott of all functions held in the Prince's honour and Bombay should wear the appearance of a deserted city on the day of his landing.

Gandhi went to Delhi and moved on November 4, at the A.I.C.C. the civil disobedience resolution which was passed in a slightly amended form after a lengthy discussion. The signal was given! The bugle was blown. The Government was challenged. The next day the A.I.C.C. reaffirmed the Karachi resolution. At the meeting of the Working Committee, Gandhi had suggested that one who proposed to undertake civil disobedience must know hand-spinning. This made Motilal Nehru burst into laughter. N. C. Kelkar and V. J. Patel burst out in loud angry protests!

Gandhi appeared to be making the country fearless and carrying on the struggle to a crescendo. Appeal to the soldiers in the Indian Army to sever their connection with it was no doubt a historic action, which, according to British rule, amounted to high treason. Gandhi was challenging the mighty empire to do its worst. The Congress leaders were pressing Gandhi to launch the struggle.

The forthcoming visit of the Prince of Wales proved to be a storm signal. The Government of India utilized the services of the Maharajah of Baroda in urging Gandhi not to involve the Prince of wales in political agitation. The disturbed political conditions were unfavourable to the visit of the Prince of Wales and Montagu was hesitating to send him to India. But Lord Reading pressed the British Government to send the Prince and remove the wrong impression that India was unsafe for his visit.

The Prince of Wales arrived in Bombay amidst angry demonstrations on November 17 when riots broke out in Bombay and Gandhi found the crowds out of control. Lord Reading, who was responsible for the visit of the Prince, broke down in the Bombay Governor's House, holding his proud head in both hands. The violent mob burnt tram-cars and liquor shops yelling Mahatma Gandhi ki jai. Hindus and Muslims fought with Christians, Jews and Parsis, assaulting even Parsi women because they joined in the welcome to the Prince.

During the riots 53 people were killed and 400 were wounded.

Gandhi described the riots as "a deep stain". He wept bitterly and said that he was bankrupt. He desperately issued to the rioters an appeal to restore peace in Bombay, helplessly resorted to a fast and then pathetically broke the fast at a gathering of Hindus, Muslims, Christians and Parsis.

Gandhi sadly declared that he proposed thenceforth to observe every Monday a twenty-four hours' fast till Swaraj was attained. He lamented that the hope of reviving civil disobedience was dashed to pieces. His resolve to start it began to waver. The riots were a red signal to him!

CHAPTER XXVI

Bardoli Misfires

The Negotiations Between the Afghan and the British Government had been going on for several months. At last Sir Henry Debbs, the envoy of the British Government, succeeded, after much effort, in winning over the Amir of Afghanistan to the side of the British. The Amir signed a Treaty of Peace with the British Government on November 1, 1921, and the King ratified the Anglo-Afghan Treaty on December 1, 1921.

Since peace had been secured on the North-West Frontier, the Viceroy felt relieved from his most pressing cause of anxiety and he could now wholly devote his attention to the Indian problem. The Khilafat agitation and the non-co-operation movement were isolated from the dangerous Afghan situation. So, in the first week of December 1921, the Viceroy girded his loins and launched an offensive against the non-co-operation movement. The Punjab and U.P. Governments also attacked the non-co-operators. In the first week of December 1921, Lajpatrai, Motilal Nehru and Jawaharlal Nehru were put in jail, and C. R. Das, who was President-elect of the Congress, was arrested on December 10, 1921. His wife and son had been arrested earlier. The battle was joined. Soon after, Rajagopalachari was arrested.

The Gujarat Provincial Congress Committee had chosen Bardoli and Anand Talukas for launching civil disobedience, but on touring the talukas, Gandhi found them unfit for the proposed action and he suspended the struggle. Although the A.I.C.C. had alerted the Provincial Congress Committee to be ready for civil disobedience to the point of refusal of taxes,

Gandhi wanted to start it in a district of his choice and, if successful, to extend it to other districts.

At this juncture, the Viceroy, Lord Reading, who had been depressed at the failure of the Prince's visit to Bombay wanted the Prince not to return home disappointed. The Viceroy hoped that the Prince's visit to Calcutta at least should be a happy one. He therefore welcomed a suggestion for a *rapprochement* with Gandhi and, with that end in view, Hridaynath Kunzru and Jamnadas Dwarkadas were sent to the Sabarmati Ashram to meet Gandhi on December 17. Lord Reading did this in consultation with Sir Tej Bahadur Sapru who was Law Member, Malaviya and Besant. Kunzru and Jamnadas Dwarkadas met Gandhi on December 18 and gave him the message. The offer contained the proposal that Lord Reading would hold a Round Table Conference of representatives of different shades of political opinion with the object of finding some way out of the existing deadlock if Gandhi called off the boycott of the Prince's visit to Calcutta and agreed to the discontinuation of the unlawful activities of the non-co-operators.

Lord Ronaldshay (afterwards Lord Zetland), Governor of Bengal, allowed C. R. Das and Abul Kalam Azad, who were in Alipore Jail, to write to Gandhi. Das agreed and urged Gandhi to accept the offer as he wanted to take tactical advantage of it. Gandhi accepted the offer and Kunzru and Jamnadas left Ahmedabad. Gandhi had given them an assurance that he would make no conditions precedent to joining the proposed Round Table Conference. But soon Gandhi had talks with some Maulavis as well as with Sardar Patel, and he changed his mind. In his telegram of December 19 to Malaviya and Das, Gandhi demanded first the release of the Ali Brothers and the *fatwa* prisoners and the withdrawal of all restrictive orders.

Subhas Chandra Bose, who was in jail with Das, wrote afterwards that C. R. Das was angry and disgusted at this. The chance of a lifetime, he said, had been lost. Besant said, "Gandhi has bungled and lost a great opportunity." Moderate opinion in India spoke of the "failure of Gandhi". The Maharashtrian Tilakite leaders had called early in December 1921, at their Akola Conference, for a revision of the non-cooperation policy and had resolved to remain fighting in the ring to the end. It was not true that the British were impatient to bestow more reforms on India. They wanted to tide over the difficult situation. Some benefits might have accrued, but Gandhi, being by nature more a mass moral leader than statesman, could not properly handle the situation. Das may have fared better, but he was in jail.

As the move for the negotiations had failed, Government resorted to drastic repression. Volunteer organizations were declared illegal, meetings and processions were forcibly dispersed and the press was muzzled. Wholesale arrests of leaders and volunteers, search of offices and prosecutions were the order of the day. Gandhi asked his followers to widen the gates of prisons and to enter them as the bridegroom enters a bride's chamber. They should use the sword of self-sacrifice. No big or swift movement could be carried on, he said, without bold risks and life would not be worth living if it was not attended with risks. No suffering was too great a price for freedom.

During the last week of December 1921, the Indian National Congress met at Ahmedabad to take the vital decision on the civil disobedience movement. The pandal was a magnificent structure with khaddar (hand-spun and hand-woven cloth) all over, khaddar to the right, khaddar to the left, khaddar overhead and khaddar below. There were no chairs or tables for the delegates. For the first time all had to squat on the floor. At Calcutta Gandhi had captured the Congress, at Nagpur transformed it into a mass organization and at Ahmedabad he completely Gandhi-ised it. The pandal called the Khadi Nagar stood on the bank of the Sabarmati, just at one end of Ellis Bridge. The whole ground was brightly lit up for eight nights. Adjoining it were the Muslim Nagar and the Khilafat Pandal. Except Mohamed Ali Jinnah, all the delegates, workers and leaders were in khadi. The chairman of the Reception Committee, Vallabhbhai Patel, took no more than twenty minutes to read his welcome address in Hindi.

Gandhi, to the embarrassment of the leaders, entered the pandal with only a loin-cloth. The rank and file in the Congress said he was a real Mahatma. He was indifferent to both fear and decorum.

THE PRESIDENT-ELECT OF the Congress, C. R. Das, was in jail. Although Hakim Ajmal Khan was elected to occupy the Presidential chair, the actual business was transacted by Gandhi! Das's speech was read by Sarojini Naidu. In his address, Das had said that untouchability was a national sin. His message was that the students were the hope and glory of the motherland. Gandhi nominated members for the Working Committee. The most important resolution was the one that bestowed dictatorship of the Congress on Gandhi till further instructions. Gandhi became a non-violent dictator ten months before Mussolini, the violent dictator, assumed power in Italy on October 28, 1922. Gandhi was given power to appoint his successor in emergency. As regards the proposal for a Round Table Conference, Gandhi said that though the Congress had passed the resolution on civil disobedience, the door was always open for such a conference.

Jinnah, Malaviya and others tried to persuade Gandhi to accept the proposal for a Round Table Conference but failed. Gandhi told a press reporter that he saw no change of heart in the British Government. It was here that he first used the words 'change of heart'. The most notable defeat was of Hazarat Mohani's resolution for a change of the Congress creed in favour of complete independence. The Muslim leader said he was shocked that even after the lapse of the year, Swaraj, which had been promised by Gandhi, had not materialized. He also said that men like Jawaharlal Nehru were supporters of his views on declaring independence.

Gandhi, opposing the resolution, replied that the failure of the promised Swaraj was due to non-fulfilment of the conditions laid down by him. "Let us not," he added, "get into waters whose depth we do not know." The proposal, if passed, would take them to unfathomable depths. Creeds were not simple things which they could change as they did their clothes.

Hazarat Mohani's resolution about independence was defeated also in the Muslim League session which was held during the same week at Ahmedabad near the Congress session. The Khilafat Conference expressed sympathy with the Moplahs in their sufferings and congratulated them on their sacrifices in the cause of religion. It condemned those Moplahs who were responsible for forcible conversion of Hindus. The Muslim League condemned the reported actions of Moplahs who had ill-treated their Hindu brethren.

It was not only the Muslims in the Khilafat Conference and the Muslim League who ignored the criminality of the barbaric Moplah action in Malabar, but the Congress under the truth-seeker Gandhi did so by declaring that there were only three cases of forcible conversions! It showed to what level the Gandhi-dominated Congress had fallen in placating the Muslims. Shraddhanand observes in his *Liberator* of August 26, 1926, that "the original resolution condemned the Moplahs wholesale for the killing of Hindus and burning of Hindu homes and the forcible conversions to Islam." But in passing such a resolution the Gandhian Hindu leaders trained in the art of surrendering and placating the Muslims had done their job to the satisfaction of their master. The Moplah leaders Maulana Fakir and Hazarat Mohani gave the go-by to the truth about the Moplah atrocities. Whenever the Muslim question arose, Gandhi was over-generous but not just.

There was an inter-caste dinner held at the time of the Ahmedabad Congress. When the orthodox from different parts of the country protested against it, Gandhi, the defender of caste, declared that he had not been consulted nor had he attended the dinner. Gandhi added that his information was that only food fried in ghee was served, which, according to Gujarati custom, was not objectionable! There was a lighter side to this atmosphere. When the leaders began to consider the next avenue for the Congress, Aney asked Gandhi: "Mahatmaji, you say in one breath Swaraj in one year, and in another you fix a date for the next year's Congress!" In this atmosphere, Mohamed Ali Jinnah asked someone what place he had in such a Congress. The most amusing thing was that on December 31, 1921, Gandhi presided over the first National Musical Conference which was convened by Vishnu Digambar Paluskar, a leading exponent of Indian classical music. The object of the conference was to popularise music in national associations.

Some more light must be shed on Gandhi's opposition to the resolution on independence. He had been shelving the fact of defining the meaning of independence for the previous twelve months. The Viceroy tried to find the meaning Gandhi attached to the word Swaraj, but he failed. The Khilafatist Muslim leaders preferred to keep the word Swaraj undefined as they were awaiting the overrunning of India by Afghan forces. At the Nagpur Congress, Gandhi and Mahomed Ali had opposed B. C. Pal's amendment to Gandhi's draft, adding the adjective 'democratic' to the word Swaraj. Pal wrote later in Mahomed Ali's *Comrade*: "I learned that Swaraj was left without any definition because the moment we tried to do so, the unity in the Congress would break up." Now that the treaty was signed between Afghanistan and India, the Muslim leaders became desperate and so Hazarat Mohani struggled hard to force the Congress to declare independence.

Explaining this point, Gandhi said in *Young India* of January 5, 1922: "But assuming that Great Britain alters her attitude as I know she will when India is strong, it will be religiously unlawful for us to insist on independence. For it will be vindictive and petulent. It would, be a denial of God."

This suggests why Gandhi was not willing to define the word Swaraj.

In a serious and pensive moment Gandhi grew prophetic and further said: "Let us see clearly what Swaraj together with the British connection means. It means undoubtedly India's ability to declare her independence if she wishes. Swaraj, therefore, will not be a free gift of the British Parliament. It will be a declaration of India's full self-expression. That it will be expressed through an Act of Parliament is true. But it will be merely a courteous ratification of the declared wish of the people of India even as it was in the case of the Union of South Africa. Not an unnecessary adverb in the Union Scheme could be altered by the House of Commons. The ratification in our case will be of a treaty to which Britain will be a party. Such Swaraj may not come this year, may not come within one generation. But I have contemplated nothing less."

In the same article, Gandhi said: "Swaraj can never be a free gift by one nation to another. It is a treasure to be purchased with a nation's best blood."

Pandit Jawaharlal, who was in Lucknow Jail, expressed his entire dissent from Maulana Hazarat Mohani's resolution. He said he was surprised to learn that his name had been mentioned in Ahmedabad amongst those who were in favour of the Maulana's resolution. If he had the good fortune, he added, to attend the Congress, he would certainly have opposed the Maulana, and he was sorry that some U.P. delegates had supported the resolution moved by Maulana Hazarat Mohani![1] It took Jawaharlal Nehru six more years to commit himself to independence in company with Subhas Bose but independently of Gandhi.

Although Gandhi had said in his article "A Puzzle and its Solution" in *Young India* of December 15, 1921, that he wanted to overthrow the Government, it was evident that during those days Gandhi was not in favour of complete independence. He was unwilling to break with the British Empire. He blamed Andrews very severely for publicly putting forward a demand for complete independence for India which Andrews had made at a meeting in Calcutta. He told Andrews that he had done a great deal of mischief by such advocacy of independence.[2]

Two months later, M. Paul Richard, a French author, declared in an interview in the *Lokamanya*, that Gandhi had said to him: "I do not work for freedom of India. I work for non-violence in the world. . . . Mr. Tilak was telling me 'I would sacrifice even truth for freedom of my country' but I am ready to sacrifice even freedom for the sake of truth."[3] Gandhi explained sorrowfully that it was sacred conversation and although he did not deny the substance of it, it was on the whole a caricature of his views on non-violence. His salvation and the salvation of India went together. These were the mystic twists and tentacles of his philosophy, often slippery but never far away from the truth. Gandhi also denied having said that Santiniketan stood for material progress and his Satyagraha Ashram for spiritual progress. Gandhi feared that the Tilakites, whom he had been trying to win over to his side, would be offended by Paul Richard's interview.

GANDHI ATTENDED THE All-Parties Conference on January 15, 1922, convened by Pandit Madan Mohan Malaviya, Jinnah, Jayakar and others in Bombay to consider the possibility of a Round Table Conference with the Government. Its President, Sankaran Nair, on obstruction from Gandhi, walked out. A compromise resolution was passed. Gandhi agreed to postpone civil disobedience till January 31, 1922, and the Congress Working Committee approved of this. The Liberals heaved a sigh of relief. Jinnah and Jayakar wrote to the Viceroy, but the Viceroy saw no basis for a profitable discussion in a Round Table Conference.

Gandhi was sounding Bardoli Taluka to see whether it was ready for civil disobedience. On January 29, 1922, the leaders had a conference at Bardoli. The Working Committee of the Congress met at Surat on January 31, 1922. As it found the people ready, the Working Committee congratulated the people of Bardoli on their determination to start mass civil disobedience. On the same day Gandhi declared at a mass meeting in Surat that he did not wish to go to jail, but would prefer to be shot. He would like, he added, to see two or three Jallianwala Baghs in Gujarat.[4] This was a wilful provocation on his part. On February 1, 1922, Gandhi gave an ultimatum to the Viceroy that mass civil disobedience would be started in Bardoli Taluka if within seven days of the publication of his manifesto he did not agree to his demands. In his slippery way Gandhi shifted the emphasis. He wanted the Viceroy to set free the non-co-operating prisoners, to free the press from all administrative control and to end Government repression.

Gandhi's manifesto was published on February 4. On the same day came the news of the "crime of Chauri Chaura".

On February 3 a procession at Chauri Chaura in the Gorakhpur district of the Uttar Pradesh, under much provocation, set fire to a police station killing 21 policemen and one sub-inspector and burning their bodies. It may be mentioned here that during Tilak's agitation in 1896 only two British officers were killed. In Gandhi's non-violent struggle about three thousand were killed up to the first quarter of the year 1922.

In his reply to Gandhi of February 6, the Viceroy said, that repressive orders were issued after the Congress passed its resolution on November 4. "Mass civil disobedience," the Viceroy stated, "is fraught with such dangers to the State that it must be met with sternness and severity."

Although Gandhi heard the news of the gruesome tragedy at Chauri Chaura which he described as a diabolical crime, he stubbornly issued his rejoinder to the Viceroy on February 7 and said: "The choice before the people is between mass civil disobedience with all its undoubted dangers and lawless repression of lawful activities of the people."

A meeting of the Working Committee was called at Bardoli on February 11, 1922, at the instance of Malaviya. Before it was held, an informal meeting was held at the Ashram of about seventy-five leaders to discuss whether civil disobedience should be started or not. Malaviya, Jayakar and N. C. Kelkar were for postponement, but the Muslim leaders were in favour of it. At the Working Committee, Vithalbhai Patel was also present. It was decided to postpone indefinitely all sorts of civil disobedience pending a meeting of the Working Committee which was expected on February 24 at Delhi.

On February 12 the Working Committee passed its resolution on Gandhi's constructive programme. With the news of this Congress surrender came the boastful statements of the English imperialists telling India that Britain had lost none of her hard fire. Gandhi pulled them up by saying the British lion was "shaking the manes", but India was prepared for all the hard fire and would be satisfied with nothing less than Śwaraj.

At the Bardoli meeting, where N. C. Kelkar was present, some leaders asked Gandhi why he issued a rejoinder to the Viceroy and made the position rather difficult even though he had received the news of the Chauri Chaura tragedy. Gandhi sorrowfully replied that he had so greatly concentrated his mind on the rejoinder that he was blind[5] to everything else at the time. After he had sent the rejoinder to the Viceroy, the truth suddenly dawned upon him. He later described it as a divine warning. From February 12, with his extreme spiritual sensitiveness and a sense of moral responsibility, he undertook a five-day fast as penance for the Chauri Chaura incidents. Yet the fact was that but for his moral influence there could have been far greater violence and more disorders.

Gandhi had said that great movements could not be stopped altogether because a Government or a people or both went wrong.[6] Although he had experienced that a movement of non-violent resistance could not long remain non-violent, he had repeated this axiom: "We may no more drop non-violent non-co-operation because of its dangers than we may stop freedom because of the dangers of its abuse."[7] Massacres and murders took place and hundreds of people were killed at Malegaon, Malabar, Bombay and Madras, yet Gandhi wanted to launch the struggle, but his political resolve broke down before his moral and spiritual stand. He rightly thought that people in Bardoli might be influenced by the violent deeds in other parts of the country.

On February 25, 1922, the A.I.C.C. meeting at Delhi, in a tense atmosphere, adopted with modifications the Working Committee's Bardoli resolution on postponement of the civil disobedience movement. Discontent and opposition reared its head at the A.I.C.C. meeting and Gandhi with great difficulty escaped being censured. Gandhi said, "I got the votes because I was Gandhi and not because the people were convinced. The drastic reversal," said Gandhi pathetically, "of practically the whole of the aggressive programme may be politically unsound and unwise, but there is no doubt that the country will have gained by my humiliation and confession of error."

Government had made all preparations for Gandhi's arrest, but in view of the Delhi resolution, they gave up the idea! Yet the British newspapers announced that he had been arrested. By now thirty thousand patriots were behind prison bars, and when the movement was at its crescendo, the dictator peremptorily gave the non-violent army orders for stand at ease.

A wave of disappointment passed over the country. The suspension of the movement angered the patriots in jail. The young men, who were courageously facing the rigours of jail life, were agitated. All despaired at the anti-climax. The feeling was that their dictator had surrendered.

Describing this surrender, Besant said, "Gandhi always flinches at the initial moment." It happened, in addition to the word blunder, bungle was the word harshly used by many to describe the surrender.

Gandhi serenely wrote to Nehru that he was sorry that all of them were terribly cut up over the resolution. The Mahatma said he was shameless, incorrigible and the only tyrant he accepted in the world was the still small voice within.[8]

Gandhi showed the courage of his conviction, which was a cardinal fact about Gandhi, and he stood supreme as a moral leader. But as a political leader he failed at the psychological moment to the despair, consternation and demoralization of his followers and of the Congress!

After the meeting of the A.I.C.C., Gandhi attended the meeting of the Gujarat Provincial Congress Committee and the Ulema's Conference at Ajmer. On March 9, 1922, the British Prime Minister accepted Montagu's resignation which was precipitated by his granting permission to Lord Reading to publish the Viceroy's despatch of February 28, 1922, for the revision of the Treaty of Sevres. Montagu, too, had given his consent to arrest the non-co-operating leaders including Gandhi. Both Montagu and Reading were Jews. Although, according to Reading, his policy was in the best interests of the Empire, his real object in pleasing the Muslims was to relieve the strain upon his Government. In the matter mentioned above, Edwin Montagu acted without consulting the Prime Minister Lloyd George and Foreign Secretary, Curzon. Montagu's political career was thus tragically cut short, the mainspring of his life was broken and this sympathizer of India died in November 1924.

The Indian Government had been discussing the question of Gandhi's arrest since October 1921. Home Member, Vincent Smith, had weighed the pros and cons, the advantages and disadvantages and advocated prosecution immediately at the risk of other dangers. Sir George Lloyd, Governor of Bombay, had told Gandhi that he would hold the latter responsible for every man, woman and child that was killed and when, after the Chauri Chaura atrocities, Gandhi met him and desperately asked him to put him in jail,[9] he retorted that he would do so when his Government got ready. The Governor was determined to arrest Gandhi and threatened the Viceroy with his resignation. The Viceroy then decided to take action against Gandhi. Lord Reading had consulted the important Governors in India. Accordingly, the District Magistrate, Ahmedabad, issued the warrant on March 6, 1922.

Gandhi knew that his arrest was imminent, for he wrote to T. Prakasam on March 7, and to M. R. Jayakar and Dr. Bhagwandas on March 10 that he would reply to their letters if he was not arrested. The article in *Young India* "If I am arrested" was a warning to the workers he had issued on March 9, 1922. Gandhi thought that his arrest would give him quiet and the physical rest which he badly needed. The Muslims thought that Gandhi was avoiding arrest. Two months earlier, the *Morning Post*,[10] London, had suggested that Gandhi should be arrested, imprisoned and even executed. Reuter's telegrams had been hinting that the British Government had decided upon Gandhi's arrest.

GANDHI RETURNED TO Ahmedabad on the afternoon of Friday, March 10, 1922. About nine o'clock at night Dan Healey, the Superintendent of Police, came in a car to the Ashram and told Shankarlal Banker, Printer and Publisher of *Young India*, who was returning home from the Ashram, that he had come to arrest him and Gandhi. Healey requested Anasuyabehn to give a message to Gandhi that he would wait till Gandhi was ready.

Hazarat Mohani and Isakhan J. Naster, who had just interviewed Gandhi were there till the arrest took place. Gandhi was told that the arrest was for four articles in *Young India*. Gandhi and the inmates of the Ashram sang the song of Narsi Mehta and the master blessed all the inmates.

It was now ten o'clock at night. With a bundle containing an extra loin-cloth, two blankets and five books, the Gita, the *Ramayana*, Rodwell's translation of the Koran, a presentation copy of the Sermon on the Mount sent by the students of a High School in California and the Ashram hymn-book, Gandhi got ready to go.

The Superintendent of Police took Gandhi, Kasturba, Anasuyabehn and Shankarlal Banker in his car to Sabarmati Jail. Some of Gandhi's disciples followed with bedding and other things. Kasturba and Anasuyabehn were sent back home.

The next day Gandhi and Banker were taken to the court by a special train. There was no excitement in Ahmedabad. Nor was peace disturbed in Bombay or elsewhere as the leaders asked the people to be quiet. Describing this peaceful atmosphere, an English autocrat contemptuously said, "Not a dog barked."[11]

The trial took place in the Divisional Commissioner's office at Shahibag before Mr. Brown, Assistant Magistrate. Gandhi called himself a farmer and weaver. Brown committed the case to the sessions.

The trial opened at 12 noon on Saturday, March 18, 1922, at the Circuit House in the court of Mr. Robert S. Broomfield. And for a wonder, the British judge, before occupying his seat on the bench, nodded respectful salutation in the court to a native in the dock! J. T. Strangman, the Advocate-General, helped by the Remembrancer and Public Prosecutor, conducted the case. The accused did not defend themselves. They were charged with three offences under section 124-A for the articles in *Young India*: Tempering with Loyalty of September 29, 1921, the Puzzle and its Solution of December 15, 1921, and Shaking the Manes of February 23, 1922. The article, Disaffection, a Virtue was dropped from the charge. The three articles were said to express disloyalty, to the Government. No counsel appeared for the grand accused. He was his own counsel. Gandhi pleaded guilty to all the charges. Banker, too, pleaded guilty. Their conduct was nonchalant and devoid of all bravado. The trial was supremely simple. Gandhi told the court that to preach disaffection towards the existing system of Government had become almost a passion with him. With a serene face he observed, "I am here, therefore, to invite and submit to the highest penalty that can be inflicted upon me." And appealing to the judge, he said, "The course open to you, Mr. Judge, is as I am just going to say in my statement, either to resign your post or inflict on me the severest penalty if you believe that the system and law you are assuring to administer are good for the people." He submitted his statement not defending his offence but justifying and aggravating it!

Giving the judgment sorrowfully on March 18, 1922, the judge, Robert Broomfield, said that even those who differed from Gandhi in politics looked upon him as a man of high ideals and of noble, or even of saintly life. He compared his case with that of Tilak "who had been sentenced to simple imprisonment for six years in 1908". "You will not consider it unreasonable, I think," the judge concluded, "that you should be classed with Mr. Tilak. That is a sentence of two years' simple imprisonment on each count of the charge, six years in all which I feel it my duty to pass upon you." The judge then passed upon Banker a sentence of simple imprisonment for one year for two counts and a fine of a thousand rupees on the third count with six months' simple imprisonment in default.

Hearing the judgment, Gandhi replied, "I would say one word since you have done me the honour of recalling the trial of the late Lokamanya Bal Gangadhar Tilak. I have just wanted to say that I consider it to be the proudest privilege and honour to be associated with his name. So far as the sentence itself is concerned, I certainly consider that it is as light as any judge would inflict upon me and so far as the whole proceedings are concerned I must say that I could not have expected greater courtesy."

"The judge," says Sarojini Naidu, "in a trembling voice full of pain felt compelled to do his duty by his own Government." "This state-trial," wrote N. C. Kelkar who witnessed the trial, "was not so much a trial by the state as a trial of the state itself."

The Advocate-General was apologetic. Broomfield's pathetic figure stole a parting glimpse of the Mahatma and walked off.

Thousands of people, who were waiting in the court and outside, were allowed to take their last look at their master. Leaders had come on behalf of their provinces from every corner of India. Men and women passed before him in mournful procession and to each he gave a cheerful look. And then with nimble feet Gandhi stepped out of the court. The guard looked more like guard of honour!

Sarojini Naidu was one among the two or three persons who were privileged to go with Gandhi to his prison to take their leave of him there. Later, while describing this scene, she told a Trichur audience that she wished that all of them who loved their wives, mothers and sisters, had seen the tenderness of this great Rishi and watched his wife as he put his arm around her and took her through the passage into the cell. Just like any ordinary man, just like any one of them, that great man who had made the Empire of Britain tremble put his arm round his wife to comfort her and said: "Do not be sad. I shall return in a free India."

As soon as Naidu, Gandhi and Kasturba entered Gandhi's cell, the jailor came, a kind old man, and said: "Oh! Mahatmaji, I was afraid that you might get rigorous imprisonment and therefore with my own hands I washed two sets of prison clothes ready for you."

Gandhi's blanket was spread in the verandah and his charkha was near the blanket. And they all sat there trying not to shed tears. But Gandhi was so happy that he was laughing like one who had received *moksha* from God.

Gandhi then spread out his feet as he always had some weakness in his legs that did not enable him to stand for long. He said: "I must rub my feet; they are very tired." Madan Mohan Malaviya, who was with him, replied: "Oh, you have been so cruel to your feet, carrying your message throughout the country. Give your feet a little rest now." Gandhi replied that for so many years he had no time to think or read. Now for six years he would read and write.[12]

During the days of the trial, peace reigned supreme throughout the country. While Gandhi was an under-trial prisoner, he was allowed to write letters and to give an interview to the representative of the *Manchester Guardian* regarding the policy of non-violence and he said that it was imperialism that was the great satan of the times. Gandhi and Shankarlal G. Banker were removed from Sabarmati Jail to Yeravda Jail on the midnight of March 20, where Gandhi said he enjoyed boundless peace.

CHAPTER XXVII

Muslims and Swarajists Turn Away

GANDHI, THE GREATEST general since Napoleon, but of a non-violent army, arrived at Yeravda Prison at five in the evening of March 21, 1922. During the journey he was treated well. The jail officer noted the marks on his body. A scar on the thigh, a small mole on the lower right eyelid, a scar about the size of a pea below the left elbow. He was five feet five inches in height and weighed 114 pounds. He was prisoner No. 8677 and was provided with two new warm heavy blankets, a coir mat and two sheets.

The next day Gandhi fasted as he was deprived of his spinning wheel, but it was returned to him in the evening. The English jailer was very rude; he touched Gandhi's utensils with his boots. The rules of the jail manual were rigorously applied to him and insults were flung at him by the jailer. Gandhi humbly observed the normal rules of jail life and protested against the acts of the jail authorities whenever they disregarded human considerations.

Rajagopalachari, accompanied by Devdas Gandhi, visited Gandhi on April 1, 1922, when the eminent prisoner was not asked to have a chair. He had to conduct the conversation standing. Rajagopalachari felt bad about it. The sight moved Devdas to tears.

Rajagopalachari said that Gandhi was treated like a common felon, jammed up in a tiny cell, deprived of ventilation and without a pillow for his head. He used books or his extra clothing as a pillow. Rajaji had just served a term of simple imprisonment for three months, and from jail he had written to Gandhi: "I hope when I come back you will have finished the Swaraj work and got back to your normal occupation of research into dietetics." Every Gandhian leader of his day believed in Gandhi achieving Swaraj by the end of the year 1921 or thereabout. They were under the spell of the Swaraj-in-one-year promise and were far from realistic about it. To their disillusionment, Gandhi, on the eve of his arrest, had said, "Swaraj after all is not a mango trick! Every moment of our activity we are gaining Swaraj!"[1]

During the interview, Gandhi told Rajagopalachari that he was given goat's milk and bread, and when he asked for fruit, oranges were provided. He had cut down his three meals to two. Raisins, which were a part of his usual diet, were not given to him, till he had exhausted the stock he had brought with him. After Rajagopalachari's visit, he was given a pillow. Yet Gandhi was provided with two cells, one to sleep in and the other to work in. His daily ration comprised bread, butter, three pounds of goat's milk, four oranges, two limes, two ounces of raisins, half a pound of flour, table salt and bicarbonate of soda.

Gandhi wrote a primer in Gujarati in April 1922 and sent it to the Ashram with a request that it should be published if approved by A. T. Gidwani of Gujarat Vidyapith and others. When it was known that Gandhi had written a Primer, Aurobindo Ghose jokingly said that he expected Gandhi's primer to contain lessons on cooking and on cleaning latrines. Gandhi did not come up to that standard!

On April 14, 1922, Gandhi wrote a letter to Hakim Ajmal Khan, but it was returned to him. He was asked to remove material parts of it. Gandhi wrote to the Government of Bombay that he would not exercise the right of sending his periodical letters unless they would forward his letters subject only to such corrections as might be found necessary. He asked for *The Times of India* weekly, the *Modern Review* which he described as a high-class monthly, and the *Saraswati. Samalochak*, a Gujarati monthly, was denied him and so he said that he was deprived of the opportunity of keeping himself in touch with Gujarati literature.

At or about this time the Government of India was thinking of transferring Gandhi to some jail in Burma in the event of any agitation.

From jail Gandhi gave advice to his relatives, friends and co-workers. He was anxious about Das's health and hoped that Motilal Nehru's asthma had left him. Ramdas was going to marry. Gandhi said he should not marry until he had tried himself for one year in the calling of his choice. Gandhi felt he continued to be 'butcher' to Kasturba because he opposed her and asked her to swallow the bitter pill of separation from Ramdas by allowing him to marry if Ramdas placed himself under the care of so good a soul as Rajagopalachari. In September 1922 he twice observed a week's silence.

When Government refused permission to Motilal Nehru and Hakim Ajmal Khan to interview Gandhi, he said that besides being his political co-workers they were his personal friends interested in his well-being. The nation was watching Gandhi in jail and as he was sentenced to imprisonment on the 18th of March, they were celebrating the 18th of every month as a day of prayer for the speedy restoration of their leader to his people. Gandhi's 53rd birthday was celebrated all over India.

Gandhi was considered a convict and criminal by the British Government. On November 10, 1922, the Parliament of the Inner Temple debarred Gandhi and removed his name from the roll of barristers, as he was convicted. What the roll of barristers lost, the eternal roll of humanity gained!

Gandhi was suffering from pyorrhoea. He had been baking *chapatis* but gave up eating *chapatis* and lived on four seers of milk, two ounces of raisins, four oranges and two lemons. In January 1923 Kasturba met him after waiting for permission to do so for twenty days. The Mulshi Petha satyagrahis were flogged on February 9, 1923 in Yeravda Jail, and Gandhi sought permission from the Jail Superintendent to meet the satyagrahis, but he was not allowed to do so.

Another incident arose from this affair. The Jail Superintendent decided to keep gossip and news from percolating into Gandhi's yard. He, therefore, imposed restrictions even on the barber convict. The barber stuck work. As a protest, Gandhi went without a shave and asked for a pair of clippers. The result was that Gandhi's colleagues in jail got their cheeks and skins badly pinched by Gandhi, who had eventually to surrender the clippers!

In April 1923 Gandhi suffered from severe pain in the stomach and the Surgeon-General Col. Maddock examined him. The Mulshi Petha prisoners resorted to fasts and they were again flogged in Yeravda Jail. Gandhi therefore threatened the Government with resorting to a fast. He discussed the matter with Col. R. M. Dalziel, the Superintendent of Yeravda Prison. At last he was allowed to have a talk with two prisoners, S. D. Dev and V. V. Dastane, and he persuaded them to break their long fast.

On August 13 Gandhi privately discussed with the

Governor, Sir George Lloyd, the classification of prisoners. It was Sir George Lloyd who had compelled Lord Reading to sanction Gandhi's arrest and in private conversation described Gandhi as a thin, spindly shrimp of a fellow. He later confessed to Drew Pearson that Gandhi had given the Government a scare and his programme had filled the jails. One could not go on arresting people forever. "And if," the Governor continued, "they had taken his next step and refused to pay tax, God knows where we would have been. Gandhi's was the most colossal experiment in world history, and it came within an inch of succeeding. But he could not control men's passions."

Some more visitors came in. Kasturba and M. G. Ranade's wife, Ramabai Ranade, met him in jail in December 1923.

In jail Gandhi framed a programme of study for himself and read about 150 books on religion, and on the social and natural sciences. He read the great Indian epics and classics and the history of India upto the Moghul period, *Satyartha Prakash*, *Rise of the Sikh Power*, *Pitt by Rosebery*, *History of Scotland*, Buckle's *History of Civilization*, Haeckel's *Evolution of Man*, Guizot's *History of Civilization* in Europe and Paul Carus's *Gospel of Buddhism*. For the first time in his life, Gandhi read ..the *Mahabharat*, *Manusmriti* and the *Upanishads* in English translation by Butler and Max-Muller, Farrar's *Seekers after God* and Mahomed Ali's *Koran*. He read Goethe's *Faust*, Plato's *Dialogues*, Tagore's *Sadhana* and George Bernard Shaw's *Man and Superman*. Some portions of *Tom Brown's School Days* by Lowell he found interesting. But *Man and Superman*, one aspect of which was designed to exhibit revolutions in attitude and change, must have left him unaffected. He read *Dr. Jekyll* and *Mr. Hyde*, but none knows his opinion of it. According to him, *Tulsi Ramayana* was the best book in the world.

On November 26, 1923, Gandhi started writing a history, *Satyagraha in South Africa*, in Gujarati, obviously to enthuse and inspire his followers with courage and the spirit of self-sacrifice. He completed writing some chapters in jail. He had started writing his autobiography in November 1921, but riots broke out in Bombay and he stopped the work. In jail he could not find time to start it again.

During 1922 and 1923, Government had to issue statements either to clarify its position or to refute rumours about Gandhi's health. During the early part of his incarceration, some tea was daily issued to him. It was stopped at Gandhi's instance." But people said the statement was false as Gandhi always condemned tea. The Government clarified the issue by stating the fact as mentioned above. Another charge they had to refute was that Gandhi was flogged in prison.

While Gandhi was thus struggling and experimenting in Yeravda Jail, his ideals were being discussed in many countries. When a leader is in jail for his principles, his cause is well advertised. Gandhi's cause became well knovn all over the world. Sir John Rees said that Gandhi in jail might prove to be more dangerous than Gandhi out of it.

Miss Blanche Watson, a well-known American writer on Indian affairs, described Gandhi as a successful failure.[2] Although, she continued, his critics characterized him as a drag on the wheel of progress" he was a mighty disturber of a powerful empire and merited a place alongside of such men as St. Francis of Assisi, Savanarola, John Brown, Wendell Phillips, Thoreau, Jaures, Tolstoy and others who were failures in their time. Like Jesus of old, Mahatma Gandhi, concluded Miss Watson, was condemned with tragic stupidity by the materialists because he insisted that means were far more important to the true progress of humanity than ends, and Gandhi believed the means would outlive every political and economic creed. The New York *Nation* said that Gandhi had given to revolution non-violent instruments which promised the release of humanity from the seeming necessity of wars for freedom.[3]

The *Communist Review*[4] observed that although Gandhi made the Indian movement for the first time truly national, the movement had outgrown Gandhi. He vainly thought to hold it back. Gandhi in jail, it added, was a powerful factor for unrest, a symbol of national martyrdom, a constant stimulation to the national cause to fight its way to freedom.

EARLY IN THE year 1924, Gandhi's health broke down. He often had a severe pain in his stomach and he passed many restless nights. So far as Gandhi's physical comfort was concerned, he was gradually provided with better facilities. On Banker's release, Mansoor Ali Sookta, Indulal Yajnik and Abdul Gani (an Urdu scholar) were sent to Gandhi as companions. Gandhi could not help performing his dietetic experiments on poor Mansoor Ali, and he himself gave up fruit as the jail authorities would not give Ali the fruit prescribed by Gandhi! At last the Superintendent yielded.

Athough Col. Dalziel, the Jail Superintendent, was very harsh, Major Jones and Col. Murray, who came after Dalziel, were courteous and kind and they never let him feel, Gandhi observed, that he was a prisoner. Gandhi was transferred to the European ward where he had superior accommodation and a garden in front of the ward. "And if," as Gandhi wrote afterwards, "I suffered from illness now and then, it is my firm belief that neither the Government nor the jail authorities could in any way be blamed." The jail authorities strictly respected all his scruples about diet. He found Major Jones often hasty but not heartless.

When Gandhi suffered from incipient dysentery, he was given emetic injections. He experienced great pain as he could not help eating more than he should have of the green figs sent by Anasuyabehn Gokhale, a staunch Gandhian from Bombay.

With such a long rigorous struggle to win mastery over palate and passion, Gandhi had so far obtained rigid control only over his time. Yet it was his dictum that failure in controlling the palate was an offence against God. Indulal Yajnik, who was with him in jail, wrote that the Mahatma was inclined to over-indulgence in eating although he tried to control his overmastering appetite with manifold vows and pledges. It is human even for a seasoned ascetic not to be always fiercely abstemious!

During the last quarter of the year 1923, Gandhi was growing weaker. He was emaciated. His hands trembled. He weighed 96 lbs. Besides fruit and milk, he took honey and increased the intake of bread to eight ounces. But his weak constitution could not bear the slightly heavier rations. And it was found that he had developed acute appendicitis. On January 11, 1924, he was taken to Sassoon Hospital, Poona, for treatment. On examination, the Surgeon-General and other medical officers came to the conclusion that any delay in performing an operation was dangerous.

Sir George Lloyd, who disliked Gandhi, had been replaced by Sir Leslie Wilson. The new Governor treated Gandhi with sympathy. Government permitted him to send for any of his medical friends. Gandhi suggested the names of Dr. Dalal and Dr. Jivraj Mehta. But the Surgeon-General Col. Maddock could not get in touch with them. Gandhi wrote this account and kept it on record in a letter to Lt. Col. Maddock who was to perform the operation and asked him to go ahead with it without delay. As Gandhi had mentioned Srinivas Sastri, Dr. Pathak and N. C. Kelkar as his friends to be present at the time of the operation, Sastri and Pathak were present. Kelkar was in Satara. While the operation room was being made ready and the doctors were outside, Gandhi whispered to Sastri that if there was any agitation for his release after the operation, which he did not wish, it should be on proper lines. If the Government thought, the Mahatma added, that they had kept him long enough, they should release him. He showed surprise at the news that he had given any message to Mahomed Ali!

On the night of January 12, 1924, Gandhi was given morphia and was operated on for appendicitis. While the operation was going on, the electricity failed on account of a thunder-storm, and the operation had to be finished with the help of a hurricane lamp. Gandhi bore the operation very well. The government press communique declared on the morning of January 13, 1924: "Mr. Gandhi was operated on for acute appendicitis last night."

Srinivas Sastri broke the news to the nation in a statement he issued on January 13 and said that the operation was successful. The next day Gandhi gave a message to the country and relieved the tension. The nation heaved a sigh of relief. The Jail Superintendent, Col. Murray, who made kind enquiries, said he was happy to see Gandhi better and hoped he would soon be released. Anxious letters and telegrams from all parts of the country poured in day and night inquiring after Gandhi's health. With the help of modern medicine, which he had called "black magic", Gandhi was making progress and had overcome the threat to his life at the age of fifty-three. Lajpatrai, Motilal Nehru and Andrews, visited Gandhi and their sadness at his ordeal gave place to gladness.

While convalescing in the hospital, Gandhi was asked through Lt. Col. Maddock what place he would choose as a health resort for him. Gandhi replied that he should be allowed to go to Tithal or Dumas in Surat District. On February 2, 1924, Gandhi gave an interview to Dilip Kumar Roy expressing his views on music. Dilip Kumar was an exponent of Indian music and was an inmate of the Aurobindo Ashram at Pondicherry. Gandhi told him that he was a lover of music as well as of the other arts. When in Africa, he was once ailing from a bruise on his upper lip, he felt soothed as soon as he heard a friend's daughter singing "Lead, Kindly Light" at his request. He maintained that asceticism was the greatest art in life, and he told Roy how happy he felt to gaze at the wonderful vault of the starry sky.

In January 1924 the Labour Party came to power in England under Ramsay MacDonald as Prime Minister. It helped to easen the situation in India. Some members in the Legislative Assembly and the Bombay Legislative Council were going to move resolutions asking for the release of Gandhi. Jinnah said Mahatma Gandhi should not be kept in jail a minute longer. Wilson had seen Lord Reading in Delhi and discussed with him the release of Gandhi. The Bombay Government thought that Gandhi's release would be a set-back to the Swaraj Party and a check on the Ali Brothers. It would greatly facilitate the smooth working of the Central Assembly and the Councils.[5]

So the Government of Bombay tactfully made Gandhi's illness an excuse for his release and issued the release order on February 4. On February 5, Col. Maddock announced, at eight in the morning, the news to Gandhi! He paused for a moment and requested Maddock to allow him to remain his patient a little longer. He was, however, grieved to know that the decision of the Government to release him was based on considerations of his health. He was released nearly four years before the expiry of his six-year sentence. Gandhi thanked the convict warders for their help and especially Gangappa who had become a most efficient nurse to him in jail.

During this jail life, Gandhi wrote 240 letters of which 24 were addressed to the jail authorities, sent 35 telegrams and granted 21 interviews. Some of the letters addressed to the Superintendent of the Prison ended with "yours obediently" or "your faithful servant," as was the practice then observed.

MEANWHILE THE INDIAN National Congress had undergone a change and had reconsidered Gandhi's programme. On June 7, 1922, the A.I.C.C. met at Allahabad. Motilal Nehru, who was out of jail now, and Rajagopalachari guided its proceedings. The A.I.C.C. appointed a Civil Disobedience Inquiry Committee which consisted of Hakim Ajmal Khan, Motilal Nehru, Rajagopalachari, Dr. Ansari, Vithalbhai Patel and Kasturiranga lyengar to tour round the country and report on the situation. It issued a questionnaire of 60 items. The Civil Disobedience Inquiry Committee met prominent leaders in all the provinces and they gave evidence. It was found that the movement had weakened since the imprisonment of Gandhi though the boycott of courts and schools had provided the Congress with a number of workers. Many advocated the entering of Councils. Leaders like Hakim Ajmal Khan and Pandit Motilal Nehru, the right and left hands of Gandhi, yielded to the demand for entry into the Council. N. C. Kelkar, who favoured Council entry and had been the spearhead of the attack on Gandhi's civil disobedience programme, demanded a modification in the old programme.

The Civil Disobedience Inquiry Committee travelled for six weeks and went to Calcutta to draft the report. Meanwhile, Das was released on August 9, 1922, and he was soon elected President of the Indian National Congress. One of the members of the C.D.I. Committee, it is said, requested him to refrain from expressing his opinion on the non-co-operation programme. The C.D.I. Committee submitted its report to Das at the end of October in which it was reverentially said: "Great, however, as is our respect and our admiration for Mahatma Gandhi, we have not allowed it to come in the way of our clear duty. We have approached his work with reverence but we have examined it with care."

The C.D. Inquiry Committee reported that the country was not prepared at that time to embark upon general mass civil disobedience. Motilal Nehru and Hakim Ajmal Khan, not to speak of Vithalbhai Patel, favoured entry into the Councils and lyengar, Ansari and Rajagopalachari opposed it. The C.D.I. Committee suggested confirmation of the suspension of boycott of schools and courts. The report noted that the times had changed and the circumstances altered. The members stated that they were inclined to believe that the policy of abstention had lost its charm. The Civil Disobedience Inquiry Committee indirectly justified Kelkar's recommendations. But it was strange that Rajagopalachari, the whole-hogger non-co-operation leader, favoured the suspension of the educational boycott! The C.D.I. Committee recommended to the non-co-operators that they should seek elections to local bodies.

Towards the end of November 1922, Das, while addressing the Calcutta Khilafat Congress, expressed himself in favour of Council entry. He had been in favour of Council entry all along, although for unity's sake he had accepted the programme of non-co-operation. As soon as Das gave expression to his views, the Gandhian no-changers refused to call him 'Desh-bandhu'. They insultingly suggested that he should resign the presidentship of the forthcoming Congress to be held at Gaya. The All-India Congress Committee met at Calcutta for five days in the third week of November 1922 and resolved that the forthcoming Congress should decide the question of Council entry.

Meantime, the Turkish Sultan fled for his life to Malta on November 17, 1922, as Turkey abolished the Sultanate. And Abdul Majid was made Khalifa. This news naturally upset the Khilafatists.

In the last week of December 1922 the 37th session of the Congress met at Gaya under the presidentship of C. R. Das, who advocated Council entry in his speech and put forth a policy of obstruction. He wanted Congressmen to oppose all measures in the Councils and create a deadlock. He said, however, that if the Khilafatists opposed his stand he would give it up.

During this session Rajagopalachari again vehemently championed the cause of the no-changers by ruthlessly overriding his own recommendations in the report of the Civil Disobedience Inquiry Committee. The no-changers led by Rajaji and Rajendra Prasad passed the Council boycott resolution by 1,740 votes against 890. The boycott of schools, colleges and courts was continued although the right of private defence in the court was conceded. The Khilafat Conference stood by their religious *fatwa* and also by the report of the Khilafat Committee which acted parallel to the Civil Disobedience Inquiry Committee, and stood for non-co-operation. The result was that the followers of Gandhi left Gaya with a sense of triumph.

It Was, However, a pyrrhic victory. There was a split in the Congress. The pro-change party leaders Das, Motilal Nehru, A. Rangaswamy Iyengar, Satyamurti, N. C. Kelkar, V. J. Patel, M. R. Jayakar, Dr. Moonje and Hakim Ajmal Khan founded on December 31, 1922, at the Gaya residence of the Maharaja of Tikari, a new party called The Congress-Khilafat Swaraj Party and decided to push forward the pro-change programme. Das was elected President and Motilal Nehru was one of the four secretaries. The party was known as the Swaraj Party. It accepted the creed and programme of the Congress and decided to work as a wing of it, hoping to win over a majority in the Congress in favour of Council entry. The Congress was divided between pro-changers and no-changers, the latter being aggressive, intolerant zealots and blind worshippers of Gandhi. The pro-changers took care to resist the temptation to cut off their moorings from the Indian National Congress. Maharashtra was a stronghold of the Swaraj Party, and for its realism Maharashtra was called crafty.

On February 4, 1923, Das came to Poona to explain the stand of his new party. When he was presented with an address by the Poona Municipality as also by the people, Das said: "As a matter of fact there is no difference between my idea of work in the Councils and responsive co-operation or Mr. Kelkar's responsive non-co-operation. I want the spirit of resistance behind the whole movement. ... In entering the Councils, we do not abandon non-co-operation. I say it is a step in advance. ... I am a dreamer, no doubt, but my dreams are not confined to dogmas and doctrines."[6]

The Congress session over, Das resigned the presidentship of the Indian National Congress, but his resignation was held over and was ultimately accepted only in May 1923. Rather than yield to the pro-changers, Rajagopalachari, Vallabhbhai Patel, Rajendra Prasad and Jamnalal Bajaj resigned their seats on the Working Committee. Dr. Ansari took over as President with Jawaharlal Nehru as one of its secretaries. After Jawaharlal's release on January 23, 1923, Motilal Nehru tried to win over his son to the Swaraj Party through Das, but to no purpose. The old order gives place to the new. Motilal Nehru and Das left the Working Committee, but Jawaharlal Nehru came in. This new Working Committee was called the Central Party, a buffer or a peace-maker or a mediator between the two warring groups. The Congressmen under Jamnalal Bajaj and Vallabhbhai Patel launched, from May to August 1923, what they called the Flag Satyagraha, at Nagpur. Volunteers from all parts of India challenged the Government because it had opposed flag processions.

During Gandhi's absence, Jamnalal Bajaj established the Gandhi Seva Sangh in 1923 to carry out the constructive programme of Gandhi. The members were believers in Truth and Non-violence. A special Congress was held under the presidentship of Maulana Azad at Delhi in September 1923, where the revolt initiated by Das, Motilal Nehru and Kelkar at Gaya became stronger. The pro-changers succeeded, and the way to the Councils was declared open. Lala Lajpatrai also was in favour of Council entry! Rajagopalachari, Rajendra Prasad and Vallabhbhai Patel yielded. The Congressmen were to enter the Councils to carry the good fight into the enemy's camp and to beard the lion in his den.

The Swaraj Party set forth its manifesto in October 1923, which pledged a policy of "uniform, continuous and consistent obstruction with a view to making the Government through Assembly and Council impossible". In December 1923 the Swarajists won a major victory in the elections to the Central Legislative Assembly, capturing 42 out of 101 elective seats, an absolute majority in the Central Provinces Council, a large number of seats in other Provincial Councils except in the Madras, the Punjab, Bihar and Orissa Councils.

Motilal Nehru, Vithalbhai Patel, M. R. Jayakar and N. C. Kelkar were elected to the Central Assembly, and Das became leader of the Swaraj Party in the Bengal Council. The Cocanada Congress session was held under the presidentship of Mahomed Ali who had been released on August 28, 1923. His brother had been released in October 1923. Mahomed Ali said in his presidential address, "Das had never meant that the Mahatma had blundered. They thought that he was something of a bungler and a blunderer where finesse was required in dealing with the bureaucrats and with a Viceroy who was supposed to have out-yankeed the Yankees during the war."

Mahomed Ali casually made a sinister suggestion to the Congress that they should divide India into two parts and allow the Muslims to convert and absorb the Untouchables in one part into the Muslim religion. If the Hindus would not absorb them into their own society, others would and must do so, he concluded. This was the price Hindus had to pay for the Hindu-Muslim unity sponsored by Gandhi. The Congress reaffirmed the resolution adopted at Delhi with regard to Council entry and added that the principle and policy of the triple boycott, too, remained unaltered!

HEARING THE NEWS of the release of their great leader, the people heaved a sigh of relief. Just after his release, while convalescing in the hospital, Gandhi wrote on February 7, 1924, to Mahomed Ali, President of the Congress, saying that his release had brought him no relief as he was ill-fitted to discharge his duties. He said that Hindu-Muslim unity had suffered a severe check, the spinning wheel was the remedy for the disease of poverty, and since he had not altered his opinion about the boycott of Councils, law-courts and Government schools, he had no data for coming to a judgment upon the vexed question of the return of Congressmen to the Councils and to the Assembly. Gandhi thanked all the numerous senders of congratulatory messages to him on his release.

On his release, Gandhi wrote to Mahadev Desai expressing his opinion about his secretarial staff. Devdas was industrious but lazy in writing letters. Pyarelal was a day-dreamer and lacked energy. Krishnadas was nervous. The inmates of the Ashram were in constant dread of thieves and so Gandhi suggested to Maganlal Gandhi that the inmates should give up all their jewellery. He requested Mahomed Yakub to desist from moving his resolution in the Central Assembly recommending Gandhi for the Nobel Prize.

In the first week of March 1924, Motilal Nehru had a talk with Gandhi but could not convert him to his views on Council entry. Gandhi began to deal with the different problems that awaited his advice. He gave an interview to a delegation from Sind. He discussed with some Sikh leaders the events in the Nabha State. He issued a statement on the Akali movement asking the reformist Sikhs to observe non-violence in their struggle in which on February 21, 1924, 21 persons were killed and 33 wounded when police fired at Jaiton on a procession of 500 Sikhs who had come to celebrate the anniversary of the Nankana incident. The Government coerced the Nabha ruler, who was a reformer and nationalist, to abdicate and the people had started satyagraha against his deposition.

Around this time the Nizam of Hyderabad was pressing the Viceroy to restore to him the Province of Berar, and he had deputed Sir Ali Imam to London to persuade the British Government to do so. The Nizam wrote to Gandhi seeking his help in the matter, but Gandhi expressed his inability to attend to the question for the time being. Gandhi's pronounced sympathy for Muslim interests might have induced the Nizam to do so.

The wound on Gandhi's stomach still bled a little occasionally. He reached Juhu, a seaside suburb of Bombay, on March 11, 1924, and stayed at Narottam Morarji's bungalow, for convalescing. He liked the place, the bungalow, the sea and its cool and gentle breezes and the coconut palms. Andrews and Gandhi took a walk along the beautiful sandy beach in Juhu.

Das and Dr. Moonje were requested by the Governors of their Provinces to form a ministry, but they declined the offer. The Montagu-Chelmsford Reforms did not transfer complete responsibility for the government to the ministers. The Governor held responsibility for certain reserved subjects such as Revenue, Law, Justice, the Police, Irrigation and Labour. The popular ministers were to be given responsibility for such transferred subjects as Local Self-Government, Education, Public Health, Public Works and Co-operative Societies.

In the Central Assembly, the Swarajists led by Motilal Nehru, with the help of Jinnah and the Liberals successfully carried through an amendment demanding that a new constitution be framed by a representative Round Table Conference. Motilal Nehru rejected also the budget grants by refusing leave to move the Finance Bill. So did Das and Dr. L. S. Moonje in their Provincial Councils.

Flushed with these victories, Das and Motilal Nehru as also Lajpatrai discussed the issue of Council entry with Gandhi at

Juhu but to no avail. Gandhi could not see eye to eye with them. He frankly told them that Council entry was inconsistent with non-co-operation as he conceived it. Neither could he convince or convert Das or Nehru. According to the Cocanada resolution, the Swarajists, he candidly observed, were justified in entering the Councils and resorting to obstruction in them. He, however, would neither actively help them nor oppose them. The no-changers should follow the constructive programmes.

Gandhi fearlessly resumed the editorship of *Young India*, the Hindi *Navajivan* and the Gujarati *Navajivan* on April 3, 1924. After his arrest, the circulation of these weeklies had declined. Although Shauib Qureshi and Rajagopalachari wielded their pens as editors of *Young India*, the number of subscribers had fallen from 21,500 to 3,000. In the very first issue edited by him, Gandhi declared that he had no new message or programme. He had hoped for his release from jail by a Swaraj Government, but that was not to be.

As Gandhi had undergone Western medical treatment, his critics and several of his friends found fault with him and reminded him of the principles he had laid down in *Hind Swaraj*. To these charges the barrister in Gandhi replied: "What is written there has reference to an ideal state. I plead guilty. But that is to admit that I am not a perfect man."[7] He held that appendicitis was a result of infirmity of thought or mind. So also he conceded that "my submission to the surgical operation was an additional infirmity of mind". On top of it all, Gandhi later fitted surgical action into non-violence. "When a surgeon," he defined, "uses a knife on a patient and makes him suffer in order to bring him relief, that is non-violence."[8]

As regards the mission of his life, Gandhi humbly said, "I do not consider myself worthy to be mentioned in the same breath with the race of prophets. I am a humble seeker of truth. I am impatient to realize myself to attain *moksha* in this very existence. ... I have no desire for the perishable kingdom of earth. I am striving for the kingdom of Heaven which is *moksha*."[9]

GANDHI DISCUSSED THE Hindu-Muslim problem with many eminent leaders. Gazi Kemal Pasha, whom the Indian Muslim leaders had been extolling to the skies, deposed the Khalifa and abolished the Khilafat on March 3, 1924, secularising Turkey. This news unnerved the Indian Muslim leaders! The bond of common interests provided by the Khilafat agitation weakened. The enthusiasm of Muslim leaders for national unity cooled down and their love of Gandhian politics and ideas began to decrease. The nationalism of Kemal Pasha discarded what the reactionary Muslims in India worshipped. Kemal Pasha described the Indian supporters of the Khilafat as foreign busy-bodies in league with the British Government.[10] Expressing its views on the tragedy of the Khilafat, *Young India*[11] shed tears and expressed the hope that either Turkey would be divorced from other Islamic countries or the new ruling classes there would be overthrown. Mahomed Ali vaingloriously roared like a clawless lion that he would fight the destroyers of the Khilafat whether English or Turkish.

Aurobindo Ghose described the imposition of the Khilafat on India as comic rather than dramatic. Azad and Yakub Hassan were satisfied with Kemal's action. Pickthall, a convert to Islam, and Fuzul Haque abused Kemal Pasha and made many accusations against him.

This was the tragic end of one plank of Gandhi's programme. He succeeded in mobilizing the Muslim orthodox masses for a time but failed in his Khilafat agitation as the Khilafat movement had no relevance to the time and to the new world. Gandhi now said that it was a question which the Muslims must settle for themselves. This was bound to affect Hindu-Muslim unity. The fiasco in Turkey brought back the attention of Indian Muslims to their situation in India and their eyes turned to communal politics.

In December 1923 Das had made a pact with the Muslim members of the Bengal Council and secured a majority in it. According to *Young India*, Das, in his desire to buy the friendship of the Mohammedans, underestimated the force of Hindu opinion or over-estimated his capacity to control it. With a generosity that seemed extravagant, Das made large promises to the Muslims and the Hindus were in a state of rebellion. B. C. Pal put himself at the head of the revolt. The communal problem which was disturbing north India assumed serious proportions in Bengal. Yet *Young India* said that it did not regard the pact as an act of folly; on the contrary, it greeted the pact as a sign of wisdom.

Just at this moment, a statement of Mahomed Ali irritated some of Swami Shraddhanand's friends who asked Mahomed Ali to resign from the Congress. This worsened the tension between Hindus and Muslims. The friends of Shraddhanand were offended by Mahomed Ali's remark that he prayed to God to illumine Gandhi's soul with the true light of Islam. This he said in reply to Muslims who charged him with being a follower of Gandhi in his religious principles. *Insaf*, a Khilafat newspaper, blamed Mahomed Ali for praising Gandhi as a Mahatma and "the most Christian-like man of the age."[12] In the aforesaid reply to Shraddhanand, Mohammed Ali explained that although he had not so far found any person who in actual character was entitled to a higher place than Mahatma Gandhi, he added that "as a follower of Islam I am bound to regard the creed of Islam as superior to that professed by the followers of any non-Islamic religion. And in this sense the creed of even a fallen and degraded Mussalman is entitled to a higher place than that of any other non-Muslim irrespective of his high character, even though the person in question be Mahatma Gandhi himself."[13] Gandhi did not mind Mahomed Ali giving him a lower place than a degraded Muslim. On the contrary, he represented this controversy as a campaign of misrepresentation. He reminded his readers that his Christian friends prayed for light for him and he added that thousands of Christians certainly held that a righteous man without belief in Jesus Christ was less than an adulterous Christian. Gandhi was living and thinking on a higher plane, and he generously exonerated Mahomed Ali from the degradation implied by his statement.

The nation had given Gandhi over a crore of rupees for the Tilak Swaraj Fund, and at Bardoli the Working Committee of the Congress outlined a constructive programme of social amelioration in February 1922. One of the features or planks of the programme was to organize the depressed classes for a better life, to improve their social, mental and moral condition. But the Congress leaders were not enthusiastic about it. Disgusted with the attitude of the Congress to the welfare of the Untouchables, Swami Shraddhanand, who had framed a programme for their amelioration, resigned from the Congress. Gandhi was in jail and the Congress selected Gangadhar Deshpande, an orthodox Brahmin, as convener of the Congress Sub-Committee to consider the problem. Then Yajnik was appointed the convener. At last, the Congress Working Committee, at its meeting in May 1923, resolved that "as this question of untouchability concerned the Hindu Community particularly, it requests the All-India Hindu Mahasabha also to take up this matter and to make strenuous efforts to remove this evil from amidst the Hindu community". Thus the responsibility for the amelioration and welfare of the depressed classes was transferred to the Hindu Mahasabha whose leaders like Lajpatrai, Swami Shraddhanand and Malaviya were in the

Congress. There was no ban on Hindu Sabhaites to be members of the Congress till the early thirties.

And how was the Tilak Swaraj Fund spent? The Congress and Gandhi were harshly criticized for the way in which the fund was handled. It was true that Gandhi was not solely responsible for the uneven disbursement of the fund, especially when he was in jail, but he should have exerted his moral influence on the leaders who made the disbursement. After there was an uproar against the alleged misappropriation of the fund by the workers, the great organizer in Gandhi as late as in June 1925, honestly but defensively observed: "Though there has been here and there misapplication of the funds and even defalcation, on the whole I am satisfied that the money has been spent for the purpose intended."[14] Yet the matter gave out a nasty smell for years.

Meanwhile the Vikom struggle was coming to a head. On the last day of March 1924, satyagraha was launched by the non-Brahmin leader, K. P. Kesava Menon, at Vikom in Travancore State for vindicating the rights of the Untouchables to use a certain road to which they were forbidden entry. The road in dispute was private property belonging to a temple which was in exclusive possession of its Brahmin trustees. They allowed the non-Brahmins, Christians and Muslims to use the road but excluded the Untouchables. The Ezhavas, the Tiyyas and the Pulayas were treated as not only Untouchables but also as Unapproachables in Travancore. Gandhi rightly supported their non-violent struggle. On the arrest of their leader Menon, George Joseph took his place. The authorities barricaded the roads. Gandhi said the satyagrahis should not scale or break fences. But he warned that the anti-untouchability movement did not aim at inter-dining or inter-marrying.[15]

CHAPTER XXVIII

Tearfully Stoops to Conquer

On May 18, 1924, Gandhi delivered at Juhu the first speech after his release on Gautama Buddha, it being Buddha Jayanti Day. In the speech he said that religion to him was a living faith in the supreme unseen force. He was more than most people endeavouring to popularize that truth for which Gautama Buddha lived and died.

Buddhism, Gandhi continued, was a part of Hinduism. Buddha did not give a new religion; he gave Hinduism a new interpretation. He taught Hindus not to take but to give life. It was Gandhi's unalterable belief that India had fallen low not because she accepted Gautama's teaching but because she failed to live up to it. A couple of days later he said that Jainism and Buddhism were mighty reforms in Hinduism.

The first thing Gandhi did while picking up the threads of his policy was to declare the futility of foreign goods. Boycott of foreign goods, he said, could not be accomplished unless every national worker religiously avoided the use of mill-made cloth. The fact was that at the Gaya Congress in 1922 the no-changers had defeated a resolution boycotting British goods, but the All-India Congress Committee had passed it at their Delhi meeting in September 1923. Gandhi wanted to wipe out that resolution.

During his illness in the hospital at Poona, an English nurse had asked Gandhi why he had saved his life with British medicines when he had proclaimed boycott of British goods. Even the umbrella that protected him from the sun was of foreign make. Gandhi had replied that he boycotted the British goods not because they were British but because they were foreign.

After an endless discussion with the Swarajist leaders, Gandhi, after the foregoing public speech, expressed his views on various political issues. In a statement he issued on May 22, 1924, he declared that Council entry was inconsistent with non-cooperation. He said he had failed to convince the Swarajist leaders of this. He would not put obstacles in their way or carry on any propaganda against their entry into the Legislatures though he could not actively help them in a project in which he did not believe. The no-changers, who were worshippers of Gandhi, declared their faith in non-co-operation. On the same day Motilal Nehru issued a statement clarifying the position of the Swarajists. He said that Gandhi's doctrine of non-violence with its implications and logical deductions had not been accepted by the Congress. Motilal also deprecated Gandhi's emphasis on the Khilafat and the Punjab wrongs. The honest thing to do, he added, was to admit failure and frankly give up the triple boycott. In the end he said that Council entry was not a negation but an extension of non-co-operation in a new field.

About this time Aurobindo Ghose criticized Gandhi's views on the Gita, brahmacharya, non-co-operation, non-violence and prayer. So Gandhi sent his son, Devdas, to Pondicherry to meet Aurobindo who sent a copy of his *Essays on the Gita* to Gandhi through Devdas and asked him for his reaction. Gandhi said he was unable to reply to this question intellectually.[1] The Mahatma and those who depended on his interpretation of the Gita propagated the view that the Gita preached non-violence and that it was an allegory.

Expressing his opinion, Aurobindo observed: "So Sri Krishna says to Arjun, 'You may kill the bad passions or evil tendencies, but do not be sorry, really they are not going to be killed! Who kills whom?' Thus the whole thing is an allegory. But is it?"

In his reply to Gandhi, Aurobindo further observed: "Nonviolence is not in the Gita. If as some people, including the Mahatma, say the Gita signifies a spiritual war or battle only, then what of *Apariharyerthe* and *Hanyamane sarire*—'inevitable circumstance' and 'body being killed'? What of *Shoka*—the sorrow—for those who are dead? To me such a reading seems the result of a defect in their mental attitude."[2] Aurobindo, a great authority on Indian philosophy, was provoked to pass this harsh remark on Gandhi's stand. Veer Savarkar, who ruthlessly criticized Gandhian views on non-violence, said that Gandhi's interpretation of Gita was irrational, as the Mahatma's mind was too unscientific to interpret the Gita. Most people deprecated Gandhi's interpretation of the Gita and some held Gandhi to be a Christian in disguise.

Just then the English translation of the French biography *Mahatma Gandhi* by Romain Rolland was published. Speaking of it, Aurobindo said that such European writers as Romain Rolland were airy, wandering in their thought. Romain Rolland appeared to Aurobindo not such a great intellect as he was reputed to be.[3] On February 24, 1924, Romain Rolland wrote to Mahadev Desai that he should be excused if there were some mistakes in the biography. Gandhi wrote to the French author that his book demonstrated once more the essential oneness of human nature though flourishing under different skies.

As regards *brahmacharya*, Gandhi said in an article at this time in *Young India* that the person who observed *brahmacharya* in thought, speech and action was totally free from disease. "Had I acquired," he added, "complete mastery over my thoughts, I would not have been during the last ten years, afflicted with the three diseases of pleurisy, dysentery and appendicitis. I believe that the body encasing a healthy *atman* is bound to be healthy." Upon this Aurobindo said that Gandhi's article did not contain consistent thought. "Once he says," he added, "that a strong mind has a strong body and then he says that as one progresses in mental development the body must get weak."[4]

Gandhi expressed his opinion that the Sikhs and Jains were a part of the Hindu community. He was sorry for those Sikhs and Jains who claimed separate identity for their sects. He advised the delegates to the Rajput Conference to devote themselves to the welfare of the poor. He offered bitter pills to Kathiawad, he said, which was a little part of Maha Gujarat. Gandhi further observed: "If Maha Gujarat did not swallow them, to which other province can I offer them, which province can I call upon to test the efficacy of my medicine?" The Kathiawad leaders, however, were far from reconciled.

Just at this time the Muslim League, which used to meet during the Congress session in a nearby pandal, now held its session at Lahore in May 1924 under the presidentship of Jinnah who had no place in Gandhi's Congress. Jinnah had helped Motilal Nehru in the Central Assembly to defeat the Government on several counts. Presiding over the Muslim League session, Jinnah declared that Swaraj was almost an interchangeable term with Hindu-Muslim unity. The Muslim League, which had been outshone by the Khilafat Committee was coming again to the front and moving away from the Gandhian Congress.

Gandhi now felt it necessary to express his views on Hindu-Muslim unity, which was proving to be a mirage. Gandhi developed his congenital fear into a thesis, and declared in his article on "Hindu-Muslim Tension: Its cause and cure" in *Young India* of May 29: "My own experience but confirms the opinion that the Mussalman as a rule is a bully, and the Hindu as a rule is a coward. But I as a Hindu am more ashamed of Hindu cowardice than I am angry at the Mussalman bullying." Thus Gandhi's misconceived ideas which he had formed in his boyhood, now fully developed into a dogma. It did not occur to Gandhi, who never studied history, that if the Hindus had been cowards they would not have been able to shake off their foreign rulers including the Muslims. Many British historians say that the British conquered India from the Marathas and not from the Muslims. But it was a fact that this attempt at Hindu-Muslim unity, although on a wrong basis, was the first notable one since that of Akbar, the Mogul emperor.

IT WAS NOW said that Gandhi's policy was responsible for the Muslim atrocities in Malabar, Multan, Saharanpur, Agra, Ajmer and elsewhere. Because he identified himself with the Khilafat question it gained an importance it would never have had otherwise. His association with it unified and awakened the Muslims and gave prestige to the Maulavis which they did not have before. Now that the Khilafat question was over, the awakened and organized Muslims proclaimed a kind of Jehad against the Hindus. Gandhi was blamed for this by foreign correspondents as well as Indian.

Unrepentant and dogmatic, Gandhi declared in *Young India* of May 29, 1924: "Had I been a prophet and foreseen all that has happened, I should have still thrown myself into the Khilafat question." He had declared his wish to sacrifice a million people for his principles and the number of Hindus killed so far was in thousands! So he said that he did not plead guilty to the charges against him.

Gandhi attributed these atrocities to a general lack of faith in non-violence and added that non-violence was the aim of all religions. The remedy against cowardice, Gandhi said, was not physical culture but the braving of dangers. "Let Hindus run risks and even, at times, get killed in so doing. They should not organize Hindu goondas for defence. The Bania and the Brahmin must learn to defend himself even violently, if not non-violently, or surrender his women folk and possessions to the goondas. The Hindus should not use the Untouchables, who generally do not fear death, as a shield against anticipated Muslim attack." This was his advice to the Hindus.

In the same article Gandhi declared that he was warned against Pandit Madan Mohan Malaviya whom the Muslims considered a friend of the Muslims. Gandhi pointed out that Malaviya was no enemy of the Muslims. He declared that Lala Lajpatrai was also distrusted, but he was no enemy of the Muslims although he doubted the immediate attainment of Hindu-Muslim unity. Gandhi then attacked Swami Shraddhanand and the Arya Samaj. He said Shraddhanand was distrusted by Muslims. He made irritating speeches, he was hasty and easily ruffled, and his bravery was unquestioned but he made his Hinduism narrow. The Arya Samajist flourished not because of the inherent merit of the teachings of *Satyarth Prakash*, but because of the grand and lofty character of the founder! He described the Arya Samajists and Shraddhanand as pugnacious, and expressed his opinion that in spite of those drawbacks, he did not regard Shraddhanand as past praying for.

This was an unworthy attack on Shraddhanand and an indirect provocation to his enemies to oppose him. Gandhi thus unjustly accused these Hindu leaders of incitement to crimes for which his own policy was mainly responsible. On them had fallen the responsibility of defending the Hindus against the Muslim fanatics. For the previous five years Gandhi and the Khilafatists had been feeding and inflaming the religious fanaticism of the Muslims through their medieval priests who raised their old-world superstitions and fanaticism to the highest pitch!

To compensate the Hindus for his attack on Hindu and Arya-Samajist leaders Gandhi had to say something about Muslim leaders also. He highly praised the Ali Brothers. According to Gandhi, they were passionately fond of Islam but were no haters of other religions, and were capable of loving the meanest of God's creatures. Their pan-Islamism was not anti-Hindu. Mahomed Ali's Cocanada address, in which he demanded an equal division of the Untouchables into Hindu and Muslim, was highly objectionable but, Gandhi added, Mahomed Ali acknowledged that it was an error. Gandhi loved the Ali Brothers in spite of their faults. Only Abdul Bari, he said, could be a dangerous friend.

Gandhi blamed the Arya Samajists for their *shuddhi* movement although he kept mum on the *tabligh.* In his opinion, there was no such thing as proselytism in Hinduism as it was understood in Christianity or to a lesser extent in Islam. The fact was that the *shuddhi* movement was a reaction to the missionary movement and to the *tabligh* movement started for the conversion of the Hindus by unlawful inducements. Gandhi was not frank enough to say so. To save the cow, the Hindus should befriend the Muslims and leave it to Muslim honour to save the cow. Hindus, living as they did in glass houses, Gandhi continued, had no right to throw stones at their Muslim neighbours. Because the Hindus denied even elementary rights to the Untouchables, God had punished them. God's ways were inscrutable, and their woes were due to the black sin of untouchability.

Gandhi then disclosed how the Agakhani movement converted the illiterate Hindus by unlawful inducements. But Gandhi did not fail to eulogize Islam to please the Muslims. He said that the history of Islam, even if it showed aberrations from its moral height, had many a brilliant page. In its glorious days it was not intolerant. When the West was sunk in darkness, a bright star rose in the Eastern firmament and gave light and comfort to a suffering world. If Islam had become gross and fanatical here, Gandhi added, let the Hindus admit that they had no small share in making it so. Gandhi, who had learnt a lesson at the hands of Muslims in South Africa, never forgot it, and playing the role of a historian which he was not, blamed the Hindus instead of blaming the gross and fanatical methods of Muslim fanatics who offered them either Islam or the sword!

The reaction of the Hindu leaders to this homily was pungent. It evoked furious criticism from them. They renewed their charge against Gandhi of partiality to Mussalmans and added that he was flattering the Mussalmans for gaining a political end. The Arya Samajists vehemently attacked him. The Hindu friends of Gandhi told him that unity was impossible so long as he trusted the Ali Brothers and Abdul Bari. Upon this Gandhi said that he had described Bari as a dangerous friend, but not vain, untruthful and unreliable. He added, however, that the Muslims were not enjoined by the Koran to slaughter cows.

Gandhi enthusiastically condemned writings like *Rangila Rasul* which were written in Urdu and were full of abuse and caricature of the Prophet, but he kept silent on the pamphlet *Sitaka Chhinal* describing the goddess Sita as a prostitute.[5] In conclusion, Gandhi asked the Hindus to buy peace from the Muslims and give peace to the Untouchables. Like borrowed clothes which do not suit us well, purchased peace does not last long. Friendship is never bought. To last long, it has to cement two hearts. Gandhi tried to bring the two religions together by praising Islam, but he fell short of bringing the hearts of the followers of the two religions together.

This time, however, he gave the proper sort of scolding to his brother cow-worshippers. He reasonably and rightly asked them to pay attention to feeding the cattle properly, to preventing cruelty, to the preservation of the fast disappearing pasture land and to improving the breed of cattle, turning the *panjrapoles* into model self-supporting dairies. Some Gandhians, like Jamnalal Bajaj, who later established Gosalas, turned to improving the breed of cattle. As Gandhi said that Hindus should give up organizing themselves, taking to the gymnasium and making preparations for fighting back against the Muslims, the Gandhian zealots took to opposing Hindu youth taking physical exercise lest they aggravate Hindu-Muslim tensions! Gandhi not only did this but also recanted his statement in relation to Muslims by stating that he did not regard every Mussalman as a bully!

JUST AT THIS moment two great contemporaries of Gandhi had started their work for the reorganization of Hindu society on the basis of social equality, reason, liberty and fraternity. One was Savarkar, who had been removed from the Andamans Cellular Jail in May 1921 to Yervada Jail and in January 1924 was interned at Ratnagiri. From jail Savarkar sent the manuscript of his immortal work *Hindutva* which was published when its author was still in jail. The book became the Bible of the All-India Hindu movement, was hailed by Indian leaders as a great book and an outstanding contribution to Hindu thought and philosophy. It gave a tremendous stimulus to Hindu nationalism and consolidation.

Savarkar's great book was both a result of his deep reflection and an intense reaction to Gandhism which had helped to revive Muslim reactionaries and fed their fanaticism. In June 1924 Savarkar started his movement for social equality and abolition of untouchability. He wrote powerful essays on the scientific and secular outlook, advocating the abolition of the caste system and exposing the injustice and hollowness of rigid customs, decayed traditions and the time-worn, scripture-born outlook. He fearlessly and unequivocally championed the cause of the Untouchables.

Savarkar started a temple-entry movement in favour of the Untouchables and bravely fought the social no-changers. He denounced Gandhism for its doctrine of absolute non-violence, and bitingly ridiculed its pro-Muslim policy. It so happened that Kaka Kalelkar and Gandhi cautioned Appasaheb Patwardhan of Ratnagiri not to be swayed by Savarkar's views. Gandhi told Patwardhan to be cautious about Savarkar's views as, according to Gandhi, Savarkar was a deep one. Patwardhan regarded Savarkar as his inspirer. Patwardhan was known in Maharashtra as one of Gandhi's chief disciples.

Another great force demanding a social revolution arose at this time in the form of the revolutionary leadership of Dr. B. R. Ambedkar. He started his movement for abolishing untouchability and the reorganization of Hindu society on the basis of social equality, fraternity and liberty. The movement launched by Savarkar for social revolution and the movement inaugurated by Ambedkar greatly counteracted the work of Gandhi in that field. Savarkar's stand on the reorganization of Hindu society and his vehement opposition to Gandhi's policy regarding Hindu-Muslim unity had repercussions in the thinking of those leaders who were opposing Gandhian policy. Gandhi's orthodox views on the uplift of Untouchables paled before the revolutionary role of Savarkar. Gandhi's lukewarm attitudes could not be sustained against Ambedkar who soon grew to be the indisputable champion of the depressed classes and the downtrodden, and his social philosophy was an antidote to Gandhism.

While putting the major blame for the disruption of Hindu-Muslim unity on some Hindu leaders, Gandhi now devoted himself more energetically to the causes that led to the failure of his non-co-operation movement. For a few days after his release, he studied the situation. He gradually realized how rigid and determined the opposition of his devotees was to Das and Motilal Nehru. His first stand was that he supported the Bardoli resolution without being opposed to Council entry. But three months later he became determined to crush the promoters of Council entry. He chose to give battle to his opponents at Ahmedabad by calling a meeting of the All-India Congress Committee at the end of June 1924. He then launched an assault on the Swaraj Party led by Das and Motilal Nehru by declaring that the executive organization of the Congress must not contain titled persons, Government schoolmasters, practising lawyers, members of Legislative bodies and persons who used foreign cloth or even cloth manufactured in Indian mills and those who dealt in such cloth.

In fact Gandhi now wanted to rid the Congress of all those who had no implicit faith in his five boycotts, namely mill-spun cloth, Government law courts, Government schools, titles and Legislative bodies. It also was his view that many Congress executive bodies did not believe in non-violence; they would not allow him to interpret peaceful to mean non-violence and "legitimate" to mean truthful. He said that those who did not believe in the five boycotts should resign from the Congress executive bodies. He did not hesitate to say that the Congress would contain two parties, but without a split.

The new interpretation of the meaning of 'peaceful' and 'legitimate' meant a change in the constitution adopted at the Nagpur session in 1920. Gandhi wanted to fit those words into his concept of non-violence. This point later proved decisive in the resignation of Gandhi from the Congress in 1934.

So the last stage of Gandhi's first phase of leadership began with this challenge. Das and Nehru accepted the challenge with proper respect for this great leader. The other side said that the practice of the five boycotts was unjust, confused and impossible. Ultimately, Gandhi had no objection to a doctor becoming a member of the All-India Congress Committee or a member of the executive, although the doctor used foreign medicines. Gandhi had no objection to an agent of foreign sugar or an agent of foreign motor-cars, becoming members of the All-India Congress Committee, but he took exception to lawyers becoming members of the All-India Congress Committee. And a person who did not spin about 10 tolas of yarn in a day was not fit for membership of the Congress. Aurobindo described this purification as absurd and humorously added, "one can follow up this kind of proposal by saying, 'All the members must produce a certificate that they have cooked their own food, cleaned their latrines, etc'."[6]

The Congress dictator was determined to purge the advocates of Council entry. By then Hakim Ajmal Khan, Dr. Ansari, Sarojini Naidu, Jawaharlal Nehru, Abul Kalam Azad and T. Prakasam had assumed the role of the central party in the Congress. Although they were in favour of Gandhi, they acted as mediators between the no-changers and the pro-changers. Would they play the same role now?

Gandhi delivered the inaugural address at the Gujarat Vidyapith on June 10. He told the students that for a slave there was no happiness even in his dreams. Knowledge was that which led to salvation. They should resolve in their mind that, if it became necessary, they would earn their livelihood by doing the work of a scavenger or a weaver, but would do nothing unworthy in their lives. They should abandon their professors if they found that they had come to make money or to show off their learning. If they had faith, they should not worry what would happen to their parents, their brothers and sisters. They would eat only after the relatives had something to eat. In the end Gandhi proudly declared that the Gujarat Vidyapith was a model for the whole country.

As the day of the A.I.C.C. meeting was drawing near, Gandhi was growing restless. He was out to defeat the Swarajists and drive them out of the Congress. So he published in *Young India* on June 16, the draft resolutions he wanted to move in the A.I.C.C. First he wanted to impose compulsory spinning on the members, secondly, to put drastic restrictions on the working of the office-bearers of the Congress, thirdly, to enforce the five boycotts and fourthly, to condemn the act of Gopinath Saha who had shot on January 12, 1924 Earnest Day, an Englishman, in a crowded street of Calcutta, mistaking him for Teggart, the Commissioner of Police.

Gandhi's arrest had led to the revival of the revolutionary movement in Bengal. The Bengal Provincial Conference held at the end of May 1924 at Serajganj paid respectful homage to the patriotism and sacrifice of Gopinath Saha who suffered capital punishment in connection with Day's murder. Das felt impelled to support the resolution. And the whole country was agog! Gandhi called Gopinath Saha a misleading patriot although he held the selflessness, defiance of death and love of the country of such revolutionaries to be unquestionable, and added that if the revolutionaries gave him their enthusiastic support, they would deserve homage not merely for their motives but also for their acts which could be emulated by the least of their countrymen.

Gandhi said that in taking decisions on the above mentioned resolutions, he should not be spared, his past services should not be considered if he was in the wrong. Without bias or false emotion or sentiment they should approach their task. This was the acid test for his followers, and a challenge to the Swarajists. He threatened that if there were equal votes on either side he would leave the Congress. He said he would not hesitate to turn the Congress into an exclusively khaddar-producing and khaddar-propaganda organization till the attainment of Swaraj. His Swaraj was to keep intact the genius of Indian civilization.

THE A.I.C.C. MET at Ahmedabad at the end of June 1924 and Gandhi moved his first resolution telling the Congress leaders that he was doing so at the risk of creating a split in the country and parting company with the dearest of his friends. "You must," he added, "either choose another leader or accept my conditions. I have stated that a constitution should be held sacred only as long as it helps us to progress." As regards khadi, he said that it was through it that they could forge a close bond with the masses in the country. If he came to see that the spinning wheel was an impediment in the winning of Swaraj, he would immediately set fire to it. That way, he concluded, he was an iconoclast, and in that sense a Muslim. He wanted, he concluded, to die as the country's purest man. That was his aspiration. And Gandhi, who talked of democracy and advised others not to leave the Congress but to convert the majority to their views, warned: "If you reject me today, you will see me walk out cheerfully, with no complaint, no bitterness. Staying outside, I shall try and raise an independent organization or body."

Motilal Nehru and Das protested against Gandhi's insistence on the penal clause directed unconstitutionally against those who did not spin and produce ten tolas of yarn. Although they accepted the utility of charkha, they decried its exaggerated importance in politics. So the Swarajists in a body walked out before the spinning resolution was put to the vote. It was carried by 67, against 37 votes. The fact was that the Swarajists who walked out plus those who voted against it formed a clear majority.

Gandhi recoiled from the situation he had created. A sense of justice and qualms of conscience troubled his mind. And he immediately got the A.I.C.C. to rescind the penal clause as he did not wish to carry his point with a false majority. This was his first defeat in the Congress. Shuaib Qureshi said that it was not proper for the dignity of the House to rescind its own resolution which it had passed a few minutes earlier! The other two resolutions were settled by compromise.

Gandhi's discomfiture did not end here. He was shocked when he faced bitter opposition in regard to his resolution on Gopinath Saha whom he had styled a misleading patriot. Das led the bitter opposition to it. Gandhi's resolution was carried by 78 votes to 70, by a narrow majority indeed! But Gandhi learnt the lesson of his life when he moved a resolution to make an inconsistent exception in favour of one of his lieutenants, Gangadhar Deshpande, who was fighting a case in court, in contravention of Resolution No. 3 regarding the observance of the five boycotts which the A.I.C.C. had passed. A point of order was raised by one of Gandhi's own disciples, and Mahomed Ali ruled out Gandhi's resolution as unconstitutional!

Gandhi's resolution was thrown out! He was utterly shocked. It was a cup of poison, he said, and he drank it. "I asked myself" he exclaimed, "O! poor creature! Do you serve God or Satan? Why do you trouble yourself in this way?"[7] He then paused a while and burst into tears. Seeing this, his lieutenants and colleagues too shed pious tears. Gandhi sighed, "Let me be relieved of the leadership." At this, all the Gandhian orthodox no-changers knelt before Gandhi and at the instance of Abul Kalam Azad entreated him not to leave them although some of them had let him down. Mahomed Ali placed his cap at the feet of Gandhi. In Gandhi's camp there were adulators and hypocrites who had utterly failed either to give effect to Gandhi's constructive programme or to stand by it irrevocably. That was the official end of Gandhi's civil disobedience movement which was brought about not only by the active opposition to it of the Swarajists but also by the inactivity and demoralization of those who professed to follow him!

Describing this tragedy, Gandhi observed in *Young India* of July 3, 1924, "Then I sank within me. I felt that God was speaking to me through them and seemed to say, 'Thou fool, knowest not thou that thou are impossible? Thy time is up'." . . . In a short speech in Hindustani, he said: "I lay bare my heart and let them see the blood oozing out of it. It takes much to make me weep. I try to suppress tears even when there is occasion for them. But, in spite of all my efforts to be brave, I broke down utterly .... It was the saddest speech I had ever made .... I saw that I was utterly defeated and humbled."

After this saddest day in his life, Gandhi said that it was his innermost wish to retire from the Congress and confine his activity merely to Hindu-Muslim unity, khaddar and untouchability. With a majority at his disposal, Gandhi was a dictator-cum-democrat. With a minority at his disposal, he was never a democrat. He then abjured democracy! Although he had desperately tried to transform the Congress politicians into a clan of spinners, he was not satisfied with that. He expected all the best Brahmins to unwind India from the coil of the mercantile cobra! In his dreams, in his sleep, while eating, he thought of the spinning wheel which he styled his non-violent sword and symbol of liberty. Aurobindo Ghose had a dig at the plight of the Gandhian politicians and said that the quota of 3,000 yards of yarn a month was possible if spinning by proxy was allowed. A leader's wife or daughter, he added, might do it for him!

Gandhi then learned that Motilal Nehru had returned to wine-drinking, and Motilal was reported to have said, "water has been called pure. But wine is made after being thrice distilled, it is, therefore, purer than water." Upon this Gandhi wrote to Motilal Nehru on July 3, 1924, "I know that if a man drinks privately, he may drink publicly too. A public man, however, may not drink publicly, if he is likely to offend. I distinguish between private drinking and secret drinking." Motilal Nehru sharply retorted, "To me, it is clear that deceiving men by keeping up false appearances is worse than offending them, and I must express my utter inability to understand how you can possibly reconcile yourself to the suggestion that I might drink privately at all. I must also respectfully differ from the distinction you draw between private drinking and secret drinking. In my humble opinion, it is a distinction without a difference." Motilal was brave and fearless and never pretended to be a saint. He hated hypocrisy.

A little while earlier, Gandhi had discussed publicly whether they should look into a leader's private life unless he committed a mistake in his public life. Since the movement they had launched was of self-purification it would be correct to think that a leader's private life was not distinct from his public life.[8] They were reformers, and it was an ancient and correct belief that a reformer's private life ought to be pure. Tilak was of the opinion that if they looked into the private life of public men and decided to admit as members of the Congress only those who were morally good, the Congress would not get even a handful of such men. They, Tilak added, should ask a man whether he wanted Swaraj.[9] Then he should be accepted as a member. How many men Gandhi would have with him if he strictly applied his test to his colleagues and his disciples was a difficult question to answer.

Gandhi failed to capture the machinery of the Congress. His belief that charkha was a panacea for all the ills of the country was rejected by the Congress. It was now also proved beyond doubt that for the Congress as a whole the non-violent method was not and could not be a religion, an unchallengeable creed or dogma. It could be a policy and a method. No political party could adopt such a creed. The author and originator of absolute non-violent non-co-operation was made to realize the stark realities, but for a decade more he held to his view and kept trying in vain to convert the Indian political intelligentsia to the ritualism of non-violence.

At the end of July 1924, Gandhi once again discussed the use of the loin-cloth. He declared that he could not lay it aside till he had won Swaraj. When he started wearing it, he did fear that it would be labelled indecent. He wished, he said, to be in tune with the life of the poorest of the poor.

Hindu-Muslim riots broke out in Nagpur and Delhi in the middle of July 1924. Gandhi was sad, lost weight to an alarming extent, and wrote to a friend, "I am seeking means of exit from the Congress without a fireworks display." The presidentship of the Congress was offered to him, but he hesitated to accept it. He wanted to capture the Maharashtra party which was, according to him, well drilled, had a determined policy and a record of great sacrifices behind it. He wrote to Motilal Nehru requesting him to consult Das and N. C. Kelkar whether he should accept the presidentship of the Congress, while he suggested the name of Sarojini Naidu for it. But Sarojini had said of him that he should not needlessly interfere in politics. He was, she added, a saint and he should be satisfied with the homage the people paid him.[10]

About this time a reporter gave out some wrong information about Gandhi's statement on Malabar floods and Gandhi wrote to Natarajan on August 6, 1924: "I felt like shooting the reporter when I saw the wire. But as it is against my creed to do so, I subsided." Yet non-violence was to be observed in thought, word and deed! After all Gandhi was a human being belonging to this world!

Another strange thing Gandhi did at this time was the opposition he offered to the scheme of compulsory primary education as all compulsion was hateful to him. Congressmen had captured the Municipalities all over India, and Jawaharlal Nehru, C. R. Das, Sardar Patel were Presidents of Municipalities in their home towns. There the question of compulsory primary education arose. Gandhi said compulsion was certainly unnecessary. Before trying compulsion, he observed, they should try voluntary primary education. At this time Gandhi criticized the immoral opium policy of the Indian Government and pleaded for the total abolition of traffic in opium for the purposes of revenue. He supported the movement launched by Miss La Motte who was trying to reduce the world's growth of opium to the level of medical necessity and had convened a conference at Geneva.

Gandhi was terribly disheartened at this time. He said it

would not be surprising if he were assassinated during the year. On August 16, 1924, he left for Delhi to bring about a settlement on the communal question. But it seems he could not do much beyond giving an interview to the Associated Press of India. He was moved by the desecration of temples. He said he was both an idolator and an iconoclast. He believed in idol-worship which uplifted the human race and broke idolatry which refused others to worship their deities. These desecrations were creating deep wounds in his heart. He asked the Muslims to remember that Islam was judged by their conduct and that religion was more than life.

On his return to Ahmedabad, Gandhi was presented with an address by the Ahmedabad Municipality and on August 29 by the Bombay Municipality. Gandhi said at a Bombay meeting held to honour him on August 31: "You regard me as a Mahatma, not because of my truth, nor for my non-violence but my deep attachment for the poorest of the poor. Whatever happens, I can never desert the poor in their rags." For him humanitarian service was religion. But his humanitarianism sprang from his devotion to God. "My movement is not atheist. It is not a denial of God." This was a reply to those who said that Gandhi was introducing revolutionary Bolshevism in India. Upon this M. N. Roy replied to Gandhi, "Bolshevism is not a gospel of God. Bolshevism is prepared to leave God alone, if He and His agents on earth agree not to meddle in things temporal. But if they do not agree to be satisfied with their super-material position and seek to make trouble on earth, Bolshevism will preach atheism to liberate the masses from the snare of ignorance woven by religion."[11]

In a rejoinder, Gandhi said that he believed in conversion of mankind and not its destruction, and he could no more tolerate the yoke of Bolshevism as described by Roy than of capitalism. Mobocracy, Gandhi concluded, was autocracy multiplied a million times. Gandhi visited Poona, where the opposition to Gandhian *charkha* was increasing rapidly. Gandhi was reluctant to accept the presidentship of the Belgaum Congress. His mind was distracted. He said that the sorrow of Goethe's Margaret represented his own. He sang with her "My peace is gone, and my heart is sore."

COMMUNAL RIOTS WERE stalking the land. Hindu-Muslim unity proved a day-dream. The Mahatma's advice fell on deaf ears. On September 9 and 10, the Muslims at Kohat in the Punjab barbarously slaughtered a number of Hindus. With great anguish in his heart, Gandhi observed: "Our non-co-operation has taken the form of non-co-operation in practice with one another instead of with the Government."

Horrified by the atrocities in Kohat, Gandhi reached Delhi on September 14, 1924. Light came to him like a flash, and he undertook a purificatory fast of 21 days at Mahomed Ali's residence in Delhi. Gandhi said he might be charged with having committed a breach of faith with the Hindus. He had asked them to settle quarrels by dying and not by killing. He said his fast was penance. He blamed only himself. Since his non-violence was imperfect, he saw violence around him. Defeated and helpless, he must submit his petition to God who had been dethroned. Opposition to his ideals was rising in the Congress. He had lost control over the situation.

Gandhi's fast naturally created a great sensation in the country. A Unity Conference was hurriedly held at Delhi on September 27 and it passed a resolution deploring the fratricidal strife. The conference laid down some principles of settlement and detailed instructions regarding the question of conversions and re-conversions, playing music before mosques, and cow-slaughter. It appointed also a Central National Panchayat of six leaders with Gandhi as the President with powers to add to their members upto 15, to inquire into and to settle all disputes and differences where necessary and desirable.

The Unity Conference and some deputations appealed to Gandhi to give up this fast but to no purpose. He promised Motilal Nehru he would break his fast if his life were at any time really in danger; for, he said, he did not want to die but to live and serve, a purer and a better man.

On October 6 Gandhi said that Napoleon found himself a prisoner and the mighty Kaiser a private gentleman. Man was nothing! He also told a student of Andrews that Oscar Wilde saw the highest art simply in outward forms and therefore succeeded in beautifying immorality.

On October 8, at twelve noon, Gandhi broke his fast with a cup of lemon juice amidst a religious atmosphere created by the chanting of Koran verses, Christian hymns, and Vedic songs. Breaking his fast, Gandhi observed: "My prayer is that God will give me the chance to cement this unity with my life, if necessary. The Hinduism that refuses to live in peace with Islam is no religion at all, and Islam is worth nothing if it refuses to tolerate Hinduism." The end of the fast was more than dramatic. Mahomed Ali presented Gandhi with a cow purchased from a butcher for being sent to a *panjrapole*.[12]

Gandhi was now turning away from direct action. The tug-of-war between the two wings of the Congress for control of the organization continued. Gandhi's hold on the Congress was slackening. He was, he said, sick of it. He wrote to Rajaji that they should not resist the Swarajists, they should abdicate power. He said that there was no fight left in him. The no-changers called it surrender. He said he was putting an undue strain upon the loyalty of his colleagues. "We must stoop," he argued, "to conquer. Service requires no power, no office, no prestige. It should be the balm to the lacerated heart of Rajaji."

Just then the Government of Bengal issued an ordinance on October 25, 1924, authorising arrest and detention without warrant or trial of persons on mere suspicion to suppress the revolutionary activities in the Province. Das described it as a lawless law. Under it, nearly eighty young men including Subhas Bose, who was Chief Officer of the Calcutta Corporation, and a large number of workers belonging to the Swarajist Party were interned. Violence begot violence and because of such legislative violence, Das said, the revolutionary crimes increased. On November 2, 1924, Gandhi left Delhi for Calcutta, and as the repression there inspired a unity between the two wings, Gandhi made a pact with Das and Motilal Nehru on November 6. The Gandhian wing allowed the Swarajists to carry on their Council entry programme and the Swarajists accepted to support the constructive programme; and the introduction of daily spinning and in case of illness by any other person, and to wearing hand-spun and hand-woven khaddar at political and Congress functions as a qualification for the membership. Gandhi declared that neither party could do without the other.

Defending this pact, he said in *Young India* of November 13: "I thank God that He gave me strength to surrender to the Swarajists all that it was possible for me to surrender, much more than I or many friends had expected." He appreciated the grit, discipline, cohesion and defiance of the Swarajists.

Gandhi's critics said that the pact was an ignominious surrender. To his dogmatic colleagues it was a lapse if not a betrayal. According to Gandhi, the pact was an admission of the fact that the Swaraj Party was a strong and growing wing of the Congress.

Having signed the pact, Gandhi accepted the presidentship

of the forthcoming Belgaum session of the Congress. As suggested in the Calcutta pact, an All-party conference was convened at Bombay on November 21 and 22 to forge an united front against the Government. The All-party Conference condemned the policy of repression and appointed a committee to consider the best way of reuniting all political parties.

At this time Gandhi tried his best to ease the tension between Jawaharlal Nehru and Motilal Nehru. The elder Nehru was in an irritable mood. Gandhi said he did not want to be the cause, direct or indirect, of the slightest breach in the wonderful affection between father and son. The thought of the mental distraction of Jawaharlal hurt Gandhi who told him that it made him unhappy to see Motilal unhappy. Gandhi firmly stood by the Nehrus in spite of his differences with them.

In the last week of December 1924, Gandhi presided over the Belgaum session of the Congress. As President, he said a few words and sat down, as copies of his presidential address had been distributed the previous day. The Congress ratified the Gandhi-Das pact, Vithalbhai Patel and Lajpatrai voting with the minority, Vithalbhai Patel said that they had no right to exclude from the Congress any man who had no faith in khaddar. Lajpatrai said that the pact was a bundle of inconsistencies. In his presidential address Gandhi said he would strive for Swaraj within the Empire, but would not hesitate to sever all connections, if severance became a necessity through Britain's own fault.

Gandhi justified the necessity for suspending the non-cooperation movement and allowing the Swarajists to be a wing of the Congress. The Swarajists accepted the spinning franchise which was shorn of its rigidities. Das said that his faith in spinning was robust and Motilal said he must confess that most of the Swarajists had a suspicion that this franchise would not work properly. When Motilal said that Gandhi was their general, all laughed! But Lajpatrai said that if Gandhi was their leader, the Swaraj Party had no right to exist at all. Gandhi attended the Hindu Mahasabha session held in the Congress pandal at Belgaum. The Congress also entertained and heard the deputation of Buddhists of Ceylon. Their leader Pereira pleaded that the possession of the Buddha temple at Buddha Gaya should vest in the hands of Buddhists. Gandhi was in favour of the demand, and Rajendra Prasad was requested to submit his report on the matter early as ordained by the Cocanada Congress.

CHAPTER XXIX

In the Doldrums

After His Struggle against them for eight months, Gandhi's surrender to Das and Motilal was so complete that Lord Reading the Viceroy wrote jubilantly, on January 1, 1925: "Gandhi is now attached to the tail of Das and Nehru although they try their utmost to make him and his supporters think that he is one of the heads, if not the head. It is pathetic to observe the rapid decline in the power of Gandhi and the frantic attempts he is now making to cling to his position as leader at the expense of practically every principle he has hitherto advocated."[1] The Viceroy believed in Gandhi's sincerity as well as his devotion to high ideals, and held him to be an ethical teacher, but he doubted the political wisdom of his leadership and felt that personal vanity still played far too important a part in his modes of thinking.

The waning in Gandhi's influence was a fact. The no-changers were depressed. There was no fight left in the masses as their enthusiasm had cooled down for want of action and guidance. Gandhi's over-emphasis on cow-protection and on the virtues of the spinning wheel (that it would bring salvation to the country) had repelled the intelligentsia. Non-co-operation was dead.

The Council-wreckers were gradually turning towards the right. Although the Swaraj Party promised in its early stage an aggressive fight like the one offered by the Irish Council-wreckers, its leaders began to turn moderate. Gandhi, who always preferred the Nehrus to Das, promised help and strength to Motilal Nehru in controlling the Congress organization. Having lost his hold on the Congress, Gandhi decided to do propaganda in favour of *charkha* and abolition of untouchability, the question of Hindu-Muslim unity being relegated to the background. Yet he resolutely repeated his living faith in it and said he did not despair of the situation and still hoped that unity was coming. At the moment he could not arrive at a workable solution and so he waited for its arrival like an old fisherman, who, tired of his long patient waiting, clings to the hope of a successful bait.

Early in January 1925, Gandhi visited Dohad, Godhra and Bhavnagar talking of yarn, khadi and untouchability. At the Kathiawad Political Conference on January 8, he declared: "Swaraj as conceived by me does not mean the end of Kingship. Nor does it mean the end of capital. Accumulated capital means ruling power. I am for the establishment of right relations between capital and labour. I do not wish for the supremacy of the one over the other."

On January 23, 1925, Gandhi presided over the meeting of the All-Party Conference Committee which considered the appointment of a sub-committee to draw up a plan for Swaraj and Hindu-Muslim unity. On the next day a sub-committee was appointed with Motilal Nehru as Secretary and Gandhi as President. It was however declared adjourned by Gandhi and Nehru till March 2.

Eminent men, who were interested in Gandhi's work, viewed his life sympathetically. Wilfred Wellock observed in the *Socialist Review* that the theory of non-violence, which Gandhi applied in a mass direction and on a gigantic scale, was his real contribution to modern civilization. He said Gandhi was first and foremost a saint, something of a thinker, and also a man of action and superior to Tolstoy in his exposition of non-violence.[2]

While Wilfred Wellock was extolling Gandhi to the skies, the orthodox Hindus, at a meeting in Bombay, declared that those who wanted to abolish untouchability were heretics. Some of the speakers wanted even to lynch the heretics, including Gandhi.

Gandhi and Shaukat Ali visited Rawalpindi in the first week of March 1925 to inquire into the causes that led to the Kohat riots. Gandhi and Shaukat Ali came to different conclusions on the same evidence and Gandhi suggested that the matter should be referred to Dr. Ansari or Hakim Ajmal Khan for their opinion. At last Gandhi published his statement on March 19, 1925, contrary to the advice of Hakim Ajmal Khan and Motilal Nehru. Gandhi could not condone the looting, arson and conversions of the Hindus but Shaukat Ali treated it all lightly. This had unhappy repercussions on the general atmosphere in the country. Many riots followed and Gandhi as Chairman of the National Arbitration Board, appointed at the All-Party Conference at Delhi in September 1924, expressed regretfully his inability to advise the conflicting parties. He claimed no longer to exercise influence over the respective communities.

Gandhi asked the Hindus not to resort to physical training so that they might not disturb the Muslims. He himself had formed a Cow-protection Sabha on January 24, 1925 and become its Chairman. A few days later, he wrote to Jawaharlal Nehru, who had protested to him against his article, "God and Congress" in which Gandhi held that cow-protection meant the protection of the weak, the helpless and the deaf. The cow was a sermon on pity. The pledge that Gandhi had drawn up started with the words: "With God as my witness . . . ."

Many agnostics and Buddhists objected to the use of the word 'God' in the pledge of the Congress. They asked him to replace 'God' by 'conscience'. Gandhi replied: "To me God is truth and love; God is ethics and morality; God is fearlessness. God is the source of light and life and yet He is above and beyond all those. God is conscience. We are not. He alone is."

Jawaharlal Nehru, who thought that the religious outlook was the enemy of clear thought, said that a religious man was concerned far more with his own salvation than with the good of society and he resisted the God-idea. He wrote to Gandhi that reason should be the sole test of the truth. Gandhi replied that he did not mind reason being the sole test even though the test often bewildered and landed one in errors that bordered on superstition. "That" Gandhi added, "which gives one the greatest solace in the midst of the severest fire is God."[3]

This time Gandhi made bold enough to tell the Muslims that even the teachings of the Koran could not be exempt from criticism. The creed of Islam as expressed in a verse from the Koran said: "There is no God but Allah and Mohammed is His apostle."[4] When Indian Muslims give up this rigid view of religion as did the Muslims in Turkey, they would march with the world.

Gandhi visited Madras on his way to Vikom. The Madras Municipality presented him with an address printed on khaddar and enclosed in a khaddar casket. In reply, Gandhi said he wanted to take to Municipal life as he called himself a scavenger and believed in sanitation from more than one point of view. However, he pointed out one omission in the address. He was a humanitarian first and wanted to remain a humanitarian to the last, and among his humble services in the cause of humanity he placed khaddar in the forefront.

GANDHI EXPRESSED HIS views on journalism when he unveiled a portrait of Kasturiranga lyengar on March 9 at the office of the *Hindu*, Madras. Journalism, he declared, should never be prostituted for selfish ends, for the sake of merely earning a livelihood or worse still for amassing money. Journalism to be useful and serviceable to the country would take its definite shape and place only when it devoted its best energy to the service of the country.

Gandhi looked upon journalism as an aid to his mission of life. A few days later, he observed: "I may not write in anger or malice. I may not write idly. . . I may not write merely to excite passion. The reader can have no idea of the restraint I have to exercise from week to week in the choice of topic. and my vocabulary. Often my vanity dictates a smart expression to my anger, a harsh adjective. It is a terrible ordeal but a fine exercise to remove these weeds. Well, let the world understand that the finesse is carefully and prayerfully cultivated."[5]

Gandhi then made a tour of Travancore. He was impressed with its beautiful scenery. It was his opinion that woman in India lived nowhere in greater freedom than in Malabar, and education among women was nowhere greater than in Travancore. He was greatly pleased with the simple living and simple dress of the dowager queen-mother of Travancore, and of the prince and the young queen. Visiting several towns and villages in Travancore, he went to Vikom on March 10, 1925, and exhorted the satyagrahis to carry on their campaign till they had achieved success. The satyagraha had been going on for a year. At Vikom Gandhi was presented with an address. Yet a registered letter questioning the representative character of the address was handed over to him by post.

Gandhi suggested an alternative proposal, an arbitration, a referendum or an examination of the issue by select pundits of the Sankar Smritis. But his orthodox opponents did not agree. At a public meeting he declared that he wanted to bring the campaign to a close in the shortest possible time. Satyagraha, he added, was a method of conversion and conviction and it sought no coercion. At this time K. Kelappan Nair had come to the front as a champion of the Untouchables.

Gandhi's non-violent struggle attracted many foreign journalists and writers. Savel Ziamand had an interview with Gandhi.

The Indian people, Gandhi observed, would adopt the doctrine of non-violence "as all our ancient traditions, our epics, our history show that we are more ready to suffer than to inflict punishment on others."[6]

About this time somebody asked Gandhi to state who paid for his living and touring expenses. He said that he gave up his former mode of dress because he wished to be in tune with the life of the poorest of the poor. Answering the query about his expenses, he said: "I do make the claim that I attempt to act as I preach. But I must confess that I am not as inexpensive in my wants as I would like to be. My food since my illness costs more than it should. By no means I can call it a poor man's food. My travels too cost more than they did before my illness. I am no longer able to travel long distance third class. Nor do I travel, as I did before, without a companion. All this means not simplicity and poverty, but the reverse of it. I draw nothing from the All-India Congress Committee or the Gujarat Committee. But friends fund my travelling expenses including food and clothing."[7]

Yet Gandhi had at his disposal the biggest fund ever collected in the world by a political party, and he spent millions on political propaganda. His was an expensive leadership. Just to humour him, first class railway saloons were sometimes termed second class. Just to satisfy his love of simplicity, palaces were called huts. It is no exaggeration to say that Gandhi's menu and living were undoubtedly expensive. Nobody would have objected to his way of life or whispered a word against it as it was necessary to keep his boundless energy fresh and flowing. But since he claimed he did nothing that would not be in tune with the condition of the poor masses of India, he was often criticized for this. Sarojini Naidu once humourously but appropriately said that it took a great deal of money to keep Gandhi living in poverty![8] That trait led to the hall-mark of hypocrisy which Gandhi's followers literally continued in respect of their food and style of living.

Early in April 1925, Gandhi toured Kathiawad addressing meetings and conferences and visiting villages on his way. He met some workers devoted to khadi propaganda, saw large crowds of people barefoot, standing unmoved in the baking dust of the barren roads. The Untouchables had insufficient water for drinking, bathing and washing, and the sight agonised Gandhi.

Towards the middle of April 1925, Gandhi visited Navsari, Broach, Jambusar and other places in Gujarat. His advice to the Municipality of Jambusar was that a Municipality which ignored the Untouchables hardly deserved the name. He also declared that no association should trouble itself to present him with an address if it could not endorse his work for and among the Untouchables. He then reached Tithal for a rest after an attack of malaria.

In One Of the two most sensational statements Gandhi made in 1925, he denounced Shivaji, Rana Pratap, Ranjit Singh, Guru Govind Singh, Washington, Garibaldi, Kemal Pasha, De Valera and Lenin as misguided patriots. "By the test of the theory," he replied feverishly in *Young India* of April 9, 1925, to a revolutionary, "I do not hesitate to say that it is highly likely that had I lived as their contemporary and in the respective countries I would have called every one of them a misguided patriot, even though a successful and brave warrior."

To soften the severity of this attack, Gandhi said, "I condemn, for all climes and for all times secret murders and unfair methods even for a fair cause. Armed conspiracies against something satanic is like matching Satans against Satan. ... I disbelieve history so far as details of acts of heroes are concerned. I accept broad facts of history and draw my lessons for my conduct."

Gandhi disagreed with the methods of the historians and said: "That which is permanent and therefore necessary eludes the historian of events. Truth transcends history." So, according to Gandhi's standard, his great contemporaries and most of the great men in history were misguided patriots and he was the only rightly guided patriot. All historians prior to Gandhi's advent into politics did not know that truth transcended history!

It was Gandhi's proud refrain that "if we are to make progress, we must not repeat history but make history". With that object in view he was denegrating these men and demolishing their influence! Gandhi called himself a crank. Some of his critics scornfully called him a madman. But he never concealed his views.

Gandhi's condemning Shivaji, Pratap and Guru Govind Singh as misguided patriots deeply hurt the delicate and sacred feelings of Maharashtra which never forgave him for it. A determined opposition to Gandhi's ideology grew in Maharashtra and expressed itself bitterly. Shivaji was regarded by Indian historians and leaders as the maker of a nation and a symbol of nationalism. In the darkest period of Hindustan he alone rose and put a self-respecting Hindustan politically on the map of the world in the real sense of the term. Gandhi's lieutenant Jawaharlal Nehru followed his leader's attack on Shivaji and later had to apologize to a righteously angry Maharashtra.

In the meanwhile, Das, the leader of the Swarajists, had given a stimulus to politics in Bengal. On January 7, 1925, he had defeated the introduction of the Bengal Criminal Law Amendment Bill, but the Governor put it on the statute book. Das and his party were suspected of having sympathy with the terrorist movement and also of financing it. In his manifesto Das said he was opposed on principle to political assassinations and violence in any shape or form.

Lord Birkenhead, Secretary of State for India, referred to Das's manifesto in the House of Lords on March 31 and requested Das to take the further step of co-operating with the Government in repressing violence. Accordingly, on April 3, Das made another statement promising active propaganda against violence and stating that his efforts in that direction were bound to be ineffective unless a favourable atmosphere was created by the Government.

When Das got himself in a tight corner, Gandhi rushed to Calcutta partly to help him out and partly to annihilate the revolutionary movement in Bengal. By the introduction of the spinning franchise he wanted to bring Bengal under the control of the no-changers. On May 2 Gandhi addressed the Bengal Provincial Young Men's Conference and told the youth that he had gone there to have a heart-to-heart talk with them and to tell them that they should banish all evil thoughts from their minds. He told the All-Bengal Hindu Conference to abolish untouchability, but he cautiously added: "The removal of untouchability does never mean destruction of Varnashram Dharma (division of society into four varnas or castes and of the individual life into four stages)."

At Faridpur the Bengal Provincial Conference was held on May 3. Addressing the conference, Gandhi said they were to attain freedom not by killing, not by dying but by plodding. Das, President of the conference, spoke in favour of the ideal of Dominion Status as against independence.

Gandhi toured Bengal studying the problem of untouchability, spreading the cult of *charkha*, and impressing upon the minds of young Bengal that they would not get Swaraj by violence but by non-violence and *charkha*.

During the Bengal tour Gandhi addressed many meetings, met prominent leaders, young and old, and students, discussed social problems with caste Hindus and Untouchables. At Barisal he advised the fallen sisters to give up their immoral trade and to spin and earn their living honestly. He said that India was lost through her businessmen, but the people would recover it through them. He asked the women to tear off the *purdah.* The important personalities he met during the tour were Prafulla Chandra Ray and Satish Babu. Das's chief political heir, Subhas Bose, was in jail. Gandhi pushed his own disciple, J. M. Sengupta, into the leadership of Bengal making him President of the Bengal Provincial Congress and Mayor of Calcutta. Thus for the time being he clipped the wings of the revolutionaries and succeeded in bringing Bengal under his influence. That is why Rajaji later proudly said that it was Gandhi who killed the terrorist movement in India and not the British.[9]

Gandhi was in Bengal for nearly four months, May, June, July, and August 1925. He paid a visit to Surendranath Banerjee and greeted Tagore on his birthday on May 7. He spoke at Noakhali on May 14 blaming both parties, Hindus and Muslims, for their disunity, and declared that no power on earth could separate them if they were determined to be united.

Meantime the Vikom satyagraha proved effective. It had a good effect on their opponents and on the Travancore Government. Towards the end of May the barricades were removed and all prohibitory orders were withdrawn. The satyagrahis continued their patient struggle in the hope that all roads would be soon thrown open for the use of the Unapproachables. Ultimately they succeeded in January 1926 when the roads surrounding the temple were declared open to the Unapproachables also. Gandhi then requested K. Kelàppan Nair, the leader of the satyagrahis, to cultivate public opinion in the matter of temple entry and work for the welfare of the Untouchables.

JUST AT THIS time a calamity overtook India. In the third week of May, Das had gone to Darjeeling for a change of air. There, for five long days, Gandhi discussed with him a number of political problems. Das was expecting some great political concessions from Lord Birkenhead, but the romantic, colourful and masterful personality of Das left the stage of this world on June 16, 1925. The nation sank into grief. Gandhi led the funeral procession of two million people. A giant among men, sighed

Gandhi, had fallen and added he had realized not only how great Deshbandhu was but also how good.

On July 28 Gandhi addressed a meeting of missionaries at the Y.M.C.A. in Calcutta and declared: "I must tell you in all humility that Hinduism, as I know it, entirely satisfies my soul, fills my whole being and I find a solace in Bhagwad Gita and *Upanishads* that I miss even in the Sermon on the Mount."[10] Thus Gandhi cut his connection with the Christian missionaries and disillusioned them!

For the previous two years, the missionaries had been requesting him to explain his views on Christianity. Early in September 1924, a Roman Catholic, who was Secretary of a Catholic Indian Association, had written to Gandhi appealing to him to disclaim the comparison of him with Christ that appeared frequently in Indian nationalist papers. They had described him as the "Modern Christ". The correspondent said that Christ preached religion and not politics, was not a married man, spoke in terms of humanity and said that physical force for a righteous cause was not incompatible with the doctrines he preached. Gandhi replied that he claimed no divinity or prophetship. He was a humble seeker after truth bent upon finding it. He could not render service to the people without entering politics. He was no master, but a struggling, erring, humble servant of India and through her of humanity. He counted no sacrifice too great for the sake of seeing God face to face.

Worship of Christ and honest glorification of His message by Gandhi resulted in giving a stimulus to the work of Christian missionaries in India for years, and that is why he was hailed as a modern Jesus. Gandhi's disciples and the nationalist press were busy extolling him to godhood as were their forefathers in this land noted for creating new gods. So they compared their new god, Gandhi, with Christ the Son of God. Christ did not dabble in politics, while Gandhi breathed politics. Gandhi indulged in sexual experiments whereas Christ was above sex. The Mahatma spent crores of rupees on political propaganda whereas Christ had nothing to do with money. Christ ate and drank with men and women of every class and race. Gandhi was not in favour of inter-dining and inter-marrying. Christ was not a vegetarian while Gandhi was one. Above all, Gandhi defended caste or Varnashram Dharma which denied the equality of man.

Motilal Nehru, who had demanded in March 1924 the holding of a Round Table Conference to reconsider the political problem, outvoted the budget grants with the help of Jinnah.

Some months later, the Labour Government of England appointed, in August 1924, a public committee under the Chairmanship of Sir Alexander Muddiman, who was at that time President of the Council of States, to examine the working of the Act. On March 9, 1925, the report of the Muddiman Committee was published. In September 1925 the report came before the Legislative Council at its Simla session. Speaking on it, Motilal Nehru again put forward the national demand and appealed to the Government to convene a Round Table Conference or any other suitable agency to decide the question of transfer of power except for defence and foreign and economic affairs which could be reserved, he said, to the Viceroy for a short transitional period.

While trying to compel the Government to resolve the political deadlock, the Swarajists not only watered down the national demand but also slipped into unabashed co-operation. In July 1925 Motilal Nehru agreed to work on the Skeen Committee with Sir Andrew Skeen as Chairman. It was to report on the setting up of a Military Training College on the model of Sandhurst. Vithalbhai Patel advised Motilal Nehru not to accept membership while Kelkar sent by wire his consent to its acceptance. Motilal Nehru and Jinnah played a very important role in the Skeen Committee and later a military college was established in Dehra Dun. In August 1925 Patel became President of 'the Legislative Assembly to better serve the nation and to prove that the Swarajists were not mere destructive critics of the Government. He added that he would attend on the Viceroy ten times a day if he wanted. Gandhi, who had nothing to do with Council entry, congratulated Patel on his being elected President of the Legislative Assembly.

Gandhi had completely lost his hold on Congress affairs. So he proposed to place the entire machinery of the Congress at Nehru's disposal and absolve him from the Belgaum Pact. Accordingly, at Patna on September 22 and 23, 1925, Gandhi gave up his insistence on the compulsory yarn franchise, and the All-India Congress Committee passed a resolution accepting the four-anna alternative franchise. Nobody except a few hardbound disciples of Gandhi were in love with the yarn franchise. Gandhi was biding his time and waiting for an opportunity to regain the leadership although he had ordered the non-co-operators to surrender the control of the party to the Swarajists.

The Congress was now converted again into a political organization and Motilal Nehru was entrusted with the leadership of the nation. What Gandhi and the country did to perpetuate the memory of Das was to erect a memorial in his name, a hospital. The Swarajists, however, were soon divided on the acceptance of a seat on the Governor's Executive Council by S. B. Tambe of the Central Provinces Legislative Council. Kelkar, Jayakar and Dr. Moonje vehemently opposed Motilal Nehru who indignantly denounced Maharashtra as the diseased bone of Indian politics. Upon this Jayakar replied to Nehru that a surgeon and not a pandit was required to cut off the diseased part! Kelkar, Jayakar, Aney and Dr. Moonje, all top Maharashtrian leaders, challenged Motilal Nehru. Kelkar, Jayakar and Moonje resigned their seats on the Executive of the Swaraj Party. Motilal Nehru then went to Bombay and made a pact with them there on December 4, 1925.

During his tour of Bengal, Bihar, U.P. and Cutch, Gandhi realized that the great disease of the people was laziness. Idleness led to destructive tendencies and it was a great disease among Indians, the consequence of which was poverty. He said religion was not opposed to economic and political questions. He told the Bengali youth that he wanted freedom of his country so that its resources might be utilized for the benefit of mankind; his country might die so that the human race should live.

TAGORE ONCE AGAIN criticized Gandhi in September 1925 for his over-emphasis on the use of the spinning wheel. "My reason and conscience," he observed, "restrain me lest I should be a party to the raising of the *charkha* to a higher place than is its due." Stung to the quick by Tagore's penetrating criticism, Gandhi apologetically observed in *Young India* of November 5, 1925 that machinery must not be allowed to displace necessary human labour. He added that he had often said that they should assimilate the best in the modern world, and all that was good in the West. The fact was that Gandhi had condemned Western civilization outright for years.

Gandhi forgetfully or perhaps calculatingly began his article by describing Tagore as 'Sir Rabindranath' although the poet had resigned his title many years earlier. The *Modern Review* of December 1925 and the *Indian Review* of the same month observed that Gandhi should not have referred in his article to the idea of "competition", "jealousy" and "Gopis" in respect of Tagore. It was not so much a reflection, they said, upon the poet as it was upon Gandhi himself. They said Gandhi's view of the poet was utterly wrong and he should not have said that "the Poet makes his Gopis dance to the tune of his flute." This was not the business of the poet, they added, but of the man who made his living by puppet shows, and that the politician's trade, rather than the poet's, was near that of the puppet showman! The greatness of great men is due to their great and good qualities, but their little foibles stick to them to the last.

Gandhi also established an All-India Spinners' Association in October 1925. One of its secretaries was Jawaharlal Nehru. Nehru was an admirer of science, the modern world, and modern civilization! Every member of the new Association was to regard the spinning movement as his principal sphere of work. Much earlier, Gandhi had offered Jawaharlal Nehru monetary help and asked him whether he would take up a professorship or would be correspondent to some paper. But Motilal told his son that he should not worry about money. The father said he would earn in a week what the son would take a year to spend. For, Motilal Nehru, the old non-co-operator, had resumed his legal practice at the age of sixty.

Gandhi undertook a fast for seven days in November 1925 when he discovered some moral lapses among the boys and girls of his Ashram. He identified himself with the sins of the young ones who were under his care. About this time Miss Madeleina Slade, tall, beautiful and thirty-three years old, arrived at the Ashram. Gandhi regarded her as his daughter and named her Mirabehn.

Sarojini Naidu, the second woman to be President of the Congress, delivered her address which was poetic in its verse. Gandhi was feeling lonely and he said he did not claim to lead any party because he was a seeker after truth and he was constantly growing. In November he wrote to Dr. Ansari: "My heart becomes sick and weary. And when I listen to the still small voice within, I derive hope and smile in spite of the conflagration raging round me."

Sarojini Naidu was advised to do everything in consultation with Motilal Nehru whom Dr. Pattabhi Sitaramayya, a rabid and aggressive no-changer, hatefully charged with being a blatant responsive co-operator. As Motilal Nehru, the Swarajists leader, was censured also by responsive co-operators like Jayakar, Moonje and Kelkar, he found himself in trouble.

The responsivist Kelkar moved two amendments recommending the abolition of even the alternative yarn franchise and the compulsory donning of khaddar at the time of voting in the Congress. Gandhi angrily replied that as it was an official resolution and could not be changed, those who were opposed to khaddar and yarn franchise should leave the Congress.

It was decided at the Kanpur session that if the Government did not respond to the national demand, the Swarajists should boycott the Councils and should only attend the Councils to reject the budget. Malaviya said humorously that the resolution was neither a man nor a woman and to the hearty laughter of the delegates Motilal Nehru said that it was both! It was neither worldly nor saintly! It was a grand display of inconsistency! Jayakar announced the resignations of Kelkar, Moonje and himself from the Legislatures.

At Kanpur Gandhi was much less an amused spectator. He spoke only once in the session and it was on the resolution regarding South Africa. But he saw that his lieutenants obtained the leadership of the Congress. On one occasion Gandhi was disturbed by the proceedings of the Congress. The original resolution observed that the country was not ready for civil disobedience. Sambamurti moved an amendment asking for the deletion of this sentence. Sarojini Naidu ruled that the amendment was lost. Thereupon, the votes were counted and it was found that each side had 49 votes. Sarojini again asked the no's to raise their hands. Gandhi was the first to raise his hand and so the amendment was lost by 70 votes! Gandhi's detachment at this Congress must have been enlivened by his matchless American admirer, the Rev. J. H. Holmes, who wore his usual American clothes but donned a Gandhi cap.

Parliamentary obstruction, owing to the feeble policy of the Swarajists, was not effective and determined. It could not prove decisive as it was not co-ordinated with agitation outside the Assembly and Councils, which the Swarajists utterly ignored. The death of Das thus marked the end of the first epoch of parliamentary opposition. Das had Parnell's dash in parliamentary opposition whereas Motilal Nehru had the moderation of Redmond.

During the days when his influence was in eclipse, Gandhi began publishing serially *The Story of My Experiments with Truth* in *Navajivan* from November 29, 1925, and in *Young India* from December 31, 1925. The serial publication of his book *Satyagraha in South Africa* was completed on November 22, 1925. This he did obviously to revive hope for success in the struggle and encourage his followers to suffer and sacrifice for the goal.

Gandhi now decided to spend the year 1926 at the Ashram in self-imposed retirement. He took a vow not to leave the

Ashram for one year, except for reasons of health or in some unforeseen circumstances. His health was impaired, and the political atmosphere was quite disappointing. He was having a rest and doing quiet work.

During this year Gandhi spoke and wrote of *charkha* and once said that Dr. Talwalkar was as crazy about tuberculosis as he himself was about *charkha*. He approvingly quoted how King George fulminated against American typewriters when he saw a Government clerk typing letters on an American typewriter. Spinning enabled him, Gandhi said, to identify himself with God in the form of the poor and the downtrodden. A cause was greater than a man and it was greater than himself. The spinning wheel was the remedy against all the ills of the nation, even against the imprisonment of Bengal patriots!

During his self-imposed retirement, Gandhi held discourses with his disciples on the Gita which went on from February 24 to November 27, 1926. These discourses were given during the morning prayers at the Ashram.

In March 1926 Gandhi broached the subject of the killing of monkeys to Kishorelal Mashruwala. He said it was difficult to get over age-old sentiments. Non-violence was not a cover for cowardice. Non-violence presupposed the ability to strike, and was a conscious, deliberate restraint on violence, but vengeance was any day superior to passive, effeminate and helpless submission. Forgiveness was higher still. Yet Gandhi boldly and frankly defended the killing of sixty stray dogs by a millowner of Ahmedabad in September 1925. When the Ahmedabad Humanitarian League asked Gandhi's opinion on it, he replied that killing stray dogs was not against his stand on non-violence, and he remained unmoved by their protest.

Some months earlier Gandhi had said that he would kiss the feet of the violator of the modesty of a sister.[11] His ahimsa now admitted of the destruction of rabid dogs and even the destruction of a man found in the act of killing people. This was quite sensible. But what else did Tilak say in this matter? Every great Indian other than Gandhi advocated killing of an aggressor who comes to kill. Thomas Masaryk had asked Tolstoy the Russian apostle of absolute non-violence why a peace-loving man void of evil instinct should be slain and not the man of evil purpose who killed.

Gandhi replied to the Humanitarians that a principle was the expression of perfection, and as imperfect beings like them could not practise perfection, they desired every moment to explore the limits of its compromise in practice. Another reasonable stand Gandhi took was his solid support to the remarriage of widows. He said he did not regard the child widow marriage as remarriage.

Gandhi Who Preached naturopathy, was sad when a disciple named D. Hanumantharao died in March 1926, without taking any medicine as a fanatical zelot of naturopathy. He had rebuked Gandhi, who, although a preacher of natural treatment, used quinine, arsenic and iron injections, even undergoing an operation to save his life. When he was in such a predicament, Gandhi said it was one thing to have an ideal and another to be able to practise it. He admitted he had not reached that stage. It is customary for most philosophers and leaders to lay down principles and for followers to die for them. It is easy for men to fight for principles but difficult to live up to them.

Meanwhile Motilal Nehru, as directed by the Kanpur Congress and the All-India Congress Committee meeting at Delhi in the first week of March 1926, made a final speech on March 8, 1926 in the Legislative Assembly. He told the Government that they had co-operated with it for two years and a half and realized that the honourable co-operation offered by Das had been rejected by the Government. They were not only humiliated but their ablest compatriots were in jails. He warned the Government that unless it changed its ways, they would find the whole country honeycombed with secret societies. And he led his party out of the Assembly chamber.

The Swarajists and Responsivists met at the Sabarmati Ashram on April 21, 1926. Kelkar, Jayakar, Lajpatrai, Sarojini Naidu, Motilal Nehru and others signed a pact to be ratified by the All-India Congress Committee to meet at Ahmedabad in the first week of May. Later the pact was called the Sabarmati Pact. Motilal, who was by nature an able but imperious and intolerant leader, proved to be an impetuous master. He had no clear ideas as a political tactician, and so the Council entry experience ended in a tragedy.

Motilal Nehru realized that to have a tussle with the Responsivists was to catch a tartar. They were men who had made sacrifices and suffered and worked longer than he had in the cause of the Freedom struggle. Kelkar had served selflessly for years and so had Jayakar who was as eminent a lawyer and as great a patriot as Motilal Nehru in respect of wealth and sacrifice. They were not men to be cowed down. Gandhi must have been pleased to find the pot calling the kettle black.

Lajpatrai, Malaviya and Responsivists were Hindu-minded and they had no faith in Motilal Nehru as he was partial to Muslims, apathetic or indifferent to Hindu interests. For the support the Muslims gave him in the Legislative Assembly at Delhi, they wanted the Hindu support in making N.W.F. Province independent.

Thus the disintegration of the Swaraj Party was fast approaching. Gandhi's civil disobedience had collapsed and the policy of Council entry had proved ineffective. A feeling of frustration among the youth was growing. Gandhi, who had always his ear to the ground, said sorrowfully, "Hope rose high in 1921 to be dashed seemingly to pieces the very moment it rose to the highest point. The tide has appeared to be ebbing ever since. We are passing through midnight gloom. Possibly we have not yet seen the worst."

Gandhi had to settle some delicate questions between Vithalbhai Patel and Motilal Nehru who wanted Patel to subscribe half the Speaker's salary to the Swaraj Party funds. When Gandhi asked Patel about it, the latter replied that there was no agreement for giving half or any portion of his salary to the Party funds. And Kelkar said Motilal Nehru credited all the money he received as allowances for his work on the Skeen Committee when the things came in for criticism. Motilal Nehru said Patel should resign the Speaker's post and the latter replied that he belonged to no party as Speaker. Motilal said he was appointed on the Skeen Committee not as a Swarajist, but owing to his personal position.

But Gandhi, the father of non-co-operation, wrote to Motilal Nehru that although he personally disliked the Skeen Committee having to be given up by the latter he should do so if they were to quit the Councils.

When things had come to such a pass, the confirmed non-co-operator Gandhi saw Sir Henry Lawrence, the acting Governor of Bombay, at the instance of the latter at Mahabaleshwar on May 18, 1926. During the interview he discussed with him agriculture, *charkha* and the cattle problem and he could not identify himself with the proposal of the Royal Commission on Agriculture. In his usual mystic way Gandhi defended his meeting with the Governor and replied to his critics: "If I turn traitor, or to put it mildly, if I alter my opinion, they must be ready to denounce me and still abide by their own convictions."

The Governor, however, asked Gandhi to give his opinion on the Sabarmati Pact. Gandhi refused to say anything for publication. He was afraid he would add to the existing bitterness if he did so, but he was criticized for it. Upon this Gandhi said in a philosophic vein that life would be burdensome if every misrepresentation had to be answered and cleared up. Gandhi's critics said that he had broken his vow of not leaving the Ashram unless absolutely essential for his health. He had not attended a meeting of the All-India Congress Committee at Ahmedabad because he did not think it worthwhile to break his vow.

Lord Irwin, the new Viceroy, succeeded Lord Reading on April 1, 1926. A man with a deep religious faith, a firmness of spirit and force of character, he had acted as Minister for Agriculture and Fisheries in the British Cabinet and was an author of a biography. His former name was Edward Wood.

Early in April 1926, it was being arranged that Gandhi should rest at Mussoorie, but the proposal was dropped in answer to the chit that was drawn. "When there is no principle at stake," Gandhi wrote to Abbas Tyabji, "and when it is difficult to decide, I find God's answer through drawing chits and it has proved for me a most valuable time and trouble-saver!" Indian village folk apply flowers to the stone image of their deity to know God's wish; their great leader did it in a similar way! About this time the confirmed non-co-operator warned a woman debtor, Gangabehn Majmudar, that if she did not return the amount of Rs. 10,000 which he had given her as a loan, he would be driven in desperation to approach a lawyer.

Gandhi wished to go to Finland to attend a conference of Christian Young Men at Helsingfors. Romain Rolland said that Young Christian Europe saw in Gandhi the purest Christian (without knowing it) of the day. It was even arranged to take a goat on board the ship. But in a lavatory (which he called his library) his inner voice told him that he should not go. Besides he felt that the invitation was not spontaneous. And in July 1926 he cancelled the trip as he did in the case of his visit to China and America at this time. He believed that if there was power in his message, it would be felt without his physical presence.

On July 5, 1926, Gandhi issued a humorous statement from his Sabarmati Ashram about what he would do if he were emperor of India. The first thing he would do was to disband the army and retain only a certain number of police for the protection of the people against thieves and robbers, cultivate the friendship of the Frontier tribes, and shut up the representatives of Hindus and Muslims in one room and open it only after they had settled their quarrels.

Motilal Nehru's Swaraj Party was defeated in the elections which were held in November 1926. It suffered a rout in Bombay, C.P., the Punjab and U.P. at the hands of the Nationalist Party led by Lala Lajpatrai and Malaviya and at the hands of the Responsivists. Vithalbhai Patel was again elected President of the Legislative Assembly in January 1927.

Jawaharlal Nehru was in Europe (from March 1926 to November 1927) looking after the health of his wife, meeting Romain Rolland, and participating in the activities of the Congress of Oppressed Nationalities at Brussels. Jawaharlal wrote to Gandhi about his work at the Congress at Brussels. Gandhi, who had made the Congress stop all foreign propaganda, misinterpreted Jawaharlal by saying that "there is the danger of our people again looking to external forces and external aid for salvation instead of seeking to achieve it by evolving internal strength". Gandhi did not attach as much importance to foreign propaganda as did Tilak, Savarkar, Subhas and Jawaharlal Nehru.

Gandhi carried on his experiments in diet and conducted his classes on the *Gita*. He described the practice of untouchability as a hydra-headed monster. Speaking of rationalism, he opined that reason and rationalism had to yield first place to faith and prayer.

At this time Gandhi opposed his son Manilal Gandhi's desire to marry 'Fatima, a Muslim girl in South Africa. "If," he said in his letter of April 3, 1926, "you stick to Hinduism and Fatima to Islam it would be like putting two swords in one sheath. And what should be your children's faith?" Manilal's inter-communal marriage, he warned, would not be in the interests of society and would have a powerful impact on the Hindu-Muslim question. Inter-communal marriages were no solution to the problem. He said he could not embolden himself to discuss the topic with Kasturba. Manilal came to India and on April 6, 1927, at Akola, married the niece of Kishorlal Mashruwala in the presence of Gandhi. The Mahatma had no daughter but some woman cheated people in Aden saying that she was the daughter of Gandhi.

CHAPTER XXX

Young India Goes Ahead

It So Happened that Gandhi the superman cut Romain Rolland his biographer to the quick. In reply to a letter from the editor of the Romain Rolland Birthday Book Gandhi described Romain Rolland as his self-chosen advertiser. Tagore sent Gandhi a message that Rolland had been offended by this term. Yet Gandhi in a letter of October 29, 1926, explained to Romain Rolland that the expression was used as a mark of respect for him. Thereon Romain Rolland wrote back to Gandhi saying that he had not said or written to Tagore or to any of his disciples anything about his remark in the *Liber-Amicorum.* He added with utter humility: "I consider it an honour of my life to have been able to place myself at your service and to have spread your thoughts in the world."![1] It is possible that Romain Rolland might have on second thoughts given a philosophic turn to the episode.

At this time communal dissensions were increasing. In those strife-stricken days Gandhi was criticized for reading the *New Testament* with the students of the Gujarat National College.

On October 10, 1926, Gandhi executed his will cancelling all previous wills and bequeathing his all to the Trustees of the Satyagraha Ashram and thereafter to the Trustees thereof from time to time as his heirs even "my rights in whatever books and whatever articles I have written or I may write hereafter". He appointed them to administer his affairs after his death when necessary.

About this time Gandhi declared his opinion that "birth control by contraceptives is a race suicide". Gandhi the moral preceptor of the Ashram detected sexual aberrations in some boys and girls of the Ashram and therefore undertook a fast from November 24 to 30, 1926. Gandhi went to Wardha on December 4 and stayed there upto December 20, 1926. He then left for the Gauhati Congress. Meanwhile Gandhi, expressing his opinion on the report of the Royal Commission on Indian Currency, said on December 2, that he did not understand it, he was in search of a teacher to explain it to him. The Commission had been announced on August 20, 1926, under Hilton Young. The Commission recommended fixing the value of the rupee at 1*s*. 6*d*. gold and the creation of a Central Bank.

Gandhi attended the Gauhati Congress session in the last week of December 1926 and hoisted the Congress flag. The atmosphere of the Congress was depressed by the gloom of the murder of Swami Shraddhanand who, on December 23, 1926, had fallen a victim to the knife of Abdul Rashid whom Gandhi called Brother Abdul Rashid. S. Srinivas lyengar, a brilliant lawyer and politician, presided. Motilal Nehru was present. Lajpatrai, Jayakar and Kelkar did not attend. Aney and Moonje were passive spectators. Pandit Malaviya's views favouring office acceptance failed. Gandhi broke a year's silence. He opposed a resolution on independence because, he added, Swaraj included independence. Malaviya and Jinnah opposed the resolution and walked out.

Addressing the Congress at Gauhati, Gandhi said: "Now you will perhaps understand why I have called Abdul Rashid a brother, and I repeat it. I do not even regard him as guilty of Swami's murder. Guilty indeed are all those who excited feelings of hatred against one another." Of Shraddhanand, Gandhi said in two obituary notes: "He lived a hero. He died a hero. He blurted out the truth as he knew it without regard to consequence. The newspaper man has become a walking plague. He spread the contagion of his calumnies."

Swami Shraddhanand in his *Liberator*, which he had started on April 1, 1926, had written a series of twenty-six articles on "The Indian National Congress", completing it on October 28, 1926. In one of these articles he had exposed Mahomed Ali's intrigue with the Afghan ruler and also the part played by Gandhi in it. It is very likely that the blurting out of the truth referred to by Gandhi related to that article. In May 1924 Gandhi had written that Shraddhanand was not past praying for!

The terror of the tragic event had some effect on Gandhi himself. His craze for self-sacrifice cooled down for a moment.

He sounded a warning to the Congress leaders saying: "Let us all be brave enough to die the death of a martyr, but let no one lust for martyrdom."

It was customary with Gandhi to call a murderer brother or Godfearing man when he happened to be a Muslim and to call the assassinator of British officers a murderer when he happened to be a Hindu. Gandhi kept up this attitude to the end. The Muslims did not lag behind in their praise of Abdul Rashid. The students and professors of the famous theological college at Deoband finished five complete recitations of the Koran so that the soul of Abdul Rashid, who was hanged on November 14, 1927, might gain merit and a place in the summit of the seventh heaven, *'a' ala-e-illeeyeen.*[2]

WHILE RETURNING FROM Gauhati, Gandhi delivered a convocation address on January 30, 1927 to the students of the Bihar Vidyapith at Patna. Then he started his tour of Maharashtra beginning with Berar and the Central Provinces. Shapurji Saklatwala met him at Yeotmal on February 5, 1927. He was a communist, a member of the British Parliament, and on a visit to India. Saklatwala told Gandhi that though there were differences between Hindus and Muslims they should declare independence, and that imperialism must be ended. Gandhi told him that his programme was impracticable in India and if he thought it was practicable he should return to India and execute it.

Gandhi later asked Saklatwala what his final message was for India. Saklatwala replied: "For God's sake, my dear Gandhi, wear a pair of trousers!"[3] Gandhi could not give up using his loin-cloth because he knew that renunciation and religion were the guiding stars of the ignorant Indian masses whom he swayed. Had he granted Saklatwala's request, more than fifty per cent of Gandhi's disciples would have deserted him. He was a perfect blend of a Bania, a barrister and a bairagi.

During Gandhi's Maharashtra tour, the Responsivists (Tilak-ites) kept aloof from receptions held in his honour. Gandhi was presented with yarn garlands and expensive silk caskets which he put to auction and his devotees were encouraged to buy them. During this tour someone asked him what had become of the crore of rupees collected for the Tilak Swaraj Fund. He explained his position and added, "I know no institution in the world which does not have dishonest agents."

At Pandhurpur there was a stir among the orthodox Hindus

when it was rumoured that Gandhi was going to enter the famous Vithoba temple in company with non-Hindus as he had entered the Benares temple with a Buddhist. With a view to dispelling these rumours, Gandhi told the audience that the lady friend who was with him at Benares was a Buddhist and "therefore a Hindu"! He hated the hypocrisy and cupidity at places of pilgrimage. He was grieved to find at these places drunkards and dissolute worshippers in charge of temples. Amidst the crowds and commotion Gandhi could steal a few minutes to auction the garlands and sell khadi and could find bidders for a yarn garland. Think of a nation's leader auctioning his own garlands and caskets for national purposes! Gandhi often said he was a Bania, and sometimes acted the part well.

Gandhi bowed to the image of Vithoba, but his sandals were stolen by a thief or a devotee. Gandhi said that the devotee did not know that his 'Mahatma' would have to wait another six months for the death of an animal at the Ashram. For he used to wear sandals made only from the skin of an animal which had died a natural death. Shantikumar Morarji, who accompanied him, said that he need not wait long for the sandals. They had simply to stop feeding an animal and its death would occur. Gandhi then inquired of Shantikumar whether Untouchables were allowed to enter the temple of Vithoba. Shantikumar had told him that it was so. But while leaving the temple they came to know that the Untouchables were allowed to enter up to the Namdeo's step only. Gandhi was sorry he had entered the temple.

Another question some of the social workers asked Gandhi was about his partiality for Muslims. The questioners cautioned Gandhi against the hypocrisy of his followers who donned khadi on the day of his visits. "If you fought for the Khilafat, why do you not fight for the Hindu Sanghatan today?" was a question often asked. This exasperated Gandhi. He angrily replied that he had done it to save the cow. Let the people, he added, rail at him and insult him if they liked, but he would not pay them back in their own coin.

At Ratnagiri, on March 1, Gandhi made a very important speech. In every district of Maharashtra he made about ten speeches. The Ratnagiri speech was significant as Gandhi knew that Savarkar since his release had been a critic of his Khilafat policy and of his opposition to the revolutionary movement and his non-violent non-co-operation. Gandhi's declaration that Shivaji was a misguided patriot had added much bitterness to the criticism, and his lukewarm policy concerning the barbarous acts of the Moplahs had given an added edge to it. Gandhi's statement that he would assist the Amir of Afghanistan if he invaded India had enraged the Hindu Sanghatanists. Gandhi, above all, had tried to suppress the revolutionary movement in Bengal.

"Lokamanya's birthplace," said Gandhi, in the course of his speech, "is a place of pilgrimage not only for me but for the whole of India." He recalled that his old friend Savarkar, whom he had known well in England and whose sacrifice and patriotism were well known, was residing at Ratnagiri.

"We had our differences then," Gandhi, befitting a great leader and a great organizer, observed: "we have them now, but they have not affected in the least our friendship. Differences of opinion should never mean hostility. If they did, my wife and I should be sworn enemies of each other. I do not know two persons in the world who had no differences of opinion, and as I am a follower of the Gita, I have always attempted to regard those who differ from me with the same affection as I have for my nearest and dearest."

Gandhi then replied to the Hindu Sanghatanists who asked him to take part in the Shuddhi movement. He said he asked Hindus, Muslims and Christians to stop the conversion movement, "I therefore say," he concluded, "to the Hindus 'Do whatever you like, but don't ask a man like me, who has come to his conclusions after the maturest thinking, to take up what he cannot'."

This shows the tempo and the embarrassment caused to Gandhi in Konkan which Savarkar had influenced tremendously with his Hindu Sanghatan ideology.

On the eve of Gandhi's visit, Congressmen desired that the Ratnagiri Municipality and the people should give Gandhi, their great leader, a fitting address. But Savarkar, it is said, frankly but ungenerously expressed his displeasure over the move. Adulators on both sides worsened the situation. Gandhian zealots tried to poison Gandhi's ears and entreated him not to visit Savarkar. Gandhi's speech was reported to Savarkar who had been ill for sometime. He hurriedly sent a note to Gandhi inviting him to his residence. Gandhi came, curtailing his other engagements. Savarkar received Gandhi and Kasturba with great cordiality. The conversation took place in Hindi.

It was after nearly eighteen years that Gandhi was now meeting Savarkar, his old opponent of their London days. Though of different moulds, great ones recognize each other's strength. The real object of Gandhi in visiting Savarkar was to see whether the revolutionary volcano was now extinct, a spent force, or whether it was still bursting. During the course of the interview, Gandhi told Savarkar with a pleasant smile that he would have stayed with him at Ratnagiri for two or three days had his programme not been already fixed. Savarkar replied that he, too, would have been glad to entertain Gandhi, but agreed that Gandhi should go on with his great mission of arousing the nation's enthusiasm for the freedom movement, as fortunately he was free to do.

For a short while they discussed political problems. But neither was convinced of the other's view. And then suddenly Savarkar asked Gandhi to clarify his attitude on untouchability and shuddhi (re-conversion). In reply, Gandhi said: "To me the view that a man loses his religion is absurd. And although I believe in reconversion of a person who was forcibly or deceitfully converted to an alien faith, I am not for reconversion of persons whose ancestors have changed their faiths decades ago. Nor do I uphold the conversion of persons from other religions."

After this discussion, Gandhi said, "We cannot have a long talk today but you know my regard for you as a lover of truth and as one who would lay down his life for the sake of truth. Besides, our goal is ultimately one and I would like you to correspond with me as regards all points of difference between us." "I thank you," said Savarkar, "but you are free and I am bound, and I don't want to put you in a difficult position. I will correspond with you."

While taking leave of Savarkar, Gandhi said: "It is clear that we disagree on some problems. But I hope you have no objection to my making experiments." Savarkar immediately replied: "You know the story of the boys and frogs. You will be making the experiment at the cost of the nation." R. K. Govande, President of the Malvan Taluka Congress Committee, intervened and said that he now realized that Gandhi plus Savarkar was equal to Swaraj! Hearing this, Gandhi laughed.

Gandhi was now doubly sure that the faith and fire in Savarkar was unaffected even by the tortures and tribulations of his jail life in the Andamans. This was the last meeting between them. Though Savarkar was released in May 1937 and made a whirlwind propaganda tour throughout the length and breadth of India as the great leader of the Hindu Mahasabha, no occasion arose for a meeting between the two leaders.

The tour of Maharashtra ended with a speech at Poona. Gandhi frankly said, "If I cannot make myself understood to Poona students, it is my misfortune, the misfortune of my country and shall I say your misfortune?"[4] For, the bitter opposition to his aims and ideals originated in Maharashtra.

GANDHI THEN VISITED Hardwar in the middle of March 1927 and delivered an address at the Silver Jubilee function of the Gurukul, Kangri. He appealed to the Gurukul students to carry on the mission of their master Swamiji and added, "Remember Abdul Rashid has not murdered Swamiji, he has made him a martyr." At the Educational Conference at Hardwar he said that it was the duty of the Muslims to learn Sanskrit because, in the final analysis, of their forebears two were Rama and Krishna and they ought to know Sanskrit in order to know them.

On returning to Bombay, Gandhi addressed meetings at Santa Cruz and Ghatkopar and went to Poona by train on March 24. In the evening he felt a sudden giddiness and it was accompanied by numbing of the left side of the body. At Poona station he was not in a condition to walk. So he was carried to the Bangalore Mail. Gandhi felt that his vision was blurring. He had a refreshing sleep in the train and he thought that the attack had subsided.

On March 24 and 25 Gandhi addressed about seven meetings at Kolhapur as it was his first visit to that state. There he preached the use of khadi. Owing to ill-health Gandhi could not make a speech at Nipani. Some programmes were gone through silently. Gangadhar Deshpande, Rajagopalachari and Kasturba addressed meetings. Ill-health detained Gandhi at Nipani for five days. Belgaum presented Gandhi with an address and a purse. Gandhi was silent, sitting in a chair on the platform. He had a mild attack of apoplexy with paralysis of the left leg and arm, and his tongue and eye were also affected. So he was advised to cancel his travelling and speaking programmes during the hot weather. His blood pressure was high (188).

On April 1, 1927, Gandhi was taken to Amboli Hill Station in Sawantwadi. There he was confined to bed. The Chief of Sawantwadi, who was a dutiful, benevolent and just ruler, made arrangements for Gandhi's stay. The place had the advantage of being by the seaside and on a hill. Gandhi's nerves were crying for rest and he felt quite relaxed in this quiet spot with its picturesque surroundings. Dr. Jivraj Mehta examined him and advised him to cancel his programme for some months, but allowed him reading in bed or writing occasional letters to friends. The Chief of Sawantwadi met him and Gandhi and his party were impressed by his simplicity, the deep interest he took in the welfare of his subjects and his popularity among his people.

Gandhi sent a message to the meeting held in Bombay on April 6, 1927, to celebrate the Golden Jubilee of Nanalal Dalpatram who was a great poet of Gujarat. Nanalal was professor at Princes College in Rajkot. Being tremendously influenced by the call of the nation in 1920, he gave up his job and came to join the Gujarat Vidyapith. He was emotional and irritable. He, could not hit it off with Vallabhbhai Patel and Gandhi. So he was not appointed. Gandhi's hypnotism gradually lost its effect upon him and he grew critical of the non-violent dictator. The message Gandhi sent described him as a milch-cow, and added: "Who would not mind the kicks and a thrust of the horns by a milch-cow?"

The poet took offence at this message and did not allow the men in charge of the function to read it out. Gandhi therefore wrote to Nanalal on April 7, 1927: "I took pains and fondly wrote a harmless little letter praising you which you did not like. Every morning I ask forgiveness of God even for an unconscious fault. Won't you pardon me this unintentional slip, for which I apologize to you? Unless you forgive me I will not stop begging pardon." Although Gandhi's message was not read out, it was published in some journals and Gandhi sadly said that it would have been better if it had not been published. Later, Gandhi tried through professor R. B. Athavale for a reconciliation, but Nanalal never reconciled himself with Gandhi. As a result Nanalal was ostracized. He stubbornly faced the ostracism but did not yield an inch. Such was the end of many a man who opposed Gandhi. It was easy for Gandhi to ask pardon humbly but difficult for him to forgive.

Under medical advice and at the instance of Rajagopalachari, Gandhi was then taken to Nandi Hills on April 20. The place is 35 miles from Bangalore. He stayed there for about one and a half months.

During his stay at Nandi Hills, many eminent men and some missionaries met him. They kindly inquired after his health. Srinivas Sastri met him and sought his advice on the matter of his appointment as India's first Agent-General to South Africa. For the previous two or three years Gandhi's emissaries, Andrews and Sarojini Naidu, had been helping to solve the problem of the Indians in South Africa. Gandhi welcomed Sastri's appointment which he had recommended.

Early in May 1927, Manchersha Avari started civil disobedience at Nagpur against the Arms Act and the Explosive Substances Act. Avari aimed at the release of the Bengali detenus. It was declared that Gandhi had consented to the satyagraha. Gandhi contradicted the report and stated that there was no proper atmosphere in the country for civil disobedience. The grave injustice inflicted upon the Bengal detenus, Gandhi added, he keenly felt, but he did not desire to make a fruitless exhibition or his powerlessness. Avari was sentenced to four years' rigorous imprisonment on June 4, 1927.

Towards the end of May the blood pressure of Gandhi went down, but his weakness lingered. His recovery from the disease was at a snail's pace. Mirza Ismail saw Gandhi at Nandi Hills in company with Vishveshvarayya, the ex-Dewan of Mysore. The Maharaja of Mysore spun daily. While expressing his opinion on the question of the cow versus the buffalo, Gandhi observed that buffalo breeding should be stopped and the cow should be protected as it had become part of the Hindu religion. Although he discussed such sundry questions, throughout the months he chiefly talked of the spinning wheel, and his politics was confined to the *charkha*. Gandhi's health improved greatly as time passed. The blood pressure dropped to 155. Mathurdas Trikamji wanted him to stay at Panchgani, but Gandhi refused to do so.

Meanwhile communal carnage raged in the Punjab, Bihar, Central Provinces and at other places. While Gandhi was ailing, about 25 riots broke out in which 250 persons were killed and more than 2,500 were injured. With a view to stopping the carnage, the A.I.C.C., at its Bombay session on May 16, supported the demand of the Muslim leaders for separate provinces as a fair and reasonable one, and also separation of Sind from Bombay Province. These demands were supported on the basis of a Muslim majority in these provinces, ostensibly on the basis of linguistic provinces but as demanded by the Muslim leaders at their Delhi Conference in March 1927. The Muslim leaders had proposed that Muslim representatives should be not less than one-third in the Central Legislative Assembly. For the national unity of Gandhi's dream anything was to be conceded. This was the price paid to Muslims for their co-operation with Motilal Nehru in the Legislative Assembly at Delhi where this proposal had been mooted.

Srinivas lyengar, President of the Congress, informed Gandhi of this victory by telegram and soon after saw Gandhi at Nandi Hills and reminded the Mahatma of his boast which he had made at Gauhati. Gandhi had said to Iyengar at Gauhati: "Many have failed but you might succeed because your faith is invincible!" And he proved it to a fault!

WHILE GANDHI WAS at Nandi Hills, Congress leaders were deciding on the choice of the candidate for the presidentship of the Congress. Jawaharlal Nehru had made a fine impression at the Brussels Congress of Oppressed Nationalities in February 1927. Motilal Nehru unhesitatingly sponsored the name of his son for the presidentship of the Congress and in the first week of May 1927 he wrote to Gandhi recommending him for the presidency. His own name was suggested by Sarojini Naidu as prompted by Jinnah and the Maharaja of Mahmudabad, as Motilal was proverbially inclined to the Muslim side. But Motilal was then a solitary figure in Indian politics, and Gandhi said too many forces were working against him.

So, on May 25, 1927, Gandhi wrote to Jawaharlal Nehru inquiring whether he would like to accept the presidency of the ensuing session of the Congress. If he did so, he would be lost for one year to the masses, Gandhi added, because the Congress leaders had lost control on the masses. "I do not myself see," he observed thoughtfully, "the way so clear as to make me force the crown on you and plead with you to wear it." As regards Jawaharlal Nehru's reports on the doings of the Oppressed Nations' Congress, Gandhi said that he did not expect much from the League.

Motilal Nehru was pressing Gandhi to put the crown of the Congress on his son's head. On May 25 Gandhi, therefore, suggested Jawaharlal for the presidency, but S. Srinivas Iyengar, who paid a visit to Gandhi at Nandi Hills, preferred Dr. Ansari and Gandhi yielded. Gandhi informed Motilal Nehru accordingly. Gandhi had kept away from the Congress, but such was his power that the candidate for the Congress presidency was not nominated without his approval. Singly, he was a major force, but jointly the Swarajists and the Nationalists dominated the field.

Gandhi now felt better. The attack of apoplexy and paralysis had passed away leaving no after-effects. The climate of Nandi Hills however became too chilly for him. So he and his party left for Bangalore on June 5, 1927. They stayed at Kumar Park, one of the palaces of the Maharaja of Mysore.

During his stay at Bangalore, Gandhi wrote in *Young India* of June 16, 1927, an article on Hindu-Muslim unity. One of his friends had remarked that if he had not dragged the Hindus into the Khilafat agitation, the recent tragic events would not have happened. Gandhi replied that he did not repent of his part in the Khilafat agitation and that he would always defend his action on the Khilafat question.

Gandhi stayed in Bangalore till the end of August 1927. During this period he gave an impetus to the propagation of khadi and *charkha*. He attended a meeting of the All-India Spinners' Association, paid visits to the Government dairy and opened a Khadi Exhibition at Bangalore during the first week of July. In order to help the spread of Hindi he attended the performance of a Hindi play, *Deenbandhu Kabir* at Bangalore, presided over the Karnatak Hindi Conference and addressed students' meetings at Bangalore and Mysore.

Gandhi visited the Indian Institute of Science at Bangalore. A man of faith entering a centre of reason! Gandhi and science came together! "There is," he said to the students, "no place here for a rustic like me who has to stand speechless in awe and wonderment." Their research, he added, would be useless if it was not allied to internal research which could link their hearts with the millions, and unless all the discoveries they made had the welfare of the poor as the end in view, all their workshops would be really no better than Satan's workshops.[5]

On July 29 Gandhi addressed a meeting of Christian Missionaries. He said they were trying to do the right thing in a wrong way. They should not undermine the faith of the people they came to serve. Several municipalities honoured Gandhi with addresses. On August 5 Mysore State celebrated the Silver Jubilee of the Maharaja's rule and Gandhi appealed to the ruler to introduce prohibition in Mysore. He spoke to the Adi-Karnatak boys and collected money for Gujarat flood relief.

Visiting Shimoga, Harihar, Sagar and Belur, Gandhi commenced his Tamil Nadu tour at the end of August, speaking on temperance, prohibition and *charkha*. Speaking at Madras at the Y.M.C.A., he said: "I do not believe in a religion bereft of economics." At Madras Gandhi told the Neill-Statue-volunteers that not even a Swaraj Government could do without an Arms Act. The volunteers were engaged in the agitation for the removal of General James George Smith Neill's statue from the city. Gandhi told them that they should leave the Congress alone and fight independently, but they should not resort to satyagraha until all other resources were exhausted.

Meanwhile Motilal Nehru was displeased with the President-designate, Dr. Ansari. Although Gandhi and Motilal Nehru requested him not to issue his statement on the policy of the Congress, Dr. Ansari did it to the embarrassment of Motilal Nehru. So he wanted Dr. Ansari to resign. Gandhi, who had championed Ansari's election, again requested him to issue another statement saying that he would not impose his personal views on the Congress. Motilal Nehru again wired to Gandhi that there was a demand for making Jawaharlal Nehru President of the Congress. But Gandhi did not let down Dr. Ansari. At the end of August 1927, Motilal Nehru left for Europe to defend a case in London and then to join Jawaharlal in Europe who was looking after his wife Kamala and taking an interest in new political movements there.

On September 15, 1927, Gandhi's reply to and review of *Mother India* by Katherine Mayo was published in *Young India*. She had levelled terrible accusations against Indian society, culture and man. The title of Gandhi's article was "Drain Inspector's Report". Gandhi said the authoress failed to show that she was uncommitted and unattached and he suggested that the work must have been subsidized. Katherine Mayo had met Gandhi at the Sabarmati Ashram on March 17, 1926. If she was not financially supported, concluded Gandhi, Miss Mayo was an avowed Indophobe and Anglophile reluctant to see anything good in Indians and anything bad in the British and their rule. Miss Mayo, the stooge of British imperialism, had written a similar book *Isles of Fear* against the independence of Philippines. Gandhi said at a meeting at Cuddalore that he had no solution to the Brahmin-non-Brahmin question. The Brahmins had not told Gandhi about their differences and Gandhi said that since he lived more with Brahmins than with others, the non-Brahmins suspected him. He held that the Brahmin was the finest flower of Hinduism and humanity and he would not have the non-Brahmins to rise on the ruin of the Brahmins.[6]

THE LEGISLATIVE ASSEMBLY passed a bill to check the communal carnage that had disfigured the face of the land. Leaders of the nation held a Unity Conference at Calcutta in October 1927, appealing to both the communities to stop the murders. Gandhi's health had improved greatly and his weight had risen to 113 pounds. He left Mangalore on October 28 and reached Bombay on the morning of October 29 by the S.S. Vegavati. As usual, Gandhi did a little business on the launch taking him to the steamer, by selling one of the gifts of the previous evening for Rs. 125.

The next day Gandhi left by the Punjab Mail for Delhi. He interviewed Lord Irwin, the new Viceroy, and discussed with him the Hindu-Muslim question, political reforms and the appointment of the Simon Commission. Several Indian leaders were invited by the new Viceroy, Lord Irwin, to a conference on October 31, whose proceedings were not published.

On November 8 Lord Irwin announced an All-white Commission to make inquiries into the working of the Indian constitution and prepare the next instalment of constitutional reforms. The Members of the All-India Statutory Commission were Members of the British Parliament. Birkenhead, the Secretary of State for India, was a die-hard British Imperialist and was afraid that if he appointed Indian Members on the Commission, they would join the Labour Members of the Commission. The Chairman of the Commission was Sir John Simon, an eminent lawyer and a liberal politician who was influenced by the opinions of Reading and Birkenhead. According to Birkenhead, it was frankly inconceivable that India would ever be fit for Dominion Status. He had even opposed to some extent the Montagu-Chelmsford Report when he was a member of the British Cabinet.

The announcement deeply angered the Indian political parties and all leading politicians denounced it. In a statement the President of the Congress on November 10 called upon the people to boycott it. Motilal Nehru was then in Europe. Jinnah denounced the Simon Commission by issuing a statement on November 16, 1927. Jinnah said, "Jallianwala Bagh was physical butchery. The Simon Commission is the butchery of our soul." Lajpatrai and Jayakar did the same thing. The Viceroy expected the Muslims to support the Commission and he thought that if they supported it, the Hindus would not boycott it. This was a miscalculation on his part.

Gandhi returned to Bombay on November 6, staying at the Sabarmati Ashram for two days, and the next day left for Colombo by the S.S. *Querimbra*. On November 12 he reached Colombo. During his tour he was received warmly by the Buddhists as well as the Christians. He called on the Governor, Herbert James Stanley, who had been Secretary to Lord Gladstone, the Governor-General of South Africa, in 1913. Gandhi visited Colombo, Negombo, Kandy and Jaffna and other places.

Gandhi was in a Buddhist country and naturally he proudly told the audiences that his eldest son accused him of being a follower of the Buddha. Some Hindus, he added, accused him of spreading Buddhistic teachings under the guise of Sanatana

Dharma. Gandhi, however, felt proud of being a follower of the Buddha. He told them that Gautama was the greatest Hindu reformer. Gautama was a Hindu of the Hindus. He never rejected the message of the Vedas, Gandhi concluded, but introduced a living reformation in the petrified faith that surrounded him.[7]

Gandhi's speeches were translated both in Sinhalese and in Tamil. He told the workers that there was no shame in honourable labour, and that drink was a devil in whose net they must not fall. He proudly told the Muslims that when he saw them he was reminded of his happy days he spent in South Africa when his life was almost wholly cast in the midst of his Muslim countrymen. He told another meeting that Swaraj was not the birthright of one country only. Swaraj was the birthright of all countries.

At one place Gandhi was asked whether Kasturba was his mother! Amused, Gandhi said, "Yes, she is my mother." The next day he explained that "for years past she had ceased to be his wife and "for the past thirty years she had filled the place of his mother. She had been his mother, nurse, cook and bottle-washer!"

Gandhi returned to Madras on December 1, 1927, and then began his tour of Orissa which was suffering from a visitation of floods. The people in Orissa were poor, but their appearance was poorer. Gandhi writhed in pain at the sight of the starving millions, and he asked them to give him a gift. It was the promise of abstaining from drink.

From Cuttack, Gandhi returned to Madras on December 22, 1927, to attend the Congress session which was to meet on December 26 under the presidentship of Dr. Ansari. Gandhi opened the khadi exhibition. The most attractive feature of the Congress was the presence of Jawaharlal Nehru who had come directly to Madras from Europe, and the presence of Subhas Chandra Bose. Jawaharlal Nehru had visited Russia and had brought the message of Socialism and Internationalism to India. He was quite a different man now, a new politician with a new outlook. The atmosphere of the proposed boycott against the Simon Commission was growing provocative and intense.

Jawaharlal Nehru moved that "This Congress declare the goal of the Indian people to be complete national independence." Gandhi was present but did not take much interest in the proceedings. He, who had been opposing the independence resolution at successive sessions of the Congress, was indignant at Nehru's resolution. Srinivas lyengar and Subhas Chandra Bose fearlessly supported Jawaharlal Nehru.

The Congress resolved to boycott the Simon Commission "at every stage and in every form". The Congress authorized the Working Committee to draft a new constitution in co-operation with similar committees appointed by other organizations, political, labour and others.

Jawaharlal Nehru expressed the thoughts of the Indian youth. Presiding over the Republican Congress at Madras on December 28 in the Congress pandal, he said, "Even though the Congress passed a resolution of independence a new organization[8] should be formed to carry on propaganda and try to convert those who had vague ideas of independence and did not know what Republicanism is."

Pandit Jawaharlal Nehru touched the right chord in the hearts of young India and the lull in Indian political atmosphere disappeared. He whipped the flagging energy of the nation.

Gandhi took very little part in the open session or the work of the committees. He was unhappy and unwell. Jawaharlal Nehru declared independence but did not say how the goal was to be achieved. Gandhi must have noticed this weakness. But he was silent. During his stay in Madras, he called on Fenner Brockway who was ailing in a Madras hospital.

On December 31, the Muslim League under the presidentship of Jinnah met at its annual session in Calcutta and declared that Muslims would give up separate electorates provided their demands for separation of Sind were met and the status of self-governing Province was given to the North-West Frontier. They soon got this but the Hindus' demand for joint electorates was never met during British rule. The separate electorate poisoned India's atmosphere with communalism and encouraged men to think in terms of religion and community, as partisans and not as countrymen or citizens of one nation.

CHAPTER XXXI

Return to Leadership

GANDHI WAS UPSET by the proceedings of the Madras Congress. He could not fail to perceive, he observed in *Young India* of January 5, 1928, that irresponsible talk and work were the order of the day. Indiscipline was not a rare feature. He expressed his anger too. He said the independence resolution which had been rejected the previous year had been passed almost without opposition. Gandhi had been opposing the resolution since the Ahmedabad session of 1921.

Gandhi described the Madras resolution, which was passed without his consent, as hastily conceived and thoughtlessly passed. By passing such resolutions, he added, they became the laughing stock of the critics and had almost sunk to the level of a schoolboys' debating society! Moreover he was utterly disappointed at the Congressmen's lack of faith in khadi. This was no doubt an attack directed at Pandit Jawaharlal Nehru who was the prime mover at the Madras Congress. Not only that, in private discussion Gandhi condemned the independence resolution with faint praise. Beasant described the independence resolution as a dignified one.

On his arrival at Ahmedabad, Gandhi wrote to Jawaharlal Nehru on January 4, 1928, that Nehru was going too fast. He should have taken time to think, and most of the resolution he had framed and got carried could have been delayed for a year. Nehru replied, and Gandhi said that when Jawaharlal Nehru was chafing under self-suppression, he overlooked the very things which appeared to him now as Gandhi's serious blemishes. "The differences", continued Gandhi, "between you and me appear to me to be so vast and radical that there seems to be no meeting ground between us. I cannot conceal from you my grief that I should lose a comrade so valiant, so faithful, so able and so honest as you have always been: but in serving a cause, comradeships have got to be sacrificed".[1]

Gandhi, who preserved his correspondence so carefully, informed Jawaharlal Nehru on January 13, that he had destroyed his first letter after reading it and if Nehru did not want to take the trouble of writing another letter, he was prepared to publish his second one. Evidently Gandhi was in an angry mood! To pass a resolution on independence ignoring the presence of the Mahatma was an insult to him and that too in the company of Subhas Bose and Srinivas lyengar! It was this resolution which had been put off for seven successive years by the Mahatma! He alone could say that he would win Swaraj in one year, but how dare these leaders make such a declaration without his consent!

On January 14, 1928, Jawaharlal Nehru issued a statement that the independence resolution was not passed in a hurry or thoughtlessly. It was the demand of all Provincial Congress Committees and for some years had repeatedly come up before the Congress in various forms. Independence, he added, was the correct legal definition of an independent country, and although it meant severance with the British connection it did not mean that there should be no alliance between India and England. *Young India* snubbed the rebellious young India.

Gandhi celebrated the wedding of his third son Ramdas with great solemnity and simplicity, the couple doing homage to Nature, the gods and the Bhagawad Gita. The bridegroom was thirty years old. Gandhi wished the new couple a long life of service.

Although Gandhi had overcome his illness, his constant exertion told upon his health and he had to lie down frequently at the Ashram. In the first week of February 1928, his blood-pressure rose, he fainted and remained unconscious for two minutes, and there was severe pain in his stomach. A little later he attended a political conference at Porbandar and on his way back laid the foundation stone of a temple for the Untouchables.

On February 10, 1928, Gandhi invited his friends to dinner at the Ashram which act seemed to be a departure from its normal rules. After the dinner Gandhi, perhaps in a spirit of fun, said that he would die[2] on March 17, thinking that the six years' imprisonment was to end on that day. Just at this time Jawaharlal Nehru met Gandhi at his Ashram as he must have felt the need of a compromise, each realizing the role of the other! The Present and Future were to be blended! Humanitarianism and humanism were to co-operate!

The Simon Commission landed in Bombay on February 3, 1928, and was greeted everywhere with black flags, and placards with the slogan, "Go back, Simon". Congressmen staged hostile demonstrations on a nation-wide scale, and the police fired on them at some places. On February 16, 1928, the Legislative Assembly passed a resolution moved by Lala Lajpatrai declaring that the constitution and scheme of the Commission were unacceptable to India and the Assembly would have nothing to do with the Commission at any stage or in any form. This boycott resolution was carried in the Assembly by 68 votes against 62. The Simon Commission returned home on March 31, 1928. Long afterwards, Lord Irwin said that the decision to exclude Indians from the Commission appeared to have been a mistake[3] although he was a party to the decision.

The Gujarat Vidyapith underwent a change in February 1928. Kaka Kalelkar was appointed President of the Committee and Vice-Chancellor of the University. The condition of the Gujarat Vidyapith was causing anxiety to Gandhi. Kalelkar was asked to take charge of it. He became Principal of the Gujarat National College. He held these two offices till January 3, 1935. Gandhi was Chancellor.

While one of Gandhi's colleagues was installed in the Gadi of the Vice-Chancellor, another colleague and disciple Maganlal Gandhi died on April 23, 1928, in Patna after an illness of nine days. He was Gandhi's nephew and had been helping him in his work since 1904. He practised Gandhi's ideals with the utmost austerity and severity. He had completely surrendered his life to the service of Gandhi and to silent and selfless constructive work. According to Gandhi, he was the watchdog of the Ashram in all its aspects—material, moral and spiritual. And as was usual with Gandhi, Maganlal's name also was honoured with a memorial fund.

Around this time, Gandhi supported an appeal for funds issued by the Karve Jubilee Committee. Karve was the founder of the Indian Women's University. Gandhi described Prof. D. K. Karve as a giant among silent and selfless workers and praised him for his self-effacement, his single-minded devotion to duty, his inexhaustible energy, his honesty in all circumstances, his faith in the midst of opposition and his irrepressible optimism.

Gandhi gave a message on Tolstoy's centenary day which was

celebrated on August 28, 1928, all over the world. He said he had many Gurus of whom Tolstoy was one. Gokhale was his political Guru. He had no spiritual Guru. But, he added, "While thus the little throne within has remained vacant, next to Rajchandra, Tolstoy is one of three moderns who had exerted the deepest spiritual influence on my life, the third being Ruskin."[4] According to Gandhi, Tolstoy was the most truthful man of his age and was "the greatest apostle of non-violence that the present age has produced".

Meanwhile the All-Parties Conference convened by the Congress Party met in February 1928 at Delhi and later in May in Bombay and appointed a committee under Motilal Nehru to draft a constitution for India. It worked from June to August 1928 and drafted a constitution. Jawaharlal Nehru was appointed Secretary of the Committee.

This was the first Indian attempt at constitution-making. It mainly aimed at closing the Muslim breach, conceding in a philosophic and wise tone the establishment of new Muslim provinces for Sind and the N.W.F. in addition to making many 'concessions to Muslims in other provinces.' It declared the goal of India to be self-governing dominion allowing Congressmen to work for independence. Subhas Bose was one of the signatories with Motilal Nehru and Sir Tej Bahadur Sapru. As regards the depressed classes, the Nehru Report said: "In our suggestions for the constitution we have not made any special provision for the representation of the depressed classes in the legislatures. This could only be done by way of special electorates or by nomination."

GANDHI CONGRATULATED MOTILAL Nehru on producing a unanimous report after strenuous efforts. He ventured to suggest that the report "represents the largest common measure possible for parties often representing opposite views". Gandhi hoped that the All-Parties Conference meeting at Lucknow in the last week of August 1928 would arrive at a workable unanimity from the national point of view, and then the people would work for the acceptance of the demands. The Nehru Report had discarded communal representation but provided for the reservation of seats for Muslim minorities in proportion to their population.

It may be noted here that Jinnah had left Bombay for London on April 3, 1928, and during the work of the Nehru Committee he was in Paris looking after the health of his wife with whom he had made a rapprochement during her illness. Dr. Besant praised the Nehru Report and said, "The day of bondage is ending and the dawn of freedom is on the eastern horizon." Lord Birkenhead, notorious for his ponderous insolence, had challenged the Indians to produce an agreed scheme for a constitution, and they had done so.

The elder Nehru carried the day at Lucknow. Gandhi said it was a brilliant victory. The protagonists of Dominion Status were in a majority at the All-Parties Conference. Motilal Nehru had to keep them united and bring about a workable unanimity. Pandit Jawaharlal was defeated at Lucknow when the report of the All-Parties Conference was adopted on August 29. On the same day the Independence for India League was formed at Lucknow. Srinivas lyengar was President and Jawaharlal Nehru and Subhas Bose, Secretaries. The father was the spokesman for Dominion Status and the son was the champion of independence!

After the founding of the ginger group, the tension between the young and the old Nehru grew more intense. The elder Nehru had founded the Indian National Union, which was still-born, and now his son had his League, having just presided over the session of the Republican Congress at Madras. As the younger Nehru was going well ahead of him, the elder Nehru asked Gandhi to restrain him.[5]

The year 1928 witnessed a great labour stir in India. The biggest mill strike in the history of Bombay began in April and lasted for six months. The workers heroically fought for their rights. Simultaneously, a heroic no-tax campaign launched by Vallabhbhai Patel in Bardoli had been going on since February 12, 1928. It was against the enhanced revenue of 25 per cent on the farmers that they were fighting. Many satyagrahis were arrested, and their property was attached. The Government used Pathans to surround the houses of the villagers, evidently with a view to provoking the people to resort to violence. Yet they showed heroic patience at the grave provocation, and such was the type of non-violent warfare used by Patel's men that ultimately the Pathans also were cowed into submission.

While the Bardoli no-tax campaign was going on, Gandhi distinguished between non-co-operation and civil resistance. "Both are included," he observed in *Young India* of July 19, 1928, "in the wider term satyagraha which covers any and every effort based on truth and non-violence." The term non-co-operation was designed to include, among other things, the items named in the programme of 1920 with the object of attaining Swaraj. The struggle at Bardoli was to seek redress of a specific grievance. It started with the conventional prayer and petition and on failure they took to civil resistance. "The civil resistance," he continued, "does not mean civil disobedience of the laws and rules promulgated by constituted authority. It simply means non-payment of a portion of tax which the aggrieved ryots contend has been improperly and unjustly imposed on."

In the end, on August 6, 1928, a compromise was arrived at. Sir Leslie Wilson, the Governor of Bombay, yielded under pressure from Delhi. His Government agreed to institute an impartial inquiry into the Bardoli Revenue settlement. The Bardoli prisoners were released, their forfeited lands were restored and the purchasers of the forfeited lands were persuaded to give them up. The Patils and Talatis were reinstated. Vallabhbhai Patel was given a hero's welcome at Ahmedabad on August 16. At the meeting Gandhi eulogized Patel's services, and said that Patel meant a leader. It was declared that an unarmed people could force the hands of a Government by resorting to truth and non-violence. Bardoli's disgrace of 1922 was wiped out by this notable achievement in 1928. Patel was given a rousing reception at several places in Gujarat. He was called Sardar after this heroic victory. The Government inquired into the matter and found that the grievances of the cultivators were justified. The Government therefore agreed to a considerable reduction in the land revenue rates.

At this juncture Gandhi was involved in a bitter controversy over the death of a calf which he had had killed by asking a doctor to give it a poisonous injection to put an end to its suffering.[6] The calf was suffering from an incurable disease and there was no hope of its recovery. Some people said that the killing of the calf was wrong and an act of violence as the cow was sacred. Gandhi was criticized, and even threatened with dire punishment. A Jain friend angrily wrote, "Gandhi, you killed that calf. You killed that cow, and if I do not kill you in return, I am no Jain." Gandhi was asked whether he would apply to human beings the same principle. He replied: "The same law holds good in both the cases." In practice, Gandhi observed, people did not cut short the lives of their relatives and dear ones by death. He further said that it was like going a step further than the surgeon to sever life from the body in the interest of the sufferer. Gandhi's critics said: "In killing the animal one might have unselfish and altruistic motives, but in killing the relatives one might not be so." So his doctrine many rejected so far at least as it related to human beings. Animals do not express their desire, but if a man expresses his desire to live, why should he be killed?

Gandhi also wrote that he was seriously considering the question of killing the monkeys, who threatened the Ashram vegetables and fruit trees with utter destruction, in case it should become unavoidable. The principle of non-violence had its searching examination and reintrospection and sometimes reason had the upper hand of it. Gandhi said: "I do not hesitate to instigate and direct an attack on the monkeys in order to save the crops."[7]

Although Gandhi believed in the sacredness of all life, he said it was impossible to find a society where there would be no agriculture and therefore no destruction of some life. The orthodox people poured curses on Gandhi by inundating him with letters full of abuse. Some of them angrily suggested that his intellect had suffered decay with the attainment of his sixtieth year and that if he had been given a poison injection in the Sassoon Hospital in 1924 and his life cut short, the monkeys and the calf would have been saved! Gandhi was roundly condemned at several meetings in Surat, Bombay and other cities for his most 'brutal' action.

The question of the presidentship of the year was to be decided. In *Young India* Gandhi said Vallabhbhai Patel's name was suggested by Motilal but Patel's hands were too full to allow his attention being diverted from Bardoli. Jawaharlal Nehru had captured by his sterling worth, the imagination of the youth of the country and although his own feeling in the matter was that Jawaharlal should wear the crown, Motilal Nehru should be made President as urged by Bengal. And the elder Nehru was elected to preside at Calcutta.

On October 11, 1928, the Simon Commission returned to India on its second visit and remained till April 13, 1929. It faced social and political boycott everywhere at the hands of the public. Though the Central Committee appointed by the Government of India, and the Provincial Committees helped the Commission by submitting their reports to it, at many places the demonstrators and boycott-leaders were manhandled by the police. On October 30, 1928, Lajpatrai received blows on his chest in such a demonstration and as the result of the blows Lajpatrai, one of India's eminent leaders and Punjab's greatest leader of the twentieth century, died on November 17. A wave of helplessness and anger swept over the country and it sank with grief. Gandhi as usual collected a memorial fund in the name of the great leader.

GANDHI ATTENDED THE All-India Convention which met on December 22, 1928, at Calcutta to finalise the Nehru Report. There Jinnah reopened the communal issue. He said he was doing it not as a Muslim but as a nationalist.

Jinnah had put forward a proposal in December 1927 demanding reservation for Muslims of a third of the seats in the Central Legislative Council. The Nehru Report made no mention of this but guaranteed reservation of seats in the provinces for ten years. As Jinnah was not given the attention and respect that was due to a great emissary of Hindu-Muslim unity, he gave up his role and gradually became a determined opponent of the Congress and its politics. After the convention he said with tears in his eyes to a friend: "This is the parting of the ways."[8] Jinnah then put forward his notorious 14 points for the consideration of the All-Muslim Conference which met at Calcutta on December 31, 1928. Mahomed Ali, an ex-President of the Congress, denounced the Nehru Report as an abject surrender on the part of the Congress Swarajists to the Liberals. The Aga Khan advocated independence for every province![9] A large section of the Muslims rejected the Nehru Report.

Gandhi was for Dominion Status and in favour of the Nehru Report. Sir C. P. Ramaswami Aiyer and Dr. Besant supported Dominion Status. But Srinivas lyengar, demanding independence, read a statement with the support of Jawaharlal Nehru, Subhas Bose and Satyamurti, and said that they disassociated themselves from the report so far as it committed them to the acceptance of Dominion Status. Gandhi, without consulting Besant, Jinnah or Motilal Nehru, shifted his position and sided with Srinivas lyengar.

The Congress session was held at Calcutta under the presidentship of Motilal Nehru. At the Subjects Committee Subhas Bose and Jawaharlal Nehru opposed Gandhi's resolution favouring the Nehru Committee's demand for Dominion Status. Gandhi then revised his resolution and his new draft declared that if Dominion Status was not granted within one year, India would demand complete independence.

While moving this resolution, Gandhi praised young Nehru's impatience for independence, but Jawaharlal was absent. Subhas Bose was gagged by the President. Thus Gandhi's revised resolution was passed in the Subjects Committee.

Subhas Bose then moved an amendment to it in the open session calling for a declaration of independence and said that young India had no faith in the British. Jawaharlal hesitatingly supported Subhas Bose. But the old guard, who were in favour of Dominion Status, whispered that if Gandhi was defeated he would retire from the Congress. The result was that Subhas Bose was defeated. His amendment was lost by 973, votes to 1,350, and Gandhi's resolution was passed.

Sure of his victory, Gandhi now rebuked the younger leaders and said: "Independence is a thing, after all, made of sterner stuff. It is not made by juggling with words."

Gandhi again seized the opportunity of bridging the gulf between the two parties, the Left wing and the Right wing of the Congress, and staged a come-back to active politics. The spirit of the young regained the strength of action and the strength of the old guard won the spirit. Gandhi skilfully fused the two camps together. He saved the prestige of both Nehrus.

When the time came for registering votes on the independence-compromise resolution, Motilal Nehru shrewdly announced that only khadi-clad delegates would be allowed to vote. The younger people were defeated. A delegate with a khadi scarf wore a mill dhoti. He removed his dhoti, wound his scarf in place of it, and exercised his right of vote!

Gandhi, then, wrote in *Young India*, January 3, 1929, that for him the meaning of independence was Swaraj. "Independence," he added, "is a word employed for European consumption" and "Swaraj" was the swadeshi word. Then why had he been for years opposing the English word Independence? The fact was that Gandhi was in favour of Dominion Status if the British Government which was partly responsible for his rise and towards which he was well-disposed from the beginning, was ready for a compromise. For the previous five years Gandhi had been watching the situation and carrying the waves of the Freedom struggle to the farthest corner of the country with the message of the spinning wheel which, for the masses, was more a symbol of Swaraj than that of economic aid. Another point worth mentioning was that Council entry no longer remained a live issue at the Calcutta session.

During the Congress week, Gandhi presided over the Hindi Prachar Conference at Calcutta, Subhas Bose being the chairman of the Reception Committee. Bose read his speech in faultless Hindi and said that Justice Sharadacharan Mitra was the father of the idea that there should be one script for all

India and that it ought to be Devanagari. Gandhi hoped that the South and Bengal would soon pick up Hindi so that the ensuing Congress would transact its business in Hindi-Hindustani. "There was no independence," Gandhi observed immediately after the conference, "for the masses if their representatives cannot conduct their proceedings in the national language. English will be and must remain the language of international diplomacy and intercourse. But it must not be allowed to usurp the function of the national language".

While in Calcutta, Gandhi called on Nagendranath Basu who had completed his Bengali encyclopedia at the age of 45, commencing it at 19. He began his Hindi Encyclopedia at the age of forty-seven. When Gandhi met him he was sixty-three and it was still incomplete. Basu was sitting in an unfurnished unpretentious room and asked Gandhi to sit on his bed as he was doing himself. Gandhi sat on a stool. Basu was a martyr to asthma. He told Gandhi that those labours of his were *sadhana*.[10] He worshipped God through them and lived for his work. Gandhi was reminded of Dr. Murray's work and said nations were made by the achievements of such giants. It shows how a great selfless work attracts great men.

Gandhi gave up the idea of a tour of Europe and declared in *Young India* of January 31, 1929: "If the Nehru Report is not accepted by or on behalf of the British people before the end of December 31 next, it will cease to have any meaning for me, I must declare myself an independencewallah." He would, he said, strain every nerve to carry out the preparatory programme. Gandhi would declare independence on the midnight of December 31, 1929, at Lahore, a declaration which he had held up since the Ahmedabad Congress of 1921. There was another reason for giving up his visit to Europe. Barring those, he observed, who out of their partiality for him would have him in Europe and America at any cost, the peoples of the West would be justified in saying, "Physician heal thyself". He was waiting for the clearest possible light and requested them to pray with him.

Gandhi quoted Napoleon to support his doctrine of nonviolence. When Napoleon was at the height of his success, he said: "There are only two powers in the world, those powers are the spirit and the sword. In the long run the sword will always be conquered by the spirit." Had Napoleon practised this, he would have occupied a place in history along with Buddha and Christ.

ABOUT THIS TIME Gandhi in his Mahatmatic way made public the faults of the inmates of his Ashram which according to him was his best creation. Chhaganlal Gandhi was caught in the act of embezzlement. Kasturba had kept to herself four rupees against the rules of the Ashram, and a widow in the Ashram had been seduced by a young inmate. Gandhi could not be content with their repentance. He grieved over their shortcomings and asked the world whether he should escape by committing suicide, by fasting or by burning himself in the Ashram.

In February 1929 Gandhi toured Sind collecting money for the Lajpatrai Memorial Fund, exhorting people to wear .khadi, to boycott foreign cloth, to eschew the drink habit and to treat Untouchables well. During his tour Gandhi found that the Congress was functioning only in name and it was full of squabbles in Sind. He found also that the Muslims were against the Nehru Report. Gandhi told some girl students at a meeting in Karachi that if he had a girl under his charge he would rather keep her a maiden all her life than give her away to one who expected a single pie for taking her for his wife.

At a depressed classes' school in one of these cities some of the children told Gandhi that he was given the purse to buy sweetmeats for a picnic. During this tour Gandhi spoke against *deti-leti*, the system of dowry, and appealed to the students to root it out.

Rasik, son of Harilal Gandhi and a grandson of Gandhi, died on February 8 at Delhi while working at the Jamia Milia. He was seventeen and Gandhi had wanted him to be a national servant. The thought that he had died at his post filled Gandhi with joy. In his mystic way Gandhi said his grandson's death brought Gandhi nearer to God. His was a death, Gandhi concluded, not to mourn but to enjoy.[11] In this mystic way he had once almost congratulated Mahomed Ali on having his daughter sick![12]

At Delhi, where Gandhi went for a Workers' Committee meeting, he attended a Speaker's party on February 19 which was also attended by the Viceroy, Jinnah, the Maharaja of Kashmir, and others. Speaker Vithalbhai Patel organised the party to break the ice as it were. But nothing important happened. Gandhi said England would never make any advance to satisfy India's aspirations till she was forced to do it. The Congress Working Committee formed the Foreign Cloth Boycott Committee as underlined in Gandhi's scheme.

Gandhi then started on his visit to Burma. On March 4, 1929, on his way, he lit a bonfire of foreign clothes at a public place in Calcutta. He refused to accept a notice which the police came to serve on him. The Police Commissioner, Charles Tegart, wanted him to attend the Court the next day and answer the charge laid against him for starting a bonfire at a public place. Gandhi was arrested at 11 p.m. But on his promise to attend the Court on March 26 he was allowed to go to Burma.[13] In return, Gandhi gave the police an undertaking that till the case was decided there should be no burning of foreign cloth in Calcutta public squares. Later he was fined Rupee 1 for the act. The fine was paid by the Bengal Provincial Congress Committee. An appeal was filed, but it was dismissed on September 13, 1929, as Gandhi was not keen on proceeding with it.

Gandhi reached Rangoon on March 8, 1929, on the *S.S. Aronda*. He was visiting Burma after a period of fourteen years. He put up at Dr. Pranjivan Mehta's. Kasturba, Mahadev Desai, Prof. Zakir Husain, Purushottam and Raghavan were with him. As a noble son of India, Gandhi was presented with an address of welcome by the Rangoon Municipality and several other Municipalities. Replying to the address by the Rangoon Municipality, Gandhi said he would feel honoured if he was claimed as a Buddhist. He said Buddhism was to Hinduism what Protestantism was to Roman Catholicism. He remonstrated with the Indians for not throwing in their lot with the Burmese. He asked them to start with the boycott of all cloth of foreign manufacture.

He advised the Phoongys to unite stainless purity with great wisdom. The representatives of the press evinced great anxiety about the question of the separation of Burma from India, and they thought that Gandhi had come there to advise them on the issue. But Gandhi told them that they had to decide the question for themselves. He was not in a position, he added, to answer their question for the time being. He visited Prome, Mandalay, Pyinmana and other places and returned to Calcutta on March 22.

AROUND THIS TIME an effective movement against war was launched by women in Europe. On January 4, 1929, a conference was held at Frankfurt-On-Main by the Women's International League for Peace and Freedom. It issued an appeal for moral support to the movement for Renunciation of War. The logical conclusion of the Renunciation of War could only be disarmament. Commenting on this appeal, Gandhi said that Indians could render moral and material support by regaining their freedom, not by warlike means but by non-violent means. "I am positive," he concluded, "that if we unflinchingly adhere to these means in the prosecution of our goal, we shall have made the largest contribution to the world peace."[14]

In March 1929 Gandhi gave an interview at Ahmedabad to Dr. John Mott who had come from America to preside over the World Students' Conference at Mysore. This was Dr. Mott's third visit, his first being thirty years earlier. Gandhi said to the leader of the students: "The most distinctive and the largest contribution of Hinduism to India's culture is the doctrine of ahimsa. It has given a definite bias to the history of the country for the last three thousand years and over and it has not ceased to be a living force in the lives of India's millions even today."[15] He further said that the teaching of the doctrine of ahimsa had so permeated the people that armed revolution had almost become an impossibility in India, not because the people were physically weak as some would have it, but because the tradition of ahimsa had struck deep roots among the people. Luckily, Dr. Mott was a leader of students and not a student of history!

During this interview Gandhi praised Islam for its belief in the oneness of God and the brotherhood of man for those who were nominally within its fold, and blamed Christianity for being a symbol of materialistic civilization and exploitation. He said, however, that Christianity drew the pointed attention of Indians to their defects.

On April 5 Gandhi left Bombay for Hyderabad *en route* to Madras. Before this extensive Andhra and Utkal tour began, Gandhi had warned the Congress leaders in that region that they must not present him, without his permission, with earmarked purses. They must not exploit his name for local work. He requested them to help him keep his body in good condition, giving it only six hours' work a day, since they regarded it as a national trust.

Gandhi visited Bezwada, Vayyur, Bandar, Guntur, Ellore, Adoni and numerous other places and villages, asking the people to boycott foreign cloth, promote khadi, put the Congress house in order, remove the stigma of untouchability and eschew drinking and gambling. He unveiled Lajpatrai's picture, hoisted the national flag and received a lot of purses.

Gandhi was unique among Indian leaders in touring the whole country so many times and seeing the hinterland with its dusty and muddy cottages and rough roads and using all sorts of conveyances. No modem leader except Gandhi, for that matter, no emperor or conqueror of the past, had seen the real Bharat and her people and their life so closely, thoroughly and anxiously.

On his way to Pedapadu, Gandhi paid a visit to a young virgin widow named Satyavatidevi who donated her ornaments to Gandhi for his khadi work. Gandhi spoke of her at a meeting and said voluntary enlightened widowhood was a great asset to any nation just as enforced ignorant widowhood was a disgrace. If a young man of 18 being widowed could marry, why a young widow should not have the same right, asked Gandhi.

While Gandhi was on the Andhra tour, two young men, Bhagat Singh and Batukeshwar Dutt, belonging to the Hindustan Socialist Republican Association, threw two bombs on April 8, 1929, at the Treasury Benches in the Central Legislative Assembly, injuring several persons. When they were arrested in the Assembly Hall, Bhagat Singh declared that the bomb was thrown "not to kill but to make the deaf hear." Motilal Nehru, leader of the Opposition, and President Vithalbhai Patel were unmoved and undisturbed. Patel was about to give his ruling on the Public Safety Bill. Sir John Simon was present in the President's gallery. The whole British Empire was rudely shocked by the explosion. It declared to the whole world the revolutionary will of the Indian people to break its shackles. It achieved what hundreds of political speeches could not do.

Referring to this bomb explosion in *Young India* of April 18, 1929, Gandhi said that Congressmen should not give, even in secret, any approval to the deed. He observed that the Government, which was indifferent to popular feeling, was in no small measure to blame for the madness of the bomb throwers. The bomb had no milieu in India, he added, and the Government could prevent its use by conceding the national demand gracefully in time. Gandhi thus condemned the action of Bhagat Singh as madness, but used it for promoting the cause of the nation.

But Gandhi unwittingly acknowledged the debt to the revolutionaries. Writing on the cult of the bomb in *Young India* of January 2, 1930, he observed: "Every time violence has occurred we have lost heavily, that is to say, military expenditure has arisen. As against this, I am willing to put the Morley-Minto Reforms, the Montagu Reforms and the like." Thus the cult of the bomb was responsible, Gandhi agreed, in bringing about the political reforms obtained before 1920. The fact was that Tilak and the revolutionaries had wrested these Reforms.

In the same article of April 18, 1929, Gandhi referred to the assassination of Rajpal, the author of *Rangila Rasul*. He was murdered by a Muslim at Lahore on April 6, 1929. Gandhi said that the assassin had discredited Islam, but he was sorry that the assassination had given Rajpal a martyrdom and a name which he did not deserve.

The A.I.C.C met in Bombay on May 25, 1929. Gandhi moved a resolution calling on the Congress organizations to making preparations for the struggle, as the Government had launched a campaign of repression. The Government was bent on arresting the national workers. It made unwarranted house searches and gave ill-treatment to labour leaders who were awaiting their trial at Meerut.

Gandhi also attended the second session of the Indian States Peoples' Conference on May 25 which was held under the presidentship of C. Y. Chintamani, the Liberal leader. On reaching Ahmedabad, Gandhi inquired after Vallabhbhai Patel's health and on June 19 reached Almora passing through Rai Bareilly, Tadikhet, Nainital, Ranikhet and other places.

At Almora, a villager, Padamsingh, was run over by Gandhi's car. Gandhi visited him in the hospital and promised him that he would take care of his son. At Nainital he said that he had no liking for delivering speeches, but in order to obtain money he would make one. Addressing the meetings in Almora, Gandhi said that his health was not in a condition to undertake long journeys, but he was obliged to tour in order to collect money.

Gandhi rested for a week at Kausanie and wrote the preface to his work *Anasaktiyoga* which was a commentary on the Gita. Every Indian leader of thought or founder of a new ideology has interpreted the Gita to suit his own outlook on life and Gandhi was no exception to this rule.

In June 1929 Dr. J. T. Sunderland's *India in Bondage*: *Her Right to Freedom* was proscribed and the publisher, Ramanand Chatterji, editor of *Modern Review*, was arrested. Gandhi condemned the Government for this action and said that the arrest was a forcible proof of Dr. Sunderland's indictment of British rule.

On his return journey, Gandhi attended the Working Committee meeting at Delhi where it was decided that Congressmen should resign their seats in Councils subject to the approval of the A.I.C.C. It met at Allahabad on July 26 and 27, 1929, and a spirited discussion followed on the subject. Gandhi made a compromise with Subhas Bose and other young leaders who were in favour of maintaining the stronghold in the Councils

Especially Maharashtra, Bengal, Madras and the United Provinces were against resigning seats in the Councils.

The compromise resolution moved by Gandhi gave the Congress members in Councils the option of leaving them at any time up to the Lahore Congress. Chandra Nath Pande, a leader from the U.P., compared Gandhi with the cows which Mohammedans were said to have placed in front of their armies in ancient times. The compromise resolution was carried.

Motilal Nehru, who had gradually changed sides, now openly joined hands with Gandhi and ruled out of order the next two resolutions which sought to congratulate Bhagat Singh and B. K. Dutt on their patriotic spirit. Motilal Nehru had supported Das in congratulating Gopinath Saha, but now he said that the Congress could not at the same time adhere to the principle of non-violence and express its appreciation of violence.[16] The selfless deeds of revolutionaries awoke the nation to heroic deeds. The Congress always exploited the waves of enthusiasm created by their deeds. Since the death of Das they had grown apathetic to their patriotism and selfless sacrifice, so much so that when Jatindra Nath Das, who died on September 13, 1929, after seventy-five days of hunger strike, Gandhi observed silence in his *Young India* on this martyr's death. Jatindra Nath Das was one of the accused in the Lahore Conspiracy Case which had started in the middle of 1929 to try Bhagat Singh and his colleagues.

CHAPTER XXXII

India Declares Independence

On Returning To Ahmedabad, Gandhi published a forceful article in *Young India* on August 1, 1929, fervently recommending Jawaharlal Nehru to the presidentship of the Congress. By his courage, determination, hard work and integrity, Jawaharlal had captivated the imagination of the youth of India. The older men had had their innings. Nehru was not a red rag to John Bull, and Gandhi himself was believed to be a back-number.

Gandhi came to Bombay on August 11 and tried to persuade Jinnah and the Ali Brothers to accept the Nehru Report. As Gandhi was suffering from dysentery, Dr. Jivraj Mehta examined him. As a result Gandhi gave up taking uncooked food. He had started an experiment of eating raw but soaked grain on May 9, 1929. In *Young India* of June 13, 1929 in a note entitled "Food Faddist" Gandhi had observed: "I have been known as a crank, faddist, mad man and I draw to myself cranks, faddists and mad men." Someone belonging to this faddish race had induced Gandhi to plunge into a new dietetic experiment.

Gandhi's lukewarm policy towards the Kathiawad States infuriated a young man and he protested against it. Gandhi replied that his efforts to obtain the redress of grievances at Bhavnagar continued, but the result was not in his hands, "but in hands of God who alone controls results". Gandhi supported the indefatigable Dr. S. Mathulaksmi Reddi in his efforts to abolish the Devadasi system by suitable legislation, although most prominent Congressmen opposed the proposed reforms and defended the infamous and immoral institution. Under the cloak of religion and devotion to God girls were bought and adopted by those so-called devotees and they made a living out of prostitution.

Although Gandhi had suggested the name of Jawaharlal Nehru for the presidentship of the Congress, the Reception Committee of Lahore selected Gandhi for the post on August 18. Declining the invitation politely, Gandhi said that he did not approve of certain things which Congressmen did in the name of the Congress. Moreover his acceptance would embarrass them. So he again appealed to them to select Jawaharlal Nehru. In the last week of August Jawaharlal Nehru met him at Ahmedabad. Gandhi was then to tour the U.P. He gave instructions in *Young India* to the workers in U.P. that he should be saved from the horror of feet-touching devotion. He had been hurt by the nails of the devotees cutting into his flesh.

Gandhi visited Bhopal, and called on the Nawab. Then on September 11, 1929, the U.P. tour began. Gandhi addressed meetings at Agra, where he visited the Taj Mahal which shocked him and did not enrapture him. At Benares he delivered the convocation address at the National University when he first put on a silk dhoti!

At this time Gandhi gave his opinion on tree worship. He saw no necessity, he said, for leading a crusade against it. "I do not," he observed, "defend tree worship because, I consider it" to be a necessary aid to devotion,[1] but only because I recognize that God manifests Himself in innumerable forms in the universe and every such manifestation commands my spontaneous reverence." This attitude is the key to Gandhi's abiding influence with the illiterate Indian masses.

Gandhi's assistants were required to account for every pie received. Money came pouring in and had to be counted up in moving trains and cars. Gandhi could not waste anything. He preserved for use all pins, and half sheets of blank paper from letters and wrote on the backs of these sheets which were written or printed on the other side.

During this tour, as usual, Gandhi acquired some information about local problems, talked to students, addressed women's meetings, sometimes held consultations with strangers or farmers.

On September 28, he attended a meeting of the A.I.C.C. which he was instrumental in calling. Pandit Malaviya pressed him to accept the presidentship of the Congress. Gandhi explained why he declined the honour. He said he had no call from within and he was too weak to lead the Congress.

There was no other alternative. Vallabhbhai Patel had said that it was impossible for a soldier to fill the place which the

General himself had given up. Motilal said that if Gandhi was a back number, he was much more so, being eight years his senior.

In July 1929 Motilal again pressed the claims of his son on Gandhi and said Gandhi was the head and Jawaharlal was the voice of the hour. On July 9, 1929, Jawaharlal Nehru wrote to Gandhi begging him not to press his name for presidentship. Jawaharlal Nehru said that he represented nobody but himself and had not the politician's flair for forming groups and parties. With all this Jawaharlal Nehru had promised Gandhi that if the thing was thrust upon him he would not reject it.[2]

Anyway Gandhi wanted to separate Jawaharlal Nehru from Subhas Bose so that the youngsters who wanted to break away from Britain could not dominate the decision at Lahore. Finally Jawaharlal was elected. He accepted it. But because he was not elected in the ordinary way, he later observed in his autobiography that he did not come to it by the main entrance or even a side-door but by a trap-door! Thus Gandhi's vigorous propaganda which he conducted in the press, in public discussions and private conversations came to a successful end. He saddled Jawaharlal Nehru with the responsibility and astutely drove a wedge between Subhas and Jawaharlal. The dream of Motilal Nehru was now to be realized. A grand historic spectacle, father to hand over the crown to son in the presence of lakhs of people. A consummation devoutly to be wished for! Gandhi left his tour incomplete and returned to Delhi on November 1, 1929.

Meanwhile Lord Irwin had been on a visit to England in June 1929 to consult Ramsay MacDonald, Prime Minister of the new Labour Government, and to find a solution to the Indian deadlock. The new Secretary of State was W. Wedgwood Benn, later Lord Stensgate. Lord Irvin returned to India on October 25. He made an announcement on October 31, 1929, promising Dominion Status and a Round Table Conference in London of representatives of the British Indian and the Indian States with the British Government and the Joint Parliamentary Committee after the publication of the Simon Commission Report.

On November 4, the Congress Working Committee met at Delhi. Gandhi and Motilal Nehru welcomed the Viceroy's announcement. An All-Parties Conference was called at Delhi and issued a joint manifesto on November 4, signed by Gandhi, Sapru, Besant, Motilal Nehru, Jawaharlal Nehru, Sarojini Naidu, Dr. Ansari, Vithalbhai Patel and Khaliquzzaman. Jawaharlal Nehru, who had signed at the instance of Gandhi, withdrew his signature on second thoughts. The manifesto said that the signatories hoped to be able to tender their co-operation to his Majesty's Government in their effort to evolve a scheme of a Dominion Constitution suitable for India's needs, but certain acts should be done and certain points should be cleared up so as to inspire trust in them and ensure their co-operation. Gandhi had his misgivings, but he was waiting for the reaction to the manifesto. The Viceroy knew that although Gandhi publicly asked for a change of heart, he privately hankered after "liberty to order our own future".

In The Meantime the second part of Gandhi's autobiography, *The Story of My Experiments with Truth*, was published in October 1929. The first part had been released in October 1927. Gandhi's autobiography is free from false modesty. But it is the fusion of the autobiographer, the teacher and the leader, and so it is not free from unwarranted vanity and justification and from the object of setting a good example to his followers. No doubt it possesses par excellence the power of self-examination and self-analysis. It may be mentioned here that Gandhi wrote his autobiography during the virtual retirement caused by his defeat in 1924 by the Swarajists.

Gandhi again went on a tour and reached Allahabad on November 15 to attend the Working Committee meeting and also to attend the All-Parties Conference and their joint sitting. Visiting Fatehpur, Jhansi and Chirgaon, he reached Ahmedabad where he met on November 26 Reginald Reynolds. On this day he converted Navajivan into a trust. Vithalbhai Patel met him on the same day. Birkenhead and Lord Reading criticized Irvin in the British Parliament for his announcement regarding the Simon Commission. Baldwin remained cold and MacDonald was silent. In India the tempo of the national struggle was rising, with several young men's movements, labour upheavals and peasants' agitations.

Gandhi went to Wardha and stayed there for a fortnight from December 7, towards the middle of the month. Jawaharlal Nehru saw him and showed him his draft presidential address wherein he had gone wholehog for independence and rejected the invitation to the Round Table Conference. This made Gandhi reconsider his position.

December dawned. The shadow of the Lahore Congress loomed even larger. Just at this time all the principal political leaders of the country expressed a desire to meet Lord Irwin.

The Viceroy wanted to meet these leaders on December 2. But Motilal had to conduct an important case in Lucknow on December 12 and on December 14 the Viceroy had to go to Mysore on a shooting expedition. So December 23 was fixed for the interview. While the Viceroy was returning to Delhi, the revolutionaries made an attempt to overthrow the white carriages of the Viceroy's train on the morning of December 23 near Delhi. Some damage was done to the train, but the Viceroy escaped unhurt.

Gandhi left Wardha to meet the Viceroy. When the correspondents asked him some questions, he replied: "Silence is golden. To talk would only be to complicate matters." Gandhi and Pandit Motilal Nehru representing the Congress, Sir Tej Bahadur Sapru, Mohamed Ali Jinnah and Vithalbhai Patel, President of the Assembly, met the Viceroy on the fateful day.

The Viceroy hoped that the train incident might have made the politicians more tractable, but he found that it had made them more intractable. The unfriendly discussions and hot debates in the British Parliament had hardened the situation and the Left wing in the Congress was bitter. It was a day of silence for Gandhi, and he broke the silence at four in the evening. Gandhi congratulated Irwin on his close escape from death and did most of the talking. Motilal Nehru, Sapru and Jinnah did not know his mind as they had no chance to talk to him earlier because of his silence.

Gandhi said that unless the British Government was willing to name an early and definite date for implementing the Dominion Status assurance, the Working Committee of the Congress which was to meet at Lahore would almost certainly be obliged to declare in favour of independence and back their words by an active campaign of civil disobedience. "As they anticipated," observes the Viceroy in his *Fullness of Days*, "I was unable to give them the kind of undertaking they wanted."[3]

So there was no settlement, and the negotiations came to an abrupt end. It proved to be a fateful day in the life of Gandhi and in the history of the British Empire. Patel was not aware of the attitude of Gandhi, and Motilal and Sapru and Jinnah too were nonplussed.

Lord Reading's prophesy that Irwin would have a comparatively quiet time, but the second half of his term would be a period of trouble and anxiety came true.[4] Gandhi and Motilal Nehru went to Lahore to attend the Congress session there. Gandhi later said that if he was a breaker of the negotiations and if he had made a hash of it, he had done so because "I was driven to it".[5] He said he spoke in accordance with the dictates of his inner voice, But the inner voice was awakened by Jawaharlal Nehru's draft speech! Had Gandhi and Motilal Nehru, who were in favour of Dominion Status, met the Viceroy on December 12, they would perhaps have agreed to his proposal and created trouble for the younger Nehru. But that was not to be. Motilal Nehru was overcome by his paternal affection and a few days before this interview he had said to Vithalbhai Patel, "All roads lead to Lahore!"

THE CONGRESS MET at Lahore in the last week of December 1929. Every shop and every stall there displayed pictures of Bhagat Singh and B. K. Dutt. This was the last Congress without a loudspeaker. The women volunteers had put on saffron saries. The Congress was largely attended by special correspondents from Britain, America and other parts of the world. The President-designate Jawaharlal Nehru was taken in a magnificent procession. His father and his mother witnessed their son seated on a white horse, receiving the salutes of the national volunteers.

After the midnight of December 31, 1929, the clock struck twelve and with it ended the Dominion Status proposal! Just at that moment Jawaharlal Nehru, standing on the Ravi River, hoisted the flag of Independence and again declared the aim of independence which the Congress had chosen two years earlier at its Madras session. Pandit Jawaharlal Nehru was beside himself with joy. He sang and danced round the flag staff. The whole nation applauded the glorious and historic announcement. Young and old India echoed with the slogan *Inquilab Zindabad*, "*Long live the Revolution!*" The Revolutionary Party led by Savarkar had already declared Indian Independence in their own way on August 22, 1907 at the Stuttgart Socialist Congress.

In his presidential address Jawaharlal Nehru said that the Congress had not acknowledged and would not acknowledge the right of the British Parliament to dictate to Indians. And in his epoch-making address he observed: "The great majority of us, I take it, judge the issue not on moral but on practical grounds, and if we reject the way of violence it is because it promises no substantial results. Violence is bad but slavery is far worse."

Moving the Independence Resolution, Gandhi told the Congress officially, after eight long years, that "the word Swaraj in article 1 of the Congress constitution shall mean complete independence." Indian political thought had gone ahead of Gandhi, and he had to fall in line with it to ride the rising tide in the nation.

The Congress also declared a boycott of the Round Table Conference and added that the whole scheme of the Nehru Committee's Report had lapsed. The Congress authorized the A.I.C.C., when it deemed fit, to launch a programme of civil disobedience including non-payment of taxes whether in selected areas or otherwise. The Congress condemned by a narrow majority of votes the attempt on the life of Lord Irwin. It was passed by 935 to 897 votes although Gandhi appealed with all his soul-force to the delegates to pass it unanimously.

Subhas Bose moved an amendment to Gandhi's resolution emphasizing severance from the British Empire and advocating a parallel Government and a programme of all-round boycott and general strike in addition to civil disobedience campaign. But he was defeated as Gandhi replied that Bose's plan was too ambitious. Jawaharlal Nehru was on Gandhi's side as he was saddled by Gandhi with the responsibility of keeping both the wings of the Congress together. Subhas Bose described young Nehru's acceptance of the presidentship as an unhappy event and added, "Since then Jawaharlal Nehru has been a consistent and unfailing supporter of the Mahatma."

According to Gandhi, Nehru's speech was extreme in conception but moderate in expression. He was a confirmed Socialist and was tempering his ideals to suit his surroundings.

Jawaharlal Nehru's heart was with Gandhi and his head with Socialism. Although a wonderful fusion of a doer and a dreamer, he tended at crucial moments to play a glorious Hamlet on the political stage of the world. But at the most opportune time the politician in him overcame all hesitancy, and Nehru rose to international glory and eminence!

At Lahore Gandhi seized the opportunity to tighten his hold on the Congress. He dropped Subhas Bose and Srinivas lyengar from the Congress Working Committee despite the uproar of the members and delegates. The second thing he achieved was to destroy the Swaraj Party which he could not do in 1924. The Congress decided to boycott the Legislative Assembly and Councils and thus the Swaraj Party was given a decent burial. By declaring 'Independence' again at Lahore, he succeeded in overriding the Madras resolution of Independence to which he was not a party.

Did the Congress provide any definite programme for the

attainment of Swaraj? They had nothing except boycott, abstention and resignations. It was left to Gandhi, and he could not see at the time any light coming out of the surrounding darkness. But the great gift of Gandhi was that he had always his ear to the ground and was in touch with the masses. He was the only mass leader in India, and his great virtue was action which brought the intelligentsia into the struggle. The party of revolutionaries was growing in strength, and action alone, Gandhi observed, had any appeal for them! In his opinion civil resistance and civil resistance alone could save the country from impending lawlessness and secret crime. He, therefore, decided to launch direct action and give them a lead so as to prevent anarchy.

With the declaration of Independence, the Congress gave a call to the nation to prepare for the struggle. On January 2, 1930, Subhas Bose founded at Lahore the Congress Democratic Party to give a more militant stimulus to the Congress in respect of the severance of the British connection. The younger Nehru with Srinivas lyengar had established two political institutions — the Republican Congress and the India League for Independence. And they were still-born. It was now Subhas Bose's turn to found a new political party and it too was still-born.

While Gandhi was returning from Lahore to Delhi by a special third-class carriage reserved for him and his party, some young Congressmen entered it. The passing of the resolution on the bomb and the clause appreciating Lord Irwin's efforts towards the solution of the national problem had given Congress youth offence and these two points rankled in their minds. So they expressed their anger and discontent in the compartments with the slogans "Bande Mataram" and "Down with Gandhism." Such anti-Gandhi slogans were raised in Bengali camps in Lahore. 'Father, Son and the Holy Ghost' was their slogan and Sengupta's men gave a counter-slogan.

In accordance with the appeal of the Lahore Congress, Gandhi asked the nation to observe January 26 as Independence Day as they had been observing the national week commencing from April 6 every year. He said that they should observe the Independence Day with discipline, restraint, reserve and dignity and flag-hoisting ceremony.

CHAPTER XXXIII

The Magic of Salt

THE REVOLUTIONARY TEMPO was rising, and Gandhi was not able to cope up with it, although he got himself again in the saddle of the leadership of India. He had no message from his God, or light from Him; nor did his inner voice respond to his environment.

On January 18 Tagore, who was said to be "on a begging mission" by *Young India*, paid a visit to Gandhi's Sabarmati Ashram. In a simple room Tagore had a talk with Gandhi. The poet told Gandhi that he was then seventy and so he was considerably older than him. Gandhi replied that when an old man of sixty could not dance, a young poet of seventy could dance.

At thousands of meetings the Independence Declaration was read out on January 26, 1930, and millions of people took the pledge to get rid of the quadruple curse of British rule—the economic, political, cultural and spiritual ruin of India.

The Ali Brothers and other Muslim leaders advised the Indian Muslims not to participate in the celebration of Independence Day. Their charge against the Congress was that it had done nothing for the achievement of Hindu-Muslim unity. It never occurred, Shaukat Ali added, to Congressmen that it was their duty to make efforts in that direction.

Gandhi was groping his way through the darkness. And suddenly he hit upon an idea on January 30. He made an offer to Lord Irwin as he had done to Lord Reading. He called it a childish offer. He requested Lord Irwin and the British Cabinet to announce the following reforms: (1) Total prohibition; (2) Reduction of the ratio to 1*s* 4*d*.; (3) Reduction of the land revenue to at least 50 per cent, making it subject to legislative control; (4) Abolition of the salt tax; (5) Reduction of military expenditure to at least 50 per cent to begin with; (6) Reduction of the salaries of the higher grade service to one-half or less so as to suit the reduced revenue; (7) Protective tariff on foreign cloth; (8) The passage of the Coastal Traffic Reservation Bill; (9) Discharge of all political prisoners save those condemned for murder or the attempt or threat of it by the ordinary judicial tribunal, withdrawal of all political prosecutions, abrogation of Section 124A, the Regulation of 1818, and the like, and permission to all the Indian exiles to return home; (10) Abolition of C.I.D. or its popular control; (11) Issue of licences to use fire-arms for self-defence subject to popular control.[1]

When the Congress had declared complete independence, who authorized Gandhi, a lawyer from Bezwada asked, to try and strike such a bargain? Gandhi's points, though perhaps good social reforms in themselves, were bewildering to Jawaharlal Nehru too. Gandhi's stand was inconsistent. But it seems he was forging his instruments from these impossible demands. Replying to critics, Gandhi of course said that conceding of these points was a preliminary to a conference about Independence.

On January 23, 1930, Subhas Bose and his comrades were sentenced to one year's rigorous imprisonment for having taken out a procession on August 21, 1929, on All-Bengal Political Sufferers' Day. Gandhi congratulated Bose on his one-year rigorous imprisonment and said that Bengal's bravery and self-sacrifice could never wane. He suggested that the Indians should honourably fill the prisons to overflowing till the Government had a surfeit of political prisoners and make it profitless to imprison any more people. Gandhi perhaps thought that if twenty lakhs of people courted jail, the Indian jails would not contain this vast number and the British Government would come to terms with India.

When the news of the Declaration of Independence was broadcast, several Englishmen, like Horace Alexander, wrote anxiously to Gandhi. Commander Kenworthy, a leader of the Labour Party in Britain, met Gandhi at his Ashram on January 30. On February 12 Jawaharlal Nehru met him at the Ashram, and the meeting of the Working Committee at Ahmedabad decided on February 16 to launch satyagraha. It invested Gandhi with full powers in regard to the satyagraha.

Gandhi published his rules for the satyagrahis and a printed circular telling his followers what they should do if he was arrested. In it he said that he had no all-India successor in view but circumstances would provide the successor. Mass movements all over the world, he added, had thrown up unexpected leaders. There should be no exception to that rule. Concluding his statement, Gandhi said that a votary of satyagraha should be either in prison or in an analogous state or engaged in civil disobedience or in constructive work advancing Swaraj. Under the rules of satyagraha, Gandhi advised the civil resisters to harbour no anger and suffer the anger of the opponent but not to salute the Union Jack. He advised them to behave in prison courteously.

Towards the middle of February, news appeared in the press that Gandhi was launching upon a non-payment of salt tax to begin with. During the nineteenth century the British Government had killed by ruthless methods the manufacture of salt in Bengal and other provinces and dumped Liverpool salt on India which could easily produce good salt with comparatively little labour. Commenting on this news item, Gandhi said that there was that truth in it, that he was contemplating some method of attacking that nefarious monopoly. "Next to water and air," observed Gandhi, "salt is perhaps the greatest necessity of life. It is the only condiment of the poor. Cattle cannot live without salt. Salt is a necessary article in many manufactures. It is also a rich manure."[2]

In the first article Gandhi wrote in his youth in *The Vegetarian* of February 2, 1891, he had described the utter poverty of the Indians and said that they lived on bread, and "salt, a heavily taxed article".[3] While in South Africa he had paid high tributes in *Indian Opinion* to Dr. Hutchinson who had said that it was a great shame for the British Government in India to continue the salt tax. Dr. Hutchinson considered the salt tax a barbarous act. Gandhi had said as early as July 1905 that salt being an essential article in the diet of Indians, the salt tax should be immediately abolished.

Gandhi had given up salt for some years. Tradition reveals that salt has something to do with sex. And sex and salt played a great role in Gandhi's life and in his experiments with truth.

The Nehrus were now on the move. They again met Gandhi on February 28. The preparations for the struggle against the salt tax were going on and the tempo was rising. On March 6 Gandhi gave in *Young India* the implications of the Penal sections of the salt tax for the knowledge of the satyagrahis, seizures, the detention, search and arrest prescribed under it.

On March 2 Gandhi sent a letter to the Viceroy, Lord Irwin,

wiih Reginald Reynolds who was his Quaker disciple. Gandhi as usual used an English messenger to do the job. According to him, Reynolds was a friend of India and had identified himself completely with the Indian cause. He had come to India some months earlier. It was Gandhi's practice to use the unselfish and unsolicited association of such cultured, well-read and devout Englishmen in the act! Gandhi thought Providence had sent Reynolds to himl

Gandhi's letter was handed over to Reynolds on March 1, but he missed the train that day and Pyarelal, who had forgotten to mention a reference to the salt tax, prepared another letter. Reynolds delivered the letter to Lord Irwin on March 4, and the news about it appeared in the press on March 6. Gandhi told the readers of *Young India* that the letter did not mean an ultimatum but a friendly, frank communication from one who considered himself to be a friend of Englishmen. In his friendly letter Gandhi, describing the Government as a curse, blamed it for reducing India politically to servitude, appealed to the 'Viceroy to remove the evil of the Salt Act and the drink and drug revenue and pave the way for a real conference between equals. He added that "he had served the British people up to 1919 blindly". After the letter was sent to the Viceroy, the Nehrus, father and son, left Ahmedabad on March 3.

The Viceroy, Lord Irwin, curtly acknowledged Gandhi's letter through his Private Secretary, G. Cunningham. The Viceroy regretted to learn that Gandhi contemplated a course of action which was clearly bound to involve violation of the law and danger to the public peace. Upon this Gandhi said: "On bended knee I asked for bread and I have received stone instead. It was open to the Viceroy to disarm me by freeing the poor man's salt."[4] Gandhi began his letter with 'Dear Friend' and the Viceroy's letter began with 'Dear Mr. Gandhi'.

The Government prepared itself for the struggle. It appointed every police officer above the rank of a constable in the Bombay Presidency, except in Sindh, as a Salt Officer. And Government struck against Gandhi first by sentencing Sardar Vallabhbhai Patel to three months' imprisonment on March 7. In jail he was treated like a common felon. He was given food which induced dysentery, to which he was prone. Commenting on Patel's arrest, Gandhi said that his right hand was cut off and he declared that in his absence Dr. Haribhai would look after the Ashram inmates. He declared: "We shall have no peace, nor shall the Government have any, until we have won Swaraj."

And when Gandhi was about to repudiate the law and challenge the Government, Gandhi's so-called elder brother Shaukat Ali condemned Gandhi's independence movement as a movement for Hindu Raj and said that it was against the Muslims, and so they should leave it alone! When Gandhi asked him as to the veracity of his statement, he telegraphically confirmed it! This was a return gift to Gandhi, the unkindest cut of all! Gandhi replied that when Shaukat Ali discovered that he was not guilty of the charges Shaukat Ali imagined against him, he hoped the Muslim leader would "restore him to his pocket!"[5]

On March 10 Gandhi addressed a meeting at the prayer grounds of the Ashram. He told the people that the Government was puzzled and perplexed by the non-violent nature of the struggle. He appealed to them to take courage in both hands and contribute in men towards the struggle which promised to be fierce and prolonged.

Numerous visitors and journalists interviewed Gandhi on the eve of his historic March. Bolton, the leader-writer of *The Times of India*, met him at the Ashram. Gandhi told him that he was not interested in the form of Government. The method alone interested him. There was a method of fraud and violence. He chose the method of non-violence and truth. He agreed that boycott of foreign cloth had fizzled out.[6]

As regards the risk of violence, Gandhi replied that his movement might lead to it, though he was trying his best to prevent that. "Today," he continued, "there is greater risk of violence, in the absence of any safety-valve in the shape of movement of non-violence like the one I am contemplating."[7] He hoped that the party of violence would give him fair play. For him it was the opportunity of a lifetime.

So Gandhi's movement was devised to serve as a safety-valve for violence and particularly for the violence of the revolutionaries whom he wanted to attract to his movement. This was one of the purposes of the campaign, Gandhi believed.

The revolutionaries, too, gave Gandhi a period of three years from March 12, 1930, to March 11, 1933, through one Colonel Bedy to conduct his non-violent battle, another chance to Gandhism to fulfil the mission of independence. Gandhi said that if the letter he received was true, he congratulated the revolutionary party on its decision. The three years' limit given to him[8] was ample and Gandhi hoped that the revolutionary party would prevent, so far as possible, sporadic violence from breaking out.

On the evening of March 11, twelve hours before the March, Gandhi stood on the sands of the Sabarmati to address the vast audience. "This will be," he calmly said, "my last speech on the sacked banks of the Sabarmati. Possibly these may be the last words of my life here."[9]

Gandhi told them that the history of the world was full of instances of men who rose to leadership, by sheer force of self-confidence, bravery and tenacity. He asked them to boycott liquor and foreign cloth. He expected the lawyers, the judges and the peons to bid good-bye to Government employment. A satyagrahi, he added, whether free or incarcerated, was victorious.

ON THE MORNING of March 12, 1930, Gandhi, the saint of Sabarmati and the greatest leader of modern India, started on his salt march to Dandi at 6.30 a.m., on foot, with 78 followers, after taking a vow that he would not return to the Ashram of Sabarmati till Independence had been won. They left the Ashram singing the famous hymn "Vaishna-va Jana", amidst the joyous company of a host of journalists, through roads decorated with green leaves, flags and bunting.

With staff in hand and a silver watch, presented by Shantikumar Morarji, tied to his waist, Gandhi at the age of sixty-one marched along at the head of his followers. His steps were firm and his look serene and shining. It was an epic march for the freedom of one-fifth of the human race.

There were no women in the batch, Gandhi said, for the presence of women might embarrass the English and thereby make the fight unequal. Besides, there might even be tortures in jail and the women's time had not yet come. All the satyagrahis were not Ashramites. There were two Mohammedans and one Christian. The rest were Hindus, including two Untouchables.

From the point of view of academic qualifications, 12 were graduates, 7 of Bombay University, 3 of the Gujarat Vidyapith, 2 of foreign universities. From Guajarat came 32, Maharashtra 13, U.P. 8, Cutch 6, Kerala 4, Punjab 3, Rajputana 3, Bombay 2, Sind 1, Nepal 1, Tamil Nadu 1, Andhra 1, Utkal 1, Karnatak 1, Bihar 1 and Bengal 1. Gandhi's son Manilal and grandson Kanti were among the 78 followers.

Gandhi and his party walked about ten miles a day through

the heat and dust. Two or three of the satyagrahis became fatigued and they had to use a bullock-cart. But Gandhi refused to ride the pony that followed him or to travel in a bullock-cart. His feet were gently massaged in the evening. At Nadiad he said, "God willing I hope to do the whole march on foot. For me this is nothing less than a holy pilgrimage!" Simple rustic men in foreign cloth ruffled him a little, but he had no time to accost them.

At his prayer meeting, Gandhi addressed the people and told them that he expected Government servants to resign, students to give up their schools and the people to give up foreign cloth. Early in the morning he finished his correspondence sometimes in the moonlight. He even signed two hundred cards for Sir Daniel Hamilton from the Sunderbuns, giving a message to his students to "be honest".

With his chosen few trudging behind him, Gandhi indefatigably marched along the dusty roads, addressing meetings of thousands of people, preaching the duty of disloyalty to the Government, advertising the cause and arousing the people to sedition and sacrifice. He had deliberately chosen such a long route as he had done during South African struggle, so that he might enthuse the people and demonstrate their woes and will to the whole world! At one place, he said: "We don't want the Salt Act even under Swaraj."

Gandhi crossed the river Malvi early in the morning on March 20 and slept on the bank. There Jawaharlal Nehru, President of the Congress, met him and discussed things with him. At Broach Gandhi crossed the Narmada. He stopped Kitson lights being carried by men. Throughout the march the Ashram rules regarding food and prayers were strictly observed. At one place Gandhi severely remonstrated with his followers against rich food and extravagance in the campaign.

In the first week of April 1930, Gandhi appealed to Indian women to participate in picketing liquor and foreign-cloth shops. They might, he said, even find themselves in prison, to be insulted or even injured bodily. To suffer such insult and injury should be a matter of pride to them.

In the beginning the Government expected the movement to peter out and even ridiculed it. But as the volume and tempo began to grow and spread, the Bombay Government began persistently to persuade Lord Irwin to take action against Gandhi. But he refused to give Sir Frederick Sykes, the Governor of Bombay, special powers to deal with the emergency. Lord Irwin had declared in the Assembly that he was only taking steps to maintain law and order. He was not in favour of Gandhi's arrest. He was marking time. For, "the Christian Viceroy" wrote on April 7, 1930, to the Secretary of State that he had been told a few days earlier that Gandhi's horoscope predicted "that lie will die this year and that is the explanation of this desperate throw. It would be a very happy solution."[10] So he left it to the Provincial Governments to deal suitably with leaders other than Gandhi. He would not arrest Gandhi before he broke the law and put on the side of the Congress those who were still undecided. Gandhi's prominent workers in Gujarat and at other places were arrested, his millionaire friend, Jamnalal Bajaj, and Gangadharrao Deshpande, Sengupta and others were also jailed.

Gandhi reached Dandi on April 5, 1930, covering a distance of 241 miles in 24 days. He stayed in Shiraz Abdullabhai's bungalow. Sarojini Naidu met him there. Gandhi nominated Abbas Tyabji and Sarojini Naidu respectively to succeed him. On April 6 Gandhi, accompanied by a procession of 2,000 people, bathed in the sea at 8.30 a.m. and broke the salt law by picking up some natural salt lying on the shore of Dandi. Sarojini Naidu, who stood near him, shouted "Hail, Thee, Deliverer!"

Government did not arrest Gandhi for breaking the law, but there were country-wide arrests. While Gandhi was at Dandi, Pandit Jawaharlal Nehru was arrested on April 14 and sentenced to six months' simple imprisonment. Before Jawaharlal Nehru's arrest Mahadeo Desai sent him, in a packet, just a pinch of salt manufactured by Gandhi on April 6 at Dandi "to be kept either as a memento or sold by auction, the upset price to be not less than a thousand rupees".

The Responsivist leaders N. C. Kelkar and Aney resigned their seats in the Central Legislative Assembly and joined the struggle, to the keenest joy of the Mahatma. Gandhi addressed women at a conference at Dandi and inspired them to picket liquor and foreign-cloth shops.

At the beginning there was no violence other than the Government's. Maunds of contraband salt was collected, manufactured, stored, and distributed in thousands of packets. The expectations of the advisers of Lord Irwin, the wishful thinking of Lord Peel and the predictions of the loyalist newspapers were entirely belied. All wars start through small causes. Salt worked wonders as the greased cartridges did in the War of Independence of 1857. Salt became the symbol of India's will to freedom. There was no violence in spite of deliberate provocations during the first stage of the struggle. Government had issued orders asking the district officers not to take action against women volunteers for the time being.

But after Gandhi broke the salt law and gave the signal, the battle for salt assumed throughout the land the fiercest look. The arrest of Jawaharlal Nehru added fuel to the fire and there was firing at Calcutta and Karachi. The nation responded to the call of Gandhi enthusiastically and beyond his expectations. The Bengali revolutionaries raided the Chittagong military arsenals on April 19, 1930. The N. W. F. was aflame with the civil disobedience movement and Abdul Ghaffar Khan and his Khudai Khidmatgars—servants of God—developed a wonderful non-violent resistance movement. And when Ghaffar Khan was arrested, there were angry demonstrations and disturbances in Peshawar. Thereafter, armoured cars were sent to cow down the demonstrators and wholesale firing was done which resulted in hundreds of deaths and casualties. Two platoons of the 39th Garhwal Rifles were ordered to quell the disturbances in Peshawar, but they refused to fire. The memory of Amritsar still hung in the air, and there was reluctance to put down the civil disobedience movement.

To meet the emergency, the Viceroy began issuing ordinances. He promulgated the Bengal Criminal Law Amendment Ordinance and revived the Press Act to cripple the patriotic Indian Press. On April 25, Vithalbhai Patel resigned the Speakership of the Central Assembly saying that thousands were prepared to lay down their lives and to court imprisonment. Commenting on these oppressive and repressive measures, Gandhi condemned the British Raj as a Black Regime and Goonda Raj. "Even," he added, "Dyerism pales into insignificance."

Men, women and children in thousands gallantly faced bullets and cavalry baton charges. People faced the mounted guard and their brutal and savage assaults. Patels and talatis resigned in hundreds. Khajur trees were cut down. There were forcible seizures of salt, more than sixty thousand detentions, prosecutions and arrests all over India.

In the Freedom struggle it was Lokamanya Tilak who made jail-going respectable among the middle classes, and it was Gandhi who made it popular among the village folk. By his magic touch, Gandhi created numerous heroes out of dust and mud. He transformed the Congress into a mass party, and it assumed a real nationalist character. Not only did he change the face of the Congress but also changed the face of India, spiritually! The intellectuals who called him an enigma, and the patriots who called him impractical and dogmatic, and the

British who called him an impostor, were all bewildered! The march was neither a ponderous joke nor a ridiculous hoax; it was an unparalleled stroke by an uncommon man with common views.

While Gandhi's march was progressing, he received cables from Mexico, the Phillippines, South Africa, East Africa and elsewhere wishing the cause success. The Executive of the War Registers' International led by A. Fenner Brockway and others sent their love and sympathy, promising assistance in Gandhi's fight for truth and justice. The Women's International League for Peace and Freedom cabled: "May Non-Violence achieve success." The women of Gujarat appealed to the Viceroy and the Rashtriya Stree Sabha devoted itself to boycotting liquor and foreign cloth.

At Last With orders from the Central Government, which was authorized on April 30 by the Secretary of State to arrest Gandhi, the Bombay Government decided on May 3 to arrest Gandhi under Regulation XXV of 1827 and restrain him in Yeravda Central Prison, "during the pleasure of the Government". To avoid strikes and closing of shops on May 5, the Government of Bombay were advised to arrest Gandhi at a late hour on May 4 and all other Provincial Governments were warned on April 29 and advised, in view of possible riots and disturbances, to maintain troops in readiness.

Accordingly, the District Magistrate of Surat and a police party went with flash-lights to Karadi where he was resting in a little cottage, surrounded Gandhi's cot and executed the warrant at midnight. The police party consisted of two police officers armed with pistols and thirty policemen armed with rifles. The police had cut off all telephonic and telegraphic communications.

Gandhi asked the Magistrate to read the orders and asked for some time for ablutions and prayer. After the ablutions, he asked Pandit Khare to recite the famous hymn 'Vaishnava Jana'. Surrounded by the ring of policemen, Gandhi and his disciples stood up, his eyes closed and head bent in mute reverence. The prayer over, all Gandhi's disciples bowed down before the master and bade him an affectionate farewell.

Gandhi was arrested at 1.45 a.m. on Monday, May 5, 1930, his day of silence. Dr. A. H. Thomas, Presidency Surgeon, Bombay, was asked to accompany Gandhi as medical officer from the time the prisoner was placed on the train. On the eve of his arrest, Gandhi had drafted a second letter to the Viceroy, informing him of his intention to take possession of the Salt Works at Dharasana.

Gandhi had kept a message ready in the event of his arrest. In it he observed: "If the struggle so auspiciously begun is continued in the spirit of non-violence to the end, not only shall we see Purna Swaraj established in our country before long, but we shall have given to the world an object lesson worthy of India and her glorious past."[11] He was taken in a car to Navsari, then by train to Borivli. The train reached Borivli at 6-40 a.m. there Gandhi was examined and then taken in a closed car to Yeravda. He was delivered to the Superintendent of Yeravda Prison at 10.30 a.m. Gandhi was in good health and excellent spirits. A Medical Board consisting of Major Martin, A. A. Thomas and R. F. Steel examined him and found that his blood pressure was systolic 140, diastolic 104.

The news of Gandhi's arrest stirred the wrath of the nation, and the mill-workers, railway workers and shop-keepers struck work. There was firing in Delhi, Peshawar and other places. French, German and American papers and sympathizers of the Indian struggle all over the world appealed to the British Government to settle the issue amicably with Gandhi.

The tide of resistance swept all over the nation. Martial law was proclaimed in Sholapur and some leaders of the people there were hanged afterwards. Disturbances occurred in Calcutta, Mymensingh, Karachi, Lucknow, Midnapur, Multan, Delhi, Rawalpindi and Peshawar. Ghaffar Khan's Red Shirt soldiers rose in large numbers against the repression. Abbas Tyabji, the ex-judge of Baroda, led the March as the successor of Gandhi, but his followers were arrested. Then Sarojini Naidu, the Indian Nightingale, rose with the spirit of Laxmibai of Jhansi and led a raid of the Dharasana Salt Depot on May 21. The police battered the skulls of the satyagrahis. Miller, an American journalist, witnessed the inhuman acts of the police who savagely kicked non-violent men in the abdomen and dragged their bleeding bodies to a ditch! These barbarous acts were repeated by the police at Wadala in Bombay and at numerous other places all over India. Hundreds of non-violent men valiantly fell in this Freedom struggle!

The boycott of foreign cloth, of liquor and of British goods was almost complete. Cloth and goods worth crores of rupees lay sealed by Congress volunteers in stores and warehouses. During this boycott women played a glorious role, facing police lathi charges in a spirit of martyrdom. Every volunteer, male or female, regarded it as a national honour to face beating, bayonet charges, jail and death!

The civil disobedience movement was at its height and repression of it reached a climax. Carrying the Congress flag or wearing the khaddar cap was met with punishment. The Madras High Court set aside the order of the District Magistrate of Guntur who had put a ban on the use of khaddar caps. The secret distribution of Congress bulletins in many cities through hosts of volunteers was a feature of the day.

Prabhat pheries were taken out, awakening the sleepers in the early morning to the call of duty. Gandhi was happy. "It was," he observed, "in the Yeravda Jail that I read of the inauguration of *Prabhat pheris*. I thought that whoever originated the idea deserved thanks for it. I felt that apart from their propaganda value, they were spiritually beautiful."[12]

The Congress Working Committee invited students, officials and lawyers to participate in the struggle and extended the field of the struggle to all those who believed in ahimsa as a matter of policy. They appealed to them to raid salt depots, break forest laws, tighten the boycott of liquor and foreign cloth shops and stop transactions with British-owned firms and banks. In June the Congress was outlawed under lawless laws! The British diehards and Churchill's brothers-in-imperialism cursed Gandhi. Lord Zetland, a rabid imperialist, described Gandhi as "a spurious saint of Gujarat". He condemned Gandhi's action as the Mahatma's blind, insensate folly. And yet the most important fact was that Gandhi did not suspend the civil disobedience campaign on account of the nationalist revolutionary activity which was resumed by several revolutionaries who had been released after 1928.

The Viceroy issued ordinance after ordinance from April to December 1930, ten in all, to suppress the Freedom struggle. With these ordinances, opportunities for breaking the laws grew. Noted arrests, firings and lathi-charges drew big processions and hartals and demonstrations in cities and towns. India became a scene of a glorious battle and the world witnessed the upsurge of a revolution! Here was a milestone, a touchstone, in human history!

WHILE IN JAIL, Gandhi was kept in the same two-room cell in the European yard as in 1922. In one of his early letters to the jail authorities he said: "I know that my food is a costly affair. It grieves me but it has become a physical necessity with me."

When the jail authorities informed him that only blood relations could see him, he replied that he recognized no distinction between blood relations and other relatives and added that it meant that his wife Kasturba would not be able to see him as she was not one of his blood relations. The order was rescinded, and the word "blood" was removed from it. He stopped, from May 22, meeting anyone in prison till the Government acceded to his request.

Government was anxious not to cause Gandhi needless hardship and was in search of a prisoner companion who would be fit to be able to massage his body. Gandhi's cells were never locked up. He could sleep in the open. The jail steward purchased fruit for him. A Maratha convict milked a goat in Gandhi's presence twice daily. A Brahmin convict cleansed his utensils, a sweeper convict attended to his needs and two European convicts daily put out and brought in Gandhi's cot. He was given all the books and periodicals he asked for. At one stage, Gandhi decided that he did not want massage any more. His artificial teeth and the carding bow were brought to him.

In one of his letters to the Ashramites, Gandhi said: "I have been quite happy and have been making up for arrears of rest. The nights are cool. I am giving as much time as I can to the *takli*. I have no hurry to go to the books. My health is all right. I rise in the morning at the Ashram hour, i.e. at 4 a.m. I rest regularly at eight in the morning and 12 noon, and thus get some two or three hours' sleep during the day." Gandhi was treated as a state prisoner or a detenue.

Gandhi said he was happy that he had seen Kasturba the evening previous to his arrest. He wanted none of the Ashramites to get nervous or troubled on his account and God above would take care of them. So let them not worry about one another. To the children, whom he called little birds, he said: "I have no wings yet I come flying to you every day in thought. And you also can come flying to me in thought." Gandhi was supplied with a sewing machine and he began learning how to sew.

Acharya Kalelkar, who was undergoing a term of imprisonment, became his companion on June 19, 1930. Gandhi began to learn Marathi with the help of Kalelkar. At this juncture the Mulsi Petha prisoners had gone on hunger strike; fetters were put on them and they were flogged. Gandhi acted in the prison not as a prisoner but as a leader of the sayagrahis. He wanted to inquire into the condition of this prisoner or that, and demanded the liberty to see the other prisoners. He threatened to go on hunger strike if he was not allowed to do so. So, at one time the Government considered the necessity of having Gandhi removed outside the Presidency. Gandhi drew up a list of persons he wanted to meet; but the list was rejected by the prison authorities. Securities were demanded from *Young India*, *Navajivan* and Navajivan Press at the end of June. After July 3 they were suppressed under the press ordinance. "Cyclostyled copies of *Young India* were then brought out. George Slocombe of the London *Daily Herald*, was allowed to interview Gandhi in jail on May 19 and 20, 1930, with a view to ascertaining from him the conditions on which he would be willing to call off the civil disobedience movement. Slocombe had an interview with Motilal Nehru in Bombay before he was sentenced to imprisonment on June 30. Motilal Nehru gave the interview at the instance of Vithalbhai Patel. Slocombe then drafted a statement on June 25 which was approved by Motilal Nehru and sent to Jayakar and Sapru.

On July 23 and 24, 1930, Jayakar and Sapru met Gandhi in jail with the consent of the Viceroy to whom they had written that they would try to restore normal conditions in the country. On July 27 Sapru and Jayakar, the peace-makers, met Jawaharlal Nehru and Motilal Nehru in Naini Jail and handed over Gandhi's note to them. Gandhi had written to Motilal: "Whatever you and Jawaharlal do is acceptable to me."

The Nehrus were unwilling to commit themselves without consulting Gandhi. They gave a note and a letter for Gandhi. Jayakar handed over these to Gandhi on July 31. It was felt that the Nehrus and Gandhi should meet and discuss the problem. So the Nehrus and Dr. Syed Mahamud were brought by train to Poona for peace talks with Gandhi. The parleys took place in the main room on the first floor of the Red Gate of the jail on August 14 and 15. Gandhi, Motilal Nehru, Jawaharlal Nehru, Sardar Patel, Sarojini Naidu, Jairamdas Daulatram, Dr. Syed Mahamud, Jayakar and Sapru discussed the problem. The elder Nehru's simple and light food cost the Bombay Government more than they were willing to pay, and they asked the Central Government to bear the expenses which amounted to rupees eighty-nine, fourteen annas and seven pies. They paid the bill after a long correspondence! The Nehrus and Dr. Mahamud were taken to Naini Jail by a special train to avoid demonstrations on the way. At this time, Sapru said: "It is my fervent belief that India has never had a greater friend than Lord Irwin."

The peace-makers reported the results of their negotiations to the Viceroy and with a letter from him again interviewed the

Nehrus on August 30 and then met Gandhi. From September 3 to 5 they discussed the possible terms of peace with Gandhi, but the negotiations finally broke down. This time A. Rangaswami lyengar was with the peace-makers.

After the breakdown of the peace talks, Gandhi became more assertive and aggressive in prison. He wanted to establish contact with civil disobedience prisoners. The prison and other Government authorities, who took the utmost care of Gandhi's health, now thought that he should not be allowed to dictate terms in prison. They feared that if they yielded on one point he might assert himself on many others.

Gandhi then threatened them openly: "I am aware, as prisoner I have no rights and no choice as to the disposal of my body. But I know also that the upkeep of my body requires my cooperation. I should no longer be interested in the preservation of a body that cannot be used for the service that the dweller within yearns after. I am human. Even as a prisoner I cannot divest of the human in me. The moral code of a civil resister requires him willingly to submit to all prison discipline that is not 'in conflict with self-respect.'

On September 30, 1930, Gandhi gave an ultimatum to the prison authorities. In a letter he protested: "I can no longer restrain myself now. The deprivation of touch with these fellow prisoners is unbearable for me. Unless therefore I get satisfaction by Saturday noon next, I must begin to withdraw my co-operation as to the keeping of my body. To what extent I shall carry the non-co-operation I am unable to say at present. It will be determined as the days proceed, by the inner urge and my courage and strength. The commencement will be made with my refusing all food except the ordinary convict diet, i.e. such of it as I can religiously take. I can take only five natural ingredients in addition to salt. The *kanji* and *chapati* I shall take on the responsibility of and at the desire of the authorities."

The Home Department yielded. It asked E. E. Doyle, Inspector-General of Prisons, to instruct Major R. V. Martin, the Jail Superintendent, to allow Gandhi to interview some of his friends undergoing imprisonment in the same prison.

On October 11 Jawaharlal Nehru was released; his father had been released a month earlier. Motilal Nehru, the great leader, next to Gandhi, had been ill for some months and still gave a lead to the nation in many matters. In the freedom struggle of India, hundreds of families suffered and sacrificed during the civil disobedience movement, but few had the power and popularity of the Nehrus. In the Freedom struggle the Nehru family rose to the peak of immortal fame by their selfless sacrifices, noble patriotism and gallant fight.

Gandhi wanted to send to the Ashram the yarn he had spun in prison to be woven into saris for his wife. He promised that he would instruct the Ashramites not to sell or auction it. But the Government turned down his request. In jail Gandhi translated the *bhajans* of his Ashram.

Gandhi developed digestive trouble as a result of his experiments in diet. As a result of fasting, he had lost ten pounds. On November 27 he weighed 101 pounds. On one occasion, he fainted and had to be assisted to regain consciousness. And although this trouble was of Gandhi's own making, J. E. B. Hotson, the Home Member of the Bombay Government, observed: "No doubt he himself is chiefly responsible for this but anything like a breakdown, however caused, would be very embarrassing to us." Upto December 19 Gandhi was allowed six interviews. Pyarelal, now a prisoner, was allowed to be a companion of Gandhi from November 29, 1930.

Several persons, internationally famous, wrote to Gandhi, but the letters were not delivered to him. They were not destroyed, but kept in the files. The jail authorities allowed Gandhi, in January 1931, to sign an appeal along with J. C. Bose, Romain Rolland and Einstein, for a Golden Book of Appreciation to be presented to Rabindranath Tagore on his 71st birthday.

THE SIMON COMMISSION Report was published in June 1930 and on November 12, 1930, the Round Table Conference was inaugurated by the King-Emperor. Ramsay MacDonald, presiding over the Round Table Conference, said to the members that they were present at the birth of a new history.

The Round Table Conference was not a Constituent Assembly entrusted with the work of drafting a constitution. It was a gathering of Indian and British statesmen including the rulers of the Indian States who met with Indian leaders at a common conference for the first time. Another salient feature of the R.T.C. was that two representatives of the depressed classes were invited to participace in discussions for the political and constitutional development of India. The Conference consisted of 89 delegates, 16 from the three political parties in the British Parliament, 16 from the Indian States and 57 from British India.[14]

The venue of the conference was shifted from the House of Lords to St. James' Palace. From November 17 to 21 Sapru, Jayakar, Moonje, Jinnah, the Maharaja of Bikaner and Ambedkar made impressive speeches. In his lucid and appealing style, the guide, friend and philosopher of the conference, Sir Tej Bahadur Sapru said: "India wants and is determined to achieve a status of equality - equality with all the three "members of the British Commonwealth equality which will give it a Government not merely responsive to, but responsible to the popular voice."

The Maharaja of Bikaner declared that the Princes were prepared to federate of their own free will with self-governing Federal British India. Jayakar, in his sweet sonorous voice, said that if the Indian delegates returned to India empty-handed from their labours in the conference, "it will be the surest way of raising in volume and in intensity his demand for independence."

Dr. Ambedkar said: "Our wrongs have remained as open sores and they have not been righted, although 150 years of British rule have rolled away." He upheld the demand for Dominion Status. He thundered before the conference: "No constitution will be workable which is not acceptable to the majority of the people. The time when you were to choose and India was to accept is gone, never to return. Let the consent of the people and not the accident of logic be the touchstone of your new constitution, if you desire that it should be worked."

After the general discussion in the Plenary session, nine sub-committees were appointed. They did much spade work. But since the different communities differed on the question of seats and on the system of elections, whether separate or joint electorates with reserved seats should be employed, the conference adjourned. But the adjournment was due to the non-co-operation of the Congress, the largest political party in India. No constitutional progress was possible when it was in revolt.

While the Round Table Conference was going on, Mahomed Ali, patriot and stormy petrel of the Muslims, breathed his last in London on January 4, 1931. He was buried in Jerusalem as he did not wish to return to India if she continued to be a slave country.

Announcing the adjournment of the Round Table Conference, on January 19, 1931, Ramsay MacDonald, the Prime Minister of Great Britain, declared: "The view of His Majesty's Government is that responsibility for the Government of India should be placed upon the legislatures, central and provincial, with such provisions as may be necessary to guarantee, during a period of transition, the observance of certain obligations and to meet other special circumstances, and also with such guarantees as are required by the minorities, to protect their political liberties and rights." "If," MacDonald added, "in the meantime, there is response to the Viceroy's appeal from those engaged at present in civil disobedience, and there is a wish to co-operate on the general lines of this declaration, steps will be taken to enlist their services."

On January 25, 1931, the Government of India decided to release unconditionally the Congress Working Committee leaders and to lift the ban on the Congress Party to allow full facilities for discussion of the Prime Minister's statement.

And then Lord Irwin 'the Christian' Viceroy, ordering the release of the Congress leaders, declared: "My Government will impose no conditions on these releases . . . our action has been taken in pursuance of a sincere desire to assist the creation of such peaceable conditions as would enable the Government to implement the undertaking given by the Prime Minister."

The Central Government instructed the Provincial Governments to release Gandhi and the members of the Working Committee on January 26, 1931, at such an hour that they would not be able to participate in the celebration of the Congress Independence Day. The local Governments were advised to avoid clashes with the Congress demonstrations and not to arrest those leaders without referring the matter to them. The gate of Yeravda Prison opened on January 26, 1931, at 10-30 p.m. and Gandhi, Pyarelal and Sarojini Naidu were taken in a car to Chinchavad. There they boarded a train and reached Bombay at 5-45 on the morning of January 27, 1931.

CHAPTER XXXIV

The Delhi Pact

BELLS OF OVATION rang all over the country at the release of the great leader, and Bombay gave Gandhi a unique welcome at Azad Maidan. Some people were crushed in the crowd. One died. Gandhi could not address the vast mass meeting.

A great man's life goes on rolling like a great river. The first thing Gandhi did was to visit the Congress hospital and look after the wounded! The Government which had underrated the power and influence of the Congress with the people, and the British statesmen who had overrated the strength and status of other Indian political parties, now realized the strength of the Congress and its grip over the people. All great movements have their setbacks and temporary defeats. Both the people and the Government knew that the Freedom struggle had suffered a temporary defeat. But it was not a moral or spiritual defeat. The spirit of the people was unbeaten and their faith was invincible.

On his release, Gandhi declared in Bombay that manufacture of salt and boycott of foreign cloth and liquor would continue, not as symbols of resistance to misrule, but because they were desirable in themselves. He was hungering for peace if it could be had with honour and he had come out with an open mind unfettered by enmity and prepared to study the whole situation.

Gandhi left Bombay for Allahabad to meet Motilal Nehru who had been seriously ill. The elder Nehru was glad to see the great leader, his son Jawaharlal, his daughter-in-law Kamala Nehru, and the other leaders of the Congress who assembled at Anand Bhavan for the meeting of the Working Committee. Motilal could not participate in the meeting. He sat up in an arm-chair and silently welcomed his colleagues. His eyes had a glitter, but his head was bowed. "We shall surely win Swaraj"," said Gandhi to the dying hero, "If you survive this crisis!" Motilal replied, "Why, you have already won it." Motilal was taken to Lucknow for X-ray treatment, and at Lucknow in the early hours of February 6 India's great, noble leader, elder statesman, great parliamentarian, a symbol of Hindu, Muslim and Western cultures, passed away leaving a great name behind him, and a still greater fortune for the nation in the form of his son and grand-daughter Indira! His body was taken to Allahabad. Gandhi said at the cremation grounds that the pyre was being dedicated to the altar of the nation, and in a press statement he said that he was more widowed than Mrs. Nehru.

Gandhi waited till the arrival of Srinivas Sastri, Jayakar and Sapru, who had cabled from London to Motilal Nehru requesting the Working Committee to defer the final decision. Gandhi now held that it was no joy to him to put thousands to suffering. He wrote a letter to the Viceroy on February 1, 1931, drawing his attention to the alleged police excesses during the civil disobedience movement and demanded an inquiry into them. Although the diehards like Churchill were adamant in the British Parliament, Lord Irwin was not averse to making a fresh approach to the Congress despite the warning voices of his advisers, H. W. Emerson, the Home Secretary, Sir James Crerar, the Home Member, and those in London. The announcement of Lord Irwin's successor, Lord Willingdon, had been made, and he was to come in April. The name of General Smuts was suggested for Viceroy, but it was later dropped. Irwin was determined to play a historic role before his departure.

The Viceroy flatly rejected Gandhi's suggestion for an inquiry into the police outrages. However, he asked Gandhi to forget the past and to consider the future. At this juncture Sastri, Sapru and Jayakar arrived in India and Gandhi met them at Allahabad in the second week of February.

Gandhi seemed to be in a blind alley. After his talks with Sapru and Jayakar, he wrote Lord Irwin a letter on February 14 and said to his "Dear Friend": "As a rule I neither wait for outward prompting nor stand on ceremony, but straightway seek personal contact with officials whenever I feel such contact is needed in the interests of a cause. But somehow or other in the present case I have missed the guidance of the inner voice. But I have received suggestions from friends whose advice I value that I should seek an interview with you before coming to any decision. I can no longer resist this advice." And before he advised the Congress to suspend the civil disobedience movement and co-operate in the Round Table Conference, he wanted to have a heart-to-heart talk with Irwin. "I would like," he appealingly concluded, "to meet not so much the Viceroy as the man in you." Irwin was persuaded by Sastri to see Gandhi if the Mahatma sought an interview. He told the Viceroy that Gandhi was like a capricious woman and that the Viceroy had to win him over. He also told the Viceroy that Gandhi's dominant quality was vanity, unconscious but not less real.[1] Sastri told Gandhi that if the Mahatma saw the Viceroy he guaranteed that "you will come out a conquered man and you will be his man henceforth." Upon this Gandhi replied: "I wish to be conquered."

The Viceroy informed the Secretary of State for India that he was taking the necessary steps to meet Gandhi. He thought that discussions about peace terms had become inevitable and he wanted enlightened opinion in Europe and in India opposed to civil disobedience.

Gandhi and Irwin were typical historic figures. Like Gandhi, Irwin was deeply religious. The one was a devout Christian whereas the other was a devout Hindu. As religion was an integral part of his life, Irwin was always careful about his prayers and whenever he was on his travels, he would break his journey in such a way as to be able to offer prayers in a wayside church. The six-foot-five Englishman was a typical product of Eton and Christ Church with a streak of Yorkshire ruthlessness and acumen in him. Gandhi, five-foot-five, was a typical product of the Inner Temple and of Porbandar with a streak of the Bania's shrewdness in him.

The one was reared on the sermons of Pusey and Keble, the other on the Gita, the Sermon on the Mount and on the teachings of Raychandbhai and Tolstoy, Ruskin and Thoreau. Gandhi was not only the leader of a party but the spokesman of the vast Indian conservative masses. The one lived in a palace. The other lived in an Ashram. A man in his forties, Irwin was a politician trying to use religion for his statesmanship whereas Gandhi in his sixties was a lawyer-politician trying to be a saint. Gandhi's mystic ways had baffled many a statesman. Sarojini Naidu called both of them Mahatmas. The senior Mahatma was the grandson of a Dewan and the junior Mahatma was the great-grandson of the Grey of the Reform Bill.

The news of the Viceroy's willingness to meet Gandhi outraged the pride of Britain's mighty imperialist, Winston Churchill. "On February 23, 1931, he said in his speech to the West Essex Conservative Association that it was "alarming and also nauseating to see Mr. Gandhi, a seditious Inner Temple lawyer, now posing as a fakir of a type well known in the East, striding half-naked up the steps of the Viceregal Palace, while he is still organizing and conducting a defiant campaign of civil disobedience, to parley on equal terms with the representative of the King-Emperor!"[2] Churchill was contempt personified—the contempt of all British imperialistic diehards, dead and alive! He had sat at the same table with rebels like Louis Botha and Michael Collins! It was his anguish that the naked fakir had blown off the clothes of all imperialists and exposed the nakedness of the British Empire.

IRWIN MET THE saint of Sabarmati who was in a loin-cloth on February 17, 1931, and again eight times for twenty-four hours in all during the four weeks that followed. During these interviews there was a gap of three or four days. The Viceroy perhaps took this much time to consult the India Office in London. The simplicity, sincerity and humility of the one impressed the other. Gandhi's starting point was, observed Irwin, always human and very simple. But it was not easy to argue with Gandhi. During these talks Sapru once observed: "Our difficulty is that we cannot get him to discuss real political problems. He is all the time putting to us moral and social conundrums."[3] Indeed it would have been an ordeal for any statesman to watch and listen to Gandhi's sudden shifting thoughts and rambling monologues, but the Viceroy had to maintain his interest in the talks and keep them going. The Viceroy became conscious of his opponent's powerful personality and exceptional character.

The first thing Irwin explained to Gandhi was that any decision made must be based on the assumption that India's goal was an All-India Federation with a responsible federal government with safeguards. Then they gradually discussed the salt laws, the conduct of the police, and the release of political prisoners in the Meerut Conspiracy Trial and those convicted under martial law in Sholapur. Irwin refused even to discuss the question of releasing men who had been convicted of crimes of violence during the civil disobedience, but those who had been arrested for other offences were about to be discharged.

After four days of close and long discussion, Gandhi gave up his point of demanding an inquiry into the alleged excesses of the police. "I had no guarantee," Irwin said, "that he might not start civil disobedience again, and if and when he did, I wanted the police to have their tails up and not down."[4] Irwin held that although there might be some cases in which discipline had collapsed, it did not justify an inquiry. The talks were likely to founder on this point, but the peace-makers, Sapru and Jayakar, averted the rupture.

In Gandhi's opinion Irwin was at first very stiff and frigid and then became friendly, courteous and frank![5] Gandhi was equally courteous. He allowed Emerson to destroy an angry letter of his without keeping a copy of it.

The salt issue was settled amicably with Sir George Schuster, the Finance Member. The inhabitants of the seaside villages could prepare or collect salt but should not sell it to people outside their areas. The subject of picketing was also discussed. Gandhi wanted to reserve the right to use economic boycott as a political weapon. It was, however, agreed that there should be no compulsion on merchants who made their living by dealing in English goods, but the right of peaceful picketing under certain conditions was granted. As regards the forfeited property, Irwin refused to abandon third party rights created by sales of forfeited property. Gandhi had to be content with having his objections entered in the clause. His heart was full of helpless anguish! All ordinances and notifications declaring certain association unlawful would be withdrawn, except those restraining terrorist activities. Fines and securities not already collected were to be remitted. The civil disobedience movement, which had toned down, was thus called off.

On the night of March 4 when the negotiations were on the point of breakdown, Gandhi got the Working Committee committed to the pact. Jawaharlal Nehru, President of the Congress and leader of young India, did not oppose Gandhi but yielded. Motilal Nehru, the one leader who could have influenced Gandhi, was dead.

The Delhi Pact was signed by Gandhi and Irwin at noon on March 5, 1931, in a free and friendly atmosphere. Irwin said that they should drink to each other's health. Gandhi was glad to do so. He took out a paper bag out of a fold in his shawl and said gleefully, "Thank you, I will put some of this salt into tea to remind us of the famous Boston Tea Party!" Both laughed and joked freely over Churchill's account of the "naked fakir". Irwin and Gandhi rose to go, and Gandhi forgot to take his shawl. Irwin picked it up and handing it to him, saying: "Gandhi you haven't much on you, you know, that you cannot afford to leave that behindl"

Irwin won a hard bargain at the risk of his political future. It was agreed that the Congress should participate in the future sessions of the Round Table Conference, and that the subject of discussion should be the future of India in an all-India Federation with a responsible federal Government with responsibility or reservations or safeguards in the interests of India, for such matters as, for instance, defence, the position of minorities, the financial credit of India, and the discharge of various obligations.

After the agreement was signed on March 5, 1931, the Secretary of State began to waver, but Irwin telegraphed to say that revision in the text of the Delhi Pact was impossible and it would be inviting disaster.

Gandhi's prestige and popularity reached the pinnacle of glory as he made the pact with the representative of the British King. A rebel rose to the position of equal status with the Viceroy, who treated him as the sole spokesman of India. Yet Lord Irwin had not yielded much from the eleven points of Gandhi except for some consolation prizes. Thus there was less bargaining and more of bartering away of Gandhi's points in the Pact.

By signing the Delhi Pact, Gandhi sprang a surprise on his colleagues. Gandhi did not gain much. Neither Dominion Status nor Independence was assured. And instead of "suspending" the civil disobedience movement, he had effectively discontinued it! A few hours after Irwin and Gandhi had signed the agreement, Gandhi went back to Irwin rather depressed, and said that Jawaharlal Nehru was unhappy about it as Nehru thought that "Gandhi had unwittingly sold India"! "I exhorted him," observed Irwin in his *Fullness of Days*, "not to let this worry him unduly, as I had no doubt that very soon I should be getting cables from England, telling me that in Churchill's opinion I had sold Great Britain."[6]

Jawaharlal Nehru was greatly shocked, dismayed and distressed. He feared that the pact would result in demoralization of the nationalist movement. "Was it for this," he ruminated, "that our people had behaved so gallantly for a year? Were all our brave words and deeds to end in this?" But he observed sorrowfully, "Our leader had committed himself; and, even if we disagreed with him, what could we do? Throw him over? Break with him? Announce our disagreement? That might bring about some personal satisfaction to an individual, but it made no difference to the final decision."[7]

The next day in his usual walk Gandhi took Nehru along and tried to convince him that no surrender of principle had been made. His interpretation seemed to be a forced one and Nehru was not convinced. Nehru told Gandhi that his way of springing surprises upon his comrades frightened him and filled him with apprehension. Gandhi admitted the presence of this unknown element in him, and said that he himself could not answer for it or foretell what it might lead to.[8] He was unpredictable.

This shows that the Working Committee helplessly accepted the pact. Gandhi had not taken his colleagues into his confidence and acted as he had done in the South African struggle in 1908.

Sardar Patel, whom Gandhi got elected President of the ensuing Congress, though overriding the usual proceedings, by the Working Committee, had promised the restoration of the lands to peasants after the settlement. He was naturally displeased and disappointed. Das had died long ago, Vithalbhai Patel had left for Europe and Subhas Bose was in jail.

This was the second time that Gandhi had fulfilled the prophecy of Gokhale, his political Guru, that Gandhi would exercise enormous influence on the masses, but when the history of political parleys would be written disinterestedly, he would go down in history as a great failure.

GANDHI'S *YOUNG INDIA* began to appear in printed form on March 12, 1931. It was now the great responsibility of Gandhi and the members of the Working Committee to secure the ratification of the Delhi Pact. So they applied themselves to this great task. At the beginning of his talks, Gandhi had paid glowing tributes in Delhi to the glorious role the women and children of India had played in the recent struggle! The cross-examination of Gandhi by the press was very severe. Gandhi told the press that it was neither possible nor wise to say which party was victorious.

Gandhi further stated that the Congress had embarked deliberately, though provisionally, on a career of co-operation. He appealed to the revolutionaries to give him a chance to work out his plan of truth and non-violence. The revolutionaries were attacking the British in their own way and Gandhi was appealing to them "to desist from their activities, if not yet out of conviction, then out of expedience."[9] He had been sending forth this appeal for the past sixteen years but to no avail!

So the claim of Rajaji that it was Gandhi and not the British Government that had killed the terrorist movement in India gave no correct picture of the situation. It was the inauguration of provincial autonomy in 1937 that had some effect on the minds of the revolutionaries.

At a meeting in Delhi, Gandhi said on March 7, 1931, to the Muslims, "Have as big a share of the spoils as you want: we will be content to serve you." To the revolutionaries he said that they should get the old leaders to abdicate if they had bungled and had been guilty of weakness.[10] Throughout the negotiations, he added, he had not acted on his own, he was backed by the whole Working Committee. He could not "in all conscience agree to anyone being sent to the gallows, much less a brave man like Bhagat Singh." "History," he concluded in his proverbial way, "records numerous instances of the truth that those who use the sword shall perish by the sword."

In Bombay, on March 17, Gandhi by way of an explanation said that the settlement in no way committed Congressmen to a position less than that implied by the Lahore Resolution.

Subhas Bose, who was released on March 8, met Gandhi in Bombay on March 16. Gandhi assured him that he would do nothing that was inconsistent with the goal of independence and would try to secure amnesty for those who had not been mentioned in the pact. The peasants in U.P. and Gujarat were distressed and displeased with the pact, and Bengal was far from pleased, as there was no amnesty for its sons who had languished in prison. Gandhi did not visit Dandi or Karadi which would have been full of drama and colour as he was not in a mood to add to the excitement of Gujarat.

Ahmedabad went mad with joy during the visit Gandhi paid, but he would not go to the Ashram as the vow prevented his visit to it. He paid tributes to the volunteers, boys and girls, who had helped the satyagrahis. Later, on July 31, he visited the Ashram at Ahmedabad.

On his way to Karachi, Gandhi met Lord Irwin at Delhi who complained that Congressmen had not kept the spirit of the pact. Two days after, Emerson, the Home Secretary, supplied Gandhi with details about the complaint made by the Viceroy.

During this interview, Gandhi, who had been pressed to save the life of Bhagat Singh, appealed on March 23 to the Viceroy on his behalf. On the previous day Irwin had rejected Bhagat Singh's appeal for a reprieve. Accordingly, Bhagat Singh was to be hanged at Lahore on the evening of March 23, 1931 when Gandhi would be on his way to Karachi for the Congress.

"Gandhi said that he greatly feared," Irwin noted, "unless I could do something about it, the effect would be to destroy our pact." Irwin stated that from his point of view it was neither possible to grant Bhagat Singh a reprieve nor to postpone a decision on his sentence and encourage people to think that there was such a chance of remission. So to let the execution proceed was the best course. Upon this, Irwin reported, Gandhi thought for a moment and then said, "Would your Excellency see any objection to my saying that I pleaded for the young man's life? I said that I saw none, if he would also add that from my point of view he did not see what other course I would have taken."[11]

The Viceroy knew that Gandhi would not break with him. Besides, the execution of Bhagat Singh and his comrades Rajguru and Sukhdeo, at a psychological moment, might cause a split in the Congress and weaken its forces. Gandhi was no leader of the Sinn Fein Party which had secured a remission for a hero who had been condemned to death.

The members of the Working Committee tried their utmost to see that those who were for the ratification of the pact should be not only elected as delegates but also not stranded for lack of funds. Those who were hostile to the pact were either in jail or were stranded for want of funds. Political parties are not averse to such tricks, and the Right wing of the Congress was no exception to it. Besides Gandhi had put Vallabhbhai Patel, his own man, into the saddle of the Congress presidentship.

When Gandhi reached Karachi, the news of Bhagat Singh's execution had reached it. Young men showered on Gandhi the slogans "Gandhi go back", "Down with Gandhism", "Gandhi's truce has sent Bhagat Singh to the gallows". Even the Red-shirts had done so at Malir station near Karachi. Gandhi was received with black flowers and black garlands. He bore it all patiently and said in the speech before the Congress that he would treasure the black flowers in the Ashram if the young men did not show repentance and that they might kill him but could not kill Gandhism as they could not kill truth and non-violence.

Gandhi told the Naujawan Bharat Sabha (Youth Movement) that he had done his best to save Bhagat Singh and he (Gandhi) had done no harm to the country. The atmosphere was tense. Gandhi used his sharpest weapons to beat his opponents into silence. He managed to bring Sardar Kishen Singh, Bhagat Singh's father, to the rostrum to speak in support of the Congress leaders.

At the Subjects Committee, Jamnadas Mehta said, "If anyone other than Gandhi had been responsible for the agreement he would have been thrown into the sea." As a concession to his opponents, Gandhi got the Congress to pass a resolution appreciating the courage and self-sacrifice of Bhagat Singh and his comrades while at the same time condemning all acts of violence. Gandhi was the author of the resolution.[12]

Gandhi, who had successfully used prayer before the Dandi March for political propaganda, did so during the Karachi session with great success. So it evoked the remark from M. N. Roy that it was not a Congress meeting but a fair! Sardar Patel, the President of the Congress, strangely enough, defended Dominion Status in order to support Gandhi's stand in respect of the Round Table Conference. The Congress passed a resolution endorsing the Delhi Pact but declared that the goal of complete independence remained intact. Was this an endorsement, or an infringement of the Delhi Pact, or both?

Nehru and Subhas Bose did not like the pact, but they decided to keep a united front under Gandhi's leadership. Nehru had refused the request of Gandhi to move the resolution ratifying the pact, but at the last moment he yielded!

The Congress passed a resolution on Fundamental Rights and offered a sop to some new socialist-minded leaders. M. N. Roy, who had been touring India under a pseudonym, was present at this session as Dr. Mohamud. The Working Committee appointed a flag committee under Sardar Patel.

On April 2 the Working Committee duly appointed Gandhi as the sole delegate to the Round Table Conference. Gandhi said this arrangement was the best, most efficacious and economical. "Not the ability of the delegation," wrote Gandhi in *Young India*, "will tell at the conference but the power behind it,"[13]

The Working Committee was dominated by Gandhians and Nehru was not expected to oppose them in this proposal. It was not a good proposal. At least one nationalist from every minority community, like Dr. Ansari, should have been selected to accompany Gandhi as a delegate. In fact, the Working Committee at one stage thought of sending a batch of about 15 delegates and Government were quite willing to accommodate up to 20. But they thought that Gandhi was going to London not to hammer out the details of a constitution but to negotiate the fundamentals of a treaty. So it was thought that he would do it better alone than many.[14]

Gandhi was asked a volley of questions concerning the pact. As for the students who had left schools and colleges, he said that they could hawk khadi! The civil resisters, who were discharged, should be employed in Congress organizations. Some should become labourers! The serious charge against Gandhi was that he had sacrificed his country for "truth,' that he considered and treated Indians like test-tubes in an experiment of non-violence[15] and truth, staked the whole nation for his individual self-evolution, and that his attitude towards the Round Table Conference was inconsistent.

The lawyer in Gandhi replied that manners changed with times; and if he was inconsistent, he was wisely so. He had not permanently boycotted the Round Table Conference! He had not sacrificed the country for truth, the decision was taken by the Working Committee. But writing pathetically, he asserted, "I have no hesitation in saying that I should, if there could be such a choice, most decidedly sacrifice the country for truth."

The Gandhi-Irwin Pact stirred the Muslim leaders. When cities and towns in India observed *hartal* as a protest against the execution of Bhagat Singh and his comrades, communal riots broke out at Kanpur, Benares, Agra and Mirzapur. Ganesh Shankar Vidyarthi, who went to pacify the rioters, was killed in Kanpur on March 24.

The Muslims were in a responsive mood, said Gandhi in public and privately, and success at the Round Table Conference depended upon the Hindu-Muslim unity. He had addressed the Jamiat-ul-Ulema-I-Hind at Karachi and conferred with the leaders of the All-India Muslim Conference in Delhi. This made the Muslim leaders feel that although Gandhi was a power and had forced the Government to make a pact with him, he had his weaknesses and inferiority complex in regard to the Muslims as before. So Shaukat Ali met Gandhi in Delhi and Bombay. In the presence of Subhas Bose the nationalist Muslims led by Dr. Ansari told Gandhi at Delhi that communal representation should go, but when Gandhi showed his usual over-anxiety over the problem, the communal Muslim leaders began to stiffen their attitude and presented him with Jinnah's fourteen points.

By not taking any nationalist Muslim as a Congress delegate to the Round Table Conference, Gandhi was increasing his own difficulties. After meeting Gandhi in Delhi, Shaukat Ali declared in Bombay on April 12 that he would fight single-handed, not with one but even with ten lakhs of Gandhis!

ON APRIL 7 Gandhi inaugurated the 4th Annual Session of the Federation of Indian Chambers of Commerce at Delhi. In his address he said that Indian civilization must not be allowed to be wiped out by inroads from the West. Some critics mischievously identified Indian civilization with the loin-cloth. Gandhi replied to the critics in *Young India* of April 30 that "Indian culture is therefore Indian. It is neither Hindu, Islamic or any other, wholly. It is a fusion of all and essentially Eastern".

Gandhi was worried over the problem of the peasants of Gujarat and the high-handed behaviour of the government officers towards them. After the Delhi Pact, the Executive had reported to their old tactics. Gandhi warned Emerson that the pact was not being honoured.

Gandhi called on Lord Irwin in Bombay on April 17 as he was leaving India the next day. Irwin, the peace-maker, had tried to humanize the Indian Government for some time and had tried to keep tempers as he put it to his military secretary.[16] Gandhi praised Lord Irwin saying that the Delhi Pact would have been impossible without the Viceroy's inexhaustible industry and equally inexhaustible and unfailing courtesy. He never allowed himself, observed Gandhi, to be betrayed into irritation, though unconsciously the Mahatma had given him causes for irritation.[17]

Lord Irwin was impressed with the force of Gandhi's great character and personality and he had written to His Majesty about it. Speaking about Gandhi, Irwin said, "He is a blend of a mystic and a politician who has long stood as the symbol of struggle for material autonomy."

The new Viceroy, Lord Willingdon, who arrived in Bombay, tactically refused to see Gandhi and confine his attention to him.

Gandhi met the collectors and the commissioner of Gujarat, but the problem of the Gujarat peasants was not solved to his satisfaction, it remained an open sore for a long time.

On May 13 Gandhi went to Simla and discussed the execution of the pact with Emerson. Two days later he called on Lord Willingdon, the new Viceroy, who had arrived in Bombay on April 18, 1931. Lord Willingdon's appointment had been welcomed by Sapru, Sir C. P. Ramaswami Aiyer, Sir Chimanlal Setalvad and others.

In May, the brother of the King of Bhutan, Father Verrier Elwin and Subhas Bose met Gandhi. He visited Borsad and Bardoli and met the local officials in the matter of the grievances of the peasants in May, June and July. Discussing the problem with Emerson, Gandhi sought interviews with the new Viceroy who wanted him to attend the Round Table Conference. The Viceroy granted as many as four interviews and discussed things, without yielding substantially on any point. Gandhi threatened him at one point, saying he would not go to attend the Round Table Conference as the situation in Gujarat was deteriorating. At the last interview Abdul Ghaffar Khan, Sardar Patel and Jawaharlal Nehru were with him. A settlement was reached. On August 28 a communique was issued declaiming that the Delhi Pact would remain operative and an inquiry would be set up to look into the Bardoli repression. Gandhi wrote to the Viceroy that he was going with the latter's blessings and on August 27 he left Simla hurriedly by a special train to Bombay. All this had more stagecraft than statecraft in it.

Before Gandhi left for London, he met, on August 14, 1931, Dr. Ambedkar, who had on behalf of the depressed classes of which he was the leader, launched a movement for social equality at Mahad in 1927 and for temple entry in particular on March 2, 1930, at Nasik. The direct action launched by Ambedkar for the liberation of the depressed classes energized and organized them all over India. Thousands gathered under Dr. Ambedkar's banner at the depressed classes Congress at Nagpur in August 1930 and declared political independence!

Dr. Ambedkar had impressed the first session of the Round Table Conference with his ability, grasp, fearlessness and patriotism. The centre of gravity in respect of the depressed classes had shifted from Gandhi to Ambedkar, and he had been hailed all over India as their champion and liberator. Up to now Gandhi thought that Ambedkar was some Brahmin who took deep interest in the Untouchables and therefore talked intemperately.[18] Gandhi had referred to the Nasik struggle for temple entry launched by Ambedkar as a disgraceful quarrel, and appealed to the Untouchables to suspend their satyagraha.

On August 6 Gandhi wrote to Ambedkar that he wanted to meet him at his residence if it was inconvenient for Ambedkar to come over to Mani Bhavan. Accompanied by his colleagues, Dr. Ambedkar met him on August 14 at Mani Bhavan in Gamdevi, Bombay. The two great leaders met for the first time.

During the course of the conversation, Gandhi told Ambedkar that it was he who incorporated the problem of Untouchables into the programme of the Congress which had spent rupees twenty lakhs on their uplift and that it was surprising that men like Dr. Ambedkar should oppose him.

Dr. Ambedkar replied that it was true that because of Gandhi the Congress gave recognition to the problem, but it did nothing more than that. The money it spent was all waste. Had the Congress been sincere, it would have surely made the removal of untouchability a condition, like wearing of khaddar, for becoming a member of the Congress. But the Congress cared more for strength than for principles. The caste Hindus, like the British Government, had not shown any change of heart. The depressed classes, Ambedkar added, had no faith in great leaders and Mahatmas. For history taught them that Mahatmas, like fleeting phantoms, raised dust but raised no level. Then Gandhi praised Ambedkar as a patriot of sterling worth, but Ambedkar said that he could not call India his homeland and Hinduism his religion wherein the depressed classes were treated worse than cats and dogs. If any harm did not come to the country through his action, it might be due to his conscience.

Then the conversation turned to the main problem. Ambedkar told Gandhi that he was striving to secure human rights for his people. The first session of the Round Table Conference, he went on, had given recognition to the political rights of the depressed classes and had recommended for them political safeguards and adequate representation. It was beneficial to them. So he asked Gandhi's opinion about it. Gandhi sharply replied that he was against the political separation of the Untouchables from the Hindus as it would be absolutely suicidal. Upon this Ambedkar thanked Gandhi for his frank opinion and took his leave.[19]

Ambedkar left the hall, his face reflecting his fiery resolve to fight out the issue with all his might and to secure human rights for his downtrodden people.

The interview thus ended in a grim atmosphere. Gandhi was the boss of Indian politics, the dictator, the uncrowned king of the Indian masses, who were dazed and electrified by his dynamic actions. A Hindu leader answering Gandhi back was unthinkable. But the die was cast. The interview sounded the beginning of a war between Gandhi and Ambedkar.

Hindu-Muslim unity, one of the main planks of Gandhi's platform, had already given way. The second plank, the removal of untouchability, now began to crack!

GANDHI LEFT BOMBAY by S.S. *Rajputana* for London on August 29. With him were Sarojini Naidu, Sir Prabhashankar Pattani, Mahadeo Desai, Pyarelal, Devdas, Mirabehn and G. D. Birla. He confessed that friends wanted him to take Jawaharlal Nehru along to keep him on the straight path and to serve him as his dictionary of reference in case of doubt. But he chose his God to accompany him and replied: "I must go to London with God as my sole guide."[20]

Gandhi started on his voyage with a staff in hand and wearing a loin-cloth. He had once declared in his *Navajivan* of April 6, 1924, that "tidiness is necessary, not as adornment, but for the sake of cleanliness and decorum. ... A proper dress keeps up decorum and shows our regard for others. ... If I had to go to a foreign land, I would by all means put away my loin-cloth in a trunk."[21] Churchill had stigmatized him as "a naked fakir", and so he preferred to discard decorum and regard for others. In his message he said: "I shall strive for a constitution, which will release India from all thraldom and patronage and give her, if need, be, the right to sin. The horizon is", he gravely observed, "as black as it possibly could be. There is every chance of my returning empty-handed."

Gandhi and his party were second-class passengers and he occupied a corner of the second-class deck despite his will to have the lowest class berths. He began to survey the contents of his cabin and was exasperated at the sight of swarthy suit cases, leather wallets, binoculars, camp-cots and costly Kashmiri shawls. On severe castigation by the master, the party sent back seven suit-cases and cabin trunks from Aden.

The little sons and daughters of the home-going English passengers made friends with Gandhi. He pulled them by the ears, patted them on the back and gave them grapes or dates.

At Aden an address was presented to Gandhi and he received greetings from Madame Zaglul Pasha and Nahas Pasha, President of the Wafd Party of Egypt. Madeline Rolland, sister of Romain Rolland, met him at Marseilles when he landed on September 11. The students of Marseilles welcomed him as the spiritual ambassador of India. Two British detectives, Sergeant Evans and Sergeant Rogers, joined Gandhi here "to watch over his safety and prevent his being annoyed by the crowds of sight seers". To a French journalist who asked him whether he would move in London in loin-cloth, he replied, "You, in your country, wear plus fours and I prefer minus fours." To a French customs officer, Gandhi declared: "I am a poor mendicant. My earthly possessions consist of six spinning wheels, prison dishes, a can of goat's milk, six home-spun loin-cloths and towels, and my reputation which cannot be worth much." Gandhi declared his "reputation" as Oscar Wilde had declared his "intellect" when he landed at New York! Gandhi did not reveal that he had God with him!

The British Conservative and Communist papers misrepresented Gandhi. One said he had prostrated himself before the Prince of Wales and Gandhi replied that he would fall at the feet of an ant but not a king. To the correspondent of the *Daily Mail* he said he would far rather India perished than that she won freedom at the sacrifice of truth. As this correspondent had misrepresented him, Gandhi said to him indignantly: "I may tell you that I have sense of humour which saves me from annoyance over these things. If I were lacking in it, I should have gone mad by now."

After visiting Paris and Boulogne, Gandhi disembarked on September 12, 1931, in the pouring rain at Folkestone and went to London by car. He was loosely wrapped in a loin-cloth and khaddar shawl. His feet were bare but for his sandals. His entourage flocked and fluttered around him. Gandhi's great devotee, John Hayness Holmes, met him in London. A few days earlier, on August 24, 1931, the Labour Government of Britain had collapsed, and a Coalition Government headed by MacDonald had come to power.

There was a big public reception at the Friends' Meeting House under the presidentship of Lawrence Housman which honoured Gandhi as the guest of the nation. Squatting on the floor, the Mahatma replied to the hosts at the reception. A few bespectacled old ladies belonging to the League Against Imperialism held up banners with slogans against him. They considered Gandhi among the enemies of freedom as he had made a pact with Irwin. Then the detectives accompanying Gandhi were followed by a row of cars to Kingsley Hall, defying all traffic signals to the surprise of van-drivers and bus-drivers. They learnt that Gandhi, the guest of His Majesty's Government, was passing by. Sarojini Naidu, accustomed to the Taj Mahal Hotel, went to a hotel in the West End. Over a thousand people led by the Mayor and the officials of Bow greeted him and welcomed him to Kingsley Hall in the East End, among the slums. Miss Muriel Lester, who had come to Gandhi's Ashram at Ahmedabad on October 2, 1926, was his host at Kingsley Hall where he was given five small rooms. With her sister Doris she had founded Kingsley Hall in 1914. Sir Samuel Hoare says that the India Office had made arrangements for Gandhi's stay in a West End Hotel, but he preferred to stay with his friends in Kingsley Hall, Bow. So the India Office provided for his regular transport between the East and the West End. Bow spontaneously took to Gandhi. Children flocked round him and called him "uncle Gandhi".

CHAPTER XXXV

The Round Table Conference

THE SECOND SESSION of the Round Table Conference began on September 7, 1931. This time the personnel of the conference was enlarged by including a few more representatives such as Sir Mohamad Iqbal, the Muslim League President; Dr. S. K. Dutta, the Christian representative; G. D. Birla, the great financier and industrialist; Pandit Madan Mohan Malaviya, the Sanatani Hindu reformer; Sarojini Naidu and Sir Ali Imam,

At this juncture Britain found itself in an unprecedented economic crisis. Panic prevailed in Britain's markets. Shortly before this session, Labour made room for a national Government, Ramsay MacDonald, remaining in the saddle. But the Secretary of State for India, Wedgwood Benn, was replaced by Sir Samuel Hoare. The tide was turning in favour of the Conservatives.

The main work of this session of the Round Table Conference was to be done in the Federal Structure Committee and the Minorities Committee. The conference was to re-examine ard amplify the reports prepared by the corresponding committees of the first session. The highlight of this session was the enigmatic personality of Mahatma Gandhi.

On Sunday, September 13, Jayakar, Sapru and Vithalbhai Patel met Gandhi. The Mahatma, sitting at Kingsley Hall, then made a broadcast to the American people which was arranged by the Columbia Broadcasting System. Gandhi approached the microphone with curiosity and trepidation and asked, "Do I have to speak into that thing?" These very words of Gandhi were heard for the first time on the other side of the Atlantic.

Gandhi delivered the message extempore. When the engineer signalled him to stop he said, "Well, that is over."[1] These words also were heard across the Atlantic. In his message Gandhi said that the Indians represented all the principal religions of the world and they wanted to abolish untouchability and banish drinks and drugs. He appealed to the conscience of the world to come to the rescue of a people dying to regain their liberty. India, he concluded, was leading a bloodless revolution through non-violence and truth, means which were unique in history.

The American press reproduced great portions of this speech on the following day, but the British press largely ignored it.

After this broadcast, Gandhi was escorted to the Dorchester Hotel where he met Prime Minister MacDonald and other British delegates to the Round Table Conference. MacDonald had a few words to say to Gandhi. Lord Sankey also met him.

The next day Gandhi attended the session of the Round Table Conference. The guards stood to attention. The Lord Chancellor welcomed the distinguished guests. Sir Samuel Hoare, Secretary of State, made a brief speech. Gandhi made no speech as it was his silence day.

On September 15, 1931, Gandhi made his first speech in the Federal Structure Committee of the Round Table Conference. He claimed that the Congress was national and represented all Indian interests and classes. He told the committee that the Congress represented the Muslims because it had had Muslims as Presidents and Muslims as members of its Working Committee. It represented the depressed classes because removal of untouchability was a plank on the political platform of the Congress. He told the Princes that Congress stood for the States also inasmuch as "even now the Congress had endeavoured to serve the Princes of India by refraining from any interference in their domestic and internal affairs". The Congress represented also women, Gandhi added, because it had had Dr. Annie Besant and Sarojini Naidu as Presidents. It had had Christian as well as Parsi Presidents. And because he was the sole representative of the Congress, it followed that he was the sole representative of the Indian nation!

Gandhi reaffirmed the Congress goal of complete independence and said that it would work for that goal, particularly so as to give the nation control over the army, external affairs, finance, fiscal and economic policy.

The same day Dr. Ambedkar spoke in the Federal Structure Committee emphasizing the point that the States' representatives to the Federal Assembly should be chosen by election and not by nomination, for it was his confirmed opinion that nomination made the Executive irresponsible to the legislature. It gave a false appearance to the outside world that the legislature was working normally on the basis of majority rule. This gave a shock to the princely order, and those who followed Dr. Ambedkar either supported or tried to refute him, a majority of them thinking Ambedkar's views radical and revolutionary.

The next day Gandhi, the sole representative of Indian nationalism, referred to Ambedkar's views on States' representation and said, "Whilst my sympathies, broadly speaking, are with Dr. Ambedkar, my reason is wholly with Gavin Jones and Sir Sultan Ahmed." Gandhi favoured the proposal for Federation, but supported the standpoint of the Princes put forward by Gavin Jones and Sultan Ahmed, which was against the States' people. "Here we have no right," Gandhi continued, "in my humble way, to say to the States what they should do and what they shall not do." He supported adult franchise irrespective of literacy and favoured the system of one chamber.

Gandhi then turned to the pivotal problem that had been haunting the delegates. He referred to the problem of special representation claimed by the different communities, and said: "The Congress has reconciled itself to special treatment of the Hindu-Muslim-Sikh tangle. There are sound historical reasons for it, but the Congress will not extend that doctrine in any shape or form. I listened to the list of special interests. So far as the Untouchables are concerned, I have not yet quite grasped what Dr. Ambedkar has to say, but of course, the Congress will share the onus with Dr. Ambedkar of representating the interests of the Untouchables. The interests of the Untouchables are as dear to the Congress as the interests of any other body or any other individual throughout the length and breadth of India. Therefore, I would most strongly resist any further special representation."

This was nothing but a declaration of war, Ambedkar observed, by Gandhi and by the Congress against the Untouchables. "With this declaration by Mr. Gandhi," he added, "I knew what Mr. Gandhi would do in the Minorities Committee which was the main forum for the discussion of this question."

After Britain departed from the gold standard, on September 21, 1931, Sir Samuel Hoare asked Gandhi in the India Office whether he would be able to explain to him the effect it would have on the Rupee. "But I understand nothing whatever about currency," Gandhi replied with great frankness. The Indian

Government was perturbed by the sudden change in the currency standard. So as to safeguard the interests of India, Lord Willingdon's Government issued an ordinance delinking the Rupee from the Pound. But Sir Samuel cabled to the Government of India to issue another ordinance linking the Rupee back to the Pound. Upon this, both the Indian and British members of the Viceroy's Executive Council protested against the policy of Sir Samuel Hoare and offered to resign. But Sir Samuel got Gandhi, the spokesman for India, through G. D. Birla, to agree to the *status quo*, and the result was that India was let down because of Gandhi's ignorance and Birla's influence. Later, some delegates told Gandhi that the departure from the gold standard was a betrayal of Indian interests. So Gandhi condemned it forthright as another instance of the economic exploitation of the dumb masses of India![2]

As Gandhi stayed at Kingsley Hall, the other delegates found it difficult to be in contact with him. They complained about it. So an old house in Knightsbridge was hired from September 21. Gandhi's friends at Kingsley Hall like Muriel Lester and Miss Mary Hughes, daughter of the author of *Tom Brown's School Days*, were determined not to let him go. Gandhi said: "But I feel happy in Miss Lester's abode because I get here a taste of the life I am pledged to live." So Gandhi preferred to spend the nights at Kingsley Hall. Visitors were divided into those who should call at Kingsley Hall and those who should call at Knightsbridge. Mirabehn (Miss Slade) wrote: "Mahadev, Devdas and Pyarelal live at Knightsbridge. Bapu and I sleep at Kingsley Hall. Bapu goes away in the morning to his work, in the West End at about 8.15 and I come along to Knightsbridge with goat's milk for the midday meal about 12.30 after having done all sweeping and dusting of rooms, washing of clothes, etc."

"Instead of 1 and 2 o'clock" Mirabehn continued, "it has been 11.30 and 12 midnight for going to bed. The rising hour for prayer (just Bapu and myself) continues to be 3 o'clock. At 5.30 a.m. he goes for his morning walk. The weather is getting decidedly cooler, and it continues fine. Bapu still wears just the two Kashmir shawls—one for shoulders and one for the legs when sitting. When walking he only uses the shoulder one. His health except for want of sleep, remains good."[3]

"For my breakfast," Gandhi explained to the editor of the *Spectator*, London, "at eight o'clock I have sixteen ounces of goat's milk and four oranges for my luncheon. At one o'clock I again have sixteen ounces of milk, grapes, pears or other fruits. My evening meal is between five and six o'clock. I eat a teaspoonful of almond paste, twenty or thirty dates, several tomatoes and a lettuce or other salad. This avoids indigestion. As you will note, I eat no starch and no cereals."

Ida Barton, who lived opposite Kingsley Hall, washed clothes for Gandhi and his party. She was the wife of a labourer in the East End of London.

It Was On September 22 that Charlie Chaplin, the world-famous Anglo-American film actor who wrote, directed and produced his own pictures, came to meet the Mahatma. Gandhi had never heard of his name. But when he was told who the visitor was and how he came from the people and lived for the people and how he had made millions laugh, Gandhi agreed to meet Chaplin. The interview took place at the house of Dr. Katial, who had placed himself and his Rolls-Royce at Gandhi's disposal during his stay in London.

Gandhi's secretary, Mahadev Desai, says that Gandhi was told that Charlie Chaplin would like to see him. But Chaplin says: "I had been asked if I would like to meet him. Of course, I was thrilled." They talked on the use of machinery. "I have always respected," Chaplin observes in *My Autobiography*, "and admired Gandhi for his political astuteness and his iron will. But I thought his visit to London was a mistake. His legendary significance evaporated in the London scene, and his religious display fell short of impressiveness. In the cold dank climate of England, wearing his traditional loin-cloth, which he gathered about him in disorderly fashion, he seemed incongruous. It made his presence in London food for glibness and caricature."[4]

About this time Dr. Felix Adler, American educator, Prof. of Ethics at Columbia University and founder of the Ethical and Cultural Movement, wrote an article, "An Evaluation of Gandhi," which attracted considerable public attention in America. According to Dr. Adler, "really great men as a rule decide upon their life purpose and aim early; whereas Gandhi, in early life, was 'changeable' and 'suggestible', did not frame for himself a philosophy of life or choose his life mission until the age of twenty-seven." Dr. Adler declared that Gandhi was inconsistent in supporting Great Britain in her wars and was also inconsistent in "sanctioning caste".[5] Besides Will Durant, Dr. Adler was the only non-Indian thinker who took note of Gandhi's views on the caste system. Dr. Adler rightly attributed

Gandhi's influence over the Indians to the fact that Gandhi stood for resistance to England.

Dr. Adler regarded Gandhi as religiously ignorant and narrow and in his opinion he was not worthy of respect as a religious teacher as he made, for his personal spiritual help, chief use only of the Gita and the Christian Gospels. Here Dr. Adler judged Gandhi wrongly for Gandhi's religious views were anything but narrow, the professor's first point, being equally untenable.

The first meeting of the Minorities Committee took place on September 28. Gandhi had met Jinnah and the Aga Khan and discussed the minority problem on the eve of this meeting of the Minorities Committee. He had also met Dr. Ambedkar at the residence of the latter before this meeting. Gandhi listened to Ambedkar but did not speak much. He told Ambedkar that he would consent to Ambedkar's demands if others agreed. The Premier admitted that the problem of minorities in India baffled them all. He observed that some of the delegates suggested arbitration by Government, but he thought that arbitration would probably be unacceptable to some of them. Thereupon the Aga Khan said that Mahatma Gandhi was going to meet the Muslim delegates that night and so he asked for an adjournment.

At this moment Dr. Ambedkar said that the depressed classes had already presented their case to the Minorities Sub-Committee on the previous occasion. He was glad, he observed, that further negotiations were going to take place for settling the communal issue. But he warned that those who were negotiating ought to understand that they were not plenipotentiaries at all; "that whatever may be the representative character of Mr. Gandhi or the Congress people, they certainly are not in a position to bind us certainly not, I say that most emphatically in the meeting." Upon this the Chairman, MacDonald, said: "Dr. Ambedkar's position has been made absolutely clear, in his usual splendid way. He has left no doubt at all about it."[6]

On October 1 Mahatma Gandhi again asked for a week's adjournment. He told the committee that he was in frequent discussions with Muslim leaders of various groups. At this Dr. Ambedkar said that as a representative of the Indian National Congress Gandhi was not prepared to give political recognition to any community other than Muslims and the Sikhs and was not prepared to recognize the depressed classes. A week earlier Gandhi had told him so and on the previous day Gandhi had told the members of the Minorities Committee in his office that the attitude he had taken in the Federal Structure Committee was his full and well-considered attitude. Ambedkar, therefore, declared that if the depressed classes were not recognized in the future constitution of India, he would neither join that particular committee nor wholeheartedly support the proposition of adjournment.

The discussion between Gandhi and the Muslim leaders went on for a week. It was reported that the discussions had reached an encouraging state and Gandhi had conceded to the Muslims their fourteen points, accepted the view that the residuary powers be vested in federating provinces, allowed the Muslims a majority in the Punjab and in Bengal and had offered the Muslims a blank cheque. The talks, however, foundered on the Sikh-Muslim question.

On October 8 Gandhi announced with deep sorrow and deeper humiliation to the Minorities Committee his utter failure in securing an integrated solution to the communal question through informal conversations amongst and with the different representatives of different groups. "The causes of failure," he added, "were inherent in the composition of the Indian delegation. We are almost all not elected representatives of the parties or groups whom we are presumed to represent; nor are those whose presence was absolutely necessary for an agreed solution to be found here." He had not a shadow of doubt that the iceberg of communal differences would melt under the warmth of the sun of freedom. As regards the demand for representation of the Untouchables he said, "What I have said and what I must repeat is that I am opposed to their special representation. I am convinced that this can do them no good and may do much harm. But the Congress is wedded to adult franchise. Therefore, millions of them can be placed on voters' roll." He agreed at the same time to the formation of the new Muslim Provinces of Sind, Baluchistan and the N. W. Frontier.

Gandhi, therefore, moved for an adjournment of the meeting *sine die*. Dr. Ambedkar, replying to Gandhi, observed in a vitriolic tone: "I say, therefore, that whether I am a nominee or not, I fully represent the claims of my community. Let no man be under any mistaken impression as regards that. The Mahatma has been claiming," Ambedkar proceeded, "that the Congress stands for the depressed classes, and the Congress represents the depressed classes more than I or my colleagues can do. To that claim I can only say that it is one of the many false claims which irresponsible people keep on making although the persons concerned with regard to those claims have been invariably denying them."[7]

And then Dr. Ambedkar showed bundles of cablegrams received from the different institutions and organizations of Untouchables from the farthest corners of India supporting his stand and challenging the stand, guardianship and leadership of Gandhi.

Dr. Ambedkar then told the Committee that either it should solve the problem or the British Government should undertake its solution. In his utter disappointment and fear he said that the depressed classes were not anxious about the transfer of power; it should be accompanied by such conditions and by such provisions that the power should not find itself in the hands of a group of people whether Mohammedans or Hindus; the solution should be such that the power should be shared by all communities in their respective proportions.

This statement by Ambedkar that he was not anxious about the transfer of power was condemned in India by the Congress press as one voiced without a blush. They said Ambedkar had cast restraint and decency to the winds.

Premier MacDonald made a speech after Ambedkar's which was rather pungent in tone; some called it ingrate, full of sideshafts against Gandhi.

Gandhi tried to isolate and stifle Dr. Ambedkar. Although he told Ambedkar that he would agree to the demands of the depressed classes if all others agreed, in private he tried to dissuade the Muslim leaders from supporting Ambedkar. In his letter of October 12, 1931, to *The Times of India* Ambedkar stated that this conduct was "unbecoming a Mahatma and to be expected only from an inveterate opponent of the depressed classes. Mr. Gandhi is not only not playing the part of a friend of the depressed classes, but he is not even playing the part of an honest foe".

The fact was, as disclosed by Ambedkar, that Gandhi went to the Aga Khan with a copy of the holy Koran in his hand and asked the Muslim leader to withdraw his support to the depressed classes, but the Aga Khan refused to do so.[8] Describing this incident, Ambedkar later indignantly said that if a 'man with God's name on his lips and a dagger under his arm deserved the title of Mahatma, Mohandas Karamchand Gandhi was a Mahatma.[9]'

Ambedkar was supported by the All India Depressed Classes Conference at their Gurgaon session, which declared that Gandhi was misrepresenting their case. It strongly denounced the claim made by Gandhi that the Congress had been taking care of the Untouchables from the beginning and had championed their cause. This onslaught by Ambedkar made Gandhi's position very delicate. His sentimental stand and assumed leadership of the Untouchables was exposed. The exposure became more pronounced by the temple entry movement launched by the depressed classes in India at Nasik and at Guruvayur.

MEANWHILE GANDHI ATTENDED a journalists party, visited India Office and gave a spiritual message for a gramophone company, drawing a royalty of £5,000. He visited Nottingham and Birmingham, met his quaker friends, including Horace Alexander, and had a talk with Sir Samuel Hoare. He called on the Archbishop of Canterbury and Lord Irwin and paid a courtesy call on Col. Maddock who had saved Gandhi's life in Sassoon Hospital in 1924. Gandhi visited Eton and addressed the students. At Oxford he met Prof. Gilbert Murray and held discussions with Henry Lawrence on the question of franchise and talked to students of the Ruskin Society. He stayed with Alec who was maternal uncle of Mirabehn. On October 28 he made a speech before Montessorie students from all countries; Madame Montessorie presided over the meeting.

Of these interviews and visits, the interviews with the Red Dean Johnson of Canterbury, Samuel Hoare and Irwin were important. The Archbishop said that there was one great interest in common between Gandhi and him, that was religion. Bertrand Russell's book on China was on his table. The Dean drove Gandhi to the sea for fresh air and said, "Many have asked me whether I was going to convert Mr. Gandhi to Christianity. 'To convert him!' I said to them indignantly: 'His is one of the most Christlike lives that I have yet come across''.[10] The Dean regarded Gandhi as St. Francis of Assisi.

The Red Dean had already interpreted Gandhi's attitude to machinery in his own way. "Machinery," he said, "ought not to enslave man, that is one thing, and machinery ought not to put out of employment and impoverish him. It is because it has impoverished masses of men in India that Mr. Gandhi asks them to go back to the wheel." The Dean asked Gandhi to bless the mission the Red Dean desired to take to China. The Mission was to consist of the Red Dean, Dr. Grenfell and Dr. Albert Schweitzer.

The most important interview Gandhi had was with Samuel Hoare, Secretary of State for India. Hoare was in a difficult position. The declaration of the goal of India as the attainment of Dominion Status by Lord Irwin on October 31, 1929 had divided Churchill, Birkenhead and Reading from Baldwin, who was instinctively liberal on Indian questions, and was convinced that if they were to keep India within the Commonwealth, they must be prepared to go much further in their concessions. Sir Samuel Hoare had argued in favour of an All-India Federation before a Business Committee at which Churchill, Chamberlain, Peel, Oliver Stanley and Hailsham were present. Churchill greatly resented any suggestions for responsibility at the Centre. He was in favour of provincial autonomy without any change at the Centre.[11]

While the Conservative diehards were wholly against real power being transferred to India, their opposition to Gandhi had sprung from another cause. Gandhi's agitation, they said, had undoubtedly though unintentionally, undermined respect for law and order and encouraged young men in India to attack and kill Government officials. The Indian leaders on their part did not know that these diehards were not in a majority in the Conservative Party. Thus the confusion and suspicion grew thicker.

Gandhi met Sir Samuel Hoare one afternoon. To Hoare he looked smaller and more bent than his pictures had shown him, but the British statesman was impressed by his sharp and penetrating eyes. He frankly told Gandhi that he could not promise immediate Dominion Status and that terrorism was as fatal to Indian aspirations as it was to British sympathy for them. There was no make-believe between them. He considered Sir Samuel to be frank and straightforward and capable of advising or approving ruthless repression. At the end of October, Britain went to the polls and the Tories came to power.

There was an afternoon party at Buckingham Palace for all the Round Table Conference delegates on November 5, 1931. Sir Samuel wondered how King George V would receive the leader of the civil disobedience movement. So he had an audience with the King. His Majesty's reaction was much as he expected. "What! Have this rebel fakir in the Palace after he has been behind all these attacks on my loyal officers?" Then he again shouted, "The little man to be in the Palace with no proper clothes on, and bare knees!" He was, however, mollified. An invitation without any conditions as to clothes was sent to Gandhi. He accepted it. Hoare presented Gandhi to the King. The King's simple sincerity and Gandhi's beautiful manners saved the situation, although the King looked at Gandhi resentfully.

At the last moment the King said in a haughty manner,

"Remember, Mr. Gandhi, I won't have any attacks on my Empire." Sir Samuel Hoare held his breath. Just then Gandhi suavely and gravely answered: "I must not be drawn into a political argument in Your Majesty's Palace after receiving Your Majesty's hospitality."[12]

Previously the King had asked Ramsay MacDonald when he was called first to Buckingham Palace, "Well, what are you Socialists going to do about me?" His gesture meant to ask Gandhi what the Indian leader was going to do about his Indian Empire! The King-Emperor asked Ambedkar about the condition of the Untouchables in India, and when he heard some harrowing tales from Ambedkar, he shuddered.

The Minorities Had made a pact and also jointly submitted a Memorandum supporting the civic rights of the Depressed Classes and demanding their recruitment to public service, as well as military and police services. When Gandhi saw this Minorities Pact which conferred on the depressed classes separate electorates, he was terribly enraged and he thundered against it in the Minorities Committee on November 13: "I would like to repeat what I have said before, that, while the Congress will always accept any solution that may be acceptable to the Hindus, the Mussalmans and the Sikhs, it will be no party to special reservation or special electorates for any other Minorities." "I can understand," he lamented, "the claims advanced by other Minorities, but the claim advanced on behalf of the Untouchables, is to me the 'unkindest cut of all'. It means perpetual bar sinister. I would not sell the vital interests of the Untouchables even for the sake of winning the freedom of India." If there was any referendum of the Untouchables, he proceeded, he would get their vote and he would top the poll.

With all his regard for Dr. Ambedkar's ability and for his desire to see the Untouchables uplifted, Gandhi said that Ambedkar was labouring under a great error. "It was not a proper claim," Gandhi added, "which is registered by Dr. Ambedkar, when he seeks to speak for the whole of the Untouchables in India". It will create a division in Hinduism which I cannot possibly look forward to with any satisfaction. I do not mind the Untouchables being converted to Islam or Christianity. I should tolerate that but I cannot possibly tolerate what is in store for Hinduism if there are these two divisions set up in every village."

Concluding, Gandhi said, "Therefore I want to say with all

the emphasis that I can command that if I was the only person to resist this thing I will resist it with my life."

While in England, Gandhi was so persistently plied with questions about the problem of the Untouchables that he had to yield to their pressure. To one questioner he replied that Dr. Ambedkar spoke for that particular part of the country where he came from. And Gandhi was the leader who defended the caste system which put the depressed classes on the lowest rung of society!

Gandhi could have clinched the issue with joint electorates and reserved seats for the depressed classes. Instead, Gandhi went on in his own way, as his stand apparently looked noble and favourable to the caste Hindus. But Dr. Ambedkar ruthlessly destroyed his platform by the interviews he gave, the statements he issued and the speeches he made at different institutions. Such an opportunity comes once in an age and Dr. Ambedkar, the natural spokesman and leader of the Untouchables, seized that opportunity and put the problem before the bar of the world. He wanted to relieve the Untouchables from their agelong slavery and to raise those crawling millions to the status of human beings.

If political slavery for a hundred and fifty years could justify the caste Hindus' extreme methods and violent means against the British Government, the Untouchables were a thousand times justified in lashing with scathing hatred the spokesman of their oppressors and their system of oppression. Oppressors never become saviours. Ambedkar's was a nobler goal and a nobler task, a mightier endeavour to win human rights for his suppressed people. And because he opposed Gandhi he was depicted by the Indian Press as a serpent in the grass, a devil, a destroyer of Hinduism, a traitor to the country and a stooge of the British Empire! He became the most hated man in India. A fellow passenger told T. A. Raman, a well-known journalist, that if he ever murdered anybody it would be Dr. Ambedkar!

Describing this conflict between Gandhi and Ambedkar, Glorney Bolton observes: "Day after day Dr. Ambedkar came into greater prominence. He spoke for the Untouchables and every speech on the welfare of India—whether from a Conservative or a Socialist platform—would contain a reference to the tragic plight of Untouchables. It was a sentimental rather than a practical concern. Gandhi, by representing the Untouchables, would have drawn eulogies from almost every pulpit in England, but now Dr. Ambedkar had destroyed his platform. He so opposed the Mahatma that the public began to believe that two personalities dominated the conference—Mr. Gandhi and Dr. Ambedkar. ... At first Mohammedans seemed to enjoy the discomfiture; but in time every delegate was wishing that Dr. Ambedkar would show Gandhi the courtesy to which his personal eminence certainly entitled him."[13]

Ambedkar's opinion about Gandhi was that a worse person could not have been chosen to guide India's destiny, and that his behaviour at the Round Table Conference showed that in the flush of victory Gandhi could be very petty-minded. An American journalist said that Gandhi should have brought a strong contingent of representatives of the nationalist sections of the minorities. Similar unfavourable opinion was expressed by Sir Chimanlal Setalvad in his *Recollections and Reflections*. Sastri said that Gandhi's reputation had not been enhanced in England by the speeches he made there. Gandhi had frankly told Setalvad that he had not read the Government of India Act of 1919.

Giving his impressions, Sir Samuel Hoare, later Viscount Templewood, who was a participant in the whole proceedings observed, "His (Gandhi's) chief opponent was Dr. Ambedkar, the representative of the depressed classes, who insisted that the millions of Untouchables needed separate constituencies and rigid protection. The two men never ceased to dispute with each other. Ambedkar was a very able advocate of the Old Bailey type, fluent, audacious and aggressive. Gandhi's reaction must have intensely irritated him."[14] Gandhi repeated, Sir Samuel Hoare observed, what he had said many times before and he was indifferent to whether his audience was bored or hostile. Gandhi believed in the truthfulness of Sir Samuel. Lord Reading watched Ambedkar with intense sympathy while he fought his battles doughtily.

The Prime Minister MacDonald saw that there was no solution to the Minorities problem, so he asked all the members of the Minorities Committee to sign a requisition authorising him to settle the communal question and to pledge themselves to accept his decision. Gandhi signed the requisition along with the other members and committed himself and the Congress to the award MacDonald was to give. Ambedkar did not sign the requisition.

After the Plenary session was over, the Prime Minister adjourned the Round Table Conference on December 1, 1931. Gandhi moved a vote of hearty and most sincere thanks to the Chairman who had conducted the proceedings in a becoming and courteous manner although he added that they had come to the parting of the ways. MacDonald presented him with a copy of his book *Wanderings and Excursions*.

Sir Samuel Hoare as Viscount Templewood afterwards said in his book: "I believe that if I had been able to say to him (Gandhi): 'Take Dominion Status at once without any safeguards,' we should not only have found him one of our best friends, but he would immediately have offered us in return all the safeguards in the Government of India Bill and many more besides if anyone had wanted them."[15]

DESPITE HIS FAILURE as a politician, the Mahatma made some important declarations while in Britain. He said that "without a control over defence and external affairs, it is no independence. It will be a mere husk not worth touching." Another was that "India will have freedom whether the communal question is solved or not." He had come to England because he had given Lord Irwin his promise to attend the R.T. Conference and discuss everything. It was the wisest decision, Gandhi observed, to have sent him alone to the Round Table Conference.

When Lady Minto told Gandhi in London that his leader and predecessor, Gokhale, had proposed separate electorates, Gandhi replied with a smile, "Gokhale was a good man, but even good men may make mistakes."[16] It implies that Gandhi accepted her statement. In London he met General Smuts twice in November 1931. He met Bernard Shaw and his wife, Lloyd George, Bishop Bell of Chichester, C. P. Scott, former editor of the *Manchester Guardian*, Brailsford, Laski, Desmond, Polak, Dr. Gilbert Murray, Dr. John Murray, Prof. Coupland and many other prominent persons.

Churchill's son Randolph met him as a journalist and Churchill's cousin Mrs. Clare Sherridan made a bust of Gandhi. Jo Davidson, who called himself a "plastic surgeon" and was called "the dean of U.S. Sculptors", did a bust of Gandhi. Bernard Shaw said that Gandhi and he belonged to a very small community on earth. When Shaw asked Gandhi whether the Round Table Conference did not try his patience, Gandhi replied that it required more than the patience of a Job.

Gandhi addressed a meeting of missionaries under the presidentship of the Archbishop of England. Eagerly and with strong emotion, Gandhi saw the Trinity College at Cambridge, where Jawaharlal Nehru had been educated. He visited Lancashire and addressed the labourers. He visited the Agricultural Exhibition of Islington Dairy Farm. A goat called Lucille supplied Gandhi with milk. About two hundred and fifty farmers accompanied Gandhi to see the goats.

Gandhi planted a tree in the compound of Kingsley Hall, visited a blind man in St. Andrew's Hospital, gave his autograph on his autobiography which was purchased by Ben Flatten for one rupee as the book was not selected for review. Gandhi used a single cake of soap for three months. The night watchman on the East End always greeted Gandhi with a good morning. He visited the family of one of the two detectives and had tea with his wife and children. A small girl in London wrote in an essay that Gandhi was a Christian Indian.

Meanwhile, the political situation in India was fast deteriorating in the North-West Frontier, U.P. and Bengal. Bengali detenus were attacked in the detention camp of Hijli. One detenu was killed and many were wounded in firing. Several officers were killed by Bengali revolutionaries. Sardar Patel cabled to Gandhi that the repression was in full swing, and Gandhi said that the happening had disturbed him. So he gave up the thought of visiting America.

Gandhi and his party left London on December 4, 1931. With him were Mrs. Polak's sister, Muriel Lester and the two detectives. While embarking, Gandhi gave a message to England: "If it falls to my lot to fight them, I will be engaged in the fight never out of hatred, but most surely out of love." In the evening he addressed meetings and was the guest of Madame Lourse Guiyesse. Then he stayed at Villeneuve with Romain Rolland for six days. Here he had long conversations with Pierre Ceresole, the founder of the International Voluntary Service for Peace. He asked Gandhi: "Tell us what qualities you think a leader for this age would need." "Realization of God every minute of the twenty-four hours,"[17] replied Gandhi.

Gandhi addressed international workers and labourers and, at Geneva, addressed a meeting at which he spoke on disarmament in the Victoria Hall. He said that the League of Nations lacked sanctions. The means adopted by India would supply the necessary sanctions. Gandhi, who asked for control over the Indian army, opined that Switzerland was really not aggressive and it did not need any army. It should give a lesson in disarmament and show the world that the Swiss were brave enough to do without arms.[18]

On December 12 Gandhi saw Mussolini who was quite cordial to him. General Moris, a friend of Romain Rolland, was his host. Italy gave Gandhi a courteous welcome. Gandhi saw that Mussolini's eyes were never still. When the Dictator asked him what he thought of the fascist state he had built, Gandhi said nonchalantly that he was building a house of cards. The Pope refused to see Gandhi. Paying a visit to the Vatican, Gandhi bowed his head before the image at the Vatican of Christ crucified, walked around it devotionally and said, "nations like individuals could only be made through the agony of the cross." Tolstoy's daughter, Madame Soukhotine (or Signora Albertini) Tolstoy, met him in Rome. Princess Maria of Italy brought Gandhi a basket of fruit.

Miss Tolstoy told him that her four brothers loved their father Tolstoy, but did not accept his principles. She said she had her differences with Romain Rolland who was in sympathy with Bolshevik methods, "the doctrine that the end justifies the means."[19]

Senior Gayda, a leading journalist, entertained the party at tea. Gandhi gave no interviews in Rome. Yet Gayda distorted his statements in conversation and issued a statement declaring that Gandhi had said in an interview that the struggle would be resumed at once. It shocked the London public and officials in India. Although Gandhi cabled a categorical denial of the report to Sir Samuel who had been horrified by it, the harm had been done.

Mussolini's Government had made arrangements for Gandhi's travel by train. At Brindisi the History and Art Society held a function in Gandhi's honour on December 14. They gave him goat's milk in a cup manufactured in the fifth century before Christ. The British detectives Evans and Rogers returned from here to London. When Gandhi asked them what present they would like to receive, they replied that they should be given watches with Gandhi's name engraved on them. Later Gandhi purchased two silver watches of British manufacture in Bombay and sent them over to Sir Samuel Hoare as presents for the detectives. He also sent Sir Samuel Hoare a letter of friendly greetings.

Gandhi wanted to meet Kemal Pasha. He would have gone to Turkey to see him if peremptory cables had not called him back to India.[20] So Gandhi left Brindisi by S.S. *Pilsna* on December 14 and reached Bombay on December 28, 1931.

Early on the night of December 27, the Congress volunteers gathered at the Mole station. About eight thousand members of the depressed classes too marched to the Mole station at half-past two on the morning of December 28. When Mahatma Gandhi got down at six in the morning, the Depressed Class people staged a black flag demonstration against him. Then there ensued a free fight, with stone-throwing, use of lathis, brick-bats and sodawater bottles, acclaiming and decrying the arrival of the apostle of non-violence to his Homeland! This was uncharitable, but Congressmen had never showed charity to Ambedkar whom they had decried as a traitor and a Charvak!

When Gandhi was asked why the Untouchables were angry with him, he merely denied they were angry with him and added that he would gladly die so that they might live. The next day, on the terrace of Mani Bhavan, Bombay, he was presented with an address by the Nationalist Depressed Class Party. He asked them to fight against separate electorates.

While on board, Gandhi had said that he returned to India not with disappointment but with hope enriched. However, he had come to the conclusion that Britain was in no mood to concede favours to India, although the British Premier had reaffirmed his Government's belief in an All-India Federation, making the Central Government responsible to the legislature subject to Defence and Foreign Affairs and granting the Muslim demands for the administrative separation of some territories and formation of N.W.F. into a Province. This was later issued as a White Paper.

During the last day of the voyage, Gandhi had told Reuter that he would take no hasty steps. He was constantly praying for God's guidance. Nehru and Abdul Ghaffar Khan had been jailed a day or two before Gandhi's arrival. In a telegram to the Viceroy, Gandhi protested against the arrests, ordinances and shootings. He made a speech at the Azad Maidan, Bombay, and alerted the nation for another ordeal. He declared: "Peace if possible, war if necessary."

Gandhi asked for an interview with the Viceroy, who turned down his request on December 29, 1931. On receipt of the Viceroy's telegram, Gandhi said he was preparing to go to jail. He appealed to the Viceroy to reconsider his request for an interview, but to no purpose. The Congress decided to restart the struggle. On January 4, 1932, the Government arrested Gandhi in Bombay at three in the morning under Regulation No. 25 of 1871. This was his fifth arrest. The Government of Bombay wanted to remove him to the Andamans or to Aden, but later changed its mind and kept him in Yeravda Jail.

CHAPTER XXXVI

The Gandhi-Ambedkar Pact

THE OFFENSIVE LAUNCHED by Lord Willingdon on January 4 by arresting Gandhi and Sardar Patel, the President of the Congress, had been practically in operation since December 26, 1931, and the Government had arrested Subhas Bose on January 2, 1932.

Although Gandhi's actions were unpredictable, he would not have been able to stave off the struggle even if Willingdon had granted him an interview. The situation was such that Gandhi's colleagues would have taken over the struggle had he shown reluctance to lead it. There was the danger of Gandhi's leadership being thrown overboard and his principles of truth and non-violence being abandoned. Gandhi was not prepared to renounce his leadership and go into the wilderness again. Willingdon on his part thought that prevention was better than cure. There was no change of heart in the Government, and after Lord Irwin's departure the British bureaucracy in India forgot his promises to India and Gandhi.

Willingdon issued the new ordinances in the morning of January 4, 1932, declaring Congress organizations illegal, but not the Congress and its flag. Kisan Sabhas, Youth Leagues and Peasants' organizations and institutions allied with and sympathetic to the Congress were all banned. The Provincial Governments resorted to new weapons of repression, suppression and oppression in every field with new ordinances and regulations.

The Bardoli inquiry had collapsed, the peasants' condition in U.P. deteriorated, tension in Bengal increased terribly and repression in the Frontier region attained white heat. Government raided Gandhi's Sabarmati Ashram. Kasturba Gandhi was first sentenced to six weeks' imprisonment, and again on March 15 to six months'. Mahadev Desai, who had been arrested, was kept with Gandhi at Yeravda from March 10, 1932. In Bengal, Veena Das shot at the Governor of Bengal on March 6, 1932, and at Midnapur a revolutionary fired at R. Douglas, District Magistrate, on March 30.

Lord Willingdon thought that he would be able to suppress the Congress satyagraha agitation within six weeks. His Government had placed orders for thousands of new lathis, clamped new ordinances on India and ruthlessly inflicted terrible punishments on the people. Action taken under ordinances was not to be challenged in Civil Courts. Special courts under special judges and special magistrates and Summary Courts were instituted. Even Lord Irwin and Sir Samuel Hoare supported Willingdon's black acts and repressive measures.

The Working Committee of the Congress invested the President with all its powers and the President in turn transferred them to his successors. This time the satyagraha methods took to secrecy. The leaders had to issue unauthorized bulletins, leaflets, news-sheets and reports which were cyclostyled, duplicated, printed without declaring the printers' names, sometimes under fictitious names of printers and persons.

Picketing of liquor shops and foreign cloth shops and of British goods, British medicines, British banks, insurance companies, foreign sugar and kerosene oil was vigorously done. Payment of rent and *chaukidari* tax were withheld. Forest laws were broken and salt laws were defied. Large numbers of people travelled on trains without tickets. Risings, strikes, disturbances took place throughout India.

The more intense the movement grew, the more heartless and ruthless the weapons used against it. More than a lakh of people were arrested, lakhs were lathi-charged. New camp jails and temporary jails were opened. Graduates, professors, lawyers, editors and philanthropists were imprisoned and crammed into 'C' class in spite of their education and social status. Congress flags were hauled down, and Union Jacks were unfurled on Municipal buildings. Heavy fines were imposed on conviction, and a punitive tax was imposed on villages and cities. Firing was resorted to in some towns and cities, many persons were killed and thousands were injured. Whipping was the order of the day.

In spite of the ban on the Congress organizations, the Congress leaders held its session under Seth Ranchhod Das Amritlal at

Delhi in April 1932. The President-elect, Pandit Madan Mohan Malaviya, was arrested.

When India was fighting the British imperialists tooth and nail, the boycott and civil disobedience movement was reaching its climax. Gandhi in jail was thinking of giving battle to the British Government over a vital constitutional point. The Franchise Committee under Lord Lothian was touring India in February, interviewing different politicians and party leaders on the issue. The caste Hindu members of the Lothian Committee violently differed from Dr. Ambedkar on his demand for separate electorates for the depressed classes.

Having sensed this move, Gandhi wrote to Sir Samuel Hoare on March 11, 1932, warning the British Government that if they created separate electorates for the depressed classes, "I must fast unto death". He also reminded him of his vow which he had taken at the last meeting of the Minorities Committee that he would resist such a decision with his life. He said his opposition to it was based on religious and moral grounds. Sir Samuel replied on April 13, that Gandhi's views would be taken into consideration before the final decision was taken. He could only say that they intended to give any decision that might be necessary, solely or only upon the merits of the case.

Dr. Ambedkar, too, was not sure of the forthcoming decision. So he left for London on May 26 to see the British Prime Minister and his Cabinet Ministers before their decision on the Communal Award was announced. He passionately pleaded his case for separate electorates and returned to Bombay on August 17. Gandhi was determined to oppose this demand. But meantime M. C. Rajah had made an agreement with Dr. Moonje about joint electorates and reserved seats, and so Ambedkar was uneasy.

The British Government announced its Communal Award on August 17, 1932, ignoring Gandhi's ultimatum. According to this Communal Award, the depressed classes were granted separate seats in the Provincial Assemblies and also the right to double votes by which they were to elect their own representatives and to vote also in the general constituencies.

The Communal Award perpetuated the divisions among the Indians. It politically balkanised India. It perpetuated separate electorates to the Muslims, Sikhs, Europeans and Christians and gave separate electorates to the depressed classes. The national majority of the Hindus was turned into a minority. The Hindus, who represented about seventy-five per cent of the whole of British India, were reduced to a minority of forty-five percent in the Central Legislature. On principle, Gandhi had no word to say against separate electorates being conceded to the Christians, Muslims, Sikhs and Europeans. On August 18 Gandhi wrote to Ramsay MacDonald informing him of his resolve to resist the scheme of separate electorates for the depressed classes by resorting to a perpetual fast unto death, which he would commence on September 20, 1932. On September 8 the Prime Minister cabled in reply: "We felt it our duty to safeguard what we believed to be the right of the depressed classes." He added that they were equally careful to do nothing that would split off the depressed classes from the Hindus. Gandhi said in a rejoinder that to say the award was for the benefit of the people of India and his fast would deprive them of it was a misinterpretation of what he had said.

As a matter of fact Gandhi was a signatory to the requisition made to the British Premier at the time of the last meeting of the Minorities Committee, empowering the British Premier to arbitrate in the matter of the final solution to the communal problem. "I was a party," he later admitted, "to the request made to the late Mr. MacDonald to arbitrate."[1] He was, therefore, morally bound by his word. Although he had expressed his determined opposition to giving separate electorates for the depressed classes, he had not mentioned this condition while signing the requisition. He had conceded separate electorates to the Muslims and Sikhs on historical grounds. But now he thought that the grant of separate electorates to the depressed classes would simply divide and disrupt Hinduism.

The governing and undying characteristic of Gandhi was action. All his power emanated from his endless action. Action had made him what he was. Even in jail he would never sit a silent witness to any declaration vitally affecting the destinies of India. So he focused the attention of the world on Yeravda Jail and made his last attempt at depriving Ambedkar of the advantages he had gained for the depressed classes. The politician in Gandhi, who had failed at the Round Table Conference, was now appealing to the Hindus in the name of nationalism and religion to unite and to consolidate themselves. And apparently it was a good stand. Sardar Patel was not in favour of Gandhi's fast and Pandit Jawaharlal Nehru was sorry Gandhi had chosen a side-issue for his "final" sacrifice. Nehru said, "And I felt angry with him at his religious and sentimental approach to a political question, and his frequent references to God in connection with it. He even seemed to suggest that God had indicated the very date of the fast. What a terrible example to set."[2] Subhas Bose, who was in jail, said that all rational thinking had been suspended.

THERE WAS CONFUSION and consternation in the country. The caste Hindus got panicky, not because they felt ashamed of their inhuman conduct towards the Untouchables but because the life of Gandhi, their great political liberator, was in danger. Dr. Rajendra Prasad said that Hinduism was on trial. Pandit Malaviya took the lead and convened a conference of the Hindu leaders in Bombay on September 19, 1932. Visitors, leaders, letters arrived at Ambedkar's Rajagriha requesting him to reconsider the issue. He frankly and fearlessly replied that he was willing to consider anything, but unwilling to allow the rights of the depressed classes to be curtailed in any way.

In a second statement Ambedkar said, "It would have been justifiable if Mr. Gandhi had resorted to this extreme step for obtaining independence for the country on which he was so insistent all through the Round Table Conference debates. It is also a painful surprise," Ambedkar proceeded, "that Mr. Gandhi should have singled out special representation for the depressed classes in the Communal Award as an excuse for his self-immolation. Separate electorates are granted not only to the depressed classes but to the Indian Christians, Anglo-Indians and Europeans as well as to Mohammedans and the Sikhs." Ambedkar was in an angry mood and he attacked the weak points in Gandhi's arguments. He added that Gandhi knew what would have happened to his life if he had resorted to a fast unto death against separate electorates for Muslims or Christians or if he had gone an a fast unto death against the British Government for immediate independence. Nor did Gandhi ever threaten a fast unto death for the immediate abolition of untouchability.

There was now endless talk about Ambedkar in every political party, in every social circle and in every religious institution. Much ill-will was directed against him.

The Hindu Leaders' Conference met in Bombay on September 19 under the presidentship of Pandit Madan Mohan Malaviya. Ambedkar was asked to speak first. Ambedkar said it was very proper that every man should try to save the precious life of Gandhi. He requested the leaders to bring alternative proposals from Gandhi; but for saving his life, Ambedkar added, he would not be a party to any proposal that was against the interests of his people. The leaders shuddered at this blunt declaration.

On September 20, 1932, Gandhi started his fast in Yeravda Jail and was allowed to carry on negotiations in connection with the Communal Award. Gandhi wrote to the Government of Bombay that he would not offer any conditions for his release. Sir Chimanlal Setalvad, leader of the delegation that had waited upon Gandhi in Yeravda Jail, told the conference on September 20 that Gandhi had no personal objection to the reservation of seats for the depressed classes. Thereupon Ambedkar said that he was placed on the horns of a dilemma, and added: "It has fallen to my lot to be the villain of the piece. But I tell you I shall not be deterred from my pious duty and betray the just and legitimate interests of my people even if you hang me on the nearest lamp-post in the street. You better appeal to Gandhi to postpone his fast about a week and then seek for the solution of the problem."

The conference adjourned till two in the afternoon. On the next day, 21st September, Sapru evolved a scheme of primary and secondary elections for the reserved seats. According to it, the depressed classes themselves were to select for every seat a panel of not less than three candidates and then out of these three candidates one was to be selected by the joint electorate of the caste Hindus and the depressed classes.

By the midnight train on September 21 the leaders went to Poona. On September 22 Ambedkar met Gandhi in Yeravda Jail. Rajagopalachari and Dr. Rajendra Prasad, too, saw Gandhi. But no compromise was reached. Gandhi's condition was becoming serious. A fierce storm was raging outside, and an entangling silence prevailed inside the jail under the thick shade of a mango tree where the Mahatma was lying on a cot. MacDonald's Award had given the depressed classes 71 seats in all Provincial Legislatures, and now the depressed classes were given 148 seats in the Provincial Legislatures and some more also in the Central Assembly.

On September 23 the negotiations broke down several times. Ambedkar was cool and collected. He insisted that the question of reserved seats should be settled by a referendum after twenty-five years. On September 24 he again met Gandhi who said: "Five years or my life!" As Gandhi's health had taken a serious turn, an agreement was reached at five on the evening of Saturday 24 between the two parties without any reference to the question of referendum. Ambedkar, then, on behalf of the depressed classes, signed the agreement known as the Poona Pact and Pandit Malaviya, Sapru, Jayakar, Dr. Rajendra Prasad and Rajagopalachari signed it on behalf of the caste Hindus. M. G. Rajah and Gavai, too, signed it.

The contents of the pact were cabled to the British Cabinet and to the Viceroy and also handed over to the Secretary of the Bombay Government by each party separately. The next day the Hindu leaders' meeting praised Ambedkar who said: "If Gandhi had shown the same consideration to my point of view then it would not have been necessary for him to go through this ordeal."[3] Here the Mahatma showed that the real benefactor of the depressed classes was Gandhi and not the British Government! On September 26 the British Government announced that it would recommend to Parliament the endorsement of the Poona Pact. On the same evening at about half-past five, Gandhi broke his fast by taking lemon juice at the hands of Kasturba amidst a gathering of two hundred disciples, admirers and colleagues, including Tagore, Sarojini Naidu, Sardar Patel and Swarup Rani Nehru. Kasturba had been brought to Yeravda Prison from Sabarmati Jail when Gandhi's health had taken a serious turn.

At the time of the Round Table Conference, the Mahatma in Gandhi had partly dominated the field, but the politician in Gandhi had virtually failed. Now at Poona the politician in Gandhi had succeeded and the Mahatma was defeated. It may be mentioned here that Tagore, who had enveloped his head in the shawl of Gandhi and burst into tears over his breast, turned out to be one of the bitter opponents of the Poona Pact when instead of 10 the depressed classes were given 30 seats in Bengal! The depressed classes lost the opportunity of bending the caste-Hindu leaders to their will as they were to participate in the general election while they had the right to elect their own representatives. The caste Hindus now had the power to elect the depressed class candidates, and the result was that those who were self-respecting and wanted to secure social equality and equal opportunity for the depressed classes, stood at the mercy of the caste Hindus who were their oppressors!

After Gandhi broke his fast, India breathed freely again, but Srinivas Sastri with his peculiar foresight, said that they would begin to perceive that the gains of the Poona Pact were dubious and some might call it a mad bargain. The tension over it, he observed, was possible only in this superstitious country. Setalvad said that Gandhi, who refused in London absolutely to agree to reservation of seats for the depressed classes, conceded in Poona not only reservation of seats but also separate primary electorates.

Besides restraining the influence of Ambedkar, the fast tried to sting the Hindu conscience into right religious action. But what it actually evoked was a little genuine sympathy and nothing more. Some temples were reported to have been thrown open to the Untouchables. The number of such temples was romanticised; but the facts were sad. Dilapidated, deserted and non-existent temples were listed to extend support and sympathy to the Mahatma. Gandhi himself had never fought for temple entry of the Untouchables and inter-dining was anathema to him. He had expressed his desire in May 1930 that Ambedkar should call off the Nasik satyagraha as, he said, the Congress would solve the question in Swaraj. Some District Congress leaders had opposed the Nasik satyagraha. All things over, Gandhi asked Nehru how he viewed the thing and wrote to Nehru later, that Indira, who had seen him during the fast, had put on flesh!

At this time K. Kelappan, who had been fighting for the temple entry of the depressed classes at Guruvayur in Kerala since November 1931, went on a fast from September 21, 1932, and declared that he would not stop it till the doors of the Krishna Temple at Guruvayur were thrown open to the depressed classes. However, he suspended his fast for three months on a telegraphic assurance from Gandhi that he would go on a fast with Kelappan from January 1, 1933, if the doors of the temple at Guruvayur were not thrown open to the Untouchables. Born at Quilandy, educated at Kozikode and Madras, Kelappan had given up his law studies in Bombay and plunged into politics at the call of Gandhi. Later he became an eminent Kerala Congress leader and courted jail several times during the Freedom struggle.

THE CONCESSION GRANTED to Gandhi by the Government to carry on negotiations and correspondence and to issue statements, to meet leaders and to lead a public, social movement was a feat of diplomacy on the part of the Viceroy. Lord Willingdon suppressed all the jail rules, perhaps for the first time in the history of the penitentiary and permitted a political prisoner to give his nation a lead in social reform. He intentionally did it to divert militant nationalist energies into "constructive" channels and shrewdly turned the youthful energies and idealism of the rising generation from the demand for independence to social reform.

A week, from September 27 to October 2, was observed as the Untouchability Abolition Week. As a result of the discussion and awakening and agitation, an Anti-Untouchability League was founded on September 30, 1932, with Delhi as its headquarters, Amritlal Thakkar as its Secretary and the multimillionaire G. D. Birla as its President. A network of Provincial Boards was set up to do the work. A public appeal was made for rupees twenty-five lakhs for the uplift of the Untouchables. The Untouchables said that the money would be lifted and they would remain where they were!

Yeravda Prison became Yeravda Mandir, the centre of a movement for the liberation of the depressed classes. At this the orthodox Hindus said: "Our religion is in danger! To abolish untouchability is irreligious and a sin!" Sanatani reformers like Prof. S. M. Mate and leaders like Kelkar favoured restricted reforms in this respect and were not on Gandhi's side. The Poona orthodox Hindus tried to prejudice the Bengali leader, Pandit Satish Das Gupta, against Gandhi by telling him false stories about him. Pandit Panchanan Tarka Ratna Bhattacharya from Bhapada in Bengal met Gandhi. He said untouchability was a part of religion; if Gandhi himself desired salvation he should abandon the question, but if he was doing it as practical politics he should do so. Pandit Rajeshwarshastri Dravid from Benares came to Poona to defend untouchability. Poona became a stronghold of all-India orthodoxy and renewed its role in the counter-revolution!

Gandhi was now in a mood of co-operation or compromise and said, "In spite of my repeated declarations it is not generally recognized that, by instinct, I am a co-operator." Leaders were agitating for his release, but the Government was adamant. Shaukat Ali was also moved to send a cordial telegram to Gandhi, his 'old chief' and Gandhi replied to him that he was still in Shaukat Ali's pocket! The Viceroy refused the request of Shaukat Ali for an interview with Gandhi.

The concessions granted to Gandhi to lead the social movement were withdrawn from September 29. Gandhi ulitimately warned the Government on October 25 that if Harijan work was not allowed, he would not co-operate with the Government and would take 'C' class diet. For one day, November 1, 1932, he actually took 'C' class diet and stopped taking it the next day at the request of the Government which yielded to him. He again went on a fast on December 3, but broke his fast the next day as Appasaheb Patwardhan was allowed to do scavenging in Ratnagiri Jail as desired by Patwardhan.

Meanwhile K. Kelappan had given up his fast on October 1, as suggested by Gandhi, and Gandhi wired from jail to Zamorin, the ruler of Cochin, urging him to act according to his promise and remove the objections to temple entry. The movement was gradually petering out.

Gandhi informed Zamorin that if a referendum in Ponnani Taluka decided by a majority against the temple entry of the Untouchables, he would refrain from his proposed fast which he was to undertake on January 1, 1933. The majority decided in the unofficial referendum in favour of temple entry, but the Zamorin would not yield. He said it was not a private temple and so not bound to respect public opinion. Gandhi sharply pointed out the decision of the Madras High Court: "The Guruvayur is not a private temple but a public temple and every Hindu has a right to worship in it." In Poona prominent Shastris like Swami Kevalanand, Narayan Shastri Marathe, Laxman Shastri Joshi, Babu Bhagawandas, Anand Shanker Dhruva of Benares, Indraraman Sastri, Keshav Laxman Daftari and P. H. Purandare supported the rights of the untouchable Hindus to temple entry, admission to educational institutions and the use of public wells, ghats, tanks and rivers on the strength of fundamental principles and the spirit of the Dharma shastras.

Just at this time two bills were prepared in Madras, one by Subbaroyan for being introduced in the Madras Legislative Council and another by Ranga lyer for being introduced in the Central Assembly. Gandhi postponed his fast as he said he was waiting for the decision of the Viceroy whose permission was required for the introduction of the bills. The hardened sanatanists, the semi-sanatani reformers like Pandit Madan Mohan Malaviya and the rabid orthodox insisted that the question of temple entry should be decided neither by a referendum nor by the interference of law. And most surprisingly, in a telegraphic outburst, Malaviya urged Gandhi that Ranga lyer's bill should be withdrawn as the Pandit was opposed on principle even to indirect interference by legislature in the management of the temples. Moreover, he added, the bill was not in accordance with the terms of the Bombay pledge which was taken by Hindu leaders after the Poona Pact! Thus hundreds of Gandhi's caste Hindu supporters were exposed as being in reality opposed to the temple entry of the Untouchables. For several years Gandhi himself had expressed disapproval of temple entry for them.

The British bureaucracy on their part suspected the motives of the Gandhi-Rajagopalachari move which nearly ushered in the Ranga lyer Bill. It was Rajagopalachari who took a keen interest in the drafting of this bill. The bureaucracy thought that it was the political design of Gandhi and Rajaji to arouse the depressed classes against the British Government. Non-intervention in religious matters being their declared policy, they feared that it would add to the bitternece of the people who were already politically estranged.

The India Office, however, at last advised Willingdon, who was in favour of the bills as a Liberal, to grant permission to the legislators to introduce them. The Viceroy refused permission to Dr. Subbaroyan and Narayan Nambiar to introduce their bills in the Madras Legislative Council as the problem underlying them was of an all-India character. However, he allowed the Central legislators to do so. Gandhi wrote to the Viceroy on January 24 that the problem of temple entry was not confined to Guruvayur only but to the whole nation. On February 18 the Viceroy replied to Gandhi that the bills would be circulated to elicit public opinion.

Meanwhile the third session of the Round Table Conference was held from November 17, 1932, to December 24, 1932. Sastri, Setalvad, Jinnah and C. Y. Chintamani were dropped from this session. The British Labour Party did not participate in it. The princes had lost their enthusiasm for these conferences and were marking time. The main business before the third session was to supplement the work so far done at the previous sessions by filling in some details and to decide the composition of the Central Government in the light of the Lothian, the Percy and the Davidson Committes. As adult franchise was found impracticable under the existing circumstances, the franchise was extended and a part of the feminine population was enfranchised. Sapru was the outstanding spokesman for India and with some others he pleaded bravely for Federation and responsibility at the Centre.

ON HIS RETURN to Bombay from London, Dr. Ambedkar was invited by Gandhi to visit him in Yeravda Prison. When he did so on February 4, 1933, as he had done before his departure to London, Gandhi asked him to support the bills introduced by Dr. Subbaroyan and Ranga lyer. Ambedkar replied that he would not support Subbaroyan's bill since it did not condemn untouchability as a sin. Besides, he said, it depended for its solution on a referendum and not on the right to worship of the depressed classes. He could not support Ranga lyer's bill either.

Yet Ambedkar sent a message to the first issue of *Harijan* a weekly started by Gandhi on February 11, 1933, under the auspices of the Servants of Untouchables Society, to propagate the cause of the Untouchables. Its editor was Ramachandra V. Sastry. In his message Ambedkar said: "The outcaste is a by-product of the caste system. There will be outcastes as long as there are castes. Nothing can emancipate the outcaste except the destruction of the caste system. Nothing can help the Hindus and ensure their survival in the coming struggle except the purging of Hindu faith of this odious and vicious dogma."

And in his famous statement of February 12, 1933, on the temple entry, Ambedkar declared that he could not support Ranga lyer's bill because it was based on the principle of majority. "Sin and immorality," Ambedkar continued, "cannot become tolerable because a majority is addicted to them or because the majority chooses to practise them." Ambedkar further stated that the surest way for the salvation of the depressed classes lay in higher education, higher employment and better ways of earning a living. Ambedkar, therefore, said to the caste Hindus: "To open or not to open temples is a question for you to consider and not for me to agitate. If you think it is bad manners not to respect the sacredness of human personality, open your temples and be a gentleman. If you rather be a Hindu than be a gentleman, then shut the doors and damn yourself. For I do not care to come."

Concluding his statement, Dr. Ambedkar asked Gandhi a pertinent question: "If I accept the temple entry now and agitate for the abolition of *chaturvarnya* and caste system, on what side Gandhi would be." Gandhi, who believed that the caste system was an answer to social needs and that Varnashram Dharma was based on the Hindu scriptures, replied to Ambedkar's message in *Harijan* of February 11, 1933, that he did not believe the caste system, even as distinguished from Varnashram, to be an odious and vicious dogma. He added: "It is as wrong to destroy caste because of the outcaste, as it would be to destroy a body because of an ugly growth in it, or of a crop because of the weeds."

Replying to Ambedkar's temple entry statement, Gandhi indicated on what side he would be if the struggle for the abolition of the caste system was launched by Ambedkar. "I am," Gandhi said, "a Hindu, not merely because I am born in the Hindu fold, but I am one by conviction and choice. There is no superiority or inferiority in the Hinduism of my conviction. But when Ambedkar wants to fight Varnashram itself, I cannot lie in his camp, because I believe Varnashram to be an integral part of Hinduism." Gandhi gave a similar reply to Stanley Jones who had asked him why he was not doing away with the caste system altogether. Gandhi had been defending the caste system for years, and although he tried to give a colour of modernity to caste, he could never be a social revolutionary. Like many orthodox social reformers he wanted to whitewash and renovate a decayed institution.

Gandhi was asked why he described the Untouchables as Harijans. He replied that Harijan meant a man of God and that the name was suggested to him by an untouchable correspondent, the word being first used by the Gujarati saint-poet, Narsi Mehta. Gandhi stated that the change of name did not bring any change in their status, but one was spared the use of a term of reproach. Besides, all religions described God, Gandhi added, as pre-eminently the Friend of the friendless and the Help of the helpless and the Protector of the weak. And in India, he observed, who could be more friendless, helpless or weaker than the forty million or more Hindus of India who were classified as Untouchables? Whatever religious men like Gandhi say, the assurance that God has been the Friend, Helper and the Protector of the poor and the weak has been a great fraud in human history. It has been the lot of the poor to live without food, shelter and clothing for ages.

On the eve of his departure to London to attend meetings of the Joint Select Committee, Dr. Ambedkar saw Gandhi in Yeravda Jail. Gandhi complained that he was called a devil by orthodox Hindus and added that he was sorry that even Ambedkar was not pleased with his work. He wished Ambedkar *bon voyage*.

Gandhi did not start his fast on January 1, 1933, although he had promised K. Kelappan that he would do so. He declared that he was awaiting the decision of the Viceroy on Ranga Iyer's bill before he did anything in the matter. The fact was that Rajaji and other colleagues of Gandhi had dissuaded him from going on a fast. They argued that if Kelappan did not go on a fast it was improper on the part of Gandhi to keep his promise to Kelappan. And they saw that Kelappan did not go on a fast. In a letter Pandit Malaviya said to Gandhi: "Take care that pride of *tapasya* does not corrupt you. There should be no more fast." In any case, Gandhi was quite exhausted. He accepted the covert suggestion and like a sinking man he caught at a straw.

Ranga lyer introduced his bill on March 24, 1933, when Rajagopalachari, tho non-co-operator, was eagerly watching from the visitors' gallery and Gandhi was anxiously following the proceedings from the jail. When Gandhi was criticized for seeking the co-operation of the Government and of the legislators, he excused himself by saying in his usual fashion "that different circumstances evoke different applications of the same doctrine". He was seeking co-operation, he added, to further his purpose which he held to be very sacred and altogether good. The other bills presented for introduction by M. C. Rajah, Gayaprasad Singh and B. C. Mitter were dropped. But the discussion on Ranga lyer's bill went on.

While Gandhi was in jail "Neela Nagini" visited him in January 1933. She was an American woman whose real name was Neela Cram Cook. She was brought up in a Bohemian family where the very name of Jesus was taboo. She had been married in Greece at the age of seventeen and had a son who was with her. She was twenty-four and she suffered from frequent moral lapses which she repented. After her divorce, she came to India, embraced Hinduism and devoted herself to the welfare of the Untouchables in Mysore.

Polak saw Gandhi in jail in March 1933. Subhas Bose was packed off to Europe for reasons of health in the third week of February 1933. Gandhi's great friend and supporter Dr. Pranjivandas Mehta died at Rangoon in July 1932.

Gandhi's son was to marry the daughter of Rajagopalachari, a Brahmin. The question was gnawing at his mind. On consulting the *shastras* he may have found that a revision in his views on caste was necessary. He had said in *Young India* of October 6, 1921 that Hinduism most emphatically discouraged inter-dining and inter-marriage between castes, but now in a statement issued to the press he said restrictions on inter-caste dining and inter-caste marriage was no part of the Hindu religion. Gandhi's adopted daughter Lakshmi was married to Marutidas on March 14 at Sabarmati when Gandhi sent his blessings. Laxman Shastri Joshi performed the marriage of Devdas with Lakshmi at the Parnakuti and Gandhi blessed the couple. The marriage was also registered at Poona on June 21, 1933.

The publication of *Harijanbandhu*, the Gujarati version of *Harijan*, commenced from March 12, 1933. The White Paper regarding the reforms was published on March 17, 1933. On

April 8 Gandhi wrote to the Viceroy that he could not give his opinion on the White Paper without consulting his colleagues.

During this imprisonment realization dawned on Gandhi that Muslims shared Iqbal's anti-nationalism and the poet at the time disowned his own song *Hindustan Hamara*, meaning India is ours. Gandhi said that anti-nationalism had nothing to do with pan-Islamism. Just as, Gandhi observed, he was a Hindu first and therefore a true Indian, so also a Muslim should be a Muslim first but a true Indian. The Muslim leadership did not understand this. "Nowadays," Gandhi sighed ruefully, "to be a Muslim is not to be a nationalist."[4] He found Kaka Kalelkar innocent of the Maharashtra spirit and had long forgotten that Vinoba Bhave was a Maharashtrian. "A teacher or Acharya is one who behaves himself and thus sets an example of good behaviour. God was visible only to the eye of faith." Gandhi now preferred the Western Calendar to the Hindu Calendar and said: "We cannot have any hatred for it." He liked the definition of science given in Maunder's *Astronomy Without A Telescope*: "Science is accurate measurement."[5] He also expressed his opinion on the dictum, 'art for art sake'. "All art is an expression or a reflection of the human soul; therefore as is the soul, so is the art. The artist's soul will be reflected in his art. The briefest and simplest definitions of happiness," he said, "is to live for the happiness of others and to see others happy." In jail Sardar Patel nursed him with the loving care of a mother.

On May 8, 1933, Gandhi started a twenty-one day fast for self-purification. It was not against anybody. He had given a week's notice to the Government. On the same day he was released at 6 p.m. and at 9 p.m. he was removed to Lady Thackersey's palatial (parnakuti) cottage. Kasturba was released on May 13 and attended on him. The same night he instructed M. S. Aney, the Congress President, to suspend satyagraha for a month or six weeks. Accordingly, Aney did so by issuing a statement on May 17. The fast continued and Gandhi broke it on May 29. As a result of the fast his weight was reduced to 100 pounds.

"It is a matter of conjecture," Subhas Bose rightly observed, "if the Government knew that the Mahatma would suspend the civil disobedience campaign if he were set free. On May 8, 1933, when the Mahatma started his fast, the Government issued a communique stating that in view of the nature of the object of the fast and the attitude of the mind which it disclosed, the Government had decided that the Mahatma should be set at liberty."[6]

CHAPTER XXXVII

Harijan Tour

Long After The end of his fast, Gandhi declared in *Harijan* of July 8, 1933, that although he believed God to be without any form, he went on the fast as God ordained him to do so. "I have always believed God to be without form. But what I did hear was like a voice from afar and yet quite near. For me," he went on, "the Voice of God, of Conscience, of Truth or the " inner Voice, or the still small voice mean one and the same thing." The sceptic, he added, was free to say that it was self-delusion or hallucination, but not the unanimous verdict of the whole world against him could shake him from the belief that "what I heard was the Voice of God".

"The hearing of the voice," Gandhi disclosed to the world, "was preceded by a terrible struggle within me. Suddenly the voice came upon me. I listened, made certain that it was the voice, and the struggle ceased. I was calm. The date and the hour of the fast were fixed. Joy came over me."

And God came to his succour and asked him to go on a fast for the uplift of the Untouchables, and though he said it was for purification of self and a penance it was also for the misbehaviour of his disciples. The civil disobedience movement, after a hard extensive struggle, had nearly petered out for want of leadership. The suspension of the struggle was criticized harshly by some leaders. Vithalbhai Patel and Subhas Bose, who were in Vienna, became furious and issued a statement on May 9, 1933, declaring that Gandhi as a political leader had failed. They added that his method of warfare based on the principle of maximum suffering for Indians and minimum suffering for the enemy could not possibly lead to success. Gandhi never forgave Subhas Bose for this angry and violent attack on his leadership.

Vithalbhai Patel died of heart-trouble on October 22, 1933, in a Swiss clinic near Geneva. Hearing the news, Gandhi wrote to the Sardar that Vithalbhai Patel's death caused him pain and he had written to Subhas appreciating his devoted service to Patel during his illness and asked the Sardar to write to him about it.

On his release, Gandhi was welcomed at several places in Poona. On June 12, 13 and 14, 1933, a conference was held there and Congress leaders from all provinces attended it. Gandhi made a short speech, asking the delegates to put forward their views frankly. While reviewing the situation, the majority of them said that the movement should be suspended. In the end Gandhi was authorized to seek an unconditional interview with the Viceroy.

Gandhi telegraphically requested the Viceroy to grant him an interview, but the Viceroy rejected his request, stating that nothing was possible unless the movement was withdrawn. Sir Samuel Hoare declared that Gandhi could not be a negotiator keeping in reserve the unconditional weapon of civil disobedience. On July 18 Gandhi made another appeal for an interview, but the Private Secretary to the Viceroy informed him that there was no question of holding conversations with the representative of an association which had not abandoned the movement.

On July 19 Gandhi returned to Ahmedabad where he visited Mirabehn in Sabarmati Jail. He announced his intention to disband the Sabarmati Ashram and asked the Bombay Government to take possession of it. Later, on September 30, 1933, Gandhi offered the Sabarmati Ashram for Harijan work to the Servants of Untouchables Society which was a new name given in July 1933 to the All-India Anti-untouchability League. Much later, on September 5, 1939, the property of the Sabarmati Ashram was vested in the Trust for the uplift of Harijans and became officially known as Harijan Ashram.

On July 26 Gandhi issued his famous statement on the methods of secrecy adopted by Congressmen during the movement. A few days earlier he had praised the bravery and sacrifice of the numerous civil resisters but had asked them to discard secrecy if the movement was to be continued.

To those who implored him not to stick to the Harijan movement alone, Gandhi replied that he could not give twenty-four hours of the day to Harijan work, and he could not give up a life principle for the sake of Harijan work. It would be pertinent to note here what Aurobindo, philosopher and spiritualist, had to say on Gandhi's views on secrecy. He said, "Gandhi talked about secrecy being a sin, but that is one of his many extravagances."[1]

Gandhi felt deeply humiliated at the Viceroy's refusal of an unconditional interview and so on July 30 he declared at Ahmedabad that he would march with thirty-three companions, the first halt being at Ras. This time there were nearly as many women as there were men with him, and he informed the Government accordingly. The Government refused to take possession of the Ashram, but Gandhi's offer showed how great men are often out to sacrifice everything for their principles, even the organizations they have established.

Gandhi, Kasturba, Mahadev Desai and thirty inmates of the Sabarmati Ashram were arrested on the morning of August 1. Gandhi was taken to Sabarmati Jail and then to Yeravda Jail. This was his sixth arrest in India. On August 4 he was released at 9 a.m. with orders requiring him to leave Poona by 9.30 a.m. but he expressed his desire to disobey the orders and was arrested for the seventh time, tried in Yeravda Jail by a magistrate and sentenced to one year's imprisonment. When the magistrate asked him about his occupation, he replied that he was a spinner, weaver and farmer, and his residence was "Yeravda Jail now". Mahadev Desai and Kasturba were also sentenced to imprisonment. After Gandhi's arrest, the campaign of civil disobedience was started again and hundreds of Congressmen were arrested in the first week of August 1933.

In jail, Gandhi wanted all the facilities of doing Harijan work that he had been given during his previous incarceration. If he did not get permission to do so, he would deny himself all nourishment except salt and water. "Life," he wrote to Government, "ceases to interest me, if I may not do Harijan work without let or hindrance." The Government replied that Gandhi courted imprisonment on a purely political issue and so would not be given any special treatment, not given to other 'A' class prisoners. If Gandhi, stated the Government on August 18, abandoned civil disobedience activities and incitements, he would be set at liberty at once so that he could devote himself wholly and without restriction to the cause of social reform. But Gandhi refused this offer of conditional release. His health deteriorated rapidly. He was removed to Sassoon Hospital, Poona, and the end seemed near. On August 23 his health became critical. He even disposed of the few articles he had with him among the members of the nursing staff, but he was released on the same day. He secured his release through a fast, a weapon he invariably used against the Government which was afraid of events consequent upon his possible death in prison.

Yet Gandhi described his release as an unexpected event which had taken place through the unscrutable ways of God! Among the prominent leaders who bitterly criticized Gandhi's retreat was K. F. Nariman.

GANDHI DECIDED TO devote himself to Harijan work till August 3, 1934, as the period of sentence would have expired on that date. "Up to the 3rd of August next," he observed, "I must not court imprisonment by offering aggressive civil resistance." On September 9 and 10, 1933, Jawaharlal Nehru met him in Poona. They discussed the aims and policy and goal of the Congress. They reiterated that the goal was Independence. Nehru was of the opinion that without a material change in the vested interest the condition of the masses could never be improved. He also told the Mahatma that the problem of India's freedom could not be separated from the vital international problems of the world and so they must range themselves with the progressive forces of the world. He plainly told Gandhi that their movement was essentially an open one, but in corresponding with each other a measure of secrecy might be necessary, but secrecy was hardly the word for it and privacy suited better.

Gandhi replied that though he might not go as far as Nehru, he agreed that without a material revision of the vested interests the condition of the masses could not be improved. He could not seek to coerce anyone; he sought to convert the vested interests. In a press statement in December 1933 Nehru said: "There is no middle road between fascism and communism, one has to choose between the two and I choose the communist ideal."[2]

These differences in the two leaders' outlook began to manifest themselves from this time. They arose from fundamental as well as temperamental attitudes and principles. Gandhi, who was not prepared to allow Nehru a chance to break from the Congress and his own ideology, later said in a reply to a note by the editor of *Madras Mail* in December 1933 that they should not be disturbed at the views of a sane and honest man like Jawaharlal Nehru who did not stand for Russian Communism. It would be Indian Socialism with a different colouring. "As regards the tenants," Gandhi continued, "they also had a right to the land, they must have a just share of the produce of their labour, and the actual holder of the land must be one who worked by the sweat of his brow."[3] Yet Gandhi defended the system of zamindars and taluks and talked of trusteeship.

On September 20, 1933, Dr. Annie Besant died at Adyar, but Gandhi, who was in Bombay, said not a word of condolence for that great and fearless friend of Indian independence.

In the last week of September 1933, Gandhi moved to the Satyagraha Ashram at Wardha. It took some time for him to get well again. His weight had decreased to 90 pounds. But he kept worrying about Sardar Patel's nose and Jamnalal Bajaj's ear!

After taking a rest for six weeks, Gandhi increased his weight to 108 pounds. Now aged sixty-five, he started on a whirlwind Harijan tour of nine months on November 7, 1933, from Wardha, declaring open some private temples to Harijans, collecting money for the Harijan Fund and telling people that it was blasphemy to say that God resided in a temple from which a particular class of the same faith was excluded. He was glad that he had started his Harijan tour from Wardha, the geographical centre of India. He pleaded that the untouchable Hindus should have access to all public institutions, such as schools, roads and public wells which had been thrown open by the Bombay Government in the Bombay presidency in pursuance of a resolution moved by S. K. Bole, a social reformer, and adopted by the Bombay Legislative Council on August 4, 1923. Dr. N. B. Khare was in charge of his Berar tour, and Gandhi complimented him on the smooth arrangements he had made for it.

Gandhi appealed to the people to support the Temple Entry Bill of Ranga lyer which, according to him, wanted to legalize the opinion of a majority.

At Nagpur Gandhi auctioned a cowrie donated by a poor man and it fetched Rs. 111. He sold caskets. He declared that about Rs. 20,00,000 had been spent for the removal of untouchability and the uplift of the Harijans. He had personally spent a sum of nearly five lakhs of rupees. At the Nagpur meeting eggs were thrown at Gandhi by Sanatanists. Pandit Lalnath, a Sanatanist leader, and his fanatic followers from north India along with other Sanatanist workers made abortive attempts to hold up Gandhi's car at Dhamangaon and Amraoti, and at Akola by even lying prostrate before it. On November 20 Gandhi rested for a day at Chikalda which is a hill station.

Then visiting Raipur, Itarsi and Anantpuri, Gandhi reached

Jubbulpore where on December 8 Dr. Ansari found that the continuous strain of his tour had caused a rise in Gandhi's blood pressure and so advised him to take the utmost precautions. Gandhi appealed to the people to take no more than four hours' work from him a day. In one of his letters from Raipur, Gandhi wrote to Sardar Patel, "The crowds are as large as before, perhaps larger, and as crazy as ever." This implied that the suspension of the civil disobedience movement had not affected his popularity. But Gandhi's health, it seems, was failing him. He wrote to Patel on December 25, 1933: "I cannot even recall what has to be written to whom, may be on account of old age." He visited Delhi and spent five days giving a fillip to Harijan work.

On December 16, 1933, Gandhi commenced his Harijan tour in southern India by addressing a meeting of the Harijan workers in Andhra. He told them that their purity and suffering would not fail to touch the hearts of the orthodox. If they missed this god-given opportunity to purge themselves of the curse of untouchability, they would have to pay for it with bitter tears. During his three-day visit to Madras, he addressed meetings of women, students and workers, exhorting them not to make distinctions of high and low between man and man, and that labour at least should have no distinctions of high and low.

While giving an interview to a Harijan deputation on the eve of his departure, Gandhi said, "Untouchability is a dead thing, but being a monster, it still seems to be taking breath. But it is the last breath." So optimistic Gandhi was and confident of his success in this great venture and mission!

Gandhi continued his Andhra tour, visiting Guntur, Ellore, Rajahmundry, Vizagapatam and other places. He addressed the Andhra villagers sitting on the hood of his motor-car and cried out, "a bangle for an autograph! If we fail in this trial," he declared, "Hinduism and Hindus will perish." On January 4, 1934, he entered the Mysore State. On his begging mission, he visited Bangalore, Mysore and Badanwala and then took three days' rest from January 6. Mahadev Desai and Kasturba were in jail and their absence, he said, moved him deeply. At Bangalore he put up at Kumar Park, the palace belonging to the Maharaja of Mysore. The Viceroy was displeased with the Maharaja at this.

On January 10, 1934, Gandhi commenced his tour of Malabar, the blackest spot on the "untouchability map" of India Swami Vivekanand had described the Malabaris as lunatics.[4] Gandhi told them that they should wipe out the shame of untouchability from Malabar. The face of the Nayadis (unapproachables) would always haunt him. At a Guruvayur meeting, some men were wounded in the scuffle that ensued between the supporters of Gandhi and the volunteers sent by the Varnashram Sangh from north India. The Sanatanists tried to break Gandhi's meetings, obstructed his movements and staged black-flag demonstrations at almost all prominent places. During the tour some women gave him bangles, some necklaces, and Gandhi's *Harijan* expressed his gratitude for and delight at these gifts. On January 16, 1934, Gandhi left for a tour of Travancore and Cochin. He visited Kottayam and Alleppey. He said that some men there defended the sin of untouchability as if it had divine sanction! If untouchability, he said, were removed, it must result in bringing all Indians together, and all humanity nearer to them.

During the tour Untouchables told him at some places that nothing was done in villages to remove untouchability, and temples were again closed against them. Gandhi agreed with their suggestion that caste Hindus should employ Harijans as domestic servants. They also told him that the temple entry movement had come to a dead stop though Gandhi believed that it was going forward.

On January 20, 1934, when he entered Trivandrum, he was glad to see that the Travancore State had already declared open public roads, wells and *chatrams* to all classes of people. Gandhi congratulated the State on the reform it had recently introduced. Everywhere Gandhi heard the wails and woes of those who were ground down by social tyranny. He said he had become a Harijan and he would like to suffer with Harijans. The Maharaja was indifferent to Gandhi, and Sir C. P. Ramaswamy Aiyer, the Dewan, did not care to meet Gandhi. "Kelappan," Gandhi wrote to Patel, "will probably marry a Christian lady, and so his connection with the Harijan Sevak Sangh will come to an end."

WHEN GANDHI WAS at Calicut on the night of January 15, 1934, the terrible calamity of earthquake overtook Bihar, destroying thousands of lives and lakhs of houses and about 6 million wells up to a distance of a thousand miles. The daily life of the people was completely shattered and paralysed. The Bihar Government released Rajendra Prasad on January 17 to help the earthquake sufferers. Gandhi was seeking God's advice but he said: "I am being crushed to pieces, still I talk, laugh and seem to enjoy, for I have to do that. But I am thinking of it all the twenty-four hours and made a public appeal for funds for the stricken Bihar." Someone asked Gandhi why he was fiddling while Bihar was burning.

Gandhi declared in a statement in *Harijan* of February 2, 1934: "Let the anti-untouchability reformers regard the earthquake as a nemesis for the sin of untouchability. I share the belief with the whole world, civilized and uncivilized, that calamities such as the Bihar one come to mankind as a chastisement for their sins. I regard untouchability as such a grave sin as to warrant divine chastisement." He must have shuddered at his own superstitious interpretation and so he extended the cause of the calamity to a wider range and whispered, "I do not interpret chastisement as an exclusive punishment for the sin of untouchability".

Gandhi did not cancel his tour programme and go to Bihar. He thought there was no immediate need for him to go there. He toured Karnatak and Orissa and then went to Bihar.

Tagore and Savarkar held up Gandhi's interpretation of the earthquake to ridicule. Tagore denounced it as an unscientific view of things. He asserted that physical catastrophes have their inevitable and exclusive origin in certain combinations of physical facts. "If," he proceeded, "we associate ethical principles with cosmic phenomena, we shall have to admit that human nature is morally superior. We are perfectly secure in the faith that our own sins and errors, however enormous, have not enough force to bring down the structure of creation to ruins." Tagore was sorry that Gandhi's views emphasized "the elements of unreason which is a fundamental source of all blind powers that drive us against freedom and self-respect".

Savarkar was sorry that superstition should hold its sway in India even during the twentieth century. The Britisher, he observed, crushed everything that was with the Indians, but not their precious possession of credulous superstition. It was, he added, quite all right when Indians did not know the causes of such things as an earthquake, a disease or a pestilence, but to stick to prayer and sacrifice of animals even when science had revealed the causes of physical calamities was simply absurd. Savarkar appealed to the Hindus to follow the cause and effect theory that is never disturbed by the thought of divine pleasure or displeasure. Later Savarkar issued a booklet in Marathi condemning the irrational outlook of Gandhi and called it *Gandhi Gondhal*—Gandhian confusion.

About Tagore's criticism of his unscientific and superstitious views, Gandhi said that Tagore wrote such things in haste and then corrected himself.[8] But in *Harijan* of February 16, 1934, replying to Tagore, he said: "I early discovered certain differences of outlook between us. God rules me in tiniest detail of my life. I believe literally that not a leaf moves but by His will."

But the philosophical basis of Gandhism is further disclosed when he observed: "Visitations like draughts, floods, earthquakes and the like, though they seem to have only physical origins, are, for me, somehow connected with man's morals. Therefore, I instinctively felt that the earthquake was a visitation for the sin of untouchability." "I admit," he continued, "my utter ignorance of the working of the laws of Nature. But even as I cannot help believing in God though I am unable to prove His existence to the sceptics, in like manner, I cannot prove the connection of sin of untouchability with Bihar visitation even though the connection is instinctively felt by me. With me," he concluded, "the cosmic phenomena and human behaviour is a living faith."

In this view Gandhi was indeed the spokesman for the ignorant masses; reason and science were not his strong points. In his opinion God poured His wrath on the people of Bihar for the sins of untouchability committed by Hindus all over India. They deserved to suffer, he thought, even the innocent children, non-Hindus and animals in that region for no sin of untouchability on their part. And if God was omniscient, kind, all-pervading, why did He punish in the earthquake persons who were not concerned with the sin of untouchability? Sometimes men of God turn their back upon science and reason. And Gandhi, who believed that not a leaf moved without God's will, did precisely that.

The Christian Harijans in Malabar and Tamilnad, who had changed their faith to escape the hardships inflicted upon them by caste Hindus, had, they told Gandhi, fared no better in the Christian fold. Gandhi consoled them by saying that they would get indirect benefits in future.

In February 1934 Gandhi used the good offices of his European emissary Muriel Lester to see the Governor of Bengal. But nothing came out of it. On the eve of Gandhi's visit to Pondicherry on February 17, 1934, Gandhi had requested Aurobindo Ghose for an interview. But he courteously refused to see him. Aurobindo granted an audience to his visitors thrice a year. Aurobindo had criticized Gandhi's views on the Gita, Hindu-Muslim unity, non-violence and secrecy in politics. It was

about this time that the American Journal *Christian Century* suggested that Gandhi should be given the Nobel Prize.

Gandhi completed his tour of Malabar and Karnatak and reached Allahabad on March 11, 1934. He called on Kamala Nehru and Swarup Rani Nehru as Jawaharlal had been sentenced to two years' imprisonment on February 16 for the three provocative speeches he had delivered at Calcutta in January 1934. Then Gandhi visited Patna and toured Bihar from March 11 to April 9, 1934, inspecting the relief work, cheering the grief-stricken people and giving them detailed instructions. He fervently appealed to them to abolish untouchability and to abolish distinctions between man and man. He then toured Assam on foot from April 10 to May 3. There he told the people that no human being could be unclean by birth and he only was pure who walked in the fear of God and His creatures.

GANDHI HAD SENSED that some of the Congressmen were eager to enter Legislative Councils. Dr. B. C. Roy, Dr. Ansari and other Congress leaders of their persuasion had met in Delhi on March 31, 1934, and had decided to revive the Swaraj Party and to fight elections to the Legislative Assembly and Councils which were to be held in November 1934. But before this Delhi Conference the Democratic Swaraj Party Conference under N. C. Kelkar and Jamnadas Mehta had resolved to fight the ensuing elections. Gandhi had sensed the change of political climate. So after "an intense introspection and searching of the heart and waiting upon God", Gandhi on Monday, April 2, his silence day, drafted a statement at an out-of-the-way place called Saharsa, without any knowledge of what had happened in Delhi, and passed it on to Rajendra Prasad. It underwent considerable revision and was abridged. Meanwhile, Dr. Ansari and Bhulabhai Desai met him at Patna. Gandhi released his statement on April 6 and made room for the Council-goers, himself remaining the sole representative of civil resistance in action.

On May 1 and 2, the Congress leaders, Bhulabhai Desai, B. C. Roy, Deepnarayan Singh, K. F. Nariman and K. M. Munshi, met Gandhi at Ranchi and discussed with him his statement of April 6. Gandhi was told by them that they were not disowning him, but that he should release the Congress from civil disobedience. Gandhi admitted that his words had lost their power, but he knew, he added, he would give a good account of himself when the time came to do so. He yielded. The Swaraj Party met in conference at Ranchi on May 3, 1934,

and decided to enter the Councils to effect reforms in matters such as labour, currency, exchange, agriculture and the constructive programme of the Congress. As the civil disobedience movement was suspended, the office of Acting President M. S. Aney terminated and in his place Jamnalal Bajaj was nominated to act as President.

On May 4 Gandhi left for a tour of Orissa and from May 5 he carried out the tour on foot. He was protected by the police and he said he could not help feeling ashamed that they had to defend him against possible mischief. At some places Harijans showered flowers on him and welcomed him with conch shells while the orthodox howled and staged black flag processions against him. On May 16 he caught a train for Patna to attend a meeting of the A.I.C.C. there.

The A.I.C.C., which had not been banned by the Government, met under the presidentship of Pandit Malaviya at Patna on May 18 and 19, and Gandhi officially suspended the civil resistance movement. He allowed Congressmen to enter the Councils but the A.I.C.C., instead of permitting the Swaraj Party to function, appointed a Board to run and control elections of members to the legislatures on behalf of the Congress. Gandhi then completed his Orissa walking tour on June 7, 1934.

On June 12, 1934, the Government lifted the ban on Congress organizations which resumed their work freely. Thus the civil disobedience campaign rose and fell. But just at this moment an event of note took place in the history of India and India declared her will to march forward with the progressive forces of the world. India stood once again at the cross-roads as in 1907 at Surat and in 1920 at Calcutta. On May 17, 1934, at Patna Congress leaders of the socialist persuasion first met in conference under Acharya Narendra Dev, Principal, Kashi Vidyapith, and decided to organize an All-India Congress Socialist Party.

The Socialists doubted the efficacy of Gandhian economic policy and methods of warfare. They were now disillusioned with Gandhi. According to them, Gandhism was a system of clemency and charity and not a system of social justice. Yet they clung to the Congress. Some leaders, who had opposed individual satyagraha at Poona in June 1933, had decided to form a separate Socialist Party independently of those who had taken a similar decision in Nasik Jail. The Nasik group was led by Jayaprakash Narayan who was one of the founders of the Bihar Socialist Party. The spirit of the Socialist Party was Jayaprakash Narayan, and the godfather was Jawaharlal Nehru,

who often tried to rationalize Gandhism. He was in jail at this time.

The Congress Socialist Party was opposed to Council entry and in order to ward off the danger that might come from it, the Congress Working Committee resolved: "It was necessary in view of all the loose talk about confiscation of private property and the necessity of class war to remind Congressmen that such ideas were contrary to the Congress creed of non-violence."

The Congress Socialists said that this was a further retreat from the Karachi resolution.

Gandhi returned to Wardha on June 9, 1934. His disciples, Mirabehn and Muriel Lester, left for England, and Miss Agatha Harrison, who had come to India, also left for England. These British emissaries of Gandhi, Mirabehn and Muriel Lester, were doing political work according to their lights, meeting leaders like Lloyd George. The Congress Working Committee met at Wardha on June 12 and 13 and again at Bombay on June 17 and, 18. It passed a resolution condemning the White Paper and another on the Communal Award. Aney and Malaviya desired the Congress to denounce both the White Paper and the Communal Award. But under the pressure of its Nationalist Muslim members, it resolved "that the Congress in view of the division of opinion can neither accept nor reject the Communal Award as long as the division of opinion lasts". Bose later said in his *Indian Struggle* that the Muslim leaders in the Congress held "a pistol at the Working Committee and because of their insistence," the Congress was forced to take up this ridiculous attitude of neither accepting nor rejecting the Communal Award. Nehru thought that the Communal Award was "merely a problem created by the middle and upper classes for the sake of a few seats in the legislature or appointments in Government service or for ministerial positions". Subhas Bose was in Europe and Nehru was in Naini Central Jail.

This equivocal and nefarious neither-accept-nor-reject policy showed how a cankerous growth was developing in the body of India's leading political party under the leadership of Gandhi. The Congress Party in the Central Assembly later allowed Jinnah to compel the Central Assembly to endorse the Communal Award which was against all democratic and secular ideals! Gandhi wrote to Sardar Patel that "the Congressmen will loyally support the policy enunciated in the resolution of the Working Committee regarding the Communal Award."[6]

Gandhi went to Poona on June 19 and was there for a week.

He visited Harijan localities, the Women's University and the Christ Seva Sangha, addressing meetings and holding discussions. "While he was on his way to attend a meeting at Vishrambag Wada on the evening of June 25, 1934, to receive a municipal address, a bomb was thrown at a motorcar which, the bomb thrower thought, was carrying Gandhi. But Gandhi was following in another motor-car and was saved.

Seven persons including the Chief Officer and two constables who were in the car were injured. The bomb fell at the feet of L. B. Bhopatkar, a municipal member, a prominent leader in Maharashtra and an ex-President of the Maharashtra Provincial Congress Committee. Bhopatkar was seriously injured.

Gandhi issued a statement on the bomb explosion and said that he could not believe any sane Sanatanist could ever encourage the insane act that was perpetrated that evening. This sorrowful incident, he observed, advanced the Harijan cause. But Gandhi had nothing to say about the suffering of Bhopatkar. His heart had no compassion for him as he differed from him in politics. Bhopatkar was a man of broader sympathies. Writing about the bomb explosion, Gandhi said to Sardar Patel that something of the sort was only to be expected. "But," he added, "not a sparrow falls without God's will." It is said that the bomb-thrower was a fanatic devotee of Sanatana Dharma which treated a section of their co-religionists as worse than dogs.

Commenting on the bomb incident, Gandhi wrote in *Harijan* of June 26, 1934: "I am not aching for martyrdom, but if it comes in my way in the prosecution of what I consider to be the supreme duty in defence of the faith I hold in common with millions of Hindus, I shall have well earned it, and it will be possible for the historian of the future to say that the vow I had taken before Harijans that I would, if need be, die in the attempt to remove untouchability literally fulfilled."

Gandhi told the Socialists in Poona that he claimed to be a socialist because of his belief and conduct and added: "Jawaharlal is my heir and successor so far as my hold on the Congress is concerned. I am discharging his stewardship."[7]

Gandhi then visited Ahmedabad, Bhavnagar, Karachi, Ajmer and Lahore. Everywhere the Sanatanists greeted him with black flags. Pandit Lalnath did not shed a grain of his inhumanity. His religion breathed hatred. He tried to break Gandhi's meetings and once received a lathi blow. Gandhi chastised his audience who thought a word to the wise would not be enough and so had given a blow to the insensate,

unsympathetic and unenlightened pundit. At Karachi a man with an axe called on Gandhi but was arrested by the police.

Gandhi then went to Lahore, Calcutta, Kanpur and Lucknow. He faced the Sanatanists; but he was mightily pleased to see the crowds larger than ever before in Lahore and elsewhere. He told the Bihar zamindars that class war was foreign to the essential genius of India and "Ramrajya of my dream ensures rights alike of prince and pauper". Supposing that there was an attempt to unjustly deprive them of their property, they would find him fighting on their side. Nehru, he added, did indeed talk of nationalization of property, but it need not frighten them.[8]

Gandhi closed his Harijan tour at Benares on July 29, 1934, where the Sanatanists led by the infamous Pandit Lalnath publicly burnt Gandhi's portrait and published inflammatory leaflets against him. The police and the social workers of the town were anxious about Gandhi's safety. Baba Kalbhairav, a rabid Sanatanist, was at the root of this trouble.

Gandhi travelled and trudged about 12,500 miles for his Harijan work and collected about eight lakhs of rupees. He concluded his tour with a press statement in which he declared enthusiastically that "the impression left on my mind is that untouchability is on its last legs". And he shared the belief of many that untouchability would soon be a thing of the past.

ON AUGUST 5, 1934, Gandhi returned to Wardha, undertook a fast and concluded it on August 14. Though the fast was primarily and nominally intended for the hurt caused to Pandit Lalnath, he wanted the Harijan workers to help the Harijan movement with greater personal purification and greater concentration. He wanted Congress workers to use clean, truthful and non-violent methods in elections, and to observe the rule about the use of khaddar. He was filled with horror and anguish at their deceit and manipulations. His conclusion was that "no fast was ever proved an insurance against human frailties. We can only mount to success through failures".

What was the result of the Harijan tour in which Gandhi canvassed support for Ranga Iyer's bill? With the connivance of the Congress members in the Central Assembly and because of lack of sympathy on the part of the Government which thought the bill to be impracticable and likely to lead to a serious invasion of private rights, the orthodox leaders smothered it by resorting to dilatory tactics. Ranga lyer withdrew the bill on August 23, 1934.

The depressed classes rightly said that if Gandhi was the uncrowned King of India, why did he require the sanction of the British Government to abolish untouchability and why could he not succeed in his object? In the temple entry movement the depressed classes themselves did not participate; they were onlookers. They knew that most of the Congress Hindus were opposed to social equality, had spent little out of the Tilak Swaraj Fund on their welfare, and that Gandhi's movement was fundamentally semi-reformist. It lacked the real urge for a social revolution. Gandhi looked at the problem from the viewpoint of a humanitarian and not that of a social revolutionary. Dr. Ambedkar had already captivated their minds and had become their saviour. That is why the applause, purses and propaganda emanating from the Gandhian Harijan movement did not prove particularly beneficial to them.

While taking a rest in Wardha, Gandhi proffered advice to village workers regarding spinning, tanning, the rearing of cows, and the use of buffaloes which Gandhi wished to discourage.

At this time Gandhi had a grave problem to solve. Kaka Kalelkar resigned the trusteeship of the Gujarat Vidyapith and Gandhi wrote to Patel, who had been released, that if anyone could keep Kaka in Gujarat, it would have Sardar's approval and blessings. So he sought Sardar's approval. Gandhi wrote again to Patel: "I have decided that even in order to get over this bitterness, Kaka should not leave Gujarat for the present." Gandhi, who once said that Patel had his protecting eye on him, was completely dominated by him. He could not do anything in Gujarat without his consent!

Gandhi received a shock from Jawaharlal Nehru who had been released temporarily on August 11, 1934, on account of his wife's illness. Nehru protested against the suspension of the civil disobedience movement. The decision gave Nehru, he said, the biggest shock he had ever had, and he felt absolutely alone, left high and dry on a deserted island! He was indignant at the thought that those who were entrusted with the flag of Indian freedom with pomp had actually hauled it down[9] at the height of the national struggle at the bidding of the enemy! The resolution of the Working Committee on the subject, Nehru added, showed such an outstanding ignorance of the elements of socialism that it was painful to read it and to realize that it might be read outside India. It was, he added, hardly becoming for a reasoned argument to be answered by sentimental appeals or by the cheap remark that the conditions in India were different and the economic laws that applied elsewhere did not function in India. In passing, Nehru reminded Gandhi that political objectives were the special province of the Congress. By this he indirectly showed his disapproval of Gandhi's Harijan movement.

On August 17 Gandhi replied that there was not enough reason for all the grief and disappointment Nehru had felt. He wanted complete independence in the full English sense of the term. As for socialism, he said that the Socialists as a body were in a hurry. He said he had looked up the dictionary meaning of socialism, but it took him no further than where he was before. However, he brought to the notice of Nehru that the latter had been hard on the members of the Working Committee. They were also his colleagues, and after an explosion he wanted construction. But on August 19 he wrote to Sardar Patel that Jawaharlal's explosion was not so dangerous as it sounded. "He only exercised his right to let off steam. I believe he is now quiet,"[10] he added.

Gandhi was now about to retire from the Congress, and his statements and sad utterances were an indication of this. In a statement he issued from Wardha on September 17, 1934, he enumerated the reasons for his retirement. It was his impression that a very large body of the Congress intelligentsia were tired of his methods and views, that he was a hindrance rather than a help to the natural growth of the Congress, and as the Congress was dominated by his personality it could not remain the most democratic and representative organization. "Many Congressmen," he observed, ''have despaired of resisting me."

After fourteen years of trial, non-violence still remained a policy with the majority of the Congress. His method for the removal of untouchability was different. "I cannot remain," he proceeded, "in the Congress." And to be in active opposition was unthinkable. As regards civil resistance, there need not be any wonder that it should have been limited only to him. Besides, many Congressmen believed that the end justified the means. He had his programme: untouchability, Hindu-Muslim unity, cent per cent swadeshi in the sense of revival of village industries. He would, he concluded, love to serve the Congress in his own humble manner, whether he was in it or outside.

Srinivas Sastri said at a meeting in Bombay: "The Congress is not meant for saints and sages. It is meant for the common man and woman." Aney and Malaviya, who differed from the Congress over the Communal Award, resigned their membership of the Congress Parliamentary Board, and on July 31, 1934, they started the Nationalist Party to combat the Communal Award and the White Paper.

As the last resort, Gandhi placed for the consideration of the ensuing Congress four amendments to the Congress creed. The first aimed at replacing the words "legitimate and peaceful" by "truthful and non-violent". The second was about four-anna franchise, to be substituted by the delivery of 2,000 rounds of a prescribed quality of yarn a month and the third was about the right of vote in the Congress elections.

Meanwhile elections were held to the Central Legislative Assembly and Gandhi said the election results were really wonderful. The Working Committee appointed on October 20, 1934, a sub-committee of Gandhi, Bhulabhai Desai, K. M. Munshi, Pattabhi Sitaramayya and Jairamdas Daulatram with power to co-opt and to report on Gandhi's amendments by the next day. The sub-committee reviewed the whole constitution and submitted its report to the Working Committee, but the amendment of the creed, as proposed by Gandhi, was not accepted by the Subjects Committee of the Congress. The words signifying the reasonable attitude of a political party "legitimate" and "peaceful" were not replaced by the spiritual pair "truthful and non-violent". This was a signal defeat for Gandhi although the other amendments were accepted in one form or another.

Three and a half years after its Karachi session, the Congress met on October 27 and 28, 1934, at Ghaffar Nagar in Bombay under the presidentship of Dr. Rajendra Prasad. The neither-accept-nor-reject policy of the Working Committee was confirmed. The Congress rejected the White Paper on which the British Government's proposals were based. The most important issue before the Bombay Congress was the change Gandhi sought to effect in the creed of the Congress; and on that issue he was resolutely and ruthlessly defeated. The Congress remained a political organization belonging to the matter-of-fact world.

The last day of the Congress witnessed a heart-breaking scene when Gandhi in his sixty-sixth year severed his official connection with the Congress. The Congress shed tears over it, reiterating its confidence in the leadership of Gandhi. In his farewell speech Gandhi hoped that the Congress would soon give effect to the khaddar clause and the labour franchise, and said that his interest in the Congress organization would thenceforth be confined to watching from a distance the enforcement of the principles for which the Congress stood. He vouched for the correctness of the Congress programme which had progressive social, moral and economic goals.

And so Gandhi, who always asked other leaders to secure a majority in the Congress for their views and not to leave it on account of defeat, left the Congress because it did not accept his doctrines of truth and non-violence even when he threatened to resign.

Gandhi was sure that neither Rajendra Prasad nor Sardar Patel would be able to assume the leadership of the Congress. After six months he wrote, early in April 1935, to Sardar Patel to tell the people in U.P. that "your real leader is Nehru. We can stand before you only as his trustees". That should be, he added, the warp, and the woof could be as Patel liked it.

CHAPTER XXXVIII

Village Uplift

After The Bombay Congress, Gandhi returned to Wardha on October 30, 1934. He immediately issued a statement in which he said he would continue taking an interest in the welfare of the Congress and would devote himself to constructive work. On November 2, 1934, he resigned from the Gujarat Provincial Congress. He stayed at Wardha for nearly a month.

The Bombay Congress did not approve Gandhi's spiritual philosophy, but accepted secular politics and rejected the Gandhian weapon of bloodless revolution. Gandhi's *Harijan* was significantly silent on this point, and on Gandhi's retirement from the Congress. As he was now deeply interested in the All-India Spinners' Association, he sang its praises in *Harijan* and said the spinners eked out their meagre earnings by twelve rupees a year.

The Government, however, looked at Gandhi's constructive work with suspicion. On November 13 Government issued a confidential circular to all Provincial Governments warning them against Gandhi's scheme to revive village industries as they were of the opinion that it was motivated by political designs. Government thought that Gandhi's contemplated revival of village life was directed towards a revival of the subversive movement on an extended scale involving the masses in the rural areas. For a few days Gandhi did not know about this circular and it would have made no difference had he known this. He wrote an exhaustive article on "Village Industries" in *Harijan* of November 16, explaining his ideas on village industries and their promotion as outlined by him at the Bombay Congress in his resolution on the subject.

As Gandhi was the only leader who had seen the villages closely, he realized that they were lifeless, their industries were slipping out of their hands and they were burdened with debts. He wrote in an article: "Mechanization is good when the hands are too few for the work intended to be accomplished. It is an evil when there are more hands than required for the work, as is the case in India." The problem in India was not how to find leisure for the teeming millions inhabiting our villages, but how to utilize their idle hours. "The new spinning and weaving mills," Gandhi added, "had deprived the villagers of a substantial means of livelihood, for they had displaced thousands of workers."

The All-India Spinners' Association established with the approval of the Congress by Gandhi in September 1925 had been doing work in about 5,000 villages. But it was not enough to universalize khadi or to rejuvenate the villages. Gandhi wanted to revive the moribund village industries and crafts and to investigate, tabulate and classify the ones that were to be revived. He chose two that were connected with cloth and food. He wanted to displace the flour-mill and rice-mill that were driving millions of women out of employment and also sugar which was replacing jaggery. He had issued a questionnaire to several well-known doctors and chemists, asking them to enlighten him on the chemical analysis and different food values of polished and unpolished rice, jaggery and sugar, but he was not satisfied with any of the replies.

This campaign for village uplift was the result of Gandhi's close study of the poverty and unhygienic conditions in Indian villages, his inborn humanitarianism, his zeal for making experiments with diet and his innate love of cleanliness. He often proudly asserted that he had been a cook all his life and had been making experiments with diet since his student days in London.

The growth of socialist trends in the Congress must have drawn Gandhi's pointed attention to the state of the village economy. But his social and economic ideas and outlook did not allow him to advocate radical social change. His profound emphasis on the village economy was right, but it suffered because of his attitude to zamindars, to modern agriculture tools, implements and fertilizers and by his hostility to modern contraceptives. His ideas of village self-sufficiency were not radical enough to secure agricultural surplus, to increase the purchasing power and living standard of the peasants and to meet the rising pressure on land. His programme was not adequate to provide non-agricultural outlets for the development of village industries. This was the new society he sincerely wanted to bring into being although it was based on an inadequate social and economic structure.

As regards landlordism, Gandhi later said that he was not for a fight against the money-lender for a reduction in the rate of interest and for a fight against the zamindar for an increased share of agricultural produce because in that case the people would not be able to make common cause in the fight for Swaraj. He said love and exclusive possession would never go together and added: "Man will ever remain imperfect, and it will be always his part to try to be perfect. You might say," he went on, "that trusteeship is a legal fiction. Absolute trusteeship is an abstraction like Euclid's definition of a point, and is equally unattainable. But if we strive for it, we will be able to go further in realizing a state of equality on earth by another method."

If the people concerned did not behave as trustees, Gandhi believed, the people would have to deprive them of their possessions through the state with minimum exercise of violence. But in his opinion the violence of private ownership was less injurious than the violence of the state and an increase of the power of the state did the greatest harm to mankind by destroying individuality, which lay at the root of progress. The solution to this problem was the law of Varna which, according to him, admitted of no distinctions of high and low and guaranteed to each the fruits of his labour.

Gandhi came to the conclusion that the people must husk their own rice and grind their own flour. The campaign had nothing to do with politics, political party or civil disobedience. Gandhi founded on December 14, 1934, the All-India Village Industries Association with the object of reorganizing and reconstructing villages. The organizers were to work under Gandhi's guidance and carry on research, publish literature, establish agencies and do propaganda. The Board of Management consisted of Dr. Prafulla Ghosh, Shankarlal Banker, Dr. Khan Sahib and others and the Board of advisers was comprised of Tagore, Sir J. C. Bose, Sir P. C. Ray, Sir C. V. Raman, Dr. Ansari and others.

The frontier leader Abdul Ghaffar Khan was arrested at Wardha on December 7 and was kept in Sabarmati Jail, having been sentenced to two years' imprisonment.

Gandhi left Wardha for Delhi on December 29, 1934, and stayed there for a month. While in Delhi, Gandhi did not attend the party given in honour of the Viceroy by Syed Reza Ali who was Agent-designate for South Africa. Gandhi later explained that as the invitation was formal, he regretted he could not attend it as it would have put the Viceroy in an awkward position.

It was in Delhi on January 11, 1935, that the confidential circular of Government against Gandhi's village reconstruction programme came to light. So on January 22, Gandhi clarified his position by stating that the A.I.V.I.A. was meant exclusively for the uplift of the villages. He should be glad, he added, if Government were to take the wind out of his sails. If they helped him, he could produce magical results. His only object was to abolish idleness, to help people turn their time to good account, to fight poor feeding habits and to stop all economic rot. Acharya Kripalani had said that the A.I.V.I.A. aimed at creating a revolution to proceed from the villages and Gandhi expected his movement to have immense political effects. But the Government thought otherwise, and in order to forestall Gandhi's activities in villages it provided in the Budget one crore of rupees for the economic development and improvement of the rural areas!

THE NON-VIOLENT struggle for Swaraj was called off and the fight in the Legislative Council began at Delhi. After the new elections to the Central Assembly, the Legislative Assembly started its work on January 21, 1935. Mohamed Ali Jinnah, who had returned to India in January 1934 after Liaquat Ali's persuasive talks, was now taking a keen interest in politics. The biography, *Grey Wolf*, by H. C. Armstrong had highly impressed him and his ideal became Mustafa Kemal. Jinnah was now a different man. In England he had talks with Mohamad Iqbal who had originated the idea of a separate nation for the Muslims, and these ideas had begun captivating him. Jinnah was naturally against federation and the report of the Joint Parliamentary Committee, but he wanted to endorse the Communal Award. The Congress President, Rajendra Prasad, had begun talks with Jinnah on January 23, 1935, for a compromise with the Muslim League when Gandhi was in Delhi. Utilizing this opportunity to further his new goal, Jinnah shrewdly co-operated with the Congress Assembly Party, which was wedded to the suicidal policy of neither-reject-nor-accept, in trying to reject the Joint Parliamentary Committee's Report; but the Congress amendment was defeated. However, for the help Jinnah rendered to the Congress Party, the Congress members deliberately remained neutral in the Central Assembly when on February 7, 1935,

Jinnah moved his amendment recommending the endorsement of the Communal Award. With this treacherous help Jinnah compelled the Assembly to do his will. And the Communal Award gave free scope to the Muslim ego and its separatist ambitions.

While the Government was making much of Gandhi's village uplift, he was really making the best of his retirement from politics. Events were moving fast. The India Bill was published and the second reading of the bill was passed by the British Parliament on February 10, 1935, while Gandhi was discussing "Green leaves and their food values" and "Cow's milk *v/s* Buffalo's milk". On August 2, 1935, the India Bill received the royal assent.

On March 23, 1935, Gandhi began a four-week silence to cope with the arrears of work. Dr. Ansari resigned from the Presidentship of the Congress Parliamentary Board for reasons of health and at or about this time Rajaji became exhausted. Gandhi said that Rajaji had been isolated and though he was working without respite the Madras leader found it impossible for him to speak his mind to anyone. Agatha Harrison had suggested that Rajaji should be sent to Britain, but Gandhi thought such a visit at that time would be useless.

During Gandhi's silence, Bhansali had an interview with him, Gandhi writing questions and Bhansali replying to him. Bhansali was an old worker of Gujarat Vidyapith. He gave up that work and was engrossed in his meditation and prayer. Gandhi made him spin and do some work. Madame Halide Edube Hanum stayed at the Wardha Ashram for three days and said, she had come to pay homage not only to the greatest man of India but to the greatest servant of the world. Gandhi said to Madame Hanum: "It is the rich men who make war and that is why the world fights them." A lady of international repute, she had come to Delhi to deliver lectures at the Jamia on the invitation of her old friend, Dr. Ansari.

The temple entry movement had almost fizzled out and the Pallas from Trichinopoly district, at a conference, threatened to desert the Hindu religion. Gandhi was annoyed and said such men could not be said to be actuated by the religious spirit. The threat to desert the faith put them out of court.

Gandhi, having broken his silence on April 19, 1935, went to Indore, opened the A.-I.V.I. Exhibition and presided over the Hindi Sahitya Sammelan (Hindi Literary Conference). He told the literary men that before the advent of the British the inter-provincial contact had been maintained through the medium of Hindi. The pilgrims and the *sadhus* had kept alive the religious tradition and maintained the fundamental unity of India. "Today," he said, "the message of the removal of untouchability, of khadi and of the revival of village industries can be carried to the farthest part of India only through the medium of Hindi." No other leader was as conscious of spreading Hindi as the future lingua franca of India as Gandhi. He had been consciously and ceaselessly propagating it for over eighteen years. And to spread it in southern India was a significant and far-sighted policy which neither the propagandists of pure Hindi nor the promoters of Hindustani understood. Indeed Gandhi proved to be the greatest protagonist in this field.

Writing about this conference in *Harijan* of May 4, 1935, Gandhi observed, "The Hindi Sahitya Sammelan, recently held in Indore, passed some useful resolutions. Among them was one giving the definition of Hindi, and another expressing the opinion that all the languages that had descended from or had been largely influenced by Sanskrit should be written in the Devanagari script." Had all the languages of India been written in the Devanagari script it would have tremendously helped the unification and emotional integration of the people.

In April and May several missionaries met Gandhi and discussed religion and Christianity with him. One of the missionaries put a number of questions to Gandhi. He was asked whether he ever got angry or not. Gandhi replied that it was not that he did not get angry. "But," he said, "I only control my anger when it comes."

At last, *Harijan* of May 11, 1935 reports, came the question of questions which missionary friends were never tired of asking and Gandhi was never tired of answering. "Would you prevent missionaries coming to India in order to baptize?"

Gandhi's reply was: "Who am I to prevent them? If I had the power and could legislate, I should certainly stop all proselytizing. It is the cause of much avoidable conflict between classes and unnecessary heart-burning among missionaries. But I should welcome people of any nationality if they came to serve here for the sake of service. In Hindu households the advent of a missionary has meant the disruption of the family coming in the wake of change of dress, manners, language, food and drink."

To another question he replied, "If Jesus came to earth again he would disown many things that are being done in the name of Christianity. It is not he who says 'Lord, Lord,' that is Christian, but 'he who doeth the will of the Lord' that is a true

Christian." He asked the missionaries, "And cannot he who has not heard the name of Christ Jesus do the will of God?"

Pierre Ceresole, friend of Romain Rolland, came to India at this time and lived with Gandhi. He told Gandhi that the author of *India in the Dark Wood* wanted "The main framework of the dominant Hindu philosophy to be shattered. India can only recover under the guidance of Christ Jesus." Ceresole referred to another book called *Jesus—Lord or Leader*. "The author Frank Lenwood regrets," Ceresole proceeded, "the claim of Christianity as the final religion and pines for a fuller and richer faith than we have yet reached."

Commenting on this, Gandhi observed: "There is a swing in the pendulum, and I have a Christian friend telling me that the Gita shows how to live the New Testament, and the many passages in the latter which used to be dark were intelligible to him through a study of the Gita."[1]

As regards the legislation against proselytization, Gandhi never instructed the provincial Congress ministries when they came into existence in 1937 to legislate on the prevention of proselytizing; nor was any active struggle launched against the missionaries who came to India with the object of Christianizing India. Had he led such an active struggle the reputation of his Mahatmaship would have definitely suffered in the long run.

In India change of religion unfortunately led always to change of nationality. Proselytization paved the way for national disintegration and disloyalty. The converts changed their culture and broke their traditional ties. It deflected the converts from Indian history and nationhood, national convictions and beliefs. Christian missionaries proselytized the hill-tribes. The sons and daughters of these converts, the Nagas in the eastern frontiers of India, the Uraons and the aboriginals in Central India, who were converted to Christianity and the Christians in Travancore and Cochin, demanded separate states such as Nagaland, Jharkhand and so on.

Gandhi's admirer, Dr. Verrier Elwin, in 1944, warned India about the dangers of the conversion of hill-tribes to Christianity. He said, "At the present rate of progress the entire aboriginal population will be converted. It will be turned into a querulous, anti-national, aggressive minority community with none of the old virtues and few of the new, which will be a thorn in the side of the future governments of India."

The Christian Missionary Activities Enquiry Committee appointed by the Madhya Pradesh Government after Independence and the Prologue to the Memoirs of the Aga Khan speak volumes on the menace and should open the eyes of Indian nationalists and the well-wishers of India. In Communist or Socialist countries such a dangerous situation is not likely to arise but under Indian secularism this danger is great. It is true that the Indian Constitution gives freedom to propagate religion to Indian citizens subject to public order, morality and health. But the right is not extended to foreign missionaries.

Mohanlal Pandya, one of the foremost revolutionaries in Gujarat, died on May 15 and Gandhi mourned his death in an editorial of *Harijan*. On May 22, 1935, Kamala Nehru went to Europe for medical treatment and Gandhi made it a point to be present in Bombay to give his blessings to her and to wish her *bon voyage*. This shows how Gandhi took care of his silken ties with the Nehru family.

GANDHI THEN LEFT Bombay and reached plague-stricken Borsad on May 23, to unhesitatingly endorse the destruction of rats and fleas carried on by Sardar Patel through Dr. Bhaskar Patel, although Gandhi said that he believed even plague-stricken rats and fleas were his kindred! Naturally Gandhi was again caught in the coils of his apostolic non-violence. He was harshly criticized for this contradiction in India and his European admirers nervously sent him newspaper cuttings for an explanation in the matter.

The apostle of non-violence aided by the barrister in him apologetically offered an explanation in *Harijan* of June 22, 1934. Gandhi said: "But why this contradiction between belief and action? Contradiction is undoubtedly there. . . . Life is an aspiration. Its mission is to strive after perfection which is self-realization. The ideal must not be lowered because of our weakness or imperfections. I am painfully conscious of both in me. The silent cry daily goes out to truth to help me to remove these weaknesses and imperfections of mine." But Gandhi was now sixty-six, and had been experimenting with non-violence for the previous thirty years, in word, thought and deed!

At this time, the Rev. Mr. Fujii from Japan stayed with Gandhi, observing the manners and customs of India as he was of the opinion that "one must observe the manners and the customs of the country whose salt we eat". Dr. Karel Hujer, a famous astronomer from Czechoslovakia, saw him at Wardha. He said: "We can reach the moon in an express train in 175 days and the sun that way only in the same number of years."

All great humanitarians, ideologues, cranks and visionaries of the world had a great fascination for Gandhi.

On May 31, 1935, an earthquake shook Quetta and the surrounding districts, involving thousands of deaths and enormous destruction. Gandhi was at Borsad and returned to Wardha on June 3, visiting Baroda and Surat. Government had refused permission to the Congress President to send a relief corps to Quetta. Rajendra Prasad discussed this with Gandhi at Wardha on June 13. Gandhi asked the Government for permission to visit Quetta, but was refused. Referring to the earthquake Gandhi said in an editorial in *Harijan* of June 8: "Let us pray. The appalling disaster in Quetta paralyses one. It baffles all attempt at reconstruction. . . . The dead cannot be recalled to life. Prayer is a call to humanity. It is a call to self-purification." And he reiterated his views: "There is a divine purpose behind every physical calamity." Again in the next issue of *Harijan* he repeated: "Prayer is a sign of repentance, a desire to become better, purer. A man of prayer regards what are known as physical calamities as divine chastisement. It is a chastisement alike for individuals and for nations." Although in his usual way he referred to the sins of Quetta, he did not enumerate them.

Gandhi then impressed upon his devotees, admirers and followers the significance of "Duty of Bread Labour". According to his theory, "if all laboured for their bread and no more, then there would be enough food and enough leisure for all. Then there would be no cry of over-population, no disease, and no such misery as we see around. There will be no rich and no poor, none high and none low, no touchable and no untouchable".

A prominent Congress leader from Andhra wrote to Gandhi describing the Hindu-Muslim tension created by the aggressive attitude of the Muslims. Gandhi replied that if the people feared their Muslim brethren, they had every right to defend themselves by physical resistance. "Not to do so," he observed, "will be cowardice which can in no way be described as nonviolence. Cowardice is a species of violence worse than open and armed violence." An English friend described these views as a dangerous doctrine and asked him to explain them. There would be no occasion to defend oneself when there would be police aid at hand and resistance in self-defence was allowed in law. "The police," Gandhi replied, "much than they prevent, much less detect crime. Self-defence, then, is the only honourable course where there is unreadiness for self-immolation."

Yet Gandhi reiterated his view that "non-violence is the

greatest force at the disposal of mankind. It is mightier than the mightiest weapon of destruction devised by the igenuity of man. The doctrine of non-violence is not for the weak and the cowardly; it is meant for the brave and the strong. The bravest man allows himself to be killed without killing."

While Gandhi was giving lessons in scavenging and shoe making he met with a difficulty in finding a remedy for a snakebite. He wrote to Col. Sokhey of the Haffkine Institute asking him questions on this point. Col. Sokhey sent him some literature which whetted his curiosity and Jamnalal brought Sant Pachalegaonkar, a well-known Hindu Sanghatanist sadhu, who kept a number of snakes and gave demonstrations to Gandhi of his power over them. In his hands a snake appeared to be innocuous. And to the consternation of the members of the Congress Working Committee who had gathered at Wardha, Pachalegaonkar put the coil of a snake around Gandhi's neck. All held their breath with painful bewilderment to see Gandhi with a snake garland round his neck. The sadhu said he would take off the poison if somebody volunteered to be bitten by the snake. Gandhi readily offered himself, but at the unanimous protest of the colleagues he desisted. Someone present offered himself as a volunteer but the snake refused to bite him.

A year later Gandhi opined that it was not proper to kill snakes at sight as one could not tell a poisonous from a non-poisonous one, and the bulk of them were non-poisonous. "The snakes," he said, "have their place in the agricultural economy. They perform a particularly useful function, in that they clear the fields of rats, vermin and other pests." The mongoose eats the snakes and the snakes eat rats, vermin and other pests. This is natural non-violence!

A. A. Paul of the Federation of International Fellowship asked Gandhi in September 1935 to define his position on conversion. Gandhi replied: "The great and rich Christian missions will render true service to India, if they can persuade themselves to confine their activities to humanitarian service without the ulterior motive of converting India or at least her unsophisticated villagers to Christianity."

THE ENTHUSIASM AND devotion with which the work of removing untouchability was undertaken had almost died out. Some critics said it was a patchwork, others that it was an advertisement. The charge against it was that the movement simply aimed at removal of touch-pollution, but it did not aim at raising the Untouchables in social status.

And just at this moment Dr. Ambedkar, saviour of the suppressed people ip India, made his famous and historic declaration on October 13, 1935, at a conference in Yeola in Nasik District. He said that the Untouchables would abjure the Hindu religion and embrace some other faith which would give them an equal status in society, a secure position and rightful treatment. For the previous ten years Ambedkar had tried in vain to create an opening for his people into Hindu society. He had to fight for securing his people the right of drinking water from public places, for liberty of wearing good clothes and of using metal utensils and for the right of receiving education. The temple entry struggle at Nasik had been going on since March 1930. Ambedkar recounted in a passionate speech the plight of the depressed classes in all spheres, economic, social, educational and political, and pointed out that the immense sacrifices made by them to secure bare human rights as members of the same community under the aegis of Hinduism had proved utterly fruitless. "I solemnly assure you," he declared, "that I will not die a Hindu."

The conference delegates resolved to devote themselves to securing an honourable status and an independent position on the basis of equality with all other classes in Hindustan.

Ambedkar's declaration was given global publicity. It proved to be a veritable bombshell. It rocked all circles, political parties and social institutions to the foundation. The decision was the last dreadful scream of a smothered, suppressed and dehumanized people who were now inspired by Ambedkar to struggle for their human rights. It gave vent to their untold sufferings, crushing humiliations and the dehumanizing conditions imposed on them for ages. Leaders of Islam, Christianity and Buddhism cast greedy eyes at Ambedkar. Their offers flowered with promises. The Nizam's pockets jingled with crores of rupees.

Gandhi also commented on the declaration of Ambedkar. He called Ambedkar's decision an unfortunate event especially when untouchability was on its last legs. He said he could understand the anger of a high-souled and highly educated person like Dr. Ambedkar over atrocities such as were committed in Kavitha and other villages, and added: "But religion is not like a house or a cloak, which can be changed at will. It is a more integrated part of one's own self than of one's body." "I am convinced," concluded Gandhi, "that the change of faith by him and those who passed the resolution will not serve the cause which they have at their heart; for the millions of unsophisticated, illiterate Harijans will not listen to him and them when they have disowned their ancestral faith; especially when it is remembered that their lives, for good or for evil, are intertwined with those of caste Hindus."[2] "Let not Dr. Ambedkar's just wrath," Gandhi said next week, "deject the reformer, let it spur him to greater effort."[3]

Some other important Hindu leaders like Dr. Rajendra Prasad and Savarkar also issued statements warning Ambedkar against his decision. On their conversion, Savarkar observed, there was no possibility of their receiving equal treatment under Christianity or Islam in India. "Ambedkar, therefore," he concluded, "should follow a religion which is based on principles that are not averse to logic and reason."

A visitor asked Gandhi why he was making a kind of fetish of work, placing so much emphasis on the gospel of work, and inquired what he would say about the Buddha and the great saints like Tukaram and Dnyaneshwar. Gandhi replied: "If I had the good fortune to be face to face with one like him, I should not hesitate to ask him why he did not teach the gospel of work in preference to one of contemplation. I should do the same thing if I were to meet these saints."

Dr. Ambedkar's powerful attack on the caste system sent the term resounding throughout the world and his threat of abjuring the Hindu religion gave a tremendous impetus to the discussions on the abolition of caste. Just at this time Sir Govindrao Madgaokar's open letter to Gandhi and other Hindu leaders on the abolition of caste, was published. In reply Gandhi wrote an article entitled, "Caste has to go" in *Harijan* of November 16, 1935. It took him nearly thirty years to say this, but there too he defended the part of the caste system which restricts the individual freedom for development according to one's mental and physical quality. Gandhi, observed: "The present caste system is the very antithesis of Varnashram. The sooner public opinion abolishes it the better. In Varnashram there was and should be no prohibition of inter-marriage or inter-dining." But he cautiously added, "Prohibition there is of change of one's hereditary occupation for purposes of gain. . . . If the law of Varnashram was observed there would naturally be a tendency, so far as marriage is concerned, for people to restrict the marital relations to their own Varna."

Thus, according to Gandhi, a Mahar and a Bhangi should do these hereditary jobs and the other lower castes their own. Only touch-pollution was to be abolished and a fifth caste was to be created! This was no new deal giving the individual equal opportunity and liberty for development, but preservation of the inherent spiritual and social superiority and the privileges of the upper classes! For hereditary occupation is another name for the gospel of caste by birth! This was the very negation of democracy! It was old wine in new bottles! No change in the *status quo*.

These views of Gandhi terribly disappointed Ambedkar and he sadly observed that his hope that Gandhi would attain dictatorship in social affairs was dashed to pieces. But Gandhi had attained that position in politics and was reading Hitler's *Main Kampf* and at the time *Lenin* by Maxton! Yet this hotch-potch attitude of Gandhi to the caste system angered his colleagues of the Harijan Sevak Sangh. Some of them raised the question whether Gandhi was justified in airing his own views in *Harijan* which was issued under the aegis of the Harijan Sevak Sangh. This was a reflection on the set-up of the Sangh. Upon this Gandhi in an apologetic tone said in *Harijan*: "Its members as individuals will no doubt take their due share in moulding those forces according to their predilection."

While these sad events were taking place and were being discussed, Rajaji, writing on the Golden Jubilee of the Congress, used his Chanakya's genius to boast, in an editorial entitled, "The Revolution is Over" which he published in *Harijan*, that the Gandhian era had achieved what the previous eras could not do. "Untouchability," Rajaji whispered, "is not yet gone. But the revolution is really over and what remains is but the removal of the debris." These were hallelujahs sung to the Gandhian era and were far away from realities, if not hallucinations.

Somebody reminded Gandhi that no progress was possible without economic and political reconstruction, and the talk of polished and unpolished rice, balanced diet and so on and so forth, was mere moonshine. Gandhi was provoked to retort that he who was not ready for small reforms would never be ready for great reforms. It was his conviction, he added, that the activities that absorbed his energies and attention were calculated to achieve freedom for the nation.

FROM JUNE 3, 1935, to January 7, 1936, Gandhi was at Wardha. He had over-worked himself as his daily routine began at two in the morning and ended at eight or nine at night, giving interviews, holding conversations during morning and evening walks, carrying on a voluminous correspondence and writing articles. He became indisposed early in December 1935 and in the first week of January 1936 he fell ill. Yet on January 7, 1936, he met Muriel Lester, Dr. Tomiko Kora of the Women's University in Japan and Mrs. Tyace from China. On January 8 Gandhi left for Bombay.

During his illness the interview he gave to Japan's eminent poet, Yone Naguchi, was interesting. The poet saw Gandhi in his bed lying with a wet-earth bandage on his head. Maybe to appease his curiosity, Gandhi explained it in a poetic vein: "I sprang from Indian earth and so it is Indian earth that crowns me!" The poet said India was a most hospitable country. Gandhi told the poet that his message was included in the message Tagore had given to the world. Gandhi's illness continued and the Japanese poet also became indisposed and there was no second meeting.

In Bombay, Gandhi got some of his teeth extracted on January 19, 1936. The stay in Bombay was restful and so quiet that even Sarojini Naidu was not denied the pleasure of making him laugh his toothless laugh. Gandhi sent his condolences through the Viceroy on the death of the King-Emperor, George V, who passed away on January 20. The German Ambassador in London objected to naming a character in a drama Hezikiyah Hitler and it was therefore given another strange name George Bernard Gandhi.[4]

At this time Gandhi gave his opinion on the use of contraceptives when, at Wardha, Margaret Sanger fully discussed the question with him in the first week of December 1935. Thereupon she wrote an article in *The Illustrated Weekly of India*, saying that Gandhi did not know the aspirations and experiences of Indian women. Gandhi had tried to impress upon her his own philosophy of life that sought self-realization through self-control and said he could not recommend the remedy of birth control to women who sought his approval. He advised women to resist their husbands, but the problem was that many did not want to resist them. It was lust and not love when a couple satisfied its animal passion. In his opinion, sexual union should take place only three or four times in an entire lifetime and so he told Sanger that people should be taught that "it is immoral to have more than three or four children." What the superman, Mahatma, could not practise, he expected the common man to do! But when they discussed the method of the avoidance of sexual union during unsafe periods, Gandhi said: "It does not repel me as the other does."

Mahadev Desai wrote an editorial in *Harijan* of January 25,

1936, attacking Sanger and attributing commercial motives to her. This drew forth a hard-hitting remark by Mrs. Sanger. She said that the birth control workers were selfless workers for a cause they considered a fundamental human right and a cause for human liberty and progress. She also exposed the wrong statement Desai had inserted in his article "that Gandhi had agreed to the method of safe period".

On February 29, 1936, Gandhi addressed a conference of the Gandhi Seva Sangh at Savli near Chanda District. His philosophy, he observed, his followers should not call it Gandhism.[5] There was no *ism* about it. And no elaborate literature or propaganda was needed for it. His life, he concluded, alone could demonstrate it.

In March 1936 Dr. Thurman, one of the alumni of the Negro Universities in America, called on Gandhi and discussed with him all kinds of questions about the Negroes. He told Gandhi that the Negroes were ready to receive Gandhi's message. He said to Dr. Thurman, the leader of the Negro delegation: "Well, if it comes true, it may be through the Negroes that the unadulterated message of non-violence will be delivered to the world."[6] Later Martin Luther King Jr. fulfilled his prophesy! Martin King said, "From my background, I gained my regulating Christian ideals. From Gandhi, I learned my operational technique."[7]

Ambedkar's threat had had wide repercussions all over India. Reacting to it, Gandhi observed in *Harijan* of March 21, 1936: "Ever since Dr. Ambedkar has thrown his bombshell in the midst of Hindu society in the shape of his threatened conversion, frantic efforts had been made to wean him from the proposed step. Dr. Ambedkar's threat has had its repercussions in Harijans too." "They have begun," he continued, "to approach Hindu institutions or reformers with a demand for posts, scholarships, or the like, accompanying it with the statement that the writer might, in the event of refusal, be obliged to change to another faith. Religion," Gandhi added, "is not a matter of barter."

On the early morning of April 30, 1936, Gandhi walked to Segaon; three miles he covered on foot and one mile in a bullock-cart. He had left the Sabarmati Ashram in 1930 and after his release in May 1933 and several tours he had lived at Wardha for about a year and a half and now made Segaon his home, a Marathi-speaking village near Wardha which afforded him many facilities for work. A few days earlier he had told a gathering that "quite a number of the Ashram inmates, old and young, had given up or had failed to live up to the vows of the Ashram".[8] The population of Segaon was 600 and 75 per cent of them were Harijans, and about ten of these could read. One of his companions asked Gandhi why he was burying himself in a village. He replied, "I have been talking theory all these days, talking and giving advice on village-work without having personally come to grips with the difficulties of village work." So he chose Segaon as his headquarters. Soon a hut of Sindhi leaves and mud was constructed for him and he went to live in it on June 16, 1936. This was the cottage which statesmen, journalists, editors and leaders from many countries of the world visited and discussed politics, religion and education with him.

The Gandhi camp had been greatly disturbed at the threat of Ambedkar. Walchand Hirachand took Ambedkar to Segaon to meet Gandhi on May 1, 1936. But they differed. Gandhi wrongly thought that there were many influences in India and London acting behind Ambedkar and the problem had been allowed to assume unduly large proportions because of his threats.

Dr. Ambedkar announced that, at the instance of Dr. Moonje, Dr. Jayakar, Vijayaraghavachari and other Hindu leaders, he was considering the possibility of embracing Sikhism. Of course, these Hindu leaders chose it as a lesser evil. Gandhi and Rajagopalachari were opposed to this proposal and so they asked M. C. Rajah to publish Dr. Moonje's confidential letter and Dr. Ambedkar's statement attached to it. Gandhi and Rajagopalachari were using the disgruntled and dissatisfied mind of Rajah as a tool to arouse Muslims, Christians and the Government against Ambedkar. Rajah did so without the permission of Dr. Moonje. In the editorial in *Harijan* of August 22, 1936, Gandhi said that Rajah had rendered public service by publishing the correspondence and there was no breach of confidence in the publication as the Moonje-Ambedkar proposal was undoubtedly dangerous. Gandhi condemned Ambedkar's proposal as "fratricide".

Dr. Ambedkar stated that if the Untouchables became Sikhs they would remain within the Hindu culture and if they embraced Islam or Christianity they would be denationalized. If they went over to Islam, the danger of Muslim domination would be real; and if they became Christians it would help to strengthen the hold of Britain over India.

Rajagopalachari, who later sponsored schemes for the

vivisection of India, dubbed Ambedkar's proposal diabolical. Gandhi, who had tried to strike a deal with Ambedkar at Yeravda, now described Ambedkar's proposal as a question of barter. Replying to Rajagopalachari and to Gandhi as mentioned earlier, Ambedkar said: "I have gone to the length of considering it as alternative, it is because I felt a certain amount of responsibility for the fate of Hindus."

Meanwhile Dr. Ambedkar published his address under the title *Annihilation of Caste* which he was to have delivered at the Jat-Pat-Todak Mandal in April 1936. In it he said that caste was the bane of Hindu society and unless it became a casteless society it would not be able to defend itself. In his opinion the real enemy was the *shastras* which taught them the religion of caste. He asked them to destroy the belief in the sanctity and divinity of the *shastras* and the Vedas, and to kill Brahminism to save Hinduism. According to him, the real remedy was inter-marriage. His thesis was provocative and explosive, a verdict on Hinduism. Although the leaders of the Jat-Pat-Todak Mandal agreed to his verdict, they asked Ambedkar to change some of his references to the Vedas and Hindu scriptures, but he said he would not change a comma. The leaders of the Mandal, therefore, did not accept him as their President.

Several Hindu leaders attacked Ambedkar's thesis. Gandhi in his own way came forward to criticize it. In his article in *Harijan* of July 11, 1936, he described Ambedkar "as a man who has carved out for himself a unique position in society and is a challenge to Hinduism". But in his unique style of condemning his rivals with faint praise he added: "Dr. Ambedkar is not the man to allow himself to be forgetten. No Hindu," he observed, "who prizes his faith above life itself can afford to underrate the importance of this, indictment." In the second article in *Harijan* of July 18, Gandhi said that learned men were not the best interpreters. Saints and seers were the best interpreters and religion lived in their experiences, in their lives and sayings. He further observed: "Caste has nothing to do with religion. Varna and Ashram are institutions which have nothing to do with castes." Thereupon the secretary of the Jat-Pat-Todak Mandal informed Gandhi that Ambedkar's diagnosis was the same as theirs and Gandhi was doing a great disservice to social reform by advocating his imaginary utility of division of varnas, because for all practical purposes in Hindu society caste and varna were one and the same thing.

Ambedkar issued a harsh rejoinder to Gandhi and said surely

persons like the Mahatma who lived in glass houses should not accuse him of a desire for publicity and caste stones at him. The texts cited by him were all from Tilak's writings. None of the saints attacked the caste system, however elevating their teachings might have been. Their noble sermons had no effect on the life and conduct of the masses as against the teachings of the *shastras*. As regards the Mahatma's interpretation of varna and caste, Ambedkar observed: "The essence of the Vedic conception is the pursuit of a calling which is appropriate to one's natural aptitude. The essence of the Mahatma's conception of varna is the pursuit of ancestral calling irrespective of natural aptitude. What is the difference between caste and varna as understood by the Mahatma? I find none." Gandhi, he added, wanted to spiritualize politics but politics was commercialized, "The reason," he concluded, "the Mahatma is always supporting caste and varna is that he is afraid that if he opposed them he will lose his place in politics."[9]

The fate of Gandhi's Harijan uplift movement was no better than its theory or blue-print. M. C. Rajah moved a temple entry bill in 1938, and Rajagopalachari as Premier of Madras compelled 28 out of 30 Harijan members of the Madras Assembly to vote against it. When Rajah appealed to Gandhi, he replied that Rajah's community had no better friends than Rajagopalachari. The bill had been introduced with the consent and support of the Congress Party. Commenting on this shameful act, the *Indian Social Reformer* of August 27, 1938, said that Rajagopalachari, who wanted to get Subbaroyan's bill passed six years earlier, then candidly avowed that he had done so with a view to giving as much trouble as possible to the Government of the day. But he now opposed the same bill. And thus the cat was out of the bag. And when Dr. Khare, Prime Minister of the Central Provinces, later included a Harijan in the Cabinet, Gandhi expressed disapproval of thus "raising absurd ambitions in the minds of Harijans"! No wonder then that after twenty years of the Gandhian Harijan movement, S. Ramanathan, a Congress Minister of Madras, said in 1943: "Gandhism has given rise to a worse evil than the Hindu-Muslim conflict. It has justified the caste system and has given it a fresh lease of life. . . . Untouchability is but a feature of the caste system, and caste draws its nourishment from the pernicious doctrine of Varnashram which is a vital part of Gandhism."[10]

CHAPTER XXXIX

Gandhism Eclipsed by Socialism

GANDHI HAD DECIDED to put Jawaharlal Nehru in the saddle of the Congress presidentship and asked his consent. Sardar Patel wanted Rajaji to accept the presidentship, but he was mentally and physically too tired to wear the crown. On the one hand, Gandhi wanted to wean Nehru from the Socialists and on the other, beguile them into believing that they had won a victory over the right wing in the Congress. Gandhi knew well the psychology of Nehru who had given strength to Gandhi and infused a new spirit in the Socialists. Moreover Nehru being a man of discipline, as President he would be able to restrain the young Socialists and keep unity in the Congress. Nehru would control the Socialists and Gandhi would control Nehru, and the effect would be that Gandhi's leadership would get the strength and enthusiasm of youth.

Nehru had lost his wife in Europe on February 28, 1936, and he returned to India with her ashes on March 10 when Gandhi was in Delhi. Nehru met him at the Harijan Colony in Delhi. On March 25 Tagore, who had come to Delhi to collect money, discussed his financial difficulties with Gandhi. As a result, Gandhi arranged through the Birla brothers a donation of Rs. 40,000 to the poet. Tagore had met Gandhi in October 1935 at Wardha and discussed the financial problem of Santiniketan. The poet differed from Gandhi but sought monetary help from some of the multi-millionaires who were Gandhi's supporters. Consequently, early in February 1937 Gandhi was nominated trustee of Santiniketan.

On March 28, 1936, Gandhi opened a Swadeshi Exhibition and a Khadi and Village Industries Exhibition at Motinagar in

Lucknow. The Congress held its session from April 12 to 15 at Lucknow where Nehru, as President of the Congress session, declared that the only key to the solution of the world's problems and India's too lay in socialism. Nehru said that he used the word socialism not in a vague humanitarian way, but in the scientific, economic sense. He looked upon it, he observed, as a philosophy of life. This was an eye-opener to all muddled humanitarians headed by the Mahatma who styled themselves socialists. Gandhi attended the session after having bought a ticket for admission to the Congress. He spoke at the Congress on swadeshi and left socialism to Nehru. The resolutions passed, carried the views of the majority and in the words of Nehru, nothing that could be called socialistic appeared in any of the resolutions at Lucknow.

Gandhi left Lucknow on April 16 for Wardha, stayed there for a week, went to Nagpur and presided over the Bharatiya Sahitya Sammelan (All-India Literary Conference) on April 24 and 25. He also addressed the annual conference of the Hindi Sahitya Sammelan. As President, he appealed to the literary men not to remain in their own linguistic and cultural wells but acquaint themselves with the language and literatures of the neighbouring provinces, extend their influence to them and spread knowledge of modern, useful literature among the villages.

As President of the Hindi Sahitya Sammelan, Rajendra Prasad in his characteristic persuasive language, applied 'a non-violent axe' at the root of the Hindi-Hindustani controversy. It was the opinion of Rajendra Prasad that the word Hindi had been coined by Muslim men of letters of old.

Gandhi's Muslim friends opposed the use of the word Hindi. They said it had specific religious and cultural associations and contained Sanskrit words which were unintelligible to the Muslims. They wanted to name it Hindustani. Gandhi did not approve of their views but said that he was a new-comer in the field and he could not ask the All-India Institution to change the word Hindi as he believed that Hindi, Hindustani and Urdu were different names for the same language. At the instance of Gandhi the Bharatiya Sahitya Parishad adopted a compromise formula, "Hindi-Hindustani". Moulvi Abdul Kadar Sahib suggested the use of either Hindustani or Hindi-Urdu instead of Hindi-Hindustani. Gandhi wanted to have the Devanagiri script as the common script for all the languages spoken in the different provinces, especially those which have a large Sanskrit vocabulary.

The Congress Hindu leaders said that Hindi was the national language and though in the names of many institutions the word Hindi was used, they sometimes used Hindustani too. This, was all hodge-podge patois. Despite this, it must be admitted that it was Gandhi who played a major part in the spread of Hindi. In those days about 200 high schools in southern India were teaching Hindi and there were nearly 8 lakhs of learners of Hindi in the Madras Presidency.

The significance of these two Hindi conferences was that Rajendra Prasad spoke against the purification of Hindi, and Gandhi took a stand against trends of communalism in the Bharatiya languages. Gandhi also declared that he would ban all obscene literature. Upon this a Marathi monthly said that if Gandhi assumed power, India would be deprived of the best of Sanskrit literature, for he would find many obscene passages in them. At the Hindi Sahitya Sammelan some delegates moved that the passages from Bhushan's *Shivabavani* should not be expunged. Because these passages were supposed to hurt the feelings of the Muslims, some had asked to have them expunged. Gandhi and his followers supported the Muslim demand and the resolution was defeated.

Then, on May 8, 1936, Gandhi left for Madras, visiting Bangalore and Nandidoorg where he rested till the end of May 1936. From Bangalore on June 2, he issued a statement concerning his son, Harilal, who had embraced Islam a fortnight earlier. Harilal had announced his acceptance of Islam in the Jumma Masjid, Bombay, amid great acclamation. Gandhi said that if this acceptance was from the heart and free from any worldly considerations, he should have no quarrel with it, but he had the gravest doubts about his son's acceptance of Islam. Harilal was nearly fifty and was an alcoholic and addicted to visiting houses of ill-fame. As regards his conversion, it was said that he went over to the highest bidder. Harilal, who took the name Abdulla, was fined in Madras in September for being drunk in a public place. On September 27 Kasturba wrote him a heart-rending letter, but the unrepentant son replied that he would give up drinking if his parents adopted Islam and added that he was not Harilal but Abdulla. This son of Gandhi preached Islam for a time, but he came to his senses eventually and re-adopted Hinduism in the second week of November 1936.

In June Gandhi addressed at Kengeri a conference of Harijan workers and presided over a convocation of the Karnatak Hindi Prachar Sabha which gave a stimulus to Hindi in southern

India. On June 13 he returned to Wardha and walked in drenching rain and chilly weather to Segaon. As forewarned by his friends he caught Malaria. He could not physically stand up to the squalor, the dirt, the dust and the hard life. He had refused to anticipate breakdowns in his health. He was admitted to hospital in Wardha on September 3 and was there till September 11, 1936.

A confirmed believer in nature-cure methods who recommended naturopathy to others, Gandhi said it went against his grain to seek admission to hospital. He wrote afterwards that C. R. Das, Motilal Nehru and Tagore had faith in homeopathy "but in the end everyone seems to end up with allopathy". That also happened many a time with Gandhi, the naturopath!

MEANWHILE THE DIFFERENCES between Jawaharlal Nehru and the Gandhian group of Rightists were coming to a head. Nehru said in Bombay that though khadi was "an important item in our present programme" he did not think that it could finally solve the problem of poverty. He believed, he added, that even with the growth of industrialization there would be considerable room for the development of cottage industries in India. He thought khadi to be a vital necessity till the country had attained freedom. The Gandhians heaved a sigh of relief.

All the seven Right wing Gandhian leaders, Sardar Patel, Rajendra Prasad, Jamnadas Doulatram, Bajaj, Kripalani and Shankarrao Deo sent in their resignations and put Nehru in a quandary. Their charge against Nehru was that he preached socialism which was not adopted by the Congress while he treated them as a drag whose time was over. They said this at the instance of Gandhi.

The Right wing in the Working Committee of the Congress was chafing under Nehru's rebukes and majesterial manner, as Gandhi pointed out to Nehru. They called his activities harmful but that was not to say that he was harmful. Gandhi asked Nehru to wear the crown of thorns though the head be bruised.[1] He should not be a careworn, irritable man ready to burst on the slightest occasion. Nehru often thought of resigning from the presidentship of the Congress, but the Right wing withdrew their resignations. Nehru also changed his mind, as a break would injure the chances of success at the forthcoming elections and would have serious consequences for all the Congress work.

It was at this juncture that Jayaprakash Narayan met Gandhi at Segaon. Discussions with him must have increased his blood pressure; for Jayaprakash Narayan held Gandhism to be a mixture of timid economic analysis, good intentions and ineffective moralizing. He thought that Gandhi was being used as a cloak for reaction and conservatism.

The friction did not stop there. Gandhi himself was involved in it. He was reported to have said, "My life work is ruined by Jawaharlal's programme." He knew for a fact that Nehru did not in Lucknow come out for the use of violence in the struggle for freedom. "My philosophy," Gandhi said, "if I can be said to have any, excludes the possibility of harm to one's cause by outside agencies." "I hope," he declared, "the world will find that we had lost sight of each other only for the moment, and only to meet again with greater mutual attraction and affection." There were differences of opinions, Gandhi observed, but they did not affect their personal relations in any way whatsoever. He could not think of himself "as a rival to Jawaharlal or him to me".[2] "There were differences of method," he concluded, "but to say they make us opponents or rivals is a caricature."[3]

There were ideological differences between Gandhi and Nehru, but Gandhi did not press them. Nehru believed in industrialism and socialism and he accepted non-violence only as a policy, not as a creed. Gandhi glorified poverty and suffering whereas Nehru disliked praise of them. The Mahatma prescribed the ascetic life and mortification of the flesh as a social ideal whereas Nehru appreciated simplicity, equality and self-control. One detested present-day civilization whereas to the other it was, though full of evils, also full of good.

Gandhi always thought in terms of religion and God, of personal salvation and of sin, whereas Nehru thought in terms of secularism, democracy and socialism. According to Nehru, Gandhi was not out to change society or the social structure. Yet Jawaharlal Nehru's pressing the differences to a division would have meant disruption of the unity. This in turn would mean dislodging Gandhi's leadership.

Nehru was no organizer and he feared that he would not be able to control such a vast party in opposition to Gandhi. He was not prepared to lose the support of Gandhi who had contributed tremendously to the cultivation and glorification of Nehru's personality in the national struggle. Although Nehru was the Indian Socialists' godfather, he never openly assumed their active leadership. The ideological struggle between Gandhi and Nehru went on for a number of years. Nehru fulminated on occasion and Gandhi restrained him on every occasion, but they clung to each other till Gandhi appointed Nehru his political heir.

About this time, Gandhi told a Chinese, Y. S. Chen of the Cotton Industry Commission of China, that he had retired from the Congress for two years. He was a kind of back number and his mind and body were buried in Segaon. "What the future has in store for me," Gandhi said, "God alone knows."[4] The fact was that though he had resigned from the Congress, the Gandhi wing had a majority in the Working Committee and he controlled the party through it.

In the first week of October Vallabhbhai Patel, Jawaharlal Nehru and Rajendra Prasad met Gandhi at Sevagram. For over four years Patel had been suffering from nose-trouble and he had just undergone an operation on his nose. Gandhi himself was in better health, and at the time of the visit of the leaders was very busy attending to some of his patients. "If you have no time," said Sardar Patel, "we better go." "But," Nehru intervened, "is it not like King Canute trying to stop the waves or like someone trying to mop the tide?" Gandhi quickly retorted, "That is why we have made you the King Canute so that you may do it better than any others."[5]

Gandhi celebrated his sixty-seventh birthday. He said he did not recognize it as his birthday, but the birth of the spinning wheel! It was at this time that Gandhi declared in *Harijan* of October 3, 1936, that the Gita was neither a treatise on nonviolence nor was it written to condemn war. It had certainly not condemned war as he did. "What," he observed, "however, I have done is to put a new but natural and logical interpretation upon the whole teaching of the Gita."

Gandhi then went to Benares and on October 25 opened the temple of "Mother India", a huge relief map carved on marble, done according to the ideas of Babu Shivaprasad. At another meeting on that day he presented a commemoration volume to Maithilisharan Gupta on his golden jubilee. It was unfortunate that this great literary personality could not be president of the Hindi Sahitya Sammelan. Speaking on the occasion, Gandhi expressed his opinion that honour should be done to a great man or to his writings after his death. He said it was his innermost conviction that a man could not be called a poet or a Mahatma or avatar so long as he was alive. He should therefore have a bone to pick with Maithilisharanji if he were to believe that he was a great poet of India. "A poet," he said, "writes under inspiration and not to the dictation of anyone. He then does not write for applause. His work is its own joy and compensation." While returning, Gandhi dutifully visited the Ansari family and condoled with Mrs. Ansari, the widow of Dr. Ansari, who was his colleague and a great nationalist Muslim.

Gandhi presided over the 12th Gujarati Literary Conference. In his concluding speech as President on November 2, Gandhi asked the literary men who, according to him, had gathered there to spend a couple of days in lotus-eating, whether they had any thought of the half-starved millions, the dumb millions and their aspirations.

As regards the Art Exhibition he said it lacked expressive paintings. "Why should I," he asked, "need an artist to explain a work of art to me? Why should it not speak out to me itself? I am," he concluded, "no speaker, neither is the pen my profession. I have written what I have, because I could not help it."

On the closing day Gandhi told the literary men that the main charge of the women's organization called Jyoti Sangh against them was that the authors of the day gave an entirely false picture of women. He was told, he added, that our literature was full of exaggerated apotheoses of women. Before the writers put their pens to paper, they should think of women as their mothers and then the chastest literature would flow from their pens. English would be empty without the Bible, Arabic without the Koran and Hindi without Tulsidas. These proved that detailed descriptions of women's physical form was not an essential part of literature. The works Gandhi referred to were religious.

On November 12, 1936, the ruler of Travancore issued a proclamation declaring, ordaining and commending that no restrictions should be placed on any Hindu entering and worshipping at temples controlled by the Government. These temples numbered about 1,600. The Indian press rang with tributes to the wisdom and statesmanship of the ruler and his Dewan Sir C. P. Ramaswami Aiyer. The *Hindu* and the *Manchester Guardian* praised the wise act of the ruler and the Dewan. But the *Bombay Chronicle* and the *Hindu Herald* ascribed the proclamation to Ambedkar's grave threat of conversion. One swallow does not make a summer; yet it can be truly said that the proclamation opened a new chapter in the history of Hinduism and Hindustan. No importance was given to Gandhi's role in the declaration by the Travancore ruler and the Travancore Assembly. Undoubtedly, his great Harijan tour deserved some credit for the stimulus it gave to the movement.

Gandhi described it as the proclamation of religious freedom of Harijans and observed that it inspired them with hope and faith in their mission. He added: "I see in it the visible prayer of the invisible God." The Deputy President of the Travancore Assembly declared that their proclamation had nothing to do with the activities of the Harijan Sevak Sangh and asked whether Gandhi had succeeded in having temples opened in Ahmedabad, Wardha or Segaon! Gandhi admitted that his failure was a fact and replied: "Mine is but to do and die."

In Gandhi's opinion it was desirable to impart to young pupils to a certain extent a knowledge about the use and functions of the generative organs. "But," he observed, "this sex education that I stand for must have for its object the conquest and sublimation of the sex passion and should automatically serve to bring home to children the essential distinction between man and brute." A teacher of sexual science, he added, must be one who had attained mastery over his passions and gone through a course in this science.[6]

On November 9, 1936, C. F. Andrews and Dr. Kalidas Nag met Gandhi at Segaon. Andrews discussed with Gandhi the question of religious conversion. He asked him what Gandhi would say to a man who after considerable thought and prayer said that he could not have his peace and salvation except by becoming a Christian. Gandhi spontaneously replied that if such a man was a Hindu, he should be asked to become a good Hindu rather than find goodness in a change of faith. He also said that the Oxford Group might change the lives of as many as they liked but should not change their religion. Proselytization would allow no peace in the world. Dr. Kalidas Nag, who had attended the P.E.N. Congress held at Buenos Aires, Brazil, narrated his experiences to Gandhi and told him that his name was familiar to the people.

In the first week of December 1936, Agatha Harrison and C. F. Andrews met Gandhi at Segaon. Dr. John Mott, the famous crusader, one of the greatest evangelists of the time, met Gandhi and asked him to give his diagnosis of the Harijan problem. Gandhi said he was asking every caste Hindu to drive away untouchability from his heart. He also explained to him. how he could not be a member of the Harijan Sevak Sangh and yet guided and directed its policy. Dr. Mott later described Gandhi as a front-rank prophet.

Gandhi was at the Congress session from December 20 to 29, 1936. Faizpur was a village in East Khandesh. The Congress session was meeting for the first time in a village at the instance of Gandhi who saw the real India in her villages. To fulfil Gandhi's desire to hold the Congress in a village, his staunch admirer and the great industrialist Seth Walchand Hirachand donated at the instance of Sardar Patel, a lakh of rupees in one sum for the Faizpur Congress.[7]

Jawaharlal Nehru was elected President when Sardar Patel withdrew his name and said that his withdrawal should not be taken to mean that he endorsed all the views Jawaharlal stood for.

On December 25 Gandhi opened an exhibition at Faizpur. He was mightily pleased with the decoration and architecture, the arrangements and the discipline of the volunteers. In his speech he praised the work of architect Baburao Mhatre and Nandalal Bose. At the instance of Gandhi the guests and delegates were served food prepared from unpolished rice, hand-ground flour, pure ghee, oil and jaggery!

The Congress President, Jawaharlal Nehru, delivered his speech on December 27, 1936. A vast crowd of about 100,000 people was assembled. Pandit Nehru referred to the rape of Abyssinia, the tragedy of Spain and the triumphant march of fascism in Europe and described British Imperialism as the handmaid of the fascist powers. But declaring the goal of the Congress with studied moderation, he observed, "The Congress today stands for full democracy in India and fights for a democratic state, not for socialism. It is anti-imperialist and strives for great changes in our political and economic structure. I hope the logic of events will lead to socialism; for that seems to me, the only remedy for India's economic ills."[8]

Gandhi did not take any part in the proceedings of the Congress, but his speech made on the exhibition grounds exploded the myth that he was a spent force. He declared that real socialism had been handed down to us by our ancestors who taught: "All land belongs to Gopal which meant God and in modern language it meant state." He also said, "Parliamentary programme is in the air. It has come to stay and rightly."

Gandhi was loudly cheered when he said, "I have not yet revealed my hand. Wait until I do so." He also said, "I am powerful as ever and will prove it when time comes."

Nehru expressed his views in a moderate way as he was influenced by the Gandhian wing. M. N. Roy, who was released on November 20, 1936, after undergoing six years' imprisonment, met Gandhi at Faizpur and had some discussions with him. Gandhi asked him whether he would participate in his prayer and Roy replied that he had no faith in prayer. Roy had told Lenin that Gandhi as a religious and cultural revivalist was bound to be reactionary socially, however revolutionary he might appear politically, whereas Lenin considered Gandhi to be a revolutionary as he was a leader of the anti-imperialist movement. Gandhi and Roy had clashed already in the press.

Harijan, which gave an account of the visit to Gandhi by missionaries like Dr. Crane, Professors like Krzenski, and Negro leaders like Dr. Tobias and Prof. Mays, was silent on Roy's first visit to Gandhi and his discussions with him.

On December 23 the Socialists also held their session at Faizpur under the Presidentship of Jayaprakash Narayan and under the guidance of Acharya Narendra Deo, their guide, philosopher and leader. Gandhism was being eclipsed by socialism.

Shortly after the session, Gandhi told an Egyptian interviewer that "communism of the Russian type, that is communism which is imposed on a people, would be repugnant to India. I believe in non-violent communism." The interviewer then asked him whether he had any difference of opinion with Jawaharlal in respect of socialism. Gandhi replied: "There is, but it is a difference in emphasis. He perhaps puts an emphasis on the result, whereas I put on the means. Perhaps according to him I am putting an over-emphasis on non-violence, whereas he, though he believes in non-violence, would want to have socialism by other means, if it was impossible to have it by nonviolence."[9] In his concept of socialism, "a millionaire may have his millions, but he will hold them for the people".

Yet Gandhi said he was a socialist. Gandhi's idea of socialism had nothing to do with the economic framework of society, and in the words of Nehru it was "a kind of muddled-humanitarianism". That was why C. E. M. Joad said, "Gandhi is one-third saint, one-third lawyer and one-third humbug."[10] Leon Trotsky had no good opinion of Gandhi. He said, "Gandhi is a first class opportunist and an arch enemy of world revolution."[11] Gandhism believes that God is the master of the world whereas socialism considers the man to be the master of the universe. Socialism has adopted a scientific mode of thought whereas Gandhism has adopted a religious mode of thought.

After The Faizpur Congress, Gandhi returned to Segaon and later left for Poona. He was there for four days, holding discussions with Haribhau Phatak and Balukaka Kanitkar, and with some Ahmedabad millowners. Justice Govindrao Madgaonkar held a reception in Gandhi's honour at his residence.

There had been unending discussions on village reconstruction. A villager of Birbhum requested Gandhi to define the ideal village of his conception. Providing an outline of his ideal, Gandhi observed: "An ideal Indian village will be so constructed as to lend itself to perfect sanitation; it will have cottages with sufficient light and ventilation built of a material obtainable within a radius of five miles of it. The cottages will have courtyards enabling householders to plant vegetables for domestic use and to house their cattle. The village lanes and streets will be free from all avoidable dust. It will have wells according to its needs and accessible to all. It will have houses of worship for all, also a common meeting place, a village common for grazing its cattle, a co-operative dairy, primary and secondary schools in which industrial education will be the central fact, and it will have panchayats for settling disputes. It will produce its own grains, vegetables and fruit and its own khadi."[12] But it was the experience of Gandhi that "the greatest tragedy is the hopeless unwillingness of the villagers to better their lot".

Gandhi left Poona on a tour of Travancore on January 10, 1937, in a spirit of pilgrimage. He visited Madras, Trivandrum, Cape Comorin, Vikom, Kottayam, Guntur and many other places, preaching his doctrine of village uplift and asking the people to translate the great proclamation issued by the Travancore Maharaja into action and to abolish untouchability. He hoped the Maharaja of Cochin would follow in the footsteps of the Travancore Maharaja. He sang the praises of the Maharaja of Travancore and enthused the people tremendously.

During his tour of Travancore, Gandhi visited a Harijan boys' hostel at Trivandrum. As the hostel did not get sufficient butter-milk for the boys, a social worker asked Gandhi to send them two good cows from Gujarat. In a humorous strain, Gandhi asked for money. The social worker replied that they had no money. Gandhi asked them to steal one of the golden pots from the great state temple and to tell the state authorities that if they can afford to pour out milk for Brahmins from those golden pots, would they not pour out a little butter-milk for Harijan boys from brass pots now that they had abolished untouchability?"[13]

Indeed, if all the god in Hindu temples all over the country were set free from the shackles of gold and diamonds, the money so obtained would be able to finance a five-year plan of education. It showed how Gandhi closely observed the temples. In a changing society this is bound to happen one day.

The elections to Provincial Assemblies were held in February 1937 under the Government of India Act of 1935. Congress was successful in six out of eleven provinces; in five provinces it had an absolute majority and in four it was the largest single party. This success was largely due to Gandhi's constructive work which automatically carried the Congress patriotic ideas and its flag to remote villages which were in turn electrified by Jawaharlal Nehru's whirlwind tour.

The Congress was jubilant over its brilliant success. Its Working Committee met at Wardha and congratulated the people on their response to the Congress call. Gandhi attended the Working Committee meeting. After the elections were over, Subhas Bose was released on March 17 after a long detention and imprisonment of more than five years by the Government.

On March 15 Gandhi reached Delhi and stayed at the Harijan colony. He attended the Working Committee meeting which resolved on March 18 to accept office in those Provinces where the Congress was in a majority, provided the Governors gave assurance not to use their special powers or to set aside the advice of their ministers in regard to their constitutional activities. This was done at the instance of Gandhi who later admitted that "I had not studied the Act when I advised office acceptance."[14] But such a promise did not come forthwith.

Nehru, Bose and the Left wing leaders were against office acceptance. On March 19 the convention of the Congress members of the Provincial Legislatures met at Delhi, and Nehru administered to them the oath of national independence and allegiance to the people of India.

Meanwhile interim ministries were formed by non-Congressmen in some provinces and one such was formed in the Bombay Province by Dhanjishah Cooper with the support of Jamnadas Mehta belonging to the Democratic Swaraj Party in Maharashtra. They released Veer Savarkar, a great achievement which redounds to their credit! After twenty-seven years Savarkar became a free man to lead his people again.

While the Congressmen were awaiting the Viceroy's assurance of non-interference by the Governors in the working of Ministers, and discussion was going on in England and in India over the legality, advisability and constitutional propriety of demanding such an assurance, Rajagopalachari, who was eager to form a ministry in Madras, had a secret interview with Lord Erskine, the Governor of Madras, and assured him of Congress co-operation. He then saw Gandhi at Tithal on May 29 to secure his consent to the assurance he had given to the Governor of Madras. Gandhi was taking a rest at Tithal, after his tour of Madras and Hubli in April. He had blessed the marriage of his granddaughter, Manu Gandhi, with Surendra Mashruwala at Hubli.

At Hubli Gandhi declared at a meeting of the Gandhi Seva Sangh that the boycott of the legislatures was not an eternal principle like that of truth or non-violence. The question was purely one of strategy. He also opened a village industries exhibition and discussed office acceptance with Shivrao, representative of the *Manchester Guardian*. Gandhi secretly consented to the offer made by Rajagopalachari, his alter ego. Upon this the Governor of Madras conveyed the assurance to Lord Linlithgow, the Viceroy. Lord Linlithgow issued a long statement from Simla on June 20, 1937, which was in accordance with Gandhi's wishes. As a result the Congress Working Committee at its meeting held in Wardha on July 7, agreed to accept office, and the Congress formed ministries in six provinces towards the middle of July. The Assemblies glittered with the 'livery of freedom'!

The Congress members took the oath of allegiance to the British crown and took up the job which they had been condemning as the job of scoundrels. As regards the oath of allegiance, Gandhi had declared that "it is not a religious oath, so far as I understand the constitution, and it is wholly consistent with the demand for immediate and concrete independence"!

Gandhi returned to Segaon from Tithal on June 11 and attended the Working Committee meetings except those on August 4 when he saw the Viceroy Lord Linlithgow at Delhi. Gandhi talked to the Viceroy about the ban on Ghaffar Khan and his own visit to the Frontier. As a result, the ban on Ghaffar Khan was lifted on August 22 and after a fortnight a Congress ministry was formed in the N.-W.F.P. Gandhi also appealed to the political prisoners of the Andamans to give up their fast. He stayed at Segaon until October 25.

A few days earlier Gandhi had paid a glowing tribute to Jawaharlal Nehru for describing khadi as the livery of freedom. He wrote to Nehru that "the expression of his will live as long as we speak the English language in India".

Another notable declaration Gandhi made at this time was

about the export of monkeys to foreign countries. He said if he had the power he would not send a single monkey abroad for vivisection or slaughter.[15] For the protection of fields aud grains he allowed the destruction of monkeys but for scientific research which also aimed at the welfare of humanity he was opposed to it.

But a few days earlier, while speaking of the visibility of non-violence, Gandhi had observed: "But if the Abyssinians had retired from the field and allowed themselves to be slaughtered,[16] their seeming inactivity would have been much more effective though not for the moment visible."

At this juncture Gandhi was involved in a long, bitter public controversy which, raged for over six months in the Bombay Presidency. At the instance of Sardar Patel the Congress members of the Legislative Assembly of the Bombay Province, deprived K. F. Nariman of his opportunity to be the leader of the Assembly Party. Nariman was a selfless, fearless, brilliant, patriotic leader and was looked upon as the natural leader of the Legislative Party. He could have been easily elected had not Patel interfered and Shankarrao Deo, Gangadharrao Deshpande, and Achyutrao Patwardhan aided Patel. Nariman had offended the Gandhian Right wing leaders by his book *Whither Congress*. Sardar Patel preferred a docile Maharashtrian solicitor, B. G. Kher, to a strong leader, Nariman, in that Patel being a Gujarati could lay claim to impartiality and keep the whole show under his control. Gandhi stood by Patel.

For months Gandhi had been assuring Sardar Patel that Nariman would come to harm, he would himself fall into the ditch he was digging for others and that Patel should not read the attacks in the newspapers.[17] And yet Gandhi wrote to Nariman that his silence had been in the interests of Nariman! Gandhi agreed to be the sole arbitrator in the dispute. Nariman helplessly agreed. Gandhi in his foregoing letter said that if on the examination by Bahadurji or Madgaonkar, his findings were against Nariman, he should have an opportunity of tendering an apology and making a full and frank confession of his weakness and the wrong done to the public, the Sardar and other colleagues. But if he found Nariman unjustly dealt with by the Sardar, Gandhi observed, he would try to undo the mischief.

Partial as he was to the Sardar, Gandhi evidently assumed that the Sardar was innocent and Nariman guilty; for he mentioned no punishment to the Sardar if he was found guilty. On September 26 he wrote to Patel that he should try to forget the

Nariman affair. "You have transferred," he replied reassuringly, "your worries to me and I have passed them to Bahadurji."

So the arbitrator fell ill and transferred the burden of arbitration to Bahadurji. Nariman was a Parsi and Bahadurji, who was a Parsi, was purposely entrusted with the work. Gandhi was confident of what his judgment would be. In the second week of October, Bahadurji decided against Nariman on both the counts, his action in the election of 1934 and his action in the present dispute. Gandhi endorsed the decision and sent it to Bahadurji who read it in his office to Nariman in the presence of Mahadev Desai.

All kinds of pressures were brought on Nariman. To increase the tempo of it, a telegram had been sent to Nariman on the previous day conveying the news that Gandhi's health was affected and would not be completely restored till this episode had satisfactorily ended. Overpowered by the anxiety for the Mahatma's health, Nariman lost his grit and balance. He signed an apology which had probably been drafted by Gandhi and signed his political death-warrant. Soon after, Nariman recanted. But it was too late. Gandhi, who had agreed that the enquiry would be private and even the Working Committee need not know about it, sent all the records to the Working Committee; and without giving Nariman a chance to reply, they all got together to guillotine Nariman politically. He was declared unworthy of holding any position of trust and responsibility in the Congress organization.

The rest of his life Nariman spent reading *What Next* and saying, "Had I served my Lord as faithfully as I served the Congress, He would not have deserted me." The Congress bosses judged him wrongly and unjustly. But Nariman, who was a brilliant lawyer, should have known whether Gandhi, well known for his partiality to Patel, would be able to administer justice in a case where Patel's reputation and position were at stake.

WHILE ENGAGED IN the Nariman controversy, Gandhi was sharply criticized in Maharashtra for not signing the "Release Savarkar memorandum" when Chimote, a public worker, met Gandhi early in December 1936 at Segaon. Gandhi knew that Savarkar had been criticizing his non-violent creed, his superstitious beliefs and politics since his internment at Ratnagiri. No wonder that Gandhi angrily told Chimote that he did not know who Savarkar was and asked him whether he was the same Savarkar who had written *The Indian War of Independence of 1857*. Gandhi flatly refused to sign the appeal which had been signed by lakhs of Indians. When Jawaharlal Nehru was approached in the matter, he, too, ignored it. Both Gandhi and Nehru did not say at that time that a new ministry under the new Act would release him.

Gandhi explained his action when N. C. Kelkar criticized Gandhi for not signing the memorandum and added that Gandhi merely hoodwinked Maharashtra by praising Tilak off and on. This angered Shankarrao Deo and he requested Gandhi to state the facts. In his letter of July 20, 1939, to Shankarrao Deo, Gandhi said that he did not sign the appeal because he knew that whoever might be the ministers under the new Act would release Savarkar and added that at least Dr. Savarkar would bear him out when he said that he had done whatever he could for the release of the Savarkar brothers.

That Gandhi had written an article in *Young India* recommending the release of the Savarkar brothers was a fact. But most of the newspapers said that Gandhi's statement that Savarkar would be released by the coming ministry was an after thought. If Gandhi, they said, sought interviews with Governors and Viceroys for pleadings and appeals, why did he refuse to sign an appeal addressed to the Government on behalf of Savarkar? Coming events cast their shadows ahead. Gandhi had now three political opponents, Savarkar, Ambedkar and M. N. Roy. After Savarkar's release, Nehru, Subhas Bose, M. N. Roy and Rajagopalachari had welcomed Savarkar back to freedom, but Gandhi had kept silent on it. Gandhi had clashes with Ambedkar and the Mahatma described M. N. Roy as his Enemy No. 1.[18]

Gandhi was very anxious to guide the Congress ministries, to regulate their activities and policies and to maintain discipline in their ranks. When complaints came from different provinces that certain Congressmen were not selected for the posts of ministers, he replied that ministerships were avenues to service and not prizes for past services. He expected the ministers to show in their conduct a sufficient measure of selflessness, discipline and faith. It was not enough that the ministers should live simply and work hard. They had to see to it that the department they controlled also responded properly. Justice should become cheap and expeditious. The police should be friends of the people instead of creating fear in them. Education should be so revolutionized as to answer the needs of the poorest villagers instead of answering those of the imperial exploiters. All categories of political prisoners should be released. The methods of the Government should be preventive and not punitive.

A conscientious minister, Gandhi opined, has no time for receiving addresses and honours, or for making speeches in return for fulsome heven if deserved, praise. All these instructions were described by the press as Instruments of Instructions. Indeed Gandhi was guide, philosopher and an iron disciplinarian of the new ministries.

Gandhi advised the Congress ministries to adopt the programme of prohibition and bring about the moral, social and material welfare of those who were addicted to intoxicants and narcotics. They should resist the lure of the "tainted revenue" from drinks and drugs. "If prohibition was to be a reality," he observed, "it should be enforced within six months." He asked the ministries to stop gambling in high quarters and also to ban horse-racing. He asked whether horse-racing could not be done without gambling; or was gambling also an aid to the good breeding of horses?

Among the host of critics of Gandhi's prohibition policy was Sir Jogendra Singh, an eminent social reformer and leader. He opined that there was bound to be illicit distillation and secret drinking, and so prohibition by compulsion would fail. The provinces would only lose revenue which they needed for rural reconstruction. But Gandhi's word prevailed and prohibition was partially introduced in the Provinces where Congress ministries had been installed.

Happy at the thought and jubilant over the event Gandhi exclaimed that prohibition had come to stay. He added that the Congress was redeeming its old pledge to the people at the very first opportunity without counting the cost. Gandhi was so hopeful of and insisted on prohibition that he said: "If we can achieve prohibition within the next three years, and if we can demonstrate to the world that we can do without the military in the Provinces, we shall have raised India's name to a height that it has never reached before and which no nation has reached."

GANDHI WANTED TO bring education in India in tune with his constructive programme. As the country was poor and backward in education it could not hope to fulfil its obligations unless education was made self-supporting. "By education," he observed, "I mean an all-round drawing out of the best in child and man—body, mind and spirit." He therefore convened through the secretary of the Silver Jubilee Committee of the Marwadi Shiksha Mandal, an Educational Conference on October 22 and 23, 1937, at Wardha. Gandhi, though delicate in health, was able to stand the strain, and he presided over the conference. Jamnalal Bajaj was the Chairman of the Reception Committee and Aryanayakam looked after the arrangements. There were ninety delegates from all parts of the country among whom were some Congress ministers and notable educationists.

Gandhi welcomed the guests and put up his proposition before the conference. He asked for a free, frank and full discussion on it. He was, he added, near death's door and would not dream of thrusting anything down people's throats. He was of the opinion that the existing system of primary education was not only wasteful but harmful. The core of his emphasis was not on occupation but on education through manual training—all education of letters, history, geography, mathematics, science, etc., should be through manual training.

Gandhi advocated education through a useful handicraft, that is, manual training or vocational training, in which the vocation should serve a double purpose to enable the pupil to pay for his tuition through the products of his labour, and at the same time to develop the whole man or woman in him or her. The state should take over the products of these schools. After the conference, Gandhi admitted that his proposition was novel although novelty was no crime. His plan to impart education through village handicrafts like spinning and carding, he considered to be the spearhead of a silent social revolution fraught with the most farreaching consequences. In his opinion his scheme aimed at equalization of status and a new economic order. While at Tolstoy Farm, he had imparted education to some boys under his charge. It consisted of vocational training in digging, cooking, scavenging and shoe-making plus separate book learning, and not regular education through handicrafts.

Dr. Zakir Husain, an eminent educationist, supported Gandhi's scheme, not because it was novel but because he claimed, it was sound. He said he did not mean any insult to Gandhi when he said that Gandhiji's scheme was not original. This remark of Zakir Husain displeased many of Gandhi's blind admirers. Dr. Husain cited the work done by Prof. John Dewey (1859-1952), the American philosopher and educator in the field, and the complex method followed in Russia. Prof. K. T Shah was totally against Gandhi's scheme as he thought that primary education could not be self-sufficient.

Dr. Zakir Husain was nominated Chairman of the Committee

which was asked to prepare a report. The committee met in the first week of November at Wardha and again in the third week of November. On December 2, 1937, Dr. Husain submitted the report to Gandhi in the stipulated time. Dr. R. A. Siddiqui of Aligarh helped him to prepare his report. Zakir Husain dressed the bare skeleton of Gandhi's scheme in the proper costume of system and culture.

Gandhi's whole idea was to resuscitate the villages of India and along with many he had realized the necessity for the reorientation of educational policy for this purpose. Gandhi explained in *Harijan* of October 30 that there was no complete precedent for his scheme. *Harijan* of September 4, 1937, however, had eloquently upheld the "Report on Vocational Education in India" by A. Abbot and S. H. Wood, two British experts. Mahadev Desai said that the basic principles laid down by Abbot and Wood were the same as those by which Gandhi was guided. Gandhi had put the emphasis on the production of yarn, on spinning and carding, as the vocational bias of primary education. Boys were to learn Arithmetic by calculating how much yarn would be required for a particular purpose and "if we can interest the boys in the growth and improving the strains of cotton, science and geography will also come in". "After a seven years' course a boy of 14 was to be discharged as an earning unit. The soul of Gandhi's scheme was the spindle! But while executing the scheme nobody laid any emphasis on carpentry, smithy work, tanning or farming. As they all in their zeal to follow the Mahatma took to the spindle, they forgot the spirit of his scheme.

Gandhi wanted to turn the attention of India from West to the East, from matter to spirit, from mill to cottage, from machinery to crafts, from steering wheel to spinning wheel! It was the result and reflection of his ideal of village reconstruction and uplift. The scheme aimed more at fulfilling the needs of the old India than the needs of the new India—the needs of a changing society.

Dr. Zakir Husain called the scheme Basic National Education while Gandhi, in his foreword to the report, purposely described it as Rural National Education. Dr. Zilliacus, Chairman of the New Education Fellowship Delegation, described the Scheme as a heroic measure, Sir Radhakrishnan approved of it and Tagore said that when the scheme was actually worked out they would discover one more testimony to the genius of the practical sage.

The emphasis of Gandhi's scheme was more on village uplift

than on education while the report by Dr. Zakir Husain aimed at educational as well as cultural development. The scheme made the teacher dependent on the earnings of his pupils and sought to create in schools the atmosphere of an industry where children would become wage-earners. The system was craft-centred with little or no accent on an intellectual, liberal, academic education.

The products of children could not compete with finished goods in the market. The state could not take over children's amateurish and useless goods, and heaps of yarn accumulated in the corners of Basic Schools. The indifference, negligence and silence on the part of those associated with the implementation of the scheme was bad enough to discourage these schools, which ultimately proved very expensive.

Some improvements were suggested in the scheme at the Poona Conference in 1939 and at Jamnagar in 1941. Gandhi after his release in 1944 declared that they must educate also the parents, and basic education must become literally education for life. Yet this scheme, which according to some was the last and precious gift of Gandhi to India, because of various reasons, failed completely. Speaking about it, after more than two decades, Dr. Zakir Husain as Vice-President of the Indian Republic, declared at Bangalore on July 5, 1963 that basic education had failed because there were no good teachers.[19] Dr. John Dewey's attempt had met the same fate earlier.

Educationists should not make a fetish of vocational or life-centred education. It should be broad-based. An American educationist rightly observes: "We need people who are at home both in the world of craft and of ideas." "A democracy," he adds, "must avoid a sharp separation of the two. They are the twin aspects of the whole education."[20] The present schemes of education take no cognizance of Gandhi's Wardha Scheme. Villages in India are being modernized and industrialized, and educational ideals are being adjusted to suit the needs of a changing society and to the shape of things to come.

After this Wardha Educational Conference, Gandhi went to Calcutta and was there from October 26 to November 17. During his stay he discussed with Sir John Anderson, the Governor of Bengal, and Minister Nalini Ranjan Sarkar the release of the political prisoners from the Andamans and of the detenus in Bengal. According to a resolution passed by the Bengal Assembly on August 7, about 1,100 detenus were released on Gandhi's promise to the Bengal Government that he would do his best to create a favourable atmosphere and public opinion in favour of non-violence. Therefore the Bengal Government reviewed the situation, and Gandhi accelerated the release of the remaining 450. Gandhi was allowed to interview individual detenus in camps and jails and on Gandhi's assurance they were released. It was a great achievement for Gandhi who was responsible for the solution of a difficult and perplexing problem, and for the release of the detenus whom Government regarded as dangerous to peace.

In the elections of 1937 the Muslim League did not fare well and there was no League Ministry in any of the Muslim majority provinces. In those Provinces there were non-League Ministers. So the Muslim League made propaganda against the Congress Ministers declaring that they had committed atrocities on the Muslims. These charges were baseless or magnified. Naturally, Hindu-Muslim tension grew and the year 1937 was full of communal riots which broke out at Panipat, in U.P., Punjab, and at Shikarpur in Sind. There was a Sikh-Muslim riot at Amritsar. Gandhi was seized with fear, and on October 19 he wrote to Jinnah seeking an interview with him when the Muslim leader's influence was at a low ebb. It was given to Gandhi to seek interviews with Jinnah and give him a fresh lease of political life whenever the latter was distressed and disappointed. Jawaharlal Nehru was against Gandhi's idea of meeting Jinnah, yet he had sought the interview. But Jinnah replied that Gandhi, instead of acting as a bridge between the Congress and the League, had identified himself with the Congress although he was not even a four-anna member of the Congress.

While in Calcutta, Gandhi attended a performance of the Seraikella dancers. About this time Nagpur University wanted to confer an honorary degree of LL.D. on Gandhi, but he humbly replied that he was not worthy of it.

On December 7, 1937, Gandhi was taken to Juhu, Bombay, for a change of air as his blood pressure had risen and there was severe cold at Segaon which was considered harmful to his health at that stage. Dr. Ansari had asked him to continue taking garlic in his food. Gandhi took too much of garlic, and visitors like Jawaharlal Nehru could not stand the smell. Nehru told him that it was difficult for people to sit by him.[21]

This time there was a setback in Gandhi's health caused by the sudden rise and fall in his blood pressure. He had proper massage and baths under the guidance of Dinsha Mehta of Poona Health Torium. Dr. Gilder and Dr. Jivraj Mehta attended on him. Prayers were offered daily by devotees for his speedy recovery. When Rajagopalachari asked Gandhi why he continued to put so much passion in his talk, he replied that he had yet to learn his lesson from the Gita on how to be passionless.

During Gandhi's stay in Bombay, the Aga Khan with his son Ali met him, and the members of the Congress Working Committee discussed some problems with him.

On his return to Segaon on January 8, 1938, Gandhi felt a little better. He condoled with Jawaharlal Nehru over the death of his heroic mother Swaruprani and said she had lived nobly and died nobly. Towards the middle of January Lord Lothian, a British statesman, paid a three-day visit to Gandhi and discussed some problems with him. He made a study of the activities at Segaon and made a contribution of £125 towards its constructive activities.

About this time, in a Patna weekly, Rahul Sankrityayana, a well-known Buddhist scholar, made a fierce attack on Gandhism. He said that Gandhism had rendered a service to the country by taking to the masses the message of the revolution and sacrifice, but it had rendered an equal, if not greater, disservice by confirming, the people's faith in "our ancient follies,"[22] and by making the capitalists as the trustees.

CHAPTER XL

Dr. Khare, Bose and Rajkot

GANDHI, THE PRESIDENT-MAKER of the Congress, had written to Sardar Patel in November 1937 that though Subhas Bose was unsteady no one but he could be the President of the Haripura Congress. He had taken this decision it seems when he stayed at Sarat Bose's as a guest and had sounded him on Subhas's views. The Bengal leader had published his book, *Indian Struggle*, in January 1935 in which he had criticized Gandhi's policy. The most striking thesis in the book was that "there is no middle road between communism and fascism . . . and the next phase in world history will produce a synthesis between communism and fascism.[1] . . . That synthesis is called by the writer *Samyavada* 'the doctrine of synthesis or equality'." Gandhi chose his critic to preside over the Congress in order to soften his attack and to keep the Left wingers under control. Responsibility restrained Nehru and the same strategy might work on Subhas also.

After Gandhi's assurance of the presidentship, Bose went to London on January 8, 1938, where he was officially informed about his election to the presidentship of the Haripura Congress. Bose returned to India after having talks with Ernest Bevin, Attlee and Emon De Valera. He sought Gandhi's advice before he prepared his presidential address.

On the eve of the Haripura Congress, Gandhi explained his Trusteeship theory through Mahadev Desai in *Harijan* of February 5, 1938. According to Gandhi, the tiller had a right to the full fruits of his labour. The zamindar had no right to exploit his labour. He was to behave as a trustee and was entitled to a commission, but if legal ownership was transferred to the state, payment to those from whom the property was taken, just enough to enable them to live decently, was necessary. But Gandhi had given an assurance to the zamindars and taluqdars-that so far as he was concerned their extinction as a class was out of the question. This was the bane of his trusteeship theory. It was a system of clemency and charity and not of justice.

One of Gandhi's early beliefs was that labour and capital need not be antagonistic. He favoured death duties since inherited property should rightly belong to the nation. But in the case of zamindars he was not in favour of abolishing the class, he aimed only at reforming them.[2] No landlord in Gandhi's lifetime ever abdicated voluntarily, nor did a single millionaire become an ideal trustee.

On February 19, 1938, the Congress session was held at Haripura on the banks of the Tapti under the presidentship of Subhas Bose. In his presidential address Bose predicted that British ingenuity would seek some constitutional device for partitioning India, and suggested that satyagraha might have to be resorted to again. He emphasized the necessity of a planning commission, the need for family planning and gradual socialization of the agricultural and industrial system. He voiced a determined opposition to the proposed scheme of Federation in India. He pleaded for the adoption of the Roman script for the nation.

While Gandhi seemed to be compromising with Subhas, he and Sardar Patel were doing their utmost to deprive him of the benefits of Vithalbhai Patel's will, and ultimately they succeeded in that effort.

Although his health was causing anxiety, Gandhi was at Haripura from February 9 to 22. Dr. Sushila Nayyar attended to his health as he suffered from a cold and a cough. As President of the All-India Spinners' Association and the guide of the All-India Village Industries Association he was glad to open the exhibition at the Haripura session. There he declared: "Not cow protection but cow service is our ideal."

The Congress, though not opposed to the idea of Federation, condemned the proposed Federal Scheme as it was not a real Federation of free units enjoying more or less the same measure of freedom, civil liberty and representation by the democratic process of election.

The people from the Princely states, the Congress resolved, should work in right earnest for the establishment of their rights but not in the name of the Congress. Out of his regard for Mirza Ismail, Dewan of Mysore, Gandhi had, in November 1937, disapproved of the A.I.C.C. resolution passed against the Mysore State. So a resolution of non-interference was adopted!

The Congress also condemned the Fascist aggression in Europe. Gandhi also got angry with Sardar Patel for being unduly severe to Socialists.[3]

After the Haripura session, Gandhi returned to Segaon and stayed there till March 12. Unrest was spreading all over India. There was labour unrest and kisan unrest and communal riots had taken place. Gandhi did not like the Congress Governments using police and military force to quell them. At this juncture the Ministries of U.P. and Bihar had resigned over the question of the release of political prisoners. The Governors thought their release a grave menace to peace in their provinces and therefore they had intervened. Gandhi issued a statement defending the rights of the Ministries, and added that it was the responsibility of the Ministry to maintain law and order in the province. The Ministers had the right to exercise their unfettered judgment. The Governors should only advise them on broad policy. The crisis was resolved at the end of February 1938, and the prisoners were released.

Gandhi was in correspondence at this time with Jinnah who, suggested that talks could be held between them if it was agreed that the Muslim League represented the Muslims and the Congress, the Hindus. Gandhi expressed his willingness to meet Jinnah at any time suitable to the latter, but in his letter of March 8, 1938, indicated that he would be representing neither the Hindus nor the Congress.

Gandhi reached Calcutta on March 16, 1938, and except for a week which he spent at Delang for the Gandhi Seva Sangh meeting, he was in Calcutta till April 13. Although he was unwell, he discussed the release of prisoners with the Governor and the Ministers and visited some prisoners in jails. In doing this his mission was the mission of non-violence and not merely that of the release of the prisoners or detenus. Gandhi wanted from those prisoners and detenus an assurance for his mere satisfaction that they had abjured the methods of violence.[4]

During this stay in Calcutta, Dr. Ajit Bose, an allopath turned naturopath, paid Gandhi a fee every day for taking up his time and treating him. When he sought Gandhi's blessings, the Mahatma said, "All mad men like you have my blessings, for I know that great things in the world have been achieved by good men madly fired with ideas. You are one such." Dr. Bidhen Chandra Roy and Dr. Sunil Bose, too, examined him.

At Delang Gandhi addressed the Gandhi Seva Sangh on April 25. He told this gathering of his devotees: "Honesty, they say in English, is the best policy, and policies might and did change but non-violence was an unchangeable creed." Gandhi added that the bravery of those who used physical force was better than emasculation, and meeting one's death fighting would be better than cowardice.

During this week Kasturba, Mahadev Desai's wife, and some other persons went to Puri from Delang and had a glimpse of Jagannath, the Lord of the Universe. This temple was not open to the untouchable Hindus and Gandhi never entered it. On their return on March 28, Gandhi came to know that they had entered the temple and was indignant. His blood pressure shot up. He passed a sleepless night. He remonstrated with Mahadev Desai and Kasturba for their breach of his moral and religious code. Mahadev Desai expressed his sorrow for it at the prayer meeting on March 30 by telling the audience how he was the cause of Gandhi's breakdown.[5] Yet Gandhi was not pacified. It was a rule for him that whosoever believed in the removal of untouchability should shun temples which were not open to Harijans. Gandhi said that Lord Jagannath was not his Lord; he was the Lord of those who exploited his name and kept Harijans out. Mahadev Desai wrote to his master a note in sheer desperation imploring Gandhi to drive him away. He would prefer death, said the master, at the hands of one who loved, to life at the hands of one who did not love him. Mahadev Desai cried:

To live with the saints in heaven
Is a bliss and a glory,
But to live with a saint on earth
Is a different story.

but added that Gandhi disclaimed saintship.

As Gandhi referred to the riots which had taken place, and appealed to the people to remain nonviolent, his critics said that his writings had become hysterical and he was expecting the impossible from human nature. He replied to his critics by suggesting a solution to the problem of the communal riots. Volunteer corps pledged to nonviolence should be raised. Gandhi said that Congress was the only political organization in the world which had, at his instance, adopted unadulterated non-violence for the attainment of Swaraj.[6] Gandhi knew well that the Congress had adopted non-violence as a deliberate policy in its resolutions but neither as a creed nor an article of faith. His attempt during the Bombay session of the Congress in 1934 to change the creed of the Congress had utterly failed.

The Congress had refused to change the terms "legitimate and peaceful" to the terms "truthful and non-violent". Yet Gandhi grumbled in *Harijan* of September 3, 1938, that he had been using these terns as synonimous.

MEANWHILE THE CONGRESS Ministry in Bombay while amending the Local Boards Act, described the Scheduled Castes as 'Harijans'. It thrust this name down the throats of the Scheduled castes though Dr. Ambedkar, their accredited leader, who had captured 13 reserved seats out of 15 in the province, had opposed it tooth and nail and even staged a walk-out on the issue. It was Gandhi's wish, and his devotees did not care for the wishes of the community concerned.

It was, however, a fact that at the second session of the Round Table Conference Dr. Ambedkar had suggested that the depressed classes should be called Protestant Hindus, Non-caste Hindus or Non-conformist Hindus. Gandhi might have picked one from these, but in such matters he behaved dictatorially. Later, Ambedkar renamed them Buddhajan and broke their connection with the god Hari, as Buddhism does not believe in God and the soul.

On April 15, 1938, Gandhi met Viceroy Linlithgow in Delhi who had written to him suggesting he pay him a visit if he passed through Delhi on his way from Calcutta. He had, the Viceroy added, no special business to discuss. Although Gandhi declared in a public statement that the interview was very cordial and dealt with general topics, he wrote to Sardar Patel that the question of confiscated lands in Gujarat had been raised in the discussion.

The problem of the lands confiscated in Gujarat during the civil disobedience movement in 1930 had been, it seems, constant worry to Gandhi since the Gandhi-Irwin Pact. He wrote to Patel that "we have to regain possession of Darbar's village not for his but for our prestige . . ." and asked Patel to write to the Premier of Bombay to get the Governor to recommend that Dhara be returned to Darbar or Gandhi would intervene if it was not handed over as soon as it was asked for. Ultimately Gandhi got the problem of the confiscated lands in Gujarat solved by the Bombay Ministry under the Expropriatory Law of October 14, 1938. He frankly declared that he had some hand in the passing of the bill. The so-called owners of the land were paid money to the extent of their outlay plus interest. The confiscated properties were purchased and returned to the original tenants. The problem of the properties of great patriots like Savarkar was never a problem of prestige to the Gandhi-dominated Congress.

The Hindu-Muslim riots had been causing anxiety to the Congress leaders. Nehru and Gandhi were trying their best to reach a settlement with Jinnah.

Jawaharlal exchanged letters with Jinnah from January to April 16, 1938. Jinnah put forward his demands and Nehru discussed them with him. One of Jinnah's demands was that the Congress should give up the Bande Mataram. The Congress Working Committee, nervous about the Muslim propaganda against Bande Mataram had resolved in October 1937 to mutilate the song by retaining only the first two stanzas of it. Gandhi had written to Nehru that the Bande Mataram controversy had not died out and many Bengalis were sore at heart over the decision of the Working Committee.[7] But Nehru wrote shortly to a Muslim correspondent that Bande Mataram had difficult words and that it was not suitable as a national song.[8] As the Congress leaders began to appease the fanaticism of the Muslims, their demands began to increase.

In his letters to Jinnah, Nehru said that Jinnah's fourteen points were out of date. He also said that the Muslim League was an important communal organization and not the only organization of Indian Muslims. On April 16, 1938, Jinnah wrote to Nehru that the Pandit's tone and language again displayed arrogance and a militant spirit and he could not even clearly understand him. Jinnah, graciously upgraded Nehru's arrogance and generously played down his own!

After this debacle Gandhi came forward to meet Jinnah in a prayerful and religious spirit and had an interview with him in Bombay which lasted three and a half hours. The talks came to nothing, but they added to the prestige of Jinnah whose influence had been declining. Gandhi then left the matter to Subhas Bose who met Jinnah more than once and corresponded with him. In May Subhas Bose met the same fate as Gandhi and Nehru. Later Bose wrote to Nehru that Jinnah was unreasonable and intransigent.

Gandhi was now terribly depressed and said that for the first time in his public and private life he seemed to have lost his self-confidence. It was not, he added, that his senses were paralysed. His intellect served him well. Nor had he lost his faith in non-violence. Although his faith was burning brighter than ever, he had lost his self-confidence.

Yet Gandhi went on a tour of the North-West Frontier and

reached Peshawar on May 1, 1938, where he was welcomed by Khan Abdul Ghaffar Khan and his followers. At some stations the noise was so great that Gandhi had to stuff his ears with cotton. The journey tired him out. He stayed at Dr. Khan Saheb's, where crowds did not disturb his work and rest. The Frontier Hindus, Sikhs and Pathans maintained admirable discipline on this occasion.

A professor of the Islamic College asked Gandhi whether he had ever seen God. Gandhi replied: "It can never be a matter for argument. If you would have me convince others by argument I am floored. But I can tell you this, that I am surer of His exisience than of the fact that you and I are sitting in this room. I can only testify that I may live without air and water but not without Him. You may pluck out my eyes, but that cannot kill me. You may chop my nose, but that will not kill me. But blast my belief in God, and I am dead. You may call this superstition, but I confess it is a superstition that I hug."[9]

To a question about Abyssinia Gandhi replied that if the Abyssinians had adopted the non-violence of the strong, i.e. the non-violence which broke to pieces but never bent, Mussolini would have had no interest in Abyssinia. "Of course," he added, "it is open to anyone to say that human nature has not been known to rise to such a height." The English pacifists, he observed, favoured the use of arms when pacifism failed.

The spiritual cloud over Gandhi's mind lifted gradually. Numerous inquiries were made about his despondency, sympathy was shown for him and prayers were said. At this time an orthodox Congressman at Salem had started a fast unto death and his wife too was on a fast. Gandhi had no sympathy for them. In reply to a telegram he said, "Tell both that the fast has no moral basis. If people fasted against wrongs, fancied or real, and there was any yielding on account of a fast, society would be disrupted."[10] This remark throws much light on the psychology of Gandhi.

ON HIS RETURN from Peshawar to Bombay on May 11, Gandhi rested for eleven days and then stayed at Segaon from May 21 to September 19, 1938. During this period he expressed his opinion on the establishment of peace-brigades to prevent communal disturbances and to promote higher education and Hindu-Muslim unity. He also had a talk with Dr. Hengchih Tao of China who wanted a message for China. But most of this time he was involved in a controversy over the working of the Central Provinces Ministry. A crisis had been brewing since May 1938 in the C.P. Three Congress Ministers, Mishra, Shukla and Mehta submitted their resignations to Dr. N. B. Khare, their leader and Prime Minister, as he had brought charges of nepotism and bribery against them. But the charges were found to be only errors of judgment, and Gandhi said in *Harijan* of June 4 that they were made recklessly and spitefully. There was a compromise and the crisis was averted.

As Dr. Khare found it impossible to pull on with those three Ministers, he went to Gandhi at Segaon on June 29 and sought his advice in the matter as he had done on two previous occasions. But Sardar Patel had met Gandhi on June 21 and briefed him against Dr. Khare. So this time Gandhi reprimanded Dr. Khare for troubling him now and then and added that he was not even a four-anna member of the Congress. Dr. Khare, while taking leave of the Mahatma, said that he would act according to the message of his own inner voice. This was indeed an affront to Gandhi.

Dr. Khare then demanded resignations from his rebel colleagues as he wanted to submit resignations of all the Ministers to the Working Committee. But the three members at the instance of Dr. Rajendra Prasad had stubbornly refused to do so. Dr. Khare, therefore, in a desperate mood, instead of referring the matter to the Parliamentary Sub-Committee, resigned on July 20 with two of his colleagues.

The three Ministers should have observed democratic conventions and resigned. Their adviser, Rajendra Prasad, was a member of the Congress Parliamentary Board but not directly concerned with the supervision of the C.P. Ministry. According to parliamentary conventions, as soon as the Premier resigns the other Ministers automatically cease to be Ministers. Naturally, under article 51 of the 1935 Act the Governor had to dismiss the three rebel Ministers who refused to resign. In doing so the Governor observed parliamentary conventions and used no special right.

On July 21 the Governor invited Dr. Khare, in conformity with parliamentary conventions, to form a new ministry, as Dr. Khare was the accredited leader of the House. He formed a new Ministry which included a Harijan Minister and then informed Sardar Patel and President Subhas Bose about it telegraphically. In doing so he was constitutionally right but from the point of view of discipline he was wrong, and so played into the hands of his opponents.

On July 22 Dr. Khare was called by the Congress bosses to

Wardha to explain his position. There he was treated as a criminal and a conspirator, and his colleagues were reprimanded. The Parliamentary Sub-committee asked him to submit his resignation and also the resignation of his colleagues. In the resignation he was made to admit: "I have come to realize that in submitting my resignation and forming a new cabinet I acted hastily and committed an error of judgment." He was marched to the phone in a building near-by and Subhas Bose made him read out the text of his resignation to the Secretary of the Governor. Bose was operating the axe at the instance of his colleagues.

On July 23 Dr. Khare was again called to Wardha by the High Command and was asked to resign his leadership of the Assembly. He agreed to do so provided his right to seek re-election was conceded. He returned to Nagpur on July 24. He was again called to Wardha on July 25 and asked not to press his proposal to contest the leadership at the party meeting which was to be held the next day. Dr. Khare told them that if they did not wish him to contest the election, they should issue a further order. As he did not yield, he was taken to Segaon in a car to Gandhi who had left Wardha that evening before Khare reached that place.

Maulana Azad, Sardar Patel, Subhas Bose and Rajendra Prasad put pressure on Dr. Khare in the presence of Gandhi who reprimanded Dr. Khare for his betrayal of the Congress and the country by entering into a conspiracy with the Governor. He said that Dr. Khare was untrustworthy and unreliable and guilty of gross indiscipline. Dr. Khare had evoked the Mahatma's anger by issuing licences for rifle classes, an unforgivable sin from the viewpoint of the Mahatma. And Patel had previously a tussle with Khare over the selection of a candidate at the All-India Parliamentary Board in Faizpur. They whispered against him and dictated the content of his resignation. Dr. Khare admitted in the resignation that he had acted hastily, but Gandhi added to the draft nearly a page and a half containing humiliating and damaging admissions. As a result Dr. Khare refused to sign his death warrant. He was brought back from Segaon to Wardha and asked to inform the Congress leaders of his decision by 3 p.m. the next day,

On July 26 Dr. Khare conveyed to the Congress leaders his firm refusal to sign the draft prepared by them. So the Congress Working Committee declared: "By all these acts, Dr. Khare has proved himself unworthy of holding positions of responsibility in the Congress organization. He should be so considered till by his services as a Congressman he has shown himself well-balanced and capable of observing discipline and discharging the duties that may be undertaken by him." The Working Committee blamed also the Governor for accepting the resignations of the three Ministers and for demanding the resignations of the other three with unseemly haste. The Congress High Command, observes John Gunther in his *Inside Asia*,[11] turned out of office one of its own Prime Ministers, Dr. Khare, when it accused him of being disobedient. The fact was that he was driven to desperation and disobedience.

In the statement Gandhi issued on July 30, 1938, he said that he simply made corrections and additions to the statement which Dr. Khare had prepared. The suggestion that Dr. Khare was made to sign a prepared draft, Gandhi added, was baseless! When Dr. Khare published the photo-block of the draft, the people were dumbfounded! A bitter attack was made in the press on Patel and Gandhi, characterising their action as fascist. Gandhi replied that his critics "forget that fascism is the naked sword. Under it Dr. Khare should lose his head". So long as, Gandhi peacefully added, demonstrators remained non-violent, under the Congress regime Dr. Khare could remain the hero of Nagpur; the students and citizens of Nagpur could execrate him and the Working Committee without a hair of the demonstrators' heads being touched! This was non-violence in thought, word and deed!

Subhas Bose who was temporarily reconciled with the Mahatma, aided the Gandhians and justified their acts by saying that the additions and alterations simply helped to make explicit what was implicit in the draft! After some months, Patel, who had deliberately ruined Khare, said to Nehru, "I think it is my lot to be abused. Bengal press is furious and they blame me for Nariman and Khare episodes, although all my colleagues were also jointly responsible for these actions. In fact in Dr. Khare's matter Subhas Bose was present from the beginning to the end and it was he who had handled the whole thing."[12] Later Subhas Bose admitted that Gandhi and the High Command had done Dr. Khare a real injustice, and being in a minority he had to support their policy.[13] Dr. Khare was bitter and sometimes unbalanced, but he was a man of truth and of an unimpeachable character

As an offshoot of the agitation over Dr. Khare's resignation, a party of young men from Nagpur protested against Gandhi and the Working Committee resolution and demanded justice for Dr. Khare. Towards the end of August 1938 some Harijans did *dharna* at Gandhi's Ashram at Segaon to compel him to instruct the C.P. Ministry to take up a Harijan Minister. Gandhi replied that it was not in his power. It was Dr. Khare's charge that Gandhi disapproved of the appointment of a Harijan Minister, as in the Mahatma's opinion it raised absurd ambitions in the minds of Harijans! Gandhi had also opposed the appointment of any Harijan on the Harijan Sevak Sangh. The Khare episode weighed heavily on Gandhi's mind and told upon his health. He observed silence for long periods. In his agony he is said to have exclaimed that Khare had desecrated his position!

In September 1938 Mahadev Desai fell ill, and Gandhi said that Harijan was a weekly representing the views of one man. Even Mahadev and Pyarelal could not write anything independently whilst he (Gandhi) was alive. He said his retirement meant non-interference even in the work of the Working Committee except when it sought his help or advice. But on October 1, 1938, making a significant declaration about the role of Jawaharlal Nehru, Gandhi said, "And I have made a rule for myself that so far as the Congress is concerned, if there is an unbridgeable gulf between him and me, his view should prevail. And this for the very good reason that I am not in the Congress and he is in the centre of it, and very much in touch with everything relating to the Congress."[14]

Gandhi had been defending Sardar Patel in public controversies and sharing his sorrows, and perhaps the thought of partiality struck him. So he made the foregoing declaration, although he dwelt on the issue of Federation in order to keep the balance of power between Jawaharlal and Patel. It seems this had an effect on Patel, and he said to Kishorlal, "Bapu has placed us in Jawaharlal's charge; so we must go on doing as he says."[15] When Kishorlal reported this to Gandhi, the Mahatma wrote to the Sardar that he hoped it was only a joke and added that he had not handed the Sardar over to anyone. There was much truth in Subhas Bose's remark when he wrote to Nehru: "Gandhi will never take a stand which will alienate you."[16] Nehru, who called himself a misfit in the existing atmosphere, was in Europe from April to November 27, 1938.

At this time Gandhi was deeply perturbed by the happenings in Travancore and commented that Sir C. P. Ramaswami Aiyer would soon lose his reputation completely. But when similar happenings took place in Mysore he blamed the Congress leaders for the resolution condemning the Mysore administration! After the Faizpur session, the Princely States' people vigorously started their struggle for the establishment of peoples' rights, and as a result, repressive measures were adopted in Mysore, Travancore and Rajkot. Mirza Ismail, the Dewan of Mysore, was a favourite with Gandhi who had a poor opinion of Sir C. P. Ramaswami Aiyer. So it was natural, though not just, for Gandhi to raise a storm against Travancore and Sir C. P. Ramaswami Aiyer.

Ravishankar Shukla, who had struggled hard and succeeded in ousting Khare, formed the new C.P. Ministry and the first thing he did was to issue on September 7 an office order instructing Government Offices to prefix the appellation Mahatma whenever Gandhi was mentioned in their correspondence. This was indeed a deserving gesture made as a return gift in gratitude to the Mahatma by Pandit Shukla. When the office order was brought to Gandhi's notice, he simply said that he had registered his protest against it. His simple name, he added, sounded sweet without the adjective. He also made the odd statement that he would support any movement to drop altogether the use, of the word Mahatma before his name. No Congress Minister could have dared act against the will of the dictator of the Congress.

Gandhi left Segaon and reached Delhi on September 20 and attended the A.I.C.C. meeting where the Civil Liberties resolution was opposed by the Leftist groups. The Left wingers staged a walk-out as a protest against the resolution. Gandhi commented that the Congress was not the homogeneous body it used to be, like an army having one will, one policy, one aim and strict discipline. Those who did not believe in the fundamental policy of the Congress should serve the Congress better by remaining outside it and converting the people to their view.

Subhas Bose had allowed the Socialists full freedom to have their say at this meeting. "If chaos is to be prevented," Gandhi therefore warned, "proper measures must be taken in time." Gandhi later said that he was the sole author of that resolution. This was the way he permitted democracy in the Congress Party! Those who did not toe the line were either crushed or driven out. For "many have despaired of opposing me" was Gandhi's proud refrain. When Nehru was critical of the Right wing, i.e. the Gandhians, Gandhi asked them to resign *en bloc* from the Working Committee. In religious matters Gandhi was often excessively tolerant and in matters of political organisation he was highly intolerant of opposition. The Congress was, in the words of Jawaharlal, assuming the role of counter-revolution and that too under the excuse of the maintenance of law and order and in the name of non-violence. It was suppressing all agitation by Kisan and the labour movement.

Gandhi left Delhi and reached Peshawar on October 5 and toured the Frontier Province till November 9. At this juncture, Nazi Germany was menacing the freedom of her neighbours. On March 11, 1938, Germany invaded Austria and occupied it. Later, Britain, France, Italy and Germany signed the Munich Pact on September 30, 1938, conceding a part of Czechoslovakia to Nazi Germany. The surrender to Nazism deeply affected Gandhi. In *Harijan* of October 8, 1938, he observed: "Europe has sold her soul for the sake of seven days' earthly existence. The peace gained at Munich is a triumph of violence; it is also its defeat." England and France, he said, quailed before the combined violence of Germany and Italy. Gandhi asked whether Germany and Italy had added anything to the moral health of the world. If the Czechs, he continued, had known the use of non-violence as a weapon for the defence of national honour, they would have faced the whole might of Germany and of Italy, too.

Gandhi expressed the same emotions and made the same suggestions to the Czechs in his article "If I were a Czech". In it he said, "Science of war leads one to dictatorship pure and simple. Science of non-violence can alone lead one to pure democracy. England, France and America have to make their choice. That is the challenge of the dictators." Democracy, he said, dreaded to spill blood, and the philosophy of the dictators called it cowardice to shrink from courage.

The Russian dictator, he added, thought he would wade to peace through a sea of blood. "If I were a Czech," he added, "I will defy the might of one who would deprive me of my independence." He presented, he concluded, Dr. Eduard Benes the President of Czechoslovakia with a weapon not of the weak but of the brave. With Gandhi's permission, Mirabehn invited Dr. Benes to Segaon.

Gandhi had said: "God has not given me the power to guide the world on the path of non-violence. But I have imagined that he has chosen me as His instrument for presenting non-violence to India for dealing with her many ills. The progress already made is good."[17] But now he seized the golden opportunity offered by a disturbed Europe and went beyond the power given by God to present his weapon to the world and gave it the message of non-violence, though it turned a deaf ear to him.

This was Gandhi's second visit to the N.W.F.P. It was purely to meet the Khudai Khidmatgars and know for himself their understanding of non-violence. Khan Abdul Ghaffar Khan, known now as Frontier Gandhi, had come to believe in non-violence independently and long before he came into contact with Gandhi. He derived, said Gandhi, his belief in non-violence from the Koran just as the Bishop of London derived his belief in violence from the Bible. Ghaffar Khan had come to realize that violence was in the blood of the Pathans. He hoped that the Khudai Khidmatgars would stick to non-violence. Gandhi told his audience at Bannu that after studying all the facts he had gained the impression that the situation in respect of border raids had grown worse since the inauguration of the Congress Government. The Congress Government had no effective control over the police, nor over the military in the N.W.F.P.

Gandhi said that the raids by the border tribes were not actuated by communal considerations. That the Hindus were more often the victims was probably due to the fact that they generally possessed more money, and the kidnappings too appeared to have the same motive. "If," he continued, "the one lakh of Khudai Khidmatgars become truly non-violent in letter and in spirit and shed their violent past completely as a snake does its outworn skin, it would be nothing short of a miracle." The Khudai Khidmatgars admitted that they fell short of the Mahatma's standard of non-violence, and their leader said that with God's help they would succeed.

During his tour, the Frontier Gandhi kept constant watch over the Mahatma as a mother protects her child. When the Mahatma was asleep, the Frontier Gandhi moved about with soft, slow steps and whisked flies hovering over the sleeping saint. He brought the pick of fruits for Gandhi who wrote to Patel that the weather was fine and there were heaps of fruit to eat. Gandhi completed the tour of the land where a blood feud never ends and then returned to Delhi on November 10, 1938.

In the *Harijan* of November 26, 1938, Gandhi wrote an article on the Jews who were being cruelly persecuted in Nazi Germany. As a humanitarian, Gandhi expressed sympathy for the Jews and said that their persecution seemed to have no parallel in history. "But," Gandhi the politician and the lifelong appeaser of the Muslims, observed, "my sympathy, does not blind me to the requirements of justice. The cry for the national home for the Jews does not make much appeal to me." "If the Jews," he continued, "have no home but Palestine, will they relish the idea of being forced to leave the other parts of the world in which they are settled or do they want a double home where they can remain at will? This cry for the national home affords a colourable justification for the German expulsion of the Jews."

Gandhi asked the German Jews to offer themselves to be shot by the Nazis and advised the Palestine Jews to offer themselves to be shot or thrown into the Dead Sea by the Arabs without raising a little finger against them. The most unbefitting thing Gandhi did three weeks after this article was to remind the Jews that "Indeed, it is a stigma against them that their ancestors crucified Jesus".[18] This was unjustly condemning a whole race for the sins of their forefathers.

While Gandhi was proffering advice to the German Jews, H. G. Wells, author, playwright and thinker, was passing through Bombay. When asked if he was an admirer of Gandhi, he replied that he did not agree with the doctrine of non-violence advocated by Gandhi. He thought that a reasonable force was necessary. "Non-violence to me," he asserted, "is a policy of the vegetable kingdom. I have seen cows eating it and other animals trampling upon it."[19]

Hitler and Gandhi were politically and philosophically the antithesis of each other. But some eminent men compared Hitler with Gandhi at this stage. Philip Spratt observed: "Any popular leader must be something of an expert at psychology." Hitler and Gandhi had something in common but they obviously differed greatly. Hitler, like Gandhi, had the intuitive faculty which enabled him to know how the masses would react to an idea. But Hitler laboriously organized even the minor details of his party propaganda. Gandhi's khadi, his poverty, his style of speech, all might have been probably or not designed to further his purpose. Gandhi, while a supremely good judge of Indian mass psychology, had little to say about it in general terms. From the eyes of the people he could tell how they would react. When the people were united and agreed with him he was buoyant and confident. When the people were divided he lost his power. He became, Spratt concluded, more sensitive to mass feeling when he fasted.

GANDHI RETURNED TO Segaon on November 11 and stayed there till the end of December 1938. He was in Bardoli from January

2 to February 1, 1939. During the first part of this period he formulated the Congress policy towards the Princely States and tendered advice to the ruler of Audh who was framing a constitution for responsible Government in his small State. Towards the middle of December, the Working Committee discussed with Gandhi the ways and means to purify the Congress and declared the Hindu Mahasabha and the Muslim League as communal organizations. Prof. N. G. Ranga, Secretary of the All-India Peasants' Union, labour leader Raikar and President Subhas Bose met him towards the end of the month.

In the last week of December 1938 several foreign missionaries including Dr. Mott, who regarded Gandhi as a prophet, met him and discussed the problem of peace. He told the missionaries that they should discard Bishop Heber's wrong notions about India and believe in the fact that India's religions too were true and India had a message to give to the world.

A Chinese delegation complained to Gandhi against Japanese aggression. Gandhi prescribed to them as to others the method of non-violence. On the first day of the new year 1939 at Segaon he told P. C. Hsu, author and philosopher, that "there is no bar to united non-violent action".

A few days later, in the third week of January 1939, Dr. Toyohiko Kagawa met him. A convert to Christianity, Dr. Kagawa took his doctorate in theology, organized labour unions and dreamed of establishing a "co-operative state" in Japan. A student of religion, Dr. Kagawa wondered how Gandhi reconciled non-violence with the Gita. He thought Gandhi's interpretation was a laboured one.[20] Later the Rev. S. S. Tema, the African negro missionary, sought Gandhi's message and Gandhi replied that they should have selfless leaders living like the common people and thinking like them. Another visitor to Gandhi was S. Radhakrishnan who requested Gandhi to advise the Madras Government to make Hindi optional in Madras.

In January 1939 Gandhi was engrossed at Bardoli in solving the state problem of Rajkot, Bhavnagar and Jaipur with the leaders of these States. For the previous two months a struggle had been going on in Rajkot of establishing a constitutional Government there. A compromise was arrived at but the ruler having broken the agreement, the struggle was restarted.

While at Bardoli, Gandhi was thinking over the question of the selection of the President for the ensuing Congress session, at Tripuri. On arrival of Nehru from Europe in November he had asked him whether he would accept the presidentship, but Nehru declined. Subhas Bose had been a silent President and had not asserted himself as President, but the latitude he gave to the Socialists at the Delhi A.I.C.C. meeting and the Planning Commission he inaugurated were the two acts which had perturbed Gandhi and his Right wing which Nehru called "Gandhi and his group". When, at this juncture, one of the members of the Economic Conference asked Gandhi what he thought of the Planning Commission, he replied that he had not studied the question and that it was not discussed in his presence. "It does not mean," Gandhi said unpleasantly, "that everything that emerges from the Working Committee bears my imprimatur or is even discussed with me."[21]

The National Planning Committee had been set up by Bose to draw up a comprehensive plan of industrialization and of national development. This meant a threat to Gandhi's ideology and his ideas about village uplift. He discussed the question of the presidency with Sardar Patel and informed him on December 21, 1938, that as Maulana Azad had flatly refused to accept the presidentship, "I feel it would be better if we consider Pattabhi Sitaramayya". Gandhi and Patel always took the decision and the Gandhi group said ditto to it.

From January 11 to 14, 1939, the Working Committee met at Bardoli. But after the business was over, President Subhas Bose left and then the remaining members of the Working Committee including Jawaharlal Nehru decided that it was unnecessary to re-elect Bose.

All this shows that there was something rotten in the state of Denmark. A group of his colleagues taking a vital decision behind the back of the President meant a determined opposition to him. As Maulana Azad, who had been hesitating to contest the election against a Bengali leader, withdrew, Pattabhi's candidature was again declared from Bardoli; for he had once withdrawn in favour of Maulana Azad.

Subhas Bose had already decided to contest the election a second time, and the Gandhi group knew it. Bose wanted to give an ultimatum to the British Government if he succeeded. So he stood for the contest. But on January 19, 1939, Gandhi wired from Bardoli requesting him to withdraw in favour of Dr. Pattabhi Sitaramayya. Bose refused to do so, and on February 21 he issued a statement declaring that he was fighting the election not for personal reasons, but on the basis of a definite programme so that the contest might help the clarification of issues. He would loyally abide, Bose concluded, by the verdict of the majority of the delegates. The next day seven Gandhi wing leaders, including Sardar Patel, Rajendra Prasad,

Shankarrao Deo, Jairamadas and Bhulabhai Desai issued, at the instance of Gandhi, a joint statement from Bardoli which declared that the Congress President's position was analogous only to that of a chairman and the policies and programmes were determined by the Working Committee. They therefore supported Dr. Pattabhi Sitaramayya and Patel wrote to Nehru urging him to sign it as Gandhi had asked him to do or issue a different statement independently. Nehru did it independently and so Gandhi was displeased.

Subhas Bose replied to the joint statement fearlessly and spiritedly but without counting the cost. The Congress President, he observed, was not a constitutional monarch, but like the President of America who nominates his cabinet. He then levelled charges against his Gandhist colleagues that " it is widely believed that there is a prospect of compromise on the federal scheme between the Right wing of the Congress and the British Government, during the coming year. Consequently the Right wing do not want a Leftist president who may be a thorn in the way of compromise". It cut the Right wing to the quick and Patel issued a rejoinder saying that Bose's re-election would be harmful to the country's cause. Nehru issued two statements supporting the case against Bose without a good word about him, but praising Maulana Azad who had withdrawn from the contest.

Subhas Bose would have done well to stop at this affront; but he added fuel to the flames. He added that it was also generally believed the prospective list of ministers for the federal cabinet had been already drawn up. This was a most damaging statement against the Gandhists. Jayaprakash Narayan, Swami Sahajanand and Acharya Narendra Dev supported Bose's candidature.

Gandhi wrote an article in *Harijan* under the title "Internal Decay" in which he said that there was indiscipline and corruption in the Congress and he saw nothing but red ruin and anarchy in the future. But he added fervently that if God willed it, "I feel that I have enough strength and energy in me to lead a battle much more strenuous than any I have fought." It was clear that he was strong enough to meet any challenge to his leadership by Bose who perhaps considered him a spent force. Bose did not take into consideration the iceberg that was below the stormy sea over which his ship was sailing.

The Gandhi wing through which Gandhi controlled the Congress organization began to canvass to secure votes for Dr. Pattabhi Sitanarayya. The Gandhi Seva Sangh, the All-India Village Industries Association and the Ministers who were under the direct control of the Right wing were persuaded to do the job. And yet the Leftists and the progressive-minded voters enthusiastically voted for Bose. On January 29 he triumphed over Pattabhi, inflicting a memorable defeat on Gandhi whose refrain was that many had despaired of defeating him. The old guard, who were aided by Nehru, were shocked.

ON JANUARY 31 Gandhi wrote in the *Harijan* of February 4, 1939, an article in which he said he rejoiced in that defeat. Since he was instrumental in inducing Dr. Pattabhi not to withdraw his name as a candidate, "the defeat is more mine than his" and "it is plain that the delegates do not approve of the principles and policy for which I stand". He said that he did not subscribe to Bose's facts or arguments in his manifestoes and he thought that Bose's references to his colleagues were unjustified and unworthy. The registers, Gandhi added, contained a very large number of bogus members.

"After all," Gandhi declared sardonically in his unique style, "Subhas Bose is not an enemy of his country. He has suffered for it. In his opinion his is the most forward and boldest policy and programme. The minority can only wish it all success. If they cannot keep pace with it, they must come out of the Congress. If they can, they will add strength to the majority. Those, therefore, who feel uncomfortable in being in the Congress may come out, not in a spirit of ill-will, but with the deliberate purpose of rendering more effective service." He asked his followers to quit the Congress because he was defeated. This was how his mind, method and democracy worked! He should have remembered how his lieutenants captured the All-India Congress Committee at Calcutta in September 1920.

Gandhi not only asked his men to come out of the Congress but also took a drastic step to corner Bose so that there would be a major crisis. He wrote to Jawaharlal Nehru on February 3, 1939: "After the election and the manner in which it was fought, I feel that I shall serve the country by absenting myself from the Congress at the forthcoming session. Moreover my health is none too good. I would like you to help me. Please do not press me to attend." But a few days later Gandhi wrote to Mahadev Desai that he was going where God was taking him.

Bose realized in his heart of hearts that he had caught a tartar in his victory. So he ruefully issued a statement on February 4 saying that it could be a tragic thing for him if he succeeded in winning the confidence of other people but failed to win the confidence of India's greatest man.

Sardar Vallabhbhai Patel wrote to Nehru that their enemies had given them credit for their honesty but not the President. Nehru who was opposed to Subhas Bose's re-election, wrote to Bose on February 4, after meeting him at Santiniketan on February 2: "As I told you, your contested election has done some good and some harm." Subhas Bose wrote to him a very comprehensive letter describing Nehru as a man who rode two horses and a leader who had done more to lower him (Bose) in the estimation than all the members of the Working Committee put together.

Bose tried to patch up the differences with Gandhi at Wardha on February 15, but it worsened the situation. Nehru felt that Bose did not seek Gandhi's co-operation from the bottom of his heart. Bose could not attend the meeting of the Working Committee on February 22 which was called to discuss the agenda for the Tripuri Congress. It was unfortunate that Bose was taken ill on his return journey to Calcutta from Wardha. He later wrote an article in *Modern Review*, "My strange Illness," which added to the suspicion about the mystery of his illness. He requested the members of the Working Committee to postpone the meeting, which they construed as lack of confidence in the Working Committee. So twelve of them, on the advice of Gandhi, resigned and Nehru acted as if he had also resigned; for he now regarded Bose's re-election as an unmixed evil. Only Subhas Bose with his brother Sarat Chandra Bose remained as members of the Working Committee. So the battle was joined to depose Bose.

On February 27 Gandhi went to Rajkot to redeem the pledge of the ruler to the people. As he and Patel could not gain their object by negotiations with Dewan Darbar Viravala and the British Resident, Gandhi on the eve of the Tripuri session, went on a fast from March 3 to coerce the ruler to keep the promise given to the people. He had appealed to the Viceroy to intervene in the matter and to write to the British Resident to restore the Pact. Nehru and Bose were sorry that Gandhi made Rajkot and Jaipur overshadow the main political issue. By his fast Gandhi attracted the attention of all politicians to Rajkot, and Tripuri was thus side-tracked.

Gandhi referred to his fast and said: "God gave me the remedy."[22] "The public," he went on, "should not laugh at my connecting God with the fact. It might be the product of my heated imagination. The weapon of fasting, I know, cannot be lightly wielded. It can easily savour of violence unless it is used by one skilled in the art. I claim to be such an artist in this subject." The fast failed to convert either the Thakore Saheb or the Dewan Viravala. It effected no change of heart in them. As expected, the Congress Ministries wired the Viceroy to intervene and prevent the crisis. On March 6 Gandhi's condition caused anxiety. The Viceroy gave up his Rajputana tour, returned to Delhi and informed Gandhi through Gibson, the Resident of Rajkot, that he offered the services of the Chief Justice of India, Sir Maurice Gwyer, to arbitrate. It was a tactful move on the part of the British Viceroy. Gandhi was grateful to the Viceroy and though his offer left many things unsaid, he broke his fast on February 7 and regarded it as a good ending and as an answer to the prayers of millions. Of course Gandhi remembered Tripuri but decided to concentrate on Rajkot and he wanted to go to Delhi. His lieutenant Jamnalal Bajaj was in Jaipur Jail.

Gandhi then wrote on Rajkot and the meaning of the breaking of the fast, and another on the philosophy of his fast and the whole Rajkot affair which had ended with the help of the Viceroy! Fasting was of no use, he said, without a living faith in God. Gandhi was in Delhi from March 15 to April 7, discussing with the Viceroy the Rajkot affair and with Nehru and Jayaprakash, Subhas Bose's presidential speech. He later spent one day at Allahabad. On April 3, 1939, Sir Maurice Gwyer, Chief Justice of the Federal Court, gave his Award in favour of Sardar Patel, and the Viceroy also promised Gandhi that Government would compel Rajkot to implement the Award.

When Gandhi returned to Rajkot on April 9, hostile demonstrations were staged against Gandhi by the Muslims and Bhayats of Rajkot at the prayer grounds near Rashtriya Shala. Dr. Ambedkar was called in by the Depressed Classes, and he met Gandhi on April 19 concerning representation for the Harijans on the Reforms Committee. While the discussion was going on, Gandhi's temperature shot up, and the interview terminated.

Gandhi called on Darbar Viravala twice, met Resident Gibson, but failed to get his way. He asked the State leaders to tear the Award to pieces and rely on the goodness of Darbar Viravala. He admitted his defeat to Viravala. It was God who had given him the remedy, but he failed though he had acted, he said, the part of a wise general. As his fast ended in a fiasco, he expressed his agony on April 24, on the train to Bombay. "And so I have left empty-handed with body shattered, hope cremated.

Rajkot has been to me a priceless laboratory. My patience has been sorely tried by the tortuous politics of Kathiawad."[23] When he started for Rajkot he had said that he was going there as God was taking him there. He knew, he had added, that he would not return from Rajkot with his hopes blasted.

In negotiations, Gandhi was always a failure. Rajkot again proved this to the hilt. Gandhi became ill. His health had fast deteriorated. There was a swelling on his feet. He had wisely given up his fast and saved his life; but he lost much that was dearer to him than life. He had denounced the proposal for Federation but accepted the authority of Sir Maurice Gwyer, the Chief Justice of the Federal Court. It was indeed a tacit recognition of the Federal Scheme. Gandhi also confessed that his fast at Rajkot was tainted with *himsa* or coercion!

If Gandhi, the apostle of non-violence, after years of renunciation, efforts at purification and determination to love his enemy was unfit to use his weapon, and failed in observing ahimsa in thought, word and deed, and in using his weapons and methods and techniques for bringing about a change of heart, what would be the fate of his ideology in other hands?

At another place Gandhi's statecraft met the same fate as in Rajkot. He advised the Arya Samajists to withdraw their satyagraha which they had been conducting for some months in collaboration with the Hindu Mahasabha against the autocratic rule of the Hyderabad State. The State Congress had stopped its struggle against the Nizam at the instance of Gandhi. Now Gandhi gave a draft resolution to the leaders of the Arya Samaj advising the withdrawal of the struggle. The Conference of the Arya Samaj met at Sholapur on April 5, 1939, and Gandhi told Dr. Moonje in Delhi that the Arya Samaj would definitely withdraw the struggle as advised by him and that Dr. Moonje should wire to Savarkar, the leader of the Hindu Mahasabha, to follow suit. The Arya Samajists were on the verge of withdrawing the struggle. But Savarkar, who after his release in 1937 burst like a bombshell on the political scene in India, foiled Gandhi's attempt by his reason and eloquence. The Arya Samajists continued their struggle and finally in July 1939 the Nizam had to introduce the reforms they wanted in the State.

CHAPTER XLI

On War and Pakistan

THE TRIPURI CONGRESS was held from March 10 to 12, 1939, under the presidentship of Subhas Bose who was seriously ill. Gandhi had revealed the real reason for his absence at Tripuri, but had written to Subhas to excuse him from attendance at Tripuri "mainly on health grounds". On the eve of the session, Gandhi had sent a message asking Subhas not to defy medical advice and desiring him to regulate the proceedings from Calcutta! By his fast unto death, Gandhi had rivetted the Congress workers' attention on him, created consternation among his opponents and anguish in his sympathisers and followers.

In his presidential address, Bose desired the Congress to give an ultimatum to the British Government. Although seriously ill, Bose tried in vain to control the Congress, but at the eleventh hour the Socialists, Royists and other leftists did not support him. The Gandhists dominated the field and took their revenge on Subhas for inflicting a crushing defeat on the Mahatma.

Most of the Congress Ministers, belonged to the Right wing and were under the direct control of the members of the Parliamentary Committee who were Gandhists. These Ministers played a vital role by canvassing against Bose. A large number of All-India Congress Committee members said that if they openly voted against the wishes of Ministers they would get into trouble. So they wanted the voting to be by ballot. The suggestion was turned down. The result was that the Congress expressed its confidence in the members of the Working Committee who had resigned. It stifled Subhas Bose and resolved overruling its constitution, that Subhas Bose, the President, must form his

Working Committee in accordance with the wishes of the Mahatma. The Congress passed a resolution on the national demand without Bose's ultimatum, declared its opposition to the proposed Federation and demanded the right of the people to frame their own constitution. The thought that without Gandhi nobody would be able to lead the approaching national struggle prevailed. Subhas Bose returned to Calcutta with body and hopes shattered.

Bose thereafter wrote to Gandhi and tried to win his support in forming the Working Committee, but Gandhi did not respond to his appeals. Nehru tried half-heartedly to bring about a compromise between Gandhi and Bose. He wrote to Gandhi: "You should accept Subhas as President. To try to push him out seems to me to be an exceedingly wrong step." Yet the Mahatma was ruthless. It was Gandhi's dictum that however you may repair it, a rift is a rift. Another of his dictums was that to forgive was not to forget. It was his observation that "Man can change his temperament, can control it, but cannot eradicate it". The worldly politician in Gandhi dominated the Mahatma and he remained unmoved.

Subhas Bose finally discussed the whole problem with Gandhi and Nehru at Calcutta, but to no avail. Bose had to resign. He was the first Congress President to do so. Gandhi and his old guard ultimately deposed him. And the words Subhas Bose used in the case of Dr. Khare, that a leader has to pay the price of leadership[1] proved prophetic. In this episode the part played by Nehru was not impartial. Long afterwards Nehru told Taya Zinkin that it was true that he had let down Subhas as he thought then that Gandhi was India.[2]

Subhas Bose then founded his party, the Forward Bloc, on May 3, 1939, which turned out to have a few pillars and no foundation.

During this crisis of physical and mental agonies, Subhas Bose behaved with dignity, decorum and responsibility. He remonstrated with those who had shouted down Nehru and Rajendra Prasad. Tagore had befittingly welcomed and blessed Bose as a chosen leader of the people of Bengal. Rajendra Prasad, one of the gentle and reliable members of the old guard, was installed in Bose's place.

On May 1, 1939, Gandhi left Calcutta and on May 3 inaugurated at Brindavan, in Champaran, Bihar, a Gandhi Seva Sangh Exhibition and its session. He stayed at Brindavan for a week. In his address he said he was developing a new technique by entering into the minds of his opponents and that Gandhians should be called ahimsaites! He went to Rajkot again, breaking his journey for a day at Bombay. He was at Rajkot till June 1. While there, he withdrew without any reservation the statement he had made against the German Jews. In his statement he had said that the Jews "called down upon the Germans the curses of mankind and they wanted America and England to fight Germany on their behalf." Some Englishmen brought the error to his notice and some criticized him for this allegation. It is regrettably true that Gandhi was highly prejudiced against the Jews whom the Muslims regarded as their enemies. Gandhi's political heirs carried that prejudice through their regimes in independent India.

A crushing reply came from a Jewish writer who said that Gandhi wanted them to be superhuman when they were treated as sub-human. He angrily added that "a Jewish Gandhi in Germany, should one arise, could 'function' for about five minutes—until the first Gestapo agent would lead him, not to a concentration camp, but directly to guillotine."[3] It is no wonder that Gandhi had once expressed his gratitude to the British Government for allowing him to make his experiments in South Africa!

At Rajkot Gandhi declared that he had committed a mistake in bringing in a third party, and renouncing the Gwyer Award. He apologized to the Viceroy, the Chief Justice Maurice Gwyer and to the Thakore. The Thakore of Rajkot then garlanded him and praised his statement. Gandhi attended a reception for Thakore Saheb and advised the Parishad to co-operate with the Thakore.

Spending the first week of June 1939 in Bombay, Gandhi again returned to Bombay to attend a Working Committee Meeting on June 21. There was hot discussion on the issue of Rajkot between Gandhi and Nehru. Nehru lost his temper and talked to Gandhi with considerable feeling on the matter of Gandhi's interview published in *Harijan*. Sardar Patel and others were perturbed at this happening. So Patel wrote to Nehru on July 3: "We were all sorry to find that you were so very angry about it and we felt that you were less than fair to Bapu. I also felt that one or two such events would drive him to a decision of going out of public life altogether. As it is he is 71, and has lost much of his energy. He feels hurt when your feelings are wounded. I don't think that he loves anybody more than he loves you and when he finds that any action of his has made you unhappy, he broods over it and feels miserable. Since that evening he has been thinking of retiring altogether."[4]

Patel, therefore, requested Nehru to write to Gandhi not to take any decision without having full consultations with him if Nehru thought it advisable.

Nehru's outburst of anger did not spare even the Mahatma who felt profound love for him. Only a short while earlier, Gandhi had told his Brindavan audience that there was a heart-union between him and Nehru and no intellectual differences could break it. Although hurt to the quick by Nehru's remark, Gandhi said: "Jawaharlal thinks that by my misdeeds in Rajkot I have set back the clock of progress by a century." All over the country the impression was that Gandhi had betrayed the cause of the Rajkot people.

Yet, in the spirit of a true mother, Gandhi suggested that the Congress should send Nehru to Ceylon as India's ambassador of peace, and he later described Nehru's Ceylon visit as glorious. Although Nehru had pulled up Gandhi, he also saved him from a difficult position when Dr. Rammanohar Lohia had a tussle with the Mahatma on the South Africa resolution at the All-India Congress Committee in Bombay in June 1939. Dr. Lohia suggested two amendments to Gandhi's draft resolution. One described the Indians in South Africa not as "British Indians" but as "Indians" and the other recommended that Indians had better make a common front with the oppressed communities like the Negroes, the Zulus, and the Arabs and even the poor whites. This enraged Gandhi and he said he would have the All-India Congress Committee pass his resolution without amendments or not at all. Nehru who had supported Dr. Lohia's amendments, faltered at this stage. He persuaded Dr. Lohia to respect the opinion of Gandhi and withdraw his amendments which had been duly passed![5] There upon Subhas Bose, who met Dr. Lohia as the former was leaving the All-India Congress Committee meeting, asked him who was the real power in Indian politics, the Congress or Gandhi. Dr. Lohia replied that he was aware of the situation. Gandhi vetoed a resolution of the Congress which it had passed four hours earlier! When it suited his views Gandhi upheld democratic ideals and when the democratic vote of the Congress went against him he flew into a fury! The All-India Congress Committee resolved, despite opposition from Subhas Bose, that nobody should start satyagraha without the permission of the Provincial Congress Committee. This was obviously a check on Subhas Bose who wanted to launch such a struggle.

As the Bombay Government was to introduce prohibition from August 1, 1939, the Parsis, Christians and the Bhandaris put their problems and difficulties in the matter before the Government. S. K. Bole put the case of the Bhandaris to Gandhi in a Memorandum in Bombay on July 5, 1939, just as Gandhi's train was moving out of the station. Gandhi replied that Government would solve the problem of the tappers but they should co-operate with the Government and not threaten it in anyway. Bole wrote to Gandhi saying that theirs was not a threat. Bole was for gradual prohibition. The hasty method being adopted, he added, would lead to illicit distillation and increase crimes. It would prove, he warned, another Himalayan blunder of the Mahatma. Subhas Bose criticized the prohibition policy of the Bombay Ministry as harmful to the Minorities. Referring to this, Gandhi said Subhas Bose was playing a dangerous game!

The Congress Ministries introduced prohibition with great enthusiasm and followed the Mahatma for years. But ultimately prohibition failed. Men like Sir Jogendra Singh, Bole and others proved prohetic, and it is part of history that the attempt of the Congress to reform a small minority accustomed to drink in Indian society ended in a tragedy as it happened in the U.S.A. The Provinces which introduced prohibition did so partially, and leaders like Jawaharlal Nehru were more indifferent to it than interested in it. The Provinces gradually scrapped it to the extent that the drink is available everywhere. It is now realized at great cost that although America is not India, human nature is the same in all climes and times and human problems are everywhere the same.

Gandhi left Bombay on July 5 for a tour of the N.W.F.P. and was there till July 26. During the tour B. Shivarao, as the representative of the Government of India, requested Gandhi to persuade Indians in South Africa not to start satyagraha there. So Gandhi asked Dr. Dadoo, leader of the Passive Resistance Committee in South Africa, to postpone the struggle. Accordingly on July 29, 1939, they postponed the struggle.

The Muslim opposition to Bande Mataram was growing and Gandhi on his own authority declared that if at a mixed gathering of Hindus and Muslims, any person objected to the singing of Bande Mataram even after the Congress expurgations had been carried out, the singing should be stopped. This policy of the Congress and Gandhi was criticized by many.

On July 23 Gandhi wrote from Abbottabad a letter to Hitler, the dictator of Nazi Germany, appealing to him to prevent a war which might reduce humanity to the savage state. He considered Herr Hitler the one person who could prevent a war and added that the appeal was from one who had deliberately shunned the method of war not without considerable success. "Anyway," he concluded, "I anticipate your forgiveness if I have erred in writing to you." But the Government did not allow the letter to go to Hitler. Gandhi later included it as a part of his statement on war policy.

On July 28 Gandhi returned to Segaon from his tour of the N.W.F.P. and on August 11, 1939, attended the Working Committee meeting which disqualified Subhas Bose from holding any post in the Congress for three years. Bose, as President of the Bengal Provincial Congress Committee, had appealed to Bengal to observe July 9 as Protest Day against the Bombay resolution of the All-India Congress Committee on satyagraha. The resolution on Bose's disqualification was drafted by Gandhi. He thus non-violently put an end to Bose's career as a Congressman.

On that very day Gandhi decided to do away with the traces of Subhas Bose's presidency. He decided to abolish the Planning Committee which Subhas Bose had inaugurated during his first presidency. He wrote to Nehru on August 11, saying that much money was wasted on the Planning Committee which would bring forth little or no fruit. Gandhi had asserted in February 1939 that the goal of the Congress was not industrialization but revival of village industries.

World War II, which had been threatening to break out, started on September 1, 1939, when Nazi Germany invaded Poland. Russia, too, invaded Poland on September 17, 1939. In doing so Nazi Germany and Communist Russia had no other motive but utter self-interest and self-aggrandizement. Nazi Germany and Communist Russia had made a ten-year Non-aggression Pact on August 23, 1939, when some of the lovers of human freedom, democracy and fair play the world over had drawn in their horns. Some rubbed their eyes in surprise and a few felt betrayed by the stunning event. On August 31 the Soviet Parliament ratified the Russo-German Pact. In accordance with the provisions of the Anglo-Polish Pact of August 25, 1939, Britain declared war on Germany on September 3, 1939, "to save the whole world from the pestilence of Nazi tyranny and in defence of all that was sacred to man and to keep ablaze the flames of human liberty, reason, democracy, and fair play".

Lord Linlithgow, the Viceroy of India, proclaimed that India was at war with Germany and said that India would fight for human freedom as against the rule of force. Obviously, he made India a belligerent nation without consulting the Legislative Assembly or the Provincial Legislatures.

On his return from Abbottabad, Gandhi stayed at Segaon from July 28 to September 2, 1939. In those days Jawaharlal Nehru often felt that he could be of more use to India outside the country. So he was in China trying to establish a link between the two ancient countries. But in the second week of August when the danger of world war arose, the Working Committee had adopted a resolution on the subject framed by Nehru, declaring its unflinching determination to oppose all attempts to impose a war on India against her will.

At that time Gandhi had withdrawn his resolution which was based on out-and-out non-violence. He realized as he had done several times previously that "the Congress has no non-violent message for the world". So Gandhi said he attended the Working Committee in pursuit of his mission of non-violence, and added, "I am content to plough a lonely furrow." He continued, "I know that many in the West believe that my word does not carry weight, but I have no hesitation in declaring my faith in reason which is another word for non-violence."

Gandhi left Segaon and met the Viceroy at Simla on September 4, 1939. He told the Viceroy that he could not contemplate, without being stirred to the very depth, the destruction of London, and he broke down as he was picturing before him the Houses of Parliament and Westminster Abbey and their possible destruction. "I am not," he truly added, "therefore, just now thinking of India's deliverance. He told the Viceroy that his sympathies were with England and France from the purely humanitarian point. Indian independence will come, but what will it be worth if England and France fall, or if they come out victorious over Germany ruined and humbled?" "Yet it seemed," he added, "as if Herr Hitler knew no God but brute force". In the statement he issued on September 5, Gandhi declared: "I have returned from Viceregal Lodge empty-handed and without any understanding, open or secret." And he included in the statement his letter to Hitler.

Jawaharlal Nehru, who was rushing back to India from China, said at Rangoon that India did not approach the problem with a view to taking advantage of Britain's difficulty. If England stood for self-determination, the proof of that should be India.

Dr. Ambedkar lamented that India had no voice in her foreign policy in declaring war or in making peace but said that India should remain within the British Commonwealth of nations and strive to achieve the status of equal partnership therein. The Muslim League offered conditional support, asking the British Government to create a sense of security and satisfaction amongst the Mussalmans and, curiously enough, also urged His Majesty's Government to satisfy Arab national demands.

As President of the Hindu Mahasabha, Savarkar declared that Britain's claim that she entered the war to safeguard the vital principles affecting human freedom was a political stunt so long as she continued to hold India in political bondage.

On September 11, 1939, the Viceroy announced the postponement of the Federation Scheme. Jinnah was overjoyed at this and hoped the future constitution would be considered *de novo*. The Congress passed a resolution on September 14, drafted by Nehru. A free, democratic India, it observed, would gladly associate herself with other free nations for mutual defence against aggression and for economic co-operation. On October 10 the All-India Congress Committee asked the British Government to state their war aims and peace aims.

The Viceroy, interviewing 52 Indian leaders, declared on October 17 Britain's war aims regarding India. He sought the assistance of India in the prosecution of the war in which, he said, higher ideals were involved. He promised that at the end of the war the British Government would enter into consultation with representatives of the several communities, parties and interests in India, and with the Indian Princes, with a view to securing their aid and co-operation in the framing of a new constitution.

The All-India Congress Committee rejected the Viceroy's offer, which conceded nothing. It refused to give support to Britain and called upon the Congress Ministers to tender their resignations.

On September 15 Gandhi expressed his opinion that he was alone in thinking that whatever support was to be given to the British should be given unconditionally. He had met the Viceroy again on September 26 and discussed with him for three and a half hours Britain's war and peace aims. With reference to the Viceroy's October announcement, Gandhi said that the Congress had asked for bread and it had got a stone. The Congress, he observed, would have to go into the wilderness again before it became strong and pure enough to reach its objective.

The Congress Ministers resigned in eight provinces, creating a first-class crisis in India and a great furore in England. The Congress members in the Central Assembly had already been asked to boycott the Central Assembly. The British statesman, Lord Zetland, who was Secretary of State, Sir Samuel Hoare and Wedgwood Benn, former Secretary of State for India, made a plethora of speeches but in the words of Nehru their talk about democracy and resistance to aggression was not meant for India.

HINDU-MUSLIM TENSION WAS increasing. There were riots upto October 1939 at Asansol, Kanpur, Benares, and Cassimpur near Calcutta. With this increasing tension, Congress leaders like Nehru, Rajendra Prasad and Gandhi felt increasingly the necessity of arriving at a settlement with the Muslim League, and in October 1939 Gandhi and Nehru tried to persuade Jinnah and to arrive at some sort of an understanding with them. Gandhi, Rajendra Prasad and Jinnah jointly saw the Viceroy who told them that they should arrive at a basis of agreement between the Congress and the Muslim League.

Gandhi, Rajendra Prasad and Nehru discussed the problem with Jinnah. But as the Congress was not prepared to recognize the Muslim League as the sole representative of the Muslims, nothing came out of the talks and correspondence. So Nehru and Jinnah did not meet again in 1939. After the Congress Ministries resigned on October 31, the Muslim League celebrated the event by observing 22nd December as a Day of Deliverance and thanksgiving. But the British Governors said that the Congress Ministers had acted with impartiality and catholicity.

Gandhi was disturbed. The sand under the feet of the Hindu-Muslim peace-makers was running out. The Congress had given up the idea of non-violent defence against armed invasion, and the Hindu-Muslim riots were causing anxiety to Gandhi. In *Harijan* of October 14, 1939, he observed: "Already, the bulk of the army is manned by the Mussalmans of the North, Sikhs and Gurkhas." If the masses of the South and the Centre wished to become militarized, the Congress would have to be party to an enormous military budget. There was, as Gandhi suggested, preponderance in the military of the Muslims, and if the Congress (Hindus) joined also the military ranks, he feared that the Congress would be lost in the crowd if it wore the same old outworn armour that the world was wearing in those days. But the Congress had a name, he thought, because it represented non-violence as a political wéapon par excellence. He wanted India to discard violence even for defending her borders. "The tragedy of the situation," Gandhi observed gravely, "is that, if the Congress is to throw in its lot with those who believe in the necessity of armed defence of India, the past twenty-five years will have been years of gross neglect of the primary duty of Congressmen to team the science of armed warfare. And I fear that history will hold me, as the general of the fight, responsible for the tragedy. The future historian will say that I should have perceived that the nation was learning not non-violence of the strong but merely passivity of the weak and should have, therefore, provided for Congressmen's military training."[6]

"Being obsessed," he continued, "with the idea that somehow or other India will learn true non-violence, it would not occur to me to invite my co-workers to train themselves for armed defence. On the contrary, I used to discountenance all sword-play and the display of stout lathis."

Yet reverting to the refrain of the non-violent ideal, he observed: "Nor am I even now repentant for the past. I have the unquenchable faith that, of all the countries in the world, India is the only country which can learn the art of non-violence."

So Gandhi said that the Muslims should see that "my principal work lies through teaching at least the Hindus[7] to learn the art of non-violence unless I can bring the Muslims to the position the Ali Brothers and their associates took up during the Khilafat days." While Gandhi, discarding his all-inclusive role, chose only the Hindus to learn the art of non-violence, Savarkar was the only statesman who had the foresight to sense the danger of the Muslim preponderance in the army, in the case of internal chaos and external pressure. In his whirlwind tour of India in 1939, Savarkar sent forth appeal upon appeal and gave an impetus to the militarization of the Hindu youth. Savarkar said: "Today it may appear that these men in the armed forces are mere slaves in the pay of a foreign Government, but there can be no doubt that when the crucial moment comes they will prove themselves real patriots and staunch Hindus." While addressing the students of Scottish College, Calcutta, Savarkar said: "Since the days of our First War of Independence in 1857, it has been the policy of the British Government to keep the army out of politics. Our policy should be to carry politics into the Indian Army by all possible means and once we succeed in this, the battle of freedom will be won."

So powerful was the effect of this propaganda that Sir

Zeauddin Ahmed, Vice-Chancellor of the Aligarh Muslim University, in a speech at Poona raised an alarm at the increasing number of Hindus enlisting in the Army, Navy and Air Force, thereby reducing the percentage of Muslims in the fighting forces. *The Eastern Times*, a prominent Muslim League newspaper, was stunned by the astonishing success of the programme for the militarization of the Hindus. In 1946, when Liaquat Ali Khan, Secretary of the All-India Muslim League, joined the Interim Government, he wrote to the Viceroy complaining about the inadequate representation of Muslims in the Armed Forces.[8]

Meanwhile, Gandhi was restless over widening differences with Nehru. He had greatly praised Nehru as the draftsman of the Congress resolution of September 14 and chose him as the Chairman of the War Sub-Committee of the Congress, since the Congress could not constitutionally make him President at that juncture.

Though Gandhi described Nehru as an artist and a humanitarian and as a person who was more English than Indian in his make-up, he wrote to Nehru on October 26, 1939: "I could see, though your affection and regard for me remain undiminished, differences in outlook between us are becoming most marked. Perhaps this is the most critical period in our history." "I feel," he added, "that I must not lead if I cannot carry you all with me. There should not be divided counsels among the members of the Working Committee. I feel that you should take full charge and lead the country, leaving me free to voice my opinion."[9]

On November 19, 1939, Gandhi visited Allahabad and laid the foundation of the Kamala Nehru Hospital. He attended a Working Committee meeting and gladly found time on this occasion to issue a certificate to a barber for giving him a fine shave without soap but with a swadeshi razor! He returned to Segaon on November 25 and stayed on till February 3, 1940. There was pressure on him for starting a struggle, but he said he had no intention to embarrass the British Government. The time had not yet arrived to do so. When it became inevitable, he said, he would start the struggle.

In November 1939 there were serious riots in Sind. Gandhi said that he could only advise the afflicted people, that is the Hindus, in terms of non-violence. If they had not the capacity for non-violence, they should learn the art of defending themselves or they should resort to migration instead of living in perpetual fear of their lives and honour of their women folk. This was all right. But Gandhi, who never tried to reform

Muslims, wrongly interpreted the situation when he said: "Hinduism has become a synonym for weakness and Muslim for physical strength." Gandhi's constant sermons directed at Hindus alone were partly responsible for the tragedy of the Hindus, and they were more confused about than resolute on defence.

In Gandhi's hut at Segaon a telephone was installed in the 1st week of December 1939. Those were war days. Gandhi was now old and had no energy to run to other places or to contact his colleagues on demand. So this mechanical device, was set up. Gandhi thus took advantage of every machine device, railway, motor-car, telephone and others. Sir Stafford Cripps had talked with Gandhi for three days and Gandhi also attended a Working Committee meeting. The effect of all the resolutions of the Working Committee was that it asked the country neither to help democracy and freedom nor to oppose them. It was a sort of deadlock. At Segaon Gandhi had discussions with Rajagopalachari and Hridaya Nath Kunzru in December and in January 1940 with Rajendra Prasad, with several Bengal leaders and with Subhas Bose. Viravala died on January 23, 1940, and Gandhi mentioned him coldly in his letter to Sardar Patel. There were some critical articles and speeches on Gandhi's addendum to the pledge to be taken on January 26, 1940. The Royists, the Socialist leaders, Jayaprakash Narayan and Sampurnanand, criticized the insistence on spinning as a condition for Congress membership. They said they had not accepted it. The Socialists, Jayaprakash observed, had drawn up a new programme based on labour and peasant organizations as the basis of a revolutionary mass movement. Gandhi said he would not be able to undertake a struggle on these conditions. God would send him a plan when he gave the word, but he was not prepared knowingly to undertake a fight that must end in anarchy and red ruin.

The Viceroy made a conciliatory speech at the Orient Club, Bombay, on January 10, 1940, declaring full Dominion Status of the Statute of Westminster variety as the British objective for India, and reconsideration of the 1935 Act as soon as practicable after the War. The Viceroy, like Lord Zetland, Secretary of State for India, told the Mahatma that Britain and not the Congress would determine the status, destiny and future of India. The Viceroy was at a great disadvantage. Gandhi talked to him in his personal capacity and created an awkward situation for the Viceroy. This time Gandhi was very stiff, uncompromising and unresponsive. The result was that he created some misunderstandings in the Viceroy's mind and Gandhi could not remove them. His mystic vein always throbbed in such a situation and even his close associates were baffled by it! Mahadev Desai and Devdas agreed on this point about Gandhi.[10] Lord Linlithgow thought that politics had made Gandhi vain and egoistical. Gandhi was to have met Jinnah in Delhi but he left Delhi without doing so.

AT THIS JUNCTURE Walchand Hirachand, who had been fighting with the Central Government for the expansion of Indian industries, wrote a letter to Sir Sivaswamy lyer in that matter and he sent a copy of his letter to Mahadev Desai on February 16, 1940, for Gandhi's perusal although Gandhi's views on large-scale industrial development were unfavourable. Gandhi had blessed the first Swadeshi venture, the mercantile shipping company launched by Walchand Hirachand and Narottam Morarjee. Both had helped Gandhi in his mission with money, Narottam Morarjee as well as his son Shantikumar with great devotion, reverence and patriotism, Walchand with practical generosity and nationalistic fervour. Their place in the hierarchy of Gandhi's friends was as high as that of Jamnalal Bajaj who was a pillar of the Gandhian movement. G. D. Birla's unending help in Gandhi's mission was solid and immense both in money and political negotiations in high circles. He was an emissary in secret-cum-open diplomacy as Gandhi's interpreter. At the instance of Walchand, Gandhi wrote in spite of his dislike of big industries, an article, "the Giant and the Dwarf" favouring Indian industrial ventures and Mahadev Desai also wrote defending the stand of the national industries. Immediately after this, Walchand contacted all members of the Working Committee, and as a result the Congress in April 1938 passed a resolution against British companies in India and particularly British expansion of industries with the added legend, "India Ltd."

In reply to Walchand's letter of February 16, 1940, Mahadev Desai said on February 25, 1940: "I know that Gandhiji could have done much for developing our merchant shipping and many other things. If he was industrial-minded and not rural-minded, it would have pleased many industrialists, but then Gandhiji would not have been the Gandhiji that he is."[11] And Mahadev Desai added that he himself wondered how long he could tread the difficult path with Gandhi.

From January 26, 1940, Segaon was renamed Sevagram.

Mahadev Desai wrote to Birla that it would have been better if it were named "Lunatic Asylum".[12] The Government recorded the change in name on March 5, 1940.

After spending the second week of February 1940 at Segaon, Gandhi visited Santineketan on his way to Malikananda. He was there for three days from February 17 to 19 and visited Tagore who requested him to take Santineketan under his protecting wing. Gandhi witnessed a play, *Chandrika*, at Santineketan. But the most important visit he paid was to his old friend Charles Freer Andrews on February 19, 1940. He sat by his bedside for a pretty long time. Andrews looked at "his Mohan" with deep affection. "Swaraj is coming, Mohan," he whispered. "I am quite reconciled to my illness,"[13] added the sage and wise Christian. Andrews died peacefully on April 5, 1940.

After meeting Andrews, Gandhi attended the meeting of the Gandhi Seva Sangh at Malikananda, opened the Khadi and Village Industries Exhibition, advised the Sangh to remain aloof from politics. The Sangh resolved to establish a small committee. It was here on February 20, 1940, that Gandhi made a will in favour of Navajivan granting it the copyright to his writings. At Srirampur on his way back to Calcutta, someone threw a shoe at him but it hit Mahadev Desai. From February 28 to March 1, Gandhi attended a Working Committee meeting at Patna. At one of the meetings he reported his talk with the Viceroy whom he had met on February 5.

For some years past, Gandhi had been criticized in some quarters and even among his disciples for his practice of putting his hands, while walking, on the shoulders of grown-up girls or women.[14] They said it offended their sense of decency and set a bad example. So, on September 12, 1935, he gave up the practice, expressing the hope that his renunciation would set right those who might have done the same thing, whether under the influence of his example or without it. But something in Gandhi revolted against the decision and he relapsed into it saying that if he did not walk with his hands on the shoulders of women his blood-pressure rose up!

In May 1936 Gandhi wrote some letters to Prema Kantak, a Maharashtrian disciple of his, discussing sex problems. He frankly said in one of his letters to her that one day while in Bombay an irrepressible desire came upon him to have sexual union when he was wide awake, and he experienced ejaculation. He had no intention of fulfilling his desire. There were occasions in his life when thousands of women, he added, were safe in his company. Certain women had passion, but God saved him and them. While in South Africa, he observed, he had wet dreams at intervals of a year, but in India he had them at intervals of a month.[15]

He described this Bombay incident to Dr. Mott in December 1936. "My darkest hour," said Gandhi, "was when I was in Bombay a few months ago. It was the hour of my temptation. Whilst I was asleep, I suddenly felt as though I wanted to see a woman. Well, a man who had tried to rise superior to the sex-instinct for nearly 40 years was bound to be intensely pained when he had this frightful experience. I ultimately conquered the feeling, but I was face to face with the blackest moment of my life and if I had succumbed to it, it would have meant my absolute undoing."

Gandhi was in Bombay in January 1936 and he referred to this experience in May 1936 as described above. At the age of 67 he confessed to this frightful experience.[16]

Gandhi could not successfully curb his sexual passion and it recoiled on him in many forms till the end of his life. His self-repression was not perfect. Passion lurked in his conduct and exposed him to caustic criticism. Stories about his sexual life were circulated in India and in England. Edward Thomson, British historian, was unreasonably blamed for it although Gandhi had been severely criticized in Maharashtra for his sexual life after the publication of Prema Kantak's book *Prasad Diksha*, in 1938. In his reply to his critics in *Harijan* of November 4, 1939, Gandhi said that he required Dr. Sushila Nayyar to give him massage and medicated bath, the two things for which she was the best qualified among those who surrounded him. Gandhi explained: "There is no privacy about these operations which took over 1½ hours and during which I often go off to sleep but during which I also transact business with Mahadev Desai, Pyarelal and other co-workers."

A high-placed Englishman, Gandhi added in his reply, had joined the chorus of criticism against him. He picked out Gandhi's freedom with women and showed up his saintliness as sinfulness. American journals, Gandhi added, indulged in cruel caricatures of him, and Mirabehn who used to look after him, was the target of their attack.

Gandhi said he wanted to be the mother of man, and so every woman at once became his sister or daughter. He slept in the Ashram, he added, surrounded by women, for they felt safe with him in every respect. "If I were sexually attracted towards women," he concluded, "I have courage enough, even at this time of life, to become a polygamist. I do not believe in free love—secret or open. Free open love I have looked upon as dog's love. Secret love is besides cowardly."[17]

But it is said that the happiest sex life is one that has no history. In this context, Gandhi stands no comparison to Christ, Buddha, Tilak or Mahatma Phooley.

There was a fresh criticism of Gandhi by a Muslim as the Mahatma assumed the role of a messenger of God. He said Gandhi was incapable of bringing to bear an open mind on anything, as he looked at and interpreted things in the light of his self-assumed principles.

Gandhi had declared to the whole world that the Voice (of God) whispered to him "Thou must go on a fast".[18] He had said: "I have imagined that God had chosen me as His instrument for presenting non-violence to India."[19] He now replied: "I have never claimed to be a messenger of God except in the sense in which all human beings are."

Gandhi left Sevagram (Segaon) on March 13 to attend the Ramgarh session of the Congress which was held on March 20, 1940, under the presidentship of Maulana Azad. The first thing Gandhi did on reaching Ramgarh was to send condolences to the bereaved family of Sir Michael O'Dwyer who was shot by Udham Singh on March 12, 1940, at a meeting in the Tudor Rooms of the famous Caxton Hall, London. The meeting was organized by the Royal Asian Society and the East India Association. Lord Zetland, who presided, was also injured along with other two eminent men, Lord Lamington and Sir Luis Dane.

A heavily-built ascetic young man, about thirty-seven years old, Udham Singh was in his boyhood a volunteer serving water at the historic meeting of Jallianwala Bagh in 1919. Later, an associate of Bhagat Singh, he had been brooding over the barbarous massacres perpetrated during the Governorship of Sir Michael O'Dwyer. The day of reckoning came after 21 years. Udham Singh openly declared that he had avenged the national wrongs and punished the culprit. Had he not done so, he added, it would have been a disgrace to the nation, and he had washed out the crime in blood by his deed!

Gandhi was always punctilious in condemning every non-Muslim revolutionary as an assassin, since he regarded him as misguided. It may be remembered that he had called the assassin of Shradhanand his "brother" Abdul Rashid, and thereafter he never condemned the Muslim murderers of Hindu leaders. Just as he said he was giving lessons to the Hindus alone in non-violence so also he applied his moral teaching to the Hindu revolutionaries alone, this time to a Sikh!

That as a teacher of non-violence, Gandhi should have regarded Udham Singh's act as an act of insanity was no wonder. Udham Singh's nonchalance in the court pained him, and Gandhi stated that the young man's action had harmed the non-violent struggle. He asked his readers to disassociate themselves in the secrecy of their hearts and also openly from such acts against humanity. The German press treated the act as a brave protest against British rule in India. On May 31, 1940, Udham Singh died bravely on the gallows.

THE RAMGARH SESSION at which was displayed a painting of a cow in front of the rostrum was in all respects a victory for Gandhi. Presiding over the session, Maulana Abul Kalam Azad declared: "We have now become an Indian nation, united and indivisible." But the Indian Muslims should not consider themselves a mere minority. So he cautiously added: "To imagine that they exist helplessly as a 'minority' is to delude oneself." He drew the attention of the Muslims to the fact that if British Baluchistan was added, there were five provinces in India with Muslim majorities. The question, he added, was not of population ratio but of the large numbers and the strength behind them![20] He said he was proud of Islam's splendid traditions and was unwilling to lose even the smallest part of that inheritance.

The printed English translation of the Maulana's Urdu speech was made by Nehru. Maulana Azad's speech indirectly suggesting that the Muslims were a nation was a solace to the Muslim Leaguers. Expressing his opinion on Azad's remark regarding the minorities, Sir Ali M. K. Dehlavi, leader of the Muslim League Party in the Bombay Assembly, observed: "There I must confess I was most agreeably surprised, and I am glad to discover that our lost brother the great Maulana is, after all, a Muslim at heart, and politically not only that but a Pan-Islamist. He has made an authoritative admission, as the duly elected and accredited President of the Congress, that the Muslims in India are a nation and not a minority."[21] The British press disposed of the speech in a short summary. The Congress demanded nothing short of independence, reiterated its confidence in the leadership of Gandhi, and also its demand for a constituent assembly based on adult suffrage.

The Ramgarh session over, India heard thundering cries for

Pakistan raised by the Muslim League in its resolution of March 26, 1940, at its Lahore session. The Muslim League declared "that the areas in which the Muslims are numerically in a majority, as in the North-Western and Eastern Zones of India should be grouped to constitute 'Independent States' in which the constituent units shall be autonomous and sovereign." What Azad cautiously indicated the Muslim League openly expressed.

Various theories are advanced about the origin of Pakistan. Sir Mohammed Iqbal in his presidential address to the Muslim League in 1930 had suggested that Punjab, N.W.F.P., Sind and Baluchistan be amalgamated into a State. Historically perhaps, the idea of Pakistan was derived from the Report of the Peel Commission appointed to settle the Jewish-Arab dispute in Palestine. The Peel Commission suggested partition of Palestine and went out of its way to suggest that the Hindu-Muslim question in India might be solved in the same way.[22]" A campaign had been launched in Cambridge in 1933 to spread the idea of Pakistan.

Gandhi now entered an important phase of his life's mission, and picked up the threads of Hindu-Muslim unity and launched a new policy of appeasement. The policy of compromise is different from the policy of appeasement. The latter always proves disastrous. The Muslims were against the idea of the Constituent Assembly, and somebody asked whether Gandhi would use British forces to compel them to submit to it. In reply, Gandhi said that whether Muslims were represented by the Muslim League or not, he hoped that their representatives would not think of cutting up India according to religions but regard India as an indivisible whole. "But if the hope is frustrated," assured Gandhi, "the Congress cannot forcibly resist the express will of the Muslims of India. Needless to say the Congress can never seek the assistance of British forces to resist the vivisection. It is the Muslims who will impose their will by force singly or with British assistance on an unresisting India. If I can carry the Congress with me, I would not put the Muslims to the trouble of using force. I would be ruled by them for it would still be Indian rule."[23]

As regards the Pakistan resolution of the Muslim League, Gandhi observed in *Harijan* of April 6, 1940: "The 'two nations' theory is an untruth. The vast majority of Muslims, of India are converts to Islam or are descendants of converts. They did not become a separate nation as soon as they became converts." He remembered how Jinnah's nationality was written on his face and in his manner and how Sir Mohamad Iqbal used to speak with pride of his Brahmanical descent. "Hindus and Muslims," Gandhi concluded, "are not two nations. Those whom God has made one, man will never be able to divide."

This was a reply to Jinnah who had now advocated the two-nation theory. In Jinnah's opinion, "the Hindus and Muslims have two different religious philosophies, social customs, literatures. They neither inter-marry nor inter-dine together and indeed they have two different civilizations which are based mainly on conflicting ideas and conceptions." A few days earlier Gandhi had told a Christian missionary how the moment a person in India turned Christian, he almost changed his nationality. "He gets a job and position," Gandhi explained, "which he could not have otherwise got. He adopts foreign dress and ways of living. He cuts himself off from his own people and begins to fancy himself a limb of the ruling class."

But Gandhi did not accept this conclusion in the case of Hindu converts to Islam who changed their ideals and ways of life, and looked to foreign Muslim nations with Pan-Islamic motives. That is why Dr. Ambedkar and Savarkar, Gandhi's two great contemporaries and leaders of thought, said that in India change of religion meant change of nationality. In fact conversion should not bring about this change, as a man can be a Muslim and an Indian, he can be a Christian and an Indian.

Gandhi was not prepared to face this bitter fact. In every country there are minorities but they never claim separate nationality, and they live under one government. It was Sir Sayed Ahmed who in 1882 "put forward a cogent demand for the separate representation of Muslims during the debate in the Imperial Legislative Council upon Ripon's proposal."[24] It was the Aga Khan who preached to the Muslims: "We must secure independent political recognition from the British as a nation within a nation."[25]

As a peace-maker, friend and brother of the Muslims, Gandhi gave Nawabzada Liaquat Ali Khan, the Muslim League leader, an assurance: "As a man of non-violence," he observed, "I cannot forcibly resist the proposed partition if the Muslims of India really insist upon it. But I can never be a willing party to the vivisection. I would employ every non-violent means to prevent it. For it means the undoing of centuries of work done by numberless Hindus and Muslims to live together as one nation. Partition means a patent untruth. My whole soul rebels against the idea that Hinduism and Islam present two antagonistic cultures and doctrines. To assent to such a doctrine is for me denial of God."[26] In the same issue of *Harijan* Gandhi observed: "The Khaksar menace is no menace in itself. As a symptom of a deeper disease it is a portent."

While answering an Englishman, Gandhi replied in *Harijan* of May 4, 1940: "I would any day prefer Muslim rule to British rule." "But supposing," Gandhi said in a prophetic vein, "the worst happened and we had a civil war, it would last for a few days and months and we would settle down to business." Gandhi did not explain how the Hindus should defend themselves during the civil war. He had drilled into the minds and ears of the Hindus for an unbroken period of twenty years his lessons in non-violence, even asking them to give up stout *lathis*.

Explaining his own position *vis-a-vias* Pakistan, Gandhi said in the same issue of *Harijan*: "The partition proposal had altered the face of the Hindu-Muslim problem. I have called it an untruth. There can be no compromise with it. At the same time I have said that, if the eight crores of Muslims desire it, no power on earth can prevent it, notwithstanding opposition, violent or non-violent." And he granted that "Pakistan cannot be worse than foreign domination." Was it an explanation of his stand or a direction for the Muslim leaders to draw up their plans?

In the meanwhile, the war took a serious turn. Russia gulped down the freedom of Finland on March 12, 1940, under the pretext of her own security and also absorbed Estonia, Lithuania and Latvia in July 1940. Towards the end of June, Hitler ran over France and the low countries of Holland and Belgium. With Hitler's rising domination of Europe, Mahadev Desai said in his letter to G. D. Birla, Hitler's stock with Gandhi was going up.[27] Gandhi thought that Britain had lost the war and was impatient enough to write a letter to Lord Linlithgow in which he said so. Mahadev Desai disapproved of his master's hasty action. In his letter to Linlithgow Gandhi said that Hitler was not a bad man and if they called the war off that day, Hitler would follow suit. Gandhi also offered his services to the British Cabinet to go to Germany and elsewhere.

Hitler's military ability and blitzkrieg might have dazzled Gandhi, since he was winning without causing much bloodshed!

ON MAY 10, 1940, Winston Churchill formed his Cabinet and Amery replaced Lord Zetland as Secretary of State for India.

It seemed now that the Tories would be more indifferent to the call of India than the previous government. In June, Subhas Bose and Rajagopalachari met Gandhi and discussed the Indian deadlock in relation to the war situation. Vallabhbhai Patel and Rajagopalachari wanted to offer co-operation to the British Government in their war effort provided it accepted the main Congress demand. So the Working Committee deserted Gandhi's leadership with great reluctance and declared at Wardha on June 21 its offer of co-operation to the British Government in respect of the war and "absolved Gandhi from the responsibility for the programme and activity which the Congress had to pursue under the conditions at present prevailing in India and the world in regard to external aggression and internal disorder".

The Congress leaders honestly declared that they were unable to extend the principle of non-violence to national defence. Non-violence was not their creed. It was a policy. For Gandhi it was a creed. Gandhi was left free to operate as a world teacher. He was happy because he could bear the strain of the break with his colleagues and unhappy because he had lost the power to carry them with him. The Socialists were enraged at the offer of co-operation to the British, and Jayaprakash wrote to Nehru expressing the view that Gandhi's support would, if not positively at least negatively, incline towards the traitors. He meant Rajagopalachari and Vallabhbhai Patel. After the meeting of the Working Committee, Gandhi explained his position and role sorrowfully to the joint meeting of his followers in the Gandhi Seva Sangh and Charkha Sangh and did much heart searching!

In March Gandhi had asked the Congress Committees to form themselves into Satyagrahi Committees. He declared that destroying rails, burning police stations, cutting telegraph wires and burning post-offices meant pure violence. He feared that the chances of non-violence being accepted as a principle of state policy were very slight. Although he knew that the Congress Governments had used police and military force to put down riots and disturbances he observed that he believed "that a state can be administered on a non-violent basis if the majority of the people are non-violent. So far as I know, India is the only country which has a possibility of being such a state". Gandhi's 'ifs' which once promised Swaraj in a year proved to be as formidable as ever.

Englishmen in general thought that non-violence was a cloak while Muslim Leaguers thought that civil disobedience was aimed at them more than at the British. Gandhi told a representative of the *New York Times* that if India became free he would play his part, though outside the official sphere, in building up the nation on a strictly non-violent basis.

Gandhi then began to operate as a world teacher. On July 2 he appealed to every Briton to fight Nazism without arms, with non-violent arms. He asked the Britishers to invite Hitler and Mussolini to occupy England by allowing British men, women and children to be slaughtered. He said his universal love prompted him to appeal to them. The Viceroy conveyed his letter to the British Government and replied that they were firmly resolved, to prosecute the war to a victorious conclusion. The Friends of Society and the Council of Christian Pacifists Groups of London jointly informed Gandhi that though few of them were fully prepared to stand up to it, to most Britons Gandhi's call was an invitation to save their lives by the surrender of the principles of liberty and justice that were dearer to them than life itself. Gandhi's indictment of Hitler that he had brutalized not only Germans but a large part of humanity must have pleased those pacifists and Friends of Society.

The Congress Working Committee met in Delhi on July 3 and announced their readiness to co-operate in the war if Britain would grant complete independence. It asked Britain to constitute a provisional national Government at the Centre commanding the confidence of the Central Legislature and of the Provincial Governments. Though Gandhi admitted that no question of external invasion had arisen in the past, he still stuck to his position. The framer of the Delhi resolution was Rajagopalachari who thought that Gandhi suffered from an obsession with ahimsa and his vision was blurred. Gandhi said Vallabhbhai Patel was Rajagopalachari's greatest prize. Gandhi was inwardly perturbed at the parting of the ways with his dearest colleague Sardar Patel. But he could not help opposing him. He appealed to Gujarat, hoping that "every Gujarati Congressite man and woman, will declare adherence to ahimsa and reassure the Sardar that they will not resort to violence".

Yet the Congress remained firm. And on 1 July 28 the All-India Congress Committee met at Poona and ratified by 95 votes to 47 the Delhi resolution and it went down in history as the Poona offer as also the sporting offer. The Socialists and Communists led by Yusuf Meher Ali bitterly opposed it, but Nehru strongly supported the old guard and saved the situation.

On July 31 Azad said at a press conference in Bombay that the Congress had tried to retain Gandhi's leadership. But it was not available in the next struggle and so Congress had to shoulder the responsibility of leadership.

Gandhi was told by his critics that the universal application of non-violence was virtually impossible and society had made very little progress towards it. Teachers like the Buddha had made some effort in that direction with little success in their lifetime. Ahimsa might be good enough to be the duty of an individual; for society it was good for nothing. Ahimsa would disappear with him. Gandhi said that Azad accepted ahimsa as a weapon against internal disturbances. It was true, he added, that Nehru had said "he would not hesitate to accept Swaraj if non-violence failed and it could be won by means of violence".

Stating that man has been speedily progressing towards ahimsa, Gandhi replied that man progressed from cannibalism to hunting and to agriculture. "Man," he observed, "has to progress towards ahimsa still further. Nothing in this world is static, everything is kinetic." But Gandhi had said a little earlier that he belonged to the tribe of Columbus and Stevenson who hoped against hopes in the face of heavy odds, and added that the days of miracles were not over.

Gandhi hoped that the Congress would retrace its step. He was sure of his position. So he observed: "I have not hesitated to advise those who think with me to leave the Congress. But this does not mean that they have to do so forthwith. It is enough if they are ready to retire when I decide upon the date."[28] This was how Gandhi functioned in the Congress!

Rajagopalachari's Poona offer could not move the Government. The Viceroy, however, declared on August 8 an expansion of his Executive Council and the establishment of a War Advisory Committee. He conceded the Congress demand for a Constituent Assembly to frame the Indian constitution which was to meet after the War was over. The moment, he observed, when the Commonwealth was engaged in a struggle for existence, was not one in which fundamentally constitutional changes could be decisively made. And to please Jinnah, the Viceroy added that the British Government would not accept any system of Indian Government whose authority was directly denied by large and powerful elements.

The Congress President refused to meet and to discuss the Viceroy's proposals. Jinnah opposed the Poona offer saying that it would be a permanent Hindu majority at the centre. He too turned down the August offer. The Hamlet in Jawaharlal Nehru swung between his loyalty to Gandhi and his distress over the fate of the democracies and of freedom in Europe. The Government answered by arresting hundreds of public workers and Congress leaders.

The Congress Working Committee rejected at its Wardha meeting, the Viceroy's August proposal. It declared that his statements and offers not only fell short of the Congress demands but were also would-be impediments to the evolution of a free and united India. The Working Committee met in Bombay and they discussed several of Gandhi's drafts of a resolution, and at last they came to an agreement on one of them. They resumed their allegiance to Gandhi. Nehru moved the resolution in the All-India Congress Committee meeting on September 15 and Sardar Patel seconded it. The resolution said that the intolerable situation created by the British Government had imposed upon the Congress a struggle and requested Gandhi to guide the Congress in the action that should be taken. It added that the Delhi resolution ratified at Poona had lapsed.

Gandhi rose to address the meeting. Though he spoke in firm and measured tones, there were trepidations and hesitations in his words. "The responsibility I am assuming," he said, "is perhaps the greatest I have ever assumed in my life. We have waited long enough. Now comes the moment when the virtue of waiting has become vice." He said he was going to see the Viceroy and he might have to face a blind wall. But if he failed, he added: "We shall be free to assert our right to carry on anti-war propaganda and take the consequences."

As regards the Hindu-Muslim problem, Gandhi said: "But there is a message I should like to reach the ears of every Mussalman. India cannot win independence if eight or more crores of Mussalmans are opposed to it. But I cannot believe that all of them are so opposed, until it is proved to me by the vote of every adult Mussalman. Let them declare that they want to have their political salvation apart from that of the Hindus. India is a poor country full of Hindus and Mussalmans and others staying in every corner of it. To divide it into two is worse than anarchy. It is vivisection which cannot be tolerated not because I am a Hindu, for I am speaking from this platform as representative of Hindus, Muslims, Parsis and all else. But I will say to them, 'vivisect me before you vivisect India'. You should not do what even the Moghuls who ruled over India for over two centuries, did not do."

Gandhi knew well that Rajagopalachari was the main target of criticism at this time. So he cautiously but hurriedly wrote that it was wrong to misjudge a public worker of Rajagopalachari's calibre. "But a nation," he observed, "may easily harm itself by misjudging its true servants and denying itself their services." They should guard, he concluded, against hard, hasty and uncharitable judgments. This thought did not occur to Gandhi when he disposed of Veer Nariman, Dr. Khare and Subhas Bose.

CHAPTER XLII

Quit India

Gandhi gave an interview to the representative of the *News Chronicle* justifying his stand and met the Viceroy at Simla on September 27 and 30, 1940, as the accredited guide and captain of the Congress. The Viceroy said that the action Gandhi proposed would amount not only to the inhibition of India's war efforts but to the embarrassment of Great Britain in the prosecution of the war which the Congress said they were anxious to avoid. Gandhi said the Congress wanted to make it clear that the vast majority of the people were not interested in the war effort. He had seen the Viceroy on June 29 at Simla and told him that there was a complete political break between him and the Congress. Under Churchill, the Tories were adamant and unmoved by Gandhi's appeals. They had suffered humiliating disasters and defeats and were prepared to face the non-violent revolt of the Congress.

While Gandhi was in Delhi on October 1, 1940, he sent with Mahadev Desai a letter to Tagore who was seriously ill and had moved from Santiniketan to Calcutta. On his way back to Wardha Gandhi met on the train Nawab Bahadur Yar Jung, President of the All-India States Muslim League. He asked the Mahatma some questions regarding the Hyderabad demand to restore its ceded territories. The Nawab said that Gandhi admitted the demand was just. Gandhi then wrote an article on Hyderabad in the *Harijan* of October 13, 1940, and said the discussion was academic. "If independence," Gandhi said, "is taken by force of arms, then the strongest power will hold sway over all India. And this may be Hyderabad for ought I know."

If there was anarchy in the land, Gandhi observed, he would try to still its flames with his tiny hands. "But if you ask me in advance," Gandhi, the unarmed prophet, added, "whether I would face anarchy in preference to foreign orderly rule, either British or any other, I would unhesitatingly plump for anarchy, say, the rule of the Nizam supported by Chiefs become feudatory to him or supported by the border Muslim tribes. In my estimation it will be cent per cent domestic. It will be home rule though far, far from self-rule or Swaraj."

Savarkar, the Hindu Mahasabha leader, severely pulled up Gandhi for this article. Gandhi did not imagine any of the Hindu princes of Gwalior, Baroda or Indore to be the head of the Government in the event of anarchy, but this great Indian leader dreamed of a Muslim emperor. Such was his bent of mind and psychological make-up! Savarkar said that it was a direct incitement to the Muslims to continue their Pakistani movement with greater force and strike in time to establish a Muslim empire in India. But Savarkar added that the Nizam would meet the fate of Batcha-i-Sakku of Afghanistan.

After three days' discussion from 11 to 13 November with the Working Committee, Gandhi declared that Vinoba Bhave, the Sanskrit scholar, perfect spinner, Guru of numerous disciples, believer in independence and abolition of untouchability, and an out-and-out war resister would start direct action to fight against the denial of the right of preaching against the participation in war. He himself was not participating in the god-guided struggle because his imprisonment would cause greater embarrassment to the Government. The next step, he said, God would make clear to him.

On October 17, Vinoba Bhave inaugurated individual civil disobedience at Paunar, a village near Wardha, and moved from village to village delivering anti-war speeches. He was arrested on October 21 and sentenced to three months' imprisonment.

Gandhi suspended the publication of *Harijan*, *Harijan Bandhu* and *Harijan Sevak* and wrote in the last issue of *Harijan* dated November 10 that he was doing so as "I cannot function freely if I have to send to the Press Adviser at New Delhi every line I write about satyagraha". The District Magistrate, Poona, had served this notice on the editor of *Harijan* on October 18, 1940. After the issue of October 20, the farewell number was published on November 10.

The second satyagrahi chosen by Gandhi for individual civil disobedience was Jawaharlal Nehru. When Nehru showed his readiness, Gandhi was overwhelmed with gratitude and wrote to him on October 24, 1940: "I know what strain you are bearing in giving me your loyalty. I prize it beyond measure."[1] Nehru met Gandhi on October 30 and on his return journey he was arrested at Chheoki on October 31, and was sentenced to four years' rigorous imprisonment. Brahmo Dutt and other representative satyagrahis were brought into the field. This group contained members of the Working Committee, the All-India Congress Committee and the legislatures. Vallabhbhai Patel, Sarojini Naidu and Maulana Azad were arrested. Vinoba Bhave was released in January 1941 and he was again arrested and sentenced on January 24, 1941.

The satyagrahis, if unarrested, were not to return home, but were to go on foot from village to village. They shouted: "It is wrong to help the British war effort with men and money. The only worthy effort is to resist all war with non-violent resistance." And yet the moral prophet in Gandhi claimed that the campaign was not intended to hamper the war effort. The British Government adopted different tactics this time. It advised its magistrates to impose fines on the satyagrahis instead of imprisonment. Gandhi assured the satyagrahis that when the struggle ended, immovable property was bound to be restored to the original owners, the satyagrahis. And when the rank and file were pushed into the arena, the Government attached little importance to these nonentities and imposed only fines on them without the option of imprisonment devaluing the electioneering importance of a prison sentence. Amery announced this in the House of Commons. The result was that Gandhi had to announce, Amery added, that the payment of fine would count as an equally meritorious sacrifice in the Congress hagiology. About 25,000 satyagrahis were either fined or imprisoned. The Indian States were kept out of the civil disobedience movement. Gandhi suspended satyagraha from December 25, 1940 to January 4, 1941, as a goodwill gesture for Christmas.

Gandhi was full of enthusiasm and was at Sevagram all the time guiding the movement. He held that it would be a long drawn struggle, but thought that "time is on our side and there is no question of losing the battle". Patel's health had deteriorated and Gandhi was worried on that count. In December 1940 Subhas Bose wrote to Gandhi expressing his readiness to join the struggle. Gandhi once thought that he had gained Subhas for all time as a son, but in his case he maintained the rift. Gandhi declined his offer. They differed. He felt Bose's way was wrong. On January 10, 1941, Bose again appealed to Gandhi to reconsider his request, but Gandhi flatly declined his offer to join the struggle. Bose then disappeared on January 17, 1941.

Gandhi paid a visit to Allahabad and performed the opening ceremony of the Kamala Nehru Hospital on February 28. He called on Tej Bahadur Sapru and Madan Mohan Malaviya on March 1 and Sapru met the Viceroy on March 7.

Sir Tej Bahadur Sapru convened a Non-Party Conference in Bombay on March 13 and 14, 1941, to solve the Indian deadlock. Prominent among those who attended the conference were Sir Jagdish Prasad, Sir N. N. Sirkar, Dr. Jayakar, Sir Chimanlal Setalvad, Lokanayak Aney, Veer Savarkar, Dr. Moonje and Dr. S. P. Mookerjee. Savarkar's valuable guidance and fine spirit, observed Sir Tej gratefully, saved the conference from a debacle. The conference, in order to solve the deadlock, demanded an immediate reconstruction of the Viceroy's Executive which then consisted of non-official Indians. It asked that a time-limit should be fixed within which India was to attain the same measure of freedom as was enjoyed by the Dominions. Leopold Amery said that the resolution was not practicable, and he took shelter under the fact that communal differences prevailed in the country. Thereupon Sapru said: "Mr. Amery is mortgaging our future with certain intractable leaders."

Jinnah opined that the Non-Party Conference was engineered by the Congress and the Hindu Mahasabha. Sapru considered the possibility of a joint meeting of Gandhi, Savarkar and Jinnah. But it did not come off. Jinnah declared in April 1941 at the Madras session of the Muslim League that the principle of Pakistan must be accepted first and then only would come the question of details. Previously he asked the Congress to accept the Muslim League as the sole representative of the Muslims. The second session of the Non-Party Conference met at Poona on July 26, 1941, and passed a resolution demanding a united India.

The military situation was growing extremely difficult for the Allies. When Nazi Germany invaded Russia on June 22, 1941, the Indian Communists, who had so far characterized the war as imperialistic, suddenly found that it had become a people's war. They now gave their willing co-operation to the British in the prosecution of the war. At this critical time, the Viceroy as promised in the August declaration, expanded his Executive Council by appointing eight Indians out of thirteen members who were responsible to the Viceroy and not to the

Legislature. He announced the formation of a National Defence Council which was merely advisory. Gandhi firmly stated that the announcement did not affect the stand taken by the Congress, nor did it meet the Congress demand. But Amery characterized it as a great step in advance.

There were riots in Ahmedabad and Dacca. In May 1941 Gandhi fasted for 72 hours because of the riots and again on June 29 for communal unity.

AT THIS TIME a controversy raged on the Atlantic Charter announced by the Allies on August 14, 1941. It stood for the sovereign rights and self-government of all nations. Although President Roosevelt stated that it applied to India also, Churchill declared on September 9, 1941 that it would not apply to India; it applied only to those countries which were then under the Nazi yoke. Thereupon Savarkar was the only Indian leader who cabled to Roosevelt asking him whether he played second fiddle to Churchill or to Churchill's dictation by words or silence.

Gandhi ignored this controversy. He said that his silence was more eloquent than any words. He had mourned the death of Tagore who died on August 8, 1941. An immortal Indian, Tagore was indeed a symbol of the universal love for which great Indians stood. About this time the Government published some documents which Jayaprakash Narayan wanted to smuggle from prison. Gandhi blamed Jayaprakash for his secret methods but justified the method as it was according to the accepted cannon of war.

Gandhi's birthday was celebrated all over India and a purse of Rs. 12,000 was presented to him. But all was not well with his movement.

Vallabhbhai Patel, Sarojini Naidu, Bhulabhai Desai, Rajagopalachari and Rajendra Prasad were released, the first three for reasons of health. Gandhi had written to Patel that he should never be released because of illness. Gandhi disclosed to the public that "those who were not whole-heartedly with the Bombay resolution have come out with their doubts confirmed". He had no doubt as to the correctness of the Bombay resolution. He could neither expand his movement into a mass movement for fear of embarrassment to the Government during the war, nor give up his individual civil disobedience. He asserted that to do so would be folly. But the movement had almost failed. So the Government released Nehru and Azad on December 3 and began to release the civil disobedience prisoners. Reacting to this, Gandhi said that it "did not evoke a single responsive or appreciative chord in him".

On December 7 Japan bombed Pearl Harbour and America declared war on Japan, Germany and Italy. Events moved fast. Gandhi felt that the Working Committee and the A.I.C.C. might now reverse the Bombay resolution. So he requested President Azad to convene a meeting of the Working Committee and the A.I.C.C. On December 8, 1941, Gandhi went to Bardoli to spend a month in the Sardar's ashram, and he stayed there till January 9, 1942. Towards the middle of December 1941 Gandhi issued a 25-page booklet giving detailed instructions, as usual, on his constructive programme for the achievement of independence and a programme for the students to follow. "If it makes no appeal to the Congressmen," Gandhi lamented, "I must be rejected. For my handling of civil disobedience without the constructive programme will be like a paralysed hand attempting to lift a person."

As the god-guided struggle had failed after nearly fourteen months, Gandhi felt that the interpretation he had put on the Bombay resolution was wrong. He opposed all wars while the Congress leaders' opposition to the war was not on the principle of non-violence. But this argument as well as the interpretation was old. It was more a pretext than the real reason. The fact was that Gandhi's movement had failed. And on December 30, 1941, the Working Committee met at Bardoli and, realizing that the situation warranted a change, reverted to the Bombay resolution, relieved Gandhi of his leadership and practically reverted to the "Poona offer" for a provisional national Government. It again offered co-operation in the defence of the country. But the deadlock continued.

The A.I.C.C. ratified the Bardoli resolution on January 15, 1942. Although Gandhi suffered defeat for the third time in his life as a leader, he told the A.I.C.C. frankly that the Bardoli resolution was undoubtedly a step backward though it reflected the Congress mind. It was a mirror in which all groups could see themselves. The Congress had not banged the door to negotiations on the impossible or unpolitical ground of nonviolence. Nehru's opposition to participation in the war effort was almost as strong as his.

As regards the reported differences between Nehru and him, Gandhi again said: "We have had differences from the moment we became co-workers, and yet I have said for some years and say now that not Rajaji but Jawaharlal will be my successor.

He says he does not understand my language, and that he speaks a language foreign to me. This may or may not be true. But language is no bar to a union of hearts. And I know this that when I am gone he will speak my language."[2]

Many non-Congress statesmen had disapproved of Gandhi's movement. Dr. Ambedkar asked Gandhi why he did not start civil disobedience immediately after the Defence of India Act had been passed a year earlier. The Congress campaign of select satyagraha had signally failed to achieve any practical objective; it had long ceased to attract attention. It was called off!

Gandhi suffered a reversal in the national struggle, but his role as a moral world teacher was undiminished. He wrote a second letter to Hitler on December 24, 1941, in which he said: "Many of your acts are monstrous and hence we cannot possibly wish success to your arms. We resist British imperialism no less than Nazism. Ours is an unarmed revolt against British rule. If not British," he observed, "some other power will certainly improve upon your method and beat you with your own weapon. If you attain success," Gandhi concluded, "it will not aprove that you were in the right."[3] From this letter it appears that Gandhi had suspended the struggle on December 24.

It may be noted here that Hitler was the target of Gandhi's writings and speeches, but he never criticized Stalin who had destroyed the freedom of several small democracies in Europe! Nehru, his adviser on world affairs, too, sometimes half-heartedly mentioned this tragedy, but neither criticized Russia for her cruel destruction of freedom and democracy!

From January 18, 1942, Gandhi started his *Harijan* as a 'Peace Organization'. Gandhi then started *Harijan* (Marathi) from March 1, 1942. On October 26, 1941, Jinnah had already started *Dawn*, a weekly, for the propagation of Pakistan.

Gandhi lost his valuable colleague Jamnalal Bajaj who died on February 11. Gandhi said that Bajaj had adopted him as his father. A pillar of Gandhism, he had established a Goseva Sangh and given himself up to cow-service! A fitting end to a patriotic businessman who moved from Tilak to Gandhi. In serving Gandhi devotedly, he had served the country. Gandhi lost temporarily another disciple. A Japanese monk, who was living at his Ashram, was arrested by the police. Gandhi repeated his prayer, "I bow to the Buddha."

After attacking Pearl Harbour on December 7, 1941, Japan sank on December 10 two mighty British warships H.M.S. *Prince of Wales* and H.M.S. *Repulse*. Hong Kong surrendered a fortnight later. The military situation for the Allies became grave in the Far East and it seemed that Japan would smash the Allied forces in the East. Thus there was a grave crisis in the war situation for the Allies in the East as well as in the West. On February 9, 1942, Madame and Generalissimo Chiang Kai-shek of China paid a historic visit to India. They were the royal guests of the Viceroy, but they had come to discuss the war with the Viceroy of India and if possible to persuade the Indian political forces to help the Allies unconditionally in the war. Singapore fell on February 15. Although Nehru was profoundly interested in China, he deeply regretted his inability to give a proper welcome to the distinguished visitors from that country.

Gandhi met Chiang Kai-shek and his wife Madame Mayling Soong Chiang in Birla's house at Calcutta on February 18. At the request of Gandhi the Chinese leader and his wife had an Indian meal at Birla's. Jinnah had met Chiang Kai-shek the previous day. Gandhi had a talk with the Chinese leader, but was not much impressed with him. After his visit to the Chinese leader and statesman, Gandhi wrote to Patel: "I would not say that I learned anything, and there was nothing we could teach him. All that he had to say was this: 'Be it as it may, help the British. They are better than the others and they will now become still better'."[4] Yet Gandhi presented him with yarn and takli. Gandhi and the Generalissimo tried to understand each other; Gandhi told him that God would give him proper guidance in case of an invasion. Chiang Kai-shek was originally a Buddhist and his wife a Christian. But after their marriage he embraced Christianity. Gandhi, who said that one should live and die in one's own religion, may not have liked Chiang's conversion to Christianity!

The Chinese leader fervently urged President Roosevelt to bring pressure on Churchill to seek a peaceful solution to the Indian problem. He himself tried his best to persuade both parties, Indians and the British Government, to see the need of a peaceful solution to their problems. He was frankly in sympathy with the aspirations of the people of India for freedom. But in his opinion, immediate British withdrawal from India was impractical. If Indians were drawn into Japan's arms, he feared there would ensue a permanent occupation of India by Japan. Such a development would be bad for Britain as well as for China. To his sorrow, the British suspected that he was helping the Indians in their struggle for freedom and the Indians suspected that he was helping the British Government against the Indian people.[5] It appears from the talks the British statesmen had with Chiang Kai-shek that Nehru was willing to accept Dominion Status on Chinese and American guarantees.

A. Harriman, Roosevelt's representative in England, met Churchill at the instance of President Roosevelt in regard to the Indian problem. Churchill told him that discussions were going on in England and in India for immediate action and for settling the future of the country. Churchill cabled to President Roosevelt stating that the British Government was earnestly considering "whether a declaration of Dominion Status after the war, carrying with it, if desired, the right to secede, should be made at this critical juncture". But he added that there were difficulties regarding the Muslims, the Princes and the Untouchables. On March 10 when Rangoon fell, Roosevelt insisted that a Provisional Government in India should be instituted and the danger of Japanese domination should be stressed together with the advantage of peaceful evolution as against chaotic revolution.

Accordingly, Churchill announced the Cripps Mission in Parliament on March 11, 1942. Cripps had joined the Cabinet on February 18, 1942. Sir Stafford Cripps was a statesman who had been partly responsible for roping in Russia to the side of the Allies. With his astute thinking and legal acumen he was known as a brilliant advocate and a front-rank British statesman. He was also well known for his sympathy with Indian aspirations and for his friendship with Nehru.

LORD PRIVY SEAL of Britain, Sir Stafford Cripps came to Delhi on March 23, 1942. According to his plans, he said there would be a national Government which would function as a cabinet, the Viceroy being the constitutional head. His scheme envisaged the creation of a new Indian union which would constitute a Dominion associated with the United Kingdom immediately after the cessation of hostilities. Secondly, the scheme granted the right to any province in British India that was not prepared to accept the new constitution framed by the constitution-making body, to retain its prevailing constitutional position, provision being made for its subsequent accession if it so desired.

Cripps interviewed in Delhi India's eminent leaders, Gandhi, Nehru, Maulana Azad, Jinnah, Savarkar, Dr. Ambedkar, Sapru and others. Gandhi, who met Cripps on April 27, described Cripps' proposals as "a post-dated cheque on a failing bank". He told Cripps that his document was an invitation to the

Muslims to create Pakistan. He admitted that the movement for Pakistan had grown tremendously in volume during the previous two years and added that it would have been better had he not come to India with a cut and dried scheme to impose upon India. "Why did you come," he asked Cripps, "if this is what you have to offer? I would advise you to take the first plane home."

It was a misfortune, Gandhi wrote later, that the bearer of the proposal should have been Sir Stafford Cripps. Gandhi's movement had failed. People must realize that no political reform or progress could come without his victory. Not the war situation but Gandhi could bring it about, his inner mind seemed to tell him.

Jawaharlal Nehru took a leading part in the negotiations and discussions, but the Britishers knew that whatever Nehru might say was useless since it would be Gandhi who would decide.[6] Gandhi's dislike of the Cripps' proposals definitely weighed with the Congress in its rejection of the scheme. That Gandhi asked the Congress leaders on the telephone to reject the scheme was not a fact.

The condition attached to the Cripps proposals, was bad enough. The political parties were to accept or reject the proposals *in toto*. Savarkar, who brilliantly turned the arguments of Cripps against him, rejected the scheme *in toto*. To him the first part was acceptable, but the second part conceding the right of separation to provinces was not. Jinnah rejected the proposal as the freedom of separation was neither full nor clear although he expressed his gratification at the possibility of Pakistan being recognized.

The Congress had accepted the scheme with its secession clause, but it strained at the gnat, the defence portfolio which was to remain in the hands of the British representative during the operation of the war. And while the list of subjects pertaining to the Defence portfolio was discussed, renewed and reconsidered, Sir Stafford backed out from his original position and no such list was offered. So the Congress, too, rejected the scheme.

Cripps wound up the discussions and returned to England on April 12. He then put the entire blame for the failure of his mission on Gandhi. This friend of India lost face in India, but he put a good face on it in England.

What Amery wrote to Lord Linlithgow, who was anxious to know the Cabinet reaction to Cripps' report, is interesting. He observed: "The answer is that there was no report and no reaction. Cripps prepared no sort of report for the Cabinet.[7] The Cripps Mission," Amery wrote, "had receded far into the back of Churchill's mind. For him, the main thing about it has been the good effect in America; for the rest, he is not interested, really disliking the whole problem as much as ever before."[8] Churchill, whose blind spot was India, had openly declared: "We mean to hold our own. I have not become His Majesty's First Minister to preside over the liquidation of the British Empire." He pulled up Cripps after the propaganda was done in America. Lord Linlithgow was very sensitive to American visitors and inquiries. It was Linlithgow's worry that Cripps conducted the talks independently of him and also that he did not pay sufficient respect to the members of his Executive Council. Both Cripps and Linlithgow were disturbed at the intervention of Col. Louis Johnson, President Roosevelt's personal envoy in India. Both Wavell, the Commander-in-Chief, and Linlithgow were against their power being reduced in this way.

Vallabhbhai Patel and Gandhi were working together at this time. They wanted to keep Nehru and Rajagopalachari in the background. Sardar Patel and Mahadev Desai had persuaded Gandhi to believe that Britain was sure to lose the war. Bhulabhai Desai later told Kanji Dwarkadas that Gandhi and Patel had miscalculated British and American strength and their will to win the war. Their miscalculations led to the rejection of the Cripps' offer.[9]

Cripps' proposals had a disastrous effect on Indian politicians who had been already affected by Dr. Ambedkar's *Thoughts on Pakistan* a year earlier. Every politician cited the principle of self-determination to another, forgetting that self-determination was given to a nation and not to a part thereof. In the heated atmosphere it was not impossible for leaders like Azad to thrust the poisonous pill of provincial self-determination down the throat of the Congress which stood for India's unity and indivisibility.

In Delhi, while the Congress leaders were negotiating with Cripps, the Congress passed a resolution early in April 1942 declaring that "the Congress could not think in terms of compelling the people of any territorial unit to join the Indian Union against their declared and established will". This was a prelude to Pakistan! Gandhi was not present when the resolution was passed but it only gave effect to his oft-repeated statements in regard to the will of the Muslims. The Congress historian and leader Dr. Pattabhi Sitaramayya had to hang the head and admit:

"It is evident that the passage concedes the division of India into more than one State and gives the go-by to the unity and integrity of India."[10]

Gandhi observed silence on this historic resolution. Savarkar alone asked the nation to note "the dangerous admission on the part of the Congress and its treacherous implications". He added that the Congress had stabbed at a stroke the unity and integrity of the Indian nation itself in the back.

Rajagopalachari, the Hindu defender of Pakistan, resigned from the Working Committee and moved at the Allahabad A.I.C.C. meeting on May 2, 1942, a resolution, which had been passed by the members of the Madras legislative party, recommending the right of separation of certain areas from united India after ascertaining the wishes of the people of such areas. Rajagopalachari's resolution was thrown out by 120 votes to 15.

Upon this some sensible patriots like Balu Jagat Narayan got the Akhand Hindustan (united India) resolution passed by the A.I.C.C. at the same (Allahabad) meeting of the A.I.C.C. In the Akhand Hindustan resolution the A.I.C.C. declared: "That (any proposal to disintegrate India by giving liberty to any component state or territorial unit to secede from the Indian union or Federation will be highly detrimental to the best interests of the people of different states and provinces and the country as a whole and the Congress therefore cannot agree to any such proposal". Mark the pious pledge of the Congress to United India! Gandhi was not present at the A.I.C.C. meeting.

Now the Working Committee brought itself to the stage of its notorious formula of "neither-reject-nor-accept". Upon this Dr. Sayyid Abdul Latif of Hyderabad asked Maulana Azad whether Jagat Narayan's resolution had in any way modified or affected the Delhi resolution of the Working Committee. Maulana Azad in his letter of August 6, 1942, replied: "No part of the Delhi resolution to which you refer has in any way been affected or modified by any subsequent resolution of the A.I.C.C."[11] To the same question of Dr. Latif, Jawaharlal Nehru also replied that Babu Jagat Narayan's "resolution does not in any way override the Delhi Working Committee resolution".[12] Another revealing feature of the Akhand Hindustan resolution was that all the Muslim members of the A.I.C.C. opposed it in the Allahabad meeting of the A.I.C.C. and issued a joint statement in regard to it.

Gandhi again expressed his opinion on the Hindu-Muslim issue which had become transformed into the Pakistan issue.

Gandhi said that there were two ways of solving it, the one was the royal way of non-violence; and the other was violence. So far as he could see, he wrote in *Harijan* of April 29, 1942, such preparations for violence were silently going on, on behalf of both parties. "I dare not contemplate the actuality. I should not like to be a living witness to it." A Muslim cited this opinion and asked Gandhi whether it was not an incitement to the Hindus. And the Hindu-minded nationalists and press said his writings were an incitement to the Muslims. But Gandhi replied that he had no special knowledge of the preparation for violence on behalf of the Hindus. He had to eat his words.

Rajagopalachari was furiously criticized for his pro-Pakistani stand and his public meetings were disturbed. Though Gandhi was not present at the Allahabad A.I.C.C. meeting, he felt sad about it and said Rajagopalachari deserved a respectful hearing as his motive was lofty. Fear of the Japanese occupation of India had blinded Rajagopalachari to the obvious truth. "I consider," Gandhi declared in *Harijan* of May 24, 1942, "the vivisection of India to be a sin. I cannot prevent my neighbour from committing sin. Shri Rajagopalchari would be party to the sin." And in *Harijan* of May 31, 1942, Gandhi held Rajagopalachari to be in the wrong. He himself wrote in it that "it should be enough to state the proposition that nothing can prevent the Muslim League from having it (the demand for separation) if the Muslims really want it. No third party," Gandhi concluded, "should decide our fate. It should be reason or the sword." And he had already said that "if I can carry the Congress with me, I would not put the Muslims to the trouble of using force".[13] The fact was that Rajagopalachari was doing his utmost by his propaganda to enable the Muslim League to translate Gandhi's proposition into action.

AFTER CRIPPS' DEPARTURE on April 12, 1942, Gandhi saw his opportunity. Before Cripps' arrival his civil disobedience struggle had ended in dark disappointment. The Congress influence with the masses had decreased greatly. The morale of the people was at a low ebb. Cripps' arrival raised their hopes, but their high expectations had ended in bitterness and frustration.

Gandhi was now seventy-three. He had been promising Swaraj in a year or in a day for the past twenty-three years. The

Congress High Command was divided. Gandhi felt he must save the Congress from internal disruption, unify it and regain the Congress hold on the people by turning their increasing bitterness and frustration against the British Government. "I waited and waited," he said desperately in *Harijan* of June 7, 1942, "until the country should develop the non-violent strength necessary to throw off the foreign yoke. But my attitude has now undergone a change. I feel that I cannot afford to wait. If I continue to wait, I might have to wait till doomsday. For the preparation that I have prayed for and worked for may never come, and in the meantime I may be enveloped and overwhelmed by the flames that threaten all of us. That is why I have decided that even at certain risks which are obviously involved I must ask the people to resist the slavery."

So he must do or die. The British must withdraw from India. In that direction his thoughts began to crystallize in the last week of April 1942.

Gandhi first expressed the idea of immediate British withdrawal from India in an article entitled "Foreign Soldiers in India" which he wrote on April 19, 1942. It was published in *Harijan* of April 26. Referring to the advent of foreign soldiers in India, Gandhi observed in his article: "If the British left India to her fate as they had to leave Singapore, non-violent India would not lose anything. Probably the Japanese would leave India alone. Whatever the consequences, therefore, to India, her real safety," he added, "and Britain's too lie in orderly and timely British withdrawal from India."

Gandhi, therefore, sent with Mirabehn a draft resolution on war for the consideration of the A.I.C.C. which met at Allahabad on April 30 and May 1, 1942. "Japan's quarrel," Gandhi said in the draft, "is not with India. She is warring against the British Empire. ... If India were freed her first step would probably be to negotiate with Japan." The draft assured Japan that India bore no enmity against her but should she attack India all Indians who looked to the Congress for guidance would be expected to offer non-violent, non-co-operation to the Japanese.

Commenting on this draft, Nehru said: "The whole thought and background of the draft is favouring Japan. It is Gandhiji's feeling that Japan and Germany will win. If Bapu's approach is accepted, we become passive partners of the Axis." But it was Rajagopalachari's statesmanship that showed amply the fallacy and illogicality of Gandhi's proposal. He said, "I do not agree that if Britain goes away India will have some scope for organizing itself even if Japan should make some headway. Japan will fill the vacuum created by the British withdrawal." The Gandhi draft revised by Rajendra Prasad was passed by a big majority. It was not acceptable to Nehru who prepared another draft resolution as requested by Azad. But it was rejected. President Azad again appealed to the Working Committee to accept Nehru's draft and Nehru' resolution was eventually passed.[14]

Japan had bombed Coconada and Vizagapatam on April 6, 1942. Evacuation of Madras and of towns on the eastern coast was carried out and there was panic from Madras to Calcutta. Mandalay was evacuated. Gandhi's theory of British withdrawal was developing. On May 3 he said in *Harijan*: "I feel convinced that the British presence is the incentive for the Japanese attack." In the next issue of *Harijan* he, therefore, demanded separation from British rule as the presence of the British in India was an invitation to Japan to invade India. "My answer now is," he asserted, "leave India to God, if that is too much, then leave her to anarchy."

As a non-violent fighter Gandhi did not like the scorched earth policy; for he said, "I see neither bravery nor sacrifice in destroying life or property for offence or defence." But so far he seemed to believe that as the Japanese thundered at the gates of India the British would come to terms as soon as his movement against them was started.

It was, however, on May 14 in his interview with the representative of the *News Chronicle*, London, that Gandhi admitted the possibility of Japan's invasion of India, despite the British withdrawal, to use her ports for strategic purposes. In that case, he said, he would ask the people to offer non-violent non-co-operation to the Japanese. The realists were warning him against his dangerous and futile policy. Till this time, Gandhi had thought his supreme act would be to make the British vacate India with all the allied troops. He was preparing the ground for this. But in the latter part of June he realized his blunder and the danger of Japanese invasion and said: "For Britain's defeat in Indian waters may mean only the loss of India but if Japan wins, India loses everything."[15] He changed his attitude and he said Free India would allow allied troops to operate from India.

Gandhi argued for eight days with the Working Committee and finally at its meeting on July 14 it declared that the Congress was agreeable to the stationing of the armed forces of the Allies in India, should they so desire it, in order to ward off and resist

Japanese or other aggression, and to protect and to help China. This was how Gandhi brought the division in the Working Committee to an end. But this was a strange solution. It implied that the civil Government would be in the hands of Indians, and there would be some form of British military rule over India, a remedy worse than the disease.

It was given to Rajagopalachari again to expose the fallacy in Gandhi's stand. In a letter to Gandhi Rajagopalachari said: "Your proposal that while the civil power may be withdrawn the British and Allied forces may continue in India in anticipation of a treaty with a problematical provisional Indian Government will only lead to the exercise of all Government functions by the military forces. This will happen if only for their own safety and effective functioning. They are further likely to be urged towards this step by local chieftains and suffering people. This would be the reinstallation of the British Government in a worse form." But Gandhi said he believed in Britain's honesty! Referring to this resolution, Savarkar, too, said that the stand that 'Quit India but keep your army here' was tomfoolery!

During the Cripps Mission the Congress leaders broke off their negotiations over details of the defence portfolio, when they were offered a provisional national Government. Meantime, early in July 1942 the Viceroy expanded his Executive Council by appointing men like Dr. Ambedkar, Sir C. P. Ramaswami Aiyer, Sir J. P. Srivastava and Sir Jogendra Singh making the strength of the Indian members eight out of thirteen.

At this juncture Gandhi cautiously but definitely made an announcement that if Subhas Bose brought in German troops to oust the British in India, "his performance can only fling India from the frying pan into the fire".[16] He replied to Edgar Snow that Free India would make common cause with the Allies.

On June 14 Gandhi wrote a letter to Chiang Kai-shek wishing him success and promising that he would not take any hasty step that would injure the interests of China. "I look forward to a day," Gandhi said, "when a free India and a free China will co-operate together in friendship and brotherhood for their own good and for the good of Asia and the world." On the eve of the August revolution, Gandhi warned the Japanese that they would have no willing welcome and added that "we are in a better position of having to resist an imperialism that we detest no less than yours and Nazism." And he expressed his hope that without World Federation and brotherhood there could be no hope for humanity.

Gandhi told a representative of the *News Chronicle* that the movement would be his biggest, but he would stand against a sudden outburst of anarchy or a state of things which might be calculated to invite Japanese aggression. However, he held it to be legitimate to make the Allied Powers responsible for all that might happen in India.[17]

Gandhi was in a state of severe fatigue at this time and the doctors advised him rest and to move to a cooler place. He replied to the B.B.C. representative who asked how he hoped to lead the impending movement if he was ill and bedridden. His view was that so long as his reason was unhampered, physical illness was no bar to the conduct of a non-violent struggle. His messengers were secretly sent to interpret his mind to the Viceroy, Amrit Kaur in May 1942, and Mirabehn in July 1942 after the Wardha resolution of July 14 was passed. The Viceroy gave an interview to Amrit Kaur but found it a barren business and refused to see Mirabehn. G. D. Birla too tried to meet the Viceroy but failed.

But Gandhi could not launch his movement without some gestures towards Jinnah. He made them but Jinnah said Pakistan was an article of faith with Muslim India and "we depend upon nobody except ourselves for the achievement of our goal." Gandhi replied to Jinnah that they should first restore the original Hindustan by removing Englishtan and then adjust all rival claims. "It may be," he concluded, "one Hindustan or many Pakistans." But a few days later, writing on the Rashtriya Seva Sangh, he said: "Free India will be no Hindu Raj. It will be Indian Raj."[18] Appealing also to the Princes, Gandhi said that if they made common cause with the nation "they can run the risk of dispossession, but they lose nothing by being liberal".

The world democratic press criticized Gandhi for his contemplated move. Even the *Daily Herald* of England and the Labour Party did so. To the Americans Gandhi said that he wanted them to look upon the immediate recognition of India's independence as a war measure of first class magnitude. His prayerful search, he added, gave him the revealing maxim, "Truth is God, instead of God is Truth". In July 1942 he had sent a letter to Roosevelt through Louis Fischer who stayed with him for a week at Sevagram. In it he asked for the withdrawal of British power, keeping the Allied troops at their own expense.

IT WAS IN his article "To American Friends" which he wrote on his way to Bombay on August 3, 1942, that he first used the slogan "Quit India" which resounded throughout the world. Shantikumar Morarjee, an unfailing devotee of Gandhi, writes in his book, *Gandhijinchya Athavani* (Marathi) that there was some discussion on what should be the correct phrase or slogan to describe the movement. And so when Yusuf Meherally who had come to see and present Gandhi with a badge on which the words 'Quit India' were carved, Gandhi at once said, 'Amen!' and used the slogan in the article which he wrote on August 3.

The Working Committee met in Bombay at Gowalia Tank in the first week of August 1942 and the All-India Congress Committee on August 7 and 8. The All-India Congress Committee ratified the Working Committee resolution of July 14. Some amendments were moved to the main resolution on war and withdrawal of British rule, but they were either withdrawn or defeated, the main resolution being opposed by 23 communist members. Gandhi, Nehru and Azad spoke on this historic occasion.

The main resolution, *inter alia*, said: "The committee approves of and endorses that resolution and is of the opinion that events subsequent to it have given it further justification, and have made it clear that the immediate ending of British rule in India is an urgent necessity, both for the sake of India and for the success of the cause of the United Nations."

"On the declaration of India's Independence" the resolution continued, "a provisional Government would be formed and a Free India will be an ally of the United Nations." Its primary function must be to defend India and resist aggression, "with all the armed as well as the non-violent forces at its command". It envisaged a federal constitution with the largest measure of autonomy for the federating units, and with the residuary powers vested in these units. The freedom of India must be the symbol of and prelude to the freedom of all other Asiatic nations under foreign domination. Burma, Malaya, Indo-China, the Dutch Indies, Iran, Iraq must also attain complete freedom.

The resolution was passed by the A.I.C.C. on August 7, 1942. Gandhi made a magnificent speech on August 8, 1942, on this momentous occasion in the life of the nation and in the last phase of his own life. The resolution had the strength of India's greatest man of the century and the spirit of the great internationalist Nehru whose portrait was put up with those of Roosevelt, Stalin and Churchill at Trafalgar Square.

Gandhi first referred to the Hindu-Muslim problem and told

the anxious audience how in his school days he had specially cultivated friendships with Muslim and Parsi co-students, how Muslims and Parsis were his colleagues and helped him in his South Africa struggle, and how he had on his arrival in India unconditionally helped the Khilafat movement.

If the Congress has incurred the wrath of the Qaid-e-Azam, Gandhi said, it was because the canker of suspicion had entered his heart. Gandhi prayed for his long life and declared that he had never betrayed Muslim interests. Muslims were free to put an end to his life whenever they wished to do so. Assaults had been made on his life in the past, but God had spared him till then, and the assailants had repented for their action.

As regards the Muslim demand for Pakistan, Gandhi said that to demand the vivisection of a living organism was to ask for its very life. The Congress could not be party to such a fratricidal war. Dr. Moonje. and Savarkar who believed in the doctrine of the sword might "seek to keep the Mussalmans under Hindu domination'. If such a warfare was to be India's lot, he would not live to witness it. Millions of Mussalmans in this country, he stated, came from Hindu stock, their Homeland was India.

Gandhi observed that he could not sit silent at this supreme hour. His *mantra* was: "We shall do or die. We shall either free India, or die in the attempt. He who loses his life gains it; he who will seek to save it shall lose it. Freedom is not for the coward or the faint-hearted. Every one of you," he proceeded, "should from this moment onwards, consider yourself a free man or woman and act as if you are free and no longer under the heel of this imperialism." Gandhi warned the princes that if they would act while he was alive they would occupy an honourable place in Free India. In Jawaharlal's scheme of Free India no privileges or privileged classes had a place, as Nehru considered all property to be state-owned, he added.

Speaking of the nature of the movement, Gandhi said that it was an open rebellion, and in such a struggle secrecy was a sin. Government servants and soldiers should act like the late Justice Ranade who openly told the Government that he belonged to the Congress. He always controlled his speech and pen, Gandhi continued, but on that day the occasion had come when he had to unburden his heart before them. Gandhi then spoke in English: "I have no weapon but love to wield any authority over anyone." He said that he sported a stick as he walked, but such a cripple was called upon to bear that greatest burden. He had forfeited his credit during the past few weeks with a large number of his friends. Gandhi claimed that he enjoyed the friendship of Lord Linlithgow.

Gandhi concluded his speech by saying that although he might have forfeited the regard and love of his friends in the West, he must not suppress the voice within him, which might be called conscience or the prompting of his inner basic nature. He had known humanity and had studied something of psychology though he had not read many books on it. "Believe me, friends," he said, "I am not anxious to die. I want to live my full span of life. According to me, it is 120 years at least."

Referring to England and America, Gandhi said that they were free countries: "They were free in their fashion, free to hold in bondage coloured races of the earth." And he hoped that they would broaden the interpretation of freedom. He said that although Chiang Kai-shek was inscrutable to him, he had not said till that day that India was wrong in demanding her freedom.

"I have therefore pledged the Congress," he concluded, "and the Congress has pledged herself that she will do or die."

After this momentous meeting, leaders returned to their respective lodgings. Gandhi returned to Birla House. He told the press that he had contemplated an interval between the passing of the resolution and the starting of the struggle. The Congress had consented to the military operations of the Allied armies. On the previous day he had placed his instructions marked "confidential" before the Congress Working Committee. What was confidential might not be secret. These instructions dealt with the observance of hartals, fasts, prayers and processions. Every Congressman was his own leader and every Indian a freedom fighter. Students above sixteen years of age should come out of schools and colleges. Payment of land tax should be refused, salt should be manufactured and the penalty against its manufacture be faced. On August 8 he had written to Jinnah[19] and to a Muslim businessman in Bombay that he had no objection to Britain handing over power to the Muslim League subject to certain provisos. The Working Committee was to have met on the morning of August 9 in Bombay. But the Government had published a statement on August 8 accepting the challenge of the Congress resolution of August 7.

Rumours were thick in the air that the arrest of Congress leaders was imminent Gandhi was so sure of his freedom that he told Mahadev Desai that considering his last night's speech they would not arrest him. But his conjecture proved wrong. On Sunday August 9, Gandhi woke up at four in the morning for his prayers. The Police Commissioner knocked at the gate of Birla House and said he wanted to see Gandhi's secretary. Gandhi was about to proceed with his daily routine after prayers. The Police Commissioner told Mahadev Desai that he had warrants of arrest and detention, under the Defence of India Rules, for Gandhi, Mahadev Desai and Mirabehn (Miss Slade). Pyarelal and Mrs. Gandhi were exempted but were told that they were allowed to accompany Gandhi under the same terms which they refused. Simultaneously, wholesale arrests were made of leading Congressmen all over India.

All telephones connected with Birla House, the Bombay Congress House and the important newspapers and agencies were cut. Gandhi was given an hour to get ready. He had his breakfast of goat milk and fruit juice as usual. His favourite hymn, *Vaishnav Jana*, was then sung by his party and the members of the Birla family. Verses from the Koran were recited by a Muslim Ashramite, Amtalsalaam. Gandhi then left with a few articles including his Gita, the Ashram Book, the Koran, an Urdu Primer and his *Dhanush-Takli* for spinning. Before he entered the car he was garlanded and auspicious kum-kum marks were put on his forehead by Mrs. G. D. Birla, his hostess. G. D. Birla requested him not to be in a hurry to go on a fast. R. D. Birla, G. D. Birla and other members of the family then bade farewell to Gandhi and he left smiling as usual, accompanied by Mirabehn and the Police Commissioner in the front car and Mahadev Desai following in another car.

Gandhi's last message was: "Every man is free to go the fullest length under ahimsa by complete deadlock, strikes and all other non-violent means. Satyagrahis should go out to die and not to live. It is only when individuals go out to seek and face death that the nation will survive. *Karenge ya marenge*—we shall do or die."

A special train carried Gandhi and the members of the Working Committee. On the way, Nehru asked Gandhi why secrecy was incompatible with ahimsa. Gandhi, tired and silent, said Nehru was free to interpret it in his own way! The leaders were lodged in Ahmednagar castle and Gandhi with his party was interned in the Aga Khan Palace at Poona. The Government had given up its earlier plan to intern Gandhi at Aden and to deport the leaders to Uganda. Later Kasturba Gandhi, too, joined the company on her arrest in an attempt to address a meeting at Shivaji Park in Bombay.

On August 2 while explaining the stand of the Hindu Mahasabha at Poona, Savarkar had offered, co-operation to the

Congress in the struggle provided it promised to stand irrevocably by the unity and integrity of the nation and would accept Hindi as the national language. But Savarkar expressed his fear that the Quit India movement would end in a Split India movement. Besides, he wanted a pre-planned revolution which would be successful, with the backing of the Army. Dr. Ambedkar despaired of it and described the all-out, open rebellion as both irresponsible and insane, showing bankruptcy of statesmanship when the barbarians were at the gates of India. He said the old man Gandhi was in a hurry. Jinnah had warned the Muslims to keep aloof from the struggle of the Congress. Sir Tej Bahadur declared that none had the right to gamble with the lives and safety of 400 million people and he suggested that Gandhi, Jinnah, Savarkar and other party leaders should meet in conference and come to a settlement for the period of the war.

CHAPTER XLIII

Split India

HARDLY HAD GANDHI been a week in the Aga Khan Palace when profound grief overtook him. He lost his secretary Mahadev Desai who was more than a son to him. Mahadev Desai died of a heart attack on August 15. The old sage stood by his bedside lamenting, "Mahadev! Mahadev!" Mahadev Desai was an incarnation of self-effacing devotion. Overwhelmed with grief, Gandhi said Mahadev had died a yogi's and a patriot's death. Gandhi performed the funeral rites himself. He was cremated in the compound of the Aga Khan Palace. Gandhi followed the body, a staff in one hand and a pot of fire in the other. He lighted the funeral pyre. Gandhi said gravely, ''Mahadev has lived up to the Do or Die *mantra*." Morning and evening Gandhi visited Mahadev's samadhi.

The open rebellion or the unarmed revolt became what Gandhi wanted it to be, a short and swift one. Gandhi had said: "It will include all that a mass movement can include. I don't want rioting as a direct result. If in spite of all precautions rioting takes place, it cannot be helped. I am not going to court imprisonment. The struggle does not involve courting imprisonment."[1] Gandhi's *Harijan* dated August 23, 1942, went further, although Gandhi was not responsible for it. "Cutting of wires," it advised, "removing rails, destroying small bridges cannot be objected to in a struggle like this."

The Congress was outlawed. As a result of the national leaders' arrests, popular discontent, mass disturbances and rigorous suppression by the British Government, the country was thrown into a turmoil. The Congress underground workers and volunteers burnt down about 500 post offices, some 250 railway stations and 150 police stations. Telegraph, railway and telephone wires were cut. Rails were removed and a few small bridges were blown up by young men actuated by patriotic motives. The workers of the Tata lron and Steel Works, one of the most important companies in India, struck work. Thus the August revolution ended, as all Gandhian non-violent mass movements had done previously in violent disorders. By the end of 1942, sixty thousand two hundred and twenty-nine persons had been arrested, 18,000 were detained, 940 were killed by police firing and 1,610 were injured by military or police firing.[2]

Well had Dr. Ambedkar said in 1930: "The civil disobedience movement is a movement of mass action; its essence is coercion; it is a method of stampede, which if carried on a sufficiently large scale, is bound to end in a revolt." There was no planning and the movement was ill-directed. It was Gandhi's dictum that "a struggle which has to be planned is not a righteous struggle. God himself plans and campaigns and conducts battle!" So the 1942 movement was not planned, and God did not provide the plan either. It failed after colossal sacrifices of valiant men who literally fulfilled the message "Do or die". This was the third time that Gandhi's non-violent mass movement ended in violence and failed. Delhi was far away, at the long distance of five years.

The movement was over by the end of September 1942. But during the first two months it burst like a volcano in non-Muslim majority provinces. The Muslims had scrupulously kept away from it. The tempo, the spirit and the disaster were so colossal that the Viceroy wrote on August 31, 1942, to Amery. "I am engaged here in meeting by far the most serious rebellion since that of 1857, the gravity and extent of which we have so far concealed from the world for reasons of military security."[3] And on September 21, 1942, the Viceroy wrote to Amery: "I think we can be pretty well content with the general situation in the country, taken as a whole things are pretty comfortable."

In an inspiring message, Jayaprakash Narayan, one of the foremost leaders of the August revolution, said: "The rebellion, no doubt, seems to have been suppressed for the moment. After the first phase of the Rising was over, there was no further programme placed before the people." He said that patriotic workers were justified in fighting Britain with arms. If that did not accord with Gandhi's principles it was not their fault, and added, "then there is our work in the Indian Army and the services".[4] Jayaprakasn Narayan seemed to have realized

Savarkar's thesis that no revolution succeeds without the backing of the army.

The Muslim League did not show sympathy for the great patriotic sacrifices of the people and the deaths of the heroes. Savarkar sympathised with them in their sufferings and sacrifices and condemned the measures adopted by the Government to quell the disturbances. He warned the Government that nothing but an immediate proclamation by the British Government granting India the status of a free and equal partner would solve the problem.

After his internment, Gandhi opened correspondence with the Governor of Bombay, Sir Roger Lumley, asking for Sardar Patel's transfer to his ward and complaining about the manhandling of a fellow-prisoner. He blamed the Government for precipitating the crisis on the eve of the struggle. It was a fact that after the passing of the resolution, Gandhi had expressed his intention of seeking an interview with the Viceroy although he had declared on the eve of the A.I.C.C. session that there was no room for negotiations in the proposal for withdrawal.

The fact was that Gandhi as Congress general, who never foresaw the action of the other side, since his movement was god-guided, was forestalled by the British Viceroy. And in his letter of August 14 to the Viceroy he pleaded now for a reconsideration of the Government's policy. "Do not disregard," Gandhi pitifully said, "this pleading of one who claims to be sincere friend of the British people. Heaven guide you!" The Viceroy's reply was an emphatic "No".

On His Internment in the Aga Khan Palace, Gandhi was given newspapers to read. It seems he observed silence from August 20 to 24. The Government had stopped him going to visit the place where Mahadev Desai was cremated. The prohibition on his visit to that place continued till September 5. Gandhi took for the first time, after thirty years, icecream prepared from goat's milk on September 26 and his 74th birthday was celebrated privately by the Jail Superintendent who presented him with a garland of 74 one-rupee notes.

Churchill wanted to crush Gandhism and all it stood for and so the Navajivan Press was seized and old and new numbers of *Harijan* since 1933 were confiscated and destroyed by the District Magistrate of Ahmedabad. On inquiry from Gandhi, the Government replied that the District Magistrate was asked to destroy all objectionable literature from the Navajivan Press such as books and leaflets but he had destroyed all numbers of the *Harijan* blindly or out of excess zeal.

Gandhi now opened correspondence with the Government. On September 26, 1942, Gandhi informed the Government that he felt that the Congress was not responsible for the destruction that had taken place. So the only right course for the Government seemed to him to be to release the Congress leaders, to withdraw all repressive measures and to explore ways and means of conciliation. Government's response was merely an acknowledgement of his letter. So Gandhi wrote a personal letter to the Viceroy, Lord Linlithgow, on December 31, 1942, saying, "I seem to be the *fons et origo* of all the evil imputed to the Congress." He had given himself six months, which period was drawing to a close, and with it his patience too. Just then Prof. Bhansali had gone on a fast over the excesses committed by the police and the military at Chimur. Gandhi wanted to contact Bhansali by telegraph and if possible to dissuade him from continuing the fast. Government did not allow him to do so. He referred to that point in his letter and added: "Have I so much fallen from grace that I could not establish contact with a dying friend?"

And giving a threat that as a satyagrahi in such moments of trial he would crucify the flesh by fasting, he asked the Viceroy to convince him of his error or errors and he would make ample amends. With this threat he ended his letter, wishing that the new year might bring peace to all.

Lord Linlithgow replied in his letter of January 13, 1943, that in the light of what had happened Gandhi should let him know whether he wished to retrace his steps and dissociate himself from the policy of the previous summer. On January 17, 1943, Gandhi replied that if his letter was a growl against the Viceroy, the latter's was a counter growl, and added: "Of course I deplore the happenings which have taken place since 9th August last. But have I not laid the whole blame for them at the door of the Government of India?" He might be able to make a positive suggestion if he was put among the members of the Working Committee and if he was convinced of his errors he need not consult anybody to make a full and open confession, and also to make ample amends.

The Viceroy said that the Government held the Congress and Gandhi responsible for the sad campaign of violence, crime and revolutionary activity. He would consider the matter further, he added, if Gandhi repudiated or dissociated himself from the resolution of 9th August and the policy advocated in it. So, on

January 29, 1943, Gandhi wrote to the Viceroy that he would undertake a fast for 21 days ending on the morning of March 2, as he could not get soothing balm for his pain. This time he would add juices of citrus fruit to make water drinkable, for his wish was not to fast unto death. On February 5, the Viceroy sharply called the fast a coercion, regarding it as an attempt to find an easy way out, and added that he considered a fast for political purposes a form of blackmail (*himsa*) for which there could be no moral justification.[5]

It was indeed nothing but a tactical move on Gandhi's part, not blackmail, to secure his release. For a politician it was justifiable, though in the ultimate analysis it might imply the interpretation the Viceroy put on it. But in the words of General Smuts, to accuse Gandhi of being a fifth columnist was dire perversity!

The British War Cabinet had discussed the likely threat of a fast in the event of Gandhi's arrest. The Indian Government had contemplated Gandhi's release "as soon as his life is in danger to avoid possibility of his death as a prisoner". But the British War Cabinet instructed the Indian Government that "Gandhi must continue in detention whatever the consequences".

So the Government discovered a middle course. It showed readiness to set Gandhi at liberty for the purpose and duration of his fast; but if he did not wish to take advantage of the offer he would fast at his own risk. Upon this Gandhi said on February 7 that he felt hurt that the Viceroy whom he called a friend should have imputed a base and cowardly motive to him. If he did not survive the ordeal he would go to the Judgment Seat with the fullest faith in his innocence. On February 8, Gandhi informed the Additional Secretary Sir Richard Tottenham that he would be quite content to go on fast as a detenu or prisoner. The impending fast had not been conceived to be undergone as a free man. "If I am released," he continued, "there will be no fast in terms of correspondence above mentioned. I have," he concluded, "no desire to be released under false pretences." And he started his fast on February 10, 1943.

Government recognized its grave responsibility. In order to ward off the possible danger arising out of the fast, it published the whole correspondence on February 12. And three days after the commencement of the fast, they kept ready a pamphlet entitled, "Congress Responsibility for the Disturbances 1942-43".

With the news of the fast the whole nation was rocked to its foundations. The Indian political sky was filled with cries of

"Release Congress leaders". But the British Government remained adamant on the issue of Gandhi's release. The Non-Party leaders under the presidentship of Sir Tej Bahadur Sapru met in conference on February 19, 1943, in Bombay, and appealed to Government to release Gandhi unconditionally. Savarkar, the President of the Hindu Mahasabha, said that Gandhi's life was a national asset, national property, and so Gandhi should break his fast in the interest of the nation instead of making the nation's leaders appeal to the alien and unsympathetic rulers. But Savarkar warned that Gandhi's fast should not be expected to bring about constitutional changes, as he rightly sensed that such a move would result in a threat to the integrity of the nation.[6]

N. C. Kelkar, the veteran writer and politician, said that Gandhi should be released unconditionally, but he also expressed a fear: "It would be a misfortune, however, if he used his release to go plump into Mr. Jinnah's arms in the ephemeral interest of the formation of a national Government as visualized by Mr. Rajagopalachari."[7] Savarkar and Kelkar knew Gandhi well and their forecast about his possible actions proved correct.

It should be noted here that Rajagopalachari met Gandhi in the Aga Khan Palace during his fast[8] and he blessed the scheme adopted by Rajagopalachari. Soon after Rajagopalachari offered it to Jinnah who did not pay much attention to it at that stage, in April 1943. This scheme or formula was nothing but the proposals offered by the Muslim League to the special committee appointed by the Hindu Mahasabha to negotiate with the principal political parties and to mobilise public opinion in support of the national demand. Maheshwar Dayal, the General Secretary of the Hindu Mahasabha, had given a copy of the League proposals to Rajagopalachari at Sir Tej Bahadur Sapru's in December 1942 when they met in conference.

The fast had another effect upon the politicians. Three Executive Councillors, H. P. Mody, N. R. Sarkar and M. S. Aney resigned from the Executive Council under political pressure and their resignations produced a faint smile on the face of the Mahatma. Dr. Ambedkar, the depressed class leader, and J. P. Srivastava of Hindu Mahasabha refused to resign under pressure. The crafty politician, Rajagopalachari, kept Gandhi's approval of his scheme a secret. Neither did the Mahatma reveal it to anybody. He was conceiving Pakistan.

The fast to capacity continued on February 10, 1943. Dr. Gilder, who was a detenu in Yeravda Jail, was brought to the Aga Khan Palace, and Dr. Bidhan Chandra Roy came to Poona on February 15 to attend on Gandhi. Numerous appeals were made to Amery and Churchill for the release of Gandhi, but to no avail. On February 21 Gandhi was seized with nausea, he almost fainted and his pulse became imperceptible. Sentries were kept at the gate of the Aga Khan Palace to ward off journalists coming from all parts of the country and also from foreign countries.

On February 22 Gandhi was very near death. He went through a severe crisis. The Government nervously feared that he would succumb and so kept sandal-wood ready and issued the pamphlet, "Congress Responsibility for the Disturbances 1942-43" to meet the tidal wave of protest that might arise out of the death of Gandhi.

The grave condition of Gandhi affected some politicians and humanitarians in other countries also. Some Ceylonese Legislators urged Gandhi's release, and in London a Labour M.P.'S delegation met Amery. The All-Parties Conference Committee urged in a cable to Churchill for the immediate release of Gandhi, but Amery and Churchill remained adamant.

Fortunately for India, Gandhi's health overcame the crisis, and he survived the self-imposed ordeal at the age of 74, virtually baffling medical science.

Gandhi ended his fast on March 3, 1943, at nine in the morning amidst the singing of songs from the Gita, the Koran, the *Gitanjali* and from the Ashram Book.

THE MAHATMA'S FAST had deeply stirred the people and plunged them in grief and anxiety. It attracted world-wide attention. This excitement gradually died down and with it the slogan "release Gandhi". *The Manchester Guardian* expressed its relief that fortunately for the friendship between India and England, Gandhi was not dead, and added that it was untrue that the political situation in India remained the same. Bernard Shaw said that the imprisonment of Gandhi was the stupidest blunder the Government had let itself be landed in by its Right wing of incurable diehards.

The Non-Party leaders again met at Bombay and resolved, on March 10, 1943, to issue a statement appealing for the release of Gandhi. It was signed by Sapru, Jayakar, K. M. Munshi, Alla Bux, Rajagopalachari, Bhulabhai Desai, Sir Ardeshir Dalal, Sir Homi Mody and others. Savarkar, who had attended the conference on the previous day at the instance of Sapru and Jayakar, had expressed his opinion that not only Gandhi but all political leaders including Sarat Bose should be released, and that Government should be urged either to release these patriots or put them on trial. Savarkar was not present when the statement was drafted and issued on March 10, as he had a toothache, and also an important interview at his residence with William Philips, personal envoy of President Roosevelt. The leaders were so nervous about approaching the Viceroy that they tried to persuade Savarkar to do so on their behalf as he had great influence on him. They wanted him to press for the release of Gandhi. But Savarkar refused to do so, and the Viceroy curtly turned down the request of the Non-Party Conference.

Amery informed the House of Commons that the Government of India had no intention of staging a trial of Gandhi and other Congress leaders who were in detention. Lord Samuel made a speech in April in which he blamed Gandhi and the Congress leaders for the impasse. Gandhi was supplied with Jinnah's *Dawn* and he read in it Jinnah's invitation to him to write him a letter. On May 4 Gandhi wrote such a letter requesting Jinnah to meet him in Jail and expressing the hope that Government would allow Jinnah to do so. Rajagopalachari had handed over the scheme to him in April but Jinnah did not reply to Rajagopalachari as the scheme had not come to him direct from Gandhi.

Jinnah, expecting such a letter, thundered that terrible consequences would follow if the Government meddled with his post. Upon this Savarkar said that Jinnah's statement was more amusing than alarming and he wondered why the League dictator did not capture the Viceroy and proclaim Pakistan at once! The Government informed Gandhi and Jinnah that the letter could not be forwarded to the addressee.

To Lord Samuel, Gandhi replied refuting his charges, but the most aggressive arguments Gandhi made at this stage were in his reply of June 15, 1943, to the Government pamphlet "Congress Responsibilities for the Disturbances 1942-43". On April 13 Gandhi had received a copy of this Government pamphlet and he prepared his reply after a profound study of it. No doubt he skilfully exposed the misquotations, though not materially, given in Government pamphlet from his writings. If Government's pamphlet read like a presentation of his case by the prosecutor, Gandhi's read like that of defence counsel laying stress on ifs and buts. The pre-May 1942 statements, interviews and articles of Gandhi did create the impression that Gandhi wanted the Congress to be left in a position in which he and the Congress would be free to make terms with Japan. And though Gandhi had not contemplated violence in the scheme, it was a fact that he had said in *Harijan* of July 19, 1942: "I don't want rioting as a direct result. If in spite of all precautions rioting does take place, it cannot be helped."

Gandhi neither refuted the Government's case successfully nor said; anything about the instructions his *Harijan* had given to the Congress agitators on destruction of telephone wires. This was a national revolt against foreign rule and such activities were natural though on the grounds of non-violent principle, his instructions might not be moral. On July 24 Gandhi said that he had become aware of his message. "There is no question of one more chance. After all it is an open rebellion." He did not contradict this statement though he was then free. Honestly speaking it cannot be denied that the disturbances followed the Government action and arrest of the Congress leaders, but it was equally true that Gandhi's propaganda preceding the A.I.C.C. resolution was responsible for the destruction committed in his name and in the name of the Congress. Government in its letter of October 14, 1943, replied to Gandhi that he was responsible for the happenings and that it could not absolve him from his responsibility.

Gandhi played ping-pong in the Aga Khan Palace with Sarojini Naidu, and Kasturba listened to devotional songs on the gramophone. Gandhi accepted soup, and the ingredients required were crushed on a stone-grinder. Shantikumar Morarjee sent him an electric grinder with a silver jug. Mirabehn had built a miniature temple of Krishna. Kasturba was a worshipper at that temple and she kept a lamp burning near the tulsi-pot every evening.

Gandhi read some important books in jail. He read Shakespeare, Browning, Bernard Shaw, Marx and Lenin. He read the first volume of *Capital* at the age of 74 and said: "I could have written it better, assuming, of course, I had the leisure for study Marx has put in.[9] I do not care," he added, "whether Marxism is right or wrong. All I know is that the poor are being crushed. Something has got to be done for them." Gandhi wanted Thomson's poem, *The Hound of Heaven*. It was with Jayasukhlal Mehta and was sent to him by Shantikumar Morarjee who acted as a devoted honorary manager of Gandhi and his party outside the prison gate. Parna Kuti of Lady Thackersey was the headquarters of doctors and other guests who came to see Gandhi.

During his internment Gandhi taught his wife Gujarati grammar, history and geography. She was unhappy as she did not like Gandhi's policy of sending thousands of persons to jail. Her only desire was to die before the great man.

While Gandhi was in jail, the Gandhian institutions supplied warm blankets to the military, and the nationalist papers prospered on military advertisements and war propaganda. Yet all of them referred to the spirited youth who had joined the army as rice soldiers. Savarkar, who with great foresight wanted youth to learn the art of defence so that they may use their weapons for the Freedom struggle, and be ready for national defence in the event of a transfer of power, was described by these Gandhians and the nationalist Press as Recruiting Veer!

On October 2, 1943, Gandhi's birthday was celebrated all over India. One of his opponents, Savarkar, offered him heartfelt felicitations and wished him a long life. Gandhi was valiantly defending his stand against Government attacks although his health was shattered. But Kasturba's illness augmented his worries. On October 20, 1943, Lord Wavell replaced Lord Linlithgow. Gandhi wrote to him about Kasturba. She had undergone extreme mental agonies and had also completed her seventy-fourth year. In December 1943 and January 1944 she suffered from chronic bronchitis with dilation of the branchia and she had had attacks of tachycardia with a heart rate of 180 per minute.

Kasturba had requested the Inspector-General of Prisons that Dr. Dinshah Mehta of Poona should examine her. Gandhi's own blood pressure was 200/110. There was some delay in providing medical help on the part of the Government and Gandhi blamed the Government for this on February 3, 1944. The Government replied that no outside doctors should be allowed in jail unless the Government medical officers considered it necessary. The Vaidyaraj, Shiv Sharma, visited the Gandhi's but could do nothing for Kasturba. During her last illness she hungered for a glimpse of her eldest son Harilal.

Harilal was found and taken to Kasturba's bedside! Gandhi refused permission to the doctors to give her penicillin which was a new drug at that time. Kasturba passed away at 7.35 on the evening of February 22, 1944, with her head on the lap of her husband. The whole nation was filled with grief. She died, as Savarkar said, in the service of Man and God. The Governor-General and the Government sent condolence messages to Gandhi. Gandhi wanted to hand over Kasturba's body to his sons and relatives so that a public funeral might be arranged, but Government refused permission. So Kasturba's body was taken to a place in the compound of the Aga Khan Palace where Mahadev Desai had been cremated. Dr. D. K. Karve, Dr. R. P. Paranjpye and a few Poona leaders attended the funeral. It was the morning of February 23. Gandhi sat in a chair under a tree. Devdas lit the pyre amidst *mantras* and hymns sung by Brahmins. Ramdas Gandhi reached the place when the corpse had been reduced to ashes. A loving mother, a dutiful wife and a staunch patriot, Kasturba had performed all her roles sincerely and nobly.

Nearly two months after Kasturba's death, Gandhi was taken seriously ill with malignant malaria. He was uneasy with hookworms too. Dr. Kalabhai Gajjar, pathologist, Dr. Col. Bhandari and Surgeon-General Dr. Candy examined him and issued bulletins about his health. Dr. B. C. Roy also attended on him. On April 30 the bulletin said: "There has been worsening of Mr. Gandhi's anaemic condition and his blood pressure has fallen further. His general condition is again giving rise to some anxiety." It is said that Gandhi had a heart attack at this stage

Without consulting his Executive Council, Lord Wavell decided to release Gandhi on the evening of May 5, 1944. The Inspector-General of Police and the Superintendent of the jail camp told Gandhi that he and his party would be released the next morning. Gandhi asked whether they were joking. They told him he could continue to stay in the Palace for some time if he liked. Dr. N. B. Khare, who was then an Executive Councillor, said that Gandhi had assured the Government he would bring the Congress back to the constitutional path. Whether it is true or not, on May 6 Gandhi was released on grounds of health. Before quitting the Palace, he wrote to the Government to acquire for him the plot where Mahadev Desai and Kasturba had been cremated. He said: "Subject to the permission of the Government, I would like to arrange for the upkeep of the sacred spot and daily prayers. I hope that necessary steps will be taken by the Government in terms of my prayer." So he quit the Palace with the ashes of Mahadev and Kasturba and with the *tulsi*-pot left behind by Kasturba

WHILE HE WAS in the Aga Khan Palace, Gandhi used to put every morning a mark on his forehead with the ash collected in a box from the pyres of Mahadev Desai and Kasturba. But somebody brought to his notice that according to the Hindu religion using the ash for this purpose was inauspicious. So he gave up the practice. He was in Poona at the Thackersey's Parna Kuti, another palatial building, for three days. On May 9 he visited the samadhis of Mahadev Desai and Kasturba. While he was in Poona, he received a telegram from Allama Mishraki, the Khaksar leader, to meet Jinnah. He had sent a similar telegram to Jinnah.

On May 11 Gandhi left Poona for Bombay and stayed at Juhu, near Bombay, in a cottage of coconut-leaves built by Jehangir Patel in the compound of Shantikumar Morarjee's house. He brought the *tulsi*-pot with him and handed it over to Shantikumar Morarjee who devotionally distributed young shoots from Kasturba's plant. Gandhi wanted to write about Mahadev Desai. He had tried to do so in the Aga Khan Palace and tried again at Juhu, but made no progress. Notebooks were kept near his pillow, but they remained blank. At this point he wired to the Khaksar leader that he was ready to meet Jinnah.

The first major work Gandhi did was to circulate on June 10, 1944, cyclostyled copies of the correspondence that had taken place between him and the Government during his imprisonment. "For fear of censorship difficulties," he said, "I did not try to have the copies printed at any printing press." He visited the Dockyard area in Bombay where damage had been caused on April 14 by an explosion. He gave autographs in eleven scripts at the request of his hostess, Mrs. Sumati Morarjee.

At Juhu Gandhi enjoyed the sea breeze and took a walk after every evening prayer. He often drank the milk of a tender coconut and sometimes sat on a chair by the sea dipping his ankle in the water. Kanji Dwarkadas, who met him at Juhu on June 10, wrote that Gandhi was unhappy, depressed, uncertain of himself and confused. Gandhi saw two films, *Mission to Moscow* and *Ram Rajya*. He met H. P. Mody, Jamnadas Dwarkadas and Kanji Dwarkadas. Jayakar discussed with him the political deadlock. He listened to devotional songs sung by Manhar Barve, Hirabai Badodekar, Pagnis, Bade Gulam Ali Khan and others. He sent a letter to Jayakar with Shantikumar Morarjee saying that he could not withdraw the August resolution as it was innocuous. He met the ailing Yusuf Meher Ali.

After a stay of 35 days, Gandhi left Bombay on June 15 for Poona, and put up at Dr. Mehta's Nature Cure Clinic. From Poona he wrote a letter on June 17 to the Viceroy, Lord Wavell, to permit him to see the members of the Working Committee and wrote a letter to Churchill on the same day requesting him to see the naked fakir for the sake of Britain and India. Gandhi told Congressmen that the authority for the August resolution had lapsed and that those who were underground should surrender to the Government. On November 2, 1944, Lord Wavell wrote to Gandhi merely stating that the Prime Minister desired him to acknowledge with thanks the receipt of his letter. Gandhi's party had left behind at Juhu his old strips of cloth which he always prepared from worn-out khadi cloth. He called for them. Shantikumar Morarjee's servants had thrown them out as rags and so he gave Gandhi new pieces of cloth. Gandhi was displeased with Shantikumar for losing these old strips of khadi cloth!

On July 1 Gandhi attended a meeting of the Kasturba Gandhi National Memorial Fund and on July 2 he left for Panchgani where he stayed till August 1, 1944.

During his stay at Panchgani, Gandhi gave an interview in the first week of July to Stuart Gelder of the *News Chronicle*, London. Gandhi expected Gelder to publish it after he had communicated his impressions of Gandhi to the Viceroy. But the interview was published in *The Times of India* of July 11. On the previous day *The Times of India* had published a statement issued by Rajagopalachari in which he had said: "The public will note from the correspondence now published that I had secured Gandhiji's personal approval even during his fast in February-March last year for the formula that I am releasing." And Rajagopalachari released along with the statement the correspondence that had passed between him and Jinnah about the formula or scheme he had handed over to Jinnah with the approval of Gandhi.

In his interviews Gandhi told Stuart Gelder that he had no intention of offering civil disobedience. It was his purpose not to hinder but to help the war effort. History could not be repeated and he could not take the country back to 1942. He would be satisfied with a national Government in full control of the civil administration and would advise the Congress to participate in such a Government if formed. Churchill, he concluded, did not want a settlement. He also said that he had approved the proposals submitted to Jinnah by Rajagopalachari, if the Muslim League would endorse the demand for independence. He further said that he regarded the Rajaji formula as being consistent with national integrity and his own opinion with the spirit of the Congress resolution After the publication of the Gelder interview, Gandhi gave pressmen interviews on July 12, 13 and 14 and explained the same points over again.

Commenting on this, 'Candidus' observed in *The Times of*

India: "The past week also witnessed the revelation that Mr Gandhi, who a couple of years ago was stoutly opposed to division of the country, is now agreeable to the principle of Pakistan. It is a reversal of his original approach that partition of India would be a 'sin'. He now concedes the principle of Pakistan, division of India."[10]

Gandhi knew that the British had successfully opened in June 1944 a second front in Normandy. Rome had fallen to the Allies on June 4, 1944, and the war had taken a definite turn in favour of the Allies. So the Viceroy was indifferent to Gandhi's proposal. When the Allies were in dire need of help, they thought, Gandhi, who stood out as a moral prophet, had hit them hard. Amery and Churchill were adamantly against yielding to him. Azad had rightly criticized this policy of Gandhi and his Right wing followers in the Congress. Wavell turned down Gandhi's request for an interview which he made from Panchgani on July 15, 1944, and asked him to submit instead a definite and concrete proposal.

Gandhi's interview to Gelder was kite-flying. Here Gandhi was defeated as a moral prophet. He preferred politics to morals by abandoning resistance to India's participation in a violent war. It was a definite departure from the doctrine of absolute non-violence. The moral prophet had descended from his high pedestal!

When Rajagopalachari's scheme was publicised, the Congress press became furious. They were stunned to see that their holy father, Gandhi, was acting as the god-father to the unholy scheme of partitioning the motherland. But soon they learnt to culpably keep silent on it.

The Liberal leaders Setalvad and Chandavarkar described Rajagopalachari's offer as a danger to India's security. Pandit Madan Mohan Malaviya said that he was entirely opposed to the idea of Pakistan. Dr. Ambedkar, who had a year and a half earlier described Gandhi as the prophet of a Dark Age, described Rajagopalachari's formula as a return to sanity and added that it would have been better if the offer had been made by Gandhi himself.

"It is really unjust" observed Savarkar, "to look upon Rajagopalachari alone as the villain of this tragedy. His fault is that he allowed himself to play a willing tool in the hands of Gandhiji." Savarkar said that the provinces of India were not the properties of Gandhi and Rajagopalachari so that they could make a gift of them to anyone they liked. The Hindu Mahasabha observed the first week of August as anti-Pakistan week.

Meetings aimed at supporting the Rajagopalachari formula ended at many places in pandemonium, and several demonstrations were held against it on a country-wide scale.

On July 22 a batch of 20 Poona Hindu Sabhaites led by N. D. Apte went to Panchgani and their leader asked Gandhi whether he had blessed the nefarious Rajagopalachari formula. He admitted it, was heckled by them, and they held black-flag demonstrations against him before they returned to Poona.

Gandhi was not to be disheartened by such demonstrations. On July 17 he had written to Jinnah, and the League leader had agreed to meet him on his return from Srinagar. Jinnah saw his life's opportunity, for his stock in Punjab politics had gone down. Gandhi placed his concrete demands before the Viceroy and again appealed to the underground workers to give themselves up.

Gandhi returned to Sevagram on August 3. At this time when he was making peace with Jinnah, Dr. Ambedkar held out the olive branch to Gandhi and sought for a settlement of the depressed classes problem. Gandhi replied on August 6 that he would love to own "Ambedkar as his colleague and co-worker" but "I know to my cost that you and I hold different views on this problem". On August 15 he finally paid his need of tribute to Mahadev Desai's idealism and devoted life. In the first week of September he discussed the constructive programme, ahimsa, charkha and hygiene with the All-India Spinners' Association.

At this time Gandhi had a long discussion with P. C. Joshi over the definition of "people's war". Before the invasion of Russia by Germany, World War II was, in the opinion of the Indian Communists, an imperialist war, but as soon as Germany invaded Russia it became a people's war! The Communists betrayed the August movement and were now busy betraying Indian unity by propagating the acceptance of Pakistan. The Communist Party was at this juncture prompted by its desire to help Soviet Russia even at the sacrifice of India's interests. The war, it said, had split the world into two camps: the freedom-loving peoples of the world and the Fascists.

P. C. Joshi wrote to Gandhi that if the patriotic leaders of the colonial people remained neutral, they indirectly aided the Fascist aggression. The fact was that the alliance of Russia with Britain and America was dictated by exigency rather than by any unity of ideals. The Communists enthusiastically claimed that they were inspired to fight for what they called "the greatest cause of mankind—a world Socialist brotherhood of free and equal peoples". Gandhi plainly told Joshi that he did not share the Communist definition of "peoples's war" as it did not include Asiatics and the Negroes. The Communists had forsworn their allegiance to the Congress and had decided to leave it. It is history that World War II ended in slavery for about a dozen neighbours of Russia and did not end in creating a community of free and equal peoples.

As Gandhi Was to meet Jinnah, L. G. Thatte, organizer of the Anti-Pakistan Front, Bombay, went to Wardha and picketed at the Sevagram Ashram with eight other volunteers and tried to prevent Gandhi from meeting Jinnah. But they were all arrested. When their leader Thatte was arrested, a dagger with a 7" blade was found on him. Thatte said that he who would assassinate Gandhi would become a martyr. Upon this the police said that this should be left to the leaders of the Hindu Mahasabha! Thatte replied that it would be too great an honour for Mahatma Gandhi and that a Jamadar would be quite enough to assassinate him. After the arrest of Thatte and his followers, Gandhi went by train to Bombay. Thatte was prosecuted under the Arms Act and the other eight volunteers were let off. Thatte's defence was that he had kept that dagger to defend himself against any possible attack on him by the Khaksar volunteers.

Nathuram Godse was definitely not among the nine men who picketed at Sevagram. He had not gone to Wardha. According to police reports there were nine volunteers and one of them was Thatte; seven belonged to Bengal and one was a Brahmin from Madras.[11] Yet Gandhi's biographer Pyarelal in his *Last Phase —I* published an untruth, maliciously implicating the names of Savarkar and Godse in this incident.

The special train carrying Gandhi left Wardha for Bombay. It was guarded by the Khaksar Muslim volunteers and protected by British soldiers who "happened" to travel in the same train. Bitter opposition to Gandhi was demonstrated all along the way. At several stations black-flag demonstrations were staged by Hindu Sanghatanists and other nationalists. The Hindus in the Punjab, the Sikhs, and the Hindus in Bengal were greatly upset and they bitterly criticized Gandhi. The Mahatma had laughed at Lord Hardinge who had police protection during his travels but now he was doing the same thing!

Gandhi reached Bombay safely on September 9 and within two hours of his arrival met Jinnah at his residence at Mount Pleasant Road. The time was 3.55 p.m. Gandhi put his arm around Jinnah's shoulder in a brotherly way and greeted him enthusiastically. It seems the pressure was not light and so Jinnah, lean and lanky, said merrily: "Take care, I might fall!" Jinnah had already rejected the Rajaji formula as 'a maimed, mutilated and moth-eaten Pakistan".

Gandhi said that Jinnah's contempt for Rajagopalachari was staggering. Gandhi offered his own scheme based on Rajagopalachari's formula and accepted the principle of the division of India in accordance with the demand of the Muslim League! Jinnah wanted him to withdraw the August resolution which contemplated a Federal Central Government on the basis of a united, democratic Government in India. According to Jinnah, this meant Hindu Raj, and he did not want any plebiscite in the Muslim majority provinces. Gandhi opposed both the points. Jinnah demanded autonomous and sovereign states for the Muslim majority provinces in the East and in the West.

The lengthy correspondence and prolonged talks between Gandhi and Jinnah took place for three weeks. Gandhi paid nineteen visits to Jinnah without receiving a single one in return, even observed his usual silence on Sundays and returned every day with an unpleasant face from Mount Pleasant Road! Both were sick men physically and politically! Yet Jinnah gained much. He got the Congress moral leader committed to the principle of the division of India. On September 24 Gandhi wrote to Jinnah: "If the vote is in favour of separation, it shall be agreed that those areas shall form a separate State as soon as India is free from foreign domination and can therefore be constituted into two sovereign Independent States." Gandhi had declared on several occasions that Pakistan was a sin, a denial of God and an untruth. He had asked the protagonists of Pakistan to vivisect him before they vivisected India. But now he conceded the principle of the vivisection of India and to undo the work of centuries. The master diplomat in Jinnah knew well that it was the British who were the final givers.

The talks terminated on September 27. Jinnah was ill. Gandhi sent Dr. Mehta to him to give him massage. According to his friend Kanji Dwarkadas, Jinnah had developed a habit of twisting and pinching his lower lip, a sign of loneliness and nervousness. Jinnah did not have a fall! Gandhi definitely had a slippery fall! A few days later Jinnah told Kanji Dwarkadas that Gandhi talked frankly but Jinnah exclaimed, "I should rather die fighting than commit suicide".[12]

Lord Linlithgow, who was in favour of the unity of India, once said that "the Hindus have made the mistake of taking Jinnah seriously about Pakistan and as a result they have given substance to the shadow". But now Gandhi and Rajagopalachari transformed the shadow into substance. Commenting on these Gandhi-Jinnah talks, the veteran politician, Sir Chimanlal Setalvad, observed: "It is really inconceivable why Mr. Gandhi, without really understanding the implications and effects of Pakistan wanted by Mr. Jinnah, said in advance that he accepted Pakistan in principle and thereby created confusion and misunderstanding which it will take a long time to clear."

With the end of these talks ended the fond hopes and false expectations raised by the nationalist press. The Mahatma stooped to conquer, but his Mahatmic methods failed against the shrewdness of Jinnah. During the previous eight years, Gandhi-Jinnah talks had been periodical features of the Indian political scene. This time the Congress forgot its oft-repeated argument that the Muslim League was not the only representative of the Indian Muslims. Jinnah had given the slogan of Pakistan to the Muslims which epitomized their age-old fears, aspirations and ambitions. Was not Gandhi's claim to speak for the whole nation vitiated? Gandhi faced a double climb-down. He regarded partition of the land as a sin, and yet he showed his willingness to be a party to it while he also lost his claim to speak for the whole nation. Gandhi made the Congress recognize the role of Jinnah as the chief spokesman of the whole Indian Muslim population, and indeed his own leadership was never accepted by the Indian Muslims. The third thing that emerged was that Gandhi, who had said that the authority invested in him had lapsed, was conducting negotiations in his personal capacity.

During the talks Rajagopalachari was with him at Birla House in Bombay, suggesting and preparing drafts for Gandhi. The Mahatma read them, corrected them or prepared his own. Sometimes Gandhi was late in returning to Birla house. Someone took his evening meal to Jinnah's house; and Gandhi ate it there, as he unfailingly took his last meal of the day before sunset.

Gandhi returned to Sevagram on September 1, 1944, and stayed there till March 30, 1945, except for three days in December 1944 and the last week of February 1945 which he spent at Wardha.

On October 2, 1944, the nation paid loving and grateful homage to Gandhi, the greatest man in India of his day. On this seventy-fifth birthday he was presented with a birthday volume entitled *Gandhiji* which included the tribute by Albert Einsten. "Generations to come," observed Einsten, "in may well be, will scarce believe that such a one as this ever in flesh and blood walked upon this earth." At Rangoon, Netaji Subhas Bose described him as the father of the nation and sought his blessings in the holy war of liberation. Bernard Shaw sent birthday greetings.

Sevagram was jubilant on that day with Congress flags flowing upon the house-tops. Sarojini Naidu applied *Kum kum* to Gandhi's forehead, garlanded him with handspun yarn and showered flowers on him. Gandhi addressed them in Hindustani and joked that he wanted to live for 125 years but Malaviyaji had cut it down by twenty-five years by wiring to him that he should live for a hundred years! Gandhi was presented, on behalf of the trustees of the Kasturba Gandhi National Memorial Fund with cheques for rupees eighty lakhs and odd. This money had to be spent in seven lakhs of villages.

Members of the Talimi Sangh met Gandhi on November 10. He objected to their including "the basic education" in the trust deed of the Kasturba Fund as he did not wish to put a strain on the trustees.

By November 1944 the Government had restored all the confiscated machinery and other articles to the Navajivan Press. From December 4 to 31 Gandhi declared a holiday for himself. No talk, no letters, no interviews, no reading of newspapers. He was thoroughly fatigued. Even after a siesta, he said, the brain seemed tired. Except for unforeseen circumstances of a grave nature he would strictly adhere to his vow of silence. During this month of silence, he visited the samadhi of Jamnalal Bajaj, the Leper Asylum at Wardha and the dairy at Pipri.

CHAPTER XLIV

From Unity to Parity

AFTER SUFFERING A defeat outside, Gandhi now turned to what his critics called his monastic order, namely the Gandhi Seva Sangh, the Hindustani Talimi Sangh, the All-India Spinners' Association, the All-India Village Industries Association, and now the Kasturba Gandhi National Memorial Trust. This monastic order nurtured and reared the hierarchy of Gandhians who were the pillars of the Congress in villages. Gandhi had woven these institutions into a new brotherhood of political Jesuits to whose power leaders like Nehru and Patel bowed and through which uncritical devotion to Gandhi and prejudices against science and modern thought were fostered in the name of social reconstruction at the cost of intellect and reason, increasing blind belief in the Mahatma's power to make miracles! The Harijan Seva Sangh did not yield much fruit as Dr. Ambedkar's powerful influence prevailed in this field.

So the year 1945 opened with a conference of the Hindustani Talimi Sangh which was held at Sevagram on January 11. Gandhi was still observing silence during the day and so his speech was read out by Dr. Zakir Husain. In it he said that true education must be self-supporting and that the delegates should become teachers of the villagers, their servants in the true sense. Sevagram was declared an ideal centre for conducting experiments in *Nayee Talim*, as Wardha was the centre for village industries experiments. Gandhi also addressed the village workers' training camp which was opened near Sevagram.

Gandhi devoted himself to constructive work. On February 18 he addressed at Sevagram about 150 workers who were engaged in Kasturba Gandhi National Memorial Trust work. Gandhi told them that the amount of one crore and twenty-four lakhs that had been collected was not to be squandered away or loosely handled. The money was to be spent in villages on medical relief for women and children. But Gandhi had not made up his mind about maternity homes and free hospitals. Poverty and ignorance were the root cause of village backwardness. So education was to be along the lines of *Nayee Talim*. And through khadi and village industries their economic condition was to be bettered.

On February 26 Gandhi attended the conference of the All-India Hindustani Prachar Sabha which he had started in 1942 with the help of Jamnalal Bajaj. His advice regarding adoption of two scripts, Hindi and Urdu, had been ignored by the Bharatiya Sahitya Sammelan. Although Gandhi had been observing silence for the previous three months, he broke his vow during the daytime thrice. He hoped that a day would soon come when Hindi and Urdu would meet and become one.

On March 17 he announced Vinoba Bhave and Kishorlal as his successors in his Ashram. At this time he declared that it was meaningless to talk of ending the political deadlock when the members of the Working Committee were in jail. He attended also a meeting of the All-India Spinners' Association and discussed the proposal made by Jaju, the Secretary of the Charkha Sangh. Unless they shed their fear, he declared, they would kill khadi.

Gandhi's observance of a prolonged silence was partly due to his physical weakness and partly to his secret involvement in a serious plan. On his release Dr. Syed Mahmud a member of the Working Committee, met Gandhi at Sevagram in October 1944. Gandhi made him write a letter to Bhulabhai Desai requesting him to see Liaquat Ali, the leader of the Muslim League in the Central Assembly, and discuss with him the formation of a composite Government consisting of the Congress and the Muslim League. After waiting for a fortnight or so, Gandhi himself wrote a letter in Gujarati to Bhulabhai Desai urging him to expedite the matter.

Bhulabhai met Liaquat Ali in Delhi and prepared a draft which was later known as the Bhulabhai-Liaquat Ali Pact. Liaquat Ali was to get Jinnah's approval and Bhulabhai Gandhi's. Bhulabhai met Gandhi with the draft and Gandhi made some changes in it, approved the draft secretly and asked Bhulabhai to meet Lord Wavell, the Viceroy. Bhulabhai met Wavell and handed over the draft to him for consideration and action. This secret pact surpassed the Rajaji formula in the harm it did to the national majority. It agreed to a percentage of fifty-fifty in all representations for the Hindus and the Muslims. The demand for parity in the alliance of the Congress with the Muslim League in the Central Assembly had ripened into a reality.

Lord Wavell expressed his fear to Bhulabhai that Gandhi would not stick to the draft in the end. Wavell, however, told him that he was going to London to consult the British Cabinet about the draft. Accordingly, he went to London on March 21, 1945, for consultations. Meanwhile, news of the secret pact leaked out and the members of the Working Committee, who were interned at Ahmednagar, were indignant at it. They expressed their anger and displeasure in a resolution about the pact.

Dr. P. C. Ghosh, one of the members of the Working Committee, met Gandhi at Sevagram after his release from Ahmednagar and gave him a copy of the resolution of the Working Committee. Gandhi took the cue and sent a female messenger to Delhi to contact Bhulabhai Desai. She told him that Gandhi would not bless a Government formed by Bhulabhai and Liaquat Ali because he did not like the agreement. In a fit of anger Bhulabhai Desai shouted: "Let Bapu go to hell. I will stand by what I have done!"[1]

Gandhi came to Bombay on March 31 and addressed meetings of the workers of the Kasturba Gandhi National Memorial Trust. He sent condolence to Mrs. Roosevelt and said the President Roosevelt was spared the humiliating spectacle of being a party to a peace which threatened to be a prelude to war, bloodier still if possible. Gandhi said later that those who had their hands dyed deep in blood could not build a non-violent order for the world. He then left Bombay on April 20 and stayed at Mahabaleshwar till the end of May. He then went to Panchgani where he remained till June 18. On June 10 he said at Panchgani that the Allied victory was not a triumph of truth over untruth.

Lord Wavell stayed in London for over nine weeks discussing the parity proposals. The Bhulabhai Desai-Liaquat Ali Pact was supported by the Sapru Conciliation Committee's findings which were cabled to Lord Wavell in London. This committee was established by Sapru and his friends in November 1944 and had the blessings of the Mahatma.

Meanwhile Hitler and Mussolini died in tragic circumstances and Germany surrendered early in May 1945. Churchill resigned in May.

Wavell returned to India on June 5 with the so-called Wavell

Plan. The British Cabinet moderated the parity proposals. They changed the parity of the Congress and the Muslim League to parity between the caste Hindu representatives and those of the Muslims and made room for the Harijans, Sikhs and others, removing the glaring injustice to the national majority and to others.

Wavell announced his plan in a broadcast on June 14, inviting Indian leaders to take counsel with him with a view to forming a new Executive Council. The plan presupposed full co-operation in the war effort against Japan by the leaders. He invited twenty-one leaders to the conference he proposed to hold on June 28 at Simla.

The Congress Working Committee members were released on June 15. On that day Gandhi issued a statement to pacify the Working Committee members and said *inter alia*: "I am not ashamed of the part I have played in advising Shri Bhulabhai Desai when he consulted me about his proposal." Gandhi, the moral teacher, did not reveal that the idea of the pact originated with him. The Working Committee held its meeting in Bombay on June 21 and 22. Gandhi had informed the Viceroy that he had no *locus standi* as the recognized representative of the Congress and suggested to him that he should invite Azad to the Simla Conference. The Viceroy did so.

The Working Committee of the Congress accepted the invitation to attend the Simla Conference. But Azad, Patel and Nehru called Bhulabhai Desai and censured him for having mooted the Bhulabhai Desai-Liaquat Ali Pact. According to them, it amounted to treachery. Bhulabhai told them that they were blaming him unnecessarily as he had done the bidding of the Mahatma. Upon this they furiously pounced upon him and said they would decide later what to do about the Mahatma, but he should not expect any important assignment in future from the Congress!

Humiliated, Bhulabhai met Gandhi and pleaded for removing the injustice done to him. Instead of protecting him from threats and attacks, Gandhi told Bhulabhai that he had wealth, reputation and position; he should not covet a post in the Viceroy's Executive Council. Not only that, Gandhi asked him as he had done in the case of Dr. Khare, to give him a statement in writing to this effect: "I, Bhulabhai Desai, consider myself incompetent to be a member of the Viceroy's Executive Council and also declare that I will never accept such a job even now or at any time in future."

Bhulabhai was stunned! He said to Gandhi angrily, "You

use a person as an instrument for your purpose and as soon as that purpose is served, you bury that individual. No one should expect any justice at your hands."[2]

ALL THE EX-PREMIERS of eleven provinces, the leaders of the parties in the Central Assembly, and the Council of State, a leader each of the Sikhs and the depressed classes, Jinnah and Gandhi as two leaders of the two main recognized parties, and Azad who was invited at Gandhi's suggestion, assembled on June 25, 1945, at Simla. The Hindu Mahasabha was deliberately dropped since it treated the Wavell Plan as anti-Hindu, anti-democratic and a negation of nationalism.

The Congress, on behalf of the caste Hindus, who formed 54 per cent of the total Indian population, was represented by its Muslim President Maulana Azad! The Muslims, 22 per cent of the population, were given parity of representation with the caste Hindus and were represented by Jinnah. The depressed classes forming 21 per cent of the total population were given one representative.

Gandhi reached Simla on June 24 and stayed there for about three weeks. He did not attend the conference but met the Viceroy on June 24 and again on July 11. On June 21 Gandhi expressed the hope that there would be a happy outcome to the Simla Conference in its efforts to form an interim nationally-based Government.

The Simla Conference assembled on June 25, 1945, at the Viceregal Lodge. The Viceroy Lord Wavell delivered the inaugural address. It began well. Within the first few hours the conference agreed to the basic item in the Wavell Plan, namely the prosecution of the war against Japan. But weeks of open and private negotiations thereafter failed to produce an agreement on the personnel of the National Government. Jinnah wanted all the Muslim representatives from the Muslim League and the Congress felt it humiliating to yield on this point. So the conference ended on July 14, 1945, keeping on record the Congress acceptance of communal parity between caste Hindus and Muslims.

The political parity sanctioned by Gandhi was transformed into communal parity. That was the gain the Muslim League secured through Lord Wavell who was blatantly partial to the Muslims, through the connivance of Nehru and Patel, and through the short-sighted dealings of Gandhi. When the nationalist press unblushingly said that parity was an interim arrangement, their statements provoked Dr. S. P. Mookerji, President of the Hindu Mahasabha, to ask, "Can you ever commit an interim suicide? If not, then suicide once committed can never be undone".

The Mahasabha, however, did nothing beyond this retort and the observance of anti-Pakistan day and a *hartal*. It did not resort to the long-promised direct action when its very existence was jeopardized by inaction and when it was forfeiting all reason to exist separately from the Congress. A very powerful section in the Congress was bringing pressure on Gandhi to prevent him from going too far in the direction of Pakistan.

This situation was the creation of Gandhi who had propelled Bhulabhai Desai to do the deed and then got himself involved in it as usual and lost ground. Patel and Nehru were rattled but were not bold enough to battle with the real author of the Bhulabhai-Liaquat Ali Pact. They made speeches and said that they were against such diplomatic efforts but perhaps only with a view to covering up breakdowns in Congress policy.

Gandhi returned to Sevagram on July 18 and resigned from the Hindi Sahitya Sammelan, as its leaders did not approve of his policy. His advice was that the national language should be neither Sanskritized nor Persianized and that it should be written both in the Nagari and in Urdu scripts. The Gandhi group left the Hindi Sahitya Sammelan and started their own institution, the Hindustani Talimi Sangh.

After staying for a month at Sevagram, Gandhi went to Poona on August 21 and except for the four days he spent with the Working Committee and All-India Congress Committee meetings in Bombay in the last week of September 1945, he was at Poona till November 18, 1945.

During the Simla Conference, Britain went to the polls and returned Labour to office with an overwhelming majority. The British are not idol-worshippers and they threw out Churchill, their war-time Prime Minister and the Conservative Party and with it the arrogant Amery too. Churchill was now their hero but not their leader! The Labour Party took office on July 26, 1945. Almost simultaneously Japan, with Hiroshima and Nagasaki atom-bombed, surrendered on August 15, 1945.

Bevin had said during his election campaign that if Labour were returned, it would close the India Office and transfer the business to the dominions. The Labour victory sent a thrill of joy through the political circles in India. In August 1945 the redoubtable Rajagopalachari rejoined the Congress with his zeal and zest for Pakistan!

Pethick-Lawrence was made Secretary of State for India. Lord Wavell went to London on August 21, 1945 for a fresh examination of the entire Indian problem and returned to India towards the middle of September 1945. He announced general elections to test the strength of the political parties, to break the ground for future political negotiations with the newly-elected representatives, to hammer out a constitution and to negotiate a treaty with the Constituent Body that would be formed.

So all the political parties prepared for the elections. Gandhi attended the Working Committee meeting and that of the A.I.C.C which congratulated the nation for the courage and endurance with which it had withstood the fierce and violent onslaught of British power in 1942. It also moved a resolution on the I.N.A. soldiers and appointed a Defence Committee consisting of Sir Tej Bahadur Sapru, Bhulabhai Desai and others to defend them. The Congress criticized the Wavell proposals, demanded release of everyone sentenced for political activities and declared that the Congress would contest the elections to demonstrate the will of the people. Gandhi was in indifferent health. So he returned to the Nature Cure Clinic of Dr. Dinshah Mehta in Poona.

GANDHI SAW THAT he had differences with Nehru on economic and social issues. So he again raised the question of differences with Nehru and added that if these differences were fundamental, the public should be made aware of them. Gandhi said that he was an old man and added: "I have therefore made you as my heir. I must, however, understand my heir and my heir should understand me. Then alone shall I be content."

Gandhi's conception of an ideal village did not appeal to Nehru. According to him "a village, normally speaking, is backward intellectually and culturally, and no progress can be made from a backward environment". Nehru replied that he stood for scientific and technological developments and observed, "I do not think it is possible for India to be really independent unless she is a technically advanced country. In the present context of the world, we cannot advance without a strong background of scientific research in every department."[3]

The puzzle and the paradox of the relations between these two great personalities, Gandhi and Nehru, baffled many a thinking man. They represented ideas and ideals of two different historical epochs, but they were leading the same movement for the independence of India.

Socially, India lived in the nineteenth century which was represented by Gandhi, and historically India lived in the twentieth century which was represented by Nehru. One stood for the old India, the other for the new. That the new India triumphed over the old one is history. Yet the world interpreted this cleavage in a different way. Lin Yutang said: "The people of India listen to Nehru, Nehru listens to Gandhi, and Gandhi listens only to God!"

On November 5, 1945, the trial of Capt. Shah Nawaz Khan, Capt. P. K. Sahgal and Lt. G. S. Dhillon of the Indian National Army began at the Red Fort in Delhi. Netaji Bose lost the battle of Imphal in May 1945 and died following an air-crash in a hospital at Taihoku on August 19, 1945. His army popularly known as the Azad Hind Fouz, undoubtedly fought a glorious war, a war of which any freedom-loving nation should be proud. It hastened the decision of the British to leave India and brought the country on the threshold of independence.

The nation's sympathy and love flowed towards Netaji's defeated soldiers. Leaders like Savarkar and Dr. Mookerjee had clamoured for their unconditional release. Congress leaders and workers led by Gandhi and Nehru, who styled them rice soldiers, changed their attitude to the I.N.A. In his appeal to the Viceroy, Gandhi said that India adored these men who were on trial. And the trial changed its colour and nature! It was transformed into a trial, India *v/s* the British Empire! Needless to say, Nehru and Gandhi were now in their favour from national pride as well as out of political opportunism. Naturally, Bhulabhai Desai, backed by Jawaharlal Nehru, Sir Tej Bahadur Sapru, Dr. K. N. Katju, Asaf Ali and Sir Dilip Singh defended the heroes who stood the trial by court martial. On January 3, 1946, they were sentenced to transportation for life, but Sir Claude Auchinlerk, the C-in-C, remitted the sentences. And the nation echoed with the name of Subhas Bose, her immortal son.

The elections to the Central Assembly were held at the end of November 1945. The Congress with its gigantic political machinery plunged into the election campaign heart and soul. Supported by the "Pakistan purse", the Muslim League entered the election arena with "Pakistan or Perish" as its slogan. The Congress manifesto stressed the Quit India demand and fully exploited the patriotic upsurge caused by the I.N.A. trials whose soldiers they had unblushingly condemned as rice soldiers. The Hindu Mahasabha with its meagre purse and scanty press entered the field with the slogans "Independence and

Integrity of India," "a vote for the Congress is a vote for Pakistan!" Unfortunately for the Hindu Mahasabha, its great leader Savarkar was ill throughout the election period.

The Muslim League routed the Congress Muslim candidates by securing all the thirty-two seats in the Central Assembly, only Asaf Ali being elected by the Hindu majority electorate at Delhi. Jinnah proudly declared that he had achieved what Hitler could not. The Hindu Mahasabha was wiped out of the political picture of the country by the Congress. Roy's Radical Democratic Party and Dr. Ambedkar's Scheduled Castes Federation suffered the same fate!

Gandhi left Poona on November 18, 1945 for Sevagram and he was at Calcutta on December 1, discussing with Governor R. G. Casey the food and famine problem of Bengal.

Gandhi then attended the wedding of Geeta, the daughter of Sarat Bose, who had met the Mahatma in Poona in September. Gandhi also met the Viceroy, Lord Wavell, who was then on a visit to Calcutta. He told the Viceroy that the British should quit rather than dispense "monkey justice". He attended the Working Committee on December 11 which decided to sack the Communists from the Congress. The Congress got rid of these parasites that had flourished on it and begun to eat into its vitals.

On December 19 Gandhi laid the foundation stone of Andrews Memorial Hospital, paid a visit to Kalabhavan of Nandlal Bose, where he said that *tapascharya* meant single-minded devotion. He added that Tagore as a person was much superior to his work "as all great and good men are better and greater than their works". Gandhi visited Santiniketan and saw again Governor R. G. Casey. During that visit he met the Governor five times and had pleasant talks with him. After his retirement, Casey wrote a book *An Australian in India* in which he describes Gandhi as lively, courteous, tactful and a good listener. According to him, Gandhi had a good sense of humour and he took pains to show that he was a man of learning which he was not. His daily prayer meetings had something of the flavour of open-air revivalist meetings. "Mr. Gandhi," Casey observes, "is credited by many of his followers with being a saint and a statesman. Whilst I have a considerable regard for him, I do not believe he is either."

"What claims," he adds, "has Mr. Gandhi to statesmanship? There is a simple criterion for determining whether a man is a statesman; the passage of time should show that he was right in his major political decisions three times out of four. I do not think Mr. Gandhi can claim this record. Perhaps," Casey concludes, "one might say that amongst saints he was a statesman, and amongst statesmen a saint."[4]

After his visit to Casey, Gandhi visited Gauhati and other places in Assam. During his tour he talked to the people about God and Marx, voluntary discipline and non-violent weapons. He told them that God was within themselves, that he appreciated Marx's acumen and industry but could not believe in his conclusions.

Gandhi told a journalist that the Bengali youth took to violence at the risk of death, and poverty to disprove Curzon's remark that the Bengalees were effeminate. The Russian example, Gandhi opined, could not suit India as he believed that India's tradition was wholly different from Russia's. The historical settings too were different. The whole Russian population was under arms. "Indian masses," Gandhi declared in a vain glow of confidence, "will not take to arms, even if they could be given the necessary training."[5] In Assam, he said it was their shame that the Adivasis should be isolated as trivial people. He felt that Assam was a vast field for constructive work.

Gandhi returned to Calcutta on January 14 and left it on January 20 for Madras where he stayed till the end of the month, talking on the importance of the Indian languages. He told the people sorrowfully that English was more in vogue in the South than Hindustani, especially in Madras, and it was their dharma (duty) to learn Hindustani. On January 26 he said that he hoped they would not have to repeat the independence pledge the following year! He presided over the jubilee celebrations of the Dakshini Hindi Prachar Sabha and its convocation and said that the national language was Hindustani and not Hindi!

By now a Parliamentary Delegation of ten members was touring India. They began their survey on their arrival on January 5, 1946, and met important leaders. They met Gandhi at Madras on January 25. The delegation returned to London on February 10. Gandhi met the Madras Governor and called twice on the ailing Srinivas Sastri. He visited the Meenakshi temple at Madura. During this stay, Sir C. P. Ramaswami Aiyer had a talk with him. A local businessman weighed Gandhi against silver and paid Gandhi the value of the silver. Gandhi told the workers that he hoped a worker would one day be the president of the Congress. He said he himself was a worker, had given up his property, and the lakhs of rupees he had with him were not his own. The London police were the best police force in the world because they had taken oath that they would be the servants of the people and not their masters. Gandhi also expressed his appreciation of those who worked for people suffering from leprosy.

Meanwhile, *Harijan* was started again on February 10, 1946. An application was made on December 3, 1945, for lifting the ban on *Harijan* and Government agreed to do so on January 30, 1946. It was now published from Ahmedabad and priced two annas.

In the Madras Presidency, Rajagopalachari had become unpopular on account of his pro-Pakistani propaganda, his apostasy in 1942 and his scheming to get the premiership of Madras. He was the alter ego of Gandhi. During his tour Gandhi said that he knew there was a clique in Tamilnadu against Rajagopalachari and he criticized it, extolling Rajagopalachari to the skies. Kamaraj Nadar protested against Gandhi's use of the word "clique" and resigned. Gandhi replied that the dictionary meaning of the word "clique" was "small exclusive party". But Gandhi did not withdraw the word! He stood by the Kautilya in Rajagopalachari. Gandhi's remark was condemned and Rajagopalachari's opponents threatened to fast as a protest against it. Gandhi then replied: "I cannot give up an opinion honestly held even if the whole world fasts against me."

Rajagopalachari sent in his resignation to Gandhi thanking him for the good opinion he had expressed about him publicly, but added: "I struggled hard to work without minding my calumniators but I give it up now."[6] Rajagopalachari declared that when he was not seeking power he was accused of doing so.

On his return to Sevagram on February 6, Gandhi delivered a sermon to the teacher-trainees on basic education, and he discussed the food problem and famine conditions with the Secretary of the Viceroy who had specially come to seek his advice. The merchant class fully exploited the situation and raised the prices of cloth. Gandhi blamed them for it. To meet the danger of a food shortage, he advised the people to grow greens in earthen pots and in discarded old tins.

Gandhi also asked the Viceroy on February 21 to give the Indian Army a unique opportunity to do constructive work. Medium-sized vessels should be used for fishing. "The dry fish," observed Gandhi, "even now forms part of the normal diet of a great number of people, who are very poor, that is, when it is available and they can afford to buy it. The distribution of food should be through the co-operative societies."[7]

Gandhi's mention of fish as a food shocked his admirers. They asked whether it did not entail violence. Gandhi replied that that kind of violence is inherent in all embodied life, therefore in man too. He did not consider it violence, he added, to permit the fish-eaters to eat fish.[8]

Gandhi then went to Bombay on February 18 when anti-British feelings in India were at white heat. The I.N.A. trials, which had shaken the steel frame of the Empire, inspired the spirit of revolt and an outburst became inevitable. It was the turn of the Royal Indian Navy and the Air Force to revolt! The British soldiers were fighting for their survival but what were the Indian soldiers fighting for, the Indian soldiers asked themselves. An act of defiance by a few educated ratings from the H.M.I.S. *Talwar*[9] set off a flaming gesture of self-assertion by all men of the Royal Indian Navy, and the Royal Air Force joined it.

The army refused to fire on their naval comrades. The revolt started on February 17 and by the 18th the British had lost all control on sections of the Armed Forces. The revolt spread to Calcutta and Karachi. Men in the wireless stations as far away as Aden and the Persian Gulf were in revolt. The backbone of the Imperial structure broke down. The Indian Army was again experiencing and expressing the pangs of freedom.

The B.B.C. broadcast the alarming news. The British statesmen were alerted. They realized the significance of the second round of revolt in the Indian Army. This revolt speeded up the process of Britain's decision to leave India which had been already accelerated by the I.N.A. soldiers! It was more than three years since the collapse of the "Quit India" movement. In the meantime much water had flowed in the Ganga. The Congress leaders were busy contesting elections to provincial Assemblies on the basis of Wavell's announcement of September 1945.

On the next day of this revolt, Lord Pethick-Lawrence, Secretary of State for India, announced on February 19, 1946 the intention of His Majesty's Government to send out a delegation of three Cabinet Members, Sir Stafford Cripps, A. V. Alexander and himself, to discuss with the Indian party leaders on the spot the question of solving the political deadlock in the country.

Vallabhbhai Patel and Jawaharlal Nehru advised these ratings to surrender unconditionally, and they obeyed them. In *Harijan* of March 3, 1946, Gandhi indignantly said: "Those who incited the mutineers did not know what they were doing. The latter were bound to submit ultimately." Aruna Asaf Ali, who had met Gandhi on several occasions when she was underground, refuted Gandhi's stand which condemned the action of the Royal Indian Navy ratings. The British intention, Gandhi said, to quit India in favour of Indian rule would be delayed because of this distressful unrest. And although he did not blame Mashruwala and Kalelkar for preaching violence, in his reply to the Government pamphlet in 1943, now after three years he blamed them for misinterpreting non-violence in their impatient zeal for the movement.

As regards the mutineers, Gandhi said that if they mutinied for the freedom of India they could not do so without a call from a prepared revolutionary party! They were thoughtless in supposing that by their might they would deliver India from foreign domination! Gandhi's critics had also blamed Gandhi for having thoughtlessly launched the "Quit India" movement without any preparation!

At Or About this time, a devotee requested Gandhi to write a treatise on the science of ahimsa. He honestly replied: "To write a treatise on the science of ahimsa is beyond my powers. I am not built for academic writings. Action is my domain."[10] He further said that Vinoba could do so, but Vinoba would not agree for want of time. Mashruwala did but it might not be correct to call his work a *shastra* and Kaka Kalelkar was an incorrigible nomad. In circles closest to him there was not a single first-rate scholar, nor an eminent man with a scientific approach. On occasion Jawaharlal Nehru tried to rationalize some of Gandhi's ideas, fondly and faithfully but falteringly. Gandhi's final reply was striking and memorable. "No man," he declared, "has been able to describe God fully. The same holds true of ahimsa."[11] Incidentally it may be mentioned here that Gandhi was the author of the *Gitapadarthakosh: Gitana Shabdona Sartha Sthalanirdesh*. It gives how many times a certain word has appeared in the Gita. The dictionary was published in 1936. At this time Gandhi expressed his wish to live to the age of 125 years and he said that the basis of his wish was the third *mantra* from *Ishopanishad* which means that a man should desire to live for 100 years while serving with detachment. The idea of death was crossing his mind. He had told the people at Madura that he would know much better how to control the crowd if next time such a visit ever came. Ill-health was causing him great distress. So Gandhi's nature-cure hobby had become a passion. He became a trustee of the All-India Nature Cure Federation with Dr. Dinshah Mehta and Jehangir Patel as co-trustees. It was the ambition of Dr. Mehta to see a full-fledged Nature Cure University established in India. Gandhi commented that, "I was a fool to think that I could ever hope to make an institute for the poor in a town". So he gave up the pursuit, and an experiment in village nature cure was started at Uruli-Kanchan near Poona. The expression "to fool" he had once used for himself in a joke with Sastri. Whatever Gandhi said about himself in a lighter mood, the truth was that his image was now worshipped in a temple. Gandhi published news of this in *Harijan* of March 24, 1946, and denounced it. "This I consider," Gandhi observed, "to be a gross form of idolatry. The person who erected the temple has wasted his resources by misusing them, the villagers who are drawn there are misled and I am being insulted in that the whole of my life has been caricatured in that temple. Gita is worshipped," he added, "not by parrot-like recitation but by following its teaching."

The Congress won a resounding victory in the middle of March 1946 in the provincial elections, completely annihilating the Roy, Savarkar and Ambedkar parties. The League won 427 out of 507 Muslim seats in the provincial legislatures with 74 per cent of the Muslim vote. The only set-back the Muslim League suffered was in the North-West Frontier Province where the Khan brothers won a clear majority. A few days later the Congress formed ministries in eight of the eleven provinces. The Muslim League did so in Sind and Bengal. The Punjab Ministry was formed by the Unionists with the support of the Congress.

Gandhi stayed at Poona from February 20 to March 10 where the Aga Khan and the Nawab of Bhopal met him, as did an Indian delegation from South Africa. He came to Bombay on March 11, and attended a Working Committee meeting in Bombay from March 12 to 16. While he was in Bombay, Captain Shah Nawaz and Sahgal met him. The Viceroy's Secretary also had a chat with him.

On March 15 the British Prime Minister, Clement Attlee, declared India's right to attain full independence within or even without the British Commonwealth, if she so desired. In respect of the minority problem of India Attlee added: "We cannot allow a minority to place their veto on the advance of the majority." Nehru welcomed the pleasant tone in Attlee's announcement. Gandhi said in Bombay that to suspect the Cabinet Mission's *bona fides* was a kind of weakness. They were coming to restore to India what was her due. Jinnah described Attlee's statement as rope-walking and accused Gandhi of spoiling the atmosphere for negotiations with the Cabinet Mission. In an outburst, Jinnah said that Gandhi's non-violence was a shelter for him and a pose to practise hypocrisy and fraud, and to bamboozle the world, especially foreign countries.

On March 16 Gandhi addressed a meeting at Shivaji Park, Bombay, and told the people that the root of satyagraha was in prayer. If they learnt the art of dying cheerfully in the performance of their duty, they would convert and control the hooligan elements in the country. To him Ramnam was the infallible remedy for all ills. He stayed from March 16 to 30 partly at Poona and at Uruli-Kanchan, returning to Bombay on March 31. He then stayed for a day at the Harijan Colony in Worli where an attempt was made by some misguided persons to burn down his hut.

The British Labour and Liberal Press applauded Attlee for the great step he proposed to take. So did the American and French Press. On March 24, 1946, the Cabinet Mission arrived in Delhi and Gandhi was invited to meet it. He stayed at the Bhangi Colony in Delhi, and later at Simla and Mussoorie before returning to Delhi where he remained till June 28. He discussed the Cabinet Mission proposals with Cripps and Pethick-Lawrence on a number of occasions at Delhi and Simla, and made statements several times at both places. He was happy and expressed his faith in the good intentions of the British Cabinet. He visited the I.N.A. internees and said: "We should be proud of the I.N.A. men." He declared in *Harijan* of March 30, 1946, that his instinct told him that Subhas Bose was alive. "But God alone knows," he went on, "for truth is God." With a view to harnessing their energy to national work, Gandhi appealed to the I.N.A. men to help people fight famine with the same courage and cohesion, doggedness and resourcefulness which they had shown on the battlefield.

Gandhi also met, at Bhangi Colony, the Ex-President of America, Herbert Hoover, then Chairman of the U.S. Famine Commission, and Jayaprakash Narayan who had been released on April 11, 1946. He also advised the Working Committee in Delhi on some important issues. The outstanding feature of the Cabinet Mission discussions was that Jinnah spoke for the Muslims, Maulana Azad, the Congress President, for the Hindus and the Nawab of Bhopal for Princely India!

Numerous official and informal series of interviews, discussions and deliberations took place in the Viceregal Lodge with leaders and Premiers of Provinces, and with Sapru, Jinnah, Azad, Gandhi and Ambedkar in Delhi and Simla. The Mission missed getting the advice of Srinivas Sastri who died on April 17, 1946. Sastri had supported Savarkar in his stand for a united India. The Hindu Mahasabha leaders, Dr. S P. Mookerjee and L. B. Bhopatkar, told the Mission that the partition of India under any guise or disguise would be economically unsound and disastrous, and politically suicidal.

JINNAH VOICED HIS opposition to the setting up of one Constituent Assembly. And the fight for Pakistan took a grim turn. On April 5, 1946, Jawaharlal Nehru thundered at Delhi: "The Congress is not going to agree to the Muslim League demand for Pakistan under any circumstances whatever, even if the British Government agrees to it."[12] Jinnah went a step ahead at the age of 70. He told the representative of *News Chronicle* that he did not consider himself an Indian. His lieutenants began to talk of civil war. H. S. Suhrawardy threatened the British Government, stating that if it entrusted the destiny of India to the Congress *Junta* the Muslim League would not allow the Central Government to function even for a day.[13] Feroz Khan Noon warned that the destruction and havoc that the Muslims would do in the country would put into the shade what Chengiz Khan had done![14] Jinnah told a reporter that it was essential to have a corridor to join the two blocs of Pakistan. He refused to meet Azad as President of the Congress. This was the first round of the last phase in the creation of Pakistan.

A Tripartite Conference consisting of the British Ministers, the Viceroy and the representatives of the Congress and the Muslim League, was held at Simla on May 12, 1946, but it failed to arrive at a decision. The Mission then came out with a new proposal now known as the State Paper of May 16. The *prima donna* on India's stage, observed the American magazine *Time*, was Jinnah and not Gandhi. And Gandhi, the adviser to the Cabinet Mission, said, "Their one purpose is to end British rule as early as may be. It is an appeal and an advice. It has no compulsion in it. Freedom to opt out is an additional safeguard."[15] He described the

State Paper of May 16 as a brave and frank document, but added that the popular and not official interpretation should prevail. Gandhi had told Cripps that where his advice would contradict Nehru's, he should follow Pandit Nehru's advice rather than his own!

The State Paper repudiated Jinnah's demand for the division of India, contemplated a central union with powers restricted only to matters of external affairs, defence and communications, gave full autonomy to the provinces and provided facilities to the provinces to form themselves into three groups, two of which designated B and C were mischievously conceived as a concession to the Muslim League. A Constituent Assembly was to be elected by the Provincial legislators of the major communities, the important minorities and the Princely States, which were freed from Crown paramountcy.

The League accepted the State Paper on May 22, hoping to arrive at Pakistan through the proposed groups. Jinnah proposed to hold out his hand of "co-operation" to the Congress. The Congress, too, accepted the plan of May 16 as it stood, and declared its willingness to join the Constituent Assembly with a view to framing the constitution of a free, united and democratic India.

On June 29 the Cabinet Mission returned to London leaving it to Lord Wavell to work out the procedure and to form an interim Government.

Gandhi returned to Bombay on June 29 and took a train to Poona the next day. A rail disaster was narrowly averted near Karjat. Gandhi was asleep but when he came to know about it said he was saved a seventh time. The first thing Gandhi did at Poona was to write an article on "Atom Bomb and Ahimsa". "The moral," he observed, "to be legitimately drawn from the supreme tragedy of the bomb is that it will not be destroyed by counter bombs as violence cannot be by violence. Mankind has to get rid of violence only through non-violence. Hatred can be overcome only by love."

Meantime Nehru had gone to Kashmir to help his friend Sheikh Abdulla who was on trial. Nehru was arrested but soon released at the intervention of the Viceroy. Nehru was President of the States People's Conference and President-elect of the Congress.

Gandhi attended the Working Committee and the A.I.C.C. which met under its new President, Pandit Nehru. Seeing the critical situation in the history of the nation and the way the negotiations were being conducted by the Congress leaders, Gandhi realized that Nehru should be their leader and speak in a representative capacity for the nation. Besides, Nehru was on friendly terms with several British statesmen. Gandhi said that "he was a fine and stable bridge between the old and the new". At the instance of Gandhi, Patel and Kripalani had withdrawn from the presidential contest. Gandhi frankly told the A.I.C.C. that he had asked Nehru to wear the crown of thorns for the sake of the nation and that he had agreed to do so. The fact was that at this time Azad had inadvertently displeased Gandhi. He had written a letter to Cripps over the heads of his colleagues and Cripps had shown the letter to Gandhi. Besides, Azad had been President of the Congress for a long period of six years and unlike Patel, Nehru was nearer to the nationalist Muslims being a secular and not a Hindu-minded leader. It was a well-known quip in Congress circles that the only genuinely nationalist Muslim was Nehru!

From July 9 to August 5, 1946, Gandhi was in Poona. During this period he rested for some days at Panchgani and at Uruli-Kanchan where he met Louis Fischer as well as the African Indian delegation. He addressed the Deccan princes on July 28 at Poona and on July 29 spoke to the Congress Education Ministers and the Congress Ministers for Industries.

The Deccan princes were thinking of forming a union. Gandhi asked them each to form first a union with their own people and then consult Nehru who was the President of the States' People's Conference. His speech was rather sharp and slashing without bad words!

Addressing the Congress Education Ministers, Gandhi said that were he in a ministerial chair, he would issue broad instructions that thereafter all educational activity of the Government would be on basic education lines. To the Congress Commerce Ministers he said that they should pay attention to the village industries. He added that he did not believe in arm-chair or armed socialism. Dr. Lohia had entered Goa at this time and the Portuguese Governor-General wrote to Gandhi referring to him as a stranger. Gandhi replied that the Portuguese, coming from Portugal, were strangers whether philanthropists or Governors. He warned the Goa Government that in Free India Goa could not be allowed to exist as a separate entity in opposition to the laws of a Free State.

In July 1943 the Scheduled Castes Federation had launched a satyagraha in Poona before the Council Hall. Dr. Ambedkar demanded a blue-print from the Congress regarding the right and interests of the six crores of Untouchables in the future constitution of India. Gandhi, who was in Poona, took note of it and said in *Harijan* of August 4, 1946, that there was a parody of satyagraha in the "show" staged by Dr. Ambedkar and added that even if the means were non-violent the cause was certainly vague.

Having been empowered as an authoritative spokesman of the Congress, Nehru told a Press Conference in Bombay on July 10 that there could finally be no grouping of provinces, as the Congress held that provinces should be considered free at the initial stage to opt out of the section or group in which they were placed. This unstatesmanlike statement of Nehru gave an opportunity to Jinnah to push forward his demands, and on July 17, 1946, the Muslim League Council resolved at its meeting in Bombay to resort to direct action, rejecting the Cabinet Mission proposal which it had previously accepted. Jinnah refused to discuss the ethics of violence and non-violence, and the League Secretary declared their determination to employ every means in their power.

On August 9 the Congress Working Committee appealed to the Sikh leaders to reconsider their decision and join the Constituent Assembly. After Congress gave them certain assurances, they decided to do so.

On August 12 the Viceroy invited Nehru, the President of the Congress, to make proposals for the immediate formation of an Interim Government, and Nehru accepted the invitation. On August 13 Nehru wrote a letter to Jinnah seeking his cooperation, but Jinnah's reply was in the negative. On August 15 Nehru met Jinnah at his Bombay residence but to no purpose.

Communal riots had been going on since May 1946. These had cast their lengthening shadows over many cities in the land as the Muslim leaders and papers recklessly encouraged communal hysteria. Any Muslim who was not a Muslim Leaguer was considered a traitor, a Hindu, a Kaffir deserving death. And as planned, organized and ordered by the Muslim League, direct action began on August 16.

Jinnah had told pressmen that Muslims would launch a struggle which would be a thousand times worse than the 1942 struggle. The League Ministry of Bengal deliberately declared August 16 as a holiday. The police were silent observers of the butchery, and the military remained inactive. Not getting Government protection, the Hindus organized and retaliated with equal vehemence.

About 10,000 men, women and children were massacred. The victims were largely Hindus. The Muslim League's terrible direct action led to an unprecedented holocaust in Calcutta. It is now known as the great killing. In a short while the virus spread over the Noakhali District in Eastern Bengal where Hindus formed 18 per cent of the population and Muslim 80 per cent. There the direct action resulted in looting, arson, kidnapping and wholesale murders, forced conversions and forced marriages of Hindu women.

"War was not like this," wrote a military officer in the *Statesman*, Calcutta. British Imperialism had physically disarmed the Hindus and, in general, Gandhi's thirty-year emphasis on non-violence had enfeebled them. The goats swore by non-violence and the wolves sprang upon them. The army was called in at Calcutta to stop the orgy of murders and to restore order. Suhrawardy, the Chief Minister of Bengal, gained 'notoriety as the great killer of Calcutta.

CHAPTER XLV

In Noakhali and Bihar

GANDHI RETURNED TO Sevagram on August 6, 1946, and attended a Working Committee meeting. At Sevagram he met Raja Mahendra Pratap, the great revolutionary patriot, who had just returned to India. On August 24, on the eve of his departure for Delhi, Gandhi said, "I am leaving for Delhi tomorrow; I do not know when I shall return from there." The last group he addressed at Sevagram was the Basic Teachers' camp. He left Sevagram on August 25 and reached Delhi the next day. The cottage he lived in at Sevagram is called *Akhirinivas*. He had noted in his *Harijan* of August 25, 1946, "Calcutta has given an ocular demonstration what direct action is and how it is to be done."

On August 25 the Viceroy declared his resolve to form an Interim Government of sixteen members of which six were to be nominees of the Congress, five of the League and five representatives of the Minorities. The Congress took office on September 2, 1946, gave one of its six seats to the depressed classes and one to a Muslim and stood by its principles. The Muslim League did not co-operate. Its main objection was that the grouping should not be disturbed and that all the Muslim members should be nominees of the League. Pandit Nehru became the Vice-President of the Cabinet. Patel, Rajagopalachari, Rajendra Prasad, Sarat Bose, Asaf Ali and Jagjivan Ram were his Congress colleagues in the Cabinet. The others were: Sardar Baldeo Singh, Dr. John Matthai, Sir Shafaat Ahmed Khan, Syed Ali Zaheer and C. H. Bhabha. Sir Shafaat was stabbed by a Muslim fanatic.

Gandhi was jubilant. Early in the morning he met the Congress Ministers, who had sought his blessings before taking the oath. Being a silence day, he wrote his message on a piece of paper: "End the Salt Act, do not forget the Dandi March. Achieve communal unity. Remove untouchability and make khadi universal." Gandhi wrote a note to Nehru. At his prayer meeting, Gandhi described the day as a red-letter day in India's history, thanked the British Government for having resolved an age-old issue between Britain and India by arriving at a peaceful settlement of the problem. "Power," he observed, "has not yet been completely transferred into our hands. The Viceroy is still here with the army. Sooner, rather than later, complete power will be in our hands, if Pandit Nehru, our uncrowned king and first Prime Minister, and his colleagues fully and worthily do their part. The Viceroy would, then, himself vacate his palace and to be sure, it will be turned into a hospital for the poor, including the Harijans who are the poorest of the poor."[1]

Gandhi stayed in Delhi from August 26 to October 27, a helpless witness to the inhuman atrocities and terrible massacres. He was busy discussing political affairs with the Viceroy and the Nawab of Bhopal. The latter was doing his utmost to bring about a compromise between the Congress and the League. Gandhi paid a return call on the Nawab of Bhopal. He attended a Working Committee meeting, gave an interview to Preston Grover, an American reporter, and met H. N. Kunzru. In *Harijan* of October 6, 1946, replying to a question about Hindu-Muslim unity, Gandhi frankly admitted: "I must own defeat on that point." Yet his advice to the Hindus was that Hindu-Muslim unity "would be a present possibility if Hindus in their lakhs offered themselves to be cut to pieces without retaliation or anger in their hearts".[2] Gandhi's critics were provoked to say that this was a monomaniacal principle, and not non-violence! Had Gandhi not told the Hindus that cows must go into the mouth of the tiger in large numbers so that its appetite might be satisfied?

In the second week of October 1946, it was found that during the negotiations with the League, the sentence "the League was the representative body of the Muslims" was written instead of the sentence "the League was the authoritative organization of an overwhelming majority of the Muslims." Nehru rectified the mistake. Gandhi openly confessed his blunder on October 12 at his prayer meeting and said he had lost confidence in himself and the belief that he would live for 125 years. He was, he added, old now and his brain was getting weak and his memory never was good. And as penance for his error he fasted for four days.

Nehru's Interim Government proved unequal to the task of putting down the organized fanaticism of the Muslims. The army was neutral. The Home Department of Patel could not prevent the butchery in Calcutta and Noakhali. Amidst this confusion Jinnah shrewdly pushed his lieutenants into the Interim Government on October 26, 1946, without raising his usual objection to the inclusion of the Congress Muslim member. They were Liaquat Ali, Chundrigar, Abdul Rab Nishtar, Ghaznafar Ali Khan and Jogendra Nath Mandal. The last was a depressed class leader who had helped to save Suhrawardy from defeat during a no-confidence motion. And Jinnah's fight for Pakistan thus continued with renewed force and fire to smash the administration and sabotage the Cabinet Mission Plan which had sought to establish an All-India Central Government.

The League leaders and their Ministers in the Central and Provincial Legislatures wrote and spoke in words of fire and all under the very eyes of Nehru and Patel. Ghaznafar Ali Khan said: "If Mohammad Bin Kasim and Muhammed of Ghazni could invade India with armies composed of a few thousands, and yet were able to overpower lakhs of Hindus, God willing, a few lakhs of Muslims will yet overwhelm crores of Hindus." On another occasion he asked the Hindus to embrace Islam to save themselves from the holocaust.

On the day the Muslim League joined the Interim Government, Gandhi left for Calcutta to establish peace and amity. About 10,000 men, women and children had been killed in Calcutta. Stones were pelted at his train in Aligarh. Nehru, Patel, Liaquat Ali and Nishtar went to Calcutta to establish peace. For a week Gandhi was in Calcutta and strove to bring about peace there till November 5. He sought the help of Suhrawardy, the keeper who had turned a poacher.

Echoes of the terrible tragedies in Bengal were on the lips of everybody in India. Bihar was in turmoil. Moved by the multitudes of Hindu refugees who were deprived of their homes, wives, children and property, the Bihari Hindus were enraged. On October 25, which Bihar had observed as Noakhali Day, they began retaliating on such a scale that Jinnah said retaliation elsewhere for the killing in Bihar would be a catastrophe. His human heart now showed signs of grief for a time. At this juncture Jinnah advocated exchange of population,[3] but the suggestion was ignored; for what would Gandhi and Nehru do with their ideal of secularism and nationalism without the Muslims?

The climax of the disturbances was reached in the first week of November 1946. Lord Wavell, the Commander-in-Chief, Nehru and Nishtar flew to the scene in Bihar. Patel too resorted to drastic action, but he had warned the Viceroy, according to a report in *Hindustan Standard* that if East Bengal did not stop the rioting, Bihar might start trouble which would be followed by disturbances in the whole of India! Nehru threatened the Bihar Hindus with bullets and with bombing from the air. He had no bullets for the butchers who bled Noakhali. There his policy of non-intervention in provincial autonomy came in his way. The police opened fire a number of times in Bihar and all the Government forces ruthlessly suppressed the Hindu retaliatory riots in Bihar. Dr. Ambedkar described this dreadful situation as a Government of one country by two nations!

Then Gandhi went a step further. On November 5 he threatened the Bihari Hindus with a fast. Moral prophet that he was, Gandhi wrote on November 6 from Sodepur, Calcutta: "Bihar of my dreams has falsified them. It is easy enough to retort that things under the Muslim League Government in Bengal were no better, if not worse and that Bihar is merely a result of the latter. A bad act of one party is no justification for a similar act by the opposing party." He added that he had already reduced his diet and this low diet would become a fast unto death. Gandhi always undertook a fast to chide the Hindus, as they naturally bore affection for him. He knew what would happen to his fast if he undertook one to chide the Muslims. Some progressive Muslims had expressed their displeasure and written to him that he never tried to reform the Muslims or criticize their religion as he did in the case of Hinduism and Hindus.

It should be noted here that there was wide discontent among the Hindus at the well-meant but contradictory attitude of the Congress which helplessly witnessed and heard about the massacres of the Hindus in Bengal. Even Congress minded newspapers resented this attitude. The *Yashoda* in its weekly issue (Vol. VI, No. 4, 78 Gandhian Era) observed in its editorial: "If Nehru's body must fall, it must fall at Noakhali. If Gandhiji is to fast, he should fast in Noakhali. The dark figures of the great tragedy enacted at Noakhali must be brought to justice." The *Yashoda* further observed that Noakhali bled, and nobody went near the place till there was no more to be bled, and added: "But the role of Gandhiji throughout is as untenable as it is incredulous. Till the communal flare in Bihar, he was passive. No other explanation can be offered for his guilty inactivity over the East Bengal affair."

Violence whenever, wherever and howsoever it occurs must be condemned by all sensible persons and leaders. The violence which provokes the subsequent violence must be curbed and condemned first. And without doubt the Congress leaders lamentably failed in this sacred duty. One cannot be a passive spectator of violence at one time and an active suppressor at another.

The general effect of Gandhi's policy was that his popularity began to wane and the circulation of *Harijan* progressively diminished from this period.

A correspondent of the Associate Press of America rightly asked Gandhi: "In view of recent Indian history of 1942 unrest, I.N.A. movement, R.I.N. mutiny, Calcutta-Bombay disturbances, movements in Indian States such as Kashmir and recent communal riots can it be said your creed of non-violence has failed, in so far as non-violence has not taken roots in Indian life?" Gandhi replied that it was a dangerous generalization!

AT SODEPUR GANDHI was worried and reserved. He lost his temper with Satish Babu and rebuked him for the kind of volunteers he had posted for special duties. Prof. Nirmal Kumar Bose was surprised to see that the Mahatma was human enough to lose his temper! So, in his book, *My Days with Gandhi*, he gave some close-ups of his outbursts! In the first week of November Gandhi declared that the ban imposed on the *Satyarth Prakash* by the Sind Government was senseless and urged its removal. None but a fanatic bans a religious book.

While Gandhi's inner voice was telling him, "You may not live to be a witness to this senseless slaughter," he and his party left Sodepur on November 6, 1946, with a heavy heart for Noakhali by a special train fitted with a microphone. During his walking tour he visited Chandipur, Dattapara, Kazirkhil and Madhupur and stayed in Srirampur from November 20 to January 1, 1947. He surveyed the sites of destruction and made a plea for sanity. His was, he said, a Do or Die mission, a venture in faith. It was a painful sight to him to see the images of his dreams reduced to ashes. According to him, ahimsa was the chief glory of Hinduism. He was proving it by his example. He wore leather sandals and walked unaided, slipping frequently.

From Noakhali, Gandhi declared in *Harijan* that Bihar had forgotten humanity. He told the Muslims of Noakhali District that the Hindus of Bihar had given way to madness. As was his wont on such occasions he harped on his memories of the Ali Brothers. He asked the Hindus, whenever he found them in any village, not to run away from their villages but to make every effort to live in peace with their Muslim neighbours. Gandhi and his party saw numerous villages in which many persons had been killed, houses burnt and property damaged. Mrs. Sucheta Kripalani who returned from her tour of Noakhali said, "Molestation of women, intimidation and encirclement were still going on in the affected areas of Noakhali District".

At Srirampur Gandhi's stenographer, Parsuram, who was most devoted and selfless, deserted Gandhi as Gandhi's experiments in sex were intolerable to him. Gandhi lay naked in bed with his granddaughter Manu. This kind of relationship he also had with his several other female associates. It is not known whether their guardians had given their consent to Gandhi to making such experiments with these women. Kishorlal Mashruwala and Narhari Parekh had objected to these experiments. The discussion went on for months.

On February 14, 1947, Gandhi wrote to Birla[4] and others asking whether there was any sin in such experiments. Gandhi wanted to issue a statement on his sex experiments but Sardar Patel was opposed to it. Patel told Gandhi that what Gandhi looked upon as dharma was really *adharma*. Devadas Gandhi was also opposed to these experiments. Others said that though perfectly spotless, Gandhi should conduct himself as the world desired him to do. Gandhi wrote to Birla: "For after all I am not God. I can commit mistakes; (for aught one knows) this may prove to be my biggest at the fag-end of my life. If that be so, all my well-wishers can open my eyes if they oppose me. If they do not (it means) I shall go from hence even as I am (unreformed). Whatever I am doing here it as a part of my *yajna* (duty)."

Gandhi was 77 at this time. "The point," he said, "we must make our friends grasp is this: when I take M. in my lap, do I do so as a pure-hearted father or as a father who has strayed from the path of virtue? What I am doing is nothing new to me; in thought I have done it for the last 50 years; in action, in varying degrees, over quite a number of years."

Prasad Diksha, a book containing Gandhi's letters to Miss Prema Kantak, was published in Marathi but it was never allowed to go into print in Gujarati, Hindi or English. This book contains letters which reveal a few of the sex whims of the Mahatma. Gandhi was overconscious of his sex. He had tried for years to suppress it. But he could not succeed in banishing it from his thoughts. It may be said that no great Indian saint ever made such experiments with women, married or unmarried. A saint who does so would not stand high in the domain of culture and religion. Let his blind devotees say that Gandhi, like some other saints, tried to be a God's eunuch or a mother to his women associates, but the fact remains.

The damp climate affected Gandhi. He suffered from catarrh. Several bottles of water were kept by his bedside. He awoke at 4.30 a.m. every morning and his mosquito curtain was removed. He brushed his gums. He had an iron bowl on his lap when doing this. At the prayers he kept time by clapping. He ate walnuts and almonds. At 5.30 a.m. he took 16 ounces of orange or *mosambi* juice, and at 7 a.m. 16 ounces of goat's milk and 8 ounces of orange or *mosambi* juice. At 12 noon he drank 16 ounces of goat's milk boiled down to 4 ounces, ate boiled vegetables, 8 ounces, raw vegetables like tomatoes, carrots, etc. 8 ounces, and a salad of green leaves like *palong* or coriander 2 ounces. At 2 p.m. he drank a glass of coconut milk. At 5 p.m. he had 16 ounces of goat's milk boiled down to 4 ounces, 19 ounces of dates boiled in milk, and a small quantity of fruit including kernel of coconut.[5] Often he used to lie down for half an hour with a mud-pack upon his abdomen and a cold mud poultice on his forehead. From the menu given above one can understand why a fellow-passenger once asked Gandhi whether his food was worth only six pice and sharply criticized him for not living up to his ideal of complete identification with the poor.[6]

At meal-time Gandhi used a set of false dentures. A patient of chronic amebiasis, he suffered also from high blood pressure, and the veins in his temples often throbbed, causing him acute discomfort.

A cotton mattress, two pillows and a bed-cover consisting of two or more shawls of wool were also with him.

Somebody gave presents to the party and when Nehru came to meet Gandhi, Bapu gave him, on December 27, 1946, a packet of cigarettes reserved for him! Every other gift was given away. Shankarrao Deo, Kripalani and Nehru had long discussions with Gandhi at Srirampur.

Nehru and Jinnah had been invited to London in the first week of December 1946 to settle the differences arising out of the grouping proposition and the set-up of the Constituent Assembly. The British Prime Minister, Attlee, and the Cabinet Mission had a conference with Wavell, Nehru, Jinnah and Baldev Singh. They failed to arrive at any decision. The British Ministry upheld Jinnah's interpretation of the grouping proposition of the State Paper. They also announced that any constitution framed without the consent of large elements of the population could not be forced on unwilling parts of the country.

Defeated at the Conference, Nehru returned to India. On December 9 the Constituent Assembly met and Dr. Rajendra Prasad was elected President on December 11, 1946. Nehru made an impressive speech in the Constituent Assembly on the declaration of objectives, declaring India's objective as an Independent Sovereign Republic. The Muslim League boycotted the Constituent Assembly.

Gandhi was groping in the dark. He said sadly:

"The night is dark and I am far from home,
Lead thou me on."

Then he explained his Do or Die mission. To do meant that Hindus and Muslims should live together in peace, otherwise he would die in the attempt. He told the Hindus that real safety could be only when they placed reliance wholly on God. According to him, true prayers never were unheard. Friends were sceptical about his success and he himself was sceptical of it. He asked himself whether his ahimsa had become bankrupt, but as was his wont he dubbed the Hindus cowards. He remarked to a friend, "I have met human monsters from my earliest youth." Everywhere there was a demand for more and more military protection. Muslims desired to drive Gandhi out of Noakhali. They objected to the Sikh volunteers accompanying him even without their Kripan. Gandhi told his opponents that he did not want to return from Bengal defeated. He would rather die, if need be, at the hands of an assassin.

Gandhi told some correspondents that any question, of exchanging populations was unthinkable and impracticable. That question never crossed his mind, he added. He found that, "my ahimsa does not seem to answer in the matter of Hindu-Muslim relations" although he positively believed that ahimsa was a perfect instrument, but he said his technique was at fault. So he had put his ahimsa to the acid test. In his very lifetime, massacres had taken place in his own country. These monstrous deeds falsified his boast that if massacres happened after his death it should be taken for granted that the ahimsa in him was narrow or false. During Gandhi's very lifetime, it was cruelly proved so.

GANDHI STARTED A 'one-night-one-village' walking tour of East Bengal on January 5, 1947, when he left Chandipur for Masimpur, and ended the tour at Haim Char on March 2, 1947. So far he had not disclosed to the world that he himself, the author of non-violence, had been moving in Noakhali under military escort. On being asked how one who was subject to fear could give courage to others, he replied, "I do happen to be moving under armed protection. I am surrounded by armed police and military, keenly alert to guard me from all danger. I am helpless in the matter as it is arranged by the Government which being responsible to the people feels that it is their duty to keep me guarded by the police and military. How can I prevent them from doing so?"[7] The Sikhs were giving him valuable assistance and, if he refused that service, he added, he would fall in his own estimate. This was how Gandhi tested his ahimsa, under the protection of armed police, the military and his brave Sikh volunteers! They were doing their duty!

Gandhi was 78 when he undertook this hazardous tour. Only a man of his boundless energy and undying enthusiasm could have attempted to perform the feat.

Nirmal K. Bose, while shaving his master Gandhi, for full five months, asked him many questions about Noakhali and showed a particularly keen interest in Gandhi's sexual experiments and attitudes. Unfortunately he shed no useful light in his book on the Noakhali adventure undertaken with a lakh of rupees and with the help of the military, armed police and Sikh volunteers. It was not the tour of a Mahatma but the procession of a Monarch!

During his tour Gandhi's ears were poisoned against Sardar Patel by some interested persons. Patel did nothing but his duty to save India from the revolts of the Muslims in Delhi, Punjab and Alwar and from rioting by the Khaksars. When Patel asked the Hindus to protect themselves with whatever weapons they could find, he was accused of inflammatory speeches and violence. Gandhi asked Patel to clarify his position and wrote to him that there were frequent differences between Patel's approach and his own to political problems.

Patel replied to Gandhi refuting his charges. When Patel was further accused of repression by the Muslims, he told Gandhi that the Khaksars wanted Delhi, Agra and Ajmer to be included in Pakistan!

What was the effect of Gandhi's military-guarded tour on the Muslims of East Bengal? While Gandhi did his peace work, the arson and the killing were going on. The Government which used the military for the protection of Gandhi had no sympathy for the tragic fate of the Hindu minority. The Muslims in East Bengal continued to carry out their atrocities. Their opposition took a vulgar turn towards the end of February 1947. They deliberately dirtied the roads every day, they boycotted his meetings. Patel informed Gandhi that the Governor of Bengal and the Bengal Ministry also wanted to oust him from Bengal.

At this sad moment, Syed Mahmud came to Gandhi's succour. He sent an urgent call to Gandhi urging him to save the Bihar Muslims. Gandhi, after a tour of nearly four months, left the Noakhali Hindus to God and went to Bihar, reaching Patna with the piece of pumice stone with which his feet were daily cleaned.

Meanwhile, the British Government announced, on February 20, 1947, complete transfer of power by June 1948. Wavell, who used his only eye to observe Muslim interests, was recalled and Lord Mountbatten was appointed Viceroy. Lord Wavell wanted the Congress to form a coalition Government even in the Provinces and create a stalemate all over India! It is said that Gandhi had cabled to the British Government to recall Lord Wavell who had done much mischief to the Indian nationalist cause.

On reaching Patna on March 5, 1947, Gandhi started his peace mission. Abdul Ghaffar Khan joined him. In the second week of March, Gandhi's close associates Swami Anand and Kedarnathji came to Patna to make private inquiries regarding Gandhi's sex experiments. They asked Nirmal K. Bose's opinion on the subject. His explanation to them displeased Gandhi, and Nirmal K. Bose left Gandhi on March 18, 1947. It was Gandhi's opinion that Nirmal K. Bose was unjust to women who shared his Guru's bed. Nirmal K. Bose's discovery was that Gandhi defended his close associates, and placed their loyalty above many other things, even national work. If one questioned Gandhi's purity, the Mahatma would fly into a temper, and when he had tremors he was held tightly to the bosom by his disciples. Bose gave a psychological justification for Gandhi's sex experiments. He said that Gandhi was trying to be a woman, and repression was a means to his lofty end, serving also as a penance for his proving untrue to his dying father. As whispers and small talk and innuendoes were going on, Gandhi told a prayer meeting at Amishapara on February 1, that he wanted to be God's eunuch and that is why he shared his bed with his granddaughter Manu Gandhi. Nirmal Bose did not ask Gandhi why it was necessary for Gandhi to share his bed with women if he believed that he could become a God's eunuch not through an operation but by prayer.[8]

Spiritual health is no more stable than bodily. The sicknesses of the soul have their ups and downs. Such was the case with Gandhi. These signs indicated that the spiritual health of Gandhi was very unsteady, although he might have been unaffected by passion as such. He did not explain the necessity of performing these sex experiments which he called *Yajna*, yet he asked the people to bless them blindfold! He afterwards wrote four articles in June 1947 in *Harijan* on *brahmacharya*, *Ramanama* and God but side-tracked the main issue of his sharing his bed regularly with women!

Gandhi tried to wean away the Hindus in Bihar from their anger and restore confidence in the Muslims. He told the Ministers that Congress rule could not be natural if Muslims were not free and safe under it. During his tour in Bihar, Dr. Daddoo and Naicker, the two Indian leaders from South Africa, met him and discussed their problems. Gandhi confessed to the Bihari Hindus that Muslims in Noakhali had not contributed towards the relief of the Hindus and that he was looked upon as enemy Number One rather than a friend by the majority of the Muslim community in India.[9] On March 19, 1947, Gandhi attended the funeral of his erstwhile colleague, Abdul Bari.

ON MARCH 22, 1947, the new Viceroy, Lord Mountbatten, arrived in Delhi to turn over India to Indians. Lord Wavell made his exit the next day. With his suave personality and persuasive optimism Lord Mountbatten resumed the threads of discussion. By now the Congress had demanded division of the Punjab into two parts and there was talk of the division of Bengal into two parts. Savarkar supported the partition of the Punjab and of Bengal, wishing the Hindu majority in East Punjab and West Bengal to join the Indian State. Gandhi was then being tricked by Suhrawardy into considering a scheme for a united Sovereign Bengal. That he considered the proposal worthy of discussion showed that Gandhi had lost his grip over political problems.

On March 26 Lord Mountbatten invited Gandhi to Delhi. He left Patna on March 30 and met the Viceroy on April 1, 1947. He believed that the Viceroy had come definitely to transfer power to Indian hands. Soon after his arrival, the Viceroy first met Gandhi, for the British statesmen did not give much importance to Patel or the President of the Congress. They knew that a settlement secured through Gandhi would be more beneficial to their nation than a settlement with other leaders. And Gandhi's consent covered Nehru's.

Although Gandhi was losing his power with the masses, he had a hold on the Congress. He attended the Inter-Asian Relations Conference on the same day at the *Purana Quila* in Delhi and, replying to some questions, he said that he would "not like to live in this world if it is not to be one". He said he would attend the conference because he could not say no to the Viceroy who had invited him to Delhi and since he had come to Delhi he would attend the conference, although he was Nehru's prisoner also. He requested the delegates not to carry to their countries, the law of the jungle which the Hindus and the Muslims had resorted to for the present. "Man can make his destiny," he added, "so far as he is allowed by the great power which overrides all our intentions, all our plans and carries out His own plans."

Gandhi told the conference with great emphasis that India, having her independence through essentially and predominantly non-violent means, would use its independence for the independence of the suppressed countries. At a prayer meeting he said that the conference was a big thing and their jewel Jawaharlal Nehru was the beloved of the delegates because of his love for them and his dream of a United Asia. It would be cruel to spoil Jawaharlal's dream of a United Asia by internal strife.

On April 2, Gandhi, addressing the conference, gave his message of love and truth and said that wisdom went to the West from the East through Zoroaster, Buddha, Jesus, Moses, and also from Mohammed who gave the message of Allah. Yet it was a pity that he was standing in the shade of a curfew order at the time of the Inter-Asian Relations Conference in Delhi which had been torn by violence.

On April 15, 1947, Gandhi and Jinnah issued a joint appeal to the communities deploring the recent acts of lawlessness and violence which had brought utmost disgrace to the fair name of

India and appealing to them to refrain from all acts of violence and disorder. There should be no violence employed, they added, in the pursuit of political aims. Gandhi was in Delhi from March 31 to April 12, 1947. His prayer meetings were disturbed. Some now opposed his reciting the Koran at his meetings. Valmiki temple was a Hindu temple and he could not recite the Koran there. He was asked whether he had sung the Gita in a mosque. Gandhi had said in his *Indian Home Rule*: "A man, whilst he is dreaming, believes in his dream; he is undeceived only when he is awakened from his sleep." He himself experienced this. He had lost the power of his charismatic leadership. He felt forsaken by his God, as people whispered that virtue had gone out of him.[10] His mission had come to an end.

Gandhi was called a fifth columnist, a slave of Jinnah and 'Mohammed Gandhi'[11] by many fanatics. He said he would willingly have prayed and hoped he would have had the courage to die at their hands with the names of Rama and Rahim on his lips if they wanted to kill him. It was because he was a sanatani Hindu, he observed, that he claimed to be a Christian, a Buddhist, a Muslim. He appealed to the Hindus and the Sikhs not to retaliate. He dared say that even if all Hindus and Sikhs died without retaliation at the hands of their Muslim brethren they would save not only Hinduism and Sikhism but also serve Islam and save the world. He had already offered a plan to the Hindus. He wanted them to fall victims to the knives of the Muslims like cows into the mouth of a tiger to appease his hunger.

Mountbatten was working with great speed to transfer power to India while Churchill was wailing about the scattering and squandering of the crown and the empire. He talked about India being shamelessly cast away. In a speech at the Primrose League he attacked Attlee's policy. Replying to it, Prime Minister Clement Attlee said at the Scottish Trade Union Council on April 25, 1947: "Churchill ignores the great movement for self-Government which has been spreading throughout Asia for decades. He abandons the democratic principle for which he fought in the war. The fact is that on the subject Mr. Churchill never thinks. He only gives way to his emotion."[12] Nehru's was the clarion call of Asian freedom while Churchill's was the last shriek of a dying empire!

Gandhi was at Patna from April 13 to April 30, 1947. On May 1 he again went to Delhi to meet the Viceroy. On May 4 Gandhi attended a Working Committee meeting and saw the

Viceroy. He was impressed by the Viceroy and he praised him for his sincerity in transferring power to India. On May 2 Gandhi had expressed his fear at the prayer meeting, "God forbid that India should ever become a military nation, which "would be a menace to the peace of the world". On May 6 Gandhi called on Jinnah at his Delhi residence. About this time Sane Guruji, a Maharashtrian Gandhist leader, went on a fast to compel the trustees of the Vithoba temple at Pandharpur to throw it open to the Harijans. Gandhi wired Sane Guruji not to go on fast, but he persisted and succeeded in his object on May 10 with all the progressive social forces backing up his cause. And the Harijans entered the temple on November 20.

Gandhi visited Calcutta and discussed the scheme for a United Sovereign Bengal with Dr. Shyama Prasad Mookerjee, Sarat Bose and Suhrawardy. The Bengali Hindus had no faith in Suhrawardy, the killer, and they demanded partition of Bengal. Gandhi asked them, "Why do you regard Pakistan as inevitable?" On May 15 Gandhi returned to Patna for his peace mission. He again visited Delhi on May 25, and put up at Bhangi Colony. During the journey he lost his watch at Kanpur which he had used for about 25 years. A British watch manufacturer presented him with a new watch.

Meanwhile, in April, Jawaharlal Nehru, Sardar Vallabhbhai Patel and Rajendra Prasad were ready to surrender the unity and integrity of India to Jinnah. Nehru declared at the U.P. Political Conference that the Muslims should have Pakistan if they wanted it. Vallabhbhai Patel said it should be done with mutual discussion and Rajendra Prasad expressed anxiety about the division of the defence forces! With these commitments of the Congress leaders the new Viceroy went to London on May 18, and secured sanction for his blue-print and also for the swift procedure of its execution.

CHAPTER XLVI

The Tragic End

LORD MOUNTBATTEN RETURNED on May 30, 1947, with the "Quit India" decision of the British Cabinet. He interviewed the Congress leaders, the Sikh leaders, Jinnah and Gandhi on June 2. Then, on June 3, the British Prime Minister from London and Mountbatten from Delhi announced simultaneously their new plan, known as the June 3rd Plan, which contemplated the creation of one or two Dominions by August 15, 1947, made provision for separate Constituent Assemblies, partition of the Punjab and Bengal provinces, and referendum for Baluchistan, the North-West Frontier Province and the Sylhet District of Assam to decide which Dominion they would join. Gandhi had come to Delhi on May 25 at the instance of Nehru and Patel.

Gandhi must have agreed to the partition of India before the Viceroy went to London, since he advised the Sind Hindus to take to migration in the event of partition and that view had appeared in *Harijan* of May 25, 1947. Both Jinnah and Gandhi had seen the Viceroy on May 4, 1947, before he went to London. It was impossible for Lord Mountbatten to go to London with his scheme for the partition of India without Gandhi's consent. And yet Gandhi asked the Bengal Hindus: "Why do you regard Pakistan as inevitable?"[1] On May 30 he told his prayer audience that if the Pakistan of Jinnah's conception was a reasonable proposition, he should have no difficulty in convincing[2] India to accept it!

During Gandhi's stay in Delhi, he sorrowfully observed: "In India as I see it shaping today there is no place for me. I have given up the hope of living 125 years. I might last a year or two. That is a different matter. But I have no wish to live if

India is to be submerged in a deluge of violence."[3] Gandhi's American disciple Richard Gregg consoled him in his sorrow and shed tears on the tragic situation in which his Indian Guru was involved. In the turmoil and the turbulent time Gandhi's voice became powerless.

In a written message on June 9, 1947, Gandhi explained the reason for his not actively opposing the vivisection of India. He was reminded of his vow that the vivisection of India would mean vivisection of himself. But he replied that he did not plead guilty to the taunts as when he made the statement he had been voicing public opinion. "But when public opinion was against him, was he to coerce it?" he asked. He admitted that he had become or rather was considered a back-number. "In any case," Gandhi concluded, "it was not dignified to swear at the Viceroy if the leaders were ill-chosen, or if the people were, so was the king."[4] His acceptance of Pakistan was a foregone conclusion. Gandhi tried to escape by throwing the blame on the people and on the leaders. Savarkar had made a desperate appeal to the Congress to seek the peoples' verdict by a plebiscite; for he said that the Congressmen had not been elected to the Legislatures on the issue of the partition of India. But to no avail!

Gandhi and Nehru now began to de-Hinduise everything. They described the Hindus as the non-Muslims of India. Gandhi said the Muslim majority provinces might call themselves Pakistan, but the rest and the largest part of India need not call itself Hindustan. Hindustan would mean the abode of Hindus, but Parsees, Jews, Christians and Anglo-Indians also lived in it. "That is why," Gandhi observed, "Pandit Nehru refused to call the non-Pakistan areas Hindustan and loved to call it by the proud name of the Union of Indian Republics."[5] The Hindus must thank Gandhi and Nehru for not calling Hindustan "non-Pakistan"! Hindustan was a political state just as Turkastan, Afghanistan, Baluchistan, Germany, Japan, France are nation states. All states and countries are named after the national majority.

Gandhi gave a timely warning to the Indian States that if they failed to take time by the forelock they would cease to be. Their declaration of freedom, he asserted, would be tantamount to war. He also said that an Indian was a citizen enjoying equal rights in every part of India, but he must submerge himself in the province where he resided. At this time Gandhi outdid himself by declaring his wish to install an ordinary Harijan girl into the Presidential chair of India. If he had really meant this, he would have asked the Congress to make Dr. Ambedkar the first President of India. Dr. Ambedkar was one of the greatest men of learning, an eminent politician and a reputed constitutionalist.

The All-India Congress Committee at its Delhi session on June 14, 1947, accepted the 3rd June Plan by a resolution supported by Nehru, the idol of the nation, who had unequivocally professed and declared in the vein of Lincoln that he would defend the integrity of India. But Nehru had not the will and the grit of Lincoln. This resolution was enthusiastically upheld by the nationalist Muslim, Maulana Azad, who had, on April 1946, insinuatingly stated that "the situation in India is such that all attempts to establish a centralized and unitary Government are bound to fail".[6]

With divine satisfaction Azad now supported the creation of Pakistan. He described the Plan as the only way to settle India's problem, as the Congress was committed, he recalled, to the principle of self-determination and was against coercing any unwilling areas to join the Union. But who got the Congress committed to that resolution? It was the crafty Azad; and Nehru had fallen a victim to it, self-determination being then a new idea in Indian politics.

The Socialists in the All-India Congress Committee culpably remained neutral in that meeting. They had no opinion to offer on such a vital issue concerning the life of the nation! The neutral action of the Socialists reflected their thoughts! The lonely member of the All-India Congress Committee opposing this nefarious move and black decision was Babu Purushottamdas Tandon. He appealed to the A.I.C.C. that though the Congress Working Committee had failed them, the A.I.C.C. had the strength of millions behind them and they must reject the resolution, the acceptance of which, he added, meant an abject surrender to the Muslim League and to the British. Sardar Patel's support to the partition of India was a complete change from the sword to surrender.

Gandhi, in his 40-minute address to the All-India Congress Committee, commended the Working Committee's resolution on the British Plan of June 3. He put an ultimatum before the A.I.C.C. He asked them either to accept the resolution conceding Pakistan or to replace the old tried Congress leaders who were responsible for all the achievements of the Congress. He advised them to accept the Plan and added that it was their duty to stand by their leaders. If they rejected the Working Committee's decision, he added, what would the world think of it? All the Parties, the British, the Congress and Muslim League had accepted it and it would not be proper for the Congress to go back on its word. The consequences of such a rejection would be the finding of a new set of leaders who could constitute not only the Congress Working Committee but also take charge of the Government. If the opponents of the resolution could find such a set of leaders they could then reject the resolution if they so felt.[7]

The goats surrendered to the wolves, to the law of the jungle, so that the land should bleed no more. It was the old, decrepit, tired Congress leaders, bred and brought up in Gandhian philosophy, and not the Hindu masses that surrendered to the force of the knife. The Congress leaders adapted themselves to the circumstance which was a creation of their policy and philosophy. Partition was an act of the Congress which yielded to the circumstances, and the Viceroy was powerless in the face of the Congress acceptance. The acceptance of partition exploded once for all the myth that Gandhi and Nehru were also the leaders of the Indian Muslims. Gandhi mishandled the question of the Muslims, got them organized on the wrong issue of the Khilafat, and turned Jinnah into an opponent—that patriot who had patriotically resigned his membership of the Imperial Legislature as a protest against the Rowlatt Act and wanted to be the Muslim Gokhale of India.

In consenting to the partition of India, Gandhi regarded the party above the country. *The Free Press Journal*, Bombay, one of the chief spokesmen of the Congress, flashed in full banner headline the news, 'Nation's Leaders Betray Country's Cause', Gandhi's movement started with the Khilafat and ended with the creation of Pakistan.

Who is a truth-seeker? One who clings to truth, even if the very heavens fall. But Gandhi the truth-seeker hit the last nail on the coffin of United India and the resolution accepting partition was passed. According to Gandhi, Pakistan was an untruth and the truth seeker became a party to untruth in broad daylight. To Gandhi, Pakistan was a denial of God, but he now deserted and denied God. Gandhi believed that nothing was impossible for a satyagrahi. Therefore, he could have easily declared with Luther, "peace if possible, but truth at any rate". The unfortunate politician in Gandhi who always failed, got the upper hand of the truth-seeker and stiffled the truth-seeker in him.

The charge which history will make against Gandhi is that he was the first national leader to accept the principle of the division of the country and was a party to the vivisection of India in spite of his declared vows and oaths. Formerly he was on the side of truth, but now he wanted truth on his side. And lo! Gandhi practised what he preached. Ten years earlier he had openly declared: "Needless to say, the Congress can never seek the assistance of British forces to resist the vivisection. It is the Muslims who will impose their will by force, singly or with British assistance on an unresisting India. If I can carry the Congress with me, I would not put the Muslims to the trouble of using force."[8] He fulfilled his promise to a letter!

The Congress leaders had grown quite old. They were thoroughly exhausted. They carried on negotiations with the Viceroy with many voices whereas the Muslim League did it through Jinnah alone. The Congress leaders proved their incapacity to rise to the occasion and show the grit of Lincoln in facing a civil war. The British ultimately sided with the Muslims, and the partition of India became a settled fact. "Had Gandhi told us not to accept partition," observed Pandit Nehru afterwards, "we could have gone on fighting and waiting." Later, on October 16, 1949, Nehru made a confession that he would have opposed the creation of Pakistan with all his might had he foreseen its effects.[10] Savarkar's prophesy came true. Savarkar, like Lincoln, was prepared to face a civil war and Ambedkar suggested transfer of population from the respective zones, but the Congress leaders accepted partition plus the massacre of two million people!

ON JULY 4, 1947, the Indian Independence Bill was introduced and passed by the British Parliament. Prime Minister Attlee had stated before the House of Commons on March 15, 1946, when he made the declaration of the proposed transfer of power, that the national idea had spread right through, not the least perhaps among some of the soldiers who had done such wonderful service in the war. Fenner Brockway, the political Secretary of the Independent Labour Party of England, gave three reasons for the transfer of power by Britain to India. He said that, the Indian people were determined to achieve independence; secondly, there was the revolt of the Royal Indian Navy and that the Indian forces could not be relied upon for serving Britain's purposes; and thirdly, Britain did not want to estrange India which was a market and a source of foodstuffs for her. Although they did not mention the I.N.A. directly, it was clear that the revolt in the Indian armed forces had bent them to the inevitable. Thus the war of independence, which was inaugurated by the heroes of 1857, and was fought heroically by revolutionaries inspired and led by Savarkar, the Anushilan Samiti and the Ghadr Party, by Subhas' I.N.A. and the men of the Royal Indian Navy and by thousands of Congressmen led by great Congress leaders like Tilak, Gandhi and Jawaharlal Nehru, came to a successful end.

The King signed the Independence Bill on July 18, 1947. India was divided and two national unions came into being, Jinnah preferred to be the Governor-General of Pakistan, and Lord Mountbatten remained the Governor-General of India. Gandhi's theory that "without Hindu-Muslim unity India cannot win freedom" was falsified and negated.

On July 7 Gandhi expressed his wish at the prayer meeting that the Hindus should swear that "they do not wish to have any army at all or, at least, refuse even to use it against their Muslim brethren whether in the union or outside it in Pakistan". Had India listened to this unarmed prophet it would have been by now under the heel of Pakistan. He regarded, Gandhi said, Pakistan as an established fact beyond dispute or discussion. On July 22 at the political-cum-prayer meeting, for every post-prayer meeting of his was political, Gandhi said that he had mistaken the Congress passive resistance for non-violence. He had been repeating this since 1934.

On July 22 some men, probably members of the Constituent Assembly, condoled with Gandhi that there was no "charkha" in the flag and that khadi was banished from it. Others again held that the "charkha was replaced by the wheel on its white surface. If the flag truly represented feeling, i.e., if the charkha and khadi were in their hearts, it was well. If not, the flag had no value for him".[11]

With the appearance of the new flag divorced from charkha and khadi and adorned with Ashoka's (wheel of law) chakra, and the silk surface, disappeared the last vestige of Gandhism. The Congress leaders themselves did it. Writing on the National Flag, in *Harijan* of August 3, Gandhi expressed his excruciating pain when he declared that "those, therefore, who say that the flag that was at one time the Congress flag has now become the National Flag are wrong". And he deeply, lamented: "I have not yet known a worthy son for whom age has disfigured his mother. It is conceivably possible to gild pure gold, but the son is yet to be born who would embellish his parent. Hence in my opinion nothing would have been lost if our councillors had never thought of interfering with the design of the original flag."

"I would refuse to salute the flag," Gandhi thundered furiously in the editorial, "that bears the foregoing interpretation, however artistic it may appear." And what was the interpretation Gandhi referred to? The promoters of the new flag chose Ashoka's disc mounted with lions and saw that the flag had no need of khadi. To them, the spinning wheel was an old woman's solace and Gandhi's toy. Gandhi again declared on August 7 that if the present design did not represent the original but something contrary, "my head would refuse to bow to the new flag". It seems Gandhi never saluted the National Flag.

At this time the South African problem had taken a serious turn and the Indians there were harassed. Gandhi urged General Smuts to resign if he could not control the unruly element in the European community.

In June Gandhi gave an interview to Prof. Colin Clark of Oxford University and told him that the Indian people were "idle". They were not really interested in spiritual or religious matters. They tended to avoid work. Indian businessmen were more interested in speculation than in production. Lastly, Gandhi expressed his categorical condemnation of contraceptives and sterilization. It was his confirmed opinion that "our real malady is not destitution but laziness, apathy and inertia. Laziness," he had once observed sorrowfully, "had been the plague of India!

Gandhi was in Delhi upto July 30, 1947, and on July 31 he left for Amritsar. At Phillaur station, a bomb was thrown at the train in which Gandhi was travelling. He visited Amritsar, Rawalpindi, Srinagar, Jammu and Lahore. He said at Lahore that the rest of his life was going to be spent in Pakistan, may be in East Bengal or West Punjab or perhaps in the N.W.F.P. He asked the people of West Punjab not to be panicky, but to be brave and courageous. "I would refuse to stop saying 'Rama' if I am forced to do so, and would prefer to be murdered. Similarly I cannot be forced to salute any flag," he added. He then went to Calcutta which was then under Congress rule. The Muslims in Calcutta were living in terror, and so he said he would like to give up his life if thereby he could contribute to the quenching of mob fury there. At Calcutta he said: "My present place is in Noakhali and I would go there even if I have to die."

On the evening of August 13, 1947, twenty-four hours before

the dawn of freedom, Gandhi moved from Sodepur locality in Calcutta to a house in Beliaghata, a riot-affected area, so as to restore peace in Calcutta. About a thousand young men staged a demonstration in front of his house in Beliaghata, and the mob which went on swelling shouted, "Gandhi, go back! Suhrawardy, go back! It demanded that Gandhi should go and settle in some area which Hindus had evacuated. Towards dusk the mob forced open the gates and climbed through the windows of the house shouting slogans. Gandhi give up his prayer, told the demonstrators that if he was convinced that he had committed a mistake in coming over there, he would move away. Shortly after, the commotion grew and the demonstrators started throwing brickbats at the windows. As a result the house was littered with broken pieces of glass and brickbats. The police used force to disperse the crowd.[12]

ON AUGUST 15, 1947, India became a free country. The historic event was celebrated by the Congress as a day of national rejoicing. Undoubtedly it was a great day in the history of the world as it saw a great liberating force released in Asia in the form of Indian Independence, and the birth of the biggest Muslim State under the Sun. And with their rise, the Sun set on the British Empire. Savarkar asked the Hindu Mahasabha not to celebrate the 15th of August, since the Motherland would be actually torn asunder on that day and the results of the disintegration were likely to lead to bitter feelings and ill-will. Gandhi, too, had said at Patna on August 8, "15th August is a day of our trial. Swaraj that has come is not worth celebrating by illumination. It is a day when we should fast and spin and pray".

Accordingly, Gandhi observed a one-day fast on August 15 at Calcutta. He did not attend the main celebrations in Delhi, They could have asked him to hoist the new flag, but he was not prepared to bow to it. He said: "I cannot afford to take part in this rejoicing, which is a sorry affair." Nor did he give any message to the press for broadcasting.

Simultaneously with the national rejoicings, a terrible wave of wholesale massacre and brutality spread over the Punjab and Sind. Unprecedented violence was let loose. The tidings that came from the Punjab were grim and blood-curdling. The massacre of men, women and children went on unabated.

Millions were uprooted from their native soil, their hearths, their homes. They were torn from their dear ones and robbed of all their possessions. Nobody was sure of the morrow. Burnt houses, looted shops, broken skulls, smoking ruins, blood-smeared corpses, and mutilated bodies, scattered all over towns and villages, spoke of the blood-bath which barbarously surpassed most others in history. The country rang with horror.

The visionary in Nehru was rudely shaken to his marrow. He admitted in his broadcast on August 19, 1947, that "nearly the whole of India celebrated the coming of independence, but not so the unhappy land of the five rivers in the Punjab". He also said that "there was sufficient disaster and sorrow, arson and murder, looting and crime of all descriptions". Shortsighted Congressmen were fiddling while West Punjab was burning and bleeding.

In this atmosphere Gandhi, at a post-prayer meeting in Calcutta, told the Hindus that the Hindu majority must be just at all costs and overlook the mistakes of the minorities. He told labour that labour was priceless and he wanted a marriage between capital and labour. He asked the nationalist Muslims to join the Muslim League if they wanted to affect the Muslim masses.

The Rev. Mr. Kellas, Principal of the Scottish Church College, asked him in Calcutta whether India would remain a secular State. Gandhi replied that it should undoubtedly be secular and he added that everyone living in it should be entitled to profess his religion without let or hindrance, so long as the citizen obeyed the common law of the land.

Next week he told a Calcutta audience that religion was a personal matter and if the people succeeded in continuing the personal plans, all would be well in our political life. "If officers of the Government," continued Gandhi, "as well as members of the public undertook the responsibility and worked whole-heartedly for the creation of a secular State, then only could we build a new India that would be the glory of the world."

In September 1946 Gandhi had expressly said: "If I were a dictator, religion and State would be separate. I swear by my religion. I will die for it. But it is my personal affair. The State has nothing to do with it."[13]

When Gandhi spoke of secularism, by this he meant religious tolerance. His ideology which was based on God, religion and a future life was opposed to secularism.

On August 24 Gandhi was given an address by the Calcutta Municipal Corporation. There was a rumour that Gandhi was fired at. Upon this he remarked on how fortunate he would have considered himself if someone were to shoot him!

Gandhi was presented with an address by Muslims on August 31. But about 10 a.m. his residence was attacked by Hindus with lathis and bricks. He was rescued when the Police Commissioner and Chief Minister Prafulla Chandra Ghosh appeared on the scene. The next day, Gandhi started a fast unto death, but broke it on September 4 when leaders of all communities undertook to try and stop the riots.

Gandhi left Calcutta on September 7 and reached Delhi on September 9 when it had become almost a city of the dead. He lived there till January 30, 1948. This time he stayed at Birla House as the Bhangi Colony was filled with refugees. He had his usual post-prayer meetings every day. He expressed his desire to go to Lahore without any protection and if he was to face death, he said he would do it with a happy smile provided things settled down in Delhi.

On September 26 Gandhi said during the post-prayer meeting that he had been an opponent of all warfare. But if there was no other way of securing justice from Pakistan and if Pakistan persistently refused to see its proved error and continued to minimize it, the Indian Government would have to go to war[14] against it. And war was not a joke. No one wanted war. That way lay destruction, he added. If there was a war, he stressed, Hindus in Pakistan could not be fifth-columnists there. No one would tolerate that. If their loyalty lay not with Pakistan, they would leave it. Similarly if the loyalty of the Muslims in the Indian Union lay with Pakistan, they should not stay in the Indian Union.

There was a time when India listened to Gandhi. Now he was a back-number, he observed. He was told he had no place in the new order, where they wanted machines, navy, air force and what not. He could never be a party to it.

The Muslims were reported to have said: "*Haske liya* Pakistan *larke lenge* Hindustan." If Gandhi had had his way, he would never let them have it by force of arms. Some dreamed of converting the whole of India to Islam. That never could happen through war. Pakistan, he said, could never destroy Hindustan.

Hindus were not in a mood to listen to Gandhi. They had lost faith in his vows, promises, actions and ideology. Gandhi declared that he would ask India to go to war to secure justice for the Hindus and the Sikhs. Nobody in the streets believed in his declaration.

The Pakistan Government gave badges to the Harijans to wear having the sign of a star and crescent, declared Jogendra Nath Mandal, a member of the Pakistan Cabinet. Gandhi said that no one should be converted against one's will. Jogendra Nath afterwards repented for keeping company with the leopards who could never change their spots.

On October 22, 1947, Pakistan invaded Kashmir which acceded to the Indian Union on October 26. Gandhi made a reference to the Kashmir invasion on October 29, 1947. On October 27 the Indian Cabinet had sent troops by air to Kashmir. Gandhi observed that "all he knew was that it was right for the Union Government to rush troops, even a handful, to Srinagar. That must save the situation. . . . The result was in the hands of God. Men could but do or die. He would not shed a tear if the little union force was wiped out, like the Spartans, bravely defending Kashmir..."[15] The Indian troops stemmed the tide of invasion which had almost reached the gate of the capital.

Gandhi's non-violent role ended here when he supported the despatch of Indian troops to Kashmir and whole-heartedly backed Nehru on the ground that India had a moral obligation to go to the aid of the victims of aggression. Gandhi, the moral and unarmed prophet, who had advised the Britons, Jews and Abyssinians to surrender their countries and lives to the aggressors, supported the military defence of Kashmir. If, according to Gandhi, war as a means of settling international disputes was wrong, this advice was wrong. Every nation can defend war on some such, moral ground. But yet Gandhi, the apostle of non-violence, had avowed that if India took up the doctrine of the sword she would cease to be the pride of his heart.[16]

On November 3, 1947, Gandhi spoke in favour of lifting food controls. He asked the people of French India to carry on a constitutional agitation to join the Indian Union of which they formed an integral part. He made a broadcast to displaced persons on November 12. This was the first and last occasion when Gandhi spoke on the radio in India. About this time Princess Elizabeth of Britain became engaged and Gandhi sent with Lord Mountbatten his best wishes and a small table-cloth woven out of yarn by himself as a present. Answering a question. Gandhi said on December 7, 1947, that religion and nationalism were two dissimilars. Each was equal to the other in its own place. "No man," he observed, "who values his religion as also his nationalism can barter away the one for the other." He paid calls on the Viceroy, visited the camps of the displaced persons, attended the meeting of A.I.V.I.A. In Delhi, he met Liaquat Ali, Prime Minister of Pakistan, on January 4, 1948. Around this time, Gandhi's statue was damaged at Karachi by Muslim fanatics.

It Is Obvious that confusion, fanaticism and violence had been reigning supreme during the last three months of 1947. Bred and brought up in an atmosphere of Gandhism, Gandhian leaders proved to be unequal to the occasion and could not face the historic necessities of the moment. People realized, that Gandhism was an illusion. Gandhi himself again and again declared that the nation followed not non-violence but passive resistance. Nehru said that the nation had had to wade through an ocean of blood and tears.

This crisis was grave, grim and unprecedented. Such were the times when people showed a profound disbelief in and dislike of Gandhism which seemed till the previous day the ruling belief of the majority. The blood that had been flowing for the previous one year, the sufferings and fears and sorrows that gripped millions proved that Gandhism was a dreamland. The situation was utterly volcanic and it disclosed that the whole range of consequences was largely the outcome of Gandhian beliefs and actions. People now seemed unwilling to sacrifice their ease or convenience in the hope of securing higher advantages for others and assuring the honour of tomorrow.

Perturbed by the atrocities, imbecilities and the holocaust that marked the course of the period, even the great Congress leaders were chilled in their Gandhian beliefs. They now realized that mere height of aim and nobility of expression could not move the matter-of-fact world.

K. M. Munshi, who claimed to have followed the Mahatma, while reviewing the situation in the freedom issue of his *Social Welfare*, observed: "Last thirty-five years, we have been brought up on a slogan: naturalness and inevitableness of Hindu-Muslim unity. That this was a wishful thinking has been proved in Noakhali, Bihar, Rawalpindi in a hundred villages, by tens of thousands of men, women and children fleeing for safety. The Muslim—a hard realist—knew and exploited the hollowness of the slogans; the Hindu cherishes it still. Hindus love words and ideals."[17] What a melancholy epitaph on Gandhism by a Gandhist! How fitting yet flagrant, how frank yet furious, how realistic though belated!

The terrific shock of events also evoked a spontaneous remark from Babu Purshottamdas Tandon. He declared while speaking at a meeting in Bareilly that Gandhi's doctrine of absolute non-violence had proved to be useless and was greatly responsible for the partition of India. Even the *Bharat Jyoti*, a leading English weekly and a strong spokesman of the Congress in Bombay, bewailed in its editorial dated October 26, 1947, under the caption "Barter not Truth": "Today Gandhiji is a living witness to the failure of his political mission. His failure is the measure of his departure from truth. Gandhiji resisted partition of India, but like Yudhishthira, by a play of words, secured the nation's ratification of partition; he, like Yudhishthira, is witnessing hell's torments. Power of truth is great; lie's punishment is greater. So, barter not truth."

People, who were now filled with a sense of and anxiety for security, spoke in terms of struggle for survival. In Calcutta and Delhi they disturbed Gandhi's meetings, shouted "Gandhi, Go Back!" The mob stoned his residence, a bomb was thrown at the train carrying Gandhi, and Nehru was confronted with the slogan "Let Gandhi Die". Gandhi's post-prayer political meetings were abandoned, disturbed, heckled and routed. Pickets had to be placed at his residence in Birla House to protect Gandhi, the symbol of non-violence. Detectives in plain clothes guarded Gandhi's post-prayer meetings.

Savarkar had nothing to do either with these violent mob demonstrations or with the newspapers' incisive criticisms of Gandhi and Gandhism. That was the growing opinion of the people and the columns of the Congress Press reflected it. There was confusion, indecision and misjudgment of the issues in the minds of the people, their leaders and their press. Vallabhbhai Patel, the Home Minister, was trying to save India from the Muslim treachery and rioting. In the first week of January 1948 he plainly said in Calcutta and Lucknow that those Muslims who were disloyal to India would have to go to Pakistan. Gandhi himself had said so, but to show his impartiality he told Patel that the Mahatma had realized that Patel and he were two, although he formerly believed that they were one. S. K. Patil, Patel's right-hand man and the Bombay boss of the Congress, once told a Bombay audience that when Patel made a complaint against Nehru, Gandhi told him that Nehru was young and the nation wanted him. When Nehru complained to Gandhi he told Nehru that Patel was practical and experienced and that nation wanted Sardar Patel.[18] But the fact was that Gandhi was prejudiced against Patel who was determined to suppress Muslim rioting.

The crisis was capped by Gandhi's famous fast which he started at Birla House in Delhi on January 13, 1948, for the reinstatement of the Muslims in their homes in Delhi; for the restoration of desecrated mosques to their former use and for five other reasons. India was to pay Pakistan rupees fifty-five crores by way of financial adjustments. Pakistan was fighting with India in Kashmir, and Patel and Nehru thought that if money was paid to Pakistan at that juncture, it would be helping her to carry on the war in Kashmir. Gandhi's fast undoubtedly aimed at pressing Patel and Nehru to make the payment and the hit was especially directed at Patel. And although on January 1, 1948, the Government of India announced its reluctance to pay the amount to Pakistan, it ultimately paid Pakistan rupees fifty-five crores which had been loudly denied and refused.

The *Modern Review*, a Calcutta monthly noted for its balanced views all over the world, began its editorial notes in its issue of January 1948 with a pertinent question: "The time has come when our trusted leaders, including the Father of the Nation, have to be asked for a clear reply to a plain question. Where does the Hindu of the Indian Union stand today and what does freedom mean for him? Does he possess along with others the democratic birth-rights by which a state has to be ruled and administered for the greatest good of the majority, or is he there merely to serve as so much fuel for a burnt sacrifice to be used as 'conscience-fodder,' so to say, by his leaders, just as the totalitarian Fuhrer used his people as cannon fodder?"

The Modern Review blamed the national leaders for sacrificing Hindu interests at every emotional impulse and for betraying the trust of hundreds of millions of the majority.

Referring to the fast of Gandhi, *The Modern Review* concluded its note in a grave judgment: "Mahatmaji's fast will, we are sure, attain its object for the time being but the results would be futile and disastrous in the long run, unless Pakistan mends its ways. Indeed, this fast will enhance communal bitterness a thousand-fold on this side when the people realize the futility of their sacrifices, and would make the ultimate and inevitable clash horrible and catastrophic beyond all measure, unless Mahatmaji can work his miracle in Pakistan as well."

Gandhi's fast continued, but on receiving as usual an assurance from the leaders of the communities, he broke his fast on January 18, 1948, taking *mosambi* juice at the hands of Maulana Azad. He learnt that Nehru had not had food for a day or two. So he wrote to him to give up his fast and added: "May you live long and continue to be the jewel of India."

Yet things had not assumed normalcy. Madanlal Pahava, a young refugee from Punjab residing in Ahmednagar, exploded a bomb during Gandhi's prayer meeting on January 20 and yet Gandhi pleaded for mercy towards Madanlal. The police could have prevented the forthcoming tragedy if they had acted speedily on the information given by Madanlal.

Gandhi's health was not good. On January 29 he wrote to K. G. Mashruwala that both the kidney and the liver were functioning badly. Gandhi was to go to Sevagram to stay there from the 3rd to 12th February 1948.

Gandhi was revolving in his mind his thoughts about the reorganization of the Congress. He wanted the Congress to cease to be a political body and devote itself to social reconstruction. He wrote a pamphlet entitled "Congress Position" on January 27, and it was published in *Harijan* of February 2, 1948. He drafted a constitution for the Congress militia as laid down in "Congress Position". It was published in *Harijan* of February 15, 1948. Gandhi was regarded as the architect of Pakistan by common men, the rank and file of almost all political parties, as he had been placating the Muslims in India for decades. The Hindu Sabhaites held him responsible for the partition of India. The tragedy of the refugees in Delhi and in other parts of India made their hatred burn against Gandhi. The payment of fifty-five crores of rupees to Pakistan ignited the spark, and the young Hindu Mahasabha leaders Nathuram Godse, N. D. Apte and their friend Karkare, an active Hindu Mahasabha leader, took it in their heads to finish off Gandhi. Madanlal was their accessary to the crime.

The tension had not eased, confusion and excitement reached white heat. And in the midst of this atmosphere of extreme gloom and disaster, Nathuram Vinayak Godse shot Gandhi with a revolver while Gandhi was going to the prayer ground in the compound of Birla House at Delhi in the evening at 5.30 on Friday, January 30, 1948, five minutes after Gandhi had had a talk with Sardar Patel for settling the differences between Patel and Nehru on the question of Muslim loyalty to India.

It was Gandhi's belief that not a blade of grass moved without God's will. "In a strictly scientific sense," he once observed, "God is at the bottom of both good and evil. He directs the assassin's dagger no less than surgeon's knife."[19] "When God feels that our work here is done," he once wrote to Patel, "He will take us away in a moment."

The 'divinely-appointed' instrument ceased its work. A great mission that had been ringing in the world for about fifty long years came to an end. The long prayer, as every prayer does, came to an end. The fascinating powerful glow in the Mahatma's eyes went out forever.

THE NEWS OF the assassination of Gandhi spread like wild fire. It was tragic and terrifying. All sensible people condemned the act of assassination. Depressed looked the whole world for a while. An earthquake of sorrow passed over the country. Mother India shed precious tears for her great son in spite of her bleeding wounds. The wise said that Gandhi belonged to the ages.

Great men die but greatness never dies. Jawaharlal Nehru sorrowfully said: "The Light has gone out of our life and there is darkness everywhere."

Gandhi, the apostle of non-violence, was honoured in his death by giving a military salute of 79 guns by a machinery which he wanted to destroy and on the evening of January 31 the funeral procession, attended by twelve lakhs of people and representatives of the different nations, saw the cremation of his last remains at Raj Ghat, Delhi, on the banks of the Jamuna at 4.45 p.m. Ramdas Gandhi lit the pyre. Jawaharlal Nehru, Sardar Vallabhbhai Patel, Dr. Rajendra Prasad, Lord Mountbatten, Sardar Baldev Singh and Acharya Kripalani were present at the cremation ground. On the 12th day Gandhi's ashes were immersed in the holy rivers of the country, at some places borne in silver urns to the rivers or the sea.

The New York Times said: "A light has gone out. The rest remained for history's inexorable hand to write down." The Danish Premier, M. Hans Bedtoft, said that Mahatma Gandhi represented to Danes the "real idealist". Prime Minister of Pakistan, Liaquat Ali Khan sent Nehru their deepest sympathy over the tragic death of Gandhi. His dastardly assassination, he added, must be condemned unreservedly by everybody.

President Truman of the U.S.A. said: "As a teacher and

leader, his influence made itself felt not only in India but everywhere in the world, and his death brings great sorrow to all peace-loving people." George Marshall, U.S. Secretary of State, described Gandhi as a spokesman for the conscience of all mankind. Sir Winston Churchill said, "I am shocked at the wicked crime." Bernard Shaw said, "It shows how dangerous it is to be too good." Smuts said, "A Prince among men has passed away."

Dr. Ambedkar's reaction was not sympathetic. It was said he was put in mind of the pithy remarks of Cicero who had exclaimed at the news of Caesar's murder that the dawn of freedom had come.

Quaid-i-Azam Mohamed Ali Jinnah, Governor-General of Pakistan, said, "I was shocked to learn of the most dastardly attack on the life of Mr. Gandhi, resulting in his death. Whatever our political differences, he was one of the greatest men produced by the Hindu community and a leader who commanded their universal confidence and respect."

With the shots fired by Nathuram Vinayak Godse disappeared one of the greatest political figures from the stage of world politics. The assassin was a bachelor of thirty-seven with medium height, fair skin, square jaws, a resolute and sober face, serious flickering eyes, a high forehead, closed cropped hair, all giving the appearance of a man of serious purpose. He was a fiery editor, a powerful speaker, a member of the All-India Committee of the Hindu Mahasabha and well known as a lieutenant of Savarkar and a vanguard in Savarkarian movement. In his early youth he was a worker of the R.S.S. He hung down his head if he heard a filthy word! But after the vivisection of India, in his fanatical love of Hindu nation he discarded the saner leadership of Savarkar.

In the name of Mahatma Gandhi, the apostle of non-violence, arson and murders were perpetrated and destruction was made of properties of Brahmins and especially of Hindu Sabhaites in Bombay, Poona, in the States of Kolhapur, Sangli, Miraj, and other places. About twenty-five thousand persons of Hindu Sabha persuasion were arrested all over the country.

Savarkar, who had condemned the assassination of Mahatma Gandhi on January 31, 1948, again issued a statement on the eve of his arrest on February 4 condemning unequivocally such fratricidal crimes whether they were perpetrated by the individual frenzy or mob fury. On May 15, after a period of nearly three and a half months, he was implicated in the crime as accused number nine. There were three more accused but they had absconded.

During the trial Savarkar said that the approver Badge's allegations were found uncorroborated hearsay and uncorroborated inferences. He was defended by the famous eminent lawyer Bhopatkar who was President of the Hindu Mahasabha and by P. R. Das, brother of C. R. Das. The special judge Atma Charan, giving his judgment on February 10, 1949, said: "There is thus no reason to suppose that Savarkar had any hand in what took place at Delhi on January 20 and 30, 1948. He is found not guilty of the offences as specified in the charge, and is acquitted thereunder."

Godse confessed that he killed Gandhi whom he considered to be the father of Pakistan and he was hanged on November 15, 1949. And along with him was hanged Apte as the brain, while Karkare, Madanlal and Gopal Godse were sentenced to transportation for life. Dr. Parchure and Kistaya were acquitted in the appeal.

Generally, great politicians and not saints fall a victim to an assassin's knife or bullet. An assassin prepares himself to perpetrate a treacherous deed and kills a great man to uphold a principle or for the sheer lust of killing or rarely to appease private vengeance or to carry out a political vendetta. Politicians from Julius Caesar to John Kennedy and several dictators were killed. Great and good men like Lincoln and Gandhi were murdered. Trotsky, Aung San, Bandarnaike, Liaquat Ali were murdered as politicians. These were political murders.

IN HIS AUTOBIOGRAPHY Jawaharlal Nehru observes that Gandhi was an extraordinary paradox. Gandhi did not gather his knowledge from history, but he learnt from his mistakes as he went on experimenting with his life. In his autobiography Gandhi avows: "What I want to achieve, what I have been striving and pining to achieve these thirty years, is self-realization, to see God face to face, to attain *moksha* (freedom from birth and death)." Yet his was one of the longest political roles on the stage of world politics. He had the soul of an ascetic and the spirit of a politician, organizer, moral teacher and leader of men. But with such a long and leading role he could not be radical or revolutionary in bringing about actual and far-reaching social changes in India.

Moreover, his rigid ascetic outlook on life, his glorification of poverty, his "belief in a future life and in the continuity of *karma* through successive births", and his faith in the doctrine that "what we sow here we must reap elsewhere—there is no escape"[20]—all these confirmed his belief in Varnashram Dharma, the doctrine of inequality and the *status quo*. Such views uphold the superstitious belief that poverty is God-made and birth as an Untouchable is the result of one's sins in a previous life. One is led to believe that that was why Gandhi did not fight for the annihilation of untouchability as valiantly and vigorously as he fought the colour bar in South Africa.

One can hardly credit Gandhi with being the first to expound the idea of non-violence in dealing with the Government of one's own country. George Fox (1621-91), too, believed in the inner voice, denounced war and opposed authority. But undoubtedly history will give credit to Gandhi for having been the first to launch the idea of non-violence in dealing with a foreign Government with a view to overthrowing it. This was an event unheard of in history. It was as unique as Gandhi's odd sort of double lower lip.

Non-violence is a political method or technique, not a condition of being, not a part of the structure of life. It is Gandhi's distinctive contribution to political science.

Gandhi's political philosophy does not try to formulate an approach and his experiments do not provide a key to the other problems of social or political conflict. For Gandhi did not express his views in an integrated or coherent system and publish a book on it. He wrote only three books, *Hind Swaraj*, *Satyagraha in South Africa* and his *Autobiography*, but they only partly deal with his theory and largely with his actions and experiments. There is an absence of a *magnum opus* on his basic theory as he was essentially a man of action and not a man of reflection. His torrential journalistic writings were unsystematic, sometimes unscientific and often inconsistent, full of repetitions, contradictions and paradoxes. No wonder then that Jawaharlal Nehru, a close associate of Gandhi, though he knew his writings and speeches well, once remarked: "In spite of the closest association with him for many years, I am not clear in my own mind about his objective."[21] Aware of this weakness, Gandhi thought it proper to declare: "As a matter of fact, my writings should be cremated with my body.

What I have done will endure, not what I have said and written."[22]

However, Gandhi's emphasis on non-violence was an eternal and formidable reminder to the strife-torn world of the evils of colour bar, of war as a means of settling questions between countries, of the greed for colonization. Positively, on a world plane, Gandhi was the greatest man since Ashoka to expound this doctrine for the sake of humanity. His message that all religions are basically true and that Swaraj is the birth-right of all nations is worthy of universal respect and value. He hoped, that like the law of gravitation, the law of love some day would prevail.

Was Gandhi a failure? Although Gandhi did not give up his mission in despair, he was convinced in the evening of his life that he had failed. Gandhi said that his only fitting epitaph would be: "He tried but signally failed."[23] Viewed against the background of human history, his life devoted to non-violence was not a failure. The task was too heavy and too high for a single man to achieve. But even if it was a failure, such glorious failures contain the ingredients of human progress. Indeed the success inherent in his failure is more thought provoking than the success of those who claim with equal justification that it is nobler to save humanity from aggressors and killers, whatever that means.

Gandhi took Gautam Buddha's compassion but not his reason. Graham Wallace once said: "India may have cause to regret for centuries Gandhi's refusal to allow his reason to cooperate with his instinct."[24] But that refusal was compensated for to some extent by Jawaharlal Nehru who was his colleague and political heir. Some said that there was more spinning than thinking in Gandhi's India. The mystic way in which he expressed himself, the symbols he used, the belief he had in the doctrine that God does everything (he causes earthquakes to punish men for their sins) gave a handle to his critics. It is true his emphasis was on man; but it was neither on his reason nor on his environment. It was on his emotion. And he was a humanist in the religious sense.

Gandhi's writings and speeches sometimes lacked logic and reason, but he was greater than his writings, and his charisma was superb. No other leader had so powerful and irresistible an influence as he had on the Indian masses. Indians as a race are peculiarly sensitive to character and more responsive to moral than to intellectual leadership. Some of his contemporaries possessed Gandhi's sincerity of purpose, purity of motive and sturdy patriotism; but Gandhi's personal renunciation had a unique hold on the masses. Renunciation and religion have a unique hold on the Indian mind which has not come out of the middle ages. And asceticism and renunciation have always constituted the greatest goal of great men in India. Pearl Buck rightly said in *My Several Worlds*[25] that Gandhi's followers devoted themselves to him because he had made the great renunciation of personal gain and advancement.

Perhaps Gandhi may be the last great man in India with a living faith in God. The present trends in the world show that men in future can be great or even saints without a belief in God. It is however not true that Gandhi opened the path to freedom for India. It had been opened before his advent on the Indian scene. Nor was he the sole author of Indian independence. He is not a living influence on the heart and life of India which has fought, after his death, three wars manfully. But he undoubtedly started a ferment in Indian society which inspired an army of patriots to fight non-violently for freedom with a new spirit and a new weapon, with intrepid courage and a sense of self-sacrifice. Gandhi was perhaps the only great man of his age who used the maximum years of his life in service and action. In the past, humanity has had several greater heroes, better thinkers, and wiser politicians than Gandhi and it may have many more in the future, but it may not have the like of Gandhi who was a peculiar product of his own age. He is in a class by himself. The greatness of Gandhi's life was in his sense of duty, and the duty of his life was undying action. He was the greatest man of his day in India and one of the greatest men in history. He belongs to the galaxy of the immortals. After all, he was a man and had his foibles. But the foibles will vanish with the passage of time and the pure gold of his virtues will shine brilliantly in history.

Abbreviations used in the References

AAC — Ambedkar, Dr. B. R., *Annihilation of Caste*
ABP — *Amrit Bazar Patrika*
ACF — Andrews, C. F., *Mahatma Gandhi's Ideas*
ACH — Campbell-Johnson, Alan, *Viscount Halifax*
ACM — Campbell-Johnson, Alan, *Mission with Mountbatten*
AD — Athavale, D. V., *The Life of Mahatma Gandhi*
AET — Purani, A. B., *Evening Talks with Sri Aurobindo*
AHM — *Sri Aurobindo on Himself and on the Mother*
AND — Chakrabarti, Atulananda, *Nehru, His Democracy and India*
ATP — Ambedkar, Dr. B. R., *Thoughts On Pakistan (1941)*

BB — Barr, F. Mary, *Bapu*
BC — *The Bombay Chronicle*
BD — Blunt, W. S., My Diaries
BH — Birkenhead, The Earl of, *Halifax : The Life of Halifax*
BIS — Bose, Subhas, *The Indian Struggle* (1920-1942)
BJ — *Bhawan's Journal*, September 1969
BM — Brij Narain, *Marxism Is Dead*
BMA — Chaturvedi, Benarsidas and Sykes, Marjorie, *Charles Freer Andrews*
BMN — Brecher, Michael, *Nehru : A Political Biography*
BN — Bose, Nirmal Kumar, *My Days With Gandhi*
BTG — Bolton, Glorney, *The Tragedy of Gandhi*

CCA — Chaplin, Charles, *My Autobiography*
CWG — *The Collected Works of Mahatma Gandhi*

DBT — Deb, J. M., *Blood and Tears*
DD — Gandhi, M. K., *Delhi Diary*
DJ — Doke, Joseah J., M. K. *Gandhi, An Indian Patriot in South Africa*
DK — Keer, Dhananjay, *Veer Savarkar*
DKA — Keer, Dhananjay, *Dr. Ambedkar : Life And Mission*

DNN	Norman, Dorothy, *Nehru : The First Sixty Years*
FLM	Fischer, Louis, *The Life of Mahatma Gandhi*
FPJ	*The Free Press Journal*
GA	Gandhi, M. K., An Autobiography or *The Story Of My Experiments With Truth* (1945)
GC	Desai, Mahadev, *With Gandhi In Ceylon*
GCD	Dalal, C. B., *Gandhi* : 1915-1948 : *Detailed Chronology*
GCG	*Gandhiji's Correspondence* with *the Government*, 1942-44, Navajivan Publishing House
GDB	Birla, G. D., *In the Shadow of the Mahatma*
GP	Gray, R. M. and Parekh, Manilal G., *Mahatma Gandhi: An Essay In Appreciation*
GPC	Manager of Publications, Government of India, Delhi, *Congress Responsibility For The Disturbances* 1942-43
GS	G. A. Natesan & Co., *Speeches of Gopal Krishna Gokhale*
HDT	*Henry David Thoreau, Selected Writings On Nature And Liberty* Edited with an Introduction by Oscar Cargill
HF	A noted Journalist (Foreword By Dr. Pattabhi Sitaramayya), *Hopes And Fears*
HFD	Earl Of Halifax, *Fullness Of Days*
HPS	Sitaramayya, Dr. Pattabhi, *The History of the Indian National Congress*
HPS (II)	Sitaramayya, Dr. Pattabhi, *The History of the Indian National Congress*, Vol. II
HR	*Harijan*
HT	*Hindustan Times*
IAR	*Indian Annual Register*
ICG	*Incidents Of Gandhiji's Life*, Edited By Chandrashanker Shukla
IFQ	Jog, N. G., *In Freedom's Quest: A Biography of Netaji Subhas Chandra Bose*
II	Independent India
INB	Ganesh & Co. Publisher, *The Indian Nation Builders*
IO	*Indian Opinion*
IP	Gwynn, Sir Charles W., *Imperial Policing*
IR	*The Indian Review*
IST	*Indian Statutory Commission*, Vol. IV
IW	*The Illustrated Weekly of India*
IY	Yajnik Indulal, *Gandhi As I Know Him* (II)
JG	Gunther, John, *Inside Asia*
JNA	Nehru, Jawaharlal, *An Autobiography*
JNG	Gandhi, M. K., *Jawaharlal Nehru*
KBP	Krishna, K. B., *The Problem Of Minorities*
KCR	*Report Of Commission Of Inquiry Into Conspiracy To Murder Mahatma Gandhi*, By J. L. Kapur.
KDI	Kanji Dwarkadas, *India's Fight For Freedom* 1913-1937
KDT	Kanji Dwarkadas, *Ten Years To Freedom*

KK	Prasad Madho, *A Political and Spiritual Biography of Kaka Kalelkar*
KKP	*'Kelkarancha Khasgi Patravyawahar* (Part I), Edited by Y. N. Kelkar
KMA	Karandikar, M. A., *Islam In India's Transition To Modernity.*
KWH	Khanolkar, G. D., *Walchand Hirachand*
LF	Fischer, Louis, *Gandhi : His Life and Message for the World*
LP	Gandhi, M. K., *Letters To Sardar Vallabhbhai Patel*
M	*Maratha* (Marathi daily)
MA	*Mahratta*
MBC	Chakrabarti, Atulananda, *The Mahatma and His Men—G. D, Birla*
MD	*The Diary Of Mahadev Desai*
MGR	*Mahatma Gandhi*, Edited by, S. Radhakrishnan
MGRL	Romain Rolland, *Mahatma Gandhi*
MID	Montagu, E. S., *An Indian Diary*
MKH	Gandhi, M. K., *Hind Swaraj Or Indian Home Rule*
MKS	Gandhi, M, K., *Satyagraha In South Africa*
MLB	Mosley, Leonard, *The Last Days Of The British Raj*
MLG	Muriel Lester, *Gandhi: World Citizen*
MR	*Modern Review*
MRP	Prasad, Dr. Rajendra, *At The Feet Of Mahatma Gandhi*
MSA	Mitra, Sisirkumar, *The Liberator Sri Aurobindo—India* And The World
MSG	Millin, Sarah Gertrude, *General Smuts*
N	*Navajivan*
NBK	Khare, Dr. N. B., *My Political Memoirs or Autobiography*
NCG	*Profiles Of Gandhi*, Edited by Norman Cousins.
NCK[1]	Kelkar, N. C., *Geli Panch Varshe* (Marathi)
NCK[2]	Kelkar, N. C., *Gata Goshti*, (Marathi Autobiography)
NCK[3]	Kelkar, N. C., *A Passing Phase Of Politics*
NOL	Nehru, Jawaharlal, *A Bunch Of Old Letters*
NPG	Bose, Nirmal Kumar and Patwardhan, P. H., *Gandhi in Indian Politics*
PB	Pearl Buck, *My Several Worlds*
PDK	*Prasad Diksha*, Edited by Kaka Kalelkar
PEF	Pyarelal, *The Epic Fast*
PH	Polak, H. S. L., An Article
PIJ	Jung, Nawab Dr. Nazir Yar, *The Pakistan Issue*
PM	Polak, Millie Graham, *Mr. Gandhi* : *The Man*
PMC	Proceedings Of Federal Structure Committee And Minorities Committees
RD	Prithwis Chandra Ray, *Life and Times of R. Das.*
RMR	The Marquess Of Reading, *Rufus Isaacs First Marquess Of Reading*
RP	*Selected Writings And Speeches Of Dr. R. P. Paranjpye*, Edited by B. M. Gore
RRP	Ranade, M. G., *Rise Of The Maratha Power*
SCO	Sanjana, J., E., *Caste And Outcaste*

SG[1] S. Gopal, *British Policy in India*, 1885-1905
SG[2] S. Gopal, *The Viceroyalty Of Lord Irwin*, 1926-1931
SIC Shraddhanand, Swami, *Inside Congress*
SM Morarjee, Shantikumar, *Gandhijinchya Athavani* (translated into Marathi)
SMF Maharashtra State Committee for a History of the Freedom Movement in India, *Source Material For A History Of The Freedom Movement In India*, Vol. III, Part I
SMG Natesan & Co., *Speeches And Writings Of Mahatma Gandhi*
SMJ Saiyed, M. H., *Mohamed Ali Jinnah*
SNS G. A. Natesan & Co., *Speeches and Writings of Sarojini Naidu*
SW *Social Welfare*

TFJ Nehru, Jawaharlal, *Towards Freedom*
TFL Tinkar, Hugh, *Foundations of Local Self-Government in India, Pakistan and Burma*
TG Orient Longmans, *Talking Of Gandhiji*
TI *The Times Of India*
TK *Lokmanya Tilakanche Kesaritil Lekh* (Part III)
TMG Tendulkar, D. G., *Mahatma*
TNY Templewood, Viscount, *Nine Troubled Years*
TPK Prabhu, R. K. and Kelekar Ravindra, *Truth Called Them Differently*
TRP Mansergh, Nicholas and Lumley E. W. R., *The Constitutional Relations Between Britain And India: The Transfer Of Power* 1942-47, Vol. II
TZR Zinkin, Taya, *Reporting India*

VDL Savarkar, V. D., *Londonchi Batami Patre*
VDW Savarkar, V.D., *The War Of Independence Of 1857*
VL Vivekanand, Swami, *Lectures From Colombo To Almora*
VV *Vividh-Vritta*

WBG Morton, Eleanor, *Women Behind Gandhi*
WP Watts & Co., *Some of Paine's Masterpieces*
WH Hunter, Sir William, *The Indian Empire : Its People, History And Problems*

YI *Young India*
YIT Gandhi, Mahatma, *Young India* 1919-1922, (Tagore & Co.)

References

CHAPTER I

1. HR 22 June 1935
2. HR 12 January 1947
3. YI 4 September 1924
4. ACF p. 246
5. YI 27 April 1921
6. GA p. 479
7. CWG Vol. XVIII, p. 414
8. HR 15 june 1947
9. CWG Vol. XXIV, p.532
10. N 10 August 1924
11. N 27 July 1924
12. MD Part IV, p. 53
13. CWG Vol. IX. P. 205
14. CWG Vol. VI, p. 433
15. CWG Vol. I, p. 55
16. CWG Vol. I, p. 54
17. CWG Vol. VI, p. 432
18. CWG Vol. I, p. 8
19. CWG Vol. VI, p. 432
20. CWG Vol. I, p. 2
21. GA p. 479
22. CWG Vol. I, p. 58
23. CWG Vol. XIII, p. 24

CHAPTER II

1. CWG Vol. I, pp. 13-16
2. MR May 1930
3. N 27 July 1924
4. GP p. 8
5. YI 31 December 1931
6. CWG Vol. I, p. 30
7. CWG Vol. VI, p. 432
8. CWG Vol. I, p.66
9. DJ p.32.
10. CWG Vol. I, p.62

CHAPTER III

1. MD Vol. I, pp. 51-52
2. CWG Vol. XIV, p.24
3. YI 1 September 1921
4. AD p.140
5. YI 23 March 1921
6. IR May 1925
7. CWG Vol. I, P.74
8. CWG Vol. I, P.74

CHAPTER IV

1. YI 27 April 1921

CHAPTER V

1. CWG Vol. I, pp. 142-163
2. CWG Vol. I, p.141
3. CWG Vol. I, p.140
4. CWG Vol. I, p.169
5. GA p. 203
6. CWG Vol. II, p. 35
7. CWG Vol. I, p. 359
8. CWG Vol. I, p. 77
9. CWG Vol. II, p. 93
10. GA p. 220

CHAPTER VI

1. CWG Vol. II, p.173
2. MKS p. 94
3. CWG Vol. II, p. 166

4. GA p. 241
5. GA p. 247
6. GA p. 247
7. FPJ 30 June 1969
8. ACF p. 364
9. MSG p. 235
10. CWG Vol. III, p. 207
11. CWG Vol. III, p. 206
12. CWG Vc . III, p. 189
13. SG[1] p. 384
14. CWG Vol. IV, p. 440
15. MD Vol. IV, p. 248
16. CWG Vol. VI, p. 432
17. GA p. 308
18. GA p. 318
19. CWG Vol. III, p. 313
20. CWG Vol. IV, p. 320

Chapter VII

1. CWG Vol. IV, p. 224
2. IO 18 June 1904
3. CWG Vol. IV, p. 225
4. PH *National Standard* 26 January 1950
5. MD Vol. I, p. 38
6. MD Vol. I, p. 38
7. IO 24 December 1904
8. PM p. 22
9. MKH p. 44
10. GA pp. 380-81
11. CWG Vol. VI, p. 360
12. PM p. 65
13. TI 2 October 1969
14. CWG Vol. IV, p. 469
15. CWG Vol. V, p. 299
16. INB p. 93
17. CWG Vol. V, p. 48
18. CWG Vol. V, pp. 56-57
19. YI 9 April 1925
20. CWG Vol V, p. 92
21. IO 11 November 1905
22. IO 2 December 1905
23. CWG Vol. V, p. 397

Chapter VIII

1. ACF p. 140
2. CWG Vol. XVI, pp. 146-47
3. CWG Vol. V, p. 418
4. CWG Vol. V, p. 421
5. CWG Vol. V, p. 443
6. CWG Vol. VI, p. 84
7. IO 7 November 1906
8. CWG Vol. VI, p. 59-60
9. CWG Vol. VI, p. 255.
10. CWG Vol. VI, pp. 33-34
11. CWG Vol. VI, p. 259
12. CWG Vol. VI, p. 269
13. CWG Vol. VI, p. 335-36
14. CWG Vol. VI, p. 486

Chapter IX

1. MKS p. 202
2. CWG Vol. VII, pp. 6-7
3. CWG Vol. VII, pp. 7-8
4. CWG Vol. VII, p. 8
5. IO 27 July 1907
6. CWG Vol. VII, p. 202
7. IO 31 August 1907
8. CWG Vol. VIII, pp. 99-100
9. CWG Vol. VIII, pp. 99-100
10. CWG Vol. VII, p. 211
11. HDT p. 71
12. CWG Vol. VII, p. 267
13. CWG Vol. VII, p. 284
14. VDL p. 45
15. VDL pp. 67-72
16. VDL p. 72
17. CWG Vol. VII, p. 361
18. MKS p. 177
19. IO 28 December 1907
20. CWG Vol. VIII, p. 66
21. CWG Vol. IX, p. 125
22. CWG Vol. IX, p. 126
23. MKS p. 246
24. MKS pp. 250-57
25. CWG Vol. VIII, p. 100
26. CWG Vol. VIII, p. 92

Chapter X

1. MSG p. 241
2. CWG Vol. VIII, p. 254
3. CWG Vol. VIII, pp. 242-46
4. CWG Vol. VIII, p. 319
5. CWG Vol. VIII, p. 348
6. CWG Vol. VIII, p. 321
7. CWG Vol. VIII, pp. 418-19

8. IO 1 August 1908
9. MKS p. 291
10. CWG Vol. IX, pp. 100-01
11. CWG Vol. IX, p. 126
12. CWG Vol. IX, p. 106
13. CWG Vol. IX, pp. 225-26
14. CWG Vol. IX, p. 227
15. CWG Vol. IX, p. 175
16. GA pp. 479-80
17. CWG Vol. IX, 218
18. CWG Vol. IX, 243

CHAPTER XI

1. CWG Vol. IX, p. 265
2. CWG Vol. IX, p. 306
3. IO 14 August 1909
4. IO 14 August 1909
5. BD Part II, p. 288
6. DK p. 63
7. WP pp. 35-36
8. VDW p. 273
9. CWG Vol. IX, p. 320
10. CWG Vol. IX, p. 343
11. CWG Vol. IX, p. 378
12. CWG Vol. IX, pp. 388-89
13. GS p. 891
14. CWG Vol. IX, pp. 444-46
15. CWG Vol. IX, p. 593
16. CWG Vol. IX, p. 415
17. CWG Vol. IX, p. 476
18. ICG p. 200
19. CWG Vol. XVII, p.387
20. CWG Vol. IX, pp. 528-29

CHAPTER XII

1. LF p. 34
2. BM p. 96
3. CWG Vol. X, p. 70
4. CWG Vol. X, p. 139
5. SMG p. 1013
6. GS p. 863
7. CWG Vol. X, p. 151
8. HR 5 February 1938
9. IO 7 May 1910
10. MKS p. 377
11. CWG Vol. X, p. 249
12. CWG Vol. X, pp. 512-13
13. CWG Vol. X, p. 398
14. CWG Vol. XI, p. 44
15. CWG Vol. XI, p. 78
16. CWG Vo1. XI, p. 118
17. CWG Vol. XI, p. 333
18. CWG Vol. XI, pp. 165-66
19. CWG Vol. XXXIII, p. 25
20. GS pp. 883-84
21. IO 28 December 1912

CHAPTER XIII

1. CWG Vol. XVI, p. 69
2. YI 20 April 1921
3. CWG Vol. XII, p. 274
4. CWG Vol. XII, p. 324
5. CWG Vol. XII, p. 380
6. CWG Vol. XXXIV, p.470
7. MSG p. 236
8. CWG Vol. XIII, p. 59
9. CWG Vol. XII, p. 126
10. CWG Vol. XII, p. 490

CHAPTER XIV

1. TG p. 40
2. CWG Vol. XIII, p. 279
3. KK p. 156
4. CWG Vol. XIII, p. 45
5. SIC p. 49
6. CWG Vol. XIII, p. 59
7. IW 6 January 1969
8. RP pp. 138-39
9. CWG Vol. XIII, p. 94
10. CWG Vol. XIII, p. 94
11. CWG Vol. XIII, p. 136
12. CWG Vol. XIII, p. 121
13. SM p. 9

CHAPTER XV

1. BJ September 1969
2. IR March 1923
3. SMF Vol. III Part I, pp. 21-22
4. CWC Vol. XIII, p. 565
5. CWG Vol. XIII, p. 220
6. YI 6 August 1925
7. CWG Vol.XIII, pp.221-23
8. CWG Vol. XIII, p. 245

9.	SMF	Vol. III, Part I, p.26
10.	CWG	Vol. XIII, pp. 294-96
11.	TI	3 November 1968
12.	MSA	pp. 171-72
13.	Kelkar N.C. in FPJ	28 June 1947
14.	TFJ	p. 44
15.	SNS	p. 78

CHAPTER XVI

1.	MGR	pp. 222-23
2.	MRP	p. 62
3.	KDI	pp. 46-47
4.	*Mouj*	March 1948
5.	CWG	Vol. XIV, p. 52
6.	MID	p. 58

CHAPTER XVII

1.	CWG	Vol. XIV, p. 161
2.	CWG	Vol. XIV, p. 206
3.	CWG	Vol. XIV, pp. 260-63
4.	CWG	Vol. XIV, p. 266
5.	CWG	Vol. XV, p. 68
6.	CWG	Vol. XIV, pp. 97, 157
7.	*Mouj*	March 1948
8.	CWG	Vol. XIV, pp. 440-41
9.	CWG	Vol. XIV, p. 511
10.	IW	25 May 1969
11.	CWG	Vol. XV, p. 71 P. 279

CHAPTER XVIII

1.	IW	9 March 1969
2.	CWG	Vol. XV, p. 168
3.	CWG	Vol. XV, p. 210
4.	SMF	Vol. Ill, Part I, pp. 114, 131
5.	IP	pp. 60-61
6.	CWG	Vol. XV, p. 219
7.	CWG	Vo,. XV, p. 253
8.	CWG	Vol. XV, p. 381
9.	CWG	Vol. XVI, p. 13
10.	MKS	p. 7
11.	MGRL	p. 17

CHAPTER XIX

1.	CWG	Vol. XVI, p. 283
2.	CWG	Vol. XVI, pp. 81-82
3.	SMF	Vol. III, Part I, p.240
4.	MBC	p. 72
5.	NCK[1]	p. 422
6.	NCK[2]	p. 437
7.	SIC	p. 111

CHAPTER XX

1.	KDI	p. 144
2.	KDI	p. 146
3.	MSA	p. 172
4.	YIT	p. 53
5.	YI	16 March 1921
6.	KDI	p. 150
7.	CWG	Vol. XVII, p. 388
8.	CWG	Vol. XIV, p. 110
9.	YI	29 June 1920
10.	KMA	p. 178
11.	YIT	p. 1069-72
12.	YI	15 August 1920
13.	IR	July 1924
14.	YI	2 June 1920
15.	YI	9 June 1920
16.	MR	July 1920
17.	YI	6 June 1920
18.	NCK[1]	p. 36

CHAPTER XXI

1.	YI	4 August 1920
2.	YI	28 April 1920
3.	YI	11 August 1920
4.	KDI	p. 152
5.	NOL	pp. 6, 17
6.	NCK[1]	p. 51
7.	KDI also ATP	p. 152 p. 147
8.	WH	p. 317
9.	RRP	p. 2
10.	CWG	Vol. XVIII, p. 34
11.	BB	p. 70
12.	CWG	Vol. XVIII, p. 489
13.	NCK[1]	pp. 80-84
14.	MR	December 1920
15.	CWG	Vol. XVIII, p. 335
16.	MR	October 1920

CHAPTER XXII

1.	YI	27 October 1920
2.	CWG	Vol. XVIII, p. 438

3. CWG Vol. XVIII, pp. 329-30
4. MR December 1920
also SMG pp. 510-12
5. YIT p. 457
6. YI 17 November1920
7. YI 17 November1920
8. TI 20 January 1925
9. CWG Vol. XIII, pp. 301-03
10. GP p. 106
11. CWG Vol. XIII, p. 94
12. YI 25 February1920
13. YI 8 December1920
14. YI 8 December1920
15. YI 29 December1920
16. GS pp. 1056-58
17. RD p. 159
18. NCK[1] pp. 345-46
19. SIC p. 123
20. IR January 1921
21. IR January 1921

CHAPTER XXIII

1. YI 2 February 1921
2. N 14 August 1921
3. MR February 1921
4. YI 2 February 1921
5. SMF Vol. III, Part I, p. 367
6. CWG Vol. XIX, p. 179
7. CWG Vol. XIX, pp. 374-75
8. BC 15 February1921
9. BC 15 February1921
10. YI 16 March 1921
11. YI 16 February1921

CHAPTER XXIV

1. YI 27 April 1921
2. CWG Vol. XIX, p. 327
3. MR June 1921
4. IR March 1921
5. IR March 1921
6. IR March 1921
7. MR April 1921
8. TPK pp. 28-29
9. SIC p. 126
10. *The Leader* 11 May 1921
11. *Shivaji And His Times* pp. 479-80
12. RMR p. 196
13. RMR p. 198
14. RMR p. 198
15. ATP pp. 150-51

CHAPTER XXV

1. YI 18 May 1921
2. YI 20 April 1921
3. YI 18 May 1921
4. CWG Vol. XX, p. 317
5. SMF Vol. III, Part I, p. 419
6. CWG Vol. XX, p. 34
7. CWG Vol. XX, p. 445
8. IR November 1923
9. SMF Vol. III, Part I, p. 435
10. IST Vol. IV, p. 99
11. ATP p. 154
12. YI 8 September1921
13. IR September 1921
14. YI 27 October 1921

CHAPTER XXVI

1. YI 19 January 1922
2. IR June 1922
3. YI 23 February1922
4. SMF Vol. Ill, Part I, p. 461
5. NCK[1] p. 351
6. YI 28 July 1920
7. YI 15 December1920
8. YI 2 March 1922
9. CWG Vol. XXIII, p. 557
10. MR February 1922
11. YI 27 February1927
12. IR May 1923

CHAPTER XXVII

1. CWG Vol. XXIII, p. 2
2. IR September 1922
3. MR April 1922
4. MR January 1923
5. SMF Vol. III, Fart II, pp. 245-46
6. NCK[3] pp. v & vi
7. YI 3 April 1924
8. CWG Vol. XXIV, p. 379
9. YI 3 April 1924
10. ABP 27 April 1947

11.	YI	20 March 1924
12.	KMA	p. 178
13.	YI	10 April 1924
14.	YI	18 June 1925
15.	YI	1 May 1924

CHAPTER XXVIII

1.	AET	p. 56
2.	AET	PP. 24, 55
3.	AET	pp. 65-66
4.	AET	p. 27
5.	KMA	p. 179
6.	AET	p. 28
7.	CWG	Vol. XXIV, p. 331
8.	N	29 June 1924
9.	TK	Part III, p. 463
10.	Lokamanya	22 August 1924
11.	YI	1 January 1925
12.	MR	November 1924

CHAPTER XXIX

1.	RMR	p. 304
2.	MR	February 1925
3.	NOL	p. 42
4.	YI	5 March 1925
5.	IR	April & August 1925
6.	MR	March 1925
7.	YI	30 April 1925
8.	WBG	p. 173
9.	TG	p. 42
10.	YI	6 August 1925
11.	N	6 July 1926

CHAPTER XXX

1.	CWG	Vol. XXXII, p. 602
2.	ATP	p. 153
3.	SCO	p. 123
4.	YI	24 March 1927
5.	YI	21 July 1927
6.	YI	9 March 192
7.	GC	P. 91
8.	IY	Part II, p. 69

CHAPTER XXXI

1.	NOL	p. 57
2.	GCD	p. 71
3.	HFD	pp. 114-15
4.	YI	20 September 1928
5.	SMF	Vol. III, Part II, p. 405
6.	YI	4 October 1928
7.	YI	13 September 1928
8.	SMJ	p. 400
9.	HPS	p. 565
10.	YI	10 January 1929
11.	YI	21 February 1929
12.	AET	p. 19
13.	YI	14 March 1929
14.	YI	21 March 1929
15.	YI	21 March 1929
16.	SMF	Part III, Part II, p. 446

CHAPTER XXXII

1.	YI	26 September 1929
2.	YI	10 January 1930
3.	HFD	p. 146
4.	SG[2]	p. 15

CHAPTER XXXIII

1.	YI	30 January 1930
2.	YI	27 February 1930
3.	CWG	Vol. I, p. 25
4.	YI	12 March 1930
5.	YI	12 March 1930
6.	YI	20 March 1930
7.	YI	20 March 1930
8.	YI	20 March 1930
9.	YI	20 March 1930
10.	BH	p. 282
11.	YI	8 May 1930
12.	YI	1 April 1931
13.	SMC	Vol. III, Part III, 530 (Page 530 Prisoner's expenses)
14.	TNT	p. 47

CHAPTER XXXIV

1.	BH	p. 281
2.	TNY	p. 54
3.	ACH	p. 292
4.	HFD	p. 149
5.	ACH	pp. 291 & 299
6.	HFD	p. 151
7.	JNA	pp. 257-58
8.	DNN	Vol. I, p. 243

9.	YI	12 March 1931
10.	YI	12 March 1931
11.	HFD	p. 150
12.	YI	16 April 1931
13.	YI	9 April 1931
14.	HPS	Vol. I, p. 784
15.	YI	26 March 1931
16.	TNY	p. 44
17.	MR	April 1931
18.	MD	p. 52
19.	DKA	pp. 165-67
20.	YI	3 September 1931
21.	CWG	Vol. XXIII, p. 385

CHAPTER XXXV

1.	NCG	pp. 12-14
2.	BTG	pp. 270-71
3.	MKI	pp. 380-81
4.	CCA	p. 371
5.	MR	September 1931
6.	PMC	p. 527
7.	PMC	p. 534
8.	*The Janata*	30 January 1932
9.	NCK[2]	p. 754
10.	YI	22 October 1931
11.	TNY	p. 61
12.	TNY	pp. 59-60
13.	BTG	pp. 266-67
14.	TNY	p. 60
15.	TNY	p. 63
16.	KBP	p. 110
17.	MLG	p. 27
18.	MKI	p. 395
19.	YI	14 January 1932
20.	HR	21 January 1939

CHAPTER XXXVI

1.	HR	4 November 1939
2.	DNN	Vol. I, p. 271
3.	PEF	p. 189
4.	MD	p. 33
5.	MD	p. 131
6.	BIS	p. 261

CHAPTER XXXVII

1.	AHM	p.342
2.	IFQ	pp.114-15
3.	JNG	p. 59
4.	VL	p. 218
5.	LP	p. 44
6.	LP	p. 77
7.	JNG	p. 61
8.	JNG	p. 61
9.	NOL	p. 114

CHAPTER XXXVIII

1.	HR	25 May 1935
2.	HR	19 October 1935
3.	HR	26 October 1935
4.	GCD	p. 115
5.	HR	28 March 1936
6.	HR	14 March 1936
7.	NCG	p. 14
8.	HR	29 February 1936
9.	AAC	AP. II, p. 25
10.	SCO	p. xiii

CHAPTER XXXIX

1.	JNG	pp. 70-71
2.	HR	25 July 1936
3.	HR	8 August 1936
4.	HR	8 August 1936
5.	HR	10 October 1936
6.	HR	21 November 1936
7.	KWH	p. 342
8.	HPS (II)	pp. 83-84
9.	HR	13 February 1937
10.	VV	23 November 1947
11.	MA	8 September 1939
12.	HR	9 January 1937
13.	HR	13 February 1937
14.	HR	4 September 1937
15.	HR	18 September 1937
16.	HR	20 March 1937
17.	LP	pp. 122, 125
18.	II	5 April 1945
19.	TI	6 July 1963
20.	TI	25 December 1971
21.	SM	p. 26
22.	HR	22 January 1938

CHAPTER XL

1.	BIS	pp. 313-14
2.	HR	31 July 1937

3.	LP	p. 130
4.	HR	23 April 1938
5.	HR	9 April 1938
6.	HR	9 April 1938
7.	NOL	p. 248
8.	MR	Octooer 1937
9.	HR	14 May 1938
10.	HR	21 May 1938
11.	JG	p. 472
12.	NOL	p. 313
13.	NBK	p. 48
14.	HR	1 October 1938
15.	LP	p. 141
16.	NOL	p. 166
17.	HR	23 July 1938
18.	HR	17 December 1938
19.	TI	17 December 1938
20.	HR	21 January 1939
21.	HR	28 February 1939
22.	HR	11 March 1939
23.	HR	29 April 1939

CHAPTER XLI

1.	TMG	Vol. IV, p. 266
2.	TZR	p. 217
3.	HR	27 May 1939
4.	NOL	p. 377
5.	IW	14 August 1960
6.	HR	14 October 1939
7.	HR	7 October 1939
8.	ACM	p. 58
9.	NOL	p. 394
10.	GDB	p. 232
11.	KWH	p. 381
12.	GDB	p. 253
13.	BMA	p. 317
14.	HR	21 September 1935
15.	PDK	pp. 129-30
16.	HR	26 December 1936
17.	HR	4 November 1939
18.	HR	28 October 1939
19.	HR	23 July 1938
20.	Printed Address	p. 17
21.	TI	22 March 1940
22.	MA	22 January 1943
23.	HR	23 March 1940
24.	TFL	p. 48
25.	TI	28 April 1968
26.	HR	13 April 1940
27.	GDB	p. 273

CHAPTER XLII

1.	NOL	p. 444
2.	HR	25 January 1942
3.	GDB	pp. 228-30
4.	LP	p. 162
5.	TRP	p. 676-77
6.	TRP	p. 674
7.	TRP	p. 42
8.	TRP	p. 42
9.	KDT	p. 65
10.	HPS	II, p. 635
11.	PIJ	p. 116
12.	PIJ	p. 119
13.	HR	23 March 1941
14.	JNG	pp. 123-39
15.	HR	14 June 1942
16.	HR	19 July 1942
17.	HR	26 July 1942
18.	HR	4 August 1942
19.	HPS	II, p. 349

CHAPTER XLIII

1.	HR	19 July 1942
2.	DBT	p. 65
3.	TRP	p. 853
4.	GPC	p. 74
5.	GCG	p. 28
6.	DK	p. 333
7.	KKP	p. 158
8.	TI	10 July 1944
9.	TMG	Vol. VI, p. 235
10.	TI	12 July 1944
11.	KCR	pp. 125-26
12.	KDT	p. 127

CHAPTER XLIV

1.	NBK	pp. 82-84
2.	NBK	pp. 80-81
3.	JNG	pp. 148-53
4.		pp. 59-60
5.	TMG	Vol. VI, p. 29.
6.	TI	23 February 1946
7.	HR	17 March 1946

8.	HR	24 March 1946
9.	TI	22 February 1970
10.	HR	3 March 1946
11.	HR	3 March 1946
12.	HF	p. xvii
13.	HF	p. 21
14.	HF	p. 22

CHAPTER XLV

1.	HR	8 September 1946
2.	HR	6 October 1946
3.	GDB	p. 259
4.	GDB	pp. 292-93
5.	BN	p. 85
6.	BN	p. 23
7.	HR	26 January 1947
8.	BN	p. 200
9.	BN	p. 167
10.	HR	27 April 1947
11.	HR	27 April 1947
12.	ABP	27 April 1947

CHAPTER XLVI

1.	HR	1 June 1947
2.	HT	1 June 1947
3.	HR	8 June 1947
4.	TI	10 June 1947
5.	TI	13 June 1947
6.	TI	14 May 1947
7.	TI	16 June 1947
8.	HR	23 March 1940
9.	MLB	p. 248
10.	AND	p. 46
11.	TI	22 July 1947
12.	TI	14 August 1947
13.	HR	22 September 1946
14.	DD	p. 40
15.	HR	9 November 1947
17.	YI	11 August 1920
18.	SC	16 August 1947
19.	M	29 January 1969
20.	HR	20 October 1946
21.	TI	2 October 1969
22.	NPG	p. 56
23.	HR	13 April 1940
24.	TSS	p. 139
25.	PB	p. 352

Preface

1.	CWG	Vol. XV, p. 53
2.	CWG	Vol. XIV, p. 199

Tilak on Gandhi

THE FIRST BIOGRAPHY of Mahatma Gandhi in Marathi was written by Avantikabai Gokhale in 1918. Along with her husband Babanrao she was sent to Champaran to assist Gandhi in his work in Bihar. The work was in progress when she penned a short biography and requested Bal Gangadhar Tilak to write a foreword.

Tilak had first met Gandhi when Barrister Gandhi had come to India to fetch his family to South Africa. Along with Gopal Krishna Gokhale, he had guided a meeting in Poona under the chairmanship of Dr R. G. Bhandarkar in support of the cause of the Indians in South Africa. Gandhi had travelled with Tilak from Bombay to Calcutta to attend the 1901 session of the Indian National Congress. Tilak's newspaper *Kesari* had made laudatory references to Gandhi on the latter's visits to India in 1896 and 1901-1902. In spite of this close connection, Gandhi acknowledged Gokhale as his political mentor. Gokhale died in 1915.

It is interesting to study the influences of Tilak and Gandhi on each other from 1915 to 1920. This foreword, that Tilak wrote in a hurry, almost as a duty, is an important document. Since this biography was published way back in 1918 in a small edition, and not reprinted since then, and as this foreword has presumably not been published in translation in any other language, this document has rarely been used by scholars. For that purpose this is now being made available in English a hundred years after it was written.

It may be relevant to refer to certain details regarding Tilak. Tilak was known for his sharp differences with his onetime close friend Gopal

Ganesh Agarkar over what should have priority — social reform or political struggle. In some way Gandhi, with his holistic approach, had shown the way. Tilak's reference to Gandhi's political work in South Africa is important in that context.

Tilak was on his way to England to file a legal case against Valentine Chirol, who had represented Tilak's activities in a seditious light. Interestingly, Tilak's foreword absolves Gandhi from any such charges while Gandhi was pointing out defects in the British rule is probably a slanting reference to his own political situation. In spite of Gandhi's differences with the Moderates Pherozeshah Mehta and Gopal Krishna Gokhale and the Extremists Bal Gangadhar Tilak, Lala Lajpat Rai and Bipin Chandra Pal, Mahatma Gandhi, with his holistic approach, became the carrier of the torches lit by all these senior leaders. It is interesting to note that Tilak refers to Gandhi as Mahatma even in 1918.

Mahatma Gandhi by Bal Gangadhar Tilak

Translated from Marathi by Ramdas Bhatkal, from *Mahatma Gandhi: Charitra Vishesh Parichay* (1918) by Avantikabai Gokhale

When I had gone to Calcutta last year in December 1917 for the Congress session, Mrs. Avantikabai Gokhale informed me that she was writing a biography of Mahatma Gandhi and requested me to write a foreword. Of course, I could not refuse this request; but at that time I did not realise that this book would be ready so soon. I had not realised at all, especially that I will have to write the foreword to this work in a hurry as I was leaving for England. But now that I am faced with such a situation I have to somehow complete this foreword. More time and leisure was needed to write a foreword to a biography of Mahatma Gandhi. I am upset that this facility is not available to me. Even so, as per the Sanskrit saying, '*Akarnat mandkarnam priyaha*' (it is better to do something than nothing at all) I am undertaking this task. And I hope the readers of this work will forgive me after taking into account these circumstances.

There is hardly anyone in India who is not familiar with Mahatma Gandhi's name. It can even be said that everyone desires to know more about him. But there was no book available in Marathi to satisfy this desire. That lacuna has been filled by this book written in a simple style by Avantikabai Gokhale. I congratulate her for this. As Avantikabai mentions, Gandhi's work is continuously in progress and someone writing on this subject afresh is likely to get new information every year. Even so, a work written at present will not come in the way of any future writer; on the other hand, Avantikabai will get the credit for introducing the contribution of this great patriot to the readers in Maharashtra. Avantikabai is currently in Champaran to assist Mahatma Gandhi by working under him. She is acquainted thoroughly with the thoughts, behaviour, personal nature, way of living and opinion on various issues of the subject of her biography, along with his relationship with other members of his family as also others, not just through books, but based on direct observation. The readers will see that this personal association has played a major role in the writing of this biography.

It does not need much effort to understand why the life of Mahatma Gandhi should be so instructive and worth emulating. There are many like Gandhi who have come back after qualifying as a barrister in England. His father was working as a Diwan and there would be many who may have had similar privileges. Or there may be many like him, with a simple straightforward nature. All these matter little. After the spread of English education in this country there are several who came out of Indian universities with expert knowledge. Achievements such as a detailed study of world history or geography, or an accurate grasp of some scientific discipline are possible through intellect and many of our intelligent people have achieved these in an excellent manner in the last hundred or may be a hundred and fifty years. Similarly, our educated class has used its brain power to think intelligently and logically about western social systems, western beliefs or social organisations. The life stories of those that actually demonstrate morality and good character, which in this land enable control over the surroundings, and can enable fulfilment of any effort made, are rarely to be seen. This is exactly what is special about Gandhi's life. Perhaps, many of us may not agree with some of his opinions on social, religious, political or other topics. There could be many who will outshine him in scholarship. But if we consider one's character as important, as mentioned above, then the life of Mahatma Gandhi is truly likely to be an ideal for the common man. I do not think there can be any dispute about this. And that is why I recommend this work, which is now available in Marathi, for close study to the people of Maharashtra.

There is little doubt that Indians, whether resident in India or elsewhere in the British Empire, are in an impoverished condition everywhere.

What has caused this impoverishment, what is the nature of the change from the previous conditions, what needs to be done to prevent this deterioration — all these issues having been discussed at great length; I would not like to write about these in this brief foreword. Moreover, I believe that is not an important lesson to be drawn from Gandhi's life. In the domestic life of an individual or in the life of a nation the conditions are usually created as a result of the acts of previous generations or earlier times. It is true that if the conditions are undesirable those living currently in those conditions cannot be blamed. But if the present conditions are bad, and, if the person trapped in those circumstances, particularly a leader of the nation, does not discuss appropriately the reasons causing these conditions and the remedy to remove these conditions after arriving at decisions based on deep thinking, then one will have to conclude that he has not lived up to his duty. Even though we may not be responsible for the creation of these conditions, even so, it is the duty, in fact a sacred duty, of every person individually or collectively, to try to improve the situation as far as possible. That is the rule of the shastras and religion. That by which the world is sustained and maintained is termed dharma. And this involves mainly improving the present position of the world and taking it progressively to the next level, and doing things, getting things done — that is both doing them oneself as well as making others do them — so as to attain perfection.

Whichever country one may be born into, one is not born to enjoy luxuriously all of one's life along with one's family on its produce; it is to accomplish higher goals in life. This is wholeheartedly accepted by *shastrakara*s and religious leaders. The possibilities of this higher ideal are so noble that the man walking this path attains unity with God, the sustainer of the world. The *shastra*s describe this as attaining divinity. Even though the *shastra*s and religious scriptures ordain this, we have to sadly observe that our compatriots have not given much attention to this aspect. Otherwise, the current situation would not have arisen. Just because our national leaders did not give as much attention as necessary in the past, it does not mean that we must also not try to tread that path. There is no time limit on what can be done for the betterment of our country. That our forefathers made no such efforts does not mean that such effort should never be made by later generations. If it has not been done today, it is not that it cannot be done tomorrow, and if not done tomorrow, it is not that it cannot be done the day after. It is our duty to make such efforts. And whenever and whoever is awakened by this sense of duty should tirelessly try to fulfil this as one's own duty selflessly and tirelessly, and without any fear of the hardships that may befall one or members of one's family, trusting the Almighty and without aspiring for any results; this, in short, is the essential truth underlying this thinking. That is the main lesson to be drawn from the life of Mahatma Gandhi.

In recent times another feeling that is gaining ground is that if the conditions in India are to improve then Indian society must first improve and when that happens then that will be the time to think of political issues. From Mahatma Gandhi's life it will be clear to the readers how this idea is far from valid. To bring about reforms in all areas in the nation, as explained in the Sanskrit saying '*Sarvarambhastundulaha prasthamulaha'* — if not the whole at least partial power has to be with the national leaders and thinkers. Without power wisdom is ineffective; not just that, even the capabilities go waste. Therefore, any efforts to improve the condition of the country, specially, must be done primarily in the field of fundamental issues necessary for all these reforms. If Mahatma Gandhi did not hold this view then he would not have dabbled in political reforms. The efforts for betterment of Indian labourers in African settlements were not just of social character, but they were also linked concerning directly with the political system in Africa. In fact it can be said that the Indian labourers faced this grave situation because of the oppressive nature of the administration in Africa. This affected Gandhi naturally into thinking that unless the political system was reformed, the condition of Indians in Africa will not improve. If we are partners in the British Empire, then the Indian subjects must have the same rights as the white subjects. This is obviously as per natural justice. But the colonisers, believing selfishly that the colonies now established by the whites have been established only for their own benefit, are unwilling to treat those in other areas with the same consideration. But, it is not that they do not need people from other lands. The colonies have abundant land and deposits but, the colonisers do not have sufficient manpower to fully utilise this wealth. Even if the few hundred or thousand colonisers work not just with two but with four hands and even if they utilise several machines having the power of a thousand hands, even so, they will not be able to reap even one percent of the monetary benefits that they potentially can derive from the colonies.

Just as they used to exploit the Negros in Africa in the past the colonisers thought of getting wealthy by borrowing from India black labourers and exploiting their strength like animals. Since the bureaucracy in India consisted of the brethren of the colonisers, the government in India did not give as much attention as they should have towards the pitiable condition of Indian labourers in the colonies. Leaders in India had noticed the pitiable political condition for the past several years. But until someone like Gandhi came forward there was hardly any effort at their amelioration. This was known, but not quite realised; and even if it was realised no attempts were being made to rectify the situation. By showing a path out of this helpless situation, Gandhi, by his own example, pointed the way towards reform. This will be clear from this biography. What Gandhi did to rescue Indians in Africa from this impoverished situation needs to be studied closely. If the political system anywhere is unjust, any effort to improve that situation cannot be considered as sedition. To call it sedition means that the rulers do not want to support justice, morality; they do not want to resist injustice or to give equal rights to all their citizens. We believe that the good of the subjects is the true objective and strength of political power. Once this proposition is accepted another rule automatically follows.

That is, wherever there is injustice, removing that by resistance is, in a way assisting the political power to implement its objective. But because of prejudices arising out of previous experiences or selfishness some specific individuals, castes or classes out of the subjects get so obsessed that they do not see the principles of justice. Actually, these groups in a way oppress others. At this juncture if the rulers suddenly step in to halt injustice then these obstinate and selfish groups, that are considered honourable by the weightage acquired through tradition, tend to be offended. And this disturbs peace that has been established over the years. Therefore, in such situations, unless those oppressed make determined efforts, the rulers do not generally involve themselves. Briefly, just as one does not pick up an active child capable of walking, unless it stumbles and falls down, we find a similar experience in political matters. So far as there is no obstruction to smooth administration why should the rulers pay any attention? It is but human nature that one does not like to unnecessarily interfere in smooth affairs.

When one actually experiences these ill-effects, and not just that, but one finds that it is absolutely necessary to point these out, only then, will a true statesman be inclined to look for improvement; not otherwise. Obviously, it is the duty of every patriot in every such situation to use every occasion to expose the sorrows and the demands of the citizens or to bring forth their oppressed situation to such an extent that finally the rulers themselves have to improve the situation. Gandhi fulfilled this duty in an excellent manner and because of that he has become fully worthy of the praise and respect of the people.

To explore the truth underlying Gandhi's strategy of obstruction we need to say a few more words. As regards the laws passed to maintain peace in the country, to fight with the ruling administrators or to rebel by disobeying their orders, however well intentioned it may be, is naturally considered as against the law. In such a situation, any patriot who wishes to bring about reforms in a lawful manner has to face several difficulties. He is boiling within, he intensely yearns for reforms. He is certain that transgression of laws is against discipline, but he cannot find any solution. The method of unarmed resistance chosen by Gandhi or non-cooperation, or to use his own language the method of Satyagraha, has suggested itself through such difficulties. And therefore it has become scientifically sound and well honed.

Though it is possible to be resorted to this method on all occasions and at all times, it may be difficult to say, with certainty whether or not it should be resorted to on each and every occasion and whether it will or will not be as successful every time. But all of us will have to admit that this is a very noble method. When a ruler lays down a law for all subjects to obey, he also lays down punishment for those who transgress that law. Normally this punishment is such that every person would tend to follow the moral path. The path of morality consists of happiness, satisfaction and peace. And if there is any possibility of deviation from this natural tendency, arising out of selfishness, then the rule of law is instrumental in removing this vacillation and reinforcing natural instinct towards the good path. But in the opposite situation, when the limitations put by the legislation are not based on religion or justice and only because of punishment prescribed by the extant laws are they made enforceable; then even the wise men face an important dilemma: to accept punishment prescribed by the laws while standing by one's loyalty to the principles of justice and truth or to reject the divine sense of justice out of fear of the punishment prescribed in this artificially made law. Principled persons committed to truth and justice lay down that in such a situation it is not proper to follow artificial restrictions in the shape of that law. But to bring in effect this advice, dedication to truth and justice is required to be so strong that one should instinctively be able to do one's duty without any thought of one's own happiness or unhappiness, or that of one's family, children or even of their strength or weakness. This is what is known as moral courage, genuine truthfulness or virtuous character, and magnanimity. This is not possible only by erudition or by being born in a respectable family. Not even by being intelligent. This is truly the soul force. And the Upanishad saying '*Naymatma pravachanen labhyo na medhaya na bahuna shruten*' which needs to be carefully noted.

Even though the proposition that such soul force cannot be acquired by mere erudition or intelligence and it should be naturally innate, is true, even then, one cannot ignore that a determined person can acquire this quality, as described in the Gita, by study and selflessness, step by step. This is the essence of the statement that the biographies of great and noble persons are useful in developing one's character. One who is naturally virtuous can understand his own nature fully and can raise it to perfection by reading the biographies of great personalities. Not just that, even if they are immature by nature or character at birth they can utilise reading of biographies to acquire maturity. Therefore, I recommend that this biography of Mahatma Gandhi should be read by all from comprehensive points of view.

Poona city, Bal Gangadhar Tilak
16, March 1918

Index

Published by :
JNANADA PRAKASHAN (P&D)
4837/2, 24, Ansari Road, Daryaganj
New Delhi-110 002, India
Phone : +91-11-23272047
Mobile : +91-9212137080

Assisted by :
Text Book Promotion Society of India
4837/2, 24, Ansari Road, Daryaganj
New Delhi-110 002, India
Phone : +91-11-23272047
Mobile : +91-9212137080

Edition : 2016

Encyclopaedic Dictionary of Computer Science

ISBN: 978-81-7139-362-6 (Set)

Typesetting by :
Vardhman Computers
New Delhi-110 017, India

Published by Mrs. S. Chowdhary for M/s. Jnanada Prakashan (P&D Daryaganj, Ansari Road, New Delhi-110002, India and printed at Balaj Offset, Navin Shahdara, Delhi-110032, India.

ENCYCLOPAEDIC DICTIO
OF
COMPUTE
SCIENCE

Volume 1

A-F

Edited by

Dr. Akshaya Kumar Nayak
Dr. Avinash Chiranjeev
Er. Haojam Rocky S.

JNANADA PRAKASHAN (P

in association with

THE GLOBAL OPEN UNIVERS

NAGALAND (INDIA)

PREFACE

As we enter the 21st century, technology involving computer science proliferates in most areas of our lives. How we work, how we study, how we run errands, how we spend our leisure time, and how we communicate all entail the use of computers. The past decade has seen an explosion of new growth on the internet and the introduction of personal computers into millions of homes. Along with this growth has come the proliferation of specialised terminology—related not just to the internet, but to software, multimedia systems, information processing, and more. The Dictionary of Computer Science includes the newest terminology and makes it accessible to anyone who works with a computer at home, school, or work. This dictionary contains over 6,000 entries in the first edition—as well as a comprehensive cross-referencing system, providing clear and concise definitions for the newest terms in computing.

The wide range of topics covered include computer applications in industry, the office, science, education, and the home; the means of achieving these applications—the hardware, software, computer organisation, telecommunications, and user interaction; security, safety, and legal issues; underlying concepts and theories in computing and associated fields; and major computer manufacturers and organisations. Special emphasis is placed on terms widely used in relation to the latest advances in personal computing, computer graphics, networking, artificial intelligence, and computer security. Full coverage is also given to the Internet, World Wide Web, and multimedia programmes.

From browser and sniffer programme to millennium bug and spam, the Dictionary of Computer Science, First Edition will prove invaluable to students and teachers of computing, and everyone who uses computers in the home, lab, or business.

— **Editors**

A

Å *n.* See angstrom.

A or a *n.* See ampere.

A: or a: *n.* In Windows and some other operating systems, the identifier used for the first, or primary, floppy disk drive. Unless otherwise specified by changing the CMOS startup instructions, this is the drive the operating system checks first for startup instructions.

AAL *n.* See ATM Adaptation Layer.

Abandonware *n.* Discontinued video or computer games. Abandonware is often collected and played by computer game enthusiasts on refurbished systems or on PCs running emulator software.

ABC *n.* 1. Acronym for Atanasoff-Berry Computer. The first electronic digital computer, created by John Atanasoff and Clifford Berry of Iowa State University in 1942. 2. Acronym for automatic brightness control. A circuit that changes the luminance of a monitor to compensate for ambient lighting conditions. 3. An imperative language and programming environment from CWI, Netherlands. This interactive, structured, high-level language is easy to learn and use. It is not a systems-programming language, but it is good for teaching or prototyping.

Abeline *n.* A high-performance network developed by Qwest Communications, Nortel, and Cisco Systems to provide a backbone network for the Internet2 project. Abeline interconnects the gigaPoPs created by the Internet2 project and its member institutions, enabling connected institutions to develop advanced network services and applications.

Abend or ABEND *n.* Abbreviation for abnormal end. The premature ending of a programme because of programme error or system failure.

ABIOS *n.* Acronym for Advanced Basic Input/Output System. A set of input/output service routines designed to support multitasking and protected mode that were built into IBM PS/2 PCs.

Abnormal end *n.* See abend.

A-Bone *n.* The Asian-Pacific Internet backbone that connects users in East and South Asian countries and Australia at T1 speeds or better, without the need to send data through North American facilities. The A-Bone was launched by Asia Internet Holding Co., Ltd. in 1996. By 1998, a total of 13 countries were connected to the A-Bone's hub in Japan. A-Bone also includes links to both Europe and the United States.

Abort *vb.* To terminate abruptly, often used in reference to a programme or procedure in progress.

Absolute address *n.* A means of specifying a precise memory location in a programme by using its address (number) rather than an expression to calculate the address. Also called: direct address, machine address, real address.

Absolute coding *n.* Programme code that uses absolute addressing rather than indirect addressing. See also absolute address, relative address.

Absolute coordinates *n.* Coordinates that are defined in terms of their distance from the origin, the point where the axes intersect. Graphs and computer graphics use absolute coordinates to locate points on a chart or display grid—for example, points in relation to the x- and y-axes on a graph or the x-, y-, and z-axes used to specify the location of a three-dimensional graphic object on the screen.

Absolute link *n.* A hyperlink to the exact location of a file on a file server, the World Wide Web, or a company intranet. Absolute links use an exact path; if you move the file containing the hyperlink or a hyperlink destination, the link breaks.

Absolute path *n.* A path to a file that begins with the drive identifier and root directory or with a network share and ends with the complete file name (for example, C:\docs\work\contract.txt or\\netshare\docs\work\contract.txt). Also called: full path.

Absolute pointing device *n.* A mechanical or physical pointing device whose location is associated with the position of the onscreen cursor. For example, if the user of a graphics tablet places the pen on the upper right corner of the tablet, the cursor moves to the upper right corner of the screen or onscreen window associated with the pen.

Absolute URL *n.* The full Internet address of a page or other World Wide Web resource. The absolute URL includes a protocol, such as "http," network location, and optional path and file name—for example, http:// example.microsoft.com/.

Absolute value *n.* The magnitude of a number, irrespective of its sign (+ or –). An absolute value is always greater than or equal to zero. For example, 10 is the absolute value of 10 and of –10. Programming languages and spreadsheet programmes commonly include functions that return the absolute value of a number.

Abstract[1] *adj.* 1. In character recognition systems, of, pertaining to, or being a type of symbol that, unlike a letter or numeral, has no intrinsic meaning and must be defined before it can be interpreted. 2. In programming, of, pertaining to, or being a data type defined by the operations that can be performed on objects of that type rather than by the properties of the objects themselves.

Abstract[2] *n.* In information processing and library science, a summary typically consisting of a paragraph or a few paragraphs at the beginning of an investigative document, such as a scientific paper.

Abstract class *n.* 1. In object-oriented programming, a class in which no objects can be created. It is, however, used to defined subclasses, and objects are created from the subclasses. See also object (definition 2). 2. In Java programming, a class that contains one or more abstract methods and therefore can never be instantiated. Abstract classes are defined so that other classes can extend them and make them concrete by implementing the abstract methods. See also class, instantiate, Java, method, object (definition 2).

Abstract data type *n.* In programming, a data set defined by the programmer in terms of the information it can contain and the operations that can be performed with it. An abstract data type is more generalised than a data type constrained by the properties of the objects it contains—for example, the data type "pet" is more generalised than the data types "pet dog," "pet bird," and "pet fish." The standard example used in illustrating an abstract data type is the stack, a small portion of memory used to store information, generally on a temporary basis. As an abstract data type, the stack is simply a structure onto which values can be pushed (added) and from which they can be popped (removed). The type of value, such as integer, is irrelevant to the definition. The way in which the programme performs operations on abstract data types is encapsulated, or hidden, from the rest of the programme. Encapsulation enables the programmer to change the definition of the data type or its operations without introducing errors to the existing code that uses the abstract data type. Abstract data types represent an intermediate step between traditional programming and object-oriented programming. See also data type, object-oriented programming.

Abstraction *n.* 1. Broadly, the use of specialised software, such as an application programming interface (API), as a means of shielding software from device dependencies or the complexities of underlying software. For instance, hardware abstraction enables programmes to focus on a task, such as communications, instead of on individual differences between communications devices. 2. In object-oriented programming, the process of reducing an object to its essence so that only the necessary elements are represented. Abstraction defines an object in terms of its properties (attributes), behaviours (functionality), and interface (means of communicating with other objects).

Abstract machine *n.* A design for a processor that is not meant for implementation but that represents a model for processing abstract machine language. Its instruction set can use instructions that more closely resemble the compiled language than the instructions used by an actual computer. It can also be used to make the implementation of the language more portable to other platforms.

Abstract machine language *n.* 1. An intermediate programming language used by an interpreter or compiler. 2. See pseudocode (definition 1).

Abstract syntax *n.* A data structure description that is independent of hardware structures and encodings.

Abstract Syntax Notation One *n.* The ISO standard notation for independent specification of data types and structures for syntax conversion. Acronym: ASN.1. See also data type, ISO, syntax.

Abstract syntax tree *n.* A treelike representation of programmes used in many integrated programming environments and structure-oriented editors.

Abstract Window Toolkit *n.* A library of Java GUIs (graphical user interfaces) that provides the connections between a Java application and the native GUI of the computer on which the application runs. Also called: AWT.

AC *n.* See alternating current.

AC adapter *n.* An external power supply that converts from a 110 VAC or 220 VAC domestic electric supply ("house current" or "main power") to low-voltage DC, which is required to operate solid-state electronic equipment (such as a laptop computer) that does not include an internal power supply.

Accelerated Graphics Port *n.* See AGP.

Accelerator *n.* 1. In applications, a key or key combination used to perform a defined function. Also called: shortcut key. 2. In hardware, a device that speeds or enhances the operation of one or more subsystems, leading to improved programme performance. See also accelerator card, Windows-based accelerator.

Accelerator card *n.* A printed circuit board that replaces or augments the computer's main microprocessor, resulting in faster performance. Also called: accelerator board. See also expansion board, graphics accelerator.

Acceptable use policy *n.* A statement issued by an ISP (Internet service provider) or an online information service that indicates what activities users may or may not engage in while logged into the service. For example, some providers prohibit users from engaging in commercial activity on the network. Acronym: AUP. See also ISP, online information service.

Acceptance test *n.* A formal evaluation of a hardware product performed by the customer, usually at the factory, to verify that the product is performing according to specifications.

Access[1] *n.* 1. The act of reading data from or writing data to memory. 2. Connection to the Internet or other network or system.

Access[2] *vb.* To gain entry to memory in order to read or write data.

Access *n.* Microsoft's relational database–management software for the Windows desktop platform. Part of the family of Microsoft Office products, Access in its most recent version (Access 2002) supports Web technology for building, managing, and sharing data. Access 2002 also includes new and improved tools for accessing and viewing information and offers integration with Microsoft's BackOffice database product, SQL Server.

Access arm *n.* A mechanical arm that moves the read/write head(s) over the surface of a disk in a disk drive. See the illustration. Also called: head arm.

ACCESS.bus *n.* A bidirectional bus for connecting peripherals to a PC. The ACCESS.bus can connect up to 125 low-speed peripherals, such as printers, modems, mice, and keyboards, to the system through a single, general-purpose port. Peripherals that support the ACCESS.bus provide a connector or port connection that is similar to a phone-jack connector and are daisy-chained together. However, the PC communicates directly with each peripheral and vice versa. Connecting an ACCESS.bus device (for example, a printer) to a system results in the system automatically identifying and configuring it for optimum performance. Peripherals can be connected while the computer is running (hot plugging) and are automatically assigned a unique address (auto-addressing). Developed from the I2 architecture designed jointly by Philips and Digital Equipment Corporation, the ACCESS.bus specification is controlled by the ACCESS.bus Industry Group and competes with Intel's USB. See also bidirectional, bus, daisy chain[1], hot plugging, input/output port, peripheral.

Access code *n.* See password.

Access control *n.* The mechanisms for limiting access to certain items of information or to certain controls based on users' identities and their membership in various predefined groups. Access control is typically used by system administrators for controlling user access to network resources, such as servers, directories, and files. See also access privileges, system administrator.

Access control list *n.* A list associated with a file or a resource that contains information about which users or groups have permission to access a resource or modify the file. Acronym: ACL.

Accessibility *n.* A quality of software, hardware, or a complete computer system that makes it usable by people with one or more physical disabilities, such as restricted mobility, blindness, or deafness.

Accessibility aids *n.* Utilities that make computers easier to use for people with disabilities. Examples of accessibility aids include screen readers, speech recognition programmes, and onscreen keyboards.

Access key *n.* A key combination, such as ALT+F, that moves the focus to a menu, a command, or a control, without using the mouse.

Access mechanism *n.* 1. The disk drive components that move the read/write head(s) to the proper track of a magnetic disk or optical disc. See also disk controller. 2. A circuit that allows one part of a computer system to send signals to another part. 3. In programming, the means by which an application can read from or write to a resource. Also called: access method.

Access method *n.* See access mechanism.

Access number *n.* The telephone number used by a subscriber to gain access to an online service.

Accessory *n.* See peripheral.

Access path *n.* See search path.

Access permission *n.* See permission.

Access point *n.* In a wireless LAN (local area network), a transceiver that connects the LAN to a wired network. See also wireless LAN.

Access privileges *n.* The type of operations permitted a given user for a certain system resource on a network or a file server. A variety of operations, such as the ability to access a server, view the contents of a directory, open or transfer files, and create, modify, or delete files or directories, can be allowed or disallowed by the system administrator. Assigning access privileges to users helps the system administrator to maintain security on the system, as well as the privacy of confidential information, and to allocate system resources, such as disk space. Also called: access rights. See also file protection, file server, permission, system administrator, write access.

Access rights *n.* See access privileges.

Access speed *n.* See access time.

Access time *n.* 1. The amount of time it takes for data to be delivered from memory to the processor after the address for the data has been selected. 2. The time needed for a read/write head in a disk drive to locate a track on a disk. Access time is usually measured in milliseconds and is used as a performance measure for hard disks and CD-ROM drives. See also read/write head, seek time, settling time, wait state.

Account *n.* 1. A record-keeping arrangement used by the vendor of an online service to identify a subscriber and to maintain a record of customer usage for billing purposes. 2. The record-keeping mechanism used by networks and multiuser operating systems for keeping track of authorised users. Network accounts are created by network administrators and are used both to validate users and to administer policies--for example, permissions—related to each user.

Accounting file *n.* A file generated by a printer controller that keeps track of the number of pages printed per job as well as the user that requested the print job.

Accounting machine *n.* 1. One of the earliest applications of automatic data processing, used in business accounting primarily during the 1940s and 1950s. The first accounting machines were nonelectronic and used punched cards and wires arranged in plugboard panels. 2. A computer in which an accounting software package starts up whenever the machine is turned on, the computer thus becoming a dedicated machine with accounting as its sole function.

Account lockout *n.* A security feature in Windows XP that locks a user account if a number of failed logon attempts occur within a specified amount of time, based on security policy lockout settings. Locked accounts cannot log on.

Account name *n.* The part of an e-mail address that identifies a user or an account on an e-mail system. An e-mail address on the Internet typically consists of an account name, followed by the @ (at) symbol, a host name, and a domain name. See also account (definition 2), domain name, e-mail address.

Account policy *n.* On local area networks and multi-user operating systems, a set of rules governing whether a new user is allowed access to the system and whether an existing user's rights are expanded to include additional system resources. An account policy also generally states the rules with which the user must comply while using the system in order to maintain access privileges.

ACCU *n.* See Association of C and C++ Users.

Accumulator *n.* A register used for logic or arithmetic, usually to count items or accumulate a sum. See also register.

Accuracy *n.* The degree to which the result of a calculation or measurement approximates the true value.

ACID *n.* Abbreviation for Atomicity, Consistency, Isolation, Durability. The four essential properties of an electronic transaction. Atomicity requires that a transaction be fully completed or else fully canceled. Consistency requires that resources used are transformed from one consistent state to another. Isolation requires all transactions to be independent of each other. Durability requires that the completed transaction be permanent, including survival through system failure. See also transaction.

ACIS *n.* Acronym for Andy, Charles, Ian's System. An object-oriented geometric modeling toolkit owned by Spatial Technology. Designed for use as a "geometry engine" within 3-D modeling applications, ACIS provides an open architecture framework for wire-frame, surface, and solid modeling from a common, unified data structure. ACIS is generally considered the de facto standard for solids modeling in the CAM/CAE industries.

ACK *n.* Short for acknowledgment. A message sent by the receiving unit to the sending station or computer indicating either that the unit is ready to receive transmission or that a transmission was received without error.

Acoustic coupler *n.* An archaic device once used in computer communications. The coupler was a cradle-like instrument into which the headset of a telephone was placed. Its function was somewhat similar to the job now done by modems.

ACPI *n.* Acronym for Advanced Configuration and Power Interface. An open specification developed jointly by Microsoft, Intel, and Toshiba for managing power consumption on mobile, desktop, and server computers. Unlike earlier, BIOS-based management solutions, ACPI provides a means of integrating power management through all parts of a PC, including applications, hardware, and the operating system (OS). ACPI enables an OS to control a computer's power state in response to input from the user, from an application, or from a device driver. For example, an

ACPI-enabled OS could turn a CD-ROM drive, a printer, or even a television on or off as needed. ACPI is part of the industry-wide OnNow initiative that allows system manufacturers to deliver computers that start at the touch of a keyboard. See also plug and play, power management.

Acrobat *n.* A programme from Adobe Systems, Inc., that converts a fully formatted document created on a Windows, Macintosh, MS-DOS, or UNIX platform into a Portable Document Format (PDF) file that can be viewed on several different platforms. Acrobat enables users to send documents that contain distinctive typefaces, colour, graphics, and photographs electronically to recipients, regardless of the application used to create the originals. Recipients need the Acrobat Reader, which is available free, to view the files. Depending on version and platform, it also includes tools such as Distiller (which creates PDF files from PostScript files), Exchange (which is used for links, annotations, and security-related matters), and PDF Writer (which creates PDF files from files created with business software).

Acrobat Reader *n.* A free programme produced and distributed by Adobe Systems, Inc., for displaying and printing documents that are in Portable Document Format (PDF).

Action query *n.* In Microsoft Access, a query that copies or changes data. Action queries include append, delete, make-table, and update queries. They are identified by an exclamation point (!) next to their name in the Database window.

Action statement *n.* See statement.

Activation *n.* In Sun Microsystem's J2EE network platform, the process of transferring an enterprise java bean (EJB) from secondary storage to memory. See also EJB, J2EE.

Activation record *n.* A data structure that represents the state of some construct (such as a procedure, a function, a block, an expression, or a module) of a running programme. An activation record is useful for the run-time management of both data and sequencing.

Active *adj.* Pertaining to the device, programme, file, or portion of the screen that is currently operational or subject to command operations. Usually the cursor or a highlighted section shows the active element on the display screen.

Active Accessibility *n.* A Microsoft initiative, introduced in 1997, that consists of programme files and conventions that make it easier for software developers to integrate accessibility aids, such as screen magnifiers or text-to-voice converters, into their application's user interface to make software easier for users with limited physical abilities to use. Active Accessibility is based on COM technologies and is supported by Windows 9x, Windows XP, Windows NT 4.0 and above, Internet Explorer 3 and above, and Office 2000 and above. Acronym: MSAA. Also called: Microsoft Active Accessibility.

Active cell *n.* The highlighted cell on a spreadsheet display that is the current focus of operation. Also called: current cell, selected cell. See also range.

Active Channel *n.* A Web site described by a Channel Definition Format (CDF) file. Developers can use Active Channels to automatically download content to a user on a subscription basis, to send content to users on a regular schedule, to deliver personalised content to individual users, and to provide content to a Windows screen saver. Active Channels were introduced in Microsoft Internet Explorer 4 and can be used to deliver information through either the Internet or an intranet. See also pull, webcasting.

Active Client *n.* The client-side set of technologies in Microsoft's Active Platform for Web-oriented, cross-platform distributed computing. The chief features of the Active Client include support for HTML and dynamic HTML, language-independent scripting, Java applets, and ActiveX objects. Active Client is operating system–independent, so it runs on multiple platforms, including Microsoft Windows, UNIX, and Apple Macintosh. See also Active Platform, Active Server.

Active content *n.* Material on a Web page that changes on the screen with time or in response to user action. Active content is implemented through ActiveX controls. See also ActiveX control.

Active data object *n.* An application programming interface (API) developed by Microsoft for applications that access databases. ADO is an easy-to-use interface to OLE Database (OLE DB), an API that accesses the data directly from a database. Also called: ActiveX data object.

Active Desktop *n.* The feature introduced with Microsoft's Internet Explorer 4 that enables end users to display active—that is, updateable, customizable—HTML content on the Windows desktop. Active content includes such items as channels, Web pages, ActiveX controls, and Java applets. See also Active Channel, ActiveX, HTML, Internet Explorer, Java.

Active Directory *n.* A Microsoft technology, part of the Active Platform, that is designed to enable applications to find, use, and manage directory resources (for example, user names, network printers, and permissions) in a distributed computing environment. Distributed environments are usually heterogeneous collections of networks that often run proprietary directory services from different providers. To simplify directory-related activities associated with locating and administering network users and resources, Active Directory presents applications with a single set of interfaces that eliminates the need to deal with differences between and among these proprietary services. Active Directory is a component of the Windows Open Services Architecture (WOSA).

Active Directory Services Interface *n.* An administrative tool known as a Microsoft Management Console (MMC) snap-in that allows administrators to manage objects in the domain.

Active file *n.* The file affected by a current command—typically a data file.

Active Framework for Data Warehousing *n.* A data warehousing solution developed by Microsoft and Texas Instruments that represents Microsoft's standard for managing metadata. Acronym: AFDW.

Active hub *n.* 1. The central computer that regenerates and retransmits all signals in an active star network. See also active star. 2. A type of hub used on ARCnet networks that both regenerates (boosts) signals and passes them along.

Active-matrix display *n.* A liquid crystal display (LCD) made from a large array of liquid crystal cells using active-matrix technology. The active matrix is a method of addressing an array of simple LC cells—one cell per pixel. In its simplest form there is one thin-film transistor (TFT) for each cell. Voltage applied selectively to these cells produces the viewable image. Active-matrix displays are often used in laptop and notebook computers because of their shallow depth and are notable for their high-quality colour displays, which are viewable from wider angles than images produced by most passive-matrix displays. Also called: TFT, TFT display, TFT LCD. See also liquid crystal display, TFT.

ActiveMovie *n.* Former name for the DirectX component now known as DirectShow. Also called: DirectShow.

Active Platform *n.* A Microsoft development platform that offers a standardised approach to incorporating Internet and distributed computing technologies in client/server applications. Microsoft Windows 9x, Microsoft Windows NT, and Microsoft Internet Explorer 4.x (and later) provide the basis for the Active Platform. On the client side, users are given a consistent interface that enables them to easily access both local and remote information. On the server side, developers can take advantage of the tools and technologies that span the client and the server. Active Platform supports development of the modular object-oriented programmes known as component software and allows creation of cross-platform applications that can run on multiple chips and operating systems. Active Platform includes support for HTML and the creation of small programmes in several languages through client-side scripting.

Active programme *n.* The programme currently in control of a microprocessor.

Active Server Pages *n.* A Web-oriented technology developed by Microsoft that is designed to enable server-side (as opposed to client-side) scripting. Active Server Pages are text files that can contain not only text and HTML tags as in standard Web documents, but also commands written in a scripting language (such as VBScript or JavaScript) that can be carried out on the server. This server-side work enables a Web author to add interactivity to a document or to customise the viewing or delivery of information to the client without worrying about the platform the client is running. All Active Server Pages are saved with an .asp extension and can be accessed like standard URLs through a Web browser, such as Microsoft Internet Explorer or Netscape Navigator. When an Active Server Page is requested by a browser, the server carries out any script commands embedded in the page, generates an HTML document, and sends the document back to the browser for display on the requesting (client) computer. Active Server Pages can also be enhanced and extended with ActiveX components. Acronym: ASP. See also Active Server, ActiveX.

Active star *n.* A form of the star network topology in which the central computer actively regenerates and retransmits all signals. See also star network.

ActiveStore *n.* A Microsoft initiative, introduced in 1998, for supporting integration of applications used in retail environments regardless of the developing vendor. Active-Store provides a common user interface, base system services (such as security and crash recovery), common access to data across applications, and communication between applications.

ActiveSync *n.* A Microsoft programme that manages synchronization of information, including e-mail, schedules, and application files, between a handheld PC and a desktop computer.

Active vision *n.* A branch of computer vision research that believes robotic vision problems can be solved by allowing a robot to collect and analyse a sequence of images dynamically from changing viewpoints. Not unlike human or animal vision, active vision uses the information derived from multiple viewpoints to gain a greater depth of perception, resolve haziness, and establish relationships between the visual representation of an action and the action itself. Active vision systems may be characterised by simple image-processing algorithms, little or no calibration, and fast real-time hardware. See also artificial intelligence, computer vision, robotics.

Active window *n.* In an environment capable of displaying multiple onscreen windows, the window containing the display or document that will be affected by current cursor movements, commands, and text entry. See also graphical user interface.

ActiveX *n.* A set of technologies that enables software components to interact with one another in a networked environment, regardless of the language in which the components were created. ActiveX, which was developed by Microsoft in the mid 1990s and is currently administered by the Open Group, is built on Microsoft's Component Object Model (COM). Currently, ActiveX is used primarily to develop interactive content for the World Wide Web, although it can be used in desktop applications and other programmes. ActiveX controls can be embedded in Web pages to produce animation and other multimedia effects, interactive objects, and sophisticated applications.

ActiveX control *n.* A reusable software component based on Microsoft's ActiveX technology that is used to add interactivity and more functionality, such as animation or a popup menu, to a Web page, applications, and software development tools. An ActiveX control can be written in any of a number of languages, including Java, C++, and Visual Basic.

Activity ratio *n.* The number of records in use compared with the total number of records in a database file. See also database, record[1].

ACTOR *n.* An object-oriented language developed by The Whitewater Group, Ltd., designed primarily to facilitate Microsoft Windows programming. See also object-oriented programming.

Actuator *n.* A disk drive mechanism for moving the read/write head(s) to the location of the desired track on a disk. See the illustration. See also disk drive, stepper motor, voice coil.

Ada *n.* A high-level programming language designed under the direction of the U.S. Department of Defence (DoD) in the late 1970s and intended to be the primary language for DoD software development. Originally based on Pascal, Ada supports real-time operations and multitasking. The language was named after Augusta Ada Byron, who assisted Charles Babbage in developing programmes for his Analytical Engine, the first mechanical computer, in the nineteenth century. See also multitasking, Pascal, real-time.

Adapter or adaptor *n.* A printed circuit board that enables a personal computer to use a peripheral device, such as a CD-ROM drive, modem, or joystick, for which it does not already have the necessary connections, ports, or circuit boards. Commonly, a single adapter card can have more than one adapter on it. Also called: interface card. See also controller, expansion board, network adapter, port[1], video adapter.

Adapter card or adaptor card *n.* See adapter.

Adaptive answering *n.* The ability of a modem to detect whether an incoming call is a fax or a data transmission and respond accordingly. See also modem.

Adaptive delta pulse code modulation *n.* A class of compression encoding and decoding algorithms used in audio compression and other data compression applications. These algorithms store digitally sampled signals as a series of changes in value, adapting the range of the change with each sample as needed, thus increasing the effective bit resolution of the data. Acronym: ADPCM. See also pulse code modulation.

Adaptive differential pulse code modulation *n.* A digital audio compression algorithm that stores a sample as the difference between a linear combination of previous samples and the actual sample, rather than the measurement itself. The linear combination formula is modified every few samples to minimise the dynamic range of the output signal, resulting in efficient storage. See also pulse code modulation.

Adaptive load balancing *n.* See load balancing.

Adaptive routing *n.* See dynamic routing.

Adaptive system *n.* An artificial intelligence system that is capable of altering its behaviour based on certain features of its experience or environment. See also expert system.

ADB *n.* See Apple Desktop Bus.

ADC *n.* See analog-to-digital converter.

A-D converter *n.* See analog-to-digital converter.

Adder *n.* 1. A component of the CPU (central processing unit) that adds two numbers sent to it by processing instructions. See also central processing unit. 2. A circuit that sums the amplitudes, or strength, of two input signals. See also full adder, half adder.

Add-in *n.* See add-on.

Addition record *n.* 1. A file that describes new record entries (such as a new customer, employee, or product) in a database so that they can later be scrutinised and posted. 2. A record in a change file specifying a new entry. See also change file.

Add-on *n.* 1. A hardware device, such as an expansion board or chip, that can be added to a computer to expand its capabilities. Also called: add-in. See also open architecture (definition 2). 2. A supplemental programme that can extend the capabilities of an application programme. See also utility programme.

Address[1] *n.* 1. A number specifying a location in memory where data is stored. See also absolute address, address space, physical address, virtual address. 2. A name or token specifying a particular computer or site on the Internet or other network. 3. A code used to specify an e-mail destination.

Address[2] *vb.* To reference a particular storage location.

Addressable cursor *n.* A cursor programmed so that it can be moved to any location on the screen, by means of the keyboard or a mouse.

Address book *n.* 1. In an e-mail programme, a reference section listing e-mail addresses and individuals' names. 2. As a Web page, an informal e-mail or URL phone book.

Address bus *n.* A bus consisting of 20 to 64 separate hardware lines that is used to carry the signals specifying memory locations for data. See also bus.

Address classes *n.* Predefined groupings of Internet addresses with each class defining networks of a certain size. The range of numbers that can be assigned for the first octet in the IP address is based on the address class. Class A networks (values 1 to 126) are the largest, with more than 16 million hosts per network. Class B networks (128 to 191) have up to 65,534 hosts per network, and Class C networks (192 to 223) can have up to 254 hosts per network.

Address decoder *n.* An electronic device that converts a numeric address to the electrical signals needed to select a specific memory location on one or more RAM chips.

Addressing *n.* The process of assigning or referring to an address. In programming, the address is typically a value specifying a memory location. See also address[1].

Address mapping table *n.* A table used by routers or DNS (Domain Name System) servers to obtain the corresponding IP (Internet Protocol) address of a text name of a computer resource, such as the name of a host computer on the Internet. Acronym: AMT. See also DNS server, IP address, router.

Address mark *n.* See index mark.

Address mask *n.* A number that, when compared by the computer with a network address number, will block out all but the necessary information. For example, in a network that uses XXX.XXX.XXX.YYY and where all computers within the network use the same first address numbers, the mask will block out XXX.XXX.XXX and use only the significant numbers in the address, YYY. See also address[1] (definition 2).

Address mode *n.* The method used to indicate an address in memory. See also absolute address, indexed address, paged address, relative address.

Address modification *n.* The process of updating an address of a location in memory during computation.

Address munging *n.* The practice of modifying an e mail address in posts to newsgroups or other Internet forums to foil computer programmes that gather e-mail addresses. The host name in an e-mail address is altered to create a fictitious address in such a way that a human can still easily determine the correct address. For example, a person with an e-mail address of Jane@myispoffers-usersfreeemail.com could modify, or "mung," her address to read Jane@remove-this-to-reply-myispoffersusersfreeemail.com. Address munging is generally used to prevent delivery of unsolicited junk e-mail or spam. Also called: munging. See also address[1] (definition 2), host name, mung, spam.

Address register *n.* A register (a high-speed memory circuit) that holds an address where specific data can be found for the transfer of information. See also register.

Address resolution *n.* The identification of a computer's IP (Internet Protocol) address by finding the corresponding match in an address mapping table. See also address mapping table.

Address Resolution Protocol *n.* See ARP.

Address space *n.* The total range of memory locations addressable by a computer.

Address translation *n.* The process of converting one kind of address to another, such as a virtual address to a physical address.

Ad-hoc network *n.* A temporary network formed by communicating stations or computers in a wireless LAN. See also wireless LAN.

ADJ *n.* Short for adjacent. A Boolean qualifier to indicate cases where two instances are adjacent to each other. In the case of a search string, "Microsoft ADJ Word" would return only instances where "Microsoft" and "Word" are adjacent in the string.

Administrative alerts *n.* Alerts that relate to server and resource use. They notify users about problems in areas such as security and access, user sessions, server shutdown due to power loss (when an uninterruptible power supply is available), directory replication, and printing. When a computer generates an administrative alert, a message is sent to a predefined list of users and computers. See also Alerter service.

ADN *n.* See Advanced Digital Network.

ADO *n.* See Active data object.

Adobe Type Manager *n.* Software from Adobe Systems, Inc., that manages PostScript fonts on a system. Acronym: ATM. See also PostScript.

ADO.NET *n.* The suite of data access technologies included in the .NET Framework class libraries that provide access to relational data and XML. ADO.NET consists of classes that make up the DataSet (such as tables, rows, columns, relations, and so on), .NET Framework data providers, and custom type definitions (such as SqlTypes for SQL Server).

ADP *n.* See data processing.

ADPCM *n.* See adaptive delta pulse code modulation.

ADSL *n.* Acronym for asymmetric digital subscriber line. Technology and equipment allowing high-speed digital communication, including video signals, across an ordinary twisted-pair copper phone line, with speeds up to 8 Mbps (megabits per second) downstream (to the customer) and up to 640 Kbps (kilobits per second) upstream. ADSL access to the Internet is offered by some regional telephone companies, offering users faster connection times than those available through connections made over standard phone lines. Also called: asymmetric digital subscriber loop.

Advanced Configuration and Power Interface *n.* See ACPI.

Advanced Digital Network *n.* A dedicated line service capable of transmitting data, video, and other digital signals with exceptional reliability, offered as a premier service by communications companies. Usually Advanced Digital Network refers to speeds at or above 56 kilobits per second (Kbps). See also dedicated line.

Advanced Encryption Standard *n.* See AES.

Advanced Interactive Executive *n.* See AIX.

Advanced Mobile Phone Service *n.* See AMPS.

Advanced Power Management (APM) *n.* An older power management technology used in mobile PCs before the implementation of Advanced Configuration and Power Interface (ACPI). Advanced Power Management is a software interface that functions between the BIOS power-management software that is specific to the hardware and a power-management policy driver that is run by the operating system.

Advanced Programme-to-Programme Communication *n.* See APPC.

Advanced Research Projects Agency Network *n.* See ARPANET.

Advanced RISC *n.* Short for Advanced reduced instruction set computing. A specification for a RISC microchip architecture and system environment designed by MIPS Computer Systems to provide binary compatibility among software applications. See also RISC.

Advanced RISC Computing Specification *n.* The minimum hardware requirements enabling a RISC-based system to comply with the Advanced Computing Environment standard. See also Advanced RISC.

Advanced RISC Machines *n.* See ARM.

Advanced SCSI Programming Interface (ASPI) *n.* An interface specification developed by Adaptec, Inc., for sending commands to SCSI host adapters. The interface provides an abstraction layer that insulates the programmer from considerations of the particular host adapter used. See also adapter, SCSI.

Advanced Streaming Format *n.* An open file format specification for streaming multimedia files containing text, graphics, sound, video, and animation. Advanced Streaming Format (ASF) does not define the format for any media streams within the file. Rather, it defines a standardised, extensible file "container" that is not dependent on a particular operating system or communication protocol, or on a particular method (such as HTML or MPEG-4) used to compose the data stream in the file. An ASF file consists of three objects: a Header object containing information about the file itself, a Data object containing the media streams, and an optional Index object that can help support random access to data within the file. The ASF specification has been submitted to the ISO (International Organisation for Standardization) for consideration. Acronym: ASF. See also streaming.

Adventure game *n.* A role-playing computer game in which the player becomes a character in a narrative. In order to complete the game, the player must solve problems and avoid or overcome attacks and other forms of interference from the game's environment and other characters. The first adventure game was called "Adventure." It was developed in 1976 by Will Crowther of Bolt, Baranek & Newman. See also arcade game, computer game, role-playing game.

AE *n.* Acronym for application entity. In the ISO/OSI reference model, one of the two software parties involved in a communications session. See also ISO/OSI reference model.

A/E/C SYSTEMS conference *n.* Annual conference of the architecture, engineering, and construction industry. The conference promotes the exchange of information on new techniques and technologies used by these industries.

.aero *n.* One of seven new top-level domain names approved in 2000 by the Internet Corporation for Assigned Names and Numbers (ICANN). .aero is meant for use with air-transport industry-related Web sites. The seven new domain names became available for use in the spring of 2001.

AES *n.* Acronym for Advanced Encryption Standard. A cryptographic algorithm specified by the National Institute of Standards and Technology (NIST) to protect sensitive information. AES is specified in three key sizes: 128, 192, and 256 bits. AES replaces the 56-bit key Data Encryption Standard (DES), which was adopted in 1976. See also DES.

AFC *n.* See Application Foundation Classes.

AFDW *n.* See Active Framework for Data Warehousing.

Affinity *n.* For Network Load Balancing, the method used to associate client requests to cluster hosts. When no affinity is specified, all network requests are load balanced across the cluster without respect to their source. Affinity is implemented by directing all client requests from the same IP address to the same cluster host. See also client request, IP address.

AFIPS *n.* Acronym for American Federation of Information Processing Societies. An organisation formed in 1961 for the advancement of computing and information-related concerns. The U.S. representative of the International Federation of Information Processing, AFIPS was replaced by the Federation on Computing in the United States (FOCUS) in 1990.

AFK *adv.* Acronym for away from keyboard. A phrase occasionally seen in live chat services on the Internet and online information services as an indication that one is momentarily unable to answer. See also chat[1] (definition 1).

AFP *n.* Acronym for AppleTalk Filing Protocol. A remote filing system protocol that provides a standard means for a workstation on an AppleTalk network to access and manipulate files on an AFP-implemented server. Also called: AppleShare File Server.

AFS *n.* Acronym for Andrew File System. A distributed file system that allows clients and servers to share resources through local-area and wide-area networks. AFS is based on a distributed file system developed at Carnegie-Mellon University, and is named for the university's founders—Andrew Carnegie and Andrew Mellon. AFS is now maintained and supplied by Transarc Corporation. See also distributed file system.

Agent *n.* 1. A programme that performs a background task for a user and reports to the user when the task is done or some expected event has taken place. 2. A programme that searches through archives or other repositories of information on a topic specified by the user. Agents of this sort are used most often on the Internet and are generally dedicated to searching a single type of information repository, such as postings on Usenet groups. Spiders are a type of agent used on the Internet. Also called: intelligent agent. See also spider. 3. In client/server applications, a process that mediates between the client and the server. 4. In Simple Network Management Protocol

(SNMP), a programme that monitors network traffic. See also SNMP.

Aggregated links *n.* See link aggregation.

Aggregation of links *n.* See link aggregation.

AGP *n.* Acronym for Accelerated Graphics Port. A high-performance bus specification designed for fast, high-quality display of 3-D and video images. Developed by Intel Corporation, AGP uses a dedicated point-to-point connection between the graphics controller and main system memory. This connection enables AGP-capable display adapters and compatible chip sets to transfer video data directly between system memory and adapter memory, to display images more quickly and smoothly than they can be displayed when the information must be transferred over the system's primary (PCI) bus. AGP also allows for storing complex image elements such as texture maps in system memory and thus reduces the need for large amounts of memory on the adapter itself. AGP runs at 66 MHz—twice as fast as the PCI bus—and can support data transfer speeds of up to 533 Mbps. See also PCI local bus.

AH *n.* Authentication Header. A form of IP packet authentication included in the IPSec security standard. AH attaches a header to the packet with authentication information but does not encrypt the packet data, which allows its use in cases where encryption is not allowed. See also ESP, IPSec.

AI *n.* See artificial intelligence.

.aiff *n.* The file extension that identifies audio files in the sound format originally used on Apple and Silicon Graphics (SGI) computers.

AIFF *n.* The sound format originally used on Apple and Silicon Graphics (SGI) computers. AIFF stores waveform files in an 8-bit monaural format. See also waveform.

AIM *n.* Acronym for America Online Instant Messenger. A popular instant-messaging service provided for free by America Online. With the AIM service, instant messages can be sent over an Internet connection using the AIM software or directly from a Web browser using AIM Express. See also America Online, instant messaging.

AirPort *n.* A wireless connectivity option introduced by Apple in 1999. AirPort provides wireless network and Internet communications to all AirPort card–equipped Macintosh computers within 150 feet of an AirPort base station. AirPort was developed around the IEEE 802.11 Direct Sequence Spectrum (DSSS) industry standard and is interoperable with other 802.11-based equipment.

AirSnort *n.* A hacking tool used to gather and decrypt passwords in data sent over wireless networks. AirSnort monitors wireless transmissions and collects packets of data. When it has collected enough data, AirSnort is able to compute the encryption key used in the transmission. AirSnort takes advantage of security flaws in the Wired Equivalent Protocol (WEP) standard. See also password sniffing.

AIX *n.* Acronym for Advanced Interactive Executive. A version of the UNIX operating system developed and maintained by IBM for its UNIX workstations and PCs.

Alarm *n.* A visual or auditory signal from a computer alerting the user to an error or a hazardous situation.

ALB *n.* See load balancing.

Alert *n.* 1. In many operating systems with GUIs (graphical user interfaces), an audible or visual alarm that signals an error or represents a warning of some sort. See also alert box. 2. In programming, an asynchronous notification sent by one thread to another. The alert interrupts the recipient thread at defined points in its execution and causes it to execute an asynchronous procedure call. See also asynchronous procedure call, thread (definition 1).

Alert box *n.* An onscreen box in a GUI (graphical user interface) that is used to deliver a message or warning.

Alerter service *n.* A service used by the server and other services to notify selected users and computers of administrative alerts that occur on a computer. The Alerter service requires the Messenger service. See also administrative alerts, Messenger service, service.

ALGOL *n.* Acronym for Algorithmic Language. The first structured procedural programming language, developed in the late 1950s and once widely used in Europe.

Algorithm *n.* A finite sequence of steps for solving a logical or mathematical problem or performing a task.

Algorithmic language *n.* A programming language, such as Ada, Basic, C, or Pascal, that uses algorithms for problem solving.

Algorithmic Language *n.* See ALGOL.

Alias *n.* 1. An alternative label for some object, such as a file or data collection. 2. A name used to direct e-mail messages to a person or group of people on a network. 3. A false signal that results from the digitization of an analog audio sample.

Aliasing *n.* In computer graphics, the jagged appearance of curves or diagonal lines on a display screen, which is caused by low screen resolution. See the illustration.

Aliasing bug *n.* A class of subtle programming errors that can arise in code that performs dynamic allocation. If several pointers address the same chunk of storage, the programme may free the storage using one of the pointers but then attempt to use another one (an alias), which would no longer be pointing to the desired data. This bug is avoidable by the use of allocation strategies that never use more than one copy of a pointer to allocated core memory, or by the use of higher-level languages, such as LISP, which employ a garbage collection feature. Also called: stale pointer bug. See also alias, dynamic allocation, garbage collection.

Align *vb.* 1. In an application such as a word processor, to position lines of type relative to some point, such as the page margin. The most common types of alignment are left- and right-aligned and centered. See the illustration. 2. To adjust some device to position it within specified tolerances, such as the read/write head relative to a track on a disk. 3. In data handling, to store multiple-byte data units so that the respective bytes fall in corresponding locations of memory.

Alignment *n.* The arrangement of objects in fixed or predetermined positions, rows, or columns. For example, the

Macintosh Finder can do automatic alignment of icons in a folder or on the desktop.

Allegro *n.* Ported to a number of operating systems, Allegro is a freeware library of functions for use in programming computer games and graphics programmes. It is written for the DJGPP compiler in a mixture of C and assembly language. The most recent release version is 4.0.0. See also assembly language, DJGPP.

Allocate *vb.* To reserve a resource, such as sufficient memory, for use by a programme.

Allocation *n.* In operating systems, the process of reserving memory for use by a programme.

Allocation block size *n.* The size of an individual block on a storage medium, such as a hard drive, which is determined by factors such as total disk size and partitioning options.

Allocation unit *n.* See cluster.

All points addressable *n.* The mode in computer graphics in which all pixels can be individually manipulated. Acronym: APA. See also graphics mode.

ALOHA *n.* See ALOHAnet.

ALOHAnet *n.* The first wireless packet-switched network and the first large network to be connected to the ARPANET. ALOHAnet was built in 1970 at the University of Hawaii by Norm Abramson and was funded by Larry Roberts. ALOHAnet enabled computers at seven campuses on four different islands to communicate bidirectionally with the central computer on Oahu using a network of radio transmitters. The ALOHA protocol was the basis for Ethernet. See also ARPANET, Ethernet, network.

Alpha[1] *adj.* Of or pertaining to software that is ready for initial testing.

Alpha[2] *n.* A software product that is under development and has enough functionality to begin testing. An alpha is usually unstable and does not have all the features or functionality that the released product is to have.

Alpha *n.* 1. Digital Equipment Corporation's (DEC) line of computers built on its 64-bit RISC-based microprocessor (Alphachip). 2. DEC's internal name for a microprocessor product introduced in February 1992 as the DECchip 21064, which evolved into DEC's current Alphachips. See also Alphachip, DECchip 21064.

Alpha AXP *adj.* Of, pertaining to, or characteristic of Digital Equipment Corporation's 64-bit RISC-based microprocessor technology implemented in its DECchip product. The designation AXP is used by DEC in its personal computer products to indicate that a product has a DECchip microprocessor.

Alphabet *n.* In communications and data processing, the subset of a complete character set, including letters, numerals, punctuation marks, and other common symbols as well as the codes used to represent them. See also ASCII, CCITT, character set, EBCDIC, ISO.

Alpha blending *n.* In 3-D computer game rendering and other digital animation applications, a graphics technique for creating realistic transparent and semi-transparent images. Alpha blending combines a transparent source colour with a translucent destination colour to realistically simulate effects such as smoke, glass, and water.

Alpha box *n.* A computer built around the DEC's DECchip 21064 processor (called Alpha internally at Digital Equipment Corporation). See also DECchip 21064.

Alpha channel *n.* The high-order 8 bits of a 32-bit graphics pixel used to manipulate the remaining 24 bits for purposes of colouring or masking.

Alphachip *n.* A 64-bit RISC-based microprocessor from Digital Equipment Corporation.

Alphageometric *adj.* In reference to computer graphics, especially videotext and teletext systems, pertaining to or being a display method that uses codes for alphanumeric characters and creates graphics using geometric primitives. Shapes such as horizontal and vertical lines and corners are alphageometric. See also alphamosaic.

Alphamosaic *adj.* In reference to computer graphics, especially videotext and teletext systems, pertaining to or being a display technique that uses codes for alphanumeric characters and creates graphics using rectangular arrangements of elements to form a mosaic. See also alphageometric.

Alphanumeric *adj.* Consisting of letters or digits, or both, and sometimes including control characters, space characters, and other special characters. See also ASCII, character set, EBCDIC.

Alphanumeric display *n.* Electronic display on a wireless phone, pager, or handheld device capable of showing both text and numbers.

Alphanumeric display terminal *n.* A terminal capable of displaying characters but not graphics.

Alphanumeric messaging *n.* Ability to receive messages containing text and numbers on a pager or digital wireless phone. Also known as short message service (SMS).

Alphanumeric mode *n.* See text mode.

Alphanumeric sort *n.* A method of sorting data, such as a set of records, that typically uses the following order: punctuation marks, numerals, alphabetic characters (with capitals preceding lowercase letters), and any remaining symbols.

Alpha test *n.* The process of user testing that is carried out on a piece of alpha software.

Altair 8800 *n.* A small computer introduced in 1975 by Micro Instrumentation Telemetry Systems (MITS) of New Mexico and sold primarily in kit form. The Altair was based on the 8-bit Intel 8080 microprocessor, had 256 bytes of random access memory, received input through a bank of switches on the front panel, and displayed output via a row of light-emitting diodes. Although it was short-lived, the Altair is considered the first successful personal computer, which was then called a home computer.

AltaVista *n.* A World Wide Web search site and portal hosted by Digital Equipment Corporation. See also portal.

Alternate circuit-switched voice/circuit-switched data *n.* A configuration option for ISDN B (bearer) channels that enables the digital transmission of either voice or data communications between two users for the duration of a call. Acronym: CSV/CSD. See also B channel, circuit-switched data, circuit-switched voice, ISDN.

Alternate key *n.* 1. Any candidate key in a database not designated as the primary key. 2. See Alt key.

Alternating current *n.* Electric current that reverses its direction of flow (polarity) periodically according to a frequency measured in hertz, or cycles per second. Acronym: AC.

Alt key *n.* A key included on PC and other standard keyboards that is used in conjunction with another key to produce some special feature or function and is typically marked with the letters Alt.

Alt. newsgroups *n.* Internet newsgroups that are part of the alt. ("alternative") hierarchy and have the prefix alt. Unlike the seven Usenet newsgroup hierarchies (comp., misc., news., rec., sci., soc., talk.) that require formal votes among users in the hierarchy before official newsgroups can be established, anybody can create an alt. newsgroup. Therefore, newsgroups devoted to discussions of obscure or bizarre topics are generally part of the alt. hierarchy.

Always on *n.* An Internet connection that is maintained continuously, whether or not the computer user is online. Always-on connections provide convenience to users who don't need to dial in or log on to access the Internet, but also provide more opportunities for hackers to attempt to access the system or use the computer to spread malicious programmes.

AM *n.* See amplitude modulation.

AMD-K6 *n.* Family of x86-compatible processors introduced by Advanced Micro Devices, Inc. (AMD) in 1997. Comparable in performance to the Intel Pentium II, the AMD-K6 family is composed of Windows-compatible processors with MMX support that run 32-bit programmes. They have 8.8 million transistors, include 64-KB (AMD-K6) L1 caches for faster execution, and are based on a technology known as RISC86 that converts x86 programme instructions into RISC operations for execution. The AMD-K6 family ranges in speed from 166 to over 500 MHz. See also MMX, Pentium, RISC.

AMD-K7 *n.* See Athlon.

American Federation of Information Processing Societies *n.* See AFIPS.

American National Standards Institute *n.* See ANSI.

American Registry for Internet Numbers *n.* See ARIN.

American Standard Code for Information Interchange *n.* See ASCII.

America Online *n.* An online information service, based in Vienna, Virginia, that provides e-mail, news, educational and entertainment services, and Internet access. America Online is one of the largest American ISPs (Internet service providers). In 2000, America Online merged with media giant Time Warner Inc. to become AOL Time Warner Inc. Intended for mass-market delivery of branded content and communication services, the merged companies form a communication and media conglomerate with the Internet's largest user base and a wide range of entertainment, publishing, and cable properties. Acronym: AOL.

America Online Instant Messenger *n.* See AIM.

AMI BIOS *n.* A ROM BIOS developed and marketed by American Megatrends, Inc. (AMI), for use in IBM-compatible computers. A popular feature is that its configuration software is stored in the ROM chip along with the BIOS routines, so the user does not need a separate configuration disk to modify system settings, such as amount of memory installed and number and types of disk drives. See also BIOS, Phoenix BIOS, ROM BIOS.

Amiga *n.* An operating system owned by Amiga, Inc. The Amiga model of desktop computer, which featured the Amiga operating system, was introduced by Commodore in 1985. The Amiga was especially strong in its ability to support sound and video, which made it popular among broadcast and multimedia producers, but it was overshadowed by the IBM

Personal Computer (and its clones) and the Apple Macintosh. The ownership of the Amiga design has been through the hands of several companies in the United States and Germany.

Amp *n.* See ampere.

Ampere *n.* The basic unit of electric current. One ampere is equivalent to a flow of 1 coulomb per second. Abbreviation: a, A, amp.

Amplitude *n.* A measure of the strength of a signal, such as sound or voltage, determined by the distance from the baseline to the peak of the waveform. See also waveform.

Amplitude modulation *n.* A method of encoding information in a transmission, such as radio, using a carrier wave of constant frequency but of varying amplitude. See the illustration. Acronym: AM.

Amplitude shift keying *n.* A form of amplitude modulation that uses two different wave heights to represent the binary values 1 and 0. See also amplitude modulation.

AMPS *n.* Acronym for Advanced Mobile Phone Service. The standard for analog cellular phone service, widely used in the United States and many other countries around the world. AMPS was introduced by AT&T in 1983. It relies on frequency division multiple access (FDMA) to divide frequencies in the 800 MHz to 900 MHz range into 30 KHz channels for sending and receiving calls. A form of AMPS based on a narrower bandwidth is known as N-AMPS. The comparable standard for digital cellular phones is known as D-AMPS. See also D-AMPS, N-AMPS.

AMT *n.* See address mapping table.

Anaglyph *n.* A 3-D effect obtained by creating two overlapping images that appear as a single three dimensional image when viewed through special lenses. Anaglyph 3-D technologies are used on the Web to produce 3-D images for a variety of virtual reality, teaching, and research applications.

Analog *adj.* Pertaining to or being a device or signal that is continuously varying in strength or quantity, such as voltage or audio, rather than based on discrete units, such as the binary digits 1 and 0. A lighting dimmer switch is an analog device because it is not based on absolute settings.

Analog channel *n.* A communications channel, such as a voice-grade telephone line, carrying signals that vary continuously and can assume any value within a specified range.

Analog computer *n.* A computer that measures data varying continuously in value, such as speed or temperature.

Analog data *n.* Data that is represented by continuous variations in some physical property, such as voltage, frequency, or pressure.

Analog display *n.* A video display capable of depicting a continuous range of colours or shades rather than discrete values.

Analog line *n.* A communications line, such as a standard telephone line, that carries continuously varying (analog) signals.

Analog modem *n.* See modem.

Analog signal generator *n.* A device that generates continuously variable signals and is sometimes used to activate an actuator in a disk drive. See also actuator.

Analog-to-digital converter *n.* A device that converts a continuously varying (analog) signal, such as sound or voltage, from a monitoring instrument to binary code for use by a computer. See the illustration. Acronym: ADC. Also called: A-D converter. See also modem.

Analysis *n.* The evaluation of a situation or problem, including review from various aspects or points of view. In computing, analysis commonly involves such features as flow control, error control, and evaluation of efficiency. Often the overall problem is divided into smaller components that can be more easily dealt with. See also flow analysis, numerical analysis, systems analysis.

Analysis graphics *n.* See presentation graphics.

Analytical Engine *n.* A mechanical calculating machine designed by British mathematician Charles Babbage in 1833 but never completed. It was the first general-purpose digital computer. See also Difference Engine.

Anchor *n.* 1. A format code in a desktop publishing or word processing document that keeps an element in the document, such as a figure or a caption or a label associated with the figure, in a certain position in the document. The anchored object is generally attached to another element in the document such as a piece of text (often a paragraph), a graphic, or a particular place in the document. As text and other objects are added to the document, the anchored object moves relative to the object to which it is anchored or remains stationary. 2. A tag in an HTML document that defines a section of text, an icon, or other element as a link to another element in the document or to another document or file. See also hyperlink.

Ancillary equipment *n.* See peripheral.

AND *n.* A logical operation combining the values of two bits (0, 1) or two Boolean values (false, true) that returns a value of 1 (true) if both input values are 1 (true) and returns a 0 (false) otherwise. See the table.

Table A.1 The Possible Combinations with a Boolean AND.

a	b	a AND b
0	0	0
0	1	0
1	0	0
1	1	1

AND gate *n.* A digital circuit whose output is a value of 1 only when all input values are 1. See the illustration. See also truth table.

Andrew File System *n.* See AFS.

Angstrom *n.* A unit of measure equal to one 10-billionth (10^{-10}) of a meter or one 250-millionth of an inch. Light wavelength, for example, is commonly measured in angstroms. Abbreviation: Å.

Animated cursors *n.* A Windows 95 and Windows NT feature that allows a series of frames, one after another, to appear at the mouse pointer location instead of a single image, thus producing a short loop of animation. The animated cursors feature is designated by the .ani suffix.

Animated GIF *n.* A series of graphic images in GIF format, displayed sequentially in a single location to give the appearance of a moving picture. See also GIF.

Animation *n.* The illusion of movement created by using a succession of static images. In computer graphics, the images can all be drawn separately, or starting and ending points can be drawn with the intervening images provided by software. See also 3-D graphic, surface modeling, tween, wire-frame model.

ANN *n.* See artificial neural network.

Annotation *n.* A note or comment attached to some part of a document to provide related information. Some applications support voice annotations or annotations accessible by icons. See also comment.

Annoybot *n.* A bot on an Internet Relay Chat (IRC) channel or a multiuser dungeon (MUD) that interacts with the user in an obnoxious manner. See also bot, IRC, MUD.

Anode *n.* In electronics, the positively charged terminal or electrode toward which electrons flow.

Anonymity *n.* The ability to send an e-mail message or an article to a newsgroup without one's identity becoming known. Ordinarily, the e-mail address of the sender appears automatically in a message's header, which is created by the client software. To achieve anonymity, a message must be sent through an anonymous remailer—which, however, maintains a record of the sender's identity to enable replies. See also anonymous remailer.

Anonymous *n.* On the Internet, the standard login name used to obtain access to a public FTP file archive. See also anonymous FTP.

Anonymous FTP *n.* The ability to access a remote computer system on which one does not have an account, via the Internet's File Transfer Protocol (FTP). Users have restricted access rights with anonymous FTP and usually can only copy files to or from a public directory, often named /pub, on the remote system. Users can also typically use FTP commands, such as listing files and directories. When using anonymous FTP, the user accesses the remote computer system with an FTP programme and generally uses anonymous or ftp as a logon name. The password is usually the user's e-mail address, although a user can often skip giving a password or give a false e-mail address. In other cases, the password can be the word anonymous. Many FTP sites do not permit anonymous FTP access in order to maintain security. Those that do permit anonymous FTP sometimes restrict users to only downloading files for the same reason. See also FTP[1] (definition 1), logon, / pub.

Anonymous remailer *n.* An e-mail server that receives incoming messages, replaces the headers that identify the original sources of the messages, and sends the messages to their ultimate destinations. The purpose of an anonymous remailer is to hide the identities of the senders of the e-mail messages.

Anonymous server *n.* 1. The software used by an anonymous remailer. See also anonymous remailer. 2. Software that provides anonymous FTP service. See also anonymous FTP.

ANSI *n.* 1. Acronym for American National Standards Institute. A voluntary, nonprofit organisation of business and industry groups formed in 1918 for the development and adoption of trade and communication standards in the United States. ANSI is the American representative of ISO (the International Organisation for Standardization). Among its many concerns, ANSI has developed recommendations for the use of programming languages including FORTRAN, C, and COBOL, and various networking technologies. See also ANSI C, ANSI.SYS, SCSI. 2. The Microsoft Windows ANSI character set. This set is includes ISO 8859/x plus additional characters. This set was originally based on an ANSI draft standard. The MS-DOS operating system uses the ANSI character set if ANSI.SYS is installed.

ANSI C *n.* A version of the C programming language standardised by ANSI. See also ANSI, K&R C.

ANSI/SPARC *n.* Acronym for American National Standards Institute Standards Planning and Requirements Committee. The ANSI committee that, in the 1970s, proposed a generalised, three-schema architecture that is used as the foundation for some database management systems.

ANSI.SYS *n.* An installable device driver for MS-DOS computers that uses ANSI commands (escape sequences) to enhance the user's control of the console. See also ANSI, driver, escape sequence, install.

ANSI X3.30-1997 *n.* A standard entitled "Representation for Calendar Date and Ordinal Date for Information Interchange" from the American National Standards Institute (ANSI) that covers date formats. Many organisations, including the U.S. federal government, have standardised date formats using this standard to facilitate work on the Year 2000 problem.

Answer mode *n.* A setting that allows a modem to answer an incoming call automatically. It is used in all fax machines. Also called: auto answer.

Answer-only modem *n.* A modem that can receive but not originate calls.

Answer/originate modem *n.* A modem that can both send and receive calls—the most common type of modem in use.

Antialiasing *n.* A software technique for smoothing the jagged appearance of curved or diagonal lines caused by poor resolution on a display screen. Methods of anti-aliasing include surrounding pixels with intermediate shades and manipulating the size and horizontal alignment of pixels. See the illustration. See also dithering.

Antiglare or anti-glare *adj.* Pertaining to any measure taken to reduce reflections of external light on a monitor screen. The screen may be coated with a chemical (which may reduce its brightness), covered with a polarising filter, or simply rotated so that external light is not reflected into the user's eye.

Anti-replay *n.* An IP packet–level security feature that prevents packets that have been intercepted and changed from being inserted into the data stream. Anti-replay creates a security association between a source and destination computer, with each agreeing on a numbering sequence for transmitted packets. The anti-replay mechanism detects packets tagged with numbers that fall outside the accepted sequence, discards them, sends an error message, and logs the event. The anti-replay protocol is included as part of the IPSec standard. See also IPSec.

Antistatic device *n.* A device designed to minimise shocks caused by the buildup of static electricity, which can disrupt computer equipment or cause data loss. An antistatic device may take the form of a floor mat, a wristband with a wire attached to the workstation, a spray, a lotion, or other special-purpose device. See also static², static electricity.

Antivirus programme *n.* A computer programme that scans a computer's memory and mass storage to identify, isolate, and eliminate viruses, and that examines incoming files for viruses as the computer receives them.

Anti-worm *n.* See automatic patching,, do-gooder virus.

Anycasting *n.* Communication between a single sender and the nearest receiver in a group. In IPv6, anycasting enables one host to initiate the updating of routing tables for a group of hosts. See also IPv6.

Any key *n.* Any random key on a computer keyboard. Some programmes prompt the user to "press any key" to continue. It does not matter which key the user presses. There is no key on the keyboard called Any.

Any-to-any connectivity *n.* The property of an integrated computer network environment where it is possible to share data across multiple protocols, host types, and network topologies.

AOL *n.* See America Online.

AOL Instant Messenger *n.* See AIM.

AOL NetFind *n.* Resident Web-finding tool of America Online (AOL) information service. Searches by keyword and concept. Using Intelligent Concept Extraction (ICE) and Excite technology, this tool finds relationships between words and ideas; for example, between "elderly people" and "senior citizen." See also Excite, Intelligent Concept Extraction.

Apache *n.* A free open-source HTTP (Web) server introduced in 1995 by the Apache Group as an extension to, and improvement of, the National Center for Supercomputing Applications' earlier HTTPd (version 1.3). Apache is popular on UNIX-based systems, including Linux, and also runs on Windows NT and other operating systems, such as BeOS. Because the server was based on existing code with a series of patches, it became known as "A Patchy server," which led to the official name Apache. See also HTTPd.

Apache Group *n.* A non-profit organisation of volunteers from around the world that operates and contributes to the Apache HTTP Server Project.

Apache HTTP Server Project *n.* A collaborative effort by the members of the Apache Group to design, develop, and maintain the Apache HTTP (Web) server. See also Apache, Apache Group.

Apache project *n.* See Apache HTTP Server Project.

APC *n.* See asynchronous procedure call.

Aperture grill *n.* A type of CRT (cathode ray tube) used in computer monitors that uses thin, closely-spaced vertical wires to isolate the individual pixels. The first aperture grill CRT was the Sony Trinitron, but several other manufacturers also produce aperture grill CRTs. See also CRT.

APEX *n.* Acronym for Assembly Process Exhibition and Conference. Exhibition and conference for members of the electronics manufacturing industry. APEX features product exhibits, speeches, technical conferences, and forums on issues that affect the industry.

API *n.* See application programming interface.

APL *n.* A Programming Language. A high-level language introduced in 1968 for scientific and mathematical applications. APL is a subprogram-based interpreted language that uses a large set of special characters and terse syntax and is available for use on PC-compatible machines. See also interpreted language.

APM *n.* See Advanced Power Management.

APNIC *n.* Acronym for Asian-Pacific Network Information Center, a nonprofit, voluntary membership organisation covering the Asia/Pacific Rim region. APNIC, like its European counterpart RIPE and its American counterpart ARIN, devotes itself to matters related to the Internet, among them such tasks as registering new members, allocating IP addresses, and maintaining database information. See also ARIN, RIPE.

app *n.* See application.

APPC *n.* Acronym for Advanced Programme-to-Programme Communication. A specification developed as part of IBM's SNA (Systems Network Architecture) model and designed to enable applications programmes running on different computers to communicate and exchange data directly. APPC extends SNA to include minicomputers and PCs.

Append *vb.* To place or insert as an attachment by adding data to the end of a file or database or extending a character string. See also file, string.

Apple II *n.* The second computer introduced by the Apple Computer Corporation, in April 1977. The Apple II featured 4 K dynamic RAM, expandable to 48 K (with 16 K chips), and used the 6502 microprocessor. The Apple II was the first computer to offer a TV video adapter as an optional alternative to a colour computer monitor. It also featured sound and eight expansion slots.

Apple Desktop Bus *n.* A serial communications pathway built into Apple Macintosh and Apple IIGS computers. Typically a flexible cord, it enables low-speed input devices, such as a keyboard or mouse, to communicate with the computer. The bus functions like a simple local area network that can connect up to 16 devices, such as light pens, trackballs, and graphics tablets, to the computer. Although there are only two external ports, more than two devices can be linked in a series called a daisy chain. Acronym: ADB. See also bus, daisy chain[2], device driver, input/output port, serial communication.

AppleDraw *n.* A shareware drawing application for Macintosh computers.

Apple Events *n.* A feature added to Mac OS System 7 that enables one application to send a command, such as save or open, to another application. See also Mac OS.

Apple Extended Keyboard *n.* A 105-key keyboard that works with the Macintosh SE, Macintosh II, and Apple IIGS computers. This keyboard marks Apple's first inclusion of function (F) keys, whose absence was long cited as a shortcoming of the Macintosh compared with IBM PCs and compatibles. This feature, along with other layout changes and the addition of new keys and lights, makes the Apple Extended Keyboard quite similar in form to the IBM enhanced keyboard. See the illustration. See also enhanced keyboard.

Apple Filing Protocol *n.* See AFP.

Apple key *n.* A key on Apple keyboards labeled with an outline of the Apple logo. On the Apple Extended Keyboard, this key is the same as the Command key, which functions similarly to the Control key on IBM and compatible keyboards. It is generally used in conjunction with a character key as a shortcut to making menu selections or starting a macro.

Apple Macintosh *n.* See Macintosh.

Apple Newton *n.* See Newton.

AppleScript *n.* A script language developed by Apple Computer, Inc., for Macintosh computers running under the Mac OS to execute commands and automate functions. See also script.

AppleShare *n.* A file server software developed by Apple Computer, Inc., that works with the Mac OS and allows one Macintosh computer to share files with another on the same network. See also file server, Mac OS.

Applet *n.* A programme that can be downloaded over the Internet and executed on the recipient's machine. Applets are often written in the Java programming language and run within browser software, and they are typically used to customise or add interactive elements to a Web page.

AppleTalk *n.* An inexpensive local area network developed by Apple Computer, Inc., for Macintosh computers that can be used by Apple and non-Apple computers to communicate and share resources such as printers and file servers. Non-Apple computers must be equipped with AppleTalk hardware and suitable software. The network uses a layered set of protocols similar to the ISO/OSI reference model and transfers information in the form of packets called frames. AppleTalk supports connections to other AppleTalk networks through devices known as bridges, and it supports connections to dissimilar networks through devices called gateways. See also bridge, frame (definition 2), gateway.

AppleTalk Phase 2 *n.* The extended AppleTalk Internet model designed by Apple Computer, Inc., that supports multiple zones within a network and extended addressing capacity.

AppleWorks *n.* A suite of productivity applications, formerly known as ClarisWorks, distributed by Apple Computer, Inc., and shipped on the iMac computer. AppleWorks/ClarisWorks is an integrated product that includes support for word processing, spreadsheets, databases, drawing, painting, charting, and the Internet.

Appliance *n.* 1. See server appliance. 2. See information appliance. 3. A device with a single or limited purpose with functionality. This functionality is similar to a simple consumer appliance.

Appliance server *n.* 1. An inexpensive computing device used for specific tasks including Internet connectivity or file-and-print services. The server is usually easy to use but does not possess the capabilities or software of a typical server for general office use. 2. See server appliance.

Application *n.* A programme designed to assist in the performance of a specific task, such as word processing, accounting, or inventory management.

Application binary interface *n.* A set of instructions that specifies how an executable file interacts with the hardware and how information is stored. Acronym: ABI.

Application-centric *adj.* Of, pertaining to, or characteristic of an operating system in which a user invokes an application to open or create documents (such as word processing files or spreadsheets). Command-line interfaces and some graphical user interfaces such as the Windows 3.x Programme Manager are application-centric.

Application developer *n.* An individual who designs and analyses the appearance and operation of an application programme.

Application development environment *n.* An integrated suite of programmes for use by software developers. Typical components of application development environments include a compiler, file browsing system, debugger, and text editor for use in creating programmes.

Application development language *n.* A computer language designed for creating applications. The term is usually restricted to refer to languages with specific high-level constructs geared toward record design, form layout, database retrieval and update, and similar tasks. See also 4GL, application, application generator.

Application development system *n.* A programming environment designed for the development of an application, typically including a text editor, compiler, and linker, and often including a library of common software routines for use in the developed programme.

Application entity *n.* See AE.

Application file *n.* See programme file.

Application Foundation Classes *n.* A set of Java class libraries developed by Microsoft that provides developers with user-interface controls and graphics tools for creating and manipulating elements such as text and fonts. The Application Foundation Classes extend the capabilities of Java's Abstract Windowing Toolkit (AWT) and are used to facilitate and expedite the creation of Java applets and applications through the use of prebuilt, customizable development components. Acronym: AFC. See also Internet Foundation Classes, Java, Java Foundation Classes, Microsoft Foundation Classes.

Application gateway *n.* Software running on a machine that is intended to maintain security on a secluded network yet allow certain traffic to go between the private network and the outside world. See also firewall.

Application generator *n.* Software for generating source or machine code for running an application based on a description of the desired functionality. Limited in scope, application generators are included with some database programmes and use built-in instruction sets to generate programme code. See also application.

Application heap *n.* A block of RAM used by an application to store its code, resources, records, document data, and other information. See also heap (definition 1), RAM.

Application layer *n.* The highest layer of standards in the Open Systems Interconnection (OSI) reference model. The application layer contains signals that perform useful work for the user, such as file transfer or remote access to a computer, as opposed to lower levels, which control the exchange of data between transmitter and receiver. See the illustration. See also ISO/OSI reference model.

Application notification *n.* An application notification starts an application at a specified time or when a system event occurs. When an application starts as the result of a notification, the system specifies a command-line parameter that identifies the event that has occurred. See also Class A IP address, Class B IP address, Class C IP address.

Application processor *n.* A processor dedicated to a single application.

Application programme *n.* See application.

Application programme interface *n.* See application programming interface.

Application programming interface *n.* A set of routines used by an application programme to direct the performance of procedures by the computer's operating system. Acronym: API. Also called: application programme interface.

Application server *n.* 1. A server programme on a computer in a distributed network that handles the business logic between users and backend business applications or databases.

Application servers also can provide transaction management, failover, and load balancing. An application server is often viewed as part of a three-tier application consisting of a front-end GUI server such as an HTTP server (first tier), an application server (middle tier), and a backend database and transaction server (third tier). Also called: appserver. 2. Any machine on which an application-server programme is running. Also called: appserver.

Application service provider *n.* A third-party company or organisation that hosts applications or services for individuals or business customers. The customer connects to a data center maintained by the application service provider (ASP) through Internet or private lines to access applications that would otherwise need to be housed on the customer's local servers or individual PCs. This arrangement allows the customer to free up disk space that would otherwise be taken by applications, as well as to access the most recent software updates. ASPs deliver solutions ranging from high-end applications to services for small and medium-sized businesses. Acronym: ASP.

Application shortcut key *n.* A key or combination of keys that when pressed will quickly perform an action within an application that would normally require several user actions, such as menu selections. Also called: keyboard shortcut.

Aqua *n.* The graphical user interface (GUI) of Macintosh OS X. Aqua was designed to maintain familiarity and a comfort level for users of the earlier Macintosh system while allowing access to newer Macintosh OS X capabilities. The Aqua GUI features updated versions of Macintosh staples such as the Finder alongside new features like the Dock, a new type of organisational tool. See also Dock,, Macintosh OS X.

Arbitration *n.* A set of rules for resolving competing demands for a machine resource by multiple users or processes. See also contention.

.arc *n.* The file extension that identifies compressed archive files encoded using the Advanced RISC Computing Specification (ARC) format. See also compressed file.

Arcade game *n.* 1. A coin-operated computer game for one or more players that features high-quality screen graphics, sound, and rapid action. 2. Any computer game designed to mimic the style of a coin-operated arcade game, such as games marketed for the home computer. See also computer game.

Archie *n.* An Internet utility for finding files in public archives obtainable by anonymous FTP. The master Archie server at McGill University in Montreal downloads FTP indexes from participating FTP servers, merges them into a master list, and sends updated copies of the master list to other Archie servers each day. Archie is a shortened form of archive. See also anonymous FTP, FTP[1] (definition 1).

Archie client *n.* See Archie.

Archie server *n.* On the Internet, a server that contains Archie indexes to the names and addresses of files in public FTP archives. See also Archie, FTP[1] (definition 1), server (definition 2).

Architecture *n.* 1. The physical construction or design of a computer system and its components. See also cache, CISC, closed architecture, network architecture, open architecture, pipelining, RISC. 2. The data-handling capacity of a microprocessor. 3. The design of application software incorporating protocols and the means for expansion and interfacing with other programmes.

Archive[1] *n.* 1. A tape or disk containing files copied from another storage device and used as backup storage. 2. A compressed file. 3. A file directory on the Internet that is available by File Transfer Protocol (FTP) or an Internet directory established for dissemination of stored files.

Archive[2] *vb.* 1. To copy files onto a tape or disk for long-term storage. 2. To compress a file.

Archive bit *n.* A bit that is associated with a file and is used to indicate whether the file has been backed up. See also back up, bit.

Archive file *n.* A file that contains a set of files, such as a programme with its documentation and example input files, or collected postings from a newsgroup. On UNIX systems, archive files can be created using the tar programme; they can then be compressed using compress or gzip. PKZIP under MS-DOS and Windows and StuffIt under Mac OS create archive files that are already compressed. See also compress1, gzip, PKZIP, StuffIt, tar1.

Archive site *n.* A site on the Internet that stores files. The files are usually accessed through one of the following ways: downloaded through anonymous FTP, retrieved through Gopher, or viewed on the World Wide Web. See also anonymous FTP, Gopher.

ARCnet *n.* Short for Attached Resource Computer Network. A form of token bus network architecture for PC-based LANs developed by Datapoint Corporation. ARCnet relies on a bus or star topology and can support up to 255 nodes. Different versions run at speeds of 1.5 Mbps, 20 Mbps (ARCnet Plus), and 100 Mbps.

ARCnet Plus *n.* See ARCnet.

Area chart *n.* A graphical presentation, such as of quarterly sales figures, that uses shading or colouring to emphasize the difference between the line representing one set of data points and the line representing a separate but related set of data points. See the illustration.

Area search *n.* In information management, the examination of a group of documents for the purpose of identifying those that are relevant to a particular subject or category.

Arg *n.* See argument.

Argument *n.* An independent variable, used with an operator or passed to a subprogram that uses the argument to carry out specific operations. See also algorithm, operator (definition 1), parameter, subprogram.

ARIN *n.* Acronym for American Registry for Internet Numbers. A nonprofit organisation formed to register and administer Internet Protocol (IP) addresses in North and South America. The American Registry for Internet Numbers separates the allocation of IP addresses from the administration of top-level

Internet domains, such as .com and .edu. Both of these tasks were previously managed by Network Solutions, Inc., as part of the InterNIC consortium. Its international counterparts are RIPE, in Europe, and APNIC, in Asia and the Pacific Rim. See also APNIC, InterNIC, IP address, RIPE.

Arithmetic[1] *adj.* Pertaining to the mathematical operations of addition, subtraction, multiplication, and division.

Arithmetic[2] *n.* The branch of mathematics dealing with the addition, subtraction, multiplication, and division of real numbers.

Arithmetic expression *n.* A series of elements, including data labels and constants as well as numbers, that are joined by arithmetic operators, such as + and –, and can be calculated to produce a value.

Arithmetic logic unit *n.* A component of a microprocessor chip used for arithmetic, comparative, and logical functions. Acronym: ALU. See also gate (definition 1).

Arithmetic operation *n.* Any of the standard calculations performed in arithmetic—addition, subtraction, multiplication, or division. The term is also used in reference to negative numbers and absolute values.

Arithmetic operator *n.* An operator that performs an arithmetic operation: +, –,*, or /. An arithmetic operator usually takes one or two arguments. See also argument, binary, logical operator, operator (definition 1), unary.

.arj *n.* The MS-DOS file extension used with archive files created with the ARJ compression programme.

ARM *n.* Short for Advanced RISC Machines. A name for any of a group of small, high-performance 32-bit RISC-based microprocessors licensed to various semiconductor manufacturers by designer ARM Limited. ARM chips are notable for their low cost and efficient use of power. They are used in a wide variety of products, including mobile phones, handheld computers, automotive and embedded solutions, and consumer electronics, including digital cameras and game systems. See also StrongARM.

ARP *n.* Acronym for Address Resolution Protocol. A TCP/IP protocol for determining the hardware address (or physical address) of a node on a local area network connected to the Internet, when only the IP address (or logical address) is known. An ARP request is sent to the network, and the node that has the IP address responds with its hardware address. Although ARP technically refers only to finding the hardware address, and RARP (for Reverse ARP) refers to the reverse procedure, ARP is commonly used for both senses. See also IP address, TCP/IP.

ARPANET *n.* A large wide area network created in the 1960s by the U.S. Department of Defense Advanced Research Projects Agency (ARPA, renamed DARPA in the 1970s) for the free exchange of information between universities and research organisations, although the military also used this network for communications. In the 1980s MILNET, a separate network, was spun off from ARPANET for use by the military. ARPANET was the network from which the Internet evolved. See also ALOHA-net, Internet, MILNET.

ARP request *n.* Short for Address Resolution Protocol. An ARP packet containing the Internet address of a host computer. The receiving computer responds with or passes along the corresponding Ethernet address. See also ARP, Ethernet, IP address, packet.

Array *n.* In programming, a list of data values, all of the same type, any element of which can be referenced by an expression consisting of the array name followed by an indexing expression. Arrays are part of the fundamentals of data structures, which, in turn, are a major fundamental of computer programming. See also array element, index[1], record[1], vector.

Array element *n.* A data value in an array.

Array processor *n.* A group of interconnected, identical processors operating synchronously, often under the control of a central processor.

Arrow key *n.* Any of four keys labeled with arrows pointing up, down, left, and right, used to move the cursor vertically or horizontally on the display screen or, in some programmes, to extend the highlight. See the illustration.

ART *n.* Acronym for Adaptive Resonance Theory. First introduced as a theory of human information processing by Stephen Grossberg, ART has evolved into several classes of self-organising neural networks that use two layers of ideal cases to predict outcome. It is a form of cluster analysis where data is classified or matched to the previously stored pattern it most closely resembles. This data is said to resonate with the ideal case layer, which is then updated to reflect the new information. The constant recategorization of input results in a powerful autonomous neural network.

Article *n.* A message that appears in an Internet newsgroup. Also called: post. See also newsgroup.

Articulation *n.* A series of adjustments applied by a synthesizer to the pitch, volume, and other parameters of an instrument sound to make it more realistic.

Artifact *n.* A visible imperfection or distortion in a digital image. Artifacts may be caused by hardware/software limitations or may be a byproduct of compression.

Artificial intelligence *n.* The branch of computer science concerned with enabling computers to simulate such aspects of human intelligence as speech recognition, deduction, inference, creative response, the ability to learn from experience, and the ability to make inferences given incomplete information. Two common areas of artificial-intelligence research are expert systems and natural-language processing. Acronym: AI. See also expert system, natural-language processing.

Artificial life *n.* The study of computer systems that simulate some aspects of the behaviour of living organisms. Artificial life includes systems in which programmes intended to perform some particular task compete for survival and reproduction based on their performance; the offspring can combine pieces of code and undergo random variations, and the programmes so modified compete in turn, until an optimal solution is found.

Artificial neural network *n.* A form of computer artificial intelligence that uses software based on concepts understood from biological neural networks to adaptively perform a task. Acronym: ANN.

AS *n.* See autonomous system.

.asc *n.* A file name extension most commonly indicating that the file contains ASCII text that can be processed by all types of word processing software, including MS-DOS Edit, Windows Notepad, Windows 9x or Windows NT WordPad, and Microsoft Word. Some systems may use this extension to indicate that a file contains image information. See also ASCII.

Ascender *n.* The portion of a lowercase letter that extends above the main body (x-height) of the letter. See the illustration. See also base line, x-height.

Ascending order *n.* The arrangement of a sequence of items from lowest to highest, such as from 1 to 10 or from A to Z. The rules for determining ascending order in a particular application can be very complicated: capital letters before lowercase letters, extended ASCII characters in ASCII order, and so on.

Ascending sort *n.* A sort that results in the arrangement of items in ascending order. See also alphanumeric sort, ascending order.

Ascii *n.* In an FTP client programme, the command that instructs the FTP server to send or receive files as ASCII text. See also ASCII, FTP client.

ASCII *n.* Acronym for American Standard Code for Information Interchange. A coding scheme using 7 or 8 bits that assigns numeric values to up to 256 characters, including letters, numerals, punctuation marks, control characters, and other symbols. ASCII was developed in 1968 to standardise data transmission among disparate hardware and software systems and is built into most minicomputers and all PCs. ASCII is divided into two sets: 128 characters (standard ASCII) and an additional 128 (extended ASCII). See also ASCII file, character, character code, control character, extended ASCII, standard ASCII.

ASCII character set *n.* A standard 7-bit code for representing ASCII characters using binary values; code values range from 0 to 127. Most PC-based systems use an 8-bit extended ASCII code, with an extra 128 characters used to represent special symbols, foreign-language characters, and graphic symbols. See also ASCII, character, EBCDIC, extended ASCII, standard ASCII.

ASCII EOL value *n.* The sequence of bytes that indicates the end of a line of text. For Windows and MS-DOS systems, this is the hexadecimal sequence 0D 0A or the decimal sequence 13 10. Data files imported from other kinds of computers might not display correctly if the software used is not capable of recognising these differences and adjusting for them. See also ASCII, EOL.

ASCII file *n.* A document file in ASCII format, containing characters, spaces, punctuation, carriage returns, and sometimes tabs and an end-of-file marker, but no formatting information. Also called: ASCII file, text file, text-only file. See also ASCII, text file.

ASCII transfer *n.* The preferred mode of electronic exchange for text files. In ASCII mode, character conversions to and from the network-standard character set are performed. See also ASCII.

ASCIIZ string *n.* In programming, an ASCII string terminated by the NULL character (a byte containing the character whose ASCII value is 0). Also called: null-terminated string.

ASF *n.* See Advanced Streaming Format.

Asian-Pacific Network Information Center *n.* See APNIC.

ASIC *n.* Acronym for application-specific integrated circuit. See also gate array.

ASK *n.* See amplitude shift keying.

ASN *n.* Acronym for a utonomous—system number. See autonomous system.

ASN.1 *n.* See Abstract Syntax Notation One.

.asp *n.* A file extension that identifies a Web page as an Active Server Page.

ASP *n.* 1. See Active Server Pages. 2. See application service provider.

Aspect ratio *n.* In computer displays and graphics, the ratio of the width of an image or image area to its height. An aspect ratio of 2:1, for example, indicates that the image is twice as wide as it is high. The aspect ratio is an important factor in maintaining correct proportions when an image is printed, rescaled, or incorporated into another document.

ASPI *n.* See Advanced SCSI Programming Interface.

ASP.NET *n.* A set of technologies in the Microsoft .NET Framework for building Web applications and XML Web services. ASP.NET pages execute on the server and generate markup (such as HTML, WML, or XML) that is sent to a desktop or mobile browser. ASP.NET pages use a compiled, event-driven programming model that improves performance and enables the separation of application logic and user interface. ASP.NET pages and XML Web services files created using ASP.NET contain server-side (rather than client-side) logic written in Visual Basic .NET, C# .NET, or any .NET-compatible language. Web applications and XML Web services take advantage of the features of the common language runtime, such as type safety, inheritance, language interoperability, versioning, and integrated security.

ASP.NET server control *n.* A server-side component that encapsulates user-interface and related functionality. An ASP.NET server control derives directly or indirectly from the System.Web.UI.Control class. The superset of ASP.NET server controls includes Web server controls, HTML server controls, and mobile controls. The page syntax for an ASP.NET server control includes a runat="server" attribute on the control's tag. See also Web server control, HTML server control, validation server controls.

ASP.NET Web application *n.* An application that processes HTTP requests (Web requests) and executes on top of the ASP.NET runtime. An ASP.NET application can include ASP.NET pages, XML Web services, HTTP handlers, and HTTP modules.

ASR *n.* 1. See automatic system reconfiguration. 2. Acronym for Automatic Speech Recognition. Technology which allows machines to recognise and respond to human voice commands. ASR systems may be used to control a computer or to operate word processing and similar applications. Many ASR products are designed for use by users with disabilities who might have difficulty using a keyboard or mouse.

Assemble *vb.* In programming, to convert an assembly language programme to equivalent machine language instructions called object code. See also assembler, assembly language, linker, object code.

Assembler *n.* A programme that converts assembly language programmes, which are understandable by humans, into executable machine language. See also assemble, assembly language, assembly listing, compiler (definition 2), machine code.

Assembly *n.* A collection of one or more files that are versioned and deployed as a unit. An assembly is the primary building block of a .NET Framework application. All managed types and resources are contained within an assembly and are marked either as accessible only within the assembly or as accessible from code in other assemblies. Assemblies also play a key role in security. The code access security system uses information about the assembly to determine the set of permissions that code in the assembly is granted.

Assembly cache *n.* A machine-wide code cache used for side-by-side storage of assemblies. There are two parts to the cache: the global assembly cache contains assemblies that are explicitly installed to be shared among many applications on the computer; the download cache stores code downloaded from Internet or intranet sites, isolated to the application that triggered the download so that code downloaded on behalf of one application/page does not impact other applications. See also global assembly cache.

Assembly language *n.* A low-level programming language using abbreviations or mnemonic codes in which each statement corresponds to a single machine instruction. An assembly language is translated to machine language by the assembler and is specific to a given processor. Advantages of using an assembly language include increased execution speed and direct programmer interaction with system hardware. See also assembler, compiler, high-level language, low-level language, machine code.

Assembly listing *n.* A file created by an assembler that includes the statements of an assembly language programme, the machine language generated by the assembler, and a list of the symbols used in the programme. See also assembler, assembly language.

Assertion *n.* A Boolean statement used in a programme to test a condition that, if the programme is operating correctly, should always evaluate as true; otherwise the programme will typically terminate with an appropriate error message. Assertions are used for debugging programmes and for documenting how a programme should operate.

Assignment operator *n.* An operator used to assign a value to a variable or data structure. See also assignment statement, operator (definition 1).

Assignment statement *n.* A programming language statement used to assign a value to a variable. It usually consists of three elements: an expression to be assigned, an assignment operator (typically a symbol such as = or :=), and a destination variable. On execution of the assignment statement, the expression is evaluated and the resulting value is stored in the specified destination. See also assignment operator, expression, variable.

Associate *vb.* To inform the operating system that a particular file name extension is linked to a specific application. When a file is opened that has an extension associated with a given application, the operating system automatically starts the application and loads the file.

Association Control Service Element *n.* An Open Systems Interconnection (OSI) method to establish a call between two applications by checking the identities and contexts of the application entities and performing an authentication security check. Acronym: ACSE. See also ISO/OSI reference model.

Association for Computing Machinery *n.* A membership society founded in 1947 and devoted to the advancement of knowledge and technical proficiency of information processing professionals. Acronym: ACM.

Association of C and C++ Users *n.* An organisation of people interested in the programming language C and its variants. Members of the association include professional programmers, manufacturers and vendors of compilers, and nonprofessional programming enthusiasts. Acronym: ACCU.

Associative storage *n.* A memory-based storage method in which data items are accessed not on the basis of a fixed address or location but by analysis of their content. Also called: content-addressed storage.

Associativity *n.* See operator associativity.

Asymmetrical transmission *n.* A form of transmission used by high-speed modems, typically those that operate at rates of 9600 bps or more, that allows simultaneous incoming and outgoing transmission by dividing a telephone line bandwidth into two channels: one in the range of 300 to 450 bps and one at a speed of 9600 bps or more.

Asymmetric modem *n.* A modem that transmits data to the telephone network and receives data from the network at different speeds. Most commonly, an asymmetric modem will have a maximum download speed substantially higher than its upload speed. See also modem.

Asynchronous *adj.* Pertaining to, being, or characteristic of something that is not dependent on timing. For example, asynchronous communications can start and stop at any time instead of having to match the timing governed by a clock.

Asynchronous chip *n.* A microprocessor chip that does not need to operate in sync with a system clock. Asynchronous chip operations do not need to be timed to clock speed and draw power only when operations are in progress. This allows asynchronous chips the potential for greater computational speed and lower power consumption than traditional chips.

Asynchronous communications *n.* Computer-to-computer communications in which the sending and receiving computers do not rely on timing as a means of determining where transmissions begin and end.

Asynchronous device *n.* A device whose internal operations are not synchronised with the timing of any other part of the system.

Asynchronous operation *n.* An operation that proceeds independently of any timing mechanism, such as a clock. For example, two modems communicating asynchronously rely upon each sending the other start and stop signals in order to pace the exchange of information.

Asynchronous procedure call *n.* A function call that executes separately from an executing programme when a set of enabling conditions exist. After the conditions have been met, the operating system's kernel issues a software interrupt and directs the executing programme to execute the call. Acronym: APC. See also function call.

Asynchronous Protocol Specification *n.* The X.445 standard. See also X series.

Asynchronous static RAM *n.* A type of static RAM (SRAM) that is not synchronised with the system clock. Like static RAM in general, asynchronous static RAM, or async SRAM, is used in a computer's L2 cache—the special portion of memory used for storing frequently accessed information. Because this type of static RAM is not synchronised with the clock, the CPU must wait for data requested from the L2 cache. Asynchronous static RAM is faster than main memory but not as fast as synchronous burst static RAM or pipeline burst static RAM. Also called: async SRAM. See also L2 cache, static RAM.

Asynchronous Transfer Mode *n.* See ATM (definition 1).

Asynchronous transmission *n.* In modem communication, a form of data transmission in which data is sent intermittently, one character at a time, rather than in a steady stream with characters separated by fixed time intervals. Asynchronous transmission relies on the use of a start bit and stop bit(s), in addition to the bits representing the character (and an optional parity bit), to distinguish separate characters. See the illustration.

Async SRAM *n.* See asynchronous static RAM.

AT&T System V *n.* See System V.

ATA *n.* Acronym for Advanced Technology Attachment. ANSI group X3T10's official name for the disk drive interface standard for integrating drive controllers directly on disk drives. The original ATA standard is commonly known as Integrated Drive Electronics (IDE). Later ATA versions include ATA-2, ATA-3, and Ultra-ATA. See the table. Also called: AT attachment. See also direct memory access, EIDE, IDE, logical block addressing, PIO, SMART system.

Table A.2 ATA Specifications.

ATA Specification	Also Called	Features
ATA	IDE	Supports PIO (Programmed Input/Output), which transfers data through the CPU. Data transfer rates are 3.3 mbps, 5.2 mbps, and 8.3 mbps.
ATA-2	Fast ATA, Enhanced IDE (EIDE)	Supports faster PIO rates and DMA (direct memory access), which bypasses the CPU. Data transfer rates are between 4 mbps and 16.6 mbps. It also supports LBA (logical block addressing), which allows support for drives larger than 528 MB.
ATA-3		Revision of ATA-2 with SMART (self-monitoring analysis and reporting technology) for greater reliability.
Ultra-ATA	ATA-33, DMA-33, Ultra-DMA, UDMA	Supports DMA burst mode (roughly, all-at-once) data transfers of 33.3 mbps.

ATA hard disk drive card *n.* Expansion card used to control and interface with an ATA hard disk drive. These cards are usually ISA cards. See also ATA, ISA.

ATA/IDE hard disk drive *n.* ATA (Advanced Technology Attachment) and IDE (Integrated Drive Electronics—or numerous other interpretations) are one and the same thing: a disk drive implementation designed to integrate the controller onto the drive itself, thereby reducing interface costs and making firmware implementations easier.

ATAPI *n.* The interface used by the IBM PC AT system for accessing CD-ROM devices.

AT Attachment *n.* See ATA.

AT bus *n.* The electric pathway used by IBM AT and compatible computers to connect the motherboard and peripheral devices. The AT bus supports 16 bits of data, whereas the original PC bus supports only 8 bits. Also called: expansion bus. See also EISA, ISA, Micro Channel Architecture.

aTdHvAaNnKcSe *n.* See TIA.

ATDP *n.* Acronym for Attention Dial Pulse, a command that initiates pulse (as opposed to touch-tone) dialing in Hayes and Hayes-compatible modems.

ATDT *n.* Acronym for Attention Dial Tone, a command that initiates touch-tone (as opposed to pulse) dialing in Hayes and Hayes-compatible modems.

Athlon *n.* Family of x86-compatible processors introduced by Advanced Micro Devices, Inc. (AMD) in 1999. Athlon, which was code-named AMD-K7, is a successor to the AMD-K6 family. Comparable to upper-end Intel Pentium III processors in performance, Athlon is distinguished by over 22 million transistors; a fully pipelined, superscalar floating-point engine, which enhances performance of graphics and multimedia programmes, Internet streaming applications, and games; a 200-MHz system bus; and a 128-KB L1 cache. Although the L2 cache is 512 KB in size, the Athlon can support L2 cache sizes up to 8 MB. The first Athlon releases featured clock speeds of 500 to 650 MHz; 800-MHz and faster versions are now available. Athlon, which runs 32-bit programmes, is compatible with most PC operating systems, including Microsoft Windows, Linux, OS/2 Warp, and NetWare. See also AMD-K6.

ATM *n.* 1. Acronym for Asynchronous Transfer Mode. A network technology capable of transmitting data, voice, audio, video, and frame relay traffic in real time. Data, including frame relay data, is broken into packets containing 53 bytes each, which are switched between any two nodes in the system at rates ranging from 1.5 Mbps to 622 Mbps (over fiber optic cable). The basic unit of ATM transmission is known as a cell, a packet consisting of 5 bytes routing information and a 48-byte payload (data). These cells are transmitted to their destination, where they are reassembled into the original traffic. During transmission, cells from different users may be intermixed asynchronously to maximise utilization of network resources. ATM is defined in the broadband ISDN protocol at the levels corresponding to levels 1 and 2 of the ISO/OSI reference model. It is currently used in LANs (local area networks) involving workstations and personal computers, but it is expected to be adopted by the telephone companies, which will be able to charge customers for the data they transmit rather than for their connect time. See also broadband, ISDN, ISO/OSI reference model. 2. Acronym for automated teller machine. A special-purpose terminal that bank customers can use to make deposits, obtain cash, and perform other transactions. 3. See Adobe Type Manager.

ATM Adaptation Layer *n.* The ATM layer that mediates between higher-level and lower-level services, converting different types of data (such as audio, video, and data frames) to the 48-byte payloads required by ATM. Acronym: AAL. See also ATM.

ATM Forum *n.* Forum created in 1991 and including more than 750 companies related to communications and computing, as well as government agencies and research groups. The forum aims to promote Asynchronous Transfer Mode for data communication. See also ATM (definition 1).

Atomicity, Consistency, Isolation, Durability *n.* See ACID.

Atomic operation *n.* An operation considered or guaranteed to be indivisible (by analogy with an atom of matter, once thought to be indivisible). Either the operation is uninterruptible or, if it is aborted, a mechanism is provided that ensures the return of the system to its state prior to initiation of the operation.

Atomic transaction *n.* A set of operations that follow an "all or nothing" principle, in which either all of the operations are successfully executed or none of them is executed. Atomic transactions are appropriate for order entry and fulfillment or for money transfers to ensure that information is fully updated. For example, if funds are transferred between accounts on two databases, one account cannot be credited if the other is not debited by the same amount. An atomic transaction would involve both recording the credit in one database and recording the corresponding debit in the other. If any operation in the transaction fails, the transaction is aborted and any information changes are undone. See also Distributed Computing Environment, TP monitor, transaction processing.

Attach *vb.* To include an external document, a file, or an executable programme with an e-mail message.

Attached document *n.* An ASCII text file or a binary file, such as a document created in a word processing system, that is included with an e-mail message as an attachment. See also ASCII, attachment, binary file, BinHex[1], MIME, uuencode.

Attached file *n.* See attachment.

Attached processor *n.* A secondary processor attached to a computer system, such as a keyboard or video subsystem processor.

Attached Resource Computer Network *n.* See ARCnet.

Attachment *n.* A file that accompanies an e-mail message. As transmitted, an attached file is an exact copy of the original file located on the sender's computer. The file can be a document, an executable programme, or a compressed file containing more than one item, among other types of files. The file is not part of the actual e-mail message, and it is generally encoded using uuencoding, MIME, or BinHex. Most e-mail programmes automatically encode an attached document for transmission with a message. The recipient of the message must have an e-mail programme capable of decoding the attached document or use a separate utility to decode it in order to read the document. Some gateways prohibit transmission of files over a certain size. Most e-mail systems permit more than one file to be attached to an e-mail message at a time.

Attachment unit interface *n.* See AUI.

Attenuation *n.* The weakening of a transmitted signal, such as the distortion of a digital signal or the reduction in amplitude of an electrical signal, as it travels farther from its source. Attenuation is usually measured in decibels and is sometimes desirable, as when signal strength is reduced electronically, for example, by a radio volume control, to prevent overloading.

Atto- prefix Metric prefix meaning 10^{-18} (one quintillionth).

Attract mode *n.* In commercial arcade games, when a coin-operated game is not in use, the screen will rotate through "attract mode." The aim is to both tempt prospective players and demonstrate game play or rules. Also, by constantly changing the screen image, attract mode avoids screen burn in. See also arcade game, burn in.

Attribute *n.* 1. In a database record, the name or structure of a field. For example, the files LASTNAME, FIRSTNAME, and PHONE would be attributes of each record in a PHONELIST database. The size of a field or the type of information it contains would also be attributes of a database record. 2. In screen displays, an element of additional information stored with each character in the video buffer of a video adapter running in character mode. Such attributes control the background and foreground colours of the character, underlining, and blinking. 3. In markup languages such as SGML and HTML, a name-value pair within a tagged element that modifies certain features of that element. See also HTML, SGML.

Attribution line *n.* In newsgroups, e-mail, and other Internet-based communications, an identification line added to material quoted from earlier postings. Some mail and messaging software will add an attribution line automatically, which might read something like "News King wrote:" and usually appears immediately before the quoted text.

ATX *n.* A specification for PC motherboard architectures with built-in audio and video capabilities, introduced by Intel in 1995. ATX supports USB and full-length boards in all sockets. See also board, motherboard, specification, USB.

Audio *adj.* Relating to frequencies within the range of perception by the human ear—from about 15 to 20,000 hertz (cycles per second). See also audio response, synthesizer.

Audio board *n.* See sound card.

Audio card *n.* See sound card.

Audiocast *n.* The transmission of an audio signal using IP protocols. See also IP.

Audio compression *n.* A method of reducing the overall loudness of an audio signal. This is accomplished by limiting the amount of apparent distortion when the signal is played back through a speaker or transmitted through a communications link.

Audio output *n.* See audio response.

Audio output port *n.* A circuit consisting of a digital-to-analog converter that transforms signals from the computer to audible tones. It is used in conjunction with an amplifier and a speaker. See also digital-to-analog converter.

Audio response *n.* Any sound produced by a computer; specifically, spoken output produced by a computer in response to some specific type of input. Such output may be generated using a combination of words from a digitized vocabulary or through the synthesis of words from tables of phonemes. See also frequency response, phoneme.

Audiotex *n.* An application allowing users to send and receive information by telephone. Users typically call an audiotex system and are presented with a series of choices or a series of questions through a voice mail system. When users select choices by pressing the buttons on the phone (rotary dial phones cannot be used for audiotex) or by speaking aloud, a database host responds by sending information to the voice mail system, which then converts the data to a spoken message for the user, or it responds by receiving and storing the information entered by the user. Also called: audiotext. See also voice mail.

Audiotext *n.* See audiotex.

Audio Video Interleaved *n.* See AVI.

Audiovisual *adj.* Relating to or being any material that uses a combination of sight and sound to present information.

Audit *n.* In reference to computing, an examination of equipment, programmes, activities, and procedures to determine how efficiently the overall system is performing, especially in terms of ensuring the integrity and security of data.

Auditing *n.* The process an operating system uses to detect and record security-related events, such as an attempt to create, to access, or to delete objects such as files and directories. The records of such events are stored in a file known as a security log, whose contents are available only to those with the proper clearance. See also security log.

Audit policy *n.* A policy that determines the security events to be reported to the network administrator.

Audit trail *n.* In reference to computing, a means of tracing all activities affecting a piece of information, such as a data record, from the time it is entered into a system to the time it is removed. An audit trail makes it possible to document, for example, who made changes to a particular record and when.

AUI *n.* 1. Acronym for attachment unit interface. A 15-pin (DB-15) connector commonly used to connect a network interface card to an Ethernet cable. 2. See aural user interface.

AUI cable *n.* Short for Attachment Unit Interface cable. A transceiver cable used to connect a host adapter within a computer to an Ethernet (10base5 or 10BaseF) network. See also 10Base5, 10Base-F, Ethernet (definition 1), transceiver cable.

AUP *n.* See acceptable use policy.

Aural user interface *n.* Voice-activated interface that allows users to issue spoken commands to electronic devices. The aural user interface is used with features such as voice recognition for computers and voice-activated dialing for wireless phones. Acronym: AUI.

Authentication *n.* In a multiuser or network operating system, the process by which the system validates a user's logon information. A user's name and password are compared against an authorised list, and if the system detects a match, access is granted to the extent specified in the permission list for that user. See also logon, password, permission, user account, user name.

Authentication center *n.* Secure database used to identify and prevent wireless phone fraud. Authentication centers verify whether a wireless phone is registered with a wireless carrier's network.

Authentication Header *n.* See AH.

Authenticode *n.* A security feature of Microsoft Internet Explorer. Authenticode allows vendors of downloadable executable code (plug-ins or ActiveX controls, for example) to attach digital certificates to their products to assure end users that the code is from the original developer and has not been altered. Authenticode lets end users decide for themselves whether to accept or reject software components posted on the Internet before downloading begins. See also ActiveX control, Internet Explorer, security.

Author[1] *vb.* 1. To create a product for implementation via computer technology. 2. To write a computer programme. 3. To assemble multimedia components, such as graphics, text, audio, and animation, in a publication or product, for delivery on a CD-ROM or DVD or online, to be viewed on a computer. 4. To create Web pages. Traditionally, to author meant to write a literary work or journalistic piece; in the cyberworld, to write is "to provide content"; thus, to author in the traditional sense is to be a "content provider."

Author[2] *n.* See Web author.

Authoring language *n.* A computer language or application development system designed primarily for creating programmes, databases, and materials for computer-aided instruction (CAI). A familiar example in relation to microcomputers is PILOT, a language used to create lessons. See also CAI, PILOT.

Authoring software *n.* A type of computer programme used for creating Web pages and other hypertext and multimedia applications. Authoring software provides a way to define relationships between different types of objects, including text, graphics, and sound, and to present them in a desired order. This type of programme is sometimes known as authorware, although the latter name is generally associated with a specific product from Macromedia. Also called: authoring tool.

Authoring system *n.* Application software that enables the operator to create and format a document for a specific kind of computer environment. An authoring system, especially for multimedia work, often consists of several applications within the framework of a single, controlling application. See also authoring language.

Authority *n.* A DNS server responsible for resolving names and IP addresses of sites and resources on the Internet at a particular level of authority: top-level domain, second-level domain, or subdomain.

Authorization *n.* In reference to computing, especially remote computers on a network, the right granted an individual to use the system and the data stored on it. Authorization is typically set up by a system administrator and verified by the computer based on some form of user identification, such as a code number or password. Also called: access privileges, permission. See also network, system administrator.

Authorization code *n.* See password.

Autoanswer *n.* See answer mode.

Autoassociative *adj.* In data reduction or clustering, autoassociative models use the same set of variables as both predictors and targets. In autoassociative neural networks, each pattern presented serves as both the input and output pattern. Autoassociative networks are typically used for tasks involving pattern completion. See also artificial intelligence, cluster analysis, neural networks, operator associativity, pattern recognition.

Autoattendant *adj.* A term used to describe a store-and-forward computer system that replaces the traditional switchboard operator, directing telephone calls to their correct extensions or voice mail. Autoattendant systems may implement voice prompts, touch-tone menus, or voice recognition features to send calls to their proper destinations.

AutoCorrect *n.* A function in Microsoft Word for Windows that automatically corrects errors and makes other substitutions as soon as a user types text. For example, AutoCorrect can be set up to fix misspellings, such as teh for the, or to change "straight" (" ") quotation marks to "smart" (" ") quotation marks. The user can select which AutoCorrect features to enable. See also smart quotes.

Autodial *n.* A feature enabling a modem to open a telephone line and initiate a call by transmitting a stored telephone number as a series of pulses or tones.

AUTOEXEC.BAT *n.* A special-purpose batch file (set of commands) that is automatically carried out by the MS-DOS operating system when the computer is started or restarted. Created by the user or (in later versions of MS-DOS) by the operating system at system installation, the file contains basic startup commands that help configure the system to installed devices and to the user's preferences.

AutoIP *n.* Short for automatic Internet Protocol addressing. A technique used by a device to obtain a valid IP address without a DHCP server or other IP-configuration authority. With AutoIP, a device randomly chooses an IP address from a set of reserved addresses and queries the local network to determine whether another client already is using that address. The device repeats the steps of picking and verifying until an unused address is found. AutoIP, based on an Internet Engineering Task Force (IETF) Internet Draft, is used in

Universal Plug and Play (UPnP) networking. See also UPnP networking.

Autokey *n.* See typematic.

Autoload *vb.* To make some type of resource available without it having to be specifically requested. A programme, for example, might autoload fonts or files as they are needed. Similarly, a CD-ROM drive might autoload audio discs or automatically start a setup programme on a software CD-ROM. See also AutoPlay.

Autoloader *n.* A device that automatically prepares a diskette, CD, or other storage medium for use.

Automagic *adj.* Slang for a process performed in some unexplained (but not inexplicable) way by a computer. An automagic process might either be too complicated to explain (such as a complex spreadsheet calculation), or it might be a complex process made to appear simple to the user (such as clicking on a heading to arrange the items in a list in alphabetical or chronological order).

Automata theory *n.* 1. The study of computing processes and their capabilities and limitations; that is, how systems receive and process input and produce output. See also cellular automata. 2. The study of the relationship between behavioural theories and the operation of automated devices.

Automated home *n.* See smart home.

Automated office *n.* A broad term used to refer to an office where work is carried out with the aid of computers, telecommunications facilities, and other electronic devices.

Automatic error correction *n.* A process that, upon detection of an internal processing or data transmission error, invokes a routine designed to correct the error or retry the operation.

Automatic IP addressing *n.* See AutoIP.

Automatic patching *n.* A process in which vulnerabilities caused by a destructive computer virus infection are tracked down and corrected by a do-gooder virus or other anti-virus programme. Automatic patching may be initiated by the user, or may be done by a virus entering a back door left by a malicious virus, without the consent of the user. See do-gooder virus. See also anti-worm.

Automatic Private IP Addressing *n.* A feature of Windows XP TCP/IP that automatically configures a unique IP address from the range 169.254.0.1 through 169.254.255.254 and a subnet mask of 255.255.0.0 when the TCP/IP protocol is configured for dynamic addressing and Dynamic Host Configuration Protocol (DHCP) is not available. Acronym: APIPA. See also DHCP server, Dynamic Host Configuration Protocol (DHCP), IP address, Transmission Control Protocol/Internet Protocol (TCP/IP).

Automatic Sequence Controlled Calculator *n.* See Mark I.

Automatic speech recognition *n.* See ASR (definition 2).

Automatic system reconfiguration *n.* Automation of configuration by the system to accommodate some change in either the software or the hardware. Acronym: ASR.

Automation *n.* 1. The implementation of a mechanical or electronic system or tool to automatically complete a task, thereby reducing or eliminating human intervention. 2. Formerly known as OLE Automation, a Microsoft-designed technology that enables an application to expose objects and their properties for use by other applications. This allows a word processor to display and manipulate a spreadsheet programme, for instance. The application that exposes an object for use is called the server; the application that manipulates the object is called the client. Automation can be either local or remote (on a computer elsewhere on a network). It is intended primarily for use by high-level languages such as Microsoft Visual Basic and Microsoft Visual C++. See also ActiveX control, OLE.

Automonitor *n.* A process or system feature capable of assessing the status of its own internal environment.

Autonomous agent *n.* A software or robotic entity that is capable of independent action in open, unpredictable environments. Often referred to as an intelligent agent, or simply agent, autonomous agents complete some kind of automatic process that can communicate with other agents or perform different kinds of directed tasks. Autonomous agents are currently being applied in areas as diverse as computer games, interactive cinema, information retrieval and filtering, user interface design, electronic commerce, auto piloting of vehicles and spacecraft, and industrial process control. Also called: intelligent agent. See also agent (definition 2).

Autonomous-system number *n.* See autonomous system.

Autonomous system *n.* A group of routers or networks controlled by a single administrative authority using a common Interior Gateway Protocol (IGP) for routing packets. Each autonomous system is assigned a globally unique number called an autonomous-system number (ASN). Acronym: AS. Also called: routing domain. See also IGP.

Auto PC *n.* An information and entertainment system for use in automobiles. Developed by Microsoft and powered by Microsoft Windows CE (a Windows-compatible operating system designed for embedded applications), Auto PC implements speech-recognition technology to enable individuals to rely on hands-free, spoken commands for tasks such as accessing a contact database (names, addresses, numbers), calling up e-mail or traffic reports, controlling an audio system, or obtaining destination directions. The Auto PC fits into the dashboard, in the space normally occupied by a radio. See also voice recognition, Windows.

AutoPlay *n.* A feature in Windows 9x and later that allows it to automatically operate a CD-ROM. When a CD is inserted into a CD-ROM drive, Windows looks for a file called AUTORUN.INF on the CD. If the file is found, Windows will open it and carry out its instructions, which are usually to set up an application from the CD-ROM on the computer's hard disk or to start the application once it has been installed. If an audio CD is inserted into the drive, Windows will automatically launch the CD Player application and play it.

Autopolling *n.* The process of periodically determining the status of each device in a set so that the active programme can process the events generated by each device, such as whether a mouse button was pressed or whether new data is available at a serial port. This can be contrasted with event-driven processing, in which the operating system alerts a programme or routine to the occurrence of an event by means of an interrupt or message rather than having to check each device in turn. Also called: polling.

Autorepeat *n.* See typematic.

Autoresponder *n.* E-mail utility that replies automatically to an incoming e-mail. Typically, an autoresponder sends a standard, pre-written message confirming the receipt of the original e-mail.

Autorestart *n.* A process or system feature that can automatically restart the system after the occurrence of certain type of errors or a power system failure.

AUTORUN.INF *n.* A file that when present on removable media, such as CD-ROMs, triggers the AutoPlay feature in Windows 9x and Windows NT. The file, located in the root directory of the inserted medium, contains information on what action the operating system is to take on the CD-ROM—generally, an instruction to run an installation programme.

Autosave *n.* A programme feature that automatically saves an open file to a disk or other medium at defined intervals or after a certain number of keystrokes to ensure that changes to a document are periodically saved.

Autosizing *n.* The ability of a monitor to accept signals at one resolution and display the image at a different resolution. A monitor capable of autosizing maintains the aspect ratio of an image but enlarges or reduces the image to fit in the space available. See also monitor, resolution (definition 1).

Autostart routine *n.* A process by which a system or device is automatically prepared for operation with the occurrence of powering up, or turning the system on, or some other predetermined event. See also AUTOEXEC.BAT, autorestart, boot, power up.

Autostereogram *n.* A computer-generated image, popularised in books and posters, that looks like an abstract design, but which emerges as a three-dimensional picture when the user looks beyond the image, without trying to focus on the hidden picture itself. Autostereograms in which the overlying design consists of a repetitive pattern are known as Single Image Stereograms (SIS). Those in which the design looks like a random pattern of coloured dots are called Single Image Random Dot Stereograms, or SIRDS. Also called: stereogram.

Autotrace *n.* A drawing programme feature that draws lines along the edges of a bitmapped image to convert the image to an object-oriented one. See also bitmapped graphics, object-oriented graphics.

AUX *n.* The logical device name reserved by MS-DOS for an auxiliary device, or peripheral. AUX usually refers to a system's first serial port, also known as COM1.

A/UX *n.* A version of the multiuser, multitasking UNIX operating system provided by Apple Computer for various Macintosh computers and based on the AT&T System V, release 2.2 of UNIX with some enhancements. A/UX incorporates a number of Apple features, including support for the Macintosh Toolbox, so that applications can provide users with the graphics-based interface characteristic of that computer. See also System V.

Auxiliary device *n.* See peripheral.

Auxiliary equipment *n.* See peripheral.

Auxiliary storage *n.* Any storage medium, such as disk or tape, not directly accessed by a computer's microprocessor, as is random access memory (RAM). In current usage, such media are typically referred to as storage or permanent storage, and the RAM chips that the microprocessor uses directly for temporary storage are referred to as memory.

Availability *n.* 1. In processing, the accessibility of a computer system or resource, such as a printer, in terms of usage or of the percentage of the total amount of time the device is needed. 2. A measure of the fault tolerance of a computer and its programmes. A highly available computer runs 24 hours a day, 7 days a week. See also fault tolerance.

Available time *n.* See uptime.

Avalanche ad *n.* One of several larger formats for online ads developed to replace traditional banner ads on the Internet. Avalanche ads are generally 120 x 800 pixels in size. See also skyscraper ad.

Avatar *n.* In virtual-reality environments such as certain types of Internet chat rooms, a graphical representation of a user. An avatar typically is a generic picture or animation of a human of either gender, a photograph or caricature of the user, a picture or animation of an animal, or an object chosen by the user to depict his or her virtual-reality "identity."

.avi *n.* The file extension that identifies an audiovisual interleaved data file in the Microsoft RIFF format.

AVI *n.* Acronym for Audio Video Interleaved. A Windows multimedia file format for sound and moving pictures that uses the Microsoft RIFF (Resource Interchange File Format) specification.

Awk *n.* A UNIX-based language designed for file processing applications, awk is a part of the POSIX Command Language and Utilities standard. It is considered a subset of PERL.

AWT *n.* See Abstract Window Toolkit.

Axis *n.* In a chart or other two-dimensional system using coordinates, the horizontal line (x-axis) or vertical line (y-axis) that serves as a reference for plotting points. In a three-dimensional coordinate system, a third line (z-axis) is used to represent depth. See the illustration. See also Cartesian coordinates.

B

b1 *adj.* Short for binary.

b2 *n.* 1. Short for bit. 2. Short for baud.

B *n.* Short for byte.

B: or b: *n.* 1. Identifier for a second floppy disk drive on MS-DOS and other operating systems. 2. Identifier for a single disk drive when used as the secondary drive.

B1FF *n.* Slang for a new online user who is prone to making mistakes in e-mail, newsgroup articles, or chats that show his or her inexperience. Examples of typical mistakes made by B1FFs include sentences ending with multiple exclamation points (!!!!) and messages typed in ALL CAPS. Although it's spelled B-1(one)-F-F, the term is pronounced "bif."

B2B *n.* Short for business-to-business. The electronic exchange of products and services between businesses without the direct involvement of consumers. B2B's effects on business include streamlining purchasing, accounting, and other administrative functions; lowering transaction costs; and simplifying the sale of excess inventory. Related businesses have collaborated on the creation of Internet-based supply-chain networks.

B2C *n.* Short for business-to-consumer. The direct electronic exchange of products and services between businesses and consumers. B2C's effects on business include improving the efficiency in delivering goods and services to consumers.

Backbone *n.* 1. A network of communication transmission that carries major traffic between smaller networks. The backbones of the Internet, including communications carriers such as Sprint and MCI, can span thousands of miles using microwave relays and dedicated lines. 2. The smaller networks (compared with the entire Internet) that perform the bulk of the packet switching of Internet communication. Today these smaller networks still consist of the networks that were originally developed to make up the Internet—the computer networks of the educational and research institutions of the United States—especially NSFnet, the computer network of the National Science Foundation in Oak Ridge, Tennessee. See also NSFnet, packet switching. 3. The wires that carry major communications traffic within a network. In a local area network, a backbone may be a bus. Also called: collapsed backbone.

Backbone cabal *n.* On the Internet, a term for the group of network administrators responsible for naming the hierarchy of Usenet newsgroups and devising the procedures for creating new newsgroups. The backbone cabal no longer exists.

Back door *n.* A means of gaining access to a programme or system by bypassing its security controls. Programmers often build back doors into systems under development so that they can fix bugs. If the back door becomes known to anyone other than the programmer, or if it is not removed before the software is released, it becomes a security risk. Also called: trapdoor.

Back end *n.* 1. In a client/server application, the part of the programme that runs on the server. See also client/server architecture. 2. In networking, a server computer or the processing that takes place on it. 3. The part of a compiler that transforms source code (human-readable programme statements) into object code (machine-readable code). See also compiler (definition 2), object code, source code.

Back-end processor *n.* 1. A slave processor that performs a specialised task such as providing rapid access to a database, freeing the main processor for other work. Such a task is considered "back-end" because it is subordinate to the computer's main function. 2. A processor that manipulates data sent to it from another processor; for example, a high-speed graphics processor dedicated to painting images on a video display operates in response to commands passed "back" to it by the main processor.

Background[1] *adj.* In the context of processes or tasks that are part of an operating system or programme, operating without interaction with the user while the user is working on another task. Background processes or tasks are assigned a lower priority in the microprocessor's allotment of time than foreground tasks and generally remain invisible to the user unless the user requests an update or brings the task to the foreground. Generally, only multitasking operating systems are able to support background processing. However, some operating systems that do not support multitasking may be able to perform one or more types of background tasks. For example, in the Apple Macintosh operating system running with multitasking turned off, the Background Printing option can be used to print documents while the user is doing other work. See also multitasking.

Background[2] *n.* 1. The colour against which characters and graphics are displayed, such as a white background for black characters. 2. The colours, textures, patterns, and pictures that comprise the surface of the desktop, upon which icons, buttons, menu bars, and toolbars are situated. See also wallpaper. 3. The colours, textures, patterns, and pictures that comprise the surface of a Web page, upon which text, icons, graphics, buttons, and other items are situated. See also wallpaper. 4. The condition of an open but currently inactive window in a windowing environment. See also inactive window.

Background noise *n.* The noise inherent in a line or circuit, independent of the presence of a signal. See also noise.

Background printing *n.* The process of sending a document to a printer at the same time that the computer is performing one or more other tasks.

Background processing *n.* The execution of certain operations by the operating system or a programme during momentary lulls in the primary (foreground) task. An example of a background process is a word processor programme printing a document during the time that occurs between the user's keystrokes. See also background[1].

Background programme *n.* A programme that can run or is running in the background. See also background[1].

Background task *n.* See background[1].

Back-lit or backlit *adj.* Having a source of light, such as a lamp or LED behind a (usually translucent) viewing surface, in order to illuminate the surface.

Back-lit display or backlit display *n.* Something illuminated from behind, rather than by a light source above or to the front.

BackOffice *n.* A suite of software developed by Microsoft that provides certain network services. Designed to work with Windows NT and Windows 2000, BackOffice includes such services as e-mail (Exchange), intranet capabilities (Site Server), network management (Systems Management Server), and high-end database development (SQL Server), among others.

Back Orifice *n.* A hostile application tool used by hackers to gain control of a remote computer. Back Orifice consists of client and server applications. The client application is used to control a computer running the server application. A target computer is taken over after an executable file, typically delivered by an e-mail attachment or a removable disk, is opened. Back Orifice then copies itself to the Windows System directory and transfers control to the machine running the client application. Back Orifice first appeared in the summer of 1998 and was quickly contained through updated security software. Its name is a play on words for the Microsoft BackOffice suite of servers.

Back panel *n.* The panel at the rear of a computer cabinet through which most of the connections to outside power sources and peripherals are made. See the illustration.

Backplane *n.* A circuit board or framework that supports other circuit boards, devices, and the interconnections among devices, and provides power and data signals to supported devices.

Backspace key *n.* 1. A key that, on IBM and compatible keyboards, moves the cursor to the left, one character at a time, usually erasing each character as it moves. 2. On Macintosh keyboards, a key (called the Delete key on some Macintosh keyboards) that erases currently selected text or, if no text is selected, erases the character to the left of the insertion point (cursor). See the illustration.

Back up *vb.* 1. To make a duplicate copy of a programme, a disk, or data. See also backup. 2. To return to a previous stable state, such as one in which a database is known to be complete and consistent.

Backup *n.* A duplicate copy of a programme, a disk, or data, made either for archiving purposes or for safeguarding valuable files from loss should the active copy be damaged or destroyed. A backup is an "insurance" copy. Some application programmes automatically make backup copies of data files, maintaining both the current version and the preceding version on disk. Also called: backup copy, backup file.

Backup and recovery *n.* A strategy available in many database management systems that allows a database to be restored to the latest complete unit of work (transaction) after a software or hardware error has rendered the database unusable. The process starts with the latest backup copy of the database. The transaction log, or change file, for the database is read, and each logged transaction is recovered through the last checkpoint on the log. See also backup, checkpoint, log (definition 1).

Backup and restore *n.* The process of maintaining backup files and putting them back onto the source medium if necessary.

Backup copy *n.* See backup.

Backup file *n.* See backup.

Backus-Naur form *n.* A metalanguage used for defining the syntax of formal languages, both for the developer of the language and for the user. A language is defined by a set of statements, in each of which a language element known as a metavariable, written in angle brackets, is defined in terms of actual symbols (called terminals) and other metavariables (including itself if necessary). See the illustration. Acronym: BNF. See also metalanguage, normal form (definition 2).

Backward chaining *n.* In expert systems, a form of problem solving that starts with a statement and a set of rules leading to the statement and then works backward, matching the rules with information from a database of facts until the statement can be either verified or proved wrong.

Bacterium *n.* A type of computer virus that repeatedly replicates itself, eventually taking over the entire system. See also virus.

BAD *adj.* Acronym for broken as designed. Derogatory jargon for a product or device that consistently fails to work.

Bad block *n.* A faulty memory location. A bad block is identified by the computer's memory controller in the self-test procedure when the computer is turned on or is rebooted. See bad sector.

Bad sector *n.* A disk sector that cannot be used for data storage, usually because of media damage or imperfections. Finding, marking, and avoiding bad sectors on a disk is one of the many tasks performed by a computer's operating system. A disk-formatting utility can also find and mark the bad sectors on a disk.

Bad track *n.* A track on a hard disk or floppy disk that is identified as containing a faulty sector and consequently is bypassed by the operating system. See also bad sector.

.bak *n.* An auxiliary file, created either automatically or upon command, that contains the second-most-recent version of a file and that bears the same file name, with the extension .bak. See also backup.

Balanced line *n.* A transmission line, such as twisted-pair cabling, that contains two conductors capable of carrying equal voltages and currents of opposite polarity and direction.

Balloon Help *n.* An onscreen help feature in the form of a cartoon dialog balloon on the Mac OS developed by Apple Computer, Inc. After activating this feature by clicking on the balloon icon on the toolbar, the user can position the cursor over an icon or other item, and a dialog balloon will appear that describes the function of the item.

Balloons *n.* In print layout view or Web layout view, markup balloons show markup elements, such as comments and tracked changes, in the margins of your document. Use these balloons to easily see and respond to reviewers' changes and comments.

Ball printer *n.* An impact printer that uses a small ball-shaped print head that bears fully formed characters in raised relief on its surface. The printer rotates and tilts the ball to line up characters and then strikes the ball against a ribbon. This method was used in the IBM Selectric typewriter.

Band *n.* 1. In printing graphics, a rectangular portion of a graphic sent by the computer to a printer. The technique of dividing a graphic into bands prevents a printer from having to reconstruct an entire image in memory before printing it. 2. In communications, a contiguous range of frequencies used for a particular purpose, such as radio or television broadcasts.

Bandpass filter *n.* An electronic circuit that passes signals that are within a certain frequency range (band) but blocks or attenuates signals above or below the band. See also attenuation.

Bandwidth *n.* 1. The difference between the highest and lowest frequencies that an analog communications system can pass as measured in Hertz (Hz) or cycles per second. For example, a telephone accommodates a bandwidth of 3000 Hz: the difference between the lowest (300 Hz) and highest (3300 Hz) frequencies it can carry. 2. The data transfer capacity, or speed of transmission, of a digital communications system as measured in bits per second (bps).

Bandwidth management *n.* The analysis and control of traffic on WAN (wide area network) and Internet links to prioritise bandwidth and improve quality of service (QoS). See also quality of service (definition 2), traffic shaping.

Bandwidth on demand *n.* In telecommunications, the capability of increasing throughput, in increments, as required by the channel to be serviced. See also bandwidth, channel (definition 2), throughput.

Bandwidth reservation *n.* Process of assigning in advance a percentage of bandwidth to each user or application served by a network. Bandwidth reservation optimises the use of available traffic by prioritising time-critical packets. Also called: bandwidth allocation, custom queuing. See also bandwidth management, traffic shaping.

Bandwidth shaping *n.* See traffic shaping.

Bandwidth test *n.* A benchmark test that determines the speed of a network connection. Bandwidth tests estimate the downstream and upstream speeds by sending a series of packets over the network and measuring how many packets are received in a given amount of time. Also called: throughput test. See also benchmark[1], throughput (definition 1).

Bandwidth trading *n.* The exchange of excess bandwidth capacity. Although considered a possible commodity market, bandwidth trading currently lacks standardised contracts and instantaneous provisioning needed to simplify the trading process. Also called: bandwidth brokerage, bandwidth exchange.

Bang *n.* The pronunciation for an exclamation point, particularly when the exclamation point is used in a file name or in a path on UNIX systems. See also bang path.

Bang path *n.* Slang for an older form of e-mail address used in UUCP (UNIX-to-UNIX copy). A bang address supplies the path that the message needs to take to reach its destination, including the name of each host through which the message is to be passed. Exclamation points called "bangs" separate the elements of the e-mail address, such as the user account and host names. The address name!location, where "name" is the user account and "location" is the host name, would be spoken as "name bang location."

Bank *n.* 1. Any group of similar electrical devices connected together for use as a single device. For example, transistors may be connected in a row/column array inside a chip to form memory, or several memory chips may be connected together to form a memory module such as a SIMM. See also SIMM. 2. A section of memory, usually of a size convenient for a CPU to address. For example, an 8-bit processor can address 65,536 bytes of memory; therefore, a 64-kilobyte (64-KB) memory bank is the largest that the processor can address at once. To address another 64-KB bank of memory requires circuitry that fools the CPU into looking at a separate block of memory. See also bank switching, page (definition 2).

Bank switching *n.* A method of expanding a computer's available random access memory (RAM) by switching between banks of RAM chips that share a range of memory addresses, which is set aside before switching begins. Only one bank is directly accessible at a time; when a bank is not active, it retains whatever is stored in it. Before another bank can be used, the operating system, driver, or programme must explicitly issue a command to the hardware to make the switch. Because switching between banks takes time, memory-intensive operations take longer with bank-switched memory than with main memory. Bank-switched memory typically takes the form of an expansion card that plugs into a slot on the motherboard.

Banner *n.* A section of a Web page containing an advertisement that is usually an inch or less tall and spans the width of the Web page. The banner contains a link to the advertiser's Web site. See also Web page, Web site.

Banner page *n.* 1. The title page that may be added to printouts by most print spoolers. Such a page typically incorporates account ID information, job length, and print spooler information, and is used primarily to separate one print job from another. See also print spooler. 2. In software, an initial screen used to identify a product and credit its producers.

Bar chart *n.* A type of graphic in which data items are shown as rectangular bars. The bars may be displayed either vertically or horizontally and may be distinguished from one another by colour or by some type of shading or pattern. Positive and negative values may be shown in relation to a zero baseline. Two types of bar charts are common: a standard bar chart, in which each value is represented by a separate bar, and a stacked bar chart, in which several data points are "stacked" to produce a single bar. See the illustration. Also called: bar graph.

Bar code *n.* The special identification code printed as a set of vertical bars of differing widths on books, grocery products, and other merchandise. Used for rapid, error-free input in such facilities as libraries, hospitals, and grocery stores, bar codes represent binary information that can be read by an optical scanner. The coding can include numbers, letters, or a combination of the two; some codes include built-in error checking and can be read in either direction.

Bar code reader *n.* See bar code scanner.

Bar code scanner *n.* An optical device that uses a laser beam to read and interpret bar codes, such as the Universal Product Codes found on grocery products and other retail items. See also bar code, Universal Product Code.

Bare board *n.* A circuit board with no chips on it; most commonly, a memory board not populated with memory chips.

Bare bones[1] *adj.* Purely functional; stripped or otherwise clean of features. Bare bones applications provide only the most basic functions necessary to perform a given task. By the same token, a bare bones computer provides a minimal amount of hardware or is sold at retail with no peripherals and just the operating system (and no other software).

Bare bones[2] *n.* 1. An application that provides only the most basic functions necessary to perform a given task. 2. A computer consisting only of motherboard (equipped with CPU and RAM), cabinet, power supply, floppy disk drive, and keyboard, to which the user must add hard disk, video adapter, monitor, and any other peripherals. See also motherboard, peripheral.

Bar graph *n.* See bar chart.

Base *n.* 1. In mathematics, a number that is raised to the power specified by an exponent. For example, in $2^3 = 2 \times 2 \times 2 = 8$, the base is 2. 2. In mathematics, the number of digits in a particular numbering system. With microcomputers, four numbering systems are commonly used or referred to—binary, octal, decimal, and hexadecimal—and each is based on a different number of digits. The binary, or base-2, numbering system, which is used to discuss the states of a computer's logic, has two digits, 0 and 1. Octal, or base-8, has eight digits, 0 through 7. The familiar decimal, or base-10, numbering system has ten digits, 0 through 9. Hexadecimal, or base-16, has sixteen digits, 0 through 9 and A through F. When numbers are written in a particular base, the base is often subscripted and enclosed in parentheses after the number, as in $24AE_{(16)} = 9{,}390$. Also called: radix. See also binary[1], decimal, hexadecimal, octal. 3. One of three terminals (emitter, base, and collector) in a bipolar transistor. The current through the base controls the current between the emitter and the collector. See also transistor. 4. The insulating foundation of a printed circuit board. See also circuit board.

Base address *n.* The part of a two-part memory address that remains constant and provides a reference point from which the location of a byte of data can be calculated. A base address is accompanied by an offset value that is added to the base to determine the exact location (the absolute address) of the information. The concept is similar to a street address system. For example, "2010 Main Street" consists of a base (the 2000 block of Main Street) plus an offset (10 from the beginning of the block). Base addresses are known as segment addresses in IBM PCs and compatibles; data in these computers is identified by its position as a relative offset from the start of the segment. See also absolute address, offset, relative address, segment.

Baseband *adj.* Of or relating to communications systems in which the medium of transmission (such as a wire or fiber-optic cable) carries a single message at a time in digital form. Baseband communication is found in local area networks such as Ethernet and Token Ring. See also Ethernet, fiber optics, Token Ring network.

Baseband network *n.* A type of local area network in which messages travel in digital form on a single transmission channel between machines connected by coaxial cable or twisted-pair wiring. Machines on a baseband network transmit only when the channel is not busy, although a technique called time-division multiplexing can enable channel sharing. Each message on a baseband network travels as a packet that contains information about the source and destination machines as well as message data. Baseband networks operate over short distances at speeds ranging from about 50 kilobits per second (50 Kbps) to 16 megabits per second (16 Mbps). Receiving, verifying, and converting a message, however, add considerably to the actual time, reducing throughput. The maximum recommended distance for such a network is about 2 miles, or considerably less if the network is heavily used. See also coaxial cable, multiplexing, packet (definition 2), throughput, time-division multiplexing, twisted-pair cable.

Base class *n.* In C++, a class from which other classes have been or can be derived by inheritance. See also class, derived class, inheritance, object-oriented programming.

Base line or baseline *n.* In the printing and display of characters on the screen, an imaginary horizontal line with which the base of each character, excluding descenders, is aligned. See the illustration. See also ascender, descender, font.

Base memory *n.* See conventional memory.

Base RAM *n.* See conventional memory.

Base station *n.* Transmission tower for wireless phone signals. Commonly known as cell towers, base stations also encompass the radio antennas and electronics that handle wireless calls. Base stations relay conversations into and out of the wired phone network and between wireless phones. Each base station covers a limited area known as a cell.

Base style *n.* The underlying or original style on which other styles in a document are dependent. When you change a formatting element of the base style in a document, all other styles that originate from the base style will also reflect the change.

Basic or BASIC *n.* Acronym for Beginner's All-purpose Symbolic Instruction Code, a high-level programming language developed in the mid-1960s by John Kemeny and Thomas Kurtz at Dartmouth College. It is widely considered one of the easiest programming languages to learn. See also True BASIC, Visual BASIC.

Basic Rate Interface *n.* See BRI.

Basic Service Set *n.* The communicating stations, or nodes, on a wireless LAN. See also wireless LAN.

Bastion host *n.* A computer which provides security by serving as a gateway between an internal network and external systems. All outside traffic attempting to connect to the internal network is routed through the bastion host, which defends against potential attacks by intercepting and screening incoming packets. The bastion host may be part of a larger security system providing multiple layers of protection.

.bat *n.* The file extension that identifies a batch programme file. In MS-DOS, .bat files are executable files that contain calls to other programme files. See also batch file.

Batch *n.* A group of documents or data records that are processed as a unit. See also batch job, batch processing.

Batch file *n.* An ASCII text file containing a sequence of operating-system commands, possibly including parameters and operators supported by the batch command language. When the user types a batch file name at the command prompt, the commands are processed sequentially. Also called: batch programme. See also AUTOEXEC.BAT, .bat.

Batch file transmission *n.* The transmission of multiple files as the result of a single command. Acronym: BFT.

Batch job *n.* A programme or set of commands that runs without user interaction. See also batch processing.

Batch processing *n.* 1. Execution of a batch file. See also batch file. 2. The practice of acquiring programmes and data sets from users, running them one or a few at a time, and then providing the results to the users. 3. The practice of storing transactions for a period of time before they are posted to a master file, typically in a separate operation undertaken at night.

Batch programme *n.* A programme that executes without interacting with the user. See also batch file.

Batch system *n.* A system that processes data in discrete groups of previously scheduled operations rather than interactively or in real time.

Batch total *n.* A total calculated for an element common to a group (batch) of records, used as a control to verify that all information is accounted for and has been entered correctly. For example, the total of a day's sales can be used as a batch total to verify the records of all individual sales.

Battery *n.* Two or more cells in a container that produce an electrical current when two electrodes within the container touch an electrolyte. In personal computers, batteries are used as an auxiliary source of power when the main power is shut off, as a power source for laptop and notebook computers (rechargeable batteries, such as nickel cadmium, nickel metal hydride, and lithium ion, are used), and as a method to keep the internal clock and the circuitry responsible for the part of RAM that stores important system information always powered up. See also lead ion battery, lithium ion battery, nickel cadmium battery, nickel metal hydride battery, RAM.

Battery backup *n.* 1. A battery-operated power supply used as an auxiliary source of electricity in the event of a power failure. 2. Any use of a battery to keep a circuit running when the main power is shut off, such as powering a computer's clock/calendar and the special RAM that stores important system information between sessions. See also UPS.

Battery meter *n.* A device used to measure the current (capacity) of an electrical cell.

Baud *n.* One signal change per second, a measure of data transmission speed. Named after the French engineer and telegrapher Jean-Maurice-Emile Baudot and originally used to measure the transmission speed of telegraph equipment, the term now most commonly refers to the data transmission speed of a modem. See also baud rate.

Baudot code *n.* A 5-bit coding scheme used principally for telex transmissions, originally developed for telegraphy by the

French engineer and telegrapher Jean-Maurice-Emile Baudot. Sometimes it is equated, although inaccurately, with the International Alphabet Number 2 proposed by the Comité Consultatif Internationale Télégraphique et Téléphonique (CCITT).

Baud rate *n.* The speed at which a modem can transmit data. The baud rate is the number of events, or signal changes, that occur in one second—not the number of bits per second (bps) transmitted. In high-speed digital communications, one event can actually encode more than one bit, and modems are more accurately described in terms of bits per second than baud rate. For example, a so-called 9600-baud modem actually operates at 2400 baud but transmits 9600 bits per second by encoding 4 bits per event (2400 x 4 = 9600) and thus is a 9600-bps modem.

Bay *n.* A shelf or opening used for the installation of electronic equipment—for example, the space reserved for additional disk drives, CD-ROM drives, or other equipment in the cabinets of microcomputers. See also drive bay.

Bayonet-Neill-Concelman *n.* See BNC.

BBL *n.* Acronym for be back later. An expression used commonly on live chat services on the Internet and online information services to indicate that a participant is temporarily leaving the discussion forum but intends to return at a later time. See also chat[1] (definition 1).

BBS *n.* 1. Acronym for bulletin board system. A computer system equipped with one or more modems or other means of network access that serves as an information and message-passing center for remote users. Often BBSs are focused on special interests, such as science fiction, movies, Windows software, or Macintosh systems, and can have free or fee-based access, or a combination. Users dial into a BBS with their modems and post messages to other BBS users in special areas devoted to a particular topic, in a manner reminiscent of the posting of notes on a cork bulletin board. Many BBSs also allow users to chat online with other users, send e-mail, download and upload files that include freeware and shareware software, and access the Internet. Many software and hardware companies run proprietary BBSs for customers that include sales information, technical support, and software upgrades and patches. 2. Acronym for be back soon. A shorthand expression often seen in Internet discussion groups by a participant leaving the group who wishes to bid a temporary farewell to the rest of the group.

BCC *n.* Acronym for blind courtesy copy. A feature of e-mail programmes that allows a user to send a copy of an e-mail message to a recipient without notifying other recipients that this was done. Generally, the recipient's address is entered into a field called "bcc:" in the mail header. Also called: blind carbon copy. See also e-mail[1] (definition 1), header (definition 1).

BCD *n.* See binary-coded decimal.

bCentral *n.* A Web site for small businesses that provides online subscription services for customer management, financial management, and e-commerce. BCentral is part of the Microsoft .NET initiative. See also MSN, .NET.

B channel *n.* Short for **bearer channel**. One of the 64-Kbps communications channels that carry data on an ISDN circuit. A BRI (Basic Rate Interface) ISDN line has two B channels and one D (data) channel. A PRI (Primary Rate Interface) ISDN line has 23 B channels (in North America) or 30 B channels (in Europe) and one D channel. See also BRI, D channel, ISDN.

BCNF *n.* Acronym for Boyce-Codd normal form. See normal form (definition 1).

Beacon *n.* On an FDDI network, a special frame generated and passed along when a node detects a problem. See also frame (definition 2).

Beam *vb.* To transfer information from one device to another through an infrared wireless connection. The term typically refers to data sharing using handheld devices such as Palm organizers, Pocket PCs, mobile phones, and pagers.

Bearer channel *n.* See B channel.

BeBox *n.* A high-performance multiprocessor computer (RISC-based PowerPC) made by Be, Inc., and loaded with Be's operating system, BeOS. Be discontinued production of the BeBox in January 1997 in order to focus on software (BeOS) development. See also BeOS, PowerPC, RISC.

BEDO DRAM *n.* Acronym for Burst Extended Data Out Dynamic RAM. A type of EDO (extended-data-out) dynamic RAM (DRAM) that handles memory transfers in bursts of four items in order to speed the process of returning data to a computer's CPU. BEDO DRAM takes advantage of the fact that memory requests typically refer to sequential addresses. BEDO DRAM does not function well with bus speeds above 66 MHz. However, once it has accessed the first memory address, it can process the remaining three items in the burst at 10 ns (nanoseconds) each. Also called: BEDO RAM. See also dynamic RAM, EDO DRAM.

Beginner's All-purpose Symbolic Instruction Code *n.* See Basic.

Beginning-of-file *n.* 1. A code placed by a programme before the first byte in a file, used by the computer's operating system to keep track of locations within a file with respect to the first byte (character) in it. 2. The starting location of a file on a disk relative to the first storage location on the disk. A data directory or catalog contains this location. Acronym: BOF.

Bell communications standards *n.* A series of data transmission standards originated by AT&T during the late 1970s and early 1980s that, through wide acceptance in North America, became de facto standards for modems. Bell 103, now mostly obsolete, governed transmission at 300 bits per second (bps) with full-duplex, asynchronous communications over dial-up telephone lines using frequency-shift keying (FSK). Bell 212A governed modem operations at 1200 bps with full-duplex, asynchronous communications over dial-up telephone lines using phase-shift keying (PSK). An international set of transmission standards, known as the CCITT recommendations, has become generally accepted as the primary source of standardization, especially for communications at speeds greater than 1200 bps. See also CCITT V series, FSK, phase-shift keying.

Bell-compatible modem *n.* A modem that operates according to the Bell communications standards. See also Bell communications standards.

Bellman-Ford distance-vector routing algorithm *n.* An algorithm that helps to determine the shortest route between two nodes on a network. The Routing Information Protocol (RIP) is based on the Bellman-Ford distance-vector routing algorithm. See also RIP (definition 2).

Bells and whistles *n.* Attractive features added to hardware or software beyond basic functionality, comparable to accessories such as electric door locks and air conditioning added to an automobile. Products, especially computer systems, without such adornments are sometimes called "plain vanilla."

Benchmark[1] *n.* A test used to measure hardware or software performance. Benchmarks for hardware use programmes that test the capabilities of the equipment—for example, the speed at which a CPU can execute instructions or handle floating-point numbers. Benchmarks for software determine the efficiency, accuracy, or speed of a programme in performing a particular task, such as recalculating data in a spreadsheet. The same data is used with each programme tested, so the resulting scores can be compared to see which programmes perform well and in what areas. The design of fair benchmarks is something of an art, because various combinations of hardware and software can exhibit widely variable performance under different conditions. Often, after a benchmark has become a standard, developers try to optimize a product to run that benchmark faster than similar products run it in order to enhance sales. See also sieve of Eratosthenes.

Benchmark[2] *vb.* To measure the performance of hardware or software.

Benign virus *n.* A programme that exhibits properties of a virus, such as self-replication, but does not otherwise do harm to the computer systems that it infects.

BeOS *n.* An operating system developed by Be, Inc., that runs on PowerPC systems and, until they were discontinued, the company's original BeBox computers. Designed as a "media OS," the BeOS was created to support the large file sizes and high-performance processing demands of digital media and the Internet. It is an object-oriented, multithreaded operating system and can be run on symmetric multiprocessing systems containing two or more processors. Like many other operating systems, the BeOS provides preemptive multitasking, virtual memory, and memory protection. It also provides high-performance input/output capabilities, a 64-bit file system that can support terabyte-sized files, and a number of Internet-related features including built-in mail and Web services. See also BeBox.

Beowulf *n.* Name for a class of virtual supercomputer created by linking numerous PCs through network connections into a single high-performance unit based on inexpensive, x86-based hardware and publicly available software, such as some versions of UNIX. This clustering technique can provide performance comparable to a traditional supercomputer at approximately 10 percent of the cost. The first Beowulf cluster was assembled at NASA's Goddard Space Flight Center in 1994. The origin of the name comes from Beowulf, the hero who fought and killed the monster Grendel in an eighth-century Old English saga.

Beowulf-class computing *n.* See Beowulf.

Berkeley Internet Name Domain *n.* See BIND.

Berkeley Sockets API *n.* See sockets API.

Bernoulli box *n.* A removable floppy disk drive for personal computers that uses a nonvolatile cartridge and has high storage capacity. Named after Daniel Bernoulli, an eighteenth-century physicist who first demonstrated the principle of aerodynamic lift, the Bernoulli box uses high speed to bend the flexible disk close to the read/write head in the disk drive. See also read/write head.

Bernoulli process *n.* A mathematical process involving the Bernoulli trial, a repetition of an experiment in which there are only two possible outcomes, such as success and failure. This process is used mostly in statistical analysis. See also Bernoulli sampling process, binomial distribution.

Bernoulli sampling process *n.* In statistics, a sequence of n independent and identical trials of a random experiment, with each trial having one of two possible outcomes. See also Bernoulli process, binomial distribution.

Best of breed *adj.* A term used to describe a product that is the best in a particular category of products.

Beta[1] *adj.* Of or relating to software or hardware that is a beta.

Beta[2] *n.* A new software or hardware product, or one that is being updated, that is ready to be released to users for beta testing in real-world situations. Usually betas have most or all of the features and functionality implemented that the finished product is to have. See also beta test.

Beta site *n.* An individual or an organisation that tests software before it is released to the public. The company producing the software usually selects these beta sites from a pool of established customers or volunteers. Most beta sites perform this service free of charge, often to get a first look at the software and to receive free copies of the software once it is released to the public.

Beta test *n.* A test of software that is still under development, accomplished by having people actually use the software. In a beta test, a software product is sent to selected potential customers and influential end users (known as beta sites), who test its functionality and report any operational or utilization errors (bugs) found. The beta test is usually one of the last steps a software developer takes before releasing the product to market; however, if the beta sites indicate that the software has operational difficulties or an extraordinary number of bugs, the developer may conduct more beta tests before the software is released to customers.

Betweening *n.* See tween.

Bezel *n.* In arcade games, the bezel refers to the glass located around the monitor. It is often silk-screened with artwork relating to the game. See also arcade game.

Bézier curve *n.* A curve that is calculated mathematically to connect separate points into smooth, free-form curves and surfaces of the type needed for illustration programmes and CAD models. Bézier curves need only a few points to define a large number of shapes—hence their usefulness over other mathematical methods for approximating a given shape. See the illustration. See also CAD.

BFT *n.* See batch file transmission, binary file transfer.

BGP *n.* See Border Gateway Protocol.

Bias *n.* 1. A uniform or systematic deviation from a point of reference. 2. In mathematics, an indication of the amount by which the average of a group of values deviates from a reference value. 3. In electronics, a voltage applied to a transistor or other electronic device to establish a reference level for its operation. 4. In communications, a type of distortion in the length of transmitted bits, caused by a lag that occurs as voltage builds up or falls off each time the signal changes from 0 to 1 or vice versa.

Bidirectional *adj.* Operating in two directions. A bidirectional printer can print from left to right and from right to left; a bidirectional bus can transfer signals in both directions between two devices.

Bidirectional parallel port *n.* An interface that supports two-way parallel communication between a device, such as a printer, and a computer. See also interface (definition 3), parallel port.

Bidirectional printing *n.* The ability of an impact or ink-jet printer to print from left to right and from right to left. Bidirectional printing improves speed substantially because no time is wasted returning the print head to the beginning of the next line, but it may lower print quality.

Bi-endian *adj.* Of, pertaining to, or characteristic of processors and other chips that can be switched to work in big endian or little endian mode. The PowerPC chip has this ability, which allows it to run the little endian Windows NT or the big endian MacOS/PPC. See also big endian, little endian, PowerPC.

BIFF *n.* Short for Binary Interchange File Format. The native file format used by Microsoft Excel.

Biff *n.* 1. A BSD utility that issues a signal when new mail has arrived. Biff was named after a University of California graduate student's dog who had a habit of barking at the mailman at the time the utility was developed. 2. See B1FF.

Biff *vb.* To provide notification of new (incoming) e-mail.

Bifurcation *n.* A split that results in two possible outcomes, such as 1 and 0 or on and off.

Big 5 *n.* Traditional Chinese encoding.

Big Blue *n.* The International Business Machines (IBM) Corporation. This nickname comes from the corporate colour used on IBM's early mainframes and still used in the company logo.

Big endian *adj.* Storing numbers in such a way that the most significant byte is placed first. For example, given the hexadecimal number A02B, the big endian method would cause the number to be stored as A02B, and the little endian method would cause the number to be stored as 2BA0. The big endian method is used by Motorola microprocessors; Intel microprocessors use the little endian method. The term big endian is derived from Jonathan Swift's Gulliver's Travels, in which the Big-Endians were a group of people who opposed the emperor's decree that eggs should be broken at the small end before they were eaten.

Big iron *n.* One or more large, fast, and expensive computers, such as a Cray supercomputer or a room-filling mainframe system.

Big red switch *n.* The power on/off switch of a computer, thought of as a kind of interrupt or last resort. On the original IBM PC and many other computers, it was indeed big and red. Using the switch is an interrupt of last resort because it deletes all the data in RAM and can also damage the hard drive. Acronym: BRS.

Billboard *n.* A primitive inserted into a 3-D scene that is oriented so that one face is toward the viewer. A texture, usually an animated sprite, is applied to the billboard to give the appearance of a 3-D object in the scene.

Billion *n.* 1. In American usage (as is usual with microcomputers), a thousand million, or 10^9. Computer terminology uses the prefixes giga- for 1 billion and nano- for 1

Billionth. 2. In British usage, a million million, or 10^{12}, which is a trillion in American usage.

Billisecond *n.* See nanosecond.

Bimodal virus *n.* See multipartite virus.

.bin *n.* A file name extension for a file encoded with MacBinary. See also MacBinary.

Binary[1] *adj.* Having two components, alternatives, or outcomes. The binary number system has 2 as its base, so values are expressed as combinations of two digits, 0 and 1. These two digits can represent the logical values true and false as well as numerals, and they can be represented in an electronic device by the two states on and off, recognised as two voltage levels. Therefore, the binary number system is at the heart of digital computing. Although ideal for computers, binary numbers are usually difficult for people to interpret because they are repetitive strings of 1s and 0s. To ease translation, programmers and others who habitually work with the computer's internal processing abilities use hexadecimal (base-16) or octal (base-8) numbers. See Appendix E. See also base (definition 2), binary-coded decimal, binary number, bit, Boolean algebra, byte, cyclic binary code, digital computer, dyadic, logic circuit.

Binary[2] *n.* In an FTP client programme, the command that instructs the FTP server to send or receive files as binary data. See also FTP client, FTP server.

Binary chop *n.* See binary search.

Binary-coded decimal *n.* A system for encoding decimal numbers in binary form to avoid rounding and conversion errors. In binary-coded decimal coding, each digit of a decimal number is coded separately as a binary numeral. Each of the decimal digits 0 through 9 is coded in 4 bits, and for ease of reading, each group of 4 bits is separated by a space. This format is also called 8-4-2-1, after the weights of the four bit positions, and uses the following codes: 0000 = 0; 0001 = 1; 0010 = 2; 0011 = 3; 0100 = 4; 0101 = 5; 0110 = 6; 0111 = 7; 1000 = 8; 1001 = 9. Thus, the decimal number 12 is 0001 0010 in binary-coded decimal notation. Acronym: BCD. See also base (definition 2), binary, binary number, decimal, EBCDIC, packed decimal, round.

Binary compatibility *n.* Portability of executable programmes (binary files) from one platform, or flavor of operating system, to another. See also flavor, portable (definition 1).

Binary conversion *n.* The conversion of a number to or from the binary number system. See Appendix E. See also binary[2].

Binary device *n.* Any device that processes information as a series of on/off or high/low electrical states. See also binary.

Binary digit *n.* Either of the two digits in the binary number system, 0 and 1. See also bit.

Binary file *n.* A file consisting of a sequence of 8-bit data or executable code, as distinguished from files consisting of human-readable ASCII text. Binary files are usually in a form readable only by a programme, often compressed or structured in a way that is easy for a particular programme to read.

Binary file transfer *n.* Transfer of a file containing arbitrary bytes or words, as opposed to a text file containing only printable characters (for example, ASCII characters with codes 10, 13, and 32–126). On modern operating systems a text file is simply a binary file that happens to contain only printable characters, but some older systems distinguish the two file types, requiring programmes to handle them differently. Acronym: BFT.

Binary format *n.* Any format that structures data in 8-bit form. Binary format is generally used to represent object code (programme instructions translated into a machine-readable form) or data in a transmission stream. See also binary file.

Binary notation *n.* Representation of numbers using the binary digits, 0 and 1.

Binary number *n.* A number expressed in binary form, or base 2. Binary numbers are composed of zeros and ones. See Appendix E. See also binary[2].

Binary search *n.* A type of search algorithm that seeks an item, with a known name, in an ordered list by first comparing the sought item to the item at the middle of the list's order. The search then divides the list in two, determines in which half of the order the item should be, and repeats this process until the sought item is found. Also called: binary chop, dichotomizing search. See also search algorithm.

Binary synchronous protocol *n.* See BISYNC.

Binary transfer *n.* The preferred mode of electronic exchange for executable files, application data files, and encrypted files.

Binary tree *n.* In programming, a specific type of tree data structure in which each node has at most two subtrees, one left and one right. Binary trees are often used for sorting information; each node of the binary search tree contains a key, with values less than that key added to one subtree and values greater than that key added to the other. See the illustration. See also binary search, tree.

Binaural sound *n.* See 3-D audio.

Bind *vb.* To associate two pieces of information with one another. The term is most often used with reference to associating a symbol (such as the name of a variable) with some descriptive information (such as a memory address, a data type, or an actual value). See also binding time, dynamic binding, static binding.

BIND *n.* Acronym for Berkeley Internet Name Domain. A domain name server originally written for the BSD version of UNIX developed at the Berkeley campus of the University of California but now available for most versions of UNIX. As a domain name server, BIND translates between human-readable domain names and Internet-friendly, numeric IP addresses. It is widely used on Internet servers. See also DNS, DNS server, IP address.

Binder *n.* A Microsoft Office programme that you can use to organise related documents. You can check spelling, number pages consecutively across all documents in the binder, and print the documents.

Binding *n.* The process by which protocols are associated with one another and the network adapter to provide a complete set of protocols needed for handling data from the application layer to the physical layer. See also ISO/OSI reference model.

Binding time *n.* The point in a program's use at which binding of information occurs, usually in reference to programme elements being bound to their storage locations and values. The most common binding times are during compilation (compile-time binding), during linking (link-time binding), and during programme execution (run-time binding). See also bind, compile-time binding, link-time binding, run-time binding.

BinHex[1] *n.* 1. Short for binary to hexadecimal. A format for converting binary data files into ASCII text so they can be transmitted via e-mail to another computer or in a newsgroup post. This method can be used when standard ASCII characters are needed for transmission, as they are on the Internet. BinHex is used most frequently by Mac users. See also MIME. 2. An Apple Macintosh programme for converting binary data files into ASCII text and vice versa using the BinHex format.

BinHex[2] *vb.* To convert a binary file into printable 7-bit ASCII text or to convert the resulting ASCII text file back to binary format using the BinHex programme.

Binomial distribution *n.* In statistics, a list or a function that describes the probabilities of the possible values of a random variable chosen by means of a Bernoulli sampling process. A Bernoulli process has three characteristics: each trial has only two possible outcomes—success or failure; each trial is independent of all other trials; and the probability of success for each trial is constant. A binomial distribution can be used to calculate the probability of getting a specified number of successes in a Bernoulli process. For example, the binomial distribution can be used to calculate the probability of getting a 7 three times in 20 rolls of a pair of dice. Also called: Bernoulli distribution.

BioAPI *n.* An open system specification for use in biometric security and authentication technologies. BioAPI supports a wide range of biometric technology, from handheld devices to large-scale networks, and applications include fingerprint identification, facial recognition, speaker verification, dynamic signatures, and hand geometry. BioAPI was developed for the BioAPI Consortium, a group of organisations with ties to biometrics. BioAPI incorporates compatibility with existing biometric standards such as HA-API, which allows applications to operate BioAPI-compliant technologies without modification.

Biometrics *n.* Traditionally, the science of measuring and analysing human biological characteristics. In computer technology, biometrics relates to authentication and security techniques that rely on measurable, individual biological stamps to recognise or verify an individual's identity. For example, fingerprints, handprints, or voice-recognition might be used to enable access to a computer, to a room, or to an electronic commerce account. Security schemes are generally categorised into three levels: level 1 relies on something the person carries, such as an ID badge with a photo or a computer cardkey; level 2 relies on something the person knows, such as a password or a code number; and level 3, the highest level, relies on something that is a part of the person's biological makeup or behaviour, such as a fingerprint, the pattern of blood vessels in a retina, or a signature. See also fingerprint reader, handwriting recognition (definition 1), voice recognition.

Bionics *n.* The study of living organisms, their characteristics, and the ways they function, with a view toward creating hardware that can simulate or duplicate the activities of a biological system. See also cybernetics.

BIOS *n.* Acronym for basic input/output system. On PC-compatible computers, the set of essential software routines that tests hardware at startup, starts the operating system, and supports the transfer of data among hardware devices, including the date and time. The operating system date is initialised from the BIOS or Real Time Clock date when the machine is booted. Many older PCs, particularly those dating before 1997, have BIOSs that store only 2-digit years and thus may have suffered from Year 2000 problems. The BIOS is stored in read-only memory (ROM) so that it can be executed when the computer is turned on. Although critical to performance, the BIOS is usually invisible to computer users. See also AMI BIOS, CMOS setup, Phoenix BIOS, ROM BIOS.

BIOS test *n.* A test to see if a PC will make the transition to the year 2000 and keep the correct date. The test can range from resetting the system time in the BIOS and rebooting to running a programme or software routine specially designed to uncover Year 2000 problems.

Bipartite virus *n.* See multipartite virus.

Bipolar *adj.* 1. Having two opposite states, such as positive and negative. 2. In information transfer and processing, pertaining to or characteristic of a signal in which opposite voltage polarities represent on and off, true and false, or some other pair of values. See also nonreturn to zero. 3. In electronics, pertaining to or characteristic of a transistor having two types of charge carriers. See also transistor.

BIS *n.* See business information system.

BISDN *n.* See broadband ISDN.

Bistable *adj.* Of, pertaining to, or characteristic of a system or device that has two possible states, such as on and off. See also flip-flop.

Bistable circuit *n.* Any circuit that has only two stable states. The transition between them must be initiated from outside the circuit. A bistable circuit is capable of storing 1 bit of information.

Bistable multivibrator *n.* See flip-flop.

BISYNC *n.* Short for binary synchronous communications protocol. A communications standard developed by IBM. BISYNC transmissions are encoded in either ASCII or EBCDIC. Messages can be of any length and are sent in units called frames, optionally preceded by a message header. BISYNC uses synchronous transmission, in which message elements are separated by a specific time interval, so each frame is preceded and followed by special characters that enable the sending and receiving machines to synchronize their clocks. STX and ETX are control characters that mark the beginning and end of the message text; BCC is a set of characters used to verify the accuracy of transmission. See the illustration. Also called: BSC.

Bit *n.* Short for binary digit. The smallest unit of information handled by a computer. One bit expresses a 1 or a 0 in a binary numeral, or a true or false logical condition, and is represented physically by an element such as a high or low voltage at one point in a circuit or a small spot on a disk magnetised one way or the other. A single bit conveys little information a human would consider meaningful. A group of 8 bits, however, makes up a byte, which can be used to represent many types of information, such as a letter of the alphabet, a decimal digit, or other character. See also ASCII, binary[1], byte.

Bit block *n.* In computer graphics and display, a rectangular group of pixels treated as a unit. Bit blocks are so named because they are, literally, blocks of bits describing the pixels' display characteristics, such as colour and intensity. Programmers use bit blocks and a technique called bit block transfer (bitblt) to display images rapidly on the screen and to animate them. See also bit block transfer.

Bit block transfer *n.* In graphics display and animation, a programming technique that manipulates blocks of bits in memory that represent the colour and other attributes of a rectangular block of pixels forming a screen image. The image described can range in size from a cursor to a cartoon. Such a bit block is moved through a computer's video RAM as a unit so that its pixels can be rapidly displayed in a desired location on the screen. The bits can also be altered; for example, light and dark portions of an image can be reversed. Successive displays can thus be used to change the appearance of an image or to move it around on the screen. Some computers contain special graphics hardware for manipulating bit blocks on the screen independently of the contents of the rest of the screen. This speeds the animation of small shapes, because a programme need not constantly compare and redraw the background around the moving shape. Also called: bitblt. See also sprite.

Bitblt *n.* See bit block transfer.

Bit bucket *n.* An imaginary location into which data can be discarded. A bit bucket is a null input/output device from which no data is read and to which data can be written without effect. The NUL device recognised by MS-DOS is a bit bucket. A directory listing, for example, simply disappears when sent to NUL.

Bit data type *n.* In an Access project, a data type that stores either a 1 or 0 value. Integer values other than 1 or 0 are accepted, but are always interpreted as 1.

Bit density *n.* A measure of the amount of information per unit of linear distance or surface area in a storage medium or per unit of time in a communications pipeline.

Bit depth *n.* The number of bits per pixel allocated for storing indexed colour information in a graphics file.

Bit flipping *n.* A process of inverting bits—changing 1s to 0s and vice versa. For example, in a graphics programme, to invert a black-and-white bitmapped image (to change black to white and vice versa), the programme could simply flip the bits that compose the bit map.

Bit image *n.* A sequential collection of bits that represents in memory an image to be displayed on the screen, particularly in systems having a graphical user interface. Each bit in a bit image corresponds to one pixel (dot) on the screen. The screen itself, for example, represents a single bit image; similarly, the dot patterns for all the characters in a font represent a bit image of the font. In a black-and-white display each pixel is either white or black, so it can be represented by a single bit. The "pattern" of 0s and 1s in the bit image then determines the pattern of white and black dots forming an image on the screen. In a colour display the corresponding description of onscreen bits is called a pixel image because more than one bit is needed to represent each pixel. See also bitmap, pixel image.

Bit manipulation *n.* An action intended to change only one or more individual bits within a byte or word. Manipulation of the entire byte or word is much more common and generally simpler. See also mask.

Bitmap *n.* A data structure in memory that represents information in the form of a collection of individual bits. A bit map is used to represent a bit image. Another use of a bit map in some systems is the representation of the blocks of storage on a disk, indicating whether each block is free (0) or in use (1). See also bit image, pixel image.

Bitmapped font *n.* A set of characters in a particular size and style in which each character is described as a unique bit map (pattern of dots). Macintosh screen fonts are examples of bitmapped fonts. See the illustration. See also downloadable font, outline font, TrueType.

Bitmapped graphics *n.* Computer graphics represented as arrays of bits in memory that represent the attributes of the individual pixels in an image (one bit per pixel in a black-and-white display, multiple bits per pixel in a colour or gray-scale display). Bitmapped graphics are typical of paint programmes, which treat images as collections of dots rather than as shapes. See also bit image, bit map, pixel image.

Bit mask *n.* A value used with bit-wise operators (And, Eqv, Imp, Not, Or, and Xor) to test, set, or reset the state of individual bits in a bit-wise field value.

BITNET *n.* Acronym for Because It's Time Network. A WAN (wide area network) founded in 1981 and operated by the Corporation for Research and Educational Networking (CREN) in Washington, D.C. Now defunct, BITNET provided e-mail and file transfer services between mainframe computers at educational and research institutions in North America, Europe, and Japan. BITNET used the IBM Network Job Entry (NJE) protocol rather than TCP/IP, but it could exchange e-mail with the Internet. The listserv software for maintaining mailing lists was originated on BITNET.

Bit. newsgroups *n.* A hierarchy of Internet newsgroups that mirror the content of some BITNET mailing lists. See also BITNET.

Bit-oriented protocol *n.* A communications protocol in which data is transmitted as a steady stream of bits rather than as a string of characters. Because the bits transmitted have no inherent meaning in terms of a particular character set (such as ASCII), a bit-oriented protocol uses special sequences of bits rather than reserved characters for control purposes. The HDLC (high-level data link control) defined by ISO is a bit-oriented protocol.

Bit parallel *adj.* Transmitting simultaneously all bits in a set (such as a byte) over separate wires in a cable. See also parallel transmission.

Bit pattern *n.* 1. A combination of bits, often used to indicate the possible unique combinations of a specific number of bits. For example, a 3-bit pattern allows 8 possible combinations and an 8-bit pattern allows 256 combinations. 2. A pattern of black and white pixels in a computer system capable of supporting bitmapped graphics. See also pixel.

Bitplane *n.* 1. One of a set of bit maps that collectively make up a colour image. Each bit plane contains the values for one bit of the set of bits that describe a pixel. One bit plane allows two colours (usually black and white) to be represented; two bit planes, four colours; three bit planes, eight colours; and so on. These sections of memory are called bit planes because they are treated as if they were separate layers that stack one upon another to form the complete image. By contrast, in a chunky pixel image, the bits describing a given pixel are stored contiguously within the same byte. The use of bit planes to represent colours is often associated with the use of a colour look-up table, or colour map, which is used to assign colours to particular bit patterns. Bit planes are used in the EGA and VGA in 16-colour graphics modes; the four planes correspond to the 4 bits of the IRGB code. See also colour look-up table, colour map, EGA, IRGB, layering, VGA. 2. Rarely, one level of a set of superimposed images (such as circuit diagrams) to be displayed on the screen.

Bit rate *n.* 1. The speed at which binary digits are transmitted. See also transfer rate. 2. The streaming speed of digital content on a network. Bit rate is usually measured in kilobits per second (Kbps).

Bit serial *n.* The transmission of bits in a byte one after another over a single wire. See also serial transmission.

Bit slice microprocessor *n.* A building block for microprocessors that are custom-developed for specialised uses. These chips can be programmed to handle the same tasks as other CPUs but they operate on short units of information, such as 2 or 4 bits. They are combined into processors that handle the longer words.

Bits per inch *n.* A measure of data storage capacity; the number of bits that fit into an inch of space on a disk or a tape. On a disk, bits per inch are measured based on inches of circumference of a given track. Acronym: BPI. See also packing density.

Bits per pixel *n.* Also known as colour depth or bit depth. The term refers to the number of bits (8, 16, 24, or 32) used to store and display the colour data for a single pixel. The number of bits per pixel determines the range of colour available to an image. Acronym: bpp.

Bits per second *n.* See bps.

Bit stream *n.* 1. A series of binary digits representing a flow of information transferred through a given medium. 2. In synchronous communications, a continuous flow of data in which characters in the stream are separated from one another by the receiving station rather than by markers, such as start and stop bits, inserted into the data.

Bit stuffing *n.* The practice of inserting extra bits into a stream of transmitted data. Bit stuffing is used to ensure that a special sequence of bits appears only at desired locations. For example, in the HDLC, SDLC, and X.25 communications protocols, six 1 bits in a row can appear only at the beginning and end of a frame (block) of data, so bit stuffing is used to insert a 0 bit into the rest of the stream whenever five 1 bits appear in a row. The inserted 0 bits are removed by the receiving station to return the data to its original form. See also HDLC, SDLC, X.25.

Bit transfer rate *n.* See transfer rate.

Bit twiddler *n.* See also hacker. Slang for someone devoted to computers, particularly one who likes to programme in assembly language.

BIX *n.* Acronym for BYTE Information Exchange. An online service originated by BYTE magazine, now owned and operated by Delphi Internet Services Corporation. BIX offers e-mail, software downloads, and conferences relating to hardware and software.

.biz *n.* One of seven new top-level domain names approved in 2000 by the Internet Corporation for Assigned Names and Numbers (ICANN), .biz is meant for use in business-related Web sites.

Biz. news groups *n.* Usenet newsgroups that are part of the biz. hierarchy and have the prefix of biz. These newsgroups are devoted to discussions related to business. Unlike most other newsgroup hierarchies, biz. newsgroups permit users to post advertisement and other marketing material. See also newsgroup, traditional newsgroup hierarchy.

BizTalk Server *n.* An application developed by Microsoft Corporation to streamline business processes within a large company's internal network and between business partners over the Internet. BizTalk Server enables the integration of business applications written in different computer languages and running on various operating systems.

BlackBerry *n.* A wireless handheld device that allows mobile users to send and receive e-mail, as well as view appointment calendars and contact lists. The BlackBerry features a display screen and a built-in keyboard operated by pressing the keys with the thumbs. BlackBerry's ease of use and its ability to send and receive messages silently have made it a popular device for wireless text messaging in a business environment.

Black box *n.* A unit of hardware or software whose internal structure is unknown but whose function is documented. The internal mechanics of the function do not matter to a designer who uses a black box to obtain that function. For example, a memory chip can be viewed as a black box. Many people use memory chips and design them into computers, but generally only memory chip designers need to understand their internal operation.

Black box testing *n.* An approach to testing software in which the tester treats the software as a black box—that is, the testing focuses on the program's functionality rather than on its internal structure. Black box testing is thus user oriented, in that the primary concern is whether the programme works, not how it is constructed. Black box testing is generally performed on software that is under development.

Black hat *n.* A hacker who operates with malicious or criminal intent. A black hat will break into a system to alter or damage data or to commit theft.

Black hole *n.* A mysterious "place" on a computer network where messages, such as e-mail and news items, disappear without a trace. The usage is derived from stellar black holes, which have such strong gravitational fields that even light cannot escape them. The term is sometimes also used to refer to projects that consume vast amounts of time with no apparent product.

Blackout *n.* A condition in which the electricity level drops to zero; a complete loss of power. A number of factors cause a blackout, including natural disasters, such as a storm or an earthquake, or a failure in the power company's equipment, such as a transformer or a power line. A blackout might or might not damage a computer, depending on the state of the computer when the blackout occurs. As with switching a computer off before saving any data, a blackout will cause all unsaved data to be irretrievably lost. The most potentially damaging situation is one in which a blackout occurs while a disk drive is reading information from or writing information to a disk. The information being read or written will probably become corrupted, causing the loss of a small part of a file, an entire file, or the entire disk; the disk drive itself might suffer damage as a result of the sudden power loss. The only reliable means of preventing damage caused by a blackout is to use a battery-backed uninterruptible power supply (UPS). See also UPS.

Blank[1] *n.* The character entered by pressing the spacebar. See also space character.

Blank[2] *vb.* To not show or not display an image on part or all of the screen.

Blanking *n.* The brief suppression of a display signal as the electron beam in a raster-scan video monitor is moved into position to display a new line. After tracing each scan line, the beam is at the right edge of the screen and must return to the left (horizontal retrace) to begin a new line. The display signal must be turned off during the time of the retrace (horizontal blanking interval) to avoid overwriting the line just displayed. Similarly, after tracing the bottom scan line, the electron beam moves to the top left corner (vertical retrace), and the beam must be turned off during the time of this retrace (vertical blanking interval) to avoid marking the screen with the retrace path.

Blast *vb.* See burn (definition 1).

Bleed *n.* In a printed document, any element that runs off the edge of the page or into the gutter. Bleeds are often used in books to mark important pages so they are easier to find. See also gutter.

Blend[1] *n.* A photo or graphic created with a software blending process.

Blend[2] *vb.* In illustration and other graphics software, to create a new combined graphic from two or more separate graphic elements. Photos, art, colours, shapes, and text may be blended together digitally. Graphic elements may be blended for artistic effect, or may be realistic enough to appear as a single photo or graphic.

Blind search *n.* A search for data in memory or on a storage device with no foreknowledge as to the data's order or location. See also linear search.

Blink *vb.* To flash on and off. Cursors, insertion points, menu choices, warning messages, and other displays on a computer screen that are intended to catch the eye are often made to blink. The rate of blinking in a graphical user interface can sometimes be controlled by the user.

Blink speed *n.* The rate at which the cursor indicating the active insertion point in a text window, or other display element, flashes on and off.

Blip *n.* A small, optically sensed mark on a recording medium, such as microfilm, that is used for counting or other tracking purposes.

Blit *vb.* To render a glyph/bitmap to the display. Also called: blitting. See also bit block transfer.

Blitter *n.* A function that copies a bitmap from memory onto the screen.

Bloatware *n.* Software whose files occupy an extremely large amount of storage space on a user's hard disk, especially in comparison with previous versions of the same product.

Block[1] *n.* 1. Generally, a contiguous collection of similar things that are handled together as a whole. 2. A section of random access memory temporarily assigned (allocated) to a programme by the operating system. 3. A group of statements in a programme that are treated as a unit. For example, if a stated condition is true, all of the statements in the block are executed, but none are executed if the condition is false. 4. A unit of transmitted information consisting of identification codes, data, and error-checking codes. 5. A collection of consecutive bytes of data that are read from or written to a device (such as a disk) as a group. 6. A rectangular grid of pixels that are handled as a unit. 7. A segment of text that can be selected and acted upon as a whole in an application. 8. In the Java programming language, any code between matching braces constitutes a block. For example, { x = 1; }. See also code, Java.

Block[2] *vb.* 1. To distribute a file over fixed-size blocks in storage. 2. To prevent a signal from being transmitted. 3. To select a segment of text, by using a mouse, menu selection, or cursor key, to be acted upon in some way, such as to format or to delete the segment.

Block cipher *n.* A private key encryption method that encrypts data in blocks of a fixed size (usually 64 bits). The encrypted data block contains the same number of bits as the original. See also encryption, private key.

Block cursor *n.* An onscreen cursor that has the same width and height in pixels as a text-mode character cell. A block cursor is used in text-based applications, especially as the mouse pointer when a mouse is installed in the system. See also character cell, cursor (definition 1), mouse pointer.

Block device *n.* A device, such as a disk drive, that moves information in blocks—groups of bytes—rather than one character (byte) at a time.

Block diagram *n.* A chart of a computer or other system in which labeled blocks represent principal components and lines and arrows between the blocks show the pathways and relationships among the components. A block diagram is an overall view of what a system consists of and how it works. To show the various components of such a system in more detail, different types of diagrams, such as flowcharts or schematics, are used. See the illustration.

Block gap *n.* The unused physical space that separates blocks of data or physical records on a tape or formatted sectors on a disk. Also called: IBG, interblock gap.

Block header *n.* Information that appears at the beginning of a block of data and serves such purposes as signaling the beginning of the block, identifying the block, providing error-checking information, and describing such characteristics as the block length and the type of data contained in the block. See also header (definition 2).

Blocking factor *n.* 1. The size of the chunks in which data is transferred to or from a block device such as a disk. If fewer bytes are requested, the disk drive will still read the whole block. Common blocking factors on personal computers are 128, 256, and 512 bytes. 2. The number of file records in one disk block. If the record length for a file is 170 bytes, a block on the disk contains 512 bytes, and records do not span blocks, then the blocking factor is 3, and each block contains 510 (170 x 3) bytes of data and 2 unused bytes.

Block length *n.* The length, usually in bytes, of a block of data. Block length typically ranges from 512 bytes through 4096 kilobytes (KB), depending on the purpose for which the block is used.

Block move *n.* Movement of a number of items of data together to a different location, as in reorganising documents with a word processor or moving the contents of cell ranges in a spreadsheet. Most CPUs have instructions that easily support block moves.

Block size *n.* The declared size of a block of data transferred internally within a computer, via FTP, or by modem. The size is usually chosen to make the most efficient use of all the hardware devices involved. See also FTP(definition 1).

Block structure *n.* The organisation of a programme into groups of statements called blocks, which are treated as units. Programming languages such as Ada, C, and Pascal were designed around block structure. A block is a section of code surrounded by certain delimiters (such as BEGIN and END or { and }), which signify that the intervening code can be treated as a related group of statements. For example, in C, each function is a separate block. Block structure also limits the scope of constants, data types, and variables declared in a block to that block. See also function (definition 2), procedure, scope (definition 1).

Block transfer *n.* The movement of data in discrete blocks (groups of bytes).

Blog[1] *n.* See weblog.

Blog[2] *vb.* To create or maintain a weblog.

Blogger *n.* One who creates or maintains a weblog.

Blow *vb.* See burn (definition 1).

Blow up *vb.* To terminate abnormally, as when a programme crosses some computational or storage boundary and cannot handle the situation on the other side, as in, "I tried to draw outside the window, and the graphics routines blew up." See also abend, abort.

Blue screen *n.* A technique used in film matte special effects, in which one image is superimposed on another image. Action or objects are filmed against a blue screen. The desired background is filmed separately, and the shot containing the action or objects is superimposed onto the background. The result is one image where the blue screen disappears.

Blue Screen of Death *n.* In a Microsoft Windows computer environment, a semi-humorous reference to the result of a fatal error in which the screen turns blue and the computer crashes. Recovery from a Blue Screen of Death error typically requires the user to reboot the computer. Acronym: BSOD. Also called: blue-screen error. See also fatal error.

Bluetooth *n.* Technology protocol developed to wirelessly connect electronic devices such as wireless phones, personal digital assistants (PDAs), and computers. Devices equipped with Bluetooth chips can exchange information within about a 30-foot range via radio waves in the 2.45 gigahertz (GHz) spectrum. Bluetooth was developed by the Bluetooth Special Interest Group, a consortium of telecommunications, computing, consumer electronics, and related industry groups.

Bluetooth Special Interest Group *n.* A group of companies from the telecommunications, computing, and networking industries that promotes the development and deployment of Bluetooth technology. See also Bluetooth.

Bluetooth wireless technology *n.* A specification for radio links between mobile PCs, mobile phones, and other portable devices. These radio links are small-form factor, low cost, and short range.

.bmp *n.* The file extension that identifies raster graphics stored in bit map file format. See also bit map.

BNC *n.* Acronym for bayonet-Neill-Concelman. Named for Paul Neill of Bell Labs and Carl Concelman (affiliation unknown), who developed two earlier types of coaxial connectors known as the N connector and C connector, BNC is a type of connector used to join segments of coaxial cable. When one connector is inserted into another and rotated 90 degrees, they lock. BNC connectors are often used with closed-circuit television. The letters BNC are sometimes also considered an acronym for British Naval Connector. See the illustration. Also called: BNC connector. See also coaxial cable.

BNC connector *n.* See BNC.

Board *n.* An electronic module consisting of chips and other electronic components mounted on a flat, rigid substrate on which conductive paths are laid between the components. A personal computer contains a main board, called the motherboard, which usually has the microprocessor on it and slots into which other, smaller boards, called cards or adapters, can be plugged to expand the functionality of the main system, allowing connections to monitors, disk drives, or a network. See also adapter, card (definition 1), motherboard.

Board computer *n.* See single-board.

Board level *n.* A level of focus in troubleshooting and repair that involves tracking down a problem in a computer to a circuit board and replacing the board. This is in contrast to the component level, which involves repairing the board itself. In many cases board-level repairs are made in order to quickly restore the device to working condition; the boards replaced are then repaired and tested for use in later board-level repairs. See also circuit board.

Body *n.* 1. In e-mail and Internet newsgroups, the content of a message. The body of a message follows the header, which contains information about the sender, origin, and destination of the message. See also header (definition 1). 2. In HTML, SGML, and XML, a section of a document that contains the content of the document, along with tags describing characteristics of the content—for example, format. 3. A segment of a data packet containing the actual data.

Body face *n.* A typeface suitable for the main text in a document rather than for headings and titles. Because of their readability, fonts having serifs, such as Times and Palatino, are good body faces, although sans serif faces can also be used as body text. See also sans serif, serif.

BOF *n.* Acronym for birds of a feather. Meetings of special interest groups at trade shows, conferences, and conventions. BOF sessions provide an opportunity for people working on the same technology at different companies or research institutions to meet and exchange their experiences. See beginning-of-file.

Boilerplate *n.* Recyclable text; a piece of writing or code, such as an organisation's mission statement or the graphics code that prints a software company's logo, which can be used over and over in many different documents. The size of boilerplate text can range from a paragraph or two to many pages. It is, essentially, generic composition that can be written once, saved on disk, and merged, either verbatim or with slight modification, into whatever documents or programmes later require it.

Boldface *n.* A type style that makes the text to which it is applied appear darker and heavier than the surrounding text. Some applications allow the buser to apply a "Bold" command to selected text; other programmes require that special codes be embedded in the text before and after words that are to be printed in boldface.

Bomb[1] *n.* A programme planted surreptitiously, with intent to damage or destroy a system in some way—for example, to erase a hard disk or cause it to be unreadable to the operating system. See also Trojan horse, virus, worm.

Bomb[2] *vb.* To fail abruptly and completely, without giving the user a chance to recover from the problem short of restarting the programme or system. See also abend, bug (definition 1), crash[2] (definition 1), hang.

Bonding *n.* 1. Acronym for Bandwidth On Demand Interoperability Group. 2. The process of combining two or more ISDN B (bearer) channels to form a single channel with a bandwidth greater than the standard B channel bandwidth of 64 Kbps. Bonding two B channels, for example, provides a bandwidth of 128 Kbps, which is four times faster than a 28.8

Kbps modem. Such high-speed channels are ideal for video conferencing, imaging, and transferring large-scale data. See also B channel, BRI, ISDN.

Bonding *vb.* See link aggregation.

Bookmark *n.* 1. A marker inserted at a specific point in a document to which the user may wish to return for later reference. 2. In Netscape Navigator, a link to a Web page or other URL that a user has stored in a local file in order to return to it later. See also Favorites folder, hotlist, URL.

Bookmark file *n.* 1. A Netscape Navigator file containing the addresses of preferred Web sites. It is synonymous with the Favorites folder in Internet Explorer and the hotlist in Mosaic. See also Favorites folder, hotlist, Internet Explorer, Mosaic. 2. A rendering of such a file in HTML format, generally posted on a Web page for the benefit of other people. See also HTML.

Boolean *adj.* Of, pertaining to, or characteristic of logical (true, false) values. Many languages directly support a Boolean data type, with predefined values for true and false; others use integer data types to implement Boolean values, usually (although not always) with 0 equaling false and "not 0" equaling true. See also Boolean algebra, Boolean operator.

Boolean algebra *n.* An algebra, fundamental to computer operations but developed in the mid-nineteenth century by English mathematician George Boole, for determining whether logical propositions are true or false rather than for determining the values of numerical expressions. In Boolean algebra, variables must have one of only two possible values, true or false, and relationships between these variables are expressed with logical operators, such as AND, OR, and NOT. Given these two-state variables and the relationships they can have to one another, Boolean algebra produces such propositions as C = A AND B, which means that C is true if and only if both A is true and B is true; thus, it can be used to process information and to solve problems. Furthermore, Boolean logic can be readily applied to the electronic circuitry used in digital computing. Like the binary numbers 1 and 0, true and false are easily represented by two contrasting physical states of a circuit, such as voltages, and computer circuits known as logic gates control the flow of electricity (bits of data) so as to represent AND, OR, NOT, and other Boolean operators. Within a computer, these logic gates are combined, with the output from one becoming the input to another so that the final result (still nothing more than sets of 1s and 0s) is meaningful data, such as the sum of two numbers. See the illustration. See also adder (definition 1), binary[1], Boolean operator, gate (definition 1), logic circuit, truth table.

Boolean expression *n.* An expression that yields a Boolean value (true or false). Such expressions can involve comparisons (testing values for equality or, for non-Boolean values, the < [less than] or > [greater than] relation) and logical combination (using Boolean operators such as AND, OR, and XOR) of Boolean expressions. Also called: conditional expression, logical expression. See also Boolean, Boolean algebra, Boolean operator, relational operator.

Boolean logic *n.* See Boolean algebra.

Boolean operator *n.* An operator designed to work with Boolean values. The four most common Boolean operators in programming use are AND (logical conjunction), OR (logical inclusion), XOR (exclusive OR), and NOT (logical negation). Boolean operators are often used as qualifiers in database searches—for example, find all records where DEPARTMENT = "marketing" OR DEPARTMENT = "sales" AND SKILL = "word processing". Also called: logical operator. See also AND, exclusive OR, NOT, OR.

Boolean search *n.* A database search that uses Boolean operators. See also Boolean operator.

Boost *vb.* To strengthen a network signal before it is transmitted further.

Boot[1] *n.* The process of starting or resetting a computer. When first turned on (cold boot) or reset (warm boot), the computer executes the software that loads and starts the computer's more complicated operating system and prepares it for use. Thus, the computer can be said to pull itself up by its own bootstraps. Also called: bootstrap. See also BIOS, bootstrap loader, cold boot, warm boot.

Boot[2] *vb*. 1. To start or reset a computer by turning the power on, by pressing a reset button on the computer case, or by issuing a software command to restart. Also called: bootstrap, boot up. See also reboot. 2. To execute the bootstrap loader programme. Also called: bootstrap. See also bootstrap loader.

Bootable *adj*. Containing the system files necessary for booting a PC and running it. See also boot[2].

Bootable disk *n*. See boot disk.

Boot block *n*. A portion of a disk that contains the operating-system loader and other basic information that enables a computer to start up. See also block[1] (definition 5).

Boot disk *n*. A floppy disk that contains key system files from a PC-compatible operating system and that can boot, or start, the PC. A boot disk must be inserted in the primary floppy disk drive (usually drive A:) and is used when there is some problem with starting the PC from the hard disk, from which the computer generally boots. Also called: bootable disk. See also A:, boot[2], boot drive, hard disk.

Boot drive *n*. In a PC-compatible computer, the disk drive that the BIOS uses to automatically load the operating system when the computer is turned on. Generally, the default boot drive is the primary floppy disk drive A: in PC-compatible computers with MS-DOS, Windows 3x, or Windows 9x operating systems. If a floppy disk is not found in that drive, the BIOS will check the primary hard disk next, which is drive C:. The BIOS for these operating systems can be reconfigured to search drive C: first by using the BIOS setup programme. See also A:, BIOS, disk drive, hard disk.

Boot failure *n*. The inability of a computer to locate or activate the operating system and thus boot, or start, the computer. See also boot[2].

Boot files *n*. The system files needed to start Microsoft Windows. The boot files include Ntldr and Ntdetect.com. See also partition boot sector.

Boot loader *n.* See bootstrap loader.

BOOTP *n.* See Bootstrap Protocol.

Boot partition *n.* The partition on a hard disk that contains the operating system and support files that the system loads into memory when the computer is turned on or restarted.

Boot record *n.* The section of a disk that contains the operating system.

Boot sector *n.* The portion of a disk reserved for the bootstrap loader (the self-starting portion) of an operating system. The boot sector typically contains a short machine language programme that loads the operating system.

Bootstrap[1] *n.* See boot[1].

Bootstrap[2] *vb.* See boot[2].

Bootstrap loader *n.* A programme that is automatically run when a computer is switched on (booted). After first performing a few basic hardware tests, the bootstrap loader loads and passes control to a larger loader programme, which typically then loads the operating system. The bootstrap loader typically resides in the computer's read-only memory (ROM).

Bootstrap Protocol *n.* A protocol used primarily on TCP/IP networks to configure diskless workstations. RFCs 951 and 1542 define this protocol. DHCP is a later boot configuration protocol that uses this protocol. The Microsoft DGCP service provided limited support for BOOTP service. Acronym: BOOTP. Also called: Boot Protocol. See also boot[2], DHCP, RFC, TCP/IP.

Boot up *vb.* See boot[2].

Border *n.* 1. In programmes and working environments that feature onscreen windows, the edge surrounding the user's workspace. Window borders provide a visible frame around a document or graphic. Depending on the programme and its requirements, they can also represent an area in which the cursor or a mouse pointer takes on special characteristics. For example, clicking the mouse on a window border can enable the user to resize the window or split the window in two. 2.

In printing, a decorative line or pattern along one or more edges of a page or illustration.

Border Gateway Protocol *n.* A protocol used by NSFnet that is based on the External Gateway Protocol. Acronym: BGP. See also External Gateway Protocol, NSFnet.

Boss screen *n.* A false display screen usually featuring business-related material that can be substituted for a game display when the boss walks by. Boss screens were popular with MS-DOS games, where it was difficult to switch to another application quickly. However, games designed for the Mac or Windows 9x generally don't need them because it is easy to switch to a different screen or application to hide the fact that one is playing a game.

Bot *n.* 1. Short for robot. A displayed representation of a person or other entity whose actions are based on programming. 2. A programme that performs some task on a network, especially a task that is repetitive or time consuming. 3. On the Internet, a programme that performs a repetitive or time-consuming task, such as searching Web sites and newsgroups for information and indexing them in a database or other record-keeping system (called spiders); automatically posting one or more articles to multiple newsgroups (often used in spamming and called spambots); or keeping IRC channels open. Also called: Internet robot. See also IRC, newsgroup, spam, spambot, spider.

Bottom-up design *n.* A programme development design methodology in which the lower-level tasks of a programme are defined first; the design of the higher-level functions proceeds from the design of the lower-level ones. See also bottom-up programming, top-down programming.

Bottom-up programming *n.* A programming technique in which lower-level functions are developed and tested first; higher-level functions are then built using the lower-level functions. Many programme developers believe that the ideal combination is top-down design and bottom-up programming. See also top-down design.

Bounce *vb.* To return to the sender, used in reference to undeliverable e-mail.

BounceKeys *n.* A feature in Windows 9x that instructs the processor to ignore double strokes of the same key and other unintentional keystrokes.

Bound[1] *adj.* Limited in performance or speed; for example, an input/output-bound system is limited by the speed of its input and output devices (keyboard, disk drives, and so on), even though the processor or programme is capable of performing at a higher rate.

Bound[2] *n.* The upper or lower limit in a permitted range of values.

Bounding box *n.* See graphic limits.

Bourne shell *n.* The first major shell, or command interpreter, for UNIX and part of the AT&T System V release. The Bourne shell scripting language, developed at AT&T Bell Laboratories by Steve Bourne in 1979, was one of the original command languages for the UNIX operating system. While the Bourne shell lacks some features common in other UNIX shells, such as command-line editing and recall of previously issued commands, it is the one that the majority of shell scripts adhere to. Also called: sh. See also shell[1], shell script, System V, UNIX.

Boutique reseller *n.* A type of VAR (value-added reseller) that specialises in providing customised software, hardware, and services to vertical, or niche, markets. In the VAR environment, boutique resellers are distinguished from master resellers, or systems integrators, which offer a much wider variety of products and services. See also value-added reseller.

Box *n.* 1. Container for a piece of electronic equipment. 2. Slang for a computer more specifically the unit holding the central processing unit, or CPU, and other "guts" of the system, as in "bet that new high-performance box really screams." See also central processing unit. 3. An IBM front-end processor. 4. A rectangular—actually, diamond-shaped—symbol, usually called a decision box, used in flowcharting to represent a point at which a process branches into more than one possible outcome, as in a yes/no situation. See also decision box. 5.

The boundary around a graphic image on screen. See also graphic limits.

Box-top license *n.* See shrinkwrap agreement.

Boyce-Codd normal form *n.* See normal form (definition 1).

Bozo *n.* A slang term used frequently on the Internet, particularly in newsgroups, for a foolish or eccentric person.

Bozo filter *n.* On the Internet, slang for a feature in some e-mail clients and newsgroup readers or a separate utility that allows the user to block, or filter out, incoming e-mail messages or newsgroup articles from specified individuals. Generally, these individuals are ones that the user does not want to hear from, such as bozos. Also called: kill file. See also bozo.

BPI *n.* See bits per inch, bytes per inch.

Bpp *n.* See bits per pixel.

Bps *n.* Short for bits per second. The measure of transmission speed used in relation to networks and communication lines. Although bps represents the basic unit of measure, networks and communications devices, such as modems, are so fast that speeds are usually given in multiples of bps—Kbps (kilobits, or thousands of bits, per second), Mbps (megabits, or millions of bits, per second), and Gbps (gigabits, or billions of bits, per second). Speed in bps is not the same as the baud rate for a modem. See also baud rate.

Braindamaged *adj.* Performing in an erratic or destructive manner. A braindamaged application or utility programme is characterised by some or all of the following traits: a mysterious and unintuitive user interface, failure to respond predictably to commands, failure to release unused memory, failure to close open files, and use of "reserved" elements of the operating system that can result in a fatal error in a programme or the operating system. Braindamaged programmes are also often responsible for causing problems across local area networks.

Brain dump *n.* A large, unorganised mass of information, presented in response to a query via e-mail or a newsgroup article, that is difficult to digest or interpret.

Branch *n.* 1. A node intermediate between the root and the leaves in some types of logical tree structure, such as the directory tree in Windows or a tape distribution organisation. 2. Any connection between two items such as blocks in a flowchart or nodes in a network. See branch instruction.

Branch instruction *n.* An assembly- or machine-level instruction that transfers control to another instruction, usually based on some condition (that is, it transfers if a specific condition is true or false). Branch instructions are most often relative transfers, jumping forward or backward by a certain number of bytes of code. See also GOTO statement, jump instruction.

Branchpoint *n.* The location at which a given branch instruction occurs if the attendant condition (if any) is true. See also branch instruction.

Branch prediction *n.* A technique used in some processors with an instruction called prefetch to guess whether or not a branch will be taken in a programme, and to fetch executable code from the appropriate location. When a branch instruction is executed, it and the next instruction executed are stored in a buffer. This information is used to predict which way the instruction will branch the next time it is executed. When the prediction is correct (as it is over 90 percent of the time), executing a branch does not cause a pipeline break, so the system is not slowed down by the need to retrieve the next instruction. See also branch instruction, buffer[1], central processing unit, pipeline processing.

BRB *n.* Acronym for (I'll) be right back. An expression used commonly on live chat services on the Internet and online information services by participants signaling their temporary departure from the group. See also chat[1] (definition 1).

Breadboard *n.* A blank, perforated board used to support prototype electronic circuits. Experimenters would put components on one side of the board and run the leads through the perforations to be connected by wires running along the underside. Today a circuit designer's breadboard is made of plastic. Its holes are small and closely spaced to accommodate the pins of chips, and connections are made by metal strips plugged into the holes. See the illustration.

Break[1] *n.* 1. Interruption of a programme caused by the user pressing the Break key or its equivalent. 2. Interruption of a communications transmission that occurs when the receiving station interrupts and takes over control of the line or when the transmitting station prematurely halts transmission. 3. In the Java programming language, a keyword used to resume programme execution at the next statement following the current statement. If the keyword is followed by a label, the programme resumes at the indicated labeled statement. See also execute, statement.

Break[2] *vb.* 1. To interrupt execution at a given spot, usually for the purpose of debugging. See also breakpoint. 2. To cause a routine, module, or programme that had previously worked to cease working correctly.

Break key *n.* A key or combination of keys used to tell a computer to halt, or break out of, whatever it is doing. On IBM PCs and compatibles under DOS, pressing the Pause/Break or Scroll Lock/Break key while holding down the Ctrl key issues the break command (as does Ctrl-C). On Macintosh computers, the key combination that sends a break code is Command-period. See the illustration.

Break mode *n.* A temporary suspension of programme execution while in the development environment. In break mode, you can examine, debug, reset, step through, or continue programme execution.

Breakout box *n.* A small hardware device that can be attached between two devices normally connected by a cable (such as a computer and a modem) to display and, if necessary, change the activity through individual wires of the cable.

Breakpoint *n.* A location in a programme at which execution is halted so that a programmer can examine the program's status, the contents of variables, and so on. A breakpoint is set and used within a debugger and is usually implemented by inserting at that point some kind of jump, call, or trap instruction that transfers control to the debugger. See also debug, debugger.

BRI *n.* Acronym for Basic Rate Interface. An ISDN subscriber service that uses two B (64 Kbps) channels and one D (64 Kbps) channel to transmit voice, video, and data signals. See also ISDN.

Bridge *n.* In terms of the Year 2000 problem, a programme, routine, or other conversion mechanism that converts date formats from 2-digit years to 4-digit years and vice versa. A bridge is used as a remedy for literally bridging the 2-digit/4-digit format gap between programmes or systems.

Bridge *n.* 1. A device that connects networks using the same communications protocols so that information can be passed from one to the other. 2. A device that connects two LANs (local area networks), whether or not they use the same protocols, and allows information to flow between them. The bridge operates at the ISO/OSI data-link layer. Also called: layer switch. See also data-link layer.

Bridge page *n.* See doorway page.

Bridge router *n.* A device that supports the functions of both a bridge and router. A bridge router links two segments of a local or wide area network, passing packets of data between the segments as necessary, and uses Level 2 addresses for routing. Also called: Brouter. See also bridge (definition 2), router.

Bridgeware *n.* Hardware or software designed to convert application programmes or data files to a form that can be used by a different computer.

Briefcase *n.* A system folder in Windows 9x used for synchronising files between two computers, usually between desktop and laptop computers. The Briefcase can be transferred to another computer via disk, cable, or network. When files are transferred back to the original computer, the Briefcase updates all files to the most recent version.

Brightness *n.* The perceived quality of radiance or luminosity of a visible object. Brightness is literally in the eye (and mind) of the beholder; a candle in the night appears brighter than the same candle under incandescent lights. Although its subjective value cannot be measured with physical instruments, brightness can be measured as luminance (radiant energy). The brightness component of a colour is different from its colour (the hue) and from the intensity of its colour (the saturation). See also colour model, HSB.

British Naval Connector *n.* See BNC.

Broadband *adj.* Of or relating to communications systems in which the medium of transmission (such as a wire or fiber-optic cable) carries multiple messages at a time, each message modulated on its own carrier frequency by means of modems. Broadband communication is found in wide area networks.

Broadband ISDN *n.* Next-generation ISDN based on ATM (Asynchronous Transfer Mode) technology. Broadband ISDN divides information into two categories: interactive services, which are controlled by the user, and distributed (or distribution) services that can be broadcast to the user. Acronym: BISDN. See also ATM (definition 1), ISDN.

Broadband modem *n.* A modem for use on a broadband network. Broadband technology allows several networks to coexist on a single cable. Traffic from one network does not interfere with traffic from another, since the conversations happen on different frequencies, rather like the commercial radio system. See also broadband network.

Broadband network *n.* A local area network on which transmissions travel as radio-frequency signals over separate inbound and outbound channels. Stations on a broadband network are connected by coaxial or fiber-optic cable, which can carry data, voice, and video simultaneously over multiple transmission channels that are distinguished by frequency. A broadband network is capable of high-speed operation (20 megabits or more), but it is more expensive than a baseband network and can be difficult to install. Such a network is based on the same technology used by cable television (CATV). Also called: wideband transmission.

Broadcast[1] *adj.* Sent to more than one recipient. In communications and on networks, a broadcast message is one distributed to all stations. See also e-mail[1] (definition 1).

Broadcast[2] *n.* As in radio or television, a transmission sent to more than one recipient.

Broadcast publishing point *n.* A type of publishing point that streams content in such a way that the client cannot control (start, stop, pause, fast forward, or rewind) the content. Content streamed from a broadcast publishing point can be delivered as a multicast or unicast stream. Formerly called a station.

Broadcast storm *n.* A network broadcast that causes multiple hosts to respond simultaneously, overloading the network. A broadcast storm may occur when old TCP/IP routers are mixed with routers that support a new protocol. See also communications protocol, router, TCP/IP.

Broken as designed *adj.* See BAD.

Brouter *n.* See bridge router.

Brownout *n.* A condition in which the electricity level is appreciably reduced for a sustained period of time. In contrast to a blackout, or total loss of power, a brownout continues the flow of electricity to all devices connected to electrical outlets, although at lower levels than the normally supplied levels (120 volts in the United States). A brownout can be extremely damaging to sensitive electronic devices, such as computers, because the reduced and often fluctuating voltage levels can cause components to operate for extended periods of time outside the range they were designed to work in. On a computer, a brownout is characterised by a smaller, dimmer, and somewhat fluctuating display area on the monitor and potentially erratic behaviour by the system unit. The only reliable means of preventing damage caused by a brownout condition is to use a battery-backed uninterruptible power supply (UPS). See also UPS.

Browse *vb.* To scan a database, a list of files, or the Internet, either for a particular item or for anything that seems to be of interest. Generally, browsing implies observing, rather than changing, information. In unauthorised computer hacking, browsing is a (presumably) nondestructive means of finding out about an unknown computer after illegally gaining entry.

Browser *n.* See Web browser.

Browser box *n.* See WebTV.

Browser CLUT *n.* A colour look-up table consisting of the 216 colours deemed safe when viewed with most Web browsers on most computer operating systems. See also CLUT, Web safe palette.

BRS *n.* See big red switch.

Brush *n.* A tool used in paint programmes to sketch or fill in areas of a drawing with the colour and pattern currently in use. Paint programmes that offer a variety of brush shapes can produce brushstrokes of varying width and, in some cases, shadowing or calligraphic effects.

Brute force *adj.* In general, any process that essentially involves "doing it the hard way." In computer technology, however, brute force typically refers to a programming style that relies on the computer's processing power rather than on skill and planning to create or find a more elegant solution to a problem. Brute-force programming also ignores available information on how similar situations were handled in the past and might depend on outmoded design methodologies. For example, a programme using brute force to crack passwords might try all the words in a dictionary (which would require huge amounts of computing power). Instead, more elegant programming would involve using special rules, history, statistics, and other available techniques or information to limit the number and types of words to try first.

BSC *n.* See BISYNC.

BSD/OS *n.* A version of the UNIX operating system based on BSD UNIX and sold by Berkeley Software Design, Inc. See also BSD UNIX.

BSD UNIX *n.* Acronym for Berkeley Software Distribution UNIX. A UNIX version developed at the University of California at

Berkeley, providing additional capabilities such as networking, extra peripheral support, and use of extended filenames. BSD UNIX was instrumental in gaining widespread acceptance of UNIX and in getting academic institutions connected to the Internet. BSD UNIX is now being developed by Berkeley Software Design, Inc. Also called: Berkeley UNIX. See also BSD/OS, UNIX.

BSOD *n.* See Blue Screen of Death.

BSS *n.* See Basic Service Set.

B-tree or btree *n.* A tree structure for storing database indexes. Each node in the tree contains a sorted list of key values and links that correspond to ranges of key values between the listed values. To find a specific data record given its key value, the programme reads the first node, or root, from the disk and compares the desired key with the keys in the node to select a subrange of key values to search. It repeats the process with the node indicated by the corresponding link. At the lowest level, the links indicate the data records. The database system can thus rapidly skip down through the levels of the tree structure to find the simple index entries that contain the location of the desired records or rows. See the illustration.

BTW or btw *n.* Acronym for by the way. An expression often used to preface remarks in e-mail and Internet newsgroup articles.

Bubble chart *n.* A chart in which annotated ovals (bubbles) representing categories, operations, or procedures are connected by lines or arrows that represent data flows or other relationships among the items represented by bubbles. In systems analysis, bubble charts, rather than block diagrams or flowcharts, are used to describe the connections between concepts or parts of a whole, without emphasizing a structural, sequential, or procedural relationship between the parts. See the illustration.

Bubble-jet printer *n.* A form of nonimpact printer that uses a mechanism similar to that used by an ink-jet printer to shoot ink from nozzles to form characters on paper. A bubble-jet printer uses special heating elements to prepare the ink, whereas an ink-jet printer uses piezoelectric crystals. See also ink-jet printer, nonimpact printer.

Bubble memory *n.* Memory formed by a series of persistent magnetic "bubbles" in a thin film substrate. In contrast to ROM, information can be written to bubble memory. In contrast to RAM, data written to bubble memory remains there until it is changed, even when the computer is turned off. For this reason, bubble memory has had some application in environments in which a computer system must be able to recover with minimal data loss in the event of a power failure. The use of and demand for bubble memory has all but disappeared because of the introduction of flash memory, which is less expensive and easier to produce. See also flash memory, nonvolatile memory.

Bubble sort *n.* A sorting algorithm that starts at the end of a list with n elements and moves all the way through, testing the value of each adjacent pair of items and swapping them if they aren't in the right order. The entire process is then repeated for the remaining n – 1 items in the list, and so on, until the list is completely sorted, with the largest value at the end of the list. A bubble sort is so named because the "lightest" item in a list (the smallest) will figuratively "bubble up" to the top of the list first; then the next-lightest item bubbles up to its position, and so on. See the illustration. Also called: exchange sort. See also algorithm, sort.

Bubble storage *n.* See bubble memory.

Bucket *n.* A region of memory that is addressable as an entity and can be used as a receptacle to hold data. See also bit bucket.

Bucket brigade attack *n.* See man-in-the-middle attack.

Buffer[1] *n.* A region of memory reserved for use as an intermediate repository in which data is temporarily held while waiting to be transferred between two locations or devices. For instance, a buffer is used while transferring data from an application, such as a word processor, to an input/output device, such as a printer.

Buffer[2] *vb.* To use a region of memory to hold data that is waiting to be transferred, especially to or from input/output (I/O) devices such as disk drives and serial ports.

Buffer pool *n.* A group of memory or storage-device locations that are allocated for temporary storage, especially during transfer operations.

Buffer storage *n.* 1. The use of a special area in memory to hold data temporarily for processing until a programme or operating system is ready to deal with it. 2. An area of storage that is used to hold data to be passed between devices that are not synchronised or have different bit transfer rates.

Bug *n.* 1. An error in coding or logic that causes a programme to malfunction or to produce incorrect results. Minor bugs, such as a cursor that does not behave as expected, can be inconvenient or frustrating, but do not damage information. More severe bugs can require the user to restart the programme or the computer, losing whatever previous work had not been saved. Worse yet are bugs that damage saved data without alerting the user. All such errors must be found and corrected by the process known as debugging. Because of the potential risk to important data, commercial application programmes are tested and debugged as completely as possible before release. After the programme becomes available, further minor bugs are corrected in the next update. A more severe bug can sometimes be fixed with a piece of software called a patch, which circumvents the problem or in some other way alleviates its effects. See also beta test, bomb[2], crash[2] (definition 1), debug, debugger, hang, inherent error, logic error, semantic error, syntax error. 2. A recurring physical problem that prevents a system or set of components from working together properly. While the origin of this definition is in some dispute, computer folklore attributes the first use of bug in this sense to a problem in the Harvard Mark I or the Army/University of Pennsylvania ENIAC that was traced to a moth caught between the contacts of a relay in the machine (although a moth is not entomologically a true bug).

Buggy *adj.* Full of flaws, or bugs, in reference to software. See also bug (definition 1).

Building-block principle *n.* See modular design.

Built-in check *n.* See hardware check, power-on self test.

Built-in font *n.* See internal font.

Built-in groups *n.* The default groups provided with Microsoft Windows NT and Windows NT Advanced Server. A group defines a collection of rights and permissions for the user accounts that are its members. Built-in groups are therefore a convenient means of providing access to commonly used resources. See also group[1].

Bulk eraser *n.* A device for eliminating all information from a storage medium, such as a floppy disk or a tape, by generating a strong magnetic field that scrambles the alignment of the ferrous materials in the media that encode stored data.

Bulk storage *n.* Any medium capable of containing large quantities of information, such as tape, fixed disk, or optical disc.

Bullet *n.* A typographical symbol, such as a filled or empty circle, diamond, box, or asterisk, used to set off a small block of text or each item in a list. Round and square bullets are used to set off different levels of information. See also dingbat.

Bulletin board system *n.* See BBS.

Bulletproof *adj.* Capable of overcoming hardware problems that, in another system, could lead to interruption of the task in progress.

Bump mapping *n.* In 3D computer game rendering and other digital animation applications, a graphic technique in which a texture is added to the surface of an image to increase the perceived detail of the object. Bump mapping gives each pixel a texture, which is calculated by the computer's video card to respond to changes in surroundings, allowing a more realistic interpretation of objects. See the illustration.

Bundle *vb.* To combine products for sale as a lot. Frequently, operating system software and some widely used applications are bundled with a computer system for sale.

Bundled software *n.* 1. Programmes sold with a computer as part of a combined hardware/software package. 2. Smaller programmes sold with larger programmes to increase the latter's functionality or attractiveness.

Burn *vb.* 1. To write data electronically into a programmable read-only memory (PROM) chip by using a special programming device known variously as a PROM programmer, PROM blower, or PROM blaster. Also called: blast, blow. See also PROM. 2. To create read-only memory compact discs (CD-ROMs). 3. To write data electronically on a flash memory chip or a PC Card Type III. Unlike PROM chips or CD-ROM, flash memory media can be burned, or flashed, repeatedly with new information. Also called: flash.

Burn in *vb.* 1. To keep a new system or device running continuously so that any weak elements or components will fail early and can be found and corrected before the system becomes an integral part of the user's work routine. Such a test is often performed at the factory before a device is shipped. 2. To make a permanent change in the phosphor coating on the inside of a monitor screen by leaving the monitor on and keeping a bright, unchanging image on the screen for extended periods. Such an image will remain visible after the monitor is turned off. Burning in was a danger with older PC monitors; it is no longer a concern with most new PC monitors. Also called: ghosting.

Burst[1] *n.* Transfer of a block of data all at one time without a break. Certain microprocessors and certain buses have features that support various types of burst transfers. See also burst speed (definition 1).

Burst[2] *vb.* To break fanfold continuous-feed paper apart at its perforations, resulting in a stack of separate sheets.

Burster *n.* A device used to burst, or break apart at the perforations, fanfold continuous-feed paper.

Burst extended-data-out RAM *n.* See BEDO DRAM.

Burst mode *n.* A method of data transfer in which information is collected and sent as a unit in one high-speed transmission. In burst mode, an input/output device takes control of a multiplexer channel for the time required to send its data. In effect, the multiplexer, which normally merges input from several sources into a single high-speed data stream, becomes a channel dedicated to the needs of one device until the entire transmission has been sent. Burst mode is used both in communications and between devices in a computer system. See also burst[1].

Burst rate *n.* See burst speed (definition 1).

Burst speed *n.* 1. The fastest speed at which a device can operate without interruption. For example, various communications devices (as on networks) can send data in bursts, and the speed of such equipment is sometimes measured as the burst speed (the speed of data transfer while the burst is being executed). Also called: burst rate. 2. The number of characters per second that a printer can print on one line without a carriage return or linefeed. Burst speed measures the actual speed of printing, without consideration of the time taken to advance paper or to move the print head back to the left margin. Almost always, the speed claimed by the manufacturer is the burst speed. By contrast, throughput is the number of characters per second when one or more entire pages of text are being printed and is a more practical measurement of printer speed in real-life situations.

Bursty *adj.* Transmitting data in spurts, or bursts, rather than in a continuous stream.

Bus *n.* A set of hardware lines (conductors) used for data transfer among the components of a computer system. A bus is essentially a shared highway that connects different parts of the system—including the processor, disk-drive controller, memory, and input/output ports—and enables them to transfer information. The bus consists of specialised groups of lines that carry different types of information. One group of lines carries data; another carries memory addresses (locations) where data items are to be found; yet another carries control signals. Buses are characterised by the number of bits they can transfer at a single time, equivalent to the number of wires within the bus. A computer with a 32-bit address bus and a 16-bit data bus, for example, can transfer 16 bits of data at a time from any of 2^{32} memory locations. Most PCs contain one or more expansion slots into which additional boards can be plugged to connect them to the bus.

Bus enumerator *n.* A device driver that identifies devices located on a specific bus and assigns a unique identification code to each device. The bus enumerator is responsible for loading information about the devices onto the hardware tree. See also bus, device driver, hardware tree.

Bus extender *n.* 1. A device that expands the capacity of a bus. For example, IBM PC/AT computers used a bus extender to add onto the earlier PC bus and allow the use of 16-bit expansion boards in addition to 8-bit boards. See also bus. 2. A special board used by engineers to raise an add-on board above the computer's cabinet, making it easier to work on the circuit board.

Business graphics *n.* See presentation graphics.

Business information system *n.* A combination of computers, printers, communications equipment, and other devices designed to handle data. A completely automated business information system receives, processes, and stores data; transfers information as needed; and produces reports or printouts on demand. Acronym: BIS. See also management information system.

Business logic *n.* A set of rules and calculations built into a business information application. The application uses business logic to sort incoming information and respond accordingly. Business logic functions as a set of guidelines that ensure the application's actions conform to the specific needs of a business.

Business software *n.* Any computer application designed primarily for use in business, as opposed to scientific use or entertainment. In addition to the well-known areas of word processing, spreadsheets, databases, and communications, business software for microcomputers also encompasses such applications as accounting, payroll, financial planning, project management, decision and support systems, personnel record maintenance, and office management.

Business Software Alliance *n.* International organisation of computer software companies that promotes the interests of the software industry. This alliance focuses on educating the public on the importance of software, advancing free and open world trade, and supporting legislation opposing software piracy and Internet theft. The Business Software Alliance has offices in the United States, Europe, and Asia, with members in more than 60 nations around the world. Acronym: BSA.

Bus mastering *n.* In modern bus architectures, the ability of a device controller card—a network adapter or a disk controller, for example—to bypass the CPU and work directly with other devices to transfer data into and out of memory. Enabling devices to take temporary control of the system bus for data transfer and bus mastering frees the CPU for other work. This in turn improves performance in tasks, such as video replay and multiple-user queries to large databases, that require simultaneous data access and intensive processing. The technology known as direct memory access (DMA) is a well-known example of bus mastering. See also bus, controller, direct memory access.

Bus mouse *n.* A mouse that attaches to the computer's bus through a special card or port rather than through a serial port. See also mouse.

Bus network *n.* A topology (configuration) for a LAN (local area network) in which all nodes are connected to a main communications line (bus). On a bus network, each node monitors activity on the line. Messages are detected by all nodes but are accepted only by the node(s) to which they are addressed. A malfunctioning node ceases to communicate but does not disrupt operation (as it might on a ring network, in which messages are passed from one node to the next). To avoid collisions that occur when two or more nodes try to use the line at the same time, bus networks commonly rely on collision detection or token passing to regulate traffic. See the illustration. Also called: bus topology, linear bus. See also collision detection, contention, CSMA/CD, token bus network, token passing.

Bus system *n.* The interface circuitry that controls the operations of a bus and connects it with the rest of the computer system. See also bus.

Bus topology *n.* See bus network.

Button *n.* 1. A graphic element in a dialog box that, when activated, performs a specified function. The user activates a button by clicking on it with a mouse or, if the button has the focus, by hitting the Return or Enter key. 2. On a mouse, a movable piece that is pressed to activate some function. Older mouse models have only one button; newer models typically have two or more buttons.

Button bomb *n.* A button on Web pages with the image of a bomb.

Button help *n.* Help information displayed via the selection of buttons or icons. Applications such as the World Wide Web, multimedia kiosks, and computer-aided instruction often use button help icons to ease system navigation.

Bypass *n.* In telecommunications, the use of communication pathways other than the local telephone company, such as satellites and microwave systems.

Byte *n.* Short for binary term. A unit of data, today almost always consisting of 8 bits. A byte can represent a single character, such as a letter, a digit, or a punctuation mark. Because a byte represents only a small amount of information, amounts of computer memory and storage are usually given in kilobytes (1024 bytes), megabytes (1,048,576 bytes), or gigabytes (1,073,741,824 bytes). Abbreviation: B. See also bit, gigabyte, kilobyte, megabyte.

Bytecode *n.* An encoding of a computer programme that a compiler produces when the original source code is processed. This encoding is in an abstract, processor-independent form that cannot be directly executed by most CPUs but is highly suitable for further analysis (for example, compiler optimization), for processing by interpreters (for example, executing Java applets within Web browsers), or for use in generation of binary instructions for the target computer's

CPU. Intermediate bytecode production is a feature of the compilers for the Pascal and Java programming languages. See also central processing unit, compiler (definition 2), interpreter, Java, Java applet, Pascal.

BYTE Information Exchange *n.* See BIX.

Byte-oriented protocol *n.* A communications protocol in which data is transmitted as a string of characters in a particular character set, such as ASCII, rather than as a stream of bits as in a bit-oriented protocol. To express control information, a byte-oriented protocol relies on control characters, most of which are defined by the coding scheme used. The asynchronous communications protocols commonly used with modems and IBM's BISYNC protocol are byte-oriented protocols.

Bytes per inch *n.* The number of bytes that fit into an inch of length on a disk track or a tape. Acronym: BPI.

C

C *n.* A programming language developed by Dennis Ritchie at Bell Laboratories in 1972. It is so named because its immediate predecessor was the B programming language. Although C is considered by many to be more a machine-independent assembly language than a high-level language, its close association with the UNIX operating system, its enormous popularity, and its standardization by the American National Standards Institute (ANSI) have made it perhaps the closest thing to a standard programming language in the microcomputer/workstation marketplace. C is a compiled language that contains a small set of built-in functions that are machine dependent. The rest of the C functions are machine independent and are contained in libraries that can be accessed from C programmes. C programmes are composed of one or more functions defined by the programmer; thus C is a structured programming language. See also C++, compiled language, library, Objective-C, structured programming.

C++ *n.* An object-oriented version of the C programming language, developed by Bjarne Stroustrup in the early 1980s at Bell Laboratories and adopted by a number of vendors, including Apple Computer, Inc. and Sun Micro-systems, Inc. See also C, Objective-C, object-oriented programming.

C2 *n.* A security class of the U.S. Department of Defense Trusted Computer System Evaluation Criteria (DOD 4200.28.STD). C2 is the lowest level of security in the U.S. National Computer Security Center's hierarchy of criteria for trusted computer systems, requiring user logon with password and a mechanism for auditing. The C2 level is outlined in the Orange Book. See also Orange Book (definition 1).

CA *n.* See certificate authority.

.cab *n.* File extension for cabinet files, which are multiple files compressed into one and extractable with the extract.exe utility. Such files are frequently found on Microsoft software (for example, Windows 9x) distribution disks.

Cabinet *n.* The box in which the main components of a computer (CPU, the hard drive, floppy and CD-ROM drives, and expansion slots for peripheral devices, such as monitors) are located. See also CPU, expansion slot.

Cable[1] *n.* A collection of wires shielded within a protective tube, used to connect peripheral devices to a computer. A mouse, a keyboard, and a printer might all be connected to a computer with cables. Printer cables typically implement a serial or a parallel path for data to travel along. See the illustration.

Cable[2] *adj.* Pertaining to the cable television (CATV) distribution system. For example, a cable modem is a modem that sends and receives digital data through a connection to a cable TV system. Because cable TV is a broadband service, it can carry data (such as an Internet connection) at a very high speed. See also CATV.

Cable connector *n.* The connector on either end of a cable. See also DB connector, DIN connector, RS-232-C standard, RS-422/423/449.

Cable matcher *n.* A device that allows the use of a cable that has slightly different wire connections from those required by the devices to which it is attached.

Cable modem *n.* A modem that sends and receives data through a coaxial cable television network instead of telephone lines, as with a conventional modem. Cable modems, which have speeds of 500 kilobits per second (Kbps), can generally transmit data faster than current conventional modems. However, cable modems do not operate at the same rate upstream (when sending information) and downstream (when receiving information). Upstream rates vary from about 2 Mbps to 10 Mbps, downstream rates from about 10 Mbps to 36 Mbps. See also coaxial cable, modem.

Cable telephony *n.* Telephone service provided over a cable TV connection rather than over traditional telephone lines. Although service is delivered over cable rather than telephone wire, the end user perceives no difference between cable telephony and normal telephone service. Proponents of cable telephony see it as part of the eventual integration of Internet, television, and telephone services into a single communication/ entertainment unit.

Cable television *n.* See CATV.

Cabling diagram *n.* A plan that shows the path of cables that attach computer system components or peripherals. Cabling diagrams are particularly important for explaining the connection of disk drives to a disk controller.

Cache *n.* A special memory subsystem in which frequently used data values are duplicated for quick access. A memory cache stores the contents of frequently accessed RAM locations and the addresses where these data items are stored. When the processor references an address in memory, the cache checks to see whether it holds that address. If it does hold the address, the data is returned to the processor; if it does not, a regular memory access occurs. A cache is useful when RAM accesses are slow compared with the microprocessor speed because cache memory is always faster than main RAM memory. See also disk cache, wait state.

Cache card *n.* An expansion card that increases a system's cache memory. See also cache, expansion board.

Cache-Coherent Non-Uniform Memory Access *n.* See ccNUMA.

Cache farm *n.* A group of servers that save copies of Web pages to caches to fulfill successive requests without calling the pages up repeatedly from the Web server. In essence, the servers are dedicated to caching. By saving Web pages where they can be accessed without increasing traffic on the Web site, the cache farm allows higher-performance Web access for the end user and a reduction in network congestion and volume. See also cache.

Cache memory *n.* See cache.

Cache poisoning *n.* Deliberate corruption of Internet Domain Name System (DNS) information through alteration of data that equates host names with their IP addresses. Misleading information of this type, when cached (saved) by one DNS server and later passed to another, exposes DNS servers to attacks in which data sent from one host to another can be accessed or corrupted. Cache poisoning has been used to redirect network requests from a legitimate server to an alternate Web site. See also DNS.

CAD *n.* Acronym for computer-aided design. A system of programmes and workstations used in designing engineering, architectural, and scientific models ranging from simple tools to buildings, aircraft, integrated circuits, and molecules. Various CAD applications create objects in two or three dimensions, presenting the results as wire-frame "skeletons," as more substantial models with shaded surfaces, or as solid objects. Some programmes can also rotate or resize models, show interior views, generate lists of materials required for construction, and perform other allied functions. CAD programmes rely on mathematics, often requiring the computing power of a high-performance workstation. See also CAD/CAM, I-CASE.

CAD/CAM *n.* Acronym for computer-aided design/computer-aided manufacturing. The use of computers in both the design and manufacture of a product. With CAD/CAM, a product, such as a machine part, is designed with a CAD programme and the finished design is translated into a set of instructions that can be transmitted to and used by the machines dedicated to fabrication, assembly, and process control. See also CAD, I-CASE.

CADD *n.* A system of hardware and software similar to CAD but with additional features related to engineering conventions, including the ability to display dimension specifications and other notes. Acronym: CADD. See also CAD.

Caddy *n.* A plastic carrier that holds a CD-ROM and is inserted into a CD-ROM drive. Some PCs, especially older models, have CD-ROM drives that require the use of a caddy. Most current CD-ROM drives do not require a caddy.

CAE *n.* Acronym for computer-aided engineering. An application that enables the user to perform engineering tests and analyses on designs created with a computer. In some instances, capabilities such as logic testing that are generally attributed to CAE applications are also part of CAD programmes, so the distinction between CAD and CAE is not a hard-and-fast one. See also CAD, I-CASE.

CAI *n.* Acronym for computer-aided (or computer-assisted) instruction. An educational programme designed to serve as a teaching tool. CAI programmes typically use tutorials, drills, and question-and-answer sessions to present a topic and to test the student's comprehension. CAI programmes are excellent aids for presenting factual material and for allowing students to pace their learning speed. Subjects and complexity range from beginning arithmetic to advanced mathematics, science, history, computer studies, and specialised topics. Also called: CAL, CAT, computer-aided learning, computer-aided teaching, computer-assisted learning, computer-assisted teaching, computer-augmented learning. See also I-CASE.

CAL *n.* 1. Acronym for computer-assisted (or computer-augmented) learning. See CAI. 2. Acronym for Common Application Language. An object-oriented communications language for controlling home-networking products. CAL, originally part of the CEBus (Consumer Electronic Bus) standard for home automation, can be implemented with various communication protocols, home-networking standards, and home electronic products. See also CEBus, home automation.

Calculator *n.* Broadly, any device that performs arithmetic operations on numbers. Sophisticated calculators can be programmed for certain functions and can store values in memory, but they differ from computers in several ways: they have a fixed set of commands, they do not recognise text, they cannot retrieve values stored in a data file, and they cannot find and use values generated by a programme such as a spreadsheet.

Calendar programme *n.* An application programme in the form of an electronic calendar, commonly used for highlighting dates and scheduling appointments. Some calendar programmes resemble wall calendars, displaying dates in blocks labeled with the days of the week; others display dates day by day and enable the user to enter appointments, notes, and other memoranda. A day-of-the-week type of calendar programme could, for example, be used to find out that Christmas 2003 will be on a Saturday. Depending on its capabilities, such a programme might cover only the current century, or it might cover hundreds of years and even allow for the change (in 1582) from the Julian to the Gregorian calendar. A calendar/scheduler programme might show blocks of dates or, like an appointment book, single days divided into hours or half hours, with room for notes. Some programmes allow the user to set an alarm to go off at an important point in the schedule. Other programmes can coordinate the calendars of different people on the same network so that a person entering an appointment into his or her calendar also enters the appointment into a colleague's calendar.

Call[1] *n.* In a programme, an instruction or statement that transfers programme execution to some section of code, such as a subroutine, to perform a specific task. Once the task is performed, programme execution resumes at the calling point in the programme. See also calling sequence.

Call[2] *vb.* 1. To establish a connection through a telecommunications network. 2. To transfer programme execution to some section of code (usually a subroutine) while saving the necessary information to allow execution to resume at the calling point when the called section has completed execution. Some languages (such as FORTRAN) have an explicit CALL statement; others (such as C and Pascal) perform a call when the name of a procedure or function appears. In assembly language, there are various names for a CALL instruction. When a subroutine call occurs in any language, one or more values (known as arguments or parameters) are often passed to the subroutine, which can then use and sometimes modify these values. See also argument, parameter.

Callback or callback security *n.* A security feature used to authenticate users calling in to a network. During callback, the network validates the caller's username and password, hangs up, and then returns the call, usually to a preauthorised number. This security measure usually prevents unauthorised access to an account even if an individual's logon ID and password have been stolen. See remote access server. See also authentication, preset-to callback.

Callback modem *n.* A modem that, instead of answering an incoming call, requires the caller to enter a touch-tone code and hang up so that the modem can return the call. When the modem receives the caller's code, it checks the code against a stored set of phone numbers. If the code matches an authorised number, the modem dials the number and then opens a connection for the original caller. Callback modems are used when communications lines must be available to outside users but data must be protected from unauthorised intruders.

Calling sequence *n.* In a programme when a subroutine call occurs, an agreement between the calling routine and the called routine on how arguments will be passed and in what order, how values will be returned, and which routine will handle any necessary housekeeping (such as cleaning up the stack). The calling sequence becomes important when the calling and called routines were created with different compilers or if either was written in assembly language. Two common calling sequences are the C calling sequence and the Pascal calling sequence. In the C calling sequence, the calling routine pushes any arguments included in the call on the stack in reverse order (right to left) and performs any stack cleanup; this permits a varying number of arguments to be passed to a given routine. In the Pascal calling sequence, the calling routine pushes any included arguments on the stack in the order in which they appear (left to right), and the called routine is expected to clean up the stack. See also argument, call[1], stack.

CALL instruction *n.* A type of programming instruction that diverts programme execution to a new area in memory (sequence of directives) and also allows eventual return to the original sequence of directives.

CALS *n.* Acronym for Computer-Aided Acquisition and Logistics Support. A U.S. Department of Defense standard for electronic exchange of data with commercial suppliers.

CAM *n.* 1. Acronym for computer-aided manufacturing. The use of computers in automating the fabrication, assembly, and control aspects of manufacturing. CAM applies to the manufacture of products ranging from small-scale production to the use of robotics in full-scale assembly lines. CAM relates more to the use of specialised programmes and equipment than it does to the use of microcomputers in a manufacturing environment. See also CAD/CAM, I-CASE. 2. See Common Access Method.

Camera-ready *adj.* In publishing, of or pertaining to the stage at which a document, with all typographic elements and graphics in place, is suitably prepared to be sent to a printing service. The printing service photographs the camera-ready copy and then uses the photograph to make plates for printing. Some applications are advertised as being able to bring documents to the camera-ready stage, eliminating the need for manual layout and pasteup of elements onto boards.

Campuswide information system *n.* Information and services distributed on a college or university campus through computer networks. Campuswide information system services typically include student and faculty directories, calendars of campus events, and access to databases. Acronym: CWIS.

Cancel *n.* A control character used in communication with printers and other computers, commonly designated as CAN. It usually means that the line of text being sent should be canceled. In ASCII, which is the basis of character sets used by most microcomputers, this is represented internally as character code 24.

Cancelbot *n.* Short for cancel robot. A programme that identifies articles in newsgroups based on a set of criteria and cancels the distribution of those articles. Although the criteria for cancellation is set by the owner of the cancelbot, most cancelbots exist to identify and eliminate spam messages posted to dozens or hundreds of newsgroups. See also spam.

Cancel message *n.* A message sent to Usenet news servers indicating that a certain article is to be canceled, or deleted, from the server. See also article, news server, Usenet.

Candidate key *n.* A unique identifier for a tuple (row) within a relation (database table). The candidate key may be either simple (a single attribute) or composite (two or more attributes). By definition, every relation must have at least one candidate key, but it is possible for a relation to have more than one candidate key. If there is only one candidate key, it automatically becomes the primary key for the relation. If there are multiple candidate keys, the designer must designate one as the primary key. Any candidate key that is not the designated primary key is an alternate key. See also key (definition 2), primary key.

Canned programme *n.* See canned software.

Canned routine *n.* A previously written routine that is copied into a programme and used as is, without modification. See also library routine.

Canned software *n.* Off-the-shelf software, such as word processors and spreadsheet programmes.

Canonical form *n.* In mathematics and programming, the standard or prototypical form of an expression or a statement.

Canonical name *n.* An object's distinguished name presented with the root first and without the LDAP attribute tags (such as: CN=, DC=). The segments of the name are delimited with forward slashes (/). For example, CN=MyDocuments,OU=MyOU,DC=Microsoft,DC=Com is presented as microsoft.com/MyOU/MyDocuments in canonical form. See also Lightweight Directory Access Protocol.

Capacitance *n.* The ability to store an electric charge. Capacitance is measured in farads. A capacitance of 1 farad will hold 1 coulomb of charge at a potential of 1 volt. In practical use, a farad is an extremely large amount of capacitance; typical capacitors have values of microfarads (10^{-6}) or picofarads (10^{-12}). See also capacitor.

Capacitor *n.* A circuit component that provides a known amount of capacitance (ability to store an electric charge). A capacitor typically consists of two conductive plates separated by an insulating (dielectric) material. If other factors remain constant, capacitance increases as the plates are made larger or brought closer together. A capacitor blocks direct current but passes alternating current to an extent that depends on its capacitance and on the frequency of the current. See also capacitance.

Capacity *n.* The amount of information a computer or an attached device can process or store. See also computer.

Caps *n.* Short for capital letters.

Caps Lock key *n.* A toggle key that, when on, shifts the alphabetic characters on the keyboard to uppercase. The Caps Lock key does not affect numbers, punctuation marks, or other symbols. See the illustration.

Capstan *n.* On a tape recorder, a polished metal post against which a turning rubber wheel (called a pinch roller) presses to move a length of magnetic tape placed between the wheel and the post. The capstan controls the speed of the tape as it moves past the recording head. See also pinch roller.

Capture *vb.* In communications, to transfer received data into a file for archiving or later analysis.

Capture board *n.* See video capture card.

Capture card *n.* See video capture card.

Carbon *n.* Code name for the Application Programme Interfaces (API) and shared libraries used to write applications for Macintosh OS X. Since Macintosh OS X is an entirely different system rather than an update of the previous Macintosh OS, Carbon bridges the gap between the systems, allowing developers to rewrite their programmes to OS X without rewriting the code for the entire application. Carbon allows OS X native applications to run under earlier versions of the Macintosh OS without modification but with OS X advantages.

Carbon copy *n.* See cc.

Carbonize *vb.* To update a Macintosh application for OS X. Although older versions of Macintosh applications will run under OS X, only those that have been carbonised will be able to use OS X–specific advantages.

Carbon ribbon *n.* A ribbon used with impact printers, especially daisy-wheel printers, and with typewriters for highest-quality output. A carbon ribbon is made of a thin strip of Mylar coated on one side with a carbon film. Characters printed with a carbon ribbon are extremely crisp and free from the fuzziness that can be associated with an inked cloth ribbon. Also called: film ribbon, Mylar ribbon. See also daisy-wheel printer.

Card *n.* 1. A printed circuit board or adapter that can be plugged into a computer to provide added functionality or new capability. These cards provide specialised services, such as mouse support and modem capabilities, that are not built into the computer. See also adapter, board, printed circuit board. 2. In programmes such as the HyperCard hypertext programme, an onscreen representation of an index card on which information can be stored and "filed" (saved) for future reference. See also hypertext. 3. A manila card about 3 inches high by 7 inches long on which 80 columns of data could be entered in the form of holes punched with a keypunch machine. The punched holes corresponded to numbers, letters, and other characters and could be read by a computer that used a punched-card reader. Also called: punched card. See also card reader (definition 2).

Card cage *n.* An enclosure area for holding printed circuit boards (cards). Most computers have an area with protective metal and mounting brackets where cards are installed. The term originally came from an external box that held rack-mounted cards or peripherals and resembled a cage.

Carder *n.* A person who engages in online credit card fraud. Specifically, a carder steals credit card numbers, either to purchase merchandise (often computer-related) from Web-based stores or to trade the stolen numbers with like-minded individuals—again, over the Internet. Carders generally obtain credit card numbers through conventional means, such as "trashing" (searching through trash) or calling individuals and posing as bank officers. See also hacker (definition 2).

Cardinal number *n.* A number that indicates how many items there are in a set—for example, "There are 27 names on that list."

Card punch *n.* See keypunch.

Card reader *n.* 1. An input device used chiefly for identification purposes that reads information that has been magnetically encoded, usually in two tracks, on a plastic card, such as a credit card or an employee badge. 2. A mechanical apparatus that reads computer data from punched cards. No longer in widespread use, card readers allow computer data to be created off line and then input to the computer for processing. This need for offline data creation was because of limited CPU resources. Reading batches of punched cards was a better use of CPU time than waiting for a human operator to key data directly into the computer's memory. Also called: punched-card reader.

Caret *n.* The small, upward-pointing symbol (^) typically found over the 6 key on the top row of a microcomputer keyboard. In some programming languages, the caret is used as an exponentiation operator. For example, the expression 3 ^ 2 represents the number 3 raised to the second power. The caret is also used to represent the Control key on the keyboard. For example, ^Z means "hold the Control key down and press the Z key."

Careware *n.* Software developed by an individual or a small group and distributed freely, with the proviso that users make a donation to a charity if they continue to use the software after trying it out. The charity is one usually designated by the software creator.

Carnivore *n.* Digital wiretap technology developed by the U.S. Federal Bureau of Investigation. Carnivore's purpose is to track and capture e-mail and other Internet-based communications sent from and received by a suspect. Carnivore copies all of an ISP's network traffic into a collection system where a filter sifts through all communications, disregarding all data but that related to the suspect.

Carpal tunnel syndrome *n.* A form of repetitive strain injury to the wrist and hand. Making the same small motions over and over can cause swelling and scarring of the soft tissue of the wrist, which then compresses the main nerve leading to the hand. Symptoms of carpal tunnel syndrome include pain and tingling in the fingers, and in advanced cases, carpal tunnel syndrome can lead to loss of functionality of the hands. Typing at a computer keyboard without proper wrist support is a common cause of carpal tunnel syndrome. Acronym: CTS. See also repetitive strain injury, wrist support.

Carriage *n.* The assembly that holds the platen of a typewriter or a typewriterlike printer. On a standard typewriter, the platen and carriage move past a fixed position within the typewriter housing, where the keys strike the paper; the platen rotates to advance the paper held in the carriage. On most impact printers for computers, however, the print head moves back and forth across a platen, which rotates but does not move horizontally; in such machines, the assembly that carries the print head is often called the print-head carriage assembly. See also carriage return, platen.

Carriage return *n.* A control character that tells a computer or printer to return to the beginning of the current line. A carriage return is similar to the return on a typewriter but does not automatically advance to the beginning of a new line. For example, a carriage-return character alone, received at the end of the words This is a sample line of text would cause the cursor or printer to return to the first letter of the word This. In the ASCII character set, the carriage-return character has the decimal value of 13 (hexadecimal 0D). See the illustration.

Carrier *n.* 1. In communications, a specified frequency that can be modulated to convey information. 2. A company that provides telephone and other communications services to consumers.

Carrier Detect *n.* See CD (definition 2).

Carrier frequency *n.* A radio-frequency signal, such as those used with modems and on networks, used to transmit information. A carrier frequency is a signal that vibrates at a fixed number of cycles per second, or hertz (Hz), and is modulated (changed) in either frequency or amplitude to enable it to carry intelligible information.

Carrier sense multiple access with collision detection *n.* See CSMA/CD.

Carrier signal *n.* See carrier frequency.

Carrier system *n.* A communications method that uses different carrier frequencies to transfer information along multiple channels of a single path. Transmission involves modulating the signal on each frequency at the originating station and demodulating the signal at the receiving station.

Carry *n.* In arithmetic, the process of moving a digit to the next higher position when the sum of two numbers is greater than the largest digit in the number system being used. Computers, based on logic circuits, and often able to add all digits in two numbers simultaneously (do parallel addition), perform carries in several exotic ways. For example, they perform complete carries, in which one carry is allowed to propagate—that is, to generate other carries in other digit positions. They can also perform partial carries, in which carries resulting from parallel addition are stored temporarily.

Carry bit *n.* The bit, associated with an adder circuit, that indicates that an addition operation has produced a carry (as in 9 + 7). Also called: carry flag.

Carry flag *n.* See carry bit.

Cartesian coordinates *n.* Points on a plane (two dimensions) or in space (three dimensions) that are located by their positions in relation to intersecting axes; named after the French mathematician René Descartes, who introduced the system in the seventeenth century. In two dimensions, points are described by their positions in relation to the two familiar axes, x (usually horizontal) and y (usually vertical). In three dimensions, a third axis, z, is added to the x- and y-axes. See the illustration. See also coordinate system.

Cartesian product *n.* See product (definition 1).

Cartridge *n.* Any of various container devices that usually consist of some form of plastic housing. See also disk cartridge, ink cartridge, memory cartridge, ribbon cartridge, ROM cartridge, tape cartridge, toner cartridge.

Cartridge font *n.* A font contained in a plug-in cartridge and used to add fonts to laser, ink-jet, or high-end dot-matrix printers. Cartridge fonts are distinguished both from internal fonts, which are contained in ROM in the printer and are always available, and from downloadable (soft) fonts, which reside on disk and which can be sent to the printer as needed. See also font cartridge.

Cascade *n.* 1. Additional elements displayed by a menu item or list box from which the user can choose in order to interact with other screen elements. 2. In newsgroup articles, the accumulation of quotation marks (often angle brackets) added by newsgroup readers each time an article is replied to. Most newsgroup readers will copy the original article in the body of the reply; after several replies, the original material will have several quotation marks. See also article, newsgroup, newsreader.

Cascade connection *n.* See pipe (definition 1).

Cascaded star topology *n.* A star network in which nodes connect to hubs and hubs connect to other hubs in a hierarchical (cascaded) parent/child relationship. This topology is characteristic of 100Base-VG networks.

Cascading hubs *n.* A network configuration in which hubs are connected to other hubs. See also hub.

Cascading menu *n.* A hierarchical graphical menu system in which a side menu of subcategories is displayed when the pointer is placed on the main category.

Cascading Style Sheet mechanism *n.* See cascading style sheets.

Cascading style sheets *n.* A Hypertext Markup Language (HTML) specification developed by The World Wide Web Consortium

(W3C) that allows authors of HTML documents and users to attach style sheets to HTML documents. The style sheets include typographical information on how the page should appear, such as the font of the text in the page. This specification also directs the way in which the style sheets of the HTML document and the user's style will blend. Cascading style sheets have been proposed for the HTML 3.2 standard. Acronym: CSS. Also called: Cascading Style Sheet mechanism, CSS1. See also HTML, style sheet (definition 2).

Cascading windows *n.* A sequence of successive, overlapping windows in a graphical user interface, displayed so that the title bar of each is visible. Also called: overlaid windows.

Case *n.* In text processing, an indication of whether one or more alphabetic characters are capitalised (uppercase) or not (lowercase). A case-sensitive programme or routine distinguishes between uppercase and lowercase letters and treats the word cat as totally distinct from either Cat or CAT. A case-sensitive programme that also separates capitalised and lowercased words would list Arkansas before aardvark or antimony, even though its alphabetic position follows both lowercased words.

CASE *n.* Acronym for computer-aided software engineering. A comprehensive label for software designed to use computers in all phases of computer programme development, from planning and modeling through coding and documentation. CASE represents a working environment consisting of programmes and other development tools that help managers, systems analysts, programmers, and others to automate the design and implementation of programmes and procedures for business, engineering, and scientific computer systems.

Case-sensitive search *n.* A search in a database in which capitalization of key words must exactly match the capitalization of words in the database. A case-sensitive search for "north and south" would fail to find a database entry for "North and South."

Case sensitivity *n.* Discrimination between lowercase and uppercase characters in a programme or a programming language. See also case.

Case statement *n.* In programming languages such as Ada, Pascal, and C, a type of control statement that executes one of several sets of instructions based on some key value. Case statements are used in evaluating situations that can have a number of different results. "Case" in this sense refers to a refinement of a basic IF-THEN type of conditional statement (if A is true, then do B), but a case statement functions more like a series of nested IFs (if A, then do this; else if B, then do that; else...). In a case evaluation, a variable (such as a number or a string of characters) is compared against one after another of a series of constants assigned by the programmer. Each constant represents a different case and defines an action to be carried out. When the programme finds a constant that matches the variable, it carries out whatever action is dictated by the case in which the match occurs. See also constant, control statement, variable.

Cassette *n.* The unit consisting of both the plastic case and the magnetic tape it contains. Cassette tapes are used for backing up large amounts of computer data.

Cassette tape *n.* 1. The tape within a cassette. 2. The unit consisting of both the plastic cassette case and the tape it contains.

Cast *n.* A programmer-specified data conversion from one type to another, such as a conversion from integer to floating point. Also called: coercion. See also data type.

CAT *n.* 1. Acronym for computer-aided testing. A procedure used by engineers for checking or analysing designs, especially those created with CAD programmes. Computer-aided testing is also used by software developers for automated regression testing. 2. Acronym for computer-assisted teaching or computer-aided teaching. See CAI. 3. Acronym for computerised axial tomography. A medical procedure in which a computer is used to generate a three-dimensional image of a body part from a series of X-rays taken as cross sections along a single axis. See CAI.

Catalog *n.* 1. In a computer, a list containing specific information, such as name, length, type, and location of files or of storage space. 2. In a database, the data dictionary. See also data dictionary.

Catch *n.* A keyword in the Java programming language used to declare a block of statements to be executed in the event that a Java exception or runtime error occurs in a preceding "try" block. See also block, exception, keyword, runtime, try.

Category 3 cable *n.* Network cable that supports frequencies up to 16 MHz and transmission speeds up to 10 Mbps (standard Ethernet). Category 3 cable has four unshielded twisted pairs (UTPs) of copper wire and RJ-45 connectors, and is used in voice and 10Base-T applications. Also called: Cat 3 cable.

Category 4 cable *n.* Network cable that supports frequencies up to 20 MHz and transmission speeds up to 16 Mbps. Category 4 cable has four unshielded twisted pairs (UTPs) of copper wire and RJ-45 connectors. Less popular than Category 3 and Category 5 cables, it is used primarily for token ring networks. Also called: Cat 4 cable.

Category 5 cable *n.* Network cable that supports frequencies up to 100 MHz and transmission speeds up to 100 Mbps (using two pairs) or 1000 Mbps (using four pairs and called gigabit over copper). Category 5 cable has four unshielded twisted pairs (UTPs) of copper wire and RJ-45 connectors, and is used for 10/100/1000 Base-T, ATM, and token ring networks. Also called: Cat 5 cable.

Category 5e cable *n.* Network cable that supports frequencies up to 100 MHz and transmission speeds up to 1000 Mbps (half-duplex mode) or 2000 Mbps (full-duplex mode). Category 5e cable has four unshielded twisted pairs (UTPs) of copper wire, RJ-45 connectors, and enhanced shielding to prevent signal degradation. Category 5e cable can be used for 10/100/1000 Base-T, ATM, and token ring networks.

Catena *n.* A series of items in a chained list—that is, a list in which one item points to the next in sequence. See also linked list.

Cathode *n.* 1. The terminal or electrode that is negatively charged and from which electrons flow. 2. The electron-emitting electrode in a vacuum tube. 3. The negative terminal of a battery.

Cathode-ray oscilloscope *n.* See oscilloscope.

Cathode-ray tube *n.* See CRT.

CATV *n.* Acronym for community antenna television or cable television. A television broadcasting system that uses coaxial or fiber-optic cable to distribute a broadband signal containing many separate television programme channels. CATV systems are also increasingly being used to carry digital data—for example, Internet connections—to and from subscribers.

CatXML *n.* Acronym for Catalogue XML. An open standard for using XML in catalogue information exchanges over the Internet. CatXML uses a flexible XML schema with multiple profiles that can be adapted to meet the needs of individual businesses. CatXML supports existing information structures and provides distributed query information grid models and dynamic output formats.

Cavity virus *n.* A type of virus that overwrites and hides within a section of the file it has infected. A cavity virus overwrites only a part of the host file filled with a constant, allowing the file to continue to function.

CBEMA *n.* Acronym for Computer and Business Equipment Manufacturers Association. An organisation of hardware vendors and manufacturers in the United States involved in standardising information processing and related equipment.

CBL *n.* Acronym for computer-based learning. Applies to either computer-aided instruction (CAI), which focuses primarily on education, or computer-based training (CBT), which is application-specific or job-oriented teaching. See also CAI, CBT.

CBT *n.* Acronym for computer-based training. The use of computers and specially developed tutorial programmes for teaching. CBT uses colour, graphics, and other attention-getting aids to help maintain interest, and it has both simple and sophisticated applications. A software developer, for example, might include a series of CBT lessons with an application to give new users a hands-on feel for the programme; a consultant might use a longer and more detailed CBT programme as a tool in a management-training seminar.

CC *n.* Acronym for courtesy copy. A directive to an e-mail programme to send a complete copy of a given piece of mail to another individual. The use of cc mail addressing, as opposed to directly addressing the mail to a person, generally implies that the recipient is not required to take any action; the message is for informational purposes only. In a cc directive, the fact that this recipient received the mail is printed in the mail header and is thus known to all other recipients. Also called: carbon copy. See also e-mail[1] (definition 1), header.

CCC *n.* Acronym for Computer Controlled Character. CCC is generally used in role-playing computer games like MUD. It refers to a character that is not played by a human player but is actually a computer-generated character built into the game itself. See also computer game, MUD, role-playing game.

CCD *n.* See charge-coupled device.

CCI *n.* See Common Client Interface.

CCITT *n.* Acronym for Comité Consultatif International Télégraphique et Téléphonique, now called the International Telecommunication Union-Telecommunication Standardisation Sector (ITU-TSS, often abbreviated as ITU-T). CCITT was the organisation that performed the standardization functions for the International Telecommunication Union (ITU). Following a reorganisation of the ITU in 1992, CCITT ceased to exist as a separate body, although several standards are still known by the CCITT prefix. See also ITU.

CCITT Groups 1–4 *n.* A set of four standards recommended by the Comité Consultatif International Télégraphique et Téléphonique (International Telegraph and Telephone Consultative Committee) for the encoding and transmission of images over fax machines. Groups 1 and 2 relate to analog devices and are generally out of use. Groups 3 and 4, which deal with digital devices, are outlined below. Group 3 is a widespread standard that supports standard images of 203 horizontal dots per inch (dpi) by 98 vertical dpi and fine images of 203 horizontal dpi by 198 vertical dpi; supports two methods of data compression, one (based on the Huffman code) reducing an image to 10 to 20 percent of the original, the second (READ, for relative element address designate) compressing images to 6 to 12 percent of the original; and provides for password protection and for polling so that a receiving machine can request transmission as appropriate. Group 4, a newer standard, supports images of up to 400 dpi; supports data compression based on a beginning row of white pixels (dots), with each succeeding line encoded as a series of changes from the line before, compressing images to 3 to 10 percent of the original; does not include error-correction information in the transmission; and requires an Integrated Services Digital Network (ISDN) phone line rather than a dial-up line.

cc:Mail *n.* An e-mail programme originally introduced by cc:mail, Inc., and currently produced by the Lotus Development Corporation. Lotus cc:Mail runs on multiple networking platforms and the Internet and is closely integrated with Lotus Notes collaborative software.

ccNUMA *n.* Acronym for Cache-Coherent Non-Uniform Memory Access. A technology that enables many symmetric multiprocessing systems to be connected by high-speed/wide-bandwidth interconnect hardware so that they function as one machine. See also symmetric multiprocessing.

CCP *n.* Acronym for Certificate in Computer Programming. A senior-level programming credential awarded by the Institute for Certification of Computer Professionals to individuals who pass an extensive set of programming examinations.

cd *n.* Acronym for change directory. In MS-DOS, UNIX, and FTP client programmes, the command that changes the current directory to the directory whose path follows cd in the command. See also directory, path (definition 5).

CD *n.* 1. An individual compact disc, such as a CD-ROM. See also CD-ROM, compact disc (definition 2). 2. Acronym for

Carrier Detect, a signal sent from a modem to the attached computer to indicate that the modem is online. See also DCD.

CD-E *n.* Acronym for compact disc-erasable. A technological improvement in CDs (compact discs) whereby information can be repeatedly changed on the CD. Contemporary CDs are "write once, read many," in that the information originally written cannot be changed.

Cdev *n.* Short for control panel device. A Macintosh utility that allows basic system settings to be customised. In Macintosh computers running System 6, a cdev is a utility programme placed in the system folder. Keyboard and mouse cdevs are preinstalled. Other cdevs are provided with software packages and utilities. In System 7, cdevs are called control panels. See also control panel, system folder.

CDF *n.* See Channel Definition Format.

CDFS *n.* 1. Acronym for CD-ROM File System. A 32-bit protected-mode file system that controls access to the contents of CD-ROM drives in Windows 9x. See also protected mode. 2. A designation used with UNIX computers to indicate that a file system resides on a read-only removable medium (that is a CD-ROM). This usually implies that the compact disc is compliant with the ISO 9660 standard. CDFS is also used as a part of commands that mount media (hard drives, tape drives, remote networked drives, and CD-ROMs) for use on a computer. See also CD-ROM, ISO 9660.

CD-I *n.* Acronym for compact disc-interactive. A hardware and software standard for a form of optical disc technology that can combine audio, video, and text on high-capacity compact discs. CD-I includes such features as image display and resolution, animation, special effects, and audio. The standard covers methods of encoding, compressing, decompressing, and displaying stored information. See also CD-ROM.

CDMA *n.* See Code Division Multiple Access.

CDN *n.* Acronym for content delivery network. A service that caches the pages of a Web site on geographically dispersed servers to enable faster delivery of Web pages. When a page is requested at a URL that is content delivery–enabled, the content delivery network routes the user's request to a cache server close to the user. See also content delivery.

CDP *n.* Acronym for Certificate in Data Processing. A certificate awarded by the Institute for Certification of Computer Professionals to individuals who pass a set of examinations on computers and related areas, including programming, software, and systems analysis.

CDPD *n.* See Cellular Digital Packet Data.

CD player *n.* Short for compact disc player. A device that reads the information stored on a CD. A CD player contains the optical equipment necessary for reading a disc's contents and the electronic circuitry for interpreting the data as it is read.

CD Plus *n.* A compact disc encoding format that allows mixing of audio recordings and computer data on the same CD, without the possibility of audio equipment becoming damaged by attempting to play the data sections.

CD-R *n.* Acronym for compact disc-recordable. A type of CD-ROM that can be written on a CD recorder and read on a CD-ROM drive. See also CD recorder, CD-ROM.

CD-R/E *adj.* Acronym for compact disc-recordable and erasable. Of or pertaining to hardware and software for interfacing computers with both CD-R (compact disc-recordable) and CD-E (compact disc-erasable) devices. See also CD-R.

CD recorder *n.* A device used to write CD-ROMs. Because a disc can be written only once on these machines, they are used most commonly to create CD-ROMs for data archives or to produce CD-ROM masters that can be duplicated for mass distribution. Also called: CD-R machine, CD-ROM burner. See also CD-ROM.

CD-R machine *n.* See CD recorder.

CD-ROM *n.* 1. Acronym for compact disc read-only memory. A form of storage characterised by high capacity (roughly 650 megabytes) and the use of laser optics rather than magnetic means for reading data. Although CD-ROM drives are strictly read-only, they are similar to CD-R drives (write once, read many), optical WORM devices, and optical read-write drives. See also CD-I, CD-R, WORM. 2. An individual CD (compact disc) designed for use with a computer and capable of storing up to 650 megabytes of data. See also CD, disc.

CD-ROM burner *n.* See CD recorder.

CD-ROM drive *n.* An electromechancial device that reads data on CD-ROMs. Most CD-ROM drives have a SCSI interface, although some are connected to a PC via a controller for a disk drive. Data is read through a small laser that is focused on the surface of the CD-ROM through optical mirrors in the read/write head. A spindle and drive motor revolve the CD-ROM, so all data, which is stored in spirals from the center, can be read. CD-ROM drives vary in the access time to locate a track on the CD-ROM and the seek time to move the read/write head. See the illustration. Also called: CD drive. See also CD-ROM, compact disc.

CD-ROM Extended Architecture *n.* See CD-ROM/XA.

CD-ROM File System *n.* See CDFS (definition 1).

CD-ROM jukebox *n.* A CD-ROM player that can contain up to 200 CD-ROMs and is connected to a CD-ROM drive in a personal computer or workstation. A user can request data from any of the CD-ROMs in the jukebox, and the device will locate and play the disk that contains the data. Although only one CD-ROM can be played at a time, if multiple CD-ROM jukeboxes are each connected to separate CD-ROM drives that are daisy-chained together to the computer, more than one CD-ROM can be used at a time. See also CD-ROM, CD-ROM drive, daisy chain.

CD-ROM/XA *n.* Short for CD-ROM Extended Architecture. An extended CD-ROM format developed by Philips, Sony, and Microsoft. CD-ROM/XA is consistent with the ISO 9660 (High Sierra) standard, with further specification of ADPCM (adaptive differential pulse code modulation) audio, images, and interleaved data. See also adaptive differential pulse code modulation, CD-ROM, High Sierra specification.

CD-RW *n.* Acronym for compact disc-rewritable. The technology, equipment, software, and media used in the production of multiple-write CDs (compact discs).

CDS *n.* See Circuit Data Services.

CDV *n.* 1. Acronym for compressed digital video. The compression of video images for high-speed transmission. 2. Acronym for compact disc video. A 5-inch videodisc. See also videodisc.

CD Video *n.* See CDV (definition 2).

CeBIT *n.* One of the world's leading tradeshows for the information technology, telecommunications, and office automation industries. Held annually in Hannover, Germany, CeBIT attracts hundreds of thousands of visitors and exhibitors from more than 60 countries.

CEBus *n.* Short for Consumer Electronic Bus. CEBus is an open architecture set of specification documents that define protocols for how to make products communicate through power line wires, low voltage twisted pairs, coax, infrared, RF, and fiber optics. Anyone, anywhere can get a copy of the plans and develop products that work with the CEBus standard.

Celeron *n.* Intel's family of budget-priced microprocessors introduced in 1998. Celeron chips are based on the same P6 microarchitecture as the Pentium II processor. They include an integrated 128-KB L2 cache and support Intel's MMX technology. Celeron chips have speeds of up to 1.3 GHz in early 2002. See also Pentium.

Cell *n.* 1. The intersection of a row and a column in a spreadsheet. Each row and column in a spreadsheet is unique, so each cell can be uniquely identified—for example, cell B17, at the intersection of column B and row 17. Each cell is displayed as a rectangular space that can hold text, a value, or a formula. 2. An addressable (named or numbered) storage unit for information. A binary cell, for example, is a storage unit that can hold 1 bit of information—that is, it can be either on or off. 3. A fixed-length packet, the basic transmission unit on high-speed networks, such as ATM. See also ATM. 4. Coverage area for wireless phones served by a single base station (cell tower), usually surrounded by six other cells. As a wireless phone moves across the boundary between cells, the conversation is handed from one cell to the next. Cells may be less than a half mile or more than 15 miles in radius, depending on the volume of wireless calls or the presence of large buildings or terrain that might interfere with signals.

Cell animation or cel animation *n.* A process performed by software that emulates traditional cell animation, which uses transparent celluloid sheets ("cells" or "cels" for short) to overlay active elements in an animation frame onto a static background. Computer cell animation is quite efficient because images can be quickly reproduced and manipulated.

Cell padding *n.* The space between the contents and the inside edges of a table cell.

Cell reference *n.* The set of coordinates that a cell occupies on a worksheet. For example, the reference of the cell that appears at the intersection of column B and row 3 is B3.

Cell relay *n.* A form of packet switching in which information is multiplexed onto a carrier and transferred in fixed-length packets (cells).

Cellular automata *n.* 1. In computer science, theoretical models of parallel computers. They enable the investigation of parallel computers without the need to actually build them. The cellular automaton is composed of a network of multiple cells, each representing a processor in the parallel computer. The cells must be identical, and they must have a finite amount of available memory. Each cell outputs a value calculated from the input values it receives from its neighboring cells, and all cells output their values simultaneously. 2. Systems in which rules are applied to multiple cells and their neighbors in a regular spatial lattice or grid that advances through time. Usually, each cell in a cellular automaton has any one state out of a finite number of states. The state changes discretely in time according to rules that depend on the condition of the individual cell and its neighbors. Thus, an individual cell in a cellular automaton takes a neighbor cell's state as input before outputting its own state. Additionally, all the cells in the lattice are updated simultaneously, while the state of the entire lattice also advances discretely in time. Many computer simulations of cellular automata are demonstrated on Web sites; the best known Web example is J.H. Conway's Game of Life.

Cellular Digital Packet Data *n.* A wireless standard providing two-way, 19.2-Kbps packet data transmission over existing cellular telephone channels. Acronym: CDPD. See also packet, wireless.

Cellular Telecommunications and Internet Association *n.* Association based in Washington, D.C. that represents the wireless telecommunications industry and its equipment manufacturers. Acronym: CTIA.

Censorship *n.* The action of preventing material that a party considers objectionable from circulating within a system of communication over which that party has some power. The Internet as a whole is not censored, but some parts of it come under varying degrees of control. A news server, for example, often is set to exclude any or all of the alt. newsgroups, such as alt.sex.* or alt.music.white-power, which are unmoderated and tend to be controversial. A moderated newsgroup or mailing list might be considered to be "censored" because the moderator will usually delete highly controversial and obscene content or content that is on a different topic from that followed by the newsgroup. Online services have identifiable owners, who often take some share of responsibility for what reaches their users' computer screens. In some countries, censorship of certain political or cultural Web sites is a matter of national policy.

Censorware *n.* Software that imposes restrictions on what Internet sites, newsgroups, or files may be accessed by the user.

Center *vb.* To align characters around a point located in the middle of a line, page, or other defined area; in effect, to place text an equal distance from each margin or border. See also align (definition 1).

Centi-prefix 1. One hundred. 2. One hundredth, as in centimeter—one hundredth of a meter.

Centralized network *n.* A network in which nodes connect to and use resources on a single central computer, typically a mainframe.

Centralized processing *n.* The location of computer processing facilities and operations in a single (centralised) place.

Central office *n.* In communications, the switching center where interconnections between customers' communications lines are made.

Central office exchange service *n.* See Centrex.

Central processing unit *n.* See CPU.

Centrex *n.* An option offered by some phone companies in which up-to-date phone facilities are available to business customers, giving the customer access to a complete range of phone services without having to purchase or maintain the necessary equipment. Customers can purchase just the lines and services they will use. The name central office exchange refers to the fact that the phone facilities for Centrex services, particularly switching services, are generally maintained at the offices of the local or central phone company. Since Centrex offers a wider range of services, it is replacing PBX for businesses. See also switching.

Centronics parallel interface *n.* A *de facto* standard for parallel data exchange paths between computers and peripherals, originally developed by the printer manufacturer Centronics, Inc. The Centronics parallel interface provides eight parallel data lines plus additional lines for control and status information. See also parallel interface.

CERN *n.* Acronym for Conseil Européen pour la Recherche Nucléaire (the European Laboratory for Particle Physics). CERN, a physics research center located in Geneva, Switzerland, is where the original development of the World Wide Web took place by Tim Berners-Lee in 1989 as a method to facilitate communication among members of the scientific community. See also NCSA (definition 1).

CERN server *n.* One of the first Hypertext Transfer Protocol (HTTP) servers, developed at CERN by Tim Berners-Lee. The CERN server is still in wide use and is free of charge. See also CERN, HTTP server (definition 1).

CERT *n.* Acronym for Computer Emergency Response Team. An organisation that provides a round-the-clock security consultation service for Internet users and provides advisories whenever new virus programmes and other computer security threats are discovered.

Certificate *n.* A certificate is sent when a message is digitally signed. The certificate proves the sender's identity and supplies the recipient with a public key with which to decrypt the sender's encrypted messages. Also called: digital certificate.

Certificate authority *n.* An issuer of digital certificates, the cyberspace equivalent of identity cards. A certificate authority may be an external issuing company (such as VeriSign) or an internal company authority that has installed its own server (such as the Microsoft Certificate Server) for issuing and verifying certificates. A certificate authority is responsible for providing and assigning the unique strings of numbers that make up the "keys" used in digital certificates for authentication and to encrypt and decrypt sensitive or confidential incoming and outgoing online information. Acronym: CA. See also digital certificate, encryption.

Certificate revocation list *n.* A document maintained and published by a certification authority that lists certificates that have been revoked. Acronym: CRL. See also certificate, certification authority.

Certificate trust list *n.* A signed list of root certification authority certificates that an administrator considers reputable for designated purposes, such as client authentication or secure e-mail. Acronym: CTL. See also certificate, certificate authority, root certificate.

Certification *n.* 1. The act of awarding a document to demonstrate a computer professional's competence in a particular field. Some hardware and software suppliers, such as Microsoft and Novell, offer certification in the use of their products; other organisations, such as the Institute for Certification of Computer Professionals (ICCP) and the Computing Technology Industry Association (CompTIA), offer more general certification. 2. The act of awarding a document to demonstrate that a hardware or software product meets some specification, such as being able to work with a certain other hardware or software product. 3. The issuance of a notice that a user or site is trusted for the purpose of security and computer authentication. Often certification is used with Web sites.

Certification authority *n.* An organisation that assigns encryption keys. See also certificate authority.

CFML *n.* Acronym for Cold Fusion Markup Language. A programming environment and proprietary, tag-based markup language for server-side processing.

CGA *n.* Acronym for Colour/Graphics Adapter. A video adapter board introduced by IBM in 1981. The CGA is capable of several character and graphics modes, including character modes of 40 or 80 horizontal characters (columns) by 25 vertical lines with 16 colours, and graphics modes of 640 horizontal pixels by 200 vertical pixels with 2 colours, or 320 horizontal pixels by 200 vertical pixels with 4 colours. See also graphics adapter, video adapter.

CGI *n.* 1. Acronym for Common Gateway Interface. The specification that defines communications between information servers (such as HTTP servers) and resources on the server's host computer, such as databases and other programmes. For example, when a user submits a form through a Web browser, the HTTP server executes a programme (often called a CGI script) and passes the user's input information to that programme via CGI. The programme then returns information to the server via CGI. Use of CGI can make a Web page much more dynamic and add interactivity for the user. See also CGI script, HTTP server (definition 1). 2. See Computer Graphics Interface.

Cgi-bin *n.* Short for Common Gateway Interface-binaries. A file directory that holds external applications to be executed by HTTP servers via CGI. See also CGI (definition 1).

CGI programme *n.* See CGI script.

CGI script *n.* Short for Common Gateway Interface script. An external application that is executed by an HTTP server machine in response to a request by a client, such as a Web browser. Generally, the CGI script is invoked when the user clicks on some element in a Web page, such as a link or an image. Communication between the CGI script and the server is carried out via the CGI specification. CGI scripts can be written in many programming languages, including C, C++, and Visual Basic. However, the most commonly used language for CGI scripts is Perl because it is a small but robust language and it is common on UNIX, which is the platform on which the majority of Web sites run. CGI scripts don't necessarily need to be scripts; they can also be batch programmes or compiled programmes. CGI scripts are used to provide interactivity on a Web page, including such features as providing a form that users can fill out, image maps that contain links to other Web pages or resources, and links that users can click on to send e-mail.

CGM *n.* See Computer Graphics Metafile.

Chad *n.* The paper removed when a hole is punched in a card, in a tape, or at the perforated edge of continuous-form paper—the computer equivalent of a doughnut hole.

Chaining *n.* 1. In computers, the linking of two or more entities so that they are dependent upon one another for operation. 2. In programming, the linking of two or more programmes so that the first programme causes the second programme to begin executing. 3. In programming, linking programme statements so that each statement, except for the first, relies on the previous statement for input. 4. With batch files, linking two or more batch files so that the completion of the first batch file causes the second batch file to begin executing. 5. With data storage, linking two or more individual units of storage. For example, a single file on a disk may actually be stored on several different sectors of the disk, each of which points to the next sector containing a piece of that file. These sectors are said to be chained together, or, more literally, to be a chain of clusters. 6. See daisy chaining.

Chain printer *n.* See line printer.

Chalkware *n.* See vaporware.

Challenge Handshake Authentication Protocol *n.* An authentication scheme used by PPP servers to validate the identity of the originator of a connection, upon connection or any time later. Acronym: CHAP. See also authentication, PPP.

Change directory *n.* See cd.

Change file *n.* A file that records transactional changes occurring in a database, providing a basis for updating a master file and establishing an audit trail. Also called: transaction log. See also addition record.

Change management *n.* 1. The process of tracking and controlling updates, revisions, and other changes to a hardware or software product or project. 2. The process of managing change during a company's restructuring or reengineering.

Channel *n.* 1. A path or link through which information passes between two devices. A channel can be either internal or external to a microcomputer. 2. In communications, a medium for transferring information. Depending on its type, a communications channel can carry information (data, sound, and/or video) in either analog or digital form. A communications channel can be a physical link, such as the cable connecting two stations in a network, or it can consist of some electromagnetic transmission on one or more frequencies within a bandwidth in the electromagnetic spectrum, as in radio and television, or in optical, microwave, or voice-grade communication. Also called: circuit, line. See also analog, band, bandwidth, digital, electromagnetic spectrum, frequency. 3. A single colour within a digital colour space. For example, the RGB colour space contains three channels—red, green, and blue—and all colours within the RGB colour space are created with a combination of one or more of those three colour channels.

Channel access *n.* 1. A method used in networked systems to gain access to the data communication channel that links two or more computers. Common methods of channel access are contention, polling, and the token ring network. See also channel, contention, polling, token ring network. 2. In wireless technology, an access method such as CDMA (Code Division Multiple Access). See also Code Division Multiple Access.

Channel adapter *n.* A device that enables hardware using two different types of communications channels to communicate.

Channel aggregator *n.* See content aggregator.

Channel capacity *n.* The speed at which a communications channel can transfer information, measured in bits per second (bps) or in baud.

Channel Definition Format *n.* A file format based on XML that describes a channel—a collection of Web pages—on a server. The Channel Definition Format is used with the Active Channel feature in Microsoft Internet Explorer to deliver selected, often personalised, information to individuals on a subscription basis. See also Active Channel, webcasting.

Channel hop *vb.* To switch repeatedly from one IRC channel to another. See also IRC.

Channel op *n.* Short for channel operator. A user on an IRC channel who has the privilege of expelling undesirable participants. See also IRC.

Channel operator *n.* See channel op.

Channel Service Unit *n.* See DDS.

CHAP *n.* See Challenge Handshake Authentication Protocol.

Character *n.* A letter, number, punctuation mark, or other symbol or control code that is represented to a computer by one unit—1 byte—of information. A character is not necessarily visible, either on the screen or on paper; a space, for example, is as much a character as is the letter a or any of the digits 0 through 9. Because computers must manage not only so-called printable characters but also the look (formatting) and transfer of electronically stored information, a character can additionally indicate a carriage return or a paragraph mark in a word-processed document. It can be a signal to sound a beep, begin a new page, or mark the end of a file. See also ASCII, control character, EBCDIC.

Character cell *n.* A rectangular block of pixels that represents the space in which a given character is drawn on the screen. Computer displays use different numbers of pixels as character cells. Character cells are not always the same size for a given font, however; for proportionally spaced fonts, such as those commonly displayed on the Apple Macintosh, the height within a given font remains the same, but the width varies with each character.

Character code *n.* A specific code that represents a particular character in a set, such as the ASCII character set. The character code for a given key depends on whether another key, such as Shift, is pressed at the same time. For example, pressing the A key alone normally generates the character code for a lowercase a. Pressing Shift plus the A key normally generates the character code for an uppercase A.

Character definition table *n.* A table of patterns that a computer can hold in memory and use as a reference for determining the arrangement of dots used to create and display bitmapped characters on the screen. See also bitmapped font.

Character density *n.* In printing or screen display, a measure of the number of characters per unit of area or of linear distance. See also pitch (definition 1).

Character device *n.* 1. A computer device, such as a keyboard or printer, that receives or transmits information as a stream of characters, one character at a time. The characters can be transferred either bit by bit (serial transmission) or byte by byte (parallel transmission) but are not moved from place to place in blocks (groups of bytes). 2. In reference to video displays, a device that handles text but not graphics. See also text mode.

Character entity *n.* In HTML and SGML, the notation for a special character. A character entity begins with an & (ampersand), followed by either a string of letters or of numbers, and ends with a semicolon. The special characters represented by character entities include acute and grave accents, the tilde, and Greek letters, among others. Also called: named entity.

Character generator *n.* A programme or a hardware device that translates a given character code, such as an ASCII code, into a matching pixel pattern for display on the screen. Such devices are typically limited in the number and range of styles of fonts they support, as compared to machines that support bitmapped characters.

Character image *n.* A set of bits arranged in the shape of a character. Each character image exists within a rectangular grid, or character rectangle, that defines its height and width. See also bitmapped font.

Characteristic *n.* In mathematics, the exponent of a floating-point number (the portion following the E that indicates the position of the decimal point) or the integer portion of a logarithm. See also floating-point notation, logarithm.

Character map *n.* In text-based computer graphics, a block of memory addresses that correspond to character spaces on a display screen. The memory allocated to each character space is used to hold the description of the character to be displayed in that space. See also alphageometric.

Character mode *n.* See text mode.

Character-oriented protocol *n.* See byte-oriented protocol.

Character printer *n.* 1. A printer that operates by printing one character at a time, such as a standard dot-matrix printer or a daisy-wheel printer. 2. A printer that cannot print graphics, such as a daisy-wheel printer or even a dot-matrix or laser printer that lacks a graphics mode. Such a printer simply receives character codes from the controlling system and prints the appropriate characters.

Character recognition *n.* The process of applying pattern-matching methods to character shapes that have been read into a computer to determine which alphanumeric characters or punctuation marks the shapes represent. Because different typefaces and text treatments, such as bold and italic, can make big differences in the way characters are shaped, character recognition can be prone to error. Some systems work only with known typefaces and sizes, with no text treatments. These systems achieve very high accuracy levels, but they can work only with text specifically printed for them. Other systems use extremely sophisticated pattern-matching techniques to learn new typefaces and sizes, achieving fairly good accuracy. See also magnetic-ink character recognition, optical character recognition, pattern recognition (definition 1).

Character rectangle *n.* The space taken up by the graphical representation (bit map) of a character. See the illustration. See also bit map.

Character set *n.* A grouping of alphabetic, numeric, and other characters that have some relationship in common. For example, the standard ASCII character set includes letters, numbers, symbols, and control codes that make up the ASCII coding scheme.

Characters per inch *n.* A measurement for the number of characters of a particular size and font that can fit into a line one inch long. This number is affected by two attributes of the type: its point size and the width of the letters in the particular font being measured. In monospace fonts, characters have a constant width; in proportional fonts, characters have varying widths. Thus, measurements of the number of characters per inch must be averaged. Acronym: cpi. See also monospace font, pitch (definition 1), proportional font.

Characters per second *n.* 1. A measure of the speed of a nonlaser printer, such as a dot-matrix or an ink-jet printer. 2. A measure of the rate at which a device, such as a disk drive, can transfer data. In serial communications, the speed of a modem in bits per second can generally be divided by 10 for a rough determination of the number of characters per second transmitted. Acronym: CPS.

Character string *n.* A set of characters treated as a unit and interpreted by a computer as text rather than numbers. A character string can contain any sequence of elements from a given character set, such as letters, numbers, control characters, and extended ASCII characters. Also called: string. See also ASCII, control character, extended ASCII.

Character style *n.* Any attribute, such as boldface, italic, underline, or small caps, applied to a character. Depending on the operating system or programme considered, the range of character styles of text might or might not include the font, which refers to the design of a group of characters in a given size. See also font family.

Character user interface *n.* A user interface that displays only text characters. Acronym: CUI. See also user interface.

Charge *n.* A property of subatomic particles, which can have either a negative charge or a positive charge. In electronics, a charge consists of either an excess of electrons (a negative charge) or a deficiency of electrons (a positive charge). The unit of charge is the coulomb, which corresponds to 6.26 x 1018 electrons.

Charge-coupled device *n.* A device in which individual semiconductor components are connected so that the electrical charge at the output of one device provides the input to the next. The light-detecting component of digital cameras and many video cameras is a charge-coupled device. Acronym: CCD.

Chart *n.* A graphic or diagram that displays data or the relationships between sets of data in pictorial rather than numeric form.

Chassis *n.* A metal frame on which electronic components, such as printed circuit boards, fans, and power supplies, are mounted. See the illustration.

Chat 1 *n.* 1. Real-time conversation via computer. When a participant types a line of text and then presses the Enter key, that participant's words appear on the screens of the other participants, who can then respond in kind. Most online services support chat; on the Internet, IRC is the usual system. See also IRC. 2. An Internet utility programme that supports chat. IRC has largely superseded it.

Chat 2 *vb.* To carry on a real-time conversation with other users by computer. See also IRC.

Chat room *n.* The informal term for a data communication channel that links computers and permits users to "converse" by sending text messages to one another in real time. Similar to the channels provided by IRC (Internet Relay Chat), chat rooms are available through online services and some electronic bulletin board systems (BBSs). Chat rooms are often devoted to a particular subject or are conducted on a certain schedule. See also BBS, chat, IRC, room.

Cheapernet *n.* See 10Base2.

Cheat code *n.* In computer games, a secret keyboard sequence or code that gives a player an advantage in the game. For example, cheat codes often confer more ammunition, lives, or the ability to fly or walk through obstacles. See also adventure games, computer games.

Check bit *n.* One of a set of bits that are added to a data message at its origin and scrutinised by the receiving process to determine whether an error has occurred during transmission. The simplest example is a parity bit. See also data integrity, parity bit.

Check box *n.* An interactive control often found in graphical user interfaces. Check boxes are used to enable or disable one or more features or options from a set. When an option is selected, an x or a check mark appears in the box. See also control (definition 2).

Check digit *n.* A digit added to an account number or other identifying key value and then recomputed when the number is used. This process determines whether an error occurred when the number was entered. See also checksum.

Checkpoint *n.* 1. A processing juncture at which the normal operation of a programme or system is momentarily suspended in order to determine its environmental status. 2. A file containing information that describes the state of the system (the environment) at a particular time.

Checksum *n.* A calculated value that is used to test data for the presence of errors that can occur when data is transmitted or when it is written to disk. The checksum is calculated for a given chunk of data by sequentially combining all the bytes of data with a series of arithmetic or logical operations. After the data is transmitted or stored, a new checksum is calculated in the same way using the (possibly faulty) transmitted or stored data. If the two checksums do not match, an error has occurred and the data should be transmitted or stored again. Checksums cannot detect all errors, and they cannot be used to correct erroneous data. See also error-correction coding.

Cheese worm *n.* An Internet worm that patches security holes created by the Lion worm. The Cheese worm searches out and infects Linux-based systems that were previously compromised by the Lion worm, repairing vulnerabilities and closing a back door left by the earlier infection. It then uses the healed computer to scan for other vulnerable computers connected to the Internet and sends itself to them.

Chernobyl packet *n.* A form of network attack in which a data packet sent by a hacker activates every available option for the protocol in use on the receiving system. The Chernobyl packet will cause a packet storm that will eventually overload and crash the network. Also called: kamikaze packet.

Chernobyl virus *n.* See CIH virus.

Chiclet keyboard *n.* A microcomputer keyboard used on the first version of the IBM PCjr home computer. Chiclet keys are small and square, resembling the chewing gum pieces, and they act like pushbuttons, without the resistance and clear feedback of traditional keys. They are also much smaller and typically are spread out, so touch typing is more difficult than on a conventional keyboard.

Child *n.* 1. A process initiated by another process (the parent). This initiating action is frequently called a fork. The parent process often sleeps (is suspended) until the child process stops executing. 2. In a tree structure, the relationship of a node to its immediate predecessor. See also generation (definition 2), tree structure.

Child process *n.* See child (definition 1).

Children's Online Privacy Protection Act *n.* See COPPA.

Chimes of doom *n.* In Macintosh computers, a series of chimes that sound as a result of serious system failure.

Chip *n.* See integrated circuit.

Chip card *n.* See smart card.

Chip set or chipset *n.* A collection of chips designed to function as a unit in the performance of some common task. The term is most commonly used to refer to the set of integrated circuits, such as the programmable interrupt controller, that support a CPU together with the CPU itself. Often a chip set will fit on one chip. See also CPU, integrated circuit, programmable interrupt controller.

Choke *n.* See inductor.

Choose *vb.* To pick a command or an option from within a graphical user interface, as by clicking a button in a dialog box or pulling down a menu and then releasing the mouse button on one of its options. Although select is often used instead of choose to describe the same action, choose is the preferred term because select has specific connotations within computing. See also select.

Chooser *n.* On the Apple Macintosh, a desk accessory that allows the user to select a printer or a device on a network, such as a file server or a printer.

Chooser extension *n.* A programme that adds items to the Macintosh Chooser desk accessory. At system startup, Chooser adds to its menu of options from the extensions available in the system extensions folder. For example, if you want to use a particular printer with your Mac OS, you must have the right Chooser extension for that printer in the extensions folder when the computer is turned on. See also Chooser, extension (definition 4).

Chroma *n.* The quality of a colour that combines hue and saturation. See also hue, saturation.

CHRP *n.* See Common Hardware Reference Platform.

Churn rate *n.* The rate of customer subscription turnover. In beeper, cell phone, and online businesses, it is common for customers to drop their monthly subscriptions, creating a churn rate as high as 2 or 3 percent per month. High churn rates are costly to companies because attracting new subscribers through advertising and promotion is expensive.

CIDR *n.* See classless interdomain routing.

CIFS *n.* See Common Internet File System.

CIH virus *n.* A highly destructive virus that first appeared in early 1998. When activated, the CIH virus code will attempt to overwrite the flash BIOS of infected machines, rendering the computer unbootable. The CIH virus is also known as the Chernobyl virus because in its original form it was set to activate on the anniversary of the Chernobyl nuclear accident. Although the CIH virus lacks stealth or sophisticated replication capabilities and is easily detected by current virus security programmes, it continues to appear regularly. Also called: Chernobyl virus. See also virus.

CIM *n.* 1. Acronym for Common Information Model. A conceptual specification supported by the Desktop Management Task Force (DMTF) for applying an object-oriented, Web-based model to describing management data in an enterprise network. Part of the DMTF's Web-Based Enterprise Management initiative, CIM is a system-independent and application-independent common framework for describing and sharing management information. It is based on a three-tiered model based on schemas—sets of classes: the Core Schema covers all areas of management; Common Schemas cover specific management areas, such as networks, applications, and devices; and Extension Schemas cover specific technologies, such as operating systems and applications. CIM is supported by a number of industry vendors, including Sun, IBM, Microsoft, and Cisco. See also DMTF, WBEM. 2. Acronym for computer-integrated manufacturing. The use of computers, communication lines and specialised software to automate both the managerial functions and the operational activiti

CIP *n.* 1. Short for Commerce Interchange Pipeline. A Microsoft technology that provides for secure routing of business dat between applications over a public network such as the Internet. CIP is independent of data format and supports encryption and digital signatures, as well as various transport protocols including SMTP, HTTP, DCOM, and EDI value-added networks. Typically, data such as invoices and purchase orders travel over a network through a transmit pipeline and are read from the network by a receive pipeline that decodes and prepares the data for the receiving application. 2. Short for Common Indexing Protocol. A protocol defined by the Internet Engineering Task Force (IETF) for enabling servers to share indexing information. CIP was developed to provide servers with a standard means of sharing information about the contents of their databases.

Cipher *n.* 1. A code. 2. An encoded character. 3. A zero.

Ciphertext *n.* The scrambled or otherwise encoded text of an encrypted message. See also encryption.

Circuit *n.* 1. Any path that can carry electrical current. 2. A combination of electrical components interconnected to perform a particular task. At one level, a computer consists of a single circuit; at another, it consists of hundreds of interconnected circuits.

Circuit analyzer *n.* Any device for measuring one or more characteristics of an electrical circuit. Voltage, current, and resistance are the characteristics most commonly measured. Oscilloscopes are circuit analyzers.

Circuit board *n.* A flat piece of insulating material, such as epoxy or phenolic resin, on which electrical components are mounted and interconnected to form a circuit. Most modern circuit boards use patterns of copper foil to interconnect the components. The foil layers may be on one or both sides of the board and, in more advanced designs, in several layers within the board. A printed circuit board is one in which the pattern of copper foil is laid down by a printing process such as photolithography. See the illustration. See also board, printed circuit board.

Circuit breaker *n.* A switch that opens and cuts off the flow of current when the current exceeds a certain level. Circuit breakers are placed at critical points in circuits to protect against damage that could result from excessive current flow, which is typically caused by component failure. Circuit breakers are often used in place of fuses because they need only to be reset rather than replaced.

Circuit card *n.* See circuit board.

Circuit Data Services *n.* A GTE service that uses circuit switching technology to provide fast data transfer using a laptop computer and cellular telephone. Acronym: CDS. See also circuit switching.

Circuit-switched data *n.* An ISDN option that can be specified for B (bearer) channels that enables an ISDN user to transmit digital data over the channel at 64 Kbps along a point-to-point, dedicated connection for the duration of a call. Acronym: CSD. See also alternate circuit-switched voice/circuit-switched data, B channel, ISDN.

Circuit-switched voice *n.* An ISDN option that can be specified for B (bearer) channels that uses the channel to set up a point-to-point, dedicated connection for the digital transmission of voice communications for the duration of a call. Acronym: CSV. See also alternate circuit-switched voice/circuit-switched data, B channel, ISDN.

Circuit switching *n.* A method of opening communications lines, as through the telephone system, by creating a physical link between the initiating and receiving parties. In circuit switching, the connection is made at a switching center, which physically connects the two parties and maintains an open line between them for as long as needed. Circuit switching is typically used on the dial-up telephone network, and it is also used on a smaller scale in privately maintained communications networks. Unlike other methods of transmission, such as packet switching, it requires the link to be established before any communication can take place.

Circular list *n.* A linked or chained list in which processing continues through all items, as in a ring, and returns to the starting point, no matter where that point is located in the list. See also linked list.

CIS *n.* 1. Acronym for CompuServe Information Service See CompuServe. 2. Short for contact image sensor. A light-sensitive mechanism used in scanners and fax machines. A CIS scanner reflects light from a row of light-emitting diodes (LEDs) onto a document or other object and converts the reflected light to digital images. CIS sensors are smaller and lighter than the charge-coupled devices (CCDs) traditionally used in scanners, but the image quality they produce is not as good as the image quality produced by CCDs. See also light-emitting diode, scanner.

CISC *n.* Acronym for complex instruction set computing. The implementation of complex instructions in a microprocessor design so that they can be invoked at the assembly language level. The instructions can be very powerful, allowing for complicated and flexible ways of calculating such elements as memory addresses. All this complexity, however, usually requires many clock cycles to execute each instruction.

CIX *n.* See Commercial Internet Exchange.

CKO *n.* Acronym for Chief Knowledge Officer. A corporate executive in charge of management and distribution of all the business and technical knowledge of a company. The CKO maximises the value of stored knowledge by ensuring that employees have access, and by avoiding knowledge loss caused by technology-based changes and upgrades in databases and other storage.

ClariNet *n.* A commercial service that distributes news articles from United Press International (UPI) and other news agencies in newsgroups that are part of the clari. hierarchy. Unlike most other newsgroups, access to the clari. newsgroups is restricted to Internet service providers who pay a subscription fee to ClariNet.

Clari. newsgroups *n.* Internet newsgroups maintained by ClariNet Communications, Inc. ClariNet newsgroups contain news articles obtained from the Reuters and United Press International wire services, SportsTicker, Commerce Business Daily, and other sources. Unlike most other newsgroups, ClariNet groups are only accessible through Internet service providers who purchase the service. See also ClariNet, ISP, newsgroup.

ClarisWorks *n.* See AppleWorks.

Class *n.* 1. In object-oriented programming, a generalised category that describes a group of more specific items, called objects, that can exist within it. A class is a descriptive tool used in a programme to define a set of attributes or a set of services (actions available to other parts of the programme) that characterise any member (object) of the class. Programme classes are comparable in concept to the categories that people use to organise information about their world, such as animal, vegetable, and mineral, that define the types of entities they include and the ways those entities behave. The definition of classes in object-oriented programming is comparable to the definition of types in languages such as C and Pascal. See also object-oriented programming. 2. For hardware, the method for grouping particular types of devices and buses according to the basic ways that they can be installed and managed by the operating system. The hardware tree is organised by device class, and Windows uses class installers to inst

Class A IP address *n.* A unicast IP address that ranges from 1.0.0.1 through 126.255.255.254. The first octet indicates the network, and the last three octets indicate the host on the network. See also Class B IP address, Class C IP address, IP address classes.

Class A network *n.* An Internet network that can define a maximum of 16,777,215 hosts. Class A networks use the first byte of an IP address to designate the network, with the first (high-order) bit set to 0. The host is designated by the last 3 bytes. Class A addressing currently allows for a maximum of 128 networks. Class A networks are best suited for sites with few networks but numerous hosts and are usually designated for use by large government or educational institutions. See also host, IP address.

Class B IP address *n.* A unicast IP address that ranges from 128.0.0.1 through 191.255.255.254. The first two octets indicate the network, and the last two octets indicate the host on the network. See also Class A IP address, Class C IP address, IP address classes.

Class C IP address *n.* A unicast IP address that ranges from 192.0.0.1 to 223.255.255.254. The first three octets indicate the network, and the last octet indicates the host on the network. See also Class A IP address, Class B IP address, IP address classes.

Classful IP addressing *n.* An IP addressing scheme where IP addresses are organised into classes: Class A, Class B, and Class C. See also IP address classes.

Classic *n.* An environment within Mac OS X that allows a user to run legacy software. Classic emulates the earlier Macintosh operating system chosen by the user and provides support for programmes that aren't compatible with Mac OS X architecture. See also Carbon, Cocoa, Mac OS X.

Classless interdomain routing *n.* An address scheme that uses aggregation strategies to minimise the size of top-level Internet routing tables. Routes are grouped with the objective of minimising the quantity of information carried by core routers. The main requirement for this scheme is the use of routing protocols that support it, such as Border Gateway Protocol (BGP) version 4 and RIP version 2. Acronym: CIDR. See also Border Gateway Protocol, communications protocol, RIP, router, supernetting.

Class library *n.* A collection of standard routines and subprogrammes that a programmer can use in object-oriented programmes. A typical class library for a graphical user interface might include routines for buttons and scroll bars; or a class library for a communications programme might include a routine for dialing a telephone line through a modem. See also class, object-oriented programming.

Classpath *n.* In Java programming, a classpath is an environmental variable that tells the Java Virtual Machine (JVM) and Java programmes where to find class libraries, including user-defined class libraries. See also class, class library, Java Virtual Machine.

Clean boot *n.* Booting or starting a computer using the minimum system files in the operating system. The clean boot is used as a troubleshooting method for isolating problems associated with software that may be calling on the same system resources at the same time, causing conflicts that lower the performance of the system, make some programmes inoperable, or crash the computer. See also boot1, crash1 (definition 1), operating system.

Clean install *n.* Reinstallation of software in a manner that ensures that no application or system files from a previous installation will remain. The procedure prevents smart installer programmes from skipping file installations where a file already exists, which could potentially keep a problem from being removed.

Clean interface *n.* A user interface with simple features and intuitive commands. See also user interface.

Clean room *n.* A room in which dust and other small particles are filtered from the air and in which protective clothing is worn to avoid contaminating electronic components and other delicate, sensitive equipment.

Clear key *n.* A key in the upper left corner of the numeric keypad on some keyboards. In many applications, it clears the currently selected menu choice or deletes the current selection. See the illustration.

Clear memory *vb.* A process that erases all data stored in RAM.

Clear To Send *n.* See CTS.

ClearType *n.* A Microsoft font technology that improves the resolution of text on LCD displays, such as those used on laptop computers. ClearType technology uses proprietary signal processing and the properties of LCD displays to produce clearer, more detailed characters and spacing, and thus significantly increase readability.

CLEC *n.* Acronym for Competitive Local Exchange Carrier. A company that sells access to the public switched telephone network, or other last mile network connections, in competition with a traditional telephone company. See also ILEC, last mile.

Click *vb.* To press and release a mouse button once without moving the mouse. Clicking is usually performed to select or deselect an item or to activate a programme or programme feature. See also right click.

Clicks and mortar *n.* A business that combines an online presence with traditional "bricks and mortar" outlets.

Click speed *n.* The maximum interval between the first and second time a user presses a button on a mouse or other pointing device that will still identify these actions as a double-click to the computer as opposed to two single-clicks. See also double-click, mouse, pointing device.

Clickstream *n.* The path a user takes while browsing a Web site. Each distinct selection made on a Web page adds one click to the stream. The further down the clickstream the user goes without finding the sought item, the more likely he or she is to depart to another Web site. Analysis of usage patterns helps Web site designers create user-friendly site structures, links, and search facilities. See also Web site.

Clickthrough *n.* The number of times that visitors to a Web site click on an advertising banner within a specified period of time. Clickthrough is one of the elements that Web site producers use to decide how much to charge advertisers. See also clickthrough rate.

Clickthrough rate *n.* The proportion of visitors to a Web site who click on a banner advertisement there, expressed as a percentage of total visitors to the Web site. Also called: click rate. See also clickthrough.

Clickwrap agreement *n.* A contract or license in software or on a Web site that sets forth conditions for use of the software or for goods and services distributed through the Web site. Users must agree to the terms in a clickwrap agreement—typically by clicking on a button that states "I Agree" or "Agree"—before they can install the software or utilise goods or services. A clickwrap agreement is an electronic version of an End-User License Agreement. Also called: clickwrap license. See also End-User License Agreement.

Clickwrap license *n.* See clickwrap agreement.

Client *n.* 1. In object-oriented programming, a member of a class (group) that uses the services of another class to which it is not related. See also inheritance (definition 1). 2. A process, such as a programme or task, that requests a service provided by another programme—for example, a word processor that calls on a sort routine built into another programme. The client process uses the requested service without having to "know" any working details about the other programme or the service itself. 3. On a local area network or the Internet, a computer that accesses shared network resources provided by another computer (called a server). See also client/server architecture, server.

Client error *n.* A problem reported by the Hypertext Transfer Protocol (HTTP) client module as the result of difficulty in interpreting a command or the inability to connect properly to a remote host.

Client/server architecture *n.* An arrangement used on LANs (local area networks) that makes use of distributed intelligence to treat both the server and the individual workstations as intelligent, programmable devices, thus exploiting the full computing power of each. This is done by splitting the processing of an application between two distinct components: a "front-end" client and a "back-end" server. The client component is a complete, stand-alone personal computer (not a "dumb" terminal), and it offers the user its full range of power and features for running applications. The server component can be a personal computer, a minicomputer, or a mainframe that provides the traditional strengths offered by minicomputers and mainframes in a time-sharing environment: data management, information sharing between clients, and sophisticated network administration and security features. The client and server machines work together to accomplish the processing of the application being used. Not only does this increase the processing power avail

Client/server network *n.* See client/server architecture.

Client-side image maps *n.* An image map that performs the processing completely within the client programme (i.e., Web browser) itself. Early Web implementations of image maps (circa 1993) transmitted user mouse click coordinates to the Web server for processing. Generally client-side image maps improve the speed of response to the user. See also image map.

Client-side programme *n.* On the Internet, a programme that is run on a client computer rather than on a server computer.

Clip *vb.* 1. To cut off the portion of a displayed image that lies beyond a certain boundary, such as the edge of a window. Certain graphics programmes also support clipping as a means of masking everything but a certain object so that painting tools, for example, can be applied to the object alone. 2. To cut a photograph, drawing, or other illustration from a clip art collection—either in a book or on a disk. See also clip art. 3. To cut off the peaks of a signal in an electronic circuit.

Clip art *n.* A collection—either in a book or on a disk—of proprietary or public-domain photographs, diagrams, maps, drawings, and other such graphics that can be "clipped" from the collection and incorporated into other documents.

Clipboard *n.* 1. A special memory resource maintained by windowing operating systems. The clipboard stores a copy of the last information that was copied or cut. A paste operation passes data from the clipboard to the current programme. A clipboard allows information to be transferred from one programme to another, provided the second programme can read data generated by the first. Data copied using the clipboard is static and will not reflect later changes. See also cut and paste, DDE. 2. A computer that uses a pen as the primary input device. See also clipboard computer, pen computer.

Clipboard computer *n.* A portable computer whose overall appearance and operation resembles that of a traditional clipboard. A clipboard computer has an LCD or similar flat display and has a pen for user input instead of a keyboard, mouse, or other input device; the user operates the computer by touching the pen to the display. Data entered in a clipboard computer is generally transferred to another computer via a cable or a modem. A clipboard computer is used as a traditional clipboard is used, as in field work, data collection, or meetings. See also pen computer, portable computer.

Clipper Chip *n.* An integrated circuit that implements the SkipJack algorithm, an encryption algorithm created by the National Security Agency that encrypts 64-bit blocks of data with an 80-bit key. The Clipper Chip is manufactured by the U.S. government to encrypt telephone data. It has the added feature that it can be decrypted by the U.S. government, which has tried unsuccessfully to make the chip compulsory in the United States. See also encryption.

Clipping path *n.* A polygon or curve that is used to mask an area in a document. Only what is inside the clipping path appears when the document is printed. See also PostScript.

Clip source tag *n.* Computer coding tag that locates a streaming digital media image for use on a Web page. The clip source tag includes the pathway to the image, which may be stored on a Web server, a Web site, or on the computer where the Web page is displayed.

Clobber *vb.* To destroy data, generally by inadvertently writing other data over it.

Clock *n.* 1. The electronic circuit in a computer that generates a steady stream of timing pulses—the digital signals that synchronise every operation. The system clock signal is precisely set by a quartz crystal, typically at a specific frequency between 1 and 50 megahertz. The clock rate of a computer is one of the prime determinants of its overall processing speed, and it can go as high as the other components of the computer allow. Also called: system clock. 2. The battery-backed circuit that keeps track of the time and date in a computer—not the same as the system clock. Also called: clock/calendar.

Clock/calendar *n.* An independent timekeeping circuit used within a microcomputer to maintain the correct time and calendar date. A clock/calendar circuit is battery powered, so it continues running even when the computer is turned off. The time and date kept by the clock/calendar can be used by the operating system (for example, to "stamp" files with the date and time of creation or revision) and by application programmes (for example, to insert the date or time in a document). Also called: clock, internal clock.

Clock doubling *n.* A technology employed by some Intel microprocessors that enables the chip to process data and instructions at twice the speed of the rest of the system. See also i486DX2.

Clocking *n.* See synchronization (definition 3).

Clockless chip *n.* See asynchronous chip.

Clock pulse *n.* An electronic pulse generated periodically by a crystal oscillator to synchronise the actions of a digital device.

Clock rate *n.* The speed at which the internal clock in an electronic device oscillates. In computers, each tick (oscillation) of the clock is called a cycle, and the clock rate is measured in megahertz, or millions of cycles per second. Also called clock speed, the clock rate determines how quickly the CPU can execute basic instructions, such as adding two numbers, and it is used to synchronise the activities of various components in the system. Between 1981, when the IBM PC was released, and early 2002, typical clock rates for personal computers increased about 1000-fold, from 4.77 MHz to 2 GHz and faster. Also called: clock speed, hertz time. See also clock (definition 1).

Clock speed *n.* See clock rate.

Clock tick *n.* See CPU cycle (definition 2).

Clone1 *n.* A copy; in microcomputer terminology, a look-alike, act-alike computer that contains the same microprocessor and runs the same programmes as a better-known, more prestigious, and often more expensive machine.

Clone2 *vb.* To copy or replicate the entire contents of a hard disk drive, including the operating system, configuration settings, and programmes, by creating an image of the hard disk drive. Hard disk drives are often cloned for batch installation on other computers, particularly those on a network, or for use as backups.

Close1 *n.* An FTP command that instructs the client to close the current connection with a server. See also FTP1 (definition 1), Web site.

Close2 *vb.* 1. To end an application's relationship with an open file so that the application will no longer be able to access the file without opening it again. 2. To end a computer's connection with another computer on a network.

Close box *n.* In the Macintosh graphical user interface, a small box in the left corner of a window's title bar. Clicking on the box closes the window.

Close button *n.* In the graphical user interface for Windows 9x, Windows NT, and the X Window System, a square button in the right corner (left corner in X Windows) of a window's title bar with an x mark on it. Clicking on the button closes the window. Also called: X button.

Closed architecture *n.* 1. Any computer design whose specifications are not freely available. Such proprietary specifications make it difficult or impossible for third-party vendors to create ancillary devices that work correctly with a closed-architecture machine; usually only its original maker can build peripherals and add-ons for such a machine. 2. A computer system that provides no expansion slots for adding new types of circuit boards within the system unit. The original Apple Macintosh was an example of a closed architecture.

Closed file *n.* A file not being used by an application. An application must open such a file before reading or writing to it and must close it afterward.

Closed shop *n.* A computer environment in which access to the computer is restricted to programmers and other specialists.

Closed system *n.* See closed architecture (definition 2).

Cloth ribbon *n.* An inked ribbon generally used with impact printers and typewriters. The print element strikes the ribbon and drives it against the paper so as to transfer ink; then the ribbon advances slightly to make fresh ink available. A cloth ribbon is wrapped onto a spool or loaded into a cartridge that is made to fit the printer used. Cloth ribbon, although adequate for most tasks, is sometimes replaced by film ribbon when the crispest possible output is called for. However, a cloth ribbon, which re-inks itself by capillary action, is usable for multiple impressions, unlike a film ribbon.

CLS *n.* Acronym for Common Language Specification. A subset of language features supported by the .NET common language runtime, comprised of features common to several object-oriented programming languages. CLS-compliant components and tools are guaranteed to interoperate with other CLS-compliant components and tools.

Cluster *n.* 1. An aggregation, such as a group of data points on a graph. 2. A communications computer and its associated terminals. 3. In data storage, a disk-storage unit consisting of a fixed number of sectors (storage segments on the disk) that the operating system uses to read or write information; typically, a cluster consists of two to eight sectors, each of which holds a certain number of bytes (characters). 4. A group of independent network servers that operate—and appear to clients—as if they were a single unit. A cluster network is designed to improve network capacity by, among other things, enabling the servers within a cluster to shift work in order to balance the load. By enabling one server to take over for another, a cluster network also enhances stability and minimises or eliminates downtime caused by application or system failure. See also client/server architecture.

Cluster analysis *n.* A technique used in data mining and knowledge discovery to group observations by identifying and extracting like or similar group conditions. Cluster analysis aims to describe the structure of a complex data set. See also ART, data mining.

Cluster controller *n.* An intermediary device that is situated between a computer and a group (cluster) of subsidiary devices, such as terminals on a network, and is used to control the cluster.

Clustering *n.* The grouping of multiple servers in a way that allows them to appear to be a single unit to client computers on a network. Clustering is a means of increasing network capacity, providing live backup in case one of the servers fails, and improving data security. See also cluster (definition 4), server.

Cluster network *n.* See cluster (definition 4).

Cluster virus *n.* A type of virus that infects once but gives the appearance of infecting every application launched. A cluster virus modifies the file system so that it is loaded before any application that the user attempts to open. Because the virus is also run when running any programme, it appears that every programme on the disk is infected.

CLUT *n.* Acronym for Colour Look Up Table. In digital graphics applications, a specific set of colours used in the creation of graphics. When a graphic is created or edited, the user may specify a CLUT that corresponds with the needs of print, Web, or other destination media. In Web design, a specific CLUT of browser-safe colours is used to be certain graphics and designs will display consistently across different platforms and with different browsers. See also browser CLUT, websafe palette.

CMI *n.* Acronym for computer-managed instruction. Any type of teaching that uses computers as educational tools. See also CAI, CBT.

CMOS *n.* 1. Acronym for complementary metal-oxide semiconductor. A semiconductor technology in which pairs of metal-oxide semiconductor field-effect transistors (MOSFETs), one N-type and one P-type, are integrated on a single silicon chip. Generally used for RAM and switching applications, these devices have very high speed and extremely low power consumption. They are, however, easily damaged by static electricity. See also MOSFET, N-type semiconductor, P-type semiconductor. 2. The battery-backed memory used to store parameter values needed to boot PCs, such as the type of disks and the amount of memory, as well as the clock/calendar time.

CMOS RAM *n.* Short for random access memory. made using complementary metal-oxide semiconductor technology. CMOS chips consume extremely little power and have high tolerance for noise from the power supply. These characteristics make CMOS chips, including CMOS RAM chips, very useful in hardware components that are powered by batteries, such as most microcomputer clocks and certain types of scratchpad RAM that are maintained by the operating system. See also CMOS (definition 1), parameter RAM, RAM.

CMOS setup *n.* A system configuration utility, accessible at boot time, for setting up certain system options, such as the date and time, the kind of drives installed, and port configuration. See also CMOS (definition 2).

CMS *n.* See colour management system.

CMY *n.* Acronym for cyan-magenta-yellow. A model for describing colours that are produced by absorbing light, as by ink on paper, rather than by emitting light, as on a video monitor. The three kinds of cone cells in the eye respond to red, green, and blue light, which are absorbed (removed from white light) by cyan, magenta, and yellow pigments, respectively. Percentages of pigments in these subtractive primary colours can therefore be mixed to get the appearance of any desired colour. Absence of any pigment leaves white unchanged; adding 100 percent of all three pigments turns white to black.

CMYK *n.* Acronym for cyan-magenta-yellow-black. A colour model that is similar to the CMY colour model but produces black with a separate black component rather than by adding 100 percent of cyan, magenta, and yellow. See also CMY.

Coaxial cable *n.* A round, flexible, two-conductor cable consisting of—from the center outwards—a copper wire, a layer of protective insulation, a braided metal mesh sleeve, and an outer shield, or jacket of PVC or fire-resistant material. The shield prevents signals transmitted on the center wire from affecting nearby components and prevents external interference from affecting the signal carried on the center wire. Coaxial cable is widely used in networks. It is the same type of wiring as that used for cable television. See the illustration.

COBOL *n.* Acronym for Common Business-Oriented Language. A verbose, English-like compiled programming language developed between 1959 and 1961 and still in widespread use today, especially in business applications typically run on mainframes. A COBOL programme consists of an Identification Division, which specifies the name of the programme and contains any other documentation the programmer wants to add; an Environment Division, which specifies the computers being used and the files used in the programme for input and output; a Data Division, which describes the format of the data structures used in the programme; and a Procedure Division, which contains the procedures that dictate the actions of the programme. See also compiled language.

Cobweb site *n.* A Web site that is far out of date. See also Web site.

Cocoa *n.* A set of object-oriented development tools and interfaces available on Mac OS X. Cocoa contains a set of frameworks, software components, and development tools used to construct applications for Mac OS X and provides programming interfaces in Java and Objective-C. Cocoa is based on NeXT's OpenStep and is integrated with Apple technologies.

CODASYL *n.* Acronym for Conference on Data Systems Languages. An organisation founded by the U.S. Department of Defense. CODASYL is dedicated to the development of data-management systems and languages, among them the widely used COBOL.

Code1 *n.* 1. Programme instructions. Source code consists of human-readable statements written by a programmer in a programming language. Machine code consists of numerical instructions that the computer can recognise and execute and that were converted from source code. See also data, programme. 2. A system of symbols used to convert information from one form to another. A code for converting information in order to conceal it is often called a cipher. 3. One of a set of symbols used to represent information.

Code2 *vb.* To write programme instructions in a programming language. See also programme.

Code access security *n.* A mechanism provided by the runtime whereby managed code is granted permissions by security policy and these permissions are enforced, limiting what operations the code will be allowed to perform. To prevent unintended code paths from exposing a security vulnerability, all callers on the call stack must be granted the necessary permissions (possibly subject to override by assertion or denial).

Codec *n.* 1. Short for coder/decoder. Hardware that can convert audio or video signals between analog and digital forms. 2. Short for compressor/decompressor. Hardware or software that can compress and uncompress audio or video data. See also compress2, uncompress. 3. Hardware that combines the functions of definitions 1 and 2.

Code conversion *n.* 1. The process of translating programme instructions from one form into another. Code may be converted at the source-language level (for example, from C to Pascal), at the hardware-platform level (for example, from working on the IBM PC to working on the Apple Macintosh), or at the language level (for example, from source code in C to machine code). See also code1 (definition 1). 2. The process of transforming data from one representation to another, such as from ASCII to EBCDIC or from two's complement to binary-coded decimal.

Code Division Multiple Access *n.* A form of multiplexing in which the transmitter encodes the signal, using a pseudo-random sequence that the receiver also knows and can use to decode the received signal. Each different random sequence corresponds to a different communication channel. Motorola uses Code Division Multiple Access for digital cellular phones. Acronym: CDMA. Also called: spread spectrum. See also multiplexing, transmitter.

Code page *n.* In MS-DOS versions 3.3 and later, a table that relates the binary character codes used by a programme to keys on the keyboard or to the appearance of characters on the display. Code pages are a means of providing support for character sets and keyboard layouts used in different countries. Devices such as the display and the keyboard can be configured to use a specific code page and to switch from one code page (such as United States) to another (such as Portugal) at the user's request.

Code profiler *n.* A tool designed to aid developers in identifying and eliminating the code inefficiencies that cause bottlenecks and degrade performance in their applications. Code profilers analyse an executing application to determine both how long functions take to execute and how often they are called. Using a code profiler is a repetitive process in that the tool must be reused after each section of inefficient code has been found and corrected.

Coder *n.* See programmer.

Code Red worm *n.* A fast-spreading and pernicious Internet worm first discovered in mid-2001. The Code Red worm propagates quickly, and any machine that was infected once is potentially vulnerable to re-infection. The Code Red worm is time sensitive, spreading in propagation mode from the 1st to the 19th of each month, attacking in flood mode from the 20th to the 27th, and finally hiding in hibernation mode until the 1st of the next month when the cycle begins again. The worm maintains a list of all computers previously infected, and all these computers will be attacked each month by every newly infected machine. This makes total eradication of the worm difficult because a single machine remaining infected from earlier propagation/attack cycles can potentially re-infect every machine on the list, and each computer might be subject to multiple attacks. At least three versions of the Code Red worm are known to exist. The Code Red worm was named for a caffeinated soft drink by the security team that first tracked the worm.

Code segment *n.* 1. A memory segment containing programme instructions. 2. A named and segregated portion of a program's code typically performing a specific class of operations. Code segments in this sense are often loaded into memory as memory segments. The main programme segment is kept in memory, and auxiliary segments are loaded only when they are required.

Code signing *n.* The process of adding a digital signature to additions and updates made to source code and applications published on the Internet. Code signing is intended to provide a level of security and trust to Internet software distribution. See also digital signature.

Code snippet *n.* 1. In a graphical user interface, programming instructions embedded in a menu option or button defined by the user. The snippet—consisting of one or more lines of source code—determines what the option or button does when chosen or clicked. 2. A small piece of programming code that is part of a larger programme. Usually the code snippet performs a specific function or task.

Coding form *n.* A sheet of paper ruled with horizontal and vertical lines to aid in writing source code for older languages that have position-dependent syntax (such as FORTRAN). Most programmers now use graph paper if they use paper at all.

Coercion *n.* See cast.

Coffee Pot Control Protocol *n.* See HTCPCP.

Coherence *n.* 1. In raster-scan technology, the assignment of the value of one pixel to the pixel next to it. 2. In optics, the property of some electromagnetic waves of being in phase with one another, as in light from a laser.

Cold boot *n.* A startup process that begins with turning on the computer's power. Typically, a cold boot involves some basic hardware checking by the system, after which the operating system is loaded from disk into memory. See also boot1.

Cold fault *n.* A fatal error that occurs immediately upon or shortly after startup as a result of the misalignment of components in the system. The process of running and shutting down any computer induces a series of thermal expansions and contractions in its internal components. Over time, these changes in the dimensions of components can create a microscopic crack in a chip or loosen a pin in a socket; thus, the system crashes when cold, but the problem seems to disappear after the machine is warm. For this reason, some users leave the system unit (but not the monitor) of a computer running from day to day, rather than turn the machine on only when needed.

Cold link *n.* A link established upon a request for data. Once the request is filled, the link is broken. The next time data is required, a link from the client to the server must be reestablished. In a client/server architecture, cold links are useful when the linked item consists of a large amount of data. Dynamic Data Exchange (DDE), used in applications such as Microsoft Excel, uses cold links for data exchange. See also client/server architecture, DDE.

Cold start *n.* See cold boot.

Collaboration data object *n.* Microsoft Exchange Server technology for creating messaging and collaboration applications. A collaboration data object consists of a scripting interface added to Microsoft Messaging Application Programming Interface (MAPI). Acronym: CDO.

Collaborative filtering *n.* A means of deriving information from the experiences and opinions of a number of people. The term was coined by Doug Terry at Xerox PARC, who first used the technique by allowing users to annotate documents as they read them and to choose which documents to read next based not only on their content but also on what others wrote about them. A common use of collaborative filtering is the creation of lists of World Wide Web pages of interest to particular people; by documenting the experiences of several people, a list of interesting Web sites can be "filtered." Collaborative filtering is also used as a marketing research tool; by keeping a database of opinions and ratings regarding several products, researchers can predict which new products the people contributing to the database will like.

Collapsed backbone *n.* See backbone (definition 3).

Collate *vb.* In data handling, to merge items from two or more similar sets to create a combined set that maintains the order or sequence of items in the original sets.

Collating sort *n.* A sort that proceeds by continuous merging of two or more files to produce a certain sequence of records or data items.

Collation sequence *n.* The ordering relationship (sequence) among objects that is to be established by a collating sort. See also collating sort.

Collector *n.* The region of a bipolar transistor into which charge carriers flow under normal operating conditions. The output of the transistor is usually taken from the collector. With respect to the base and emitter, the collector is positive in an NPN transistor and negative in a PNP transistor. See also NPN transistor, PNP transistor.

Collision *n.* The result of two devices or network workstations trying to transmit signals at the exact same time on the same channel. The typical outcome is a garbled transmission.

Collision detection *n.* 1. The process by which a node on a local area network monitors the communications line to determine when a collision has occurred; that is, when two nodes have attempted to transmit at the same time. Although network stations usually avoid collisions by monitoring the line and waiting for it to clear before transmitting, the method is not foolproof. When a collision does occur, the two nodes involved usually wait a random amount of time before attempting to retransmit. See also contention, CSMA/CD. 2. The process by which a game or simulation programme determines whether two objects on the screen are touching each other. This is a time-consuming, often complicated procedure; some computers optimised for graphics and games, such as the Amiga, have special hardware built in specifically to detect collisions.

Colocation or co-location *n.* The operation of a server, router, or other device in a facility that provides a dedicated Internet connection, physical space in a secured cage, and regulated power. Colocation services often include fire detection and extinguishing, backup power, technical support, and additional security measures to ensure high availability.

Colour *n.* In physics, the component of the human perception of light that depends on frequency. For light of a single frequency, colour ranges from violet at the high-frequency end of the visible-light band (a small portion of the total electromagnetic spectrum) to red at the low-frequency end. In computer video, colour is produced by a combination of hardware and software. Software manipulates combinations of bits that represent the distinct shades of colour that are destined for particular positions on the screen (characters or individual dots, called pixels). The video adapter hardware translates these bits into electrical signals, which in turn control the brightnesses of different-coloured phosphors at the corresponding positions on the screen of the monitor CRT. The user's eye unites the light from the phosphors to perceive a single colour. See also colour model, colour monitor, CRT, HSB, monitor, RGB, video, video adapter.

Colour bits *n.* A predetermined number of bits assigned to each displayable pixel that determine the pixel's colour when it is displayed on a monitor. For example, two colour bits are required for four colours; eight colour bits are required for 256 colours. See also pixel image.

Colour box *n.* In the Windows NT and Windows 9x Paint accessory, a graphic screen element in the form of a paint box that is used to select foreground and background colours.

Colour burst *n.* A technique used to encode colour in a composite video signal, originally developed so that black-and-white television monitors could display programmes broadcast in colour. The colour burst consists of a combination of the red, green, and blue intensities (used by black-and-white displays) and two colour-difference signals that determine separate red, green, and blue intensities (used by colour displays). See also colour look-up table.

Colour cycling *n.* A technique used in computer graphics for changing the colour of one or more pixels on the screen by changing the colour palette used by the video adapter rather than by changing the colour bits for each pixel. For example, to cause a red circle to fade away to a black background colour, the programme need only change the set of signal values corresponding to "red" in the video adapter's colour look-up table, periodically making it darker until it matches the black background. At each step, the apparent colour of the whole circle changes instantly; it appears to fade rather than to be painted over and over. The speed at which and the degree to which the circle fades are entirely up to the programmer.

Colour depth *n.* The number of colour values that can be assigned to a single pixel in an image. Also known as bit depth, colour depth can range from 1 bit (black and white) to 32 bits (over 16.7 million colours). See also bit depth.

Colour gamut *n.* The particular range of colours that a device is able to produce. A device such as a scanner, monitor, or printer can produce a unique range of colours, which is determined by the characteristics of the device itself. See also rendering intent.

Colour/Graphics Adapter *n.* See CGA.

Colourimeter *n.* A device that evaluates and identifies colours in terms of a standard set of synthesised colours.

Colour look-up table *n.* A table stored in a computer's video adapter, containing the colour signal values that correspond to the different colours that can be displayed on the computer's monitor. When colour is displayed indirectly, a small number of colour bits are stored for each pixel and are used to select a set of signal values from the colour look-up table. Also called: colour map, colour table, video look-up table. See also colour bits, palette (definition 2), pixel.

Colour Look Up Table *n.* See CLUT.

Colour management *n.* The process of producing or reproducing accurate, consistent colour across any of a variety of colour input, output, and display devices. Colour management includes, but is not limited to, accurate conversion of RGB input from input devices such as a scanner or a camera or from display devices such as a monitor to CMYK output for an output device such as a printer. Colour management also encompasses application of a device profile, which contains information on colour behaviour for the printer or other device on which the image will be reproduced, and allowance for environmental variations such as humidity and lighting. See also CMYK, RGB.

Colour management system *n.* A technology designed to calibrate, characterize, and process colour production and reproduction across a variety of colour input, output, and display devices. See also colour management.

Colour map *n.* See colour look-up table.

Colour model *n.* Any method or convention for representing colour in desktop publishing and graphic arts. In the graphic arts and printing fields, colours are often specified with the Pantone system. In computer graphics, colours can be described using any of several different colour systems: HSB (hue, saturation, and brightness), CMY (cyan, magenta, and yellow), and RGB (red, green, and blue). See also CMY, HSB, Pantone Matching System, process colour, RGB, spot colour.

Colour monitor *n.* A video display device designed to work with a video card or an adapter to produce text or graphics images in colour. A colour monitor, unlike a monochrome display, has a screen coated internally with patterns of three phosphors that glow red, green, and blue when struck by an electron beam. To create colours such as yellow, pink, and orange, the three phosphors are lighted together in varying degrees. A video card that uses large groups of bits (6 or more) to describe colours and that generates analog (continuously variable) signals is capable of generating an enormous potential range of colours on a colour monitor. See also colour, colour model, Cycolour.

Colour palette *n.* See palette (definition 1).

Colour plane *n.* See bit plane.

Colour printer *n.* A computer printer that can print full-colour output. Most colour printers can also produce black-and-white output.

Colour saturation *n.* The amount of a hue contained in a colour; the more saturation, the more intense the colour. See also colour model, HSB.

Colour scanner *n.* A scanner that converts images to a digitized format and is able to interpret colour. Depth of colour depends on the scanner's bit depth—its ability to transform colour into 8, 16, 24, or 32 bits. High-end colour scanners, commonly used when output is to be printed, are able to encode information at a high resolution or number of dots per inch (dpi). Low-end colour scanners encode information at a resolution of 72 dpi and are commonly used for computer screen images not intended for printing. See also resolution (definition 1), scanner.

Colour separation *n.* 1. The process of printing the colours in a document as separate output files, each of which is to be printed using a different-coloured ink. There are two types of colour separation: spot colour separation and process colour separation. See also colour model, process colour, spot colour. 2. One of the output files produced by a colour document, to be printed in its own colour of ink.

Colour space *n.* A means of describing colour in digital environments. RGB is the most common colour space on the Web, and with other colour, the most common colour space viewed on computer displays, while CMYK is the main colour space for desktop publishing and other digital print media.

Colour supertwist nematic display *n.* See supertwist display.

Colour table *n.* See colour look-up table.

Column *n.* 1. A series of items arranged vertically within some type of framework—for example, a continuous series of cells running from top to bottom in a spreadsheet, a set of lines of specified width on a printed page, a vertical line of pixels on a video screen, or a set of values aligned vertically in a table or matrix. 2. In a relational database management system, the name for an attribute. The collection of column values that form the description of a particular entity is called a tuple or row. A column is equivalent to a field in a record in a nonrelational file system. See also entity, field (definition 1), row, table (definition 2).

Column chart *n.* A bar chart in which values are displayed and printed as vertical bars. See the illustration. See also bar chart.

.com *n.* 1. In the Internet's Domain Name System, the top-level domain that identifies addresses operated by commercial organisations. The domain name .com appears as a suffix at the end of the address. See also DNS (definition 1), domain (definition 3). 2. In MS-DOS, the file extension that identifies a command file. See also COM (definition 3).

COM *n.* 1. A name reserved by the MS-DOS operating system for serial communications ports. For example, if a modem is connected to one serial port and a serial printer to another, the devices are identified as COM1 and COM2 by the operating system. 2. Acronym for Component Object Model. A specification developed by Microsoft for building software components that can be assembled into programmes or add functionality to existing programmes running on Microsoft Windows platforms. COM components can be written in a variety of languages, although most are written in C++, and can be unplugged from a programme at runtime without having to recompile the programme. COM is the foundation of the OLE (object linking and embedding), ActiveX, and DirectX specifications. See also ActiveX, component (definition 2), DirectX, OLE. 3. The extension reserved by MS-DOS for a type of executable binary (programme) file limited to a single 64-kilobyte (KB) segment. COM files are often used for utility programmes and short routines. They are not supp

COM1 *n.* A serial communications port in Wintel systems. COM1 is usually specified by the I/O range 03F8H, is usually associated with interrupt request line IRQ4, and in many systems is used to connect an RS232 serial mouse. See also IRQ.

COM2 *n.* A serial communications port in Wintel systems. COM2 is usually specified by the I/O range 02F8H, is usually associated with interrupt request line IRQ3, and in many systems is used to connect a modem. See also IRQ.

COM3 *n.* A serial communications port in Wintel (Windows running on an Intel chip) systems. COM3 is usually specified by the I/O range 03E8H, is usually associated with interrupt request line IRQ4, and in many systems is used as an alternative to COM1 or COM2 if the latter is being used by some other peripheral. See also IRQ, port, Wintel.

Combinatorial explosion *n.* A condition inherent in certain types of mathematical problems in which small increases in the problem's size (number of data items or parameters of the operation) lead to enormous increases in the time required to obtain a solution. See also combinatorics.

Combinatorics *n.* A branch of mathematics related to probability and statistics, involving the study of counting, grouping, and arrangement of finite sets of elements. Combinatorics involves the two concepts of combinations and permutations. A combination is the grouping of elements taken from a larger set without regard to the order of the elements in each group; for example, taking two elements at a time from a set of four objects (A, B, C, and D) creates six combinations of objects: AB, AC, AD, BC, BD, and CD. A permutation is a grouping of elements taken from a larger set with regard to the order of the elements. For example, in making permutations of two objects from the same set of four objects, there would be four candidates to choose from for the first selection (A), and three left over to choose from for the second selection (B), or 12 permutations in all: AB, AC, AD, BA, BC, BD, CA, CB, CD, DA, DB, DC. See also combinatorial explosion.

COM callable wrapper *n.* A proxy object generated by the runtime so that existing COM applications can use managed classes, including .NET Framework classes, transparently. Acronym: CCW.

COMDEX *n.* Any of a series of annual computer trade shows operated by Softbank COMDEX, Inc. One of these shows takes place in Las Vegas each November and is the largest computer trade show in the United States.

Comma-delimited file *n.* A data file consisting of fields and records, stored as text, in which the fields are separated from each other by commas. Use of comma-delimited files allows communication between database systems that use different formats. If the data in a field contains a comma, the field is further surrounded with quotation marks.

Command *n.* An instruction to a computer programme that, when issued by the user, causes an action to be carried out. Commands are usually either typed at the keyboard or chosen from a menu.

Command buffer *n.* An area in memory in which commands entered by the user are kept. A command buffer can enable the user to repeat commands without retyping them completely, edit past commands to change some argument or correct a mistake, undo commands, or obtain a list of past commands. See also history, template (definition 4).

Command button *n.* A control shaped like a pushbutton in a dialog box in a graphical user interface. By clicking a command button, the user causes the computer to perform some action, such as opening a file that has just been selected using the other controls in the dialog box.

COMMAND.COM *n.* The command interpreter for MS-DOS. See also command interpreter.

Command-driven *adj.* Accepting commands in the form of code words or letters, which the user must learn.

Command-driven system *n.* A system in which the user initiates operations by a command entered from the console.

Command interpreter *n.* A programme, usually part of the operating system, that accepts typed commands from the keyboard and performs tasks as directed. The command interpreter is responsible for loading applications and directing the flow of information between applications. In OS/2 and MS-DOS, the command interpreter also handles simple functions, such as moving and copying files and displaying disk directory information. See also shell1.

Command key *n.* On the original Macintosh keyboard, a key labeled with the special symbol, sometimes called the propeller or puppy foot. This key is found on one or both sides of the Spacebar, depending on the version of the Apple keyboard. The key serves some of the same functions as the Control key on IBM keyboards. See also Control key.

Command language *n.* The set of keywords and expressions that are accepted as valid by the command interpreter. See also command interpreter.

Command line *n.* A string of text written in the command language and passed to the command interpreter for execution. See also command language.

Command-line interface *n.* A form of interface between the operating system and the user in which the user types commands, using a special command language. Although systems with command-line interfaces are usually considered more difficult to learn and use than those with graphical interfaces, command-based systems are usually programmable; this gives them flexibility unavailable in graphics-based systems that do not have a programming interface.

Command mode *n.* A mode of operation in which a programme waits for a command to be issued.

Command prompt window *n.* A window displayed on the desktop used to interface with the MS-DOS operating system. MS-DOS commands are typed at an entry point identified by a blinking cursor. See also MS-DOS.

Command shell *n.* See shell1.

Command state *n.* The state in which a modem accepts commands, such as a command to dial a telephone number.

Comment *n.* Text embedded in a programme for documentation purposes. Comments usually describe what the programme does, who wrote it, why it was changed, and so on. Most programming languages have a syntax for creating comments so that they can be recognised and ignored by the compiler or assembler. Also called: remark. See also comment out.

Comment out *vb.* To disable one or more lines of code from a programme temporarily by enclosing them within a comment statement. See also comment, conditional compilation, nest.

Commerce Interchange Pipeline *n.* See CIP.

Commerce server *n.* An HTTP server designed for conducting online business transactions. Data is transferred between the server and Web browser in an encrypted form to keep information such as credit card numbers reasonably secure. Commerce servers are typically used by online stores and companies that are set up for mail order business. The wares or services offered by the store or company are described and displayed in photographs on the store or company Web site and users can order directly from the site using their Web browser. A number of companies market commerce servers, including Netscape, Microsoft, and Quarterdeck. See also HTTP server (definition 1), Secure Sockets Layer, Web browser.

Commercial access provider *n.* See ISP.

Commercial Internet Exchange *n.* A nonprofit trade organisation of public Internet service providers. In addition to the usual representational and social activities, the organisation also operates an Internet backbone router that is accessible to its members. Acronym: CIX. See also backbone (definition 1), ISP, router.

Commercial off-the-shelf board *n.* A hardware board or platform that is readily available in the industry for purchase and can be used for development or test purposes. Also called: COTS board.

Common Access Method *n.* A standard developed by Future Domain and other SCSI vendors allowing SCSI adapters to communicate with SCSI peripherals regardless of the particular hardware used. See also SCSI.

Common Application Language *n.* See CAL.

Common carrier *n.* A communications company (e.g., a telephone company) that provides service to the public and is regulated by governmental organisations.

Common Client Interface *n.* A control interface begun with the X Windows version of NCSA Mosaic whereby other programmes can control the local copy of a Web browser. The X Windows and Windows versions of NCSA Mosaic can communicate with other programmes via TCP/IP. The Windows version is also capable of OLE communication. Acronym: CCI. See also Mosaic, OLE, TCP/IP, X Window System.

Common Gateway Interface *n.* See CGI (definition 1), CGI script.

Common Hardware Reference Platform *n.* A specification describing a family of machines, based on the PowerPC processor, that are capable of booting multiple operating systems, including Mac OS, Windows NT, AIX, and Solaris. Acronym: CHRP. See also PowerPC.

Common Indexing Protocol *n.* See CIP.

Common Information Model *n.* See CIM (definition 1).

Common Internet File System *n.* A standard proposed by Microsoft that would compete directly with Sun Microsystems' Web Network File System. A system of file sharing of Internet or intranet files. Acronym: CIFS.

Common language runtime *n.* The engine at the core of managed code execution. The runtime supplies managed code with services such as cross-language integration, code access security, object lifetime management, and debugging and profiling support.

Common language runtime host *n.* An unmanaged application that uses a set of APIs, called the hosting interfaces, to integrate managed code into the application. Common language runtime hosts often require a high degree of customization over the runtime that is loaded into the process. The hosting interfaces allow common language runtime hosts to specify settings that configure the garbage collector, select the appropriate build for their environment (server versus workstation), and so on. Common language runtime hosts often support an extensibility model that allows the end user to dynamically add new pieces of functionality, such as a new control or a user-written function. These extensions are typically isolated from each other in the process using application domains and custom security settings. Examples of common language runtime hosts include ASP.NET, Microsoft Internet Explorer, and a host to run executables launched from the Windows Shell.

Common Language Specification *n.* See CLS.

Common LISP *n.* Short for Common List Processing. A formalised and standardised version of the LISP programming language.

Because LISP is in the public domain, a number of different versions of the language have evolved, and Common LISP was made a standard to give programmers a definitive source for LISP. See also LISP, programming language, standard (definition 1).

Common Object Request Broker Architecture *n.* See CORBA.

Common type system *n.* The specification that determines how the runtime defines, uses, and manages types.

Common User Access *n.* A set of standards for management of user interfaces as part of IBM's Systems Application Architecture (SAA). Common User Access is designed to facilitate development of applications that are compatible and consistent across different platforms. Acronym: CUA. See also standard (definition 1), user interface.

Communications *n.* The vast discipline encompassing the methods, mechanisms, and media involved in information transfer. In computer-related areas, communications involves data transfer from one computer to another through a communications medium, such as a telephone, microwave relay, satellite link, or physical cable. Two primary methods of computer communications exist: temporary connection of two computers through a switched network, such as the public telephone system, and permanent or semipermanent linking of multiple workstations or computers in a network. The line between the two is indistinct, however, because microcomputers equipped with modems are often used to access both privately owned and public-access network computers. See also asynchronous transmission, CCITT, channel (definition 2), communications protocol, IEEE, ISDN, ISO/OSI model, LAN, modem, network, synchronous transmission.

Communications Act of 1934 *n.* See FCC.

Communication Satellite Corporation *n.* Corporation created by the U.S. government to provide international satellite services for telecommunications. Acronym: COMSAT.

Communications channel *n.* See channel (definition 2).

Communications controller *n.* A device used as an intermediary in transferring communications to and from the host computer to which it is connected. By relieving the host computer of the actual tasks of sending, receiving, deciphering, and checking transmissions for errors, a communications controller helps to make efficient use of the host computer's processing time—time that might be better used for noncommunications tasks. A communications controller can be either a programmable machine in its own right or a nonprogrammable device designed to follow certain communications protocols. See also front-end processor (definition 2).

Communications link *n.* The connection between computers that enables data transfer.

Communications network *n.* See network.

Communications parameter *n.* Any of several settings required in order to enable computers to communicate. In asynchronous communications, for example, modem speed, number of data bits and stop bits, and type of parity are parameters that must be set correctly to establish communication between two modems.

Communications port *n.* See COM.

Communications programme *n.* A software programme that enables a computer to connect with another computer and to exchange information. For initiating communications, communications programmes perform such tasks as maintaining communications parameters, storing and dialing phone numbers automatically, recording and executing logon procedures, and repeatedly dialing busy lines. Once a connection is made, communications programmes can also be instructed to save incoming messages on disk or to find and transmit disk files. During communication, these types of programmes perform the major, and usually invisible, tasks of encoding data, coordinating transmissions to and from the distant computer, and checking incoming data for transmission errors.

Communications protocol *n.* A set of rules or standards designed to enable computers to connect with one another and to exchange information with as little error as possible. The protocol generally accepted for standardising overall computer communications is a seven-layer set of hardware and software guidelines known as the OSI (Open Systems Interconnection) model. A somewhat different standard, widely used before the OSI model was developed, is IBM's SNA (Systems Network Architecture). The word protocol is often used, sometimes confusingly, in reference to a multitude of standards affecting different aspects of communication, such as file transfer (for example, XMODEM and ZMODEM), handshaking (for example, XON/XOFF), and network transmissions (for example, CSMA/CD). See also ISO/OSI model, SNA.

Communications satellite *n.* A satellite stationed in geosynchronous orbit that acts as a microwave relay station, receiving signals sent from a ground-based station (earth station), amplifying them, and retransmitting them on a different frequency to another ground-based station. Initially used for telephone and television signals, communications satellites can also be used for high-speed transmission of computer data. Two factors affecting the use of satellites with computers, however, are propagation delay (the time lag caused by the distance traveled by the signal) and security concerns. See also downlink, uplink.

Communications server *n.* A gateway that translates packets on a local area network (LAN) into asynchronous signals, such as those used on telephone lines or in RS-232-C serial communications, and allows all nodes on the LAN access to its modems or RS-232-C connections. See also gateway, RS-232-C standard.

Communications slot *n.* On many models of the Apple Macintosh, a dedicated expansion slot for network interface cards. Acronym: CS.

Communications software *n.* The software that controls the modem in response to user commands. Generally such software includes terminal emulation as well as file transfer facilities. See also modem, terminal emulation.

Communications system *n.* The combination of hardware, software, and data transfer links that make up a communications facility.

Communications Terminal Protocol *n.* A terminal protocol that enables a user at a remote location to access a computer as if the remote computer were directly connected (hardwired) to the computer. Acronym: CTERM.

Community antenna television *n.* See CATV.

COMNET Conference & Expo *n.* Conference and exposition for the communications networking industry. The conference features educational sessions and exhibitions on technical and business issues affecting communications networks.

Compact disc *n.* 1. An optical storage medium for digital data, usually audio. A compact disc is a nonmagnetic, polished metal disc with a protective plastic coating that can hold up to 74 minutes of high-fidelity recorded sound. The disk is read by an optical scanning mechanism that uses a high-intensity light source, such as a laser, and mirrors. Also called: optical disc. 2. A technology that forms the basis of media such as CD-ROM, CD-ROM/XA, CD-I, CD-R, DVI, and PhotoCD. These media are all compact disc–based but store various types of digital information and have different read/write capabilities. Documentation for compact disc formats can be found in books designated by the colour of their covers. For example, documentation for audio compact discs is found in the Red Book. See also CD-I, CD-R, CD-ROM, CD-ROM/XA, DVI, Green Book (definition 2), Orange Book (definition 2), PhotoCD, Red Book (definition 2). 3. See CD.

CompactFlash *n.* Plug-in memory devices designed by the CompactFlash Association for use in digital cameras and, eventually, other devices for storing and transporting digital data, sound, images, and video. CompactFlash devices are small cards 1.7 x 1.4 x 0.13 inches (43 x 36 x 3.3 mm) in size. They are based on nonvolatile flash technology, so they do not rely on batteries or other power to retain information. See also digital camera.

CompactFlash Association *n.* A nonprofit association that developed and promotes the CompactFlash specification. Founded in October 1995, it has a membership that includes 3COM, Eastman Kodak Company, Hewlett-Packard, IBM, and NEC, among other corporations. See also CompactFlash.

Compaction *n.* The process of gathering and packing the currently allocated regions of memory or auxiliary storage into as small a space as possible, so as to create as much continuous free space as possible.

Compact model *n.* A memory model of the Intel 80x86 processor family. The compact model allows only 64 kilobytes (KB) for the code of a programme but up to 1 megabyte (MB) for the program's data. See also memory model.

CompactPCI *n.* An open bus specification for industrial computing needs developed by the PCI Industrial Computer Manufacturers Group (PICMG). CompactPCI is based on the desktop-computing PCI bus but differs in a number of respects, including a pin-and-socket connector and a design that allows for front loading and removal of cards. CompactPCI is intended for applications such as industrial automation, military systems, and real-time data acquisition. It is suitable for high-speed communications devices, such as routers, and allows for hot-plugging. See also hot plugging, PCI local bus.

Comparator *n.* A device for comparing two items to determine whether they are equal. In electronics, for example, a comparator is a circuit that compares two input voltages and indicates which is higher.

Compare *vb.* To check two items, such as words, files, or numeric values, so as to determine whether they are the same or different. In a programme, the outcome of a compare operation often determines which of two or more actions is taken next.

Comparison criteria *n.* A set of search conditions that is used to find data. Comparison criteria can be a series of characters that you want to match, such as "Northwind Traders", or an expression, such as ">300".

Compatibility *n.* 1. The degree to which a computer, an attached device, a data file, or a programme can work with or understand the same commands, formats, or language as another. True compatibility means that any operational differences are invisible to people and programmes alike. 2. The extent to which two machines can work in harmony. Compatibility (or the lack thereof) between two machines indicates whether, and to what degree, the computers can communicate, share data, or run the same programmes. For example, an Apple Macintosh and an IBM PC are generally incompatible because they cannot communicate freely or share data without the aid of hardware and/or software that functions as an intermediary or a converter. 3. The extent to which a piece of hardware conforms to an accepted standard (for example, IBM-compatible or Hayes-compatible). In this sense, compatibility means that the hardware ideally operates in all respects like the standard on which it is based.

Compatibility box *n.* See DOS box (definition 1).

Compatibility mode *n.* A mode in which hardware or software in one system supports operations of software from another system. The term often refers to the ability of advanced operating systems designed for Intel microprocessors (for example, OS/2 and Windows NT) to run MS-DOS software or to the ability of some UNIX workstations and of some Apple Macintosh systems to run MS-DOS software.

Competitive Local Exchange Carrier *n.* See CLEC.

Compile *vb.* To translate all the source code of a programme from a high-level language into object code prior to execution of the programme. Object code is executable machine code or a variation of machine code. More generally, compiling is sometimes used to describe translating any high-level symbolic description into a lower-level symbolic or machine-readable format. A programme that performs this task is known as a compiler. See also compiler (definition 2), compile time, high-level language, machine code, source code.

Compile-and-go *adj.* Of, pertaining to, or characteristic of a development environment that automatically runs a programme after compiling it. See also compile, execute.

Compiled Basic *n.* Any version of Basic that is translated into machine code prior to execution by a compiler. Basic has traditionally been an interpreted language (translated and executed statement by statement); because compiled Basic generally produces faster-executing programmes, it is the technology of choice for professional Basic programmers. See also Basic, compiled language, interpreted language.

Compiled language *n.* A language that is translated into machine code prior to any execution, as opposed to an interpreted language, which is translated and executed statement by statement. See also compiler (definition 2).

Compiler *n.* 1. Any programme that transforms one set of symbols into another by following a set of syntactic and semantic rules. 2. A programme that translates all the source code of a programme written in a high-level language into object code prior to execution of the programme. See also assembler, compile, high-level language, interpreted language, language processor, object code.

Compile time *n.* 1. The amount of time required to perform a compilation of a programme. Compile time can range from a fraction of a second to many hours, depending on the size and complexity of the programme, the speed of the compiler, and the performance of the hardware. See also compiler (definition 2). 2. The point at which a programme is being compiled (i.e., most languages evaluate constant expressions at compile time but evaluate variable expressions at run time). See also link time, run time.

Compile-time binding *n.* Assignment of a meaning to an identifier (such as a function name or a constant) in a programme at the time the programme is compiled rather than at the time it is run.

Complement *n.* Loosely, a number that can be thought of as the mirror image of another number written to the same base, such as base 10 or base 2. Complements are commonly used to represent negative numbers. Two types of complements are encountered in computer-related contexts: radix-minus-1 complements and true complements. A radix-minus-1 complement is known in the decimal system as a nine's complement and in the binary system as a one's complement. True complements are known in the decimal system as ten's complement and in binary as two's complement—a form commonly used to represent negative numbers in processing. See also complementary operation, nine's complement, one's complement, ten's complement, two's complement.

Complementary metal-oxide semiconductor *n.* See CMOS.

Complementary operation *n.* In Boolean logic, an operation that produces the opposite result from that of another operation performed on the same data. For example, if A is true, NOT A (its complement) is false. See also Boolean algebra.

Completeness check *n.* A survey to determine that all data required in a record is present.

Complex instruction set computing *n.* See CISC.

Complex number *n.* A number of the form a + bi, where a and b are real numbers and i is the square root of -1, called the imaginary unit. Complex numbers can be plotted as points on a two-dimensional plane called the complex plane. The a number is plotted along the plane's horizontal axis (the real axis), and the b number is plotted along the vertical axis (the imaginary axis).

Comp. newsgroups *n.* Usenet newsgroups that are part of the comp. hierarchy and have the prefix comp. These newsgroups are devoted to discussions of computer hardware, software, and other aspects of computer science. Comp. newsgroups are one of the seven original Usenet newsgroup hierarchies. The other six are misc., news., rec., sci., soc., and talk. See also newsgroup, traditional newsgroup hierarchy, Usenet.

Component *n.* 1. A discrete part of a larger system or structure. 2. An individual modular software routine that has been compiled and dynamically linked, and is ready to use with other components or programmes. See also compile, component software, link (definition 1), programme, routine. 3. In Sun Microsystem's J2EE network platform, an application-level software unit supported by a container. Components are configurable at deployment time. The J2EE platform defines four types of components: enterprise java beans, Web components, applets, and application clients. See also applet, container (definition 3), Enterprise JavaBeans, J2EE.

Component Object Model *n.* See COM (definition 2).

Component Pascal *n.* A Pascal derivative designed for programming software components for .NET and JVM platforms. See also Oberon, Pascal.

Component software *n.* Modular software routines, or components, that can be combined with other components to form an overall programme. A programmer can use and reuse an existing component and not have to understand its inner workings, just how to have another programme or component call it and pass data to and from it. Also called: componentware. See also component, programme, routine.

Componentware *n.* See component software.

COM port or comm port *n.* Short for communications port , the logical address assigned by MS-DOS (versions 3.3 and later) and Microsoft Windows (including Windows 9x and Windows NT) to each of the four serial ports on an IBM Personal Computer or a PC compatible. COM ports also have come to be known as the actual serial ports on a PC's CPU where peripherals, such as printers, scanners, and external modems, are plugged in. See the illustration. See also COM (definition 1), input/output port, serial port.

Composite display *n.* A display, characteristic of television monitors and some computer monitors, that is capable of extracting an image from a composite signal (also called an NTSC signal). A composite display signal carries on one wire not only the coded information required to form an image on the screen but also the pulses needed to synchronise horizontal and vertical scanning as the electron beam sweeps back and forth across the screen. Composite displays can be either monochrome or colour. A composite colour signal combines the three primary video colours (red, green, and blue) in a colour burst component that determines the shade of colour displayed on the screen. Composite colour monitors are less readable than either monochrome monitors or the RGB colour monitors that use separate signals (and wires) for the red, green, and blue components of the image. See also colour burst, colour monitor, monochrome display, NTSC, RGB monitor.

Composite key *n.* A key whose definition consists of two or more fields in a file, columns in a table, or attributes in a relation.

Composite video display *n.* A display that receives all encoded video information (including colour, horizontal synchronisation, and vertical synchronization) in one signal. A composite video signal under NTSC (National Television System Committee) standards is generally required for television sets and videotape recorders. See also NTSC.

Compound document *n.* A document that contains different types of information, each type created with a different application; for example, a report containing both charts (created with a spreadsheet) and text (created with a word processor) is a compound document. Although a compound document is visually a single, seamless unit, it is actually formed of discrete objects (blocks of information) that are created in their own applications. These objects can either be physically embedded in the destination document, or they can be linked to it while remaining in the originating file. Both embedded and linked objects can be edited. Linked objects, however, can be updated to reflect changes made to the source file. See also ActiveX, OLE, OpenDoc.

Compound statement *n.* A single instruction composed of two or more individual instructions.

Compress1 *n.* A proprietary UNIX utility for reducing the size of data files. Files compressed with this utility have the extension .Z added to their names.

Compress2 *vb.* To reduce the size of a set of data, such as a file or a communications message, so that it can be stored in less space or transmitted with less bandwidth. Data can be compressed by removing repeated patterns of bits and replacing them with some form of summary that takes up less space; restoring the repeated patterns decompresses the data. Lossless compression methods must be used for text, code, and numeric data files; lossy compression may be used for video and sound files. See also lossless compression, lossy compression.

Compressed digital video *n.* See CDV (definition 1).

Compressed disk *n.* A hard disk or floppy disk whose apparent capacity to hold data has been increased through the use of a compression utility, such as Stacker or Double Space. See also data compression.

Compressed drive *n.* A hard disk whose apparent capacity has been increased through the use of a compression utility, such as Stacker or Double Space. See also compressed disk, data compression.

Compressed file *n.* A file whose contents have been compressed by a special utility programme so that it occupies less space on a disk or other storage device than in its uncompressed (normal) state. See also installation programme, LHARC, PKUNZIP, PKZIP, utility programme.

Compressed Read-Only File System *n.* See cramfs.

Compressed SLIP *n.* Short for Compressed Serial Line Internet Protocol. A version of SLIP using compressed Internet address information, thereby making the protocol faster than SLIP. Acronym: CSLIP. See also SLIP.

Compression *n.* See data compression.

Compressor *n.* A device that limits some aspect of a transmitted signal, such as volume, in order to increase efficiency.

CompuServe *n.* An online information service that is a subsidiary of America Online. CompuServe provides information and communications capabilities, including Internet access. It is primarily known for its technical support forums for commercial hardware and software products and for being one of the first large commercial online services. CompuServe also operates various private network services.

Computational intelligence *n.* The study of the design of intelligent agents whose reasoning is based on computational methods. The central scientific goal of computational intelligence is to understand the principles that make intelligent behaviour possible, in natural or artificial systems. An intelligent agent is flexible to changing environments and changing goals—it learns from experience, and it makes appropriate choices given perceptual limitations and finite computation. The central engineering goal of computational intelligence is to specify methods for the design of useful, intelligent artifacts. See also agents (definition 2), artificial intelligence, autonomous agent.

Computation-bound *adj.* Of, pertaining to, or characteristic of a situation in which the performance of a computer is limited by the number of arithmetic operations the microprocessor must perform. When a system is computation-bound, the microprocessor is overloaded with calculations. Also called: CPU-bound.

Compute *vb.* 1. To perform calculations. 2. To use a computer or cause it to do work.

Computer *n.* Any device capable of processing information to produce a desired result. No matter how large or small they are, computers typically perform their work in three well-defined steps: (1) accepting input, (2) processing the input according to predefined rules (programmes), and (3) producing output. There are several ways to categorise computers, including class (ranging from microcomputers to supercomputers), generation (first through fifth generation), and mode of processing (analog versus digital). See the table. See also analog, digital (definition 2), integrated circuit, large-scale integration, very-large-scale integration.

Computer art *n.* A broad term that can refer either to art created on a computer or to art generated by a computer, the difference being whether the artist is human or electronic. When created by human beings, computer art is done with painting programmes that offer a range of line-drawing tools, brushes, shapes, patterns, and colours. Some programmes also offer predrawn figures and animation capabilities.

Table C.1 Ways to Categorise Computers

Class	Computers can be classified as supercomputers, mainframes, superminicomputers, minicomputers, workstations, microcomputers, or PDAs. All other things (for example, the age of the machine) being equal, such a categorization provides some indication of the computer's speed, size, cost, and abilities.
Generation	First-generation computers of historic significance, such as UNIVAC, introduced in the early 1950s, were based on vacuum tubes. Second-generation computers, appearing in the early 1960s, were those in which transistors replaced vacuum tubes. Third-generation computers, dating from the 1960s, were those in which integrated circuits replaced transistors. Fourth-generation computers, appearing in the mid-1970s, are those, such as microcomputers, in which large-scale integration (LSI) enabled thousands of circuits to be incorporated on one chip. Fifth-generation computers are expected to combine very-large-scale integration (VLSI) with sophisticated approaches to computing, including artificial intelligence and true distributed processing.
Mode of processing	Computers are either analog or digital. Analog computers, generally used in scientific pursuits, represent values by continuously variable signals that can have any of an infinite number of values within a limited range at any particular time. Digital computers, the type most people think of as computers, represent values by discrete signals—the bits representing the binary digits 0 and 1.

Computer-assisted diagnosis *n.* The use of computers by physicians in diagnosing patient conditions. Medical application programmes can help to determine the cause, symptoms, and treatment of a problem as well as to maintain a record of a patient's medical history and test results. See also expert system.

Computer-based learning *n.* See CBL.

Computer-based training *n.* See CBT.

Computer center *n.* A centralised location that contains computers, such as mainframes or minicomputers, along with associated equipment for providing data processing services to a group of people.

Computer conferencing *n.* Person-to-person interaction through the use of computers located in different places but connected through communications facilities.

Computer control console *n.* See system console.

Computer crime *n.* The illegal use of a computer by an unauthorised individual, either for pleasure (as by a computer hacker) or for profit (as by a thief). See also hacker (definition 2).

Computer-dependent *adj.* See hardware-dependent.

Computer Emergency Response Team *n.* See CERT.

Computer engineering *n.* The discipline that involves the design and underlying philosophies involved in the development of computer hardware.

Computer family *n.* A term commonly used to indicate a group of computers that are built around the same microprocessor or around a series of related microprocessors and that share significant design features. For example, the Apple Macintosh computers, from the original Macintosh (introduced in 1984) to the Quadra, represent a family designed by Apple around the Motorola 68000, 68020, 68030, and 68040 microprocessors. Computer families tend to parallel microprocessor families, but this is not always the case. For instance, Macintoshes are no longer made with 680x0 processors, and the Macintosh family has "extended" to another generation: the Power Macs, based on the PowerPC microprocessor.

Computer game *n.* A class of computer programme in which one or more users interacts with the computer as a form of entertainment. Computer games run the gamut from simple alphabet games for toddlers to chess, treasure hunts, war games, and simulations of world events. The games are controlled from a keyboard or with a joystick or other device and are supplied on disks, on CD-ROMs, as game cartridges, on the Internet, or as arcade devices.

Computer graphics *n.* The display of "pictures," as opposed to only alphabetic and numeric characters, on a computer screen.

Computer graphics encompasses different methods of generating, displaying, and storing information. Thus, computer graphics can refer to the creation of business charts and diagrams; the display of drawings, italic characters, and mouse pointers on the screen; or the way images are generated and displayed on the screen. See also graphics mode, presentation graphics, raster graphics, vector graphics.

Computer Graphics Interface *n.* A software standard applied to computer graphics devices, such as printers and plotters. Computer Graphics Interface is an offshoot of a widely recognised graphics standard called GKS (Graphical Kernel System), which provides applications programmers with standard methods of creating, manipulating, and displaying or printing computer graphics. Acronym: CGI. See also Graphical Kernel System.

Computer Graphics Metafile *n.* A software standard related to the widely recognised GKS (Graphical Kernel System) that provides applications programmers with a standard means of describing a graphic as a set of instructions for re-creating it. A graphics metafile can be stored on disk or sent to an output device; Computer Graphics Metafile provides a common language for describing such files in relation to the GKS standard. Acronym: CGM. See also Graphical Kernel System.

Computer-independent language *n.* A computer language designed to be independent of any given hardware platform. Most high-level languages are intended to be computer-independent; actual implementations of the languages (in the form of compilers and interpreters) tend to have some hardware-specific features and aspects. See also computer language.

Computer-input microfilm *n.* See CIM (definition 2).

Computer instruction *n.* 1. An instruction that a computer can recognise and act on. See also machine instruction. 2. The use of a computer in teaching. See also CAI.

Computer-integrated manufacturing *n.* See CIM (definition 1).

Computer interface unit *n.* See interface (definition 3).

Computerized axial tomography *n.* See CAT (definition 3).

Computerized mail *n.* See e-mail1.

Computer language *n.* An artificial language that specifies instructions to be executed on a computer. The term covers a wide spectrum, from binary-coded machine language to high-level languages. See also assembly language, high-level language, machine code.

Computer letter *n.* See form letter.

Computer literacy *n.* Knowledge and an understanding of computers combined with the ability to use them effectively. On the least specialised level, computer literacy involves knowing how to turn on a computer, start and stop simple application programmes, and save and print information. At higher levels, computer literacy becomes more detailed, involving the ability of power users to manipulate complex applications and, possibly, to programme in languages such as Basic or C. At the highest levels, computer literacy leads to specialised technical knowledge of electronics and assembly language. See also power user.

Computer-managed instruction *n.* See CMI.

Computer name *n.* In computer networking, a name that uniquely identifies a computer to the network. A computer's name cannot be the same as any other computer or domain name on the network. It differs from a user name in that the computer name is used to identify a particular computer and all its shared resources to the rest of the system so that they can be accessed.

Computer network *n.* See network.

Computer-output microfilm *n.* See COM (definition 4).

Computerphile *n.* A person who is immersed in the world of computing, who collects computers, or whose hobby involves computing.

Computer power *n.* The ability of a computer to perform work. If defined as the number of instructions the machine can carry out in a given time, computer power is measured in millions of instructions per second (MIPS) or millions of floating-point operations per second (MFLOPS). Power is measured in other ways too, depending on the needs or objectives of the person evaluating the machine. By users or purchasers of computers, power is often considered in terms of the machine's amount of random access memory (RAM), the speed at which the processor works, or the number of bits (8, 16, 32, and so on) handled by the computer at one time. Other factors enter into such an evaluation, however; two of the most important are how well the components of the computer work together and how well they are matched to the tasks required of them. For example, no matter how fast or powerful the computer, its speed will be hampered during operations involving the hard disk if the hard disk is slow (for example, with an access time of 65 millise

Computer Press Association *n.* A trade organisation of journalists, broadcasters, and authors who write or report about computer technology and the computer industry.

Computer Professionals for Social Responsibility *n.* See CPSR.

Computer programme *n.* A set of instructions in some computer language intended to be executed on a computer so as to perform some task. The term usually implies a self-contained entity, as opposed to a routine or a library. See also computer language.

Computer-readable *adj.* Of, pertaining to, or characteristic of information that can be interpreted and acted on by a computer. Two types of information are referred to as computer-readable: bar codes, magnetic tape, magnetic-ink characters, and other formats that can be scanned in some way and read as data by a computer; and machine code, the form in which instructions and data reach the computer's microprocessor.

Computer revolution *n.* The societal and technological phenomenon involving the swift development and widespread use and acceptance of computers—specifically single-user personal computers. The impact of these machines is considered revolutionary for two reasons. First, their appearance and success were rapid. Second, and more important, their speed and accuracy produced a change in the ways in which information can be processed, stored, and transferred.

Computer science *n.* The study of computers, including their design, operation, and use in processing information. Computer science combines both theoretical and practical aspects of engineering, electronics, information theory, mathematics, logic, and human behaviour. Aspects of computer science range from programming and computer architecture to artificial intelligence and robotics.

Computer security *n.* The steps taken to protect a computer and the information it contains. On large systems or those handling financial or confidential data, computer security requires professional supervision that combines legal and technical expertise. On a microcomputer, data protection can be achieved by backing up and storing copies of files in a separate location, and the integrity of data on the computer can be maintained by assigning passwords to files, marking files read-only to avoid changes to them, physically locking a hard disk, storing sensitive information on floppy disks kept in locked cabinets, and installing special programmes to protect against viruses. On a computer that many people have access to, security can be maintained by requiring personnel to use passwords and by granting only approved users access to sensitive information. See also bacterium, encryption, virus.

Computer simulation *n.* See simulation.

Computer system *n.* The configuration that includes all functional components of a computer and its associated hardware. A basic microcomputer system includes a console, or system unit, with one or more disk drives, a monitor, and a keyboard. Additional hardware, called peripherals, can include such devices as a printer, a modem, and a mouse. Software is usually not considered part of a computer system, although the operating system that runs the hardware is known as system software.

Computer telephone integration *n.* A process allowing computer applications to answer incoming calls, provide database information onscreen at the same time the call comes in, automatically route and reroute calls by drag-and-drop, automatically dial and speed-dial outgoing calls from a computer-resident database, and identify incoming customer calls and transfer them to predetermined destinations. See also drag-and-drop.

Computer Telephony Expo *n.* See CT Expo.

Computer typesetting *n.* Typesetting operations that are partially or totally controlled by computers. Partial control can involve the transmittal of text directly from the source to the typesetter, without a paste-up stage. Full computerization can include the digitization of all graphics, which would then also be transmitted directly to the typesetter and regenerated without paste-up.

Computer users' group *n.* See user group.

Computer utility *n.* See utility.

Computer virus *n.* See virus.

Computer vision *n.* The processing of visual information by a computer. Computer vision is a form of artificial intelligence that creates a symbolic description of images that are generally input from a video camera or sensor in order to convert the images to digital form. Computer vision is often associated with robotics. Acronym: CV. See also artificial intelligence, robotics.

Computer Vision Syndrome *n.* A change in a user's vision caused by prolonged exposure to computer monitors. Symptoms of Computer Vision Syndrome (CVS) can include blurred vision, dry, burning eyes, focusing problems, and headaches. CVS may be controlled with regular breaks from the computer, use of monitor filters or colour adjustments, or adjustments to eyeglass prescriptions. Acronym: CVS.

COM recorder *n.* Short for computer output microfilm recorder. A device that records computer information on microfilm.

COMSAT *n.* See Communication Satellite Corporation.

CON *n.* The logical device name for console; reserved by the MS-DOS operating system for the keyboard and the screen. The input-only keyboard and the output-only screen together make up the console and represent the primary sources of input and output in an MS-DOS computer system.

Concatenate *vb.* To join sequentially (for example, to combine the two strings "hello" and "there" into the single string "hello there"). See also character string.

Concatenated data set *n.* A group of separate sets of related data treated as a single unit for processing.

Concentrator *n.* A communications device that combines signals from multiple sources, such as terminals on a network, into one or more signals before sending them to their destination.

Conceptual schema *n.* In a database model that supports a three-schema architecture (such as that described by ANSI/X3/SPARC), a description of the information contents and structure of a database. A conceptual schema (also known as a logical schema) provides a model of the total database, thus acting as an intermediary between the two other types of schemas (internal and external) that deal with storing information and presenting it to the user. Schemas are generally defined using commands from a DDL (data definition language) supported by the database system. See also internal schema, schema.

Concordance *n.* A list of words that appear in a document, along with the contexts of the appearances.

Concrete class *n.* In object-oriented programming, a class in which objects can be created. See also class (definition 1).

Concurrent *adj.* Of, pertaining to, or characteristic of a computer operation in which two or more processes (programmes) have access to the microprocessor's time and are therefore carried out nearly simultaneously. Because a microprocessor can work with much smaller units of time than people can perceive, concurrent processes appear to be occurring simultaneously but in reality are not.

Concurrent execution *n.* The apparently simultaneous execution of two or more routines or programmes. Concurrent execution can be accomplished on a single process or by using time-sharing techniques, such as dividing programmes into different tasks or threads of execution, or by using multiple processors. Also called: parallel execution. See also parallel algorithm, processor, sequential execution, task, thread (definition 1), time-sharing.

Concurrent operation *n.* See concurrent.

Concurrent processing *n.* See concurrent.

Concurrent programme execution *n.* See concurrent.

Concurrent Versions System *n.* See CVS (definition 2).

Condensed *adj.* Of, pertaining to, or characteristic of a font style, supported in some applications, that reduces the width of each character and then sets the characters closer together than their normal spacing. Many dot-matrix printers have a feature that causes the printer to reduce the width of each character and print them closer together, resulting in more characters fitting on a single line.

Condition *n.* The state of an expression or a variable (for example, when a result can be either true or false, or equal or not equal).

Conditional *adj.* Of, pertaining to, or characteristic of an action or operation that takes place based on whether or not a certain condition is true. See also Boolean expression, conditional statement.

Conditional branch *n.* In a programme, a branch instruction that occurs when a particular condition code is true or false. The term is normally used in relation to low-level languages. See also branch instruction, condition code.

Conditional compilation *n.* Selective compilation or translation of source code of a programme based on certain conditions or flags; for example, sections of a programme specified by the programmer might be compiled only if a DEBUG flag has been defined at compilation time. See also comment out.

Conditional expression *n.* See Boolean expression.

Conditional jump *n.* In a programme, a jump instruction that occurs when a particular condition code is true or false. The term is normally used in relation to low-level languages. See also condition code, jump instruction.

Conditional statement *n.* A programming-language statement that selects an execution path based on whether some condition is true or false (for example, the IF statement). See also case statement, conditional, IF statement, statement.

Conditional transfer *n.* A transfer of the flow of execution to a given location in a programme based on whether a particular condition is true. The term is usually used in relation to high-level languages. See also conditional statement.

Condition code *n.* One of a set of bits that are set on (1, or true) or off (0, or false) as the result of previous machine instructions. The term is used primarily in assembly or machine language situations. Condition codes are hardware-specific but usually include carry, overflow, zero result, and negative result codes. See also conditional branch.

Conditioning *n.* The use of special equipment to improve the ability of a communications line to transmit data. Conditioning controls or compensates for signal attenuation, noise, and distortion. It can be used only on leased lines, where the path from sending to receiving computer is known in advance.

Conductor *n.* A substance that conducts electricity well. Metals are good conductors, with silver and gold being among the best. The most commonly used conductor is copper.

Conference on Data Systems Languages *n.* See CODASYL.

CONFIG.SYS *n.* A special text file that controls certain aspects of operating-system behaviour in MS-DOS and OS/2. Commands in the CONFIG.SYS file enable or disable system features, set limits on resources (for example, the maximum number of open files), and extend the operating system by loading device drivers that control hardware specific to an individual computer system.

Configuration *n.* 1. In reference to a single microcomputer, the sum of a system's internal and external components, including memory, disk drives, keyboard, video, and generally less critical add-on hardware, such as a mouse, modem, or printer. Software (the operating system and various device drivers), the user's choices established through configuration files such as the AUTOEXEC.BAT and CONFIG.SYS files on IBM PCs and compatibles, and sometimes hardware (switches and jumpers) are needed to "configure the configuration" to work correctly. Although system configuration can be changed, as by adding more memory or disk capacity, the basic structure of the system—its architecture—remains the same. See also AUTOEXEC.BAT, CONFIG.SYS. 2. In relation to networks, the entire interconnected set of hardware, or the way in which a network is laid out—the manner in which elements are connected.

Configuration file *n.* A file that contains machine-readable operating specifications for a piece of hardware or software or that contains information on another file or on a specific user, such as the user's logon ID.

Congestion *n.* The condition of a network when the current load approaches or exceeds the available resources and bandwidth designed to handle that load at a particular location in the network. Packet loss and delays are associated with congestion.

Connect charge *n.* The amount of money a user must pay for connecting to a commercial communications system or service. Some services calculate the connect charge as a flat rate per billing period. Others charge a varying rate based on the type of service or the amount of information being accessed. Still others base their charges on the number of time units used, the time or distance involved per connection, the bandwidth of each connected session, or some combination of the preceding criteria. See also connect time.

Connection *n.* A physical link via wire, radio, fiberoptic cable, or other medium between two or more communications devices.

Connection-based session *n.* A communications session that requires a connection to be established between hosts prior to an exchange of data.

Connectionism *n.* A model in artificial intelligence that advocates using highly parallel, specialised processes that compute simultaneously and are massively connected. Thus, the connectionist approach would not use a single high-speed processor to compute an algorithm, but would break out many simple specialised processing elements that are highly connected. Neural networks are classic examples of connectionism in that each "neuron" in the network may be assigned to a single processor. See also algorithm, artificial intelligence, neural network.

Connectionless *adj.* In communications, of, pertaining to, or characteristic of a method of data transmission that does not require a direct connection between two nodes on one or more networks. Connectionless communication is achieved by passing, or routing, data packets, each of which contains a source and destination address, through the nodes until the destination is reached. See also node (definition 2), packet (definition 2).

Connectionless session *n.* A communications session that does not require a connection to be established between hosts prior to an exchange of data.

Connection-oriented *adj.* In communications, of, pertaining to, or characteristic of a method of data transmission that requires a direct connection between two nodes on one or more networks.

Connection pooling *n.* A resource optimization feature of ODBC (Open Database Connectivity) 3 that results in more efficient sharing of database connections and objects. Connection pooling maintains open collections (pools) of database connections that can be used and reused by applications without the need to open and close a connection for each request. This is particularly important for Web-based applications. Connection pooling enables sharing among different components, maximises performance, and minimises the number of idle connections. See also ODBC.

Connectivity *n.* 1. The nature of the connection between a user's computer and another computer, such as a server or a host computer on the Internet or a network. This may describe the quality of the circuit or telephone line, the degree of freedom from noise, or the bandwidth of the communications devices. 2. The ability of hardware devices or software packages to transmit data between other devices or packages. 3. The ability of hardware devices, software packages, or a computer itself to work with network devices or with other hardware devices, software packages, or a computer over a network connection.

Connectoid *n.* In Windows 9x and Windows NT, an icon representing a dial-up networking connection that will also execute a script for logging onto the network dialed.

Connector *n.* 1. In hardware, a coupler used to join cables or to join a cable to a device (for example, an RS-232-C connector used to join a modem cable to a computer). Most connector types are available in one of two genders—male or female. A male connector is characterised by one or more exposed pins; a female connector is characterised by one or more receptacles—sockets or jacks—designed to accept the pins on the male connector. See also DB connector, DIN connector. 2. In programming, a circular symbol used in a flowchart to indicate a break, as to another page.

Connect time *n.* The amount of time during which a user is actively connected to a remote computer. On commercial systems, the connect time is one means of calculating how much money the user must pay for using the system. See also connect charge.

Consistency check *n.* A survey to verify that items of data conform to certain formats, bounds, and other parameters and are not internally contradictory.

Console *n.* 1. A control unit, such as a terminal, through which a user communicates with a computer. In microcomputers, the console is the cabinet that houses the main components and controls of the system, sometimes including the screen, the keyboard, or both. With the MS-DOS operating system, the console is the primary input (keyboard) and primary output device (screen), as evidenced by the device name CON. See also CON, system console. 2. See game console.

Console game *n.* A special-purpose computer system designed specifically for the home user to play video games. A game console typically includes a CPU, one or more game controllers, audio output, and a video output that connects to a television set. Individual games and memory cards are supplied on plug-in cartridges or compact discs. Many recent versions are 128-bit systems and also include a modem for online gaming over the Internet. Well-known console games include Microsoft Xbox, Sony PlayStation 2, Nintendo GameCube, and Sega Dreamcast. Also called: game console. See also computer game, Dreamcast, GameCube, PlayStation, Xbox.

Constant *n.* A named item that retains a consistent value throughout the execution of a programme, as opposed to a variable, which can have its value changed during execution.

Constant expression *n.* An expression that is composed only of constants and, hence, whose value does not change during programme execution.

Constellation *n.* In communications, a pattern representing the possible states of a carrier wave, each of which is associated with a particular bit combination. A constellation shows the number of states that can be recognised as unique changes in a communications signal and thus the maximum number of bits that can be encoded in a single change (equivalent to 1 baud, or one event). See the illustration.

Constraint *n.* In programming, a restriction on the solutions that are acceptable for a problem.

Consultant *n.* A computer professional who deals with client firms as an independent contractor rather than as an employee. Consultants are often engaged to analyse user needs and develop system specifications.

Consumer Electronics Show *n.* Annual tradeshow of the consumer electronics industry, held in Las Vegas, Nevada. CES features exhibits of the latest consumer electronics products and conference events that focus on consumer trends and business strategies. Acronym: CES.

Contact manager *n.* A type of specialised database that allows a user to maintain a record of personal communication with others. Contact managers are widely used by salespeople and others who want to keep track of conversations, e-mail, and other forms of communication with a large number of current and prospective customers or clients. See also database.

Container *n.* 1. In OLE terminology, a file containing linked or embedded objects. See also OLE. 2. In SGML, an element that has content as opposed to one consisting solely of the tag name and attributes. See also element, SGML, tag. 3. In Sun Microsystem's J2EE network platform, an entity that provides life cycle management, security, deployment, and runtime services to components such as beans, Web components, applets, and application clients. Each type of container created (for example, EJB, Web, JSP, servlet, applet, and application client) also provides component-specific services. See also applet, component (definition 3), enterprise java bean, JSP, servlet.

Container object *n.* An object that can logically contain other objects. For example, a folder is a container object. See also noncontainer object, object.

Content *n.* 1. The data that appears between the starting and ending tags of an element in an SGML, XML, or HTML document. The content of an element may consist of plain text or other elements. See also element (definition 2), HTML, SGML, tag (definition 3). 2. The message body of a newsgroup article or e-mail message. 3. The "meat" of a document, as opposed to its format or appearance.

Content-addressed storage *n.* See associative storage.

Content aggregator *n.* 1. Broadly, an organisation or business that groups Internet-based information by topic or area of interest—for example, sports scores, business news, or online shopping—to provide users with a means of accessing that content from a single location. 2. In terms of push technology and multicasting, a service business that mediates between subscribers ("customers") and content providers by gathering and organising information for broadcast over the Internet.

Content aggregators supply subscribers with client software through which content providers broadcast (push) information via "channels" that allow users both to choose the kind of information they receive and to decide when they want it updated. Also called: channel aggregator. See also push, webcasting.

Content caching *n.* See content delivery.

Content delivery *n.* The process of caching the pages of a Web site on geographically dispersed servers to enable faster delivery of Web pages. When a page is requested at a URL that is content-delivery enabled, the content-delivery network routes the user's request to a cache server closer to the user. Content delivery frequently is used for high-traffic Web sites or for specific high-traffic events. Also called: content distribution, content caching.

Content distribution *n.* See content delivery.

Contention *n.* On a network, competition among nodes for the opportunity to use a communications line or network resource. In one sense, contention applies to a situation in which two or more devices attempt to transmit at the same time, thus causing a collision on the line. In a somewhat different sense, contention also applies to a free-for-all method of controlling access to a communications line, in which the right to transmit is awarded to the station that wins control of the line. See also CSMA/CD.

Content Management Server *n.* Automated software application developed by Microsoft Corporation to assist nontechnical users in creating, tracking, and publishing content for Web sites. A workflow system delineates the tasks each user can perform, assigns content to individuals or groups, and allows users to monitor the status of content with which they are associated.

Content Protection for Recordable Media *n.* See CPRM.

Content provider *n.* 1. Broadly, an individual, group, or business that provides information for viewing or distribution on the Internet or on private or semiprivate intranets or extranets.

Content in this sense includes not only information but also video, audio, software, listings of Web sites, and product-specific materials such as online catalogs. 2. A service business that makes Internet information resources available to users. Content providers include online services such as America Online and CompuServe, Internet service providers (ISPs), and an increasing number of media companies representing television, long-distance telephone, and publishing industries. See also ISP, online information service.

Content Scrambling System *n.* See CSS.

Contents directory *n.* A series of queues that contain the descriptors and addresses of routines located within a region of memory.

Context-dependent *adj.* Of, pertaining to, or characteristic of a process or a set of data characters whose meaning depends on the surrounding environment.

Context-sensitive help *n.* A form of assistance in which a programme that provides onscreen help shows information to the user concerning the current command or operation being attempted.

Context-sensitive menu *n.* A menu that highlights options as available or unavailable depending on the context in which the option is called. The menus on Windows' menu bar, for example, are context sensitive; options such as copy are grayed out if nothing is selected.

Context switching *n.* A type of multitasking; the act of turning the central processor's "attention" from one task to another, rather than allocating increments of time to each task in turn. See also multitasking, time slice.

Contextual search *n.* A search operation in which the user can direct a programme to search specified files for a particular set of text characters.

Contiguous *adj.* Having a shared boundary; being immediately adjacent. For example, contiguous sectors on a disk are data-storage segments physically located next to one another.

Contiguous data structure *n.* A data structure, such as an array, that is stored in a consecutive set of memory locations. See also data structure.

Continuous carrier *n.* In communications, a carrier signal that remains on throughout the transmission, whether or not it is carrying information.

Continuous-form paper *n.* Paper in which each sheet is connected to the sheets before and after it, for use with most impact and ink-jet printers and some other printing devices designed with an appropriate paper-feed mechanism. The paper usually has holes punched along each side so that it can be pulled by a tractor-feed device. See the illustration. See also pin feed, sprocket feed, tractor feed.

Continuous processing *n.* The processing of transactions as they are input to the system.

Continuous speech recognition *n.* A type of automatic speech recognition (ASR) technology that responds to strings of words. Continuous speech recognition allows a user to speak in a natural voice without the need to slow down and enunciate each word separately. Continuous speech recognition software takes advantage of context in recognising words, and thus will not operate at full efficiency if each word is spoken with distinct separation. See also ASR (definition 2).

Continuous-tone image *n.* An image, such as a photograph, in which colour or varying shades of gray are reproduced as gradients rather than as clustered or variably sized dots, as in traditional book or newspaper printing. Continuous-tone images can be viewed on an analog monitor (such as a television monitor), which accepts input as a continuously variable signal. They cannot be viewed on a digital monitor, which requires input broken into discrete units, nor can they be printed in books or newspapers, which represent illustrations as groups of dots. See also scan (definition 2), video digitizer.

Continuous-tone printer *n.* A printer that produces an image using smoothly blended levels of continuous ink for gradations of gray or colour.

Contouring *n.* 1. In computer graphics, such as CAD models, the representation of the surface of an object—its bumps and crannies. See the illustration. 2. In image processing, the loss of detail that occurs in a shaded image when too few gradations of gray are used to reproduce a graphic, such as a photograph. In photography and graphic arts, this phenomenon is sometimes called posterization.

Contrast *n.* 1. The degree of difference between light and dark extremes of colour on a monitor or on printed output. 2. The control knob by which the contrast of a monitor is changed.

Control *n.* 1. Management of a computer and its processing abilities so as to maintain order as tasks and activities are carried out. Control applies to measures designed to ensure error-free actions carried out at the right time and in the right order relative to other data-handling or hardware-based activities. In reference to hardware, control of system operations can reside in a data pathway called a controi bus. In reference to software, control refers to programme instructions that manage data-handling tasks. 2. In a graphical user interface, an object on the screen that can be manipulated by the user to perform an action. The most common controls are buttons, which allow the user to select options, and scroll bars, which allow the user to move through a document or position text in a window.

Control break *n.* A transition in control of the computer that typically gives control of the CPU (central processing unit) to the user console or to some other programme.

Control-Break *n.* See Break key.

Control bus *n.* The set of lines (conductors) within a computer that carry control signals between the CPU (central processing unit) and other devices. For example, a control bus line is used to indicate whether the CPU is attempting to read from memory or to write to it; another control bus line is used by memory to request an interrupt in case of a memory error.

Control character *n.* 1. Any of the first 32 characters in the ASCII character set (0 through 31 in decimal representation), each of which is defined as having a standard control function, such as carriage return, linefeed, or backspace. 2. Any of the 26 characters Control-A through Control-Z (1 through 26 in decimal representation) that can be typed at the keyboard by holding the Control key down and typing the appropriate letter. The six remaining characters with control functions, such as Escape (ASCII 27), cannot be typed using the Control key.

Control code *n.* One or more nonprinting characters used by a computer programme to control the actions of a device, used in printing, communications, and management of display screens. Control codes are mainly employed by programmers or by users to control a printer when an application programme does not support the printer or one of its specialised features. In video, control codes are sent from a computer to a display unit to manipulate the appearance of text or a cursor on the screen. Popular video control code sets are ANSI and VT-100. Also called: escape sequence, setup string. See also control character.

Control console *n.* See console.

Control data *n.* Data that consists of information about timing and switching, used to synchronise and route other data or to manage the operation of a device such as a bus or a port.

Control flow *n.* The tracing of all possible execution paths in a programme, often represented in the form of a diagram. See the illustration.

Control key *n.* A key that, when pressed in combination with another key, gives the other key an alternative meaning. In many application programmes, Control (labeled CTRL or Ctrl on a PC keyboard) plus another key is used as a command for special functions. See the illustration. See also control character (definition 2).

Controller *n.* A device that other devices rely on for access to a computer subsystem. A disk controller, for example, controls access to one or more disk drives, managing physical and logical access to the drive or drives.

Control logic *n.* The electronic circuitry that generates, interprets, and uses control data.

Control panel *n.* In Windows and Macintosh systems, a utility that allows the user to control aspects of the operating system or hardware, such as system time and date, keyboard characteristics, and networking parameters.

Control panel device *n.* See cdev.

Control sequence *n.* See control code.

Control signal *n.* An electronic signal used to control internal or external devices or processes.

Control statement *n.* A statement that affects the flow of execution through a programme. Control statements include conditional statements (CASE, IF-THEN-ELSE), iterative statements (DO, FOR, REPEAT, WHILE), and transfer statements (GOTO). See also conditional statement, iterative statement, statement, transfer statement.

Control strip *n.* 1. An equipment calibration tool used to determine the corrections needed to restore accuracy by comparing recorded data against known values. 2. A utility that groups shortcuts to commonly used items or information, such as time, battery power level, desktop items, and programmes, in an easily accessible place. See also shortcut.

Control structure *n.* A portion of a programme defined by the relationship between the statements, used in structured programming. There are three basic control structures: sequence, where one statement simply follows another; selection, where programme flow depends on which criteria are met; and iteration, where an action is repeated until some condition occurs.

Control unit *n.* A device or circuit that performs an arbitrating or regulating function. For example, a memory controller chip controls access to a computer's memory and is the control unit for that memory.

Control variable *n.* In programming, the variable in a control statement that dictates the flow of execution. For example, the index variable in a FOR loop controls the number of times a group of statements are executed. See also control statement.

Convenience adapter *n.* See port replicator.

Convention *n.* Any standard that is used more or less universally in a given situation. Many conventions are applied to microcomputers. In programming, for example, a language such as C relies on formally accepted symbols and abbreviations that must be used in programmes. Less formally, programmers usually adopt the convention of indenting subordinate instructions in a routine so that the structure of the programme is more easily visualised. National and international committees often discuss and arbitrate conventions for programming languages, data structures, communication standards, and device characteristics. See also CCITT, ISO, NTSC, standard (definition 1).

Conventional memory *n.* The amount of RAM addressable by an IBM PC or compatible machine operating in real mode. This is typically 640 kilobytes (KB). Without the use of special techniques, conventional memory is the only kind of RAM accessible to MS-DOS programmes. See also protected mode, real mode.

Convergence *n.* A coming together. Convergence can occur between different disciplines and technologies, as when telephone communications and computing converge in the field of telecommunications. It can also occur within a programme, such as a spreadsheet, when a circular set of formulas are repeatedly recalculated (iterated), with the results of each iteration coming closer to a true solution.

Conversational *adj.* Of, pertaining to, or characteristic of the mode of operation, typical of microcomputers, in which the computer user and the system engage in a dialogue of commands and system responses. See also interactive.

Conversational interaction *n.* Interaction in which two or more parties alternately transmit and receive messages from each other. See also interactive processing.

Conversational language *n.* Any programming language that allows the programmer to instruct the computer in a conversational mode, as opposed to more formal, structured languages. For example, in a COBOL programme, in order to execute a procedure called CHECK 10 times, a programme would use the following statement: PERFORM CHECK 10 TIMES.

Conversational mode *n.* See conversational.

Conversion *n.* The process of changing from one form or format to another; where information is concerned, a changeover that affects form but not substance. Types of conversion include data (changing the way information is represented), file (changing a file from one format to another), hardware (changing all or part of a computer system), media (transferring data from one storage media to another), software (changing a programme designed for one platform so that it runs on another), and system (changing from one operating system to another).

Conversion table *n.* A table listing a set of characters or numbers and their equivalents in another coding scheme. Common examples of conversion tables include ASCII tables, which list characters and their ASCII values, and decimal-to-hexadecimal tables. Several conversion tables are in Appendixes A-E.

Converter *n.* Any device that changes electrical signals or computer data from one form to another. For example, an analog-to-digital converter translates analog signals to digital signals.

Converter box *n.* See converter.

Cookbook1 *adj.* Of, pertaining to, or characteristic of a book or manual that presents information using a step-by-step approach. For example, a cookbook approach to programming might present a series of sample programmes that the reader could analyse and adapt to his or her own needs.

Cookbook2 *n.* A computer book or manual that presents information using a step-by-step approach. Most often, cookbook refers to a programming guide, but it can refer to a book that shows how to accomplish specialised tasks in an application.

Cooked mode *n.* One of two forms (the other being raw mode) in which an operating system such as UNIX or -MS-DOS "sees" the handle, or identifier, for a character-based device. If the handle is in cooked mode, the operating system stores each character in a buffer and gives special treatment to carriage returns, end-of-file markers, and linefeed and tab characters, sending a line of data to a device, such as the screen, only after it reads a carriage-return or end-of-file character. In cooked mode, characters read from standard input are often automatically echoed (displayed) on the screen.

Cookie *n.* 1. A block of data that a server returns to a client in response to a request from the client. 2. On the World Wide Web, a block of data that a Web server stores on a client system. When a user returns to the same Web site, the browser sends a copy of the cookie back to the server. Cookies are used to identify users, to instruct the server to send a customised version of the requested Web page, to submit account information for the user, and for other administrative purposes. 3. Originally an allusion to fortune cookie, a UNIX programme that outputs a different message, or "fortune," each time it is used. On some systems, the cookie programme is run during user logon.

Cookie filtering tool *n.* A utility that prevents a cookie on a Web browser from relaying information about the user requesting access to a Web site. See also cookie (definition 2).

Cookies policy *n.* A statement that describes a Web site's policy regarding cookies. The policy usually defines a cookie, explains the types of cookies used by the Web site, and describes how the Web site uses the information stored in the cookies.

.coop *n.* One of seven new top-level domain names approved in 2000 by the Internet Corporation for Assigned-Names and Numbers (ICANN), .coop is meant for use with the Web sites of nonprofit cooperatives. The seven new domain names became available for use in the spring of 2001.

Cooperative multitasking *n.* A type of multitasking in which one or more background tasks are given processing time during idle times in the foreground task only if the foreground task allows it. This is the primary mode of multitasking in the Macintosh operating system. See also background1, context switching, foreground1, multitasking, time slice.

Cooperative processing *n.* A mode of operation characteristic of distributed systems in which two or more computers, such as a mainframe and a microcomputer, can simultaneously carry out portions of the same programme or work on the same data.

Coordinate *n.* Any element in a group of references to a particular location, such as the intersection of a certain row and column. In computer graphics and displays, coordinates specify such elements as points on a line, the corners of a square, or the location of a pixel on the screen. In other computer applications, coordinates specify cells on a spreadsheet, data points on a graph, locations in memory, and so on. See also Cartesian coordinates, polar coordinates.

Coordinate dimensioning *n.* A form of spatial positioning in which a point is described, relative to a fixed reference, in terms of its distance and direction along predefined axes. See also Cartesian coordinates, three-dimensional model, two-dimensional model.

Coordinated universal time format *n.* See Universal Time Coordinate.

Coordinate pair *n.* A pair of values representing the x-coordinate and y-coordinate of a point that are stored in a two-dimensional array that can contain coordinates for many points.

COPPA *n.* Acronym for Children's Online Privacy Protection Act. A U.S. federal law enacted in April 2000 and designed to protect the online privacy of children under the age of 13. COPPA requires Web sites that collect personal information from children under 13 to receive permission from parents or guardians first, and to monitor and supervise children's experiences with interactive Web elements such as chat rooms and e-mail.

Copper chip *n.* A microprocessor that uses copper (rather than the more common aluminum) to connect transistors in a computer chip. Copper chip technology, which was developed by IBM and introduced in 1997, can be expected to boost the speed of a microprocessor by as much as 33 percent.

Coprocessor *n.* A processor, distinct from the main microprocessor, that performs additional functions or assists the main microprocessor. The most common type of coprocessor is the floating-point coprocessor, also called a numeric or math coprocessor, which is designed to perform numeric calculations faster and better than the general-purpose microprocessors used in personal computers. See also floating-point processor.

Copy *vb.* To duplicate information and reproduce it in another part of a document, in a different file or memory location, or in a different medium. A copy operation can affect data ranging from a single character to large segments of text, a graphics image, or from one to many data files. Text and graphics, for example, can be copied to another part of a document, to the computer's memory (by means of a temporary storage facility such as the Windows or Macintosh Clipboard), or to a different file. Similarly, files can be copied from one disk or directory to another, and data can be copied from the screen to a printer or to a data file. In most cases, a copy procedure leaves the original information in place.

Copy disk *n.* An MS-DOS command to duplicate the contents of a floppy disk on a second disk. See also floppy disk, MS-DOS.

Copy holder *n.* An inclined clipboard or other such device designed to hold printed material so that it can be easily viewed by someone working at a computer keyboard.

Copyleft *n.* See General Public License.

Copy programme *n.* 1. A programme designed to duplicate one or more files to another disk or directory. 2. A programme that disables or circumvents the copy-protection device on a computer programme so that the software can be copied, often illegally, to another disk. See also copy protection.

Copy protection *n.* A software lock placed on a computer programme by its developer to prevent the product from being copied and distributed without approval or authorization.

Copyright *n.* A method of protecting the rights of an originator of a creative work, such as a text, a piece of music, a painting, or a computer programme, through law. In many countries the originator of a work has copyright in the work as soon as it is fixed in a tangible medium (such as a piece of paper or a disk file); that rule applies in the United States for works created after 1977. Registration of a copyright, or the use of a copyright symbol, is not needed to create the copyright but does strengthen the originator's legal powers. Unauthorised copying and distribution of copyrighted material can lead to severe penalties, whether done for profit or not. Copyrights affect the computer community in three ways: the copyright protection of software, the copyright status of material (such as song lyrics) distributed over a network such as the Internet, and the copyright status of original material distributed over a network (such as a newsgroup post).

CORBA *n.* Acronym for Common Object Request Broker Architecture. A specification developed by the Object Management Group in 1992 in which pieces of programmes (objects) communicate with other objects in other programmes, even if the two programmes are written in different programming languages and are running on different platforms. A programme makes its request for objects through an object request broker, or ORB, and thus does not need to know the structure of the programme from which the object comes. CORBA is designed to work in object-oriented environments. See also IIOP, object (definition 2), Object Management Group, object-oriented.

Core *n.* One of the types of memory built into computers before random access memory (RAM) was available or affordable. Some people still use the term to refer to the main memory of any computer system, as in the phrase core dump—a listing of the raw contents of main memory at the moment of a system crash.

Core class *n.* In the Java programming language, a public class or interface that is a standard member of the language. Core classes, at minimum, are available on all operating systems where the Java platform runs. A programme written entirely in the Java programming language relies only on core classes. See also class (definition 1), object, object-oriented programming.

Core programme *n.* A programme or programme segment that is resident in random access memory (RAM).

Coresident *adj.* Of or pertaining to a condition in which two or more programmes are loaded in memory at the same time.

Corona wire *n.* In laser printers, a wire though which high voltage is passed to ionize the air and transfer a uniform electrostatic charge to the photosensitive medium in preparation for the laser.

Coroutine *n.* A routine that is in memory at the same time as, and frequently executed concurrently with, another.

Corrective maintenance *n.* The process of diagnosing and correcting computer problems after they occur.

Correspondence quality *n.* See print quality.

Corruption *n.* A process wherein data in memory or on disk is unintentionally changed, with its meaning thereby altered or obliterated.

Cost-benefit analysis *n.* The comparison of benefits to costs for a particular item or action. Cost-benefit analysis is often used in MIS or IS departments to determine such things as whether purchasing a new computer system is a good investment or whether hiring more staff is necessary. See also IS, MIS.

Coulomb *n.* A unit of electrical charge equivalent to roughly 6.26 x 1018 electrons, with a negative charge being an excess of electrons and a positive charge being a deficiency of electrons.

Counter *n.* 1. In programming, a variable used to keep count of something. 2. In electronics, a circuit that counts a specified number of pulses before generating an output. 3. A device that keeps track of the number of visitors to a World Wide Web site.

Counting loop *n.* In a programme, a group of statements that are repeated, thereby incrementing a variable used as a counter (for example, a programme might repeat a counting loop that adds 1 to its counter until the counter equals 10). See also loop1 (definition 1).

Country code *n.* See major geographic domain.

Country-specific *adj.* Of, pertaining to, or characteristic of hardware or software that uses characters or conventions unique to a particular country or group of countries. Country-specific does not necessarily refer to spoken languages, although it does allow for special characters (such as accent marks) that are language-specific. Generally, the features considered country-specific include keyboard layout (including special-character keys), time and date conventions, financial and monetary symbols, decimal notation (decimal point or comma), and alphabetic sorting order. Such features are handled either by a computer's operating system (for example, by the Keyboard and Country commands in MS-DOS) or by application programmes that offer options for tailoring documents to a particular set of national or international conventions.

Courseware *n.* Software dedicated to education or training.

Courtesy copy *n.* See cc.

CPA *n.* See Computer Press Association.

CPCP *n.* See HTCPCP.

CPI *n.* See characters per inch.

CP/M *n.* Acronym for Control Programme/Monitor. A line of operating systems from Digital Research, Inc. (DRI), for microcomputers based on Intel microprocessors. The first system, CP/M-80, was the most popular operating system for 8080- and Z80-based microcomputers. Digital Research also developed CP/M-86 for 8086/8088-based computers, CP/M-Z8000 for Zilog Z8000-based computers, and CP/M-68K for Motorola 68000-based computers. When the IBM PC and MS-DOS were introduced, common use of CP/M by end users dwindled. DRI continues to enhance the CP/M line, supporting multitasking with the Concurrent CP/M and MP/M products. See also MP/M.

CPM *n.* See critical path method.

CPRM *n.* Acronym for Content Protection for Recordable Media. Technology developed to control the use of copyrighted digital music and video material by blocking the transfer of protected files to portable media such as zip disks and smart cards. CPRM would be added to storage devices and provide data scrambling and identification codes to block the copying of copyrighted files.

CPS *n.* See characters per second.

CPSR *n.* Acronym for Computer Professionals for Social Responsibility. A public advocacy organisation of computer professionals. CPSR was originally formed out of concern over the use of computer technology for military purposes but has extended its interest to such issues as civil liberties and the effect of computers on workers.

CPU *n.* Acronym for central processing unit. The computational and control unit of a computer. The CPU is the device that interprets and executes instructions. Mainframes and early minicomputers contained circuit boards full of integrated circuits that implemented the CPU. Single-chip central processing units, called microprocessors, made possible personal computers and workstations. Examples of single-chip CPUs are the Motorola 68000, 68020, and 68030 chips and the Intel 8080, 8086, 80286, 80386, and i486 chips. The CPU—or microprocessor, in the case of a microcomputer—has the ability to fetch, decode, and execute instructions and to transfer information to and from other resources over the computer's main data-transfer path, the bus. By definition, the CPU is the chip that functions as the "brain" of a computer. In some instances, however, the term encompasses both the processor and the computer's memory or, even more broadly, the main computer console (as opposed to peripheral equipment). See the illustration.

CPU-bound *adj.* See computation-bound.

CPU cache *n.* A section of fast memory linking the CPU (central processing unit) and main memory that temporarily stores data and instructions the CPU needs to execute upcoming commands and programmes. Considerably faster than main memory, the CPU cache contains data that is transferred in blocks, thereby speeding execution. The system anticipates the data it will need through algorithms. Also called: cache memory, memory cache. See also cache, CPU, VCACHE.

CPU cycle *n.* 1. The smallest unit of time recognised by the CPU (central processing unit)—typically a few hundred-millionths of a second. 2. The time required for the CPU to perform the simplest instruction, such as fetching the contents of a register or performing a no-operation instruction (NOP). Also called: clock tick.

CPU fan *n.* An electric fan usually placed directly on a CPU (central processing unit) or on the CPU's heat sink to help dissipate heat from the chip by circulating air around it. See also CPU, heat sink.

CPU speed *n.* A relative measure of the data-processing capacity of a particular CPU (central processing unit), usually measured in megahertz. See also CPU.

CPU time *n.* In multiprocessing, the amount of time during which a particular process has active control of the CPU (central processing unit). See also CPU, multiprocessing.

CR *n.* See carriage return.

Crack *vb.* 1. To gain unauthorised access to a network by breaching its security. 2. To decipher encrypted information.

Cracker *n.* A person who overcomes the security measures of a computer system and gains unauthorised access. The goal of some crackers is to obtain information illegally from a computer system or use computer resources. However, the goal of the majority is only to break into the system. See also hacker (definition 2).

Cradle *n.* A receptacle used to recharge the batteries in some handheld or palm-size PCs or PDAs (personal digital assistants). Some cradles also serve as a means to connect these smaller devices with a desktop PC. Not all of these devices require a cradle to recharge or connect to a desktop system. Also called: dock, docking station.

Cramfs *n.* Short for Compressed Read-Only File System and cram a File System onto a small ROM. A filesystem feature available with Linux version 2.4 systems. Cramfs are used in handheld Linux devices to compress and write applications to ROM or Flash memory.

Crash1 *n.* The failure of either a programme or a disk drive. A programme crash results in the loss of all unsaved data and can leave the operating system unstable enough to require restarting the computer. A disk drive crash, sometimes called a disk crash, leaves the drive inoperable and can cause loss of data. See also abend, head crash.

Crash2 *vb.* 1. For a system or programme, to fail to function correctly, resulting in the suspension of operation. See also abend. 2. For a magnetic head, to hit a recording medium, with possible damage to one or both.

Crash recovery *n.* The ability of a computer to resume operation after a disastrous failure, such as the failure of a hard drive. Ideally, recovery can occur without any loss of data, although usually some, if not all, data is lost. See also crash1.

Crawl *vb.* To compile and organise entries for a search engine by reading Web pages and related information. Crawling is typically performed by programmes called "spiders."

Crawler *n.* See spider, Web browser.

Cray-1 *n.* An early supercomputer developed in 1976 by Seymour Cray. Extremely powerful in its day, the 64-bit Cray-1 ran at 75 MHz and was capable of executing 160 million floating-point operations per second. See also supercomputer.

CRC *n.* Acronym for cyclical (or cyclic) redundancy check. A procedure used in checking for errors in data transmission. CRC error checking uses a complex calculation to generate a number based on the data transmitted. The sending device performs the calculation before transmission and includes it in the packet that it sends to the receiving device. The receiving device repeats the same calculation after transmission. If both devices obtain the same result, it is assumed that the transmission was error free. The procedure is known as a redundancy check because each transmission includes not only data but extra (redundant) error-checking values. Communications protocols such as XMODEM and Kermit use cyclical redundancy checking.

Create method *n.* In Java programming, a method defined in the home interface and invoked by a client to create an enterprise java bean. See also enterprise java bean, method.

Creator *n.* On the Apple Macintosh, the programme that creates a file. Files are linked to their creators by creator codes; this link enables the operating system to open the creator application when a document file is opened.

Credentials *n.* A set of information that includes identification and proof of identification that is used to gain access to local and network resources. Examples of credentials are user names and passwords, smart cards, and certificates.

Creeping featurism *n.* The process by which features are added to a new version of a programme by software developers until the programme becomes unduly cumbersome and difficult to use. Generally, creeping featurism occurs as developers attempt to enhance the competitiveness of the programme with each new release by adding new features.

Crippled version *n.* A scaled-down or functionally reduced version of hardware or software, distributed for demonstration purposes. See also demo.

Critical error *n.* An error that suspends processing until the condition can be corrected either by software or by user intervention (for example, an attempt to read to a nonexistent disk, an out-of-paper condition on the printer, or a checksum fault in a data message).

Critical-error handler *n.* A software routine that attempts to correct or achieve a graceful exit from a critical or threatening error. See also critical error, graceful exit.

Critical path method *n.* A means of evaluating and managing a large project by isolating tasks, milestone events, and schedules and by showing interrelationships among them. The critical path for which this method is named is a line connecting crucial events, any of which, if delayed, affects subsequent events and, ultimately, completion of the project. Acronym: CPM.

Crop *vb.* In computer graphics, to cut off part of an image, such as unneeded sections of a graphic or extra white space around the borders. As in preparing photographs or illustrations for traditional printing, cropping is used to refine or clean up a graphic for placement in a document.

Crop marks *n.* 1. Lines drawn at the edges of pages to mark where the paper will be cut to form pages in the final document. See the illustration. See also registration marks. 2. Lines drawn on photographs or illustrations to indicate where they will be cropped, or cut. See also crop.

Cross-assembler *n.* An assembler that executes on one hardware platform but generates machine code for another. See also assembler, compiler, cross-compiler, cross development.

Cross-check *vb.* To check the accuracy of a calculation by using another method to verify the result.

Cross-compiler *n.* A compiler that executes on one hardware platform but generates object code for another. See also assembler, compiler (definition 2), cross-assembler, cross development.

Cross development *n.* The use of one system to develop programmes for a different type of system, often because the software development tools of the development system are superior to those of the target system.

Cross-foot *vb.* To check the accuracy of a total, as on a ledger sheet, by adding across columns and down rows, all figures contributing to the total.

Cross hairs *n.* Intersecting lines used by some computer input devices to locate a particular x-y-coordinate.

Cross-hatching *n.* Shading made up of regularly spaced, intersecting lines. Cross-hatching is one of several methods for filling in areas of a graphic. See the illustration.

Cross-linked files *n.* In Windows 9x, Windows 3.x, and MS-DOS, a file-storage error occurring when one or more sections, or clusters, of the hard drive or a floppy disk have been erroneously allocated to more than one file in the file allocation table. Like lost clusters, cross-linked files can result from the ungraceful exit (messy or abrupt termination) of an application programme. See also file allocation table, lost cluster.

Crossover cable *n.* A cable used to connect two computers together for file sharing and personal networking. Crossover cables may be connected to Ethernet or FireWire ports.

Cross-platform *adj.* Of, pertaining to, or characteristic of a software application or hardware device that can be run or operated on more than one system platform.

Cross-post *vb.* To copy a message or news article from one newsgroup, conference topic, e-mail system, or other communications channel to another—for example, from a Usenet newsgroup to a CompuServe forum or from e-mail to a newsgroup.

Cross-site scripting *n.* A security vulnerability of dynamic Web pages generated from a database in response to user input. With cross-site scripting, a malicious user introduces unwanted executable script or code into another user's Web session. Once running, this script could allow others to monitor the user's Web session, change what is displayed on the screen, or shut down the Web browser. Web sites that allow visitors to add comments or make other additions or changes to the pages are the most vulnerable to this flaw. Cross-site scripting is not restricted to the products of a particular vendor or a particular operating system. See also script.

Crosstab query *n.* A query that calculates a sum, an average, a count, or other type of total on records, and then groups the result by two types of information—one down the left side of the datasheet and the other across the top.

Crosstalk *n.* Interference caused by a signal transferring from one circuit to another, as on a telephone line.

CRT *n.* Acronym for cathode-ray tube. The basis of the television screen and the standard microcomputer display screen. A CRT display is built around a vacuum tube containing one or more electron guns whose electron beams rapidly sweep horizontally across the inside of the front surface of the tube, which is coated with a material that glows when irradiated. Each electron beam moves from left to right, top to bottom, one horizontal scan line at a time. To keep the screen image from flickering, the electron beam refreshes the screen 30 times or more per second. The clarity of the image is determined by the number of pixels on the screen. See the illustration. See also pixel, raster, resolution (definition 1).

CRT controller *n.* The part of a video adapter board that generates the video signal, including the horizontal and vertical synchronization signals. See also video adapter.

Cruise *vb.* See surf.

Crunch *vb.* To process information. See also number crunching.

Cryoelectronic *adj.* Involving the use of superconducting electronics kept in a cryogenic environment at very low temperatures.

Crypto *n.* See cryptography.

Cryptoanalysis *n.* The decoding of electronically encrypted information for the purpose of understanding encryption techniques. See also cryptography, encryption.

CryptoAPI *n.* An application programming interface (API) that is provided as part of Microsoft Windows. CryptoAPI provides a set of functions that allows applications to encrypt or digitally sign data in a flexible manner while providing protection for the user's sensitive private key data. Actual cryptographic operations are performed by independent modules known as cryptographic service providers (CSPs). See also application programming interface (API), cryptographic service provider, private key.

Cryptographic service provider *n.* An independent module that performs cryptographic operations, such as creating and destroying keys. A cryptographic service provider consists of, at a minimum, a DLL and a signature file. Acronym: CSP.

Cryptography *n.* The use of codes to convert data so that only a specific recipient will be able to read it using a key. The persistent problem of cryptography is that the key must be transmitted to the intended recipient and may be intercepted. Public key cryptography is a recent significant advance. Also called: crypto. See also code1 (definition 2), encryption, PGP, private key, public key.

CSD *n.* See circuit-switched data.

C shell *n.* One of the command-line interfaces available under UNIX. The C shell is very usable but is not on every system.

CSLIP *n.* See Compressed SLIP.

CSMA/CA *n.* Acronym for Carrier Sense Multiple Access with Collision Avoidance, a protocol for controlling network access similar to CSMA/CD, in that nodes (stations) listen to the network and transmit only when it is free. But in CSMA/CA, nodes avoid data collisions by signaling their intention with a brief Request to Send (RTS) signal and then waiting for acknowledgment before actually transmitting.

CSMA/CD *n.* Acronym for Carrier Sense Multiple Access with Collision Detection. A network protocol for handling situations in which two or more nodes (stations) transmit at the same time, thus causing a collision. With CSMA/CD, each node on the network monitors the line and transmits when it senses that the line is not busy. If a collision occurs because another node is using the same opportunity to transmit, both nodes stop transmitting. To avoid another collision, both then wait for differing random amounts of time before attempting to transmit again.

CSO *n.* Acronym for Computing Services Office. An Internet directory service that matches users' own names with e-mail addresses, generally at colleges and universities. The CSO service, which can be reached through Gopher, was originally developed at the Computing Services Office at the University of Illinois.

CSO name server *n.* A facility that provides e-mail directory information through the CSO system. See also CSO.

CSS *n.* 1. See cascading style sheets. 2. Acronym for Content Scrambling System. An encryption feature added to DVDs distributed with approval of the MPAA. CSS looks for a matching region code on the DVD and the playback device. If the codes do not match (such as for a DVD purchased in Japan and a DVD player purchased in the United States), CSS will not allow the DVD to play. CSS also will not allow a DVD to be played on playback equipment not approved by the MPAA. See also deCSS, region code.

CSS1 *n.* See cascading style sheets.

CSTN display *n.* See supertwist display.

CSU *n.* See DDS.

.csv *n.* The file extension for a comma-delimited text file.

CSV *n.* 1. See circuit-switched voice. 2. See alternate circuit-switched voice/circuit-switched data. 3. Acronym for comma separated values. Filename extension assigned to text files containing tabular data of the sort stored in database fields. As the name indicates, individual data entries are separated by commas.

CTERM *n.* See Communications Terminal Protocol.

CT Expo *n.* Acronym for Computer Telephony Expo. Annual exposition on data and communications issues involving the computer, telecommunications, and Internet industries. Held in Los Angeles, California, CT Expo features exhibits by hundreds of companies displaying their latest products and services, as well as conferences on a range of subjects affecting computer telephony.

CTI *n.* Acronym for computer-telephony integration. The practice of using a computer to control one or more telephone and communications functions.

CTIA *n.* See Cellular Telecommunications and Internet Association.

CTIA Wireless *n.* Annual conference of the wireless data, mobile Internet, and handheld computing industries. Sponsored by the Cellular Telecommunications and Internet Association, CTIA Wireless showcases products and technical developments in the field of wireless communications and data.

CTL *n.* Short for control. See control character (definition 2), Control key.

CTO *n.* Acronym for Chief Technology Officer. A corporate executive in charge of managing a company's information technology (IT) architecture and other technological assets. The CTO's responsibilities may include oversight of IT centers, networks and intranet, applications, databases, Web presence, and other technological resources.

CTRL or Ctrl *n.* Short for control. A designation used to label the Control key on computer keyboards. See also control character (definition 2), Control key.

Ctrl+Alt+Delete *n.* A three-key combination used with IBM and compatible computers to restart (reboot) the machine. Pressing Ctrl+Alt+Delete (Control+Alternate+Delete) causes a warm boot in MS-DOS—the computer restarts but does not go through all of the internal checks involved when power to the system is switched on (cold boot). In Windows 9x and Windows NT, Ctrl+Alt+Delete provides a dialog box from which the user may choose to shut down the computer or end any current tasks.

Ctrl+C *n.* 1. In UNIX, the key combination used to break out of a running process. 2. The keyboard shortcut recognised by many programmes (as in Windows) as an instruction to copy the currently selected item.

Ctrl+S *n.* 1. On systems in which a software handshake is used between terminals and a central computer, the key combination used to suspend output. Ctrl+Q will resume output after a Ctrl-S suspension. See also software handshake, XON/XOFF. 2. A keyboard shortcut recognised by many programmes as an instruction to save the current document or file.

CTS *n.* Acronym for Clear To Send. In serial communications, a signal sent, as from a modem to its computer, to indicate that transmission can proceed. CTS is a hardware signal sent over line 5 in RS-232-C connections.

CUA *n.* See Common User Access.

cube *n.* An OLAP data structure. A cube contains dimensions (like Country/Region/City) and data fields (like Sales Amount). Dimensions organise types of data into hierarchies with levels of detail, and data fields measure quantities.

Cube *n.* A personal computer design introduced by Apple in 2000. The Cube featured a unique 8-by-8-by-8-inch transparent curved cube shape with the power supply outside the chassis to create a small and extremely quiet computer. The Cube offered the same G4 processor and features available on other Macintosh computers, but with fewer expansion options. Although the unique design drew notice for innovation, Apple discontinued manufacture of the Cube in 2001 after only one year of production.

CUI *n.* See character user interface.

CUL8R *n.* A fanciful shorthand notation meaning "See you later," sometimes seen in Internet discussion groups as a farewell by a participant temporarily leaving the group.

Curly quotes *n.* See smart quotes.

Current *n.* The flow of electric charge through a conductor, or the amount of such flow. Current is measured in amperes. See also ampere, coulomb.

Current cell *n.* See active cell.

Current directory *n.* The disk directory at the end of the active directory path—the directory that is searched first for a requested file, and the one in which a new file is stored unless another directory is specified. See also path (definition 2).

Current drain *n.* 1. The current taken from a voltage source by its load (the object receiving the current). Also called: drain. 2. The load itself. For example, a flashlight bulb takes current from the battery; this current is the drain on the battery, and the bulb itself may also be called the drain.

Current location counter *n.* See programme counter.

Current-mode logic *n.* A type of circuit design in which the transistors operate in unsaturated (amplifying) mode.

Cursor *n.* 1. A special onscreen indicator, such as a blinking underline or rectangle, that marks the place at which a keystroke will appear when typed. 2. In reference to digitizing tablets, the stylus (pointer or "pen"). 3. In applications and operating systems that use a mouse, the arrow or other onscreen icon that moves with movements of the mouse.

Cursor blink speed *n.* The rate at which a cursor on a screen flashes on and off. See also cursor (definition 1).

Cursor control *n.* The ability of a computer user to move the cursor to a specified location on the screen. Keys dedicated to cursor control include the left, right, up, and down arrow keys and certain others, such as Backspace, Home, and End. Pointing devices such as the mouse can also control cursor movements, often helping the user move the cursor long distances from place to place in a document.

Cursor key *n.* See arrow key.

CUSeeMe *n.* A video conferencing programme developed at Cornell University. It was the first programme to give Windows and Mac OS users the ability to engage in real-time video conferencing over the Internet, but it requires a lot of bandwidth (at least 128 Kbps speed) to function properly.

Custom control *n.* A control authored by a user or a third-party software vendor that does not belong to the .NET Framework class library. This is a generic term that includes user controls. A custom server control is used in Web Forms (ASP.NET pages). A custom client control is used in Windows Forms applications.

Customize *vb.* To modify or assemble hardware or software to suit the needs or preferences of the user. Traditionally, hardware customising ranges from designing an electronic circuit for a particular customer to putting together a computer facility tailored to a customer's special need. Software customising usually means modifying or designing software for a specific customer.

Custom queuing *n.* A form of queuing on Cisco routers where the wide area network (WAN) link is divided into micropipes based on a percentage of the total bandwidth available on the pipe. See also bandwidth reservation.

Custom software *n.* Any type of programme developed for a particular client or to address a special need. Certain products, such as dBASE and Lotus 1-2-3, are designed to provide the flexibility and tools required for producing tailor-made applications. See also CASE.

Cut *vb.* To remove part of a document, usually placing it temporarily in memory so that the cut portion can be inserted (pasted) elsewhere.

Cut and paste *n.* A procedure in which the computer acts as an electronic combination of scissors and glue for reorganising a document or for compiling a document from different sources. In cut and paste, the portion of a document to be moved is selected, removed to storage in memory or on disk, and then reinserted into the same or a different document.

Cut-through switch *n.* A network switch that routes packets immediately to the port associated with the packet's recipient. See also packet.

CV *n.* See computer vision.

CVS *n.* 1. See Computer Vision Syndrome. 2. Acronym for Concurrent Versions System. An open-source network-transparent version control system which allows multiple developers to view and edit code simultaneously. Popular because the client-server function allows operation over the Internet. CVS maintains a single copy of the source code with a record of who initiated changes and when the changes were made. CVS was developed for the UNIX operating system and is commonly used by programmers working with Linux, Mac OS X, and other UNIX-based environments.

CWIS *n.* See campuswide information system.

cXML *n.* Acronym for commerce XML. A set of document definitions for Extensible Markup Language (XML) developed for use in business-to-business e-commerce. cXML defines standards for product listings, allows for electronic requests and responses between procurement applications and suppliers, and provides for secure financial transactions via the Internet.

Cyber- prefix A prefix attached to "everyday" words in order to give them a computer-based or online meaning, as in cyberlaw (the practice of law either in relation to or through the use of the Internet) and cyberspace (the virtual online world). The prefix is derived from the word cybernetics, which refers to the study of mechanisms used to control and regulate complex systems, either human or machine.

Cyberart *n.* The artwork of artists who use computers to create or distribute their efforts.

Cybercafe or cyber café *n.* 1. A coffee shop or restaurant that offers access to PCs or other terminals that are connected to the Internet, usually for a per-hour or per-minute fee. Users are encouraged to buy beverages or food to drink or eat while accessing the Internet. 2. A virtual café on the Internet, generally used for social purposes. Users interact with each other by means of a chat programme or by posting messages to one another through a bulletin board system, such as in a newsgroup or on a Web site.

Cybercash *n.* See e-money.

Cyberchat *n.* See IRC.

Cybercop *n.* A person who investigates criminal acts committed online, especially fraud and harassment.

Cyberculture *n.* The behaviour, beliefs, customs, and etiquette that characterise groups of individuals who communicate or socialise over computer networks, such as the Internet. The cyberculture of one group can be vastly different from the cyberculture of another.

Cyberdog *n.* Apple's Internet suite for Web browsing and e-mail, based on OpenDoc for easy integration with other applications. See also OpenDoc.

Cyberlawyer *n.* 1. An attorney whose practice involves the law related to computers and online communication, including elements of communications law, intellectual property rights, privacy and security issues, and other specialties. 2. An attorney who advertises or distributes information over the Internet and the World Wide Web.

Cyberlife *n.* In the gaming world, a technology that mimics biological DNA. See also digital DNA.

Cybernaut *n.* One who spends copious time online, exploring the Internet. Also called: Internaut. See also cyberspace.

Cybernetics *n.* The study of control systems, such as the nervous system, in living organisms and the development of equivalent systems in electronic and mechanical devices. Cybernetics compares similarities and differences between living and nonliving systems (whether those systems comprise individuals, groups, or societies) and is based on theories of communication and control that can be applied to either living or nonliving systems or both. See also bionics.

Cyberpunk *n.* 1. A genre of near-future science fiction in which conflict and action take place in virtual-reality environments maintained on global computer networks in a worldwide culture of dystopian alienation. The prototypical cyberpunk novel is William Gibson's Neuromancer (1982). 2. A category of popular culture that resembles the ethos of cyberpunk fiction. 3. A person or fictional character who resembles the heroes of cyberpunk fiction.

Cybersex *n.* Communication via electronic means, such as e-mail, chat, or newsgroups, for the purpose of sexual stimulation or gratification. See also chat1 (definition 1), newsgroup.

Cyberspace *n.* 1. The advanced shared virtual-reality network imagined by William Gibson in his novel Neuromancer (1982). 2. The universe of environments, such as the Internet, in which persons interact by means of connected computers. A defining characteristic of cyberspace is that communication is independent of physical distance.

Cyberspeak *n.* Terminology and language (often jargon, slang, and acronyms) relating to the Internet (computer-connected) environment, that is, cyberspace. See also cyberspace.

Cybersquatter *n.* A person who registers company names and other trademarks as Internet domain names in order to force the named companies or owners of the trademarks to buy them at an inflated price.

Cyberwidow *n.* The spouse of a person who spends inordinate amounts of time on the Internet.

Cybrarian *n.* Software used at some libraries that allows one to query a database through the use of an interactive search engine.

Cycle power *vb.* To turn the power to a machine off and back on in order to clear something out of memory or to reboot after a hung or crashed state.

Cycle time *n.* The amount of time between a random access memory (RAM) access and the earliest time a new access can occur. See also access time (definition 1).

Cyclical redundancy check *n.* See CRC.

Table C.2 Cyclic Binary Code Compared to Other Numeral Systems

Cyclic binary	"Plain" binary	Decimal
0000	0000	0
0001	0001	1
0011	0010	2
0010	0011	3
0110	0100	4
0111	0101	5
0101	0110	6
0100	0111	7
1100	1000	8
1101	1001	9

Cyclic binary code *n.* A binary representation of numbers in which each number differs from the one that precedes it by one unit (bit), in one position. Cyclic binary numbers differ from "plain" binary numbers, even though both are based on two digits, 0 and 1. The numbers in the cyclic binary system represent a code, much like Morse code, whereas "plain" binary numbers represent actual values in the binary number system. Because sequential numbers differ by only 1 bit, cyclic binary is used to minimise errors in representing unit measurements. See the table.

Cycolour *n.* A colour printing process that uses a special film embedded with millions of capsules filled with cyan, magenta, and yellow dyes. When exposed to red, green, or blue light, the respective capsules become hard and unbreakable. The film is then pressed against specially treated paper, and the capsules that have not hardened in the previous process break, releasing their colours onto the paper.

D

DA *n.* See desk accessory.

DAC *n.* See digital-to-analog converter.

DACL *n.* See discretionary access control list.

Daemon *n.* A programme associated with UNIX systems that performs a housekeeping or maintenance utility function without being called by the user. A daemon sits in the background and is activated only when needed, for example, to correct an error from which another programme cannot recover.

Daisy chain1 *n.* A set of devices connected in series. In order to eliminate conflicting requests to use the channel (bus) to which all the devices are connected, each device is given a different priority. SCSI (Small Computer System Interface) and the newer USB (Universal Serial Bus) both support daisy-chained devices. See also SCSI, USB.

Daisy chain2 *vb.* To connect a series of devices, one to another, like daisies in a chain of flowers.

Daisy wheel *n.* A print element consisting of a set of formed characters with each character mounted on a separate type bar, all radiating from a center hub. See also daisy-wheel printer, thimble, thimble printer.

Daisy-wheel printer *n.* A printer that uses a daisy-wheel type element. Daisy-wheel output is crisp and slightly imprinted, with fully formed characters resembling typewriter quality. Daisy-wheel printers were standard for high-quality printing until being superseded by laser printers. See also daisy wheel, thimble, thimble printer.

Damping *n.* A technique for preventing overshoot (exceeding the desired limit) in the response of a circuit or device.

D-AMPS *n.* Acronym for Digital Advanced Mobile Phone Service. The digital form of the analog AMPS cellular phone service. D-AMPS, sometimes spelled DAMPS, differs from AMPS in being digital and in tripling the number of available channels by using time division multiple access (TDMA) to divide each of the 30 AMPS channels into three separate channels. See also AMPS, FDMA, TDMA.

DAO *n.* See Data Access Objects.

DAP *n.* See Directory Access Protocol.

DaratechSUMMIT *n.* Conference on emerging engineering and technology developments in the information technology industry. The DaratechSUMMIT focuses on how information technology affects business practices and assists in manufacturing and production.

dark fiber *n.* Unused capacity in fiber-optic communications.

Darlington circuit *n.* An amplifier circuit made of two transistors, often mounted in the same housing. The collectors of the two transistors are connected, and the emitter of the first is connected to the base of the second. Darlington circuits provide high-gain amplification. Also called: Darlington pair.

Darlington pair *n.* See Darlington circuit.

DARPA *n.* See Defense Advanced Research Projects Agency.

DARPANET *n.* Short for Defense Advanced Research Projects Agency NETwork. See ARPANET.

Darwin *n.* Apple Computer's open-source operating system, which forms the core of Mac OS X. Darwin is a processor-independent BSD UNIX operating system based on FreeBSD and Mach 3.0 technologies. Darwin offers advanced networking, protected memory, preemptive multitasking, and support for Macintosh and UNIX file systems. Darwin can be run on both the Power PC Macintosh and Intel processor-based computers. See also Mac OS X.

DAS *n.* See dual attachment station.

DASD *n.* Acronym for direct access storage device. A data storage device by which information can be accessed directly, instead of by passing sequentially through all storage areas. For example, a disk drive is a DASD, but a tape unit is not, because, with a tape unit, the data is stored as a linear sequence. See also direct access.

.dat *n.* A generic file extension for a data file.

DAT *n.* See digital audio tape, dynamic address translation.

data *n.* Plural of the Latin datum, meaning an item of information. In practice, data is often used for the singular as well as the plural form of the noun. See also datum.

Data Access Objects *n.* A data access interface that communicates with Microsoft Jet and ODBC-compliant data sources to connect to, retrieve, manipulate, and update data and the database structure. Acronym: DAO.

Data acquisition *n.* The process of obtaining data from another source, usually one outside a specific system.

Data aggregate *n.* A collection of data records. It usually includes a description of the placement of the data blocks and their relation to the entire set.

Data attribute *n.* Structural information about data that describes its context and meaning.

Data bank *n.* Any substantial collection of data.

Database *n.* A file composed of records, each containing fields together with a set of operations for searching, sorting, recombining, and other functions. Acronym: DB.

Database administrator *n.* One who manages a database. The administrator determines the content, internal structure, and access strategy for a database, defines security and integrity, and monitors performance. Acronym: DBA. Also called: database manager.

Database analyst *n.* One who provides the analytic functions needed to design and maintain applications requiring a database.

Database designer *n.* One who designs and implements functions required for applications that use a database.

Database engine *n.* The programme module or modules that provide access to a database management system (DBMS).

Database machine *n.* 1. A peripheral that executes database tasks, thereby relieving the main computer from performing them. 2. A database server that performs only database tasks.

Database management system *n.* A software interface between the database and the user. A database management system handles user requests for database actions and allows for control of security and data integrity requirements. Acronym: DBMS. Also called: database manager. See also database engine.

Database manager *n.* See database administrator, database management system.

Database publishing *n.* The use of desktop publishing or Internet technology to produce reports containing information obtained from a database.

Database server *n.* A network node, or station, dedicated to storing and providing access to a shared database. Also called: database machine.

Database structure *n.* A general description of the format of records in a database, including the number of fields, specifications regarding the type of data that can be entered in each field, and the field names used.

Data bit *n.* In asynchronous communications, one of a group of from 5 to 8 bits that represents a single character of data for transmission. Data bits are preceded by a start bit and followed by an optional parity bit and one or more stop bits. See also asynchronous transmission, bit, communications parameter.

Data buffer *n.* An area in memory where data is temporarily stored while being moved from one location to another. See also buffer1.

Data bus *n.* See bus.

Data cable *n.* Fiber-optic or wire cable used to transfer data from one device to another.

Data capture *n.* 1. The collection of information at the time of a transaction. 2. The process of saving on a storage medium a record of interchanges between a user and a remote information utility.

Data carrier *n.* See carrier (definition 1).

Data Carrier Detected *n.* See DCD (definition 1).

Data chaining *n.* The process of storing segments of data in noncontiguous locations while retaining the ability to reconnect them in the proper sequence.

Data channel *n.* See channel (definition 1).

Data closet *n.* See wiring closet.

Data collection *n.* 1. The process of acquiring source documents or data. 2. The grouping of data by means of classification, sorting, ordering, and other organising methods.

Datacom *n.* See communications. Short for data communications.

Data communications *n.* See communications.

Data compaction *n.* See data compression.

Data compression *n.* A means of reducing the amount of space or bandwidth needed to store or transmit a block of data, used in data communications, facsimile transmission, file storage and transfer, and CD-ROM publishing. Also called: data compaction.

Data conferencing *n.* Simultaneous data communication among geographically separated participants in a meeting. Data conferencing involves whiteboards and other software that enable a single set of files at one location to be accessed and modified by all participants. See the illustration. See also desktop conferencing, whiteboard.

Data control *n.* The aspect of data management concerned with tracking how and by whom data is used, accessed, altered, owned, and reported on.

Data conversion *n.* Changing the way information is represented in a document or file—for instance, changing binary representation to decimal or hexadecimal.

Data corruption *n.* See corruption.

Data declaration *n.* A statement in a programme that specifies the characteristics of a variable. The requirements for data declarations vary among different programming languages but can include such values as variable name, data type, initial value, and size specification. See also array, data type, record, variable.

Data definition language *n.* A language that defines all attributes and properties of a database, especially record layouts, field definitions, key fields, file locations, and storage strategy. Acronym: DDL.

Data description language *n.* A language designed specifically for declaring data structures and files. See also data definition language.

Data dictionary *n.* A database containing data about all the databases in a database system. Data dictionaries store all the various schema and file specifications and their locations. They also contain information about which programmes use which data and which users are interested in which reports.

Data directory *n.* See catalog, data dictionary.

Data-driven attack *n.* A form of attack in which malicious code is hidden in a programme or other innocuous data. When the data is executed, the virus or other destructive code is activated. A data-driven attack is typically used to bypass a firewall or other security measures.

Data-driven processing *n.* A form of processing where the processor or programme must wait for data to arrive before it can advance to the next step in a sequence.

Data element *n.* A single unit of data. Also called: data item. See also data field.

Data encapsulation *n.* A method of dealing with computers with Year 2000 problems that entailed modifying the input and output logic of a programme, leaving the actual data unchanged as it was processed. The input logic was modified to reflect a date in the past that the computer could handle that paralleled the current calendar. When output was generated, the output logic changed the data to reflect the correct date.

Data encryption *n.* See encryption.

Data encryption key *n.* A sequence of secret information, such as a string of decimal numbers or binary digits, that is used to encrypt and decrypt data. Acronym: DEK. See also decryption, encryption, key (definition 3).

Data encryption standard *n.* See DES.

Data entry *n.* The process of writing new data to computer memory.

Data/fax modem *n.* A modem that can handle both serial data and facsimile images to either send or receive transmissions.

Data field *n.* A well-defined portion of a data record, such as a column in a database table.

Data field masking *n.* The process of filtering or selecting part of a data field to control the way it is returned and displayed.

Data file *n.* A file consisting of data in the form of text, numbers, or graphics, as distinct from a programme file of commands and instructions.

Data flow or dataflow *n.* 1. The movement of data through a system, from entry to destination. 2. In parallel processing, a design in which a calculation is made either when all necessary data is available (data-driven processing) or when other processors request the data (demand-driven processing). See also parallel processing.

Data fork *n.* In Macintosh files, the part of a stored document that contains user-supplied information, such as the text of a word-processing document. A Macintosh file can have a data fork, a resource fork (which contains information such as programme code, font data, digitized sound, or icons), and a header. All three parts are used by the operating system in file management and storage. See also resource (definition 2), resource fork.

Data format *n.* The structure applied to data by an application programme to provide a context in which the data can be interpreted.

Data frame *n.* A packet of information transmitted as a unit on a network. Data frames are defined by the network's data-link layer and exist only on the wire between network nodes. See also data-link layer, frame (definition 2).

Data glove *n.* A data input device or controller in the form of a glove fitted with sensors that convert movement of the hand and fingers into commands. See also virtual reality.

Datagram *n.* One packet, or unit, of information, along with relevant delivery information such as the destination address, that is sent through a packet-switching network. See also packet switching.

Data independence *n.* The separation of data in a database from the programmes that manipulate it. Data independence makes stored data as accessible as possible.

Data integrity *n.* The accuracy of data and its conformity to its expected value, especially after being transmitted or processed.

Data interchange format *n.* A format consisting of ASCII codes in which database, spreadsheet, and similar documents can be structured to facilitate their use by and transfer to other programmes. Acronym: DIF. See also ASCII.

Data item *n.* See data element.

Data library *n.* A cataloged collection of data files on disk or in another storage medium.

Data link *n.* A connection between any two devices capable of sending and receiving information, such as a computer and a printer or a main computer and a terminal. Sometimes the term is extended to include equipment, such as a modem, that enables transmission and receiving. Such devices follow protocols that govern data transmission. See also communications protocol, data-link layer, DCE (definition 1), DTE.

Data Link Connection Identifier *n.* A virtual circuit on frame relay networks that permanently identifies the path to a particular destination. See also frame relay, virtual circuit.

Data Link Control *n.* See DLC.

Data link escape *n.* In data transmission, a control character that changes the meaning of the characters immediately following it.

Data-link layer *n.* The second of seven layers in the ISO/OSI reference model for standardising computer-to-computer communications. The data-link layer is one layer above the physical layer. Its concern is packaging and addressing data and managing the flow of transmissions. It is the lowest of the three layers (data-link, network, and transport) involved in actually moving data between devices. See the illustration. See also ISO/OSI reference model.

Data management *n.* The control of data from acquisition and input through processing, output, and storage. In microcomputers, hardware manages data by gathering it, moving it, and following instructions to process it. The operating system manages the hardware and ensures that the parts of the system work in harmony so that data is stored safely and accurately. Application programmes manage data by receiving and processing input according to the user's commands, and sending results to an output device or to disk storage. The user also is responsible for data management by acquiring data, labeling and organising disks, backing up data, archiving files, and removing unneeded material from the hard disk.

Data manipulation *n.* The processing of data by means of programmes that accept user commands, offer ways to handle data, and tell the hardware what to do with the data.

Data manipulation language *n.* In database management systems, a language that is used to insert data in, update, and query a database. Data manipulation languages are often capable of performing mathematical and statistical calculations that facilitate generating reports. Acronym: DML. See also structured query language.

Data mart *n.* A scaled-down version of a data warehouse that is tailored to contain only information likely to be used by the target group. See also data warehouse.

Data medium *n.* The physical material on which computer data is stored.

Data migration *n.* 1. The process of moving data from one repository or source, such as a database, to another, usually via automated scripts or programmes. Often data migration involves transferring data from one type of computer system to another. 2. In supercomputing applications, the process of storing large amounts of data off line while making them appear to be online as disk-resident files.

Data mining *n.* The process of identifying commercially useful patterns, problems, or relationships in a database, a Web server, or other computer repository through the use of advanced statistical tools. Some Web sites use data mining to monitor the efficiency of site navigation and to determine changes in the Web site's design based on how consumers are using the site.

Data model *n.* A collection of related object types, operators, and integrity rules that form the abstract entity supported by a database management system (DBMS). Thus, one speaks of a relational DBMS, a network DBMS, and so on, depending on the type of data model a DBMS -supports. In general, a DBMS supports only one data model as a practical rather than a theoretical restriction.

Data network *n.* A network designed for transferring data encoded as digital signals, as opposed to a voice network, which transmits analog signals.

Data Over Cable Service Interface Specification *n.* See DOCSIS.

Data-overrun error *n.* An error that occurs when more data is being acquired than can be processed. See also bps.

Data packet *n.* See packet.

Data path *n.* The route that a signal follows as it travels through a computer network.

Data point *n.* Any pair of numeric values plotted on a chart.

Data processing *n.* 1. The general work performed by computers. 2. More specifically, the manipulation of data to transform it into some desired result. Acronym: DP. Also called: ADP, automatic data processing, EDP, electronic data processing. See also centralised processing, decentralised processing, distributed processing.

Data Processing Management Association *n.* See DPMA.

Data projector *n.* A device, similar to a slide projector, that projects the video monitor output of a computer onto a screen.

Data protection *n.* The process of ensuring the preservation, integrity, and reliability of data. See also data integrity.

Data rate *n.* The speed at which a circuit or communications line can transfer information, usually measured in bits per second (bps).

Data record *n.* See record1.

Data reduction *n.* The process of converting raw data to a more useful form by scaling, smoothing, ordering, or other editing procedures.

Data segment *n.* The portion of memory or auxiliary storage that contains the data used by a programme.

Data Service Unit *n.* See DDS.

Data set *n.* 1. A collection of related information made up of separate elements that can be treated as a unit in data handling. 2. In communications, a modem. See also modem.

Data Set Ready *n.* See DSR.

Data sharing *n.* The use of a single file by more than one person or computer. Data sharing can be done by physically transferring a file from one computer to another, or, more commonly, by networking and computer-to-computer communications.

Data signal *n.* The information transmitted over a line or circuit. It consists of binary digits and can include actual information or messages and other elements such as control characters or error-checking codes.

Data sink *n.* 1. Any recording medium where data can be stored until needed. 2. In communications, the portion of a Data

Terminal Equipment (DTE) device that receives transmitted data.

Data source *n.* 1. The originator of computer data, frequently an analog or digital data collection device. 2. In communications, the portion of a Data Terminal Equipment (DTE) device that sends data.

Data stream *n.* An undifferentiated, byte-by-byte flow of data.

Data structure *n.* An organisational scheme, such as a record or array, that can be applied to data to facilitate interpreting the data or performing operations on it.

Data switch *n.* A device in a computer system that routes incoming data to various locations.

Data Terminal Equipment *n.* See DTE.

Data Terminal Ready *n.* See DTR.

Data traffic *n.* The exchange of electronic messages—control and data—across a network. Traffic capacity is measured in bandwidth; traffic speed is measured in bits per unit of time.

Data transfer *n.* The movement of information from one location to another, either within a computer (as from a disk drive to memory), between a computer and an external device (as between a file server and a computer on a network), or between separate computers.

Data transfer rate *n.* See data rate.

Data transmission *n.* The electronic transfer of information from a sending device to a receiving device.

Data type *n.* In programming, a definition of a set of data that specifies the possible range of values of the set, the operations that can be performed on the values, and the way in which the values are stored in memory. Defining the data type allows a computer to manipulate the data appropriately. Data types are most often supported in high-level languages and often include types such as real, integer, floating point, character, Boolean, and pointer. How a language handles data typing is one of its major characteristics. See also cast, constant, enumerated data type, strong typing, type checking, user-defined data type, variable, weak typing.

Data validation *n.* The process of testing the accuracy of data.

Data value *n.* The literal or interpreted meaning of a data item, such as an entry in a database, or a type, such as an integer, that can be used for a variable.

Data warehouse1 *n.* A database, frequently very large, that can access all of a company's information. While the warehouse can be distributed over several computers and may contain several databases and information from numerous sources in a variety of formats, it should be accessible through a server. Thus, access to the warehouse is transparent to the user, who can use simple commands to retrieve and analyse all the information. The data warehouse also contains data about how the warehouse is organised, where the information can be found, and any connections between data. Frequently used for decision support within an organisation, the data warehouse also allows the organisation to organise its data, coordinate updates, and see relationships between information gathered from different parts of the organisation. See also database, decision support system, server (definition 1), transparent (definition 1).

Data warehouse2 *vb.* To acquire, collect, manage, and disseminate information gathered from various sources into a single location; or to implement an informational database used to store sharable data. Data warehousing is a four-step process: gathering data; managing the data in a centralised location; providing access to the data along with tools for interpreting, analysing, and reporting on the data; and producing reports on the data to be used for decision making. See also downflow, inflow, metaflow, upflow.

Date and time stamp *n.* See time stamp.

Date counter overflow *n.* A problem that may occur in systems or programmes when the value in a date variable exceeds allowable values. A date counter overflow can occur when an incremental date produces a number that the system interprets as zero or a negative number. This is likely to cause the system or programme to post an error message in turn or to revert to the original starting point. Although this was largely considered a Year 2000 problem, such an error is not necessarily confined to the year 2000.

Date dependency *n.* In terms of the Year 2000 problem, the need many programmes have for date-related input or output data and the way dates are represented in that data. This dependency affects whether the programme can run correctly when the turn of the century is reached.

Date expansion *n.* A method of dealing with programmes with Year 2000 problems that entails changing data, data descriptions, and (if necessary) programme logic that pertains to dates by expanding date fields from two digits to four digits—for example, from DDMMYY to DDMMYYYY.

Date format *n.* The manner in which dates are formatted in a computer system or programme. While some organisations require that the same format be used throughout their systems and programmes, many organisations have not, which can make tracking down potential date problems, such as the Year 2000 problem, difficult. In addition, date formats can vary widely from organisation to organisation, although many have opted to standardise on formats specified in ANSI X3.30-1997 or ISO8601:1988.

Date horizon *n.* A period of time that a programme uses to determine the beginning or ending point in performing its functions. A programme that tracks inventory may have one date horizon that trails the current date by two months (a trailing date horizon) to process returned merchandise and another that precedes it by another two months (a leading date horizon) for planning purposes. If the programme logic doesn't account for any date horizons it may have, for example, if the year was 1999, the programme could experience Year 2000 problems when the leading date horizon enters January 1, 2000. See also event horizon.

Date-in-key problem *n.* A potential problem in computer systems that depend on indexed files using a two-digit date as part of the key, such as certain databases. If the files need to be in chronological order, the files beginning with the year 2000 will be out of sequence—for example, (19)99 would be interpreted as more recent than (20)00.

Date rollover *n.* See Year 2000 rollover.

Date stamp *n.* See time stamp.

Date stamping *n.* A software feature that automatically inserts the current date into a document.

Datum *n.* Singular of data; a single item of information. See also data.

Daughterboard *n.* A circuit board that attaches to another, such as the main system board (motherboard), to add extra capabilities. See also motherboard.

DAV connector *n.* See digital audio/video connector.

Day-of-the-week problem *n.* A reference to an inaccuracy that could occur after the Year 2000 in computers that calculate the day of the week based on the last two digits of the year, assuming that the dates they calculate fall in the 1900s. Because January 1, 1900 was a Monday, but January 1, 2000 was Saturday, those computers may not be able to correctly determine the day of the week. This is particularly problematic in computers that regulate timed systems based on the business week, such as a door or vault that unlocks during business hours.

DB *n.* See database.

dB *n.* See decibel.

DBA *n.* See database administrator.

DB connector *n.* Any of various connectors that facilitate parallel input and output. The initials DB (for data bus) are followed by a number that indicates the number of lines (wires) within the connector. For example, a DB-9 connector has nine pins and supports up to nine lines, each of which can connect to a pin on the connector.

.dbf *n.* A file extension for a dBASE database file.

DBMS *n.* See database management system.

DBS *n.* See direct broadcast satellite.

dbXML *n.* Acronym for database XML. A native XML database server designed to manage large collections of XML documents. dbXML may be embedded in custom applications or run as a stand-alone database.

DC *n.* See direct current.

DCA *n.* 1. Acronym for Document Content Architecture. A formatting guideline used in IBM's Systems Network Architecture (SNA) that enables the exchange of text-only documents between differing types of computers. DCA provides for two types of document formatting: Revisable-Form-Text DCA (RFTDCA), which allows for modification of formatting, and Final-Form-Text DCA (FFTDCA), which cannot be modified. See also DIA, SNA. 2. Acronym for Directory Client Agent. See DUA.

DCD *n.* 1. Acronym for Data Carrier Detected. A signal in serial communications that is sent from a modem to its computer to indicate that the modem is ready for transmitting. Also called: RLSD. See also RS-232-C standard. 2. Acronym for Document Content Description. A specification governing the rules for defining the structure and content of XML documents. The specification was created by IBM and Microsoft in 1998 and was submitted to the World Wide Web Consortium for approval. See also XML.

DCE *n.* 1. Acronym for Data Communications Equipment. The term used in RS-232 and X.25 specifications for a device, such as a modem, that provides another device (known as the Data Terminal Equipment or DTE) with access to a communications line. A DCE is an intermediary device that often transforms input from a DTE before sending it to a recipient. See also RS-232-C standard, X series.

D channel *n.* Short for data channel. In the ISDN communications architecture, the channel dedicated to carrying control signals, such as packet-switching information; and user-related data, such as phone numbers. The basic ISDN connection, called the Basic Rate Interface (BRI), is composed of two B (bearer) channels, which carry as much as 64 Kbps of actual data each, and one D channel, which transmits at either 16 Kbps or 64 Kbps. The faster Primary Rate Interface (PRI) is composed of one 64-Kbps D channel and either 23 or 30 B channels operating at 64 Kbps. See also B channel, BRI, ISDN.

DCOM *n.* Acronym for Distributed Component Object Model. The version of Microsoft's Component Object Model (COM) specification that stipulates how components communicate over Windows-based networks. It permits the distribution of different components for a single application across two or more networked computers, running an application distributed across a network so that the distribution of components is not apparent to the user, and remotely displaying an application. Also called: Distributed COM. See also COM (definition 2), component (definition 2).

DCS *n.* Acronym for Desktop Colour Separation. The primary format for preparing digital publication text and graphics for printing. DCS layouts consist of five files, one for each of the CMYK colours, and a master file which, includes the display version of the page and information on the other four files. See also OPI.

DCTL *n.* See direct-coupled transistor logic.

DDBMS *n.* See distributed database management system.

DDC *n.* Acronym for Display Data Channel. A VESA standard that allows software control of graphical computer monitors. Under DDC, monitor characteristics are provided to the graphics subsystem, which uses the data to configure the display and provide a bidirectional communication channel between the monitor and computer. Also called: VESA DDC. See also VESA2.

DDCP *n.* See direct digital colour proof.

DDE *n.* Acronym for Dynamic Data Exchange. An interprocess communication method featured in Microsoft Windows and OS/2. DDE allows two or more programmes that are running simultaneously to exchange data and commands. In Windows 3.1, DDE was largely supplanted by OLE, which is an extension of DDE. In Windows 95 and Windows NT, OLE and ActiveX are more commonly used. See also ActiveX, interprocess communication, OLE.

DDK *n.* Acronym for Driver Development Kit. A set of tools used to create software that enables an operating system to work with hardware devices. With a DDK, a software developer can build drivers to support network, storage, print, sound, video, input, and other devices. Also called: Device Driver Kit, Device Driver Developer Kit. See also driver.

DDL *n.* See data definition language.

DDoS *n.* Acronym for distributed denial of service attack. A form of denial of service attack (DoS) originating from several computers that seeks to disrupt Web access by overwhelming a target with connection requests that cannot be completed. A DDoS attack involves cracking into a number of computers and planting programmes that lie dormant until sent a signal to attack. At that point the computers send a steady stream of data packets to the targeted Web site, overwhelming the ability of the Web server to respond. Because the attack is coming from many computers, security features that might otherwise recognise the attack and stop accepting data packets from a single source are unable to shut down connections to all the attackers. See also DoS, packet, zombie.

DDR SDRAM *n.* Short for Double Data Rate Synchronous Dynamic RAM (SDRAM). A form of SDRAM that essentially doubles memory throughput to 200 megahertz or better. DDR SDRAM gets a boost in data transfer rates by producing output on both the rising and falling of the system clock—that is, twice for each clock cycle. See also SDRAM.

DDS *n.* Acronym for digital data service, a dedicated communications line that provides transmission at speeds up to 56 Kbps. DDS lines use a device known as a CSU/DSU rather than a modem for connecting two networks. The CSU, or Channel Service Unit, connects the network to the transmission line; the DSU, or Data Service Unit, converts data for transmission by the CSU and controls data flow.

Dead code *n.* Programme code that never gets executed, possibly because the programmer has eliminated all references to it, or possibly because the programme is written in such a way that the instruction(s) will never be needed—for example, an ELSE statement would never be needed in an IF condition that always proved to be true. Dead code can slow programme execution and increase the size of the programme in memory. Also called: grunge, software rot.

Dead halt *n.* A machine stop with no hope of recovery by either the programme or the operating system. The only choice after a dead halt is to reboot. Also called: drop-dead halt. See also hang.

Dead key *n.* A key used with another key to create an accented character. When pressed, a dead key produces no visible character (hence its name) but indicates that the accent mark it represents is to be combined with the next key pressed. See also key (definition 1).

Dead-letter box *n.* In e-mail or message systems, a file to which undeliverable messages are sent.

Deadlock *n.* 1. A situation that occurs when two programmes or devices are each waiting for a response from the other before continuing. Also called: deadly embrace. 2. In operating systems, a situation in which two or more processes are prevented from continuing while each waits for resources to be freed by the continuation of the other. 3. In computer games, a deadlock occurs when the resources needed to continue the game become unavailable to the player. The deadlock condition could be intentional, such as a loss condition, or a design error on the part of the game developer. See also computer games.

Deadly embrace *n.* See deadlock.

Deallocate *vb.* To free previously allocated memory. See also pointer.

Deblock *vb.* To remove one or more logical records (units of stored information) from a block. Application or database systems must often deblock information to make specific units of information available for processing.

Debounce algorithm *n.* A set of instructions that makes an assumption about how fast a user can press and release a switch and then ensures that only one press is registered in the time specified.

Debug *vb.* To detect, locate, and correct logical or syntactical errors in a programme or malfunctions in hardware. In hardware contexts, the term troubleshoot is the term more often used, especially when the problem is a major one. See also bug, debugger.

Debugger *n.* A programme designed to aid in debugging another programme by allowing the programmer to step through the programme, examine the data, and monitor conditions such as the values of variables. See also bug (definition 1), debug.

Deca- prefix Metric prefix meaning 10—that is, 10 to the first power, or 101.

Decay *n.* A decrease in the amplitude of a signal over time.

DECchip 21064 *n.* A Digital Equipment Corporation microprocessor introduced in February 1992. The DECchip 21064 is a 64-bit, RISC-based, superscalar, superpipelined chip with 64-bit registers, a 64-bit data bus, a 64-bit address bus, and a 128-bit data path between the microprocessor and memory. It also has a built-in 8-KB instruction cache, a built-in 8-KB data cache, and a floating-point processor. The DECchip 21064 contains 1.7 million transistors and operates at 3.3 volts. The 200-MHz version runs at a peak rate of 400 MPS. The chip's architecture is SMP compliant, so that several chips can be used in a parallel (multiprocessor) configuration. See also floating-point processor, MIPS, pipelining (definition 1), RISC, superpipelining, superscalar.

Deceleration time *n.* The time required for an access arm to come to a stop as it approaches the desired portion of a disk. The faster the arm moves, the more momentum it gains and the greater the deceleration time.

Decentralized processing *n.* The distribution of computer processing facilities in more than one location. Decentralised processing is not the same as distributed processing, which assigns multiple computers to the same task to increase efficiency.

Deci- prefix Metric prefix meaning 10–1 (one-tenth).

Decibel *n.* One tenth of a bel (named after Alexander Graham Bell), a unit used in electronics and other fields to measure the strength of a sound or signal. Decibel measurements fall on a logarithmic scale and compare the measured quantity against a known reference. The following formula gives the number of decibels between two values: dB = n log (x/r) where x is the measured quantity, r is the reference quantity, and n is 10 for voltage and current measurements and 20 for power measurements.Abbreviation: dB.

Decimal *n.* The base-10 numbering system. See also base (definition 2).

Decision box *n.* A diamond-shaped flowchart symbol denoting a decision that results in a branching in the process being considered. See the illustration.

Decision support system *n.* A set of programmes and related data designed to help with analysis and decision making. A decision support system provides more help in formulating decisions than a management information system (MIS) or an executive information system (EIS). It includes a database, a body of knowledge about the subject area, a "language" used to formulate problems and questions, and a modeling programme for testing alternative decisions. Acronym: DSS.

Decision table *n.* A tabular listing of possible conditions (inputs) and the desired result (output) corresponding to each condition. A decision table may be used in the preliminary analysis of programme flow, or it may be converted and incorporated into the programme itself.

Decision tree *n.* Similar to a decision table, an analysis instrument where possible outcomes of some condition are represented as branches, which may in turn generate other branches. See the illustration. See also branch, tree structure.

Deck *n.* A storage device, such as a tape deck, or a group of such devices.

Declaration *n.* A binding of an identifier to the information that relates to it. For example, to make a declaration of a constant means to bind the name of the constant with its value. Declaration usually occurs in a program's source code; the actual binding can take place at compile time or run time. See also bind, constant, data declaration, data type, identifier, instruction, routine, type declaration, variable.

Declarative markup language *n.* In text processing, a system of text-formatting codes that indicates only that a unit of text is a certain part of a document. Document formatting is then done by another programme, called a parser. SGML and HTML are examples of declarative markup languages. Acronym: DML. Also called: data manipulation language. See also HTML, SGML.

Declare *vb.* To specify the name and type of a variable that will be used in a programme. In most high-level programming languages, variables are declared at the beginning of sections of code. See also variable.

DECnet *n.* A hardware, software, and protocol stack designed by Digital Equipment Corporation for its Digital Network Architecture (DNA).

Decoder *n.* 1. A device or programme routine that converts coded data back to its original form. This can mean changing unreadable or encrypted codes into readable text or changing one code to another, although the latter type of decoding is usually referred to as conversion. 2. In electronics and hardware, a type of circuit that produces one or more selected output signals based on the combination of input signals it receives.

Decollate *vb.* To separate copies in a multipart continuous paper form.

Decompiler *n.* A programme that attempts to generate high-level source code from assembly language code or machine code. This can be a difficult task, as some assembly language code has no corresponding high-level source code. See also disassembler.

Decompress *vb.* See uncompress.

Decrement 1 *n.* The amount by which a number is decreased.

Decrement 2 *vb.* To decrease a number by a given amount.

Decryption *n.* The process of restoring encrypted data to its original form. See also data encryption key.

deCSS *n.* Decrypt CSS. A utility capable of cracking the CSS encryption system used on DVD discs. By decrypting the CSS code, DVD movies and other copyrighted material can be used with any DVD playback device without regard to license or region coding. The origin of deCSS can be traced to a number of individuals interested in creating a DVD player for the Linux OS. The term deCSS is sometimes used generically for any software capable of defeating CSS technology. See also CSS, region code.

DECstation *n.* 1. A small computer system used primarily for word processing, introduced by Digital Equipment Corporation in 1978. 2. A personal computer, part of a series, introduced by Digital Equipment Corporation in 1989. 3. A single-user UNIX workstation introduced by Digital Equipment Corporation in 1989 and based on RISC processors. See also RISC.

Dedicated *adj.* Of, pertaining to, or being a device, programme, or procedure devoted to a single task or function.

Dedicated channel *n.* A communications link reserved for a particular use or a particular user.

Dedicated line *n.* 1. A communications channel that permanently connects two or more locations. Dedicated lines are private or leased lines, rather than public ones. T1 lines, which are used by many organisations for Internet connectivity, are examples of dedicated lines. Also called: dedicated connection, leased line, private line. 2. A telephone line that is used for one purpose only, such as to receive or send faxes or to serve as a modem line.

Dedicated server *n.* A computer—usually quite powerful—that is used solely as a network server. See also server.

Deep copy *n.* A copy of the contents of a data structure, including all its substructures.

Deep hack *n.* A state of total concentration on and preoccupation with a programming effort. Also called: deep hack mode.

De facto standard *n.* A design, programme, or language that has become so widely used and imitated that it has little competition, but whose status has not been officially recognised as standard by an organisation such as the American National Standards Institute (ANSI) or the International Organisation for Standardization (ISO). See also standard.

Default1 *n.* A choice made by a programme when the user does not specify an alternative. Defaults are built into a programme when a value or option must be assumed for the programme to function.

Default2 *vb.* In reference to programmes, to make a choice when the user does not specify an alternative.

Default button *n.* The control that is automatically selected when a window is introduced by an application or operating system, typically activated by pressing the Enter key.

Default drive *n.* The disk drive that an operating system reads to and writes from when no alternative is specified.

Default home page *n.* On a Web server, the file that is returned when a directory is referenced without a specific filename. This is specified by the Web server software and is typically the file called index.html or index.htm.

Default printer *n.* The printer to which a computer sends documents for printing unless an alternative is specified.

Defense Advanced Research Projects Agency *n.* The U.S. government agency that provided the original support for the development of the interconnected networks that later grew into the Internet. Acronym: DARPA. See also ARPANET.

Deferral time *n.* The length of time that nodes on a CSMA/CD network wait before trying to retransmit after a collision. See also CSMA/CD.

Deferred address *n.* An indirect address (memory location) whose calculation is delayed until a programme is run. See also relative address.

Deferred processing *n.* Processing of data after it has been received and stored in blocks.

Deflection coils *n.* See yoke.

Deflection routing *n.* See hot potato routing.

Deformation *n.* In multimedia and computer-aided design applications, the process of altering a model via certain tools, such as stretch, shatter, bend, and twist. See also CAD, multimedia.

Defrag *vb.* Slang for defragment. To rearrange data on a disk drive so that whole files are stored in contiguous sectors and the drive heads do not have to travel to scattered locations on the disk in order to read or write portions of a particular file. See also defragmentation.

Defragger *n.* A software utility for reuniting parts of a file that have become fragmented through rewriting and updating. A defragger physically restores the file to contiguous sectors on a hard disk to speed up access as much as 75 percent. See also defragmentation, fragmentation, optimizer.

Defragmentation *n.* The process of rewriting parts of a file to contiguous sectors on a hard disk to increase the speed of access and retrieval. When files are updated, the computer tends to save these updates on the largest continuous space on the hard disk, which is often on a different sector than the other parts of the file. When files are thus "fragmented," the computer must search the hard disk each time the file is accessed to find all of the file's parts, which slows down response time. See also optimization (definition 1).

Degausser *n.* A device used to remove magnetization from a video monitor or tape recorder head and to erase information from magnetic storage media, such as tapes and disks.

Degradation *n.* 1. In communications, a deterioration of signal quality, as from line interference. 2. In computer systems, a reduction in level of performance or service. Degradation in microcomputer performance is indicated by slow response times or frequent pauses for disk access because memory is insufficient to hold an entire programme plus the data the programme is using.

Deinstall *vb.* See uninstall.

Deinterlace *n.* To combine two interlaced fields into a single frame that is not interlaced. Deinterlacing is done to remove artifacts and improve the quality of encoded video.

Dejagging *n.* Smoothing of the jagged, "stairstep" appearance of diagonal lines and curves in graphical images. Also called: anti-aliasing.

De jure standard *n.* A standard for hardware or software development that has been issued or approved through a formal process by a standards organisation. See also standard.

DEK *n.* See data encryption key.

Deka- prefix See deca-.

Delay distortion *n.* See envelope delay.

Delete *vb.* To eliminate text, a file, or part of a document with the intention of removing the information permanently. There are several ways to delete. Onscreen characters and parts of documents can be deleted with the Delete key, the Backspace key, or with a program's Delete command. Files can be deleted through a command to the operating system.

Delete key *n.* 1. On IBM and PC-compatible computers, a key whose function changes depending on the application programme. Usually it erases the character under the cursor, although in some applications it can erase selected text or graphics. See the illustration. Also called: Del key. 2. On Apple Macintosh computers, a key on the ADB and Extended keyboards that erases the character preceding the insertion point or erases highlighted text or graphics.

Deletia *n.* Omitted material. The term is used in responses to Usenet or mailing list messages to indicate that some unnecessary material has been excluded from the incorporated message being answered.

Delimit *vb.* To set the limits of some entity, generally by using a special symbol called a delimiter. Programming languages typically delimit such variable-length elements as comments, strings, and programme blocks. See also delimiter.

Delimiter *n.* A special character that sets off, or separates, individual items in a programme or set of data. Special characters often used include commas, semi-colons, tabs, and paragraph marks. See also delimit, field (definition 1), record1.

Del key *n.* See Delete key.

Delta channel *n.* See ISDN.

Demand-driven processing *n.* The processing of data immediately as it becomes available or ready. Such real-time processing avoids the need to store data that has not been processed.

Demand paging *n.* The most common implementation of virtual memory, in which pages of data are read into main memory from an auxiliary storage device only in response to interrupts that result when software requests a memory location that the system has saved to auxiliary storage and reused for other purposes. See also paging, swap (definition 2), virtual memory.

Demand priority *n.* A network access method in which hubs control network access; a feature of 100Base-VG Ethernet networks. With demand priority, nodes send requests to hubs and the hubs give permission to transmit based on priority levels assigned to the requests by the nodes. See also 100Base-VG.

Demand publishing *n.* Producing print copies of publications on an as-needed basis rather than in a single long press run. Demand publishing is a by-product of desktop publishing and advancements in printer capabilities.

Demo *n.* 1. Short for demonstration. A partial or limited version of a software package distributed free of charge for advertising purposes. Demos often consist of animated presentations that describe or demonstrate the program's features. See also crippled version. 2. A computer in a store that is available for customers to test, to see if they wish to buy it.

Demodulation *n.* In communications, the means by which a modem converts data from modulated carrier frequencies (waves that have been modified in such a way that variations in amplitude and frequency represent meaningful information) over a telephone line. Data is converted to the digital form needed by a computer to which the modem is attached, with as little distortion as possible.

Demon dialer *n.* See war dialer.

Demonstration programme or demo programme *n.* 1. A prototype that shows the onscreen look and sometimes the proposed capabilities of a programme under development. See also prototyping. 2. A scaled-down version of a proprietary programme offered as a marketing tool.

Denial of service attack *n.* See DoS.

Denizen *n.* A participant in a Usenet newsgroup.

Dense wavelength division multiplexing *n.* A data transmission technique in which multiple optical signals, each assigned to a separate colour (wavelength frequency), are multiplexed onto a single strand of optical fiber. Because each signal travels separately in its own colour band on the fiber, dense wavelength division multiplexing allows for the simultaneous transmission of different types of signals, such as SONET and ATM, each traveling at its own rate of speed. Dense wavelength division multiplexing can greatly increase the carrying capacity of a single optical fiber. Depending on the number, type, and rate of the signals involved, bandwidth can range from more than 40 Gbps to projected highs of 200 Gbps or more. Acronym: DWDM. Also called: wave divisision multiplexing, WDM.

Dependence *n.* The state in which one entity relies upon specific hardware, software, or specific events for its own definition or functionality. See also context-dependent, dependent variable, device dependence, hardware-dependent, software-dependent.

Dependent variable *n.* A variable in a programme whose value relies on the outcome of another operation.

Deployment descriptor *n.* In the Java J2EE network platform, a deployment descriptor is an XML file provided for each module or application describing how it should be deployed. The deployment descriptor directs a deployment tool to deploy a module or application with specific container options. It also describes the specific configuration requirements that an administrator must resolve when installing modules and J2EE applications into an operational environment. See also container, J2EE, module, XML.

Depth queuing *vb.* 1. In computer graphics and modeling, giving a two-dimensional object a three-dimensional appearance through such techniques as shading and -hidden-line removal. 2. Drawing objects from background to foreground to ease in the task of hidden-line removal.

Deque *n.* Short for double-ended que. A form of the queue data structure that can have elements added to or removed from either end of the list. See also queue.

Dequeue *vb.* To remove from a queue. See also queue.

Dereference *vb.* In programming, to access information at the address contained by a pointer. The syntax for dereferencing varies among computer languages. See also double-dereference, handle (definition 1), pointer.

Derived class *n.* In object-oriented programming, a class created from another class, called the base class. A derived class inherits all the features of its base class. It can then add data elements and routines, redefine routines from the base class, and restrict access to base-class features. See also base class, class, inheritance (definition 1), object-oriented programming.

Derived font *n.* A font that has been scaled or modified from a previously existing font. For example, the Macintosh operating system can generate characters in font sizes other than the installed range of sizes. See also font.

Derived relation *n.* A relation produced as the result of one or more relational-algebra operations on other relations. See also relational algebra, view (definition 2).

DES *n.* Acronym for Data Encryption Standard. A specification for encryption of computer data developed by IBM and adopted by the U.S. government as a standard in 1976. DES uses a 56-bit key. See also encryption, key (definition 3).

Descendant *n.* 1. In object-oriented programming, a class (group) that is a more specialised form of another, higher-level class. See also class, object-oriented programming. 2. In computing, a process (roughly, a programme or task) that is called by another process and inherits certain of the originator's properties, such as open files. See also child (definition 1), inheritance (definition 2).

Descendent key *n.* All the subkeys that appear when a key in the registry is expanded. A descendent key is the same as a subkey. Also called: descendant key. See also key, subkey.

Descender *n.* The portion of a lowercase letter that falls below the baseline. See the illustration. See also baseline, x-height.

Descender.

Descending sort *n.* A sort that arranges items in descending order—for example, with Z preceding A and higher numbers preceding lower ones. See also alphanumeric sort.

Descriptor *n.* 1. In information retrieval, a word, similar to an index entry in a book, that identifies a significant topic or element in a stored document or group of documents. It is used as a key in rapid search and retrieval of information. See also keyword (definition 1). 2. In programming, a piece of stored information used to describe something else, often in terms of structure, content, or some other property.

Deselect *vb.* To reverse the action of selecting an option, a range of text, a collection of graphical objects, and so on.

Deserialize *vb.* To change from serial (by bit) to parallel (by byte); to convert a single (serial) stream of bits to parallel streams representing the same information.

Design by Contract *n.* An approach to building reusable systems where a software system is viewed as a set of communicating components whose interaction is based on precisely defined specifications of the mutual obligations, also known as contracts.

Design cycle *n.* All the phases involved in developing and producing new hardware or software, including product specification, creation of prototypes, testing, debugging, and documentation.

Desk accessory *n.* A type of small programme on Macintosh computers and in windowing programmes for IBM and PC-compatible machines that acts as the electronic equivalent of a clock, calendar, calculator, or other small appliance found on a typical desktop. Desk accessories are conveniences that can be activated when needed and then either put away or moved to a small part of the screen. A special type of desk accessory, a control panel, provides the user with the ability to change the date and time as well as to control screen colours, mouse movements, and other parameters. Acronym: DA. Also called: desktop accessory. See also control panel.

Desktop *n.* An onscreen work area that uses icons and menus to simulate the top of a desk. A desktop is characteristic of the Apple Macintosh and of windowing programmes such as Microsoft Windows. Its intent is to make a computer easier to use by enabling users to move pictures of objects and to start and stop tasks in much the same way as they would if they were working on a physical desktop. See also graphical user interface.

Desktop accessory *n.* See desk accessory.

Desktop Colour Separation *n.* See DCS.

Desktop computer *n.* A computer that fits conveniently on the surface of a business desk. Most personal computers as well as some workstations can be considered desktop computers.

Desktop conferencing *n.* The use of computers for simultaneous communication among geographically separated participants in a meeting. This communication may include input to and display from application programmes as well as audio and video communication. See also data conferencing, teleconferencing, video conferencing.

Desktop enhancer *n.* Software that adds functionality to a windows-based operating system such as Microsoft Windows or Mac OS—for example, an enhanced file browser, clipboard, or multimedia player.

Desktop environment *n.* The appearance and user interface of a computer operating system (OS). An OS may offer the user opportunities to customise the desktop environment, or sometimes a choice of alternate desktop environments, with the OS underneath remaining the same.

Desktop file *n.* A hidden file maintained on a particular volume (roughly equivalent to a disk) by the Macintosh operating system for storing information about the files on it, such as version data, lists of icons, and file references.

Desktop Management Interface *n.* See DMI.

Desktop publishing *n.* The use of a computer and specialised software to combine text and graphics to create a document that can be printed on either a laser printer or a typesetting machine. Desktop publishing is a multiple-step process involving various types of software and equipment. The original text and illustrations are generally produced with software such as word processors and drawing and painting programmes and with photograph-scanning equipment and digitizers. The finished product is then transferred to a page-makeup programme, which is the software most people think of as the actual desktop publishing software. This type of programme enables the user to lay out text and graphics on the screen and see what the results will be; for refining parts of the document, these programmes often include word processing and graphics features in addition to layout capabilities. As a final step, the finished document is printed either on a laser printer or, for the best quality, by typesetting equipment.

Desktop video *n.* The use of a personal computer to display video images. The video images may be recorded on video tape or on a laser disc or may be live footage from a video camera. Live video images can be transmitted in digital form over a network in video conferencing. Acronym: DTV.

Destination *n.* The location (drive, folder, or directory) to which a file is copied or moved.

Destructive read *n.* An attribute of certain memory systems, notably core systems. In a destructive read of a memory location, the data is passed on to the processor, but the copy in memory is destroyed by the process of reading. Destructive memory systems require special logic to rewrite data back to a memory location after it is read. Also called: destructive readout. See also core.

Detail file *n.* See transaction file.

Detection *n.* Discovery of a certain condition that affects a computer system or the data with which it works.

Determinant *n.* In database design theory, any attribute or combination of attributes on which any other attribute or combination of attributes is functionally dependent.

Determinism *n.* In computing, the ability to predict an outcome or to know in advance how data will be manipulated by a processing system. A deterministic simulation, for example, is one in which a certain input always produces the same output.

Developer *n.* 1. One who designs and develops software. 2. See programmer.

Developer's toolkit *n.* A set of routines (usually in one or more libraries) designed to allow developers to more easily write programmes for a given computer, operating system, or user interface. See also library (definition 1), toolbox.

Development cycle *n.* The process of application development from definition of requirements to finished product, including the following stages: analysis, design and prototyping, software coding and testing, and implementation.

Device *n.* A generic term for a computer subsystem. Printers, serial ports, and disk drives are often referred to as devices; such subsystems frequently require their own controlling software, called device drivers. See also device driver.

Device address *n.* A location within the address space of a computer's random access memory (RAM) that can be altered either by the microprocessor or by an external device. Device addresses are different from other locations in RAM, which can be altered only by the microprocessor. See also device, input/output, RAM.

Device control character *n.* See control character.

Device controller *n.* See input/output controller.

Device dependence *n.* The requirement that a particular device be present or available for the use of a programme, interface, or protocol. Device dependence in a programme is often considered unfortunate because the programme either is limited to one system or requires adjustments for every other type of system on which it is to run.

Device driver *n.* A software component that permits a computer system to communicate with a device. In most cases, the driver also manipulates the hardware in order to transmit the data to the device. However, device drivers associated with application packages typically perform only the data translation; these higher-level drivers then rely on lower-level drivers to actually send the data to the device. Many devices, especially video adapters on PC-compatible computers, will not work properly—if at all—without the correct device drivers installed in the system.

Device Driver Developer Kit *n.* See DDK.

Device Driver Kit *n.* See DDK.

Device independence *n.* A characteristic of a programme, interface, or protocol that supports software operations that produce similar results on a wide variety of hardware. For example, the PostScript language is a device-independent page description language because programmes issuing PostScript drawing and text commands need not be customised for each potential printer.

Device-independent bitmap *n.* See DIB.

Device manager *n.* A software utility that allows viewing and changing hardware configuration settings, such as interrupts, base addresses, and serial communication parameters.

Device Manager *n.* In Windows 95, a function within the System Properties utility that indicates device conflicts and other problems and allows a user to change the properties of the computer and each device attached to it. See also property, property sheet.

Device name *n.* The label by which a computer system component is identified by the operating system. MS-DOS, for example, uses the device name COM1 to identify the first serial communications port.

Device partnership *n.* A registry key, stored on the Windows CE device, that a desktop computer uses to identify that Windows CE device when it is connected to the desktop. The key defines values for synchronization, file conversions, and backup and restore information, which enable multiple Windows CE devices to connect to the same desktop computer. A device partnership is created the first time you connect a Windows CE device to a desktop computer.

Device resolution *n.* See resolution (definition 1).

DFP *n.* See digital flat panel port.

DFS *n.* See distributed file system.

DGIS *n.* Acronym for Direct Graphics Interface Specification. An interface developed by Graphics Software Systems. DGIS is firmware (generally implemented in ROM on a video adapter) that allows a programme to display graphics on a video display through an extension to the IBM BIOS Interrupt 10H interface.

DHCP *n.* Acronym for Dynamic Host Configuration Protocol. A TCP/IP protocol that enables a network connected to the Internet to assign a temporary IP address to a host automatically when the host connects to the network. See also IP address, TCP/IP.

Dhrystone *n.* A general-performance benchmarking test, originally developed by Rheinhold Weicker in 1984 to measure and compare computer performance. The test reports general system performance in dhrystones per second. It is intended to replace the older and less reliable Whetstone benchmark. The Dhrystone benchmark, like most benchmarks, consists of standard code revised periodically to minimise unfair advantages to certain combinations of hardware, compiler, and environment. Dhrystone concentrates on string handling and uses no floating-point operations. Like most benchmarking tests, it is heavily influenced by hardware and software design, such as compiler and linker options, code optimising, cache memory, wait states, and integer data types. See also benchmark2.

DHTML *n.* See dynamic HTML.

DIA *n.* Acronym for Document Interchange Architecture. A document exchange guideline used in IBM's Systems Network Architecture (SNA). DIA specifies methods of organising and addressing documents for transmission between computers of different sizes and models. DIA is supported by IBM's Advanced Programme-to-Programme Communication (APPC) and by Logical Unit (LU) 6.2, which establish the capabilities and types of interactions possible in an SNA environment. See also DCA (definition 1), SNA.

Diacritical mark *n.* An accent mark above, below, or through a written character—for example, the acute (´) and grave (`) accents.

Dialect *n.* A variant of a language or protocol. For example, Transact-SQL is a dialect of structured query language (SQL).

Dialog *n.* 1. In computing, the exchange of human input and machine responses that forms a "conversation" between an interactive computer and the person using it. 2. The exchange of signals by computers communicating on a network.

Dialog box *n.* In a graphical user interface, a special window displayed by the system or application to solicit a response from the user. See also windowing environment.

Dial-up *adj.* Of, pertaining to, or being a connection that uses the public switched telephone network rather than a dedicated circuit or some other type of private network.

Dial-up access *n.* Connection to a data communications network through a public switched telecommunication network.

Dial-up boot loader *n.* A tool for upgrading a version of an operating system on a target device. Acronym: DUB.

Dial-up networking *n.* Connection to a remote network through use of a modem. Dial-up networking is typically used in reference to telecommuting, although the term is equally applicable to connecting to the Internet.

Dial-up service *n.* A telephone connection provider for a local or worldwide public switched telephone network that provides Internet or intranet access, advertisement via a Web page, access to news services, or access to the stock market and other resources.

DIB *n.* 1. Acronym for device-independent bitmap. A file format designed to ensure that bitmapped graphics created using one application can be loaded and displayed in another application exactly the way they appeared in the originating application. See also bitmapped graphics. 2. Acronym for Directory Information Base. A directory of user and resource names in an X.500 system. The DIB is maintained by a Directory Server Agent (DSA). Also called: white pages.

DIBengine *n.* Software, or a combination of hardware and software, that produces

DIB files. See also DIB (definition 1).

Dibit *n.* A set of 2 bits representing one of four possible combinations: 00, 01, 10, and 11. In communications, a dibit is a kind of transmission unit made possible by the modulation technique known as differential phase-shift keying, which encodes data by using four different states (phase shifts) in the transmission line to represent each of the four dibit combinations. See also phase-shift keying.

Dichotomizing search *n.* See binary search.

Dictation software *n.* Computer programmes that can recognise spoken words as input. Used as an alternative to keyboard input, dictation software cannot comprehend the spoken language; it can only convert and transmit the sounds to the computer. Speaker-dependent dictation software requires the user to "train" the computer to become familiar with his or her voice patterns and accent. First-generation discrete speech systems require the user to speak slowly and distinctly, with pauses between words. Next-generation continuous speech systems can interpret natural speech patterns and speeds. See also voice recognition.

Dictionary attack *n.* Originally a method of guessing a user's password or PIN by trying every word in the dictionary until successful. Currently used to identify any attack that tries known words or alphanumeric character strings to break a simple password.

Dielectric *n.* Insulating material, such as rubber or plastic, that does not conduct electricity.

DIF *n.* See data interchange format.

Difference *n.* 1. The amount by which two values differ. In electronics, differences in physical elements, such as waveforms or voltages, are used in the operation of circuits, amplifiers, multiplexers, communications equipment, and so on. 2. In database management, it is an operator in relational algebra that is used in sorting record sets (tuples). For example, given two relational tables, A and B, that are union-compatible (contain the same number of fields, with corresponding fields containing the same types of values), the statement DIFFERENCE A, B builds a third relation containing all those records that appear in A but not in B. See also relational algebra, tuple.

Difference Engine *n.* An early computerlike mechanical device designed by British mathematician and scientist Charles Babbage in the early 1820s. The Difference Engine was intended to be a machine with a 20-decimal capacity capable of solving mathematical problems. The concept of the Difference Engine was enhanced by Babbage in the 1830s in the design of his more famous Analytical Engine, a mechanical precursor of the electronic computer. See also Analytical Engine.

Differential *adj.* In electronics, a reference to a type of circuit that makes use of the difference between two signals rather than the difference between one signal and some reference voltage.

Differential backup *n.* A backup that copies files created or changed since the last normal or incremental backup. It does not mark files as having been backed up (in other words, the archive attribute is not cleared). If you are performing a combination of normal and differential backups, restoring files and folders requires that you have the last normal, as well as the last differential, backup.

Differential phase-shift keying *n.* See phase-shift keying.

Differentiator *n.* A circuit whose output is the differential (first derivative) of the input signal. The differential measures how fast a value is changing, so the output of a differentiator is proportional to the instantaneous rate of change of the input signal.

Diffie-Hellman *n.* Diffie-Hellman key agreement protocol. A public-key cryptography method that allows two hosts to create and share a secret key. Diffie-Hellman is used for key management by virtual private networks (VPNs) operating on the IPSec standard. See also IPSec.

Digerati *n.* Cyberspace populace that can be roughly compared to literati. Digerati are people renowned as or claiming to be knowledgeable about topics and issues related to the digital revolution; more specifically, they are people "in the know" about the Internet and online activities. See also guru, techie, wizard (definition 1).

Digest *n.* 1. An article in a moderated newsgroup that summarises multiple posts submitted to the moderator. See also moderator, newsgroup. 2. A message in a mailing list that is sent to subscribers in place of the multiple individual posts that the digest contains. If the mailing list is moderated, the digest may be edited. See also moderated.

Digicash *n.* See e-money.

Digit *n.* One of the characters used to indicate a whole number (unit) in a numbering system. In any numbering system, the number of possible digits is equal to the base, or radix, used. For example, the decimal (base-10) system has 10 digits, 0 through 9; the binary (base-2) system has 2 digits, 0 and 1;

and the hexadecimal (base-16) system has 16 digits, 0 through 9 and A through F.

Digital *adj.* 1. A reference to something based on digits (numbers) or their representation. 2. In computing, analogous in use, though not in meaning, to binary because the computers familiar to most people process information coded as different combinations of the binary digits (bits) 0 and 1.

Digital Advanced Mobile Phone Service *n.* See D-AMPS.

Digital audio disc *n.* An optical storage medium for recording digitally encoded audio information. See also compact disc (definition 1).

Digital audio tape *n.* A magnetic tape storage medium for recording digitally encoded audio information. Acronym: DAT.

Digital audio/video connector *n.* An interface on some high-end video cards or TV tuner cards that allows the simultaneous transmission of digital audio and video signals. Also called: DAV connector. See also interface (definition 3), video adapter.

Digital broadcast satellite *n.* See direct broadcast -satellite.

Digital camera *n.* A type of camera that stores photographed images electronically instead of on traditional film. A digital camera uses a CCD (charge-coupled device) element to capture the image through the lens when the operator releases the shutter in the camera; circuitry within the camera then stores the image captured by the CCD in a storage medium such as solid-state memory or a hard disk. After the image has been captured, it is downloaded by cable to the computer using software supplied with the camera. Once stored in the computer, the image can be manipulated and processed much like the image from a scanner or related input device. See also charge-coupled device, digital photography.

Digital cash *n.* See e-money.

Digital certificate *n.* 1. An assurance that software downloaded from the Internet comes from a reputable source. A digital certificate provides information about the software—such as the identity of the author and the date on which the software was registered with a certificate authority (CA), as well as a measure of tamper-resistance. 2. A user identity card or "driver's license" for cyberspace. Issued by a certificate authority (CA), a digital certificate is an electronic credential that authenticates a user on the Internet and intranets. Digital certificates ensure the legitimate online transfer of confidential information, money, or other sensitive materials by means of public encryption technology. A digital certificate holder has two keys (strings of numbers): a private key held only by the user, for "signing" outgoing messages and decrypting incoming messages; and a public key, for use by anyone, for encrypting data to send to a specific user. See also certificate authority, encryption, private key, public key.

Digital communications *n.* Exchange of communications in which all information is transmitted in binary-encoded (digital) form.

Digital computer *n.* A computer in which operations are based on two or more discrete states. Binary digital computers are based on two states, logical "on" and "off," represented by two voltage levels, arrangements of which are used to represent all types of information—numbers, letters, graphics symbols, and programme instructions. Within such a computer, the states of various circuit components change continuously to move, operate on, and save this information.

Digital Darkroom *n.* A Macintosh programme developed by Silicon Beach Software for enhancement of black-and-white photographs or scanned images.

Digital data service *n.* See DDS.

Digital data transmission *n.* The transfer of information encoded as a series of bits rather than as a fluctuating (analog) signal in a communications channel.

Digital display *n.* A video display capable of rendering only a fixed number of colours or gray shades. Examples of digital displays are IBM's Monochrome Display, Colour/Graphics Display, and Enhanced Colour Display. See also CGA, EGA, MDA.

Digital divide *n.* The gap between those who have the opportunity to take advantage of the Internet and related information resources, and those who do not. Differences in income, education, and comfort levels with technology are contributing factors to the separation between those with access to technological resources and those without.

Digital DNA *n.* 1. Broadly, a reference to the bits that comprise digital information. 2. In the gaming world, a technology called "Cyberlife" that mimics biological DNA in the creation and development of trainable creatures known as Norns. Like real DNA, digital DNA is passed from parent to offspring and determines the artificial creature's characteristics and adaptability.

Digital fingerprinting *n.* See digital watermark.

Digital flat panel port *n.* An interface designed to allow direct connection between a flat panel monitor and a computer without requiring an analog-to-digital conversion. Acronym: DFP.

Digital home *n.* See smart home.

Digital light processing projector *n.* See DLP.

Digital line *n.* A communications line that carries information only in binary-encoded (digital) form. To minimise distortion and noise interference, a digital line uses repeaters to regenerate the signal periodically during transmission. See also repeater.

Digital linear tape *n.* A magnetic storage medium used to back up data. Digital linear tape allows for faster transfer of data compared with other tape technologies. Acronym: DLT.

Digital Micromirror Device *n.* The circuit technology behind Texas Instruments' Digital Light Processing, used in image projectors. A Digital Micromirror Device, or DMD, consists of an array of individually addressable, hinged mirrors on a chip. Each chip, which is less than 0.002 mm wide, rotates in response to a digital signal to reflect light into the lens of the projection system and thus create a bright, full-colour display. Displays can be combined to create high-definition systems of 1920 ¥ 1035 (1,987,200) pixels with 64 million colours. Acronym: DMD.

Digital modem *n.* 1. A communications device that acts as the intermediary between a digital device such as a computer or terminal and a digital communications channel, such as a high-speed network line, an ISDN circuit, or a cable TV system. Although a digital modem supports standard (analog) modem protocols, it is not a "typical" modem in the sense of being a device whose primary function is to modulate (convert digital to analog) before transmission and demodulate (convert analog to digital) after transmission. It uses advanced digital modulation techniques for changing data frames into a format suitable for transmission over a digital line. See also terminal adapter. 2. A 56 Kbps modem. Such a modem is not purely digital but does eliminate the traditional digital-to-analog conversion for downstream transmissions—that is, transmissions moving from the Internet to the end user. A 56 Kbps modem is also digital in that it requires a digital connection, such as T1, between the telephone company and the user's Internet Servic

Digital Network Architecture *n.* A multilayered architecture and set of protocol specifications for networks. Designed by the Digital Equipment Corporation, Digital Network Architecture is implemented in the set of products known by the name DECnet. Acronym: DNA. See also DECnet.

Digital photography *n.* Photography by means of a digital camera. Digital photography differs from conventional photography in that a digital camera does not use a silver halide–based film to capture an image. Instead, a digital camera captures and stores each image electronically. See also digital camera.

Digital picture frame *n.* Electronic device used in displaying digital photos and graphics while giving the outward appearance of a traditional picture frame. Digital picture frames allow users to rotate photos within the frame at specified intervals, display a series of photos as a slide show, or use an Internet connection to download photos, order prints, or send customised photo sets to others.

Digital Print Order Format *n.* See DPOF.

Digital proof *n.* See direct digital colour proof.

Digital recording *n.* The storage of information in binary-encoded (digital) format. Digital recording converts information—text, graphics, sound, or pictures—to strings of 1s and 0s that can be physically represented on a storage medium. Digital recording media include computer disks and tapes, optical (or compact) discs, and ROM cartridges of the type used for some software and many computer games.

Digital Rights Management *n.* See DRM.

Digital satellite system *n.* A high-powered satellite system with the capability to deliver high-quality transmissions of hundreds of channels directly to television receivers. A DSS broadcast begins as a digital signal sent from a service provider's station to a satellite. From there, it is directed to a satellite dish (typically 18 inches) at the user's premises. The dish next transmits the signal to a converter box, which changes it to an analog signal before sending it to the television set. Acronym: DSS.

Digital Services *n.* See DS.

Digital signal *n.* A signal, such as one transmitted within or between computers, in which information is represented by discrete states—for example, high and low voltages—rather than by fluctuating levels in a continuous stream, as in an analog signal.

Digital Signal *n.* See DS.

Digital signal processor *n.* An integrated circuit designed for high-speed data manipulation and used in audio, communications, image manipulation, and other data acquisition and data control applications. Acronym: DSP.

Digital signature *n.* A security mechanism used on the Internet that relies on two keys, one public and one private, that are used to encrypt messages before transmission and to decrypt them on receipt.

Digital Signature Algorithm *n.* The U.S. government standard for digital signatures, as specified by the National Institute of Standards and Technology, in FIPS 186, Digital Signature Standard. DSA is based on signature encryption based on a public and a private key. Acronym: DSA. See also digital signature.

Digital Signature Standard *n.* A public key cryptographic standard issued in 1994 by the United States National Institute of Standards and Technology (NIST) to authenticate electronic documents. The DSS uses a Digital Signature Algorithm (DSA) to generate and verify digital signatures based on a public key, which is not secret, and a private key, which is known or held only by the person generating the signature. A digital signature serves to authenticate both the identity of the signer and the integrity of the transmitted information. Acronym: DSS. See also public key encryption.

Digital Simultaneous Voice and Data *n.* A modem technology by Multi-Tech Systems, Inc., that allows a single telephone line to be used for conversation together with data transfer. This is accomplished by switching to packet-mode communications when the need for voice transfer is detected; digitized voice packets are then transferred along with data and command packets. Acronym: DSVD.

Digital sort *n.* A type of ordering process in which record numbers or their key values are sorted digit by digit, beginning with the least significant (rightmost) digit. Also called: radix sort.

Digital speech *n.* See speech synthesis.

Digital subscriber line or Digital Subscriber Line *n.* See DSL.

Digital Subscriber Line Access Multiplexer or Digital Subscriber Line Multiplexer *n.* See DSLAM.

Digital-to-analog converter *n.* A device that translates digital data to an analog signal. A digital-to-analog converter takes a succession of discrete digital values as input and creates an analog signal whose amplitude corresponds, moment by moment, to each digital value. See the illustration. Acronym: DAC.

Digital versatile disc *n.* See digital video disc.

Digital video *n.* Video images and sound stored in a digital format. Acronym: DV.

Digital TV or digital television *n.* The transmission of television signals using digital rather than the conventional analog signals. A digital TV standard for the United States was approved by the FCC in 1996. Digital TV provides a better television experience and new information services. Digital signals produce higher quality pictures and CD-quality sound, compared to the analog signals used with today"s television. Digital TV can support interactive television, electronic programme guides, and a variety of digital services, such as Internet channel broadcasting and data services. Acronym: DTV.

Digital video disc *n.* The next generation of optical disc storage technology. With digital video disc technology, video, audio, and computer data can be encoded onto a compact disc (CD). A digital video disc can store greater amounts of data than a traditional CD. A standard single-layer, single-sided digital video disc can store 4.7 GB of data; a two-layer standard increases the single-sided disc capacity to 8.5 GB. Digital video discs can be double-sided with a maximum storage of 17 GB per disc. A digital video disc player is needed to read digital video discs; this player is equipped to read older optical storage technologies. Advocates of the digital video disc intend to replace current digital storage formats, such as laser disc, CD-ROM, and audio CD, with the single digital format of the digital video disc. Acronym: DVD. Also called: digital versatile disc. See also digital video disc–ROM.

Digital video disc–erasable *n.* A proposed extension to the digital video disc recording format to allow multiple re-recording by a consumer. Acronym: DVD-E. Also called: digital video disc–ROM.

Digital video disc–recordable *n.* A proposed extension to the digital video disc recording format to allow one-time recording by a consumer. Acronym: DVD-R.

Digital video disc–ROM *n.* A computer-readable version of a digital video disc containing either 4.7 or 8.5 GB of storage per side, the larger if 3M's dual-layer "2P" technology is used. Acronym: DVD-ROM. Also called: digital video disc–erasable. See also digital video disc.

Digital Video–Interactive *n.* A hardware/software system developed by RCA, General Electric, and Intel that implements compression of digital video and audio for microcomputer applications. Acronym: DV-I.

Digital Video Interface *n.* See DVI.

Digital video recording *n.* See DVR.

Digital watermark *n.* A unique identifier embedded in a file to deter piracy and prove file ownership and quality. Digital watermarking is often used with graphics and audio files to identify the owner's rights to these works. See also fingerprint (definition 2).

Digiterati *n.* See digerati.

Digitize *vb.* To convert any continuously varying (analog) source of input, such as the lines in a drawing or a sound signal, to a series of discrete units represented in a computer by the binary digits 0 and 1. Analog-to-digital converters are commonly used to perform this translation. See also aliasing, analog-to-digital converter.

Digitizing tablet *n.* See graphics tablet.

DikuMUD *n.* 1. Multiuser dungeon (MUD) software developed by five individuals at the Computer Science Institute at Copenhagen University (whose acronym in Danish is DIKU). DikuMUD uses multimedia and is object-oriented, but the classes are hard-coded. The software is covered by a license agreement that forbids its distribution for money. See also MUD, multimedia, object-oriented. 2. A game that uses the DikuMUD software.

Dimensioning *n.* In CAD programmes, a means of specifying and possibly controlling the measurements and spatial relationships of elements in a modeled object, such as using lines, arrows, and text (that is, measurements) to indicate the length, height, and thickness of each of the walls in a modeled room or house. See also CAD.

DIMM *n.* Acronym for dual inline memory module. A type of memory board comprised of RAM chips mounted on a circuit board, similar to the more commonly used SIMM (Single Inline

Memory Module). DIMMs are characterised by a 64-bit data path and pins (connectors) on each side that are on different circuits and that respond to different signals. SIMMs, in contrast, have a 32-bit data path, and their connectors are on the same circuit and respond to the same signal. While SIMMs must be added in pairs, DIMMs can be added to a computer one at a time. See also memory chip.

Dimmed *adj.* Shown on the screen in gray characters instead of black characters on white or white characters on black. Menu options appear dimmed in a graphical user interface to indicate that under current circumstances they are not available—for example, "Cut" when no text has been highlighted or "Paste" when there is no text in the clipboard.

DIN connector *n.* A multipin connector conforming to the specification of the German national standards organisation (Deutsch Industrie Norm). DIN connectors are used to link various components in personal computers.

Dingbat *n.* A small graphical element used for decorative purposes in a document. Some fonts, such as Zapf Dingbats, are designed to present sets of dingbats. See also font.

Diode *n.* A device that passes current in only one direction. A diode is usually a semiconductor. See the illustration. See also semiconductor.

Diode. The drawings (top) show two of the many types of diode packages. The band on the right end of each indicates polarity. At bottom is a schematic representation of a diode.

Diode-transistor logic *n.* A type of circuit design that employs diodes, transistors, and resistors to perform logic functions. Acronym: DTL.

DIP *n.* Acronym for dual inline package. A standard for packaging integrated circuits in which the microminiature electronic circuits etched on a silicon wafer are enclosed in a rectangular housing of plastic or ceramic and connected to downward-pointing pins protruding from the longer sides of the chip. Designed to facilitate circuit board manufacturing, this design does not work well for modern chips requiring very large numbers of connections. See document image processing.

Dipole *n.* A pair of opposite electric charges or magnetic poles of opposite sign separated by a small distance.

DIP switch *n.* Short for Dual Inline Package switch. One or more small rocker- or sliding-type toggle switches contained in the plastic or ceramic housing of a dual inline package (DIP) connected to a circuit board. Each switch on a DIP switch can be set to one of two positions, closed or open, to control options on the circuit board. See also DIP.

DIR *n.* An MS-DOS command that instructs a computer to display a list of files and subdirectories in the current directory or folder. If the command is followed by a path, the computer displays a list of files and subdirectories in the specified directory or folder. See also command, MS-DOS, path (definition 2).

Direct3D *n.* See DirectX.

Direct access *n.* The ability of a computer to find and go straight to a particular storage location in memory or on disk to retrieve or store an item of information. Note that direct access is not the same as direct memory access (DMA), which is the ability to transfer information directly between an input/output channel and memory rather than taking the longer and more circuitous route of I/O channel to microprocessor to memory. See also random access.

Direct access storage device *n.* See DASD.

Direct address *n.* See absolute address.

DirectAnimation *n.* See DirectX.

Direct broadcast satellite *n.* A digital telecommunications service that delivers television programming via the Digital Satellite System (DSS). Direct broadcast satellite technology uses a geostationary orbit satellite (GEO) to receive digitized signals sent by ground-based uplink centers; the satellite then beams the signal across a wide swath on Earth. Subscribers within that swath use small (18-inch) satellite dishes to bring the signal into a set-top box decoder for playback. Although primarily used for television broadcasts, the technology is seen as having potential to also deliver high-quality, digital communications and multimedia content in the future. Acronym: DBS. Also called: digital broadcast satellite. See also digital satellite system, geostationary orbit satellite, webcasting.

Direct cable connection *n.* A link between the I/O ports of two computers that uses a single cable rather than a modem or other active interface device. In most cases, a direct cable connection requires a null modem cable.

Direct-connect modem *n.* A modem that uses standard telephone wire and connectors and that plugs directly into a telephone jack, eliminating the need for an intermediary telephone.

Direct-coupled transistor logic *n.* A circuit design that uses transistors and resistors only, with the transistors directly connected to each other. This design was used in the earliest commercial integrated circuits. The switching speed and power consumption of such circuits are about average. Acronym: DCTL.

Direct current *n.* Electrical current whose direction of flow does not reverse. The current may stop or change amplitude, but it always flows in the same direction. Acronym: DC.

Direct digital colour proof *n.* A test sheet produced by a lower-cost output device, such as a colour laser printer, to serve as an approximation of what the final image will look like when produced on professional-quality printing equipment. A direct digital colour proof does not involve colour separation, as in traditional proofs. Instead, a direct digital colour proof is printed in all colours at one time on a single page, resulting in somewhat lower quality compared with traditional separation methods but having the advantages of increased speed and reduced cost. Acronym: DDCP. Also called: digital proof. See also colour separation (definition 1).

DirectDraw *n.* See DirectX.

Direct Graphics Interface Specification *n.* See DGIS.

DirectInput *n.* An API (application programming interface) developed by Microsoft for joysticks and similar pointing devices in Windows 9x. See DirectX.

Direction key *n.* See arrow key.

Direct memory access *n.* Memory access that does not involve the microprocessor and is frequently used for data transfer directly between memory and an "intelligent" peripheral device, such as a disk drive. Acronym: DMA.

DirectMusic *n.* See DirectX.

Directory *n.* 1. A catalog for filenames and other directories stored on a disk. A directory is a way of organising and grouping the files so that the user is not overwhelmed by a long list of them. The uppermost directory is called the root directory; the directories within a directory are called subdirectories. Depending on how an operating system supports directories, filenames in a directory can be viewed and ordered in various ways—for example, alphabetically, by date, by size, or as icons in a graphical user interface. What the user views as a directory is supported in the operating system by tables of data, stored on the disk, that indicate characteristics and the location of each file. In the Macintosh and Windows 9x operating systems, directories are called folders. 2. On a network, an index of names and pertinent information related to authorised users and network resources.

Directory Access Protocol *n.* The protocol that governs communications between X.500 clients and servers. See also CCITT X series.

Directory Client Agent *n.* See DUA.

Directory Information Base *n.* See DIB (definition 2).

Directory Mozilla *n.* See Open Directory Project.

Directory path *n.* See pathname.

Directory replication *n.* The copying of a master set of directories from a server (called an export server) to specified servers or workstations (called import computers) in the same or other domains. Replication simplifies the task of maintaining identical sets of directories and files on multiple computers because only a single master copy of the data must be maintained. See also directory, server.

Directory Server Agent *n.* See DSA.

Directory service *n.* A service on a network that returns mail addresses of other users or enables a user to locate hosts and services.

Directory System Agent *n.* See DSA.

Directory tree *n.* A graphic display listing the directories and subdirectories on a hard disk in tree form, with subdirectories shown as branches of the main directory. See also branch (definition 1), directory, tree structure.

Directory User Agent *n.* See DUA.

DirectPlay *n.* See DirectX.

Direct processing *n.* Processing of data as it is received by the system, as opposed to deferred processing, in which data is stored in blocks before processing.

Direct read after write *n.* See DRAW.

Direct read during write *n.* See DRDW.

Direct sequence *n.* In spread spectrum communication, a form of modulation in which a carrier is modulated by a series of binary pulses. See also modulation (definition 1), spread spectrum.

DirectShow *n.* See DirectX.

DirectSound *n.* See DirectX.

Direct view storage tube *n.* A type of cathode-ray tube (CRT) in which the screen can retain images for a long time and in which a beam of electrons from an electron gun can be moved arbitrarily across the screen surface (as opposed to a standard cathode-ray tube, in which the electron beam is moved in a specific pattern). This type of CRT is capable of displaying a precise, detailed image without requiring any screen refresh. However, once the image is drawn, it cannot be changed without a complete erasing of the screen. Acronym: DVST. Also called: storage tube.

DirectX *n.* A set of Microsoft technologies that provide developers with the tools needed to create sophisticated multimedia applications on Windows-based computers. DirectX consists of components making up two integrated layers. The Foundation layer provides low-level functions, such as support for input devices, designed to ensure that applications can run on—and take full advantage of—Windows-based hardware. The Media layer, above the Foundation layer, provides high-level services, such as support for media streaming and animation, that are needed in creating applications incorporating such features as surround sound, video, and 3-D animation. DirectAnimation, DirectSound, and other similarly named application programming interfaces (APIs) are members of the DirectX family. See the table. See also application programming interface.

DirectX Transform *n.* See DirectX.

Dirty *adj.* Of, pertaining to, or characteristic of a communications line that is hampered by excessive noise, degrading the quality of the signal. See also noise (definition 2).

Dirty bit *n.* A bit used to mark modified data in a cache so that the modifications may be carried over to primary memory. See also bit, cache.

Dirty power *n.* A power source that can cause damage to electronic components, due to noise, voltage spikes, or incorrect voltage levels.

Dirty ROM *n.* Short for dirty read-only memory. In the earlier versions of the Macintosh (Mac II, IIx, SE/30, and IIcx), a memory system that simulates a 32-bit system but is not a true (clean) 32-bit system. Among other flaws, a dirty ROM machine can access only 8 megabytes of memory under Mac OS System 7. System extensions such as MODE32 and the 32-bit enabler are available to allow a dirty ROM machine to function like a true, 32-bit clean machine.

Disable *vb.* To suppress something or to prevent it from happening. Disabling is a method of controlling system functions by disallowing certain activities. For example, a programme might temporarily disable nonessential interrupts (requests for service from system devices) to prevent interruptions during a critical point in processing.

Table D.1 ATA Specifications.

DirectX Component	Part Of	Supports
Direct3D Immediate Mode	Foundation layer	Access to 3-D video hardware
Direct3D Retained Mode	Media layer	Creation and animation of onscreen 3-D worlds
Direct-Animation	Media layer	Interactive animation and integration of different multimedia types
DirectDraw	Foundation layer	Access to display -memory and hardware capabilities
DirectInput	Foundation layer	Direct access to various input devices, including force-feedback -joysticks
DirectMusic	Foundation layer	Real-time music -composition
DirectPlay	Foundation layer	Multiplayer online gaming and other networked applications
DirectShow	Media layer	Capture and playback of streaming multimedia
DirectSound	Foundation layer	Direct access to sound cards; wave sound capture and playback
Direct-Sound3D	Foundation layer	3-D sound positioning
DirectX - Transform	Media layer	Extensibility of the DirectX platform to include value-added products

Disabled folders *n.* In the Mac OS, several folders in the System folder that contain system extensions, control panels, and other items that have been removed from the system by the extension manager. Items currently in disabled folders will not be installed upon system startup; they may, however, later be moved back to their regular folders automatically by the extension manager. See also extension manager, System folder.

Disassembler *n.* A programme that converts machine code to assembly language source code. Most debuggers have some kind of built-in disassembler that allows the programmer to view an executable programme in terms of human-readable assembly language. See also decompiler.

Disassociate *vb.* In Windows 95 and Windows NT, to remove an association between a file and some application.

Disaster dump *n.* A dump (transfer of memory contents to a printer or other output device) made when a programme fails without hope of recovery.

Disc *n.* A round, flat piece of nonmagnetic, shiny metal encased in a plastic coating, designed to be read from and written to by optical (laser) technology. It is now standard practice to use the spelling disc for optical discs and disk in all other computer contexts, such as floppy disk, hard disk, and RAM disk. See also compact disc.

Disconnect *vb.* To break a communications link.

Discrete *adj.* Separate; individual; identifiable as a unit. For example, bits are discrete elements of data processed by a computer.

Discrete multitone *n.* In telecommunications, a technology that uses digital signal processors to split available bandwidth into a number of subchannels, allowing over 6 Mbps of data to be carried over one copper twisted-pair wire. Acronym: DMT.

Discrete speech recognition *n.* Computer speech recognition format in which each word is recognised as a distinct individual unit, requiring a pause between each word spoken.

Discretionary access control list *n.* The part of an object's security descriptor that grants or denies specific users and groups permission to access the object. Only the owner of an object can change permissions granted or denied in a DACL; thus, access to the object is at the owner's discretion. Acronym: DACL. See also distribution group.

Discretionary hyphen *n.* See hyphen.

Discussion group *n.* Any of a variety of online forums in which people communicate about subjects of common interest. Forums for discussion groups include electronic mailing lists, Internet newsgroups, and IRC channels.

Dish *n.* See satellite dish.

Disk *n.* 1. A round, flat piece of flexible plastic coated with a magnetic material that can be electrically influenced to hold information recorded in digital (binary) form and encased in a protective plastic jacket to protect the disk from damage and contamination. Also called: floppy, floppy disk, microfloppy disk. 2. See hard drive.

Disk access time *n.* See access time (definition 2).

Disk buffer *n.* A small amount of memory set aside for the purpose of storing data read from, or soon to be written to, a disk. Because disk devices are slow compared with the CPU, it is not efficient to access the disk for only one or two bytes of data. Instead, during a read, a large chunk of data is read and stored in the disk buffer. When the programme wants information, it is copied from the buffer. Many requests for data can be satisfied by a single disk access. The same technique can be applied to disk writes. When the programme has information to store, it writes it into the disk buffer area in memory. When the buffer has been filled, the entire contents of the buffer are written to the disk in a single operation.

Disk cache *n.* A portion of a computer's random access memory (RAM) set aside for temporarily holding information read from disk. A disk cache does not hold entire files, as does a RAM disk (a portion of memory that acts as if it were a disk drive). Instead, a disk cache is used to hold information that either has recently been requested from disk or has previously been written to disk. If the required information remains in a disk cache, access time is considerably faster than if the programme must wait for the disk drive mechanism to fetch the information from disk. See also cache.

Disk cartridge *n.* A removable disk enclosed in a protective case. A disk cartridge can be used by certain types of hard disk drives and related devices, such as the external data storage units known as Bernoulli boxes.

Disk controller *n.* A special-purpose chip and associated circuitry that directs and controls reading from and writing to a computer's disk drive. A disk controller handles such tasks as positioning the read/write head, mediating between the drive and the microprocessor, and controlling the transfer of information to and from memory. Disk controllers are used with floppy disk drives and hard disks and can either be built into the system or be part of a card that plugs into an expansion slot.

Disk copy *n.* The process of duplicating a source disk's data and the data's organisational structure onto a target disk. See also backup.

Disk crash *n.* The failure of a disk drive. See also crash.

Disk directory *n.* An index of the files on a disk, analogous to a card catalog. A disk directory includes information about the files, such as their names, sizes, dates of creation, and physical locations on the disk. See also directory.

Disk drive *n.* An electromechanical device that reads from and writes to disks. The main components of a disk drive include a spindle on which the disk is mounted, a drive motor that spins the disk when the drive is in operation, one or more read/write heads, a second motor that positions the read/write heads over the disk, and controller circuitry that synchronizes read/write activities and transfers information to and from the computer. Two types of disk drives are in common use: floppy disk drives and hard disk drives. Floppy disk drives are designed to accept removable disks in either 5.25-inch or 3.5-inch format; hard disk drives are faster, high-capacity storage units that are completely enclosed in a protective case.

Disk driver *n.* A device driver that is added to a system to support a specific manufacturer's disk device. See also device driver.

Disk duplexing *n.* See disk mirroring.

Disk envelope *n.* The paper container that holds a 5.25-inch floppy disk and its attached jacket. The disk envelope protects exposed surfaces of the disk from dust and other foreign material that can scratch and otherwise damage the surface, resulting in the loss of recorded data. See also disk jacket.

Diskette *n.* See floppy disk.

Disk farm *n.* A number of disk drives in a single location used together to store or process vast quantities of information, such as scientific data, years' worth of corporate sales figures, large numbers of graphic images, or telephone company billing records. Current disk farms consist of magnetic or optical disks and can hold terabytes of information. In older usage, disk farms were sometimes known as "Laundromats" because they contained large drives referred to in jargon as "washing machines." See also server farm.

Disk interface *n.* 1. The circuitry that connects a disk drive to a computer system. 2. A standard for connecting disk drives and computers. For example, the ST506 standard for connecting hard disks to computers is a disk interface standard.

Disk jacket *n.* The protective plastic sheath that covers a floppy disk.

Diskless workstation *n.* A station on a computer network that is not equipped with a disk drive and that uses files stored in a file server. See also file server.

Disk memory *n.* See virtual memory.

Disk mirroring *n.* A technique in which all or part of a hard disk is duplicated onto one or more other hard disks, each of which ideally is attached to its own controller. With disk mirroring, any change made to the original disk is simultaneously made to the other disks so that if the original disk becomes damaged or corrupted, the mirror disks will contain a current, undamaged collection of the data from the original disk. Also called: disk duplexing. See also fault tolerance.

Disk operating system *n.* See DOS.

Disk pack *n.* A collection of disks in a protective container. Used primarily with minicomputers and mainframe computers, a disk pack is a removable medium, generally a stack of 14-inch disks in a plastic housing.

Disk partition *n.* A logical compartment on a physical disk drive. A single disk might have two or more logical disk partitions, each of which would be referenced with a different disk drive name. Multiple partitions are divided into a primary (boot) partition and one or more extended partitions.

Disk server *n.* A node on a local area network that acts as a remote disk drive shared by network users. Unlike a file server, which performs the more sophisticated tasks of managing network requests for files, a disk server functions as a storage medium on which users can read and write files. A disk server can be divided into sections (volumes), each of which appears to be a separate disk.

Disk striping *n.* The procedure of combining a set of same-size disk partitions that reside on separate disks (from 2 to 32 disks) into a single volume, forming a virtual stripe across the disks that the operating system recognises as a single drive. Disk striping enables multiple I/O operations in the same volume to proceed concurrently, thus offering enhanced performance. See also disk striping with parity, input/output.

Disk striping with parity *n.* The technique of maintaining parity information across a disk stripe so that if one disk partition fails, the data on that disk can be re-created using the information stored across the remaining partitions in the disk stripe. See also disk striping, fault tolerance, parity.

Disk unit *n.* A disk drive or its housing.

Dispatcher *n.* In some multitasking operating systems, the set of routines responsible for allocating CPU (central processing unit) time to various applications.

Dispatch table *n.* A table of identifiers and addresses for a certain class of routines such as interrupt handlers (routines carried out in response to certain signals or conditions). Also called: interrupt vector table, jump table, vector table. See also interrupt handler.

Disperse *vb.* To break up and place in more than one location—for example, to disperse results among several sets of data or to disperse items (such as fields in records) so that they appear in more than one place in the output.

Dispersion *n.* The degree to which, at any given time, data in a distributed (interconnected) system of computers is stored at different locations or on different devices.

Display *n.* The visual output device of a computer, which is commonly a CRT-based video display. With portable and notebook computers, the display is usually an LCD-based or a gas plasma-based flat-panel display. See also flat-panel display, liquid crystal display, video adapter, video display.

Display adapter *n.* See video adapter.

Display attribute *n.* A quality assigned to a character or an image displayed on the screen. Display attributes include such features as colour, intensity, and blinking. Users of applications can control display attributes when programmes allow them to change colour and other screen elements.

Display background *n.* In computer graphics, the portion of an onscreen image that remains static while other elements change; for example, window borders on a screen, or a palette of shapes or patterns in a drawing programme.

Display board *n.* See video adapter.

Display card *n.* See video adapter.

Display cycle *n.* The complete set of events that must occur in order for a computer image to be displayed on the screen, including both the software creation of an image in a computer's video memory and the hardware operations required for accurate onscreen display. See also refresh cycle.

Display Data Channel *n.* See DDC.

Display device *n.* See display.

Display element *n.* See graphics primitive.

Display entity *n.* See entity, graphics primitive.

Display face *n.* A typeface suitable for headings and titles in documents, distinguished by its ability to stand out from other text on the page. Sans serif faces such as Helvetica and Avant Garde often work well as display faces. See also sans serif.

Display frame *n.* One image in an animation sequence. See also frame (definition 3).

Display image *n.* The collection of elements displayed together at a single time on a computer screen.

Display page *n.* One screenful of display information stored in a computer's video memory. Computers can have enough video memory to hold more than one display page at a time. In such instances, programmers, especially those concerned with creating animation sequences, can update the screen rapidly by creating or modifying one display page while another is being viewed by the user. See also animation.

Display port *n.* An output port on a computer that provides a signal for a display device such as a video monitor. See the illustration. Also called: monitor port.

Display port.

Display PostScript *n.* An extended version of the PostScript language intended to provide a device-independent language for displaying images and text on bitmapped displays. See also PostScript.

Display Power Management Signaling *n.* See DPMS.

Display screen *n.* The part of a video unit on which images are shown. See also CRT.

Display terminal *n.* See terminal (definition 1).

Distance learning *n.* Broadly, any educational or learning process or system in which the teacher/instructor is separated geographically or in time from his or her students, or in which students are separated from other students or educational resources. Contemporary distance learning is effected through the implementation of computer and electronics technology to connect teacher and student in either real or delayed time or on an as needed basis. Content delivery may be achieved through a variety of technologies, including satellites, computers, cable television, interactive video, electronic transmissions via telephone lines, the World Wide Web and other Internet technology, and others. Distance learning does not preclude traditional learning processes; frequently it is used in conjunction with in-person classroom or professional training procedures and practices.

Distance Vector Multicast Routing Protocol *n.* An Internet routing protocol that provides an efficient mechanism for connectionless datagram delivery to a group of hosts across an Internet network. It is a distributed protocol that dynamically generates IP multicast delivery trees using a technique called Reverse Path Multicasting (RPM). Acronym: DVMRP.

Distance-vector routing algorithm *n.* See Bellman-Ford distance-vector routing algorithm.

Distortion *n.* An undesirable change in the waveform of a signal. Distortion can occur during signal transmission, as when a radio broadcast becomes garbled, or when a signal passes through a circuit, as when a stereo system is turned up too loud. Distortion often results in loss of information. It is mainly a problem in analog signals; digital signals are not affected by moderate distortion.

Distribute *vb.* To allocate among locations or facilities, as in a data-processing function that is performed by a collection of computers and other devices linked together by a network.

Distributed bulletin board *n.* A collection of newsgroups distributed to all computers in a wide area network. See also newsgroup, Usenet.

Distributed COM *n.* See DCOM.

Distributed Component Object Model *n.* See DCOM.

Distributed computing *n.* See distributed processing.

Distributed Computing Environment *n.* A set of standards from the Open Group (formerly the Open Software Foundation) for development of distributed applications that can operate on more than one platform. Acronym: DCE. See also distributed processing.

Distributed database *n.* A database implemented on a network. The component partitions are distributed over various nodes (stations) of the network. Depending on the specific update and retrieval traffic, distributing the database can significantly enhance overall performance.

Distributed database management system *n.* A database management system capable of managing a distributed database. Acronym: DDBMS. See also distributed database.

Distributed denial of service attack *n.* See DDoS.

Distributed file system *n.* A file management system in which files may be located on multiple computers connected over a local or wide area network. Acronym: DFS.

Distributed intelligence *n.* A system in which processing ability (intelligence) is distributed among multiple computers and other devices, each of which can work independently to some degree but can also communicate with the other devices to function as part of the larger system. See also distributed processing.

Distributed network *n.* A network in which processing, storage, and other functions are handled by separate units (nodes) rather than by a single main computer.

Distributed processing *n.* A form of information processing in which work is performed by separate computers linked through a communications network. Distributed processing is usually categorised as either plain distributed processing or true distributed processing. Plain distributed processing shares the workload among computers that can communicate with one another. True distributed processing has separate computers perform different tasks in such a way that their combined work can contribute to a larger goal. The latter type of processing requires a highly structured environment that allows hardware and software to communicate, share resources, and exchange information freely.

Distributed services *n.* See BISDN.

Distributed system *n.* A noncentralised network consisting of numerous computers that can communicate with one another and that appear to users as parts of a single, large, accessible "storehouse" of shared hardware, software, and data.

Distributed System Object Model *n.* IBM's System Object Model (SOM) in a shared environment, where binary class libraries can be shared between applications on networked computers or between applications on a given system. The Distributed System Object Model complements existing object-oriented languages by allowing SOM class libraries to be shared among applications written in different languages. Acronym: DSOM. See also SOM (definition 1).

Distributed transaction processing *n.* Transaction processing that is shared by one or more computers communicating over a network. Acronym: DTP. See also distributed processing, transaction processing.

Distributed workplace *n.* An environment other than the traditional office or factory, in which work is carried out on a regular basis. The flexibility afforded by the combination of communications and computing technologies enables many workers to conduct business anywhere the appropriate computer and data communications infrastructure has been set up. See also SOHO, telecommute.

Distribution group *n.* A group that is used solely for e-mail distribution and that is not security-enabled. Distribution groups cannot be listed in discretionary access control lists (DACLs) used to define permissions on resources and objects. Distribution groups can be used only with e-mail applications (such as Microsoft Exchange) to send e-mail messages to collections of users. If you do not need a group for security purposes, create a distribution group instead of a security group. See also discretionary access control list, security group.

Distribution list *n.* A list of recipients on an e-mail mailing list. This can be in the form of either a mailing list programme, such as LISTSERV, or an alias in an e-mail programme for all recipients of an e-mail message. See also alias (definition 2), LISTSERV, mailing list.

Distribution services *n.* See BISDN.

Distributive sort *n.* An ordering process in which a list is separated into parts and then reassembled in a particular order. See also sort algorithm.

Distro1 *n.* 1. A distribution of software (usually a version of Linux), digital music, or an online magazine or e-zine. See also e-zine, Linux. 2. A company or individual that sells items, typically software, music CDs, or books, via the Web.

Distro2 *vb.* To distribute or sell software releases, digital music, or text items via the Web.

Dithering *n.* A technique used in computer graphics to create the illusion of varying shades of gray on a monochrome display or printer, or additional colours on a colour display or printer. Dithering relies on treating areas of an image as groups of dots that are coloured in different patterns. Akin to the print images called halftones, dithering takes advantage of the eye's tendency to blur spots of different colours by averaging their effects and merging them into a single perceived shade or colour. Depending on the ratio of black dots to white dots within a given area, the overall effect is of a particular shade of gray. Dithering is used to add realism to computer graphics and to soften jagged edges in curves and diagonal lines at low resolutions. See the illustration. See also aliasing, halftone.

Divergence *n.* A moving apart or separation. On computer displays, divergence occurs when the red, green, and blue electron beams in a colour monitor do not collectively light the same spot on the screen. Within a programme, such as a spreadsheet, divergence can occur when a circular set of formulas is repeatedly recalculated (iterated), with the results of each iteration moving further from a stable solution.

Divide overflow *n.* See overflow error.

Division by zero *n.* An error condition caused by an attempt to divide a number by zero, which is mathematically undefined, or by a number that is sufficiently near to zero that the result is too large to be expressed by the machine. Computers do not allow division by zero, and software must provide some means of protecting the user from programme failure on such attempts.

DIX *n.* Acronym for Digital Intel Xerox, the companies that developed the AUI connector for thicknet Ethernet cable. See also AUI.

DJGPP *n.* A compiler and a set of tools used by some game programmers to produce 32-bit protected-mode programmes that run on Windows operating systems. DJGPP is a complete 32-bit C/C++ development system for PCs running MS-DOS; it includes ports of many GNU development utilities. In most cases, programmes produced using DJGPP can be sold commercially without license or royalties. See also 32-bit, Allegro, GNU.

Djinn *n.* A group of devices, resources, and users joined by Sun Microsystem's JINI technology. The group, controlled by the JINI technology infrastructure, agrees on basic specifications for administration, trust, identification, and policy. See also JINI.

DLC *n.* Acronym for Data Link Control. An error-correction protocol in the Systems Network Architecture (SNA) responsible for transmission of data between two nodes over a physical link. Supported by Microsoft Windows NT and Windows 2000, DLC is designed to provide access to IBM mainframe computers and to Hewlett-Packard printers connected to the network. See also HDLC, SNA.

DLCI *n.* See Data Link Connection Identifier.

.dll *n.* A file extension for a dynamic-link library. See also dynamic-link library.

DLL *n.* See dynamic-link library.

DLL hell *n.* A problem occurring in versions of Microsoft Windows prior to Windows Me and Windows 2000 in which a newly installed application overwrites shared dynamic-link library (DLL) files with the (older or newer) versions it needs in order to run. If the replaced files are incompatible with those needed by other applications, those applications may exhibit buggy behaviour or crash when they access the incompatible DLL files. The latest versions of the Windows operating system, Windows 2000 and Windows XP, incorporate a feature called Windows File Protection that eliminates this situation by monitoring and correcting installation and replacement of DLL files. See also dynamic-link library.

DLP *n.* Short for Digital Light Processing. a digital projection technology developed by Texas Instruments in which a signal sent from a computer to a DLP projector is projected onto a screen by means of light reflected from a Digital Micromirror Device, or DMD, that consists of thousands of tiny hinged mirrors, each representing one pixel, attached to a chip. The chip acts as a bank of switches, one switch per mirror. These switches, in turn, rotate the mirrors in response to the digital signal to reflect light through a projection lens to create the image. DLP projectors represent a newer technology than the LCD projectors also used to display images on screen. See also Digital Micromirror Device.

DMI *n.* Acronym for Desktop Management Interface. A system for managing the configurations and status of PCs on a network from a central computer. In DMI an agent programme runs in the background on each machine and returns information or performs some action (as specified by a file on that machine) in response to a query received from the central computer. The actions to be performed by the agent might include watching for errors and reporting them to the central computer as they occur; for example, a printer might be set up to report to the central computer when paper runs out or jams. DMI was developed by the DMTF (Desktop Management Task Force), a consortium of computer equipment manufacturers, and competes with SNMP (although the two can coexist on the same system). See also agent (definition 1), DMTF.

DMQL *n.* Acronym for Data Mining Query Language. Any query language developed and used for data mining relational databases. DMQLs provide a syntax for specifying the kind of knowledge to be mined, pattern presentation and visualization, conceptual hierarchies, and task relevant data. See also data mining.

DMTF *n.* Acronym for Desktop Management Task Force. A consortium formed in 1992 to develop standards for PC-based stand-alone and networked systems based on user and industry needs.

DNA *n.* See digital DNA, Digital Network Architecture, distributed network, Windows DNA.

DNS *n.* 1. Acronym for Domain Name System. The hierarchical system by which hosts on the Internet have both domain name addresses (such as bluestem.prairienet.org) and IP addresses (such as 192.17.3.4). The domain name address is used by human users and is automatically translated into the numerical IP address, which is used by the packet-routing software. DNS names consist of a top-level domain (such as .com, .org, and .net), a second-level domain (the site name of a business, an organisation, or an individual), and possibly one or more subdomains (servers within a second-level domain). See also domain name address, IP address. 2. Acronym for Domain Name Service. The Internet utility that implements the Domain Name System. DNS servers, also called name servers, maintain databases containing the addresses and are accessed transparently to the user. See also Domain Name System (definition 1), DNS server.

DNS name server *n.* See DNS server.

DNS server *n.* Short for Domain Name System server. a computer that can answer Domain Name System (DNS) queries. The DNS server keeps a database of host computers and their corresponding IP addresses. Presented with the name apex.com, for example, the DNS server would return the IP address of the hypothetical company Apex. Also called: name server. See also DNS (definition 2), IP address.

DNS zone transfer *n.* See zone transfer.

.doc *n.* A file extension that identifies document files formatted for a word processor. This is the default file extension for Microsoft Word document files.

Dock *vb.* 1. To connect a laptop or notebook computer to a docking station. See also docking station, laptop, portable computer.

2. To move a toolbar to the edge of an application window so that it attaches to and becomes a feature of the application window.

Dock *n.* An organisational feature of Mac OS X that keeps track of frequently used applications, documents, and windows. Users can drag icons to the dock for easy access or can minimise an active window to the Dock and still see the application running while working with other windows. The Dock can run along the bottom or either side of the screen. See also Mac OS X.

Docking mechanism *n.* The portion of a docking station that physically connects the portable computer with the station. See also docking station.

Docking station *n.* A unit for housing a laptop or notebook computer that contains a power connection, expansion slots, and connections to peripherals, such as a monitor, printer, full-sized keyboard, and mouse. The purpose of a docking station is to turn the laptop or notebook computer into a desktop machine and allow users the convenience of using such peripherals as a monitor and a full-sized keyboard. See the illustration. See also expansion slot, laptop, peripheral, portable computer.

DOCSIS *n.* Acronym for Data Over Cable Service Interface Specification. The International Telecommunications Union standard (ITU Recommendation J.112) that specifies functions and internal and external interfaces for high-speed, bidirectional transfer of digital data between cable television networks and subscribers. DOCSIS-compliant equipment ensures interoperability between cable modems and the cable television infrastructure, regardless of manufacturer or provider. Initially developed by a group of cable television providers, including Time Warner and TCI, DOCSIS was designed to support data, video, and rapid Internet access. Data rates are 27 Mbps to 36 Mbps downstream (from the cable network) and 320 Kbps to 10 Mbps upstream (to the cable network). See also cable modem.

Doctype *n.* A declaration at the beginning of an SGML document that gives a public or system identifier for the document type definition (DTD) of the document. See also SGML.

Document 1 *n.* Any self-contained piece of work created with an application programme and, if saved on disk, given a unique filename by which it can be retrieved. Documents are generally thought of as word-processed materials only. To a computer, however, data is nothing more than a collection of characters, so a spreadsheet or a graphic is as much a document as is a letter or report. In the Macintosh environment in particular, a document is any user-created work named and saved as a separate file.

Document 2 *vb.* To explain or annotate something, such as a programme or a procedure.

Documentation *n.* The set of instructions shipped with a programme or a piece of hardware. Documentation usually includes necessary information about the type of computer system required, setup instructions, and instructions on the use and maintenance of the product.

Document-centric *adj.* Of, pertaining to, or characteristic of an operating system in which the user opens document files and thus automatically invokes the applications (such as word processors or spreadsheet programmes) that process them. Many graphical user interfaces, such as the Macintosh Finder, as well as the World Wide Web, are document-centric.

Document Content Architecture *n.* See DCA (definition 1).

Document Content Description *n.* See DCD (definition 2).

Document file *n.* A user-created file that represents the output of a programme. Also called: data file.

Document image processing *n.* A system for storing and retrieving information for an enterprise in the form of bitmapped images of paper documents input with a scanner rather than in the form of text and numeric files. Document image processing takes more memory than purely electronic data processing, but it more readily incorporates signatures, drawings, and photographs and can be more familiar to users without computer training. See also paperless office.

Document Interchange Architecture *n.* See DIA.

Document management *n.* The full spectrum of electronic document creation and distribution within an organisation.

Document management system *n.* A server-based network facility designed for the storage and handling of an organisation's documents. A document management system, or DMS, is built around a central library known as a repository and typically supports controlled access, version tracking, cataloging, search capabilities, and the ability to check documents in and out electronically. The open interface specification known as ODMA (Open Document Management API) enables desktop applications that support ODMA to interface with a DMS so that users can access and manage documents from within their client applications. Acronym: DMS. Also called: EDMS, electronic document management system.

Document Object Model *n.* A World Wide Web Consortium specification that describes the structure of dynamic HTML and XML documents in a way that allows them to be manipulated through a Web browser. In the Document Object Model, or DOM, a document is presented as a logical structure rather than as a collection of tagged words. In essence, DOM is a means of defining a document as a treelike hierarchy of nodes in which the document is an object containing other objects, such as images and forms. Through DOM, programmes and scripts can access these objects in order to change aspects such as their appearance or behaviour. DOM is a vehicle for adding depth and interactivity to what would otherwise be a static Web page. Acronym: DOM.

Document processing *n.* The act of retrieving and manipulating a document. In terms of the way a computer works, document processing involves three main steps: creating or retrieving a data file, using a programme to manipulate the data in some way, and storing the modified file.

Document reader *n.* A device that scans printed text and uses character recognition to convert it to computer text files. See also character recognition.

Document retrieval *n.* A capability built into some application programmes that enables the user to search for specific documents by specifying items of information, such as date, author, or previously assigned keywords. Document retrieval depends on an indexing scheme that the programme maintains and uses. Depending on the program's capabilities, document retrieval might allow the user to specify more than one condition to refine a search.

Document source *n.* The plain-text HTML form of a World Wide Web document, with all tags and other markup displayed as such rather than being formatted. Also called: source, source document. See also HTML.

Document Style Semantics and Specification Language *n.* An ISO standard derived from SGML that addresses the semantics of high-quality composition in a manner independent of particular formatting systems or processes. Like CSS and XSL, it can be used to format XML documents. Acronym: DSSSL. See also ISO, SGML.

Document type definition *n.* See DTD.

Document window *n.* In windowing environments, such as the Apple Macintosh and Microsoft Windows, an onscreen window (enclosed work area) in which the user can create, view, or work on a document.

DoD *n.* See U.S. Department of Defense.

Do-gooder virus *n.* A virus or worm that has been released with the intention of correcting problems caused by other, more malicious viruses. The do-gooder virus typically looks for computers that have been compromised and then infects the system and fixes back doors and other vulnerabilities left behind by the malicious programme. The do-gooder virus may then use the repaired computer as a platform to infect other computers. See also anti-worm, automatic patching.

DO loop *n.* A control statement used in programmes that executes a section of code a number of times until a specified condition is met. DO loops are found in FORTRAN and Basic, among other languages. See also iterative statement.

DOM *n.* See Document Object Model.

Domain *n.* 1. In database design and management, the set of valid values for a given attribute. For example, the domain for the attribute AREA-CODE might be the list of all valid three-digit numeric telephone area codes in the United States. See also attribute (definition 1). 2. For Windows NT Advanced Server, a collection of computers that share a common domain database and security policy. Each domain has a unique name. 3. In the Internet and other networks, the highest subdivision of a domain name in a network address, which identifies the type of entity owning the address (for example, .com for commercial users or .edu for educational institutions) or the geographical location of the address (for example, .fr for France or .sg for Singapore). The domain is the last part of the address (for example, www.acm.org). See also domain name.

Domain controller *n.* In Windows NT, the master server that holds the directory services database that identifies all network users and resources.

Domain name *n.* An address of a network connection that identifies the owner of that address in a hierarchical format: server.organisation.type. For example, www.whitehouse.gov identifies the Web server at the White House, which is part of the U.S. government.

Domain name address *n.* The address of a device connected to the Internet or any other TCP/IP network, in the hierarchical system that uses words to identify servers, organisations, and types, such as www.logos.net. See also TCP/IP.

Domain slamming *n.* The practice of transferring ownership of domain names from one customer to another without the permission of the first customer.

Domino *n.* See Lotus Domino.

Dongle *n.* 1. See hardware key. 2. An adapter device or cable enabling a nonstandard interface between a computer and a peripheral device or between two disparate items of computer hardware.

Do-nothing instruction *n.* See no-operation instruction.

Doorway page *n.* A Web page that functions as a doorway into a Web site. Usually a doorway page contains keywords, which Internet search engines seek when they scan the Internet. Placing the correct keywords on a doorway page can increase the number of viewers visiting a site.

Dopant *n.* An impurity that is added in small quantities to semiconductor material during the manufacture of diodes, transistors, and integrated circuits. The resistance of a semiconductor falls between the resistance of a conductor and the resistance of an insulator (hence its name); dopants are added to the semiconductor to increase its conductivity. The type and amount of dopant determine whether the semiconductor will be N-type (in which current is conducted by free electrons) or P-type (in which current is conducted by electron vacancies, called holes). Common dopants include arsenic, antimony, bismuth, and phosphorus. See also N-type semiconductor, P-type semiconductor.

DoS *n.* Acronym for denial of service attack. A computerised assault, usually planned, that seeks to disrupt Web access. A denial of service attack can occur in a number of forms. The most common form of attack is to overwhelm an Internet server with connection requests that cannot be completed. This causes the server to become so busy attempting to respond to the attack that it ignores legitimate requests for connections. One example of this type of attack, known as a SYN flood, inundates the server's entry ports with false connection messages. Another, known as the Ping of Death, sends a ping command with an oversized IP packet that causes the server to freeze, crash, or restart. Other forms of denial of service attacks include the destruction or alteration of a server's configuration data, such as router information; unauthorised access to physical components of a system; and the sending of large or invalid data that causes a system to crash or freeze. See also packet, Ping of Death, SYN flood.

DOS *n.* 1. Acronym for disk operating system. A generic term describing any operating system that is loaded from disk devices when the system is started or rebooted. The term originally differentiated between disk-based systems and primitive microcomputer operating systems that were memory-based or that supported only magnetic or paper tape. 2. See MS-DOS.

DOS box *n.* 1. An OS/2 process that supports the execution of MS-DOS programmes. Also called: compatibility box. 2. A computer that uses the MS-DOS or PC-DOS operating system, as opposed to one that runs some other operating system, such as UNIX.

DOS extender *n.* A programme designed to extend the 640 KB of conventional memory available for use by DOS and DOS-based applications. A DOS extender works by claiming a portion of reserved memory (memory used by other parts of the system, such as the video adapter, the ROM BIOS, and the I/O ports).

DOS prompt *n.* The visual indication from the MS-DOS command processor that the operating system is ready to accept a new command. The default DOS prompt is a path followed by a greater-than sign (for example, C:>); the user can also design a custom prompt with the PROMPT command.

DOS Protected Mode Interface *n.* A software interface, originally developed for Microsoft Windows version 3, that enables MS-DOS-based application programmes to run in the protected mode built into 80286 and later microprocessors. In protected mode, the microprocessor can support multitasking and use of memory beyond 1 MB—capabilities otherwise unavailable to programmes designed to run under MS-DOS. See also protected mode, real mode, Virtual Control Programme Interface.

Dot *n.* 1. In the UNIX, MS-DOS, OS/2, and other operating systems, the character that separates a filename from an extension as in TEXT.DOC (pronounced "text-dot-doc"). 2. In computer graphics and printing, a small spot combined with others in a matrix of rows and columns to form a character or a graphic element in a drawing or design. The dots forming an image on the screen are called pixels. The resolution of a display or printing device is often expressed in dots per inch (dpi). Dots are not the same as spots, which are groups of dots used in the halftoning process. See also pixel, resolution (definition 1). 3. In an Internet address, the character that separates the different parts of the domain name, such as the entity name from the domain. See also domain (definition 3), domain name.

Dot address *n.* An IP address in dotted quad form. See also IP address.

Dot-addressable mode *n.* A mode of operation in which a computer programme can address ("point to") individual dots on the screen or in a printed character. See also all points addressable.

Dot-bomb *n.* An Internet-based company or organisation that has failed or downsized significantly. See also dot-commed.

Dot-com *n.* A company doing business primarily or entirely on the Internet. The term is derived from the top-level domain, .com, at the end of the Web addresses of commercial Web sites.

Dot command *n.* A formatting command typed into a document and preceded by a period (dot) to distinguish it from printable text. Text formatting programmes such as the XENIX nroff editor and word processing programmes such as WordStar use dot commands for formatting.

Dot-commed *adj.* Losing a job because of the downsizing or failure of an Internet-based company or organisation. See also dot-bomb.

Dot file *n.* A file under UNIX whose name begins with a period. Dot files do not appear in ordinary listings of the files in a directory. Dot files are often used to store programme setup information for the particular user; for example, .newsrc in a user's account indicates to a newsreader which newsgroups the user subscribes to.

Dot-matrix 1 *adj.* Referring to video and print hardware that forms character and graphic images as patterns of dots.

Dot matrix 2 *n.* The rectangular grid, or matrix, of tiny "cells" in which dots are displayed or printed in the patterns required to form text characters, circles, squares, and other graphical images. Depending on the frame of reference, the size of a dot matrix varies from a few rows and columns to an invisible grid covering an entire display screen or printed page. See also dot-matrix printer, raster.

Dot-matrix printer *n.* Any printer that produces characters made up of dots using a wire-pin print head. The quality of output from a dot-matrix printer depends largely on the number of dots in the matrix, which might be low enough to show individual dots or might be high enough to approach the look of fully formed characters. Dot-matrix printers are often categorised by the number of pins in the print head—typically 9, 18, or 24.

Dot pitch *n.* 1. In printers, the distance between dots in a dot-matrix. See also dot matrix. 2. In video displays or CRTs, a measure of image clarity. A video display's dot pitch is the vertical distance, expressed in millimeters, between like-coloured pixels. A smaller dot pitch generally means a crisper image, although the difference between two displays can vary because some manufacturers use different methods to determine the dot pitch of their products. A display's dot pitch is an integral part of the product and so cannot be altered. See also CRT, display.

Dots per inch *n.* A measure of screen and printer resolution that is expressed as the number of dots that a device can print or display per linear inch. Acronym: dpi.

Dotted decimal notation *n.* The process of formatting an IP address as a 32-bit identifier made up of four groups of numbers, with each group separated by a period. For example, 123.432.154.12.

Double buffering *n.* The use of two temporary storage areas (buffers) rather than one to hold information coming from and going to a particular input/output device. Because one buffer can be filled while the other is being emptied, double buffering increases transfer speed. Also called: ping-pong buffer.

Double-byte characters *n.* A set of characters in which each character is represented by two bytes. Some languages, such as Japanese, Chinese, and Korean, require double-byte character sets.

Double-click *vb.* To press and release a mouse button twice without moving the mouse. Double-clicking is a means of rapidly selecting and activating a programme or programme feature.

Double dabble *n.* A method of converting binary numbers to decimals by a process of doubling sums and adding successive bits: doubling the bit farthest to the left, adding the next bit and doubling the sum, adding the next bit and doubling the sum, and so on until the rightmost bit has been included in the total.

Double-density disk *n.* A disk created to hold data at twice the density (bits per inch) of a previous generation of disks. Early IBM PC floppy disks held 180 KB of data. Double-density disks increased that capacity to 360 KB. Double-density disks use modified frequency modulation encoding for storing data. See also floppy disk, microfloppy disk, , modified frequency modulation encoding.

Double-dereference *vb.* To dereference a pointer that is pointed to by another pointer; in other words, to access the information pointed to by a handle. See also dereference, handle (definition 1), pointer (definition 1).

Double leap year *n.* The mistaken idea that the year 2000 would have two leap days—February 29 and February 30—instead of one. In actuality, there was a potential leap year problem in 2000, but it was based on three rules for calculating leap years: (1) A year is a leap year if it is divisible by 4, but (2) not if it is divisible by 100, unless (3) it is also divisible by 400. Thus, 1900 was not a leap year, but 2000 is, although systems based on incorrect algorithms may not recognise it as a leap year and so may have difficulties functioning correctly after February 28, 2000.

Double posting *n.* In newsgroup discussions, the practice of replying to one's own posts. Because it may be seen as the digital equivalent to talking to one's self, double posting is considered an undesirable practice.

Double-precision *adj.* Of, pertaining to, or characteristic of a number stored in twice the amount (two words—typically 8 bytes) of computer memory that is required for storing a less precise (single-precision) number. Double-precision numbers are commonly handled by a computer in floating-point form. See also floating-point number.

Double-sided disk *n.* A floppy disk that can hold data on both its top and bottom surfaces.

Double slash *n.* See //.

Double-strike *n.* On an impact printer, such as a daisy-wheel printer, the process of printing twice over a word, producing text that appears darker and heavier, or bolder, than it normally appears. On dot-matrix printers, double striking with a slight offset can be used to fill in the space between the dots, producing smoother and darker characters.

Double supertwist nematic display *n.* See supertwist display.

Double word *n.* A unit of data consisting of two contiguous words (connected bytes, not text) that are handled together by a computer's microprocessor.

Doubly linked list *n.* A series of nodes (items representing discrete segments of information) in which each node refers to both the next node and the preceding node. Because of these two-way references, a doubly linked list can be traversed both forward and backward, rather than in a forward direction only, as with a singly linked list.

Down *adj.* Not functioning, in reference to computers, printers, communications lines on networks, and other such hardware.

Downflow *n.* One of the four stages of the data warehousing process, during which stored information is delivered and archived. See also data warehouse.

Downlink *n.* The transmission of data from a communications satellite to an earth station.

Download *vb.* 1. In communications, to transfer a copy of a file from a remote computer to the requesting computer by means of a modem or network. 2. To send a block of data, such as a PostScript file, to a dependent device, such as a PostScript printer.

Downloadable font *n.* A set of characters stored on disk and sent (downloaded) to a printer's memory when needed for printing a document. Downloadable fonts are most commonly used with laser printers and other page printers, although many dot-matrix printers can accept some of them. Also called: soft font.

Downloadable Sounds *n.* A standard for synthesizing wave sounds from digital samples stored in software. The DLS level 1 and level 2 standards are published by the MIDI Manufacturers Association. Acronym: DLS.

Downsample *n.* To decrease the number of audio samples or pixels, by applying an operation such as averaging. Popular internet music formats, such as MP3, use downsampling to reduce file size.

Downsizing *n.* In computing, the practice of moving from larger computer systems, such as mainframes and minicomputers, to smaller systems in an organisation, generally to save costs and to update to newer software. The smaller systems are usually client/server systems composed of a combination of PCs, workstations, and some legacy system such as a mainframe, connected in one or more local area networks or wide area networks. See also client/server architecture, legacy system.

Downstream 1 *n.* The direction in which information, such as a news feed for a newsgroup or data from an http (Web) server, is passed from one server to the next. See also news feed, newsgroup, server.

Downstream 2 *adv*. 1. The location of a client computer in relation to a server. 2. The direction in which data moves from the server to the client.

Downstream 3 *adj*. Refers to data that moves from a remote network to an individual computer. In some Internet-related communications technologies, data flows more quickly downstream than upstream; cable modems, for example, can transfer data as fast as 30 Mbps downstream but support much slower rates, from 128 Kbps to around 2 Mbps, upstream.

Downtime *n*. The amount or percentage of time a computer system or associated hardware remains nonfunctional. Although downtime can occur because hardware fails unexpectedly, it can also be a scheduled event, as when a network is shut down to allow time for maintenance.

Downward compatibility *n*. The capability of source code or programmes developed on a more advanced system or compiler version to be executed or compiled by a less advanced (older) version.

DP *n*. See data processing.

dpi *n*. See dots per inch.

DPMA *n*. Acronym for Data Processing Management Association. A trade organisation of information systems (IS) professionals. DPMA was founded in 1951 as the National Machine Accountants Association.

DPMI *n*. See DOS Protected Mode Interface.

DPMS *n*. Acronym for VESA Display Power Management Signaling. A VESA standard for signals that put a video monitor into "standby" or suspend mode to reduce power consumption. See also green PC, VESA.

DPOF *n*. Short for Digital Print Order Format. A printing specification developed by Canon Computer Systems, Inc., Eastman Kodak Company, Fuji Photo Film Co., Ltd., and Matsushita Electric Industrial Co., Ltd. DPOF is intended to ease the process of printing images stored on digital camera memory cards by enabling users to select the images to print, as well as specify the number of copies desired, on the card.

The images ordered can then be printed by a professional photofinishing service or on a home printer.

DPSK *n.* Acronym for differential phase-shift keying. See phase-shift keying.

Draft mode *n.* A high-speed, relatively low-quality print mode offered by most dot-matrix printers. See also dot-matrix printer, draft quality, print quality.

Draft quality *n.* A low grade of printing generated by the draft mode on dot-matrix printers. Draft quality varies among printers, ranging from suitable for most purposes to nearly useless. See also draft mode, print quality.

Drag *vb.* In graphical user interface environments, to move an image or a window from one place on the screen to another by "grabbing" it and pulling it to its new location using the mouse. The mouse pointer is positioned over the object, and the mouse button is pressed and held while the mouse is moved to the new location.

Drag-and-drop *vb.* 1. In general, to delve into something in increasing detail. 2. More specifically, to perform operations in a graphical user interface by dragging objects on the screen with the mouse. For example, to delete a document, a user can drag the document icon across the screen and drop it on the trashcan icon (Macintosh OS) or in the Recycle Bin (Windows). See also drag, graphical user interface.

Drain *n.* 1. In an FET, the electrode toward which charge carriers (electrons or holes) move from the source under control of the gate. See also FET, gate (definition 2), MOSFET, source (definition 2). 2. See current drain.

DRAM *n.* See dynamic RAM.

DRAW *n.* Acronym for direct read after write. A technique used with optical discs to verify the accuracy of information immediately after it has been recorded (written) on the disc.

Drawer *n.* In the Mac OS X Aqua interface, small child windows containing extra information that slide out of the side of main parent windows. Drawers are intended to reduce clutter on the computer desktop by enabling more information to be displayed without opening additional full-sized windows. Also called: Drop Drawer.

Drawing interchange format *n.* See DXF.

Drawing programme *n.* A programme for manipulating object-oriented graphics, as opposed to manipulating pixel images. In a drawing programme, for example, the user can manipulate an element, such as a line, a circle, or a block of text, as an independent object simply by selecting the object and moving it. See also object-oriented graphics, pixel image, vector graphics.

DRDW *n.* Acronym for direct read during write. A technique used with optical discs to verify the accuracy of information at the time it is being recorded on the disc.

Dreamcast *n.* A console game system designed by the Sega corporation. It features a Hitachi 128-bit graphics engine with an on-board SH-4 RISC processor (operating frequency of 200 MHz 360 MIPS/1.4 GFLOPS) and a customised OS using Windows CE as its base (supporting DirectX). Game developers for the Dreamcast platform use an environment supported by Microsoft Visual Studio and refined Visual C++. See also computer game, console game, DirectX, gigaflops, MIPS, OS, RISC, Visual C++.

Dribbleware *n.* Updates, patches, and new drivers for a software product that are released one at a time, as they become available, rather than being issued together in a new version of the product. A company using the dribbleware technique might distribute new and replacement files on diskette or CD-ROM, or make them available for download through the Internet or a private network. See also driver, patch1.

Drift *n.* The movement of charge carriers in a semiconductor caused by an applied voltage. The term is also used to refer to any slow, unwanted change in a parameter; for example, the value of a resistor might change, or drift, slightly as the resistor warms or cools.

Drill down *vb.* To start at a top-level menu, directory, or Web page and pass through several intermediate menus, directories, or linked pages, until the file, page, menu command, or other item being sought is reached. Drilling down is common practice in searching for files or information on the Internet, where high-level Gopher menus and World Wide Web pages are frequently very general and become more specific at each lower level. See also Gopher, menu, Web page.

Drive *n.* See disk drive.

Drive bay *n.* A hollow, rectangular area in a computer chassis designed to hold a disk drive. A drive bay always has side walls, usually made of metal, that generally contain holes to facilitate installation of a disk drive. Some drive bays, such as those intended to hold hard disks, are not visible to the user. Most drives are located on the front of the chassis so that the user can interact with the drive.

Drive letter *n.* The naming convention for disk drives on IBM and compatible computers. Drives are named by letter, beginning with A, followed by a colon.

Drive mapping *n.* The assignment of a letter or name to a disk drive so that the operating system or network server can identify and locate it. For example, in PCs, the primary drive mappings are A: and B: for floppy disk drives and C: for the hard disk. See also A:, disk drive, hard disk.

Drive number *n.* The naming convention for Macintosh disk drives. For example, a two-drive system calls its drives 0 and 1.

Driver *n.* A hardware device or a programme that controls or regulates another device. A line driver, for example, boosts signals transmitted over a communications line. A software driver is a device-specific control programme that enables a computer to work with a particular device, such as a printer or a disk drive. Because the driver handles device-specific features, the operating system is freed from the burden of having to understand—and support—the needs of individual hardware devices. See also device driver.

Driver Development Kit *n.* See DDK.

DRM *n.* Acronym for Digital Rights Management. A group of technologies developed to protect intellectual property from online piracy by controlling who can view protected content and in what form. A DRM package may allow the purchaser to view protected content, but prevent printing or forwarding. Content may also be set to expire after a set amount of time or if distributed to multiple users. DRM technology is meant to protect multiple forms of digital and analog content, and includes encryption, digital watermarking, and content tracking software.

DRO *n.* Acronym for destructive read out. See destructive read.

Drop cable *n.* A cable, also known as a transceiver cable, that is used to connect a network interface card (NIC) to a Thick Ethernet network.

Drop cap *n.* A large capital letter at the beginning of a text block that occupies the vertical depth of two or more lines of regular text. See the illustration.

Drop-dead halt *n.* See dead halt.

Drop-down menu *n.* A menu that drops from the menu bar when requested and remains open without further action until the user closes it or chooses a menu item.

Drop in *vb.* To read a spurious signal during a data read/write operation, producing erroneous data.

Droplet *n.* 1. An extension for Quark XPress that allows files to be dragged onto a page from the finder. 2. A feature from Frontier that allows scripts to be embedded within an application and run when the application is double-clicked. 3. A general name for any AppleScript programme that allows files to be dragged and dropped into it for processing. See also AppleScript.

Drop out *vb.* To lose the signal momentarily during a data read/write operation, thus producing erroneous data.

Drum *n.* A rotating cylinder used with some printers and plotters and (in the early days of mainframe computing) as a magnetic storage medium for data. In laser printers, a rotating drum is coated with a photoelectric material that retains a charge when struck by a laser beam. The electrically charged spots on the drum then attract toner particles that the drum transfers to the paper as the paper passes by.

Drum plotter *n.* A plotter in which paper is wrapped around a large revolving drum, with a pen that moves back and forth at the uppermost point on the drum. The paper is rolled with the drum to align the correct point on the paper with the pen. Drums take up a fraction of the space required by flatbed plotters that can handle the same paper size. They also effectively have no limit on the length of the paper they can handle, which can be an advantage in some applications. See also plotter.

Drum scanner *n.* A type of scanner where the medium being scanned, such as a sheet of paper, is rotated around a stationary scan head. See also scanner.

.drv *n.* The file extension for a driver file. See also driver.

Dry run *n.* Running a programme intended to have a dramatic effect, such as formatting a disk or printing a book, with the effect disabled, thus avoiding formatting a disk with data on it or wasting paper.

DS *n.* Acronym for Digital Services or Digital Signal, a category used in referencing the speed, number of channels, and transmission characteristics of T1, T2, T3, and T4 communications lines. The basic DS unit, or level, is known as DS-0, which corresponds to the 64 Kbps speed of a single T1 channel. Higher levels are made up of multiple DS-0 levels. DS-1 represents a single T1 line that transmits at 1.544 Mbps. For higher rates, T1 lines are multiplexed to create DS-2 (a T2 line consisting of four T1 channels that transmits at 6.312 Mbps), DS-3 (a T3 line consisting of 28 T1 channels that transmits at 44.736 Mbps), and DS-4 (a T4 line consisting of 168 T1 channels that transmits at 274.176 Mbps).

DSA *n.* 1. Acronym for Directory System Agent or Directory Server Agent. An X.500 server programme that looks up the address of a user on the network when requested by a DUA (Directory User Agent). See also agent (definition 3), CCITT X series, DUA. 2. See Digital Signature Algorithm.

DSL *n.* Acronym for Digital Subscriber Line, a recently developed (late 1990s) digital communications technology that can provide high-speed transmissions over standard copper telephone wiring. DSL is often referred to as xDSL, where the x stands for one or two characters that define variations of the basic DSL technology. Currently, ADSL (Asymmetric DSL) is the form most likely to be provided, but even it is, as yet, available only to limited groups of subscribers. See also ADSL, DSL Lite, HDSL, RADSL, SDSL, VDSL.

DSLAM *n.* Acronym for Digital Subscriber Line Access Multiplexer. A device in a telephone company central office that splits DSL subscriber lines and connects them to Internet network hosts and to the public telephone network. The use of a DSLAM makes it possible to provide both voice and data service through a single pair of copper wires.

DSL Lite *n.* Short for Digital Subscriber Line Lite. A variation of ADSL currently under development that simplifies installation but transmits more slowly, at 1.544 Mbps. See also ADSL, DSL.

DSO *n.* Acronym for Dynamic Shared Object. An Apache HTTP server module that supports all UNIX-based platforms. DSO uses a dynamically linked shared library of resources that are loaded and executed only at run time when necessary. DSO is most commonly used with Linux and is included in most Linux distributions.

DSOM *n.* See Distributed System Object Model.

DSP *n.* See digital signal processor.

DSR *n.* Acronym for Data Set Ready. A signal used in serial communications sent, for example, by a modem to the computer to which it is attached, to indicate that it is ready to operate. DSR is a hardware signal sent over line 6 in RS-232-C connections. See also RS-232-C standard.

DSS *n.* See decision support system, digital satellite system, Digital Signature Standard.

DSSSL *n.* See Document Style Semantics and Specification Language.

DSTN display *n.* Acronym for double supertwist nematic display. See supertwist display.

DSU *n.* See DDS.

DSVD *n.* See Digital Simultaneous Voice and Data.

DTD *n.* Acronym for document type definition. A separate document that contains formal definitions of all of the data elements in a particular type of HTML, SGML, or XML document, such as a report or a book. By consulting the DTD for a document, a programme called a parser can work with the markup codes that the document contains. See also HTML, SGML.

DTE *n.* Acronym for Data Terminal Equipment. In the RS-232-C and X.25 specifications, a device, such as a PC, that has the ability to transmit information in digital form over a cable or a communications line to a mediating device (known as the DCE). See also RS-232-C standard.

DTL *n.* See diode-transistor logic.

DTMF *n.* Acronym for Dual Tone Multiple Frequency. See touch tone dialing.

DTP *n.* See desktop publishing, distributed transaction processing.

DTR *n.* Acronym for Data Terminal Ready. A signal used in serial communications sent, for example, by a computer to its modem to indicate that the computer is ready to accept an incoming transmission. See also RS-232-C standard.

DTV *n.* Acronym for desk top video. The use of digital cameras over a network for video conferencing. See also video conferencing.

DUA *n.* Acronym for Directory User Agent. An X.500 client programme that sends a request to a DSA for the address of a user on the network. Also called: DCA, Directory Client Agent. See also agent (definition 3), DSA.

Dual attachment station *n.* An FDDI node with two connections to the network—either through a node and a concentrator or through two concentrators.

Dual-band phone *n.* Wireless phone that broadcasts and receives signals on both 800-MHz (digital cellular) and 1900-MHz (personal communications service, or PCS) networks.

Dual boot *n.* A computer configuration in which two different operating systems are installed and either can be loaded at start-up. A user might set up a dual boot system to take advantage of specific applications and functions in each operating system. A dual boot system might also be set up with each operating system in a different language. A dual boot system is not limited to only two operating systems, and when more than two are installed, it may be called a multi-boot system. See also boot1.

Dual channel controller *n.* A circuit or device that governs signal access to two pathways.

Dual density *adj.* Of, pertaining to, or characteristic of floppy disk drives that can read from and write to disks in more than one density format.

Dual disk drive *n.* A computer that has two floppy disk drives.

Dual homing *n.* A form of fault tolerance used with critical network devices on FDDI networks, in which such devices are attached to both the primary and secondary (backup) rings through two concentrators to provide the maximum possible security in case the primary ring fails.

Dual inline memory module *n.* See DIMM.

Dual inline package or dual in-line package *n.* See DIP.

Dual-mode phone *n.* Wireless phone that broadcasts and receives signals on both analog and digital networks. Dual-mode phones allow wireless phone users with digital service to send and receive calls on analog networks in areas where wireless carriers do not provide digital service.

Dual processors *n.* Two processors used in a computer to speed its operation—one processor to control memory and the bus, and another to manage input/output. Many personal computers use a second processor to perform floating-point mathematical operations. See also coprocessor, floating-point notation.

Dual-ring topology *n.* A token-passing ring topology implemented in FDDI networks that consists of two rings in which information travels in opposite directions. One ring, the primary ring, carries information; the second ring is used for backup. See also FDDI.

Dual-scan display *n.* A passive matrix LCD-type display used in laptop computers. The screen refresh rate is twice as fast in dual-scan displays as in standard passive matrix displays. Compared with active matrix displays, dual-scan displays are more economical in terms of power consumption but have less clarity and a smaller viewing angle. See also passive matrix display.

Dual-sided disk drive *n.* A disk drive that can read or write information to both the top and bottom sides of a double-sided disk. Dual-sided disk drives have two read/write heads, one for each disk surface.

Dual Tone Multiple Frequency *n.* See touch tone dialing.

DUB *n.* See dial-up boot loader.

Dumb quotes *n.* Quotation marks that have the same appearance (usually upright like the apostrophe and quotation marks on a typewriter) whether they stand before or after the material being quoted.

Dumb terminal *n.* A terminal that does not contain an internal microprocessor. Dumb terminals are typically capable of displaying only characters and numbers and responding to simple control codes.

Dummy *n.* A placeholder, usually a character, a record, or a variable, that is used to reserve space until the intended item is available. See also stub.

Dummy argument *n.* In programming, an argument that does not convey any information into or out of the called routine and is usually used to hold a place for an argument that will be used in a future revision of the routine. See also argument.

Dummy instruction *n.* See no-operation instruction.

Dummy module *n.* A module, or group of routines, that performs no function but will do so in some future revision—essentially, a collection of dummy routines. See also dummy routine.

Dummy routine *n.* A routine that performs no action but that can be rewritten to do so at some future time. Top-down programme development usually involves the creation of dummy routines that are turned into functional routines as development proceeds. Also called: stub. See also dummy argument, dummy module, top-down programming.

DUN *n.* See dial-up networking.

Duplex 1 *adj.* Capable of carrying information in both directions over a communications channel. A system is full-duplex if it can carry information in both directions at once; it is half-duplex if it can carry information in only one direction at a time.

Duplex 2 *n.* 1. Simultaneous communications, in both directions, between the sender and receiver. Also called: duplex transmission, full-duplex transmission. See also half-duplex transmission. 2. Photographic paper on which an image can be printed on both sides.

Duplex channel *n.* A communications link that allows for duplex (two-way) transmission.

Duplex printer *n.* A printer capable of printing on both sides of the page.

Duplex system *n.* A system of two computers, one of which is active while the other remains on standby, ready to take over processing if the active machine malfunctions.

Duplex transmission *n.* See duplex2 (definition 1).

Duplicate key *n.* A value assigned to an indexed field in one record in a database that duplicates a value assigned to the same field in another record in the database. For example, a key (or index) composed of ZIP-CODE would necessarily contain duplicate values if the file contained a number of addresses from a single ZIP Code. A field in which duplicate values are permitted cannot serve as a primary key because the primary key must be unique, but it can serve as a component of a composite primary key. See also field (definition 1), key (definition 2), primary key.

Duplication check *n.* 1. A survey made to determine whether duplicate records or keys exist in a file. See also key. 2. The use of separate independent calculations to establish the accuracy of a result.

DV *n.* See digital video.

DVD *n.* See digital video disc.

DVD decoder *n.* A hardware or software component that allows a digital video disc.

(DVD) drive to display movies on your computer screen. See also digital video disc.

DVD-E *n.* See digital video disc–erasable.

DVD-R *n.* See digital video disc–recordable.

DVD-ROM *n.* See digital video disc–ROM.

DVI *n.* Acronym for Digital Video Interface. A hardware-based compression/decompression technique for storing full-motion video, audio, graphics, and other data on a computer or on a CD-ROM. DVI technology was developed by RCA in 1987 and acquired by Intel in 1988. Intel has since developed a software version of DVI, called Indeo. Also called: digital video–interactive.

DV-I *n.* See digital video–interactive.

DVMRP *n.* See Distance Vector Multicast Routing Protocol.

Dvorak keyboard *n.* A keyboard layout developed by August Dvorak and William L. Dealey in 1936 as an alternative to the overwhelmingly popular QWERTY keyboard. The Dvorak keyboard was designed to speed typing by placing the characters on the keyboard for easiest access to the most frequently typed letters. In addition, pairs of letters that often occur sequentially were separated so that the hands could alternate typing them. See the illustration. See also ergonomic keyboard, keyboard.

DVR *n.* Acronym for Digital Video Recording. Technology allowing broadcast television programming to be digitized and played back immediately. Television signals are routed through a hard drive, converted to a digital format and displayed in real-time or, at the viewer's option, on a delayed basis. DVR technology can be used like a VCR to record favorite programmes in advance, with the user picking the programmes to be recorded from an online programming guide. DVR capabilities can also be added to products that have related digital technologies and components, such as set-top boxes and digital TV converters.

DVST *n.* See direct view storage tube.

DWDM *n.* See dense wavelength division multiplexing.

DXF *n.* Short for drawing interchange format. A computer-aided design file format originally developed by Autodesk; for use with the AutoCAD programme to facilitate transfer of graphics files between different applications

Dyadic *adj.* Of, pertaining to, or characteristic of a pair—for example, a dyadic processor, which contains two processors controlled by the same operating system. The term is usually limited to describing a system with two microprocessors. Dyadic Boolean operations are those such as AND and OR in which the outcome depends on both values. See also Boolean algebra, operand.

Dye-diffusion printer *n.* See continuous-tone printer.

Dye-polymer recording *n.* A recording technology used with optical discs in which dye embedded in a plastic polymer coating on an optical disc is used to create minute bumps on the surface that can be read by a laser. Dye-polymer bumps can be flattened and re-created, thus making an optical disc rewritable.

Dye-sublimation printer *n.* See continuous-tone printer.

Dylan *n.* Short for Dynamic Language. An object-oriented programming language developed by Apple Computer in the mid-1990s for application and systems development. It includes garbage collection, type-safety, error recovery, a module system, and programmer control over runtime extensibility of programmes.

Dynalink *n.* Short for dynamic link. See dynamic-link library.

Dynaload drivers *n.* Device drivers that are supported by Dynaload. Dynaload is a command that can be run from a DOS prompt under IBM's PC DOS 7 and will load compliant device drivers without modification of the CONFIG.SYS file. See also CONFIG.SYS.

Dynamic *adj.* Occurring immediately and concurrently. The term is used in describing both hardware and software; in both cases it describes some action or event that occurs when and as needed. In dynamic memory management, a programme is able to negotiate with the operating system when it needs more memory.

Dynamic address translation *n.* On-the-fly conversion of memory-location references from relative addresses (such as "three units from the beginning of X") to absolute addresses (such as "location number 123") when a programme is run. Acronym: DAT.

Dynamic allocation *n.* The allocation of memory during programme execution according to current needs. Dynamic allocation almost always implies that dynamic deallocation is possible too, so data structures can be created and destroyed as required. See also allocate, deallocate.

Dynamic binding *n.* Binding (converting symbolic addresses in the programme to storage-related addresses) that occurs during programme execution. The term often refers to object-oriented applications that determine, during run time, which software routines to call for particular data objects. Also called: late binding.

Dynamic caching *n.* A technique for storing recently used data in memory where cache size is based on how much memory is available rather than how much memory is assigned to the application currently running.

Dynamic Data Exchange *n.* See DDE.

Dynamic dump *n.* A listing, either stored on disk or sent to a printer, of memory contents generated at the time of a break in the execution of a programme—a useful tool for programmers interested in knowing what is happening at a certain point in the execution of a programme.

Dynamic Host Configuration Protocol *n.* See DHCP.

Dynamic HTML *n.* A technology designed to add richness, interactivity, and graphical interest to Web pages by providing those pages with the ability to change and update themselves dynamically—that is, in response to user actions, without the need for repeated downloads from a server. This is done by enabling the interaction of HTML, cascading style sheets (CSS), and JavaScript. Examples of dynamic HTML actions include moving graphics on the page and displaying information, such as menus or tables, in response to mouse movements or clicks. Interoperability is governed by the World Wide Web Consortium (W3C) Document Object Model (DOM) specification, a platform- and language-neutral interface to ensure that programmes and scripts can dynamically access and update the content, structure, and style of documents. Acronym: DHTML.

Dynamic keys *n.* An encryption technique in which messages are encrypted differently for each transmission based on different keys so that if a key is captured and decrypted, it would never be useful again. See also encryption, key (definition 3).

Dynamic-link library *n.* A feature of the Microsoft Windows family of operating systems and OS/2 that allows executable routines to be stored separately as files with DLL extensions and to be loaded only when needed by a programme. A dynamic-link library has several advantages. First, it does not consume any memory until it is used. Second, because a dynamic-link library is a separate file, a programmer can make corrections or improvements to only that module without affecting the operation of the calling programme or any other dynamic-link library. Finally, a programmer can use the same dynamic-link library with other programmes. Acronym: DLL.

Dynamic memory allocation *n.* The allocation of memory to a process or programme at run time. Dynamic memory is allocated from the system heap by the operating system upon request from the programme.

Dynamic page *n.* An HTML document that contains animated GIFs, Java applets, or ActiveX controls. See also ActiveX control, GIF, HTML, Java applet.

Dynamic RAM *n.* A form of semiconductor random access memory (RAM). Dynamic RAM stores information in integrated circuits containing capacitors. Because capacitors lose their charge over time, dynamic RAM boards must include logic to refresh (recharge) the RAM chips continuously. While a dynamic RAM is being refreshed, it cannot be read by the processor; if the processor must read the RAM while it is being refreshed, one or more wait states occur. Despite being slower, dynamic RAM is more commonly used than RAM because its circuitry is simpler and because it can hold up to four times as much data. Acronym: DRAM. See also RAM.

Dynamic random access memory *n.* See dynamic RAM.

Dynamic relocation *n.* The relocation in memory of data or of the code of a currently running programme by an internal system routine. Dynamic relocation helps a computer use memory efficiently.

Dynamic routing *n.* Routing that adjusts automatically to the current conditions of a network. Dynamic routing typically uses one of several dynamic-routing protocols such as Routing Information Protocol (RIP) and Border Gateway Protocol (BGP).

Dynamic scheduling *n.* The management of concurrently running processes (programmes), usually by the operating system.

Dynamic Shared Object *n.* See DSO.

Dynamic SLIP *n.* Short for dynamic Serial Line Internet Protocol. Internet access under SLIP in which the user's IP address is not permanent but is reassigned from a pool each time the user connects. The number of IP addresses an Internet service provider needs to offer is reduced to the number of connections that can be in use at once, rather than the total number of subscribers. See also IP address, ISP, SLIP.

Dynamic storage *n.* 1. Information storage systems whose contents will be lost if power is removed from the system. RAM (random access memory) systems are the most common form of dynamic storage, and both dynamic RAM (DRAM) and static RAM (SRAM) are considered forms of dynamic storage. See also dynamic RAM, static RAM. 2. In programming, blocks of memory that can be allocated, deallocated, or freely changed in size.

Dynamic Web page *n.* A Web page that has fixed form but variable content, allowing it to be tailored to a customer's search criteria.

E

E *n.* The symbol for the base of the natural logarithm 2.71828. Introduced by Leonhard Euler in the mid-eighteenth century, e is a fundamental mathematical constant used in calculus, science, engineering, and programming languages, as in logarithmic and exponential functions in C and Basic.

E-prefix Short for electronic. A prefix indicating that a word refers to the computer-based version of some traditionally nonelectronic term, as e-mail, e-commerce, and e-money.

E3 *n.* Acronym for Electronic Entertainment Expo. A major convention where game industry developers, manufacturers, and publishers demonstrate their latest wares.

EAI *n.* Acronym for Enterprise Application Integration. The process of coordinating the operation of the various programmes, databases, and existing technologies of a business or enterprise so that they function as an efficient, business-wide system.

Early binding *n.* See static binding.

EAROM *n.* Acronym for electrically alterable read-only memory. See EEPROM.

Easter egg *n.* A hidden feature of a computer programme. It may be a hidden command, an animation, a humorous message, or a list of credits for the people who developed the programme. In order to display an Easter egg, a user often must enter an obscure series of keystrokes.

Eavesdropper *n.* See lurker.

EBCDIC *n.* Acronym for Extended Binary Coded Decimal Interchange Code. An IBM code that uses 8 bits to represent

256 possible characters, including text, numbers, punctuation marks, and transmission control characters. It is used primarily in IBM mainframes and minicomputers.

E-bomb *n.* Short for e-mail bomb. A technique used by some hackers in which a target is put on a large number of mailing lists so that network traffic and storage are tied up by e-mail sent by other mailing list subscribers to the lists' recipients.

E-book *n.* Format allowing books and other large texts to be downloaded from a Web site and viewed digitally. Typically, reading an e-book requires using a small computer appliance that is about the size of a paperback book and consists of a display screen and basic controls. Users can bookmark, highlight, or annotate text, but rights management features may prevent users from e-mailing, printing, or otherwise sharing e-book contents. Also called electronic book.

Echo 1 *n.* In communications, a signal transmitted back to the sender that is distinct from the original signal. Network connections can be tested by sending an echo back to the main computer.

Echo 2 *vb.* To transmit a received signal back to the sender. Computer programmes, such as MS-DOS and OS/2, can be commanded to echo input by displaying data on the screen as it is received from the keyboard. Data communications circuits may echo text back to the originating terminal to confirm that it has been received.

Echo cancellation *n.* A technique for eliminating unwanted incoming transmissions in a modem that are echoes of the modem's own transmission. The modem sends a modified, reversed version of its transmission on its receiving path, thus erasing echoes while leaving incoming data intact. Echo cancellation is standard in V.32 modems.

Echo check *n.* In communications, a method for verifying the accuracy of transmitted data by retransmitting it to the sender, which compares the echoed signal with the original.

Echo loop attack *n.* A form of denial of service (DoS) attack in which a connection is established between User Datagram

Protocol (UDP) services on two or more host machines that bounce an increasing volume of packets back and forth. The echo loop attack ties up the host machines and causes network congestion.

Echoplex *n.* In communications, a technique for error detection. The receiving station retransmits data back to the sender's screen, where it can be displayed visually to check for accuracy.

Echo suppressor *n.* In communications, a method for preventing echoes in telephone lines. Echo suppressors inhibit signals from the listener to the speaker, creating a one-way channel. For modems that send and receive on the same frequency, the echo suppressor must be disabled to allow two-way transmission. This disabling produces the high-pitched tone heard in modem-to-modem connections.

ECL *n.* See emitter-coupled logic.

ECMA *n.* Acronym for European Computer Manufacturers Association. An organisation based in Geneva, Switzerland, whose American counterpart is CBEMA (Computer and Business Equipment Manufacturers Association). Its standard, ECMA-101, is used for transmitting formatted text and graphical images while retaining their original formatting.

ECMAScript *n.* A standardised, object-oriented scripting language specification defined by the European Computer Manufacturers Association (ECMA) 262 specification. This language was originally designed to perform computations and manipulate objects within a Web environment. Microsoft implements ECMAScript as JScript, and Netscape implements ECMAScript as JavaScript.

ECML *n.* See Electronic Commerce Modeling Language.

E-commerce *n.* Short for electronic commerce. Commercial activity that takes place by means of computers connected through a network. Electronic commerce can occur between a user and a vendor through the Internet, an online information service, or a bulletin board system (BBS), or between vendor and customer computers through electronic data interchange (EDI). Also called: e-tail. See also EDI.

ECP *n.* Acronym for Enhanced Capabilities Port. A protocol, developed by Microsoft and Hewlett Packard, for bidirectional, high-speed communication between a computer and a printer or scanner. ECP is part of the IEEE 1284 standard, which specifies enhanced parallel ports that are compatible with the older, de facto standard Centronics parallel ports. See also EPP, IEEE 1284.

E-credit *n.* See electronic credit.

E-currency *n.* See e-money.

Edge *n.* 1. In graphics, a border joining two polygons. 2. In data structures, a link between two nodes on a tree or graph. See also graph, node (definition 3), tree.

EDGE *n.* Acronym for Enhanced Data Rates for Global Evolution or Enhanced Data Rates for GSM and TDMA Evolution. A third-generation enhancement to the Global System for Mobile Communications (GSM) wireless service, which allows data, multimedia services, and applications to be delivered on broadband at rates up to 384 Kbps.

Edge connector *n.* The set of wide, flat, metallic contacts on an expansion board that is inserted into a personal computer's expansion slot or a ribbon cable's connector. It connects the board with the system's shared data pathway, or bus, by means of a series of printed lines that connect to the circuits on the board. The number and pattern of lines differ with the various types of connectors. See also expansion board, ribbon cable.

EDI *n.* Acronym for Electronic Data Interchange. A standard for exchanging bundles of data between two companies via telephone lines or the Internet. EDI transmits much larger bundles of data than can be transmitted via e-mail. For EDI to be effective, users must agree on certain standards for formatting and exchanging information, such as the X.400 protocol. See also CCITT X series, standard (definition 1).

Edit 1 *n.* A change made to a file or a document.

Edit 2 *vb.* 1. To make a change to an existing file or document. Changes to the existing document are saved in memory or in a temporary file but are not added to the document until the programme is instructed to save them. Editing programmes typically provide safeguards against inadvertent changes, such as by requesting confirmation before saving under an existing filename, by allowing the user to assign a password to a file, or by giving the option of setting the file to read-only status. 2. To run software that makes extensive, predictable changes to a file automatically, such as a linker or a filter for graphics.

Editing keys *n.* A set of keys on some keyboards that assists in editing. Located between the main keyboard and the numeric keypad, editing keys consist of three pairs: Insert and Delete, Home and End, and Page Up and Page Down.

Edit key *n.* In a software application, a predefined key or combination of keys that, when pressed, causes the application to enter edit mode.

Edit mode *n.* The mode of a programme in which a user can make changes to a document, as by inserting or deleting data or text.

Editor *n.* A programme that creates files or makes changes to existing files. An editor is usually less powerful than a word processor, lacking the latter's capability for text formatting, such as use of italics. Text or full-screen editors allow the user to move through the document using direction arrows. In contrast, line editors require the user to indicate the line number on which text is to be edited. See also Edlin.

Edlin *n.* An outdated line-by-line text editor used in MS-DOS through version 5. Its OS/2 counterpart is SSE. See also editor.

EDMS *n.* Acronym for electronic document management system. See document management system.

EDO DRAM *n.* Acronym for extended data out dynamic random access memory. A type of memory that allows for faster read times than DRAM of comparable speed by allowing a new read cycle to begin while data is being read from a previous cycle. This allows for faster overall system performance.

EDO RAM *n.* Acronym for extended data out random access memory. A type of dynamic RAM that keeps data available for the CPU while the next memory access is being initialised, resulting in increased speed. Pentium-class computers using Intel's Triton chip set are designed to take advantage of EDO RAM. See also central processing unit, dynamic RAM.

EDP *n.* 1. Acronym for electronic data processing. See data processing. 2. Acronym for Enhanced Capabilities Port. A protocol, developed by Microsoft and Hewlett Packard, for bidirectional, high-speed communication between a computer and a printer or scanner. ECP is part of the IEEE 1284 standard, which specifies enhanced parallel ports that are compatible with the older, de facto standard Centronics parallel ports. See also EPP, IEEE 1284.

.edu *n.* In the Internet's Domain Name System, the top-level domain that identifies addresses operated by four-year, degreed educational institutions. The domain name .edu appears as a suffix at the end of the address. In the United States, schools that offer kindergarten through high school classes use the top-level domain of .k12.us or just .us. See also DNS (definition 1), domain (definition 3), .k12.us, .us.

Edutainment *n.* Multimedia content in software, on CD-ROM, or on a Web site that purports to educate the user as well as entertain. See also multimedia.

EEMS *n.* Acronym for Enhanced Expanded Memory Specification A superset of the original Expanded Memory Specificatio (EMS). Version 3.0 of EMS allowed only storage of data an supported 4-page frames. EEMS allowed up to 64 pages alon with executable code to be stored in expanded memory. Th features of EEMS were included in EMS version 4.0. See als EMS, page frame.

EEPROM *n.* Acronym for electrically erasable programmabl read-only memory. A type of EPROM that can be erased wit an electrical signal. It is useful for stable storage for lon periods without electricity while still allowing repro gramming. EEPROMs contain less memory than RAM, tak longer to reprogram, and can be reprogrammed only a limite number of times before wearing out. See also EPROM, ROM

EFF *n.* See Electronic Frontier Foundation.

E-form *n.* Short for electronic form. An online document that contains blank spaces for a user to fill in with requested information and that can be submitted through a network to the organisation requesting the information. On the Web, e-forms are often coded in CGI script and secured via encryption. See also CGI (definition 1).

EGA *n.* Acronym for Enhanced Graphics Adapter. An IBM video display standard introduced in 1984. It emulates the Colour/Graphics Adapter (CGA) and the Monochrome Display Adapter (MDA) and provides medium-resolution text and graphics. It was superseded by Video Graphics Display (VGA).

Ego-surfing *n.* The practice of using a Web search engine to search for one's own name on the Internet.

EGP *n.* See exterior gateway protocol.

E-home *n.* See smart home.

EIA *n.* Acronym for Electronic Industries Association. An association based in Washington, D.C., with members from various electronics manufacturers. It sets standards for electronic components. RS-232-C, for example, is the EIA standard for connecting serial components. See also RS-232-C standard.

EIDE or E-IDE *n.* Acronym for Enhanced Integrated Drive Electronics. An extension of the IDE standard, EIDE is a hardware interface standard for disk drive designs that house control circuits in the drives themselves. It allows for standardised interfaces to the system bus while providing for advanced features, such as burst data transfer and direct data access. EIDE accommodates drives as large as 8.4 gigabytes (IDE supports up to 528 megabytes). It supports the ATA-2 interface, which permits transfer rates up to 13.3 megabytes per second (IDE permits up to 3.3 megabytes per second), and the ATAPI interface, which connects drives for CD-ROMs, optical discs and tapes, and multiple channels. Most PCs have EIDE drives, which are cheaper than SCSI drives and provide much of the same functionality. See also IDE, SCSI.

Eiffel *n.* An advanced object-oriented programming language with a syntax similar to C, developed by Bertrand Meyer in

1988. Eiffel runs on MS-DOS, OS/2, and UNIX. Its major design features are the ability to use modules in multiple programmes and software extensibility.

Eiffel# *n.* Pronounced "Eiffel Sharp." A subset language of Eiffel specifically designed to target the .NET Framework and embody the full extent of Design by Contract. See also Design by Contract.

Eight dot three *n.* See 8.3.

EIP *n.* See enterprise information portal.

EIS *n.* See executive information system.

EISA *n.* Acronym for Extended Industry Standard Architecture. A bus standard for the connection of add-on cards to a PC motherboard, such as video cards, internal modems, sound cards, drive controllers, and cards that support other peripherals. EISA was introduced in 1988 by a consortium of nine computer industry companies. The companies—AST Research, Compaq, Epson, Hewlett-Packard, NEC, Olivetti, Tandy, Wyse, and Zenith—were referred to collectively as "the Gang of Nine." EISA maintains compatibility with the earlier Industry Standard Architecture (ISA) but provides for additional features introduced by IBM in its Micro Channel Architecture bus standard. EISA has a 32-bit data path, and it uses connectors that can accept ISA cards. However, EISA cards are compatible only with EISA systems. EISA can operate at much higher frequencies than the ISA bus and provides much faster data throughput than ISA. See also ISA, Micro Channel Architecture.

EJB *n.* See Enterprise JavaBeans.

Electroluminescent *adj.* Giving off light when electric current is applied. Electroluminescent panels are used in portable computers to backlight the liquid crystal displays. A thin phosphor layer is sandwiched between two thin electrode panels, one of which is nearly transparent. See also liquid crystal display.

Electroluminescent display *n.* A type of flat-panel display used in laptops in which a thin phosphor layer is set between vertical and horizontal electrodes. These electrodes form xy-coordinates; when a vertical and a horizontal electrode are charged, the phosphor at their intersection emits light. Electroluminescent displays provide a sharp, clear image and a wide viewing angle. They were replaced by active matrix LCD screens. See also flat-panel display, liquid crystal display, passive-matrix display.

Electrolysis *n.* A process in which a chemical compound is broken down into its constituent parts by passing an electric current through it.

Electromagnet *n.* A device that creates a magnetic field when electric current passes through it. An electromagnet typically contains an iron or steel core with wire wrapped around it. Current is passed through the wire, producing a magnetic field. Electromagnets are used in disk drives to record data onto the disk surface.

Electromagnetic radiation *n.* The propagation of a magnetic field through space. Radio waves, light, and X rays are examples of electromagnetic radiation, all traveling at the speed of light.

Electromagnetic spectrum *n.* The range of frequencies of electromagnetic radiation. In theory, the spectrum's range is infinite. See the illustration.

Electromotive force *n.* The force that causes movement in charge carriers (the electrons) in a conductor. Acronym: EMF. Also called: potential, voltage. See also ampere, coulomb.

Electron beam *n.* A stream of electrons moving in one direction. An electron beam is used in a cathode-ray tube (CRT) to produce an image as it is passed across the phosphor coating inside the tube. See also CRT.

Electron gun *n.* A device that produces an electron beam, typically found in television or computer monitors. See also CRT.

Electronic bulletin board *n.* See BBS (definition 1).

Electronic cash *n.* See e-money.

Electronic circuit *n.* See circuit.

Electronic commerce *n.* See e-commerce.

Electronic Commerce Modeling Language *n.* A computer language developed by leading e-commerce companies as a standard for inputting e-wallet information into the payment fields of Web sites. This allows for one-click transfer of e-wallet information at compatible Web sites. Acronym: ECML.

Electronic credit *n.* A form of electronic commerce involving credit card transactions carried out over the Internet. Also called: e-credit. See also e-commerce.

Electronic data interchange *n.* See EDI.

Electronic data processing *n.* See data processing.

Electronic form *n.* See e-form.

Electronic Frontier Foundation *n.* A public advocacy organisation dedicated to the defense of civil liberties for computer users. The organisation was founded in 1990 by Mitchell Kapor and John Perry Barlow as a response to U.S. Secret Service raids on hackers. Acronym: EFF.

Electronic funds transfer *n.* The transfer of money via automated teller machine, telephone lines, or Internet connection. Examples of electronic fund transfers include using a credit card to make purchases from an e-commerce site, or using an automated teller machine or automated telephone banking system to move funds between bank accounts. Acronym: EFT.

Electronic Industries Association *n.* See EIA.

Electronic journal *n.* See journal.

Electronic mail *n.* See e-mail1.

Electronic mail services *n.* Services that allow users, administrators, or daemons to send, receive, and process e-mail. See also daemon.

Electronic mall *n.* A virtual collection of online businesses that affiliate with the intention of increasing the exposure of each business through the fellow businesses.

Electronic money *n.* See e-money.

Electronic music *n.* Music created with computers and electronic devices. See also MIDI, synthesizer.

Electronic office *n.* A term used especially in the late 1970s to mid-1980s to refer to a hypothetical paperless work environment to be brought about by the use of computers and communications devices.

Electronic paper *n.* Technology allowing a computer display to imitate the look and feel of traditional paper media. Electronic paper consists of thin, flexible sheets of plastic containing millions of small beads called microcapsules. Each microcapsule contains both a black and a white pigment and displays the proper colour in response to an electrical charge. It retains this pattern until a new screen of text or images is requested.

Electronic photography *n.* See digital photography.

Electronic Privacy Information Center *n.* See EPIC.

Electronic publishing *n.* A general term for distributing information via electronic media, such as communications networks or CD-ROM.

Electronics *n.* The branch of physics dealing with electrons, electronic devices, and electrical circuits.

Electronics Industries Association *n.* See EIA.

Electronic software distribution *n.* A means of directly distributing software to users online over the Internet. Electronic software distribution is analogous to direct-mail ordering. Acronym: ESD.

Electronic spreadsheet *n.* See spreadsheet programme.

Electronic storefront *n.* A business that displays its merchandise on the Internet and has provisions for contact or online sales.

Electronic text *n.* See e-text.

Electron tube *n.* A device for switching and amplifying electronic signals. It consists of a sealed glass container with electronic elements, such as metallic plates and grids, inside. In most applications, tubes have been replaced by transistors, although they are still used in cathode-ray tubes and in some radio frequency circuits and audio amplifiers. Also called: vacuum tube, valve. See also CRT.

Electrophotographic printers *n.* Printers in a category including laser, LED, LCD, and ion-deposition printers. In such a printer, a negative image is applied to an electrically charged, photosensitive drum. A photosensitive drum develops a pattern of electrostatic charge on its surface representing the photo negative of the image the drum will print. Powdered ink (toner) adheres to the charged areas of the drum, the drum presses the ink onto the paper, and then heat binds the toner to the paper. The printer types vary mainly in how they charge the drum. See also ion-deposition printer, laser printer, LCD printer, LED printer.

Electrophotography *n.* The production of photographic images using electrostatic charges. This method is used in photocopiers and laser printers. Also called: xerography. See also electrophotographic printers.

Electroplating *n.* The use of electrolysis for depositing a thin layer of one material onto another material. See also electrolysis.

Electrostatic *adj.* Of or relating to electric charges that are not flowing along a conducting path. Electrostatic charges are used in copiers and laser printers to hold toner particles on a photoconducting drum and in flatbed plotters to hold the plot medium in place.

Electrostatic discharge *n.* The discharge of static electricity from an outside source, such as human hands, into an integrated circuit, often resulting in damage to the circuit. Acronym: ESD.

Electrostatic plotter *n.* A plotter that creates an image from a dot pattern on specially coated paper. The paper is electrostatically charged and exposed to toner, which adheres to the dots. Electrostatic plotters can be up to 50 times faster than pen plotters but are more costly. Colour models produce images through multiple passes with cyan, magenta, yellow, and black. See also plotter.

Electrostatic printer *n.* See electrostatic plotter.

Elegant *adj.* Combining simplicity, terseness, efficiency, and subtlety. On the academic side of computer science, elegant design (say, of programmes, algorithms, or hardware) is a priority, but in the frenetic pace of the computer industry, elegant design may be sacrificed for the sake of speeding a product's development, sometimes resulting in bugs that are difficult to correct.

Element *n.* 1. Any stand-alone item within a broader context. For example, a data element is an item of data with the characteristics or properties of a larger set; a picture element (pixel) is one single dot on a computer screen or in a computer graphic; a print element is the part of a daisy-wheel printer that contains the embossed characters. See also daisy-wheel printer, data element, graphics primitive, pixel, thimble. 2. In markup languages such as HTML and SGML, the combination of a set of tags, any content contained between the tags, and any attributes the tags may have. Elements can be nested, one within the other. See also attribute (definition 3), HTML, markup language, SGML.

Elevator *n.* The square box within a scroll bar that can be moved up and down to change the position of text or an image on the screen. See the illustration. Also called: scroll box, thumb. See also scroll bar.

Elevator seeking *n.* A method of limiting hard disk access time in which multiple requests for data are prioritised based on the location of the data relative to the read/write head. This serves to minimise head movement. See also access time (definition 2), hard disk, read/write head.

Elite *n.* 1. A size of fixed-width type that prints 12 characters to the inch. 2. A fixed-width font that may be available in various type sizes. See also monospace font.

ELIZA *n.* A programme, modeled on Rogerian psychotherapy, that conducts simulated conversations with humans by echoing responses and posing questions based on key words in earlier comments. It was created by Dr. Joseph Weizenbaum, who considered it a bit of a joke and was alarmed that people took it seriously. See also artificial intelligence, Turing test.

Ellipsis *n.* A set of three dots (...) used to convey incompleteness. In many windowing applications, selection of a command that is followed by an ellipsis will produce a submenu or a dialog box. In programming and software manuals, an ellipsis in a syntax line indicates the repetition of certain elements. See also dialog box, syntax.

Elm *n.* Short for electronic mail. A programme for reading and composing e-mail on UNIX systems. The elm programme has a full-screen editor, making it easier to use than the original mail programme, but elm has largely been superseded by pine. See also e-mail1.

E-mail 1 or email or E-mail *n.* 1. Short for electronic mail. The exchange of text messages and computer files over a communications network, such as a local area network or the Internet, usually between computers or terminals. 2. An electronic text message.

E-mail 2 or email or E-mail *vb.* To send an e-mail message.

E-mail address *n.* A string that identifies a user so that the user can receive Internet e-mail. An e-mail address typically consists of a name that identifies the user to the mail server, followed by an at sign (@) and the host name and domain name of the mail server. For example, if Anne E. Oldhacker has an account on the machine called baz at Foo Enterprises, she might have an e-mail address aeo@baz.foo.com, which would be pronounced "A E O at baz dot foo dot com."

E-mail filter *n.* A feature in e-mail-reading software that automatically sorts incoming mail into different folders or mailboxes based on information contained in the message. For example, all incoming mail from a user's Uncle Joe might be placed in a folder labeled "Uncle Joe." Filters may also be used either to block or accept e-mail from designated sources.

E-mail management system *n.* An automated e-mail response system used by an Internet-based business to sort incoming e-mail messages into predetermined categories and either reply to the sender with an appropriate response or direct the e-mail to a customer service representative. Acronym: EMS.

Embed *vb.* To insert information created in one programme, such as a chart or an equation, into another programme. After the object is embedded, the information becomes part of the document. Any changes made to the object are reflected in the document.

Embedded *adj.* In software, pertaining to code or a command that is built into its carrier. For example, application programmes insert embedded printing commands into a document to control printing and formatting. Low-level assembly language is embedded in higher-level languages, such as C, to provide more capabilities or better efficiency.

Embedded chip *n.* See embedded system.

Embedded command *n.* A command placed in a text, graphics, or other document file, often used for printing or page-layout instructions. Such commands often do not appear on screen but can be displayed if needed. In transferring documents from one programme to another, embedded commands can cause problems if the programmes are incompatible.

Embedded controller *n.* A processor-based controller circuit board that is built into the computer machinery. See also controller.

Embedded hyperlink *n.* A link to a resource that is embedded within text or is associated with an image or an image map. See also hyperlink, image map.

Embedded interface *n.* An interface built into a hardware device's drive and controller board so that the device can be directly connected to the computer's system bus. See also controller, interface (definition 3).

Embedded system *n.* Microprocessors used to control devices such as appliances, automobiles, and machines used in business and manufacturing. An embedded system is created to manage a limited number of specific tasks within a larger device or system. An embedded system is often built onto a single chip or board and is used to control or monitor the host device—usually with little or no human intervention and often in real time. See also microprocessor.

Em dash *n.* A punctuation mark (—) used to indicate a break or interruption in a sentence. It is named for the em, a typographical unit of measure that in some fonts equals the width of a capital M.

EMF *n.* See electromotive force.

Emitter *n.* In transistors, the region that serves as a source of charge carriers.

Emitter-coupled logic *n.* A circuit design in which the emitters of two transistors are connected to a resistor so that only one of the transistors switches at a time. The advantage of this design is very high switching speed. Its drawbacks are the high number of components required and susceptibility to noise. Acronym: ECL.

EMM *n.* See Expanded Memory Manager.

E-money or emoney *n.* Short for electronic money. A generic name for the exchange of money through the Internet. Also called: cybercash, digicash, digital cash, e-cash, e-currency.

Emotag *n.* In an e-mail message or newsgroup article, a letter, word, or phrase that is encased in angle brackets and that, like an emoticon, indicates the attitude the writer takes toward what he or she has written. Often emotags have opening and closing tags, similar to HTML tags, that enclose a phrase or one or more sentences. For example: <joke>You didn't think there would really be a joke here, did you?</joke>. Some emotags consist of a single tag, such as <grin>. See also emoticon, HTML.

Emoticon *n.* A string of text characters that, when viewed sideways, form a face expressing a particular emotion. An emoticon is often used in an e-mail message or newsgroup post as a comment on the text that precedes it. Common emoticons include :-) or :) (meaning "I'm smiling at the joke here"), ;-) ("I'm winking and grinning at the joke here"), :-(("I'm sad about this"), :-7 ("I'm speaking with tongue in cheek"), :D or :-D (big smile; "I'm overjoyed"), and :-O (either a yawn of boredom or a mouth open in amazement).

EMS *n.* Acronym for Expanded Memory Specification. A technique for adding memory to PCs that allows for increasing memory beyond the Intel 80x86 microprocessor real-mode limit of 1 megabyte (MB). In earlier versions of microprocessors, EMS bypassed this memory board limit with a number of 16-kilobyte banks of RAM that could be accessed by software. In later versions of Intel microprocessors, including the 80386 and 80486 models, EMS is converted from extended memory by software memory managers, such as EMM386 in MS-DOS 5. Now EMS is used mainly for older MS-DOS applications because Windows and other applications running in protected mode on 80386 and higher microprocessors are free of the 1-MB limit. Also called: LIM EMS. See also expanded memory, protected mode.

Em space *n.* A typographical unit of measure that is equal in width to the point size of a particular font. For many fonts, this is equal to the width of a capital M, from which the em space takes its name.

Emulate *vb.* For a hardware or software system to behave in the same manner as another hardware or software system. In a network, for example, microcomputers might emulate terminals in order to communicate with mainframes.

Emulation *n.* The process of a computer, device, or programme imitating the function of another computer, device, or programme.

Emulator *n.* Hardware or software designed to make one type of computer or component act as if it were another. By means of an emulator, a computer can run software written for another machine. In a network, microcomputers might emulate terminals in order to communicate with mainframes.

Emulsion laser storage *n.* A method for recording data in film by selective heating with a laser beam.

Enable *vb.* To activate or turn on.

Encapsulate *vb.* 1. To treat a collection of structured information as a whole without affecting or taking notice of its internal structure. In communications, a message or packet constructed according to one protocol, such as a TCP/IP packet, may be taken with its formatting data as an undifferentiated stream of bits that is then broken up and packaged according to a lower-level protocol (for example, as ATM packets) to be sent over a particular network; at the destination, the lower-level packets are assembled, re-creating the message as formatted for the encapsulated protocol. See also ATM (definition 1). 2. In object-oriented programming, to keep the implementation details of a class a separate file whose contents do not need to be known by a programmer using that class. See also object-oriented programming, TCP/IP.

Encapsulated PostScript *n.* See EPS.

Encapsulated type *n.* See abstract data type.

Encapsulation *n.* 1. In object-oriented programming, the packaging of attributes (properties) and functionality (methods or behaviours) to create an object that is essentially a "black box"—one whose internal structure remains private and whose services can be accessed by other objects only through messages passed via a clearly defined interface (the programming equivalent of a mailbox or telephone line). Encapsulation ensures that the object providing service can prevent other objects from manipulating its data or procedures directly, and it enables the object requesting service to ignore the details of how that service is provided. See also information hiding. 2. In terms of the Year 2000 problem, a method of dealing with dates that entails shifting either programme logic (data encapsulation) or input (programme encapsulation) backward into the past, to a parallel year that allows the system to avoid Year 2000 complications. Encapsulation thus allows processing to take place in a "time warp" created by shifting to an earlier t

Encipher *vb.* See encrypt.

Encode *vb.* 1. See encrypt. 2. In programming, to put something into code, which frequently involves changing the form—for example, changing a decimal number to binary-coded form. See also binary-coded decimal, EBCDIC.

Encoder *n.* 1. In general, any hardware or software that encodes information—that is, converts the information to a particular form or format. For example, the Windows Media Encoder converts audio and video to a form that can be streamed to clients over a network. 2. In reference to MP3 digital audio in particular, technology that converts a WAV audio file into an MP3 file. An MP3 encoder compresses a sound file to a much smaller size, about one-twelfth as large as the original, without a perceptible drop in quality. Also called: MP3 encoder. See also MP3, WAV.

Encoding *n.* 1. See Huffman coding. 2. A method of dealing with computers with Year 2000 problems that entails storing a four-digit year in date fields designed to hold only two digits in a programme or system. This can be accomplished by using the bits associated with the date field more efficiently—for example, by converting the date field from ASCII to binary or from decimal to hexadecimal, both of which allow storage of larger values.

Encrypt *vb.* To encode (scramble) information in such a way that it is unreadable to all but those individuals possessing the key to the code. Encrypted information is known as cipher text. Also called: encipher, encode.

Encryption *n.* The process of encoding data to prevent unauthorised access, especially during transmission. Encryption is usually based on one or more keys, or codes, that are essential for decoding, or returning the data to readable form. The U.S. National Bureau of Standards created a complex encryption standard, Data Encryption Standard (DES), which is based on a 56-bit variable that provides for more than 70 quadrillion unique keys to encrypt documents. See also DES.

Encryption key *n.* A sequence of data that is used to encrypt other data and that, consequently, must be used for the data's decryption. See also decryption, encryption.

End-around carry *n.* A special type of end-around shift operation on a binary value that treats the carry bit as an extra bit; that is, the carry bit is moved from one end of the value to the other. See also carry, end-around shift, shift.

End-around shift *n.* An operation performed on a binary value in which a bit is shifted out of one end and into the other end.

For example, a right-end shift on the value 00101001 yields 10010100. See also shift.

En dash *n.* A punctuation mark (–) used to show ranges of dates and numbers, as in 1990–92, and in compound adjectives where one part is hyphenated or consists of two words, as in pre–Civil War. The en dash is named after a typographical unit of measure, the en space, which is half the width of an em space. See also em space.

End key *n.* A cursor-control key that moves the cursor to a certain position, usually to the end of a line, the end of a screen, or the end of a file, depending on the programme.

Endless loop *n.* See infinite loop.

End mark *n.* A symbol that designates the end of some entity, such as a file or word processing document.

End-of-file *n.* 1. A code placed by a programme after the last byte of a file to tell the computer's operating system that no additional data follows. In ASCII, end-of-file is represented by the decimal value 26 (hexadecimal 1A) or the Ctrl+Z control character. Acronym: EOF. 2. An indicator of some sort in a computer programme or database that indicates that the end of a file has been reached. If older systems that have the capacity to store only two-digit years in the date field also use end-of-file markers such as 99, they can be susceptible to date-related problems. See also 99 or 9999.

End-of-text *n.* In data transmission, a character used to mark the end of a text file. End-of-text does not necessarily signify the end of transmission; other information, such as error-checking or transmission control characters, can be included at the end of the file. In ASCII, end-of-text is represented by the decimal value 3 (hexadecimal 03). Acronym: ETX.

End-of-transmission *n.* A character representing the end of a transmission. In ASCII, the end-of-transmission character has the decimal value 4 (hexadecimal 04). Acronym: EOT.

Endpoint *n.* The beginning or end of a line segment.

End-to-end delivery *n.* A communications process in networks in which packets are delivered and then acknowledged by the receiving system.

End-to-end examination *n.* An inspection of all of the processes and systems in place at an organisation that affect the computer systems. The examination begins with the data or information that flows into the system, continues with how the data is manipulated and stored, and ends with how the data is output. For example, end-to-end examination is one technique that was employed to ferret out Year 2000 problems in computer systems of an organisation.

End user *n.* The ultimate user of a computer or computer application in its finished, marketable form.

End-User License Agreement *n.* A legal agreement between a software manufacturer and the software's purchaser with regard to terms of distribution, resale, and restricted use. Acronym: EULA.

Energy Star *n.* A symbol affixed to systems and components that denotes lower power-consumption design. Energy Star is the name of an Environmental Protection Agency programme that encourages PC manufacturers to build systems that are energy efficient. Requirements dictate that systems or monitors be capable of automatically entering a "sleep state" or lower power-consumption state while the unit is inactive, where the low-power state is defined as 30 watts or less. Systems and monitors that comply with these guidelines are marked with an Energy Star sticker.

Engine *n.* A processor or portion of a programme that determines how the programme manages and manipulates data. The term engine is most often used in relation to a specific use; for example, a database engine contains the tools for manipulating a database, and a Web search engine has the ability to search World Wide Web indexes for matches to one or more key words entered by the user.

Enhanced Capabilities Port *n.* See ECP.

Enhanced Category 5 cable *n.* See Cat 5e cable.

Enhanced Data Rates for Global Evolution *n.* See EDGE.

Enhanced Data Rates for GSM and TDMA Evolution *n.* See EDGE.

Enhanced Expanded Memory Specification *n.* See EEMS.

Enhanced Graphics Adapter *n.* See EGA.

Enhanced Graphics Display *n.* A PC video display capable of producing graphic images with resolutions ranging from 320 x 200 through 640 x 400 pixels, in colour or in black and white. Resolution and colour depth depend on the vertical and horizontal scanning frequencies of the display, the capabilities of the video display controller card, and available video RAM.

Enhanced IDE *n.* See EIDE.

Enhanced Integrated Device Electronics *n.* See EIDE.

Enhanced keyboard *n.* An IBM 101/102-key keyboard that replaced the PC and AT keyboards. It features 12 function keys across the top (rather than 10 on the left side), extra Control and Alt keys, and a bank of cursor and editing keys between the main keyboard and number pad. It is similar to the Apple Extended Keyboard.

Enhanced Parallel Port *n.* See EPP.

Enhanced serial port *n.* A connection port for peripheral devices, commonly used for mice and external modems. Enhanced serial ports utilize 16550-type or newer high-speed UART circuits for faster data throughput. Enhanced serial ports are capable of transferring data at speeds as high as 921.6 Kbps. Acronym: ESP. See also input/output port, UART.

Enhanced Small Device Interface *n.* See ESDI.

ENIAC *n.* An 1800-square-foot, 30-ton computer containing about 18,000 vacuum tubes and 6000 manual switches. Developed between 1942 and 1946 for the U.S. Army by J. Presper Eckert and John Mauchly at the University of Pennsylvania, ENIAC is considered to have been the first truly electronic computer. It remained in operation until 1955.

Enlarge *vb.* In Windows and other graphical user interfaces, to increase the size of a window. See also maximize.

E notation *n.* See floating-point notation.

ENQ *n.* See enquiry character.

Enquiry character *n.* Abbreviated ENQ. In communications, a control code transmitted from one station to request a response from the receiving station. In ASCII, the enquiry character is designated by decimal value 5 (hexadecimal 05).

En space *n.* A typographical unit of measure that is equal in width to half the point size of a particular font.

Enter key *n.* The key that is used at the end of a line or command to instruct the computer to process the command or text. In word processing programmes, the Enter key is used at the end of a paragraph. Also called: Return key.

Enterprise Application Integration *n.* See EAI.

Enterprise computing *n.* In a large enterprise such as a corporation, the use of computers in a network or series of interconnected networks that generally encompass a variety of different platforms, operating systems, protocols, and network architectures. Also called: enterprise networking.

Enterprise information portal *n.* A portal or gateway that allows internal and external users in a business or enterprise to access information from intranets, extranets, and the Internet for business needs. An enterprise information portal provides a simple Web interface that is designed to help users sift through large amounts of data quickly to find the information they need. By organising all internal information from company servers, databases, e-mail, and legacy systems, the enterprise information portal exercises control over the company's information availability and presentation. Acronym: EIP. See also portal.

Enterprise JavaBeans *n.* An application programming interface (API) designed to extend the JavaBean component model to cross-platform, server-side applications that can run on the various systems usually present in an enterprise environment. Enterprise JavaBeans are defined in the Enterprise JavaBean specification released by Sun Microsystems, Inc. The goal of the API is to provide developers with a means of applying Java technology to the creation of reusable server components for business applications, such as transaction processing. Acronym: EJB. See also Java, JavaBean.

Enterprise network *n.* In a large enterprise such as a corporation, the network (or interconnected networks) of computer systems owned by the enterprise, which fills the enterprise's various computing needs. This network can span diverse geographical locations and usually encompasses a range of platforms, operating systems, protocols, and network architectures.

Enterprise networking *n.* See enterprise computing.

Enterprise Resource Planning *n.* An approach to business information management that relies on integrated application software to provide data on all aspects of the enterprise, such as manufacturing, finance, inventory, human resources, sales, and so on. The objective of Enterprise Resource Planning software is to provide data, when and as needed, to enable a business to monitor and control its overall operation. Acronym: ERP.

Entity *n.* In computer-aided design and object-oriented design, an item that can be treated as a unit and, often, as a member of a particular category or type. See also CAD, object-oriented design.

Entry *n.* 1. A unit of information treated as a whole by a computer programme. 2. The process of inputting information.

Entry point *n.* A place in a programme where execution can begin.

Enumerated data type *n.* A data type consisting of a sequence of named values given in a particular order.

Envelope *n.* 1. In communications, a single unit of information that is grouped with other items, such as error-checking bits. 2. The shape of a sound wave, caused by changes in amplitude. See the illustration.

Envelope delay *n.* In communications, the difference in travel times of different frequencies in a signal. If the frequencies reach their destination at different times, signal distortion and errors can result. Also called: delay distortion.

Environment *n.* 1. The configuration of resources available to the user. Environment refers to the hardware and the operating system running on it. For example, Windows and Macintosh are called windowing environments because they are based on screen regions called windows. 2. In microcomputing, environment refers to a definition of the specifications, such as command path, that a programme operates in.

EOF *n.* See end-of-file.

EOL *n.* Acronym for end of line. A control (nonprinting) character that signals the end of a data line in a data file.

EOT *n.* See end-of-transmission.

EPIC *n.* 1. Short for Explicitly Parallel Instruction Computing. A technology developed jointly by Intel and Hewlett-Packard as the foundation of the 64-bit instruction set architecture incorporated in IA-64, the basis of the Merced chip. EPIC technology is designed to enable IA-64 processors to execute instructions efficiently and extremely quickly. Core elements include explicit parallelism based on software identification of instructions that the processor can execute concurrently; improved execution of branch paths; and earlier loads from memory. See also IA-64, Merced. 2. Short for Electronic Privacy Information Center. A public-interest research center based in Washington, D.C., dedicated to directing public attention toward civil liberties and online privacy related to electronic communication, cryptography, and related technologies.

Epitaxial layer *n.* In semiconductors, a layer that has the same crystal orientation as the underlying layer.

EPP *n.* Acronym for Enhanced Parallel Port, a high-speed port for peripheral devices other than printers and scanners—that is, for devices such as external drives. Specified in the IEEE 1284 standard, EPP describes bidirectional parallel ports that provide data throughput of 1 Mbps or more, as opposed to the 100 Kbps to 300 Kbps typical of the older, de facto standard Centronics ports. See also IEEE 1284, input/output port.

EPP IEEE standard *n.* An IEEE standard relating to the Enhanced Parallel Port (EPP) protocol. This protocol was originally developed by Intel, Xircom, and Zenith Data Systems as a means to provide a high-performance parallel port link that would still be compatible with the standard parallel port.

This protocol capability was implemented by Intel in the 386SL chip set (82360 I/O chip), prior to the establishment of the IEEE 1284 committee and the associated standards work. The EPP protocol offered many advantages to parallel port peripheral manufacturers and was quickly adopted by many as an optional data transfer method. A loose association of about 80 interested manufacturers was formed to develop and promote the EPP protocol. This association became the EPP Committee and was instrumental in helping to get this protocol adopted as one of the IEEE 1284 advanced modes. See also communications protocol, IEEE 1284, parallel port.

EPROM *n.* Acronym for erasable programmable read-only memory. A nonvolatile memory chip that is programmed after it is manufactured. EPROMs can be reprogrammed by removing the protective cover from the top of the chip and exposing the chip to ultraviolet light. Though EPROMs are more expensive than PROM chips, they can be more cost-effective if many changes are required. Also called: reprogrammable read-only memory (RPROM). See also EEPROM, PROM, ROM.

.eps *n.* The file extension that identifies Encapsulated PostScript files. See also EPS.

EPS *n.* Acronym for Encapsulated PostScript. A PostScript file format that can be used as an independent entity. The EPS image must be incorporated into the PostScript output of an application such as a desktop publisher. Many high-quality clip-art packages consist of such images. See also PostScript.

EPSF *n.* Acronym for Encapsulated PostScript file. See EPS.

Equality *n.* The property of being identical, used most often in reference to values and data structures.

Equalization *n.* A form of conditioning used to compensate for signal distortion and delay on a communication channel. Equalization attempts to maintain the amplitude and phase characteristics of a signal so that it remains true to the original when it reaches the receiving device.

Equation *n.* A mathematical statement that indicates equality with the use of an equal sign (=) between two expressions. In programming languages, assignment statements are written in equation form. See also assignment statement.

Erasable programmable read-only memory *n.* See EPROM.

Erasable storage *n.* Storage media that can be used repeatedly because the user has the ability to erase whatever data was previously there. Most forms of magnetic storage, such as tape and disk, are erasable.

Erase *vb.* To remove data permanently from a storage medium. This is usually done by replacing existing data with zeros or meaningless text or, in magnetic media, by disturbing the magnetic particles' physical arrangement, either with the erase head or with a large magnet. Erase differs from delete in that delete merely tells the computer that data or a file is no longer needed; the data remains stored and is recoverable until the operating system reuses the space containing the deleted file. Erase, on the other hand, removes data permanently. See also erase head.

Erase head *n.* The device in a magnetic tape machine that erases previously recorded information.

Eratosthenes' sieve *n.* See sieve of Eratosthenes.

Ergonomic keyboard *n.* A keyboard designed to reduce the risk of wrist and hand injuries that result from prolonged use or repetitive movement. An ergonomic keyboard can include such features as alternative key layouts, palm rests, and shaping designed to minimise strain. See also Dvorak keyboard, keyboard, Kinesis ergonomic keyboard.

Ergonomics *n.* The study of people (their physical characteristics and the ways they function) in relation to their working environment (the furnishings and machines they use). The goal of ergonomics is to incorporate comfort, efficiency, and safety into the design of keyboards, computer desks, chairs, and other items in the workplace.

Erlang *n.* A concurrent functional programming language. Originally developed for controlling telephone exchanges, Erlang is a general-purpose language best suited for applications where rapid development of complex systems and robustness are essential. Erlang has built-in support for concurrency, distribution, and fault tolerance. The most widely implemented version of Erlang is the open source version.

ERP *n.* See Enterprise Resource Planning.

Error *n.* A value or condition that is not consistent with the true, specified, or expected value or condition. In computers, an error results when an event does not occur as expected or when impossible or illegal maneuvers are attempted. In data communications, an error occurs when there is a discrepancy between the transmitted and received data. See also critical error, error message, error rate, error ratio, fatal error, hard error, inherent error, intermittent error, logic error, machine error, overflow error, parity error..

Error analysis *n.* The art and science of detecting errors in numeric calculations, especially in long and involved computations, where the possibility of errors increases.

Error checking *n.* A method for detecting discrepancies between transmitted and received data during file transfer.

Error control *n.* 1. The section of a programme, procedure, or function that checks for errors such as type mismatches, overflows and underflows, dangling or illegal pointer references, and memory-use inconsistencies. 2. The process of anticipating programme errors during software development.

Error-correcting code *n.* See error-correction coding.

Error-correction coding *n.* A method for encoding that allows for detection and correction of errors that occur during transmission. Data is encoded in such a way that transmission errors may be detected and corrected by examination of the encoded data on the receiving end. Most error-correction codes are characterised by the maximum number of errors they can detect and by the maximum number of errors they can correct. Error-correction coding is used by most modems. Also called: error-correcting code. See also error detection and correction.

Error detection and correction *n.* A method for discovering and resolving errors during file transfer. Some programmes only detect errors; others detect and attempt to fix them.

Error-detection coding *n.* A method of encoding data so that errors that occur during storage or transmission can be detected. Most error-detection codes are characterised by the maximum number of errors they can detect. See also checksum.

Error file *n.* A file that records the time and type of data processing and transmission errors.

Error handling *n.* The process of dealing with errors (or exceptions) as they arise during the running of a programme. Some programming languages, such as C++, Ada, and Eiffel, have features that aid in error handling. See also bug (definition 1).

Error message *n.* A message from the system or programme indicating that an error requiring resolution has occurred.

Error rate *n.* In communications, the ratio of the number of bits or other elements that arrive incorrectly during transmission. For a 1200-bps modem, a typical error rate would be 1 in every 200,000 bits. See also parity, parity bit, Xmodem, Ymodem.

Error ratio *n.* The ratio of errors to the number of units of data processed. See also error rate.

Error trapping *n.* 1. The process by which a programme checks for errors during execution. 2. The process of writing a function, programme, or procedure such that it is capable of continuing execution despite an error condition.

Escape character *n.* See ESC character.

Escape code *n.* A character or sequence of characters that indicates that a following character in a data stream is not to be processed in the ordinary way. In the C programming language, the escape code is the backslash \.

Escape key *n.* A key on a computer keyboard that sends the escape (ESC) character to the computer. In many applications, the Escape key moves the user back one level in the menu structure or exits the programme. See the illustration. See also Clear key.

Escape sequence *n.* A sequence of characters that usually begins with the ESC character (ASCII 27, hexadecimal 1B), which is followed by one or more additional characters. An escape sequence escapes from the normal sequence of characters (such as text) and issues an instruction or command to a device or programme.

ESC character *n.* One of the 32 control codes defined in the ASCII character set. It usually indicates the beginning of an escape sequence (a string of characters that give instructions to a device such as a printer). It is represented internally as character code 27 (hexadecimal 1B). Also called: escape character.

Esc key *n.* See Escape key.

ESD *n.* See electronic software distribution, electrostatic discharge.

ESDI *n.* Acronym for Enhanced Small Device Interface. A device that allows disks to communicate with computers at high speeds. ESDI drives typically transfer data at about 10 megabits per second, but they are capable of doubling that speed. Although fast, ESDI has been superseded by interfaces such as SCSI and EIDE. See also EIDE, SCSI.

ESP *n.* See enhanced serial port.

ESP IEEE standard *n.* Short for Encapsulating Security Payload IEEE standard. A standard for providing integrity and confidentiality to IP (Internet Protocol) datagrams. In some circumstances, it can also provide authentication to IP datagrams. See also authentication, datagram, IEEE, IP.

ESRB *n.* Acronym for Entertainment Software Rating Board. An independent, self-regulatory body providing ratings to the public and support to companies in the interactive software entertainment industry. The ESRB provides ratings for computer games and other interactive products such as Web sites, online games, and interactive chat.

E-tail *n.* See e-commerce.

E-text *n.* Short for electronic text. A book or other text-based work that is available online in an electronic media format.

An e-text can be read online or downloaded to a user's computer for offline reading. See also e-zine.

Ethernet *n.* 1. The IEEE 802.3 standard for contention networks. Ethernet uses a bus or star topology and relies on the form of access known as Carrier Sense Multiple Access with Collision Detection (CSMA/CD) to regulate communication line traffic. Network nodes are linked by coaxial cable, by fiberoptic cable, or by twisted-pair wiring. Data is transmitted in variable-length frames containing delivery and control information and up to 1500 bytes of data. The Ethernet standard provides for baseband transmission at 10 megabits (10 million bits) per second and is available in various forms, including those known as Thin Ethernet, Thick Ethernet, 10Base2, 10Base5, 10Base-F, and 10Base-T. The IEEE standard dubbed 802.3z, or Gigabit Ethernet, operates at 10 times 100 Mbps speed. See also ALOHAnet, baseband, bus network, coaxial cable, contention, CSMA/CD, Gigabit Ethernet, IEEE 802 standards, twisted-pair cable. 2. A widely used local area network system developed by Xerox in 1976, from which the IEEE 802.3 standard was dev

Ethernet/802.3 *n.* The IEEE standard for 10- or 100-Mbps transmissions over an Ethernet network. Ethernet/802.3 defines both hardware and data packet construction specifications. See also Ethernet.

E-time *n.* See execution time.

Etiquette *n.* See netiquette.

ETX *n.* See end-of-text.

Eudora *n.* An e-mail client programme originally developed as freeware for Macintosh computers by Steve Dorner at the University of Illinois, now maintained in both freeware and commercial versions for both Macintosh and Windows by Qualcomm, Inc.

EULA *n.* See End-User License Agreement.

Euphoria *n.* Acronym for End User Programming with Hierarchical Objects for Robust Interpreted Applications. An interpreted programming language intended for general application development and game programming on MS-DOS, Windows, and Linux platforms.

European Computer Manufacturers Association *n.* See ECMA.

European Laboratory for Particle Physics *n.* See CERN.

EUV lithography *n.* Acronym for Extreme UltraViolet lithography. Manufacturing process allowing smaller circuits to be etched onto chips than is possible with traditional lithographic techniques. With this process, it is possible to economically produce chips that are much faster than those that are created using traditional processes. In EUV lithography, the image of a map of circuits to appear on a chip is bounced off a series of mirrors that condense the image. The condensed image is projected onto wafers containing layers of metal, silicon, and photosensitive material. Because EUV light has a short wavelength, extremely intricate circuit patterns can be created on the wafers.

Evaluation *n.* The determination, by a programme, of the value of an expression or the action that a programme statement specifies. Evaluation can take place at compile time or at run time.

Even parity *n.* See parity.

Event *n.* An action or occurrence, often generated by the user, to which a programme might respond—for example, key presses, button clicks, or mouse movements. See also event-driven programming.

Event-driven *adj.* Of, pertaining to, or being software that accomplishes its purpose by responding to externally caused events, such as the user pressing a key or clicking a button on a mouse. For example, an event-driven data entry form will allow the user to click on and edit any field at any time rather than forcing the user to step through a fixed sequence of prompts.

Event-driven processing *n.* A programme feature belonging to more advanced operating-system architectures such as the Apple Macintosh operating system, Windows, and UNIX. In times past, programmes were required to interrogate, and effectively anticipate, every device that was expected to interact with the programme, such as the keyboard, mouse, printer, disk drive, and serial port. Often, unless sophisticated programming techniques were used, one of two events happening at the same instant would be lost. Event processing solves this problem through the creation and maintenance of an event queue. Most common events that occur are appended to the event queue for the programme to process in turn; however, certain types of events can preempt others if they have a higher priority. An event can be of several types, depending on the specific operating system considered: pressing a mouse button or keyboard key, inserting a disk, clicking on a window, or receiving information from a device driver (as for managing the transfer of data from the serial

Event-driven programming *n.* A type of programming in which the programme constantly evaluates and responds to sets of events, such as key presses or mouse movements. Event-driven programmes are typical of Apple Macintosh computers, although most graphical interfaces, such as Windows or the X Window System, also use such an approach. See also event.

Event handler *n.* 1. A method within a programme that is called automatically whenever a particular event occurs. 2. A core function in JavaScript that handles client-side events. It is the mechanism that causes a script to react to an event. For example, common JavaScript event handlers coded in Web pages include onClick, onMouseOver, and onLoad. When the user initiates the action, such as a mouse over, the event handler executes, or carries out, the desired outcome. 3. In Java applets, rather than having a specific starting point, the applet has a main loop where it waits for an event or series of events (keystroke, mouse click, and so on). Upon occurrence of the event, the event handler carries out the instructions specified. See also applet, client, JavaScript.

Event horizon *n.* The time at which hardware or software began to have the potential to encounter a Year 2000 problem. For instance, the event horizon in an accounting system in a company whose fiscal year ended on June 30, 1999, would be six months dating from January 1, 1999. Also called: time horizon to failure.

Event log *n.* A file that contains information and error messages for all activities on the computer.

Event logging *n.* The process of recording an audit entry in the audit trail whenever certain events occur, such as starting and stopping, or users logging on and off and accessing resources. See also event, service.

Event procedure *n.* A procedure automatically executed in response to an event initiated by the user or programme code, or triggered by the system.

Event property *n.* A characteristic or parameter of an object that you can use to respond to an associated event. You can run a procedure or macro when an event occurs by setting the related event property.

E-wallet *n.* A programme used in e-commerce that stores a customer's shipping and billing information to facilitate Web-based financial transactions. An e-wallet allows customers to instantly enter encrypted shipping and billing information when placing an order, rather than manually typing the information into a form on a Web page.

Exa- prefix A prefix meaning 1 quintillion (1018). In computing, which is based on the binary (base-2) numbering system, exa- has a literal value of 1,152,921,504,606,846,976, which is the power of 2 (260) closest to one quintillion.Abbreviation: E.

Exabyte *n.* Roughly one quintillion bytes, or a billion billion bytes, or 1,152,921,504,606,846,976 bytes. Abbreviation: EB.

Excel *n.* Microsoft's spreadsheet software for Windows PCs and Macintosh computers. Excel is part of the family of Office products. The most recent version, part of Office XP, includes the ability to access and analyse live data from the Web by simply copying and pasting Web pages into Excel. The first version of Excel was introduced for the Macintosh in 1985. Excel for Windows was released in 1987.

Exception *n.* In programming, a problem or change in conditions that causes the microprocessor to stop what it is doing and handle the situation in a separate routine. An exception is similar to an interrupt; both refer the microprocessor to a separate set of instructions. See also interrupt.

Exception handling *n.* See error handling.

Exchangeable disk *n.* See removable disk.

Exchange sort *n.* See bubble sort.

Excite *n.* A World Wide Web search engine developed by Excite, Inc. After conducting a search, Excite provides both a summary of each matching Web site it has located and a link to more information of the same type.

Exclusive NOR *n.* A two-state digital electronic circuit in which the output is driven high only if the inputs are all high or all low.

Exclusive OR *n.* A Boolean operation that yields "true" if and only if one of its operands is true and the other is false. See the table. Acronym: EOR.

.exe *n.* In MS-DOS, a filename extension that indicates that a file is an executable programme. To run an executable programme, the user types the filename without the .exe extension at the prompt and presses Enter. See also executable programme.

Executable1 *adj.* Of, pertaining to, or being a programme file that can be run. Executable files have extensions such as .bat, .com, and .exe.

Executable2 *n.* A programme file that can be run, such as file0.bat, file1.exe, or file2.com.

Executable programme *n.* A programme that can be run. The term usually applies to a compiled programme translated into machine code in a format that can be loaded into memory and run by a computer's processor. In interpreter languages, an executable programme can be source code in the proper format. See also code (definition 1), compiler (definition 2), computer programme, interpreter, source code.

Execute *vb.* To perform an instruction. In programming, execution implies loading the machine code of the programme into memory and then performing the instructions.

Execute in place *n.* The process of executing code directly from ROM, rather than loading it from RAM first. Executing the code in place, instead of copying the code into RAM for execution, saves system resources. Applications in other file systems, such as on a PC Card storage device, cannot be executed in this way. Acronym: XIP.

Execution time *n.* The time, measured in clock ticks (pulses of a computer's internal timer), required by a microprocessor to decode and carry out an instruction after it is fetched from memory. Also called: E-time. See also instruction time.

Executive *n.* The set of kernel-mode components that form the base operating system for Microsoft Windows NT or later. See also operating system.

Executive information system *n.* A set of tools designed to organise information into categories and reports. Because it emphasizes information, an executive information system differs from a decision support system (DSS), which is designed for analysis and decision making. Acronym: EIS.

Exerciser *n.* A programme that exercises a piece of hardware or software by running it through a large set of operations.

Exit *vb.* In a programme, to move from the called routine back to the calling routine. A routine can have more than one exit point, thus allowing termination based on various conditions.

Expanded *adj.* A font style that sets characters farther apart than the normal spacing.

Expanded memory *n.* A type of memory, up to 8 MB, that can be added to IBM PCs. Its use is defined by the Expanded Memory Specification (EMS). Expanded memory is not accessible to programmes in MS-DOS, so the Expanded Memory Manager (EMM) maps pages (blocks) of bytes from expanded memory into page frames in accessible memory areas. Expanded memory is not needed in Windows 9x, all versions of Windows NT, and Windows 2000. See also EEMS, EMS, Expanded Memory Manager, page frame.

Expanded Memory Manager *n.* A driver that implements the software portion of the Expanded Memory Specification (EMS) to make expanded memory in IBM and compatible PCs accessible. Acronym: EMM. See also EMS, expanded memory, extended memory.

Expanded Memory Specification *n.* See EMS.

Expansion *n.* A way of increasing a computer's capabilities by adding hardware that performs tasks that are not part of the basic system. Expansion is usually achieved by plugging printed circuit boards (expansion boards) into openings (expansion slots) inside the computer. See also expansion board, expansion slot, open architecture (definition 2), PC Card, PCMCIA slot.

Expansion board *n.* A circuit board that is plugged into a computer's bus (main data transfer path) to add extra functions or resources to the computer. Typical expansion boards add memory, disk drive controllers, video support, parallel and serial ports, and internal modems. For laptops and other portable computers, expansion boards come in credit card-sized devices called PC Cards that plug into a slot in the side or back of the computer. Also called: expansion board, extender board. See also expansion slot, PC Card, PCMCIA slot.

Expansion bus *n.* A group of control lines that provide a buffered interface to devices. These devices can be located either on the system board or on cards that are plugged into expansion connectors. Common expansion buses included on the system board are USB, PC Card, and PCI. See also AT bus.

Expansion card *n.* See expansion board.

Expansion slot *n.* A socket in a computer, designed to hold expansion boards and connect them to the system bus (data pathway). Expansion slots are a means of adding or enhancing the computer's features and capabilities. In laptop and other portable computers, expansion slots come in the form of PCMCIA slots designed to accept PC Cards. See also expansion board, PC Card, PCMCIA slot.

Experience points *n.* Often used in role-playing games (RPGs), experience points are a way of measuring how much a player has experienced or learned. As a player moves through a game, additional benefits, often in the form of increased statistics or skills, are earned. These points are frequently spent or used by the player to increase his or her score. See also computer game, role-playing game.

Expert system *n.* An application programme that makes decisions or solves problems in a particular field, such as finance or medicine, by using knowledge and analytical rules defined by experts in the field. It uses two components, a knowledge base and an inference engine, to form conclusions. Additional tools include user interfaces and explanation facilities, which enable the system to justify or explain its conclusions as well as allowing developers to run checks on the operating system. See also artificial intelligence, inference engine, intelligent database, knowledge base.

Expiration date *n.* The date on which a shareware, beta, or trial version of a programme stops functioning, pending purchase of the full version or the entry of an access code.

Expire *vb.* To stop functioning in whole or in part. Beta versions of software are often programmed to expire when a new version is released. See also beta2.

Explicitly Parallel Instruction Computing *n.* See EPIC.

Exploded view *n.* A form of display that shows a structure with its parts separated but depicted in relation to each other. See the illustration.

Explorer *n.* See Internet Explorer, Windows Explorer.

ExploreZip *n.* A destructive virus that attacks computers running Windows, where it first appears as an e-mail attachment named zipped_files.exe. ExploreZip affects local drives, mapped drives, and accessible network machines and destroys both document and source-code files by opening and immediately closing them, leaving a zero-byte file. Described as both a Trojan horse (because it requires the victim to open the attachment) and a worm (because it can propagate itself in certain instances), ExploreZip spreads by mailing itself to the return address of every unread e-mail in the inbox of the computer's e-mail programme, as well as by searching for—and copying itself to—the Windows directory on mapped drives and networked machines. See also Trojan horse, virus, worm.

Exponent *n.* In mathematics, a number that shows how many times a number is used as a factor in a calculation; in other words, an exponent shows that number's power. Positive exponents, as in 23, indicate multiplication (2 times 2 times 2). Negative exponents, as in 2-3, indicate division (1 divided by 23). Fractional exponents, as in 81/3, indicate the root of a number (the cube root of 8).

Exponential notation *n.* See floating-point notation.

Exponentiation *n.* The operation in which a number is raised to a given power, as in 23. In computer programmes and programming languages, exponentiation is often shown by a caret (^), as in 2^3.

Export *vb.* To move information from one system or programme to another. Files that consist only of text can be exported in ASCII (plain text format). For files with graphics, however, the receiving system or programme must offer some support for the exported file's format. See also EPS, PICT, TIFF.

Export *n.* In NFS, a file or folder made available to other network computers using the NFS mount protocol. See also NFS.

Expression *n.* A combination of symbols—identifiers, values, and operators—that yields a result upon evaluation. The resulting value can then be assigned to a variable, passed as an argument, tested in a control statement, or used in another expression.

Extended ASCII *n.* Any set of characters assigned to ASCII values between decimal 128 and 255 (hexadecimal 80 through FF). The specific characters assigned to the extended ASCII codes vary between computers and between programmes, fonts, or graphics characters. Extended ASCII adds capability by allowing for 128 additional characters, such as accented letters, graphics characters, and special symbols. See also ASCII.

Extended Binary Coded Decimal Interchange Code *n.* See EBCDIC.

Extended characters *n.* Any of the 128 additional characters in the extended ASCII (8-bit) character set. These characters include those used in several foreign languages, such as accent marks, and special symbols used for creating pictures. See also extended ASCII.

Extended data out random access memory *n.* See EDO RAM.

Extended Edition *n.* A version of OS/2 with built-in database and communications facilities, developed by IBM. See also OS/2.

eXtended Graphics Array *n.* An advanced standard for graphics controller and display mode design, introduced by IBM in 1990. This standard supports 640 x 480 resolution with 65,536 colours, or 1024 x 768 resolution with 256 colours, and is used mainly on workstation-level systems. Acronym: XGA.

Extended Industry Standard Architecture *n.* See EISA.

Extended memory *n.* System memory beyond 1 megabyte in computers based on the Intel 80x86 processors. This memory is accessible only when an 80386 or higher-level processor is operating in protected mode or in emulation on the 80286. To use extended memory, MS-DOS programmes need the aid of software that temporarily places the processor into protected mode or by the use of features in the 80386 or higher-level processors to remap portions of extended memory into conventional memory. Extended memory is not an issue in Windows 9x, all versions of Windows NT, Windows 2000, and Windows XP. See also EMS, extended memory specification, protected mode.

Extended memory specification *n.* A specification developed by Lotus, Intel, Microsoft, and AST Research that defines a software interface allowing real-mode applications to use extended memory and areas of memory not managed by MS-DOS. Memory is managed by an installable device driver, the Expanded Memory Manager (EMM). The application must use the driver to access the additional memory. Acronym: XMS. See also Expanded Memory Manager, extended memory.

Extended VGA *n.* An enhanced set of Video Graphics Array (VGA) standards that is capable of displaying an image of from 800 x 600 pixels to 1600 x 1200 pixels and that can support a palette of up to 16.7 million (224) colours. This palette approaches the 19 million colours that a normal person can distinguish, so it is considered a digital standard for colour realism that parallels analog television. Also called: Super VGA, SVGA. See also analog-to-digital converter, CRT, VGA.

Extender board *n.* See expansion board.

Extensible Firmware Interface *n.* In computers with the Intel Itanium processor, the interface between the operating system and the computer's low-level booting and initialization firmware. The interface is made up of data tables that contain platform-related information, plus boot and run-time service calls that are available to the operating system and its loader to provide a standard environment for booting an operating system and running preboot applications. Acronym: EFI.

Extensible Forms Description Language or eXtensible Forms Description Language *n.* See XFDL.

Extensible Hypertext Markup Language *n.* See XHTML.

Extensible language *n.* A computer language that allows the user to extend or modify the syntax and semantics of the language. In the strict sense, the term relates to only a few of the languages actually used that allow the programmer to change the language itself, such as Forth. See also computer language, semantics (definition 1), syntax.

Extensible Markup Language or eXtensible Markup Language *n.* See XML.

Extensible style language *n.* See XSL.

eXtensible Stylesheet Language *n.* See XSL.

eXtensible Stylesheet Language Formatting Objects *n.* See XSL-FO.

Extensible Stylesheets Language-Transformations *n.* See XSLT.

Extension *n.* 1. A set of characters added to a filename that serves to extend or clarify its meaning or to identify a file as a member of a category. An extension may be assigned by the user or by a programme, as, for example, .com or .exe for executable programmes that MS-DOS can load and run. 2. A supplemental set of codes used to include additional characters in a particular character set. 3. A programme or programme module that adds functionality to or extends the effectiveness of a programme. 4. On the Macintosh, a programme that alters or augments the functionality of the operating system. There are two types: system extensions, such as QuickTime, and Chooser extensions, such as printer drivers. When a Macintosh is turned on, the extensions in the Extensions folder within the System folder are loaded into memory. See also Chooser extension, QuickTime, System folder.

Extension Manager *n.* A Macintosh utility developed by Apple that allows the user to determine which extensions are loaded when the computer is turned on. See also extension (definition 4).

Extent *n.* On a disk or other direct-access storage device, a continuous block of storage space reserved by the operating system for a particular file or programme.

Exterior gateway protocol *n.* A protocol used by routers (gateways) on separate, independent networks for distributing routing information between and among themselves—for example, between hosts on the Internet. Acronym: EGP. Also called: external gateway protocol.

External command *n.* A programme included in an operating system such as MS-DOS that is loaded into memory and executed only when its name is entered at the system prompt. Although an external command is a programme in its own right, it is called a command because it is included with the operating system. See also XCMD.

External function *n.* See XFCN.

External Gateway Protocol *n.* A protocol for distributing information regarding availability to the routers and gateways that interconnect networks. Acronym: EGP. See also gateway, router.

External gateway protocol *n.* See exterior gateway protocol.

External hard disk *n.* A free-standing hard disk with its own case and power supply, connected to the computer with a data cable and used mainly as a portable unit. See also hard disk.

External interrupt *n.* A hardware interrupt generated by hardware elements external to the microprocessor. See also hardware interrupt, internal interrupt, interrupt.

External modem *n.* A stand-alone modem that is connected via cable to a computer's serial port. See also internal modem.

External reference *n.* A reference in a programme or routine to some identifier, such as code or data, that is not declared within that programme or routine. The term usually refers to an identifier declared in code that is separately compiled. See also compile.

External storage *n.* A storage medium for data, such as a disk or tape unit, that is external to a computer's memory.

External viewer *n.* A separate application used to view documents that are of a type that cannot be handled by the current application. See also helper programme.

Extract *vb.* 1. To remove or duplicate items from a larger group in a systematic manner. 2. In programming, to derive one set of characters from another by using a mask (pattern) that determines which characters to remove.

Extra-high-density floppy disk *n.* A 3.5-inch floppy disk capable of holding 4 MB of data and requiring a special disk drive that has two heads rather than one. See also floppy disk.

Extranet *n.* An extension of a corporate intranet using World Wide Web technology to facilitate communication with the corporation's suppliers and customers. An extranet allows customers and suppliers to gain limited access to a company's intranet in order to enhance the speed and efficiency of their business relationship. See also intranet.

Extrinsic semiconductor *n.* A semiconductor that conducts electricity due to a P-type or N-type impurity that allows electrons to flow under certain conditions, such as heat application, by forcing them to move out of their standard state to create a new band of electrons or electron gaps. See also N-type semiconductor, P-type semiconductor, semiconductor.

Eyeballs *n.* The individuals or the number of individuals who view a Web site or its advertising.

E-zine or ezine *n.* Short for electronic magazine. A digital publication available on the Internet, a bulletin board system (BBS), or other online service, often free of charge.

F

F2F *adv.* Short for face-to-faceIn person, rather than over the Internet. The term is used in e-mail.

Face *n.* 1. In geometry and computer graphics, one side of a solid object, such as a cube. 2. In printing and typography, short for typeface.

Face time *n.* Time spent dealing face-to-face with another person, rather than communicating electronically.

Facsimile *n.* See fax.

Factor *n.* In mathematics, an item that is multiplied in a multiplication problem; for example, 2 and 3 are factors in the problem 2 x 3. The prime factors of a number are a set of prime numbers that, when multiplied together, produce the number.

Factorial *n.* Expressed as n! (n factorial), the result of multiplying the successive integers from 1 through n; n! equals n x (n–1) x (n – 2) x ... x 1.

Failback *n.* In a cluster network system (one with two or more interconnected servers), the process of restoring resources and services to their primary server after they have been temporarily relocated to a backup system while repairs were implemented on the original host. See also cluster, failover.

Failover *vb.* In a cluster network system (one with two or more interconnected servers), to relocate an overloaded or failed resource, such as a server, a disk drive, or a network, to its redundant, or backup, component. For example, when one server in a two-server system stops processing because of a power outage or other malfunction, the system automatically fails over to the second server, with little or no disruption to the users. See also cluster, failback.

Fail-safe system *n.* A computer system designed to continue operating without loss of or damage to programmes and data when part of the system breaks down or seriously malfunctions.

Fail-soft system *n.* A computer system designed to fail gracefully over a period of time when an element of hardware or software malfunctions. A fail-soft system terminates nonessential functions and remains operating at a diminished capacity until the problem has been corrected.

Failure *n.* The inability of a computer system or related device to operate reliably or to operate at all. A common cause of system failure is loss of power, which can be minimised with a battery-powered backup source until all devices can be shut down. Within a system, electronic failures generally occur early in the life of a system or component and can often be produced by burning in the equipment (leaving it turned on constantly) for a few hours or days. Mechanical failures are difficult to predict but are most likely to affect devices, such as disk drives, that have moving parts.

Failure rate *n.* The number of failures in a specified time period. Failure rate is a means of measuring the reliability of a device, such as a hard disk. See also MTBF.

Fair queuing *n.* A technique used to improve quality of service that gives each session flow passing through a network device a fair share of network resources. With fair queuing, no prioritisation occurs. Acronym: FQ. See also quality of service, queuing.

Fair use *n.* A legal doctrine describing the boundaries of legitimate use of copyrighted software or other published material.

Fallout *n.* Any failure of components that occurs while equipment is being burned in, especially when the test is done at the factory. See also burn in (definition 1).

Family *n.* A series of hardware or software products that have some properties in common, such as a series of personal computers from the same company, a series of CPU chips from the same manufacturer that all use the same instruction set, a set of 32-bit operating systems based on the same API (for example, Windows 95 and Windows 98), or a set of fonts that are intended to be used together, such as Times New Roman. See also central processing unit, font, instruction set, operating system.

Fan 1 *n.* The cooling mechanism built into computer cabinets, laser printers, and other such devices to prevent malfunction due to heat buildup. Fans are the main source of the continuous humming associated with computers and other hardware.

Fan 2 *vb.* To flip through a stack of printer paper to ensure that the pages are loose and will not stick together or jam the printer.

Fanfold paper *n.* Paper with pin-feed holes on both margins designed to be fed into the tractor-feed mechanism of a printer, page by page, in a continuous, unbroken stream. Also called: z-fold paper.

Fan-in *n.* The maximum number of signals that can be fed to a given electronic device, such as a logic gate, at one time without risking signal corruption. The fan-in rating of a device depends on its type and method of construction.

Fan-out *n.* The maximum number of electronic devices that can be fed by a given electronic device, such as a logic gate, at one time without the signal becoming too weak. The fan-out rating of a device depends on its type and method of construction.

Fanzine *n.* A magazine, distributed on line or by mail, that is produced by and devoted to fans of a particular group, person, or activity. See also ezine.

FAQ *n.* Acronym for frequently asked questions. A document listing common questions and answers on a particular subject. FAQs are often posted on Internet newsgroups where new participants tend to ask the same questions that regular readers have answered many times.

Farad *n.* The unit of capacitance (the ability to hold a charge). A 1-farad capacitor holds a charge of 1 coulomb with a potential difference of 1 volt between its plates. In practical use, a farad is an extremely large amount of capacitance; capacitance is usually expressed in terms of microfarads (10–6) or picofarads (10–12). Abbreviation: F.

FARNET *n.* See Federation of American Research Networks.

Fast Ethernet *n.* See 100BaseX.

Fast Fourier transform *n.* A set of algorithms used to compute the discrete Fourier transform of a function, which in turn is used for solving series of equations, performing spectral analysis, and carrying out other signal-processing and signal-generation tasks. Acronym: FFT. See also Fourier transform.

Fast infrared port *n.* See FIR port.

Fast packet *n.* A standard for high-speed network technology that utilises fast switching of fixed-length cells or packets for real-time transmission of data. Also called: Asynchronous Transfer Mode, ATM. See also packet (definition 2), packet switching.

Fast packet switching *adj.* Of, describing, or pertaining to high-speed packet-switching networks that perform little or no error checking. The term is often, however, restricted to high-speed networking technologies, such as ATM, that transmit fixed-length cells rather than including those, such as frame relay, that transmit variable-length packets.

Fast page-mode RAM *n.* See page mode RAM.

Fast SCSI *n.* A form of the SCSI-2 interface that can transfer data 8 bits at a time at up to 10 megabytes per second. The Fast SCSI connector has 50 pins. Also called: Fast SCSI-2. See also SCSI, SCSI-2.

Fast/Wide SCSI *n.* A form of the SCSI-2 interface that can transfer data 16 bits at a time at up to 20 megabytes per second. The Fast/Wide SCSI connector has 68 pins. Also called: Fast/Wide SCSI-2. See also SCSI, SCSI-2.

FAT *n.* See file allocation table.

Fatal error *n.* An error that causes the system or application programme to crash—that is, to fail abruptly with no hope of recovery.

Fatal exception error *n.* A Windows message signaling that an unrecoverable error, one that causes the system to halt, has occurred. Data being processed when the error occurs is usually lost, and the computer must be rebooted. See also error handling.

Fat application *n.* An application that can be used on both PowerPC processor–based Macintosh computers and 68K-based Macintosh computers.

Fat binary *n.* An application format that supports both PowerPC processor–based Macintosh computers and 68K-based Macintosh computers.

Fatbits *n.* 1. Originally (as FatBits), a feature of the Apple MacPaint programme in which a small portion of a drawing can be enlarged and modified one pixel (FatBit) at a time. 2. A similar feature in any programme that allows pixel-by-pixel modification through a zoom feature.

Fat client *n.* In a client/server architecture, a client machine that performs most or all of the processing, with little or none performed by the server. The client handles presentation and functions, and the server manages data and access to it. See also client (definition 3), client/server architecture, server (definition 2), thin server.

FAT file system *n.* The system used by MS-DOS to organise and manage files. The FAT (file allocation table) is a data structure that MS-DOS creates on the disk when the disk is formatted. When MS-DOS stores a file on a formatted disk, the operating system places information about the stored file in the FAT so that MS-DOS can retrieve the file later when requested. The FAT is the only file system MS-DOS can use; OS/2, Windows NT, and Windows 9x operating systems can use the FAT file system in addition to their own file systems (HPFS, NTFS, and VFAT, respectively). See also file allocation table, HPFS, NTFS, OS/2, VFAT, Windows.

Father *n.* See generation (definition 1).

Father file *n.* A file that is the last previously valid set of a changing set of data. The father file is immediately preceded by a grandfather file and immediately succeeded by its son. The pairs father and son, parent and child (or descendant), and independent and dependent are synonymous. See also generation (definition 1).

Fat server *n.* In a client/server architecture, a server machine that performs most of the processing, with little or none performed by the client. Applications logic and data reside on the server, and presentation services are handled by the client. See also client (definition 3), client/server architecture, server (definition 2), thin client.

Fatware *n.* Software that monopolises hard disk space and power due to an overabundance of features or inefficient design. Also called: bloatware.

Fault *n.* 1. A physical defect, such as a loose connection, that prevents a system or device from operating as it should. 2. A programming error that can cause the software to fail. 3. As page fault, an attempt to access a page of virtual memory that is not mapped to a physical address. See also page fault.

Fault resilience *n.* See high availability.

Fault tolerance *n.* The ability of a computer or an operating system to respond to a catastrophic event or fault, such as a power outage or a hardware failure, in a way that ensures that no data is lost and any work in progress is not corrupted. This can be accomplished with a battery-backed power supply, backup hardware, provisions in the operating system, or any combination of these. In a fault-tolerant network, the system has the ability either to continue the system's operation without loss of data or to shut the system down and restart it, recovering all processing that was in progress when the fault occurred.

Favourite *n.* In Microsoft Internet Explorer, a user-defined shortcut to a page on the World Wide Web, analogous to a bookmark in Netscape Navigator. See also Favourites folder, hotlist.

Favourites folder *n.* In Microsoft Internet Explorer, a collection of shortcuts to Web sites that a user has selected for future reference. Other Web browsers refer to this collection by other names, such as bookmarks or hotlists. See also bookmark file (definition 1), Internet Explorer, URL.

Fax *n.* Short for facsimile. The transmission of text or graphics over telephone lines in digitised form. Conventional fax machines scan an original document, transmit an image of the document as a bit map, and reproduce the received image on a printer. Resolution and encoding are standardised in the CCITT Groups 1–4 recommendations. Fax images can also be sent and received by microcomputers equipped with fax hardware and software. See also CCITT Groups 1–4.

Fax machine *n.* Short for facsimile machine. A device that scans pages, converts the images of those pages to a digital format consistent with the international facsimile standard, and transmits the image through a telephone line. A fax machine also receives such images and prints them on paper. See also scan (definition 2).

Fax modem *n.* A modem that sends (and possibly receives) data encoded in a fax format (typically CCITT fax format), which a fax machine or another modem decodes and converts to an image. The image must already have been encoded on the host computer. Text and graphic documents can be converted into fax format by special software usually provided with the modem; paper documents must first be scanned in. Fax modems may be internal or external and may combine fax and conventional modem capabilities. See also fax, modem.

Fax on demand *n.* An automated system that makes information available for request by telephone. When a request is made, the system faxes the information to the telephone number given in the request. Acronym: FOD.

Fax programme *n.* A computer application that allows the user to send, receive, and print fax transmissions. See also fax.

Fax server *n.* A computer on a network capable of sending and receiving fax transmissions to and from other computers on the network. See also fax, server (definition 1).

FCB *n.* See file control block.

FCC *n.* Acronym for Federal Communications Commission. The U.S. agency created by the Communications Act of 1934, which regulates interstate and international wire, radio, and other broadcast transmissions, including telephone, telegraph, and telecommunications.

F connector *n.* A coaxial connector, used primarily in video applications, that requires a screw-on attachment. See the illustration.

FDDI *n.* Acronym for Fiber Distributed Data Interface. A standard developed by the American National Standards Institute (ANSI) for high-speed fiber-optic LANs (local area networks). FDDI provides specifications for transmission rates of 100 megabits (100 million bits) per second on networks based on the token ring standard. See also token ring network.

FDDI II *n.* Acronym for Fiber Distributed Data Interface. An extension of the FDDI standard, FDDI II contains additional specifications for the real-time transmission of analog data in digitised form for high-speed fiber-optic LANs (local area networks). See also FDDI.

FDHP *n.* Acronym for Full Duplex Handshaking Protocol. A protocol used by duplex modems to determine the source type of the transmission and match it. See also duplex1, handshake.

FDM *n.* Acronym for Frequency Division Multiplexing. A means of loading multiple transmission signals onto separate bands of a single communications channel so that all signals can be carried simultaneously. FDM is used in analog transmissions, as on a baseband network or in communications over a telephone line. In FDM the frequency range of the channel is divided into narrower bands, each of which can carry a different transmission signal. For example, FDM might divide a voice channel with a frequency range of 1400 hertz (Hz) into four subchannels—820–990 Hz, 1230–1400 Hz, 1640–1810 Hz, and 2050–2220 Hz—with adjacent subchannels separated by a 240-Hz guard band to minimise interference.

FDMA *n.* Acronym for Frequency Division Multiple Access. A method of multiplexing in which the set of frequencies assigned to cellular phone service is divided into 30 separate channels, each of which can be used by a different caller. FDMA is the technology used in the AMPS phone service, which is widespread in North America and in other countries around the world. See also AMPS.

Fear, uncertainty, and doubt *n.* See FUD.

Feasibility study *n.* An evaluation of a prospective project for the purpose of determining whether or not the project should be undertaken. Feasibility studies normally consider the time, budget, and technology required for completion and are generally used in computing departments in large organisations.

Feature *n.* A unique, attractive, or desirable property of a programme or of a computer or other hardware.

Feature extraction *n.* The selection of significant aspects of a computer image for use as guidelines in computerised pattern matching and image recognition. See also image processing.

Featuritis *n.* Jargon for a tendency to add new features to a programme at the expense of its original compact size or elegance. Creeping featuritis describes the accretion of feature upon feature over time, eventually resulting in a large, unwieldy, generally inelegant programme that is, or appears to be, a collection of ad-hoc additions. The result of featuritis is a programme condition known as software bloat. Also called: creeping featuritis, creeping featurism, feeping creaturism. See also bloatware.

Feb-30 n. See double leap year.

Federal Communications Commission *n.* See FCC.

Federal Information Processing Standards *n.* A system of standards, guidelines, and technical methods for information processing within the U.S. federal government. Acronym: FIPS.

Federal Internet Exchange *n.* See FIX.

Federated database *n.* A database to which scientists contribute their findings and knowledge regarding a particular field or problem. A federated database is designed for scientific collaboration on problems of such scope that they are difficult or impossible for an individual to solve. See also database.

Federation of American Research Networks *n.* A nonprofit association of internetworking technology companies in the United States that serves as a national advocate for internetworking, with a primary focus on the education, research, and related communities. Acronym: FARNET. See also internetwork.

Federation on Computing in the United States *n.* The U.S. representative of the International Federation of Information Processing (IFIP). Acronym: FOCUS. See also IFIP.

Feed 1 *n.* See news feed.

Feed 2 *vb.* 1. To advance paper through a printer. 2. To supply media to a recording device, as by inserting disks into a disk drive.

Feedback *n.* The return of a portion of system output as input to the same system. Often feedback is deliberately designed into a system, but sometimes it is unwanted. In electronics, feedback is used in monitoring, controlling, and amplifying circuitry.

Feedback circuit *n.* Any circuit or system that returns (feeds back) a portion of its output to its input. A common example of a feedback system, although it is not completely electronic, is a thermostatically controlled household heating system. This self-limiting or self-correcting process is an example of negative feedback, in which changes in output are fed back to the source so that the change in the output is reversed. In positive feedback, an increase in output is fed back to the source, increasing the output further, which creates a snowballing effect. An example of unwanted positive feedback is the "screech" that occurs when the microphone of a public address system is brought too close to its loudspeaker.

Feed scanner *n.* See sheet-fed scanner.

Feeping creaturism *n.* See featuritis.

Female connector *n.* A connector that has one or more receptacles for the insertion of pins. Female connector part numbers often include an F (female), an S (socket), a J (jack), or an R (receptacle). For example, a female DB-25 connector might be labeled DB-25S or DB-25F. (Note that although the letter F can denote a female connector, it does not have that meaning in F connector, which is a type of coaxial cable connector.) See the illustration.

Femto- prefix Metric prefix meaning 10–15 (one quadrillionth).

Femtosecond *n.* One quadrillionth (10–15) of a second. Abbreviation: fs.

FEP *n.* See front-end processor.

Ferric oxide *n.* The chemical substance Fe2O3, an oxide of iron used with a binding agent in the magnetic coating applied to disks and tapes for data storage.

Ferric RAM *n.* See FRAM.

Ferromagnetic domain *n.* See magnetic domain.

Ferromagnetic material *n.* A substance that can become highly magnetised. Ferrite and powdered iron are ferromagnetic materials commonly used in electronics, for example, as cores for inductors to increase their inductance, and as part of the coating on floppy and hard disks and magnetic tape.

FET *n.* Acronym for field-effect transistor. A type of transistor in which the flow of current between the source and the drain is modulated by the electric field around the gate electrode. FETs are used as amplifiers, oscillators, and switches and are characterised by an extremely high input impedance (resistance) that makes them particularly suitable for amplification of very small signals. Types of FETs include the junction FET and the metal-oxide semiconductor FET (MOSFET). See the illustration. See also MOSFET.

Fetch *vb.* To retrieve an instruction or an item of data from memory and store it in a register. Fetching is part of the execution cycle of a microprocessor; first an instruction or item of data must be fetched from memory and loaded into a register, after which it can be executed (if it is an instruction) or acted upon (if it is data).

Fetch time *n.* See instruction time.

Fiberoptic cable or fiber-optic cable *n.* A form of cable used in networks that transmits signals optically, rather than electrically as do coaxial and twisted-pair cable. The light-conducting heart of a fiberoptic cable is a fine glass or plastic fiber called the core. This core is surrounded by a refractive layer called the cladding that effectively traps the light and keeps it bouncing along the central fiber. Outside both the core and the cladding is a final layer of plastic or plastic-like material called the coat, or jacket. Fiberoptic cable can transmit clean signals at speeds as high as 2 Gbps. Because it transmits light, not electricity, it is also immune to eavesdropping.

Fiber optics *n.* A technology for the transmission of light beams along optical fibers. A light beam, such as that produced in a laser, can be modulated to carry information. Because light has a higher frequency on the electromagnetic spectrum than other types of radiation, such as radio waves, a single fiber-optic channel can carry significantly more information than most other means of information transmission. Optical fibers are thin strands of glass or other transparent material, with dozens or hundreds of strands housed in a single cable. Optical fibers are essentially immune to electromagnetic interference. See also optical fiber.

Fiber to the curb *n.* See FTTC.

Fiber to the home *n.* See FTTH.

Fibonacci numbers *n.* In mathematics, an infinite series in which each successive integer is the sum of the two integers that precede it—for example, 1, 1, 2, 3, 5, 8, 13, 21, 34, ... Fibonacci numbers are named for the thirteenth-century mathematician Leonardo Fibonacci of Pisa. In computing, Fibonacci numbers are used to speed binary searches by repeatedly dividing a set of data into groups in accordance with successively smaller pairs of numbers in the Fibonacci sequence. For example, a data set of 34 items would be divided into one group of 21 and another of 13. If the item being sought is in the group of 13, the group of 21 is discarded, and the group of 13 is divided into groups of 5 and 8; the search would continue until the item was located. The ratio of two successive terms in the Fibonacci sequence converges on the Golden Ratio, a "magic number" that seems to represent the proportions of an ideal rectangle. The number describes many things, from the curve of a nautilus shell to the proportions of playing cards.

Fiche *n.* See microfiche.

Fidonet *n.* 1. A protocol for sending e-mail, newsgroup postings, and files over telephone lines. The protocol originated on the Fido BBS, initiated in 1984 by Tom Jennings, and maintaining low costs has been a factor in its subsequent development. Fidonet can exchange e-mail with the Internet. 2. The network of BBSs, private companies, NGOs (nongovernment organisations), and individuals that use the Fidonet protocol.

Field *n.* 1. A location in a record in which a particular type of data is stored. For example, EMPLOYEE-RECORD might contain fields to store Last-Name, First-Name, Address, City, State, Zip-Code, Hire-Date, Current-Salary, Title, Department, and so on. Individual fields are characterised by their maximum length and the type of data (for example, alphabetic, numeric, or financial) that can be placed in them. The facility for creating these specifications usually is contained in the data definition language (DDL). In relational database management systems, fields are called columns. 2. A space in an onscreen form where the user can enter a specific item of information.

Field-effect transistor *n.* See FET.

Field expansion *n.* See date expansion.

Field Programmable Gate Array *n.* See FPGA.

Field-programmable logic array *n.* An integrated circuit containing an array of logic circuits in which the connections between the individual circuits, and thus the logic functions of the array, can be programmed after manufacture, typically at the time of installation in the field. Programming can be performed only once, typically by passing high current through fusible links on the chip. Acronym: FPLA. Also called: PLA, programmable logic array.

Field separator *n.* Any character that separates one field of data from another. See also delimiter, field (definition 1).

FIFO *n.* See first in, first out.

Fifth-generation computer *n.* See computer.

Fifth normal form *n.* See normal form (definition 1).

File *n.* A complete, named collection of information, such as a programme, a set of data used by a programme, or a user-created document. A file is the basic unit of storage that enables a computer to distinguish one set of information from another. A file is the "glue" that binds a conglomeration of instructions, numbers, words, or images into a coherent unit that a user can retrieve, change, delete, save, or send to an output device.

File allocation table *n.* A table or list maintained by some operating systems to manage disk space used for file storage. Files on a disk are stored, as space allows, in fixed-size groups of bytes (characters) rather than from beginning to end as contiguous strings of text or numbers. A single file can thus be scattered in pieces over many separate storage areas. A file allocation table maps available disk storage space so that it can mark flawed segments that should not be used and can find and link the pieces of a file. In MS-DOS, the file allocation table is commonly known as the FAT. See also FAT file system.

File attribute *n.* A restrictive label attached to a file that describes and regulates its use—for example, hidden, system, read-only, archive, and so forth. In MS-DOS, this information is stored as part of the file's directory entry.

File backup *n.* See backup.

File compression *n.* The process of reducing the size of a file for transmission or storage. See also data compression.

File control block *n.* A small block of memory temporarily assigned by a computer's operating system to hold information about an opened file. A file control block typically contains such information as the file's identification, its location on a disk, and a pointer that marks the user's current (or last) position in the file. Acronym: FCB.

File conversion *n.* The process of transforming the data in a file from one format to another without altering the data—for example, converting a file from a word processor's format to its ASCII equivalent. In some cases, information about the data, such as formatting, may be lost. Another, more detailed, type of file conversion involves changing character coding from one standard to another, as in converting EBCDIC characters (which are used primarily with mainframe computers) to ASCII characters. See also ASCII, EBCDIC.

File extension *n.* See extension (definition 1).

File extent *n.* See extent.

File format *n.* The structure of a file that defines the way it is stored and laid out on the screen or in print. The format can be fairly simple and common, as are files stored as "plain" ASCII text, or it can be quite complex and include various types of control instructions and codes used by programmes, printers, and other devices. Examples include RTF (Rich Text Format), DCA (Document Content Architecture), PICT, DIF (Data Interchange Format), DXF (Data Exchange File), TIFF (Tagged Image File Format), and EPSF (Encapsulated PostScript Format).

File fragmentation *n.* 1. The breaking apart of files as they are stored by the operating system into small, separate segments on disk. The condition is a natural consequence of enlarging files and saving them on a crowded disk that no longer contains contiguous blocks of free space large enough to hold them. File fragmentation is not an integrity problem, although it can eventually slow read and write access times if the disk is very full and storage is badly fragmented. Software products are available for redistributing (optimising) file storage to reduce fragmentation. 2. In a database, a situation in which records are not stored in their optimal access sequence because of accumulated additions and deletions of records. Most database systems offer or contain utility programmes that resequence records to improve efficiency of access and to aggregate free space occupied by deleted records.

File gap *n.* See block gap.

File handle *n.* In MS-DOS, OS/2, and Windows, a token (number) that the system uses to identify or refer to an open file or, sometimes, to a device.

File-handling routine *n.* Any routine designed to assist in creating, opening, accessing, and closing files. Most high-level languages have built-in file-handling routines, although more sophisticated or complex file-handling routines in an application are often created by the programmer.

File header *n.* See header (definition 2).

File layout *n.* In data storage, the organisation of records within a file. Frequently, descriptions of the record structure are also included within the file layout.

File librarian *n.* A person or process responsible for maintaining, archiving, copying, and providing access to a collection of data.

File maintenance *n.* Broadly, the process of changing information in a file, altering a file's control information or structure, or copying and archiving files. A person using a terminal to enter data, the programme accepting the data from the terminal and writing it to a data file, and a database administrator using a utility to alter the format of a database file are all forms of file maintenance.

File management system *n.* The organisational structure that an operating system or programme uses to order and track files. For example, a hierarchical file system uses directories in a so-called tree structure. All operating systems have built-in file management systems. Commercially available products implement additional features that provide more sophisticated means of navigating, finding, and organising files. See also file system, hierarchical file system.

File manager *n.* A module of an operating system or environment that controls the physical placement of and access to a group of programme files.

File name *n.* The set of letters, numbers, and allowable symbols assigned to a file to distinguish it from all other files in a particular directory on a disk. A file name is the label under which a computer user saves and requests a block of information. Both programmes and data have file names and often extensions that further identify the type or purpose of the file. Naming conventions, such as maximum length and allowable characters of a file name, vary from one operating system to another. See also directory, path (definition 5).

File name extension *n.* See extension (definition 1).

Filename globbing *n.* A Linux command-line feature, available on most FTP servers, which allows a user to refer to sets of files without individually listing each file name. Filename globbing can be used to select or delete all files in a working directory with a single command. At the discretion of the user, globbing can match all files, or only those with filenames containing a specific character or range of characters. See also wildcard character.

File property *n.* A detail about a file that helps identify it, such as a descriptive title, the author name, the subject, or a keyword that identifies topics or other important information in the file.

File protection *n.* A process or device by which the existence and integrity of a file are maintained. Methods of file protection range from allowing read-only access and assigning passwords to covering the write-protect notch on a disk and locking away floppy disks holding sensitive files.

File recovery *n.* The process of reconstructing lost or unreadable files on disk. Files are lost when they are inadvertently deleted, when on-disk information about their storage is damaged, or when the disk is damaged. File recovery involves the use of utility programmes that attempt to rebuild on-disk information about the storage locations of deleted files. Because deletion makes the file's disk space available but does not remove the data, data that has not yet been overwritten can be recovered. In the case of damaged files or disks, recovery programmes read whatever raw data they can find, and save the data to a new disk or file in ASCII or numeric (binary or hexadecimal) form. In some instances, however, such reconstructed files contain so much extraneous or mixed information that they are unreadable. The best way to recover a file is to restore it from a backup copy.

File retrieval *n.* The act of accessing a data file and transferring it from a storage location to the machine where it is to be used.

File server *n.* A file-storage device on a local area network that is accessible to all users on the network. Unlike a disk server, which appears to the user as a remote disk drive, a file server is a sophisticated device that not only stores files but manages them and maintains order as network users request files and make changes to them. To deal with the tasks of handling multiple—sometimes simultaneous—requests for files, a file server contains a processor and controlling software as well as a disk drive for storage. On local area networks, a file server is often a computer with a large hard disk that is dedicated only to the task of managing shared files.

File Server for Macintosh *n.* An AppleTalk network integration service that allows Macintosh clients and personal computers clients to share files. Also called: MacFile. See also Print Server for Macintosh, Services for Macintosh.

File sharing *n.* The use of computer files on networks, wherein files are stored on a central computer or a server and are requested, reviewed, and modified by more than one individual. When a file is used with different programmes or different computers, file sharing can require conversion to a mutually acceptable format. When a single file is shared by many people, access can be regulated through such means as password protection, security clearances, or file locking to prohibit changes to a file by more than one person at a time.

File size *n.* The length of a file, typically given in bytes. A computer file stored on disk actually has two file sizes, logical size and physical size. The logical file size corresponds to the file's actual size—the number of bytes it contains. The physical size refers to the amount of storage space allotted to the file on disk. Because space is set aside for a file in blocks of bytes, the last characters in the file might not completely fill the block (allocation unit) reserved for them. When this happens, the physical size is larger than the logical size of the file.

Filespec *n.* See file specification (definition 1).

File specification *n.* 1. The path to a file, from a disk drive through a chain of directory files to the file name that serves to locate a particular file. Abbreviated filespec. 2. A file name containing wildcard characters that indicate which files among a group of similarly named files are requested. 3. A document that describes the organisation of data within a file.

File structure *n.* A description of a file or group of files that are to be treated together for some purpose. Such a description includes file layout and location for each file under consideration.

File system *n.* In an operating system, the overall structure in which files are named, stored, and organised. A file system consists of files, directories, or folders, and the information needed to locate and access these items. The term can also refer to the portion of an operating system that translates requests for file operations from an application programme into low-level, sector-oriented tasks that can be understood by the drivers controlling the disk drives. See also driver.

File transfer *n.* The process of moving or transmitting a file from one location to another, as between two programmes or over a network.

File Transfer Protocol *n.* See FTP1 (definition 1).

File type *n.* A designation of the operational or structural characteristics of a file. A file's type is often identified in the file name, usually in the file name extension. See also file format.

Fill 1 *n.* In computer graphics, the coloured or patterned "paint" inside an enclosed figure, such as a circle. The portion of the shape that can be coloured or patterned is the fill area. Drawing programmes commonly offer tools for creating filled or nonfilled shapes; the user can specify colour or pattern.

Fill 2 *vb.* To add colour or a pattern to the enclosed portion of a circle or other shape.

Fill handle *n.* The small black square in the lower-right corner of a cell selection. When you point to the fill handle, the pointer changes to a black cross.

Film at 11 *n.* A phrase sometimes seen in newsgroups. An allusion to a brief newsbreak on TV that refers to a top news story that will be covered in full on the 11 o'clock news, it is used sarcastically to ridicule a previous article's lack of timeliness or newsworthiness. See also newsgroup.

Film recorder *n.* A device for capturing on 35-mm film the images displayed on a computer screen.

Film ribbon *n.* See carbon ribbon.

Filter *n.* 1. A programme or set of features within a programme that reads its standard or designated input, transforms the input in some desired way, and then writes the output to its standard or designated output destination. A database filter, for example, might flag information of a certain age. 2. In communications and electronics, hardware or software that selectively passes certain elements of a signal and eliminates or minimises others. A filter on a communications network, for example, must be designed to transmit a certain frequency but attenuate (dampen) frequencies above it (a lowpass filter), those below it (a highpass filter), or those above and below it (a bandpass filter). 3. A pattern or mask through which data is passed to weed out specified items. For instance, a filter used in e-mail or in retrieving newsgroup messages can allow users to filter out messages from other users. See also e-mail filter, mask. 4. In computer graphics, a special effect or production effect that is applied to bitmapped images

Filtering programme *n.* A programme that filters information and presents only results that match the qualifications defined in the programme.

FilterKeys *n.* A Windows 9x accessibility control panel feature that enables users with physical disabilities to use the keyboard. With FilterKeys, the system ignores brief and repeated keystrokes that result from slow or inaccurate finger movements. See also accessibility.

Final-Form-Text DCA *n.* A standard in Document Content Architecture (DCA) for storing documents in ready-to-print form for interchange between dissimilar programmes. A related standard is Revisable-Form-Text DCA (RFTDCA). Acronym: FFTDCA. See also DCA (definition 1).

Finally *n.* A keyword used in the Java programming language that executes a block of statements regardless of whether a Java exception, or run-time error, occurred in a previous block defined by the "try" keyword. See also block, exception, keyword, try.

Find *vb.* See search2.

Finder *n.* The standard interface to the Macintosh operating system. The Finder allows the user to view the contents of directories (folders); to move, copy, and delete files; and to launch applications. Items in the system are often represented as icons, and a mouse or similar pointing device is used to manipulate these items. The Finder was the first commercially successful graphical user interface, and it helped launch a wave of interest in icon-based systems. See also MultiFinder.

Finger 1 *n.* An Internet utility, originally limited to UNIX but now available on many other platforms, that enables a user to obtain information on other users who may be at other sites (if those sites permit access by finger). Given an e-mail address, finger returns the user's full name, an indication of whether or not the user is currently logged on, and any other information the user has chosen to supply as a profile. Given a first or last name, finger returns the logon names of users whose first or last names match.

Finger 2 *vb.* To obtain information on a user by means of the finger programme.

Fingerprint 1 *vb.* To scan a computer system to discover what operating system (OS) the computer is running. By detecting a computer's OS through fingerprinting, a hacker is better able to specify attacks on system vulnerabilities and therefore better able to plan an attack on that system. A hacker may use several different fingerprinting schemes separately and in tandem to pinpoint the OS of a target computer.

Fingerprint 2 *n.* Information embedded or attached to a file or image to uniquely identify it.

Fingerprint reader *n.* A scanner that reads human fingerprints for comparison to a database of stored fingerprint images.

Fingerprint recognition *n.* A technology used to control access to a computer, network, or other device or to a secure area through a user's fingerprints. The patterns of an individual's fingers are scanned by a fingerprint reader or similar device and matched with stored images of fingerprints before access is granted. See also biometric.

FIPS *n.* See Federal Information Processing Standards.

FIPS 140-1 *n.* Acronym for Federal Information Processing Standard 140-1. A U.S. Government standard, issued by the National Institute of Standards and Technology (NIST), entitled Security Requirements for Cryptographic Modules. FIPS 140-1 defines four levels of security requirements related to cryptographic hardware and software modules within computer and telecommunications systems used for sensitive but unclassified data. The four security levels range from basic module design through increasingly stringent levels of physical security. The standard covers such security-related features as hardware and software security, cryptographic algorithms, and management of encryption keys. FIPS 140-1products can be validated for federal use in both the United States and Canada after independent testing under the Cryptographic Module Validation (CMV) Programme, developed and jointly adopted by NIST and the Canadian Communication Security Establishment. See also cryptography.

Firewall *n.* A security system intended to protect an organisation's network against external threats, such as hackers, coming from another network, such as the Internet. Usually a combination of hardware and software, a firewall prevents computers in the organisation's network from communicating directly with computers external to the network and vice versa. Instead, all communication is routed through a proxy server outside of the organisation's network, and the proxy server decides whether it is safe to let a particular message or file pass through to the organisation's network. See also proxy server.

Firewall sandwich *n.* The use of load-balancing appliances on both sides of Internetworked firewalls to distribute both inbound and outbound traffic among the firewalls. The firewall sandwich architecture helps to prevent firewalls from degrading network performance and creating a single point of network failure. See also firewall, load balancing.

FireWire *n.* A high-speed serial bus from Apple that implements the IEEE 1394 standard. See also IEEE 1394.

Firmware *n.* Software routines stored in read-only memory (ROM). Unlike random access memory (RAM), read-only memory stays intact even in the absence of electrical power. Startup routines and low-level input/output instructions are stored in firmware. It falls between software and hardware in terms of ease of modification. See also RAM, ROM.

FIR port *n.* Short for fast infrared port. A wireless I/O port, most common on a portable computer, that exchanges data with an external device using infrared light. See also infrared, input/output port.

FIRST *n.* Acronym for Forum of Incident Response and Security Teams. An organisation within the Internet Society (ISOC) that coordinates with CERT in order to encourage information sharing and a unified response to security threats. See also CERT, Internet Society.

First-generation computer *n.* See computer.

First in, first out *n.* A method of processing a queue, in which items are removed in the same order in which they were added—the first in is the first out. Such an order is typical of a list of documents waiting to be printed. Acronym: FIFO. See also queue.

First normal *n.* See normal form (definition 1).

Fishbowl *n.* A secure area within a computer system in which intruders can be contained and monitored. A fishbowl is typically set up by a security administrator to impersonate important applications or information so that the system administrator can learn more about hackers who have broken into the network without the hacker learning more about or damaging the system. See also honeypot.

Fitting *n.* The calculation of a curve or other line that most closely approximates a set of data points or measurements. See also regression analysis.

Five-nines availability *n.* The availability of a system 99.999 per cent of the time. See also high availability.

FIX *n.* Acronym for Federal Internet Exchange. A connection point between the U.S. government's various internets and the Internet. There are two Federal Internet Exchanges: FIX West, in Mountain View, California; and FIX East, in College Park, Maryland. Together, they link the backbones of MILNET, ESnet (the TCP/IP network of the Department of Energy), and NSInet (NASA Sciences Internet) with NSFnet. See also backbone (definition 1), MILNET, NSFnet, TCP/IP.

Fixed disk *n.* See hard disk.

Fixed-length field *n.* In a record or in data storage, a field whose size in bytes is predetermined and constant. A fixed-length field always takes up the same amount of space on a disk, even when the amount of data stored in the field is small.

Fixed-pitch spacing *n.* See monospacing.

Fixed-point arithmetic *n.* Arithmetic performed on fixed-point numbers. See also fixed-point notation.

Fixed-point notation *n.* A numeric format in which the decimal point has a specified position. Fixed-point numbers are a compromise between integral formats, which are compact and efficient, and floating-point numeric formats, which have a great range of values. Like floating-point numbers, fixed-point numbers can have a fractional part, but operations on fixed-point numbers usually take less time than floating-point operations. See also floating-point notation, integer.

Fixed space *n.* A set amount of horizontal space used to separate characters in text—often, the width of a numeral in a given font. See also em space, en space, thin space.

Fixed spacing *n.* See monospacing.

Fixed storage *n.* Any nonremovable storage, such as a large disk that is sealed permanently in its drive.

Fixed-width font *n.* See monospace font.

Fixed-width spacing *n.* See monospacing.

Fixed-word-length computer *n.* A description that applies to almost all computers and refers to the uniform size of the data units, or words, that are processed by the microprocessor and shuttled through the system over the hardware lines composing the main data bus. Fixed-word-length computers, including IBM and Macintosh personal computers, commonly work with 2 or 4 bytes at a time.

F keys *n.* See function key.

Flag *n.* 1. Broadly, a marker of some type used by a computer in processing or interpreting information; a signal indicating the existence or status of a particular condition. Flags are used in such areas as communications, programming, and information processing. Depending on its use, a flag can be a code, embedded in data, that identifies some condition, or it can be one or more bits set internally by hardware or software to indicate an event of some type, such as an error or the result of comparing two values. 2. In the HDLC communications protocol, a flag is the unique series of bits 01111110, used to start and end a transmission frame (message unit). See also HDLC.

Flame 1 *n.* An abusive or personally insulting e-mail message or newsgroup posting.

Flame 2 *vb.* 1. To send an abusive or personally insulting e-mail message or newsgroup posting. 2. To criticise personally by means of e-mail messages or newsgroup postings.

Flame bait *n.* A posting to a mailing list, newsgroup, or other online conference that is likely to provoke flames, often because it expresses a controversial opinion on a highly emotional topic. See also flame1, flame war.

Flamefest *n.* A series of inflammatory messages or articles in a newsgroup or other online conference.

Flamer *n.* A person who sends or posts abusive messages via e-mail, in newsgroups and other online forums, and in online chats. See also chat1 (definition 1), newsgroup.

Flame war *n.* A discussion in a mailing list, newsgroup, or other online conference that has turned into a protracted exchange of flames. See also flame1.

Flash *n.* A vector graphics file format (extension .swf) developed by Macromedia to enable designers to add animation and interactivity to multimedia Web pages. Flash files can be played back with a downloadable Shockwave plug-in or a Java programme. The file format has been released by Macromedia as an open standard for the Internet.

Flash *vb.* See burn.

Flash memory *n.* A type of nonvolatile memory. Flash memory is similar to EEPROM memory in function but it must be erased in blocks, whereas EEPROM can be erased one byte at a time. Because of its block-oriented nature, flash memory is commonly used as a supplement to or replacement for hard disks in portable computers. In this context, flash memory either is built into the unit or, more commonly, is available as a PC Card that can be plugged into a PCMCIA slot. A disadvantage of the block-oriented nature of flash memory is that it cannot be practically used as main memory (RAM) because a computer needs to be able to write to memory in single-byte increments. See also EEPROM, nonvolatile memory, PC Card, PCMCIA slot.

Flash ROM *n.* See flash memory.

Flat address space *n.* An address space in which each location in memory is specified by a unique number. (Memory addresses start at 0 and increase sequentially by 1.) The Macintosh operating system, OS/2, and Windows NT use a flat address space. MS-DOS uses a segmented address space, in which a location must be accessed with a segment number and an offset number. See also segmentation.

Flatbed plotter *n.* A plotter in which paper is held on a flat platform and a pen moves along both axes, traveling across the paper to draw an image. This method is slightly more accurate than that used by drum plotters, which move the paper under the pen, but requires more space. Flatbed plotters can also accept a wider variety of media, such as vellum and acetate, because the material does not need to be flexible. See also plotter.

Flatbed scanner *n.* A scanner with a flat, transparent surface that holds the image to be scanned, generally a book or other paper document. A scan head below the surface moves across the image. Some flatbed scanners can also reproduce transparent media, such as slides. See the illustration.

Flat file *n.* A file consisting of records of a single record type in which there is no embedded structure information that governs relationships between records.

Flat-file database *n.* A database that takes the form of a table, where only one table can be used for each database. A flat-file database can only work with one file at a time.

Flat file directory *n.* A directory that cannot contain subdirectories but simply contains a list of file names.

Flat file format *n.* An image file format in which individual objects cannot be edited. Files stored in JPEG, GIF, and BMP formats, for example, are all flat files.

Flat file system *n.* A filing system with no hierarchical order in which no two files on a disk may have the same name, even if they exist in different directories.

Flat memory *n.* Memory that appears to a programme as one large addressable space, whether consisting of RAM or virtual memory. The 68000 and VAX processors have flat memory; by contrast, 80x86 processors operating in real mode have segmented memory, although when these processors operate in protected mode, OS/2 and 32-bit versions of Windows access memory using a flat memory model. Also called: linear memory.

Flat pack *n.* An integrated circuit housed in a flat rectangular package with connecting leads along the edges of the package. The flat pack was a precursor of surface-mounted chip packaging. See also surface-mount technology.

Flat-panel display *n.* A video display with a shallow physical depth, based on technology other than the CRT (cathode-ray tube). Such displays are typically used in laptop computers.

Common types of flat-panel displays are the electroluminescent display, the gas discharge display, and the LCD display.

Flat panel monitor *n.* A desktop computer monitor that uses a liquid crystal display (LCD) rather than a cathode ray tube (CRT) to display data. Flat panel monitors are not as deep as CRT monitors and so occupy much less physical space.

Flat screen *n.* See flat-panel display.

Flatten *vb.* In digital graphic creation and manipulation programmes, to combine all layers of text, images, and other graphic elements into a single layer. Elements cannot be edited after the graphic is flattened, so a graphic is not usually flattened until the final step when all adjustments have been made to the individual layers. Flattening an image significantly reduces its file size and allows it to be saved in a wider range of formats. Flattening is similar to grouping in that both actions combine a set of objects. However, flattening is a permanent action, whereas a group of objects can be ungrouped. See also layering.

Flavor *n.* One of several varieties of a system, having its own details of operation. UNIX in particular is found in distinct flavors, such as BSD UNIX or AT&T UNIX System V.

Flex circuit *n.* A circuit printed on a thin sheet of flexible polymer film that can be used in applications requiring circuits to curve and bend. Flex circuits offer space and weight savings over traditional circuits, and are used extensively for medical, industrial, and telecommunications applications.

Flexible disk *n.* See floppy disk.

Flexible transistor *n.* See plastic transistor.

Flicker *n.* Rapid, visible fluctuation in a screen image, as on a television or computer monitor. Flicker occurs when the image is refreshed (updated) too infrequently or too slowly for the eye to perceive a steady level of brightness. In television and raster-scan displays, flicker is not noticeable when the refresh rate is 50 to 60 times per second. Interlaced displays, in which the odd-numbered scan lines are refreshed on one sweep and even-numbered lines on the other, achieve a flicker-free effective refresh rate of 50 to 60 times per second because the lines appear to merge, even though each line is actually updated only 25 to 30 times per second.

Flies *n.* In Web development and marketing, individuals who spend significant time on the Web and who are the targets of specific Web content or advertising.

Flight simulator *n.* A computer-generated recreation of the experience of flying. Sophisticated flight simulators costing hundreds of thousands of dollars can provide pilot training, simulating emergency situations without putting human crews and planes at risk. Flight simulator software running on personal computers simulates flight in a less realistic fashion; it provides entertainment and practice in navigation and instrument reading.

Flip-flop *n.* A circuit that alternates between two possible states when a pulse is received at the input. For example, if the output of a flip-flop is high and a pulse is received at the input, the output "flips" to low; a second input pulse "flops" the output back to high, and so on. Also called: bistable multivibrator.

Flippy-floppy *n.* An outmoded 5.25-inch floppy disk that uses both sides for storage but is used in an older drive that can read only one side at a time. Thus, to access the opposite side, the disk must be physically removed from the drive and flipped over. See also double-sided disk.

Float *n.* The data type name used in some programming languages, notably C, to declare variables that can store floating-point numbers. See also data type, floating-point number, variable.

Floating-point arithmetic *n.* Arithmetic performed on floating-point numbers. See also floating-point notation, floating-point number.

Floating-point constant *n.* A constant representing a real, or floating-point, value. See also constant, floating-point notation.

Floating-point notation *n.* A numeric format that can be used to represent very large real numbers and very small real numbers.

Floating-point numbers are stored in two parts, a mantissa and an exponent. The mantissa specifies the digits in the number, and the exponent specifies the magnitude of the number (the position of the decimal point). For example, the numbers 314,600,000 and 0.0000451 are expressed respectively as 3146E5 and 451E-7 in floating-point notation. Most microprocessors do not directly support floating-point arithmetic; consequently, floating-point calculations are performed either by using software or with a special floating-point processor. Also called: exponential notation. See also fixed-point notation, floating-point processor, integer.

Floating-point number *n.* A number represented by a mantissa and an exponent according to a given base. The mantissa is usually a value between 0 and 1. To find the value of a floating-point number, the base is raised to the power of the exponent, and the mantissa is multiplied by the result. Ordinary scientific notation uses floating-point numbers with 10 as the base. In a computer, the base for floating-point numbers is usually 2.

Floating-point operation *n.* An arithmetic operation performed on data stored in floating-point notation. Floating-point operations are used wherever numbers may have either fractional or irrational parts, as in spreadsheets and computer-aided design (CAD). Therefore, one measure of a computer's power is how many millions of floating-point operations per second (MFLOPS or megaflops) it can perform. Acronym: FLOP. Also called: floating-point operation. See also floating-point notation, MFLOPS.

Floating-point processor *n.* A coprocessor for performing arithmetic on floating-point numbers. Adding a floating-point processor to a system can speed up the processing of math and graphics dramatically if the software is designed to recognise and use it. The i486DX and 68040 and higher microprocessors have built-in floating-point processors. Also called: math coprocessor, numeric coprocessor. See also floating-point notation, floating-point number.

Floating-point register *n.* A register designed to store floating-point values. See also floating-point number, register.

Flooding *n.* The networking technique of forwarding a frame onto all ports of a switch except the port on which it arrived. Flooding can be used for robust data distribution and route establishment. Also called: flood routing.

Floppy disk *n.* A round piece of flexible plastic film coated with ferric oxide particles that can hold a magnetic field. When placed inside a disk drive, the floppy disk rotates to bring different areas, or sectors, of the disk surface under the drive's read/write head, which can detect and alter the orientation of the particles' magnetic fields to represent binary 1s and 0s. A floppy disk 5.25 inches in diameter is encased in a flexible plastic jacket and has a large hole in the center, which fits around a spindle in the disk drive; such a disk can hold from a few hundred thousand to over one million bytes of data. A 3.5-inch disk encased in rigid plastic is also called a floppy disk or a microfloppy disk. In addition, 8-inch floppy disks were common in DEC and other minicomputer systems. See also microfloppy disk.

Floppy disk controller *n.* See disk controller.

Floppy disk drive *n.* An electromechanical device that reads data from and writes data to floppy or microfloppy disks. See the illustration. See also floppy disk.

FLOPS *n.* Acronym for floating-point operations per second. A measure of the speed at which a computer can perform floating-point operations. See also floating-point operation, MFLOPS.

Floptical *adj.* Using a combination of magnetic and optical technology to achieve a very high data density on special 3.5-inch disks. Data is written to and read from the disk magnetically, but the read/write head is positioned optically by means of a laser and grooves on the disk.

Flow analysis *n.* A method of tracing the movement of different types of information through a computer system, especially with regard to security and the controls applied to ensure the integrity of the information. See also flowchart.

Flowchart *n.* A graphic map of the path of control or data through the operations in a programme or an information-handling system. Symbols such as squares, diamonds, and ovals represent various operations. These symbols are connected by lines and arrows to indicate the flow of data or control from one point to another. Flowcharts are used both as aids in showing the way a proposed programme will work and as a means of understanding the operations of an existing programme. See the illustration.

Flow control *n.* The management of data flow in a network to ensure that the receiver can handle all the incoming data. Flow-control mechanisms, implemented in both hardware and software, prevent a sender of traffic from sending it faster than the receiver can receive it.

Flush 1 *adj.* Aligned in a certain way on the screen or on paper. Flush left, for example, means aligned on the left side; flush right means aligned on the right side. See also align (definition 1).

Flush 2 *vb.* To clear a portion of memory. For example, to flush a disk file buffer is to save its contents on disk and then clear the buffer for filling again.

Flux *n.* 1. The total strength of a magnetic, electric, or radiation field over a given area. 2. A chemical used to aid the binding of solder to electrical conductors.

Flux reversal *n.* The change in orientation of the minute magnetic particles on the surface of a disk or tape toward one of two magnetic poles. The two different alignments are used to represent binary 1 and binary 0 for data storage: a flux reversal typically represents a binary 1, and no reversal represents a binary 0.

Fly swapping *n.* See swap-on-the-fly.

FM *n.* See frequency modulation.

FM encoding *n.* See frequency modulation encoding.

Focus *vb.* In television and raster-scan displays, to make an electron beam converge at a single point on the inner surface of the screen.

FOCUS *n.* See Federation on Computing in the United States.

FOD *n.* See fax on demand.

Folder *n.* In the Mac OS, 32-bit versions of Windows, and other operating systems, a container for programmes and files in graphical user interfaces, symbolised on the screen by a graphical image (icon) of a file folder. This container is called a directory in other systems, such as MS-DOS and UNIX. A folder is a means of organising programmes and documents on a disk and can hold both files and additional folders. It first appeared commercially in Apple Computer's Lisa in 1983 and in the Apple Macintosh in 1984. See also directory.

Folio *n.* A printed page number.

Follow-up *n.* A post to a newsgroup that replies to an article. The follow-up has the same subject line as the original article, with the prefix "Re:" attached. An article and all of its follow-ups, in the order they were received, constitute a thread, which a user can read together using a newsreader.

Font *n.* A set of characters of the same typeface (such as Garamond), style (such as italic), and weight (such as bold). A font consists of all the characters available in a particular style and weight for a particular design; a typeface consists of the design itself. Fonts are used by computers for onscreen displays and by printers for hard-copy output. In both cases, the fonts are stored either as bit maps (patterns of dots) or as outlines (defined by a set of mathematical formulas). Even if the system cannot simulate different typefaces on the screen, application programmes may be able to send information about typeface and style to a printer, which can then reproduce the font if a font description is available. See also bit map, font generator.

Font card *n.* See font cartridge, ROM card.

Font cartridge *n.* A plug-in unit available for some printers that contains fonts in several different styles and sizes. Font cartridges, like downloadable fonts, enable a printer to produce characters in sizes and styles other than those created by the fonts built into it. Also called: font card. See also ROM cartridge.

Font/DA Mover *n.* An application for older Apple Macintosh systems that allows the user to install screen fonts and desk accessories.

Font editor *n.* A utility programme that enables the user to modify existing fonts or to create and save new ones. Such an application commonly works with a screen representation of the font, with a representation that can be downloaded to a PostScript or other printer, or with both. See also PostScript font, screen font.

Font family *n.* The set of available fonts representing variations of a single typeface. For example, Times Roman and Times Roman Italic are members of the same font family. When the user indicates italic, the system selects the correct italic font for the font family, with its characteristic appearance. If there is no italic font in the family, the system simply slants, or "obliques," the corresponding roman character. See also italic, roman.

Font generator *n.* A programme that transforms built-in character outlines into bit maps (patterns of dots) of the style and size required for a printed document. Font generators work by scaling a character outline to size; often they can also expand or compress the characters they generate. Some font generators store the resultant characters on disk; others send them directly to the printer.

Font number *n.* The number by which an application or operating system internally identifies a given font. On the Apple Macintosh, for example, fonts can be identified by their exact names as well as their font numbers, and a font number can be changed if the font is installed in a system already having a font with that number. See also font.

Font page *n.* A portion of video memory reserved for holding programmer-specified character definition tables (sets of character patterns) used for displaying text on the screen on IBM Multi-Colour Graphics Array video systems.

Font size *n.* The point size of a set of characters in a particular typeface. See also point1 (definition 1).

Font suitcase *n.* A file on Macintosh computers that contains one or more fonts or desk accessories. Such files are indicated in early versions of the operating system with the icon of a suitcase marked with a capital A. From System 7.0 onward, this icon is used to denote individual fonts.

Foo *n.* A string used by programmers in place of more specific information. Variables or functions in code examples intended to demonstrate syntax, as well as temporary scratch files, may all appear with the name foo. Likewise, a programmer may type foo to test a string input handler. If a second placeholder string is needed, it will often be bar, suggesting that the origin of both is the U.S. Army phrase FUBAR (an acronym which, in discreet language, represents Fouled Up Beyond All Recognition/Repair). However, other origins have been claimed.

Footer *n.* One or more identifying lines printed at the bottom of a page. A footer may contain a folio (page number), a date, the author's name, and the document title. Also called: running foot.

Footprint *n.* The surface area occupied by a personal computer or other device.

Force *vb.* In programming, to perform a particular action that would normally not occur. The term is most often used in the context of forcing data to be within a particular range of values—for example, forcing a divisor to be nonzero. See also cast.

Force feedback *n.* A technology that generates push or resistance in an input/output device. Force feedback enables an input/output device, such as a joystick or a steering wheel, to react to the user's action in appropriate response to events displayed on the screen. For example, force feedback can be used with a computer game to react to a plane rising in a steep ascent or a race car turning a tight corner. See also input/output device.

Foreground 1 *adj.* Currently having control of the system and responding to commands issued by the user. See also multitasking.

Foreground 2 *n.* 1. The colour of displayed characters and graphics. 2. The condition of the programme or document currently in control and affected by commands and data entry in a windowing environment.

Forest *n.* A collection of one or more domains in Microsoft Windows that share a common schema, configuration, and global catalog and are linked with two-way transitive trusts. See also domain, global catalog, schema, transitive trust, two-way trust.

Fork 1 *n.* One of the two parts of a file recognised by the Mac OS. A Macintosh file has a data fork and a resource fork. Most or all of a typical user-produced document is in the data fork; the resource fork usually contains application-oriented information, such as fonts, dialog boxes, and menus. See also data fork, resource fork.

Fork 2 *vb.* To initiate a child process in a multitasking system after a parent process has been started. See also multitasking.

Fork bomb *n.* In UNIX-based systems, a programme or shell script that locks up the system by recursively spawning copies of itself using the Unix system call "fork(2)" until they occupy all the process table entries. Also called: logic bomb.

FOR loop *n.* A control statement that executes a section of code a specified number of times. Actual syntax and usage vary from language to language. In most cases, the value of an index variable moves through a range of values, being assigned a different (and usually consecutive) value each time the programme moves through the section of code. See also iterative statement, loop1 (definition 1).

Form *n.* 1. A structured document with spaces reserved for entering information and often containing special coding as well. 2. In some applications (especially databases), a structured window, box, or other self-contained presentation element with predefined areas for entering or changing information. A form is a visual filter for the underlying data it is presenting, generally offering the advantages of better data organisation and greater ease of viewing. 3. In optical media, a data storage format used in compact disc technology.

4. In programming, a metalanguage (such as Backus-Naur form) used to describe the syntax of a language. See also Backus-Naur form.

Formal language *n.* A combination of syntax and semantics that completely defines a computer language. See also Backus-Naur form, semantics (definition 1), syntax.

Formal logic *n.* A study of the logical expressions, sequences, and overall construction of a valid argument, without regard to the truth of the argument. Formal logic is used in proving programme correctness.

Format 1 *n.* 1. In general, the structure or appearance of a unit of data. 2. The arrangement of data within a document file that typically permits the document to be read or written by a certain application. Many applications can store a file in a more generic format, such as plain ASCII text. 3. The layout of data storage areas (tracks and sectors) on a disk. 4. The order and types of fields in a database. 5. The attributes of a cell in a spreadsheet, such as its being alphabetic or numeric, the number of digits, the use of commas, and the use of currency signs. 6. The specifications for the placement of text on a page or in a paragraph.

Format 2 *vb.* 1. To change the appearance of selected text or the contents of a selected cell in a spreadsheet. 2. To prepare a disk for use by organising its storage space into a collection of data "compartments," each of which can be located by the operating system so that data can be sorted and retrieved. When a previously used disk is formatted, any preexisting information on it is lost.

Format bar *n.* A toolbar within an application used for modifying the format of the document being displayed, such as changing font size or type.

Formatting *n.* 1. The elements of style and presentation that are added to documents through the use of margins, indents, and different sizes, weights, and styles of type. 2. The process of initialising a disk so that it can be used to store information. See also initialize.

Form control *n.* On a Web site, an individual box or button with which you enter information on an electronic form.

Form factor *n.* 1. The size, shape, and configuration of a piece of computer hardware. The term is often applied to subcomponents such as disk drives, circuit boards, and small devices, such as handheld PCs. It can also be used more broadly to include the arrangement and positioning of external switches, plugs, and other components of the device, or it can refer to the footprint of an entire computer. 2. A term used in computer graphics, specifically with reference to a method of rendering known as radiosity, which divides an image into small patches for calculating illumination. The form factor is a calculated value that represents the amount of energy radiated by one surface and received by another, taking into account such conditions as the distance between the surfaces, their orientation with respect to one another, and the presence of obstructions between them. 3. When used to describe software, refers to the amount of memory required, the size of the programme, and so on.

Form feed *n.* A printer command that tells a printer to move to the top of the next page. In the ASCII character set, the form-feed character has the decimal value 12 (hexadecimal 0C). Because its purpose is to begin printing on a new page, form feed is also known as the page-eject character. Acronym: FF.

Form letter *n.* A letter created for printing and distribution to a group of people whose names and addresses are taken from a database and inserted by a mail-merge programme into a single basic document. See also mail merge.

Formula *n.* A mathematical statement that describes the actions to be performed on numeric values. A formula sets up a calculation without regard to the actual values it is to act upon, such as A + B, with A and B representing whatever values the user designates. Thus, a formula is unlike an arithmetic problem, such as 1 + 2, which includes values and must be restated if any value is changed. Through formulas, users of applications such as spreadsheets gain the power to perform "what-if" calculations simply by changing selected values and having the programme recalculate the results. Sophisticated programmes include many built-in formulas for performing standard business and mathematical calculations.

Forte *n.* Sun Microsystems integrated development environment (IDE) for Java developers. See also integrated development environment.

Fortezza *n.* A cryptographic technology developed by the United States National Security Agency (NSA) for enabling secure communication of sensitive information. Fortezza is based on encryption, authentication, and other technologies built into a personalised card known as the Fortezza Crypto Card that can be inserted into a PCMCIA slot on a computer. This card works with Fortezza-enabled hardware and software to secure applications such as e-mail, Web browsing, e-commerce, and file encryption. An RS-232 token can also be used with legacy systems that do not have card-reading capability. The technology is supported by a number of commercial vendors.

Forth *n.* A programming language originated by Charles Moore in the late 1960s. Moore chose the language's name, a shortened version of the word fourth, because he believed it was a fourth-generation language and his operating system would allow him to use only five letters for a programme name. Forth is an interpreted, structured language that uses threading, which lets programmers easily extend the language and enables Forth to fit a great deal of functionality into limited space. Unlike most other programming languages, Forth uses postfix notation for its mathematical expressions and requires the programmer to work with the programme stack directly. See also 4GL, interpreted language, postfix notation, stack, threading.

FORTRAN or Fortran *n.* Short for formula translation. The first high-level computer language (developed over the period 1954–58 by John Backus) and the progenitor of many key high-level concepts, such as variables, expressions, statements, iterative and conditional statements, separately compiled subroutines, and formatted input/output. FORTRAN is a compiled, structured language. The name indicates its roots in science and engineering, where it is still used heavily, although the language itself has been expanded and improved vastly over the last 35 years to become a language that is useful in any field. See also compiled language, structured programming.

Fortune cookie *n.* A proverb, prediction, joke, or other phrase chosen at random from a collection of such items and output to the screen by a programme. Fortune cookies are sometimes displayed at logon and logoff times by UNIX systems.

Forum *n.* A medium provided by an online service or BBS for users to carry on written discussions of a particular topic by posting messages and replying to them. On the Internet, the most widespread forums are the newsgroups in Usenet.

Forum of Incident Response and Security Teams *n.* See FIRST.

Forward *vb.* In e-mail, to send a received message, either modified or in its entirety, to a new recipient.

Forward chaining *n.* In expert systems, a form of problem solving that starts with a set of rules and a database of facts and works to a conclusion based on facts that match all the premises set forth in the rules. See also expert system.

Forward error correction *n.* In communications, a means of controlling errors by inserting extra (redundant) bits into a stream of data transmitted to another device. The redundant bits are used by the receiving device in detecting and, where possible, correcting errors in the data. See also error-correction coding.

Forward pointer *n.* A pointer in a linked list that contains the address (location) of the next element in the list.

FOSDIC *n.* Acronym for film optical sensing device for input to computers. A device used by the U.S. government to read documents on microfilm and store them digitally on magnetic tape or on a disk that can be accessed by a computer.

Fourier transform *n.* A mathematical method, developed by the French mathematician Jean-Baptiste-Joseph Fourier (1768–1830), for signal processing and signal generation tasks such as spectral analysis and image processing. The Fourier transform converts a signal value that is a function of time, space, or both into a function of frequency. The inverse Fourier transform converts a function of frequencies into a function of time, space, or both. See also fast Fourier transform.

Four-nines availability *n.* The availability of a system 99.99 per cent of the time. See high availability.

Fourth-generation computer *n.* See computer.

Fourth-generation language *n.* See 4GL.

Fourth normal form *n.* See normal form (definition 1).

FPGA *n.* Acronym for Field Programmable Gate Array. A type of programmable logic chip that can be configured for a wide range of specialised applications after manufacture and delivery. FPGAs can be reprogrammed to incorporate innovations and upgrades. Because of their flexibility and adaptability, FPGAs are used in devices from microwave ovens to supercomputers.

FPLA *n.* See field-programmable logic array.

FPM RAM *n.* See page mode RAM.

FPU *n.* Acronym for floating-point unit. A circuit that performs floating-point calculations. See also circuit, floating-point operation.

FQ *n.* See fair queuing.

Fractal *n.* A word coined by mathematician Benoit Mandelbrot in 1975 to describe a class of shapes characterised by irregularity, but in a way that evokes a pattern. Computer graphics technicians often use fractals to generate naturelike images such as landscapes, clouds, and forests. The distinguishing characteristic of fractals is that they are "self-similar"; any piece of a fractal, when magnified, has the same character as the whole. The standard analogy is that of a coastline, which has a similar structure whether viewed on a local or continental scale. Interestingly, it is often difficult to measure the length of the perimeter of such a shape exactly because the total distance measured depends on the size of the smallest element measured. For example, one could measure on a given coastline the perimeter of every peninsula and inlet, or at a higher magnification the perimeter of every small promontory and jetty, and so on.

Fractional T1 *n.* A shared connection to a T1 line, in which only a fraction of the 24 T1 voice or data channels are used. Acronym: FT1. See also T1.

FRAD *n.* See frame relay assembler/disassembler.

Fraggle attack *n.* See smurf attack.

Fragmentation *n.* The scattering of parts of the same disk file over different areas of the disk. Fragmentation occurs as files on a disk are deleted and new files are added. Such fragmentation slows disk access and degrades the overall performance of disk operations, although usually not severely. Utility programmes are available for rearranging file storage on fragmented disks.

FRAM *n.* Acronym for ferromagnetic random access memory. A form of data storage technology in which data is recorded semipermanently on small cards or strips of material coated with a ferric oxide (iron-based) magnetic film. As with tape or disk, the data persists without power; as with semiconductor RAM, a computer can access the data in any order.

Frame *n.* 1. In asynchronous serial communications, a unit of transmission that is sometimes measured in elapsed time and begins with the start bit that precedes a character and ends with the last stop bit that follows the character. 2. In synchronous communications, a package of information transmitted as a single unit. Every frame follows the same basic organisation and contains control information, such as synchronising characters, station address, and an error-checking value, as well as a variable amount of data. For example, a frame used in the widely accepted HDLC and related SDLC protocols begins and ends with a unique flag (01111110). See the illustration. See also HDLC, SDLC. 3. A single screen-sized image that can be displayed in sequence with other, slightly different, images to create animated drawings. 4. The storage required to hold one screen-sized image of text, graphics, or both. 5. A rectangular space containing, and defining the proportions of, a graphic. 6. The part of an onscreen window (title

Frame buffer *n.* A portion of a computer's display memory that holds the contents of a single screen image. See also video buffer.

Frame grabber *n.* See video digitizer.

Frame rate *n.* 1. The speed at which full, single-screen images are transmitted to and displayed by a raster-scan monitor. Frame rate is calculated as the number of times per second (hertz) the electron beam sweeps the screen. 2. In animation, the number of times per second an image is updated. When the frame rate exceeds about 14 frames per second, animation seems to blend into smooth motion. See also animation.

Frame relay *n.* A packet-switching protocol for use on WANs (wide area networks). Frame relay transmits variable-length packets at up to 2 Mbps over predetermined, set paths known as PVCs (permanent virtual circuits). It is a variant of X.25 but dispenses with some of X.25's error detection for the sake of speed. See also ATM (definition 1), X.25.

Frame relay access device *n.* See frame relay assembler/disassembler.

Frame relay assembler/disassembler *n.* A combination channel service unit/digital service unit (CSU/DSU) and router that connects an internal network to a frame relay connection. The device converts data (which may be in the form of IP packets or conform to some other network protocol) into packets for transmission over the frame relay network and converts such packets back to the original data. Since this type of connection is direct—without a firewall—other network protection is necessary. Acronym: FRAD. See also firewall, frame relay, IP.

Frame source *n.* In the HTML frames environment, a contents document that will look for the source document to display within a frame drawn by the local browser. See also HTML.

Frames page *n.* A Web page that divides a Web browser window into different scrollable areas that can independently display several Web pages. One window can remain unchanged, while the other windows change based on hyperlinks that the user selects.

Frames per second *n.* See frame rate.

Framework *n.* In object-oriented programming, a reusable basic design structure, consisting of abstract and concrete classes, that assists in building applications. See also abstract class, object-oriented programming.

FRC *n.* See functional redundancy checking.

Fred *n.* 1. An interface utility for X.500. See also CCITT X series. 2. A placeholder string used by programmers in syntax examples to stand for a variable name. If a programmer has used fred, the next placeholder needed is likely to be barney.

Free block *n.* A region (block) of memory that is not currently being used.

FreeBSD *n.* A freely distributed version of BSD UNIX (Berkeley Software Distribution UNIX) for IBM and IBM-compatible PCs. See also BSD UNIX.

Free-form language *n.* A language whose syntax is not constrained by the position of characters on a line. C and Pascal are free-form languages; FORTRAN is not.

Freenet or free-net *n.* A community-based computer BBS and Internet service provider, usually operated by volunteers and providing free access to subscribers in the community or access for a very small fee. Many freenets are operated by public libraries or universities. See also ISP.

Free software *n.* Software, complete with source code, that is distributed freely to users who are in turn free to use, modify, and distribute it, provided that all alterations are clearly marked and that the name and copyright notice of the original author are not deleted or modified in any way. Unlike freeware, which a user might or might not have permission to modify, free software is protected by a license agreement. Free software is a concept pioneered by the Free Software Foundation in Cambridge, Massachusetts.

Free Software Foundation *n.* An advocacy organisation founded by Richard Stallman, dedicated to eliminating restrictions on people's right to use, copy, modify, and redistribute computer programmes for noncommercial purposes. The Free Software Foundation is the maintainer of GNU software, which is UNIX-like software that can be freely distributed. See also GNU.

Free space *n.* Space on a floppy disk or a hard drive not currently occupied by data. See also floppy disk, hard disk.

Freeware *n.* A computer programme given away free of charge and often made available on the Internet or through user groups. An independent programme developer might offer a product as freeware either for personal satisfaction or to assess its reception among interested users. Freeware developers often retain all rights to their software, and users are not necessarily free to copy or distribute it further.

Freeze-frame video *n.* Video in which the image changes only once every few seconds.

Frequency counter *n.* 1. An item of engineering test equipment that measures and displays the frequencies of electronic signals. 2. An electronic circuit, often found embedded in process-control computers, that counts the frequency of occurrence of an activity.

Frequency Division Multiple Access *n.* See FDMA.

Frequency-division multiplexing *n.* See FDM.

Frequency hopping *n.* The switching of frequencies within a given bandwidth during a point-to-point transmission. Frequency hopping reduces the chance of unauthorised signal interception or the effects of single-frequency jamming.

Frequency modulation *n.* A way of encoding information in an electrical signal by varying its frequency. The FM radio band uses frequency modulation, as does the audio portion of broadcast television. See the illustration. Acronym: FM.

Frequency modulation encoding *n.* A method of storing information on a disk in which both data and additional synchronising information, called clock pulses, are recorded on the surface. FM encoding is relatively inefficient because of the extra disk space required by the clock pulses. It has been generally superseded by a more efficient method called modified frequency modulation (MFM) encoding and by the complex but extremely efficient technique called run-length limited (RLL) encoding. Abbreviation: FM encoding.

Frequency response *n.* The range of frequencies an audio device can reproduce from its input signals. See also frequency.

Friction feed *n.* A means of moving paper through a printer in which the paper is pinched either between the printer's platen and pressure rollers or (in printers that do not have a platen) between two sets of rollers. Friction feed is available on most printers, for use with paper that does not have pin-feed holes. In printers that have tractor feed as well as friction feed, the friction-feed mechanism should be left disengaged when the tractor is being used, to avoid unnecessary stress on the tractor gears. See also platen.

Friendly *adj.* Referring to features built into hardware or software that make a computer or computer programme easy to learn and easy to use. Friendliness is emphasised by most developers and sought after by most users. See also user-friendly.

Fringeware *n.* Freeware whose reliability and value are questionable. See also freeware.

Front end *n.* 1. In a client/server application, the part of the programme that runs on the client. See also client/server architecture. 2. In applications, software or a feature of software that provides an interface to another application or tool. Front ends are often used to supply a common interface for a range of tools produced by a software manufacturer. A front end generally offers a more user-friendly interface than that of the application running "behind" it. 3. In networking, a client computer or the processing that takes place on it.

Front-end processor *n.* 1. Generally, a computer or processing unit that produces and manipulates data before another processor receives it. 2. In communications, a computer that is located between communications lines and a main (host) computer and is used to relieve the host of housekeeping chores related to communications; sometimes considered synonymous with communications controller. A front-end processor is dedicated entirely to handling transmitted information, including error detection and control; receipt, transmission, and possibly encoding of messages; and management of the lines running to and from other devices. See also communications controller.

Front panel *n.* The faceplate of a computer cabinet through which the control knobs, switches, and lights are available to an operator. See also console.

Fry *vb.* To destroy a circuit board or another component of a computer by applying excessive voltage. Even when applied voltage is not excessive, an electronic component can become fried when it breaks down, conducting more current than its design permits.

Fs *n.* See femtosecond.

FSK *n.* Acronym for frequency-shift keying. A simple form of modulation in which the digital values 0 and 1 are represented by two different frequencies. FSK was used by early modems running at 300 bits per second.

FT1 *n.* See fractional T1.

FTAM *n.* Acronym for File-Transfer Access and Management. A communications standard for transferring files between different makes and models of computer.

FTP1 *n.* 1. Acronym for File Transfer Protocol, a fast, application-level protocol widely used for copying files to and from remote computer systems on a network using TCP/IP, such as the Internet. This protocol also allows users to use FTP commands to work with files, such as listing files and directories on the remote system. See also TCP/IP. 2. A common logon ID for anonymous FTP.

FTP2 *vb.* To download files from or upload files to remote computer systems, via the Internet's File Transfer Protocol. The user needs an FTP client to transfer files to and from the remote system, which must have an FTP server. Generally, the user also needs to establish an account on the remote system to FTP files, although many FTP sites permit the use of anonymous FTP. See also FTP client, FTP server.

FTP client or ftp client *n.* A programme that enables the user to upload and download files to and from an FTP site over a network, such as the Internet, using the File Transfer Protocol. See also FTP1 (definition 1).

FTP commands *n.* Commands that are part of the File Transfer Protocol. See also FTP1 (definition 1).

FTP programme or ftp programme *n.* See FTP client.

FTP server *n.* A file server that uses the File Transfer Protocol to permit users to upload or download files through the Internet or any other TCP/IP network. See also file server, FTP1 (definition 1), TCP/IP.

FTP site *n.* The collection of files and programmes residing on an FTP server. See also FTP1 (definition 1), FTP server.

FTTC *n.* Acronym for fiber to the curb. The installation and use of fiber-optic cable from the central office (CO) to within a thousand feet of a user's home or office. With FTTC, coaxial cable or another medium carries the signals from the curb into the home or office. FTTC is a replacement for Plain Old Telephone Service (POTS) that enables the distribution of telephony, cable TV, Internet access, multimedia, and other communications over one line.

FTTH *n.* Acronym for fiber to the home. The installation and use of fiber-optic cable from the central office (CO) directly into a user's home or office. FTTH is a replacement for Plain Old Telephone Service (POTS) that enables the distribution of telephony, cable TV, Internet access, multimedia, and other communications over one line.

FUD *n.* Acronym for fear, uncertainty, and doubt. Derogatory slang used to express disagreement or displeasure with a vendor's public statements, particularly when the vendor is speaking of a competitor's products. If a vendor is perceived as implying that buying from a competitor is obviously the wrong choice, that vendor is said to be using FUD as a marketing technique.

Fuel cell *n.* An electrochemical device, similar to a battery in function, in which the chemical energy of a fuel, such as hydrogen, and an oxidant, usually oxygen, are converted directly into electrical energy. Unlike batteries, however, fuel cells do not store energy, and they never run down or need recharging as long as the fuel and oxidant are supplied continuously. The principle of fuel cell technology was discovered more than 100 years ago, but until recently it had found use only in laboratories and in space travel (the Apollo missions and the space shuttle). Today, large and small fuel cells are being developed that will power portable devices such as laptop computers and cellular phones, generate electricity and heat, and replace automotive combustion engines.

Fulfillment *n.* The process of delivering goods and services ordered by a consumer. Fulfillment involves establishing a reliable procedure for tracking orders and delivering products.

Fulfillment service provider *n.* A company that provides fulfillment services for an e-commerce Web site by tracking, packing, and shipping goods ordered via the e-commerce site. A fulfillment service provider allows an e-business to save time, costs, and labour by outsourcing order processing.

Full adder *n.* A logic circuit used in a computer to add binary digits. A full adder accepts three digital inputs (bits): 2 bits to be added and a carry bit from another digit position. It produces two outputs: a sum and a carry bit. Full adders are combined with two-input circuits called half adders to enable computers to add 4 or more bits at a time. See also carry bit, half adder.

Full-duplex *adj.* See duplex1.

Full-duplex transmission *n.* See duplex(definition 1).

Full justification *n.* In typesetting, word processing, and desktop publishing, the process of aligning text evenly along both the left and right margins of a column or page. See also justify (definition 2).

Full mode *n.* The default operational state of Windows Media Player in which all of its features are displayed. The Player can also appear in skin mode. See also skin mode.

Full-motion video *n.* Video reproduction at 30 frames per second (fps) for NTSC signals or 25 fps for PAL signals. Also called: continuous motion video. See also frame (definition 1).

Full-motion video adapter *n.* An expansion card for a computer that can convert motion video from devices such as a video cassette recorder to a digital format that a computer can use, such as AVI, MPEG, or Motion JPEG. See also AVI, Motion JPEG, MPEG.

Full name *n.* A user's complete name, usually consisting of last name, first name, and middle initial. The full name is often maintained by the operating system as part of the information that identifies and defines a user account. See also user account.

Full-page display *n.* A video display with sufficient size and resolution to show at least one 81/2-by-11-inch image. Such displays are useful for desktop publishing applications. Acronym: FPD. See also portrait monitor.

Full path *n.* In a hierarchical filing system, a pathname containing all the possible components of a pathname, including the network share or drive and root directory, as well as any subdirectories and the file or object name. For example, the MS-DOS full path c:\book\chapter \myfile.doc indicates that myfile.doc is located in a directory called chapter, which in turn is located in a directory called book in the root directory of the C: drive. Also called: full pathname. See also path (definition 2), root directory, subdirectory.

Full pathname *n.* See full path.

Full-screen *adj.* Capable of using or being displayed on the full area of a display screen. Applications running in windowing environments, although they might use the entire area of the screen, commonly allocate different areas to different windows, any of which can be enlarged to fill the entire screen.

Full-text search *n.* A search for one or more documents, records, or strings based on all of the actual text data rather than on an index containing a limited set of keywords. For example, a full-text search can locate a document containing the words "albatrosses are clumsy on land" by searching files for just those words without the need of an index containing the keyword "albatross." See also index.

Fully formed character *n.* A character formed by striking an inked ribbon with a molded or cast piece of type in the manner of a typewriter. Impact printers that produce fully formed characters use letters attached to wheels (daisy wheels), balls, thimbles, bands, or chains, rather than dot-matrix wires. See also daisy wheel, near-letter-quality, thimble.

Fully populated board *n.* A printed circuit board whose integrated circuit (IC) sockets are all occupied. Memory boards in particular may have fewer than the maximum possible number of memory chips, leaving some IC sockets empty. Such a board is said to be partially populated.

Function *n.* 1. The purpose of, or the action carried out by, a programme or routine. 2. A general term for a subroutine. 3. In some languages, such as Pascal, a subroutine that returns a value. See also function call, procedure, routine, subroutine.

Functional design *n.* The specification of the relationships between working parts of a computer system, including details of logical components and the way they work together. Functional design is shown graphically in a functional diagram, which uses special symbols to represent the elements of the system.

Functional programming *n.* A style of programming in which all facilities are provided as functions (subroutines), usually without side effects. Pure functional programming languages lack a traditional assignment statement; assignment is usually implemented by copy and modify operations. Functional programming is thought to offer advantages for parallel-processing computers. See also side effect.

Functional redundancy checking *n.* A method of preventing errors by having two processors execute the same instructions on the same data at the same time. If the results produced by the two processors do not agree, an error has occurred. The Intel Pentium and higher processors have built-in support for functional redundancy checking. Acronym: FRC.

Functional specification *n.* A description of the scope, objectives, and types of operations that are to be considered in the development of an information-handling system.

Function call *n.* A program's request for the services of a particular function. A function call is coded as the name of the function along with any parameters needed for the function to perform its task. The function itself can be a part of the programme, be stored in another file and brought into the programme when the programme is compiled, or be a part of the operating system. See also function (definition 2).

Function key *n.* Any of the 10 or more keys labeled F1, F2, F3, and so on, that are placed along the left side or across the top of a keyboard (or both) and are used for special tasks by different programmes. The meaning of a function key is defined by a programme or, in some instances, by the user. Function keys are used in application programmes or the operating system to provide either a shortcut for a series of common instructions (such as calling up a program's onscreen help facility) or a feature that is not otherwise available. See also key (definition 1).

Function library *n.* A collection of routines compiled together. See also function (definition 2), library (definition 1), toolbox.

Function overloading *n.* The capability of having several routines in a programme with the same name. The different functions are distinguished by their parameter types, return value types, or both; the compiler automatically selects the correct version, based on parameter types and return types. For example, a programme might have one trigonometric sine function that uses a floating-point parameter to represent an angle in radians, and another that uses an integer parameter to represent an angle in degrees. In such a programme, sin(3.14159/2.0) would return the value 1.0 (because the sine of p/2 radians is 1), but sin(30) would return the value 0.5 (because the sine of 30 degrees is 0.5). See also operator overloading.

Function procedure *n.* A procedure that returns a value and that can be used in an expression. You declare a function with the

Function statement and end it with the End Function statement.

Fuse *n.* A circuit element that burns out or breaks when the current passing through it exceeds a certain level. A fuse protects a circuit from damage caused by excess current. It performs the same function as a circuit breaker, but it cannot be reset, so it must be replaced if it breaks. A fuse consists of a short length of wire of a specific composition and thickness; the thicker the wire, the more current it can pass before the wire melts and breaks the circuit.

Fusible link *n.* A circuit component, often part of an integrated circuit, that is designed to break, or burn like a fuse, when a relatively high current is applied. Rather than protecting against excessive current flow, fusible links allow intentional circuit modification in the field. Fusible links were used in PROM chips, and they form the foundation of a kind of integrated circuit known as a field-programmable logic array. One can customise such a circuit "in the field," after it has been made in the factory, by selectively programming high current through certain fusible links and breaking them. See also field-programmable logic array, PROM.

Fuzzy computing *n.* 1. A computing technique that deals with vague, incomplete, or ambiguous data in a precise mathematical way while providing solutions based on the human way of thinking. The term fuzzy relates to the type of data it processes, not to the technique itself, which is very exact. Fuzzy computing is also known as fuzzy set theory or fuzzy logic, and covers fuzzy control and fuzzy expert systems, for example. 2. A computing technology in which the computer interprets data by looking for patterns in problems while completing tasks. Using fuzzy computing, the computer is able to examine patterns in the data it receives and to make inferences based on that data, and act accordingly.

Fuzzy logic *n.* A form of logic used in some expert systems and other artificial-intelligence applications in which variables can have degrees of truthfulness or falsehood represented by a range of values between 1 (true) and 0 (false). With fuzzy logic, the outcome of an operation can be expressed as a probability rather than as a certainty. For example, an outcome might be probably true, possibly true, possibly false, or probably false. See also expert system.

Fuzzy set *n.* A set constructed using the principles of fuzzy logic. It is used in artificial intelligence to deal with vague or continuous data that cannot be expressed by conventional set theory. In a fuzzy set, the membership function for the set of objects is not binary but continuous, such that an object may be a member of the set to a specific degree or arbitrary value. In computer programming, a fuzzy set is usually effectively represented by an array. See also array, artificial intelligence, fuzzy logic.

FWIW *adv.* Acronym for for what it's worth. An expression used in e-mail and newsgroups.

FYI *n.* 1. Acronym for for your information. An expression used in e-mail and newsgroups to introduce information that is thought to be useful to the reader. 2. An electronic document distributed through InterNIC like a request for comments (RFC), but intended to explain an Internet standard or feature for users rather than to define it for developers, as the RFC does.